WHERE to SKI AND SNOWBOARD 2013

Published in Great Britain by
NortonWood Publishing

tel 0844 9911 123
email w17@wtss.co.uk

Editors Chris Gill and Dave Watts
Assistant editors Mandy Crook, Chris Allan, Sheila Reid, Rebecca Miles
Contributors Minty Clinch, Alan Coulson, Nicky Holford, James Hooke, Eric Jackson, Tim Perry, Ian Porter, Adam Ruck, Helena Wiesner, Fraser Wilkin

Advertising manager
Dave Ashmore

Design by Val Fox
Production by Guide Editors
Contents photos generally by Snowpix.com / Chris Gill
Production manager
Sarah Carreck
Ad production manager
Ian Stratford
Proofreader Lynda Watson
Printed and bound in Italy by Lego SpA

10 9 8 7 6 5 4 3 2 1

ISBN-13: 978–0–9558663–4–0

A CIP catalogue entry for this book is available from the British Library.

Book trade sales are handled by
Faber Factory Plus
Bloomsbury House
74–77 Great Russell Street
London WC1B 3DA

tel 020 7927 3800
bridgetlj@faber.co.uk

Individual copies of the book can be bought (for delivery anywhere in the world) at a discount price by going to our website: www.wheretoskiandsnowboard.com

This edition published 2012

WHERE *to* SKI AND *Snowboard* 2013

The Definitive Guide

to the 1,000 Best Winter Sports Resorts in the World

Edited by

Chris Gill

and

Dave Watts

This edition is dedicated to the memory of Wendy King

NortonWood

Contents 1

DOPPELMAYR

LAGRANGE

EUROTUNNEL

BEN RILEY

That's the start of it – turn the page for the heart of it ...

Contents 2

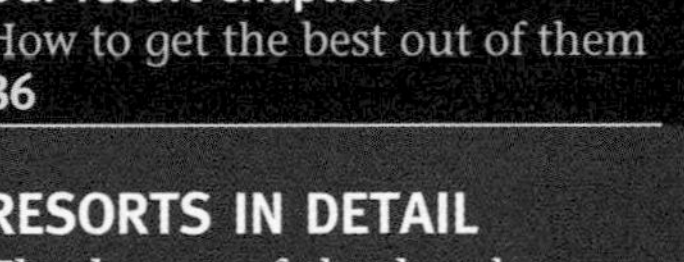

Resort chapters

About this book

It's simply the best

Dave Watts

Chris Gill

This is the 17th edition of *Where to Ski and Snowboard* – Britain's only established annual guidebook to ski resorts worldwide. It is the very best resort guide you can buy. Here's why:

- Every edition is the result of a thorough, painstaking process of **checking, updating and reviewing** the book's contents. We visit countless resorts every season, but even those we can't get to are reconsidered with the same care. In any one year, some chapters change hugely as a result, others hardly at all. But that just reflects what needs to change, and what doesn't.
- The book also benefits enormously from the **hundreds of reports** that readers send in on the resorts they visit. Every year, the 100 best reports are rewarded by a free copy of the book, and one of the readers awarded a book wins a free week in a smart French resort apartment. Read page 12 for more about this.
- By making the most of technology we are able to publish at the right time while going to press very late by conventional book publishing standards – so we can include the late-breaking news that makes the book **up to date for the season ahead**. The earliest editions of this book went to press in June; this year, it's 30 July, only about five weeks ahead of publication day.
- We work hard to make our information **reader-friendly**, with clearly structured text, comparative ratings and no-nonsense verdicts for the main aspects of each resort.
- We don't hesitate to express **critical views**. We learned our craft at Consumers' Association, where Chris became editor of *Holiday Which?* magazine and Dave became editor of *Which?* itself – so a consumerist attitude comes naturally to us.
- Our resort chapters give an **unrivalled level of detail** – including scale plans of each major resort, so that you get a clear idea of size – and all the facts you need.
- We use **colour printing** fully – we include not only piste maps for every major resort but also scores of photographs, carefully chosen so that you can see for yourself what the resorts are like.

Our ability to keep on investing in *Where to Ski and Snowboard* is largely due to the support of our advertisers – many of whom have been with us since the first edition in 1994. We are grateful for that support, and hope readers will in turn support our advertisers. It also helps if you tell them that you saw their ads in these pages: we know advertising in the book works, but advertisers can't be reminded too often.

We are absolutely committed to helping you, our readers, to make an informed choice; and we're confident that you'll find this edition the best yet. Enjoy your skiing and riding this season.

Chris Gill and Dave Watts
30 July 2012

Win a free week in France with Lagrange

Send us reports on the resorts you visit!

There are too many resorts for us to visit them all every year, and too many hotels, bars and mountain restaurants for us to visit them all. So we are always keen to encourage readers to send in reports on their holiday experiences. Every year, we give 100 copies of the new edition to the writers of the best reports. But now there's an extra incentive: all book winners will automatically be entered for a draw to win a week in a Lagrange apartment.

Your resort reports must be based on visits made during the 2012/13 season, and must be received by the end of April 2013. We much prefer to receive reports in digital form. Ideally, we'd like you to use our online form reached via www.wheretoskiandsnowboard.com. If you prefer, you can send an email to reports@wtss.co.uk – but please give your report a clear structure, using the same headings that we use in our resort chapters. If you don't, we'll find it much harder to make much use of your report. And it's vital that you give us the date of your trip, so that we can interpret your report sensibly – plus your postal address, to send your book to if you win.

The winner of the draw will get a week in a Lagrange residence. The details of the range of options will be made clear on our website. With the exception of Christmas/New Year and the period around February half term, you'll be able to choose your preferred dates (subject to availability).

LAGRANGE

Two of Lagrange's top properties – Les Fermes Emiguy in Les Gets (new last year) and Les Chalets de l'Adet in St-Lary ↓

Wendy King 1967–2012

A dream cut short

This edition is dedicated to the memory of Wendy King, who for many years acted as an assistant editor of this book and for some years as editor of our website. She died on 27 April at the age of 44.

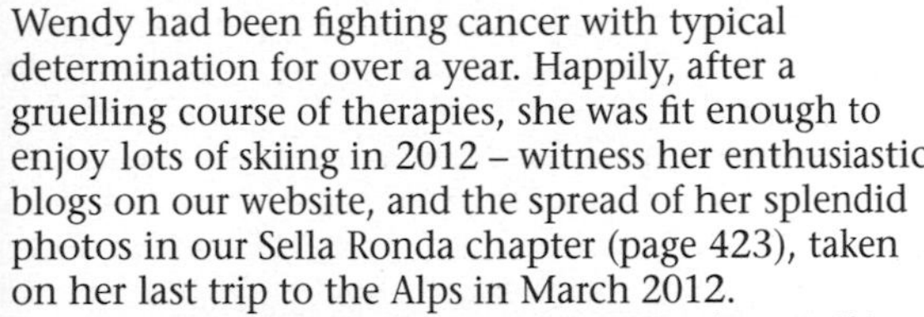

Wendy had been fighting cancer with typical determination for over a year. Happily, after a gruelling course of therapies, she was fit enough to enjoy lots of skiing in 2012 – witness her enthusiastic blogs on our website, and the spread of her splendid photos in our Sella Ronda chapter (page 423), taken on her last trip to the Alps in March 2012.

Wendy loved skiing, and she loved *Where to Ski and Snowboard*; working on it was her dream job. So she lived her dream, and it's not everyone who can say that. She worked for us – specifically for Chris, as his regular assistant editor – for nine years. Right up to the end, Wendy's appetite for work was fierce, provided that work was on the book or the website that she loved. She insisted on playing a major part in editing the 2012 edition, although she was affected by her illness and therapies. Later in 2011 Wendy made a huge contribution to the development of the apps we are still working on.

Wendy took a degree in English and translated literature; she loved writing, and learning how to improve her writing. She was a keen outdoors person, and did a lot of summer hill-walking and climbing as well as skiing. As well as exploring the UK and Europe, she hiked in Nepal, the USA and Australia.

Wendy's death came just as we were knuckling down to the job of preparing this edition. We have missed Wendy hugely, of course. But the team here has pulled together to produce the book, and we thank them all for that. We hope the result would meet Wendy's demanding standards.

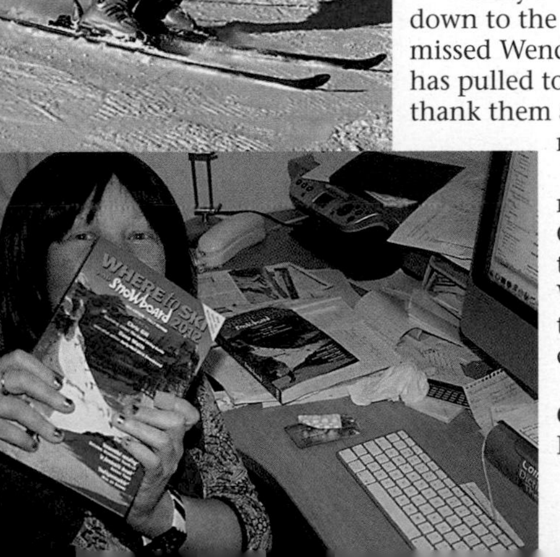

Anyone who feels so inclined can make a donation in Wendy's memory to Cancer Research UK, an organization that develops the therapies that gave Wendy one last season on the slopes. Go to: http://donateinmemory.cancerresearchuk.org/0002684

Chris Gill
Dave Watts

The editorial

The editors have their say

THE TEMPERATURE'S RISING, AGAIN

As we assemble this edition in late July 2012, the temperatures in southern England are for the first time this year approaching those we last encountered in the Aosta valley back in March – that is, around 25°C. Another strange season, then, but a very different one from the previous year and generally a more satisfactory one, as Fraser Wilkin spells out in his annual bulletin:

What a difference a year makes! The northern Alps were due a big one, and they certainly got it, despite an early scare. Autumn was the warmest and driest on record but, just as everyone feared the worst, it finally began to snow ... and snow ... and snow. In fact it didn't stop snowing for most of December, so much so that by the end of the month Val d'Isère had racked up over 4m of the stuff, nearly twice what it managed in the whole of the previous season. The Southern Alps were less fortunate – as they were for most of the season – but even here there was some good piste skiing thanks to artificial help. Further north, however, the blizzards continued into January, and snow depths approached record levels in places. February was quieter, but exceptionally cold mid-month, with Tignes recording –30°C, a new record at resort level. By contrast March was balmy, but thanks to the massive early season snowfalls, most resorts held up well and April saw a return to winter – at altitude, at least.

Had the second half of the season been anything like average then many resorts would have broken their snowfall records. In any event there were still some impressive figures – 7.4m for La Plagne is nearly 2m above average, as is 8.6m for Arosa and 9m for Lech. Snowiest of all, however, was Obertauern with a massive 12.2m!

With some notable exceptions it was a different story across the pond. Colorado's season never really got going – Vail managed just 5.2m, some 4m below average and Snowbird (Utah) was also way below par with 7m (average 12m). Only the north-west excelled. Here Whistler managed a whopping 13.8m at its mid-mountain Roundhouse measuring station, and Banff surpassed its all-time snowfall record with 7.1m.

SNOWPIX.COM / CHRIS GILL

March got seriously hot in the Alps, and where the earlier snowfall was thin, artificial snow saved the day – this is Montgenèvre, in southern France ↓

FRENCH LIFT SYSTEMS? PAH!

It's surprising how many people cling to the idea that France sets the standard for modern, efficient lift systems. It was true 20 years ago, but no longer. Here is a quote from a reader report on Saalbach, in Austria:

'The best resort I've ever visited for the numbers of fast 4-, 6- and 8-man chairs, heated seats, covers, moving carpets, the lot. Mainly gondolas out of the valley supplemented by chairs above mid-mountain – very well thought through. Only one slow chair, a three-man, that we came across. I think we used only two drags in the whole week. Better than some of the mega resorts in France, eg Tignes, which still has many slow lifts.'

Well, yes, Mr Patrick. But ... why so surprised? Do you not read and digest our every word? We've

↑ An extract from our own piste map for Saalbach. We use chair symbols to mark only fast lifts – slow ones get no symbol. As you can see, fast lifts rule!

been saying for years that Austrian resorts like Ischgl and Saalbach now set the standard, leaving big French resorts floundering in their wake. Three years ago we gave Saalbach an award for its achievements in this area. Each year the resort inches closer to the effective abolition of the slow lift – this year another T-bar gives way to a six-pack. Leaving aside nursery drags and the like, only five slow lifts remain in an area with over 50 in total. Amazing.

GOING SOFT

We seem to get an ever-increasing number of complaints – well, let's call them whinges – from readers about resorts' failure to provide covers on newly installed fast chairlifts. We have no sympathy with these wimps. Covers? Heated seats? When we were lads in Yorkshire (Gill) and Lancashire (Watts) you were lucky if t'chairlifts had chairs at all – half the time, we had to hang from ropes, and when it were real bad we used to hang from t'chairlift by our teeth ...

SWISS SPECIALITIES

We have not hesitated to make clear to our readers, over the last edition or two, that Switzerland is at present scarily expensive for British visitors (or, for that matter, any visitors from outside Switzerland). So it seems only fair to highlight positive aspects of the place when appropriate.

In this edition, we have made a bit of an effort to spruce up the 'feature panels' in our resort chapters. These are panels that we place in the chapters where we think there is something special that readers would be interested to hear about in more than the usual detail. What we've done is put pictures in most of them. And in the course of doing so we've noticed, for the first time, how many of these feature panels are in Swiss resort chapters. Of 15 such panels in the book, a disproportionate 7 are in Swiss resorts.

What does this tell you? Well, it underlines the fact that Switzerland is just a little bit special. It has revolving mountaintop restaurants; super-high railways that burrow through spectacular, precipitous mountains; world-famous toboggan runs; super-long pistes accessible to adventurous first-week skiers; the best mountain restaurants in the world. In other words, it has a lot more than just routine holiday skiing. Is it worth the current cost? Your call. Read our chapter on resort prices, on page 28. For most people, a holiday in Switzerland certainly calls for tight control of the lunch budget.

SWISS-IMAGE.CH / CHRISTIAN PERRET

Swiss specialities include some exceptionally long toboggan runs ↓

RUN ROMANCE EST MORT, MALHEUREUSEMENT

We don't envy lift companies the job of naming runs. Imagine those Monday-morning meetings in the boardroom convened, in the wake of a decision to build a new lift, to agree half a dozen new run names to add to the existing 50. They

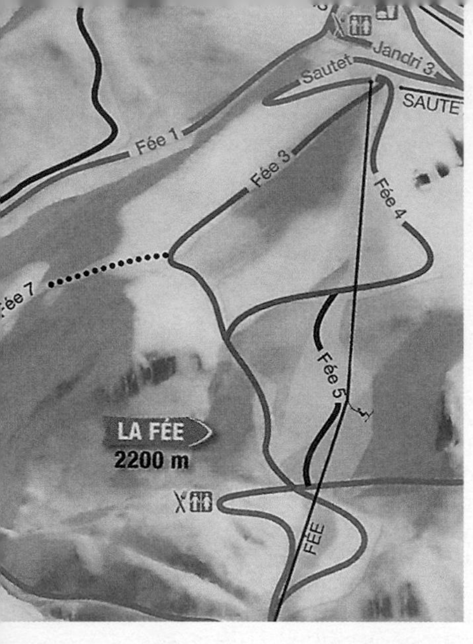

have to be distinctive, memorable, preferably rooted in the history or geography of the mountain. 'So, Jean-Nicole, what are your proposals ... ?'

Well, in the southern French resort of Les Deux-Alpes, the Monday-morning meetings will be a lot shorter in future because they've invented a system where runs inherit their names from the lifts they descend to. L2A has renamed all its runs, adopting a system that is supremely logical but in our view slightly bonkers (as well as boring). All runs leading to the Fée chair, for example, are now called Fée X, where X is a number from 1 to 7. So yes, it's easy to find a run down to the Fée lift. But will you be able to remember the runs you liked and the ones you didn't? No. Does this new system address a problem with the old system? No. So ... is it a good idea? Sorry, no. It's almost as unimaginative as Breckenridge naming its mountains Peaks 7, 8, 9 and 10.

↑ How long, we wonder, before Les Deux-Alpes drops its new run-naming system?

SPRING SNOW, ANYONE?

Our visit to Les Deux-Alpes did, however, throw up another innovation that we welcome. This was in March, when temperatures in the Alps were summer-like, resulting in some rock-hard pistes in the morning, even in super-high L2A. What we found was that some runs were kept closed in the morning because they were considered dangerously hard, and opened only once they had softened, towards lunchtime. This is an excellent scheme that should be copied elsewhere. Just after opening, some of the runs concerned were sublime – super-soft spring snow on a smooth base: the stuff of dreams.

GIVE US BACK OUR GROOMING MAPS

On another March trip, to Courchevel, it was important to ski groomed runs first thing until the rock-hard, ungroomed snow had softened. So we were dismayed to find that the US-style grooming maps that Courchevel and Méribel used to hand out, showing which runs had been groomed the previous night, no longer existed. Instead you had to search out a notice near the main lift station listing the previous night's grooming and memorize it or write it down. What a retrograde step – and one that made us miserable on a couple of occasions when we descended mogul fields of rock-hard frozen slush. We were told that next season there'll be a free smartphone app listing all the groomed runs – but not everyone has a smartphone, and not everyone wants to pay 'roaming' data charges, even if they have come down at long last. Give us back our photocopies, please!

EVER SAFER CHAIRLIFTS?

We also discovered on our Courchevel trip that many of the chairlifts there and in Méribel have now been fitted with a system that locks the safety bar closed until very near the end of the ride. This scared us a couple of times – they release very late (much later than we would normally open the bar). But we fear it may give some American visitors heart attacks – many US chairlifts don't

have safety bars, and even on a chair that has a bar, you will find Americans curiously reluctant to use it, and eager to raise it as soon as the top station is in view. They worry about being trapped, not falling off – so they are likely to be petrified by this new system.

COURCHEVEL GOES DOWN IN THE WORLD

Sorry about this, but ... while we are on Courchevel: the resort has quietly changed the names of all its villages. Its flagship Courchevel 1850 is now called just Courchevel – in itself a bonkers idea because Courchevel is also the collective name for all its villages. It was, of course, done on the advice of a marketing agency that was presumably paid a fortune for the idea. 1650 has reverted to the name of the old village it is based on, and is now Courchevel Moriond. 1550 becomes Courchevel Village. Le Praz (sometimes called 1300) is Courchevel Le Praz. We suspect that the reason for doing all this is that the old altitude-related names actually exaggerate all the altitudes; we hear that roadside altitude markers installed to help Tour de France riders track their progress made the deceit painfully obvious.

Way back in *Where to Ski and Snowboard 2000* we pointed out that the ice rink in the centre of 1850m is at 1740m, the gondola station in 1650 is below 1600m, the middle of 1550 is at 1480m, and the lake at 1300/Le Praz is at 1260m. It has taken them 13 years to respond to our remarks but we're claiming victory.

SIZE MATTERS

We're also claiming victory in another, rather more important matter: resorts coming clean on the real length of their pistes. For years we have expressed doubts about the piste km claimed by many resorts, and this year we have some results to report.

Ever since we started publishing this book 18 years ago, Courmayeur in Italy has claimed 100km of pistes, and we have been unconvinced about the figure. Last season, at last, it changed its mountain statistics to reveal that it actually has 36km of pistes to which it casually adds 64km of off-piste runs. Quite how they measure the available off-piste runs is, of course, another mystery, but 36km of pistes puts Courmayeur more or less at the bottom of the piste extent league table, where it undoubtedly belongs.

Then there's Monterosa, also in Italy. We and readers alike have been shaking our heads in disbelief for years at the claimed total for the linked three-valley system of 135km. Helpfully, the lift company publishes very clear data on individual lifts and runs, and a couple of years back we spent a bit of time poring over topographical maps of the area to see how well the published figures matched up. We came to the view, which

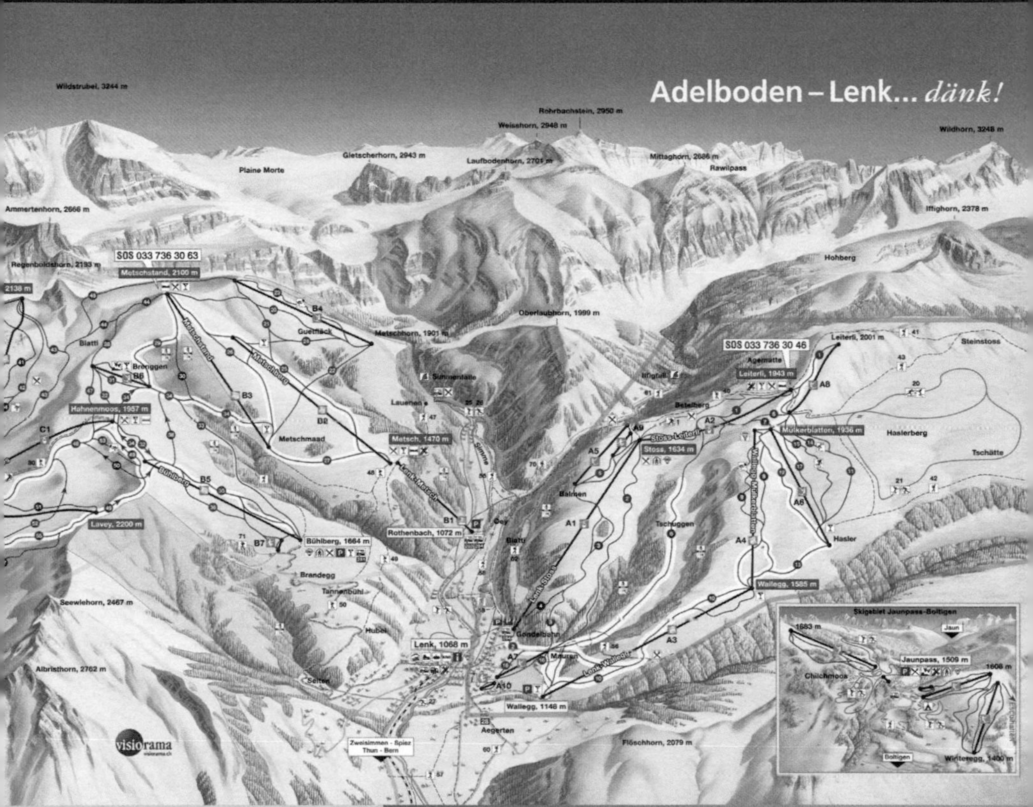

we've been expressing with increasing confidence, that when you look closely, the lift company piste lengths seemed to be about twice the real lengths.

Well, what do you know? At some point since we prepared the last edition, the lift company has sneaked into its website and quietly halved the run lengths, almost exactly. The total has come down from 135km – comfortably inside our middle-rank three-star category – to 73km. Adding on the slopes of nearby Antagnod, covered by the Monterosa lift pass and enjoyed by some readers, lifts the figure just enough to scrape into our two-star category. Ironically, the Monterosa area is actually huge – bigger, end to end, than the Trois Vallées. It just doesn't have many pistes.

All this has fired us up to try to nail exaggerated resort claims once and for all, and we think we may have found a way to do it. Watch this space.

NO END IN SIGHT TO CROWDS AND COLLISIONS

We continue to get reports of overcrowded pistes and reckless skiers causing collisions. For example, Mike Dunkley says of Mayrhofen's Penken area: 'Never in my 40 years of skiing have I skied on such dangerous, overcrowded pistes with people skiing far too fast for the conditions. Three of our group got scythed down from behind during the week.' And Mary Jo Peters says of Chamonix: 'We have never experienced such disregard for safety, especially in areas which were signposted as designated for beginners. We saw at least two very nasty collisions and one guy knocked unconscious in the middle of the piste, receiving assistance while skiers zoomed over the tips of people trying to help.'

Regular reporter Carlos Lins was prompted by his crowded day out in St Anton (from quieter, more civilized Lech) to suggest: 'Some kind of mountain ski patrol to catch skiers totally out of control and endangering the others would be very useful.' We agree. They have it in North America, so why not in Europe?

SNOWPIX.COM / CHRIS GILL

Piste crowds somehow never look as bad in pics as they are in the flesh – this run above La Plagne was virtually unskiable. We headed off-piste at the first opportunity ↓

NORTH AMERICA MOVES OUT OF REACH

Not so long ago readers were sending us around 150 reports a year about visits to American and Canadian ski resorts. This year we received just 34. It seems that fewer of our readers are venturing across the pond, despite the advantages of quieter pistes and active piste patrols, and safe, steep ungroomed runs. The main reason, fairly obviously, will be cost. Transatlantic air fares have soared (partly because of increased fuel prices and partly because of increased taxes), and local prices are much higher now in terms of pounds because of exchange rate changes – 45% higher in Canada and 35% higher in the US, compared with five years ago.

SMOKE GETS IN YOUR EYES – STILL, IN AUSTRIA

'Smoking in Austrian bars comes as a bit of a shock after four years tobacco-free in UK,' said a reporter this year. Too right. Every time we go to Austria we are amazed by the fuggy atmosphere in bars and even restaurants and hotels. In theory, only places with just one room and a floor area of

↑ The Folie Douce at Val d'Isère, now replicated not only in Val Thorens but also in Méribel
DAVE WATTS

less than 80sqm are allowed to get away without having a dedicated room for non-smokers. In practice, we frequently end up with sore throats and smelly clothes after a night or two in Austria. The Austrian government should get its act together and ban smoking completely from enclosed public places – otherwise they may well lose skiers and other tourists to rival countries.

PARTY TIME IN FRANCE

Not so long ago late afternoon partying up the mountain in France was unheard of; but now it's becoming big business. It all started with the Folie Douce in Val d'Isère (at the top of the gondola from La Daille), which adopted Austrian-style après-ski with live bands and DJs from mid-afternoon onwards. Three seasons ago the Folie Douce formula was successfully replicated above Val Thorens, and this season a replica will open above Méribel – competing for business with the established resort-level party spot at Rond-Point. There are also attempts to shift some afternoon beer on the mountain in Les Deux-Alpes, although our impression last season was that things were not going with a great swing. Still, it does seem things are at last looking up for those who like French skiing but hanker for Austrian après.

BUT TAKING THE P**S IN FRANCE TOO

Readers are still, quite rightly, getting annoyed at having to pay to use the loo at some mountain restaurants in French resorts – even if they are customers and simply peeing away the overpriced beer they have just consumed. Val d'Isère and Tignes are the key culprits, but we've had complaints from elsewhere too. One Val d'Isère visitor this year wrote that restaurants were charging 'from 30c to 2 euros. I even witnessed a woman who had not paid being followed into a toilet by the "bog bouncer". Although she was clearly desperate and had no change, she was made to leave and go to get money'. In the Trois Vallées they have built lots of public loos on the mountain and marked them on the piste map; L'Espace Killy should follow suit.

THANKS TO YOU

We are grateful to all the hundreds of readers who sent in a report on the resort they visited last season. These reports are crucial to our annual updating and revision process. As usual, the 100 readers whose reports proved most useful have won a free copy of this edition. And as last year their names have gone into the hat for a free week in a smart Pierre & Vacances apartment in the French Alps. And the lucky winner is ... Ed Ferrari.

We also have a prize for the best resort photo submitted by a reader and used in the book – a week in a smart Lagrange apartment. This year we are using photos from nine readers – the photo credits tell you who they are – and the winner is John Scott for his picture of the 'front de neige' at Avoriaz on page 223.

Congratulations to both our winners. Please consider sending in a report and some photos next season – details of what we want, and of next year's report prize, are on page 12.

What's new?

New lifts and other major developments in top resorts

In this chapter we summarize major developments in ski resorts last season and those planned for 2012/13. Most major resort chapters have a 'News' panel near the start; you'll find many more news items in those panels. To keep up to date with resort developments and regular news items, go to www.wheretoskiandsnowboard.com and sign up for our email newsletters.

Andorra

Soldeu makes off-piste more accessible

A short draglift at Pic d'Encampadana above El Tarter opened in 2011/12 to serve off-piste routes there and new red and blue runs.

Austria

Alpbach and Wildschönau linked to form Ski Juwel

An eight-seat gondola is to open for 2012/13 from Inneralpbach to Schatzberg above Auffach in the adjacent Wildschönau area, linking the two ski areas. Auffach is 7km by road from better-known Niederau, covered by the joint lift pass but not linked.

Higher speeds at Hintertux

In 2011/12 a 10-person gondola replaced the double chair from Tuxer Fernerhaus on the glacier. At Finkenberg, a six-pack replaced the Katzenmoos double chair, on the upper slopes of Penken.

Easier for beginners at Ischgl

In 2011/12 a six-pack replaced a T-bar on the nursery slopes.

Even more fast chairs for Kitzbühel

On Resterhöhe the Zweitausender double chair is to be replaced by an eight-seater for 2012/13. In the Hahnenkamm sector the Walde T-bar is to be replaced by a six-pack. In 2011/12 a six-pack replaced the Resterhöhe double chair and Moseralm T-bar.

More luxury in Lech

In 2011/12 a chondola (a fast hybrid lift of chairs and gondola cabins) replaced the Weibermahd quad above Oberlech.

Zillertal adds six-packs

Above Zell am Ziller, the Kreuzwiese drag is due to be replaced by a six-pack for 2012/13. Last season a six-pack replaced the Katzenmoos double chair on Penken, above Finkenberg.

More uplift at Obertauern

For 2012/13 a chondola is due to replace the Grünwaldkopfbahn quad from the valley. And a six-pack will replace the Hochalmbahn quad above that. Carrying capacities will increase by over 50%.

Saalbach-Hinterglemm installs yet more fast lifts

The T-bar on Bernkogel from the Hinterglemm sector is to be replaced by a six-pack with covers for 2012/13. Last season two slow chairlifts on the way up from Saalbach to Reiterkogel were replaced by an eight-seat gondola and a six-pack.

Not such a drag in Schladming

At Hauser Kaibling last season, a six-pack replaced the Almlift drag serving an isolated blue run.

More power to the glacier at Stubai

On the Stubai glacier, the Rotadl slow quad is to be moved to serve Daunjoch for 2012/13 – and is to be replaced by a fourth six-pack.

Vorarlberg – Alpenregion Bludenz: new chair and park

For 2011/12, at Sonnenkopf a new quad chair replaced a T-bar; at Brandnertal a new terrain park was built above Brand.

France

Alpe-d'Huez improves access to Auris-en-Oisans

In 2011/12 a six-pack replaced the long, slow Fontfroide chair on Signal de l'Homme. And a new blue run, Pré-Rond, was created.

Les Arcs lodging and lift improvements

For 2012/13 the second phase of the Edenarc development above Arc 1800 is to open. Last season a six-pack replaced the slow Mont Blanc chair and a drag lift from Arc 1600 towards Les Deux Têtes.

Easier access to Avoriaz

For 2012/13 the Prodains cable car from Morzine is to be replaced by a gondola, and a big aquatic centre will be opened.

Quicker link from Châtel to Avoriaz

In 2011/12 a six-pack replaced the Rochassons double chair from Plaine Dranse towards Avoriaz.

Courchevel adds more six-packs

At 1850, the Biollay quad is due to be replaced by a six-pack. Last season a six-pack replaced the Plantrey quad at 1850.

Les Deux-Alpes to replace old 'devil' gondola

For 2012/13 the Diable gondola is to be replaced by a six-pack.

New gondola for Flaine

The old Aup de Veran gondola from village level is to be replaced by a faster eight-seater for 2012/13. Last season a new six-pack from mid-mountain, the Désert Blanc, replaced two old chairs.

New chairs for Megève

Last season a six-pack replaced the old Mt Rosset chair on Mont d'Arbois, and a new quad, Ravine, opened at the top of Le Jaillet.

Quicker access to Reberty at Les Menuires

In 2012/13, a six-pack is due to replace the old bucket-lift from the bottom of La Masse to Reberty.

Modern gondolas and a new party venue for Méribel

The first two sections of the Plattières gondola are due to be upgraded, halving the ride time. The lower stage of the Saulire gondola is also to be upgraded, again halving the ride time. The Choucas restaurant is to become a new Folie Douce (like those in Val d'Isère and Val Thorens).

Montgenèvre lift improvements

There are plans to upgrade the Chalvet chair for the coming season. Last season a fast quad replaced the Montquitaine chair from Claviere towards Montgenèvre.

Six-pack and gondola for Morzine

The Troncs chairlift, useful for returning from Les Gets, will become a six-pack for 2012/13, and the Prodains cable car up to Avoriaz is to be replaced by a gondola.

Big revamps on and off the mountain at La Plagne

The Biolley sector is being revamped, with a six-pack replacing the Becoin chair, the Biolley chair and three drags. Phase two of the

Plagne-Centre renovation project will be completed. Last season a six-pack replaced the slow Verdons Sud chair from Champagny to Les Verdons above Plagne-Centre.

Faster access to Italy from La Rosière

For 2012/13 a six-pack is due to replace the slow Fort quad to Col de la Traversette, making access to La Thuile quicker.

Easier way home at St-Martin-de-Belleville

The home run was modified to allow you to bypass a tricky section.

Old village rebuilt below Tignes

The old village of Tignes-les-Boisses is being redeveloped on a big scale and rebranded Tignes 1800. The first phase is due to open at the end of 2013.

Val d'Isère gathers pace

The slow Fontaine Froide quad chairlift on Bellevarde is to be replaced by a six-pack, and there are plans for a new jumbo gondola from the resort to Solaise, but not until 2014/15. The Atelier d'Edmond restaurant at Le Fornet gained a Michelin star.

Gondolas galore at Val Thorens

The Péclet gondola will be revamped for 2012/13. Last season the new Thorens jumbo gondola opened above the Portette chair, opening up new red and blue runs.

Quicker link from Risoul to Vars

In Risoul, a quad replaced the slow Razis chair (which accesses the Vars sector) last season.

Germany

Glacial delights at Garmisch-Partenkirchen

For 2012/13 a six-pack is due to replace T-bars on the glacier.

Italy

New black runs for Cervinia

For last season, the Plateau Rosa cable car was renovated and three new black runs above Salette in the Valtournenche sector opened.

Double chairlift makes big news in Cortina d'Ampezzo

A new red slope is due to open in the Faloria sector in 2012/13. In 2011/12 in the Cinque Torri sector, a new double chairlift replaced the ancient single-person chair and subsequent rope tow from mid-mountain to the Averau Refuge.

Short-term pain for long-term gain at Courmayeur

A two-stage cable car with rotating cabins to Punta Helbronner on Mont Blanc is under construction and due to open by 2014/15. But the top section of the existing cable car here will be closed till then.

Livigno now loves off-piste

Last season new freeride zones were introduced on Mottolino, overturning the resort's previous blanket ban on off-piste skiing.

Major expansion at Madonna di Campiglio

For 2012/13 a new quad chair is due to open on the upper slopes of the Cinque Laghi sector, opening up new pistes. Last season the long-awaited gondola link between the Cinque Laghi sector and Pinzolo opened, and on Monte Spinale a fast quad replaced the Boch chair.

Good and bad news for Monterosa Ski

In 2011/12, at Gressoney, a new gondola replaced the existing one from Stafal to Gabiet. The historic Rifugio Guglielmina above Alagna burnt down, and it is not clear if it will be rebuilt.

Sauze d'Oulx makes it easy to get to Sportinia

Next season a new easy piste from Rif Mollino to Sportinia is to open. Last season two fast quads (Triplex and Pian della Rocca) on the upper part of Sauze's ski area were moved to replace two old chairs and make moving around the mountain easier.

Lots of upgrades in the Sella Ronda

In Arabba, a new chair is planned for the Porta Vescovo area. In Corvara, the Boè cable car is to be upgraded. At La Villa, the Gran Risa piste is to be enlarged. Last season the Bamby quad between San Cassiano and La Villa became a six-pack, a new quad replaced one of the double chairs from Passo Campolongo to Monte Cherz, and the Costes da l'Ega lift at Corvara was replaced by a quad.

New six-pack for Selva

A six-pack replaced a triple chair at Passo Sella for 2011/12.

Sestriere to have new pistes and a Club Med

Two new easy pistes and a Club Med in Pragelato are due to open.

Switzerland

Another blue run for Adelboden

A blue run from Sillerenbühl to Aebi is planned for 2012/13.

Andermatt about to be transformed

A huge luxury development of hotels and apartments is being built, with the first properties due to open in 2013.

Quicker access to France from Swiss side of Portes du Soleil

At Les Crosets, a six-pack replaced the slow Grand Conche chair towards Avoriaz in 2011/12.

New quad and trendy hotel for Davos

On Jakobshorn last season, a fast quad replaced the Brämabüel draglift up from Jschalp. A new room-only designer hotel opened.

New six-packs at Laax

For 2012/13 a six-pack at Lavadinas will replace an old double, and another six-pack will open from Treis Palas to Crap Masegn. Last season a six-pack replaced two draglifts from Alp Dado to the ridge above Crap Sogn Gion.

Saas-Fee mountain restaurant improvements

Last season the Spielboden mountain restaurant was taken over by the Michelin-starred Fletschorn hotel, and the revolving restaurant at Allalin was refurbished and renamed Threes!xty. For 2013/14 a new eight-person gondola is planned from the car park at the edge of the village to Spielboden.

Verbier due for lift link to Bruson

For 2012/13 a new gondola linking Bruson to Le Châble is planned. Last season a six-pack replaced the two successive slow chairs from just above the Verbier nursery slopes to Les Ruinettes.

Old chair replaced at Villars

A six-pack replaced the slow chair to Petit Chamossaire for 2011/12.

Ancient chair at last replaced in Wengen

The Wixi chair will be replaced by a six-pack for 2012/13.

Zermatt gains new ski and toboggan runs

Last season a new red run from Grunsee to the mid-station of the Findeln chairlift and a toboggan run at Furi opened.

USA – California

More Heavenly trails

In 2011/12 three new blue trails were built on the Nevada side.

Good and bad news at Mammoth

In 2011/12, a fast quad replaced the slow triple Chair 5 at mid-mountain. Sister resort June Mountain will not open this winter.

New owners modernize Squaw Valley

Last season, for the first time, all trails were named and classified for difficulty, and signposting was installed. For 2012/13 a triple chair at High Camp is to be replaced by a six-pack for quicker access to the terrain parks and the Granite Chief and Silverado areas. The lift pass now covers the next-door Alpine Meadows ski area too.

USA – Colorado

New quad on Aspen's easy mountain

At Tiehack on Buttermilk, a new fast quad replaced the existing slow lifts last season.

Yet another fast chair for Beaver Creek

Last season a fast quad replaced the Rose Bowl triple chairlift.

Bigger mountain restaurant for Snowmass

At the top of the Elk Camp gondola a new, much bigger restaurant is due to open in 2012/13 to replace Café Suzanne.

Vail trades in chairlift for gondola

In 2012/13 a new gondola is to replace the Vista Bahn chair from Vail Village to mid-mountain.

USA – Utah

Deer Valley installs new quad

A high-speed quad is due to replace the slow Deer Crest chair on Little Baldy Peak next season.

Better park and pipe access at Park City

At Resort Base last season a triple chair replaced the Three Kings double that serves the terrain park and super-pipe.

Upgrade for old Snowbird chairlift

For 2012/13 the Little Cloud double chairlift is due to be replaced by a high-speed quad. In 2011/12, a new expert bowl, Zone 5, opened near the top of the Peruvian chair.

USA – Rest of the West

Big Sky builds more deserted trails

For 2011/12 five new trails opened on Andesite Mountain.

Jackson Hole's lift improvements continue

For 2012/13 a new fast quad is to replace the Casper triple chairlift. Last season a new double chair was installed from the base of the Thunder quad to the top of the Bridger gondola.

Canada – Western Canada

More lift-served terrain for Fernie

Last season, a new triple chairlift to the top of Polar Peak opened up more terrain entirely above the treeline, including 22 new runs.

Kicking Horse improvements at base and at altitude

In 2011/12 a new beginner area at the base and a new groomed trail along Redemption Ridge and into Feuz Bowl were built.

Cutting your costs

We name the resorts where your pound will go further

by **Chris Gill**

RPI	115
lift pass	£220
ski hire	£130
lessons	£135
food & drink	£170
total	**£655**

RPI	100
lift pass	£200
ski hire	£115
lessons	£120
food & drink	£125
total	**£560**

RPI	85
lift pass	£190
ski hire	£90
lessons	£80
food & drink	£120
total	**£480**

FOOD & DRINK

Our budget figure is for six days' modest consumption of food and drink – each day, a cheap pasta or pizza lunch with a quarter-litre of house wine, a small beer, a coke and a large coffee or cappuccino.

By including four different drinks, we have tried to be fair to countries where one kind of drink may be more expensive than others. Bear in mind that if you're not happy with simple lunches day after day, you may spend much more than our budget figure, especially in resorts where the budget figure itself is quite high (ie top French and most Swiss resorts).

Three years back, in response to the declining power of the pound and resulting high cost of staying in a top ski resort, we introduced our Resort Price Index figures, designed to make it simple to see which resorts were affordable, and which were not. Last year, we extended it to cover the costs of lift passes, ski hire and lessons. Our RPI figures are now based on a total of all four costs. But, as you can see from the examples in the margin, we also show the separate costs that feed into the RPI calculation.

The food and drink element of the RPI, as in earlier years, is based on prices noted mainly by our faithful readers. If you find this survey helpful, please contribute to the exercise next season, via our website.

Exchange rate movements affected our RPIs a year ago, and have done so again. The pound buys 13% more euros than a year ago, and 10% more Swiss francs. While the rate against the Canadian dollar is unchanged, the pound buys 6% fewer American dollars. Skiing in North America now looks very expensive compared to Europe.

The margin panels explain exactly what we have included in our 'basket' of items. One particular thing to be aware of is that many people will spend a lot more on food and drink than our modest budget figure – so beware resorts where our figure is high, because yours is going to be two or three times as big.

In margin boxes in each resort chapter we present these budget figures, and a total. And at the top of the box, we give the resulting RPI. This index compares the total budget for the resort to the average across all European resorts; 100 represents the average resort. (Given the relatively small number of people going to North America, and the high costs for all resorts there, we decided a European basis made sense.) As shown in the margin on the left, high index figures (115 up) are coloured red, low ones (85 down) green; ones in between are blue. Note than the overall RPI is only part of the picture, though; in particular, the overall figures don't always reflect the cost of food and drink.

The group of resorts with roughly average RPIs (from 95 to 105) is largely French, with quite a few Austrian and Italian resorts and just Val d'Anniviers in Switzerland. The low-cost group has eastern European countries at the bottom, but then includes a healthy mix of resorts in Austria, France and Italy, with resorts from all three countries cropping up near the bottom of the RPI league. Cheapest

LIFT PASSES

Our lift pass figures are for the pass we reckon you're most likely to buy.

In Europe, where a resort sells a pass covering other linked resorts, we have used that pass price.

Where available, in America we have used special passes aimed at the international market (such as the Tri Area Pass, around Park City in Utah).

LESSONS

Our budget figure is half the cost of a four hour private lesson for two people.

Generally, we have taken prices from the main schools. You may pay more at other schools (Brit-run outfits especially) or sometimes less.

Some schools, eg the ESF in France, quote an hourly rate, easily multiplied by four. Where the standard offering is a lesson of 2.5 hours or 3.5 hours or whatever, we scaled the cost up to four hours.

in the main Alpine countries are Passo Tonale in Italy, a great place to learn to ski on good snow, and Puy-St-Vincent and Ste-Foy in France, two more excellent small resorts. The pricey group is dominated by resorts in North America and Switzerland, with just the most fashionable resorts in France and Austria – Courchevel and Lech – getting red RPIs. In the top slot is Aspen in Colorado followed by neighbouring Snowmass.

THE PICTURE BY COUNTRY

Because the pound has strengthened against the Swiss franc and particularly the euro in the past year, the average budget on which our RPIs are based is quite a bit lower than it was a year ago.

Swiss prices remain high. Only two Swiss resorts fall outside our high-cost group when you look at the overall RPI. All Swiss resorts are expensive for eating and drinking, with budget figures, even for our very modest 'basket', ranging from £170 to £235 – that is, £30 to £40 a day. You could easily spend £100 a day. For lift passes, too, many resorts are pricey. For lessons and ski hire, the picture is much more mixed. In one of our tables over the page we look at Switzerland in isolation, to identify relative bargains.

Canadian RPIs have gone up, not because prices have changed much but because the average budget for Europe that our calculations are based on has gone down. American RPIs have gone up more, because the American dollar has strengthened against the pound. All resorts in North America fall well inside the pricey group overall, because of expensive lift passes and lessons (the latter particularly in the US). Ski hire costs are generally high, though there are a few resorts that match Europe in this respect. But the picture is completely different when you come to look at your daily food and drink budget. Most places compare well with Europe, and some are positively cheap. So what you shell out every day is not going to feel too bad. As with Switzerland, we have assembled a table of North American resorts, to identify relative bargains.

Although France doesn't stand out from our overall RPI figures as expensive, compared with Austria and Italy it is way more

WAYS TO KEEP HOLIDAY COSTS UNDER CONTROL

A good way of avoiding the full impact of high resort restaurant prices is to go on a catered chalet holiday. With chalet holidays you get a filling breakfast and afternoon tea, as well as a substantial dinner, so your lunchtime needs can be minimized. Some tour ops offer 'piste picnic' packed lunches for a small extra charge. Crucially, in a chalet you get wine included with dinner – and you can organize your own aperitifs, or buy beer and mixers in the chalet at modest cost.

It's no coincidence that in these difficult times the demand for chalet holidays is soaring, and that operators have expanded their programmes to meet that demand – particularly last season. Ski Total added 25 new chalets, for example, while Inghams' programme expanded from a modest 20 properties to an impressive 63 chalets and chalet hotels across the Alps and in Finland.

Chalet holidays are not the only way to keep costs under control. A few tour operators such as Ski 2 offer 'all inclusive deal' options, quoting a price that includes half-board, vouchers for lunch at mountain restaurants, lift pass, and more. Club Med is a well-established operator of big hotels where everything is included, with lunch either back at the hotel or at dedicated mountain restaurants. Crystal has two deals in selected resorts, one including ski/board hire and lift pass, the other including a packed lunch and early-evening drinks. And yes, you can combine the two.

And of course there is self-catering. Now that it is so easy to find comfortable apartments with room to prepare meals and a dishwasher to deal with the aftermath – and with attached spas and pools of hotel standard, in many cases – self-catering is very attractive, especially for families.

46 RESORTS WHERE YOU CAN SAVE MONEY: THE ONES WITH BELOW-AVERAGE RPI FIGURES

RPI	Resort	Country	Page	RPI	Resort	Country	Page
35	Poiana Brasov etc	Romania	653	85	Bregenzerwald	Austria	192
45	Bansko etc	Bulgaria	650	85	Alpenregion Bludenz	Austria	195
70	Puy-St-Vincent	France	316	90	Bad Gastein	Austria	111
70	Passo Tonale	Italy	416	90	Saalbach-Hinterglemm	Austria	158
70	Kranjska Gora etc	Slovenia	654	90	Les Deux-Alpes	France	252
75	Ste-Foy-Tarentaise	France	337	90	Cervinia	Italy	387
80	Alpbach	Austria	107	90	Courmayeur	Italy	398
80	Vars / Risoul	France	375	90	La Grave	France	267
80	Livigno	Italy	403	90	Madonna di Campiglio	Italy	407
80	La Rosière	France	321	90	Serre-Chevalier	France	327
80	Garmisch-Partenkirchen	Germany	380	95	Châtel	France	237
80	Monterosa Ski	Italy	412	95	Megève	France	269
80	Sauze d'Oulx	Italy	418	95	Obertauern	Austria	155
85	Hintertux / Tux valley	Austria	117	95	Kitzbühel	Austria	129
85	Sestriere	Italy	439	95	Avoriaz 1800	France	222
85	Ellmau	Austria	114	95	Flaine	France	258
85	Mayrhofen	Austria	145	95	Morzine	France	296
85	Schladming	Austria	164	95	Selva / Val Gardena	Italy	432
85	Söll	Austria	173	95	Les Gets	France	265
85	Arinsal	Andorra	90	95	Samoëns	France	325
85	La Thuile	Italy	441	95	Stubai valley	Austria	189
85	The Pyrenees	France	318	95	Sella Ronda	Italy	423
85	Montgenèvre	France	292	95	Formigal etc	Spain	643

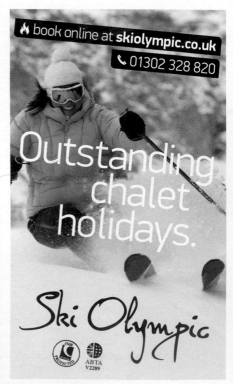

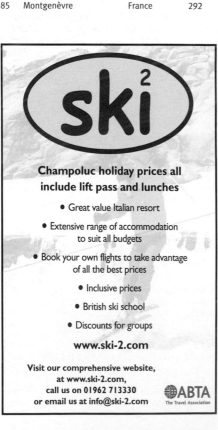

expensive for food and drink, with nearly all resorts coming in with budget figures of £120 or more – £20 a day – and most of the resorts most popular on the UK market coming in at £135 or more – for very modest consumption, remember.

Both Austria and Italy have more resorts where the costs overall are below average, and have plenty of resorts with below-average food and drink costs. We have put together some food and drink comparisons below.

In Andorra, Soldeu comes in above average, with Arinsal below. Spain costs less than average, and Slovenia appreciably less. But Bulgaria and Romania retain a firm grip on the real budget end of the market.

SKI HIRE

Our budget figures are for 'performance' skis that a keen intermediate or advanced skier might choose; not a beginner or top end demo ski. We looked at several shops.

If you book in advance online, many shops will offer a serious discount.

EUROZONE

In these tables of budget figures for food and drink and for lift passes we show the lowest and highest figures in Austria, France and Italy, and add in a top Swiss resort for comparison.

EXCHANGE RATES

We converted prices to £££ using tourist rates published in July 2012:
€1.21
SFr1.44
US$1.48
CAN$1.50

EUROZONE EXTREMES: FOOD/DRINK

Resort	Country	Budget
LOW		
Monterosa Ski	Italy	£85
Passo Tonale	Italy	£90
Livigno	Italy	£90
Schladming	Austria	£90
Sauze d'Oulx	Italy	£95
Sestriere	Italy	£95
Garmisch-Partenk'n	Germany	£95
Sella Ronda	Italy	£95
Selva / Val Gardena	Italy	£95
Alpbach	Austria	£100
Bad Gastein	Austria	£100
Ellmau	Austria	£100
Söll	Austria	£100
HIGH		
Alpe-d'Huez	France	£130
Les Arcs	France	£130
Avoriaz 1800	France	£130
Chamonix	France	£135
Flaine	France	£135
Lech	Austria	£135
La Plagne	France	£135
Samoëns	France	£135
Tignes	France	£135
Val Thorens	France	£135
Megève	France	£145
Méribel	France	£145
Val d'Isère	France	£145
Courchevel	France	£155
AND A SWISS COMPARISON		
Zermatt	Switzerland	£210

EUROZONE EXTREMES: LIFT PASSES

Resort	Country	Budget
LOW		
Ste-Foy-Tarentaise	France	£90
Puy-St-Vincent	France	£110
La Rosière	France	£140
La Thuile	Italy	£140
Vars / Risoul	France	£140
Passo Tonale	Italy	£150
Sauze d'Oulx	Italy	£150
Sestriere	Italy	£150
HIGH		
Obergurgl	Austria	£190
Sölden	Austria	£190
Tignes	France	£190
Val d'Isère	France	£190
Cortina d'Ampezzo	Italy	£200
Courchevel	France	£200
Les Arcs	France	£200
Les Menuires	France	£200
La Plagne	France	£200
La Tania	France	£200
Méribel	France	£200
Sella Ronda	Italy	£200
Selva / Val Gardena	Italy	£200
St-Martin-de-B'ville	France	£200
Val Thorens	France	£200
AND A SWISS COMPARISON		
Zermatt	Switzerland	£260

SKY HIGH

In these tables we show the lowest and highest RPI figures in Switzerland and North America. Remember that an RPI of 100 is for the European average resort, and that isn't cheap (not least because the average includes Swiss resorts).

SWISS EXTREMES: OVERALL RPI

Resort	Country	RPI
LOW		
Val d'Anniviers	Switzerland	100
Engelberg	Switzerland	110
Andermatt	Switzerland	115
Villars	Switzerland	115
HIGH		
Davos	Switzerland	130
Saas-Fee	Switzerland	130
Crans-Montana	Switzerland	135
Verbier	Switzerland	140
Zermatt	Switzerland	140
St Moritz	Switzerland	150

AMERICAN EXTREMES: OVERALL RPI

Resort	Country	RPI
LOW		
Big White	Canada	135
Silver Star	Canada	135
Revelstoke	Canada	140
Sun Peaks	Canada	140
Big Sky	USA	140
HIGH		
Vail	USA	165
Deer Valley	USA	165
Beaver Creek	USA	170
Snowmass	USA	180
Aspen	USA	185

Short breaks

Making the most of a quick snow-fix

Mini ski-trips to La Tania last December and to Courchevel the previous December each gave the editorial team three excellent days on the slopes. Whether you travel independently or as part of a package (we've done both), short-stay trips are easier to arrange now; the choice of airlines, destination airports and onward transfers is wider than ever. Midweek trips can be even better than weekends: cheaper deals and, in some resorts, quieter slopes.

With just a few days, you'll need to plan your short break carefully; but that's all part of the fun. We sum up the options here, with a few handy tips to help you to maximize your slope time.

WHERE SHALL WE GO?

Resorts closest to your arrival airport may seem the obvious starting point, but travelling a bit further can avoid any weekend crowds. You could also try smaller resorts that you might not normally bother with for a week's holiday.

Geneva is the classic gateway to the western Alps, with Chamonix just over an hour away, and other major French resorts such as Megève, Flaine and Morzine close by. Allow extra time for the Trois Vallées and the Tarentaise resorts. You could also head into Switzerland and visit Villars, Verbier or Crans-Montana.

In Italy, Turin is an underused alternative approach to the Aosta Valley, with Courmayeur, Champoluc and La Thuile conveniently reached; Sauze d'Oulx and Montgenèvre in the Milky Way are even nearer.

Further east, in Switzerland, Engelberg and Andermatt are popular options easily accessible from Zürich. So are the Austrian resorts of the Voralberg – such as Bregenzerwald and Alpenregion Bludenz (for a quiet, family-oriented time) – and the upmarket Lech and Zürs, with St Anton nearby. Also in Austria, Innsbruck provides a fantastic opportunity to combine a city break with doorstep skiing. There are lots of resorts surrounding the city, and the Stubai Valley with its reliable glacier is nearby too. Similarly Salzburg has lots of resorts within an hour or two.

The Pyrenees offer short-break opportunities too: flights into Pau (where we flew to for two days' skiing last season) and Lourdes put you close to Cauterets, Barèges-La Mongie and St-Lary-Soulan. And for a budget break, you could explore Slovenia very cheaply with flights to Ljubljana – the nearest ski area is just 8km from the airport.

WHERE TO STAY?

The range of short-stay accommodation is improving, but can still be limited in some major resorts – places such as Chamonix, Crans-Montana and Morzine, with big summer or conference business, are easier. From Salzburg or Innsbruck you could take the daily shuttles to different resorts. If you have a rental car, valley towns such as Chur, Sion and Interlaken in Switzerland, Aosta in Italy, Moûtiers and Bourg-St-Maurice in France and Radstadt in Austria are cheaper bases from which you can visit different resorts nearby.

PRICING THE OPTIONS

Costs vary enormously. Tour operators have special deals with hotels and can organize the essentials to save you time.

Around 50% of Ski 2's business is short breaks to Champoluc (at one end of Italy's Monterosa ski area). Three nights' B&B in a 3-star hotel, private transfers from any of six airports within striking distance (meeting any flight), a three-day lift pass, first-day guiding and lunches costs from £485 (£500 for a half-board package); you book your own flights.

Stanford Skiing offers three- and four-night stays in catered chalets or self-catered apartments in Megève starting on Sunday, Wednesday or Thursday; prices for a catered chalet are from £275 excluding flights and transfers. Skiweekends.com features major resorts in France, Italy and Switzerland, and offers overnight coach travel or flight options. A four-night half-board coach package to Brides-les-Bains (for Méribel) – two nights on the coach, two nights in the hotel, three days of skiing – costs from £249 per person. Momentum offers flights, car hire and three nights' B&B in a 3-star hotel from £429 in Courmayeur. Momentum, STC and Alpine Weekends will tailor-make short breaks for you.

TIPS FOR THE TRIP

Unless booking at short notice, avoid low resorts – where snow may be unreliable – and high, treeless resorts – where slopes may close in bad weather. Go for early or late flights to get the most slope-time, but note that Sunday evening traffic can be horrendous with locals going home. Book a transfer or rental car in advance; it's often cheaper and saves time on arrival. And choosing a different car hire company from the one your airline promotes can avoid queuing with others from your flight too. Taxis are generally very expensive, and public transport times between airports and resorts are rarely convenient (though Switzerland has good rail links). Rather than taking your own equipment, consider renting: most airlines impose hefty fees for ski/board carriage.

New gear for 2013

Lots of exciting new gear to improve your holiday

by **Dave Watts**
snowboard expert:
Mark Harries

Every year, new developments mean that skis, boots and snowboards get better and better. This year is no exception, with some great leaps forward for every type of equipment. The key innovations are designed to improve versatility, ease of use and comfort.

↑ The test centre in Kühtai, Austria, where over 750 pairs of skis were available to test

Last March I went on a week-long test of all the new skis for 2012/13 in Kühtai near Innsbruck, at 2020m one of Austria's highest resorts. The test was organized by the Snowsports Industries of Great Britain (a trade body of ski distributors and retailers), and there were over 750 pairs available.

ROCKING ON

The major trend is the continued march of 'rocker technology' that was introduced four seasons ago. Basically, this means that the tips of skis (and often the tails too) are lifted up from the snow, and this has a threefold effect: it improves floatation in powder and crud, it makes landing jumps easier, and it makes turning easier.

Nearly all skis now have rocker technology to some extent – from full tip and tail rockers on most freeride skis to much smaller tip-only rockers on most piste skis. Fischer even has a new 'Hybrid' range of skis where you can flick a switch on the front part of the ski and change the tip from conventional to rocker and vice versa.

WIDTH WARS

Over the last few years, skis have been getting wider. I personally now have a distinct preference for using a ski that is at least 80mm underfoot because I find it gives a much more stable platform and is easier to ski off-piste in chopped-up powder and crud. If you choose the right ski, it can work very well on hardpacked snow too.

In general Snow+Rock divides skis into four main groups based on the width underfoot: on-piste 63mm to 73mm; all mountain 74mm to 81mm; freeride 82mm to 102mm; and big mountain 103mm and more. But the boundaries between categories are becoming blurred. Ross McCloy, Snow+Rock's equipment buyer, points out that, for example, 'Völkl says its RTM 75 (75mm underfoot) is an all-mountain ski while Rossignol counts its Pursuit 16 (74mm underfoot) as a piste ski. That's because the Völkl has more rocker and therefore better off-piste performance, and the Rossignol has less rocker and is therefore better suited to on-piste skiing.'

SNOW+ROCK TIP

TOP ON-PISTE SKIS

FOR EXPERTS
Rossignol Pursuit 16 Ti/BSLT

FOR EXPERT WOMEN
K2 Superburnin

FOR RED RUN SKIERS
K2 Charger

FOR RED RUN WOMEN
Rossignol Attraxion 3

Top men's/unisex skis include (left to right): Scott Reverse K2 Sideshow Blizzard Bonafide Atomic Bent Chetler →

THIS YEAR'S WINNERS

Of the piste skis aimed at decent skiers, the Rossignol Pursuit range stood out, and our testers loved the Pursuit 16 and Pursuit 18. Others that did well include the Atomic Redster D2 SL and the Nordica Spitfire range. First-time buyers should take a look at the Rossignol Pursuit 14, Atomic Vario Scandium and Head Integrale 007. Snow+Rock is offering a special package aimed at first-time buyers: Fischer Viron 2.2 skis (or for women Fischer Inspire) plus bindings, poles, ski bag and a pair of Salomon Mission 4 boots (or for women Salomon Divine 4) for just £320 – an amazing bargain compared with the £540 it would cost to buy them all separately (the ski and binding alone would normally sell for £340).

All-mountain skis are designed to be skied off-piste as well as on-piste, and for many readers of this book who like to do both, this is the type of ski they should be looking for (it is certainly the type that I look for). And there is a huge choice of excellent skis available, including the Salomon Enduro and BBR ranges, the Völkl RTM range, Scott Reverse and the Nordica Fire Arrow range.

With freeride skis (for people who want to ski mostly off-piste but some on-piste), top performers included the Blizzard Bonafide, Scott Venture, K2 Sideshow, K2 Hardside and Völkl Mantra. Big-mountain skis are for people who spend a lot of time in the mountains and want a great ski for powder days. The Atomic Automatic, Atomic Bent Chetler, Blizzard Cochise and Rossignol Squad 7 did well at the test.

Kästle skis were not on the test, but Snow+Rock has an exclusive deal to be the only Kästle stockist in the UK; I have had rental pairs a few times and thought they were great and gave a really smooth ride. Snow+Rock also has exclusive UK rights to sell White Doctor skis, which were developed by a guy who spent 20 years working for top French ski brands. Ross McLoy, Snow+Rock's equipment buyer, says, 'Both Kästle and White Doctor produce classic skis that perform really well without any gimmicks or gizmos and are ahead of the game in ski development.'

SNOW+ROCK TIP

ALL-MOUNTAIN SKIS

FOR EXPERTS
Salomon BBR 8.9

FOR EXPERT WOMEN
Atomic Affinity Storm

FOR ADVANCED SKIERS
Head REV 80 Pro

FOR ADVANCED WOMEN
Salomon BBR Sunlite

Snow+Rock's exclusive brands, White Doctor and Kästle, perform really well without any gimmicks or gizmos →

Top women's skis include (top to bottom): Fischer Koa 84 Rossignol S7 W Salomon Rockette 90 Völkl Viola ↓

SKIS SPECIALLY FOR WOMEN

Nearly every manufacturer now produces a range of skis designed specifically for women (from novice to expert), taking account of their different physical make-up to men. In general, women tend to be lighter and less powerful, so manufacturers give their women's skis a different

SNOW+ROCK TIP

TOP SKI BOOTS

FOR EXPERTS
Salomon X Max 120

FOR EXPERT WOMEN
Lange RX 100 W

FOR RED RUN SKIERS
Atomic Hawx 80

FOR RED RUN WOMEN
Rossignol Vita Sensor2 80

construction, flex and shape. All this makes for skis that are easier to turn. At the test, favourites for good skiers in the on-piste category included Atomic Cloud D2, K2 Superburnin, Salomon Bamboo, Völkl Viola and Völkl Allura (first-time buyers should look at the Rossignol Attraxion 3). All-mountain: K2 SuperGlide, Fischer Koa 78, Salomon BBR Sunlite, Salomon Rockette 90 and Völkl Kenja. Freeride: Völkl Kiku and Aura, Rossignol S3 Women and S7 Women, K2 Brightside and Salomon Geisha.

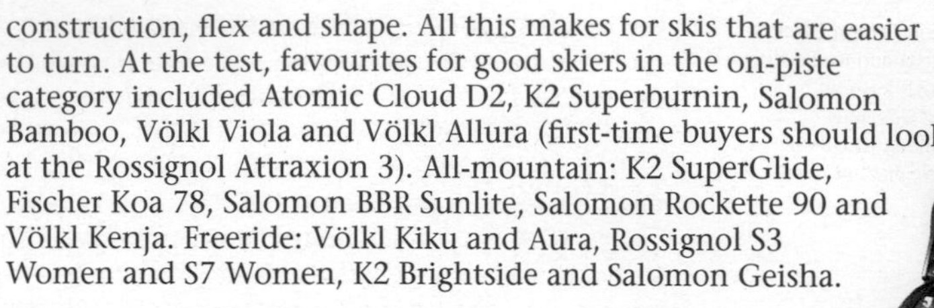

Salomon Guardian: a touring binding with downhill performance →

BIG NEWS ON BOOTS AND BINDINGS

The big news this year is another breakthrough by Salomon. It introduced its Custom Shell concept four years ago. The boot is warmed up in an oven in the shop, you step in to it, and the plastic outer shell as well as the liner is moulded to the individual shape of your foot, especially the widest part of the forefoot where most people have the greatest problems. The boot is then allowed to cool down and you have a perfect fit. All in 20 minutes. This year Salomon has a new Max version of the Custom Shell boots: the boot has a twin frame and an oversized pivot (a larger area of overlap where the top and bottom of the boot meet), which is designed to increase both performace and comfort. And the whole boot can be moulded to your foot (Salomon calls it the 360º Custom Shell). Snow+Rock will be stocking six models of boot with this new technology.

Last season, Fischer launched a new Vacuum Fit boot. This features a new type of plastic that is 15% lighter than normal and when heated in a special oven becomes very soft and malleable. It can then be moulded, using special equipment and compressed air, to the exact shape of your foot. Fischer says that this heating and moulding can be repeated up to five times if you are not happy with it when you go skiing. This year it has extended the number of boots in this range from five to twelve, going down to boots that suit good intermediate skiers.

Boots that mould to fit your foot: Salomon Max Custom Shell (top) Fischer Vacuum (bottom) ↓

There are revolutionary new bindings, too. The Salomon Guardian and Atomic Tracker bindings are designed to combine the precision and performance of a conventional downhill binding with the convenience of a touring binding, allowing the bindings to be switched from ski to walk mode with the help of your ski pole.

THE LATEST SNOWBOARDING BREAKTHROUGHS

As with skis, 'rocker technology' has had a huge influence on snowboard design in the last few years. Most recently, the trend has been away from full-on rocker designs back to conventional camber boards with a slight amount of rocker. Whilst all designs have their benefits, the type of board that you'll prefer will depend on the kind of

Gnu Carbon Credit (left) and K2 Raygun (right) are both rocker boards and can be ridden by newbies and pros alike →

SNOW + ROCK TIP

ULTIMATE ALL-MOUNTAIN SNOWBOARD SET-UP

FOR MEN

BOARD
Lib Tech TRS

BINDINGS
Ride Capo

BOOTS
ThirtyTwo Lashed Fast Track

FOR WOMEN

BOARD
Burton Déjà Vu Flying V

BINDINGS
Burton Scribe Reflex

BOOTS
Burton Bootique

snowboarding you like to do and your ability. For a lot of professional riders, particularly those whose focus is on fast riding, hitting big obstacles and steep lines, the key quality needed is stability. So they often choose a board that is built strong and has plenty of response. These kinds of boards are usually hybrid rocker, flat or regular camber depending on the brand. Conversely, some pros whose focus is freestyle (park and rails) might favour a rocker design to make board control easier and more fun. However, for normal holiday boarders, rocker-design snowboards can be a great help to improving your riding and getting the most from your holidays. And a lot of people say that from the moment they tried a rocker board they knew they would never turn back.

Snowboards such as the Gnu Carbon Credit and the K2 Raygun feature a rocker design that can be ridden by newbies and pros alike. Lifting the tip and tail away from the snow not only makes the board float better in powder but also makes it far less likely that you'll catch an edge, so novices will build confidence a lot more quickly and have more energy to snowboard for longer.

If you've tried both camber and rocker and are torn between the two, then it makes sense to go for a board with the best of both worlds. Lib Tech's latest design on the Phoenix snowboard features C3 BTX technology. This is where hybrid rocker design gets closest to camber, so it's great for aggressive riders who want plenty of stability with enhanced float and play.

But the most interesting – and potentially the most promising – design in snowboarding right now comes from a little-known German brand called Silbaerg. It uses a secret construction to alter how the board reacts when you flex it. When you carve the snowboard, the edges protrude downward into the snow giving you more grip, like a big claw. When you flex the board the other way, eg over a rail or box, the edges lift upward leaving them clear of the obstacle. This ingenious design has a lot of potential for both carving and freestyle and can be found on the Carvomat Pro, which is classic camber in design, or the flat-based Jibbomat Pro.

Flow's NX2 SE bindings have a clever design which makes them easy to step into and use ↓

Bindings are an often overlooked piece of equipment, but choosing the right pair can make a massive difference to how your snowboard reacts. Generally there are two kinds; regular strap bindings and speed entry. From the latter category Flow has a great high-end binding with a brand new design. The NX2 SE features a brand new chassis that has a simple, yet ingenious design feature that lifts the straps out of the way as you recline the drop-down highback. This means you don't have to alter the tension of the straps; you simply kick

With clothing the trend is towards colour blocking and mixing classic muted navy, grey or black with bright, vivid colours. This is an Arc'teryx Rush jacket with Arc'teryx Sabre pants ↓

your foot in, lock the highback and you're away with no fuss. If you're looking for light bindings, consider the Union Charger. If cushioning is more important, the Burton EST series such as the Cartel EST gives another level in comfort and feel. And Ride's Capo bindings feature a thick EVA foam footbed with canting, so not only do you have plush levels of cushioning, the angle of the footbed can improve your alignment on the board, which is kinder on the knees – great for anyone with dodgy knees.

Snowboard boots keep getting lighter and lace systems quicker. The Salomon F4.0 has a one-lace-pull design that wraps your foot in an instant. It's also designed to get you as low to the ground as possible using a thin, yet cushioned sole. The Burton Ambush is one the lightest boots out there and has the very fast and precise Speed Zone lacing system that controls lower and upper zone tightening separately.

BRIGHT CLOTHING AND NEW GOGGLE OPTIONS

With ski clothing, the trend is towards colour blocking, mixing classic muted navy, grey or black with a bright palette of colours such as vivid greens, brilliant blues, vibrant yellows, raspberry reds and bright orange. Design details accent bright colours. Fit varies from slim and sporty using four-way stretch fabrics to longer jackets and looser and baggier freeride and snowboard clothing. And Columbia has an amazing new Circuit Breaker electric jacket that you can heat up to the temperature that suits you.

There's a new Recon MOD Live system that comes ready-fitted into a Scott goggle (and can be fitted into a Smith goggle). It has a built-in GPS and gives you a futuristic 'James Bond' type display on a screen, showing things like your altitude, speed and exact position on the mountain (shown on a piste map that can be displayed); it's compatible with a smartphone and can display text messages too; MOD stands for Micro Optics Display. Another goggle – the Anon M1 – uses magnets to make changing lenses to suit different light a breeze.

↑ The Recon MOD Live display sits in your goggles and can tell you your speed, altitude, vertical descent, airtime of a jump and a whole lot more

As helmets have become more and more popular, the major ski brands have increased their share of the market; brands such as K2, Rossignol and Salomon are making helmets that are lighter and cheaper than those of many helmet specialists such as Smith and Giro. The latest technology to make helmets even more effective is MIPS (Multi-directional Impact Protection System); this has been developed by a Swedish company and protects your brain better in a fall. Brands such as Red, Poc, Scott and Sweet are now using it.

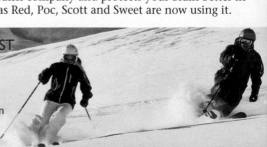

Smart apartments

Enjoy full independence in comfortable surroundings

by **Dave Watts**

Apartment holidays used to be the budget option for most people – at least on holidays to France. Shoehorn six people into a studio advertised for six and you'd have a cheap but not very comfortable time. Now things have changed, especially in France where lots of plush new apartment blocks have been built in recent years. Most have dishwashers, and many share a pool, sauna, steam room and gym to add to the pampering. Some even have comfortable furniture to relax in, too. Sure, the budget option still exists, but now you can have a comfortable apartment holiday with all the other advantages that it brings (see below). We've looked for smart apartments to recommend throughout the Alps and included them in the resort chapters.

I've been taking my annual ski holiday with my wife and a couple of friends in apartments for around 20 years. That's because we value the freedom an apartment gives you. You don't have to stick to meal times (and meals) dictated by the hotel or chalet staff; you can slob around in whatever clothes you want; you can go out and come back in whenever you choose. And, crucially in our case, you are free to have a big lunch up the mountain without worrying about having to eat a huge meal – which your chalet staff or hotel will have prepared for you – in the evening; if you lack the appetite for a full meal in the evening, you can buy snacks such as oysters, smoked salmon, pâté and local cheeses along with a good bottle of wine or two from the supermarket. If you are hungry, you can go out to a restaurant to eat. Staying in an apartment doesn't mean having to cook big meals – not for us anyway.

When we started this apartment lark, we couldn't find the sort of thing we were looking for in tour operators' brochures – all the

SKI COLLECTION

Some smart places are now well finished and furnished – this is a room in Pierre & Vacances' new 5-star Amara residence in Avoriaz ↓

apartments were of the 'cram 'em in and make it cheap' variety. So we ended up booking independently.

Now, at least in France – the country that used to have the smallest, most sordid apartments – a few tour operators (including those advertising in this chapter) offer some really smart and spacious places, mostly with leisure facilities such as pools, saunas and steam rooms. The French smart apartment concept was kick-started by apartments built by or opened in the Montagnettes and MGM names. Now they've been joined by other brands. PV Holidays launched its Pierre & Vacances Premium brand a couple of winters ago, and it now features residences in 11 resorts in the French Alps. Lagrange has 18 Alpine and six Pyrenean residences in its Prestige range.

So why the sudden change? Xavier Schouller of Peak Retreats and Ski Collection says, 'A lot of smart new residences have been built in the last five years because of tax breaks for people buying them – you get the VAT back if you agree to rent them out for several years, and French residents can set costs against income tax too. This is good news for people wanting to rent an apartment for a holiday – we now have over 200 residences on our books.' And a new classification scheme came fully into force in July 2012 and includes, for the first time, a 5-star rating (awarded, for example, to Pierre & Vacances' new Amara residence – see the Avoriaz chapter).

Ski Amis is best known as a catered chalet company, but it has moved into apartments in a big way. Instead of offering big residences such as the companies mentioned above do, it offers privately owned apartments and chalets, mainly in the Tarentaise, which includes the Trois Vallées, Paradiski and Espace Killy resorts.

↑ Many 4- and 5-star apartments have access to pool, hot tub, sauna, steam room and fitness facilities. This is Cîmes Blanches in La Rosière

PEAK RETREATS

It will have a staggering 6,000 to 8,000 available this winter from budget to luxury. Christine Van Zadelhoff, a director of Ski Amis, says, 'They will all be on our website, and you can access a selection by putting in either a budget and the number of people or more specific requirements such as three bedrooms, dishwasher, Wi-Fi, hot tub. You can book many online.'

Sadly, although there are luxurious apartments to be found in the other Alpine countries, few of them are featured by UK tour operators. Exceptions include the Swiss resorts of Grimentz (see the Val d'Anniviers chapter – bookable through Mountain Heaven, which also has French apartments in Courchevel, La Plagne and La Rosière), Champéry and Laax (the last two bookable through Erna Low as well as direct). As well as contacting local agencies to rent independently there are some good websites to try, such as www.holiday-rentals.co.uk and www.holidaylettings.co.uk. Interhome also has a wide selection.

WHAT TO CHECK BEFORE BOOKING

So what do you need to look for if you're booking what you hope is a smart apartment? Most importantly, you still need to check whether the space is enough to meet your expectations – and whether the number it's advertised for involves anyone sleeping in the living room, in bunk beds, on a mezzanine or in a cabin (which can mean an alcove). Also check the number of bathrooms and toilets. If the leisure facilities such as a pool, sauna, steam room and gym are important to you, check whether there is a charge for using these; sadly, there often is. And while most smart apartments come with a modern design, dishwasher and smartish furniture, we're sometimes disappointed by the lack of really comfy sofas and easy chairs – often because sofas double up as beds and are more comfortable to sleep in than sit on – so check that if you can.

Luxury chalets

Relax and enjoy a comfortable mountain home

by **Dave Watts**

The catered chalet holiday is a uniquely British idea. The deal, in case you're new to it, is that tour operators install their own cooks and housekeepers in chalets for the season and provide half-board plus teatime cake and, usually, travel from the UK. So you get the privacy and relaxed atmosphere of a temporary home in the mountains, without the hassle of self-catering or the cost of eating out in restaurants every night. In the beginning, in the 1960s and 70s, chalet holidays meant creaky old buildings with spartan furniture and paper-thin walls. My, how things have changed. When we first visited Méribel in 1974, en suite bathrooms were unheard of. They are now the norm. Spacious and plush living rooms with log fires are common (but spacious and plush bedrooms are less so). Spa facilities such as a sauna, steam room and hot tub are common too; some chalets even have a swimming pool. And all at prices we ordinary mortals can contemplate paying. It's these chalets that this chapter is about.

Because of the huge number of chalet holidays available, choosing the right one can be difficult. Some very helpful websites have been set up by agents, allowing you to sift out chalets that suit you best; some advertise in this chapter and elsewhere in the book.

The greatest concentration of smart chalets is found – surprise, surprise – in the British skier's favourite French resort, **Méribel**. Ski Total has a wide range of properties here, including three with the firm's top Platinum rating; they have hot tubs, of course – and a cinema and billiard room in the case of chalet Isba. Alpine Action has eight smart-looking chalets in various parts of the resort, most with sauna and/or hot tub and all with Freeview TV. Purple Ski has five top-notch and highly individual chalets – in good positions, with lovely interiors and outdoor hot tubs. Ski Olympic took a big step into the luxury market a few years back with the acquisition of

LE SKI

Study the brochures and websites and quiz the tour operator if you want a spacious and plush bedroom like this one in Le Ski's La Bouclia chalet in Val d'Isère ↓

the Parc Alpin, formerly run as a boutique hotel – 12 luxurious rooms, dinky swimming pool and sauna. Skiworld has two very swish places, especially La Ferme. Inghams has several chalets, including a few with sauna or hot tub. Other companies to consider include Consensio, Meriski and VIP.

Over the hill is **Courchevel**, a resort of parts (it has just renamed these parts – see p243 – but we are using the old names here). 1850 is well established as the 'smartest' resort in France, with the highest prices and the swankiest hotels and chalets. Operators such as Supertravel, Kaluma, Consensio and Scott Dunn have some lovely properties here. Ski Total has some chalets bordering on the luxury category. The big UK chalet centre is 1650, where Le Ski now has 17 chalets, sleeping from two to 22. Thirteen of them have sauna, steam or hot tub. And their flagship Scalottas Lodge even has a pool with a current to swim against. One of Ski Olympic's flagship Gold Collection chalets is here – chalet Monique, with TVs in the rooms and an outdoor hot tub. Skiworld has some smart-looking chalets here too – the 21-bed Estrella is one of its top places, with outdoor hot tub. Down in Le Praz, Mountain Heaven has a couple of chalets, including the very luxurious-looking Jardin d'Angele with sauna and outdoor hot tub.

La Tania, not far away off the road towards Méribel, has developed quite a range of comfortable chalet properties. Ski Amis has seven smart-looking places, all but one with outdoor hot tub and some with its Premium service. Le Ski has three neat-looking properties here. Alpine Action has three smart chalets near the centre, two with outdoor hot tubs.

In **Les Menuires** there are smart places on offer in the recently developed areas. Ski Olympic has four with saunas and hot tubs in Reberty; Ski Amis has several chalets with outdoor hot tubs in Les Bruyères and others with hot tubs and saunas in Le Bettex. And in **St-Martin** the Alpine Club has two luxurious chalets in the quiet hamlet of Villarabout, one newly built in traditional style with a

THE CHALET HOLIDAY – A PRIMER

Generally, you can either book a whole chalet (the smallest typically sleep six or eight) or share a larger chalet with others. This works surprisingly well, usually.

In the beginning, the cooking and cleaning was done by your chalet girl – often straight out of college or finishing school, and mainly intent on having a fun season. Chalet girls still exist, but now there are just as many boys, and grown-ups, including couples. It would be an exaggeration to say that service is generally professional, but training standards have certainly improved.

Breakfast is usually a buffet with the option of some cooked items. At teatime, cakes and tea are put out. Often beer and soft drinks are sold at modest prices, on an honesty basis. Dinner is a no-choice affair at a communal table, including wine – unlimited in quantity but often severely limited in quality. In 'luxury' chalets the wine may be better and you may be able to pay extra for better stuff. Once a week, the staff have a day off, and you're left to your own devices – most people like to dine in a restaurant, but you can buy in a picnic.

In chalet hotels you may have individual tables, or large ones you share with others; there may be a choice of dishes at dinner and there will usually be a bar.

double-height, open-plan living room and the other a beautiful 100-year-old farmhouse with spectacular views.

Val d'Isère is the great rival to Méribel in the French chalet business. The local specialist, YSE, has several very swish places. At the top end of Le Ski's programme are two very attractive places sharing a hot tub – La Bouclia and Pierre de Compia. Skiworld's 12 chalets include two of their top properties: Tolima, with sauna and steam room, and newly refurbished Madeleine, with outdoor hot tub. Ski Total has 15 smart places, including three very swanky chalets in their Platinum range – one with outdoor hot tub, two with saunas. Crystal's range includes three of its Finest properties, with saunas. Other companies to look at include Scott Dunn, Consensio and Le Chardon Mountain Lodges.

In **Tignes** Skiworld's programme includes some chalets with sauna and hot tub, and a swanky chalet hotel with pool and sauna. Ski Total has some very smart places with pool, hot tub and sauna, including two in their Platinum range. Crystal and Ski Olympic have some smart chalets too.

The other great French mega-area, Paradiski, offers lots of chalets in **La Plagne** and growing numbers at **Peisey-Vallandry**, on the Les Arcs side of the cable car from La Plagne. Few chalets stand out, but Ski Amis has a Premium service chalet in each of these resorts.

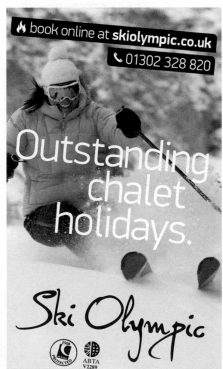

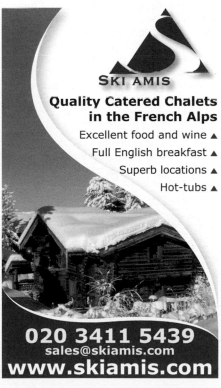

There are lots of chalets in **La Rosière**, but few notable ones. As well as Mountain Heaven's smart-looking Penthouse, with grand top-floor living space and outdoor hot tub, Ski Olympic has two chalets in a development with its own pool, sauna, steam room and hot tub. Skiworld has five smart mid-sized properties which, it is planned, will share a hot tub, steam room and two saunas for this winter. Crystal has three chalets in its Finest programme with access to saunas, hot tubs and in one case a pool.

Chalets are not common in **Avoriaz**, so it's good to see that Ski Total's handful includes one of its Platinum chalets, with sauna and log fire. Down the hill in **Les Gets**, the Ferme de Montagne is a lovely cross between a small hotel and a chalet – a beautifully renovated farmhouse with eight luxury bedrooms and gourmet food. They take short-break as well as week-long bookings.

Further south in **Alpe-d'Huez**, Ski Total, Skiworld and Inghams all have smart places with outdoor hot tub.

In Switzerland, **Verbier** is the chalet capital. Ski Total has the very smart chalet hotel Montpelier with panoramic pool, sauna and steam room, separate top-floor chalet within it and another separate smart chalet with floor-to-ceiling windows and a steam room. Other companies to look at include Ski Verbier.

Curiously, **Zermatt** has not traditionally been a great chalet resort, but Ski Total now has a remarkable 18 properties there – mostly with six or eight beds, a couple with more and some with sauna, steam room or hot tub. Skiworld has four chalet-apartments, including three very smart modern ones in the same building. Other companies to consider include Scott Dunn and Supertravel. In nearby **Saas-Fee**, Ski Total's chalet hotel Ambassador is right at the foot of the slopes with indoor pool. And Alpine Life has a lovely-looking chalet that we've had very good reports on, with hot tub, sauna and steam room. In cute little **Grimentz** (covered in our Val d'Anniviers chapter), Mountain Heaven has the very smooth slope-side Cole Ridge, with outdoor hot tub.

In Austria, **St Anton** is chalet central. Ski Total leads the pack, with a dozen places ranging from six beds to the cool 32-bed Inge, with wellness area. Crystal has some good places in Nasserein. Just over the hill in **St Christoph**, Inghams has its flagship chalet hotel – ski-in/ski-out, with a good-sized pool. Ski Total also has two smart chalet hotels (one with an indoor pool) in nearby **Lech**. Others to look at in this area include Flexiski, Kaluma and Scott Dunn.

In North America, only Skiworld now has much of a chalet programme, with good places in Aspen, Vail, Breckenridge, Winter Park and Whistler. Ski Independence has a chalet in Vail.

Smart hotels

For the perfect relaxing break

by **Dave Watts**

Much as we like staying in comfortable chalets and apartments, we also enjoy staying in good ski hotels – not poncy 5-star palaces but friendlier, comfortable well-run places with good food and good service. You'll find plenty of those in the 'Staying there' sections of the resort chapters which follow. Here we pick out a few of the best in both Europe and North America, including some of our own favourites.

Let's start with France. In many high, purpose-built resorts – Flaine and Avoriaz are prime examples – comfortable, friendly hotels of the type we like don't exist. But there are honourable exceptions. Tignes, for example, has the smartly rustic Campanules, upgraded to a 4-star last year. Les Menuires has the chalet-style 3-star Isatis with 17 suites, each with a hot tub on its balcony. Val Thorens has several really nice hotels. A favourite with our readers is the cosy, woody, ski-in/ski-out 3-star Sherpa, but we also like the elegant, very central 4-star Fitz Roy and the Val Thorens next door, which is being renovated this summer and is to reopen as a 4-star rather than a 3-star, we hear. The resort's first 5-star, the Altapura, opened last season, and a trusted reporter liked its 'unfussy atmosphere with tip-top food and service' but found it 'ferociously expensive'.

Courchevel has lots of extremely swanky places, but most leave us cold. Megève, where the old money still goes, excels in the rustic chic that seems to elude Courchevel – places like the Chalet St Georges, Fer à Cheval and Coeur de Megève. In Méribel, the Grand Coeur and the Allodis are the editorial favourites. In Val d'Isère the Christiania and Blizzard are our hotels of choice.

Lower resorts have many more traditional, family-run hotels, some featured in the advertisement opposite (as are a couple of those mentioned above) – we can personally vouch for the Macchi in Châtel and the Dahu and Bergerie in Morzine.

HOTELS-CHALETS DE TRADITION

Smartly rustic hotels with good food and service but no pretensions to grandeur – that's what we like ↓

TRADITIONAL OR MODERN – TAKE YOUR PICK

Austria has lots of reliable, traditional, family-run 4-star hotels where you can be sure of a comfortable time, substantial 4-, 5- or 6-course dinners and fabulous breakfast buffet spreads. Check out, for example, those advertising in our Lech and St Anton chapters. But Austria is also leading the way, along with some Swiss resorts, with 'hip hotels' (or 'design hotels' as it prefers to call them) where minimalism rules, along with smooth, hard surfaces of hardwood and glass. There are hotels like this in all sorts of resorts from glitzy Ischgl – the Madlein claims to have been the first 'design hotel' in the Alps – to rustic Mellau in the Vorarlberg-Bregenzerwald region, where we've enjoyed staying in the 4-star Sonne Lifestyle, and traditional Obergurgl, where we loved the 4-star Josl. In Switzerland, Zermatt is something of an Alpine design hot spot. Cool places there include the 5-star Omnia, reached by a lift that goes up through a rock, and the 4-star Cervo.

ITALIAN HIGHLIGHTS

A lot of Italian 3- and 4-star hotels can be pretty ordinary, so you have to know where to choose – read our chapters to find the best places. But some resorts have lots of good hotels. In Courmayeur, we've really enjoyed staying at two 4-stars, the Auberge de la Maison in Entrèves and the Villa Novecento a short walk from the centre; and reporters consistently praise the 3-star Bouton d'Or. Tiny Champoluc in the Monterosa region has the very comfortable and woody Breithorn and the Rouja, both 4-stars that we have stayed in very happily. And it has some great places up the hill too: Stadel Soussun, Rascard Frantze and the Aroula are all essentially mountain restaurants with charming rooms, and the new Hotellerie de Mascognaz is a lovingly restored group of stone chalets in a very isolated spot reached by skidoo. And we've had wonderful stays in two hotels in the Sella Ronda area of the Dolomites: La Perla in Corvara and the Rosa Alpina in San Cassiano – both have superb Michelin-starred food, lovely spacious and well-furnished rooms, fabulous service and a great relaxed atmosphere.

HOTELS-CHALETS DE TRADITION

Even high, purpose-built French resorts have some very comfortable hotels. This is the Campanules in Tignes ↓

NORTH AMERICAN OPTIONS

Not surprisingly, North America has its share of deeply comfortable lodgings, but some of it is too corporate and impersonal for us. In Aspen, we like the Little Nell, the historic Jerome and the boutique Lenado. At Deer Valley in Utah, Stein Eriksen Lodge is the place to go. Big chains sometimes deliver: the Four Seasons in Jackson Hole takes some beating. In Whistler, the Fairmont Chateau Whistler has the edge – but at Lake Louise another Fairmont Chateau comes second to the perfectly relaxing Post hotel.

A home in the snow

Make your dream of a bolt-hole in the snow come true

by **Dave Watts**

Buying a place in a ski resort is an ambition for lots of keen skiers and snowboarders. The last few years have been difficult times for the Alpine property market because of the economic problems – and for UK buyers it has been made even more difficult by the weakness of the pound. But in the last year or so the pound has strengthened against both the euro and the Swiss franc, so property prices have become more affordable again. And now may be your last chance to buy a new property in Switzerland before tough new laws effectively banning the building of second homes begin to bite.

Last March, the Swiss voted by a wafer-thin majority in a nationwide referendum to restrict the number of second homes in all communes to 20% of the total housing stock. New legislation is expected to be introduced that will effectively mean that after 1 January 2013 no new planning permits for second homes will be granted in most ski resorts (much to the annoyance of locals and many Swiss themselves because the ban applies not just to foreign-owned second homes but to Swiss-owned ones too).

Simon Malster, managing director of Investors in Property, has been selling property in the Alps for over 25 years. He says, 'The advice to potential buyers must be to buy now, as this will be the last opportunity to buy a new ski property in Switzerland. New properties can still be built after 1 January, as long as the building permits are processed this year. The new law may still allow communes to give building permits for schemes where the owner is obliged to rent their property out when not using it as these will be classed as investment properties, but we do not know for sure yet.' Prices are expected to rise in the next few years because the new law will reduce the supply of new properties coming on the market.

Investors in Property has properties for sale in several different

INVESTORS IN PROPERTY

Several resorts where Investors in Property has places for sale have fabulous views over the Rhône valley. This is the view from Veysonnaz ↓

↑ There are new-build apartments and chalets available in Grimentz – the rustic old village is just below these ski-in/ski-out places
INVESTORS IN PROPERTY

villages that link into the Verbier skiing area (see the end of our Verbier chapter). Malster says, 'These start at around SF800,000 for a three-bedroom chalet in Les Collons and go up to around SF3 million for a large four-bedroom chalet on the piste above Nendaz.' He also has apartments available in Veysonnaz, with fabulous views over the Rhône valley. Nick Barnes, a hotel and restaurant-owner from Long Melford, Suffolk, and a keen snowboarder, bought a place there a couple of years ago. Nick told me, 'We are absolutely delighted with it. My wife Angela and I go there several times a year; my dad uses it too and we rent it out when we aren't using it.'

Investors in Property also has apartments and chalets in and near the lovely old village of Grimentz (see our Val d'Anniviers chapter), with prices from around SF500,000, and in the brand new Titlis Resort near the gondola base in Engelberg, with prices from around SF300,000 for a studio to SF1 million for three bedrooms.

The company has been selling an increasing number of properties in Austria too. Until recently, foreigners were banned from buying in most of Austria, but new rules mean that some properties are now available to foreigners as long as they agree to make them available for renting when not using them personally – this also means that you save up to 20% VAT on the purchase price. Jessica Delaney of Investors in Property says, 'By far our most popular development has been one on the edge of Bramberg at the foot of the local Wildkogel ski area (with 55km of pistes) and right next to a gondola that opened a couple of seasons ago.' It is also just three minutes' drive from a gondola into the Kitzbühel ski area and within easy reach of many other areas such as Gerlos/Zell am Ziller and Kaprun (both around 30 minutes); prices start at 400,000 euros for two-bedroom penthouse apartments and around 500,000 euros for three- or four-bedroom chalets built to order.

France remains a favourite place for British skiers and boarders to buy property. Joanna Yellowlees-Bound, CEO of Erna Low Property, says: 'We are largely focusing on Arc 1950, which was built in the early to mid-2000s and is a traffic-free, ski-in/ski-out mini-resort with attractive buildings, outdoor pools and hot tubs, restaurants, bars, shops and ski school. Some of the original buyers find their

Pretty Kalinda Village will have gondola access to the snow-sure slopes of Tignes →

INVESTORS IN PROPERTY

circumstances have changed and now need to sell. Current prices are a bargain for purchasers, and UK sellers are still making a profit in £ terms because of the exchange rate change. We now have an office in Arc 1950 and currently have properties ranging from studios to two-bedroom duplexes.' A two-bedroom apartment might cost around 300,000 euros if, as with most, there is an agreement for a few years that you use it for a certain number of weeks a year and it goes in a rental pool the rest of the time. Erna Low also has apartments in a 4-star residence in Ste-Foy with prices for two- and three-bedroom places ranging from around 240,000 to 500,000 euros. It also has proper four- to six-bedroom chalets in Val d'Isère for 2.6 million to 9 million euros.

Simon Malster of Investors in Property says: 'The fastest-selling new development in the French Alps is Kalinda Village at Tignes 1800 (used to be called Tignes-les-Boisses). These are very high-quality apartments built by MGM with excellent leisure facilities and pool and a fast gondola into the slopes. You'll have all the advantages of Tignes' skiing without having to look at Tignes' older ugly buildings. And you are only 15 minutes by taxi from Val d'Isère, so you can enjoy its lively nightlife.' Prices range from around 210,000 euros for a one-bedroom apartment to 525,000 euros for four bedrooms, and there's an obligation to allow your property to be rented when you are not using it.

CONTACTS

Investors in Property
020 8905 5511
www.investorsinproperty.com

Erna Low Property
020 7590 1624
www.ernalowproperty.co.uk

WHAT TO LOOK FOR WHEN BUYING A HOME IN THE SNOW

First, you need to decide whether you want somewhere just for the skiing or whether you want a place in a resort that is attractive in the summer as well. Many French resorts developed after the 1950s can be deadly dull in summer, whereas others are attractive for summer as well as winter use. Second, if you want the place primarily for skiing and snowboarding, you will want reliable snow. And with global warming likely to continue, that means going for somewhere with access to high, snow-sure slopes and with good snowmaking. Third, if you intend to use the place frequently yourself, you will probably want somewhere within a couple of hours of an easily accessible airport. Fourth, make sure you understand the legal and taxation aspects – buying and running costs, all types of taxes and any resale restrictions. It is highly advisable to get professional advice on these. Fifth, make sure you understand any arrangements that you may be offered for 'sale and leaseback' or 'guaranteed return' from renting it out – these can vary enormously and may enable you to save money on the purchase price in some circumstances. Sixth, if you are intending to rent the property out yourself, don't overestimate the income you will get from it.

Some observations on skiing with children in tow

by Chris Gill

As regular readers will know, I am gradually coming to accept that my family skiing days are now over. I certainly hope to ski with my kids again but, with one of them now embarked on a career and the other recently graduated in philosophy and English, my interest in nurseries and snow gardens is dwindling towards zero. Applications are welcome from literate parents who would like to pick up the mantle of 'family skiing expert' in future editions. The pay's not great, let me tell you.

For the moment though, I remain in charge here, and have sifted through a mountain of email to pick out and then answer some of the questions readers have sent in during the year. Most of them seem to have a cost-cutting theme – not surprising in these hard times.

YOUR QUESTIONS ANSWERED

IM, Tonbridge My husband and I don't like the idea of handing over two-year-old Tamsin and four-year-old Freddy to a kindergarten, so we plan to take turns looking after them while the other goes off skiing with our friends and their older children. Is there any alternative to buying ski passes by the day?

CG You're insane. All you need are earplugs (easily found in any branch of Boots) so that you can't hear the screams as you walk away from the kindergarten. But I will address your question. If you were to go away for a decent period, some of the 'ski any X days out of Y' passes might help. But a smarter solution, and one that should be widely adopted, is the pass now offered in Austria's SkiWelt (Söll, Ellmau and neighbours), which is transferable between husband and wife. The wife is limited to skiing on sunny days. Sorry, made that bit up.

SB, Leeds We're planning to take our two kids to the France, and not looking forward to the cost. To keep the cost down, my wife wants to go to a tiny off-the-beaten-track resort. I want to go to Méribel, as usual. Please arbitrate.

CG Your wife has a point, but that's not to say you should cave in. Stand your ground for a while, and then grudgingly compromise. Suggest a chalet holiday in Les Menuires, a couple of lift rides from Méribel but with much lower prices. There are some excellent family specialist tour operators here, too. You might find the chalet people will do you packed lunches, in which case you'll be excited to hear that there is now information on picnic rooms at the end of our mountain restaurants sections in many resort chapters.

SR, Fulham Even with 'concessions', buying lift passes for our brood of three – all of skiing age – would be a big expense. How can we get round it?

CG Infants generally ski free – the trick is to find resorts where your kids qualify as infants. The age limit is typically five in France but as high as eight in Italy. If the kids are older, but beginners, look for resorts with free lifts which might be all they need for the first day or three. Then you're looking at concessions, where the discounts and age limits vary, and special family tickets.

NB, Dundee I'm appalled at the cost of children's ski clothing, particularly because the kids will of course grow out of whatever I buy. What are our options?

THE PERFECT FAMILY HOLIDAY? THE LOW-DOWN ON CHALET HOTELS

The catered chalet holiday is as popular as ever, especially with families. Since en suite bathrooms and comfy sofas became the norm rather than the exception, the attractions of the chalet – more private and less formal than hotels – have increased considerably. Now, more people are discovering the merits of the chalet's bigger cousin, the chalet hotel.

Chalet operators have for years set the pace in childcare. It was a natural extension of hiring British gels as cooks and housekeepers to hire a few as nannies, too; then all the operator had to do was identify a suitable room in a suitable chalet, and bingo – a crèche was born. For British parents unable to handle the brutality of French nurseries, the chalet was the obvious solution.

Chalet hotels are a larger version of the same thing, with some additional advantages. Some are purpose-built, but usually they are based on buildings that have operated as proper hotels. As a result, bedrooms typically are more generous than in chalets. Facilities are often better – there is likely to be a bar (with prices below resort norms, if you're lucky), and there may be a swimming pool, spa or gym, for example. There may be a menu choice at dinner.

Two of the most long-established tour operator firms dominate the family chalet hotel market. Esprit Ski was the original family chalet specialist; its programme is still dominated by standard-size chalets – in total about 50 – but it now also includes five chalet hotels. Mark Warner has always focused on chalet hotels, and has crèches in most of its 11 properties. The editorial Gill family took several successful holidays with these firms in the days when the kids needed even more attention than they do now.

Strikingly, these firms major on top resorts. They both have chalet hotels with childcare in Courchevel 1850, Méribel, Val d'Isère and La Plagne. Esprit's flagship is the super-cool Deux Domaines at Belle-Plagne, which has a decent pool and spa – young children are not allowed in the latter – and a good ski-in/ski-out location on the edge of the village. The other Esprit resorts are Saas-Fee and Alpe-d'Huez. Mark Warner also has family-oriented properties in Tignes, Les Deux-Alpes and St Anton.

CG First, a winter sun holiday. But if that's not on ... three suggestions. Bear in mind that jackets, in particular, don't need to be made specially for skiing; look at what's available in cheaper outdoor shops. Find out when your local branch of Aldi is getting its annual delivery of ski wear, and what they will be offering. And get on the internet to find people selling secondhand kit nearby.

WHO TO GO WITH?

You can, of course, have family skiing holidays more or less completely unaided. Or you can call on the support of resort nurseries, and childcare facilities associated with resort ski schools. But huge numbers of British families are wedded to the comfortable childcare arrangements offered by British tour operators.

The firms advertising in this chapter are mostly small, specialized companies going to a small range of resorts that they know inside out (only one resort, in the cases of Snowbizz and Ski 2). They are basically owner-operated, so you can expect them to be very responsive. Most operate catered chalets (explained in our chapter on luxury chalets, on page 44). Esprit Ski is a bit different – a chalet operator on a much bigger scale, offering holidays in 10 French resorts plus an interesting sprinkling across the rest of the Alps. And don't forget that there are mainstream operators such as Crystal, which operate childcare in a selection of the many resorts where they sell holidays.

The list on the facing page shows who goes to which resorts; it covers the advertisers in this chapter and Crystal, to give you an idea of your options. Note that some of the smaller operators don't have full childcare facilities in every chalet or even every resort.

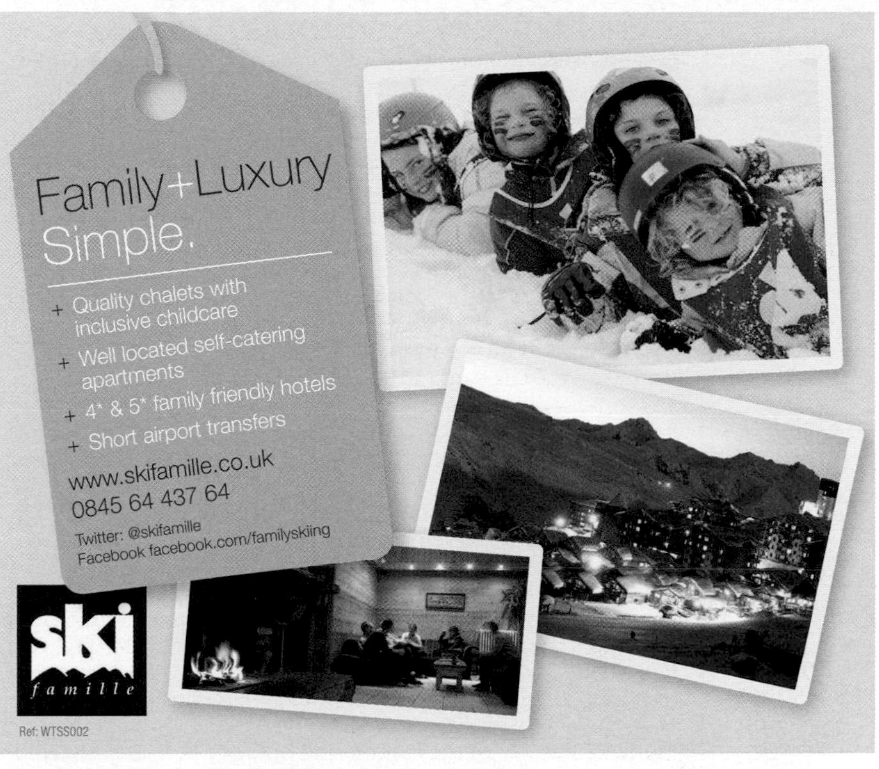

SKI 2 RACING – COACHING FOR YOUR KIDS?

The recent success of Ryan, Alysha and Charlotte Brown (the children of one of Ski 2's directors) in ski races across Europe is testimony to the expertise of their outstanding Italian race coaches in the Monterosa resort of Champoluc.

Ski 2 can now offer other youngsters the chance to benefit from the same training routine, while continuing their schooling in Champoluc.

Children joining the Ski 2 Racing programme will spend their mornings race training with local coaches and their afternoons furthering their education with two fully trained English teachers. 'House parents' will supervise the youngsters at other times, and the Ski 2 resort team will offer any other support and guidance the youngsters might need to make the most of their experience.

Accommodation will be in the family-run 3-star Hotel Petit Prince, which offers doorstep skiing at the ski area of Antagnod, close to Champoluc.

Prices – including airport transfers, full board accommodation, educational tuition, leisure supervision, full ski race programme and full area lift pass – will start at around £1,200 per week, with reductions for longer stays.

WHO GOES WHERE?

Austria

Obergurgl Esprit Ski. **Niederau** Crystal. **Scheffau** Crystal. **St Anton** Esprit Ski.

France

Alpe-d'Huez Esprit Ski, Crystal. **Les Arcs** Esprit Ski, Ski Amis. **Ardent (Avoriaz)** Family Ski. **Les Coches (La Plagne)** Family Ski. **Courchevel** Esprit Ski, Ski Amis, Mountain Heaven. **Les Gets** Esprit Ski, Ski Famille. **Les Menuires** Family Ski, Ski Amis, Ski Famille. **Méribel** Esprit Ski, Ski Amis. Morzine Mountain Heaven. **Peisey-V'dry (Les Arcs)** Esprit Ski, Mountain Heaven, Ski Amis. **La Plagne** Crystal, Esprit Ski, Family Ski, Mountain Heaven, Ski Amis. **Puy-St-Vincent** Snowbizz. **La Rosière** Esprit Ski, Mountain Heaven. **St-Martin-de-B'ville** Ski Amis. **La Tania** Ski Amis. **Tignes** Crystal, Esprit Ski, Ski Amis. **Val d'Isère** Esprit Ski, Ski Amis. **Val Thorens** Ski Amis.

Italy

Champoluc (Monterosa) Ski 2. **Claviere (Montgenèvre)** Crystal. **Selva** Esprit Ski. **Val di Fassa** Crystal.

Switzerland

Grimentz Mountain Heaven. **Saas-Fee** Esprit Ski, Family Ski.

Corporate ski trips

A great way to motivate your staff and clients

by **Dave Watts**

The market for corporate ski trips used to be big. A few seasons ago we had 13 advertisers in this chapter. Now we have one. Obviously, in difficult economic times, companies cut back on expenditure; and corporate hospitality is an easy target. It is still happening, but companies aren't spending as much and there aren't as many 'jollies' where staff and clients just go away to bond and enjoy themselves.

Amin Momen of Momentum Ski, which does a lot of corporate business, says, 'The banks have dropped out, but we still do well with corporate business from other sectors – both entertaining clients and training and motivating staff internally. Human resources people are keen to take staff away for a few days for team building and to try out new experiences (like skiing or snowboarding) as well as having productive meetings to generate sales development ideas, for example. They come back refreshed and better at their jobs.' Last season the trips Momentum organized included one for staff from an insurance company to Grindelwald in Switzerland and another for managers from a restaurant chain to Courmayeur in Italy; one financial group took clients to Megève in France, and another went to St Anton in Austria. 'Typically there are around 20 in a group,' says Momen, but each year Momentum runs a three-day trip on behalf of Lambert Smith Hampton for around 250 people in the commercial property industry; it includes an invitation-only forum that takes place before the ski day.

Mountain Heaven is a company that has catered chalets and self-catering accommodation in four French resorts and in Grimentz in Switzerland. Nick Williams, its MD, says, 'For the last four winters we've pioneered a new concept of great-value corporate trips. A firm of management consultants takes over all our self-catered accommodation in La Plagne Montalbert for its staff. They arrive from all over – the UK, Spain, Germany, Italy, France, USA – and we organize transfers from whatever airport suits them or from Aime railway station. They hold a two-day conference in Montalbert's own conference centre midweek but are free to arrive early or leave late to enjoy time on the slopes – they have the apartments for the whole week. We also deliver breakfast each day and organize lunches and dinners – including a dinner up the mountain.'

Roger Walker of Ski 2 (a company that specializes in Champoluc in the Monterosa area of the Italian Alps) says, 'Our corporate clients tend to be different from those of other companies. Most are very budget conscious, nearly all want to go out over a weekend, and the whole thing is based more on internal team bonding than on entertaining clients. Most don't want us to organize meeting facilities for them either – so we are going against the trend of cutting down on "jollies". But with some of the companies, the staff contribute to the cost – they may pay for the accommodation themselves while the company arranges the flights, picks up the tab for wine with dinner, or pays for lift passes, ski rental and lessons, for example. We'll pick guests up from any of six airports within striking distance – companies like the flexibility we offer.'

THE MOMENTUM SKI FESTIVAL – CRANS-MONTANA, VALAIS, 14 TO 17 MARCH 2013

The Momentum Ski Festival will be held again this season after its very successful launch in 2012. It will incorporate the City Ski Championships, which Momentum Ski has been running for 14 seasons, and two new events: the Financial Times Alpine Business Forum – which will be chaired by FT Weekend Editor Caroline Daniel with a panel discussing current affairs, global issues and the state of the markets – and a comedy and music festival, which is co-hosted by Marcus Brigstocke. A full programme of après-ski, stand-up comedy, live bands and big-name DJs will be organized, as well as drinks parties hosted by Cavendish Ware and the Valais, and three dinners with entertainment, each at a different venue and culminating in the prize-giving dinner on the Saturday.

Celebrity guests attending the festival are likely to include Damon Hill, Colin Jackson, Heston Blumenthal, Frank Gardner, Olympic gold medallists Tommy Moe and Antoine Dénériaz, and leading UK ski figures Graham Bell, Konrad Bartelski and Matt Chilton.

With the City Ski Championships, two races are held on the Friday: the Radar Trap Challenge (speed skiing) and the Accenture Dual Parallel Slalom. But the main event is the Saturday GS race on the World Cup Piste Nationale. On both days there'll be a race-side buffet in the Savills Alpine Homes race paddocks. And on the Saturday there'll be a DJ on the hill. Sunday will be free for skiing. The Montana Ski School will run performance clinics, and exclusive Zai skis will be available to test.

For more details call 020 7371 9111 or visit www.cityskichampionships.com.

MOMENTUM SKI / MARTIN BOND

HOW TO ORGANIZE IT AND WHERE TO GO

Organizing the whole thing yourself is a real hassle. People based in different areas of the country are likely to want to fly from different airports and at different times of day. And many hotels in the Alps don't want to take bookings for just a few days, or to provide the number of single rooms that you might want. Numbers are likely to change as people drop out for various reasons. Your group is likely to have skiers and boarders of widely differing ability and maybe some complete beginners or non-skiers, so you need to organize ski instructors or guides to teach or lead different groups. You need to organize equipment (and maybe clothing) rental and lift passes. You might want to organize 'jollies' such as dinner up the mountain and a torchlit descent back or a lunchtime BBQ on the piste, or a 'treasure hunt' event for teams on the slopes. And you might need rooms to hold business meetings in.

But that's what you use a tour operator or event organizer for – to deal with all the hassle and organize things on your behalf. And the great thing is that they don't charge you any extra for doing all that – it's part of the business to them.

Because corporate trips tend to be short, you'll want to keep the travel time to the minimum. Transfer times from airports to resorts generally range from one to four hours, and you'll probably want to operate at the lower end of that range if you can. That's why resorts such as Courmayeur and Champoluc in Italy (close to Geneva and Turin airports), Engelberg in Switzerland (close to Zürich), Kitzbühel in Austria (close to Salzburg and Innsbruck) and Garmisch in Germany (close to Munich) are popular. All these resorts have hotels that are happy to offer short break bookings too.

Flying to the snow

Flights and transfers for independent travellers

by **Rebecca Miles**

There are lots of flights to the Alps and Pyrenees; and you can often avoid the crowds by opting for quieter, queue-free regional airports. But finding your way through the minefield of routes and extra charges is hard work – and the extras can double or triple the basic cost.

So-called budget airlines go to mainstream airports such as Geneva and Milan but also to smaller places, making it easier to get to many resorts in places such as Austria, the Dolomites, the Pyrenees, Slovenia and eastern Europe. You'll find a wide choice of affordable transfers too. National carriers can be competitive, both on cost and destination, so don't ignore them when planning a trip. But note that some winter routes stop operating before the season ends.

THE LEADING GROUP

EasyJet has a big range of flights, many to Geneva, from a broad choice of UK hubs. Other key destination airports include Zürich, Innsbruck, Munich and Salzburg. From Stansted, Ljubljana is handy for Slovenian resorts and eastern Austria.

Ryanair operates mainly from Stansted, with a few flights from other UK airports. Routes/frequency change regularly, but a wide choice is offered – including Lourdes (for the western and central Pyrenees) and Memmingen (western Germany and Austria). New for 2012/13 is a weekly flight from Birmingham to Milan Bergamo.

Jet2.com has flights to Geneva, Salzburg, Chambéry and Toulouse – mainly from northern England, but also from Edinburgh, Glasgow and Belfast – available through its dedicated ski website. New for 2012/13 are Leeds Bradford and Manchester flights to Grenoble, up to twice a week, and the reintroduction of a weekly service from East Midlands to Geneva and Chambéry.

Flybe serves Geneva, Salzburg, Berne, Milan, Chambéry, Nice and, unusually, Stuttgart (handy for Germany and western Austria) – mainly from Southampton but also from Exeter and Birmingham. New for 2012/13 are flights from Newcastle to Bergen, Norway.

British Airways goes to lots of relevant airports, including Innsbruck, from a variety of UK ones. **Swiss** has lots of flights to Zürich and Geneva, some to Basel.

Monarch is launching new scheduled routes to Grenoble, Friedrichshafen and Munich, from Gatwick, Luton, Manchester, Birmingham and Leeds Bradford, up to four times a week. In addition to these new routes, Monarch operates year-round flights to Milan, Venice and Verona for the southern Alps and Dolomites.

PRICING IT UP ...

Charges and rules for baggage and for equipment carriage vary and change frequently, so it's important to check the detail. We noted EasyJet charging different fees for the first bag, dependent on destination (£18-£34 return). Ryanair permits either a standard 15kg for a first bag, priced at from £30 return, or 20kg from £50; but skis/board carriage will set you back from £50 return. BA effectively charges for skis: one checked-in bag is free up to 23kg; additional bags on European flights cost from £68 return.

ONLINE BOOKING

Most budget airlines expect you to book online, and many charge less if you book such 'extras' as hold baggage and ski carriage online too. The web addresses of the airlines we list are given as links on our website (click on Directory).

THE EXTRAS

Charges on top of basic flight costs vary between airlines. In July 2012, we looked at three (Jet2, EasyJet and Flybe) for flights to Geneva for a week in February 2013. Basic return fares varied from £96 to £231. Extra charges included:

1 checked-in 20kg (22kg for Jet2) bag return .... £14-£25

1 skis/snowboard/ boots return.. £50-£60

Check-in fee ... £0-£12

Credit card payment fee ..... £5-£9

These can add over £100 to the original cost, and the priciest of our three flights worked out at £328.52.

Also, you might be offered priority check-in/boarding for, say, £21.50 and insurance for, say, £12 (which may not cover winter sports adequately – do check). Packing ski boots separately is considered a second bag and costs extra – though most airlines allow boots too if you pay extra for ski carriage.

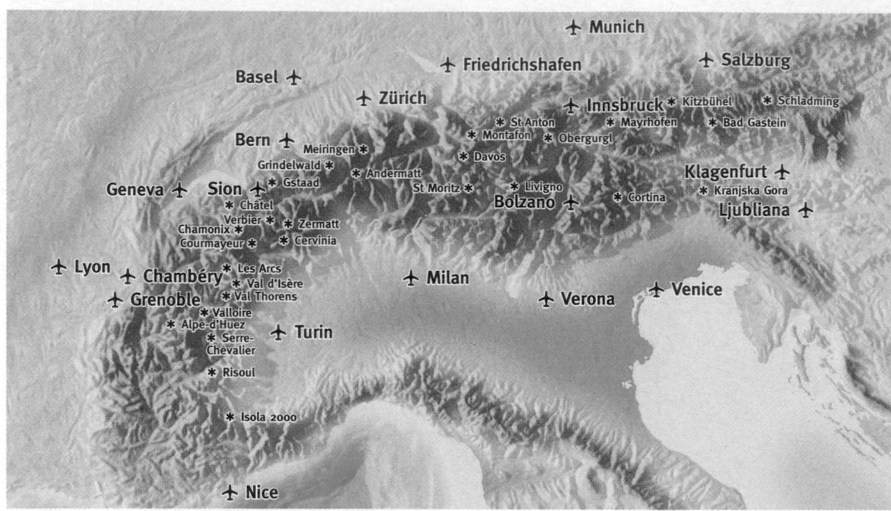

Swiss and Lufthansa still allow one set of skis and boots free in addition to a 23kg bag.

There are other extras that inflate the price too (see margin panel). And with some airlines you can now reserve seats or pre-book a meal on board – all for a fee, of course. Airport costs such as drop-off and trolley fees can also add to the overall spend.

As we went to press, we heard that one airline is experimenting on one non-ski route with charging for hand baggage unless it is small and will fit under the seat in front. Let's hope this doesn't catch on (but we fear it might).

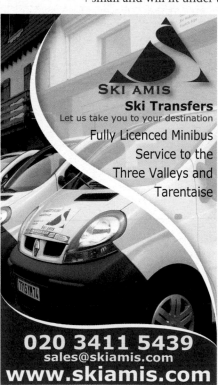

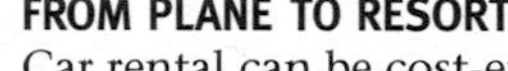

FROM PLANE TO RESORT

Car rental can be cost-effective for a short break or with a group – but, again, watch for hidden extras.

Most Swiss and Austrian airports have good public transport links to lots of resorts. Special rail passes may be cheaper than return tickets (see page 450) for Swiss passes). In Italy, buses run to the Dolomites from Verona and Innsbruck, and to the Aosta valley from Turin.

Reaching French resorts is slightly trickier, but private minibus transfers are plentiful. Tour operator Ski Amis offers a public shared minibus service from Geneva and Chambéry to the Three Valleys, La Plagne Montalbert and Peisey-Vallandry on Saturdays. Prices start at £65 per person return. Holiday Taxis (www.holidaytaxis.com) covers over 400 resorts from major airports and some stations. Transfer companies and their relevant links are listed on our website: www.wheretoskiandsnowboard.com (click on Directory).

Travelling by rail

Make tracks to the snow (greener ones)

by **Rebecca Miles**

Whether you're an enthusiast or not, rail travel has its advantages for travelling to the snow. As well as the leisurely journey aspect, taking the train can avoid overcrowded airports, traffic congestion and high baggage charges to fly. There are efficient high-speed links between London and Paris, and daytime services to French resorts can take as little as 7.5 hours (with Eurostar direct). Some French resorts have their own railway stations, so transfers can be relatively straightforward. Here we sum up the main options.

The starting point of most European rail trips is likely to be the Eurostar high-speed train from London St Pancras or from Ashford or Ebbsfleet stations in Kent.

DIRECT SERVICES TO THE FRENCH ALPS

The fastest way to France is Eurostar's direct services to the Tarentaise region – such as to Moûtiers (for the Trois Vallées) and to Bourg-St-Maurice (for Les Arcs, La Rosière, Ste-Foy, Tignes and Val d'Isère). Overnight services allow you eight days on the slopes. Daytime services give you the regular six days, the same as flying. Generally allow an hour or so for onward bus transfers, depending on the resort – though Moûtiers to Méribel takes a lot less.

Overnight trains are expected to depart from London every Friday evening from 21 December 2012 to 12 April 2013. Last season, these left at 7.38pm and arrived at Bourg at 6.41am. The return service left Bourg at 10.15pm on Saturdays and arrived in London at 7.16am. There are no special sleeping arrangements – you doze (or not) in your seat. The daytime service is expected to run on Saturdays from 15 December 2012 until 13 April 2013. Last season, it departed at 10am, arriving in Bourg by 7pm. The return service left Bourg at 9.48am and arrived at 4.11pm.

A Standard adult return cost from £149 (non-flexible) last season. A Standard Premier ticket (non-flexible) – which gets you a bigger seat pitch and basic meals – cost £229. There were discounts for the under-25s and over-60s, and semi-flexible fares were available. Seats can also be booked as part of a package holiday.

INDIRECT SERVICES TO THE FRENCH ALPS

The French regular rail network (SNCF) can get you to lots of places such as Chambéry, Briançon and Grenoble for onward buses to more southerly resorts. For Chamonix, an overnight train from Paris Austerlitz, via St-Gervais, would put you in resort by 10am next morning; prices from £150 to £200 return. A pre-bookable taxi service to get you between the Paris stations is offered through snowcarbon.co.uk; you ring or email to reserve a place, and the driver will meet your train. It costs 50 euros each way for up to eight people; ski carriage is included. SNCF has saver cards for young and older travellers. The 12-25 Card costs about £45 and entitles you to 25% or 60% discount, depending on times/days and peak periods. The Senior Card (for over 60s) costs £50 and gets you 25% to 50% discount.

HIGH-SPEED TO SWITZERLAND

The Swiss do rail travel very well, with lots of options. Allow travel times of around 10–12 hours from London. High-speed trains from Paris can get you in resort by evening – assuming a lunchtime departure. Lots of resorts, such as Andermatt, Davos, Engelberg, Grindelwald, Klosters and Zermatt, have convenient local railway stations. It's easy to get to others, such as Saas Fee and Verbier, by a combination of train and post bus. Eurostar has connecting fares to five major Swiss cities, including Geneva, Zürich and Basel; journeys are also bookable (via Rail Europe) from Paris to 18 other Swiss hubs – such as Chur, Sion and Visp. Two high-speed Lyria des Neiges routes will run this winter. The first, from Paris Gare de Lyon, will stop at Sion, Aigle and Brig, which give access to lots of resorts. The second, in conjunction with Eurostar, will run from London to Lille then Brig. Times and prices were yet to be confirmed at the time of going to press.

It is most likely to be cheaper to buy a return ticket to the Swiss border and a Swiss Transfer ticket (from £90) for onward travel rather than a straightforward return ticket to your destination resort. This Transfer ticket allows one return journey from the point of entry into Switzerland to any other station in the country, regardless of distance – you have to buy it in the UK before you travel. For more about Swiss train ticket options, see page 450.

AUSTRIA AND GERMANY

The great advantage of rail travel to Austria is that many resorts have their own convenient stations. City Night Line is part of a large network of European rail services, with weekend sleeper trains departing from Paris and Amsterdam. Winter services from Paris Est include trains direct to Innsbruck or Wörgl (Fridays), arriving late morning; or via Munich (Sat, Sun, Mon). Onward connections can get you to resorts such as St Anton, Zell am See, Mayrhofen and the SkiWelt. From Munich it's an easy hop to Garmisch-Partenkirchen. Typical fares start from £200, including Eurostar to Paris. Check out www.citynightline.de for more details.

THE ITALIAN JOB

Most Italian resorts are hard work to reach by train, but there are exceptions. The Dolomites are close to the line through Trento and Bolzano, reachable from Munich (as an onward connection from the City Night Line), from Innsbruck to the north, or from Verona to the south. Resorts of the Val di Susa are easily reached via trains from Paris Gare de Lyon to Turin and Milan. These run twice a day and stop at Bardonecchia and Oulx – 15 minutes by bus from Sauze d'Oulx and a bit further from Sestriere. A flexi-return fare from Paris starts at £90. Journeys can be booked through Rail Europe.

PLANNING AND BOOKING

Rail fares have few of the extra charges that you have to watch for with air fares. But the cheapest fares are best secured early. Booking is normally only up to 90 days in advance. Main sites include: Rail Europe (www.raileurope.co.uk), Eurostar (www.eurostar.com), Swiss railways (www.sbb.ch/en) or Austrian railways (www.oebb.at). Some local lines such as Martigny to Le Châble (for Verbier) and Bex up to Villars may have to be organized separately. Other useful websites include www.seat61.com and www.snowcarbon.co.uk.

Drive to the Alps

And ski where you please

by **Chris Allan**

Because the Channel gets in the way, because many of us habitually take package holidays by air, and because the British Isles are the centre of the low-cost airline business, we're inclined to travel to the Alps by air. The French, the Germans and the Dutch, in contrast, mainly go by car. But for British skiers, too, driving to the Alps can have lots of advantages.

Even for those going on a pretty standard week in the Alps, many people find driving is less hassle than taking flights. For families (especially those going self-catering), it simplifies the job of moving half the contents of your house to the Alps. If there are four or five people in your party, the cost can be low. If you fancy something a bit more adventurous than a standard week in one resort, taking a car opens up the exciting possibility of visiting several resorts in one trip – maybe even making up your plans as you go, so that you go wherever the snow is looking best.

The experience of driving out can be a pleasant one. Crossing the Channel is slick and painless using the fast and frequent Eurotunnel Le Shuttle trains through the tunnel – read the feature panel below. And although cross-Channel ferries can't compete with Le Shuttle in terms of crossing time, they are faster than they have ever been (as well as more comfortable).

EASY DOES IT WITH EUROTUNNEL LE SHUTTLE

We had a lot of skiing to cram into March last season, so for the first time for a while we drove out to the Alps, using the tunnel. We'd forgotten just how painless Le Shuttle is.

The terminal at Folkestone is very straightforward to reach. Junction 11A of the M20 takes you directly to the check-in gates. We left north London about 6am, and had checked in by 8.15am.

Check-in deadline is half an hour before departure. The check-in system recognizes your number plate and without human intervention prints your boarding pass. After a quick visit to the shops in the terminal to pick up the stuff you've forgotten, it's into the marshalling yard until you're called forward to drive on to the train.

If you're near the front of the queue, once on the train you drive almost the whole length of it before parking – and that will mean a quick exit at the other end. Within minutes you're gliding into the tunnel. If you might want a quick nap during the crossing, you'll probably appreciate earplugs.

We were on the autoroute south of Calais 75 minutes after we arrived at Folkestone, and on course for a dinner date in Geneva at 7.30. Heavy rain and Friday night traffic in the city delayed us a bit, but we still made it to Megève in time for a drink in the hotel bar before bed.

EUROTUNNEL

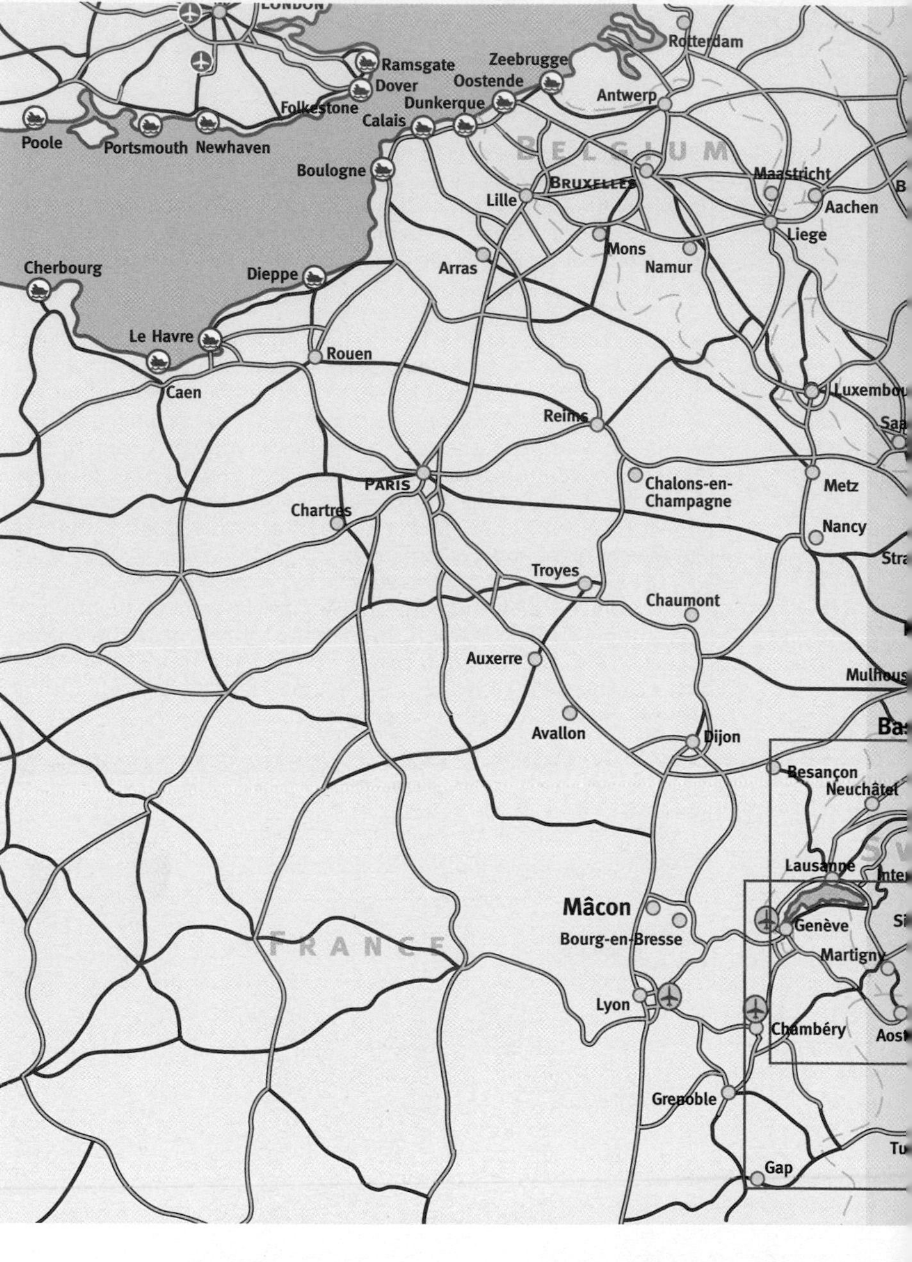

This map should help you plan your route to the Alps, at least in outline. All the main routes from the Channel and all the routes up into the mountains funnel through (or close to) three 'gateways', picked out on the map in larger type – Mâcon in France, Basel in Switzerland and Ulm in Germany.

Decide which gateway suits your destination, and pick a route to it from your planned arrival port at the Channel. Occasionally, using different Channel ports will lead you to use different gateways.

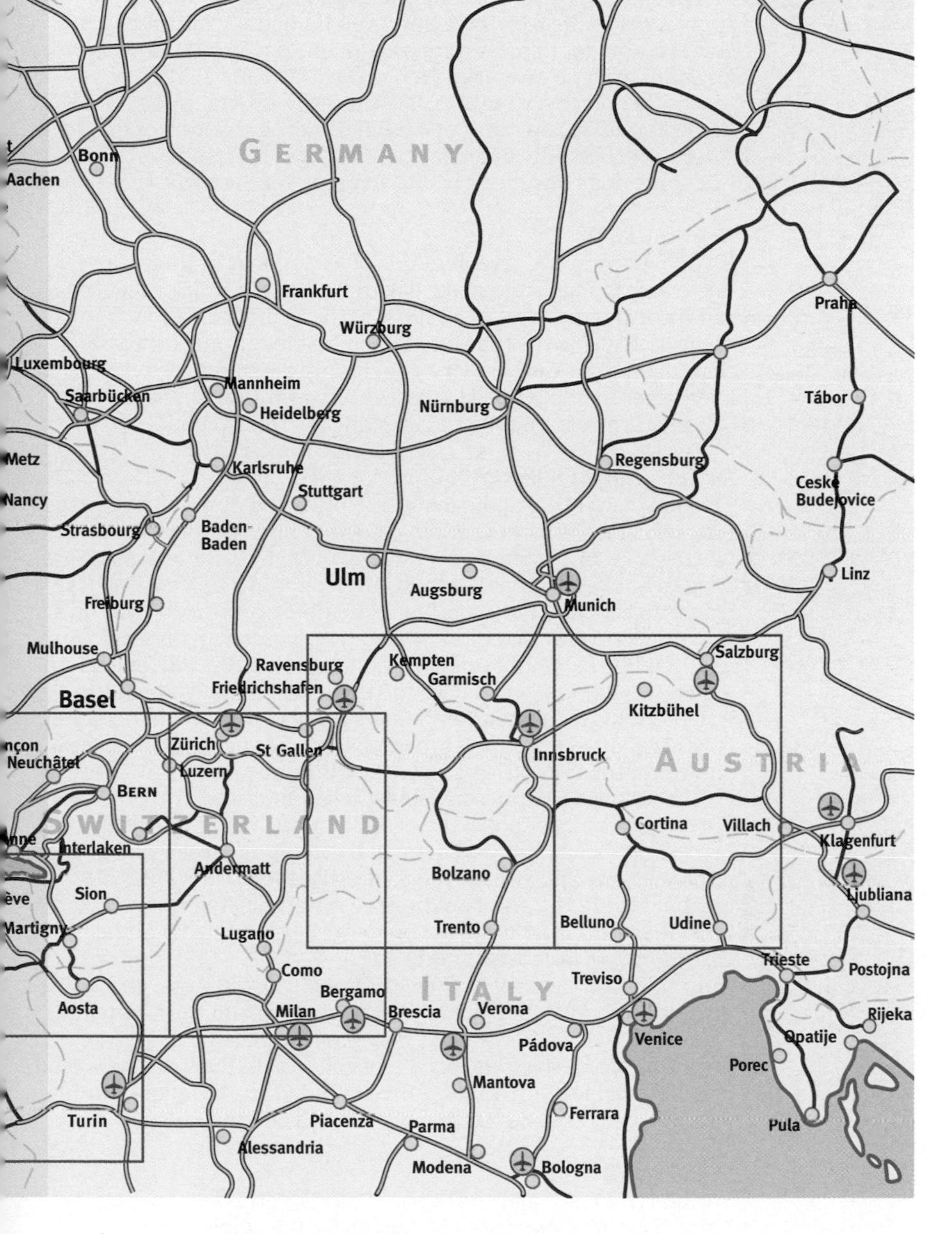

The boxes on the map correspond to the areas covered by the more detailed maps in our introductory chapters on the four main Alpine countries, starting on these pages:

Austria page 98
France page 198
Italy page 382
Switzerland page 448

The motorway networks in north-eastern France and on the approaches to the Alps have improved immensely over the years. You can now get to most resorts easily in a day from south-east England, in some cases using motorways virtually all the way.

Another plus point is that you can easily extend the standard six-day holiday. You can spend a full day on the slopes on the final Saturday (a blissfully quiet day on the slopes of most resorts) and then drive for a few hours before stopping for the night.

AS YOU LIKE IT

If you fancy visiting several resorts, you can do it in three ways: use one resort as a base and make day trips to others; use a valley town as a base, and make resort visits from there; or go on a tour, moving on every day or two. There are some notable regional lift passes that might form the basis of a trip, in Austria especially – cheaper and slicker than buying day passes each morning. Check out the Ski Amadé pass in our Austria introduction, for example.

AROUND THE ALPS IN SEVEN DAYS

The most rewarding approach to exploring the Alps – although the least relaxing – is to go touring, enjoying the freedom of going where you want, when you want. Out of high season there's no need to book accommodation in advance. And a touring holiday doesn't mean you'll be spending more time on the road than on the piste, provided you plan your route carefully. An hour's drive after the lifts have shut is all it need take, normally. It does eat into your après-ski time, of course. The major thing that you have to watch out for with a touring holiday is the cost of accommodation. Checking into a resort hotel for a night or two doesn't come cheap, and can seem a rip-off. But valley hotels can be very good value.

The following chapter has some suggestions for a trip to France. Austria offers lots of possibilities. In the west, you could take in the best skiing the country has to offer, by combining the Arlberg resorts with Ischgl, and maybe Sölden. Further east, it is easy to combine Hintertux and Mayrhofen with the SkiWelt resorts and Kitzbühel. And the Ski Amadé pass is a cheap way to combine the Gastein valley with Schladming, say.

In Italy you can stay in the beautiful old city of Aosta and visit a different resort (such as Courmayeur, Cervinia and the Monterosa resorts) each day. Elsewhere in Italy, touring makes more sense.

Switzerland also offers lots of possibilities. In the west, you could combine Verbier with Val d'Anniviers and Crans-Montana. Further east, you could start in Davos/Klosters and end up in Flims.

BE PREPARED

Winter tyres make a big difference to a car's grip on ice and snow. These tyres are compulsory in Austria for the whole winter period. In other Alpine countries, we understand that they are not; but many 'experts' warn that if you go without them and have an incident you could be in trouble. You may still need chains in really deep snow. But winter tyres will keep you going in surprisingly difficult conditions if your car also has traction control, to stop the wheels spinning. This usually forms part of the electronic stability systems now fitted to many new cars (sometimes as an option).

Cars hired in Austria and Switzerland should always be equipped with winter tyres. Cars hired elsewhere may not be.

ATTENTION SVP!

The UK motoring organizations say that when driving in France you must now carry:

- a warning triangle
- a reflective jacket that you can put on in the event of a breakdown or an accident, kept in the main passenger compartment – not stowed in the boot
- an unused, in-date, French-certified breathalyser – the advice is to carry two, in practice, in case you want to use one.

If you have a satnav, it must not be capable of displaying French speed camera locations. They say software updates are available with this data removed. A set of spare light bulbs is recommended.

But there is also some good news. Well, sort of. You can now buy an electronic tag for your car so that you can use the Télépéage lanes at autoroute toll barriers, with your tolls being automatically debited to your bank account. Sadly, the charges are non-trivial, and a bit complex; we are expecting to pay a setup cost of €30 and an annual charge of about €20, plus a 2% 'foreign exchange finance charge' added to the tolls. The tag can be used in any car, so no problem if you decide to take the Cayenne instead of the Beemer. Go to www.saneftolling.co.uk.

Drive to the French Alps

To make the most of them

by **Chris Gill**

If you've read the preceding chapter, you'll have gathered that we are pretty keen on driving to the Alps in general. But we're particularly keen on driving to the French Alps. The drive is a relatively short one, whereas many of the transfers to major French resorts from Geneva airport are relatively long.

Of course, the route from the Channel to the French Alps is through France rather than Germany, which for Francophiles like us means it's a pleasant prospect rather than a vaguely off-putting one. Especially if you are using Eurotunnel or a short ferry crossing, rather than a ferry to one of the Normandy ports, the drive is pleasantly low-pressure. Not only because you don't have to tangle with Paris but also because you don't have to use the always-busy Paris-Lyon autoroute.

The French Alps are the number-one destination for British car-borne skiers. The journey time is surprisingly short, at least if you are starting from south-east England. From Calais, for example, you can comfortably cover the 900km/560 miles to Chamonix in about nine hours plus stops – with the exception of the final few miles, the whole journey is on motorways. And except on peak weekends when half the population of Paris is on the move, the traffic is relatively light, if you steer clear of Paris.

With some exceptions in the southern Alps, all the resorts of the French Alps are within a day's driving range, provided you cross the Channel early in the day (or overnight). Saturday is still the main changeover day for resorts, and Saturday traffic into and out of many resorts can be heavy. This is especially true between Albertville and the Tarentaise resorts (from the Trois Vallées to Val d'Isère). Things are nothing like as bad as they were 25 years ago, before road improvements for the 1992 Olympics removed some of the main bottlenecks; but the resorts have expanded further in that time, and sadly the jams are back – on peak-season Saturdays you can encounter serious queues around Moûtiers. There are traffic lights placed well away from the town, to keep the queues and associated pollution away from Moûtiers.

DAY TRIP BASES

As we explained in the previous chapter, a car opens up different kinds of holiday for the adventurous holidaymaker – day tripping from a base resort, for example.

In the southern French Alps, Serre-Chevalier and Montgenèvre are ideal bases for day tripping. They are within easy reach of one another, and Montgenèvre is at one end of the Milky Way lift network, which includes Sauze d'Oulx and Sestriere in Italy – you can drive on to these resorts, or reach them by lift and piste. On the French side of the border, a few miles south, Puy-St-Vincent is an underrated resort that is well worth a visit for a day – as is the Vars/Risoul area, a little further south. The major resorts of Alpe-d'Huez and Les Deux-Alpes are also within range, as is the cult off-piste resort of La Grave. Getting to them involves crossing the high Col du Lautaret, but it's a major through-route and is not allowed to close for very long in normal winter conditions.

The Chamonix valley is an ideal destination for day tripping. The Mont Blanc Unlimited lift pass covers all the Chamonix areas, plus Courmayeur in Italy (easily reached through the Mont Blanc tunnel) and Verbier in Switzerland (a bit of a trek, even if the intervening passes are open). Megève and Les Contamines are close by, and Flaine and its satellites are fairly accessible. You could stay in a valley town such as Cluses, to escape resort prices – but Chamonix itself is not an expensive town.

In the Tarentaise region, Bourg-St-Maurice is an excellent base for visiting several resorts – Les Arcs is accessible by funicular, and La Plagne is of course linked to Les Arcs. La Rosière is only a short drive away, with a link to La Thuile. Ste-Foy is just up the valley. And at the end of the valley are Val d'Isère and Tignes. We had a great week skiing all of these from Bourg a couple of seasons ago.

MOVING ON

An alternative approach in the Tarentaise region if you want to include the famous Trois Vallées area is to stay in a series of different resorts for a day or two each, moving on from one to the next in the early evening; this way, you could have the trip of a lifetime. Compagnie des Alpes, owner of the lift systems in many of the big-name resorts of this area, sells a Holiski pass that gets discounts on day passes at most of them.

GETTING THERE

There are three 'gateways' to the different regions of the French Alps. For the northern Alps – Chamonix valley, Portes du Soleil, Flaine and neighbours – you want to head for Geneva. If coming from Calais or another short-crossing port, you no longer have to tangle with the busy A6 from Paris via Beaune to Mâcon and Lyon. The relatively new A39 autoroute south from Dijon means you can head for Bourg-en-Bresse, well east of Mâcon. For the central Alps – the mega-resorts of the Tarentaise, from Valmorel to Val d'Isère, and the Maurienne valley – you want to head for Chambéry. For the southern Alps – Alpe-d'Huez, Les Deux-Alpes, Serre-Chevalier – you want to head for Grenoble. And for either of these gateways first head for Mâcon and turn left at Lyon.

If you are taking a short Channel crossing, there are plenty of characterful towns for an overnight stop between the Channel and Dijon – Arras, St-Quentin, Laon, Troyes, Reims. All have plenty of choice of budget chain hotels, some of them in central locations where you can easily enjoy the facilities of the town (ie the brasseries), others on bleak commercial estates on the outskirts, where at least you can hope to find the compensation of extremely low room rates.

From the more westerly Channel ports of Le Havre or Caen, your route to Geneva or Mâcon sounds dead simple: take the A13 to Paris then the A6 south. But you have to get through or around Paris in the process. The most direct way around the city is the notorious périphérique – a hectic, multi-lane urban motorway close to the centre, with exits every few hundred yards and traffic that is either worryingly fast-moving or jammed solid. If the périphérique is jammed, getting round it takes ages. The more reliable alternative is to take a series of motorways and dual carriageways through the south-west fringes of Greater Paris. The route is not well signed, so it's a great help to have a competent navigator.

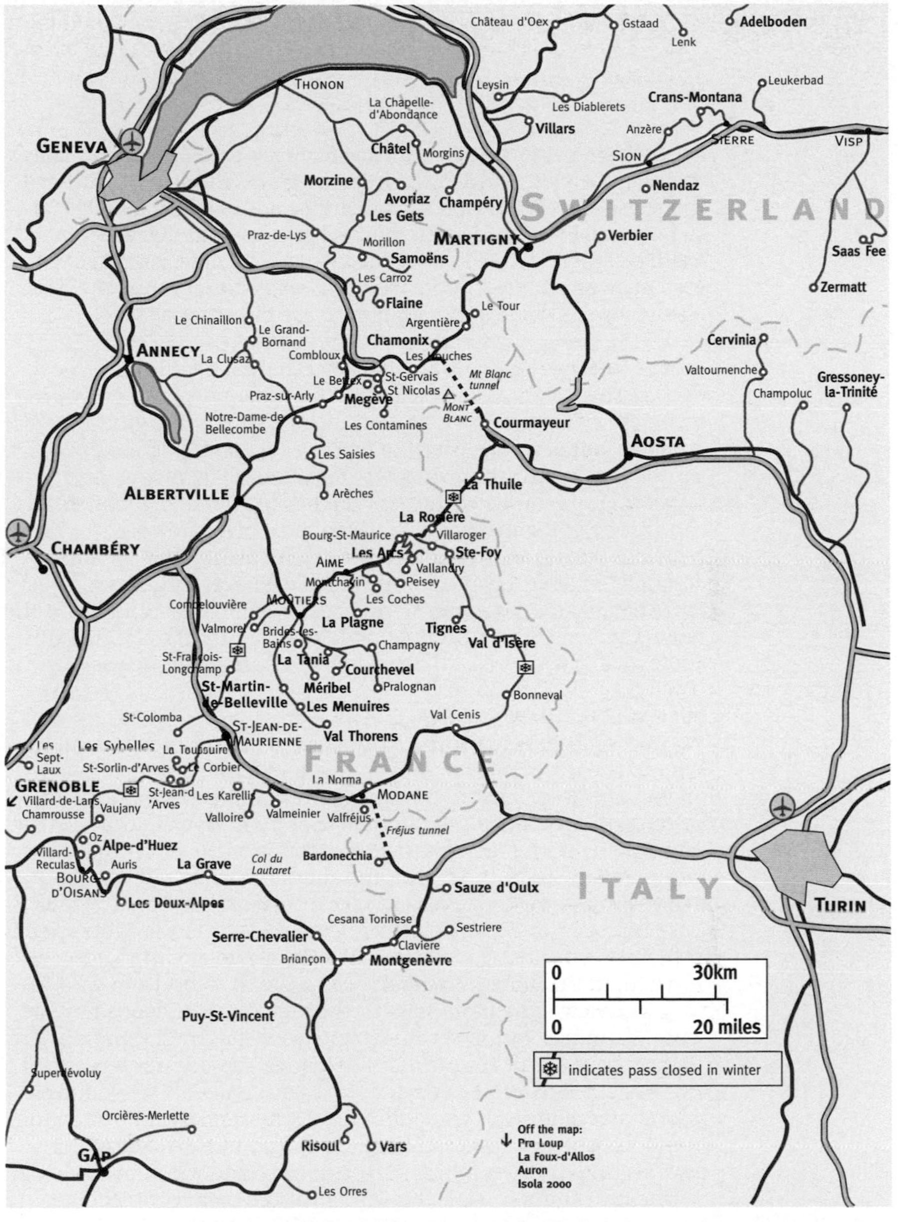

Pick the right gateway – Geneva, Chambéry or Grenoble – and you can hardly go wrong. Generally, there are no mountain passes involved. The exception is the approach to Serre-Chevalier and Montgenèvre, which involves the 2060m Col du Lautaret; the road is a major one and is ploughed frequently, but we felt the need for chains here on one occasion. Crossing the French-Swiss border between Chamonix and Verbier involves two closure-prone passes – the Montets and the Forclaz. When necessary, one-way traffic runs beside the tracks through the rail tunnel beneath the passes.

Choosing your resort

Get it right first time

Most people get to go skiing or boarding only once or twice a year, so choosing the right resort is crucially important. Chamonix, Châtel and Courchevel are all French resorts, but they are as similar as Cheddar and Camembert. Consider resorts in other countries – Kitzbühel in Austria, say, or Zermatt in Switzerland – and the differences become even more pronounced. For readers with limited experience of different resorts, here is some advice on how to use our information.

Lots of factors need to be taken into account when making your choice. The weight you attach to each of them depends on your own personal preferences, and on the make-up of the group you are going on holiday with. Starting on page 83 you'll find about 20 shortlists of resorts that we rate as outstanding in various key respects. And by now we hope you'll be able to build your own shortlist by going to www.wheretoskiandsnowboard.com.

Minor resorts and regions not widely known in the UK are described in short chapters of two or three pages. Major resorts get more detail, and more pages. Each resort chapter is organized in the same way. This short introduction takes you through the structure and explains what you will find under each heading we use.

GETTING A FEEL FOR THE PLACE

We start each chapter with a two-line verdict, in which we aim to sum up the resort in a few words. If you like the sound of it, you might want to go next to our unique Resort Price Index (RPI), in the margin. Explained fully in the chapter on page 28, this tells you how expensive the resort is, taking account of the prices of lift passes, private lessons, ski hire and simple lunches and drinks; figures around the European average of 100 are presented in blue, low ones of 85 or less are in green, high ones of 115 or more are in red. The figures that go into the RPI calculation are listed, too.

Then, in the 'Ratings' section, we rate each resort from various points of view – the more stars the better. Longer chapters have a set of 19 ratings, but in shorter chapters we have room for only the 10 most important. Following this chapter, these 10 ratings are set out for all resorts in one chart, so that you can easily track down resorts that might suit you. Still looking at the margin information, in most chapters we have a 'News' section; this is likely to be of most use and interest in resorts you already know from past visits.

The next thing to look at is our list of the main good and bad points about the resort and its slopes, picked out with + and −. This is followed by a summary in **bold type**, in which we've aimed to weigh up the pros and cons, coming off the fence and giving our view of who might like the resort. These sections should give you a good idea of whether the resort is likely to suit *you*, and whether it's worth reading our detailed analysis of it.

You'll know by now, for example, whether this is a high, hideous, convenient, purpose-built resort with superb, snow-sure, challenging slopes but absolutely no nightlife; or a pretty, traditional village with gentle wooded slopes, ideal for beginners on the rare occasions when it has some decent snow.

THE RESORT

In this first section of each chapter, we try to sort out the character of the place for you. Later, in the 'Staying there' section, we tell you more about the hotels, restaurants, bars and so on. Resorts vary enormously in some key respects and we have separate sections for each of the following headings. These match our star ratings.

Village charm At the extremes of the range are the handful of really hideous modern apartment-block resorts thrown up in France in the 1960s, and the ancient, captivating mountain villages of which Switzerland has an unfair number. But it isn't simply a question of old versus new. Some purpose-built places can have a much friendlier feel than some long-established resorts with big blocky buildings. Some places are working towns. Some are full of bars, discos and shops; others are peaceful backwaters. Traffic may choke the streets; or the village may be traffic-free.

Convenience This means how easy it is to get around the resort once you are there (not how easy the resort is to get to from the UK). Some places can be remarkably strung out, whereas others are surprisingly compact; our village plans are drawn to a standard scale, to help you gauge this. And of course proximity of lodgings to pistes determines how much walking or bussing you do.

Scenery Mountains are of course generally scenic, but there are differences, from the routinely hilly Colorado to the jaw-droppingly marvellous scenery of the Italian Dolomites and the Swiss Jungfrau region, to name two favourites.

THE MOUNTAINS

Extent of slopes Some mountains and lift networks are vast and complex, while others are much smaller and lacking variety.

Fast lifts Gondolas and fast chairlifts travel at three times the speed of slow chairlifts – cable cars and funicular railways even faster; these lifts offer short ride times, and most also shift queues quickly. We summarize the kinds of lifts you'll spend your time on. On our piste maps, we use a chair symbol to identify only fast chairs; lifts not marked with a symbol are slow chairs or draglifts.

Queues Monster queues are largely a thing of the past, but it still pays to avoid the resorts with the worst queues, especially in high season. Crowding on the pistes is more of a worry in many resorts, and we mention problems of this kind under this heading.

Terrain parks We summarize here the specially prepared fun parks and other terrain features most resorts now arrange for freestylers.

Snow reliability This is a crucial factor for many people, and one that varies enormously. In some resorts you don't have to worry at all about a lack of snow, while others are notorious for treating their paying guests to ice, mud and slush. Whether a resort is likely to have decent snow on its slopes normally depends on the height, the direction most of the slopes face (north good, south bad), its snow record and how much snowmaking it has. But bear in mind that in the Alps, high resorts tend to have rocky terrain, where the runs will need more snow than those on the pasture land of lower

resorts. Many resorts have increased their snowmaking capacity in recent years; in the 'Key facts' section we list the latest amount they claim to have, and comment on it in the snow reliability text.

For experts, intermediates, beginners Most (though not all) resorts have something to offer beginners, but relatively few will keep an expert happy for a week's holiday. As for intermediates, whether a resort will suit you really depends on your standard and inclinations. Places such as Cervinia and Obergurgl are ideal for those who want easy cruising runs, but have little to offer intermediates looking for more challenge. Others, such as Sölden and Val d'Isère, may intimidate the less confident intermediate who doesn't know the area well. Some areas linking several resorts, such as the Trois Vallées and Portes du Soleil, have vast amounts of terrain, so you can cover different ground each day. But some other well-known names, such as Mürren and Courmayeur, and many North American resorts, have surprisingly small areas.

For boarders In earlier editions we had a special panel in longer chapters but now deal with boarders' requirements in the main text, commenting on things like flat areas (bad) and the main types of lifts – gondolas, cable cars and chairs (all good) or draglifts (bad).

For cross-country We don't pretend that this is a guide for avid cross-country skiers. But we do try to help.

Mountain restaurants Here's a subject that divides people clearly into two opposing camps. To some, having a decent lunch served at your table in civilized surroundings – either in the sun, contemplating amazing scenery, or in a cosy hut, sheltered from the elements – makes or breaks the holiday. Others regard a long midday stop as a waste of valuable skiing time, as well as valuable spending money. We are firmly in the former camp. We get very disheartened by places with miserable restaurants and miserable food (eg many resorts in America); and there are some resorts that we go to partly because of the cosy huts and the food (eg Zermatt).

Schools and guides This is an area where we rely heavily on readers' reports of their own or their friends' experiences.

For families We sum up the merits of the resort, where possible evaluating the childcare arrangements. But, again, to be of real help we need first-hand reports from people whose children have actually used the facilities.

STAYING THERE

Chalets, hotels, apartments Some resorts have few hotels or few chalets. Note that we also have feature chapters on notably good chalets, hotels and apartments. If there are interesting options for staying in isolation on the slopes above the resort village, or in valley towns below it, we pick them out at the end of this section.

Eating out The range of restaurants varies widely. Even some big resorts have little choice because most visitors dine in their apartments or hotels. Most US resorts offer lots of choice.

Après-ski Tastes and styles vary enormously. Most resorts have pleasant places in which to have an immediate post-skiing beer or hot chocolate. Some then go dead. Others have noisy bars and discos until the early hours.

Off the slopes This is largely aimed at assessing how suitable a resort is for someone who doesn't intend to use the slopes, such as a non-skiing spouse. But of course it is also of interest to anyone who wants some variety of evening entertainment.

Resort ratings at a glance

The RPI figures in the second row for each resort are our Resort Price Index figures, based on a comparison of the costs of food and drink, lift passes, ski hire and a private ski lesson. An average European resort has an RPI of 100.

ANDORRA				AUSTRIA				
	Arinsal	Soldeu		Alpbach-Wildschönau	Bad Gastein	Ellmau	Hintertux / Tux valley	
Page	90	92		107	111	114	117	
RPI	**85**	**110**		**80**	**90**	**85**	**85**	
Extent	*	***		***	***	****	***	
Fast lifts	**	**		****	***	****	***	
Queues	***	***		****	***	****	***	
Snow	****	***		**	***	**	*****	
Expert	*	*		**	***	*	***	
Intermediate	**	****		***	****	****	***	
Beginner	****	****		***	**	****	**	
Charm	*	*		****	***	***	***	
Convenience	***	***		***	**	***	**	
Scenery	***	***		***	***	***	***	

	Ischgl	Kitzbühel	Lech	Mayrhofen	Obergurgl	Obertauern		
Page	122	129	137	145	150	155		
RPI	**105**	**95**	**115**	**85**	**100**	**95**		
Extent	****	***	****	***	**	**		
Fast lifts	*****	****	****	****	*****	*****		
Queues	****	***	****	*	*****	****		
Snow	****	**	****	***	*****	****		
Expert	****	***	****	**	**	***		
Intermediate	****	****	****	***	***	****		
Beginner	**	**	****	**	****	****		
Charm	***	****	****	***	****	**		
Convenience	***	**	***	*	****	****		
Scenery	***	***	***	***	***	***		

	Saalbach-Hinterglemm	Schladming	Sölden	Söll	St Anton	Stubai valley		
Page	158	164	168	173	180	189		
RPI	**90**	**85**	**100**	**85**	**105**	**95**		
Extent	***	***	***	****	****	***		
Fast lifts	*****	****	****	****	***	***		
Queues	****	****	***	***	***	***		
Snow	**	****	*****	**	****	*****		
Expert	**	**	***	*	*****	***		
Intermediate	****	****	****	****	***	***		
Beginner	***	***	***	**	*	**		
Charm	****	***	**	***	****	****		
Convenience	****	***	**	**	***	**		
Scenery	***	***	***	***	***	****		

The RPI figures

The figures in the second row for each resort are our Resort Price Index figures, based on a comparison of the costs of food and drink, lift passes, ski hire and a private ski lesson. An average European resort has an RPI of 100.

FRANCE

	Alpe-d'Huez	Les Arcs	Avoriaz 1800	Chamonix	Châtel	Courchevel	Les Deux-Alpes
Page	202	212	222	227	237	242	252
RPI	**100**	**100**	**95**	**100**	**95**	**120**	**90**
Extent	****	***	*****	***	*****	*****	***
Fast lifts	****	****	****	***	**	****	****
Queues	****	****	***	**	***	****	**
Snow	****	****	***	****	**	****	****
Expert	****	*****	***	*****	***	****	****
Intermediate	****	****	****	**	****	*****	**
Beginner	*****	***	****	**	***	****	***
Charm	**	**	**	****	***	**	**
Convenience	***	****	*****	*	**	****	***
Scenery	****	***	***	*****	***	***	****

	Flaine	Les Gets	La Grave	Megève	Les Menuires	Méribel	Mont-Genèvre
Page	258	265	267	269	276	282	292
RPI	**95**	**95**	**90**	**95**	**100**	**110**	**85**
Extent	****	*****	*	*****	*****	*****	**
Fast lifts	***	***		**	****	*****	**
Queues	***	***	****	****	****	****	****
Snow	****	**	***	**	****	***	****
Expert	****	***	*****	**	****	****	***
Intermediate	*****	****	*	****	*****	*****	****
Beginner	*****	****	*	***	***	****	*****
Charm	*	****	***	****	**	***	***
Convenience	*****	***	***	**	*****	***	***
Scenery	****	***	****	*****	***	***	***

	Morzine	La Plagne	Puy-St-Vincent	La Rosière	Samoëns	Serre-Chevalier	Ste-Foy-Tarentaise
Page	296	304	316	321	325	327	337
RPI	**95**	**105**	**70**	**80**	**95**	**90**	**75**
Extent	*****	****	**	***	****	****	*
Fast lifts	***	**	**	*	**	**	**
Queues	***	**	***	****	****	***	*****
Snow	**	****	***	***	***	***	***
Expert	***	****	***	**	****	***	****
Intermediate	****	*****	***	***	*****	****	***
Beginner	***	****	***	*****	**	****	**
Charm	***	**	**	***	****	***	***
Convenience	**	*****	*****	***	*	***	***
Scenery	***	***	****	****	****	***	***

Want to see the full set?

Major resort chapters in the book have an additional nine ratings shown at the start of each chapter. And you can see the full set of ratings for 200 resorts on our website.

www.wheretoskiandsnowboard.com

	St-Martin-de-Belleville	La Tania	Tignes	Val d'Isère	Val Thorens	Vars / Risoul		
Page	340	343	347	358	368	375		
RPI	100	100	100	100	100	80		
Extent	*****	*****	*****	*****	*****	***		
Fast lifts	****	****	***	****	*****	*		
Queues	****	****	****	****	***	****		
Snow	***	***	*****	*****	*****	***		
Expert	****	****	*****	*****	****	**		
Intermediate	*****	*****	*****	*****	*****	****		
Beginner	**	***	**	***	****	****		
Charm	****	***	*	***	**	**		
Convenience	***	****	****	***	*****	****		
Scenery	***	***	***	***	***	***		

GERMANY

ITALY

	Garmisch-Partenkirchen		Cervinia	Cortina d'Ampezzo	Courmayeur	Livigno	Madonna di Campiglio	
Page	380		387	393	398	403	407	
RPI	80		90	105	90	80	90	
Extent	*		***	***	*	**	***	
Fast lifts	***		****	***	***	****	****	
Queues	***		****	****	****	****	***	
Snow	***		*****	***	****	****	***	
Expert	****		*	**	***	***	**	
Intermediate	***		****	***	****	***	****	
Beginner	*		*****	*****	*	****	***	
Charm	***		**	****	****	***	****	
Convenience	**		***	*	*	**	***	
Scenery	****		****	*****	****	***	****	

	Monterosa Ski	Passo Tonale	Sauze d'Oulx	Sella Ronda	Selva / Val Gardena	Sestriere	La Thuile	
Page	412	416	418	423	432	439	441	
RPI	80	70	80	95	95	85	85	
Extent	**	**	****	*****	*****	****	***	
Fast lifts	*****	****	***	****	****	***	***	
Queues	****	****	***	***	***	***	****	
Snow	****	****	**	****	****	****	****	
Expert	****	*	**	**	***	***	**	
Intermediate	****	***	****	*****	*****	****	****	
Beginner	**	*****	*	****	***	***	****	
Charm	***	**	**	***	***	*	***	
Convenience	***	***	**	***	***	***	***	
Scenery	****	***	***	*****	*****	***	***	

The RPI figures

The figures in the second row for each resort are our Resort Price Index figures, based on a comparison of the costs of food and drink, lift passes, ski hire and a private ski lesson. An average European resort has an RPI of 100.

SWITZERLAND

	Adelboden	Andermatt	Champéry	Crans-Montana	Davos	Engelberg		
Page	454	457	459	462	464	471		
RPI	120	115	120	135	130	110		
Extent	***	**	*****	***	****	**		
Fast lifts	***	**	*	****	****	***		
Queues	***	**	****	***	***	**		
Snow	***	****	**	**	****	***		
Expert	**	****	***	**	****	****		
Intermediate	***	**	****	****	*****	***		
Beginner	****	*	**	***	**	**		
Charm	****	****	****	**	**	**		
Convenience	**	***	*	**	**	*		
Scenery	****	***	****	****	****	****		

	Grindel-wald	Klosters	Laax	Mürren	Saas-Fee	St Moritz		
Page	473	477	479	482	486	491		
RPI	125	125	125	125	130	150		
Extent	***	****	****	*	**	*****		
Fast lifts	****	****	*****	*****	****	****		
Queues	**	**	****	***	***	***		
Snow	**	****	***	***	*****	****		
Expert	**	****	***	***	**	****		
Intermediate	****	*****	*****	***	****	****		
Beginner	***	***	****	***	*****	**		
Charm	****	****	***	*****	*****	**		
Convenience	**	**	***	***	**	*		
Scenery	*****	****	***	*****	****	****		

	Val d'Anniviers	Verbier	Villars	Wengen	Zermatt			
Page	498	502	513	515	520			
RPI	100	140	115	125	140			
Extent	**	*****	***	***	****			
Fast lifts	*	****	**	****	*****			
Queues	****	***	***	***	***			
Snow	****	***	**	**	****			
Expert	****	*****	**	**	****			
Intermediate	***	***	***	****	****			
Beginner	***	**	****	***	**			
Charm	*****	***	***	*****	****			
Convenience	**	**	**	***	**			
Scenery	****	****	***	*****	*****			

Want a shortlist shortcut?

Our website will build a shortlist for you: you specify your priorities, and the system will use our resort ratings to draw up a shortlist – confined to one area or country, if you like.

www.wheretoskiandsnowboard.com

USA

	California Heavenly	Mammoth Mountain	Squaw Valley	Colorado Aspen	Beaver Creek	Breckenridge	Snowmass	
Page	535	540	545	548	555	557	562	
RPI	160	155	145	185	170	150	180	
Extent	***	***	***	****	**	**	****	
Fast lifts	****	****	***	****	*****	****	*****	
Queues	****	****	****	****	*****	****	****	
Snow	****	****	****	*****	*****	*****	*****	
Expert	***	****	****	*****	****	****	*****	
Intermediate	****	****	**	*****	****	****	*****	
Beginner	****	****	****	*****	*****	*****	*****	
Charm	*	**	***	****	**	***	**	
Convenience	*	**	****	**	****	***	****	
Scenery	****	***	***	***	***	***	****	

	Vail	Winter Park	Utah Alta	Canyons	Deer Valley	Park City	Snowbird	
Page	564	571	576	578	580	582	587	
RPI	165	150	150	160	165	160	155	
Extent	****	***	***	***	**	***	***	
Fast lifts	*****	****	****	***	****	***	****	
Queues	**	****	***	****	****	****	***	
Snow	*****	*****	*****	****	****	****	*****	
Expert	****	****	*****	****	***	****	*****	
Intermediate	*****	****	***	****	****	****	***	
Beginner	***	*****	***	**	****	****	**	
Charm	***	**	**	**	***	***	*	
Convenience	***	***	****	****	****	**	*****	
Scenery	***	***	***	***	***	***	***	

	Rest of the West Big Sky	Jackson Hole						
Page	590	595						
RPI	140	155						
Extent	****	***						
Fast lifts	**	****						
Queues	*****	***						
Snow	*****	****						
Expert	****	*****						
Intermediate	****	**						
Beginner	*****	***						
Charm	**	***						
Convenience	****	****						
Scenery	***	***						

Want to keep up to date?

Our website has weekly resort news throughout the year, and you can register for our monthly email newsletter – with special holiday offers, as well as resort news highlights.

www.wheretoskiandsnowboard.com

CANADA

	Banff	Big White	Fernie	Kicking Horse	Lake Louise			
Page	605	612	615	620	622			
RPI	**150**	**135**	**145**	**145**	**155**			
Extent	***	***	***	***	***			
Fast lifts	****	****	**	***	****			
Queues	****	*****	****	****	****			
Snow	****	*****	****	****	***			
Expert	****	***	*****	****	****			
Intermediate	****	****	**	***	****			
Beginner	***	****	****	***	***			
Charm	***	**	**	**	***			
Convenience	*	****	****	****	*			
Scenery	****	***	***	***	****			

	Revelstoke	Silver Star	Sun Peaks	Whistler				
Page	627	629	631	633				
RPI	**140**	**135**	**140**	**160**				
Extent	***	***	***	****				
Fast lifts	*****	****	**	*****				
Queues	*****	*****	*****	**				
Snow	****	****	****	****				
Expert	*****	****	***	*****				
Intermediate	**	***	****	*****				
Beginner	*	****	****	***				
Charm	**	***	***	***				
Convenience	***	*****	****	****				
Scenery	****	***	***	***				

www.wheretoskiandsnowboard.com

Our website is designed to complement this book. We like to think it's one of the best in the ski business. On the site you'll find lots of interest to the keen skier/boarder:

- twice-weekly news and updates on all the major resorts in Europe and North America
- full editors' ratings for 200 resorts
- interactive shortlist builder – you plug in what you want most from a resort (eg village charm, extensive slopes) and up pops a shortlist to suit you
- snow reports and resort weather forecasts
- links to thousands of useful sites such as resorts, tour operators, ski schools, airlines
- free competitions with great prizes
- special offers from leading tour operators
- blogs from the editors on their travels
- dozens of background feature articles
- forums where you can exchange views, seek advice, give vent to those grumbles
- a resort reporting system, where you can file a report and maybe win a prize
- a signup for monthly e-newsletters (essential reading for all keen skiers and boarders)

Resort shortlists

To help you spot resorts that will suit you

To streamline the job of spotting the ideal resort for your own holiday, here are lists of the best ten or so resorts for 22 different categories. Some lists embrace European and North American resorts, but many we've confined to Europe, because the US has too many qualifying resorts (eg for beginners) or because the US does things differently, making comparisons invalid (eg for off-piste).

SOMETHING FOR EVERYONE

Resorts with everything from reassuring nursery slopes to real challenges for experts

Alpe-d'Huez, France 202
Les Arcs, France 212
Aspen, Colorado 548
Courchevel, France 242
Flaine, France 258
Mammoth, California 540
Vail, Colorado 564
Val d'Isère, France 358
Whistler, Canada 633
Winter Park, Colorado 571

INTERNATIONAL OVERSIGHTS

Resorts that deserve as much attention as the ones we go back to every year, but don't get it

Alta, Utah 576
Andermatt, Switzerland 457
Bad Gastein, Austria 111
Big Sky, Montana 590
Laax, Switzerland 479
Monterosa Ski, Italy 412
Sella Ronda, Italy 423
Sölden, Austria 168
Val d'Anniviers, Switzerland 498
Vars/Risoul, France 375

HIGH-MILEAGE PISTE-BASHING

Extensive intermediate slopes with big lift networks

Alpe-d'Huez, France 202
Davos/Klosters, Switz 464/477
Flaine, France 258
Laax, Switzerland 479
Milky Way: Sauze d'Oulx (Italy), Montgenèvre (France) 418/292
Paradiski, France 302
Portes du Soleil, France/Switz 315
Sella Ronda, Italy 423
Selva, Italy 432
SkiWelt/Kitzbühel, Austria 114/129/173
St Moritz, Switz 491
Trois Vallées, France 356
Val d'Isère/Tignes, France 358/347
Whistler, Canada 633

RELIABLE SNOW IN THE ALPS

Alpine resorts where snow is rarely in short supply

Bregenzerwald, Austria 192
Chamonix, France 227
Cervinia, Italy 387
Courchevel, France 242
Hintertux, Austria 117
Lech/Zürs, Austria 137
Obergurgl, Austria 150
Obertauern, Austria 155
Saas-Fee, Switzerland 486
Sölden, Austria 168
Val d'Isère/Tignes, France 358/347
Val Thorens, France 368
Zermatt, Switzerland 520

OFF-PISTE WONDERS

Alpine resorts where, with the right guidance and equipment, you can have the time of your life

Alpe-d'Huez, France 202
Andermatt, Switzerland 457
Chamonix, France 227
Davos/Klosters, Switz 464/477
La Grave, France 267
Lech/Zürs, Austria 137
Monterosa Ski, Italy 412
St Anton, Austria 180
Val d'Isère/Tignes, France 358/347
Verbier, Switzerland 502

DRAMATIC SCENERY

Resorts where the mountains are not just high and snowy, but spectacularly scenic too

Chamonix, France 227
Cortina, Italy 393
Courmayeur, Italy 398
Heavenly, California 535
Jungfrau resorts (Grindelwald, Mürren, Wengen), Switzerland 473/482/515
Lake Louise, Canada 622
Megève, France 269
Sella Ronda, Italy 423
Selva, Italy 432
St Moritz, Switz 491
Zermatt, Switzerland 520

BACK-DOOR RESORTS
Cute little Alpine villages linked to big, bold ski areas, giving you the best of two different worlds
Les Brévières (Tignes), France 347
Champagny (La Plagne), France 304
Leogang (Saalbach), Austria 158
Montchavin (La Plagne), France 304
Peisey (Les Arcs), France 212
Le Pré (Les Arcs), France 212
Samoëns (Flaine), France 325
St-Martin (Three Valleys), France 340
Stuben (St Anton), Austria 180
Vaujany (Alpe-d'Huez), France 202

VILLAGE CHARM
Resorts with traditional character – from mountain villages to mining towns
Champéry, Switzerland 459
Courmayeur, Italy 398
Les Gets, France 265
Lech, Austria 137
Megève, France 269
Mürren, Switzerland 482
Saas-Fee, Switzerland 486
Val d'Anniviers, Switzerland 498
Wengen, Switzerland 515
Zermatt, Switzerland 520

BLACK RUNS
Resorts with steep, mogully, lift-served slopes within the safety of the piste network
Alta/Snowbird, Utah 576/587
Andermatt, Switzerland 457
Argentière/Chamonix, France 227
Aspen, Colorado 548
Beaver Creek, Colorado 555
Courchevel, France 242
Jackson Hole, Wyoming 595
Whistler, Canada 633
Winter Park, Colorado 571
Zermatt, Switzerland 520

POWDER PARADISES
Resorts with the snow, the terrain and (ideally) the lack of crowds that make for powder perfection
Alta/Snowbird, Utah 576/587
Andermatt, Switzerland 457
Big Sky, Montana 590
Big White, Canada 612
Fernie, Canada 615
La Grave, France 267
Jackson Hole, Wyoming 595
Kicking Horse, Canada 620
Monterosa Ski, Italy 412
Revelstoke, Canada 627
Ste-Foy, France 337

CHOPAHOLICS
Resorts where you can have a day riding helicopters or cats
Aspen, Colorado 548
Courmayeur, Italy 398
Fernie, Canada 615
Lech/Zürs, Austria 137
Monterosa Ski, Italy 412
Revelstoke, Canada 627
La Thuile, Italy 441
Verbier, Switzerland 502
Whistler, Canada 633
Zermatt, Switzerland 520

TOP TERRAIN PARKS
Alpine resorts with the best parks and pipes for freestyle thrills
Les Arcs, France 212
Avoriaz, France 222
Cervinia, Italy 387
Davos, Switzerland 464
Les Deux-Alpes, France 252
Ischgl, Austria 122
Laax, Switzerland 479
Lech, Austria 137
Livigno, Italy 403
Mayrhofen, Austria 145
Méribel, France 282
La Plagne, France 304
Saalbach-Hinterglemm, Austria 158
Saas Fee, Switzerland 486
St Moritz, Switzerland 491

WEATHERPROOF SLOPES
Alpine resorts with fairly snow-sure slopes if the sun shines, and trees in case it doesn't
Les Arcs, France 212
Courchevel, France 242
Courmayeur, Italy 398
Laax, Switzerland 479
Schladming, Austria 164
Selva, Italy 432
Serre-Chevalier, France 327
Sestriere, Italy 439
La Thuile, Italy 441

MOTORWAY CRUISING
Long, gentle, super-smooth pistes to bolster the frail confidence of those just off the nursery slope
Les Arcs, France 212
Breckenridge, Colorado 557
Cervinia, Italy 387
Cortina d'Ampezzo, Italy 393
Courchevel, France 242
Megève, France 269
La Plagne, France 304
Snowmass, Colorado 562
La Thuile, Italy 441
Vail, Colorado 564

RESORTS FOR BEGINNERS

European resorts with gentle, snow-sure nursery slopes and easy, longer runs to progress to

Alpe-d'Huez, France 202
Cervinia, Italy 387
Courchevel, France 242
Flaine, France 258
Montgenèvre, France 292
Passo Tonale, Italy 416
La Plagne, France 304
La Rosière, France 321
Saas-Fee, Switzerland 486
Soldeu, Andorra 92

SPECIALLY FOR FAMILIES

Alpine resorts where you can easily find accommodation surrounded by snow, not by traffic and fumes

Les Arcs, France 212
Avoriaz, France 222
Flaine, France 258
Lech, Austria 137
Montchavin (La Plagne), France 304
Mürren, Switzerland 482
Puy-St-Vincent, France 316
La Rosière, France 321
Saas-Fee, Switzerland 486
Ste-Foy, France 337
Vars/Risoul, France 375
Wengen, Switzerland 515

SNOW-SURE BUT SIMPATICO

Alpine resorts with high-rise slopes, but low-rise, traditional-style buildings

Andermatt, Switzerland 457
Arabba (Sella Ronda), Italy 423
Argentière (Chamonix), France 227
Ischgl, Austria 122
Lech/Zürs, Austria 137
Monterosa Ski, Italy 412
Obergurgl, Austria 150
Saas-Fee, Switzerland 486
Val d'Anniviers, Switzerland 498
Zermatt, Switzerland 520

SPECIAL MOUNTAIN RESTAURANTS

Alpine resorts where mountain restaurants can really add an extra dimension to your holiday

Alpe-d'Huez, France 202
Serre-Chevalier, France 327
Cortina d'Ampezzo, Italy 393
Courmayeur, Italy 398
Kitzbühel, Austria 129
Megève, France 269
La Plagne, France 304
Saalbach, Austria 158
Selva, Italy 432
Zermatt, Switzerland 520

MODERN CONVENIENCE

Alpine resorts where there's plenty of slope-side accommodation where you can ski from the door

Les Arcs, France 212
Avoriaz, France 222
Courchevel, France 242
Flaine, France 258
Les Menuires, France 276
Obertauern, Austria 155
La Plagne, France 304
Puy-St-Vincent, France 316
La Tania, France 343
Tignes, France 347
Val Thorens, France 368

LIVELY NIGHTLIFE

European resorts where you'll have no difficulty finding somewhere to boogie

Chamonix, France 227
Ischgl, Austria 122
Kitzbühel, Austria 129
Mayrhofen, Austria 145
Méribel, France 282
Saalbach, Austria 158
Sauze d'Oulx, Italy 418
Sölden, Austria 168
St Anton, Austria 180
Val d'Isère, France 358
Verbier, Switzerland 502
Zermatt, Switzerland 520

OTHER AMUSEMENTS

Alpine resorts where those not interested in skiing or boarding can still find plenty to do

Bad Gastein, Austria 111
Chamonix, France 227
Cortina d'Ampezzo, Italy 393
Davos, Switzerland 464
Kitzbühel, Austria 129
Megève, France 269
St Moritz, Switzerland 491

AFFORDABLE FUN

Resorts towards the bottom of our RPI league table that have good reasonably extensive slopes

Bad Gastein, Austria 111
Monterosa Ski, Italy 412
Pyrenees (Baqueira-Beret, Formigal), Spain 643
Pyrenees (La Mongie, St-Lary-Soulan), France 318
Sauze d'Oulx, Italy 418
Schladming, Austria 164
Sella Ronda, Italy 423
SkiWelt (Ellmau, Söll), Austria 114/173
Vars/Risoul, France 375

Our resort chapters

How to get the best out of them

FINDING A RESORT

The bulk of the book consists of the chapters listed on the facing page, devoted to individual major resorts, plus minor resorts that share the same lift system or pass. Sometimes we devote a chapter to an area not dominated by one resort – then we use the area name (eg Monterosa Ski in Italy, Stubai valley in Austria, Val d'Anniviers in Switzerland).

Chapters are grouped by country: first, the six major European countries (now including Germany); then the US and Canada (where resorts are grouped by states or regions); then minor European countries; and finally Japan. Within each group, resorts are ordered alphabetically. In Austria, the main skiing regions of Vorarlberg, the westernmost 'land', are dealt with under that name.

Short cuts to the resorts that might suit you are provided (on the pages preceding this one) by a table of comparative **star ratings** and a series of **shortlists** of resorts with particular merits.

At the back of the book is an **index** to the resort chapters, combined with a **directory** giving basic information on hundreds of other minor resorts. If the resort you are looking up is covered in a chapter devoted to a bigger resort, the page reference will be to the start of the chapter, not to the exact page on which the minor resort is described.

There's further guidance on using our information in the chapter 'Choosing your resort', on page 74 – designed to be helpful particularly to people with little or no experience of ski resorts, who may not appreciate how big the differences between one resort and another can be.

READING A RESORT CHAPTER

There are various standard items at the start of each resort chapter. In the left margin, **star ratings** summarize our view of the resort, including its suitability for different levels of skill. The more stars, the better. In major resort chapters we give an expanded set of 19 ratings. Then comes our **Resort Price Index** – explained in outline on the facing page and in detail in the feature chapter on page 28.

We give web addresses of the **tourist office** (in North America, the ski lift company) and phone numbers for recommended **hotels**. We give star ratings for hotels – either official ones or ones awarded by major tour operators. The UK tour operators offering **package holidays** in major resorts are listed in the chapter, along with those of minor resorts that are covered in the same chapter.

Our **mountain maps** show the resorts' own classification of runs. On some maps we show black diamonds to mark expert terrain without defined runs. We do not distinguish single diamond terrain from the steeper double diamond.

We include on the map any lifts definitely planned for construction for the coming season.

MAJOR LIFTS

On our piste maps we use the following symbols to identify **fast lifts**. Slow chairlifts do not get a chair symbol.

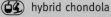

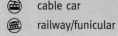

- fast chairlift
- gondola
- hybrid chondola
- cable car
- railway/funicular

THE WORLD'S BEST WINTER SPORTS RESORTS
To find a minor resort, or if you are not sure which country you should be looking under, consult the index/directory at the back of the book, which lists all resorts alphabetically.

RESORT PRICE INDEX BOXES
Our RPI figures show how prices in each resort compare with the average European resort, taking account of food and drink, lift pass, ski hire and lessons. RPIs around the average figure of 100 are in blue boxes. RPIs of 85 or less get a green box. RPIs of 115 or more get a red box. Our price survey is fully explained, and some of the results are summarized, in our chapter on 'Cutting your costs', on page 28.

RPI 85

RPI 100

RPI 115

Andorra

NEWS

2011/12: In Arcalis a new terrain park with natural wooden features opened.

LIFT PASSES

Ski Andorra
The Ski Andorra pass covers all Andorran areas and allows skiing at any single one of them each day: €198 for five non-consecutive days

Andorra is a tiny, almost entirely mountainous state sandwiched between France and Spain. It has built its prosperity on the twin pillars of tax-haven status and low-cost tourism – particularly winter tourism, and particularly in the UK market. Andorra used to be seen primarily as a cheap and cheerful holiday destination, attracting singles and young couples looking for a good time in the duty-free bars and clubs, as well as learning to ski or snowboard. But the place has changed radically over the last 25 years and has tried to move upmarket.

Soldeu, the main resort, is no longer cheap. Our price survey shows it to be as expensive as many high-profile Alpine resorts that it is not in the same league as. Not surprisingly, its popularity has fallen. According to the Crystal Ski Industry Report, Andorra's share of the UK ski market was 14% eight years ago; last season it was 6.5%.

The main resorts – **Soldeu** and **Pas de la Casa** (which share the 205km Grandvalira ski area) and **Arinsal** (linked to **Pal** to form a 53km area) – are covered in the two chapters that follow this. The other main ski area is **Arcalis,** tucked away at the head of a long valley with no accommodation at its base. Most British visitors never bother with it. But for non-beginners it makes a very worthwhile day trip, particularly from Arinsal and Pal. The terrain is varied and scenic, the slopes are usually deserted except at weekends (when locals pour in), and the snow is usually the best around. There is excellent intermediate and beginner terrain, but what marks it out is the expert terrain, including lots of off-piste between the marked runs. 'A real jewel – the boarder in our group was in heaven,' said a reporter.

The capital, **Andorra la Vella**, is choked by traffic and fumes but worth a visit for its duty-free shopping and the splendid Caldea spa, with a fantastic array of pools, baths and treatments, at Escaldes-Engordany, just outside the centre.

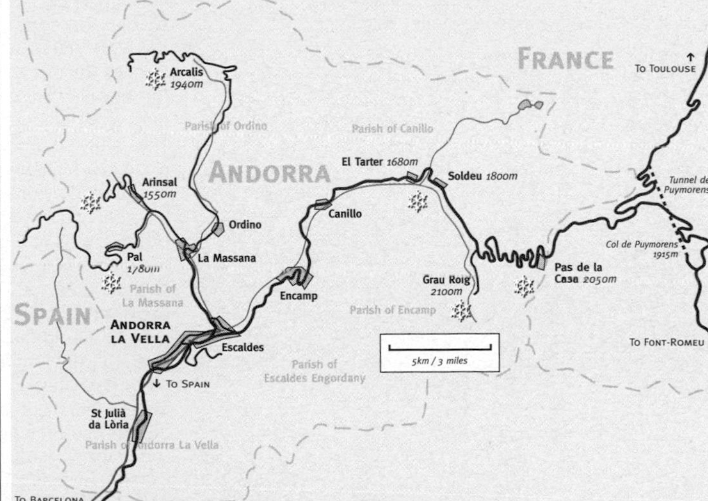

TOURIST OFFICES

Ski Andorra
www.skiandorra.ad

Arcalis
www.vallnord.com

GRANDVALIRA

← Grandvalira is by far Andorra's biggest and best ski area. This is a good shot of the pistes down to Soldeu (our favoured place to stay)

Arinsal

Lively base that suits beginners best, with a cable car link to Pal to keep intermediates amused

TOP 10 RATINGS

Extent	*
Fast lifts	**
Queues	***
Snow	****
Expert	*
Intermediate	**
Beginner	****
Charm	*
Convenience	***
Scenery	***

RPI 85

lift pass	£140
ski hire	£100
lessons	£70
food & drink	£110
total	**£420**

NEWS

2011/12: In Arinsal, a new cafe opened near the beginner slopes. In Pal, more non-ski activities were introduced to the Caubella area.

VALLNORD

Pal's slopes are the most densely wooded in Andorra and more interesting and varied than Arinsal's ↓

- + Lively bars
- + Ski school geared to British needs
- + Cable car link with Pal and shared Vallnord lift pass with Arcalis
- + Pretty, treelined slopes in Pal

- − Arinsal slopes are bleak and very confined (though this does mean children can't stray far)
- − Long, dour village with no focus
- − Poor bus link to Arcalis

Tour operators are able to tempt British beginners here in large numbers. The Brit-oriented ski school must be the key factor; prices are no longer greatly different from those in more attractive Austrian and Italian resorts.

THE RESORT

Arinsal sits near the head of a steep-sided valley north of Andorra la Vella. Pal has a more open setting in another valley. The two are linked by cable car.

The lower town of La Massana is linked by gondola to Pal's slopes, and makes a better base for competent skiers and riders wanting to spend some time at Arcalis (read the Andorra introduction). The Vallnord lift pass covers all of these areas.

Village charm The resort is a long, narrow village of grey, stone-clad buildings. The atmosphere is friendly and relaxed.

Convenience The main gondola starts from the village centre, and staying close to it is convenient; the alternative is a six-pack 1km from the centre at Cota, with a piste to return. There are free buses running through the village linking the lift bases.

Scenery Shady valleys and nicely wooded slopes dominate.

THE MOUNTAINS

The area above Arinsal is an open but narrow, east-facing bowl. Pal has the most densely wooded slopes in Andorra. Most face east; those down to the link with Arinsal face north. The piste map has lost its ghastly sepia tint but is still poor, covering distant Arcalis as well as Arinsal and Pal – nuts! Signposting is good though.

Slopes Arinsal's slopes consist essentially of a single, long, narrow bowl above the upper gondola station at Comallempla, served by a network of chairs and drags, including a quad and a six-pack. Almost at the top is the cable car link with Pal. Pal's slopes are widely spread around the mountain, with four main lift bases, all reachable by road. The main one, La Caubella, at the opposite extreme from the Arinsal link, is the arrival point of the gondola from La Massana.

Fast lifts Access is by gondola or fast chairlift. Other fast chairs exist, but there are still many slow lifts too.

Queues Reporters note few problems. But downloading on Arinsal's gondola may generate queues at peak times. The cable car link with Pal can be closed by high winds.

Terrain parks Arinsal's big freestyle area is regularly upgraded. It has its own lift, rails and jumps, a boardercross, a beginner zone and a chill-out area.

Snow reliability With most runs above 1950m, the north-easterly orientation and a decent amount of snowmaking, snow is relatively assured. In 2011 the pistes were 'kept in excellent shape', despite the prolonged drought. Grooming is good.

Experts This isn't a great area for experts, but there is some good tree

KEY FACTS

Resort	1475m 4,840ft
Slopes	1550-2560m 5,090-8,400ft
Lifts	31
Pistes	63km 39 miles
Green	16%
Blue	36%
Red	38%
Black	10%
Snowmaking	296 guns

UK PACKAGES

Crystal, Inghams, Neilson, Skitracer, STC, Thomson

Phone numbers
From abroad use the prefix +376

TOURIST OFFICE

Arinsal and Pal
www.vallnord.com

skiing in Pal. Arcalis has more to offer.

Intermediates Arinsal offers a fair range of difficulty, but competent intermediates will want to explore the much more interesting, varied and extensive Pal slopes, and perhaps make a day trip or two to Arcalis.

Beginners Around half the guests here are beginners. A special pass is available (15 euros per day), though we guess most people will book ski/ pass/tuition packs from their tour operators. The wide, gentle nursery slopes set apart from the main runs are 'great, exactly what my beginner girlfriend needed'. They can get crowded at peak times, though. There are long easy runs to progress to, as well.

Snowboarding It's a fine place to learn, but over half the lifts are drags and some of them are vicious. There are some flat sections in Pal.

Cross-country There isn't any.

Mountain restaurants These are mainly uninspiring self-service snackeries, and crowded.

Schools and guides A key factor in the appeal of the resort; over half the instructors are native English speakers. A recent reporter was very impressed with the group lessons: 'The instructor was excellent and very encouraging.' He was also impressed by the school's low prices, though again many people will book through tour operators. Private snowboard lessons were also rated 'good value'.

Families There are themed ski kindergartens for four- to eight-year-olds and nurseries for children aged one to four at both Pal and Arinsal.

STAYING THERE

Hotels The Princesa Parc (736500) is a big, glossy 4-star place near the gondola – 'a lovely hotel, with good rooms and exceptional staff'; swanky spa (open to non-residents) and a bowling alley. Rooms in the hotel Arinsal (838889) are not large, but the hotel is ideally placed and has a pleasant bar. The 3-star Crest (738020) is at the bottom of the run to Cota, handy for the fast chair up to the slopes: 'spacious apartment, perfectly good meals'. The Xalet Verdú (737140) is a smooth little 3-star. The Micolau (737707) is a characterful stone house near the centre with a jolly, beamed restaurant.

Apartments There is a reasonable choice of places.

Eating out The Surf disco-pub comes highly recommended for 'the best steaks ever'. The Sidreria Pub Herri also does steaks and grills. El Cisco is a Tex-Mex place in a lovely wood and stone building.

Après-ski Arinsal has plenty of lively bars and discos. The hotel Arinsal has good-value pints. The Derby Irish pub is a 'good place to relax and watch your ski school video'. Quo Vadis is tipped for a 'pint and pizza'.

Off the slopes There are helicopter rides, dog sledding, snowmobiling, snowshoeing, tobogganing, snow bikes and ice-diving. But a past reporter found family entertainment limited in the evenings. Andorra la Vella is half an hour away by taxi or infrequent bus.

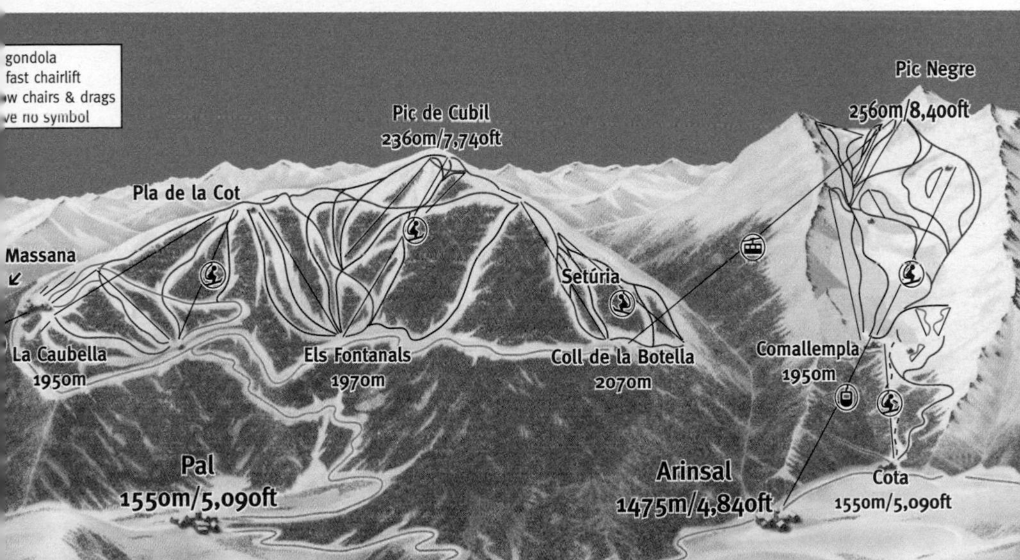

SNOWPIX.COM / CHRIS GILL

Soldeu

Our favourite place to stay in Andorra: not an attractive village, but centrally placed in the impressive Grandvalira ski area

RATINGS

The mountains	
Extent	***
Fast lifts	**
Queues	***
Terrain p'ks	****
Snow	***
Expert	*
Intermediate	****
Beginner	****
Boarder	****
X-country	*
Restaurants	**
Schools	*****
Families	**
The resort	
Charm	*
Convenience	***
Scenery	***
Eating out	***
Après-ski	****
Off-slope	*

RPI	110
lift pass	£190
ski hire	£140
lessons	£90
food & drink	£135
total	**£555**

NEWS

2011/12: A short new draglift at Pic d'Encampadana above El Tarter now serves the off-piste routes there plus new red and blue runs. A new freestyle ski school opened at the Sunset Park Peretol terrain park. And a small beginner terrain park opened above Encamp. Snowmaking was increased, and a children's themed slope opened at Grau Roig – where the children's facilities were also improved. The Espiolets restaurant was revamped to include a new cafe area downstairs.

+ Grandvalira area including Pas de la Casa rivals major Alpine resorts in terms of size
+ Excellent beginner and early intermediate terrain
+ Ski school has excellent British-run section for English-speaking visitors

− Village is spread along a busy through-road, lacking atmosphere
− Slopes can get very crowded
− Very little to interest experts
− Expensive lift pass, and beginners may be charged the full cost
− Not much to do off the slopes

If we were planning a holiday in Andorra, it would be in Soldeu (or the isolated hotel at Grau Roig, up the road – covered in Pas de la Casa at the end of this chapter). It is best placed to explore the extensive Grandvalira area. But the village is a difficult place to like, and beginners are forced to buy one of Europe's most pricey passes.

THE RESORT

Soldeu is set on a steep hillside facing the ski area across the valley. It is on the busy road that runs down the valley from France to Andorra la Vella and on to Spain. Pas de la Casa, near the French border, is the major alternative base; El Tarter, a few miles down the valley from Soldeu, and Canillo, a few miles further, are other alternatives with major lifts. All these resorts share the Grandvalira ski area and are covered at the end of this chapter. Outings to other resorts in Andorra are possible – Arcalis (see the Andorra introduction chapter) in particular is worth the trip, but it's easiest by car. The Ski Andorra lift pass covers all the resorts.

VILLAGE CHARM *

An urban ribbon

The village is an ever-growing ribbon of modern hotels, apartments and bars, with the occasional shop; the buildings have traditional stone cladding and mostly chalet-style roofs. Sounds OK, but it isn't; this is not a place to wander about at teatime – there is no focus or atmosphere, and traffic on the through-road can be heavy and sometimes fast.

CONVENIENCE ***

Over the river

A steep hillside leads down from the village to the river, and the slopes are on the opposite side. A gondola from village level or a six-pack takes you to the heart of the slopes at Espiolets, and a wide bridge across the river forms the end of the piste home, with elevators to take you up to street level. There are ski lockers at the bottom or top of the gondola. Along the road down to El Tarter, hotels and apartments are sold by tour operators under the Soldeu banner – so check where your proposed accommodation is if you want to avoid long walks or lots of bus rides. There is a valley bus running every 20 minutes (1.40 euros).

SCENERY ***

Unremarkable

Soldeu sits in a long, quite attractively wooded valley, and from the slopes there are wide mountain views, but they don't include much drama.

THE MOUNTAINS

Soldeu's main local slopes are on open mountainsides; there are runs in the woods back to most of the lift bases, but they can be challenging, especially when conditions are not particularly good. Reporters praise signposting, but classification of the runs often overstates difficulty.

EXTENT OF THE SLOPES ***

Pleasantly varied but crowded

The gondola rises over wooded, north-facing slopes to **Espiolets**, a broad shelf that is virtually a mini-resort – the ski school is based here, and there are extensive nursery slopes. From Espiolets, a gentle run to the east takes you to an area of long, easy runs served by a six-pack. Beyond that

KEY FACTS

Resort	1800m 5,910ft

Grandvalira (Soldeu/El Tarter/Pas/Grau Roig)

Slopes	1710-2560m 5,610-8,400ft
Lifts	67
Pistes	205km 127 miles
Green	15%
Blue	38%
Red	28%
Black	19%
Snowmaking	60%

LIFT PASSES

Prices in €

Age	1-day	6-day
under 12	32	157
12 to 17	39	201
18 to 64	43	227
65 plus	19	111

Free under 6, 70 plus

Beginner pass €26 per day in Canillo, El Tarter, Grau Roig and Pas de la Casa

Notes
Covers all lifts in Soldeu, El Tarter, Canillo, Grau Roig and Pas de la Casa; pedestrian and half-day passes available

Alternative passes
The Ski Andorra pass covers all Andorran areas and allows skiing at any single one of them each day; €198 for five non-consecutive days

is an extensive area of more varied slopes that links with the Pas de la Casa area. Going west from Espiolets takes you to the open bowl of **Riba Escorxada** and the arrival point of the gondola up from El Tarter. From here, another six-pack serves sunny slopes on Tosa dels Espiolets, and a fourth goes to the high point of Tossal de la Llosada and the link with **El Forn** above Canillo.

FAST LIFTS ★★★★★
Fine access but ...

Most of Grandvalira's key lifts are high-speed chairs or gondolas, but there are a lot of slow lifts too.

QUEUES ★★★★★
Some bottlenecks

The lift system generally copes. There can be morning queues for the gondola, but the next-door chair offers a choice. Up the mountain, the chairlifts in both directions out of Grau Roig are the main bottleneck; the quad at Cubil and access to Tosa Espiolets are also 'awful', says a February visitor. You may find crowds on some blue slopes (including lots of school classes snaking along) – the reds and blacks are much quieter.

TERRAIN PARKS ★★★★★
Now there are two

The main park – Snowpark El Tartar – above Riba Escorxada has a good reputation, but a 2012 reporter was disappointed: 'The parks were not as good as normal because of lack of snow.' A park-only day pass is available. Features normally include a triple line of kickers, huge gap jump, jib and giant airbag. There's a great selection of rails, including a big rainbow rail and wave-box and two wall rides. For beginners there are three small jumps, a 5m medium jump and a couple of fun boxes. A half-pipe is built when conditions permit. A draglift serves the park, and a fast quad nearby takes you slightly higher up. The new Sunset Park Peretol, above Bordes d'Envalira, opened in 2011 and caters for all levels. It is floodlit in the evenings, with music.

SNOW RELIABILITY ★★★★★
Much better than people expect

Despite its name (Soldeu means Sun God) the slopes generally enjoy reliable snow. Most slopes are north-facing, with a good natural snow record; there's extensive snowmaking, and excellent grooming helps maintain good snow – 'Snow machines and piste-bashers worked wonders,' said a 2012 reporter.

FOR EXPERTS ★★★★★
Hope for good snow off-piste

It's a limited area for experts – on-piste, at least. The Avet black run down to Soldeu deserves its grading, but most of the other blacks would be no more than reds (or even blues) in many resorts. The blacks on Tosa dels Espiolets are indistinguishable from the neighbouring (and more direct) red and blue, for example. And don't go

GRANDVALIRA

Most of the slopes are above the treeline and gentle – best suited to intermediates and beginners ➔

SCHOOLS

Soldeu
t 735191

Classes
5 3hr days: from €122

Private lessons
From €84 for 2hr

looking for moguls – the grooming is too thorough. But there is plenty of off-piste potential, notably in the bowl above Riba Escorxada – with off-piste routes (dotted on our map) served by a draglift that was new for last season – in the Espiolets and Solanelles areas –we've had a great time there in fresh powder – and above El Forn – with more off-piste routes. And the off-piste remains untouched for days because most visitors are beginners and early intermediates. There's no explanation on the piste map of whether off-piste routes/freeride areas are avalanche controlled, marked or patrolled.

FOR INTERMEDIATES ★★★★★
Lots to explore

There is plenty to amuse intermediates. The area east of Espiolets is splendid for building confidence, and those already confident will be able to explore the whole mountain. Riba Escorxada is a fine section for mixed-ability groups. The Canillo/El Forn sector has an easy, little-used blue run along the ridge with excellent views all the way to Pal and Arinsal and an easy black in the valley. Many of the blues and reds have short steeper sections, preceded by a 'slow' sign and netting in the middle of the piste to slow you down.

FOR BEGINNERS ★★★★★
Good, but not ideal

In some respects this is an excellent place to start, particularly because of the school. But it's not ideal: you have to go up the mountain to the nursery slopes, which is not only inconvenient but also expensive. There is no special beginner pass here (unlike other base villages in the area). If you buy a ski pack through your tour operator, you may not care, of course. Soldeu's Espiolets nursery area is vast, and there's a smaller area at Riba Escorxada, above El Tarter – each with a moving carpet. They are relatively snow-sure, and there are numerous easy pistes to move on to (though the crowds can be off-putting). The runs to resort level can be quite challenging because of crowds and snow conditions. Near-beginners are often better off riding a lift down.

FOR BOARDERS ★★★★★
Pick of the Pyrenees

Soldeu has become the home of snowboarding in the Pyrenees. This is a perfect place for beginners to learn

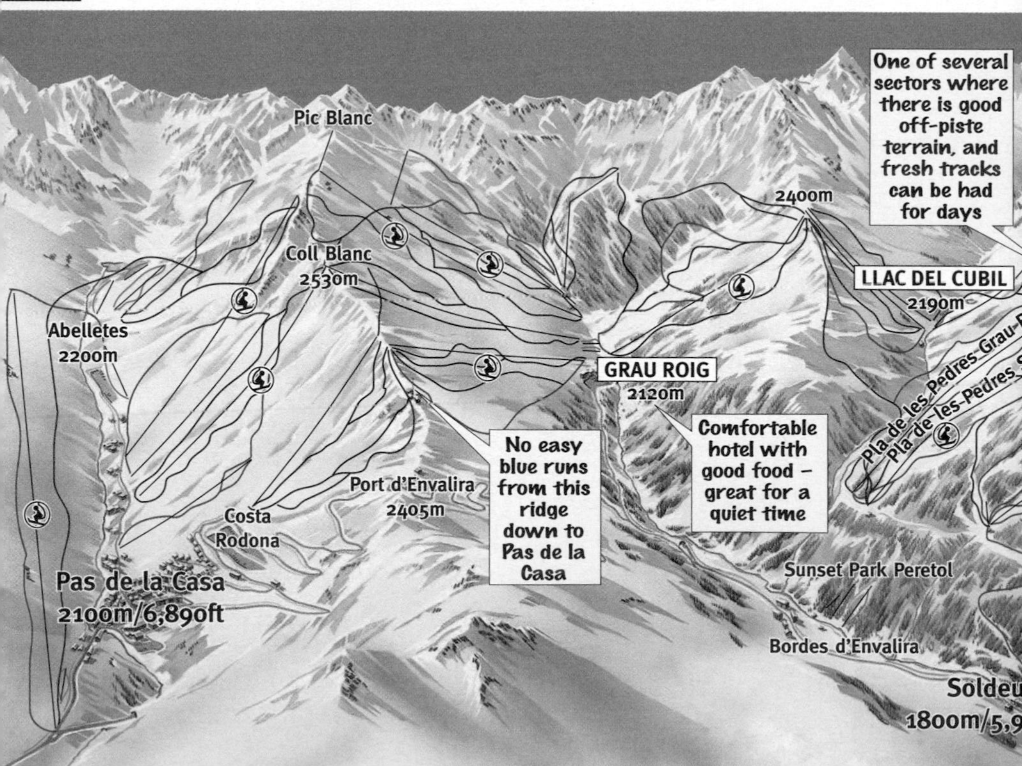

CHILDCARE

Nurseries run by ski school
Ages 1 to 4

Snow gardens run by ski school
Ages 3 to 6

Ski school
For ages 6 to 11;
15hr: from €113

on wide, gentle slopes that are served mainly by chairs, not drags. Just be wary of the plentiful flat spots. For the more advanced, Soldeu offers some good off-piste and the best terrain parks in the Pyrenees. Backcountry enthusiasts should also visit Arcalis, which has the steepest terrain and heli-boarding, and Pal, for the tree boarding. Loaded is a snowboard shop run by pro rider Tyler Chorlton.

FOR CROSS-COUNTRY ★☆☆☆☆
Head for Grau Roig

The nearest loops are at Grau Roig (see the Pas de la Casa section), reachable by bus.

MOUNTAIN RESTAURANTS ★★☆☆☆
Not a highlight

A 2012 reporter said bluntly: 'poor – head to the village'. But an earlier reporter enjoyed 'really nice Catalan sausage, roast cod, beef shank and pasta' at various places. The table-service section of Pi de Migdia at the top of the El Tarter gondola has a 'relaxed atmosphere and courteous staff'. Not far away, the Riba Escorxada restaurant includes a trattoria-pizzeria with a neat little terrace. At Espiolets, the Gall de Bosc (steakhouse) has table-service. But the best places are over towards Pas de la Casa – read that section. There is a picnic room at the Espiolets restaurant.

SCHOOLS AND GUIDES ★★★★★
One of the best for Brits

The school is well set up to deal with the huge numbers of beginner Brits, with a dedicated team of mostly native English-speaking instructors led by an Englishman. Reporters are almost all extremely positive (only one dissenting voice in the last few years), and a 2012 visitor said the school was 'brilliant – catered for our mixed ability group well, and our eight year old progressed quickly'.

FOR FAMILIES ★★☆☆☆
Unconvincing

Soldeu doesn't strike us as a great place for families, with its busy through-road and remote slopes. Whether skiing or not, children are looked after at the mid-mountain stations. There are nurseries and snow gardens for children aged three to six at various points, and a kids' circuit with themed runs at Riba Escorxada above El Tarter.

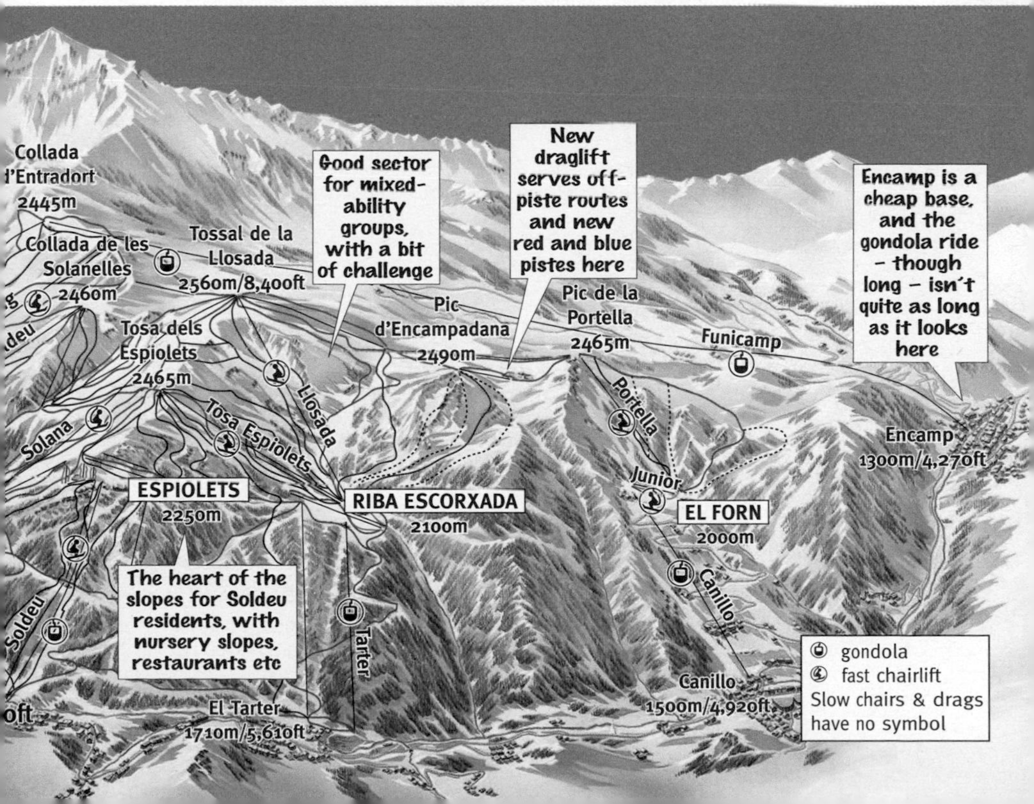

Good sector for mixed-ability groups, with a bit of challenge

New draglift serves off-piste routes and new red and blue pistes here

Encamp is a cheap base, and the gondola ride – though long – isn't quite as long as it looks here

The heart of the slopes for Soldeu residents, with nursery slopes, restaurants etc

Collada d'Entradort 2445m
Collada de les Solanelles 2460m
Tossal de la Llosada 2560m/8,400ft
Pic d'Encampadana 2490m
Pic de la Portella 2465m
Funicamp
Tosa dels Espiolets 2465m
Llosada
Tosa Espiolets
Solana
Portella
Junior
ESPIOLETS 2250m
RIBA ESCORXADA 2100m
EL FORN 2000m
Encamp 1300m/4,270ft
Canillo
Soldeu
Tarter
Canillo 1500m/4,920ft
El Tarter 1710m/5,610ft

gondola
fast chairlift
Slow chairs & drags have no symbol

↑ The gondola from the village goes up over the area's steepest piste to the main nursery slopes at Espiolets

GRANDVALIRA

ACTIVITIES

Indoor Spas, pools, hot tubs (in hotels), bowling (at Pas)

Outdoor Helicopter rides, paragliding snowmobiling, dog sledding, ballooning, snowshoeing (not all in Soldeu itself)

GETTING THERE

Air Toulouse 170km/110 miles (2hr45)

Rail L'Hospitalet-Près-L'Andorre (25km/16 miles); buses and taxis to Soldeu

UK PACKAGES

Soldeu Absolutely Snow, Crystal, Elegant Resorts, Inghams, Lagrange, Neilson, Skitracer, STC, Thomson
El Tarter Neilson
Pas de la Casa Absolutely Snow, Crystal, Independent Ski Links, Inghams, Lagrange, Neilson, Skitracer, Thomson

STAYING THERE

Accommodation is mainly in hotels, but some apartments are available.
Hotels Beware hotels sold under the Soldeu name that are actually some way out of town.
*****Sport Hotel Hermitage** (870670) At the foot of the slopes; all bedrooms are suites with mountain views. A huge spa is part of the hotel.
****Euro Esquí** (736666) On road to El Tarter but hotel 'provides a minibus and is comfortable with large rooms and good buffet food'.
****Himàlaia** (878515) Central, with sauna, steam and hot tub. Impressed a reporter with 'good rooms, excellent food, helpful staff'.
****Piolets Park** (871787) Beside the gondola, with a pool and spa. 'Good buffet-style food.'
****Sport** (870600) Over the road from the other two Sports. Lively, comfortable bar and disco-bar.
****Sport Hotel Village** (870500) Right by the Hermitage. Stylish public areas – comfortable chairs and sofas, high ceilings, beams and picture windows.
Bruxelles (851010) Recommended by a 2012 reporter for its helpful staff and cleanliness; 50m from the lift.

EATING OUT ★★★

Some atmospheric places

Most of Soldeu's restaurants are hotel-based. But we've enjoyed meals in two atmospheric old restored buildings: Fat Albert's (steaks, fish, burgers) and Borda del Rector (Andorran cuisine), nearer to El Tarter than Soldeu. The Bruxelles hotel does 'delicious food at reasonable prices'.

APRES-SKI ★★★★

No shortage of live music

A reporter last year who 'enjoyed the live music at the Villager' but little else pressed for a cut to 3 stars for this traditionally lively resort. But others seem to have more fun: 'great atmosphere'; 'live music at the Aspen'; 'people of all ages until the early hours' at the 'very busy' Fat Albert's. A 2012 reporter complained about the amount of smoke in the bars.

OFF THE SLOPES ★

Head downhill

Soldeu has lots of sporting activities, including snowmobiling, dog sledding, 4x4 driving, ice scuba-diving and ballooning, but is otherwise not great in this respect. The Sport Hotel Hermitage (pricey) and Piolets Park (cheaper) both have excellent spas. Down in Canillo is the Palau de Gel. Andorra la Vella has good shopping and the Caldea spa – see the introduction to Andorra chapter.

LINKED RESORT – 1710m

EL TARTER

El Tarter has grown over recent years and is rather sprawling, with no real centre. It is 'dull' at night. But it's otherwise a good base for the area.

LINKED RESORT – 1500m

CANILLO

This acceptably pleasant spot has no runs to valley level, but has the impressive Palau de Gel – an Olympic ice rink plus pool, gym, tennis etc.

Pas de la Casa 2100m

- ⊕ Some conveniently placed hotels
- ⊕ Andorra's liveliest nightlife
- ⊕ Attractive hotel at Grau Roig

- ⊖ Village an eyesore and traffic-choked
- ⊖ Weekend crowds from France
- ⊖ Few trees for poor-weather days

Pas has the reputation as Andorra's wildest party resort, and we don't doubt it. Having driven through it and skied down to it, we are quite happy to stay over the hill in Soldeu – or, for doorstep access to the Grandvalira slopes, at secluded Grau Roig. So are you, it seems: reports are rarely sighted.

Village charm Pas is a sizeable collection of dreary concrete-box-style apartment blocks and hotels, a product of the late 1960s and early 1970s. The central area at the base of the slopes is traffic-free, but elsewhere traffic and fumes are intrusive. By contrast, the mini-resort of Grau Roig (pronounced 'Rosh' and over the ridge from Pas) has an isolated hotel in an attractively wooded setting.
Convenience Most accommodation is conveniently placed near the lift base and slopes. There are plenty of shops and bars, as well as a sports centre.
Scenery Pas has a bleak position near the top of a high mountain pass, but there are fine views from the ridges.

THE MOUNTAIN

Slopes The slopes above Pas are all open, and vulnerable to bad weather. But there is some attractively wooded terrain over the ridge in the Grau Roig valley. From there a single lift goes on further west to the rest of the Grandvalira ski area. In the opposite direction out of Pas, a six-pack serving two runs heads towards another ridge and the French border.
Fast lifts Fast chairs exist, but they are outnumbered by slow ones and drags.
Queues Queues are rarely serious during the week, except at key bottlenecks. But at weekends and French school holidays some can develop, especially at Grau Roig.
Terrain parks There's one on the Pas side, together with a boardercross, and another at Grau Roig.
Snow reliability The combination of height and lots of snowmaking means good snow reliability, but we've generally found snow quality to be better in the Soldeu sector.
Experts There are few challenges on-piste, but there seem to be plenty of off-piste slopes inviting exploration – above Grau Roig, in particular.
Intermediates The local slopes suit confident intermediates best; more timid intermediates would be better off based in Soldeu or Grau Roig.
Beginners There are beginner slopes in Pas and Grau Roig. The Pas area is a short but inconvenient bus ride out of town. Progression to longer runs is easier in the Grau Roig sector.
Snowboarding Boarding is popular with the young crowd that the resort attracts. Drags are usually avoidable.
Cross-country There are 13km of loops near Grau Roig.
Mountain restaurants The Rifugi dels Llacs dels Pessons above Grau Roig at the head of the bowl is our favourite: a cosy, beamed table-service place with good local food.
Schools and guides The ski school has a high reputation, but a 2012 reporter complains of big classes ('16 in one').
Families There are ski kindergartens at Pas and Grau Roig, and a non-ski one at the latter.

STAYING THERE

Hotels Himàlaia-Pas (735 515) is in a good position, with a nice bar, reasonable food, comfy rooms and a pool and sauna. The Grau Roig hotel (755 556) is in a league of its own; very comfortable and smart, with a spa and 'lovely food', says a reporter.
Apartments Those in the Frontera Blanca are simple, but in pole position at the foot of the slopes.
Eating out It's not a resort for gourmets – but there is a wide enough choice of places to eat. Local tips include Cal Padrí (Catalan food) and KSB (good steakhouse).
Après-ski Après-ski can be very lively, at least at peak holiday times. Popular places include Deja Beer, a quirky pub with tapas and Wi-Fi, Paddy's Irish Pub and the Underground.
Off the slopes You can go dog sledding, snowmobiling and snowshoeing; otherwise there's visiting the leisure centre, shopping, or taking a trip to Andorra la Vella for more serious and stylish shopping and the Caldea spa (more about this in the introduction to Andorra).

Phone numbers
From abroad use the prefix +376
Central reservations phone number
Call 801074

TOURIST OFFICE
www.grandvalira.com

VOR
ARL
BERG

Austria

Austria's holiday recipe is quite distinctive. It doesn't suit everybody, but for many holidaymakers nothing else will do; in particular, French resorts will not do. Austria is the land of cute little valley villages clustered around onion-domed churches – there are no monstrous modern apartment blocks here. It's the land of friendly wooded mountains, reassuring to beginners and timid intermediates in a way that bleak snowfields and craggy peaks will never be. It's the land of friendly, welcoming people who speak good English. And it's the land of jolly, alcohol-fuelled après-ski action – in many resorts starting in mid-afternoon with dancing in mountain restaurants, and going on as long as you have the legs for it.

Back in the 1980s, Austria dominated the British skiing market. But gradually the powerful allure of the high, snow-sure French mega-resorts began to exert itself. By 1995, France had taken the lead and has kept it ever since. But the pendulum is now swinging back, with the gap between the two countries gradually closing. The latest Crystal Ski Industry Report shows that Austria's market share has risen to 28% (compared with just 20% eight years ago). Why? There are three key factors: lift systems – these days, the most efficient lift systems in Europe are not in France but in Austria; snowmaking, which in Austria is now top-notch, and means that skiers who want reliable snow can now get it even at low altitude; and on-the-spot prices. As our price survey shows, Austrian resorts are generally cheaper than French resorts – and a lot cheaper than the priciest French places.

Being the land of cute valley villages and friendly wooded mountains does have a downside: resorts that conform to this pattern are at low altitude, and as a result don't offer reliably good natural snow. Of course, you may be lucky – and recent seasons have included some bumper natural snow years for much of Austria. But the snowmaking is key; most low resorts have radically increased their snowmaking capacity in the last decade. Of course, it does require low temperatures; but in midwinter, especially, lack of snow generally coincides with low night-time temperatures, even at low altitudes, and snowmaking comes into its own.

There are some resorts that don't conform to the Austrian pattern, including some excellent high-altitude ski areas – notably Obergurgl, Ischgl and Obertauern – and some excellent glacier areas, including what we reckon are the world's best, at Hintertux and in the Stubai valley. Western Austria also has areas that get huge amounts of snow – Lech/ Zürs and especially Bregenzerwald, the snowiest corner of the Alps.

THE WORLD'S BEST LIFT SYSTEMS

The improvement in Austrian lift systems over the last decade comes as a surprise to many people. When we invented our 'fast lifts' rating a few years back, we certainly got some surprises. The resorts with the highest proportions of fast lifts in their networks are Saalbach-Hinterglemm and Ischgl, both in Austria. Obergurgl and Obertauern also get five stars. And all four have higher proportions than any other Alpine resort except Monterosa in Italy.

Always up to date
with Facebook
www.facebook.com/skiamade
You Tube
Get inspired!
Video Fans check out
www.youtube.com/skiamadetv
Ski amadé GUIDE
You're in – with the App „Ski amadé Guide"
• Free for iPhone and Android Phones
• Download it at the App Store or Android Market
Ski amadé free W-LAN
You're in - with FREE WiFi
• 250 Access Points in Ski amadé
(No Roaming in a Radius of 50 meter)
• Access Points Finder in the Mobile App „Ski amadé Guide"
KATSCHBERG
OBERTAUERN
GAMSKOGEL 2188
GALSTERBERGALM 1986 m
HAUSER KAIBLING 2015 m
PLANAI 1894 m
HOCHWURZEN 1850 m
REITERALM 1860 m
FAGERALM 1885 m
ZAUCHENSEE
KEMAHDHÖHE 1571 m
PRUGGERN 680 m
AICH 750 m
ROHRMOOS
HAUS/ENNSTAL 752 m
SCHLADMING 745 m
PICHL 765 m
FORSTAU 930 m
RADSTADT 862 m
ALTENMARKT
MANDLING 820 m
RAMSAU AM DACHSTEIN 1100 - 1300 m
RITTISBERG 1582 m
ROSSBRAND 1600 m
TANNKOPPEN 1678 m
DACHSTEINGLETSCHER 2700 m
FILZMOOS 1057 m
NEUBERG
BISCHOFSMÜTZE
SCHLADMING-DACHSTEIN
SALZBURGER SPORTWELT
FLACHAU, WAGRAIN, ST.JOHANN/ALPENDORF, ZAUCHENSEE, FLACHAUWINKL, KLEINARL, RADSTADT

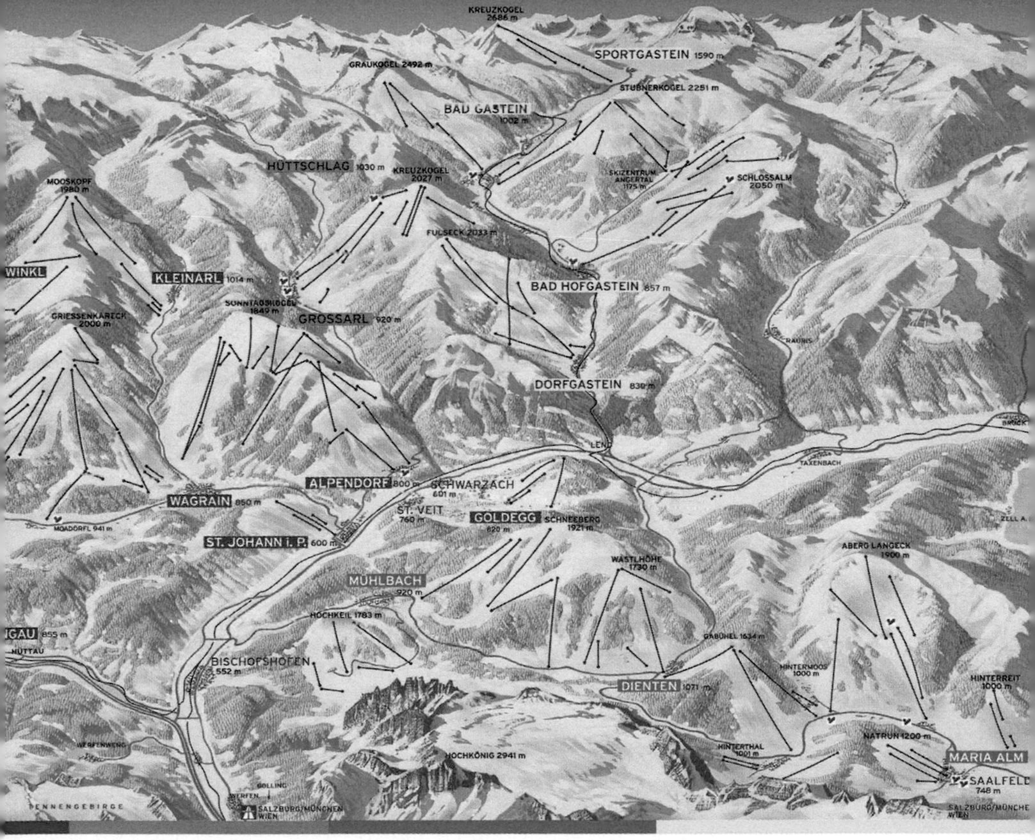

↑ Austria has some of the world's best skiable glaciers. Sölden has two glaciers, plus great viewing platforms at the top – this one overlooking the excellent glacier at Pitztal

SNOWPIX.COM / CHRIS GILL

SKI ROUTE CONFUSION

In many resorts you have to deal with chaotic handling of the concept of 'ski routes'. If a resort's piste map explains what a ski route is (and some don't), it often says a ski route is a run that is marked and avalanche controlled but not groomed or patrolled. Officially, we are told, the rule throughout Austria is that a ski route is 'marked, protected against avalanche hazards and can be groomed and patrolled'. In practice, many routes are groomed; they may or may not be patrolled. This is madness. If such a run is groomed *and* patrolled, it is a piste, and should be identified as such so that people skiing solo can confidently go down it. If it is groomed *but not* patrolled, it opens up the insane possibility that people skiing solo might descend it by mistake.

THE PARTY STARTS EARLY

These days, one of the things that annoys us most about Austrian skiing is the strange business of opening hours, or strictly speaking closing hours. As spring approaches, lift closing times in the rest of the Alps, even for some high-altitude cable cars, drift towards 5pm or even later. In Austria, basically things shut at around 4pm, even if there are three hours of daylight remaining. Nuts.

You're welcome to stay on the mountain drinking, and descend at leisure, and it has crossed our minds that the lift companies may be in the pay of the breweries. Instead of skiing on, people pack into mountain restaurants well before the end of the day and gyrate in their ski boots on the dance floor, on the tables, on the bar, on the roof beams. There are open-air ice bars, umbrella bars and transparent 'igloo' bars in which to shelter from bad weather. Huge quantities of beer and schnapps are drunk, often to the accompaniment of German drinking songs or loud Europop music. In many resorts the bands don't stop playing until after darkness falls, when the happy punters slide off in the general direction of the village to find another watering hole.

SKI AMADÉ – ONE PASS, 270 LIFTS, 860KM OF PISTES, 25 VILLAGES

Salzburgerland's Ski Amadé lift pass is one of the world's biggest in terms of the amount of terrain and number of lifts covered. What's more, with a car you really could aim to get around most of the resorts it covers – they are clustered close together, no high passes are involved in getting from one resort to another, and many areas are geared to people arriving by car, with out-of-town lifts and car parks. (They are also conveniently close to Salzburg airport – we have taken early flights from the UK and been on the slopes here well before lunchtime; come departure day, we have skied until close of play, had a leisurely drive to the airport and still had time to kill before a flight home.)

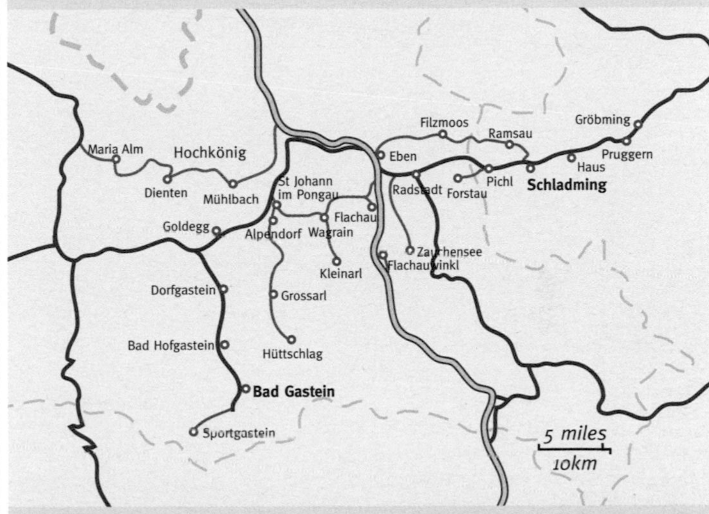

Some of the major resorts covered by the pass have their own chapters in the book. In the Schladming chapter we also cover the smaller linked resorts of Haus and Pichl, as well as Schladming's elevated satellite resort of Rohrmoos. Also close to Schladming is Ramsau in Dachstein, which has slopes at village level but also a lift up to the lip of the Dachstein glacier.

In the Bad Gastein chapter we cover not only the resorts in the Gastein valley but also the next-door valley of Grossarl, which shares a lift and piste network with Dorfgastein.

Another big region is the Salzburger Sportwelt. The largest linked area here is the 200km three-valley system linking Wagrain to Flachau in one direction and to Alpendorf/St Johann im Pongau in the other. This area also embraces an extensive lift network linking Zauchensee, Flachauwinkl and Kleinarl, plus more modest lift systems at Filzmoos, Radstadt-Altenmarkt, Eben and Goldegg. Zauchensee often has the best snow in the region because of its height and north-facing slopes.

The Hochkönig area has 150km of linked pistes running from Maria Alm in the west to Mühlbach in the east, via the smaller villages of Hinterthal and Dienten.

Considering the extent of the lift networks it covers (and the generally impressive efficiency of the lifts) the Ski Amadé pass is not expensive – 218 euros for a six-day high-season pass in 2012/13. Prices on the spot are cheap as well. In our eating and drinking price survey, resorts in the Ski Amadé region came out among the cheapest in the Alps – with prices some 20% or even 30% cheaper than the average resort. This means big savings for families, in particular, in comparison with costs in more expensive resorts.

After dinner (for those who pause for dinner, that is) the drinking and dancing starts again and carries on in town in bars and clubs until the early hours.

Of course, not all resorts conform to this image. Lech and Zürs, for example, are full of rich, cool, 'beautiful' people enjoying the comfort of 4- or 5-star hotels. And villages such as Westendorf and Alpbach are pretty, quiet, family resorts. But lots of big-name places with the best and most extensive slopes are also big party towns – notably St Anton, Saalbach-Hinterglemm, Ischgl and Sölden.

Nightlife is not limited to drinking and dancing. There are lots of floodlit toboggan runs, and UK tour operator reps organize folklore, bowling, fondue, karaoke and other evenings.

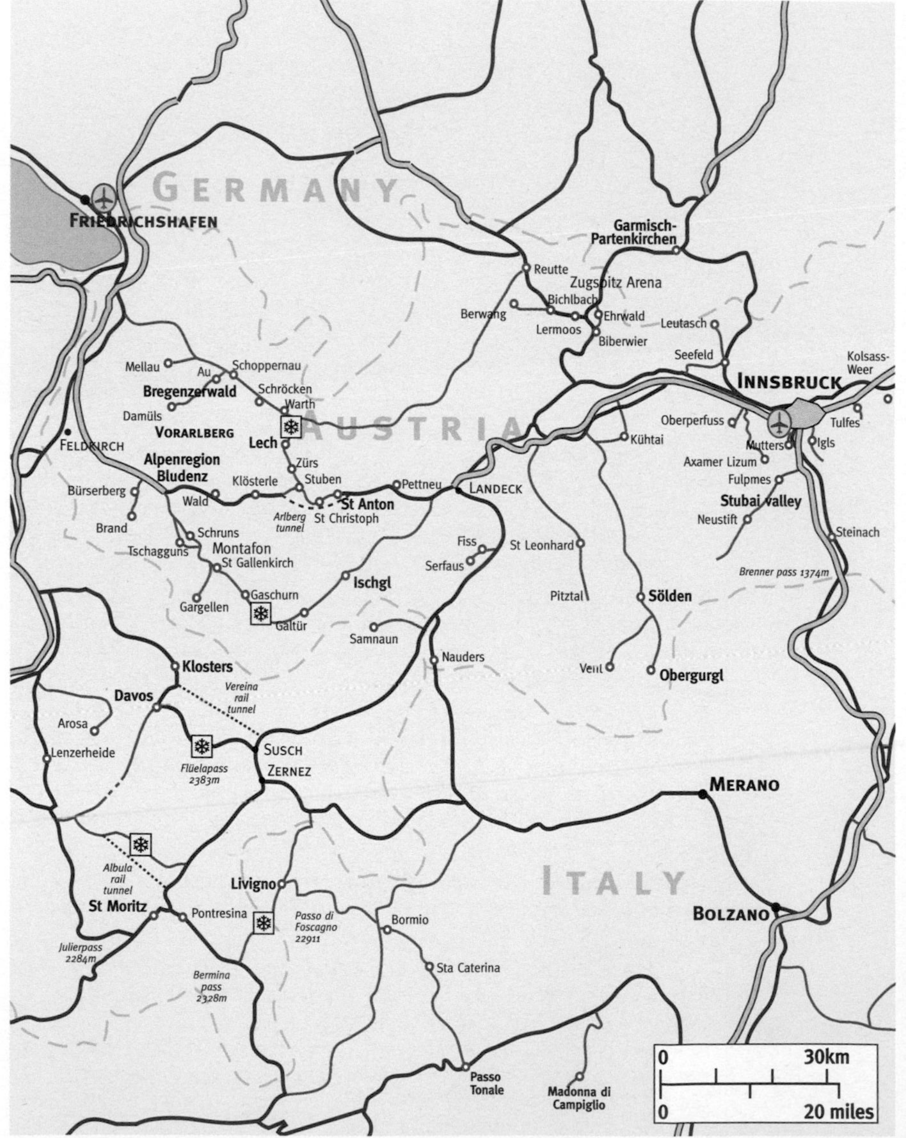

GOOD-VALUE, HIGH-QUALITY LODGING

One thing that all Austrian resorts have in common is reliably comfortable accommodation – whether it's in 4- or 5-star hotels with pools, saunas and spas or in great-value, family-run guest houses, of which Austria has thousands. Catered chalets and self-catering apartments are in general much less widely available than in French resorts.

The Germanic aversion to credit cards causes problems for many of our reporters. Many establishments do not accept cards – even quite upmarket hotels, as well as many ski lift companies. So check well in advance, or be prepared to pay in cash.

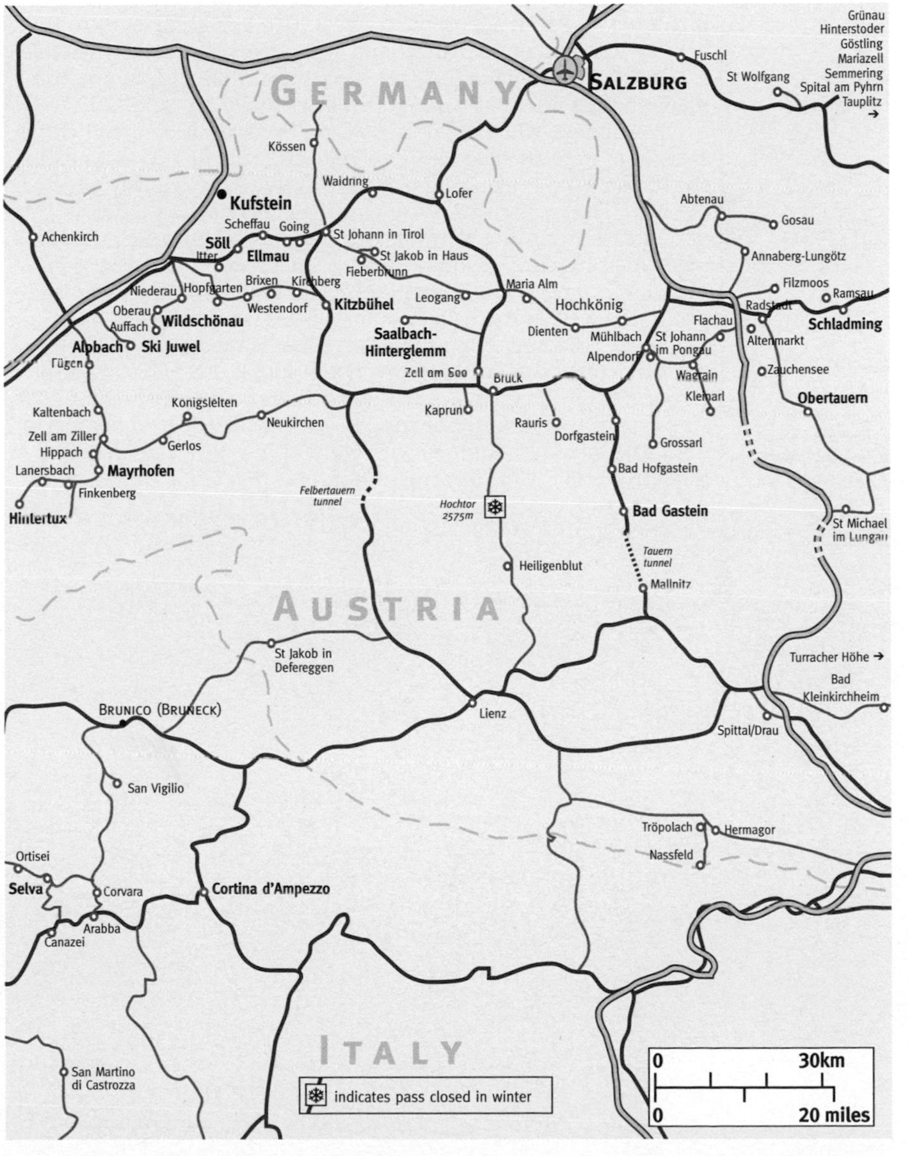

BUT STILL PUTTING UP WITH SMOKING

As other parts of the Alps have cut out smoking in bars and restaurants, Austria has lagged behind, much to the displeasure of many British visitors. In theory, there is progress. In 'multiple room establishments' the 'main room' now has to be non-smoking. In places with only one room, it's only in small places where you should now have to put up with smoke. But in practice, we find annoying smoke in most bars and some restaurants wherever we go.

GETTING AROUND THE AUSTRIAN ALPS

Austria presents few problems for the car-borne visitor, because practically all the resorts are valley villages, which involve neither steep, winding approach roads nor high-altitude passes.

The motorway along the Inn valley runs from Kufstein via Innsbruck to Landeck and, with one or two breaks, extends to the Arlberg pass and on to Switzerland. This artery is relatively reliable except in exceptionally bad weather – the altitude is low, and the road is a vital link that is kept open in virtually all conditions.

The Arlberg – which divides the Tirol from Vorarlberg, but which is also the watershed between Austria and Switzerland – is one of the few areas where driving plans are likely to be seriously affected by snow. The east–west Arlberg pass itself has a long tunnel underneath it; this isn't cheap, and you may want to take the high road when it's clear, through Stuben, St Christoph and St Anton. The Flexen pass road to Zürs and Lech branches off northwards, just to the west of the Arlberg summit; this is often closed by avalanche risk even when the Arlberg pass is open.

All cars must display a motorway toll sticker, available at petrol stations, post offices and newsagents. There's a 10-day one for 7.90 euros and a two-month one for 23 euros. From 1 November to 15 April cars must be equipped with winter tyres. Be aware that cars hired in Germany or Italy might not meet this requirement.

SNOWPIX.COM / CHRIS GILL

Most Austrian ski resorts are pretty villages with chalet style architecture – this is Lech ↓

ALPBACH TOURIST OFFICE

Alpbachtal-Wildschönau – Ski Juwe

A worthwhile new ski area is born, bringing together two small areas with a tradition of attracting British visitors

TOP 10 RATINGS	
Extent	***
Fast lifts	****
Queues	****
Snow	**
Expert	**
Intermediate	***
Beginner	***
Charm	****
Convenience	***
Scenery	***

RPI	80
lift pass	£160
ski hire	£80
lessons	£70
food & drink	£100
total	**£410**

NEWS

2012/13: An eight-seat gondola from Inneralpbach to Schatzberg is to open for 2012/13, linking the Alpbach and Auffach ski areas. A red piste will run down the top stage of the gondola, but it will not go down to valley level.

KEY FACTS

Resort	1000m 3,280ft
Ski Juwel	
Slopes	670-2025m 2,200-6,640ft
Lifts	47
Pistes	128km 80 miles
Blue	22%
Red	65%
Black	13%
Snowmaking	60%

- + Charming, traditional, relaxed villages, good for families
- + Convenient nursery slopes in Alpbach and Inneralpbach
- + Very low local prices
- + Good intermediate terrain, not without challenges

- – A lot of bus riding if you choose to stay in cute central Alpbach
- – Few long easy runs to build confidence – and hardly any in the Wildschönau resorts
- – Lower slopes can suffer from poor snow, despite snowmaking help

Alpbach is an old British favourite – it even has a British ski club. Wildschönau is best known in Britain as the area that includes the smaller resort of Niederau, although its major resort in skiing terms is Auffach. A two-stage gondola is all it has taken to link Alpbach and Auffach. Reith, like Niederau, isn't linked to the others resorts; we deal with these two separately at the end. Oberau, another possible base, is rather limited in appeal and appears in our directory.

The linked area offers an appealing mix of small, friendly villages and fairly extensive intermediate slopes. We're expecting a flood of reports from you, dear readers – and we'll be there next season, for sure.

THE RESORTS

These resorts are just a few km south of the Inn valley, a short drive east of Innsbruck. The two adjacent valleys have been linked by building a two-stage gondola from Inneralpbach, in the Alpbach valley, to the top of the Wildschönau slopes. Together they form a fair-sized area, but note that they are also part of the Kitzbüheler Alpen All Star pass area, which includes the SkiWelt (Söll, Ellmau etc), Kitzbühel, Saalbach and others. This is a great basis for a bit of day tripping, especially with a car.

Village charm Alpbach is an exceptionally pretty, captivating place; hotels and guest houses in traditional woody, chalet style crowd around the pretty church. Auffach is a more diffuse affair, but still a pleasantly rustic, traditional-style place.

Convenience Inneralpbach, once a backwater hamlet, is now the obvious place to stay, with gondolas to the top of both mountains. From the more remote bits of Inneralpbach you get to

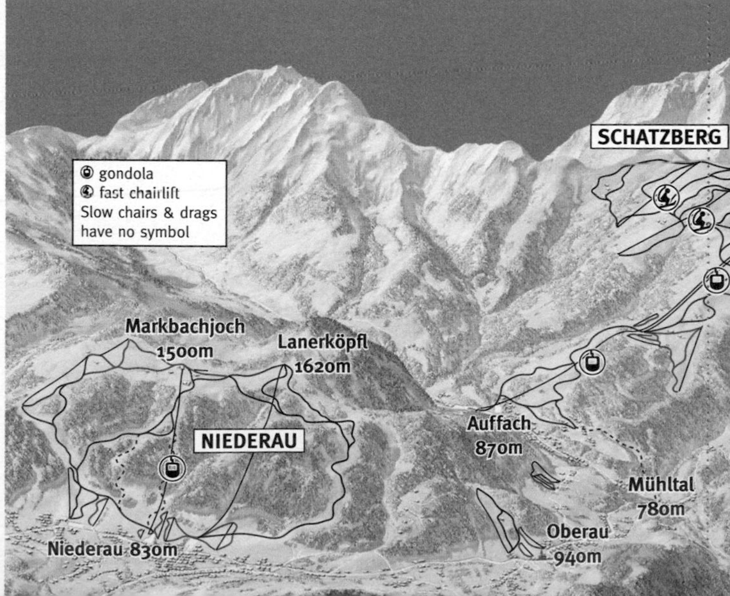

the main lifts by riding a drag and skiing down. If you stay in central Alpbach, you need to use a free shuttle-bus to Inneralpbach or to Alpbach's original gondola at Achenwirt. Auffach is centred on its gondola, but it spreads quite widely, and of course it's not very handy for the Alpbach slopes. Ski-buses link Niederau, Oberau and Auffach.
Scenery The pretty valleys and low, partly wooded ridges are picture-postcard Tirol.

THE MOUNTAINS

Throughout the area, the upper slopes are open, the lower slopes wooded.
Slopes From Inneralpbach, a two-stage gondola takes you up to open, north-east-facing slopes on the pointy Wiedersbergerhorn, served by short chairs and drags, and longer runs descending into trees towards the mid and bottom stations of a second gondola, rising from Achenwirt – the usual starting point for those staying in downtown Alpbach. There is a red run back to Inneralpbach taking you right past the base station of the new linking gondola. This goes in two stages to Schatzberg, the top of the Auffach slopes. There is a red run back to the mid-station, but no piste back to Inneralpbach – we guess the lower section is too sunny to be viable.

The pre-existing Auffach slopes follow much the same pattern as the Alpbach ones, but with better lifts.

The pistes total 128km – 145km if you were to include ski routes.
Fast lifts The access lifts are all gondolas, and Auffach has two six-packs on its upper slopes – but the upper lifts at Alpbach are all slow.
Queues The gondolas are generally able to meet the demand.
Terrain parks There are parks and pipes on both mountains, but a reporter says the Auffach one, at least, was 'absolute rubbish' last season.
Snow reliability These resorts cannot claim great snow reliability; but the slopes all face somewhere between north and east, and the altitudes are not the lowest in the Tirol. There is extensive snowmaking.
Experts The reds and the blacks (often groomed) are not without challenge, and there are runs of 1000m vertical on both mountains when snow is good. There are one or two ski routes, and more adventurous routes including the Gern run from Schatzberg down a deserted valley to the road a little way from Auffach. The schools take the top classes off-piste.
Intermediates There is plenty of fine red-run terrain; but blue-run skiers wanting to build their confidence are not well catered for at Alpbach, and not catered for at all at Auffach.
Beginners Alpbach beginners love the sunny nursery slopes beside the village. Inneralpbach has a good slope at valley level, too. The main slopes are not ideal for confidence-building – there are few satisfactory blues. But you are much better off here than in Auffach, where beginners are effectively confined to the nursery

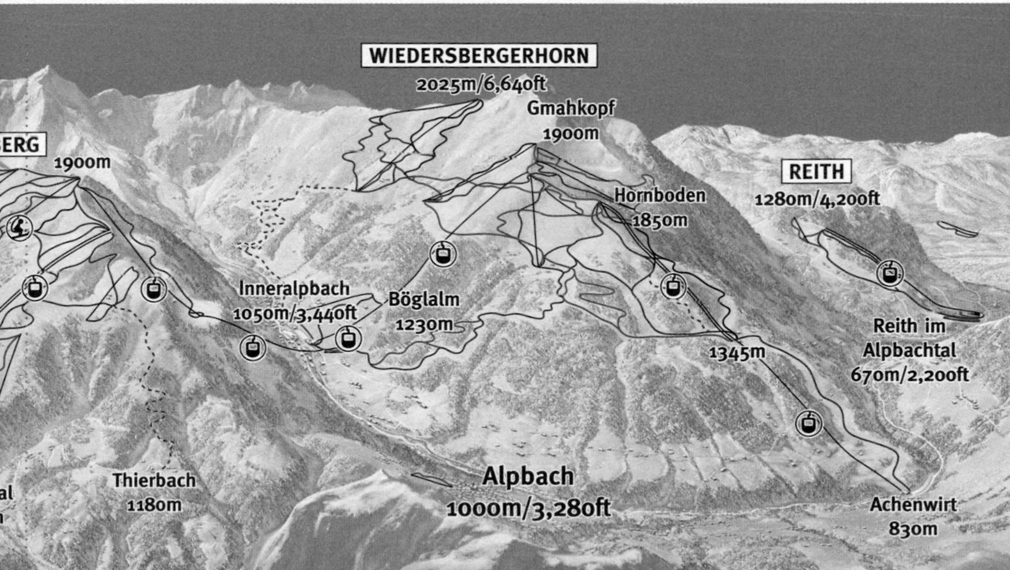

UK PACKAGES

Alpbach Alpine Answers, Crystal, Inghams, Ski Solutions, Thomson
Auffach Inghams
Niederau Crystal, Independent Ski Links, Inghams, Neilson, Skitracer, Thomson

Phone numbers
From elsewhere in Austria, for Alpbach add the prefix 05336 (from abroad +43 5336); and for the Wildschönau resorts add the prefix 05339 (from abroad +43 5339)

TOURIST OFFICE

www.alpbachtal.at
www.wildschoenau.com
www.skijuwel.com

slopes at mid-mountain, reached by the first stage of the gondola.
Snowboarding There's some good freeride terrain, plus parks.
Cross-country There are 20km of pretty cross-country trails up the valley beyond Inneralpbach.
Mountain restaurants There is an adequate supply dotted over both mountains, all named on the piste map. Reports, please. There's a picnic room at the top of Alpbach's Achenwirt gondola.
Schools and guides There's a choice of schools in each of the main villages. We lack recent reports.
Families Reporters find the compact, relaxed village and adjacent nursery slopes of Alpbach very child-friendly. The schools have excellent facilities.

STAYING THERE

Hotels There are several appealing 4-star places in central Alpbach, but we'll be aiming for Inneralpbach and the Wiedersbergerhorn (5612) or the Galtenberg (5610). In Auffach the 4-star Platzl (8928) and Auffacherhof (88370) are good central spots.
Apartments You can book some through the tourist office websites.
Eating out Mostly in hotels and guest houses. In Alpbach, tips have included the Post, the Alphof and the Jakober.
Après-ski At peak times this is typically Tirolean, with lots of noisy teatime beer swilling in the bars of central hotels. Joe's Salettl at Inneralpbach is popular.
Off the slopes There are pretty walks, and tobogganing – including a 5km run at Auffach, from the mid-station of the gondola. Trips to Innsbruck and Salzburg are possible.

875m

NIEDERAU

Niederau is 7km from Auffach, at the foot of a wooded mountain that rises to only 1600m. The village is not notably cute – it is quite spread out, with a cluster of restaurants and shops around the gondola station forming the nearest thing to a focal point. But few hotels are more than five minutes' walk from a main lift.

The main lifts are an eight-person gondola to Markbachjoch and a fast quad a few minutes' walk away, going slightly higher on Lanerköpfl. The whole area is very small – you can ski most of it in an hour or two. There are a couple of ungroomed ski routes, and three pistes to the village – an easy black, a proper red and, on skier's right, a relatively easy red. So near-beginners have to be prepared to tackle a red if they want to progress. There are excellent nursery slopes at the top and bottom, but the low ones don't get much sun in midwinter.

The 4-star Sonnschein (8353) and the 3-star Austria (8188) are central hotel tips. The village has a nice balance of après-ski – neither too noisy for families nor too quiet for the young and lively. Some bars are quite lively both at teatime and at night. Several hotel swimming pools are open to the public.

705m

REITH IM ALPBACHTAL

Reith's mountain is basically a one-run affair, but its access lift is a modern gondola rising almost 600m, and there is a top-to-bottom toboggan run.

ALPBACH TOURIST OFFICE

When the snow is good, there is nothing to beat a low, wooded Tirolean resort →

BAD GASTEIN TOURIST OFFICE

Bad Gastein – Ski Amadé

If you fancy 'taking the cure', there are few better resorts; even if you don't, you're likely to be impressed by the slopes

TOP 10 RATINGS	
Extent	***
Fast lifts	***
Queues	***
Snow	***
Expert	***
Intermediate	****
Beginner	**
Charm	***
Convenience	**
Scenery	***

RPI	90
lift pass	£160
ski hire	£80
lessons	£110
food & drink	£100
total	**£450**

Ski amadé
www.skiamade.com

- \+ Excellent, testing long runs for confident intermediates
- \+ Some relatively high slopes
- \+ Good mountain restaurants
- \+ Excellent thermal spas, but ...

- − Main resorts are spa towns, lacking the usual Austrian resort ambience
- − Valley slopes are split into five areas, and having a car helps
- − Lacks genuinely easy runs

With its essentially red-gradient mountains and spa-town resorts, the Gastein valley is a bit different from Austrian ski resort norms. We prefer spacious Bad Hofgastein to steeply tiered, rather urban Bad Gastein. But little rustic Dorfgastein, down the valley, is our favourite. All three are covered here.

THE RESORT

Bad Gastein is an old spa town near the head of the Gastein valley. At its heart is the original spa area, laid out in a compact horseshoe on steep slopes. Above this, at the level of the railway and the gondola station, is a modern suburb with more lodgings.

The Stubnerkogel slopes above the town link with Bad Hofgastein, down the valley. Beyond that, a separate area of slopes above Dorfgastein links with Grossarl in the next valley. Up the valley is another separate area at Sportgastein. Various ski-bus routes and trains connect the villages and lift stations, and 'run as per timetable' – though many bus services stop earlier than keen après-skiers would wish.

Lots of resorts in this region are covered by the Ski Amadé lift pass (read the Austria intro), and are easily reached.

Village charm The core is a curious mix of towny buildings – some grand, some modest. Away from here, the more modern hotels and guest houses have more of a normal ski resort feel.

Convenience The higher part of the resort is handy for the Stubnerkogel gondola, but the resort as a whole spreads widely, and the double chair to the separate Graukogel area is on the opposite side of town.

Scenery The resort is set in virtually a gorge, steeply tiered and wooded. The slopes are higher than many Austrian resorts (particularly at Sportgastein), with wide views as a result.

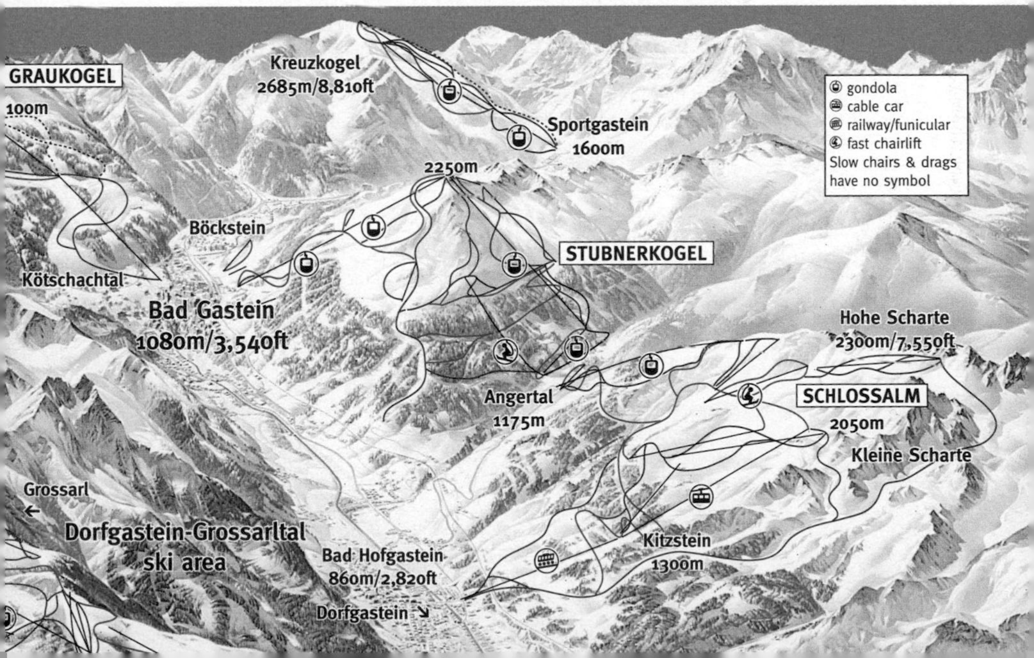

NEWS

2012/13: The snowmaking on Stubnerkogel will be improved. Plans are afoot for Schlossalm – four new lifts plus new slopes, possibly for 2014.

2011/12: Snowmaking was improved. The terrain park was enlarged.

KEY FACTS

Resort	1080m 3,540ft
The Gastein valley and Grossarl areas	
Slopes	840-2685m 2,760-8,810ft
Lifts	42
Pistes	216km 134 miles
Blue	26%
Red	60%
Black	14%
Snowmaking	57%
Bad Gastein, Bad Hofgastein, Sportgastein only	
Slopes	860-2685m 2,820-8,810ft
Lifts	25
Pistes	129km 80 miles

THE MOUNTAINS

Most of the runs are on open slopes; this is a quite exposed region, and wind can affect both the snow and the lifts. Sportgastein is especially vulnerable. Graukogel is wooded. The piste map tries to cover all the areas and is difficult to follow.

Slopes From the Stubnerkogel gondola a long blue run goes back to base, but most runs head for Angertal, which links with Bad Hofgastein.

Fast lifts There are quite a few gondolas, but also plenty of slow chairlifts and draglifts.

Queues There are few major problems.

Terrain parks There is a 'quiet and well-run' park on Stubnerkogel.

Snow reliability The slopes go a bit higher than many Austrian rivals – Sportgastein much higher – and there is snowmaking on crucial sections. Reporters in 2011 said the snow was better at Dorfgastein-Grossarl than at Stubnerkogel-Schlossalm.

Experts The few black runs are not severe, but many reds are long and satisfying. Graukogel has some of the most testing pistes. There is plenty of good off-piste – by the Jungeralm chair on the shady side of Stubnerkogel, for example. Sportgastein has an itinerary route from top to bottom.

Intermediates Confident intermediates, will find long, leg-sapping red runs in all sectors. The valley in general and Stubnerkogel in particular are not nearly so good for blue-run skiers. Sportgastein has a good range of runs, up to an easy black.

Beginners There are adequate nursery areas near the gondola station and at Angertal. But progression is awkward – the mountains are essentially steep. The few easy long runs are boring paths. There are no free lifts.

Snowboarding The valley hosts snowboard events, and there is good freeriding. Draglifts are dotted around.

Cross-country There are 90km of trails, but most are low down.

Mountain restaurants There are lots of pleasant huts doing decent food; but they can get crowded. Reader tips include Stubneralm, Jungerstube, Waldgasthof and Hirschenhütte.

Schools and guides Past reports on the school have been favourable.

Families Facilities are quite good. Angertal has a snow adventure park.

STAYING THERE

Most lodging is in hotels.

Hotels There are lots of smart 4- and 3-star hotels with spa facilities. The Grüner Baum (25160) is a lovely retreat, but wildly inconvenient except for langlauf (though they do have a shuttle-bus). Reader tips include the quite grand Elizabeth Park (25510) and the quirky, friendly Mozart (26860).

Eating out Choice is reasonable. The traditional Jägerhäusl has been tipped for its lovely food and large portions. The Amici is a good-value Italian.

Après-ski The bars are lively at close of play; evenings are more subdued. The Silver Bullet and Haeggbloms are among the most popular. Bars for a quiet late drink include the Bellini and Ritz. There are a couple of discos and a casino.

Off the slopes The thermal spa/pool facilities are excellent and extensive – but expensive. There's ice climbing, and there are quite a few shops. Excursions to Salzburg are possible.

Bad Hofgastein 860m

- ⊞ Sunny, spacious setting
- ⊞ Lovely long runs
- ⊟ Lacks ski resort ambience
- ⊟ Funicular from base can be crowded

Bad Hofgastein is a sizeable, spacious, quiet spa town set on flat ground in the widest part of the valley, with funicular access to the slopes.

Village charm The pedestrianized centre is compact and pleasant enough to stroll around, with lots of shops and restaurants. But it does feel like a town; there's little traditional Austrian rustic charm. There is a sizeable park next to the centre.

Convenience The resort spreads widely; the funicular is a long walk or ski-bus ride away from many lodgings. It's a longer ski-bus ride to Angertal.

Scenery Good valley views.

THE MOUNTAINS

Schlossalm is a broad, open bowl, with runs through patchy woods both to Bad Hofgastein and Angertal. As at Stubnerkogel, wind can be a problem.

Slopes The funicular to Kitzstein is followed by a cable car to the Schlossalm slopes. These link to Stubnerkogel via Angertal.

↑ The slopes of Stubnerkogel, seen here from Angertal, are mainly wooded and quite steep

SNOWPIX.COM / CHRIS GILL

UK PACKAGES

Alpine Answers, Crystal, Crystal Finest, Ski Line, Ski Miquel, STC, White Roc

Bad Hofgastein Crystal, Crystal Finest, Ski Club Freshtracks, Ski Line, Skitracer, STC

Phone numbers
From elsewhere in Austria add the prefix 06434 (Bad Gastein), 06432 (Bad Hofgastein), 06433 (Dorfgastein); from abroad use the prefix +43 and omit the initial '0'

TOURIST OFFICE

For all resorts in the Gastein valley:
www.gastein.com

Fast lifts Getting up the mountain can be slow, and a few old chairs remain.
Queues The access lifts are queue-prone at peak times – and the cable car can be closed by wind.
Terrain parks There isn't one.
Snow reliability Snowmaking is fairly extensive, but snow-cover down to the bottom is unreliable, especially on the sunny Angertal slopes.
Experts There are no real challenges on the local pistes, but there is ample opportunity to go off-piste.
Intermediates The Schlossalm slopes offer a good range of red runs, from easy to testing; the few blues are not all entirely easy. There are splendid long reds to the valley floor (we loved the away-from-the-lifts Hohe Scharte-Nord (10.4km long, 1440m vertical).
Beginners There is a small nursery area at the funicular station. You have to catch a bus to the bigger nursery area at Angertal. And then you have few options for progression.
Snowboarding Good freeriding. Draglifts are dotted around though.
Cross-country Bad Hofgastein makes a fine base for cross-country when its lengthy valley-floor trails have snow.
Mountain restaurants Reader favourites are the self-service Aeroplanstadl and the table-service Pyrkerhof hotel. Other tips are Haitzingalm and Bärsteinalm.
Schools and guides 'Good teaching that pushed us,' says a recent report.
Families See Bad Gastein.

STAYING THERE

Hotels We enjoyed a stay in 2010 at the 4-star Bismarck (66810) – excellent food, fairly central. Reader tips include the St Georg (61000; 200m to lift) and Palace (67150).

Apartments The Alpenparks resort is still 'excellent', says a repeat visitor.
Eating out There's plenty of choice. Piccola Italia is a good-value, popular choice. Other reader tips: the Salzburgerhof, the 'inexpensive' Chinese and Dino's (for pizza).
Après-ski Quiet by Austrian standards. The Aeroplanstadl on the hill and central Piccolo ice bar are popular at close of play. Head to Cafe Weitmoser, a historic little castle, for cakes. There are said to be a couple of disco bars.
Off the slopes The huge Alpen Therme Gastein spa has excellent pools etc. Other amenities include good shops, walking and a full-size ice rink.

DOWN-VALLEY VILLAGE – 830m

DORFGASTEIN

Dorfgastein is a quiet, rustic village. It has its own extensive slopes, shared with Grossarl in the next valley. A two-stage gondola and alternative chairlift start a little way outside the village. There is a nursery slope here, and another at the gondola mid-station. Like the other sectors, the mountain is essentially of red gradient, and best suits confident intermediates. On the front side there is one good long blue, but it doesn't go all the way to the valley. There is a terrain park. There are pleasant huts. We endorse readers' support for the excellent table-service Wengeralm. A 2011 visitor likes the Gipflstadl: 'Good food and excellent sun terrace.' The village ski schools get good reviews. Off-slope amenities are limited, but there's a pool with sauna and steam. Evenings are quiet. Reporters love the 4-star hotel Römerhof (7777) – 'superb food, great spa, extremely good value'.

Wow! What's new in Austria? See p168.

Ellmau

A good base on the extensive SkiWelt circuit, combining charm with reasonable convenience – good value too

TOP 10 RATINGS	
Extent	****
Fast lifts	****
Queues	****
Snow	**
Expert	*
Intermediate	****
Beginner	****
Charm	***
Convenience	***
Scenery	***

RPI	85
lift pass	£170
ski hire	£60
lessons	£105
food & drink	£100
total	**£435**

NEWS

2012/13: Snowmaking is to be further improved. The toboggan run is to be floodlit.

2011/12: Parents can now buy one pass between two, which either can use.

- + Part of the SkiWelt, Austria's largest linked ski area
- + Excellent nursery slopes
- + Quiet, charming family resort – more appealing than Söll
- + Cheap, even by Austrian standards
- + Snowmaking is now more extensive and well used; even so ...

- – Low altitude can mean poor snow
- – Main lift a bus or drag from village
- – Runs on upper slopes mostly short
- – Few challenges on-piste
- – Limited range of nightlife
- – The slopes can get crowded
- – Appallingly inadequate piste map

If you like the sound of the large, undemanding SkiWelt circuit, Ellmau has a lot to recommend it as your base – as does Scheffau, also covered here. But consider Brixen, Hopfgarten and Westendorf too – covered in the Söll chapter.

THE RESORT

Ellmau sits at the north-eastern corner of the SkiWelt – an area of 279km of linked slopes that's an impressive 15km across. Other parts of it are covered in our chapter on Söll. You can also progress (via Brixen) to the slopes of Kitzbühel; these and various other ski areas within easy reach are covered by the Kitzbüheler Alpen AllStarCard ski pass.

Village charm Although sizeable, the village remains quiet, with traditional chalet-style buildings, welcoming bars and shops, and a pretty church.

Convenience Accommodation is scattered; there is some out by the funicular to the main slopes, but we prefer to stay in the compact centre of the village. There is a frequent bus service, but the buses are very crowded at peak times.

Scenery The village and the slopes enjoy great close-up views of the craggy Wilder Kaiser, across the valley.

THE MOUNTAINS

The piste map is hopelessly over-ambitious in trying to show the whole area in a single view. There's a mix of short runs at altitude and much longer ones to the villages. Lots of trees.

Slopes The funicular railway on the edge of the village takes you up to Hartkaiser, from where a fine long red leads down to Blaiken (Scheffau's lift base station). Here, one of two

↑ The funicular, curling up gently rounded Hartkaiser on the right, starts a little way from the centre, which is clustered around the church

TVB WILDER-KAISER

KEY FACTS

Resort	800m 2,620ft
Entire SkiWelt	
Slopes	620-1890m 2,030-6,200ft
Lifts	91
Pistes	279km 173 miles
Blue	44%
Red	46%
Black	10%
Snowmaking	75%

LIFT PASSES

SkiWelt Wilder Kaiser-Brixental

Prices in €

Age	1-day	6-day
under 16	21	100
16 to 17	33	160
18 plus	41	200

Free under 7

Senior no deals

Beginner points cards

Notes
Ski-bus included; single ascent and part-day options

Alternative passes
Kitzbüheler Alpen AllStarCard covers: Schneewinkel (St Johann), Kitzbühel, SkiWelt, Wildschönau, Alpbachtal, Skicircus Saalbach-Hinterglemm and Zell am See-Kaprun

gondolas takes you up to Brandstadl. Immediately beyond Brandstadl, the slopes become rather bitty; an array of short runs and lifts link Brandstadl to Zinsberg. From Zinsberg, long, south-facing pistes lead down to Brixen, where a gondola goes up to Choralpe in Westendorf's area and a lovely north-facing red piste comes back down. From Choralpe you can also head off towards the Kitzbühel slopes. Part-way down to Brixen you can head towards Söll, and if you go up Hohe Salve, you get access to a long, west-facing run to Hopfgarten.

Ellmau and Going share a pleasant little area of slopes on Astberg, slightly apart from the rest of the area, and well suited to the unadventurous and to families. One piste leads to the funicular for access to the rest of the SkiWelt. The main Astberg chair is rather inconveniently positioned, midway between Ellmau and Going.

Fast lifts The main access lift is a fast funicular. Fast chairs are increasingly common on the upper slopes; a couple of seasons ago the Osthang eight-pack clinched a ★★★★ rating.

Queues Lift upgrades have greatly improved this once queue-prone area, and most reporters find few queues. But there are several bottlenecks at slow chairs around the mountain, and when snow is poor the links between Zinsberg and Eiberg get crowded.

Terrain parks Ellmau has its own terrain park, the Kaiserpark, with beginner and expert boxes, rails and kickers, as well as a chill-out zone.

Snow reliability With a low average height, and important links that get a lot of sun, the snowmaking that the SkiWelt has installed is essential; the Ellmau-Going sector now claims 80% of slopes are covered. Snowmaking can, of course, only be used when temperatures are low enough. The north-facing Eiberg area above Scheffau holds its snow well. Grooming is excellent, and reports have praised the snowmaking.

Experts There are steep plunges off the Hohe Salve summit, a ski route from Brandstadl down to Scheffau and a little mogul field between Brandstadl and Neualm, but the area isn't really suitable unless you go off-piste.

Intermediates With good snow, the SkiWelt is a paradise for those who love easy cruising. There are lots of blue runs, and many of the reds deserve a blue classification. It is a big area, and you get a feeling of travelling around. In good snow the long red runs to the valley – down the Hartkaiser funicular, for example – are excellent. The main challenge arises when ice and slush can make even gentle lower slopes tricky. For timid intermediates the easy slopes of Astberg are handy.

Beginners Ellmau has an array of good nursery slopes covered by snow-guns. The main ones are at the Going end, but there are some by the road to the funicular. The Astberg chair opens up a more snow-sure plateau at altitude. The Brandstadl area has a section of short easy runs.

Snowboarding Ellmau is a good place to learn as its local slopes are easy.

Cross-country The SkiWelt area has a total of 170km of trails, including long and challenging ones, but trails at altitude are lacking.

Mountain restaurants There are many small places providing good-value

Where is Austria's Golden Gate? Answer on p168.

UK PACKAGES

Crystal, Neilson, Ski Line, Skitracer, STC, Thomson
Scheffau Crystal, STC, Thomson

Phone numbers
From elsewhere in Austria add the prefix 05358; from abroad use the prefix +43 5358

TOURIST OFFICES

Wilder Kaiser
(Ellmau, Söll, Scheffau, Going)
www.wilderkaiser.info

SkiWelt
www.skiwelt.at

food in pleasant surroundings. The Rübezahl Alm above Ellmau is one of our favourites – a lovely old hut with good food (the ribs have been recommended) and lots of different rooms and areas which make it very cosy; but it gets very busy. Other reporter tips include: the Jägerhütte (below Hartkaiser) for 'a lovely atmosphere and good food' before enjoying the home run, and the 'jolly' Hartkaiser ('loos accessed by escalator!'). The Jochstub'n has a self-service part and a 'cute, lively' bar: 'good for an end of afternoon drink'. The Bergkaiser has 'efficient service, good-value food' and the Blattlalm on Astberg 'super views'. Read the Söll chapter, too.

Schools and guides There are three schools and a specialist boarding school in Ellmau, a couple in Scheffau and another in Going. We have no recent reports.

Families Ellmau is an attractive resort for families: 'Probably the best family resort I have visited – from ski school to alternative attractions,' says a 2012 visitor. Both the Ellmauer and the Top schools have their own fun parks and play areas. The leisure centre and toboggan run are popular.

STAYING THERE

Ellmau is essentially a hotel and guest house resort, though there are apartments that can be booked locally.

Hotels The Bär (2395) is an elegant, relaxed luxury place. The Kaiserhof (2022) is another luxury option. The Sporthotel (3755) is 'incredible for the price', with 'huge five-course meals, gorgeous pool/spa facilities, huge lounge'. The Hochfilzer (2501) is central and well equipped (with outdoor hot tub, indoor pool, sauna, steam); the simpler Pension Claudia is under the same ownership. The Kaiserblick (2230) has good spa facilities and is right by the piste.

Apartments There is a wide variety. The Landhof apartments – with pool, sauna and steam room – have impressed a regular visitor.

Eating out There is quite a wide choice. The jolly Lobewein is a splendid, big, central chalet, with cheerful service in countless rooms. The Ellmauer Alm has been tipped: 'good service despite being very busy'. A reporter's young children loved the 'no nonsense food' in the village's Tex-Mex place.

Après-ski Bettina is good for coffee and cakes. Memory is the early-evening riotous party pub. Pub 66 and Ötzy Bar have regular events such as karaoke and 'erotic dancers'. The Ellmauer Alm has live entertainment. Tour operator reps organize events such as sleigh rides and tubing, and bowling and Tirolean folklore evenings in Söll. Ski night and the Instructors' Ball have a party atmosphere each week. The toboggan run from the Astberg lift is also recommended.

Off the slopes A guest card entitles you to various discounts, including entry to the KaiserBad leisure centre. There's a pool and an ice rink. There are many excursions available, including to Innsbruck, Salzburg and Vitipeno. Valley walks are spoiled by the busy main road.

LINKED RESORT – 745m

SCHEFFAU

Little Scheffau is one of the most attractive of the region's villages and well placed for quick access to most parts of the SkiWelt area – though the village itself is not convenient for the lifts. You can ski down to the gondolas at Blaiken, but it's a bus ride back. The village spreads up quite a steep slope. Reporters recommend the 3-star Alpin (85560) and the central Gasthof Weberbauer (8115). There aren't many village restaurants; the Weberbauer has been recommended. Après-ski is 'non-existent', says one happy reporter, but there are a couple of bars. The Sternbar, nearest to the gondolas, is lively after the lifts close. There's bowling and tobogganing but little else to do off the slopes.

LINKED RESORT – 775m

GOING

Going is a tiny, attractively rustic village, ideal for families looking for a quiet time. It is well placed for the limited but quiet slopes of the Astberg and for the vast area of nursery slopes shared with Ellmau. Prices are low, but as it's at one extreme end of the SkiWelt, it's not an ideal base for covering the whole of the region on the cheap unless you have a car to speed up access to Scheffau and Söll (or you're happy to take buses). The Lanzenhof (2428) is a cosy central pension where we have enjoyed an excellent dinner.

Hintertux / Tux valley

Small, unspoiled, traditional villages, high snow-sure glacier slopes and lots of other areas covered by the valley lift pass

TOP 10 RATINGS

Extent	***
Fast lifts	***
Queues	***
Snow	*****
Expert	***
Intermediate	***
Beginner	**
Charm	***
Convenience	**
Scenery	***

RPI	85
lift pass	£170
ski hire	£70
lessons	£85
food & drink	£105
total	**£430**

NEWS

2011/12: A 10-person gondola replaced the double chair from Tuxer Fernerhaus on the glacier.

At Finkenberg, a six-pack replaced the Katzenmoos double chair, on the upper slopes of Penken.

- + Hintertux has one of the best year-round glaciers in the world
- + Lanersbach's slopes form part of an extensive area, linked to Mayrhofen
- + Wide-ranging area lift pass
- + Some excellent off-piste
- + A choice of quiet, unspoiled, traditional villages to stay in

- − Not the place for shops and throbbing nightlife
- − Not ideal for beginners or timid intermediates
- − Still some draglifts and slow chairs on the glacier slopes
- − Glacier can be cold and bleak in midwinter

For guaranteed good snow, Hintertux is simply one of the best places to go. Its glacier is not only extensive; it arguably has the most challenging and interesting runs of any lift-served Alpine glacier area. But the quieter, friendlier, non-glacial slopes down the valley, linked to the slopes of Mayrhofen, are also well worth exploring (check out the Mayrhofen chapter too).

The Tux valley, effectively the top end of the Zillertal, offers a variety of small villages. At the end of the valley, directly below the glacier, is **Hintertux**; a few km down the valley, the major resorts are **Lanersbach** and next-door **Vorderlanersbach**. Lower down still is **Finkenberg**. There is also lodging in Juns and Madseit, which are villages between Hintertux and Lanersbach.

The higher villages are linked by frequent free ski-buses. A cheap (one euro) night-bus runs until 2.30am. Finkenberg is less well served.

There are some good rustic restaurants and bars and a few places along the valley with discos or live music. But nightlife tends to be

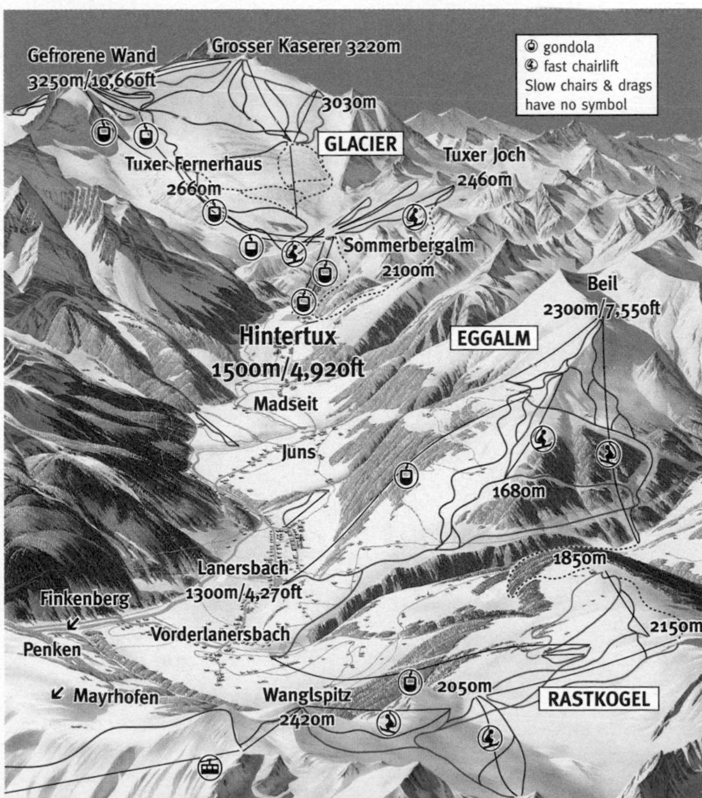

KEY FACTS

Resort	1500m 4,920ft
Ziller valley	
Slopes	630-3250m 2,070-10,660ft
Lifts	172
Pistes	668km 415 miles
Blue	26%
Red	63%
Black	11%
Snowmaking	75%
Ski and Glacier World Zillertal 3000	
Slopes	630-3250m 2,070-10,660ft
Lifts	74
Pistes	245km 152 miles
Blue	26%
Red	58%
Black	16%
Snowmaking	86%
Hintertux only	
Slopes	1500-3250m 4,920-10,660ft
Lifts	20
Pistes	86km 53 miles

quieter than in many bigger Austrian resorts (Mayrhofen, for example).

All the major resort villages have gondolas into the local slopes: the Finkenberg one goes up to the Penken slopes shared with Mayrhofen; the Vorderlanersbach one goes to Rastkogel, which is linked with the Penken slopes; and the Lanersbach one goes to Eggalm, from which you can ski to Vorderlanersbach.

The Tux valley and Mayrhofen lifts form what is called the Ski and Glacier World Zillertal 3000. The Superski lift pass also covers other Ziller valley resorts (see the Mayrhofen chapter).

Hintertux 1500m

- + Departure point for the excellent high glacier slopes
- + Liveliest of the villages for après-ski
- − Quiet later in the evening
- − Remote setting
- − Not much to do off the slopes

Life in Hintertux revolves around the glacier; staying at the base gets you up the mountain early, and means you don't have far to stagger after joining in the teatime revelry. But later on, it may feel too quiet for some.

Village charm The resort is little more than a small collection of hotels and guest houses, in traditional style. Well, two collections actually – see below.
Convenience The main village is a 15-minute walk away from the lifts, across a car park that fills with day-visitors' cars and coaches (especially when snow is poor in lower resorts); but there is a smaller group of hotels at the lift base – the obvious place to stay in our view.
Scenery There are fabulous views from the high points of the glacier.

THE MOUNTAINS

Hintertux's slopes are fairly extensive and, for a glacier, surprisingly varied and occasionally challenging. Only the final ski route to the valley is in trees.
Slopes A series of three big twin-cable gondolas go from the base to the top of the glacier in around 30 minutes. The second and third stages are linked by a short slope at Tuxer Fernerhaus. A second smaller gondola also goes to Tuxer Fernerhaus, and a 10-seat gondola replaced the Gefrorene Wand double chair above it last season. Above Tuxer Fernerhaus there are further chairs and draglifts with links across to another 1000m-vertical chain of lifts below Grosser Kaserer. Behind Gefrorene Wand is the area's one sunny piste, served by a triple chair.

Descent to the valley involves a short six-pack ride to Sommerbergalm and then a ski route to the base. At Sommerbergalm a fast quad serves short, easy slopes below Tuxer Joch and accesses a second ski route to the base, this one down a deserted valley.

SNOWPIX.COM / CHRIS GILL

In the distance, the gentle slopes of Tuxer Joch, from the top of which there's a lovely ski route down a deserted valley to the base ↓

LIFT PASSES

Super-skipass Zillertal

Prices in €

Age	1-day	6-day
under 15	20	92
15 to 18	34	164
over 19	43	205

Free under 6

Senior no deals

Beginner no deals

Notes

1-day pass covers Hintertux glacier, Eggalm, Rastkogel and Penken areas; 4-day and over passes include all Ziller valley lifts; part-day passes available

Fast lifts There are high-capacity gondolas all the way to the top, but the shorter lifts serving most of the slopes are T-bars and slow chairs.

Queues The gondolas make light work of any queues. But the main runs can get crowded, and then it is best to go to the quieter lifts on skier's left.

Terrain parks Europe's highest World Cup half-pipe is on the glacier (a popular summer hang-out), and there is a terrain park for all levels with jumps, fun boxes and rails.

Snow reliability Snow does not come more reliable than this. Even off the glacier, the other slopes are high and face north, making for very reliable snow-cover. The runs from Tuxer Fernerhaus and Tuxer Joch down to Sommerbergalm have snowmaking, as does the longer ski route to the valley – bizarre, for a ski route.

Experts There is more to amuse experts here than on any other glacier, with a proper black run at glacier level and steep slopes beneath. A lot of the off-piste is little used.

Intermediates The area particularly suits good, confident intermediates. The long runs down from Gefrorene Wand and Kaserer are fun. And the ski routes to the valley are very satisfying. Moderate intermediates will love the slopes served by drags up on the glacier, and the Tuxer Joch area.

Beginners There is a short nursery slope at valley level, but then you're riding the gondola up to and back from Sommerbergalm, where there are blue runs served by drags and a chair. You'll need a full lift pass.

Snowboarding There are some great off-piste opportunities, but boarders complain about the number of T-bars.

Cross-country See Lanersbach.

Mountain restaurants There are two big, functional self-service places at the main lift junctions, but also more attractive options. The 104-year-old Spannagelhaus is a simple refuge with self-service. Our favourite is the Gletscherhütte, at the top of the area – cosy inside, with good shielded terraces. Tuxer Joch Haus has great views of the glacier.

Schools and guides The three schools serve all the resorts in Tux, but we lack reports. Tux 3000 has guiding, touring and freeriding programmes.

Families Most of the ski schools run classes for children from age four, and lunch is provided. There's a children's fun area on the glacier.

STAYING THERE

Most hotels are large and comfortable and have spa facilities, but there are also more modest pensions.

Hotels If you are going to stay in a remote spot like this, you may as well stay close to the lifts, rather than in the village proper. Our regular reporter uses the 4-star Neuhintertux (8580) ('unusually good half-board food, large spa and pool') or failing that the more intimate Vierjahreszeiten (8525) ('pleasant, good food, smaller spa').

Apartments There are plenty of self-catering apartments.

Eating out Mainly hotel-based.

Après-ski There can be a lively après-ski scene both at mid-mountain (Sommerbergalm) and at the base; the Hohenhaus Tenne has several different bars and 'is great fun – the dance floor gets packed', the Rindererhof has a popular tea dance, and there are a couple of local bars.

Off the slopes Lots of ice activities on the glacier – climbing, natural ice palace, etc. The hotel spa facilities are excellent, including a thermal pool at the Kirchler, but there are many more options in Mayrhofen.

Lanersbach 1300m

- ⊞ Pleasant, compact village
- ⊞ Well placed for skiing the glacier and for the Mayrhofen slopes
- ⊟ Village fairly quiet by Austrian standards
- ⊟ Few easy local runs for novices

Lanersbach and neighbouring Vorderlanersbach are attractive bases for accessing both the glacier and the valley resorts.

Village charm Lanersbach is small, attractive, spacious and traditional. The quiet centre near the pretty church is delightfully unspoiled and is bypassed by the busy road up to Hintertux that passes the main lift. Vorderlanersbach is a mini version.

Convenience Lanersbach has everything you need in a resort. The centre is within walking distance of the Eggalm gondola. Vorderlanersbach has its own gondola up to Rastkogel.

Scenery These are attractive villages in a long, pretty and varied valley.

Mountain restaurants are not a highlight – this is the 104-year-old Spannagelhaus refuge's terrace →

SNOWPIX.COM / CHRIS GILL

GETTING THERE

Air Salzburg 195km/120 miles (3hr); Munich 210km/130 miles (3hr30); Innsbruck 90km/55 miles (1hr45)

Rail Local line to Mayrhofen; regular buses from station

UK PACKAGES

Hintertux Snoworks
Finkenberg Crystal

THE MOUNTAINS

A 2012 visitor found the piste map 'probably the least helpful ever' and the signposting 'confusing' as well.

Slopes The slopes of Eggalm, accessed by the gondola from Lanersbach, offer a small network of pleasantly varied intermediate pistes, usually delightfully quiet. You can descend on red or blue runs back to the village or to Vorderlanersbach, where a gondola goes up to the higher, open Rastkogel slopes; here, two fast chairlifts serve some very enjoyable long red and blue runs, and link with Mayrhofen's slopes. The linking run has red and black variants; both can get very mogulled, and many people opt to ride the jumbo cable car down; a short rope-tow cuts out the need to hike up to the top station. The lower half of the run back from Rastkogel to Eggalm is a ski route, but is really quite easy and is served by snowmaking. The alternative is to ride the gondola down to Vorderlanersbach (there are no pistes to the village) and catch the bus to Lanersbach.

Fast lifts 'Great' – gondolas are the access lifts, and Eggalm and Rastkogel each have two six-packs.

Queues We have no reports of any problems. Indeed, Eggalm can be delightfully quiet.

Terrain parks The nearest parks are at Mayrhofen and Hintertux.

Snow reliability Snow conditions are usually good, at least in early season; by Austrian standards these are high slopes, and snowmaking covers some runs on both Eggalm and Rastkogel. But Rastkogel is basically south-facing, so snow quality can suffer. The grooming was 'OK – not great', said a 2012 reporter.

Experts There are no pistes to challenge experts, but there is a fine off-piste route starting a short hike from the top of the Eggalm slopes and finishing at the village.

Intermediates The local slopes suit intermediates best – and you have Mayrhofen's slopes to explore, too.

Beginners Lanersbach has a nursery slope (as do Madseit and Juns), but there are few ideal progression slopes on Eggalm – most of the easy runs are on the higher lifts of Rastkogel.

Snowboarding The area isn't great for novices – there are draglifts dotted around, some in key places.

Cross-country There are 28km of cross-country trails around Madseit and Vorderlanersbach.

Mountain restaurants There's no shortage but most, though fairly rustic, are self-service with simple food; the small Lattenalm near the, er, Lattenalm chair on Eggalm is a table-service exception with splendid views of the Tux glacier; Heidi's Schistadl on run 3 at Rastkogel also has good views and is the 'best-value hut I've visited', says a 2012 reporter; and nearby Berghaus Lämmerbichl is a 'good self-service'.

Schools and guides There are three schools in the valley, but we lack recent reports on them.

Families The Playarena in Vorderlanersbach nursery takes newborn babies up to teenagers, and most of the schools take children from four upwards. There's a children's garden on Eggalm.

STAYING THERE
Both villages are essentially hotel-based resorts.
Hotels The better places tend to be on the main road, but complaints of noise are few. The Lanersbacherof (87256) is a good 4-star with a pool, sauna, steam room and hot tub close to the lifts ('friendly; and the food and wine are outstanding'). The 3-star Pinzger (87541) and Alpengruss (87293) are cheaper alternatives. In Vorderlanersbach the 3-star Kirchlerhof (8560) has been recommended; it has a new wellness area.
Apartments Quite a lot are available.
Eating out Mainly hotel-based, busy, and geared to serving dinner early. The Forelle is noted for its trout dishes, not surprisingly.
Après-ski Nightlife is generally quiet by Austrian standards. Try the Kleine Tenne or Bergfriedalm – an old wooden building with traditional Austrian music ('worth staying in Lanersbach just for this bar', says a 2012 reporter). Gletscherspalte is a disco ('more commercial and with a younger crowd than Bergfriedalm').
Off the slopes Facilities are fairly good for small resorts, and the bus service throughout the valley is 'extensive'. Some hotels have pools, hot tubs and fitness rooms open to non-residents. Innsbruck and Salzburg are possible excursions.

Finkenberg 840m

- ⊞ Fast lift access to the main slopes
- ⊞ Pleasant, uncrowded village that appeals to families but ...
- ⊟ Lodging sprawls along a steep and busy main road
- ⊟ No pisted runs to resort level

If you want to ski Mayrhofen's extensive area but avoid the après-ski crowds, Finkenberg makes a quieter alternative – and with direct access to the slopes.

Village charm The resort is no more than a collection of traditional-style hotels, bars, cafes and private homes. There is a central pretty area around the church.
Convenience Most of the buildings (and hotels) are spread along the busy, steep, winding main road up to Lanersbach. Beware slippery pavements. Some hotels are within walking distance of the gondola, and many of the more distant ones run their own minibuses; there is also an inefficient village minibus service.
Scenery Steep mountainsides rise up on both sides.

THE MOUNTAIN
Slopes A two-stage gondola gives direct access to the Penken slopes – and in good conditions you can ski back to the village on a ski route (though it is often closed).
Fast lifts See Mayrhofen.
Queues Few problems reported. The gondola to and from the Penken may have queues at peak times.
Terrain parks The Mayrhofen park is easily accessed.
Snow reliability The local slopes are not as well endowed with snowmaking as those on Mayrhofen's side.
Experts Not much challenge, except off-piste and the Harakiri piste.
Intermediates The whole area opens up from the top of the gondola.
Beginners There are nursery areas at the top of the gondola, on Penken, but Mayrhofen is a better base.
Snowboarding See Mayrhofen.
Cross-country Cross-country skiers have to get a bus up to Lanersbach.
Mountain restaurants See the Mayrhofen chapter.
Schools and guides The Finkenberg school has a good reputation.
Families The Finkenberg school takes children from age four.

STAYING THERE
Hotels The Sporthotel Stock (6775 410), owned by the family of former downhill champion Leonard Stock, is near the gondola station. It has great spa facilities and was upgraded from a 4-star to a 5-star in March 2012; there are several 4-stars. The Eberl (62667) has been recommended in the past, and the Kristall (62840) is 150m from the gondola with good wellness/spa facilities. The 3-star B&B hotel Harpfner (62094) is 'absolutely excellent and great value'.
Eating out Mainly in hotels, notably the Eberl. But Cafe Sennhütt'n is 'very good and reasonably priced'.
Après-ski The main après-ski spots are the lively Laterndl Pub at the foot of the gondola and Finkennest.
Off the slopes OK for the active: curling, ice skating, swimming and good local walks.

Phone numbers
From elsewhere in Austria use the prefix 05287; from abroad use the prefix +43 5287

TOURIST OFFICE
www.tux.at

Ischgl

Ischgl is unique: high, snow-sure slopes, a superb lift system, and a traditional-style Tirolean village. Perfection? Well, not quite ...

RATINGS

The mountains

Extent	★★★★
Fast lifts	★★★★★
Queues	★★★★
Terrain p'ks	★★★★★
Snow	★★★★
Expert	★★★★
Intermediate	★★★★
Beginner	★★
Boarder	★★★★★
X-country	★★★
Restaurants	★★★★
Schools	★★★
Families	★★

The resort

Charm	★★★
Convenience	★★★
Scenery	★★★
Eating out	★★★★
Après-ski	★★★★★
Off-slope	★★★

RPI	105
lift pass	£170
ski hire	£130
lessons	£105
food & drink	£125
total	**£530**

NEWS

2011/12: A six-pack replaced the Sonnenlift T-bar on the nursery slopes at Idalp. And a covered moving carpet was installed in the same area. There's a new umbrella bar at the Panorama restaurant at Idalp. Some 200 more snow-guns were installed.

KEY FACTS

Resort	1400m 4,590ft
Slopes	1400-2870m 4,590-9,420ft
Lifts	44
Pistes	238km 148 miles
Blue	20%
Red	64%
Black	16%
Snowmaking	1000 guns

- ➕ Compact, traditional-style village with a traffic-free core
- ➕ High slopes with reliable snow
- ➕ Broad area of slopes linked to Samnaun in Switzerland
- ➕ Superb modern lift system
- ➕ Après-ski like nowhere else, with an unmatched number of exceptionally lively places

- ➖ Village is densely developed, and has a rather urban, glitzy feel
- ➖ Not ideal for beginners or timid intermediates, for various reasons
- ➖ Few seriously steep runs
- ➖ Very little wooded terrain
- ➖ Treks to the gondolas for some
- ➖ Après-ski can be a bit tacky

Ischgl is at last becoming better known to Brits. It's about time – the mountain is one of Austria's best, and we love it (except in a snowstorm).

The village? We're less convinced. We visited a couple of seasons ago as part of a Tirolean tour and, looking back, Ischgl came in seventh out of seven as a place to stay. Yes, it has clear merits. But it's all a bit high-pressure, with thousands of cars and scores of coaches piling in to its parking lots, and little room to breathe.

THE RESORT

Ischgl is a compact village tucked away south of St Anton in the long, narrow Paznaun valley on the Swiss border; the ski area is shared with Samnaun in Switzerland. The Silvretta ski pass also covers Galtür further up the valley (see the end of this chapter) and Kappl and See down the valley (covered in the resort directory, at the back). All are linked by ski-buses and worth visiting; they make cheaper, quieter bases too. A car makes trips to St Anton viable. But beware: heavy snowfalls can close the valley road for days until avalanche danger is cleared.

VILLAGE CHARM ★★★
More town than village

The buildings are predominantly in traditional chalet style, with one or two modern exceptions, but this is no rustic backwater – the narrow streets have a towny feel, and the style is swanky and brash rather than tasteful. There's a selection of lively bars and a better-than-usual selection of fashion shops – 'more luxury shops than Lech', an experienced observer of these matters points out. The narrow main street plus a couple of side streets are mostly traffic-free – the valley road up to Galtür bypasses the village.

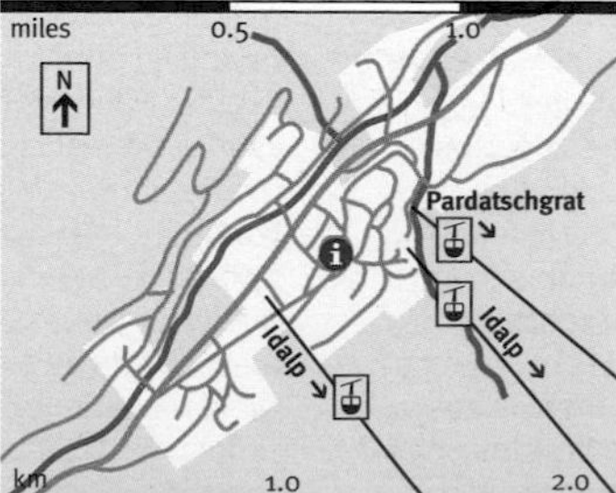

CONVENIENCE ★★★
Beware of the bypass

As our village plan suggests, it is not a big place; but it's big enough for some of the lodgings to be a good walk from the nearest lift – beware lodgings on the wrong side of the bypass road. You can leave your kit up at Idalp. Gondolas go up to mid-mountain from two points about 500m apart. The best location, overall, is on or near the main pedestrian street between the two. The eastern gondola station is separated from the main street by a low hill but is reached by an underground moving walkway.

SCENERY ★★★
Good at the top

The wooded flanks of the valley rise steeply from the village, which gets almost no sun in January. But above the treeline, the Silvretta range is revealed in all its glory.

↑ Just one of Ischgl's 23 high-speed chairlifts – this one carries a mere eight people per chair

WENDY-JANE KING

THE MOUNTAINS

Ischgl is a fair-sized, relatively high, snow-sure area. Practically all the slopes are above the treeline, the main exception being the steep lower slopes above the village and a couple of short runs low in the Fimbatal.

The piste map is good. But we have found signposting inadequate and the run numbering confusing: a run may have multiple tributaries, or may split part-way down, with the variants having the same number.

There are two varieties of ski route – plain and 'extreme' – clearly stated to be 'not monitored'.

EXTENT OF THE SLOPES ★★★★★

Extensive cross-border cruising

The sunny **Idalp** plateau, reached by the 24-person Silvrettabahn or the eight-seat Fimbabahn, is the hub of the slopes. It can be very crowded. Pardatschgrat, reached by a third gondola, is about 300m higher. From Idalp, lifts radiate to a wide variety of mainly north-west- and west-facing runs and to the Swiss border.

The red runs back down to Ischgl provoke regular complaints. Neither is easy, conditions can be tricky, and countless imbeciles skiing too fast make these runs even more hazardous. Both have final stretches that probably should be black. The wide, quiet piste down the Velilltal looks better, but turns rather nasty lower down and joins the steep 'black' bottom part of run 1A. Quite a few people ride the gondolas down.

A short piste brings you from Idalp to the lifts serving the **Höllenkar** bowl, leading up to the area's south-western end and a high point at Palinkopf. Runs of 900m vertical from here lead down to the **Fimbatal**. On the Swiss side, the hub of activity is **Alp Trida**, surrounded by south- and east facing runs with great views. From here a scenic red goes down to Compatsch, for buses to Ravaisch (for the cable car back up) and Samnaun. From Palinkopf there is a long red run down a beautiful valley to Samnaun – not difficult, but very sunny in parts and prone to closure by avalanche risk. There is a long flat stretch at the end.

FAST LIFTS ★★★★★

One of the best

Ischgl is near the top of our fast league table and about 80% of its main lifts are fast – mainly fast chairs. Not surprisingly, reporters praise the lifts – 'best resort I've been to in 20 years', 'superb', say 2012 reporters.

QUEUES ★★★★★

OK up the mountain

Queues out of the valley are not the problem they once were, since two of the access lifts were upgraded. But peak-time queues still exist. A new jumbo gondola to replace the Pardatschgat one is planned but not imminent. Crowds on the runs are an issue, especially at Idalp, and on the easier runs on the Swiss side.

TERRAIN PARKS ★★★★★
One of Europe's best
Ischgl is a top place for freestylers. The huge 'excellent' PlayStation Vita park above Idalp is the big draw – 1600m long, and always well maintained. It has beginner, public and pro lines, revamped each year. Overall, the park obstacles have an impressive creative flair. It has five kickers, 15 elements in a row and an airbag jump. There is another park at Velillscharte and a small park on the Swiss side.

SNOW RELIABILITY ★★★★
Very good
All the slopes apart from the runs back to the resort are above 1800m, and many on the Ischgl side are north-west-facing. So snow conditions are generally reliable; many reporters comment on excellent early/late season conditions. Snowmaking now covers over half the slopes, including the descents to Ischgl and Samnaun. Reporters praise the grooming.

FOR EXPERTS ★★★★
Plenty to do
Ischgl can't compare with St Anton for exciting slopes. But by general Tirolean standards it serves experts well. All the blacks are genuine ones and in combination with testing reds offer excellent, challenging descents. Head first for Palinkopf, Greitspitz and Pardatschgrat – piste 4 is a favourite. One of the branches of run 14a on Greitspitz (read our earlier remarks) includes a good steep pitch (70%, they claim). The wooded lower slopes of the Fimbatal are delightful in a storm. There is plenty of off-piste, and powder doesn't get tracked out too quickly, particularly on the Swiss side. We had an excellent day a couple of

LIFT PASSES

VIP Skipass

Prices in €

Age	1-day	6-day
under 17	26	124
17 to 59	41	207
60 plus	39	176

Free under 8

Beginner no deals

Notes
Covers Ischgl and Samnaun and local buses; half-day pass and non-skier pass available; family reductions; 2-day-plus pass available only to those with a guest card staying in Ischgl or Mathon

Alternative passes
Regional pass covers Ischgl, Samnaun, Galtür, Kappl and See

seasons ago that included exploration of the shady side of Velilltal. There are also ski routes. Ski route 39 from Palinkopf offers a testing 1000m descent.

FOR INTERMEDIATES ★★★★★
Something for everyone

Most of the slopes are wide, forgiving and ideal for intermediates – and there are plenty of them.

At the tough end of the spectrum our favourite runs are those from Palinkopf down to Gampenalp at the edge of the ski area, with great views of virgin slopes. But there are lots of other options on Palinkopf, Greitspitz and Pardatschgrat. The reds down the beautiful Velilltal and the red from Greitspitz into Switzerland are great for quiet, high-speed cruising.

For easier motorway cruising, there is lots of choice, including the runs

down around Alp Trida on the Swiss side – but these can get crowded.

FOR BEGINNERS ★★★★★
Up the mountain

Up the mountain at Idalp there are good, sunny, snow-sure nursery slopes served by a moving carpet, drags and two fast chairs, but there are no special deals for beginners – you must

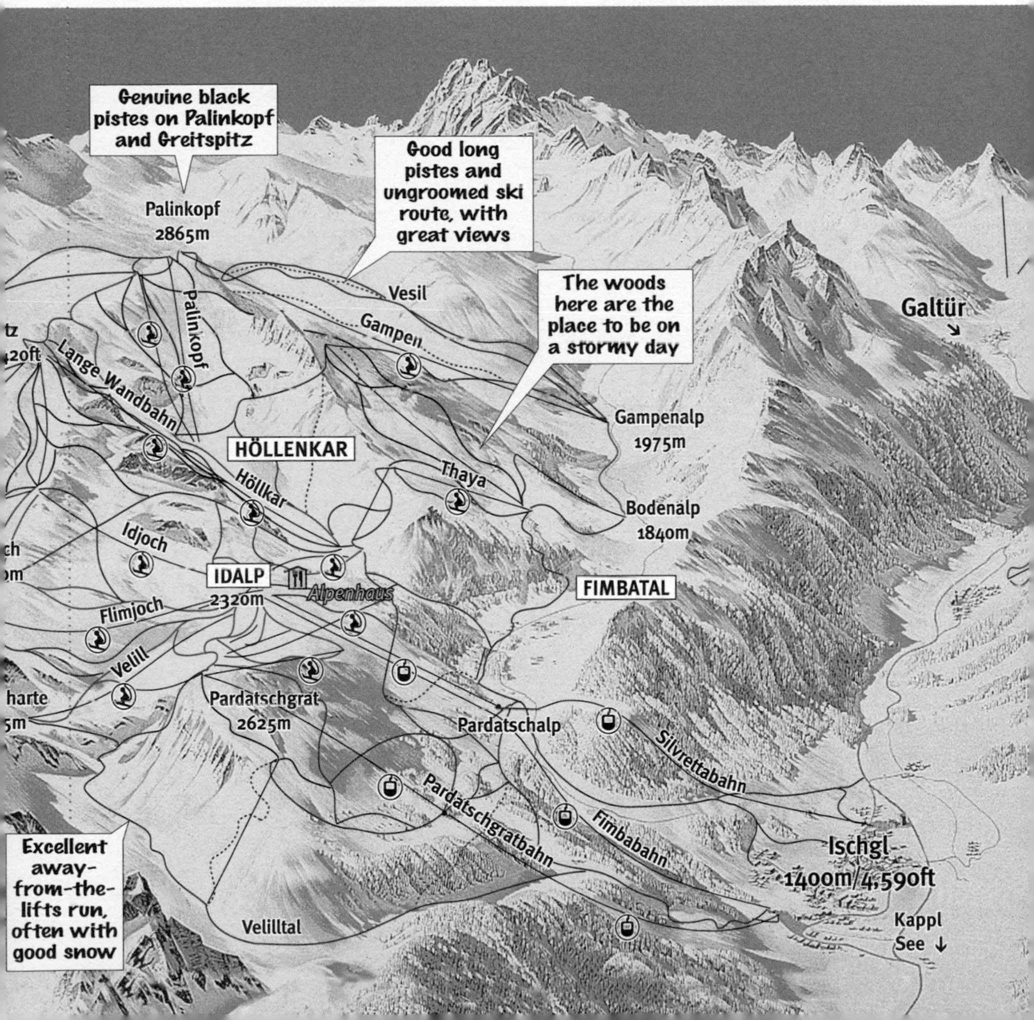

↑ Almost all the slopes are above the treeline – great on sunny days but not in a white-out

TVB PAZNAUN-ISCHGL

Hot news in Austria's hottest resort, p168.

buy a full lift pass to reach them. The blue runs on the east side of the bowl offer pleasant progression, and from there it's a small step to Switzerland.

FOR BOARDERS ★★★★★
Pretty much perfect

Ischgl has long been a popular spot for snowboarders, with its long, wide, well-groomed slopes served by snowboard-friendly gondolas and fast chairlifts. Although the off-piste terrain is less steep than in some other resorts, its above-the-treeline, easily accessible nature and good snow record makes for great riding for most ability levels. Ischgl is home to one of Austria's best terrain parks, and Silvretta Sports and Intersport Mathoy are recommended snowboard shops.

FOR CROSS-COUNTRY ★★★★★
Plenty in the valley

There are 74km of loops in the Ischgl, Galtür and Wirl area. Some trails tend to be shady, especially in early season, and are away from the main slopes, which makes meeting downhillers for lunch inconvenient.

MOUNTAIN RESTAURANTS ★★★★★
Good modern choices

Mountain restaurants generally offer good quality and choice. But capacity can be stretched at peak times. They are clearly marked on the piste map.
Editors' choice On the Austrian side at Idalp, the Alpenhaus (6840) is very much a designer place, with both table-service (upstairs) and self-service areas. We're interested only in the Nformer, obviously, although service is itself a bit slack. Food is good though, particularly the tarts, and the relaxed ambience is great; a 2012 reporter confirms our view. On the Swiss side at Alp Trida the Marmotte (+41 81 868 5221) wins no prizes for interior design but does good food in calm and comfortable surroundings.
Worth knowing about In the Fimbatal the 'lovely' Paznauner Thaya has self-service with famously good pizza, and table-service upstairs for 'fab chicken salad and spicy prawns'; often with live bands or throbbing disco music. Bodenalpe is a bit of a relic but has 'good, simple, cheap food'. From Gampenalp you can be towed 5km by snowmobile to the remote Heidelberger hütte – the way back is quite hard work, though. At Pardatschgrat, the glass-sided Pardorama complex is impressive, and less crowded than lower places. A 2011 visitor made it a regular haunt – 'very reasonable prices, excellent rösti'; there's table-service upstairs.

On the Swiss side the woody Alp Bella is good value and a consistent favourite with reporters for traditional food and 'old hut' atmosphere. Recent reports on the Alp Trida are enthusiastic. The newish glass-sided Salaas is very stylish and spacious, but otherwise unremarkable.

SCHOOLS AND GUIDES ★★★★★
No worries

The school meets up at Idalp. Recent reporters have been very happy, with instructors speaking sufficient English and giving 'good advanced lessons'. One visitor's group was smaller than the 10-12 norm. The school also organizes off-piste tours.

SCHOOLS

Schneesport-Akademie
t 5257/5404

Classes
5 days (3hr) €175

Private lessons
€115 for 90min; each additional person €25

CHILDCARE

Kindergarten (ski school)
t 5257/5404
Non-skiing children 10am to 4pm; ski-kindergarten for ages 3 to 5

Ski school
From age 5 (5 days €175)

GETTING THERE

Air Innsbruck 95km/60 miles (1hr45); Zürich 240km/150 miles (3hr30); Munich 300km/185 miles (4hr)

Rail Landeck (30km/19 miles); frequent buses from station

FOR FAMILIES ★★

High-altitude options

Children can have lunch with their ski instructor; but small kids would be better off in Galtür or Kappl, where there are good play areas – see the end of this chapter.

STAYING THERE

Chalets Ski Total broke into Ischgl a couple of seasons ago with the 58-bed chalet hotel Abendrot, in a central position, and last year it added the 22-bed Zita, near the Fimbabahn.

Hotels There is a good selection from luxurious and pricey to simple B&Bs.

*****Trofana Royal** (600) One of Austria's most luxurious hotels, with prices to match. A celebrity chef runs the kitchen. Sumptuous spa facilities.

****Christine** (5346) The best B&B in town? 'Huge rooms, central location, helpful owners, splendid spa.' Pool.

****Elisabeth** (5411) Right by the Pardatschgrat gondola, with lively après-ski. Pool, sauna and steam.

****Goldener Adler** (5217) Central, combining traditional ambience with designer rooms; 'surprisingly good food'. Sauna and spa.

****Gramaser** (5295) Near the Trofana Royal. We had a comfortable stay here in 2010; friendly staff, excellent food.

****Jägerhof** (5206) Friendly, good food, large rooms. Sauna, steam, spa. 'Splendid food and wine.'

****Lamtana** (5609) Near the Silvrettabahn. 'Spacious, modern rooms.' Wellness area.

****Madlein** (5226) Convenient, 'terribly chic', modern hotel. 'Excellent' pool, sauna, steam room. Nightclub.

****Post** (5232) 'Excellent central position; very nice staff.' Spa.

***Alpenglühn** (5294) Convenient, central and good value.

Apartments Some attractive apartments are available. The Golfais by the Pardatschgrat gondola and the apartments in the hotel Solaria (with use of its spa) have been suggested.

EATING OUT ★★★★

Plenty of choice

Most restaurants are hotel-based, but not all. We enjoyed excellent, varied meals at the popular Grillalm in hotel Gramaser, which also has a steakhouse. Reporters tip the Salnerhof and Jägerhof ('splendid food and wine') – offering five-course meals and themed evenings. For lighter meals try the Bära Falla ('great pizza and Tirolean food') and Allegra (burgers etc). The Trofana Alm, which is as much a bar as a restaurant, and the Kitzloch, with its galleries over the dance floor, are best for grills and fondue. For Italian, try the Toscana ('very good') and Salz & Pfeffer.

APRES-SKI ★★★★★

Very lively

Ischgl is the liveliest resort in the Alps, we've concluded after a lot of in-depth research. The fun starts in the early afternoon – mountain restaurants such as Paznauner Thaya slide into après mode directly after lunch – and it doesn't stop; lots of people are still in ski boots late in the evening.

The obvious ports of call in the village are the Trofana Alm near the Silvrettabahn and the Schatzi bar of the hotel Elisabeth by the Pardatschgratbahn – with scantily clad dancing girls ('supremely good fun'). Next door is Freeride, with 'friendly staff, good ski movies and no dancing girls'. Across the river the Kitzloch is one of the places for dancing on the tables in ski boots. Niki's Stadl offers 'surreal madness' thanks to its lively DJs. Feuer & Eis and the basement Kuhstahl are packed all evening – the latter is one reporter's all-time favourite après-bar. The Golden Eagle pub is popular with Brits looking for somewhere to sit. We enjoyed a quiet drink at the Kiwi and cocktails at pricey Guxa.

Later on, we enjoyed dancing to a live band in the huge Trofana Arena, which also has pole dancing, as does the Coyote Ugly. Other nightclubs include Pacha (as in Ibiza and London), Living Room and Posthörndl, with an ancient Rome theme.

OFF THE SLOPES ★★★

No sun but a nice pool

The village gets little sun in the middle of winter, and the resort is best suited to those keen to hit the slopes. But there's no shortage of off-slope activities. There are lots of maintained paths including many at altitude (the tourist office claims an astonishing 1140km in the valley), a 7km floodlit toboggan run and a splendid sports centre. And you can browse upmarket shops. It's easy to get around the valley by bus, and the Smuggler Card for pedestrians enables them to use specially selected lifts.

UK PACKAGES

Alpine Answers, Crystal, Crystal Finest, Independent Ski Links, Inghams, Interactive Resorts, Momentum, Ski Bespoke, Ski Expectations, Ski Independence, Ski Solutions, Ski Total, Skitracer, Snow Finders, STC, Zenith

Galtür Crystal, Independent Ski Links, Inghams, Neilson, Ski Independence, STC

ACTIVITIES

Indoor Silvretta Centre (bowling, billiards, swimming pool, tennis, sauna, solarium, massage), museums, concerts

Outdoor Ice rink, curling, sleigh rides, hiking tours, 7km floodlit toboggan run

Phone numbers

Calling long-distance

Add the prefix given below for each resort; when calling from abroad use the country code +43 and omit the initial '0'

Ischgl
05444

Galtür
05443

Samnaun (Switzerland)
From elsewhere in Switzerland add the prefix 081; from abroad use the prefix +41 81

TOURIST OFFICES

Ischgl
www.ischgl.com

Samnaun (Switzerland)
www.samnaun.ch

Galtür
www.galtuer.com

LINKED RESORT – 1840m

SAMNAUN

Small, quiet duty-free Samnaun is in a corner of Switzerland more easily reached from Austria. We know of no UK tour operators going here, but a reporter last year reckons more Brits are finding their way here.

There are four small components, roughly 1km apart: Samnaun-Dorf, prettily set at the head of the valley and the main focus, with some swanky hotels and duty-free shops; Ravaisch, where the cable car goes up; tiny Plan; and the hamlets of Laret and Compatsch, at the end of the main piste to the valley. We've stayed happily on the edge of Dorf in the Waldpark B&B (8618310), and a 2011 visitor highly recommends the hotel Montana (8619000) for 'comfy rooms, fab pool, three great restaurants'. Other tips: 4-star Muttler (8618130) (with a good spa and complimentary ski-bus), and Des Alpes (8685273). There's the smart AlpenQuell spa-pool-fitness centre.

The Schmuggler Alm at the bottom of the long run from Palinkopf is a popular lunch and après-ski spot. The Almraus (hotel Cresta) at Compatsch has been recommended for drinks. The school is 'first class', says a reporter.

UP-VALLEY VILLAGE – 1585m

GALTÜR

Galtür is a charming, peaceful, traditional village clustered around a pretty little church, amid impressive mountain scenery at the head of Ischgl's Paznaun valley. Many visitors find the resort very quiet – there are just a few shops, restaurants, and a 'fantastic bakery for coffee and cakes', but a 2012 visitor 'loved the contrast from bustling Ischgl'.

Sunnier and cheaper than Ischgl, Galtür is a good base for families and mixed-ability groups. Galtür's own slopes rise to 2295m above a lift base at Wirl, a short bus ride from the village. The free buses to Ischgl are regular and quick, but they get overcrowded at peak times even in January, and they stop at around 6pm. Taxis to Ischgl's nightlife are economic if shared. But a January 2012 visitor warns that the roads to both Wirl and Ischgl were closed due to avalanche danger for two days – meaning he was unable to ski.

Galtür's Silvapark ski area has six 'sectors' to help guests make the most of the mountain; there are freestyle and family sectors, for example. The slopes can be bleak in poor weather, and are limited in extent. There are two fast chairs and a gondola, but still some long draglifts. Queues are rare. The slopes are fairly high, so pretty snow-sure; we had good snow on a warm March visit.

Most runs are classified red, though some would be blue elsewhere. Run 8 is one of our favourites; a broad, long cruise with great views of the frozen dam below. The main blue piste can get crowded and has a steeper section at the top, but it is a long, pretty cruise to the valley. There are some challenges – reds and a black served by the fast Ballunspitze chair are short and steep. And there are a couple of ski routes to try. The area on the far right of the piste map, served by a slow double chair and a T-bar, is quiet, shady and has some good off-piste in a bowl and among well-spaced trees. There's a terrain park, and a fine nursery area at the lift base.

The school is 'excellent and well organized' and offers small classes. Kinderland has its own tow, carousel, moving carpet and cartoon characters. There are 74km of cross-country loops in the Galtür, Ischgl and Wirl area. The cosy, wooden Wieberhimml mountain hut is a lively, sunny spot for drinks. And we had good food at the table-service Panorama Tenne, beside the gondola. The Addis Abeba is a hip bar near the Soppalift drag.

There are good hotels, including the 'comfortable' 4-star Almhof (8253) – 'excellent evening meals, every course a work of art' – the Alpenhotel Tirol (8206) – 'excellent', 'wonderful service and food' – Flüchthorn (8202), Ballunspitze (8214) and 3-star Alpenrose (8201).

Off-slope facilities are limited, apart from the impressive Alpinarium, an avalanche-protection structure and exhibition centre built after the avalanche that devastated the village in 1999. Much of the information is in German, but it's worth a visit; they supply slippers if you turn up in ski boots. There's a sports centre with pool, tennis and squash – and night skiing and sledding on Wednesdays.

Kitzbühel

Despite the racy image, the slopes are mostly pretty tame; the town at the base, though, is something special – cute and lively

RATINGS

The mountains

Extent	★★★
Fast lifts	★★★★
Queues	★★★
Terrain p'ks	★★★
Snow	★★
Expert	★★★
Intermediate	★★★★
Beginner	★★
Boarder	★★
X-country	★★★
Restaurants	★★★★
Schools	★★★★
Families	★

The resort

Charm	★★★★
Convenience	★★
Scenery	★★★
Eating out	★★★★
Après-ski	★★★★
Off-slope	★★★★★

RPI	95
lift pass	£170
ski hire	£105
lessons	£105
food & drink	£110
total	**£490**

NEWS

2012/13: On Resterhöhe the Zweitausender double chair is to be replaced by an eight-seater. In the Hahnenkamm sector the Walde T-bar is to be replaced by a six-pack. Snowmaking is to be increased in several areas.

2011/12: A six-pack replaced the Resterhöhe double chair and Moseralm T-bar. The Hahnenkamm gondola got heated seats. Snowmaking was improved.

- + Extensive, attractive, varied slopes offering a sensation of travel – with trips to the SkiWelt also possible
- + Beautiful medieval town centre
- + Vibrant nightlife
- + Lots to do off the slopes
- + Plenty of cheap lodgings
- + Excellent mountain restaurants

- − Low altitude means snow is often poor low down (though snowmaking is fairly extensive)
- − Surprisingly few challenges on-piste
- − Disappointing resort-level nursery area
- − Some crowded pistes

Kitzbühel is one of the big names of the ski world, largely thanks to its spectacular Hahnenkamm downhill race course – the most exciting on the World Cup circuit. Hahnenkamm race weekend is one of the key dates on the Alpine social calendar. But the place also has powerful attractions for the rest of us.

We quite like the slopes, too – especially since the huge 3S cross-valley gondola made the link to Jochberg and Pass Thurn in 2004. The lift system as a whole is at last being brought up to scratch, with worthwhile new lifts in 2010, 2011 and planned for construction for the coming season.

It's just a pity the place isn't 300m higher. In countless visits over a 25-year period we've encountered good snow down to the village just once. Our advice is to book late, when you know the conditions are good.

THE RESORT

Kitzbühel is a large, animated valley town with its major ski area on one side and its minor one on the other. The major area, spreading south-west from the famous Hahnenkamm directly above the town, is shared with another substantial resort, Kirchberg, covered at the end of the chapter.

The 'still great value' Kitzbüheler Alpen AllStarCard lift pass covers seven separate ski areas in the region – see 'Lift passes'. One of those – the SkiWelt – is accessible by the Ki-West gondola, a short bus ride from Skirast.

VILLAGE CHARM ★★★★

A historic town

The largely car-free medieval centre is delightful. And many visitors love the sophisticated, towny ambience and swanky shops and cafes. But the resort spreads widely, and busy roads surround the old town. Visitors used to peaceful little Austrian villages are likely to be surprised by its urban feel.

CONVENIENCE ★★

Choose your spot carefully

A gondola from the edge of the town goes up to the Hahnenkamm, start of the main area of slopes. Across town,

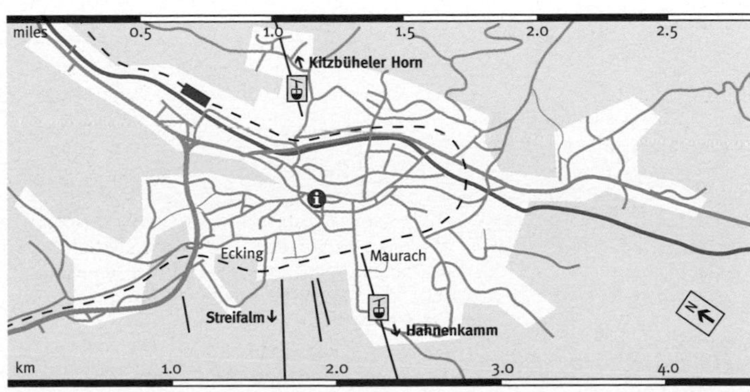

KEY FACTS	
Resort	760m
	2,490ft
Slopes	800-2000m
	2,620-6,560ft
Lifts	53
Pistes	170km
	106 miles
Blue	40%
Red	46%
Black	14%
Snowmaking	58%

close to the railway station but some way from the centre, another gondola accesses the much smaller Kitzbüheler Horn sector.

The size of Kitz makes choice of location important. Many visitors prefer to be in the centre of town and close to the Hahnenkamm gondola. Beginners should bear in mind that the Hahnenkamm nursery slopes are often lacking in snow, and then novices are taken up the Horn. Views vary on the free buses that circle the town. The circular route and high-season crowding led some recent reporters to walk instead. There are ski/boot depots at appropriate points.

SCENERY ★★★★★

Attractive valley views

Kitzbühel is set at a junction of broad, pretty valleys, among partly wooded mountains. There are good views from Pengelstein across both valleys (the minor peak of Gr Rettenstein is prominent) and to the SkiWelt.

THE HAHNENKAMM DOWNHILL

Kitzbühel's Hahnenkamm Downhill race, held in mid-January each year (25 to 27 January in 2013), is the toughest as well as one of the most famous on the World Cup circuit. On the race weekend the town is packed, and there is a real carnival atmosphere, with bands, people in traditional costumes and huge (and loud) cowbells everywhere. The race itself starts with a steep icy section before you hit the famous Mausfalle and Steilhang, where even Franz Klammer used to get worried. The course starts near the top of the Hahnenkamm gondola and drops 860m to finish amid the noise and celebrations right on the edge of town. The course is normally closed from the start of the season until after the race, but after the race weekend ordinary mortals can now try most of the course, if the snow is good enough – it's an unpisted ski route mostly. We found it steep and tricky in parts, even when going slowly – it must be terrifying at race speeds of 80mph or more.

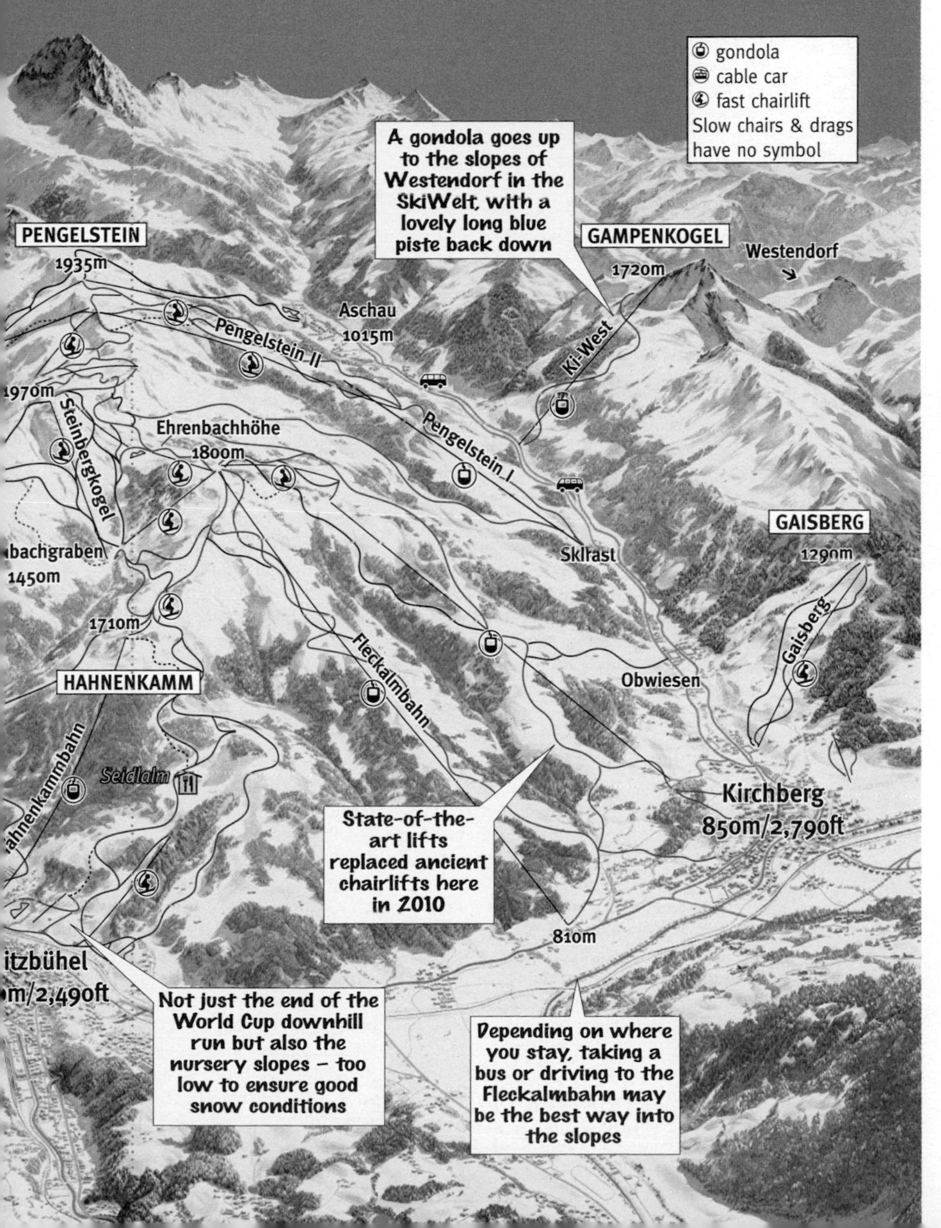
gondola
cable car
fast chairlift
Slow chairs & drags have no symbol
A gondola goes up to the slopes of Westendorf in the SkiWelt, with a lovely long blue piste back down
PENGELSTEIN
1935m
GAMPENKOGEL
1720m
Westendorf
Aschau
1015m
Pengelstein II
Ki-West
1970m
Steinbergkogel
Ehrenbachhöhe
1800m
Pengelstein I
GAISBERG
1290m
bachgraben
1450m
Skirast
Gaisberg
1710m
Fleckalmbahn
HAHNENKAMM
Obwiesen
ahnenkammbahn
Seidlalm
Kirchberg
850m/2,790ft
State-of-the-art lifts replaced ancient chairlifts here in 2010
810m
itzbühel
m/2,490ft
Not just the end of the World Cup downhill run but also the nursery slopes – too low to ensure good snow conditions
Depending on where you stay, taking a bus or driving to the Fleckalmbahn may be the best way into the slopes

LIFT PASSES

Prices in €

Age	1-day	6-day
under 16	22	106
16 to 18	35	169
19 plus	44	211

Free under 7

Senior 60+: day pass €35 on Tue & Thu; 80+: season pass €20

Beginner reduced pass for Gaisberg and Ganslern chairs only; for under-18s, seven free lifts (three in Kitzbühel)

Notes

Covers Kitzbühel, Kirchberg, Jochberg, Pass Thurn, Mittersill/ Hollersbach; hourly and pedestrian tickets; family reductions; 50% reduction on pool entry; for passes of 2+ days, additional €15 a day to ski in the SkiWelt area and reduced price to ski at St Moritz, Arosa, Adelboden, Gstaad

Alternative passes

Kitzbüheler Alpen AllStarCard covers Kitzbühel, Schneewinkel (St Johann), SkiWelt, Alpbach, Wildschönau, Skicircus Saalbach, Zell-Kaprun; Salzburg Super Ski Card covers 22 ski areas in the Salzburg province

THE MOUNTAINS

Kitzbühel's extensive slopes – shared with Kirchberg and other villages – offer some open runs higher up but soon run into patchy forest lower down. Most face north-east or north-west. The piste map is praised as clear and easy to use by the majority. Many readers find that run classifications exaggerate difficulty – though not everyone agrees, and at least one reporter reckons that the Zweitausender red run at Resterhöhe should still be classified black.

EXTENT OF THE SLOPES ★★★

Big but bitty

The slopes can be divided into several identifiable areas. The **Hahnenkamm** gondola takes you to the bowl of Ehrenbachgraben, a major lift bottleneck in the past but transformed by the installation of not only a six-pack to Ehrenbachhöhe, the arrival point of lifts from Kirchberg, but also an eight-pack to the high point of Steinbergkogel. These days, this is a place you might want to do laps.

Beyond is the slightly lower peak of **Pengelstein**, with an eight-pack up to it from the Steinbergkogel area. Several long west-facing runs go down to Skirast, where there is a gondola back up, or to Aschau. Ski-buses from these points will take you to the Ki-West gondola towards Westendorf and to Kirchberg. It takes up to an hour to reach the heart of the Westendorf slopes, including the bus.

Pengelstein is also the start of the impressive 30-person cross-valley 3S gondola to **Wurzhöhe** above Jochberg. This peak-to-peak link has fabulous views (especially if you hit the cabin with the partial glass floor) and is worth the ride just for the scenery.

Further lifts then take you to the **Resterhöhe** sector above Pass Thurn – well worth the excursion, for better snow and fewer crowds. There is a long, scenic, sunny red run to Breitmoos, mid-station of the gondola up from Hollersbach, beyond Pass Thurn. Runs are otherwise short, but mostly served by fast chairs.

The **Kitzbüheler Horn** gondola second stage leads to the sunny Trattalm bowl, with an alternative cable car taking you up to the summit of the Horn, from where a fine, solitary piste leads down into the Raintal on the east side. There's a blue piste and two ski routes back towards town.

The separate **Bichlalm** area, which used to offer lift-served off-piste, has reopened for guided snowcat skiing. There is still no date for construction of the new gondola planned here for some years.

Ski Austria's Big Three. Where? See p168.

FAST LIFTS ★★★★

Continuing to improve

The improvements that two years ago lifted Kitzbühel into our ★★★★ category continue, and the resort is now right on the brink of moving into the top class. Some problems remain: the trip back from Resterhöhe still involves two slow lifts, the lifts above Jochberg are slow, and the Horn has no fast lifts apart from the access gondola and a cable car.

QUEUES ★★★

Still some problems

There can still be peak-time queues for the Hahnenkamm gondola out of the town. The chair upgrades at Ehrenbachgraben have solved the bottleneck there. But there can still be occasional queues elsewhere on the Hahnenkamm/Pengelstein sectors, especially if good weather at the weekend attracts Germans. The Zweitausender chair (unavoidable en route to Resterhöhe) is being upgraded to an eight-seater for 2012/13, which should deal with that long-standing bottleneck. Both the Horn and the Hahnenkamm can have crowded pistes at times – though the cross-valley 3S gondola to Wurzhöhe has helped by encouraging people to use the Pass Thurn slopes.

TERRAIN PARKS ★★★

Double the fun

The DC Snowpark Hanglalm is aimed at advanced riders and has several kicker lines, from big to huge, as well as advanced rails, a plethora of butter boxes and a visually pleasing wooden obstacle section. Pro riders love the park's centrepiece, a huge gap jump. In 2011/12 a new area of the park was built, aimed at beginners and intermediates, but the park is on the Hanglalm run in the Resterhöhe sector so it is rather remote. The original park on the Kitzbüheler Horn has been renamed the Horn-Min-New-School-

↑ The slopes are at low altitude, and prettily wooded

WENDY-JANE KING

Park (snappy eh?) and is now specifically a beginner area. The park in nearby Westendorf is excellent – well worth the trip for aficionados.

SNOW RELIABILITY ★★★★★
More snowmaking now
The problem is that Kitzbühel's slopes have one of the lowest average heights in the Alps, and the Horn is also sunny. Even in an exceptionally good snow year some reporters complain of worn patches, ice and slush on the lower slopes. In a normal year, the lower slopes can be very tricky or bare at times (though the snow at the top is often OK). The expansion of snowmaking has improved matters when it's cold enough to make snow – runs down to Kitzbühel, Kirchberg, Klausen and Jochberg are covered. A 2011 visitor found conditions 'better than feared' because of this. But many slopes still remain unprotected. If snow is poor, head for Resterhöhe.

FOR EXPERTS ★★★★★
Plan to go off-piste
Steep slopes – pistes and off-piste terrain – are mostly concentrated in the Steinbergkogel-Ehrenbachgraben area, equipped with three fast chairs. Direttissima is seriously steep, but sometimes groomed – fabulous. The other blacks dotted around are easier. There are plenty of long, challenging reds. When conditions allow, there is plenty of gentler off-piste to be found – some of it safely close to pistes, some requiring a guide. And the long ski routes from Pengelstein towards Jochberg and Hechenmoos are delightful in good snow.

FOR INTERMEDIATES ★★★★★
Lots of alternatives
The Hahnenkamm area is prime terrain but can get crowded. Good intermediates will want to do the World Cup downhill run, of course (see the feature panel earlier in the chapter). And the long blues of around 1000m vertical to Klausen, KIrchberg and Skirast are satisfying. The black to Aschau is not difficult, and a lovely way to end the day (check the bus times first).

The Wurzhöhe runs are good for mixed abilities, and the short, high runs at Resterhöhe are ideal if you are more timid. There are easy reds down to Pass Thurn and Jochberg (but heed our earlier note about the tricky red Zweitausender run). The whole of this area tends to be much quieter than Hahnenkamm and Pengelstein. Much of the Horn is good cruising, and the east-facing Raintal is excellent (but, again, it has a slow chair back).

FOR BEGINNERS ★★★★★
Not ideal
The Hahnenkamm nursery slopes are no more than adequate, and prone to poor snow conditions – but at least

UK PACKAGES

Alpine Answers, Alpine Weekends, Carrier, Crystal, Crystal Finest, Elegant Resorts, Independent Ski Links, Inghams, Momentum, Neilson, Ski Line, Ski Solutions, Skitracer, Snow Finders, Snowscape, STC, Thomson
Kirchberg Ski Bespoke, Snowscape

KITZBÜHEL TOURISMUS

Hahnenkamm race weekend in January (read the feature panel two spreads back) is a big event, attracting huge, lively crowds ↓

they have some free lifts. There are nursery areas with free lifts at Jochberg, Pass Thurn and Aschau, too. The Horn has a high, sunny, nursery-like section, and quick learners will soon be cruising home from there on the long Hagstein piste. There are some easy runs to progress to if the snow is OK. Day and two-day lift passes just for the Horn slopes are available. But there are better resorts to learn in.

FOR BOARDERS ★★
Gaining recognition
Kitzbühel was never known as a snowboarders' hub, but it is growing in popularity, year on year. There are two decent parks and some good off-piste runs and fun natural obstacles on the Hahnenkamm and around Pengelstein. All the major lifts are now gondolas or chairlifts – so the area suits beginners and intermediates well. But a couple of reporters have drawn attention to the many flat linking runs, on which boarders struggle – one versatile chap ditched his board after a day, and rented skis instead.

FOR CROSS-COUNTRY ★★★
Plentiful but low
There are around 60km of trails scattered around. Most are at valley level and prone to lack of snow, but a 2012 reporter who visited when there was lots of snow highly recommends them.

MOUNTAIN RESTAURANTS ★★★★
A highlight
There are many attractive restaurants, most offering table-service. One of our Kitz regulars says again this year: 'They just get better! Yes, we will go back just for the restaurants!' Pick up a copy of the local restaurant guide. Helpfully, restaurants are named and marked on the piste map – 57 in total.
Editors' choice On our most recent visit, we had a delicious lunch of oriental beef strip salad and crispy pork ribs at Bärenbadalm (0664 855 7994), halfway to Resterhöhe. This hut has a cool, modern bar area with flat-screen TVs, a roaring log fire and comfy armchairs and sofas; you can eat there or in various dining areas with a more rustic feel. Endorsed by reporters. Seidlalm (63135), right by the lower part of the downhill course, is quiet and delightfully rustic.
Worth knowing about In the Hahnenkamm sector we had a jolly meal at Berghaus Tyrol ('try the woks', says a 2012 visitor). Readers have also suggested Hahnenkammstüberl ('particularly good gröstl'), Melkalm, Hockeckhütte, Hochkitzbühel ('wonderfully light and airy', 'good menu, food quality and table service'), Hochbrunn, Schutzhütte Steinbergkogel ('wonderful blutwurstgröstl and so welcoming'), and Ehrenbachgraben. On our 2012 visit we had a fabulous strudel at the Sonnenbühel – lovely situation, sheltered and with a good view.

SCHOOLS

Rote Teufel
t 62500

Alpin Experts
t 0664 125 5171

Element3
t 72301

Snowsports
t 0664 390 0090

Classes
(Rote Teufel prices)
6 days (2hr am and pm) €180

Private lessons
€150 for 2hr

CHILDCARE

There is no non-ski nursery, but babysitters and nannies can be hired

Ski school
From age 3 (6 days €180 – Rote Teufel)

ACTIVITIES

Indoor Aquarena Centre (pools, slides, sauna, solarium, steam baths – discounted entry with lift pass); Sportpark (tennis, bowling, climbing wall), fitness studios, beauty centres, museums, casino, cinema

Outdoor Ice rink (curling and skating), tobogganing, ballooning, 65km of cleared walking paths

GETTING THERE

Air Salzburg 75km/45 miles (1hr30); Munich 165km/105 miles (2hr30); Innsbruck 95km/60 miles (1hr30)

Rail Mainline station in resort. Post bus every 15min from station

On Pengelstein, the Usterweis is a nice woody traditional place that 'neither enthused nor disappointed' a 2012 visitor, and Schroll has 'good food and service'. The Gauxerstad'l has 'a limited menu but good service and mountainous portions', says a 2012 visitor.

At Wurzhöhe/Resterhöhe, try Hanglalm, Sonnalm or Bruggeralm ('cheap and cheerful with a very pleasant verandah'). But a regular reporter rates the Panoramaalm 'quite simply the best; the options plus the quality of food is unrivalled'.

On the Horn, there's the Hornköpfl-Hütte, and also Gipfelhaus, which is quieter, with 'super views'. The Adlerhütte is 'a favourite'.

On the pistes down to Kirchberg the Fleckalm 'offers better service and food than some of the smarter places', says a 2012 visitor. We visited the Maieralm on our 2012 visit, and we can recommend the meaty gulaschsuppe.

SCHOOLS AND GUIDES ★★★★

Red Devils rule

The Kitzbühel Rote Teufel (Red Devils) is the largest. The other schools emphasize their small scale. Element3 is an adventure company offering ski/snowboard classes. Reports please.

FOR FAMILIES ★

Not an ideal choice

It's a spread-out resort for a family. Rote Teufel takes kids from age three.

STAYING THERE

Kitzbühel is essentially a hotel resort.
Chalets Crystal has a 35-bed chalet close to the Hahnenkamm gondola.
Hotels There is an enormous choice.
*****Schloss Lebenberg** (6901) Modernized 'castle' with smart wellness centre; inconvenient location but free shuttle-bus.
*****Tennerhof** (63181) Luxurious former farmhouse, with renowned restaurant. Beautiful panelled rooms. Relais et Châteaux.
****Best Western Kaiserhof** (75503) By the Hahnenkamm gondola. Spa, pool.
****Goldener Greif** (64311) Elegant, historic inn; vaulted lobby-sitting area, panelled bar, sauna, steam.
****Maria Theresia** (64711) Central. 'Food good, rooms well appointed and staff very helpful.'

****Rasmushof** (652520) Right on the slopes by the race finish area, close to centre of town.
****Schwarzer Adler** (6911) Traditional hotel, remodelled as a boutique hotel within. Roof-top pool, spa.
****Schweizerhof** (62735) Comfortable chalet right by Hahnenkamm gondola.
****Tiefenbrunner** (66680) Traditional, family-run. Pool, spa. 'Well appointed rooms, first-class service, highly recommended.'
***Edelweiss** (75252) Close to centre. 'Most welcoming hotel we've ever stayed at; supply bags for you to take food from breakfast table for lunch.'
***Strasshofer** (62285) Central. 'We keep going back: great location, friendly, good food, excellent value.'
Mühlbergerhof (62835) Small, friendly pension in good position.
Apartments Many of the best are attached to hotels.

EATING OUT ★★★★

Something for everyone

There is a wide range of restaurants to suit all pockets, including pizzerias and fast-food outlets (even McDonald's). The Neuwirt in the Schwarzer Adler hotel is regarded as the best in town and wins awards in food guides. The Chizzo offers fine dining in one of the oldest buildings in Kitzbühel. Good, cheaper places include the traditional Huberbräu-Stüberl, Eggerwirt and, a little out of town with great views, Hagstein (traditional farm food). The Goldene Gams in the hotel Tiefenbrunner has a wide menu. Both the Centro and the Barrique are recommended for their pizzas. On Fridays you can dine at the top of the Hahnenkamm gondola at the Hochkitzbühel. For something different take a taxi to Rosi's Sonnbergstub'n. Choose the speciality lamb or duck and expect to be serenaded by Rosi herself.

APRES-SKI ★★★★

A main attraction

Nightlife is one of Kitz's great selling points, though one reporter this year notes that the bars are not as boisterous as they once were.

Immediately after the slopes close, the town is jolly without being much livelier than many other Tirolean resorts. The Streifalm bar at the foot of the slopes is popular. 'The outside bar at Chizzo was great fun,' says a recent reporter whose favourite bar was the Pavillion – 'great staff and a great party atmosphere'. Praxmair and Rupprechter are among the most atmospheric cafes for teatime cakes and pastries. The Centro and the 'quaint' Ursprung are recommended by a 2012 visitor for pre-dinner drinks.

The Seidlalm is the place for a jolly Tirolean evening. The Lichtl Pub has thousands of lights hanging from the ceiling. The Londoner Pub is described by 2012 visitors as 'a pub for young Brits', 'a good venue for live music', and 'the bar staff were fine' – quite an improvement on previous years' reports. Another 2012 reporter recommends the Sporthotel Reisch, opposite the Londoner, for being 'good fun, with a slightly older, but no less drunken/sober crowd and friendly local (not British) bar staff'. The Python, Highways and Take Five are discos.

OFF THE SLOPES ★★★★★

Plenty to do

The lift pass gives a reduction for the pools in the Aquarena leisure centre. There's skating, ice hockey, bowling etc) at the Sports Centre. There's a museum and a casino. The railway makes excursions easy (eg Salzburg, Innsbruck).

LINKED RESORT – 850m

KIRCHBERG

Kirchberg is a large, busy, spread-out place, with plentiful restaurants and shops and an unremarkable but pleasant centre. The traffic is surprisingly intrusive.

The slopes it shares with Kitzbühel are accessed via a choice of three gondolas – two on the fringe of the village and the third way out at Skirast. All require the use of 'regular and efficient' ski-buses or affordable taxis. A bit further on from Skirast is a gondola into Westendorf's slopes, and Brixen (a couple of miles away and with a gondola into the main SkiWelt slopes) can be easily reached by train or bus – read the chapter on Söll for more on these. There is a small nursery slope at the bottom of the separate Gaisberg sector, with a free lift, but it's at low altitude, and so prone to poor snow.

The village has a wide choice of lodging; the 4-star Klausen (2128) is convenient for the gondola there, and a 2012 visitor recommends the 'cosy' Haus Alpenblick (2234), a five-minute walk from the town centre. Most restaurants are hotel-based, but there are a couple of pizzerias, a Chinese and a steakhouse.

Kirchberg is a pretty lively place, both at teatime and later on. The London Pub is the main après-ski venue, but is rated by a highly experienced observer of these matters as the most filthy and depressing place he has visited. A 2012 visitor recommends the Rohrerstadl at the bottom of Piste 31 near Skirast for 'animated' après-ski: 'live group; staff very attentive', and reckons the Boomerang is 'the most lively and welcoming bar, with pool table and efficient table service'. Several places operate as discos later, and the VIP offers table-dancing.

Off the slopes there's floodlit tobogganing on Gaisberg and a leisure centre – and some hotels have swimming pools.

LINKED RESORT – 925m

JOCHBERG

Jochberg – 10km south of Kitzbühel – is not so much a village as a straggle of accommodation along a very busy road – it has nothing you could call a centre. There's a church, a bank, a post office, a ski depot, a supermarket, half a dozen restaurants and a couple of bars – and that's it. But if you're after accommodation close to the lifts, it's worth considering.

Access to the slopes is via an old, slow double chair halfway along the village, then a quite long T-bar.

Most of the lodgings are small pensions and apartments, but there are a couple of grander hotels. Of the restaurants the Alpenland is recommended by a 2012 visitor: 'Good value for money, friendly service, superb food.'

Phone numbers

From elsewhere in Austria add the prefix 05356 for Kitzbühel and 05357 for Kirchberg; from abroad use the prefixes +43 5356 / +43 5357

TOURIST OFFICES

Kitzbühel
www.kitzbuehel.com
Kirchberg
www.kirchberg.at

LECH TOURIST OFFICE

Lech

If you can afford it, simply one of the best: a captivating village with exceptionally snowy slopes – plus St Anton just over the hill

RATINGS

The mountains	
Extent	****
Fast lifts	****
Queues	****
Terrain p'ks	****
Snow	****
Expert	****
Intermediate	****
Beginner	****
Boarder	****
X-country	***
Restaurants	***
Schools	****
Families	*****
The resort	
Charm	****
Convenience	***
Scenery	***
Eating out	***
Après-ski	****
Off-slope	***

RPI	115
lift pass	£180
ski hire	£150
lessons	£110
food & drink	£135
total	**£575**

NEWS

2011/12: A chondola (a fast hybrid lift of chairs and gondola cabins) replaced the Weibermahd quad above Oberlech. The hotel Krone was refurbished; a new rooftop sun terrace was built, and it was promoted from 4-star to 5-star status.

- + Picturesque traditional village
- + Sunny but quite high slopes with excellent snow record
- + Sizeable area of intermediate pistes, plus extensive off-piste
- + Easy access by bus to the slopes of St Anton and other Arlberg resorts
- + Some very smart hotels
- + Lots of lovely heated chairlifts
- + Lively après-ski scene

- – Pricey, by Austrian standards
- – Surprisingly limited shopping
- – Few non-hotel bars or restaurants
- – Local traffic intrudes on main street
- – Very few challenging pistes
- – Nearly all slopes above treeline
- – Blue runs back to Lech are rather steep for nervous novices
- – Still a few slow, old lifts

Lech and its higher, linked neighbour Zürs are the most fashionable resorts in Austria, each able to point to a string of celebrity visitors, and to pull in Porsche-borne Germans by the thousand. Don't worry: we don't feel out of place here in our VWs, and neither would you.

The real point about Lech is that it offers excellent skiing on- and off-piste (with one of the best snow records in the Alps) combined with a village that is a pleasure to inhabit – particularly if you can afford to stay in one of its lovely top hotels. And Zürs? In its bleak setting, it is never going to be a match for Lech; but the real problem is the through-traffic. The road to Lech needs to be buried in a tunnel. A whip-round among the owners of the four 5-star hotels should be enough to raise the necessary.

THE RESORT

Lech is an old farming village set in a high valley that spent long periods of winter cut off from the outside world until the Flexen Pass road through Zürs was constructed at the end of the 19th century. Even now, the road can be closed for days on end after an exceptional snowfall.

Not far from the centre is the cable car up to Oberlech: a small, traffic-free collection of 4-star hotels set on the mountainside, with pistes running through it.

Zug is a hamlet 3km from Lech, with a lift into the Lech slopes. It's not ideal for sampling Lech's nightlife, but there is an evening bus service.

Lech is linked by lifts and runs to higher Zürs, described at the end of this chapter. There is a free and regular – but often very crowded – ski-bus service between the two resorts.

Buses (also crowded) run to St Anton, St Christoph and Stuben, too, all covered by the Arlberg pass. The post bus offers a less crowded option, but is not free. The Sonnenkopf area at Klösterle, reached by ski-bus from Stuben, is also covered (see the Vorarlberg – Alpenregion Bludenz chapter). There are plans to link the Lech area to the Warth-Schröcken area (see the Vorarlberg – Bregenzerwald chapter), possibly for 2013/14.

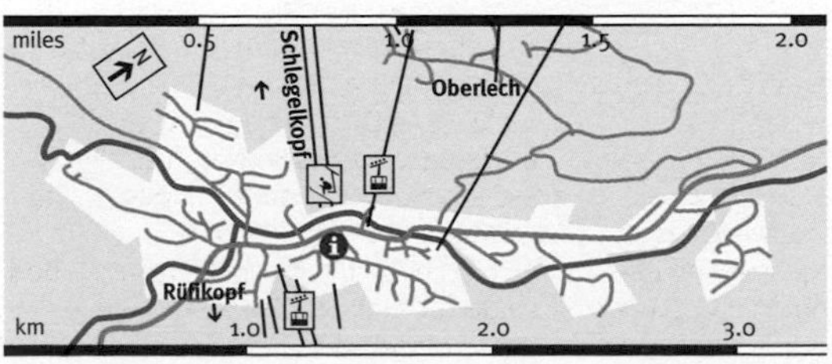

VILLAGE CHARM ****

Busy main street

The village is attractive, with upmarket hotels built in traditional chalet style, a gurgling river plus bridges, and a high incidence of snow on the streets. But don't expect a rustic idyll: away from the central area the place is fairly ordinary, and the appeal is somewhat dimmed by traffic on the main street, especially at weekends when car-borne German and Austrian visitors arrive and depart.

CONVENIENCE ★★★
It's a long village

The heart of the village is a short stretch of the main street beside the river, with most of the main hotels, the main shop (Strolz) and the Rüfikopf cable car, for access to the Zürs slopes. Just across the river are the chairlifts for Lech's main area of slopes. Chalets, apartments and pensions are dotted around the valley, and the village spreads for 2km. Some of the cheaper accommodation is quite a walk from the lifts.

Oberlech is a tiny place with pistes where you would expect streets, and an underground tunnel system linking the hotels and cable car station – used routinely to move baggage, and by guests in bad weather. The cable car works until 1am, allowing access to the mother resort's nightlife.

SCENERY ★★★
In a bright spot

Lech is in a fairly sunny position at the junction of two attractive valleys, with adequately impressive scenery, largely thanks to the Omeshorn looming to the south. It is high and open, with very few trees. From the top slopes there are views to the Valluga above St Anton in one direction, and to Warth-Schröcken in the other.

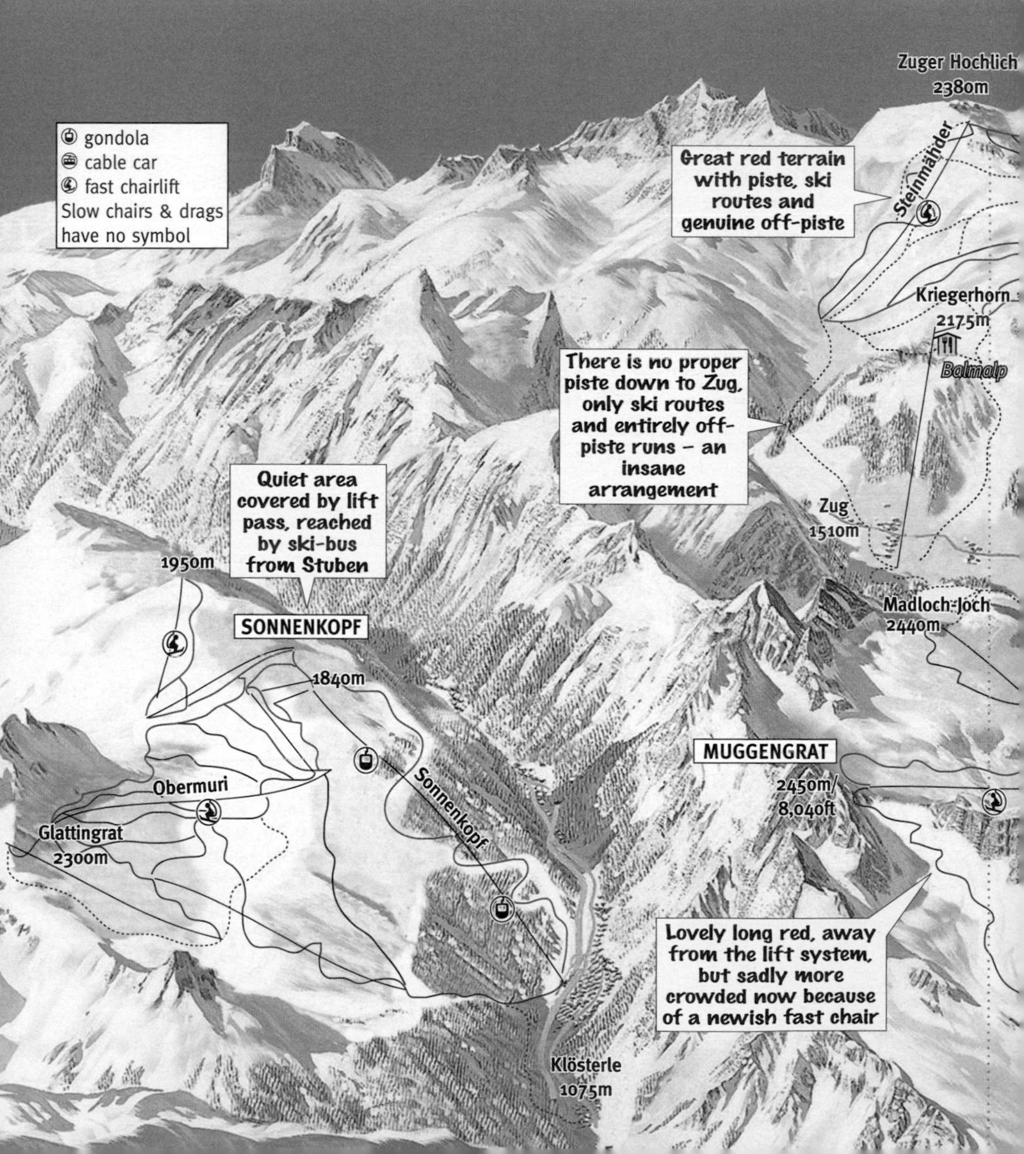
gondola
cable car
fast chairlift
Slow chairs & drags have no symbol
Zuger Hochlich
2380m
Great red terrain with piste, ski routes and genuine off-piste
Steinmähder
Kriegerhorn
2175m
Balmalp
There is no proper piste down to Zug, only ski routes and entirely off-piste runs – an insane arrangement
Zug
1510m
Quiet area covered by lift pass, reached by ski-bus from Stuben
1950m
SONNENKOPF
1840m
Madloch-Joch
2440m
Obermuri
Glattingrat
2300m
Sonnenkopf
MUGGENGRAT
2450m/
8,040ft
Lovely long red, away from the lift system, but sadly more crowded now because of a newish fast chair
Klösterle
1075m

THE MOUNTAINS

Practically all the slopes are treeless, the main exception being the lower runs just above Lech. Most are quite sunny – very few are north-facing.

The toughest runs are called 'ski routes' or 'high-alpine touring runs'. The touring runs are simply off-piste runs that would not appear on the piste map at all in most resorts. No problem – if you fancy these, hire a guide. The piste map says the ski routes are marked and avalanche controlled but not groomed or patrolled. We applaud the clear explanation (lacking in many resorts), but we think many of them should be patrolled pistes. Ski routes form the only ways down to Zug and Lech as part of the popular Lech-Zürs-Lech 'White Ring' circuit and are treated like pistes, as are several other ski routes. To add to the confusion, some of the routes are sometimes groomed (this happened on our recent visits).

The piste map, which covers the whole of the Arlberg region in one view, is unclear and misleading in places – particularly around Oberlech

Don't miss the latest in Austria. Check out p168.

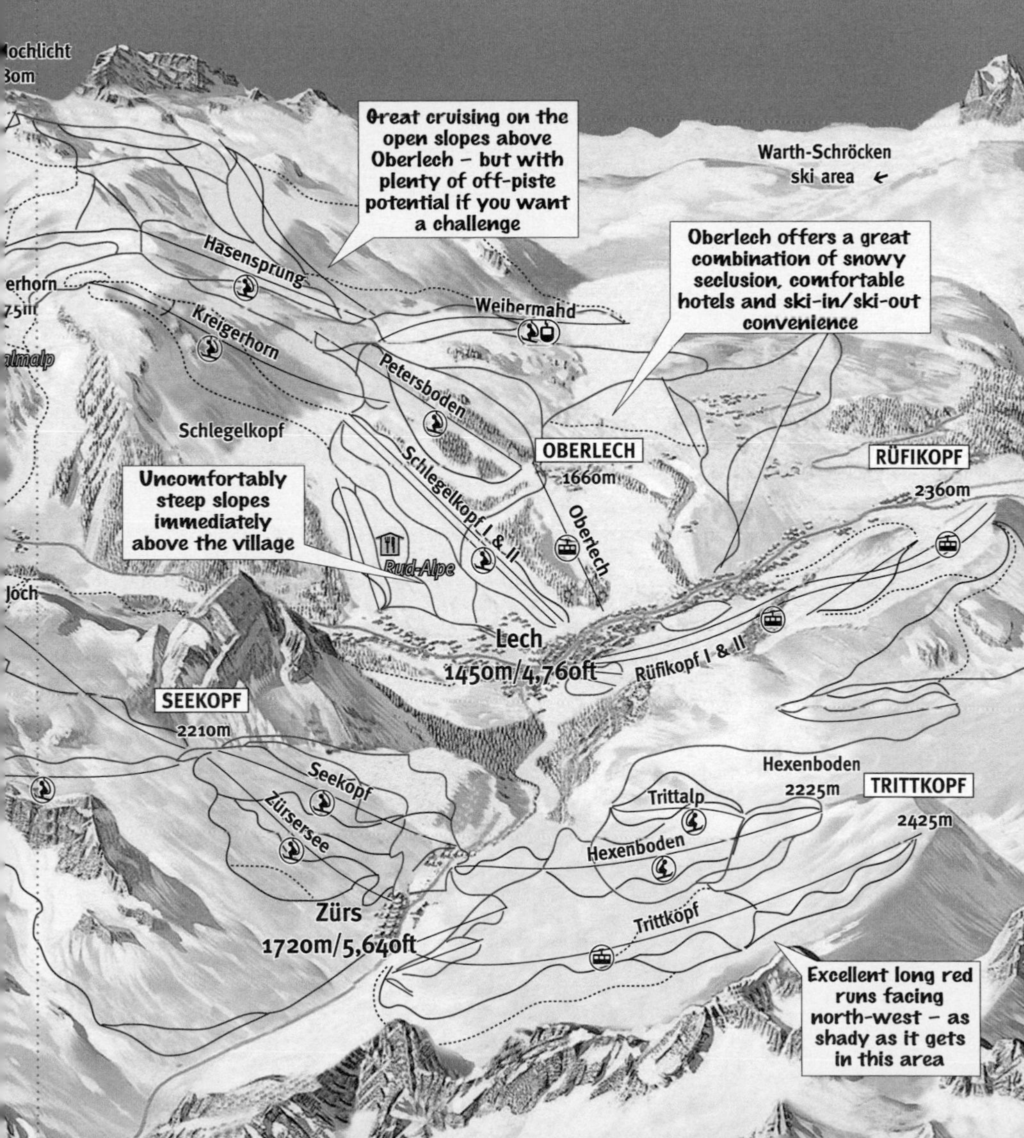
Great cruising on the open slopes above Oberlech – but with plenty of off-piste potential if you want a challenge
Warth-Schröcken ski area
Oberlech offers a great combination of snowy seclusion, comfortable hotels and ski-in/ski-out convenience
Hasensprung
Kreigerhorn
Weibermahd
Petersboden
Schlegelkopf
OBERLECH
1660m
Oberlech
RÜFIKOPF
2360m
Uncomfortably steep slopes immediately above the village
Schlegelkopf I & II
Rud-Alpe
Lech
1450m/4,760ft
Rüfikopf I & II
SEEKOPF
2210m
Seekopf
Zürsersee
Hexenboden
2225m
TRITTKOPF
2425m
Trittalp
Hexenboden
Zürs
1720m/5,640ft
Trittkopf
Excellent long red runs facing north-west – as shady as it gets in this area

↑ The area gets huge amounts of snow: this restaurant is almost at the foot of the Zürs slopes

SIMON PHILP

KEY FACTS

Resort	1450m 4,760ft
Arlberg region	
Slopes	1075-2650m 3,530-8,690ft
Lifts	84
Pistes	283km 176 miles
Blue	40%
Red	48%
Black	12%
Snowmaking	65%
For Lech-Zürs only	
Slopes	1450-2450m 4,760-8,040ft
Lifts	32
Pistes	122km 76 miles
Blue	39%
Red	48%
Black	13%

and down from Zürs to Zug and Lech. They should really have one piste map for Lech-Zürs and separate ones for St Anton-St Christoph-Stuben and for Sonnenkopf. Piste marking is OK in general. But, confusingly, the same number is given to several pistes in places. Piste classification understates the difficulty of some pistes.

EXTENT OF THE SLOPES ★★★★☆
One-way traffic

The main slopes centre on **Oberlech**, 250m above Lech (just below the treeline), and can be reached by cable car or chairlifts. The wide, open pistes above here are perfect intermediate terrain, and there is also lots of off-piste. Zuger Hochlicht, the high point in the sector, gives stunning views.

The **Rüfikopf** cable car takes Lech residents to the west-facing slopes of Zürs and the start of the Lech-Zürs-Lech circuit, which can only be done in a clockwise direction and is now called the 'White Ring'. This mountainside, with its high point at **Trittkopf**, is a mix of quite challenging intermediate slopes and flat/uphill bits. On the other side of Zürs the east-facing mountainside is of a more uniform gradient. Chairs go up to **Seekopf** with intermediate runs back down.

A six-pack goes from near here up to **Muggengrat** (the highest point of the Zürs area). This has a good blue run back under it and the long, scenic, lift-free Muggengrat Täli red run back to Zürs – this used to be delightfully quiet, but we've had reports of crowds since the six-pack arrived. It starts with a choice between a cat track and a mogul field, but develops into a fine, varied red with lots of nearby off-piste options on the way down; at the bottom you can take lifts up the other side or walk through the village to the Zürsersee chair back up to Seekopf.

From Seekopf you can ski down to the Madloch chair – slow and liable to closure by wind – which leads to the long, scenic ski route (often busy, with some tricky sections) back to the fringes of Lech, completing a clockwise circuit. You can peel off part-way down and head for Zug and the slow chairlift up to the Kriegerhorn above Oberlech.

FAST LIFTS ★★★★☆
Hot stuff

A high proportion of lifts are now fast, including a new hybrid chondola above Oberlech for last season. Seven chairlifts have the luxury bonus of heated seats. But there are still a few slow, old lifts (in particular, the chairs to Madloch-Joch above Zürs and from Zug to Kriegerhorn need modernizing) – Lech-Zürs is still some way behind Austrian pacesetters such as Ischgl and Saalbach in this respect.

QUEUES ★★★★☆
Still a few bottlenecks

There have been significant lift improvements, and feedback is generally positive, but there are still one or two bottlenecks – the Schlegelkopf fast quad out of Lech and the crucial Madloch double chair mentioned under 'Fast lifts' generate peak-time queues – so can the Rüfikopf cable cars to Zürs. The resort proudly boasts that it limits numbers on the slopes to 14,000, to ensure a more enjoyable experience – and the slopes certainly seem much quieter than those over the hill in St Anton.

LIFT PASSES

Arlberg

Prices in €

Age	1-day	6-day
under 16	27	132
16 to 19	42	191
20 to 64	46	219
65 plus	42	191

Free no one; day pass €10 if under 8, €20 if over 75

Beginner points ticket

Notes
Covers St Anton, St Christoph, Lech, Zürs and Stuben lifts, and linking bus between Rauz and Zürs; also Sonnenkopf (10 lifts) at Klösterle, 7km west of Stuben (bus link); single ascent, half-day and pedestrian options

TERRAIN PARKS ★★★★

In Lech only

The park, beside the Schlegelkopf chairlift, is one of the better terrain parks in Austria and was enjoyed by a 2012 reporter. There are over 20 features spread across easy, medium and pro lines, with kickers, two kinked boxes and a 9m-wide wall ride. The rails are also set in lines so you can hit several in a row. There's a fun box, a 4m down rail and a rainbow rail. There is also a designated Easy Park area made of little banks and jumps, great for getting used to air time.

SNOW RELIABILITY ★★★★

One of Austria's best

Lech and Zürs both get a lot of snow. Lech gets an average of almost 8m of snow between December and March, almost twice as much as St Anton and three times as much as Kitzbühel; but Zürs gets 50% more than Lech. The altitude is high by Austrian resort standards, and there is excellent snowmaking, helping to counter the sunny exposure. This combination, together with good grooming ('perfect' said a 2012 reporter), normally means good snow coverage until late April.

FOR EXPERTS ★★★★

Off-piste is the main attraction

There is only one (very short) black piste on the map, and there is no denying that for the competent skier who prefers to stick to patrolled runs the area is very limited. But the two types of off-piste route explained earlier offer lots to enjoy. There is also plenty of other excellent off-piste, much of it accessed by long traverses, and, in comparison with St Anton, fresh powder lasts well here.

Many of the best runs start from the top of the fast Steinmähder chair, which finishes just below Zuger Hochlicht. Some routes involve a short climb to access bowls of untracked powder. From the Kriegerhorn there are shorter off-piste runs down towards Lech and a very scenic long ski route down to Zug (followed by a slow chair and a rope tow to pull you along a flat area). Most runs, however, are south- or west-facing and can suffer from sun. At the end of the season, when the snow is deep and settled, the off-piste off the shoulder of the Wöstertäli from the top of the Rüfikopf cable car down to Lech can be superb, as can Zuger Hochlicht.

UK PACKAGES

Alpine Answers, Alpine Weekends, Crystal, Crystal Finest, Elegant Resorts, Erna Low, Flexiski, Independent Ski Links, Inghams, Interactive Resorts, Jeffersons, Kaluma, Luxury Chalet Collection, Momentum, Oxford Ski Co, Powder Byrne, Powder White, Scott Dunn, Ski Bespoke, Ski Club Freshtracks, Ski Expectations, Ski Independence, Ski Solutions, Ski Total, Skitracer, Skiworld, Snow Finders, STC, Supertravel, White Roc
Oberlech Kaluma, Ski Bespoke
Zürs Alpine Answers, Alpine Weekends, Carrier, Crystal, Crystal Finest, Inghams, Kaluma, Momentum, Powder Byrne, Scott Dunn, Ski Bespoke, Ski Solutions, STC

CHILDCARE

Mini-clubs
t 0664 123 9993

Kinderland Lech
From age 3

Kinderland Oberlech
From age 2

Babysitting list
Held by tourist office

Ski school
From 4½ to 12:
6 days €216

There are also good runs from the Trittkopf cable car in the Zürs sector, including a tricky one down to Stuben.

The steeper red runs (notably on Zuger Hochlicht and both sides of Zürs) are well worth a try, as is the lovely away-from-the-lifts Langerzug ski route back to Lech on the Rüfikopf side (steep start, then a gentle cruise, flattish run-out). And you'll want to visit St Anton during your stay (see separate chapter). Heli-skiing is also available, at least on weekdays.

FOR INTERMEDIATES ★★★★
Flattering variety for all

The pistes in the Oberlech area are nearly all immaculately groomed blue runs, the upper ones above the trees, the lower ones in wide swathes cut through them. It is ideal territory for cruisers not wanting surprises. But timid intermediates may find the final blue-run descents to Lech (as opposed to Oberlech) uncomfortably steep.

Strong intermediates will want to do the circuit to Zürs and back. Whether it's wise for less confident intermediates to tackle the beautiful red ski route from Madloch depends on the conditions. It is not steep, and part or all of it may be groomed despite its non-piste status, but parts can be heavily mogulled and busy, and lots of people find the run a struggle.

More adventurous intermediates will want to spend time on the fast Steinmähder chair on Zuger Hochlicht – a choice of satisfying pistes and ski routes, and from there take the scenic red run all the way to Zug (the latter part on an easy ski route rather than a piste). They may even want to give the Langerzug ski route (see 'For experts') a go. Lech is an excellent place to try skiing deep snow for the first time.

Zürs has many more interesting red runs, on both sides of the village. We like the north-west-facing reds from Trittkopf and the excellent Muggengrat Täli (see 'Extent of the slopes').

FOR BEGINNERS ★★★★
Easy slopes in all areas

The main nursery slopes are at Oberlech, but there is also a nice dedicated area in Lech. There are good, easy runs to progress to. You can buy a points card rather than a full lift pass.

FOR BOARDERS ★★★★
Easy riders, but mind the flats

Lech's upper-crust image has not stood in the way of its snowboarding development, and it is a popular destination for freeriders. There are few draglifts to deter novices; but beware of the west-facing slopes at Zürs, which have many flat/uphill sections.

FOR CROSS-COUNTRY ★★★
Picturesque valley trail

A 21km trail starts from the centre of Lech and leads through the beautiful but shady valley, along the river to Zug and back. In Zürs there is a 4km track to the Flexen Pass and back.

MOUNTAIN RESTAURANTS ★★★
Still not a strong point

The restaurants of the hotels in Oberlech have traditionally dominated the lunch scene here, but the options are widening. Restaurants are clearly marked on the piste map (except the ones in Oberlech, not surprisingly).
Editors' choice Rud-Alpe (418250) is not far above Lech, but far enough to count as a mountain restaurant – it would be an energetic non-skier who walked up. It's a welcoming, rustic place, lovingly built using timbers from other old huts. We had excellent gröstl and desserts there in 2011, efficiently served in a cosy, wood-built room – 'very good strudel', says a 2012 report. We and reporters have also enjoyed the modern, woody Balmalp, above Zug: cool music (loud on the terrace, quieter inside); simple food (pasta, pizza, ribs, salad); good views.
Worth knowing about Kriegeralpe above Oberlech is rustic and charming. Above Zürs, Seekopf offers table-service and has been praised for quality and price ('very good pasta'). At Oberlech there are several big sunny terraces set prettily around the piste. Quite often you'll find a live band playing outside one. Reader

SCHOOLS

Lech
t 2355

Oberlech
t 2007

Zürs
t 2611

Exklusiv
t 2719

Omeshorn Alpincenter
t 39880

Classes
(Lech prices)
6 days (2hr am and 2hr pm) €235

Private lessons
€280 for 4hr; each additional person €25

recommendations include Burgwald ('good chicken burgers'), Petersboden ('good pasta and great chicken salad'), Ilga Stüble, the lovely old Alter Goldener Berg and the Mohnenfluh.

SCHOOLS AND GUIDES ★★★★

Excellent in parts

The ski schools of Lech, Oberlech and Zürs all have good reputations, and the instructors speak good English. Many instructors are booked every year by regular visitors. We get good reports; one regular visitor has been satisfied for several years, and a 2012 reporter says, 'All the kids enjoyed it – lots of piste fun and park action.' Omeshorn Alpincenter and Exklusiv are alternative schools, also with guiding.

FOR FAMILIES ★★★★★

Oberlech's fine, but expensive

Oberlech makes an excellent choice for families who can afford it, particularly as its hotels are so conveniently placed for the slopes. Reporters have praised the family-friendly approach, especially to children using the lifts: 'staff really polite and helpful'. There's a kids' club in Oberlech, and Goldener Berg has an in-house kindergarten.

STAYING THERE

Chalets There are a few chalets run by UK tour ops, including two chalet hotels by Ski Total, one with pool and both with sauna, and two chalets in Zug by Skiworld, both with sauna.

Hotels There are five 5-stars, over 40 4-stars and countless other places.

LECH

*******Arlberg** (21340) Elegantly rustic central chalet, widely thought to be the best in Lech. Pool.

*******Post** (22060) Lovely old Relais & Châteaux place on the main street; pool, sauna. One of our favourites.

*******Krone** (2551) By the river. Refurbished in 2011 and now 5-star. Repeatedly tipped. Pool and spa.

******Filomena** (2211) Central aparthotel with rooms and apartments. Breakfast buffet available. Pool, sauna, steam, hot tub, solarium, massage.

******Monzabon** (2104) 'Excellent location, good food, helpful staff, attractive stube.' Pool, indoor ice rink.

******Schwarzwand** (2469) By the separate nursery slope so perfectly positioned for beginners. Sauna, steam room, solarium. Food, service and value for money are praised.

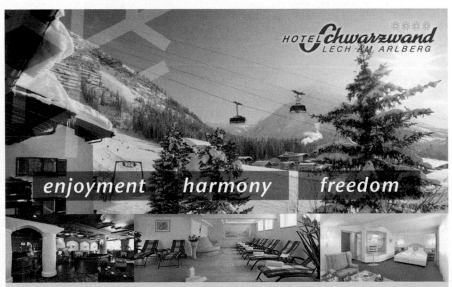

GETTING THERE

Air Zürich 200km/ 125 miles (2hr30); Innsbruck 120km/ 75 miles (1hr30); Friedrichshafen 130km/80 miles (1hr45)

Rail Langen (17km/ 10 miles); regular buses from station; buses connect with international trains

ACTIVITIES

Indoor Sports park (fitness studios, tennis, bowling, climbing wall, sauna), hotel swimming pools, museum, galleries, library, ice rink (in hotel Monzabon)

Outdoor Cleared walking paths, ice rink, curling, toboggan run (from Oberlech), paragliding, snowshoeing, horse-drawn sleigh rides

Phone numbers
From elsewhere in Austria add the prefix 05583; from abroad use the prefix +43 5583

TOURIST OFFICE

www.lech-zuers.at

******Tannbergerhof** (22020) Splendidly atmospheric inn on the main street, with outdoor bar and popular disco (teatime as well as later). Pool.
******Plattenhof** (25220) Slightly out of town. 'Great food, wonderful service, nice pool with waterfalls and eight different types of sauna.'
*****Lärchenhof** (2300) Neat B&B hotel with spa: 'Excellent breakfast, nice modern rooms and friendly owners.'

OBERLECH

******Bergkristall** (2678) Smart, family-run, on slopes. Comfortable rooms, hot tub, steam, sauna, solarium, massages. Own in-house nanny. Good reputation for food (including fresh fish daily); lovely lunch terrace.
******Burg** (22910) Smart, with pool, saunas, steam and umbrella bar.
******Montana** (2460) Welcoming chalet run by the family of Patrick Ortlieb. Pool, smart wellness centre.
******Pension Sabine** (2718) Regular haunt of an American reporter – 'great service and wonderful spa'.
Apartments There are lots available to independent bookers.

EATING OUT ★★★★★

Mainly hotel-based

There are over 50 restaurants in Lech, but nearly all of them are in hotels. Reporter recommendations include the Krone, Post, Almhof Schneider, Don Enzo Due (Italian) and Fux (Asian fusion). Hûs Nr 8 is one of the best non-hotel restaurants for traditional Austrian food. The Olympia has been suggested for cakes and coffee, and Backstüble for apple strudel. Café Fritz is cosy and relatively good value.

In Zug, the Rote Wand is excellent for traditional Austrian food ('beautiful old fashioned restaurant, attentive but not fussy service'), but is pricey. Reporters also tip the 'cosy and pleasant' Alphorn and the Klösterle.

APRES-SKI ★★★★★

Good but expensive

At Oberlech, the umbrella bar of the Burg hotel is popular at close of play, as is the champagne bar in hotel Montana. Readers also like the Ilga.

Down in Lech the outdoor bars of hotels Krone (in a lovely, sunny setting by the river) and Tannbergerhof (where there's an afternoon as well as a late-night disco) are popular. Later on, the K Club (Krone hotel) and Archiv Bar liven up. Readers like the Fux Jazzbar (with live music and a huge wine list).

Zug makes a good night out: you can take a sleigh ride for a meal at the Rote Wand, Klösterle or Auerhahn, and have drinks at the Vinothek wine bar at the s'Achtele restaurant.

After 7.30pm the free resort bus becomes a pay-for bus called James, which runs until 3am.

OFF THE SLOPES ★★★★★

At ease

For a resort where many visitors don't ski, the range of shops is surprisingly limited – Strolz's plush emporium (including a champagne bar) right in the centre is the main attraction.

It's easy for pedestrians to get to Oberlech or Zug for lunch. The village outdoor bars are ideal for posing. There are 28km of walking paths – the one along the river to Zug is 'outstandingly' beautiful; the tourist office produces a good map. There's a sports centre (no pool).

The floodlit sledging run from Oberlech to town is popular with families and highly recommended (but beware of toboggan theft – one reporter had three stolen).

LINKED RESORT – 1720m

ZÜRS

Some 10 minutes' drive towards St Anton from Lech is Zürs. Austria's first recognizable ski lift was built here in 1937. Zürs is a rare thing: a highly fashionable and expensive resort where the main occupation of visitors is skiing rather than parading. It has some excellent hotels (including four 5-stars); once inside them, all is well with the world. But the village as a whole doesn't have much appeal – it has nothing resembling a centre, few shops and a lot of intrusive traffic to/ from Lech on the central through-road. We stayed at the 5-star Zürserhof (25130) and found it excellent – great service, food and spa facilities. There are ten 4-stars, and three humble 3-stars for the impoverished.

Toni's Einkehr (a rustic hut at the foot of the Trittkopf slopes) is one of the few non-hotel restaurants and has been recommended. Nightlife is quiet: Vernissage is said to be the best spot. There's a disco in the Edelweiss hotel, a piano bar in the Alpenhof and the bar at the Hirlanda is 'pleasant'.

Many of the local Zürs instructors are booked up for private lessons for the entire season by regular clients.

TVB MAYRHOFEN / A DÄHLING

Mayrhofen

Large, lively resort with relatively reliable snow on local slopes and access to other good areas nearby, including a glacier

RATINGS

The mountains	
Extent	***
Fast lifts	****
Queues	*
Terrain p'ks	*****
Snow	***
Expert	**
Intermediate	***
Beginner	**
Boarder	****
X-country	**
Restaurants	***
Schools	****
Families	**
The resort	
Charm	***
Convenience	*
Scenery	***
Eating out	***
Après-ski	****
Off-slope	****

RPI	85
lift pass	£170
ski hire	£80
lessons	£70
food & drink	£105
total	**£425**

NEWS

2012/13: Above Zell am Ziller, the Kreuzwiese drag is due to be replaced by a fast six-pack.

2011/12: A six-pack replaced the Katzenmoos double chair on Penken, above Finkenberg. A skier services centre opened at the newly renovated gondola base station at Hippach. The terrain park was extended.

- ➕ Good for confident intermediates
- ➕ High, snow-sure slopes by local standards – plus glacier nearby
- ➕ Several worthwhile nearby areas on the same lift pass
- ➕ Lively après-ski
- ➕ Excellent children's amenities

- ➖ Long queues for the main gondola
- ➖ Slopes can be crowded
- ➖ Many lodgings a bus ride from lifts
- ➖ Runs mostly short
- ➖ Few steep pistes, although they do include Austria's steepest
- ➖ No pistes to the valley from Penken

Like so many popular Tirolean resorts, Mayrhofen manages to meet the needs of young people bent on partying and families looking for a quieter time. What marks it out is its relatively high, relatively snow-sure slopes.

Bear in mind that you can access those slopes from quieter villages between Mayrhofen and Hintertux, covered in the Hintertux chapter. And don't forget that the valley lift pass covers lots of other places that are well worth exploring – it covers over 170 lifts and more than 640km of pistes.

THE RESORT

Mayrhofen is a fairly large resort sitting in the flat-bottomed, steep-sided Zillertal. Most shops, bars and restaurants are on one long street, with hotels and pensions spread over a wider area.

Free buses and trains linking the Zillertal resorts mean you can easily have an enjoyably varied week visiting different areas on the Ziller valley lift pass including the excellent glacier at Hintertux (which has its own chapter). At the end of this chapter we cover the Zillertal Arena area, which starts at Zell am Ziller. The other major Zillertal area is Hochzillertal/Hochfügen above Kaltenbach, dealt with in the directory at the back of the book. There's a good train service to Salzburg, Innsbruck and Munich.

VILLAGE CHARM ***

Traditional and spacious

As the village has grown, architecture has been kept traditional, and the place merges with the surrounding fields in a rather charming way. The valley road bypasses the village, but it is not traffic-free.

CONVENIENCE *

Pick your spot

The original centre, around the church, the tourist office and the road out to the bus/railway stations, is now on the edge of things. The main lift to the major Penken sector of slopes is set at the opposite end of the main street, 1km away, and the Ahorn cable car is 200m further along, over the river. You can leave equipment at the lift station. The 'excellent' and 'efficient' free bus service can be crowded, and it finishes early (5.30), so location is important. The most convenient area is on the main street, close to the Penken gondola station.

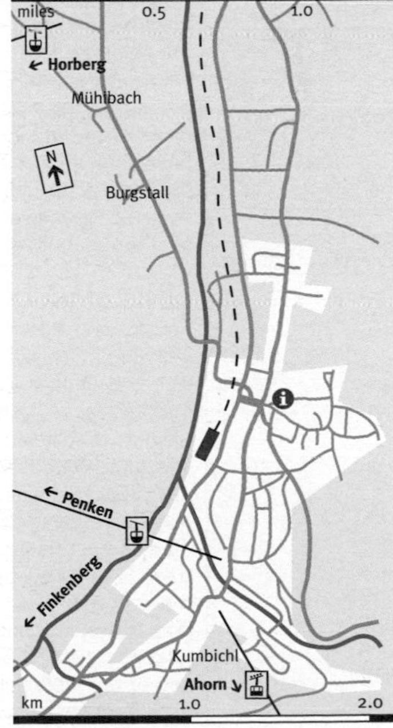

↑ Most of Mayrhofen's slopes suit confident intermediates best; there are few easy cruises

SNOWPIX.COM / CHRIS GILL

KEY FACTS

Resort	630m 2,070ft
Ziller valley	
Slopes	630-3250m 2,070-10,660ft
Lifts	172
Pistes	666km 415 miles
Blue	26%
Red	63%
Black	11%
Snowmaking	75%
Mayrhofen-Lanersbach only (ie excluding Hintertux glacier)	
Slopes	630-2500m 2,070-8,200ft
Lifts	54
Pistes	159km 99 miles
Snowmaking	123 guns

SCENERY ★★★
Views to the glacier
Mayrhofen is set between its two steep-sided mountains. From the top of each there are good views to the Hintertux glacier.

THE MOUNTAINS

Practically all Mayrhofen's slopes are above the treeline. Many are challenging reds, and some reporters note that the blues are not the easiest. Reporters praise signposting at the start of runs, but 'it is patchy lower down and at junctions', and the piste map is poor, particularly around the complex Penken summit. We very nearly ended up in Finkenberg, with our car in Hippach.

As elsewhere in Austria, there are unexplained 'ski routes', including all the runs to the valley. You may find some are groomed, but we presume all are unpatrolled. Take care.

EXTENT OF THE SLOPES ★★★
Fair-sized but inconvenient
The larger of Mayrhofen's two areas of slopes is **Penken-Horberg**, accessed by the main gondola from one end of town. It is also accessible via gondolas at Hippach and Finkenberg, both a bus ride away. You cannot get back to Mayrhofen on snow – you can catch the main gondola down or, if snow cover is good enough (it rarely is), you can descend to either Finkenberg or Hippach on ski routes (though the Finkenberg route was not marked on one of the piste maps we saw). Buses back from Finkenberg are hourly.

A big cable car links the Penken area with the **Rastkogel** slopes above Vorderlanersbach, which is in turn linked to **Eggalm** above Lanersbach – read the Hintertux chapter. Getting back from Rastkogel on skis means braving a busy mogul field with red and black variants, but you can avoid it by taking the cable car down.

The **Ahorn** area is pleasant but very small, and tends to be neglected – despite being accessed by Austria's largest cable car (carrying 160) with an eight-pack above it. There is a lovely, long red run to the valley.

FAST LIFTS ★★★★
Not enough from town
Look at the map and you'll see that a good proportion of the lifts are fast – gondolas and high-speed chairs. Readers are impressed. But that doesn't help getting people up from town first thing (see 'Queues' below).

QUEUES ★
Still a problem
Reporters in 2012 tell of waits of 15 to 30+ minutes for the Penken gondola in the morning, and more queues to ride down in the afternoon. One way to deal with them is to stroll over to the queue-free Ahorn cable car and do a few warm-up laps of 1300m vertical on that. Or you can catch a bus to one of four alternative access gondolas.

Up the mountain, queues are not so much of a problem as overcrowded pistes. One 2012 reporter said, 'Never in 40 years of skiing have I skied on such dangerous, overcrowded pistes.'

TERRAIN PARKS ★★★★★
Something for everyone
One of the finest parks in the Alps (www.vans-penken-park.com) lies beneath the Sun-Jet chairlift on Penken. There's a separate kids' park and intermediate, advanced, fun and pro areas, with a total of 11 kickers, two hips and 34 boxes and rails; a detailed plan is distributed. The half-pipe is not too big and is perfect for learning the ropes. Experts should bear in mind the 360m-long World Cup pipe at Hintertux.

SNOW RELIABILITY ★★★
Good by Tirolean standards
The area is better than most Tirolean resorts for snow because the slopes are relatively high – mostly above 1500m. Snowmaking covers the whole

LIFT PASSES

Superskipass Zillertal

Prices in €

Age	1-day	6-day
under 15	20	92
15 to 18	34	164
over 19	43	205

Free under 6

Senior no deals

Beginner no deals

Notes

1-day pass covers Mayrhofen areas only; 2-day+ passes include all Zillertal valley lifts; part-day passes

Ahorn area, all the main slopes on Penken-Horberg and some on Rastkogel and Eggalm. Hintertux is one of the best glaciers in the world. Grooming is praised.

FOR EXPERTS ★★★★★
Commit Harakiri

Austria's steepest piste, called Harakiri and under the Knorren chair, has a gradient of 78% (or 38°). It is certainly steep for a European piste; on both our recent visits, the run was mogul-free but rock hard; not surprisingly, it was delightfully deserted. It does offer a worthwhile challenge for the brave but is quite short. The black run under the Schneekar chair on Horberg is a good, fast cruise when groomed, but there are few other steepish pistes. The long unpisted trail to Hippach is quite challenging but rarely has good snow because of its low altitude. There is, however, quite a lot of decent off-piste to be found, such as from the Horbergjoch chair at the top of Rastkogel and under the cable car linking to that area.

FOR INTERMEDIATES ★★★★★
On the tough side

Most of Mayrhofen's slopes are on the steep side of the usual intermediate range – great for confident intermediates; many of the runs in the main Penken area are quite short, though, with verticals in the 300m/400m region. With access to the Lanersbach slopes, there is quite a bit of ground to cover, including delightfully quiet runs on Eggalm. Don't overlook Ahorn, mainly for its excellent run back to the valley. There are few really gentle blue runs, making the area less than ideal for nervous intermediates or near-beginners. The overcrowding on many runs can add to the intimidation factor. Ahorn offers a sanctuary, but is very limited.

FOR BEGINNERS ★★★★★
OK if it works for you

Despite its reputation for teaching, Mayrhofen is not ideal for beginners. You have to ride up the mountain to the nursery slopes, and there are no special lift passes so you'll need the full one. The Ahorn nursery slopes are excellent – high, extensive, sunny and crowd-free. But if you are with non-beginner mates, they will want to be on Penken. There are very few easy blues to progress to.

Not one but two glaciers on p168.

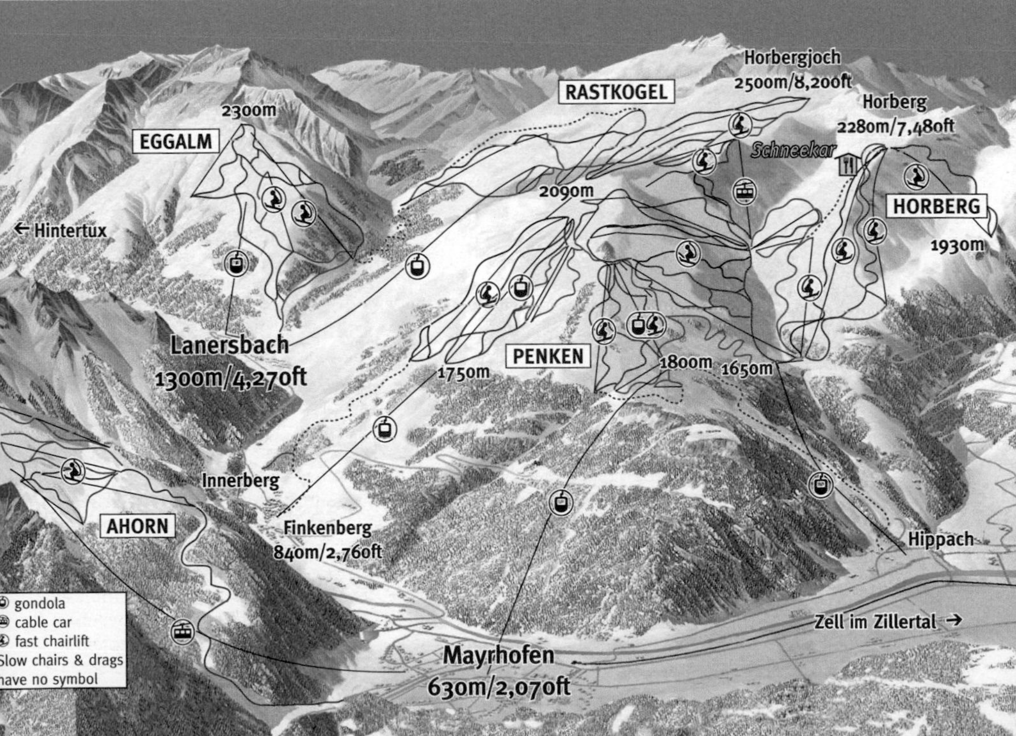

SCHOOLS

Skimayrhofen.com
t 62829

Die Roten Profis
t 63900

SMT
t 63939

Mayrhofen 3000
t 64015

Classes
(Skimayrhofen prices)
6 4hr days €155

Private lessons
From €55 for 1 hour

CHILDCARE

Wuppy's Kinderland
t 63612
Ages 3mnth to 7yr

Crèche (SMT school)
t 63939
From age 2

Babysitting list
at tourist office

Ski school
For ages 4 or 5 to 14. (6 days including lunch €167)

ACTIVITIES

Indoor Leisure pool, (pool, sauna, massage), fitness centre

Outdoor Ice rink, curling, 40km of paths, ice climbing, horse-drawn sleigh rides, paragliding, tobogganing

FOR BOARDERS ★★★★

A popular hangout

Mayrhofen has long been popular with snowboarders. But beginners may have a hard time getting around, as the terrain tends to be relatively steep, the nursery slopes are inconvenient, and the area still has quite a few draglifts. Intermediates and upwards, however, will relish the abundance of good red runs and easily accessible off-piste. The terrain park is one of the best in Europe. The Snowbombing music festival is held here each year, as well as a 5-star TTR event, the Ästhetiker Wängl Tängl.

FOR CROSS-COUNTRY ★★

Head up the valley

There are 28km of trails in the area. Snow in the valley is not reliable but higher Vorderlanersbach has a much more snow-sure trail.

MOUNTAIN RESTAURANTS ★★★

Plenty of them

Most of Penken's many mountain restaurants are attractive and are clearly marked on the piste map. Recent visitors have been impressed with the quality and value for money.
Editors' choice The Schneekar (64940) at the top of the Horberg is our kind of place – beams and open fire inside, individual bookable tables on the terrace, charming service, good view, excellent food. We had a good cheese, onion and bacon tart here, and a 2012 reporter had 'excellent' pizza.
Worth knowing about The table-service Jausenstation Tappenalm below Horberg has 'great traditional food in bright surroundings'. Higher up, Grillhofalm is tipped as the 'cheapest we found and a great place to watch the park action'. The 'modern' Panorahma by the draglifts down from the Finkenberg gondola offers 'lovely pizzas' as well as wonderful views and the 'world's best loos'. Christa's Skialm, nearby, is 'self-service but atmospheric with simple Tirolean specialities'. Also see the Lanersbach part of the Hintertux chapter.

SCHOOLS AND GUIDES ★★★★

Excellent reputations

Mayrhofen's ski schools have good reputations. Mayrhofen 3000 offered 'very good value and very good instruction' for a 2012 visitor's group, but a reporter was 'disappointed with the quality' of SMT's instructors. An off-piste guide from the Skimayrhofen.com school provided 'good service and good value' for a 2011 visitor.

FOR FAMILIES ★★

Good but inconvenient

Mayrhofen majors on childcare, and the facilities are excellent. But children have to be bussed around and ferried up and down the mountain.

STAYING THERE

Chalets There are several large places in or approaching the chalet hotel category. Skiworld has the Stoanerhof near the Ahorn cable car. Crystal has the Haus Tirol in the main street, close to the gondola. Inghams has the St Lukas, a short walk from the centre.
Hotels Note that the Penken gondola is 1km from the real centre, so 'central' does not mean 'close to lifts'. You can stay at the White Lounge ice-hotel on Ahorn too.
*****Elisabeth** (6767) The only 5-star, slightly out of the centre.
****Gutshof Zillertal** (8124) A 2011 reporter was delighted to have found this place on the southern outskirts, which offers 'almost free' hire cars. 'Good meals, great deal.' Pool, spa.
****Kramerwirt** (6700) Lovely hotel, oozing character, central.
****Neue Post** (62131) An old favourite, central. Pool, sauna, steam.
****Strass** (6705) By the gondola. Lively bars, disco, wellness centre, pool; but big, with low marks for style, and we've had complaints of noise keeping people awake.
****Zillertalerhof** (62265) 'Excellent food and service, great pool, sauna,' said a reader last year. Central.
****Sporthotel Manni** (63301) On the main street halfway between the train station and the gondola. Tipped by a 2012 reporter for 'large comfortable rooms, good steaks, excellent beer'.

UK PACKAGES

Crystal, Crystal Finest, Independent Ski Links, Inghams, Interactive Resorts, Mountain Wave, Neilson, Rude Chalets, Ski Expectations, Ski Line, Ski Solutions, Skitracer, Skiworld, STC, Thomson

Zell im Zillertal Crystal

GETTING THERE

Air Salzburg 175km/110 miles (2hr15); Munich 195km/120 miles (2hr45); Innsbruck 70km/45 miles (1hr15)

Rail Local line through to resort; regular buses from station

Phone numbers
From elsewhere in Austria add the prefix 05285 (Mayrhofen), 05282 (Zell), 05284 (Gerlos), 06564 (Königsleiten); from abroad use the prefix +43 and omit the initial '0'

TOURIST OFFICES

Mayrhofen
www.mayrhofen.at

Zillertal Arena

Zell im Zillertal
www.zell.at

Gerlos
www.gerlos.at

Königsleiten
www.wald-koenigsleiten.info

Apartments There are plenty available; Landhaus Gasser is central and was recommended by a 2012 reporter.

EATING OUT ★★★
Wide choice

There's a wide range of restaurants, from local specialities to Chinese. We've had good, satisfying meals at the jolly, friendly Tiroler Stuben near the station. Mo's is 'lively, with good food', American-style. Wirtshaus zum Griena is a lovely rustic old building on the edge of town, with a traditional menu – too much like a mountain restaurant for our taste, but popular with families. The Kramerwirt has 'excellent food with large portions'. The set menu at the Gasthof Brücke was 'excellent quality and value'.

APRES-SKI ★★★★
Lively

Après-ski is a great selling point – 'unpretentious and friendly, with little of the lager lout mentality that can prevail elsewhere'. At close of play, the umbrella bar at the top of the Penken gondola, the Ice Bar at the hotel Strass and Brück'n Stadl (Gasthof Brücke) get packed out, the latter proving particularly popular with readers for its great atmosphere. Some of the other bars in the Strass are rocking places later on, including the Speak Easy Arena, with live music and dancing until 4am. The Coup & More has 'a lively atmosphere without the rowdiness of some other places'. Mo's American theme bar is 'lively but not too noisy', has live music and is 'stylish', as is the Hara Kiri bar. Scotland Yard is popular with Brits but 'expensive and tatty', reckons a 2011 visitor. For a quiet drink we head to the bars of the big central hotels – the Neuhaus or the Neue Post.

OFF THE SLOPES ★★★★
Good for all

Innsbruck and other resorts are easily reached by train or bus. There are also good walks and sports amenities, including the swimming pool complex – with saunas, steam room and solarium. Pedestrians have no trouble getting up the mountain to meet friends for lunch. 'Several cafes and an ice-cream parlour make just walking the streets a very pleasant experience,' says a 2012 visitor. 'We had a non-skier in our party and they found plenty to do,' says another reporter.

DOWN-VALLEY AREA

ZILLERTAL ARENA

The Zillertal Arena was created in 2000 by linking the slopes of Zell am Ziller, 10km down the valley from Mayrhofen, to those above the villages of Gerlos and Königsleiten. They now share an area about as big as the Mayrhofen-Lanersbach area. The slopes are quite high, as in Mayrhofen, but they also get a lot of sun, so the snow message is a mixed one. The slopes suit intermediates best. You can really get a sense of travelling around: the trip from one end to the other is 17km and takes you over several peaks and ridges. A reporter said: 'Starting from Zell, a return trip is a full day's skiing. We did the tour over two days to fit in all the other runs.' Most runs are short – the longest, down to Gerlos, is 4km.

Zell is the main town in the Zillertal, and a real working town rather than just a resort. There are some good hotels, including the 4-star Zapfenhof (2349) on the outskirts (with pool) and the Brau (2313) in the centre. The town is a bus ride from the two gondolas into the ski area. You have to ride these down as well as up. Après-ski centres around a few bars near the base of the gondolas.

Gerlos has the advantage of being centrally situated in the ski area, allowing you to explore in either direction each day. It is a bustling resort that straddles the road up to the Gerlos pass and is a bus ride from the gondola into the slopes. Après-ski is lively and there are several good local hotels, including the 4-star Gaspingerhof (52160) with a very smart spa.

Königsleiten is very spread out, in a scenic wooded setting above a dam, with half a dozen hotels including the 4-star Königsleiten (82160). It has more extensive local slopes than Gerlos, on either side of the Gerlospass road, but less vertical. On the north side (reached by a gondola from the village) the runs are mostly genuine reds, radiating from the peak of Königsleitenspitze (2315m). The lower southern sector has a row of quad chairs serving easier slopes. The Obermoser ski school has been praised. But note that the draglift on the village nursery slope is not covered by the regional lift pass.

Both Gerlos and Königsleiten attract a lot of Dutch visitors.

OBERGURGL TOURIST OFFICE

Obergurgl

A combination of high altitude and traditional Tirolean atmosphere keeps regulars going back, despite the drawbacks

RATINGS

The mountains	
Extent	★★☆☆☆
Fast lifts	★★★★★
Queues	★★★★★
Terrain p'ks	★★☆☆☆
Snow	★★★★★
Expert	★★☆☆☆
Intermediate	★★★☆☆
Beginner	★★★★☆
Boarder	★★☆☆☆
X-country	★★☆☆☆
Restaurants	★★★☆☆
Schools	★★★★☆
Families	★★★★☆
The resort	
Charm	★★★★☆
Convenience	★★★★☆
Scenery	★★★☆☆
Eating out	★★★☆☆
Après-ski	★★★★☆
Off-slope	★★☆☆☆

RPI	100
lift pass	£190
ski hire	£125
lessons	£100
food & drink	£105
total	**£520**

NEWS

2011/12: Hochgurgl snowmaking was improved. A new beginner lift pass was introduced, and children up to nine years old can ski for free. The frequency of bus transport along the valley was improved. Night skiing was introduced in Hochgurgl.

- + Glaciers apart, one of the most snow-sure resorts in the Alps; good for a late-season holiday
- + Excellent area for beginners, timid intermediates and families
- + Mainly queue- and crowd-free
- + Traditional, quiet, chalet-style village with little traffic
- + Jolly Tirolean teatime après-ski

- − Limited area of slopes, with no tough pistes
- − Exposed setting, with very few sheltered slopes for bad weather
- − Little to do outside the hotels
- − Village is fragmented, and lacking a real centre
- − For a small Austrian resort, hotels are rather expensive

Obergurgl has never quite floated our boat. If we're going to a bleak, remote resort where there is little to do but ski, we'd rather go somewhere with rather more skiing to do.

But a loyal band of visitors go back time after time to Obergurgl or its higher satellite Hochgurgl, booking a year in advance to avoid disappointment, and it's not difficult to see why. If the list of plus-points above is what you're looking for, there really is nowhere else to beat it.

THE RESORT

Obergurgl has grown out of a traditional mountain village, set in a remote spot near the head of its valley – the highest parish in Austria and usually under a blanket of snow.

Although it's a small place, the village is split into three main parts. First you come to a cluster of hotels near the Festkogl gondola. The road then passes another group of hotels set on a little hill (beware steep, sometimes icy walks here). Finally you reach the nearest thing to a centre – a little square with the church, a fountain, the hotel Edelweiss und Gurgl and an underground car park.

Even higher Hochgurgl, linked by a mid-mountain gondola, is little more than a handful of hotels at the foot of its own area of slopes.

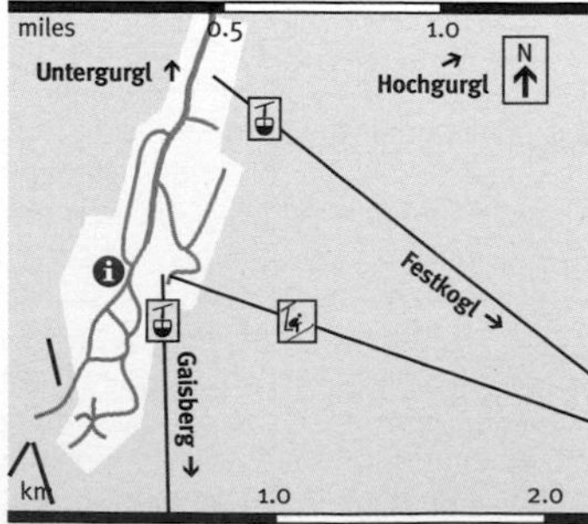

The lift pass is quite pricey, for a small resort. You can make it pricier still by paying 10 euro extra (at the time of buying your main pass) for a day in Sölden, a short bus ride down the valley (buses every half hour).

VILLAGE CHARM ★★★★☆
On the quiet side

Obergurgl has no through traffic and few day visitors, so the place is calm and relaxed. The village 'centre' is mainly traffic-free, and entirely so at night. It's quite jolly immediately after the slopes close, but rather subdued later; most people stay in their hotels.

CONVENIENCE ★★★★☆
Lifts at both ends

Obergurgl is a small place, and there are lifts at both ends. The Hohe Mut gondola station is close to the 'centre', and nowhere is a long walk from a lift. But you may need to use the free shuttle-buses (eg to get to ski school), and they are not very frequent. Hochgurl looks like a convenient ski-in/ski-out resort, but nearly all the hotels are separated from the snow by roads and/or stairs.

SCENERY ★★★☆☆
High and bleak

Obergurgl's altitude and position mean good panoramic views from the top of the lifts.

LIFT PASSES

Prices in €

Age	1-day	6-day
under 16	29	126
16 to 18	34	174
18 to 59	45	232
60 plus	39	202

Free under 9

Beginner limited pass covering nursery lifts

Notes

Covers Obergurgl and Hochgurgl, and local ski-bus; part-day passes and non-skier tickets available

KEY FACTS

Resort	1930m 6,330ft
Slopes	1795-3080m 5,890-10,100ft
Lifts	24
Pistes	110km 68 miles
Blue	32%
Red	50%
Black	18%
Snowmaking	99%

SNOWPIX.COM / CHRIS GILL

The small village spreads quite a way along the high valley, with no real centre ↓

THE MOUNTAINS

Most of the slopes are very exposed – with few woodland runs to head to in poor conditions. Wind and white-outs can shut the lifts, and severe cold can limit enthusiasm, especially in early season. If the weather is bad but not that bad, another problem arises: in our view, and that of many reporters, piste edge marking is dangerously slack – there are huge drop-offs that are not marked, and slopes seem to be marked either on one side only (often the uphill side) or in the middle only. Crazy. Reporters seem content with the piste map though. Classification of runs can overstate difficulty.

EXTENT OF THE SLOPES ★★★★★

Limited cruising

The total area of slopes is quite limited. A gondola links the Obergurgl and Hochgurgl ski areas at mid-mountain level. It closes absurdly early at 4pm. There are no piste links.

Obergurgl is the smaller of the two linked areas. It is in two sections, with a link at altitude in only one direction. The gondola from the village entrance and the Rosskar fast quad chair go to the higher **Festkogl** section. This is served by a short drag and a longer chair up to 3035m. From here you can head down to the gondola base or over to the **Hohe Mut** sector, also reached from the village via a gondola, which goes on to the sector high point at Hohe Mut. Lower down are slopes served by a slow quad and a six-pack.

There are two ski routes, which were ungroomed on our recent visit, but their status is not explained on the piste map.

The slopes of **Hochgurgl** consist of high, gentle bowls, with fast lifts serving the main slopes above the village, but drags serving the more testing outlying slopes. From the top stations there are spectacular views to the Dolomites. A single run leads down through the woods to Untergurgl.

There's night skiing on 8km of slopes in Obergurgl once a week, and on 3km in Hochgurgl twice a week.

FAST LIFTS ★★★★★

Among the best

The system is pretty impressive. Most lifts are now high-capacity gondolas or fast chairs.

QUEUES ★★★★★

Few problems

Major lift queues are rare. 'Fantastic,' say reporters. 'Surprisingly quiet and uncrowded, even in the Easter holidays.'

TERRAIN PARKS ★★★★★

Park life returns

There's now a park on Festkogl with jumps, kickers and rails.

Ski a high altitude resort with low prices - see p168

SNOW RELIABILITY ★★★★★
Excellent

Obergurgl has high slopes and is about the most snow-sure of Europe's non-glacier resorts – even without its snowmaking, which is claimed to cover all the pistes. The resort has a long season by Austrian standards. Piste grooming is generally fine.

FOR EXPERTS ★★
Not generally recommendable

There are few challenges on-piste – most of the blacks could easily be red, and where genuinely black it's only for short stretches (for example, at the very top of Wurmkogl). The ski routes are more challenging, particularly the one from Hohe Mut when mogulled. There is a lot of easy off-piste to be found – the top school groups often go off-piste when conditions are right. Slopes around the Kirchenkar draglift are good for untracked powder. And there are more serious routes – a reporter this year found 'glorious' untracked powder in the Königstal, on skier's left from Wurmkogl.

FOR INTERMEDIATES ★★★
Good but limited

There is some perfect intermediate terrain here, made even better by the normally flattering snow conditions. The problem is, there's not much of it. Keen piste-bashers will quickly tire of skiing the same runs and be itching to catch the free bus to Sölden.

Hochgurgl has the bigger area of easy runs, and these make good cruising. For more challenges, head to the Vorderer Wurmkogl lift, on the right as you look at the mountain.

The Obergurgl area has more red than blue runs but most offer no great challenge to a confident intermediate. There is some easy cruising around mid-mountain on Festkogl. The blue run from the top of this sector to the village, via the Hohe Mut sector, is 1100m vertical. And there's another long enjoyable run down the length of the gondola, with a scenic black run and ski route variant (neither of them very steep) in the adjoining valley.

On Hohe Mut, there are very easy runs in front of the Nederhütte and back towards the village. The red run from Hohe Mut is narrow and in places winding – timid intermediates beware.

FOR BEGINNERS ★★★★
You pays your money

There is one lift free only to ski school pupils, and three other beginner lifts (covered by a special cheap day pass) serving adequate slopes, at each end of Obergurgl, and just above Hochgurgl – an awkward walk from most of the hotels, but otherwise satisfactory. After that you require a

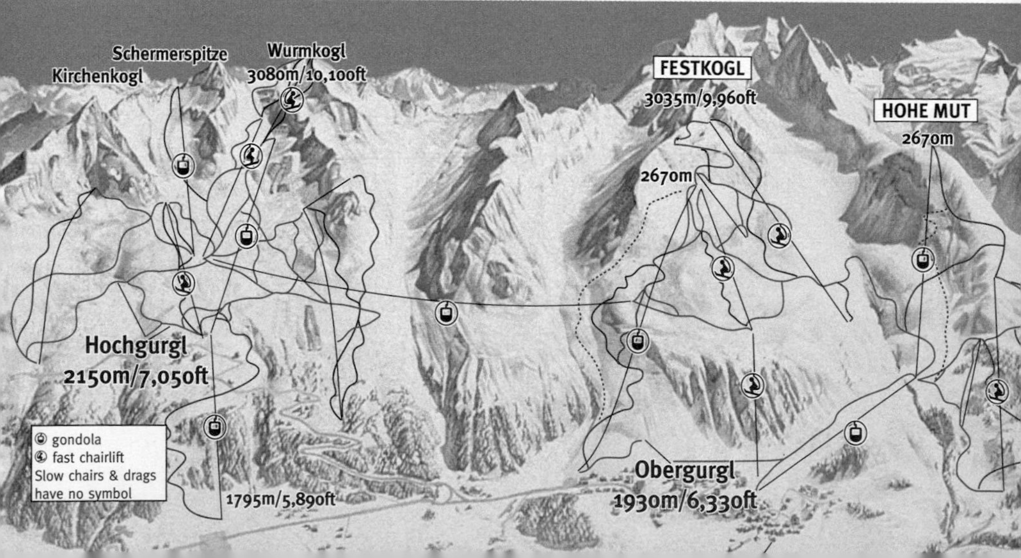

↑ There are few trees up here; this pic is taken from the Hohe Mut ski route

SNOWPIX.COM / CHRIS GILL

SCHOOLS

Obergurgl
t 6305
Hochgurgl
t 626599
Exclusiv
t 0664 182 6969
Alpinsport
t 6322

Classes
(Obergurgl prices)
6 days (2hr am and pm) €226
Private lessons
From €142 for 2hr

CHILDCARE

Alpina & Hochfirst hotel kindergartens
From age 3
Kindergarten (Obergurgl school)
t 6305
From age 3

Ski schools
From age 4 (6 days €226)

full lift pass. The gentle run under the gondola from the mid-station of the Hohe Mut gondola to the village is ideal to move on to as soon as control has been achieved. The easy broad slopes served by the Bruggenboden chair are also suitable. And then there are good longer slopes to move on to, particularly at Hochgurgl.

FOR BOARDERS ★★☆☆☆
Lacks challenge

Beginners can access most of the slopes without having to ride draglifts. There's some good off-piste potential for more advanced riders; a recent visitor singles out the area around the Steinmann chair in the Hohe Mut sector; and things have improved now that a fun park has been built.

FOR CROSS-COUNTRY ★★☆☆☆
Limited but snow-sure

Three small loops, two at Obergurgl and one at Hochgurgl, amount to just 12km of trail. At Hochgurgl 1km is floodlit. All are relatively snow-sure and pleasantly situated but, like the slopes, very exposed in bad weather. Lessons are available.

MOUNTAIN RESTAURANTS ★★★☆☆
Fair choice

Hut choice is limited, but most reports are positive.

Editors' choice No contest, really. Hohe Mut Alm (639632) has table-service, fabulous glacier views from the big terrace, a woody interior, impressively efficient service, and good hearty food on our 2011 visit – endorsed by a reporter. But it gets packed early and doesn't take bookings. The jolly Nederhütte (6425), not far above village level, is hugely popular with readers: 'great atmosphere, great traditional food'; 'excellent service, choice and reasonable prices'.
Worth knowing about The Top Mountain Star at Wurmkogl looks like an air traffic control tower, has great 360° views, a varied menu but a modern bar ambience. Kirchenkarhütte by contrast is a simple rustic hut – very small, and often crowded.

SCHOOLS AND GUIDES ★★★★☆
Positive reports

We continue to receive positive reports of the Obergurgl school and guides, with good English spoken, a maximum of nine per group except at busy times and excellent lessons and organization. Reporters find the instruction is 'exceptionally good', progression 'genuine' and the standard of teaching 'very high'; 'superb' for children. Demand for private instruction appears to be increasing, and it is advisable to book ahead during all peak periods.

FOR FAMILIES ★★★★☆
Check out your lodgings

Children's ski classes start at four years and children from age three can either join Bobo Mini Club (outdoor activities) or Bobo kindergarten (indoor). There's lunchtime supervision for ski school and kindergarten children alike. Many hotels offer childcare of one sort or another (the Alpina has been recommended), and Ski Esprit is a family-specialist UK chalet operator here.

STAYING THERE

Most tour operators feature hotels and pensions. Demand exceeds supply, and for once it is true that you should book early to avoid disappointment.
Chalets Ski Total has a big chalet here, and family-specialist sister company Esprit has two.
Hotels Accommodation is of high quality: most hotels are 4-stars, and none is less than a 3-star.

GETTING THERE

Air Innsbruck 95km/ 60 miles (2hr); Salzburg 285km/ 175 miles (4hr15); Munich 245km/ 150 miles (4hr30)

Rail Train to Ötz; regular buses from station

ACTIVITIES

Indoor Pools, saunas, whirlpools, steam baths and massage in hotels; bowling, indoor golf, indoor horse riding

Outdoor Natural ice rink, curling, snowshoeing, winter hiking paths, tobogganing

UK PACKAGES

Alpine Answers, Crystal, Crystal Finest, Esprit, Independent Ski Links, Inghams, Interactive Resorts, Momentum, Neilson, Oxford Ski Co, Ski Expectations, Ski-Monterosa, Ski Solutions, Ski Total, Skitracer, Snow Finders, Thomson

Hochgurgl Crystal Finest, Inghams, Ski Expectations, Skitracer, Snow Finders, Thomson

Phone numbers
From elsewhere in Austria add the prefix 05256; from abroad use the prefix +43 5256

TOURIST OFFICE

www.obergurgl.com

Obergurgl

****Alpina de Luxe** (6000) Big, smart; excellent children's facilities. 'Wonderful, well-run, traditional hotel with fantastic pool/sauna/spa' and a 'Brit-friendly cozzie-on' zone.

****Bergwelt** (6274) We stayed here in 2011. Very well run, with excellent food and charming service. Indoor, outdoor pools and spa facilities.

****Edelweiss und Gurgl** (6223) The focal hotel; on the central square, near the main lifts. Indoor/outdoor pool and sauna.

****Gotthard-Zeit** (6292) Convenient for skiing, but uphill from the village. 'One of the best and friendliest hotels I have stayed in,' says a recent visitor. Spa and pool.

****Hochfirst** (63250) Five minutes from gondola. Ski-bus stop outside. Indoor/outdoor pool, spa, hot tub.

****Josl** (6205) Uber-modern, convenient – close to the gondola. Big rooms, lots of storage, glass walls to bathrooms. Top-floor spa. We've stayed here and loved it.

***Pension Hohenfels** (6281) Opposite the Festkogl gondola. Basic, but 'extremely friendly staff, very good breakfasts', says a recent visitor.

Hochgurgl

*****Top Hotel Hochgurgl** (6265) Relais & Châteaux – the only 5-star in the area. Good position.

****Riml** (6261) Ski-in/ski-out location. 'Excellent pool, amazing wellness area, friendly staff, the most stunning hotel I've stayed in.'

****Sporthotel Olymp** (6491) Near the Grosse Karbahn chair. 'Excellent food and service.'

Apartments The Lohmann (6201) is modern and well placed for the slopes. The 3-star Pirchhütt (6390) has apartments close to the Festkogl gondola.

EATING OUT ★★★

Wide choice, limited range

Hotel à la carte dining rooms dominate almost completely. The independent and rustic Krumpn's Stadl (where staff dress in traditional clothing) has a good choice, including rib specials. The Romantika at the hotel Madeleine and the Belmonte are popular pizzerias. For a varied menu, the restaurants in the Edelweiss und Gurgl and the Josl (Austrian, vegetarian) have been recommended. Other tips are the Hexenkuchl in the Jenewein (Austrian food) and the Angerer Alm at Hochgurgl for more of a gourmet offering. Some evenings you can eat on the hill, at Hohe Mut Alm or at David's Skihütte – both popular snowmobile destinations.

APRES-SKI ★★★★

Lively early, quiet later

Obergurgl is more animated than you might expect, at least in the early evening. Nederhütte at the Hohe Mut mid-station is the place to be when the lifts close, which in practice means getting there well before then. 'It rocks from the first anthem until the time you want to leave. Dancing on your table/chair is obligatory and schnapps compulsory – great atmosphere, great party, great fun. Go for it!' The dancing is enhanced several times a week by live music, said to be 'enjoyed by all age groups'. You ski home afterwards (or ride down on a snowmobile). All the bars at the base of the Rosskar and Hohe Mut lifts are also popular at close of play – try the Pic-Nic ('can get smoky'), or the Hexenkuchl at the Jenewein. The newish Eisloch (ice dome bar) outside the hotel Alpina is popular.

Later on, the crowded Krumpn's Stadl barn is the liveliest place in town with a DJ most nights. Josl's Keller is popular with all ages – 'good fun'. You can usually find an atmospheric bar at one of the hotels. Reporters have enjoyed the Tuesday ski school display/mountain party/night ski on Festkogl ('worth a visit', but a 2012 visitor laments its 9pm start as he has young children) and the 'thoroughly entertaining' night-time tobogganing.

Hochgurgl is very quiet at night except for live music in Toni's Almhütte bar (Sporthotel Olymp).

OFF THE SLOPES ★★

Very limited

There isn't much to do during the day – hardly any shops, limited facilities of other kinds. There is an ice rink. Innsbruck is over two hours away by post bus. Sölden (20 minutes away) has a leisure centre and some shops. There are now buses every 15 minutes to Längenfeld (for the thermal spa). Pedestrians can ride gondolas to some of the restaurants for lunch, or walk part-way up the Hohe Mut area; there are 12km of 'pretty' hiking paths. The spas at the Crystal and Bergwelt hotels are open to non-residents for about 30 euros.

TVB OBERTAUERN

Obertauern

French-style convenience and snow-sure slopes meet Austrian après-ski – an unusual combination. Great for a short break

TOP 10 RATINGS

Extent	**
Fast lifts	*****
Queues	****
Snow	****
Expert	***
Intermediate	****
Beginner	****
Charm	**
Convenience	****
Scenery	***

RPI	95
lift pass	£160
ski hire	£95
lessons	£105
food & drink	£125
total	**£485**

NEWS

2012/13: A chondola (a mix of 10-seat gondola cabins and eight-seat chairs) is due to replace the Grünwaldkopfbahn quad from the valley. And a six-pack will replace the Hochalmbahn quad above that. Carrying capacities will increase by over 50%.

KEY FACTS

Resort	1740m 5,710ft
Slopes	1630-2315m 5,350-7,600ft
Lifts	26
Pistes	100km 62 miles
Blue	60%
Red	36%
Black	4%
Snowmaking	90%

- + Excellent snow record
- + Quite a lot of ski-in/ski-out lodging
- + Efficient modern lifts
- + Good mountain restaurants
- + Lively but not intrusive après-ski

- – Village not notably charming, and spreads along the pass a long way
- – Slopes limited in extent – and in vertical, in particular
- – Bleak, exposed setting
- – Few off-slope diversions

Obertauern's combination of attractions is unique. If you're hooked on Austrian après-ski but looking for a change from slush and ice, moving up in the world by 1000m or so could be just the ticket. But note the minus points above.

THE RESORT

In the land of picture-postcard resorts grown out of rustic valley villages, Obertauern is different – a mainly modern development at the top of the Tauern pass. The slopes and lifts form a snow-sure circuit around the village.

Village charm Built in (high-rise) chalet style mixed with stylish modern architecture, the resort is not unattractive and has an upmarket feel to it. Most accommodation is set either side of the through-road and sprawls some distance. Close to one end, another road leads off it at 90°, and some of the best après-ski bars and smart ski shops are here – it is the nearest thing to a central focus.

Convenience Check your location carefully – lifts go up either side of the access road at various points.

Scenery The setting is satisfyingly rugged, with some long views from the high points of the area.

THE MOUNTAINS

Most of the slopes are above the treeline, and bad weather can make skiing impossible (as we found on our last visit). Reporters praise the signposting and map but give mixed views on piste classification.

Slopes The circuit can be travelled either way in a couple of hours. The major share of the skiing is in the wide sunny basin to the north of the road and village. Visitors used to big areas will soon start to feel they have seen it all. Runs are short, and vertical is limited – most major lifts are in the 200m to 400m range. There is floodlit skiing twice a week.

Fast lifts There are fast chairs all over the place, and lifties reportedly manage to fill them.

Psst! Wanna see Austria's best-kept secret? Check out p168.

TVB OBERTAUERN

Obertauern has mainly short snow-sure runs served by fast modern lifts →

UK PACKAGES

Alpine Answers, Crystal Finest, Inghams, Snow Finders, STC, Thomson

Queues Crowded pistes can be more of a problem than queues. The Sonnenlift chair can have problems at ski school time.
Terrain parks The small Longplay Park is above the Almrausch hut, on the far left on our piste map.
Snow reliability Excellent because of altitude and extensive snowmaking. A reporter found grooming 'very good'.
Experts There are genuinely steep black pistes from the top Gamsleiten chair, but it is prone to closure. The icy race course under the Schaidbergbahn is a challenge. And try the black run from Seekarspitze and the ski route from Hundskogel (flat to start, steep moguls later).
Intermediates Most of the circuit is of intermediate difficulty. Stay low for easier pistes, or try the tougher runs higher up; you can't do the whole circuit without skiing reds.
Beginners There are good nursery slopes in several places, notably by the car parks at the western end of the resort. The Schaidberg chair leads to a high-altitude beginners' slope, and there is an easy run down.
Snowboarding Draglifts are optional except for beginners. Blue Tomato is a specialist school.
Cross-country 26km of trails locally.
Mountain restaurants Mountain restaurants are numerous but often crowded. Reader favourites are the Hochalm for its lively party atmosphere, the Sonnhof ('good food brought very quickly'), the Kringsalm self-service and Treff 2000. Mankei Alm is cosy, with table service.

Schools and guides We have no recent reports of the six schools, but past reviews of both Krallinger and Koch have been positive.
Families The resort isn't particularly family-oriented, and nursery slopes can be inconvenient, but most ski schools do take children. The kindergarten takes children from 10 months to four years.

STAYING THERE

Hotels Practically all accommodation is in hotels (mostly 3-star and 4-star) and guest houses. Two places are regularly tipped by readers: the Latschenhof (7334) – 'best food in Austria', 'great spa, 50m from a run' – and the Marietta (7262) – 'friendly, well-run; lovely spa'.
Eating out The choices are mostly hotels (the Latschenhof is highly recommended). Some of the après-ski bars turn themselves into restaurants – the Almrausch does 'superb food'.
Après-ski There are several cute woody chalets at the base that throb at teatime – Latsch'n Alm, Lürzer Alm, Gruber Stadl. WeltcupSchirm is a 'superb' lively umbrella bar. The Tauernkönig hotel, hidden away off the 8a home run, has 'a cosy outdoor après area'. Later on, Monkey's Heaven and the People bar have dancing. We had a quiet beer and used the free Wi-Fi in the modern, glass-fronted Mund Werk (part of a big ski shop).
Off the slopes There's an excellent, large sports centre (no pool). There are marked walks up to Kringsalm. Salzburg is an easy trip.

Phone numbers
From elsewhere in Austria add the prefix 06456; from abroad use the prefix +43 6456

TOURIST OFFICE

www.obertauern.com

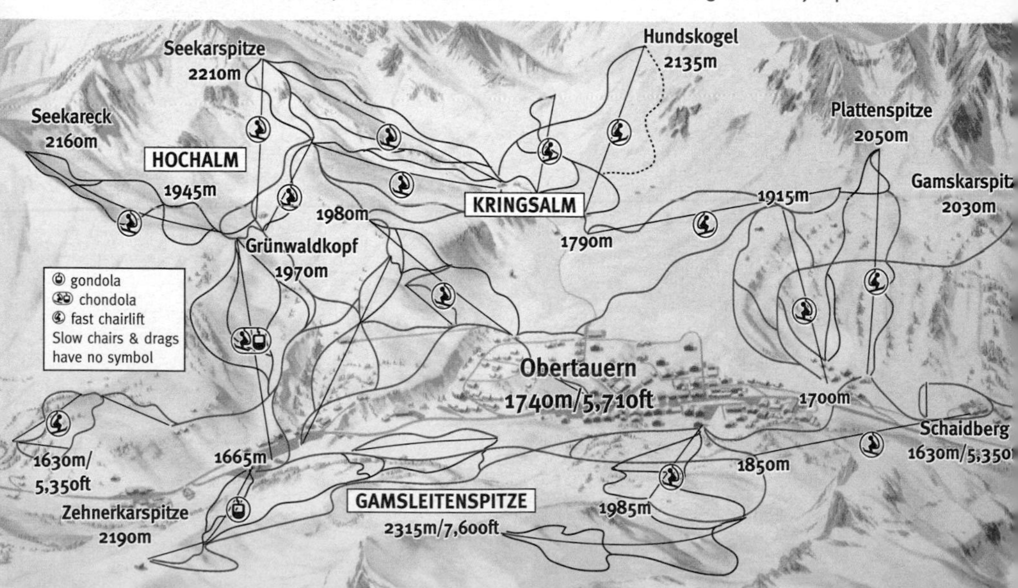

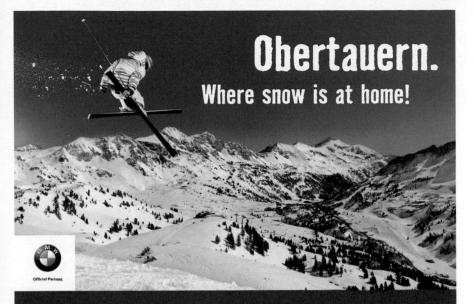

SAALBACH-HINTERGLEMM TOURIST OFFICE

Saalbach-Hinterglemm

Lively, noisy, traditional-style villages and extensive, varied, prettily wooded slopes; pity they are mostly so sunny

RATINGS

The mountains	
Extent	***
Fast lifts	*****
Queues	****
Terrain p'ks	****
Snow	**
Expert	**
Intermediate	****
Beginner	***
Boarder	*****
X-country	**
Restaurants	****
Schools	****
Families	***
The resort	
Charm	****
Convenience	****
Scenery	***
Eating out	***
Après-ski	*****
Off-slope	**

RPI	90
lift pass	£180
ski hire	£100
lessons	£80
food & drink	£105
total	**£465**

- ➕ Large, well-linked, intermediate circuit, good for mixed groups
- ➕ Impressive lift system
- ➕ Saalbach is a pleasant, lively village, largely car-free in the centre
- ➕ Dozens of good mountain huts
- ➕ Extensive snowmaking but ...

- ➖ Most slopes are sunny as well as low, and the snow suffers
- ➖ Limited steep terrain
- ➖ Nursery slopes in Saalbach are sunny, and crowded in parts
- ➖ Both villages spread widely
- ➖ Both are noisy from 4pm and Saalbach can get rowdy at night

Saalbach-Hinterglemm gets ever closer to completing its mission to abolish the slow lift. The vital link between the two villages over Reiterkogel and Bernkogel was hugely improved in one direction last season, and will be similarly improved in the other direction this coming season. Leaving aside baby drags and the like, only five slow lifts remain. Amazing.

The valley has a lot going for it in other respects, too. Sadly, good snow isn't one of them. The altitudes are modest, but the bigger problem is that most of the slopes face south. The snowmaking is good enough to make a midwinter visit here a fairly safe bet, but problems can arise as spring approaches.

THE RESORT

Saalbach and Hinterglemm are separate villages, their centres 4km apart, which have expanded along the floor of their dead-end east-west valley. They haven't quite merged, but some years back they adopted a single marketing identity. A 'ski-circus' links the two villages, with lifts and runs on both sides of the valley. At the eastern end is a link to Leogang, in the next valley to the north.

Saalbach has a justified reputation as a party town – but those doing the partying seem to be a strangely mixed bunch. Big-spending BMW and Mercedes drivers staying in the smart, expensive hotels that line the main street share the bars with teenagers spending more on alcohol than on their cheap and cheerful pensions.

Hinterglemm is a more diffuse collection of hotels and holiday homes, where prices are lower and less cash is flashed.

Several resorts in Salzburgerland are reachable by road. The obvious nearby targets are Hochkönig to the north and Zell am See to the south. There are two regional passes to consider – read the 'Lift passes' panel in the margin.

miles 0.5 1.0 1.5 2.0
Bernkogel ↖
Kohlmaiskopf ↗
Saalbach
↓ Schattberg
km 1.0 2.0 3.0

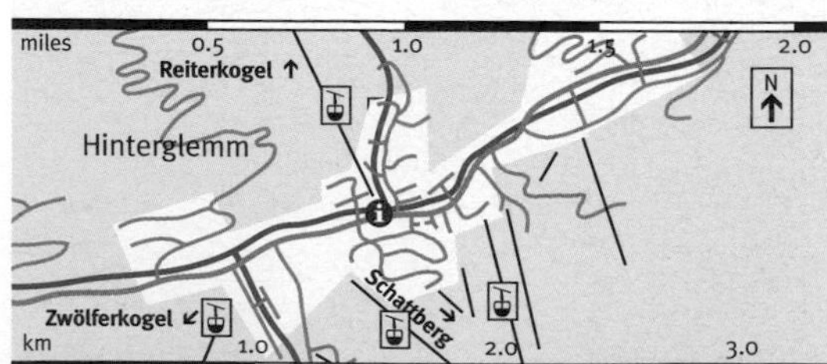

VILLAGE CHARM ****

Very appealing

Saalbach is an attractive, typically Tirolean village, with traditional-style (although mostly modern) buildings huddled together around a classic onion-domed church. Hinterglemm is less cute, with a rather featureless centre spread along a single main street. Both villages are free of through traffic.

Both villages are lively from mid-afternoon until the early hours. Saalbach in particular can get rowdy, with drunken revellers still in their ski

NEWS

2012/13: The T-bar on Bernkogel that impeded progress from Hinterglemm to Saalbach is to be replaced by a six-pack with bubbles.

2011/12: Two slow chairlifts on the way up from Saalbach to Reiterkogel were replaced, one by an eight-seat gondola and the other by a six-pack.

boots late in the evening. If you are not among them, you might find this an undesirable feature.

CONVENIENCE ★★★★

Lifts near the centre

Saalbach is more convenient than most Austrian villages, with lifts into three sectors of the slopes starting close to the traffic-free village centre; the result, if staying centrally, is near to an ideal blend of Austrian charm with French convenience. Hinterglemm also has lifts and runs close to the centre, and offers quick access to some of the most interesting slopes – and, importantly, to most of the north-facing runs. In both, the amount of walking depends on where you stay.

The valley bus service is fine, but not perfect: it finishes early, gets very busy at peak times and doesn't reach the hotels or lifts in central Hinterglemm, or hotels set away from the main road. A Nightliner bus runs infrequently between the two resorts in the evening.

SAALBACH-HINTERGLEMM

This must be midwinter, quite early in the day, when Schattberg casts a shadow over the middle part of the valley ↓

SCENERY ★★★

Pleasant rather than dramatic

The villages are flanked by modest, broad mountain ridges. The high points give more dramatic views of the mountains to the north.

THE MOUNTAINS

The runs form a 'circus' almost entirely composed of broad slopes between swathes of forest, so this is a good area in bad weather. Reporters comment on 'very good' signposting, 'good piste map and accurate classification'.

EXTENT OF THE SLOPES ★★★

User-friendly circuit

Travelling anticlockwise, you can make a complete circuit of the valley on skis, crossing from one side to the other at Vorderglemm and Lengau – if you wish you can stick to blues almost the whole way. Going clockwise, you have to do a shorter circuit – there is no lift at Vorderglemm – and there is more red-run skiing to do.

On the south-facing side, five sectors can be identified, each served by a lift from the valley – named on our map. The links across these slopes work well: when traversing the whole hillside you need to descend to the valley floor only once – at Saalbach, where the main street separates Bernkogel from Kohlmaiskopf. The Wildenkarkogel sector connects via Seidl-Alm to the slopes of **Leogang**; a small, high, open area served by fast lifts leads to a long, north-facing slope down to the base of an eight-seat gondola near Hütten, 3km from Leogang village.

Back in the main valley, the north-facing slopes are different in character: two widely separated and steeper mountains, one split into twin peaks. An eight-seat gondola rises from Saalbach to **Schattberg Ost**, where the high, open, sunny slopes behind the peak are served by a fast quad. The slightly higher peak of **Schattberg West** is reached by gondola from Hinterglemm. Another gondola makes the link from Schattberg Ost to Schattberg West. The second north-facing hill is **Zwölferkogel**, served by a two-stage eight-seat gondola from

Wow! What's new in Austria? See p168.

KEY FACTS	
Resort	1000m 3,280ft
Slopes	930-2095m 3,050-6,870ft
Lifts	55
Pistes	200km 124 miles
Blue	45%
Red	48%
Black	7%
Snowmaking	90%

Hinterglemm. A six-pack and draglift serve open slopes on the sunny side of the peak, and a second gondola from the valley provides a link from the south-facing Hochalm slopes.

The Hinterglemm nursery slopes are well used, and floodlit every evening.

FAST LIFTS ★★★★★

The world's best

Saalbach-Hinterglemm has the highest proportion of fast lifts of any major resort in the world (almost 90%). The already impressive lift system gained another gondola in 2010 and two further upgrades were made for last season – both on Bernkogel (read 'News'). An efficient lift in that direction from Saalbach was way overdue, and the parallel drags above it seem to be coping with people flooding up the new gondola. This season, the draglift you take to Bernkogel from the Hinterglemm side is being replaced. It's relentless.

QUEUES ★★★★

High season mostly

Given what we say about fast lifts, it's not surprising that the system copes well. The only recent complaints relate to peak season – a '20-minute wait on a sunny day' for the Schönleitenbahn at Vorderglemm and (last year) some delays in the morning peak getting in to the main circuit from Leogang.

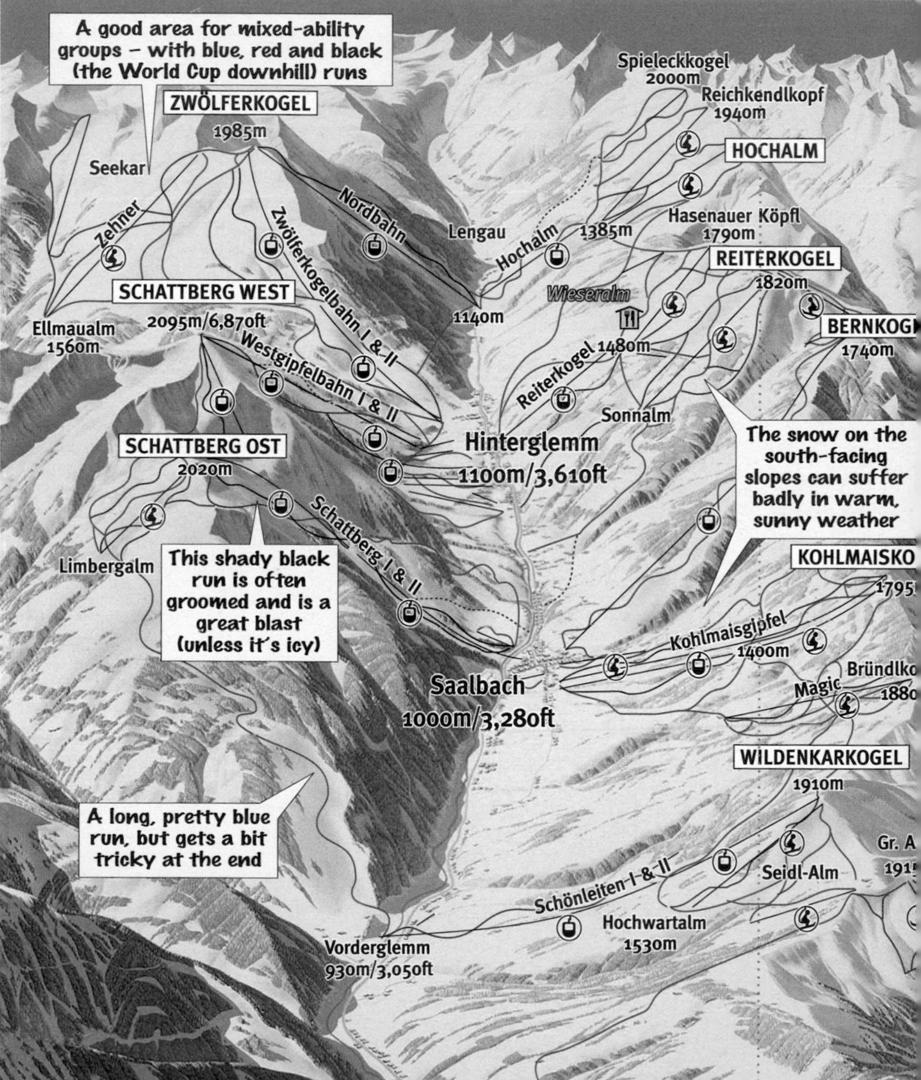

LIFT PASSES

Prices in €

Age	1-day	6-day
under 16	22	106
16 to 18	33	159
over 19	44	212

Free under 6

Senior no deals

Beginner points card

Notes
Covers Saalbach, Hinterglemm and Leogang, and the ski-bus; also Reiterkogel toboggan run at night; part-day and non-skier passes

Alternative passes
Salzburg SuperSkiCard covers 22 ski areas in the Salzburg province; Kitzbüheler Alpen All Star Card covers Kitzbühel, Schneewinkel (St Johann), Ski Welt, Alpbach, Wildschönau, Skicircus Saalbach, Zell-Kaprun

TERRAIN PARKS ★★★★
Now with its own gondola

The popular Nightpark just above Hinterglemm is served by a newish heated gondola. The park is floodlit until 9.30pm and includes Big Air, kickers, wall ride and rails, plus a beginner line. To access the park, there's a handy passenger lift up from Hinterglemm to the base of the gondola. There's another park below Kl. Asitz towards Leogang, and a park for beginners on Bernkogel.

SNOW RELIABILITY ★★
A tale of two sides

Most slopes are below 1900m and the south-facing slopes are in the majority; they can suffer when the sun comes out (we've encountered strips of machine-made snow amid green and brown fields). The north-facing slopes keep their snow better but can get icy. The long north-facing run down to Leogang often has the best snow in the area. Piste maintenance is good and snowmaking covers 90% of the area, including many top-to-bottom runs; but the fundamental problems won't go away.

FOR EXPERTS ★★
Little steep stuff

There are a few challenging slopes on the north-facing side. The long (4km) Nordabfahrt run beneath the Schattberg Ost gondola is a genuine black – a fine fast bash first thing in the morning if it has been groomed and is not icy. The Zwölferkogel Nordabfahrt at Hinterglemm is less consistent, but its classification is justified by a few short, steeper pitches. The World Cup downhill run from Zwölferkogel is interesting, as is the 5km Schattberg West–Hinterglemm red (and its scenic 'ski route' variant). Snow conditions and forest tend to limit the off-piste potential. Given decent snow, however, you can have a good time.

FOR INTERMEDIATES ★★★★
Paradise for most

The sunny side of the area is ideal for both the mileage-hungry piste-basher and the more leisurely cruiser, although many of the blues can be quite testing. For those looking for more of a challenge, the long red runs to the valley ranged along the north side are good fun. The otherwise delightful blue run from Bernkogel to Saalbach can get really crowded.

The north-facing area has some more challenging runs, with excellent relentless reds from both Schattberg West and Zwölferkogel, and a section of relatively high, open slopes around Zwölferkogel – good for mixed-ability groups wishing to ski together. None of the black runs is beyond an adventurous intermediate, unless icy. The long, pretty blue to Vorderglemm gets you right away from lifts – but it gets a bit steep and tricky towards the end, and probably should be red.

Our favourite intermediate run is the long cruise, off the circuit, to Leogang.

↑ The black run from Schattberg down to Saalbach is not super-steep

SAALBACH-HINTERGLEMM

SCHOOLS

Saalbach

Fürstauer
t 8444

Snow Academy
t 668256

Zink
t 0664 162 3655

Board.at
t 20047

easySki
t 0699 111 80010

Hinterglemm

Snow & Fun
t 7511

Activ
t 0676 517 1325

Alpin
t 74145

Total
t 560 0669

Classes
(Fürstauer prices)
5 days (4.5hr) from €168

Private lessons
From €139 for 3hr, for 1 or 2 people; extra person €15

CHILDCARE

Several hotels have nurseries

Ski schools
Some take children in mini-clubs from about age 3; from about age 4, children join ski school

FOR BEGINNERS ★★★
Head for Hinterglemm

Saalbach's two sunny nursery slopes are right next to the village. The upper one is served by a short six-pack but gets a lot of through-traffic. There are short, easy runs to progress to at Bernkogel and Schattberg.

Hinterglemm's spacious nursery area faces north, so lacks sun in midwinter but is more reliable for snow later on. It is separate from the main slopes, and preferred by reporters. Progression is aided by a gondola serving the blue slope that is also used for night skiing. There are lots of other easy blue runs to move on to, especially on the south-facing side of the valley.

FOR BOARDERS ★★★★★
Good all-rounder

Saalbach is great for boarding. Slopes are extensive, lifts are mainly chairs and gondolas, and there are pistes to appeal to beginners, intermediates and experts alike – with few flats to negotiate. For experienced boarders, there's off-piste terrain between the lifts if snow conditions permit.

FOR CROSS-COUNTRY ★★
Go to Zell am See

In mid-winter the 10km of valley trails get very little sun, and are not very exciting. There is a high trail on the Reiterkogel. But the area beyond nearby Zell am See is better.

MOUNTAIN RESTAURANTS ★★★★
Excellent quality and quantity

The area is liberally scattered with huts – about 40 in total – most of them pleasant, lively, rustic places serving good food. All are marked and named on the piste map.

Editors' choice The Wieseralm (6939), at the heart of the Hinterglemm south-facing slopes, is a welcoming woody chalet doing table-service of satisfying dishes; fine views from the terrace.
Worth knowing about Reporters regularly tip the Alte Schmiede above Leogang, a lovely wood hut with table-service, a big fireplace, huge terrace and DJ; 'superb value, delicious food appears within two minutes of ordering'. A brewery museum/ restaurant opened next door last season. Westernstadl on Bernkogel has a saloon theme, 'built around a stable with horses'; but also 'great food and friendly service'.

There's a picnic room an the top station of the Schattberg Xpress.

SCHOOLS AND GUIDES ★★★★
More reports would be good ...

There's plenty of choice. We lack reports again this year but past feedback on the Fürstauer school has been positive.

FOR FAMILIES ★★★
Hinterglemm tries harder

Saalbach doesn't go out of its way to sell itself to families, although it does have a ski kindergarten. Hinterglemm probably makes a better family base, with some good hotel-based nursery facilities – at the Theresia for example. And its nursery slope is better.

STAYING THERE

Chalets This isn't a major chalet resort, but last year Inghams introduced an 80-bed chalet hotel in a prime position in Hinterglemm.
Hotels Both villages have lots of hotels, mainly 3-star and above. Be aware that some central hotels suffer from disco noise, and front rooms from street noise into the early hours.

SAALBACH
****Alpenhotel** (6666) Central place with countless bars and restaurants, open-fire lounge, nightclub; small pool, hot tub.
****Kendler** (62250) Position second to none, beside the Bernkogel lift. Classy, expensive, good food.
****Kristiana** (6253) Near enough to lifts but away from night-time noise. Sauna, steam bath.
****Saalbacher Hof** (71110) Major central hotel, renovated in 2010, with new restaurants and wellness centre.
***Haider** (6228) Best-positioned of

ACTIVITIES

Indoor In hotels: swimming pools, sauna, massage, solarium, tennis, museum, gallery, bowling, casino

Outdoor Ice rink, curling, tobogganing, sleigh rides, snowshoeing, snowmobiling, quad bikes, ice karts, 40km of cleared paths, archery, paragliding

UK PACKAGES

Alpine Answers, BoardnLodge, Crystal, Crystal Finest, Independent Ski Links, Inghams, Interactive Resorts, Neilson, Rocketski, Ski Expectations, Ski Miquel, Skitracer, Snow Finders, Snowscape, STC, Thomson
Leogang Interactive Resorts, Zenith

GETTING THERE

Air Salzburg 90km/55 miles (2hr); Munich 225km/140 miles (3hr30)

Rail Zell am See 19km/12 miles; hourly buses

Phone numbers
From elsewhere in Austria add the prefix 06541 (Saalbach), 06583 (Leogang); from abroad use the prefix +43 and omit the initial '0'

TOURIST OFFICES

Saalbach
www.saalbach.com

Leogang
www.leogang-saalfelden.at

the 3-stars, right next to the main lifts.
*****Peter** (6236) Main street location. Recently renovated.

HINTERGLEMM
******Theresia** (74140) Hinterglemm's top hotel, good for families. On road to Saalbach, but at foot of a red run and close to a draglift into the circus. Superb food and friendly staff, say past reports. Pool and spa.
*****Sonnblick** (6408) Convenient and in a quiet location.
Apartments There's a big choice for independent travellers.
At altitude Some mountain restaurants have rooms. One reader greatly enjoyed the 3-star Sonnhof (6295) at the top of the Hochalmbahn, where in the mornings you get two six-packs all to yourself for half an hour.

EATING OUT ★★★

Wide choice of hotel restaurants

This is essentially a half-board resort, with strikingly few restaurants other than those in hotels. In Saalbach, the Kohlmais Stub'n (Aparthotel Astrid) at the foot of the slopes has friendly service, a warm woody ambience and creative, regional food. The hotel Peter's restaurant, at the top of the main street, is atmospheric and serves excellent meat dishes cooked on hot stones. Of the Alpenhotel's several eateries, we've enjoyed pizza and other stuff at La Trattoria, and like the look of its Vitrine 'wok restaurant'.

APRES-SKI ★★★★★

It rocks from early on

'The best après-ski in the Alps,' claims the resort website, and it is certainly among the best. The site lists over 20 venues. Saalbach, in particular, is very lively from mid-afternoon until the early hours, and can get quite wild.

On the hill above Saalbach, the rustic Hinterhag Alm is an institution 'Everybody meets here at 4pm', they say, and that's how it seems; live bands ensure a great atmosphere until people start to slide down to the already packed Bauer's Schi-Alm – an old cow shed with attached umbrella bars. Both are 'noisy, drunken places, but good fun'. There are alternatives: Bäckstättstall and the main bar of Berger's Sporthotel have dancing when the lifts close. Jack-in has Wi-Fi and big screen TVs for the sports fans. Bobby's Pub 'resembles a drunken youth club', but is cheap, has bowling, games machines, sport on TVs and serves Guinness. A tireless reporter reckoned that 'you can just about hold a conversation' in Zum Turm (a converted medieval jail) or Spitzbub (a converted garage), but recommends the Eva,Alm for a quiet drink. Later on, there are clubs under various central hotels, and several pole dancing dives.

We get fewer reports on the après-ski in Hinterglemm, which possibly attracts more families and fewer night-owls – 'seems very limited', said a 2012 visitor – but the Hinterhag Alm role is clearly played by the lively and rustic goat-themed Goasstall. Road King in the hotel Dorfschmiede is a lively Harley-Davidson biker-themed bar where one reporter enjoyed 'an acoustic trio doing Dylan covers' one night of the week. Later on, hit the Tanzhimmel and Hexenhäusl.

OFF THE SLOPES ★★

Surprisingly little to do

The resort is not very entertaining if you're not into winter sports. There are few shops other than supermarkets and ski shops. There are some walking paths, and the gondolas can be used (you pay by the trip). Many good restaurants are reachable by lift, for lunchtime meetings. At Hinterglemm a floodlit treetop walk opened recently, and the Reiterkogel toboggan run is said to be great fun (and good value for multiple runs). There are excursions to Salzburg.

LINKED RESORT – 800m

LEOGANG

Leogang sits in a pretty valley beneath the impressive Birnhorn. It is quietly attractive but is set on a busy through-road.

It may seem to offer a good budget base for skiing the slopes of Saalbach-Hinterglemm, but in practice it suits best those who are content with the good, generally quiet local slopes, plus the runs at the eastern end of the main circuit; getting to the best slopes beyond Hinterglemm takes quite a time. There are good nursery slopes by the village, and short runs to progress to.

Lodging is widely scattered, but there are good hotels and quiet apartments available. Restaurants are hotel-based. The rustic old chalet Kraller Alm is the focal teatime and evening rendezvous. Activities off the slopes are very limited.

SCHLADMING TOURIST OFFICE

Schladming – Ski Amadé

Pleasant old valley town in Styria, with a famous racing hill directly above, links to three other mountains and other areas nearby

RATINGS

The mountains	
Extent	★★★
Fast lifts	★★★★
Queues	★★★★
Terrain p'ks	★★★
Snow	★★★★
Expert	★★
Intermediate	★★★★
Beginner	★★★
Boarder	★★★
X-country	★★★★
Restaurants	★★★★
Schools	★★★
Families	★★★★
The resort	
Charm	★★★
Convenience	★★★
Scenery	★★★
Eating out	★★★
Après-ski	★★★
Off-slope	★★★

RPI	85
lift pass	£170
ski hire	£75
lessons	£90
food & drink	£90
total	**£425**

Ski amadé
www.skiamade.com

NEWS

2012/13: The 2013 Alpine World Ski Championships will be held here from 4 to 17 February.

2011/12: At Hauser Kaibling, a six-pack replaced the Almlift draglift serving an isolated blue run. More car parking and a media building were built beside Planet Planai.

- + Ideal for intermediate cruising
- + Very sheltered slopes, among trees
- + Lots of good mountain restaurants
- + Appealing town with friendly people
- + Very cheap for meals and drinks
- + Extensive snowmaking and shady slopes mean generally good piste conditions, but ...

- − The mainly north-facing runs can be cold in early season
- − Slopes lack variety
- − Very little to entertain experts
- − Nursery slopes not central and may involve a bus ride
- − Runs to valley level are not easy
- − Après-ski not a highlight

One slope may be rather like another here, but with its four linked mountains Schladming offers the keen intermediate a real sense of travelling around on the snow. And its solid, valley-town ambience makes it a pleasant change from the Austrian rustic-village norm.

THE RESORT

The old town of Schladming sits at the foot of Planai, one of four linked ski mountains. It has a long skiing tradition: the town has hosted many World Cup races and is this season hosting the 2013 Alpine World Ski Championships – in the lead up to that, it built a new ultra-modern skier services building, Planet Planai, at the lift base, not far from the focal square of the town.

From the western suburbs, a slow chairlift followed by a six-pack serves the next peak to the west, Hochwurzen, passing through Rohrmoos – a quiet, scattered village set on an elevated slope that forms a giant nursery area. From Hochwurzen you can progress to the most westerly of the four areas, Reiteralm. To the east of Schladming is the small, attractively rustic village of Haus, where a cable car and gondola go up to the highest of the four linked mountains, Hauser Kaibling.

Timetabled 'efficient' free ski-buses link the villages and lift bases. A night bus runs until 1am (3 euros one way, 5 euros for the evening).

There are several other separate mountains nearby covered by the local lift pass – including Fageralm (only slow chairlifts and T-bars, but lovely quiet, wide, easy cruising pistes and rustic huts – a very relaxing change of pace), Galsterbergalm, the Dachstein glacier and Stoderzinken. The Ski Alliance Amadé lift pass also covers many other resorts. A car is useful for getting the most out of this pass: trips are feasible to Bad Gastein, Wagrain/Flachau, Zauchensee and Hochkönig (and to Obertauern – not on the pass).

There are direct trains from Salzburg, so Schladming makes an excellent short break destination.

VILLAGE CHARM ★★★

Pleasant car-free centre

Most of Schladming's buildings are solid and traditional, and at its heart there's a pleasant, traffic-free main square, prettily lit at night, around which you'll find most of the shops,

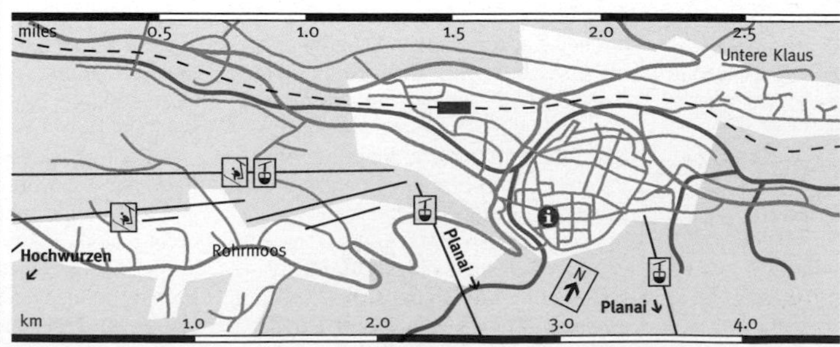

KEY FACTS

Resort	745m 2,440ft
Schladming's four linked mountains	
Slopes	745-2015m 2,440-6,610ft
Lifts	45
Pistes	125km 78 miles
Blue	34%
Red	62%
Black	4%
Snowmaking	99%

LIFT PASSES

Ski Amadé

Prices in €

Age	1-day	6-day
under 17	23	107
17 to 19	35	168
over 20	43	210

Free under 6

Senior no deals

Beginner no deals

Notes
Day-pass price is for Schladming-Dachstein only; part-day tickets available; 2-day-plus passes cover the 860km of pistes and 270 lifts in five regions: Schladming-Dachstein; Gastein; Salzburger Sportwelt; Grossarl; Hochkönig

Alternative pass
Salzburg Super Ski Card: all lifts in Salzburgerland including Zell am See, Kaprun and Saalbach-Hinterglemm

restaurants, bars and some appealing hotels. The ultra-modern Planet Planai area at the base of the gondola is a complete contrast. The busy main road bypasses the town.

CONVENIENCE ★★★☆☆
Pleasantly compact

Much of the accommodation is close to the town centre; the sports centre and tennis halls are five minutes' walk away, as is the gondola to Planai. There is also accommodation out by the Planai-Hochwurzen lift link, and further down the valley (eg Pichl). A 2012 reporter warns that the overflow car park for skiers is a 30-minute walk from the Planai gondola.

SCENERY ★★★☆☆
Four points of view

All four mountains are broadly similar, pleasantly wooded and share decent views along the Ennstal and to the more dramatic Dachsteingruppe, across the valley to the north.

THE MOUNTAINS

Most pistes are on the wooded north-facing slopes above the main valley, with some going into the side valleys higher up; there are a few short open slopes above the trees.

On our last visit we found a confusing variety of piste maps. Even for the linked four-mountain area there were at least two, plus maps for individual mountains as well, plus maps aimed primarily at showing where mountain restaurants are. All very confusing. As in many Austrian

Where is Austria's Golden Gate? Answer on p168.

areas, you may also encounter multiple pistes identified by the same number. Add to this poor signposting, and finding your way around can be tricky.

EXTENT OF THE SLOPES ★★★☆☆
Four linked sectors

The pistes now total 125km in length – a modest figure, but enough to gain the resort our ★★★ rating. Each of the sectors has a variety of runs to play on and you get a satisfying feeling of travelling around a lot. **Planai** is the main mountain, reached directly by gondola from the edge of the town centre. It is linked to **Hauser Kaibling** at altitude via the high, wooded bowl between them. But the links to **Hochwurzen** and **Reiteralm** are at valley level (and the first involves riding a gondola both ways). Our favourite area is Reiteralm – a hi-tech lift system and nicely varied terrain, extended down into Preuneggtal in 2010/11 by a new gondola and runs.

Several lower runs go across poorly signposted roads – care is needed.

FAST LIFTS ★★★★☆
Some neglected links

Each linked sector has gondola access from the car parks at the bases, and there are now lots of fast chairs. But the slow chairlift from Schladming to Hochwurzen, and the one from Pichl to Reiteralm are obvious weaknesses.

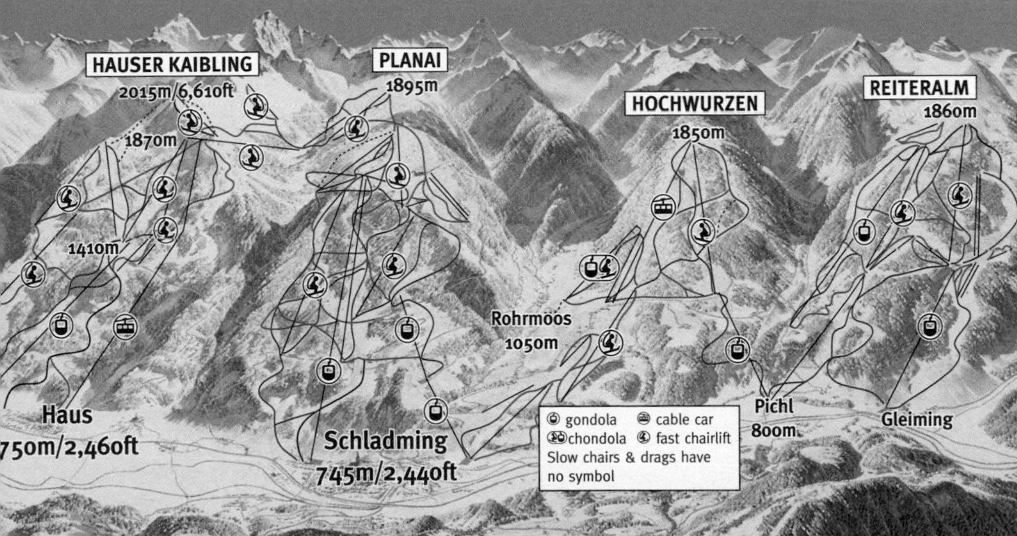

ACTIVITIES

Indoor Swimming pool, sauna, fitness club, bowling, museum, cinema

Outdoor Ice skating, curling, tobogganing, snowshoeing, sleigh rides, 50km of cleared paths

GETTING THERE

Air Salzburg 95km/ 60 miles (1hr15); Munich 255km/160 miles (3hr30)

Rail Main line station in resort

PLANAI BAHNEN / SIMON VANHAL

Schladming has three terrain parks to try. This is Horsefeathers Superpark, which is on Planai ↓

QUEUES ★★★★

New lifts helping

Queues for the Planai gondola at peak times are the only issue. New lifts built in recent years between Hauser Kaibling and Planai are now 'clearing the queues fast', says a 2012 reporter.

TERRAIN PARKS ★★★

Three to try

Planai has a park above Larchkogel, with medium and pro kicker lines, jumps, boxes and rails. Reiteralm's park is similarly well equipped; there's also a half-pipe. Hochwurzen's Playground park is floodlit until 10pm.

SNOW RELIABILITY ★★★★

Excellent in cold weather

The northerly orientation of the slopes and good maintenance help keep the pistes in better shape than in some neighbouring resorts. The serious snowmaking operation makes it a particularly good choice for early holidays; coverage is comprehensive and the system is put to good use. But at this altitude poor conditions on the lower slopes are a natural hazard.

FOR EXPERTS ★★

Strictly intermediate stuff

Schladming's status as a racing venue doesn't make it macho. The steep black finish to the Men's Downhill course and the mogul runs at the top of Planai and Hauser Kaibling are the only really challenging slopes there. Reiteralm has two steep black runs (one very short) at the top and some good tree runs. Hauser Kaibling's off-piste is good, but limited.

FOR INTERMEDIATES ★★★★

Red runs rule

The area is ideal for intermediate cruising. The majority of runs are red but the gradient of many is similar to the blues. The final section of the red below Rohrmoos is steep though (if in doubt, take the alternative blue).

New lifts have improved access to more challenging slopes at the top of Planai and Hauser Kaibling, as well as a short but pretty blue from the high point. The black racing pistes in these sectors, and the red alternatives, are ideal for fast cruising but can get very icy and tricky on the lower sections (a 2012 reporter found 'little difference' between the black and red at the bottom of Planai).

Hauser Kaibling has a lovely blue running from top to bottom, and Reiteralm has some gentle blues.

FOR BEGINNERS ★★★

Good slopes but poorly sited

The ski schools generally take beginners to the extensive but low-altitude Rohrmoos nursery area – fine if you are based there. For residents of central Schladming, it's a discouraging bus ride away.

FOR BOARDERS ★★★

Fine for all but experts

Schladming is popular with boarders. Most lifts on the spread-out mountains are gondolas or chairs, with some short drags around. The area is ideal for beginners and intermediates, except when the lower slopes are icy, though there are few exciting challenges for expert boarders bar the off-piste tree runs. The Blue Tomato snowboard shop runs the 'impressive' specialist snowboard school.

FOR CROSS-COUNTRY ★★★★

Huge network of trails

There are almost 500km of trails in the region, and the World Championships have been held at nearby Ramsau.

SCHOOLS

Tritscher
t 61142

Hopl (Hochwurzen-Planai)
t 61525

Blue Tomato (snowboard)
t 24223 16

Classes
(Tritscher prices)
5 days €169

Private lessons
€99 for 2hr; each additional person €20

CHILDCARE

Mini club (Tritscher school)
t 22647
For ages 3 and 4

Nannies
Details at tourist office

Ski school
From age 4 (€224 for 5 days including lunch – Tritscher price)

UK PACKAGES

Alpine Answers, Crystal, Crystal Finest, Skitracer, STC, Zenith

Phone numbers
From elsewhere in Austria add the prefix 03687; from abroad use the prefix +43 and omit the initial '0'

TOURIST OFFICE

www.schladming-dachstein.at
www.skiamade.com

MOUNTAIN RESTAURANTS ★★★★

A real highlight

There are plenty of attractive rustic huts; most get enthusiastic reports. Some of the piste maps mark them.

On Hauser Kaibling, Schoarlhütte has a real mountain hut atmosphere and is renowned for its ribs. For 'a very good gröstl' try Krummholzhütte. Harry's Lärchenpavillion is good for drinks and snacks.

On Planai, reporters love Onkel Willy's Hütte – 'lovely atmosphere, great staff, good soup, sausages, goulash and the best gröstl of the holiday'. Schafalm has a wide menu and 'lovely pizza'. We've enjoyed good food at the pleasant Weitmoosalm.

On Hochwurzen, the large self-service Hochwurzenhütte and cosy Hochwurzenalm just below it have been tipped. On Reiteralm the Schnepf'n Alm does 'outstanding food'. Gasselhöh Hütte has been tipped for good spare ribs.

On outlying Fageralm, we had delicious stew in the tiny Zeffererhütte, and a reporter had 'superb gröstl' at Unterbergalm.

SCHOOLS AND GUIDES ★★★

A choice – how was it for you?

There's a choice of schools but we lack recent reports.

FOR FAMILIES ★★★★

Rohrmoos is the place

The extensive gentle slopes of Rohrmoos are ideal for building up youngsters' confidence. There are Kinderlands on Planai, Reiteralm and Fageralm.

STAYING THERE

Packaged accommodation is in hotels and pensions, but there are plenty of apartments for independent travellers.

Hotels Most lodging is mid-range but a few upmarket places exist.

****__Almdorf-Reiteralm__ (72444) Ski-in/ski-out village at Hochalm, above Pichl. Individual chalets as well as hotel Edelweiss; restaurant, shop and spa facilities.

****__Sporthotel Royer__ (200) Big and comfortable, a few minutes from the Planai gondola. Pool, sauna, steam.

***__Aqi__ (23536) Cool modern place, built in 2008 and supposedly the first of a chain. Opposite Planai gondola. 'Helpful staff, spacious quiet room, good food, breakfast plentiful.'

***__Kirchenwirt__ (22435) Off the main square. 'Quaint, rooms a good size, staff friendly and helpful, food was simple but good,' says a 2012 visitor.

***__Neue Post__ (22105) Large rooms, friendly, good food, central.

Apartments Schütter (23230) at Planai West are said to be spacious.

EATING OUT ★★★

Some good places

Most of the best places are in hotels; tips include the Alte Post in the Posthotel (cosy and wood-panelled with imaginative food and good service), the Kirchenwirt and Neue Post. Friesacher Lanstuberl is a small, family-run steakhouse near the church. Maria's Mexican makes a change from Austrian food. Biochi specializes in organic and vegetarian food. We liked the Lasser Cafe and the Stadttor for coffee and cakes, and the Schwalbenbräu brewery.

APRES-SKI ★★★

Hohenhaus gets lively

Some of the mountain huts have live or loud music in the afternoon. On Hochwurzen, Tauernalm at Rohrmoos 'has a good atmosphere'. In town, the focus is the huge Hohenhaus Tenne by the Planai gondola station, which has injected life into the Schladming après scene; fabulous main bar, dance floor and regular live music – 'lively and great fun'. Later on there's a disco and various other bars to entertain. Charly's Treff (with umbrella bar) opposite also gets busy. Many of the central bars stay open until the early hours; but this isn't Ischgl. Cult and Angels are nightclubs.

OFF THE SLOPES ★★★

A few things to do

The town has a few shops, museum, pool and an ice rink. Hochwurzen has a floodlit 7km toboggan run. Some mountain restaurants are accessible to pedestrians. Trips to Salzburg are easy.

LINKED RESORT – 750m

HAUS

Haus is a fairly self-contained village, with its own ski schools, kindergartens and railway station. Hotel prices are generally lower here. The user-friendly nursery slopes are between the centre and the gondola. Excursions are easy, but off-slope activities and nightlife are very limited.

FRANK HEUER

Sölden

The resort could do with a bypass, but slopes reaching glacial heights and an ever-improving lift system offer compensation

RATINGS

The mountains	
Extent	★★★
Fast lifts	★★★★
Queues	★★★
Terrain p'ks	★★★
Snow	★★★★★
Expert	★★★
Intermediate	★★★★
Beginner	★★★
Boarder	★★★★
X-country	★
Restaurants	★★★
Schools	★★★
Families	★★
The resort	
Charm	★★
Convenience	★★
Scenery	★★★
Eating out	★★★
Après-ski	★★★★★
Off-slope	★★

RPI	**100**
lift pass	£190
ski hire	£125
lessons	£85
food & drink	£105
total	**£505**

KEY FACTS

Resort	1380m 4,530ft
Slopes	1350-3250m 4,430-10,660ft
Lifts	35
Pistes	150km 93 miles
Blue	46%
Red	34%
Black	20%
Snowmaking	67%

- ➕ Excellent snow reliability, with access to two glaciers
- ➕ Fairly extensive network of slopes suited to adventurous intermediates
- ➕ Impressive lift system
- ➕ Wide choice of huts for its size
- ➕ Very lively après-ski/nightlife

- ➖ Towny resort is spread along a road that is busy with through-traffic
- ➖ You may need a bus to the lifts
- ➖ Main runs are almost all above the trees; only a couple are sheltered
- ➖ English not universally spoken
- ➖ Town centre can get rowdy

'We were very surprised that we were the only people getting off the transfer coach in Sölden, while the other 50 went on to Obergurgl,' said a reporter last year. Yes: the resort's low profile in the UK is curious, given the powerful appeal of its snow-sure mountains and (if you like that kind of thing) its very lively après-ski scene. We always enjoy visits here, most recently in 2012, and so do the readers we hear from. And perhaps things are changing: two major chalet companies introduced big properties here last season.

THE RESORT

Sölden is a long, towny place in the Ötz valley leading up to Obergurgl. Gondolas from opposite ends of town go up to the peak of Gaislachkogl and the lift junction of Giggijoch, with most of the shops, restaurants and hotels in between them. A road winds its way above the town through various hamlets up to Hochsölden – a group of 4-star hotels and little else.

When buying a six-day lift pass you can opt to pay 10 euro extra for a day in nearby Obergurgl (the half-hourly buses are included in the lift pass). You can also get buses down the valley to Längenfeld where there is a big thermal spa. With a car you could make trips to St Anton or Ischgl.

VILLAGE CHARM ★★

Not a strong point

Despite its traditional Tirolean buildings, a pretty church among them, Sölden is no charmer. There's a good selection of shops and bars, but the ambience is towny (prominent ads for strip clubs don't help), and it is strung along the valley road running through it, lacking a central focus. More seriously, the central strip is badly affected by traffic on the road. The place attracts a lively crowd, and the partying can spill into the street. Across the river there's a quieter area, mainly of hotels and guest houses. Hochsölden offers splendid traffic-free isolation up the mountain.

CONVENIENCE ★★

Lifts at either end

It's a long town, and the gondola stations are almost a mile apart. So you may face a good walk to the lifts, or a ride on the free, efficient shuttle buses. Don't dismiss places over the river from the main street – they aren't necessarily remote from the lifts. Hochsölden is basically ski-in/ski-out.

SCENERY ★★★

Get up on Gaislachkogl

Sölden's top heights offer splendid wide views, especially south to the Italian border.

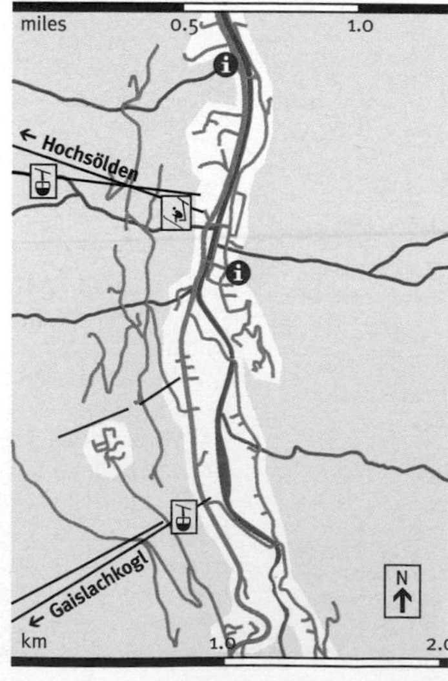

LIFT PASSES

Prices in €

Age	1-day	6-day
under 15	29	126
15 to 19	37	162
20 to 63	45	232
64 plus	39	192

Free under 5; day pass €1 if under 8

Senior min. age for senior women is 59

Beginner no deals

Notes
Part-day and pedestrian options

THE MOUNTAINS

Practically all the slopes you spend your days on are above the treeline, though there are red and black runs through trees to the village.

There are two versions of the piste map – an adequate compact Z-card and a much bigger sheet on which a slightly larger version of the map is surrounded by huge amounts of other stuff, some of it useful.

EXTENT OF THE SLOPES ★★★

Long run network

The ski area is not enormous, but it does go high. All sectors offer serious vertical and some long runs, which the piste map sets out in juicy and only occasionally misleading detail. It's 1880m vertical and a claimed 15km from the top of the glacier to the village; the runs from Gaislachkogl and Hainbachjoch are in the same league.

There are two similar-sized sectors above the town, linked by fast six-seater chairlifts out of the intervening Rettenbachtal. At the south end of town, a newish gondola leads up to an impressive three-cable gondola above it to **Gaislachkogl**. The terrain above the mid-station is served by slow chairs. There are links south towards Gaislachalm and north towards the Rettenbachtal. Another gondola from the north end of the resort goes to **Giggijoch**. Fast lifts from here serve wide, open slopes below Rotkogljoch, from where a series of fast chairs and gondolas (one a cross-valley affair with no piste beneath it) leads to Sölden's glaciers – first the **Rettenbach**, and then the **Tiefenbach**. It may be a long journey (at least five lifts to reach the top) but with luck the reward will be quiet slopes with excellent powdery winter snow. Below Giggijoch, and reached by red and black runs, is Hochsölden – also reachable by a slow single-seat chair.

FAST LIFTS ★★★★

Well-linked system

There are still some slow lifts around – including (avoidable) T-bars on the glaciers, but most of the area is very well served by fast chairs and gondolas, and the resort hovers on the brink of a 5-star rating.

QUEUES ★★★

Giggijoch's not so great

The Giggijoch gondola at one end of town still generates big queues in the morning peak. If running, the nearby antique single chair to Hochsölden is worth seeking out to avoid them. By contrast, the newish Gaislachkogl gondola seems to be relatively queue-free. Key lifts to and from the glacier,

ACTIVITIES

Indoor Freizeit Arena (swimming, sauna, fitness centre, bowling, indoor tennis, climbing wall)

Outdoor Ice rink, sleigh rides, snowshoeing, 30km of walking trails, tobogganing, paragliding, ice climbing, snowmobiling

SNOWPIX.COM / CHRIS GILL

The nursery slopes have an attractive setting on a shelf above the village – also the arrival of the gentle blue home run from Gaislachalm ↓

such as the Einzeiger chair and Seiterkar chair, get busy. The chairs to Rotkogljoch are bottlenecks but shift crowds fast. There is a weekend influx, which adds to problems.

TERRAIN PARKS ★★★★★
Sufficiently equipped

The Swatch Snowpark above Giggijoch is well-established and regularly upgraded. As well as beginner, intermediate and pro kickers, there are rails and various types of boxes. There's also a chill-out zone. The 'Swatch Shoot my ride' gives you the chance to watch and analyse your tricks on a big video wall at the bottom of the park – unfortunately it wasn't in operation this year. But there's snowcross on blue 15 and just off it the BMW slalom where you get your time recorded. The Tiefenbach glacier has an early-season park.

SNOW RELIABILITY ★★★★★
Rarely a problem

The slopes are high and roughly east-facing; and there are two extensive glaciers. Snowmaking covers 67% of the area, including all slopes on Giggijoch. Grooming is fine. Even in a generally poor season, such as 2011, you can generally count on coverage to resort level – we certainly found that on our March visit.

FOR EXPERTS ★★★★★
Off-piste challenges

None of the black pistes dotted around Sölden's map is serious, and some are silly; but there are quite a few non-trivial reds, notably on Gaislachkogl – with some steeper pitches above the mid-station – and the length and vertical of some of the runs present their own challenges. There are extensive off-piste possibilities, eg into Rettenbachtal.

FOR INTERMEDIATES ★★★★★
Serious verticals

Most of Sölden's main slopes are genuine red runs ideal for adventurous intermediates; there are several easy blacks, too. Keen piste-bashers will love the serious verticals and long runs to be done (notably from Gaislachkogl) – but after a couple of days may wonder whether the claimed extent of 150km is entirely justified.

There are two obvious targets for less confident intermediates. The long, quiet run above Gaislachalm, now reclassified blue, is great for cruising, and below it a gentle blue through the trees offers way the most friendly return to the resort. And the blues above Giggijoch offer gentler gradients, though life can be complicated by crowds here.

The glaciers are accessible to blue-run skiers, and are almost entirely of blue-run gradient – the red runs down the Seiterkar chair offer a bit of a challenge. But it's best to return via the linking gondola to the Giggijoch slopes – the blue run down the Rettenbachtal is narrow (it's a road) can get very busy, includes long flat bits where you have to pole or skate and eventually turns into a tricky red.

FOR BEGINNERS ★★★★★
Crowded nursery slopes

The beginners' slopes, served by a pair of parallel draglifts, are situated

SCHOOLS

Sölden-Hochsölden
t 2364

Yellow Power
t 2203

Freeride Center
t 0650 415 3505

Vacancia Tirol
t 3100

Ötztal
t 3821

Classes (Sölden prices) 5 days (4hr per day) €185

Private lessons
From €130 for 2hr for 1-2 persons; each additional person €30

just above the village at Innerwald and reached by a newish free shuttle lift that replaced the old chairlift. Progression to longer runs usually means using the gondola to go to and from the blues at Giggijoch; these are wide and gentle, although very busy in places. Hochsölden just below Giggijoch is on a steep slope – avoid at all costs.

FOR BOARDERS ★★★★☆
Long, wide runs

Sölden is quite popular with boarders. The nursery slope involves drags, but after that draglifts can be avoided and you'll enjoy the wide, open blue runs above Giggijoch. Intermediates will relish the abundance of long runs and open terrain, and there's great freeriding for experienced boarders. There are some flat sections of piste in the Rettenbachtal and on the runs to the resort. There's a decent terrain park.

FOR CROSS-COUNTRY ★☆☆☆☆
Little to entertain

There are a couple of loops by the river to Hof (back end of town) and another 5km trail to Rechenau.

MOUNTAIN RESTAURANTS ★★★☆☆
Few notable places

There are nearly 30 huts listed, all usefully marked on the piste map and summarized in a separate leaflet. Most offer traditional food. But those in the main area can get crowded. We like the rustic Gampe Thaya – simple food, table service, lovely terrace, cosy interior; a 2011 visitor warmly agrees. We've also enjoyed good käsespätzle at the peaceful Heidealm above Gaislachalm. Both places have fab views towards Obergurgl. Hühnersteign in the Rettenbachtal is 'cosy' and famous for its chicken (Hühne!), and the Stabele just below it is equally famous for its gigantic burgers. The self-service at Giggijoch is huge; the smaller Wirthaus table-service option looked nice. Below Hochsölden, a reader preferred the Panorama Alm, which is bright with 'excellent food'.

SCHOOLS AND GUIDES ★★★☆☆
Wide choice, lacking feedback

Sölden has five schools; all restrict class sizes. We lack recent reports, though past feedback has been positive. The newish Ötztal school provides specialist race training.

↑ The short, groomed black run at the bottom of the Rettenbach glacier is good fun

SNOWPIX.COM / CHRIS GILL

CHILDCARE

Kindergarten (run by Sölden school)
t 2364
Age 6mnth to 3yr

Ski school
From 3 to 14 (6 4hr days €190)

GETTING THERE

Air Innsbruck 85km/ 55 miles (1.15hr); Zürich 275km/170 miles (3.45hr); Munich 285km/175 miles (3hr)

Rail Train to Innsbruck or Öetz (30km); buses from station

UK PACKAGES

Crystal, Crystal Finest, Independent Ski Links, Interactive Resorts, Momentum, Neilson, Ski Solutions, Ski Total, Skitracer, Skiworld, Snow Finders, STC

Phone numbers
Except for the tourist office, from elsewhere in Austria add the prefix 05254; from abroad use the prefix +43 5254

TOURIST OFFICE

www.soelden.com

FOR FAMILIES ★★★★★
Few special facilities

Sölden does not go out of its way to cater to families. The intrusive main road traffic and possibly lengthy walks make it less attractive. But there are kindergartens at two schools and children aged four to seven pay a euro per day to use all the slopes.

STAYING THERE

Most packaged accommodation is in hotels or pensions, but there are also apartments and now catered chalets run by UK operators.

Chalets Skiworld has a 30-bed chalet a short walk from the Giggijoch lift and the town centre, and Ski Total has its newish chalet hotel Hermann above the village; two 2012 reporters were very happy with the food, wine, staff and the chalet itself, one of them less so with its location.

Hotels There is one 5-star hotel but most are good 3- or 4-stars. Take care if looking at very central places – there are noisy bars.

*****Central Spa** (22600) Fairly central but also the biggest and best in town – the only 5-star; warmly welcoming; major spa, fitness room, pool.

****Bergland** (22400) Hip, recently built place next to shuttle lift to Innerwald, with big fifth-floor spa, outdoor hot tub and decent pool.

****Erhart** (2020) Across the river 500m from the Gaislachkogl gondola. 'Excellent location, superb food,' says a 2011 reporter. Spa/fitness facilities.

****Grauer Bär** (2564) Near the Gaislachkogl lift. Spa area.

****Stefan** (2237) By the Giggijoch gondola. We've stayed happily here – good food. Fair-sized wellness area.

****Valentin** (2267) Next to the Gaislachkogl lift. 'Reasonable prices; good food, small spa, no pool,' says a 2011 visitor.

Apartments The Gaislachkogl apartments (2246) are close to the gondola, with wellness facilities. Guests also get free entry to the Freizeitarena leisure centre.

EATING OUT ★★★★★
A reasonable choice

Many of the hotels have à la carte restaurants, serving traditional Austrian food. And there are various pizzerias – Gusto is recommended this year – and a steakhouse – Joe's Höhle in hotel Castello. We usually end up in the Tavola in the hotel Rosengarten, because it doesn't take reservations, and haven't been disappointed. s'Pfandl, above the town at Ausserwald, makes a jolly evening outing for traditional Tirolean food.

APRES-SKI ★★★★★
Throbbing until late

Sölden's après-ski is justly famous. It starts up the mountain, notably at Giggijoch at the 'cosy' Eugen's Obsterhütte, or at Bubi's Schihütte on Gaislachkogl ('men come round the tables with accordions singing Austrian songs') and progresses (possibly via Philipp's Eisbar at Innerwald) to packed bars in and around the main street. The hotel Liebe Sonne's Schirmbar is 'the place to be' – lively and packed, usually overflowing into the road. Fire and Ice is a two-storey glass-fronted place that parties from 3pm to 3am. There are countless other places with live bands and throbbing discos, some with table dancing and/ or striptease. And if you've any energy left, Kuhstall 'parties till 5-6am'. Reader tips for quieter places include Grizzly's ('rustic interior, plenty of seats') and Die Alm ('sometimes with folk music').

OFF THE SLOPES ★★★★★
Disappointing for its size

There's a leisure centre, a swimming pool and an ice rink. Ice climbing and sleigh rides can be arranged. There's also a 5km floodlit toboggan run. A 2011 reporter enjoyed the Wednesday-night ski show on Gaislachkogl. Trips to Innsbruck are possible. Aqua Dome is a thermal spa centre at Längenfeld, now reached by regular buses (free with a lift pass).

Söll

The ski area is big, but the attractive village is surprisingly small and intimate; shame it is not set right by the lifts

RATINGS

The mountains	
Extent	****
Fast lifts	****
Queues	***
Terrain p'ks	***
Snow	**
Expert	*
Intermediate	****
Beginner	**
Boarder	**
X-country	***
Restaurants	***
Schools	***
Families	***
The resort	
Charm	***
Convenience	**
Scenery	***
Eating out	**
Après-ski	****
Off-slope	**

RPI	85
lift pass	£170
ski hire	£75
lessons	£95
food & drink	£100
total	**£440**

NEWS

2012/13: Snowmaking is being further extended.

2011/12: The 3.5km toboggan run is now floodlit till 10.30 every night. Parents can buy one pass between two, which either can use. The Hopfgarten home run was improved, with snowmaking to valley level.

- + Part of the SkiWelt, Austria's largest linked ski and snowboard area
- + Local slopes are north-facing, so they keep their snow relatively well
- + Pretty village with lively après-ski
- + Cheap, even by Austrian standards
- + Snowmaking is now very extensive and well used; even so ...

- − Low altitude can mean poor snow
- − Long walk or inadequate bus service from the village to the lifts
- − Runs on upper slopes mostly short
- − Few challenges except Hohe Salve
- − Not ideal for beginners
- − The SkiWelt slopes can get crowded
- − Appallingly inadequate piste map

Söll has long been popular with British beginners and intermediates, attracting both youths looking for fun and families looking for a quiet time. The resort is in fact far from ideal for beginners, but the SkiWelt can be a great area for intermediates who like easy cruising. Whether it is depends on the snow. If the weather is coming from Russia, this area can have the best snow in the Alps; but usually it isn't. If you want to be sure of good conditions, book late.

Many visitors are surprised by the small size of the village (in particular, there aren't many shops) and the long trek out to the slopes. You may prefer to stay near the lifts and trek into the village in the evening. Or you may prefer, like us, to stay in one of the other SkiWelt resorts – Ellmau along the valley (which has its own chapter) or Brixen or Westendorf over the hill (covered at the end of this chapter), which have quicker access to the Kitzbühel slopes.

THE RESORT

Söll is a pleasant, friendly village, bypassed by the main valley road; although its chalets spread quite widely, the core is compact – you can explore it on foot thoroughly in a few minutes.

The resort is part of the vast SkiWelt area, with a claimed 279km of slopes. You can also progress (via Brixen) to the slopes of Kitzbühel; these and various other ski areas within easy reach, such as Waidring, Fieberbrunn and St Johann, are covered by the Kitzbüheler Alpen AllStarCard ski pass.

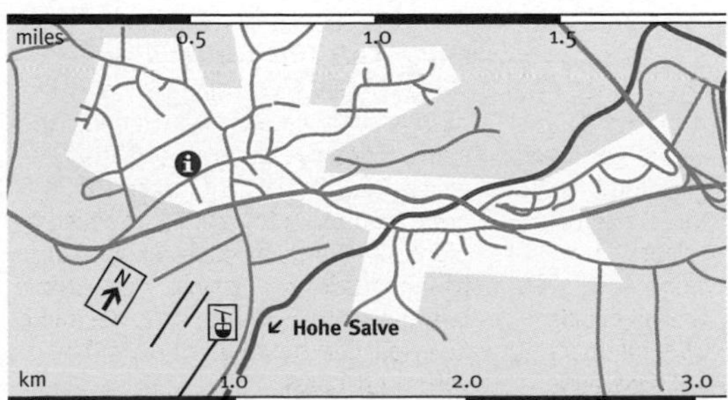

VILLAGE CHARM ***

Follows tradition

Söll is quite attractive, with chalet-style buildings and a huge church near the centre (its graveyard prettily lit by candles at night).

CONVENIENCE **

Not for the slopes

The slopes are well outside the village, on the other side of a busy road crossed by a pedestrian tunnel. You can leave your equipment at the bottom of the gondola for a small charge. There is some accommodation out near the lifts, but most is in or around the village centre. From there, it's the ski-bus or a 15-minute walk to the lifts. A base on the far side of the village may mean that you can board the bus before it gets too crowded. But the bus does not serve every corner of the community.

SCENERY ***

Head for Hohe Salve

Söll sits in a woody valley, below the distinctive dome-shaped peak of Hohe Salve. From the top, there are good views to the whole SkiWelt and the craggy Wilder Kaiser ridges.

KEY FACTS

Resort	700m 2,300ft
Entire SkiWelt	
Slopes	620-1890m 2,030-6,200ft
Lifts	91
Pistes	279km 173 miles
Blue	44%
Red	46%
Black	10%
Snowmaking	75%

THE MOUNTAINS

Although there are some open slopes high up, and the prominent high-point of Hohe Salve is noticeably bare, most of the slopes are heavily wooded.

The piste map is hopelessly over-ambitious in trying to show the whole area in a single view; the result is a map that is no doubt a very effective marketing tool but appallingly inadequate for route finding, especially on the Zinsberg side of Hohe Salve and between Eiberg and Brandstadl. The map needs to be broken down into separate maps for the main sectors.

Signposting is also criticized by readers, but we found it OK once you realize that the signs point out the direction to the next lift you want and that the signs use the number of the lift to indicate the colour of the run.

EXTENT OF THE SLOPES ★★★★

Short run network

The SkiWelt is the largest piste network in Austria, linking eight resorts. It will easily keep an average intermediate amused for a week. The peaks are not high – with the exception of Hohe Salve they are all under 1700m. In good snow there are long red runs to be done to the valley, but most of the skiing is on the upper slopes where most runs are very short (often less than 300m vertical).

A gondola takes all but complete beginners up to the mid-mountain shelf of Hochsöll, where there are a couple of short lifts and connections in several directions. These include an eight-seat gondola to the high point of Hohe Salve. From here there are runs down to Kälbersalve, Rigi and Hopfgarten. Rigi can also be reached by chairs and runs without going to

GETTING THERE

Air Salzburg 90km/ 55 miles (1hr30); Innsbruck 80km/ 50 miles (1hr15); Munich 260km/160 miles (3hr45)

Rail Wörgl (13km/ 8 miles) or Kufstein (15km/9 miles); bus to resort

Hohe Salve – to which it is itself linked by chairs. Rigi is also the start of runs down to Itter and to Hopfgarten. From Kälbersalve you can head down south-facing runs to Brixen or up to Zinsberg and on towards Ellmau – if you can decipher the piste map. From Brixen, a gondola goes up to Choralpe in Westendorf's area and a lovely north-facing red piste comes back down. From Choralpe you can also head off towards the Kitzbühel slopes.

FAST LIFTS ★★★★★
Gradual improvement

Lifts from the valley are mainly gondolas, with a growing number of fast chairs on the upper slopes; an eight-pack that opened for 2010/11 shifted the resort to a ★★★★ rating, at last. But there are still plenty of slow lifts around.

QUEUES ★★★★★
Some high-season waits

Lift upgrades have greatly improved this once queue-prone area. Again, this year's reports relate to January or March, and mention few problems. But in peak season getting out of Söll at ski-school time in the mornings remains a problem, and there are still some bottlenecks on the mountain. When snow is poor, the links between Zinsberg and Eiberg get crowded.

TERRAIN PARKS ★★★★★
Local and floodlit

Söll has its own park below Hochsöll with beginner and expert lines; features include boxes, frames and rails. It's floodlit for night riding.

Hot news in Austria's hottest resort, p168.

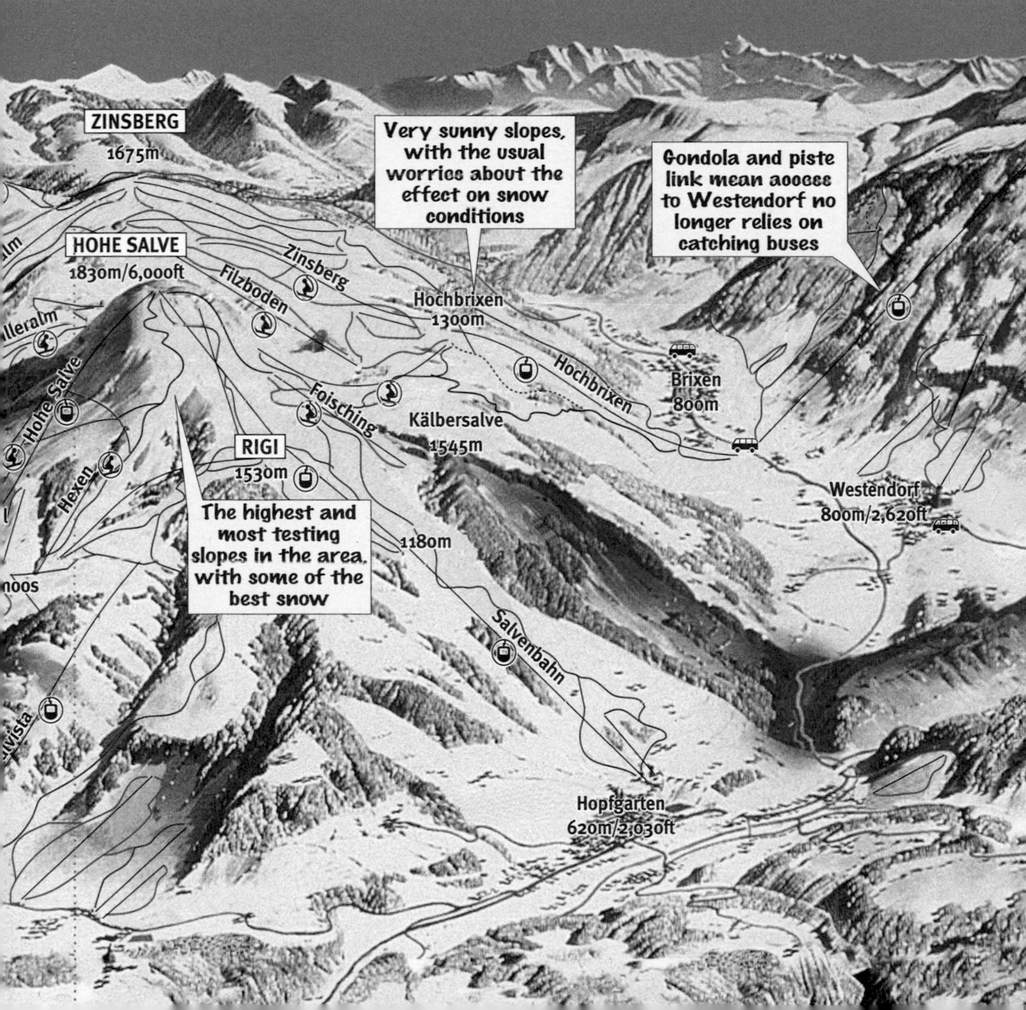

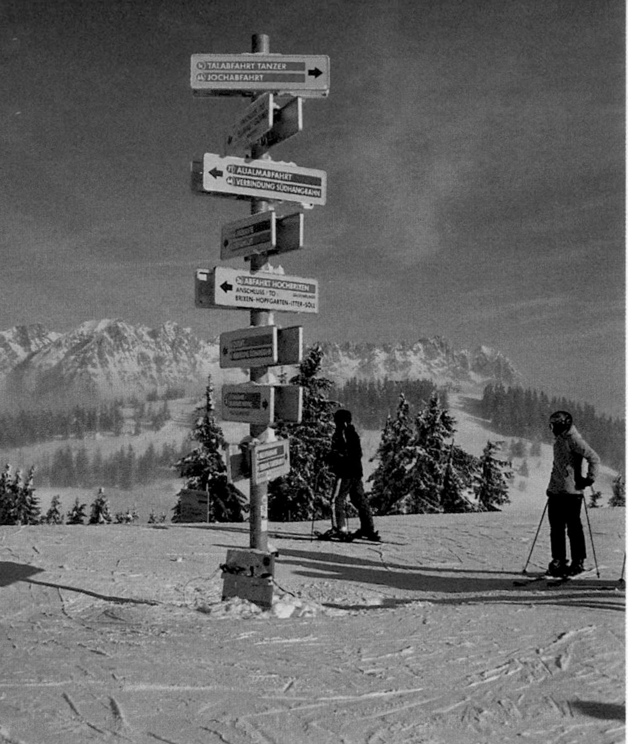

↑ You'll need to get to grips with signposts like this because the piste map isn't much help
WENDY-JANE KING

LIFT PASSES

SkiWelt Wilder Kaiser-Brixental

Prices in €

Age	1-day	6-day
under 16	21	100
16 to 17	33	160
over 18	41	200

Free under 7

Senior no deals

Beginner points cards

Notes
Ski-bus included; single ascent and part-day options; family discounts; 6-day pass can be transferable between parents

Alternative passes
Kitzbüheler Alpen AllStarCard covers: Schneewinkel (St Johann), Kitzbühel, SkiWelt, Wildschönau, Alpbachtal, Skicircus Saalbach-Hinterglemm and Zell am See-Kaprun

SNOW RELIABILITY ★★☆☆☆
Erratic – but has artificial help

The SkiWelt has had some good seasons of late, with several reporters experiencing good fresh powder for much of their holidays. But it is not always like that, and with a low average height, and important links that get a lot of sun, the snow can suffer badly in warm weather. So the snowmaking that the SkiWelt has installed is essential. At 210km and covering about 75% of the area's pistes, it is Austria's biggest snowmaking installation. Reporters have been impressed by its use and by the grooming. We were there one January before any major snowfalls, and snowmaking was keeping the links open well. Warm weather is a more serious problem.

FOR EXPERTS ★☆☆☆☆
Not a lot

The two black runs from Hohe Salve towards Hochsöll and Kälbersalve and the black run alongside the Brixen gondola are the only challenging pistes. There are further blacks in Scheffau and Ellmau, but the main challenges are gentle off-piste routes – from Brandstadl down to Söll, for example.

FOR INTERMEDIATES ★★★★☆
Mainly easy runs

When blessed with good snow the SkiWelt is a paradise for those who love easy cruising and don't mind short runs. It is a big area and you really get a feeling of travelling around. There are lots of blue runs and many of the reds could be blue. In general the most difficult slopes are those from the mid-stations to the valleys – to Blaiken, Brixen and Söll, for example. For more challenging reds head for Westendorf (and don't miss the excellent red back down from there to Brixen).

FOR BEGINNERS ★★☆☆☆
Not ideal

The big area of nursery slopes between the main road and the gondola station is fine when snow is good – gentle, spacious, uncrowded and free from good skiers whizzing past. But it can get icy or slushy. In poor snow the Hochsöll area may be used. None of the lifts is free, but points cards are available. Progression to longer runs is likely to be awkward – there aren't many blue runs in this part of the SkiWelt. One is the narrow blue from Hochsöll, on which fast learners can get home when the run is not too icy.

FOR BOARDERS ★★☆☆☆
Great cruising

Söll is a good place to try out boarding: slopes are gentle and there are plenty of gondolas and chairs. And it has its own terrain park. For competent boarders it's more limited – the slopes of the SkiWelt are tame.

FOR CROSS-COUNTRY ★★★☆☆
Neighbouring villages are better

Söll has 30km of local trails, but they are less interesting than those between Hopfgarten and Kelchsau and around and beyond Ellmau. There is a total of 170km in the SkiWelt area. Lack of snow-cover can be a problem.

MOUNTAIN RESTAURANTS ★★★☆☆
Good, but crowded

There are quite a few jolly little chalets.

Editors' choice We've enjoyed lunch at Tanzbodenalm near Brandstadl (43150) – pleasantly woody, serving delicious deer stew; 'great service, good food and wide choice'. Another favourite is Rübezahlalm (see the Ellmau chapter).

SCHOOLS

Söll-Hochsöll
t 5454

Knolin
t 0676 64 85060

Black Sheep Ski
t 06991 712871

Classes
5 4hr days: €150 (Söll prices)

Private lessons
€55 for 1hr; each additional person €20

CHILDCARE

Mini-club Hexenstube
t 05333 6377
ages 6mnth to 4yr

Monti's Kinderwelt (bambinis)
t 5454
for ages 3 to 5

Ski school
Takes children from 5 to 14 for 4hr daily (5 days €150)

ACTIVITIES

Indoor Swimming pool with sauna, solarium and massage (refurbished and due to reopen Dec 2012); bowling, squash

Outdoor Natural ice rink (skating, curling), sleigh rides, 3km of floodlit toboggan runs, walks, snowshoeing, snow tubing, paragliding

Worth knowing about Just below Hochsöll the atmospheric converted cow shed Stöcklalm is recommended by reporters. The highly rated Hohe Salve (top of the gondola) offers a large revolving terrace and good views (from the loos as well, say reporters). Other reporter recommendations include the Stoagrub'nhütte above Hopfgarten, the Aualm below Zinsberg for cakes and glühwein, the Brandstadl and the 'pleasantly rustic' Neualm above Scheffau, and, a bit lower down, Bavaria – which has a 'lovely comfy bar' and 'great value lunch specials'.

SCHOOLS AND GUIDES ★★★

Reports please

Söll-Hochsöll and Knolin are the main schools but we lack recent reports. A visitor had a 'very good' carving clinic with Black Sheep Ski.

FOR FAMILIES ★★★

A range of options

Söll has fairly wide-ranging facilities – the focus is the Söll-Hochsöll school's Monti's Kinderwelt (and day care) at the gondola mid-station, which takes children from age three. It is well equipped with play areas and nursery slopes. There's a special kids-only drag and slope on the opposite side of the village to the main lifts. As from the 2011/12 season parents can buy one pass between them, which either can use while the other minds the kids.

STAYING THERE

Chalets Crystal has two big ones.

Hotels There is a wide choice of simple gasthofs, pensions and B&Bs, plus better-quality hotel accommodation – mainly 3-star.

****Alpenpanorama** (5309) Far from lifts but with own bus stop; wonderful views; pleasant rooms.

****Bergland** (5454) Well placed between the village and lifts. Apartments as well as rooms.

****Greil** (5289) Attractive, but out of the centre and far from the lifts. Indoor pool.

****Postwirt** (5081) Attractive, central, traditional, with stube; outdoor pool.

***Eggerwirt** (5236) Between centre and main road, bus stop outside.

***Feichter** (5228) Newly renovated for 2011/12. Spa.

***Feldwebel** (5224) Central.

***Hexenalm** (5544) Next to the lifts.

***Tulpe** (5223) Next to the lifts.

Apartments The central Aparthotel Schindlhaus has nice accommodation. Some of the best apartments in town are in the Bergland hotel.

EATING OUT ★★

A fair choice

Some of the best restaurants are in hotels – the Postwirt and the Feldwebel are recommended by reporters. Dorf Stub'n offers traditional dishes and steaks, and the Venezia is a pizzeria.

APRES-SKI ★★★★

Still some very loud bars

Söll is not as raucous as it used to be, but it's still very lively and a lot of places have live music.

The Salvenstadl (Cow Shed) bar is recommended by reporters ('great après-ski bar'). Moonlight at the gondola base is 'less Brit-dominated and has dancing on the tables even in low season', and the Hexenalm bar, just down from the gondola, is recommended. The Whisky-Mühle is a large disco that can get 'wild', especially after the bars close. The hotel Austria bar is 'boisterous' with pool tables and quiz evenings. Rossini is good for cocktails and live music.

OFF THE SLOPES ★★

Not bad for a small village

You could spend a happy day in the splendid Panoramabad: taking a sauna, swimming, lounging about. It was closed for refurbishment last season, but is due to reopen in December 2012. There's a 3.5km toboggan run from the top of the gondola that's now floodlit until 10.30 every night. The large baroque church is worth a visit. Coach excursions include trips to Salzburg, Innsbruck and even Vipiteno, over the Brenner in Italy.

UK PACKAGES

Crystal, Independent Ski Links, Inghams, Neilson, Ski Line, Ski Solutions, Skitracer, STC, Thomson
Hopfgarten Contiki
Westendorf Crystal, Inghams, Interactive Resorts, Thomson

LINKED RESORT – 700m

ITTER

Itter is a tiny village half-way between Söll and Hopfgarten, with a gondola starting some way outside the village that goes up to mid-mountain. There's a hotel and half a dozen gasthofs and B&Bs. The school has a rental shop, and there are nursery slopes close to hand but few easy longer runs to progress to locally. Here, as elsewhere, the home run is red.

LINKED RESORT – 620m

HOPFGARTEN

Hopfgarten is an unspoiled, friendly, traditional resort set off the main road at the western extremity of the SkiWelt and with a two-stage gondola (largely queue-free, to judge by reports) from the village to the top of Hohe Salve.

When snow is good, the runs down to Hopfgarten are some of the best in the SkiWelt, but they get the afternoon sun. There is a beginners' slope in the village, but it is sunny as well as low. Hopfgarten is one of the best cross-country bases in the area. There are fine trails to Kelchsau (7km) and the Itter-Bocking loop (15km) starts nearby.

Cheap and cheerful gasthofs, pensions and little private B&Bs are the norm, and most are within five minutes' walk of the gondola.

Restaurants are mostly hotel-based, but there is a Chinese and a pizzeria. Après-ski is generally quiet. There's a reasonable range of off-slope activities, and trains run to Kitzbühel and Innsbruck (or Salzburg).

LINKED RESORT – 800m

BRIXEN IM THALE

Brixen im Thale spreads a long way along the valley running along the south side of the SkiWelt area. It is not particularly cute, but it is traditional in style and is pretty quiet now that it is bypassed by the main valley road. From the skiing point of view it has a great location, with lifts going up both sides of the valley. On the north side, a gondola goes to Hochbrixen and the main SkiWelt slopes; lifts diverge for Hohe Salve and Söll, or Astberg and Ellmau. In the opposite direction, a gondola goes up to Choralpe above Westendorf, which links to the slopes of Kitzbühel. The local slopes suit confident intermediates best, on both sides of the valley. The nursery area is secluded, but a bus ride away.

There are plenty of hotels and pensions but not many restaurants – most are hotel-based. Après-ski is not a highlight though there are two or three bars by the gondola station. Brixen is on the same railway line as Hopfgarten.

Westendorf 800m

- ⊞ Pleasant, traditional village
- ⊞ Challenging local slopes
- ⊞ Good local beginner slopes but ...
- ⊟ Local slopes not ideal territory for progression from the nursery slopes
- ⊟ Getting to main SkiWelt takes time

Westendorf is a quiet, attractive village with good local slopes for confident intermediates; it is slightly off the main SkiWelt circuit, but has easy access to Kitzbühel's area – so an appealing base if you plan to spend time on both.

Village charm The village is small with traditional buildings, including an attractive onion-domed church. It has a relaxed, rustic atmosphere. The quite lively late-night scene can mean a bit of noise in the streets.

Convenience The centre is close to the nursery slopes, and a five-minute walk or free ski-bus ride from the main lift. There are also regular buses to the lifts at Brixen, for quick access to the SkiWelt circuit.

Scenery The slopes here offer a bit more drama than some of the other hills nearby, and the views include the craggy Wilder Kaiser to the north.

THE MOUNTAIN

The local slopes are separated by one valley from the main SkiWelt circuit to the north and by another valley from the Kitzbühel slopes to the east. There's a pleasant mix of open and wooded slopes.

Slopes A two-stage gondola goes to Talkaser, one of the four minor peaks that make up the local area. From there, you can head for Choralpe and Brixen (via a splendid 5.5km-long red run of over 1000m vertical), or for Fleiding and Gampenkogel. All the local peaks have short east- or west-facing runs. A longer blue run of

Easy intermediate slopes, and restaurants all over the shop – this is between Eiberg and Brandstadl ➔

WENDY-JANE KING

around 800m vertical goes from Gampenkogel to the Kitzbühel connection (which involves a short shuttle-bus ride to the Pengelstein gondola at Skirast).

Fast lifts The two newish gondolas have vastly improved access but once up the mountain there are still a lot of slow lifts on the local slopes.

Queues We have no reports of any significant problems with queues.

Terrain parks There's an excellent park with something for all levels including jumps, boxes, kickers, rails and a half-pipe (www.boardplay.com).

Snow reliability Not a strong point of the region, because of the low altitude. But snowmaking is extensive and grooming excellent.

Experts The pistes are among the most testing in the SkiWelt area, and there is off-piste to be explored.

Intermediates Great for confident intermediates: nearly all Westendorf's terrain is genuinely red in gradient.

Beginners The village nursery slopes are extensive and excellent. There are a couple of genuine blues to progress to on the lower mountain, but further progression can be challenging.

Snowboarding Most lifts are chairs and gondolas, and the park is great. But some runs have tedious flat sections.

Cross-country There are lots of trails, but snow-cover is unreliable.

Mountain restaurants There are good table- and self-service places. On our 2012 visit we particularly liked Ki-West – good location, atmosphere and food. Alpenrosenhütte, Brechhornhaus and the Gassnerwirt are popular. A 2012 visitor found the self-service Talkaser busy at peak times.

Schools and guides There are three schools: Westendorf ('very good', says a 2012 visitor), Top and Snow&Co.

Families Westendorf sells itself as a family resort. The ski school kindergartens take children from the age of three.

STAYING THERE

There are plentiful hotels and guest houses, both near the village centre and further afield.

Hotels The Jakobwirt (6245) and Schermer (6268) are good 4-stars; the 3-star Post (6202) is 'basic and friendly' with 'good food'. Pension Cafe Elisabeth (8940) is central and recommended as 'very hospitable'. The small Glockenstuhl (6175) is a short walk away with a good spa. There are places out near the gondola.

Apartments The Schermerhof apartments are of good quality.

Eating out Most of the best restaurants are in hotels. The Wastlhof, Klinglers and Berggasthof Stimmlach (a taxi ride out) are other possibilities.

Après-ski There are more lively spots than you might expect in a small, cute village. The Liftstüberl and Gerry's Inn are packed at close of play. Bruchtall 'caters for kids too'. The Kibo bar near the bottom of the nursery slopes is 'friendly' with 'a great atmosphere'. In's Moment (aka Campbell's Bar) in the basement of the Jakobwirt hotel is 'terrific', with Mr Campbell himself described as 'a very genial host'. The funky Moskito Cafe Bar has live music. Karat is a smart lounge bar.

Off the slopes There are excursions to Innsbruck and Salzburg, plus pretty walks and sleigh rides.

Phone numbers
From elsewhere in Austria add the prefix 05358 (Wilder Kaiser), 05333 (Söll), 05332 (Hohe Salve), 05335 (Hopfgarten, Itter), 05334 (Brixen, Westendorf); from abroad use the prefix +43 and omit the initial '0'

TOURIST OFFICES

WILDER KAISER
(Söll, Scheffau, Going, Ellmau)
www.wilderkaiser.info

HOHE SALVE
(Hopfgarten, Itter)
www.hohe-salve.com

KITZBÜHELER ALPEN
(Brixen, Westendorf)
www.kitzbuehel-alpen.com

SKIWELT
www.skiwelt.at

TVB ST ANTON AM ARLBERG

St Anton

If what you seek is dumps, bumps, boozing and bopping, there's nowhere quite like it – and with a neat Tirolean town as a bonus

RATINGS

The mountains

Extent	****
Fast lifts	***
Queues	***
Terrain p'ks	***
Snow	****
Expert	*****
Intermediate	***
Beginner	*
Boarder	****
X-country	**
Restaurants	***
Schools	***
Families	****

The resort

Charm	****
Convenience	***
Scenery	***
Eating out	****
Après-ski	*****
Off-slope	**

RPI	105
lift pass	£180
ski hire	£130
lessons	£110
food & drink	£120
total	**£540**

NEWS

2011/12: The Mooser hotel, adjoining the Mooserwirt bar on the slopes, opened in December 2011, with luxury rooms and suites, spa, pool and restaurant. And two cool new 4-star hotels (Anthony's and M3) opened in the resort centre.

- ＋ Varied terrain for experts and adventurous intermediates
- ＋ Heavy snowfalls, lots of snow-guns
- ＋ Car-free village centre retains solid traditional charm
- ＋ Very lively après-ski
- ＋ Improved lift system has cut queues from the base areas, but ...

- − Some pistes dangerously crowded
- − Slopes can be tough for near-beginners and timid intermediates
- − Most tough runs are unpatrolled
- − Snow quality can suffer from sun
- − Resort sprawls, with long treks from some lodgings to key lifts and bars
- − Centre can be noisy at night

St Anton is one of the world's best resorts for competent skiers and riders, particularly those with the energy to après-ski as hard as they ski. If you want to, you can party from 3pm to 3am. Good luck!

But the place doesn't suit everyone. If you are thinking of trying an Austrian change from a major French resort, or of going up a gear from Kitzbühel or Söll, be sure that you are not going to get thrown by blues that get heavily mogulled, reds that might be black and runs that are dangerously crowded. We have been saying for years that the resort urgently needs to create an alternative piste to the busy run down from its main mountain. There is a ski route already there; it just needs a bit of a makeover.

THE RESORT

St Anton is the western extremity of the Tirol, at the foot of the road up to the Arlberg pass. It is at one end of a lift network that spreads across to St Christoph and over the pass to Stuben. These two tiny villages are described at the end of the chapter.

The resort is a long, sprawling place, almost a town rather than a village, squeezed into a narrow valley. As it spreads down the valley, it thins out before broadening again to form the suburb of Nasserein.

Development spreads up the hill to the west, towards the Arlberg pass – first to Oberdorf, then Gastig, 10 minutes' walk from the centre.

The ski pass covers Lech and Zürs, reached by regular free ski-buses from Alpe Rauz, where the slopes meet the Arlberg pass road, and the less well-known Sonnenkopf area above Klösterle (see the Vorarlberg – Alpenregion Bludenz chapter). But these buses can get crowded; the post bus offers a less crowded alternative and means you can start or end your outing in St Anton, but it is not free. Taxis can be economic if shared. Serfaus, Ischgl and Sölden are feasible outings by car.

VILLAGE CHARM ****
Traditional but lively

Although it is crowded and commercialized, St Anton is full of character, its traffic-free main street lined by traditional-style buildings. It is an attractively bustling place, day and night. Its shops offer little in the way of entertainment, but meet everyday needs well – a well-stocked Spar, for example, a watchmender who stocks batteries that fit our altimeters, and an excellent bookshop that sells good numbers of this book.

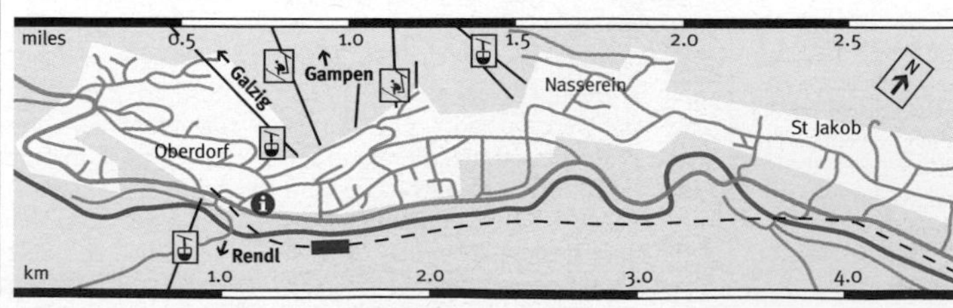

KEY FACTS

Resort	1305m 4,280ft
Arlberg region	
Slopes	1075-2650m 3,530-8,690ft
Lifts	84
Pistes	283km 176 miles
Blue	40%
Red	48%
Black	12%
Snowmaking	65%
St Anton, St Christoph and Stuben	
Slopes	1305-2650m 4,280-8,690ft
Lifts	42
Pistes	127km 79 miles

CONVENIENCE ★★★
Not bad for a large resort

The hub of the resort is at the western end of the main street, close to the base stations of the lifts to Gampen (a fast quad chair), to Galzig and to Rendl (modern gondolas). Staying on or close to this main street is ideal to keep treks to the lifts short.

Nasserein has an eight-seater gondola up to Gampen, and makes an appealing base for a quiet time. The nightlife action is a short bus ride or 15-minute walk away. Staying between the centre and Nasserein is fairly convenient, too, as the Fang chairlift gives access to all the base lifts.

SCENERY ★★★
Head for the Valluga

St Anton squeezes into a narrow, partly wooded valley. The scenery becomes more impressive as you ride up the lifts, either towards the dramatic Valluga, or across the valley up to Rendl, which opens up a splendid panorama.

THE MOUNTAINS

The main slopes are essentially open: only the lower Gampen runs and the run from Rendl to the valley offer much shelter from bad weather.

St Anton vies with Val d'Isère for the title of 'resort with most underclassified slopes'. Many of the blue runs would be better classified as red; there are also plenty of reds that could be black.

But paradoxically, none of the blacks is seriously steep; this is because the toughest runs are called 'ski routes' or 'high-alpine touring runs'. The touring runs (at Rendl and Stuben) are simply off-piste runs that would not appear on the piste map at all in most resorts – if you want to try these runs, hire a guide.

The piste map says the ski routes are marked and avalanche controlled but not groomed or patrolled. We applaud the clear explanation (lacking in many resorts), but we think many of these runs should be patrolled pistes. In several areas (notably Schindler Spitze and Rendl) they are popular runs, treated like pistes. To add to the confusion, some of the routes are sometimes groomed (this happened on our recent visits).

The piste map is designed for marketing rather than navigation, covering the whole of the Arlberg region in one view; it is unclear and misleading in places and provokes complaints from reporters. What's needed, really, is one piste map for St Anton-St Christoph-Stuben and separate ones for Lech-Zürs and for Sonnenkopf. The local TV shows the state of the pistes and queues – very useful. Several 2012 visitors had issues with piste marking – 'We went wrong more than once,' says one.

EXTENT OF THE SLOPES ★★★★
Large linked area

St Anton's slopes fall into three main sectors, two of them linked. The major sector is that beneath the local high spot, the **Valluga**, accessed by the jumbo gondola to Galzig, then a cable car. The tiny top stage of the cable car to the Valluga itself is mainly for sightseeing – you can take skis or a

TVB ST ANTON IM ARLBERG

Tiny St Christoph is a good place to stay for a quiet time; and you can ski home to it without braving the crowded piste to St Anton at the end of the day →

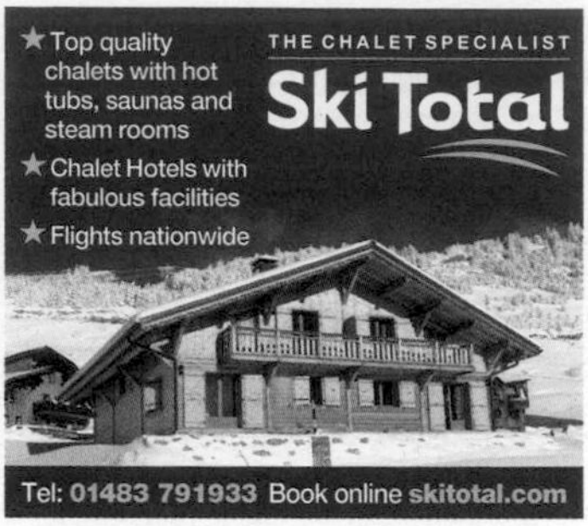

board up only if you have a guide to lead you down the tricky off-piste run to Zürs. The first stage of the cable car ends at Valluga Grat and gives access to St Anton's famous high, sunny bowls, and to the long, beautiful red/blue run to Alpe Rauz. From here there's a six-pack, the Valfagehr, to return, or you can go on to explore the rather neglected slopes of **Stuben**, described at the end of the chapter. The run to Alpe Rauz and the high Valluga runs can also be accessed by riding the Schindlergrat triple chair, though some also involve a hike. Other runs from Galzig go south-west to St Christoph and east into the Steissbachtal.

Beyond this valley, with lift and piste links in both directions, is the **Kapall-Gampen** sector, reachable by chairlift from central St Anton or gondola from Nasserein. From Gampen at mid-mountain, pistes lead back to St Anton and Nasserein. Or you can ride a six-pack on up to Kapall to ski the treeless upper mountain.

Rendl is a separate mountain, reached by a newish gondola from the centre of town. A handful of lifts serve the west-facing upper runs, and there's a good north-facing piste to the valley.

Underused area of worthwhile runs, though you have to put up with slow lifts (cold ones on the front side)
Excellent long red/blue down towards Stuben – over 1000m vertical
Albonagrat 2400m
Lech / Zurs
Flexen Pass
ALBONA
Stuben 1405m
1840m
Valfagehr
Arlenmähder
St Christoph
GAL 218
Rauz 1620m
Rauz is the key to the ski-bus services – you can ski to here and catch a free bus to Zürs
St Christoph 1800m/5,910ft
Hospiz Alm
gondola
cable car
fast chairlift
Slow chairs & drags have no symbol

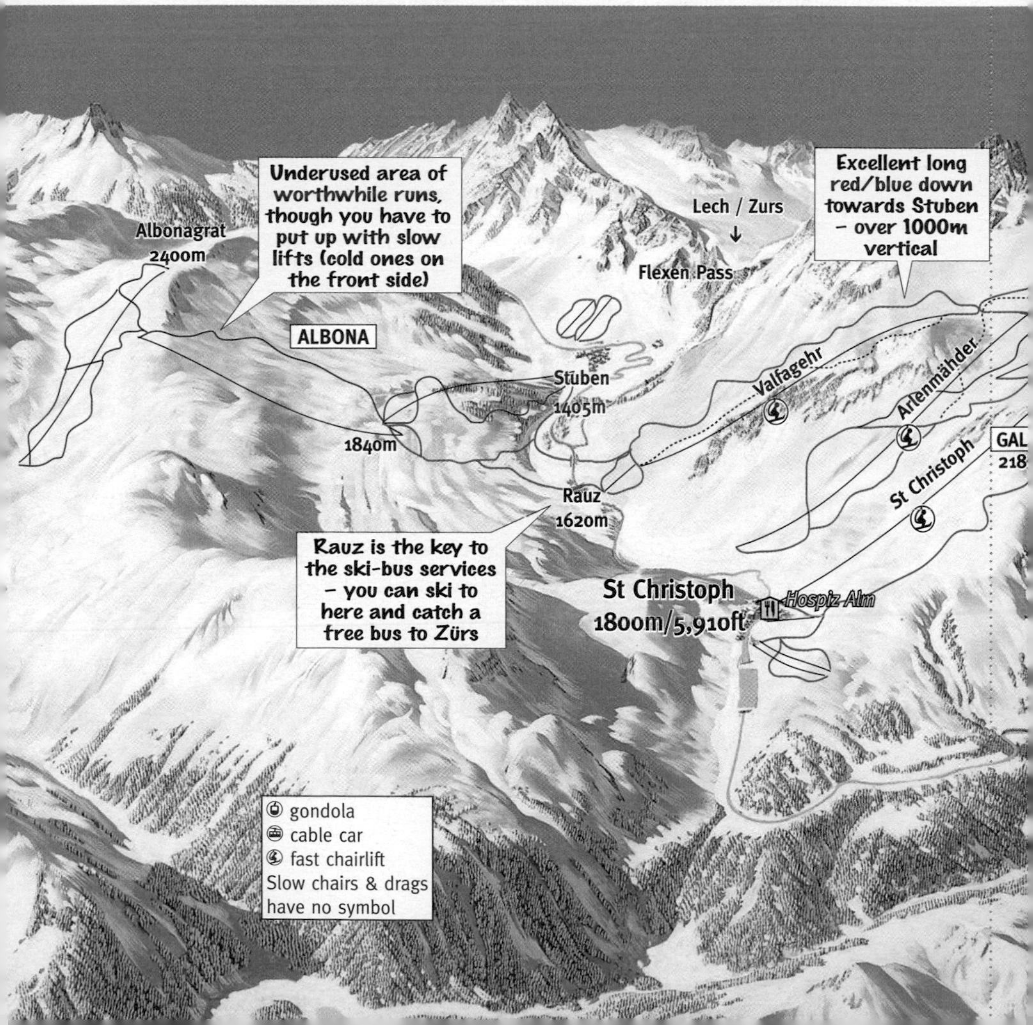

FAST LIFTS ★★★
Fast access, patchy higher up
Access from the village is by smart gondolas or fast chairs. But while the Gampen and Galzig sectors have a lot of fast chairs higher up, Rendl and Stuben still have a lot of slow ones.

QUEUES ★★★
Much improved, but ...
Queues are not the problem they once were, and 2012 reporters had few problems. But there can be queues for key lifts, including the Valluga cable car from Galzig ('average of 25 minutes', said a 2012 report), the alternative Schindlergrat chair to Schindler Spitze, the Zammermoos chair out of the Steissbachtal and the gondola from Nasserein first thing.

But more of a worry than queues are the crowded pistes – see the feature panel later in this chapter.

TERRAIN PARKS ★★★
Small, but perfectly formed
The 340m-long Stanton park on Rendl, just below the top of the gondola, has been vastly improved by Q-Parks (www.qparks.com). While it doesn't match Lech's park for quantity, it has lots of quality – including a jib line, intermediate and pro lines, beginner area, fun-cross for the kids, chill area and daily maintenance. And you get a great view of all the action from the restaurant terrace above.

SNOW RELIABILITY ★★★★
Generally very good cover
If the weather is coming from the west or north-west (as it often is), the Arlberg region gets it first, and as a result St Anton gets heavy falls of snow – and neighbouring Lech and Zürs get even more. These resorts often have much better conditions

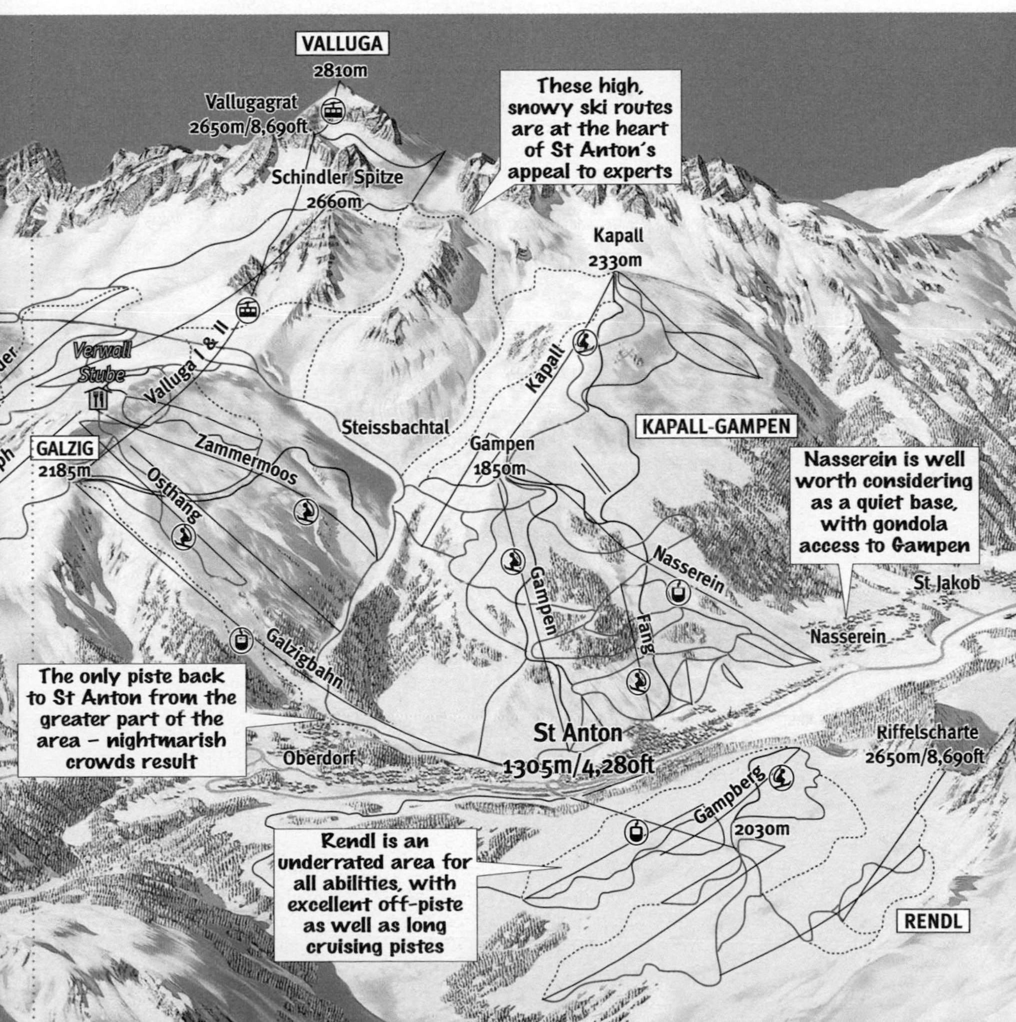
VALLUGA
2810m
Vallugagrat
2650m/8,690ft
These high, snowy ski routes are at the heart of St Anton's appeal to experts
Schindler Spitze
2660m
Kapall
2330m
Verwall Stube
Valluga I & II
Kapall
Steissbachtal
KAPALL-GAMPEN
GALZIG
2185m
Zammermoos
Gampen
1850m
Nasserein is well worth considering as a quiet base, with gondola access to Gampen
Osthang
Nasserein
Gampen
St Jakob
Fang
Nasserein
Galzigbahn
The only piste back to St Anton from the greater part of the area – nightmarish crowds result
St Anton
1305m/4,280ft
Riffelscharte
2650m/8,690ft
Oberdorf
Gampberg
2030m
Rendl is an underrated area for all abilities, with excellent off-piste as well as long cruising pistes
RENDL

GETTING THERE

Air Innsbruck 95km/ 60 miles (1hr15); Zürich 210km/ 130 miles (2hr45); Friedrichshafen 135km/85 miles (1hr45); Munich 210km/130 miles (3hr)

Rail Mainline station in resort

ACTIVITIES

Indoor Swimming pool (also hotel pools open to the public, with sauna and massage), fitness centre, tennis, squash, bowling, climbing wall, museum, library

Outdoor Cleared walking paths, natural ice rink (skating, curling), sleigh rides, snowshoeing, tobogganing, climbing, paragliding

than other resorts of a similar height, and we've had great fresh powder here as late as mid-April. But many slopes face south or south-east, causing icy or heavy conditions at times. As spring approaches, in particular, it's vital to time descents of the steeper runs off the Valluga to get decent conditions, or you can find yourself in trouble.

The lower runs are well equipped with snowmaking, which generally ensures the home runs remain open.

FOR EXPERTS ★★★★★
One of the world's great areas

St Anton vies with Chamonix, Val d'Isère and a handful of other resorts for the affections of experts. There are countless opportunities for going off-piste; see the feature panel opposite for some of them. The runs in the huge bowls below the Valluga are justifiably world-famous, and immediately after a fresh snowfall you can see tracks going all over the mountain; there are ski routes in the bowls too. Lower down, there are challenging runs in many directions from both Galzig and Kapall-Gampen. These lower runs can be doubly tricky if the snow has been hit by the sun.

Don't overlook the Rendl area, which has plenty of open space served by the top lifts, and several quite challenging runs. This is a great area for a mixed group and usually quieter than the main sector. The Sonnenkopf area, down-valley from Stuben, is even quieter and has several ski routes – and more serious off-piste, including an 'excellent' route to Langen. Read the Stuben section, too.

FOR INTERMEDIATES ★★★★★
Some real challenges

St Anton is well suited to good, adventurous intermediates. As well as lots of testing pistes, they will be able to try some of the ski routes in the Valluga bowls. The run from Schindler Spitze to Rauz is very long (over 1000m vertical), varied and ideal for good intermediates. Alternatively, turn off from this part-way down and take the Steissbachtal to the lifts back to Galzig or Gampen. The Kapall-Gampen section is also interesting, with sporty bumps among trees on the lower half. Good intermediates may enjoy the men's downhill run from the top of this sector to the town.

Timid intermediates will find St Anton less to their taste. There are few easy cruising pistes; most blue runs here would be red in most other resorts, and get bumpy, especially if there is fresh snow (the blue 1 home run often has testing moguls at the end of the day). The gentlest cruisers are the short blues on Galzig and the Steissbachtal, but they get extremely crowded. The blue from Kapall to Gampen is wide and cruisey.

The underrated Rendl area has a variety of trails suitable for good and moderate intermediates, including the long and genuinely blue Salzböden. The long treelined run to the valley (over 1000m vertical from the top) is the best run in the area when visibility is poor, but it has some awkward sections and can get very busy at the end of the day. You should take the bus to Lech-Zürs at least once during a week's stay.

FOR BEGINNERS ★★★★★
Far from ideal

The best bet for beginners is to start at Nasserein, where the nursery slope is less steep than the one close to the main lifts. There are further slopes up at Gampen and a short, gentle blue run at Rendl, served by an easy draglift. But there are no other easy, uncrowded runs for beginners to progress to. A mixed party including novices would be better off choosing a base in Lech or Zürs; those who want to explore St Anton can do so by getting on the bus.

FOR BOARDERS ★★★★★
Freeriding heaven

For many, St Anton is the Mecca of Austrian freeriding and expert boarders flock here. The terrain is far from ideal for beginners, but there are few T-bars to contend with. The Arlberg Snowboard Academy has a reputation for showing all levels where best to apply their skills.

LIFT PASSES

Arlberg

Prices in €

Age	1-day	6-day
under 16	27	132
16 to 19	42	191
20 to 64	46	219
65 plus	42	191

Free no one; day pass €10 if under 8, €20 if over 75

Beginner points ticket

Notes

Covers St Anton, St Christoph, Lech, Zürs and Stuben lifts, and linking bus between Rauz and Zürs; also Sonnenkopf (10 lifts) at Klösterle, 7km west of Stuben (bus link); single ascent, half-day and pedestrian options

FOR CROSS-COUNTRY ★★★★★

A decent amount

Trails total around 40km, and snow conditions are usually good.

MOUNTAIN RESTAURANTS ★★★★★

Lots of options

Editors' choice The Verwallstube at Galzig (2352501) is in a class of its own – an expensive table-service place with all the trimmings and splendid views. We've had seriously good lunches here a couple of times – including truffle risotto (beware: they shave the truffle until you tell them to stop, then charge by weight). We often lunch on the fringe of St Christoph at the atmospheric Hospiz Alm (3625), famed for its slide down to the toilets as well as its satisfying table-service food and amazing wine cellar. Service gets stretched at times, and it can be expensive. Recent visitors approve: 'the ribs are great to share'.

Worth knowing about The Rodelalm on Gampen is not marked on the piste map, but is beside black run 25 on the way to Nasserein. It has a lovely beamed interior, and we had good traditional food here; a reader enjoyed 'terrific roasted chicken'. On Galzig, the Ulmer Hütte, near the top of the Arlenmähder chair, has 'good service and food'. Just above the village, the après-ski bars (Mooserwirt, Griabli, Heustadl and Krazy Kanguruh) serve typical Austrian food and burgers. On Rendl, we've had good stir fry cooked to order at the spacious self-service Rendl restaurant; and the terrace (aka Rendl Beach) has great views of the terrain park action. Or head down the valley run to the small, rustic Bifang-Alm for regional specialities.

SCHOOLS AND GUIDES ★★★★★

Good reports

The St Anton and the Arlberg schools are under the same ownership but operate separately. Recent reports have been positive, and a 2012 visitor had an 'excellent private lesson with a patient and careful instructor'; but a past reporter complained of large classes with too wide a range of abilities. Piste to Powder is a specialist

OFF-PISTE RUNS IN ST ANTON

The Arlberg region is an off-piste skier's dream – renowned for its consistently high snowfall record and enormous diversity of terrain. We invited Piste to Powder Mountain Guides to give us an introduction to the possibilities. Remember you should never explore far off-piste without a guide.

Runs from Rendl

After initial practice close to the pistes, the natural progression is to go beyond the furthest lift to access the wide rolling bowls of powder of Rossfall.

More serious routes from Rendl take you well away from all lifts. The North Face, accessed from the Gampberg six-seat chair, offers challenging terrain to the intermediate/confident off-piste skier. The Riffel chairlifts access the imposing Hinter Rendl – a gigantic high-mountain bowl offering a huge descent down to St Anton, often in deep powder. A variant involves a climb to Rendl Scharte and a demanding descent with sections of 35° down the remote Malfontal to the village of Pettneu and a taxi back to St Anton.

Runs from Albona, above Stuben

Stuben's outstanding terrain, reached from the Albonagrat chair, is suited to the more experienced off-piste skier, as the descents are long. The open treelines of the Langen forest, where the powder is regularly knee to waist deep, form some of the world's finest tree skiing. A 30-minute climb from Albonagrat, with skis on your shoulder, opens up further outstanding terrain from Maroikopfe – either west, down undulating open slopes to Langen, or east, down steep 40° slopes to Verwalltal, where this glorious run ends with a glass of wine at an old hunting lodge.

Runs from the Valluga

The legendary runs from the summit cable car of the Valluga must be on the tick list of all keen and experienced off-piste skiers – the North Face, Bridge Couloir or East Couloir. Your pulse will race as you trace a steep ski line between cliff bands in the breathtaking scenery of the Pazieltal, leading down to Zürs. Here, at the top of the Madloch chairlift and after a short hidden climb, you can be roped down into the steep Valhalla Couloir, accessing 1200m vertical of open slopes ending in the hamlet of Zug, close to Lech.

MOMENTUM SKI

Weekend & a la carte ski holiday specialists

100% Tailor-Made

Premier hotels & apartments

Flexible travel arrangements

020 7371 9111

www.momentumski.com

SCHOOLS

Arlberg
t 3411

St Anton
t 3563

Alpine Faszination
t 0676 630 2136

Classes
(Arlberg prices)
6 days (2hr am and 2hr pm) €241

Private lessons
€166 for 2hr; each additional person €20

GUIDES

Piste to Powder
t 0664 174 6282

CHILDCARE

Kindergartens (run by ski schools)
t 2526 / 3563
From age 30mnth; must be toilet trained

Ski schools
Both Austrian schools take children aged from 5 (6 days including lunch €331)

BOOKSHOP

Bookshop (Anton Eiter)
Dorfstrasse 28
6580 St Anton
t +43 676 5859 152
On the main street and stocks this guidebook

off-piste outfit run by British guide Graham Austick. Most reports are very enthusiastic, and a 2012 reporter (an experienced off-piste skier) said, 'The guides are excellent; you get tips and tactics for the conditions as well as guiding; I definitely rate them.' Past comments include: 'one of the best days ever on a mountain', 'a great operation', 'exactly the right balance of instruction and guiding'. We've had reports that ability levels sometimes vary too much, though, and heard mixed views of the success of groups for beginners to off-piste.

FOR FAMILIES ★★★★
Nasserein 'ideal'

The youth centre attached to the Arlberg school is excellent, and the special slopes both for toddlers (at the bottom) and bigger children (at Gampen) are well done. Children's instruction is reportedly very good. At Nasserein there is a moving carpet on the baby slope. There's also a good children's area by the Gampen fast quad. Nasserein makes a good base, and family chalet specialist Esprit Ski has its own facilities here.

STAYING THERE

There's a wide range of places to stay, from quality hotels to cheap and cheerful pensions and apartments, and a good choice of chalets.

Chalets This is by a wide margin Austria's catered chalet capital; some places are quite luxurious with sauna, steam or hot tub. Chalet operators include Ski Total with a dozen places ranging from six beds to the cool 32-bed Inge. Skiworld has 10 places, with 10 to 40 beds; Crystal has half a dozen properties; Inghams has eight ranging from eight to 35 beds; family specialist Esprit has three big chalets in Nasserein, one next to the gondola.

Hotels There are dozens of 4- and 3-star places. For 2011/12, three cool new places opened: the Mooser at the Mooserwirt (2644) on the slopes, and Anthony's (42600) and M3 (2968) in town – see 'News'.

*****Raffl's St Antoner Hof** (2910) The one 5-star. Position less than ideal. Pool, sauna, steam.

****Bergschlössl** (2220) Charming 10-room B&B right by lifts. 'Beautifully furnished, excellent value.'

****Best Western Alte Post** (2553) Atmospheric central place with lively après-ski bar.

****Galzig** (42770) Cool modern 'skihotel' by the lifts, tipped by a regular visitor.

****Montjola** (2302) In Oberdorf. 'Good sized room, excellent food, shuttle-bus,' says a 2011 reporter.

****Pepi's Skihotel** (283060) Stylish, modern B&B right by the Rendl lift.

****Post** (2213) Ancient place bang in the centre, with good spa and pool.

****Schwarzer Adler** (22440) Centuries-old inn on main street. Varying bedrooms. Nice pool.

***Parseierblick** (3374) In Nasserein. 'Loved it; next to lift; apartment fantastic for a family.'

***Nassereinerhof** (3366) Close to the Nasserein gondola; sauna, steam room. 'Very pleasant, with good food.'

***Fahrner** (22360) Up the hill. 'Unpretentious, clean rooms, friendly, first-rate food, good wine cellar.'

Steffeler (2872) B&B in excellent central spot. Simple but welcoming; good breakfasts.

Haus Olympia (2520) 'Comfortable' guest house five minutes from the town centre. 'Good breakfasts.'

Apartments There are plenty available, but few package deals. Past tips include the Bachmann apartments in Nasserein and Haus Rali at the western end of St Anton.

EATING OUT ★★★★
Some excellent spots

There's a lot of half-board lodging in St Anton, so the restaurant scene is not huge. Our standard port of call for a drink or two and a relaxed meal is the cool Hazienda (now part of the new M3 hotel) – a basement place in the main street, with a wide-ranging menu (steaks, seafood, pasta). For more of a blowout, it's up the hill to the village museum's restaurant – excellent, sophisticated food served in elegant panelled rooms. Other

UK PACKAGES

Alpine Answers, Alpine Elements, Alpine Weekends, Bramble Ski, Carrier, Crystal, Crystal Finest, Elegant Resorts, Erna Low, Esprit, Flexiski, Friendship Travel, Independent Ski Links, Inghams, Interactive Resorts, Kaluma, Mark Warner, Momentum, Mountain Wave, Neilson, Oxford Ski Co, Powder White, Scott Dunn, Ski Bespoke, Ski Club Freshtracks, Ski Expectations, Ski Independence, Ski Line, Ski Solutions, Ski Total, Skitracer, Ski-Val, Skiworld, Snow Finders, Snoworks, Snowscape, STC, Supertravel, Thomson, VIP, White Roc

Stuben Alpine Answers, Kaluma

St Christoph Alpine Answers, Carrier, Crystal Finest, Flexiski, Inghams, Jeffersons, Kaluma, Momentum, Powder Byrne, Scott Dunn, Ski Bespoke, Thomson

favourites: Underground on the Piste ('great steaks, great music, great night out'), Fuhrmannstube (traditional food), and Pomodoro ('tasty pizzas').

Two 2012 reporters tip Fahrnerstube up the hill in Oberdorf ('pretty decor, good hearty food'). In Nasserein, the Tenne attracted a recent visitor to go 'three out of six nights – good honest Austrian food, lovingly prepared'.

APRES-SKI ★★★★★
Throbbing till late

St Anton's bars rock from mid-afternoon until the early hours. It all starts in a collection of bars on the slopes above the village. The Krazy Kanguruh is probably the most famous, but the Mooserwirt is the favourite with many reporters – 'brilliant atmosphere', 'pure fun'. It fills up as soon as the lunch trade finishes – and reputedly dispenses more beer than any other bar in Austria. Griabli, opposite, is quieter, and the terrace gives you a good view of the goings-on at the Mooserwirt; we enjoyed a live band there, and a 2012 visitor 'loved the owner's taste in rock music'. The Heustadl is still the place for 'great German cover bands'. The Sennhütte also has 'a great atmosphere'. All this is followed by a slide down the piste in the dark.

The bars in town are in full swing by 4pm, too. Most are lively, with loud music; sophisticates looking for a quieter time are less well provided for. But Jacksy's, tucked away in a side street, is good for a quiet drink. And we like the Bodega tapas bar for pre-dinner drinks and, er, tapas. Base Camp is a lot of fun and 'attracts a mixed crowd and ski instructors'. Underground on the Piste is 'characterful, presided over by a flame-haired English grande-dame'. Later on, the Piccadilly ('pick of the live music') and Bar Cuba are popular clubs. Other tips: Scotty's (in Mark Warner's chalet hotel Rosanna), Kandahar and, in Nasserein, the Fang House.

OFF THE SLOPES ★★☆☆☆
Some entertainment

We and reporters love the excellent but pricey Arlberg-well.com, a leisure centre with great indoor and outdoor pools – including one with jets that propel you around at lightning speed – plus three types of sauna and a huge steam room. A separate sports centre has an indoor climbing wall and an outdoor ice climbing wall. The village is lively during the day, but has few diverting shops. Getting to the other Arlberg resorts by bus is easy, as is visiting Innsbruck by train. Some of the better mountain huts are accessible by lift or bus. There are 70km of good walking trails, and it's worth considering Lech for 'more interesting walks'. The ski museum opens at 3pm.

Ski Austria's Big Three. Where? See p168.

BEWARE OF DANGEROUSLY OVERCROWDED PISTES

We have been saying for years that some of St Anton's pistes are often dangerously overcrowded – especially (but not only) the Steissbachtal (aka Happy Valley) and the home run below it. Bravos going recklessly fast add to the danger. So acute is this problem that several reporters have preferred to catch a bus home from Rauz or St Christoph. Other alternatives are to ride the gondola down from Galzig or to use the quite testing ski route beneath it. Our picture shows just one of several runs that feed into the home piste.

The run to Rauz can get very busy too; indeed editor Watts once abandoned skiing for the day because this piste was so crowded with reckless skiers that he felt he needed to look over his shoulder before making each turn – wing mirrors would have been handy.

We get a continual flow of similar complaints from visitors: 'dangerously crowded', 'reckless skiers', 'people, people and, er, people everywhere; the pistes are simply dangerous'; 'the number of high-speed skiers can frighten you'; 'very crowded at the end of the day with reckless skiers and lots of moguls'. We could go on …

If this was North America, the mountain would have been planned with enough pistes to cope with the people the lifts can carry, and there would be high-profile staff on duty to give reckless skiers a dressing down (or worse). Why not here?

A KÄRKKÄINEN

LINKED RESORT – 1800m

ST CHRISTOPH

St Christoph is a small collection of smart hotels, restaurants and bars just down from the summit of the Arlberg pass. There are decent beginner slopes served by draglifts and a fast quad chairlift to the heart of St Anton's slopes at Galzig, but the blue back down is not an easy run to progress to. St Christoph is quiet at night. You can't miss the huge 5-star Arlberg-Hospiz (2611). A more affordable but still excellent place is the 4-star Maiensee (2804), right on the slopes by the chair up to Galzig, with health and spa facilities and treatments. We've had good reports of the Inghams flagship 136-bed chalet hotel here – ski-in/ski-out, with good-sized pool and sauna.

LINKED RESORT – 1405m

STUBEN

Stuben is linked by lifts and pistes over the Arlberg pass to St Anton. It's a tiny, unspoiled village, with an old church, a few unobtrusive hotels, two or three bars and a few little shops. Heavy snowfalls add to the charm.

The Albona area makes a welcome change from the busy slopes of St Anton, with some lovely scenic runs. The shady slow old chair from the village can be a cold ride, but blankets are available. The reward is north-facing slopes that hold powder well and some wonderful, deserted off-piste descents, including beautiful long runs down to Langen and to St Anton.

The Albonagratstube at the very top is a simple hut serving simple food. Lower down, the Albona self-service place gets packed, even on a quiet day. Reporters recommend heading back to the village for lunch at Willi's (pizza, ribs) or the Post hotel ('lovely dining room, great food').

Stuben has sunny nursery slopes separate from the main slopes, but lack of easy runs to progress to makes it unsuitable for beginners. We've had good reports of the school.

Evenings are quiet, but several places have a pleasant atmosphere. The charming old Post (761) and Albona (712) are very comfortable. The Hubertushof (7710) is 'welcoming, efficient; excellent food and facilities'.

Phone numbers
From elsewhere in Austria add the prefix 05446 (St Anton and St Christoph), 05582 (Stuben); from abroad use the prefix +43 and omit the initial '0'

TOURIST OFFICES

St Anton
www.stantonamarlberg.com

St Christoph
www.tiscover.com/st.christoph

Stuben
www.stuben.com

TOURISM ASSOCIATION NEUSTIFT

Stubai valley

Austria's biggest glacier area, they say, and certainly one of the best; down the valley, a string of appealing village bases

TOP 10 RATINGS

Extent	★★★
Fast lifts	★★★
Queues	★★★
Snow	★★★★★
Expert	★★★
Intermediate	★★★
Beginner	★★
Charm	★★★★
Convenience	★★
Scenery	★★★★

RPI	95
lift pass	£190
ski hire	£105
lessons	£90
food & drink	£105
total	**£490**

NEWS

2012/13: On the glacier, the Rotadl slow quad is being moved to serve Daunjoch, and replaced by a fourth six-pack.

- ➕ High, snow-sure glacier slopes plus lower bad-weather options
- ➕ Quiet, pretty Tirolean villages
- ➖ A lot of shuttling up and down the valley to and from the glacier
- ➖ Few challenging pistes

The Stubaier Gletscher ranks alongside Hintertux as one of the most extensive and rewarding glacier ski areas in the Alps. Neustift is the nearest major village, 20km away. But another 5km down-valley, livelier Fulpmes is at the base of the Stubaital's best low-altitude area, Schlick 2000.

The 30km-long Stubai valley lies a short drive south of Innsbruck (there's also an antique tram to Fulpmes). The glacier is of course at the head of the valley. There are countless hamlets dotted along the valley; there is simple accommodation to be had in places like Falbeson (10km from the glacier) or Krössbach (15km). But three bigger villages – Neustift, Fulpmes and Mieders – have wooded ski areas, covered along with the glacier (and linking buses) by the Stubai Super Skipass. These resorts, described over the page, amount to a sizeable area of mostly intermediate terrain. All the villages have impressive toboggan runs – the valley has 11 in total.

The Stubaier Gletscher offers an extensive area of runs between 3200m and 2300m. Two gondolas go up from the huge car park at Mutterberg to a mid station at Fernau, and then to the two mid-mountain stations of Eisgrat and Gamsgarten. A third gondola from Eisgrat goes to the top of the slopes. Elsewhere, there is a mix of the usual glacier drag lifts and six-packs – a fourth is being added this year.

The slopes are broken up by rocky peaks giving more sense of variety than is normal on a glacier. There are lots of fabulous long blue and red cruising runs. The two short black pistes are very much at the easy end of the spectrum. But for more challenges there are numerous ski routes (not explained, but presumably unpatrolled) in several areas. Much the toughest is the 4km Fernau-Mauer at the eastern extremity of the area – after the gentlest and widest of starts this drops steeply towards the Fernau mid-station. There is also a lovely 10km ski route (Wilde Grub'n) from Gamsgarten to the valley – start with a cruise from the top of the glacier for a total of 1450m vertical. And there's proper off-piste to be explored. There are good beginner slopes at Eisgrat and Gamsgarten, where there is also a major children's area with childcare.

The area is popular with snowboarders. There are lots of natural hits and kickers across the mountain, and the big terrain park has all the usual features.

Queues are not a serious problem. The gondola and Eisjoch six-pack can get busy at weekends.

Gamsgarten has a huge self-service place, and excellent food in the table service Zur Goldenen Gams. Eisgrat has a cool newish building including a serious table-service section, Schaufelspitz. At Jochdohle, Austria's highest restaurant (3150m) gives long views. The Dresdner Hütte is a proper climbing refuge. There are picnic rooms at Eisgrat and Gamsgarten.

Après-ski starts up the mountain in the lively Gamsgarten bar and Ice Cube bar at Fernau.

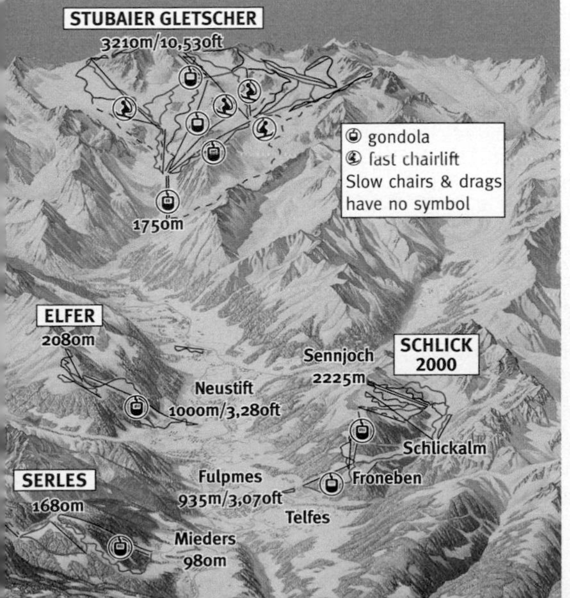

↑ There are great views – and some short slopes – at the very top of the area

SNOWPIX.COM / CHRIS GILL

KEY FACTS

Resorts	935-1000m
	3,070-3,280ft
Slopes	935-3210m
	3,070-10,530ft
Lifts	45
Pistes	147km
	91 miles
Blue	40%
Red	31%
Black	29%
Snowmaking	87%

UK PACKAGES

Neustift Crystal, Crystal Finest, Inghams, Momentum, Snowscape, Zenith
Fulpmes Crystal, Snowscape

Phone numbers
From elsewhere in Austria add the prefix 05226; from abroad use the prefix +43 5226

TOURIST OFFICE

www.stubai.at

1000m

NEUSTIFT

The major village closest to the glacier, 20km away. It's an attractive, traditional Tirolean village, with limited local slopes at Elfer.

The slopes at Elfer consist of a narrow chain of runs and lifts from Elferhütte at 2080m down to the village. The pistes are all red, and it is a quiet place for intermediates to practise. This area is north-east-facing; there is a sunny nursery slope at village level, on the other side. There are some 27km of cross-country trails.

There is a big 5-star Relais & Chateaux hotel, and lots of 4-stars and 3-stars spread around the area. In the outlying hamlet of Neder, the glacier lift company runs the family-oriented 4-star Happy Stubai (2611).

Nightlife is focused on the Dorf and Bierfassl bars and the Nachtkastl and Scala Club (formerly Rumpl) discos. Most restaurants are hotel-based. Neustift has quite a lot to offer off the slopes, including a big leisure centre with two pools, saunas and bowling.

935m

FULPMES

Fulpmes (with its satellite village of Telfes) sits at the foot of Schlick 2000, the most extensive of the lower ski areas. It is an attractive, sizeable working village not dominated by skiing (there is a downside: the shops close early). The glacier is 25km away.

Uphill from the village a two-stage gondola takes you to Kreuzjoch (2135m), opening up excellent views across the Stubaital and across the Schlick slopes to the dramatic Kalkkogel range. Most of the skiing is below the top gondola station – essentially a single open slope centred on a quad chair rising 580m, with draglifts serving the outermost runs. It is north-facing, so keeps snow well, and grooming is good. There are about five different pistes down, mostly of red difficulty with some easier blue options. There is also a ski-route – challenging at the best of times, very much so if snow is poor. And there is a fair amount of off-piste ('relatively safe', notes a regular).

Below the main slopes is a long easy run-out to the gondola mid-station at Froneben (1365m). This is the location of the nursery slopes, including Ronny's Kinderland, with moving carpets and fun features, and a couple of thumping après-ski bars. The blue run winding through woods to the village from here is good fun or tricky, depending on conditions and your competence. There is a terrain park. Queues are rare but the gondola gets busy at peak times.

There are some good huts, with table-service options at the top of the gondola and at Zirmachalm ('shared tables; great gulaschsuppe'). You can be towed by snowcat to Galtalm, in woods below Kreuzjoch, for 'great food and views'.

There's a good choice of 3- and 4-star hotels, most with pools and spa facilities. The 4-star Stubaierhof (62266) is central. Café Dorfkrug has 'good quality food, friendly service and a great Austrian folk band'.

The nearest leisure centre is in Neustift, but Fulpmes has ice skating, snowshoeing and tobogganing.

980m

MIEDERS

Mieders is near the entrance to the Stubai valley, 15 minutes' drive from Innsbruck. It's an unspoiled village with its own tiny area of slopes.

The slopes of Serles are limited to four blues and two short reds. A gondola takes you to Kopponeck at 1680m, where a couple of T-bars serve the upper runs. There are a couple of mountain restaurants and 45km of cross-country tracks above 1600m. The village has a small selection of hotels and guest houses.

SNOWPIX.COM / CHRIS GILL

Vorarlberg

Lech and Zürs are not the only resorts west of the Arlberg pass, above St Anton – the others include Europe's snowiest

Ski from St Anton to Stuben, and you cross over the Arlberg pass, moving from the Tirol to the province of Vorarlberg. Here, the melting snow drains into the Rhine, not the Inn and the Danube. It's a famously snowy area, catching the full force of storms sweeping in across the Bodensee. Fashionable and expensive Lech and Zürs are the resorts that are well known internationally, but there are small family resorts elsewhere that deserve attention.

Vorarlberg is small – the smallest 'land' in the Austrian federation (unless you count the city of Vienna). Its capital is Bregenz, down on the shores of the Bodensee.

Lech, Vorarlberg's best-known resort internationally, gets full coverage in its own chapter a few pages back, which also covers its linked close neighbour **Zürs**.

Those resorts aside, there are several other skiing regions. The first two mentioned below are covered in their own chapters following this introductory one.

Bregenzerwald, to the north-west of the Arlberg, is a delightfully unspoiled area, very proud of its cheeses – and it's here that two small resorts, Damüls and Warth, vie for the title of snowiest resort in the Alps. Warth is linked to Schröcken, and a couple of seasons ago, Damüls was linked to Mellau. The briefly named village of Au and next-door Schoppernau share the third-biggest ski area, Diedamskopf.

The **Alpenregion Bludenz**, west of the Arlberg, is based around the medieval town of Bludenz. Close to the Swiss border is one of the region's two main ski areas, Brandnertal, shared by the neighbouring resorts of Brand and Bürserberg. Its other main ski area, Sonnenkopf, above Klösterle, is further east and covered by the Arlberg lift pass, so it's a popular outing from the Arlberg resorts.

Then there are three other areas with skiing to offer. By far the biggest is the **Montafon** valley, to the south-west of the Arlberg. The biggest lift-linked ski area (with nearly 160km of pistes and a top height of 2395m) is shared by Gaschurn, St Gallenkirch and Schruns. It was created last season when a new gondola opened from St Gallenkirch (which already has one into the Nova area of slopes) into the Hochjoch area. Golm, above Vandans, is popular with families; Gargellen is a bit of a backwater. At the top of the valley is famously good ski touring terrain. In total, the valley has 243km of slopes served by over 60 lifts.

In the north-east corner of the province is a real curiosity. **Kleinwalsertal** is cut off from the rest of Austria, at the head of a German valley. It is close to one of the main German resorts, Oberstdorf, and is described briefly in the introduction to our section on Germany.

Finally, the **Bodensee-Vorarlberg** area in the north-west corner of Vorarlberg has some small areas. The largest, Laterns, has six lifts and 27km of runs, and a top height of 1780m.

Vorarlberg – Bregenzerwald

An unspoiled region that is hardly heard of on the British market, with a lot of relatively small ski areas covered on one big pass

RPI	85
lift pass	£150
ski hire	£80
lessons	£100
food & drink	£100
total	**£430**

NEWS

2012/13: At Au/Schoppernau, more snowmaking is planned.

2011/12: At Warth a new ski school building with play and climbing areas for children aged three to six years was built.

Bregenzerwald is tucked away between Germany and Switzerland at the western end of Austria, in Vorarlberg. Skirted by all the major road and rail links, it has remained remarkably unspoiled and is still primarily a farming community famous for its cheeses. But it is also the snowiest region in the Alps and has mountains rising up to over 2400m, with over 270km of pistes served by almost 100 lifts in 15 skiing areas. There is some seriously good skiing here, especially for intermediates, and the area is well worth considering for a quiet holiday exploring several different ski areas or for a family holiday. And prices are lower than in many better-known, more fashionable resorts.

Skiing began in Bregenzerwald in 1894 when the parish priest, Father Johann Müller, sent away to Norway for some newfangled 'Hickoryskis' and then careered down the slopes garbed in his flowing robes, amazing the local farmers. Until then, if you absolutely had to get around in winter, you wore a type of snowshoe. Father Johann established a trend that has transformed the region's economy.

This transformation has been greatly aided by abundant snowfall. One resort in the region, Warth, is supposed to have the best annual average snowfall in the Alps. Another, Damüls, is supposed to be the most snow-sure resort in the world. Eh? Let's just say the whole region gets huge amounts of snow. To put it in perspective: about four times as much as Kitzbühel, three times as much as Chamonix and twice as much as St Anton and Val d'Isère.

There is a ski lift in almost every village. But few of the ski areas are large. They are all covered by the 3-Valley ski pass, which also covers areas outside Bregenzerwald. The pass is valid in 29 ski areas and covers around 340km of slopes served by around 140 lifts. There are bus services between resorts, but having a car is useful: a recent reporter confirmed that getting around on buses is time consuming and that some journeys involve changing buses. There are some excellent deals for families, and nearly all the resorts offer activities other than skiing, with lots of cleared paths, tobogganing and cross-country skiing.

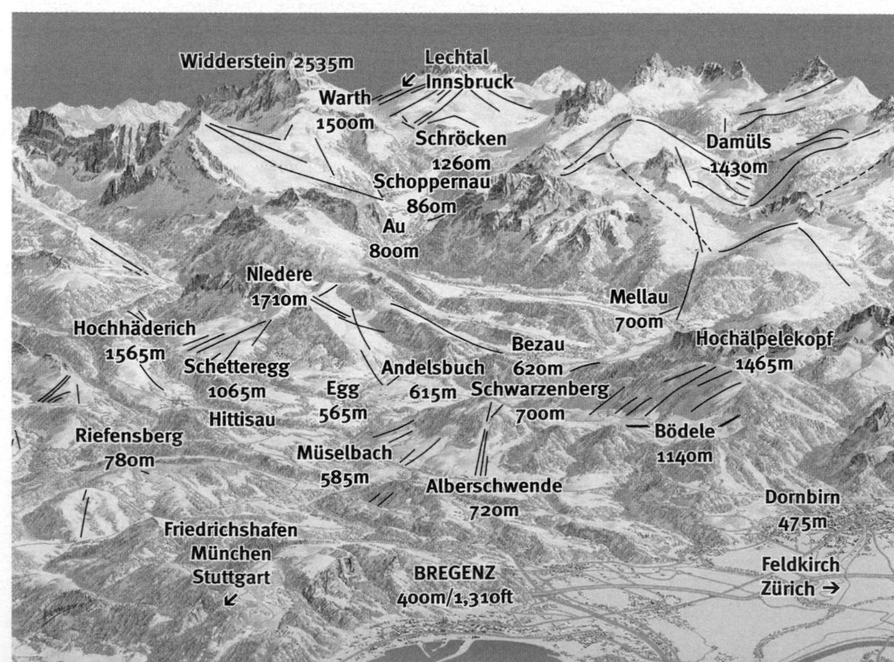

Since 2009/10 the Mellau and Damüls ski areas have been linked to form the biggest area of pistes in Bregenzerwald ➔

BREGENZERWALD TOURISMUS

THE BIGGEST SKI AREAS

Damüls and **Mellau** are now linked to form the biggest single ski area in Bregenzerwald, with 109km of runs. Just under half of these are red runs, around a quarter are blue, and the rest are blacks and ski routes. And there's a good terrain park in Damüls. Altogether there are 31 lifts – these include two gondolas and 14 chairs (with six six-packs and a fast quad).

Damüls is quite high (the base area is at 1430m), and the sunny but snow-sure slopes go up to 2000m. Most runs are quite short, above the treeline and of genuine red steepness, and some of the blues are quite narrow, so it's best for adventurous rather than timid intermediates. On our visit, all of the ski routes we tried had been groomed and were of red run steepness – and some were busier than the pistes. Damüls has 16km of cross-country tracks and over 20km of winter walking trails.

Mellau's ski area is reached by an old gondola from the edge of the village and is on the more shady side of the mountain (most of the slopes are north-facing). There's a steep black run that deserves its grading, as do the reds, and a ski route that is short but enjoyable. Most of the blues have fairly steep sections at the top – not good for timid intermediates. There's a long red through the trees right back to the village – enjoyable but narrow (it's a summer road for much of the way) – plus winter walking trails and over 20km of cross-country tracks.

Damüls has no real village centre – it consists of a series of small collections of hotels (six 4-stars, 11 3-stars), inns and gasthofs, scattered along the edge of the slopes; most of the accommodation is ski-in/ski-out.

Mellau, on the other hand, is much lower (690m) but a proper little village, quiet and peaceful (it's bypassed by the valley road). There's little more to it than a few hotels – two 4-stars, four 3-stars – some gasthofs and a couple of bars. We enjoyed our stay at the 4-star Sonne Lifestyle (5518 20100) – modern, minimalist, spacious rooms, friendly staff, good food and spa facilities.

Warth and **Schröcken** are at opposite ends of their shared 66km of slopes, which are mainly between 1500m and 2000m and served by 15 lifts, including five fast chairs. Thanks to the exceptional snowfall record, the pistes are almost always in excellent condition, and the off-piste powder gets tracked out much less quickly than in better-known resorts; a 2012 reporter found the off-piste 'virtually limitless' and lists nine highlights of his week there, mostly done with a guide. The marked runs include several easy blacks and ski routes as well as reds and blues, and there's a terrain park with three lines from easy to pro. Most of the pistes are ideal for high-speed cruising and were very quiet on our January visit. Queues are rare. Piste marking is good.

Warth is only a few kilometres along the valley from much better-known Lech (see separate chapter). The road between the villages is closed in winter because of the danger of avalanches, but you can see the Lech ski area from the top of the slopes, and you can ski there and back off-piste (the schools organize excursions twice a week). There are plans to build a lift link between the two, possibly for 2013/14. The Warth school is 'excellent for everything from children's group lessons to off-piste guiding', says a 2012 reporter.

There are 21km of cross-country loops, 20km of walking trails and tobogganing two evenings a week.

The villages are small, pretty and unspoiled. There are six 4-star hotels, two 3-stars and one 2-star, plus inns and gasthofs. The 4-stars include the 'modern, well-run and friendly' Sporthotel Steffisalp (5583 3699) with 'excellent' rooms, an après-ski hut, an umbrella bar and an 'impressive' spa area; right by the pistes and main lift (a fast quad, followed by a six-pack) in Warth. Schröcken can be reached on skis only by a ski route, and there are no lifts there – you have to drive or catch a bus to the Hochtannberg pass, where a six-pack whisks you into the centre of the ski area. The Gasthof Tannberg (5519 268) in Schröcken was 'a real find: amazing food, good service and value', says a 2012 visitor.

Au and **Schoppernau** are neighbouring villages sharing the **Diedamskopf** ski area, which boasts Bregenzerwald's highest lift station (reached by a two-stage gondola) at 2060m and fabulous 360° views from the top (and the Panorama restaurant). The sunny slopes (most face south or south-west) also have good views of the surrounding peaks and are popular with families. The eight lifts serve 44km of slopes, of which around 32% are blue pistes, 32% red, 16% black and 20% ski routes. The terrain park is the biggest in Bregenzerwald. There's night skiing twice a week.

The slopes suit good intermediates best; the blacks are quite serious, and some of the blues should be classified red, especially the blue from the top chair (which had moguls on it the afternoon we skied it). On the other hand, the reds in the Breitenalpe sector were easy and should really be classified blue. The runs are short, except for the 10km runs back to the valley station at 820m, which have a vertical of over 1200m. The lower section of this is served only by one red run and a ski route (the route was closed on our visit and the lowest section of the red run was stony; many people take the gondola down from mid-station). The rest of the pistes are above 1470m.

At the top of the mountain, the Kids Adventure Land takes children aged three to eight years old.

Cross-country enthusiasts will find over 60km of trails. There are 40km of cleared walks and a natural ice rink.

Au and Schoppernau between them have 10 4-star and four 3-star hotels, plus gasthofs and plenty of dining options. Both are a ski-bus ride or drive from the ski area and are rather spread out. We preferred Schoppernau, which is off the main road, on the same side as the slopes, and has nice snow-covered lanes and chalets.

SMALLER SKI AREAS

Andelsbuch and **Bezau** share the local **Niedere** ski area with eight lifts (including a smart newish cable car from Bezau) serving three short blue runs, a 7km-long red, a short black and several ski routes – 15km in total. It's a family ski area, and, given good snow, the ski routes offer more experienced skiers a challenge too. The top height is 1715m, and there's a panoramic restaurant at the top of the cable car. Andelsbuch has a 3-star inn plus a few gasthofs, and Bezau has three 4-star hotels and one 3-star.

Alberschwende has 18km of runs, served by a chairlift and six T-bars, and is popular with beginners. There are 16km of cross-country tracks and an ice rink. The village has a 4-star hotel, a 3-star, plus a few gasthofs.

Riefensberg has the tiny **Hochlitten** ski area, with just 5km of easy blue and red runs and four T-bars. It shares with neighbouring **Hittisau** the **Hochhäderich** ski area. This has 9km of runs (mainly blue and red but with a couple of blacks) served by four T-bars and a quad chair specially designed to be appropriate for children. It also has 16km of cross-country tracks at altitude and 12km of walking paths. Hittisau has two 4-star hotels and two 3-stars, while Riefensberg has two 2-star inns.

Egg is the biggest village in Bregenzerwald, with around 3,500 inhabitants and a small ski area at **Schetteregg**, with six lifts and 10km of easy blue and red runs between 1100m and 1400m. There are 15km of cleared walks, a 3-star hotel, and six inns.

Schwarzenberg's local **Bödele** mountain has 24km of runs (mainly easy blues and reds) served by nine lifts (nearly all draglifts). There are also 10km of cross-country tracks and 35km of walking trails. Schwarzenberg has two 4-star and two 3-star hotels.

UK PACKAGES

Damüls Ski Club Freshtracks
Mellau Ski Bespoke, Ski Club Freshtracks
Au Ski Bespoke

Phone numbers
From abroad use the prefix +43 and omit the initial '0'

TOURIST OFFICE

www.bregenzerwald.at

Vorarlberg – Alpenregion Bludenz

Two small, family-friendly ski areas set either side of a medieval town – with easy access to several other nearby ski areas

RPI	85
lift pass	£140
ski hire	£80
lessons	£105
food & drink	£105
total	**£430**

NEWS

2011/12: At Sonnenkopf a new quad chair replaced an ancient T-bar, and a new table-service restaurant with a big terrace was built at the top of it.

At Brandnertal a new terrain park was built above Brand, and a new toboggan run opened above Bürserberg.

Alpenregion Bludenz is centred on the medieval mountain town of Bludenz, in the west of Austria, and the region borders on to Switzerland. It has two main ski areas: Brandnertal to the west and Sonnenkopf in the Klostertal to the east. The latter is covered by the Arlberg ski pass (which covers St Anton and Lech too) as well as having its own pass.

Getting to the Bludenz region is easy by train or car after flying in to Zurich (155km) or Innsbruck (135km). And if you base yourself in Bludenz, it's easy to ski both the local main ski areas plus the Arlberg, Montafon and Bregenzerwald resorts. Both Brandnertal and Sonnenkopf are popular with families.

BRANDNERTAL

Two separate villages with their own ski areas that have recently been linked by a new cable car at altitude.
Brand (1040m) is strung along the valley floor near the head (the south-western end) of the Brandnertal. Eight-seater gondolas (served by free ski-buses) go up from each end of town into the bigger part of the ski area it shares with Bürserberg (890m), which is down the valley to the north-east and has a double chairlift into its own smaller area of slopes. The two areas were linked at altitude in 2007 when the Panoramabahn cable car opened. You can ski on an easy blue run from the Bürserberg area to the Brand area and catch the cable car the other way.

The area above Brand is served by two recently built six-packs, a couple of short draglifts and an old double chair. One of the six-packs reaches the area's high point of 2000m. Above Bürserberg, the area is served by a couple of old chairs and a couple of drags, one of which takes you to the blue piste linking the two areas.

Most of the runs are red, though there are a few blues and ski routes, and a solitary black run (above Bürserberg); there's a new terrain park and half-pipe above Brand (see www.backyards.at). In total there are 55km of mainly east-facing pistes that suit intermediates best; 75% of the pistes are covered by snowmaking. The area is well supplied with mountain huts.

There's excellent cross-country here, with 72km of prepared tracks including some at the top of Bürserberg and a glorious 15km circular route at 1250m.

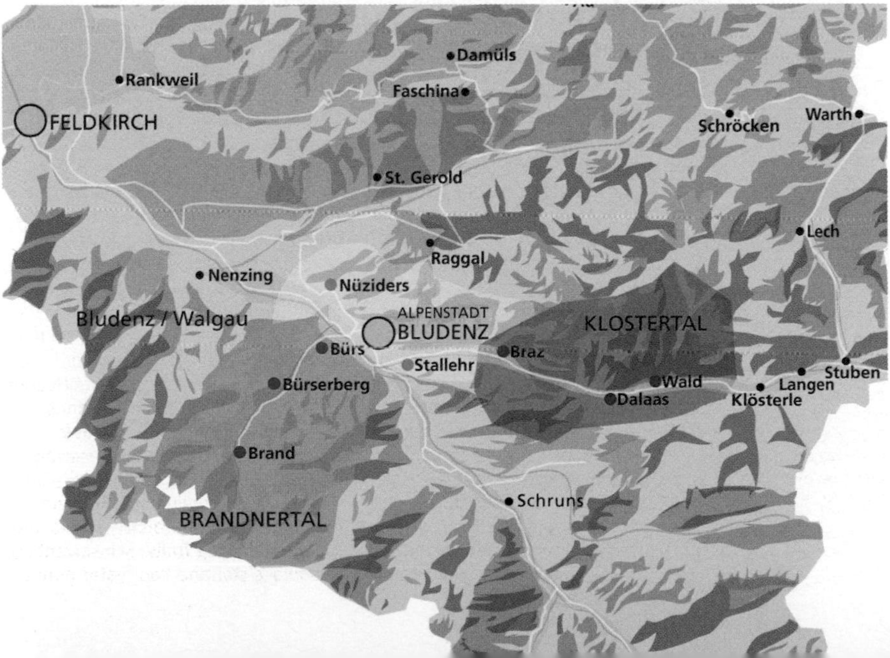

↑ Most of the region's slopes are gentle and family-friendly

ALPENREGION BLUDENZ

There's also snowshoeing and extensive winter walking trails that go right to the top of Bürserberg, plus ice skating on natural rinks.

The area goes out of its way to be family-friendly, and there's a special Kinderland area in the middle of Brand village where the two ski schools teach three- to five-year olds. Children aged eight and under ski free, and there are discounts up to age 18; from 23 March to 7 April 2013 children up to 14 ski free. There are two good toboggan runs, one 6km long above Brand and a new 1.4km one above Bürserberg. And the area is big on dog sledding; you can learn to mush huskies (including a special course for children) and take excursions (including one where you camp overnight on the mountain).

Hotels range from several 4-stars to family-run pensions, and some have a special 'Family Friendly' accreditation. Apartments are plentiful too.

SONNENKOPF

A small family-friendly ski area set off the road between Bludenz and St Anton. You can buy the local lift pass or the Arlberg lift pass, which covers the better-known resorts of St Anton, Lech and Zürs as well.

The Klostertal has various small villages lining the road to the Arlberg pass, and a roadside eight-person gondola with big car parks nearby goes up to its Sonnenkopf ski area from near the village of Wald (see map on the previous page). This has 30km of pistes served by nine lifts and suits beginners, intermediates and families best; it is often remarkably quiet here when nearby St Anton and Lech are packed.

At the top of the gondola is a good beginner area and gentle blue runs served by T-bars and a quad chair that was new for the 2011/12 season and has a new table-service mountain restaurant with a big sun terrace at the top (2000m). There's also a children's area near the top of the gondola, where there's another mountain restaurant. Children under eight ski free.

Two of the T-bars lead you to pistes down to the bigger sector of pistes, which are served by a fast quad and two double chairs, one of which leads to the area's high point of 2300m. This sector has mainly red runs plus a couple of ski routes and a solitary, seriously steep, 1.5km black run. One of the reds goes all the way back to the valley floor and to either the village of Klösterle or back to the base of the gondola. There's also good off-piste to be explored with a guide.

The 1.8km-long toboggan run goes from the top to the mid-station of the gondola. There's cross-country on the valley floor and glorious winter walking trails at altitude, including one up to Muttjöchle (2075m) beyond the new mountain restaurant.

There is good-value accommodation in villages along the valley floor and two restaurants with especially good reputations – in the 3-star Gasthof Rössle and 4-star Traube Braz, both in the village of Braz.

UK PACKAGES

Brand STC

Phone numbers
From abroad use the prefix +43 and omit the initial '0'

TOURIST OFFICE

www.en.alpenregion.at

France

Last year around a third of British skiers and snowboarders chose France for their holidays – that's more than for any other country. It's not difficult to see what attracts us to France. The country has the biggest lift and piste networks in the world; for those who like to cover as many miles in a day as possible, these are unrivalled. Most of these big areas are also at high altitude, ensuring good snow for a long season. The best of them have state-of-the-art lift systems, too – but it's a myth that all French lift systems are wonderfully efficient. In quite a few big-name areas, draglifts and slow chairlifts still rule.

Another myth is that French resort villages are all soulless, purpose-built service stations, thrown up without concern for appearance during the 1960s and 1970s. We come back to this theme below. Many French resorts are now distinctly lively in the evening – a great change over the last 20 years. And some now have the on-mountain afternoon party scene that is so common in Austria, mainly thanks to the Folie Douce chain that started several years ago in Val d'Isère, opened above Val Thorens in 2009/10 and is expanding to Méribel for 2012/13.

Although France is not expensive overall compared to its main Alpine rivals (as shown by our RPI figures), many resorts are expensive for eating and drinking – especially major ones such as Val d'Isère, Courchevel and Méribel, where prices now far exceed their Austrian and Italian rivals. This leads to many complaints from readers (along with complaints about the ludicrous practice of some mountain restaurants charging customers to use the loos). But UK tour operators do a great job in keeping catered chalet holidays affordable, with lots of food and wine included in the price. And local prices have become cheaper in terms of £s in the last year because of exchange rate changes – in July 2011 we were getting around 1.07 euros for £1, in July 2012 around 1.21 euros; let's hope the £ continues to rise.

KEEPING COSTS DOWN

Chalet holidays are not the only way of economizing, of course. Renting one of the new generation of genuinely comfortable and stylish apartments and catering for yourself is an attractive option – see our smart apartments chapter on page 39. Other ideas include staying in a relatively cheap valley town such as Bourg-St-Maurice or Brides-les-Bains and on-mountain picnic lunches, with which the Gill family experimented on their last stay in Courchevel.

ANY STYLE OF RESORT YOU LIKE

The main drawback to France, hinted at above, is the nature of some of the high-altitude purpose-built resorts. It's partly that the worst of them look hideous, but also that they were designed to cram in the maximum number of beds (and shops – we really hate the claustrophobic indoor malls) and that they are holiday camps rather than real communities. But even the worst places have learned from past mistakes, and newer developments are being built in a traditional chalet style. And the later generation of purpose-built resorts, such as La Rosière, La Tania and Arc 1950, are built in much more sympathetic style.

If you prefer, there are genuinely old mountain villages to stay in,

SNOWPIX.COM / CHRIS GILL

← Many high altitude French resorts, purpose-built in the 1960s and 70s, are plug ugly. But they are snow-sure and the new parts of them are being built in much more sympathetic chalet style – look at the contrast in this pic of Tignes

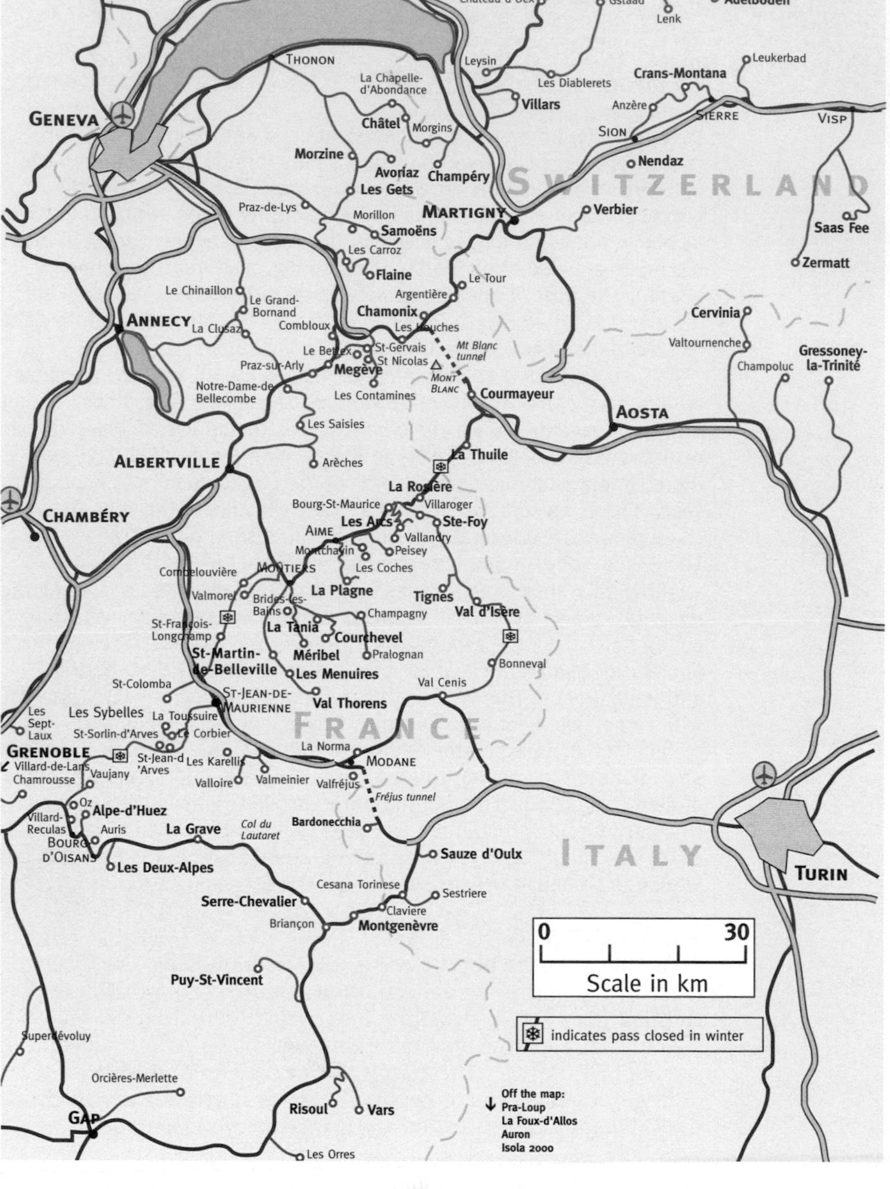

Getting around the French Alps

Pick the right gateway city as your initial Continental target – Geneva, Chambéry or Grenoble – and you can hardly go wrong. The only high pass you need worry about is on the approach to Serre-Chevalier and Montgenèvre – the 2060m Col du Lauteret; but even here the road is a major one, and kept clear of snow or reopened quickly after a fall (or you can fly to Turin and avoid that pass). Crossing the French-Swiss border between Chamonix and Verbier involves two closure-prone passes – the Montets and the Forclaz. When necessary, one-way traffic runs beside the tracks through the rail tunnel beneath the passes.

linked directly to the big lift networks. These are not usually as convenient for the slopes, but they give you a feel of being in France rather than in a winter-holiday factory. Examples include Montchavin or Champagny for La Plagne, Vaujany for Alpe-d'Huez and St-Martin-de-Belleville for the Trois Vallées. There are also old villages with their own slopes that have developed as resorts while retaining at least some rustic ambience – such as Serre-Chevalier.

Two other resorts deserve a special mention. Megève is an exceptionally charming little town combining rustic style with sophistication. And then there is Chamonix, a big, bustling town sitting literally in the shadow of Mont Blanc, Europe's highest peak, and the centre of the most radical off-piste terrain in the Alps.

SKI SCHOOL COMPETITION

Gone are the days when the ESF was the only school in town. Most resorts now have lots of competing schools, which has lifted standards enormously. And many schools are now run and staffed by highly qualified British instructors – examples include New Generation and BASS, both of which have branches in several resorts and both of which reporters speak highly of.

PERFECT PISTES

France remains unusual among European countries in rating pistes on a four-point scale. The very easiest runs are classified green; except in Val d'Isère, they are reliably gentle. This is a genuinely helpful system, which ought to be used more widely. Some French resorts, sadly, make little use of it – notably Les Arcs and La Plagne.

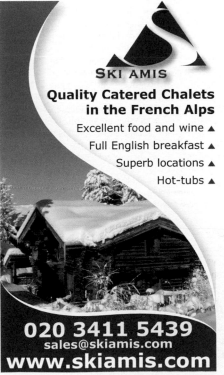

PLAT DU JOUR

Despite the prices, France has advantages in the gastronomic stakes. Table service in mountain restaurants is common, and most places do food – often including a plat du jour – that is in a different league from what you'll find in Austria or North America. In the evening, most resorts have restaurants serving good traditional French food and regional specialities.

DRIVING AMBITION?

The French Alps are easy to get to by car. Starting on page 71 there is a chapter on driving to the French Alps. Driving is still popular, despite the growth of budget airlines; for self-caterers it has the advantage of being able to stock up in good-value valley supermarkets.

AVOID THE CROWDS

French school holidays mean crowded slopes, so they are worth avoiding. The country is divided into three zones, with fortnight holidays staggered between 16 February and 17 March 2013. Avoid 2 to 17 March in particular, when Paris is on holiday.

OT ALPE-D'HUEZ / AGENCE NUTS

Alpe-d'Huez

Impressive and sunny slopes above a hotchpotch of a purpose-built village, but with attractive alternative bases

RATINGS

The mountains	
Extent	★★★★
Fast lifts	★★★★
Queues	★★★★
Terrain p'ks	★★★
Snow	★★★★
Expert	★★★★
Intermediate	★★★★
Beginner	★★★★★
Boarder	★★★★
X-country	★★★
Restaurants	★★★★
Schools	★★★★
Families	★★★
The resort	
Charm	★★
Convenience	★★★
Scenery	★★★★
Eating out	★★★★
Après-ski	★★★★
Off-slope	★★★★

RPI	100
lift pass	£180
ski hire	£115
lessons	£75
food & drink	£130
total	**£500**

KEY FACTS

Resort	1860m 6,100ft
Slopes	1100-3330m 3,610-10,920ft
Lifts	81
Pistes	250km 155 miles
Green	31%
Blue	26%
Red	31%
Black	12%
Snowmaking	32%

- + Extensive, high, sunny slopes, split interestingly into different sectors
- + Vast, gentle, sunny nursery slopes
- + Efficient access lifts from villages
- + Some good mountain restaurants
- + Livelier than many French resorts
- + Pleasant alternative bases

- − Some main intermediate runs get badly overcrowded in high season
- − Many runs get too much sun
- − Many of the tough runs are very high, and closed in bad weather
- − Practically no woodland runs
- − Spread out resort

There are few places to rival Alpe-d'Huez for extent and variety of terrain – in good wintery conditions it's one of our favourites. But as the season progresses the effects of the strong southern sun become more and more of a problem.

If you don't fancy staying in Alpe-d'Huez, think about the smaller bases described at the end of this chapter – especially Vaujany and Villard-Reculas.

THE RESORT

Alpe-d'Huez is a large, modern resort on a high, open, sunny plateau east of Grenoble. Although developed for skiing, it has grown in a seemingly unplanned, sprawling fashion.

The lift pass gives days in some other resorts. There are buses twice a week to Les Deux-Alpes, but the proper thing to do is go by helicopter – 'fantastic fun' (only 65 euros).

VILLAGE CHARM ★★

Bit of a hotchpotch

The nearest thing to a central focus is the main Avenue des Jeux in the middle, with an ice rink, indoor-outdoor swimming pool, shops, bars and restaurants. The buildings come in all shapes, sizes and designs but most new development is now in a pleasant chalet style. Reporters have remarked on the warm welcome from the locals.

CONVENIENCE ★★★

Good in clusters

The resort spreads down a gentle slope in a triangular shape from the main lift station at the top corner. Very few lodgings are ski-in/ski-out. Access roads enter at the two lower corners.

Various 'quarters' have been identified – the main village is divided into three. Vieil Alpe includes the original chalet-style part, at the bottom of the slope. During the day there's a bucket-lift (with a piste beneath it) running through the resort from here to the main lifts. This seems handy, but it opens too late in the morning, builds queues at peak times and goes slowly; some people don't like jumping on and off. Then there are four satellite 'quarters'. These are a bit of a trek from the centre but have their own lifts, bars and restaurants. The one where you are most likely to be offered lodgings is Les Bergers, beyond the eastern entrance to the resort; a chalet suburb is expanding this quarter uphill – convenient for skiing but even more remote from the village centre. A reader points out that there are no proper footways from these quarters to the main resort centre.

The free ski-bus service around the resort is infrequent but reliable.

SCENERY ★★★★

Splendid panoramic views

The resort has a fabulous high setting on a sunny plateau. There are splendid views of the southern Alps.

NEWS

2012/13: In Vaujany, a new ice rink is scheduled to open.

2011/12: A six-pack replaced the long, slow Fontfroide chair on Signal de l'Homme. And a new blue run, Pré-Rond, was created from the top towards Auris-en-Oisans. An old drag in the same area was removed. At Oz-en-Oisans a new blue slope and 16 more snow-guns were added.

A new 4-star hotel, the Alpenrose, opened in Les Bergers, near the lifts, and a CGH 4-star residence and spa, Le Cristal de l'Alpe, was new in the village centre.

More free off-slope activities were added to the lift pass. The Premium card is available as an extension, which includes equipment hire and use of the indoor pool and sports centre.

THE MOUNTAINS

Practically all the slopes are above the treeline, and so there may be little to do when a storm socks in or the wind picks up. Piste classification is very unreliable and provokes regular complaints from readers. The main problem is that some of the blues are too tough, but in some areas it's the opposite – reds that might be blue. Reporters generally find the piste map and signposting good.

EXTENT OF THE SLOPES ★★★★

Several well-linked areas

Alpe-d'Huez is a big-league resort, ranking alongside giants such as Val d'Isère or La Plagne for the extent and variety of its slopes. A notable feature is that it is possible to do many long runs with big verticals.

The slopes divide into four sectors, with good connections between them.

The biggest sector is directly above the village, on the slopes of **Pic Blanc**. The huge two-stage Grandes Rousses gondola, aka the DMC (a reference to its technology) and on the piste map marked as 'First Stage' and 'Second Stage', goes up from the top of the village. Above it, a cable car goes up to 3330m on Pic Blanc itself – the top of the small Sarenne glacier and start of the longest piste in the Alps (read our feature panel). The glacier is also reached via the Marmottes six-pack, then a two-stage gondola (the first stage of which also serves lower runs from Clocher de Macle).

The alternative from Pic Blanc is to take a 300m tunnel through the ridge

Mega-resort skiing from a quiet base? Check out Vaujany p211.

to the front face, where a west-facing black mogul field awaits you.

The Sarenne gorge separates the main resort area from **Signal de l'Homme**. It is crossed by a down-and-up fast chairlift from the Bergers part of the village. From the top you can take excellent north-facing slopes towards the gorge, or head south to Auris or west to tiny Chatelard.

On the other side of town from Signal de l'Homme is the small **Signal** sector, which is reached by draglifts next to the main gondola or by a couple of chairs lower down. Runs go down the other side of the hill to the old village of Villard-Reculas. One blue run back to Alpe-d'Huez is floodlit twice a week.

The **Vaujany-Oz** sector consists largely of north-west-facing slopes, accessible from Alpe-d'Huez via red runs. At the heart of this sector is Alpette, the mid-station of the cable car from Vaujany; it can also be reached by a gondola from Oz. A very sunny blue/red (now with much-needed snowmaking) goes down from Alpette to Oz, another blue (which boarders will find a bit flat in places) goes north to the Vaujany home slopes around Montfrais, and a shady black plunges down to L'Enversin, just below Vaujany. Using different black, red and blue pistes and ending up at L'Enversin gives an on-piste descent of 2230m vertical from Pic Blanc – one of the biggest in the world. The links

OT ALPE-D'HUEZ / LAURENT SALINOX

The world's longest run, the Sarenne, has fabulous panoramic views from the top →

back to Alpe-d'Huez are by cable car from Alpette, or a second gondola from Oz. You can also reach Oz from the top of the first stage of the DMC, followed by a long red run with a blue variant on the lower half.

FAST LIFTS ★★★★☆
Pretty efficient overall

Gondolas and fast chairs are the main access lifts and serve most areas adequately, but there are some old chairs and draglifts scattered around.

QUEUES ★★★★☆
Mainly at village level

Even in French holiday periods, there are few long hold-ups. Queues can build up for the lifts out of the village, but the DMC shifts its queue quickly. The Marmotte chairlift from the lower end of the village can cause bigger delays. The village bucket-lift is said to generate lengthy queues first thing. There can also be waits for the cable car up to Pic Blanc.

Over much of the area a greater problem than lift queues is that the main pistes can be unbearably crowded. We and many reporters rate the Chamois and Couloir runs from the top of the DMC gondola among the most crowded we've seen, anywhere. Really, something needs to be done about these runs, which are just getting worse and worse. The red runs to Vaujany and Oz can also be much too busy for comfort – 'carnage all the way', said one recent reporter of the Oz run.

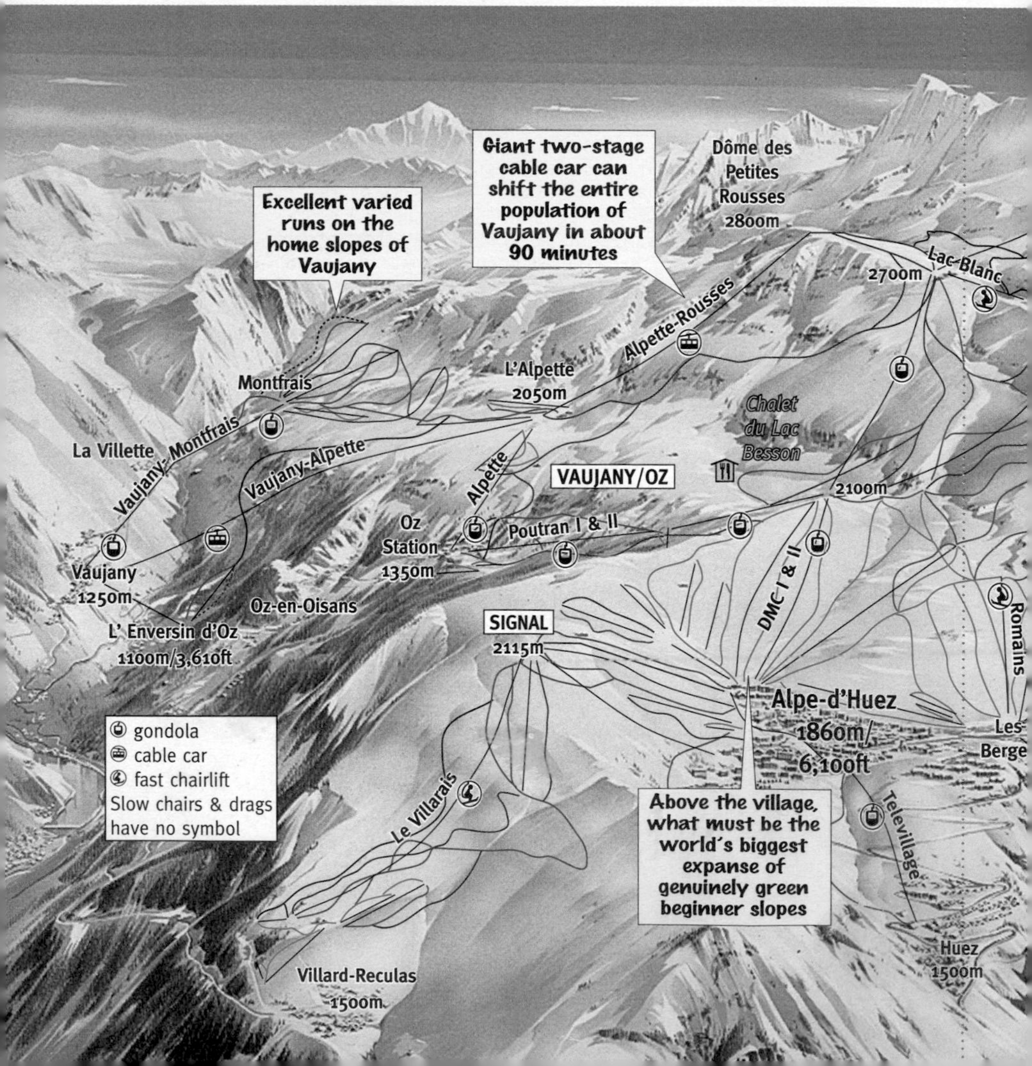

TERRAIN PARKS ★★★★★
Big and varied
A big park stretches almost all the way down the first stage of the DMC. One of our keen 'park rat' reporters says, It is definitely the best placed and possibly the best designed park I've seen. It has everything from an easy beginner line to enormous jumps and an airbag, with lots of rails too.' Other 2012 reporters praised it as well. There's a half-pipe and boardercross ('good; fast and aggressive') too. There's also a beginners' park above Vaujany. The ESF runs some freestyle courses for teenagers.

SNOW RELIABILITY ★★★★★
Affected by the sun
Alpe-d'Huez is unique among major purpose-built resorts in the Alps in having mainly south- or south-west-facing slopes. The strong southern sun means that late-season conditions may alternate between slush and ice on most runs, with some lower runs closed altogether. There are shady slopes above Vaujany and at Signal de l'Homme. The glacier area is small.

Mega-resort skiing from a quiet base? Check out Vaujany p211.

In midwinter the runs are relatively snow-sure, thanks to extensive snowmaking on the main runs above Alpe-d'Huez, Vaujany and Oz. In 2011 a reader pointed out that the piste through the resort, down the bucket-lift, does not have snowmaking and often needs it. A 2012 reader agrees but says, 'The pisteurs did a great job

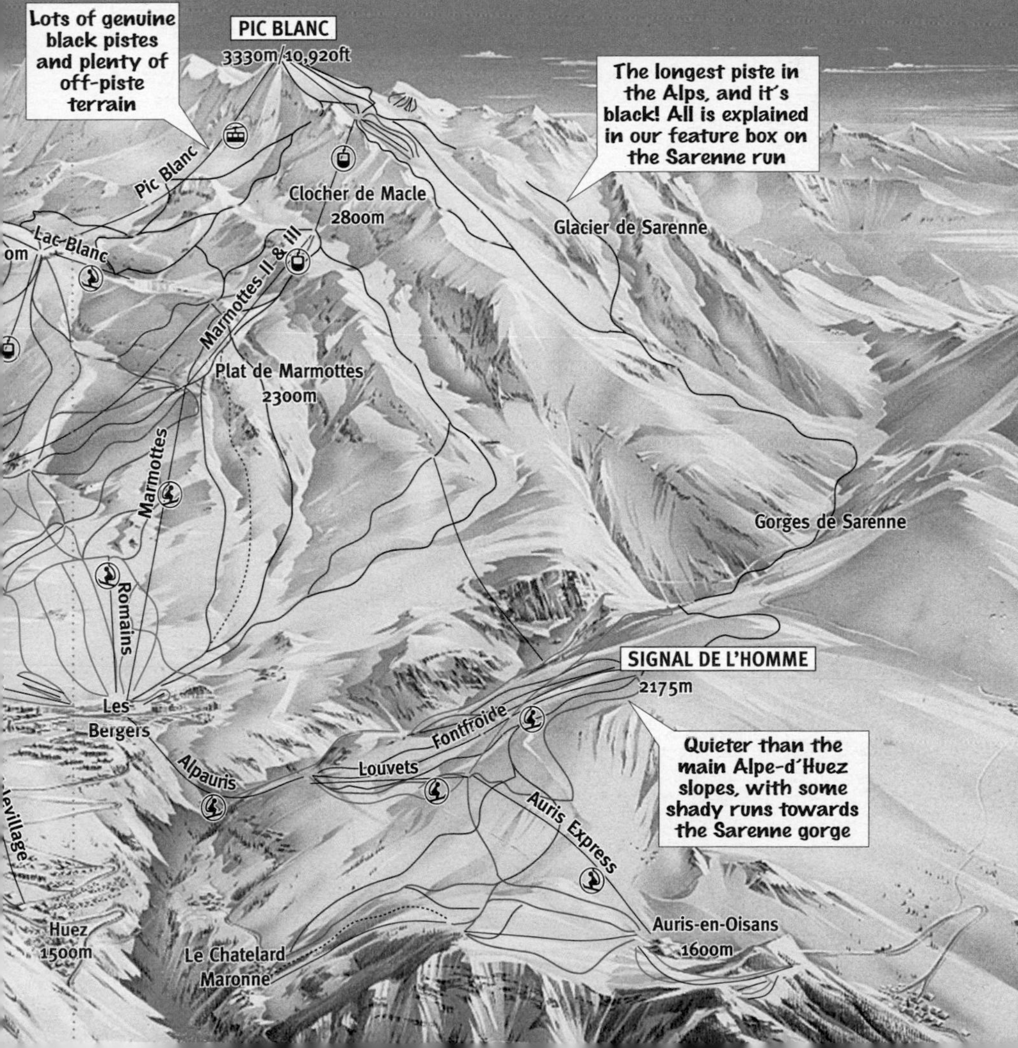

THE LONGEST PISTE IN THE ALPS – AND IT'S BLACK?

It's no surprise that most ski runs that are seriously steep are also seriously short. The really long runs in the Alps tend to be classified blue, or red at the most. The Parsenn runs above Klosters, for example – typically 12km to 15km long – are manageable in your first week on skis.

So you could be forgiven for being sceptical about the 'black' Sarenne run from the Pic Blanc: even with an impressive vertical of 2000m, a run 16km in length means an average gradient of only 11% – typical of a blue run. But the Sarenne is a run of two halves. The bottom half is virtually flat (boarders beware), but the top half is a genuine black if you take the direct route – a demanding and highly satisfying run (with stunning views) that any keen, competent and fit skier will enjoy. The steep mogul field near the top can be avoided by taking an easier option (or by using the Marmottes III gondola); and the whole run can be tackled by an adventurous intermediate. It gets a lot of sun, so pick your time with care – there's nothing worse than a sunny run with no sun. Occasionally during the season you can ski the Sarenne by moonlight or wearing a head torch: take the last lift up, have a 'simple meal', then ski down with guides. The cost is 65 euros per person.

pushing epic amounts of snow on to it every night.'

FOR EXPERTS ★★★★

Plenty of blacks and off-piste

There are long and challenging pistes as well as some serious off-piste routes. The black slope beneath the Pic Blanc cable car will be on your agenda. Despite improvements to the tunnel exit, the start of the actual slope is often awkward. The slope is of ordinary black steepness, but can be very hard in the mornings because it gets the afternoon sun. Get information on its condition. The long Sarenne run on the back of Pic Blanc is described in the panel above.

Thanks to snowmaking, we've been able to ski the black Fare piste to L'Enversin on each of our last two visits – a highly enjoyable and varied long run, away from the lifts but not steep (really of red gradient with some blue sections, we thought). The Marmottes II gondola serves genuine black runs and a red from Clocher de Macle; Balcons is steep and quiet, often with good snow; Clocher de Macle is easier but busier; don't miss the beautiful, long, lonely Combe Charbonnière (but there's a fairly long traverse on moderately steep ground at the start). The Lièvre Blanc chairlift serves further testing slopes – Balme, looping away from the lifts, is a black, and one or two reds would be classified black in many resorts, especially when grooming is poor or non-existent. In good snow conditions, the steep La Fuma run down to Le Chatelard Maronne is worth trying. And the Col de Cluy from Signal de l'Homme is long and gets away from all the lifts.

The off-piste possibilities are immense, and some are described in the feature panel later in the chapter. Some of these routes away from the lifts are shady, in contrast to the pistes of the main sector.

FOR INTERMEDIATES ★★★★

Fine selection of runs

Good intermediates have a fine selection of runs all over the area. In good snow conditions the variety of runs is difficult to beat.

Every section has some challenging red runs to test the adventurous intermediate. The Canyon run is one of the most challenging. There are lovely long runs down to Oz – the Champclotury blue from the mid-station of the gondola above Oz is a lovely, gentle run and usually quiet – and to Vaujany, with space for some serious carving. The Villard-Reculas and Signal de l'Homme sectors also have long challenging reds. Those at Signal de L'Homme are quieter, which keeps their snow better. The Chamois red from the top of the gondola down to the mid-station is quite narrow, and miserable when busy and icy and/or heavily mogulled. Fearless intermediates should enjoy the super-long Sarenne black run.

For less ambitious intermediates, there are usually blue alternatives, except on the upper part of the mountain. The main Couloir blue from the top of the big gondola is a lovely run, well served by snowmaking, but like the red Chamois it does get scarily crowded at times.

There are some great cruising runs above Vaujany; but the red runs between Vaujany and Alpe-d'Huez can be too much for early intermediates.

LIFT PASSES

Ski+

Prices in €

Age	1-day	6-day
under 13	34	161
13 to 64	43	215
65 to 71	34	161
72 plus	13	65

Free under 5

Beginner four free lifts; Première Glisse pass covers 19 lifts

Notes
Covers Alpe-d'Huez, Auris, Oz, Vaujany and Villard-Reculas; half-day passes; discounts for families and regular visitors; 2-day+ passes cover ice rink, swimming pool, night skiing and sledding, two museums; 6-day-plus passes allow one day's skiing at each of Serre-Chevalier, Puy-St-Vincent and the Milky Way in Italy, and two days in Les Deux-Alpes

Alternative passes
Alpe-d'Huez only, Auris only, Oz-Vaujany only, Villard-Reculas only; pedestrian

GETTING THERE

Air Lyon 155km/ 95 miles (2hr30); Geneva 210km/ 130 miles (3hr30); Grenoble, 105km/ 65 miles (2hr15)

Rail Grenoble (63km/ 39 miles); daily buses from station

You can travel via Oz on gondolas if you are that keen to get around.

Early intermediates will also enjoy the gentle slopes leading back to Alpe-d'Huez from the main mountain, and the Signal sector. But the unreliable piste grading (see remarks under 'The mountains') can make life scary for early intermediates, never knowing what to expect.

FOR BEGINNERS ★★★★★

Good facilities

The large networks of green runs immediately above the village and above the Les Bergers area form nursery areas as good as you will find anywhere. Sadly, these slopes get very crowded and carry a lot of fast through-traffic. Both areas have been declared low-speed zones, but the restrictions are not policed and so achieve very little. Four beginner lifts are free, and a special lift pass covers more lifts to progress to.

FOR BOARDERS ★★★★

Suits the adventurous

The resort suits experienced boarders well – the extent and variety of the mountains mean that there's a lot of good freeriding to be had; the off-piste is vast and varied and well worth checking out with a guide. The terrain park is good, too. There are quite a few flat areas to beware of though. The nursery slopes are excellent for learning but accessed mainly by draglifts (which can be avoided once a modicum of control has been achieved). Planète Surf is the main snowboard shop.

Mega-resort skiing from a quiet base? Check out Vaujany p211.

FOR CROSS-COUNTRY ★★★

High-level and convenient

There are 50km of trails, with three loops of varying degrees of difficulty, all at around 2000m and consequently relatively snow-sure.

MOUNTAIN RESTAURANTS ★★★★

Some excellent rustic huts

Mountain restaurants are generally good – even self-service places are pleasant, and there are more rustic places with table-service than is usual in high French resorts. But the restaurants in the more obvious positions get over-busy, and some charge for the toilets. The piste map does not identify restaurants. Get hold of the resort's pocket restaurant guide, which covers 15 places, and marks them on a tiny piste map.

Editors' choice Compared with the main places, the cosy little Chalet du Lac Besson (0476 806537) is an oasis of calm – tucked away on the cross-country loops north of the DMC gondola mid-station (and reached by a special access piste, the Boulevard des Lacs). Food and service are excellent. It's repeatedly endorsed by reporters and worth the effort to get to.

Worth knowing about There are a couple of good spots low down – not mountain restaurants as such, but very popular targets nonetheless. The pretty little Forêt de Maronne hotel at Chatelard, below Signal de l'Homme, does good food and has 'very reasonable prices, charming staff'. The

OT ALPE-D'HUEZ / MARK BUSCAIL

The piste through the resort links the main lifts to the old part of the resort and goes right past the lovely outdoor pool and ice rink →

SCHOOLS

ESF
t 0476 803169

Easyski International
t 0476 804277

Masterclass
t 0679 673456

Stance
t 0680 755572

Classes (ESF prices)
6 days (3hr am and 2½hr pm) €224

Private lessons
€44 for 1hr, for 1 or 2 people

GUIDES

Mountain guide office
t 0476 804255

CHILDCARE

Les Intrépides
t 0476 112161
Ages 3mnth to 4yr

Les Eterlous (ESF)
t 0476 803169
Ages 2½ to 5

Tonton Mayonnaise
(Easysky)
t 0476 804277
Ages 2½ to 3½

Ski schools
From 4 to 12 (ESF 6 days €224)

'cosy' Bergerie at Villard-Reculas is an old farmhouse with 'outstanding' views, and 'inexpensive' food.

The Combe Haute, at the foot of the Chalvet chair in the gorge towards the end of the Sarenne run has reportedly been refurbished and now 'serves lovely food in charming, rustic surroundings', but gets busy. The Signal is quieter and has great views. The Perce Neige, just below the Oz-Poutran gondola mid-station, has a wood-burning stove inside and good terrace, and does 'terrific salads and a lovely speciality chocolate cake'.

The restaurants in the Oz and Vaujany sectors tend to be cheaper, but no less satisfactory. At Montfrais, the Airelles is a rustic hut, built into the rock, with a roaring log fire; we get repeated enthusiastic reports – 'excellent plat du jour', 'lovely food, fast service, friendly staff'. Nearby, Au P'tit Truc is 'good value with well prepared food'. The Auberge de l'Alpette and the Grange at Alpette have also been recommended by recent reporters.

SCHOOLS AND GUIDES ★★★★

Plenty of choice

We get mixed reports on the ESF. A 2012 reporter's three-year-old had his first lesson and enjoyed it. Last year, we heard of an excellent private lesson but of a beginner class receiving 'minimal' tuition. We've also heard of a good off-piste group for a week but of intermediate classes spoilt by poor allocation of pupils to classes and an instructor who could speak very little English.

A 2012 visitor used two competing smaller schools – ESI ('enjoyable boarding with good progress') and Masterclass, which is made up of British instructors and run by Stuart Adamson ('the two English guys made skiing enjoyable for the kids, but it's not cheap'). Stance is run by two experienced instructors and specializes in teaching British clients.

FOR FAMILIES ★★★

Positive reports

There's Les Intrépides day care centre for children aged three months to four years – 'first class'. The children's garden and nursery (for children aged six months to five years) at Vaujany have been recommended. Family specialist Esprit now operates here (read 'Chalets' in the next section).

OFF-PISTE FOR ALL STANDARDS

There are vast amounts of off-piste terrain in Alpe-d'Huez, from fairly tame to seriously adventurous. Here we pick out just a few of the many runs to be explored – always with guidance, of course.

There are lots of off-piste variants on both sides of the Sarenne run that are good for making your first turns off-piste. The ***Combe du Loup,*** *a beautiful south-facing bowl with views over the Meije, has a black-run gradient at the top, and you end up on long, gentle slopes leading back to the Sarenne gorge.* ***La Chapelle Saint Giraud,*** *which starts at Signal de l'Homme, includes a series of small, confidence-boosting bowls, interspersed with gentle rolling terrain.*

For more experienced and adventurous off-piste skiers, the ***Grand Sablat*** *is a classic that runs through a magnificently wild setting on the eastern face of the Massif des Grandes Rousses. This descent of 2000m vertical includes glacial terrain and some steep couloirs. You can either ski down to the village of Clavans, where you can take a pre-booked helicopter or taxi back, or traverse above Clavans back to the Sarenne gorge. In the* ***Signal*** *sector, there are various classic routes down towards the village of Huez or to Villard-Reculas.*

The north-facing Vaujany sector is particularly interesting for experienced off-piste enthusiasts. Route finding can be very tricky, and huge cliffs and rock bands mean this is not a place to get lost. From the top of Pic Blanc, a 40-minute hike takes you to Col de la Pyramide at 3250m, the starting point for the classic route ***La Pyramide*** *with a vertical of over 2000m. Once at the bottom of the long and wide Pyramide snowfield, you can link into the Vaujany pistes.*

ACTIVITIES

Indoor Sports centre (tennis, gym, squash, aerobics, swimming, shooting range, climbing wall, adventure trail), sauna, cinemas, concerts, theatre, library, museum

Outdoor Ice rink, curling, cleared walking paths, tobogganing, dog sledding, snowshoeing, snowmobiling, microlight flights, sightseeing flights, ice cave, skijoring, off-road vehicle tours, hang-gliding, paragliding, ice driving school, snowkiting

Phone numbers
From abroad use the prefix +33 and omit the initial '0' of the phone number

TOURIST OFFICE

www.alpedhuez.com

STAYING THERE

There's quite a good range here. There is a Club Med in the Bergers quarter, which a recent reporter praised.

Chalets Skiworld leads the pack with half a dozen chalets including some with hot tub and sauna and one 30-bed property. Crystal has three chalets plus a central 34-bed chalet hotel. Ski Total has five chalets, most with sauna and one with outdoor hot tub. Inghams has two chalets (one with outdoor hot tub, one with sauna) plus a 70-bed chalet hotel. Family specialist Esprit has a 60-bed chalet hotel in the old village: 'Childcare top-notch, location perfect; staff were troopers,' said a 2012 reporter.

Hotels There are more hotels than is usual in a high French resort – mainly 3-star – but we get few reports from readers. More reports welcome.

******Alpenrose** (0427 042804) New 4-star in Les Bergers, opened for the 2011/12 season. Near the lifts.

******Au Chamois d'Or** (0476 803132) Good facilities, modern rooms, one of the best restaurants in town and well placed for the main gondola.

*****Pic Blanc** (0476 114242) Across the car park from the Les Bergers lifts. Comfortable; on a recent visit we stayed in a big ('superior') room.

*****Royal Ours Blanc** (0476 650765) Heart of the village; pool, sauna, steam, hot tub. 'Great little hotel, warm rooms, good food, nice staff.'

Apartments There are lots available, though few are notable. The big news last season was the opening of the very smart residence Cristal de l'Alpe with pool, hot tubs, fitness stuff etc, and a prime central location. The Pierre & Vacances residence Ours Blanc is central and recently refurbished; reporters have also been happy with P&V's residence Les Bergers, with outdoor pool. Ski Collection and Erna Low offer these properties, and also have individual chalets to rent. Skiworld has a flexible catered chalet – where you can choose what catering (if any) you want – and apartments.

EATING OUT ★★★★

Good value

Alpe-d'Huez has dozens of restaurants, some of high quality; many offer good value by resort standards.

Widely thought to be about the best is Au P'tit Creux. We've had a fabulous meal here (foie gras, carré d'agneau, mango tatin), and over several years we've had rave reviews from reporters, too. Last year's reporters tip more modest places: Smithy's Tavern ('great place for reasonably priced food – Tex-Mex') and Au Trappeur ('super and good-value pizza'). A recent reporter who worked his way round the resort rated the set menu at the Grenier 'fantastic value' and also approved of the Pomme de Pin and the Taverne.

APRES-SKI ★★★★

Plenty going on

There's a wide range of bars, some of which get fairly lively later on. There are several British-run bars in chalet hotels. One is the Underground in Vieil Alpe – 'very pleasant, with live music most nights', according to a reporter. Smithy's Tavern has plenty of atmosphere. Other places tipped by reporters include Lounge21, O'Bar and the Pacific (sister bar to the one in Val d'Isère). There are reportedly three late-night places: the Sporting (pricey though – '10 euros for a beer'), the Igloo and the Caves des Alpes.

OFF THE SLOPES ★★★★

Good by high-resort standards

There is a wide range of facilities, praised by recent non-skiers, including a big and very popular indoor-outdoor pool ('warm, with friendly staff') and an Olympic-size ice rink – both covered by the lift pass – plus an indoor pool and a splendid sports centre. There's also an ice driving school and a toboggan run. You can try paragliding and snowmobiling. Visits to the Ice Cave are highly recommended by reporters. Shopping is not impressive.

The helicopter excursion to Les Deux-Alpes is exciting, though you may want to establish exactly where it drops you. There are 250km of well-marked walkers' trails (map available), the lifts 'cope well with pedestrians', and there's a special lift pass. The better mountain restaurants are widely spread though – and some are too remote for pedestrians. You can take a sleigh ride, there are weekly church organ concerts, and there's a museum.

Don't miss the latest in Austria. Check out p168.

UK PACKAGES

Alpine Answers, Club Med, Crystal, Erna Low, Esprit, Independent Ski Links, Inghams, Interactive Resorts, La Source, Lagrange, Mountain Wave, Neilson, Oxford Ski Co, Pierre & Vacances, Powder White, PowderBeds, Richmond Holidays, Rocketski, Ski Collection, Ski Expectations, Ski France, Ski Independence, Ski Line, Ski Solutions, Ski Supreme, Ski Total, Skitracer, Skiworld, Thomson, VIP, Zenith

Villard-Reculas La Source

Oz-en-Oisans AmeriCan Ski, Erna Low, Lagrange, Peak Retreats, Ski France

Vaujany AmeriCan Ski, Erna Low, Peak Retreats, Pierre & Vacances, PowderBeds, Ski France, Ski Independence, Ski Peak

LINKED RESORT – 1500m

VILLARD-RECULAS

Villard-Reculas is a charming, secluded village just over the hill (Signal) from Alpe-d'Huez, complete with an old church and set on a small shelf between open snowfields above and tree-filled hillsides below. A fast quad takes you up to Signal.

Accommodation is mainly in apartments and chalets, booked either through the tourist office or La Source – an English-run agency that also runs a comfortable catered chalet in a carefully converted stone barn with outdoor hot tub. It is highly recommended by reporters: 'Charming chalet, excellent food, superb views, personal service, minibus transfers to and from slopes,' says a 2012 reporter. There is a 2-star hotel, the Beaux Monts (0476 804314), and a couple of restaurants and bars. The village is very quiet in the evenings.

The local slopes have something for everyone, including a nursery slope at village level. But more than one reporter has warned that the blue runs above the village are not entirely easy, especially when snow is not good, making this an awkward place for beginners and near-beginners. A recent visitor found the ESF 'excellent'.

LINKED RESORT – 1350m

OZ-EN-OISANS STATION

The small purpose-built ski station above the old village of the same name has been built in an attractive style, with much use of wood and stone, and has nursery slopes, skating rink, bars, restaurants, supermarket and two mid-range hotels. The pool in the Villages Club du Soleil is open to all. But nightlife is quiet.

Two gondolas whisk you out of the resort: one goes to Alpette, above Vaujany; the other goes in two stages to the mid-station of the DMC above Alpe-d'Huez. The main run home is liberally endowed with snow-guns, but it needs to be. One clear advantage of staying here is that the slopes above Oz are about the best in the area when heavy snow is falling – and those based elsewhere may not be able to reach them.

The smart Chalet des Neiges apartments have a pool, sauna, fitness area, bar and restaurant. Available via Peak Retreats, Lagrange and Erna Low.

LINKED RESORT – 1600m

AURIS-EN-OISANS

Auris-en-Oisans is another small, purpose-built ski station – a series of wood-clad, chalet-style apartment blocks with a few shops, bars and restaurants set just above the treeline. It's a compact family resort, with a ski school, nursery and ski kindergarten. Unsurprisingly, evenings are quiet. The Beau Site (0476 800639) looks like an apartment block but is the only hotel.

Beneath the resort is the original old village of Auris, with traditional buildings, a church and a few hotels, including the traditional Auberge de la Forêt (0476 800601).

Phone numbers
From abroad use the prefix +33 and omit the initial '0' of the phone number

TOURIST OFFICES

Villard-Reculas
www.villard-reculas.com

Oz-en-Oisans
www.oz-en-oisans.com

Auris-en-Oisans
www.auris-en-oisans.com

Vaujany
www.vaujany.com

Access to the slopes of Alpe-d'Huez is no problem and returning to Auris should be easier for novices with the new Pré-Rond blue. There are plenty of local slopes to explore, for which there is a special lift pass. Most runs are intermediate, though Auris is also the best of the local hamlets for beginners.

LINKED RESORT – 1250m

VAUJANY

Vaujany is a quiet, rapidly growing village, perched on a sunny hillside opposite its own sector of the domain. Hydroelectricity riches have financed huge investment in lifts and other infrastructure.

A giant 160-person two-stage cable car whisks you up into the heart of the Alpe-d'Huez lift system. Alternatively, a two-stage gondola takes you less dramatically to the local slopes at Montfrais via a mid-station below the tiny hamlet of La Villette.

As you enter the village, you come to a couple of small, simple hotels. The Rissiou is well run by British tour operator Ski Peak: 'delicious food and helpful staff'. Ski Peak also has half a dozen luxurious catered chalets in Vaujany and La Villette plus ten 5-star apartments. It runs a minibus service for guests. Peak Retreats (no relation) has a wide choice of apartments.

You then come to a recently built complex around a small pedestrian square, Place Centre Village, with spacious, mid-range apartments built in traditional style. There's a good ski shop, restaurants, food shops, a cafe/bar and a cavernous underground car park – and an escalator down to the nearby cable car and gondola stations. An elevator takes you further down the hill to the superb sports centre with 'fantastic pool and big slide'. A new ice rink will be ready for 2012/13. A bowling alley is planned, too.

An impressive enclosed escalator goes up the hillside past chalets and farm buildings to the top of the village, where sizeable apartment buildings are grouped around the Place de la Fare – a small car-free zone with a small supermarket, a food shop, a couple of bars and a couple of restaurants. Since most of the visitor beds are up here, it is naturally the focus of evening activity.

There are no slopes leading directly to the village. But there is a 'pulse' gondola up from L'Enversin, below the village, where the Fare black run finishes (a great run and not steep – read 'For experts' earlier in this chapter), or you can take a blue to the mid-station of the Montfrais gondola and ride down the lower stage.

Beginner children are taken to a gentle roped-off area at the top of the gondola and adult beginners to the nursery slope at Alpette, the cable car mid-station. There's a good self-service restaurant with sunny terrace right by the children's learning area. The children's ski school has been praised ('well organized by a local Brit') as has the nursery ('as good as it gets, good English spoken, not expensive').

SNOWPIX.COM / CHRIS GILL

Les Arcs

Three first-generation purpose-built villages plus a cute modern alternative – with an exceptional variety and extent of slopes

RATINGS

The mountains	
Extent	***
Fast lifts	****
Queues	****
Terrain p'ks	****
Snow	****
Expert	*****
Intermediate	****
Beginner	***
Boarder	****
X-country	**
Restaurants	**
Schools	****
Families	****
The resort	
Charm	**
Convenience	****
Scenery	***
Eating out	***
Après-ski	**
Off-slope	*

RPI	100
lift pass	£200
ski hire	£110
lessons	£80
food & drink	£130
total	**£520**

KEY FACTS

Resort	1600-2120m 5,250-6,960ft
Slopes	1200-3225m 3,940-10,580ft
Lifts	51
Pistes	200km 124 miles
Green	1%
Blue	51%
Red	30%
Black	18%
Snowmaking	226 guns
Paradiski area	
Slopes	1200-3250m 3,940-10,660ft
Lifts	144
Pistes	425km 264 miles
Green	4%
Blue	52%
Red	28%
Black	16%
Snowmaking	755 guns

- + Varied pistes, easy-to-reach off-piste
- + Lots of genuinely challenging skiing
- + Some excellent woodland runs
- + Car-free, mainly convenient villages, including cute 1950
- + Some quiet alternative bases
- + Fast cable car link to La Plagne

- − Original village centres lack charm, and aren't the most convenient
- − Some areas still blighted by slow old chairlifts
- − Fairly quiet nightlife
- − Lots of flat linking runs
- − Accommodation in high villages is nearly all in apartments

We've always liked Les Arcs' slopes: they offer long descents, plenty of steep stuff, and woods to head to in a storm. And for those who really like to travel on skis, the link to La Plagne takes you into the Trois Vallées league.

We've never been keen on the functional main villages. We're aware that their various architectural styles are highly regarded by some; we're not among them, but our real objection is to their dreary, depressing mall-style shopping centres. Newer Arc 1950 is something else: a resort that's not only more pleasant to inhabit than the others, but also very conveniently arranged.

THE RESORT

Les Arcs is made up of four modern resort units, all purpose-built, traffic-free and apartment-dominated.

Arc 1600 and 1800 stand a couple of km apart, roughly at the treeline on a broad, steepish mountainside overlooking the town of Bourg-St-Maurice (covered at the end of this chapter). Both consist mainly of large apartment blocks sitting below their slopes, with some development beside the slopes. 1600 was the first Arc, built at the top of a funicular up from Bourg. 1800 is much the largest Arc.

Arc 2000 is quite separate – on the far side of the mountain ridge, at the bottom of a high, treeless bowl. It consists of half a dozen huge, linked apartment blocks, plus more recently built chalet-style blocks. Just below Arc 2000 and linked to it by a short gondola, the newish mini-village of Arc 1950 is built in traditional style – read the margin panel.

The numbers in the village names relate only loosely to their altitudes. 'Arc 2000' was dreamt up in the 60s to evoke the millennium – the future; its altitude is actually over 2100m.

At the southern end of the area is Peisey-Vallandry, from where a cable car links with La Plagne, covered by the Paradiski passes. Even from Arc 1950 you can be at the cable car in 20 minutes. At the northern end of the ski area, at much lower altitude, is the rustic hamlet of Villaroger. These outlying villages are described at the end of the chapter.

Day trips by car to Val d'Isère-Tignes are possible. La Rosière and

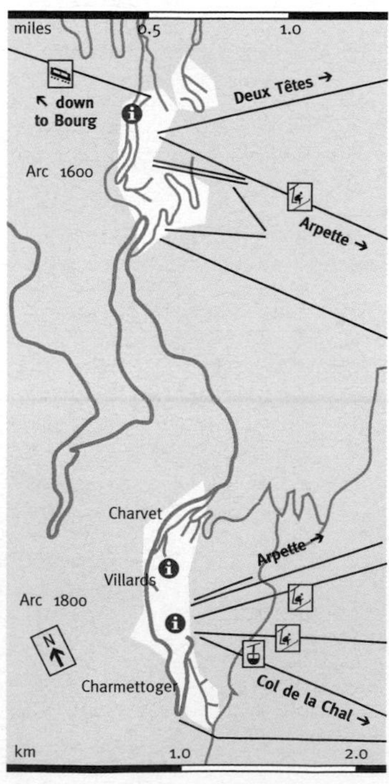

NEWS

2012/13: The second phase of the smart new Edenarc development above Arc 1800 is expected to open, plus a new 4-star hotel at 1800, the Chalets de l'Aiguille Grive.

2011/12: A six-pack replaced the slow Mont Blanc chair and a drag lift above it, from Arc 1600 to Les Deux Têtes. A drag was removed at the 1600 base. Snowmaking was added in the Villaroger, Peisey-Vallandry and Mont Blanc areas. A new spa and swimming pool complex opened in Arc 1950. And the first apartments opened in the Edenarc residence. There's also a new toboggan run at Col de la Chal.

Ste-Foy-Tarentaise are closer. Be warned: you have to pay for parking at Arcs 1950 and 2000 – the only free parking is throughout 1600 and before the entrance to 1800.

VILLAGE CHARM ★★★★★
Head for 1950

Reporters repeatedly comment on the friendliness of the locals.

The apartment blocks of Arc 1600 and 1800 are low-rise, and not hugely intrusive when seen from the slopes. Arc 1600 is set in the trees and has a friendly, small-scale atmosphere. Bigger Arc 1800 has three main parts. Le Charvet and Les Villards are focused on small shopping centres, mostly open-air but still seeming claustrophobic. Big apartment blocks run across and down the mountain. Charmettoger has apartment blocks, too, but also smaller, wood-clad buildings. Le Charvet has spread up the hill in recent years, and now has an identifiable suburb, Le Chantel. At the very top, the new Edenarc development is taking shape.

Arc 2000 consists of futuristic large blocks with swooping roof lines, plus some large chalet-style blocks.

Arc 1950 has been designed to be cute; its smaller apartment buildings have been finished in traditional style, and they are clustered around a pleasant, traffic-free square and street – quite lively at close of play.

CONVENIENCE ★★★★★
Generally very good

Arcs 1600 and 1800 offer some very convenient lodgings, a few yards from the lifts, but also some that are less convenient than they look – you can walk miles within the apartment buildings to get to (and from) the snow. The central area in Arc 1600 is good for families: uncrowded, compact, and set on even ground. Arc 1800 is more spread out, and some lodging is further up the hill, well above the village itself. The main lifts depart from Les Villards.

Arc 2000 and Arc 1950 are compact, ski-in/ski-out places, with lifts starting below them as well as above. But getting around Arc 2000 on foot can be quite an effort, reporters tell us. All the bits of Arc 1950 we've looked at are genuinely ski-in/ski-out. You park directly under the apartment buildings, which is a rare bonus at the start and end of your stay.

SCENERY ★★★★★
Attractively varied

Arcs 1600 and 1800, and the slopes, enjoy views across the valley to Mont Blanc. The lower villages enjoy good views along the Nancroix valley and to La Plagne's splendid north face of Bellecôte. Higher up, Arc 2000 and Arc 1950 sit beneath the Aiguille Rouge, high-point of the slopes – great views from the top.

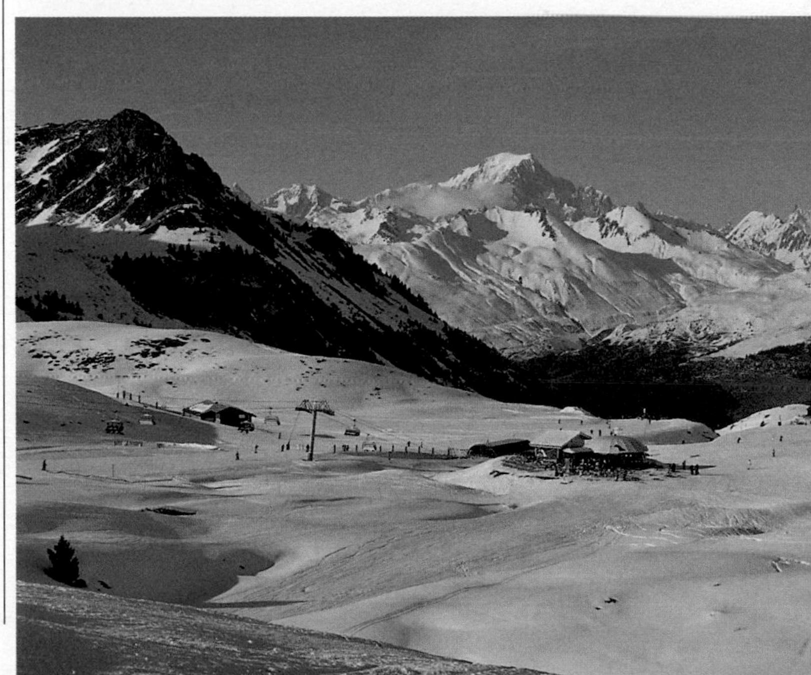

SNOWPIX.COM / CHRIS GILL

Fine views from the Arc 2000 bowl of Mont Blanc (and La Rosière – the village is just on the snow line) →

THE MOUNTAINS

Les Arcs' terrain is notably varied; it has a good mixture of high, open, snow-sure slopes and lower woodland runs (notably above Peisey-Vallandry). The piste map attempts a kind of photo-realism, and is unclear in places as a result.

EXTENT OF THE SLOPES ★★★

Well planned and varied

Our rating relates to just the Les Arcs area; the whole Paradiski area easily scores five stars.

Arc 1600 and Arc 1800 share a west-facing mountainside laced with runs down to one or other village. At the southern end is an area of woodland runs above Peisey-Vallandry.

From various points on the ridge above 1600 and 1800 you can head down into the wide Arc 2000 bowl. From there, lifts take you to the high points of the area, the Aiguille Rouge and the Grand Col. As well as a variety of steep runs back to Arc 2000, the Aiguille Rouge is the start of an epic run (over 2000m vertical and 7km long) down to Villaroger.

The resort identifies nine black runs and one red as Natur' (never groomed) pistes. On the lower half of the Aiguille Rouge is a speed-skiing run, which is sometimes open to the public.

FAST LIFTS ★★★★

Steady progress

Each of the four main villages has fast chair or gondola access to the slopes and a new six-pack from Arc 1600 was built for 2011/12, replacing not one but two slow lifts. The main irritants now are the chairs on both sides of Les Deux Têtes, between Arc 1600 and Arc 2000, and the chain of three chairs up from Villaroger.

QUEUES ★★★★

Not without problems

Queues aren't generally an issue in low season, and peak-time queues are

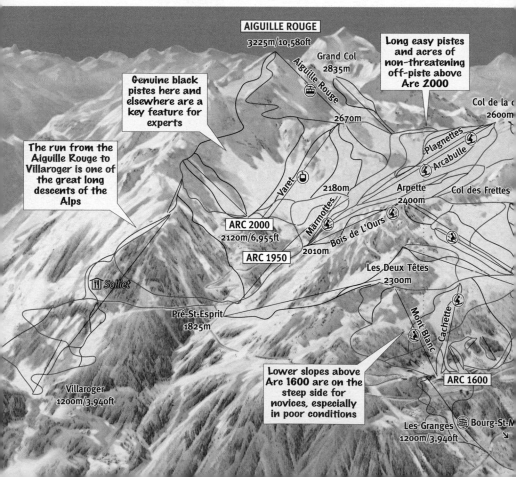

AIGUILLE ROUGE 3225m/10,58oft

Grand Col 2835m

Long easy pistes and acres of non-threatening off-piste above Arc 2000

Genuine black pistes here and elsewhere are a key feature for experts

The run from the Aiguille Rouge to Villaroger is one of the great long descents of the Alps

Aiguille Rouge

Col de la 2600m

2670m

Plagnettes

Arcabulle

Varet

2180m

Arpette 2400m

Col des Frettes

Marmottes

Bois de L'Ours

ARC 2000 2120m/6,955ft

2010m

ARC 1950

Les Deux Têtes 2300m

Solliet

Pré-St-Esprit 1825m

Mont Blanc

Cachette

Lower slopes above Arc 1600 are on the steep side for novices, especially in poor conditions

ARC 1600

Villaroger 1200m/3,940ft

Les Granges 1200m/3,940ft

Bourg-St-M

improving. But the lifts above Arc 2000 present problems, especially on sunny days. The Varet gondola to the shoulder of the Aiguille Rouge is always busy but shifts its queue quickly because it has lifties pulling people out of the queue to fill the cabins – excellent. Queues for the cable car to the top can be serious in clear weather; go at lunchtime, or late in the day, to avoid them. The Arcabulle chair has the potential for 'five-to-ten-minute waits'. At 1800 the Transarc gondola is queue prone, especially late in the day. At 1600 the Cachette chair has had difficulty coping with morning crowds arriving on the funicular from the valley – but these will presumably have been relieved by the new six-pack next to it (we lack high-season reports that might confirm this). At Plan Peisey, morning queues for the Peisey chair (and for the Derby above it) are not unknown, partly because of arrivals on the cable car from La Plagne.

At peak periods dangerously crowded pistes can be more of a problem than the queues.

TERRAIN PARKS ★★★★

One excellent park

The Apocalypse Parc is between Arc 1600 and 1800, and served by a snowboarder-friendly J-bar lift. For years, this has been one of the most advanced parks in the Alps – on a par with the main park at Avoriaz. Three

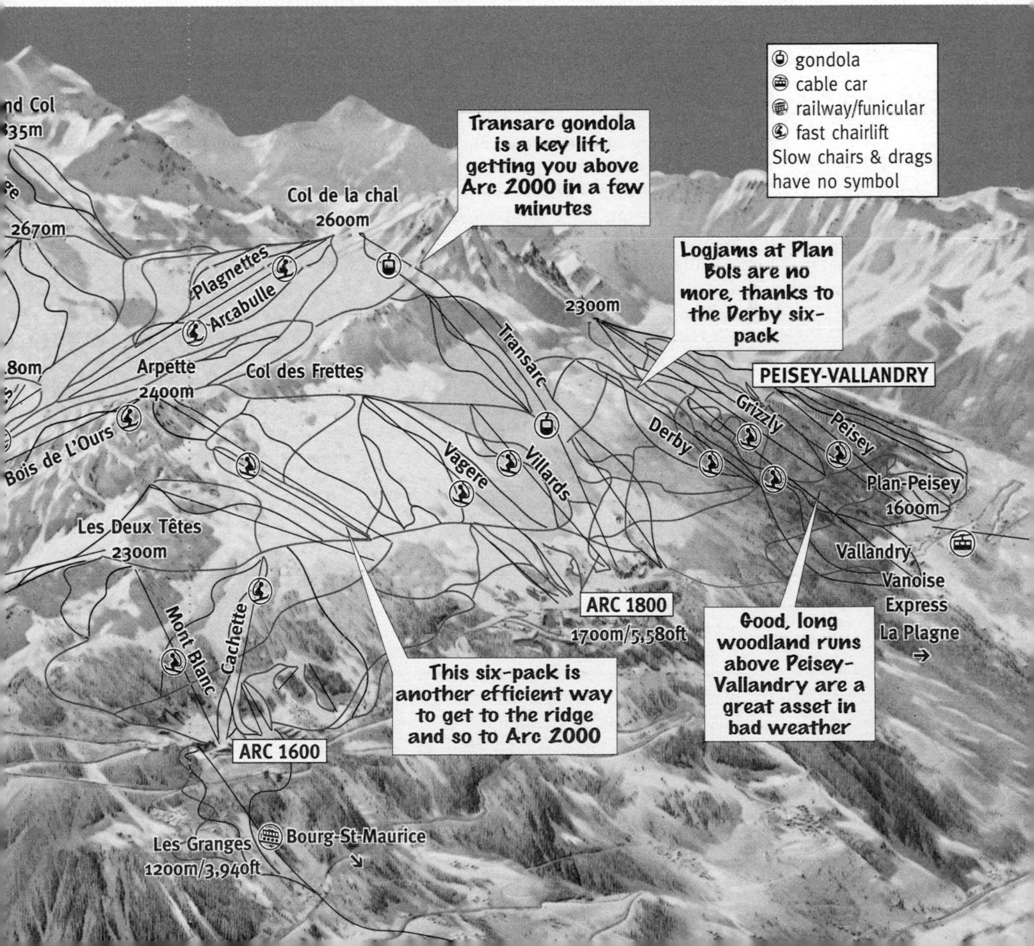

Resort news and key links: www.wheretoskiandsnowboard.com

LIFT PASSES

Les Arcs / Peisey-Vallandry

Prices in €		
Age	1-day	6-day
under 14	34	163
14 to 64	45	217
65 plus	34	163

Free under 6

Beginner Points card for one lift in each of Arc 1600/1800/2000

Senior 72 plus: 1-15 days €6

Notes
Les Arcs areas; half-day pass; family reductions; one-day Paradiski extension

Paradiski Découverte

Prices in €	
Age	6-day
under 14	181
14 to 64	241
65 plus	181

Free under 6

Beginner no deals

Notes
Les Arcs areas with one day in Paradiski

Paradiski Unlimited

Prices in €		
Age	1-day	6-day
under 14	38	193
14 to 64	51	258
65 plus	38	193

Free under 6

Beginner no deals

Senior 72 plus: 1-15 days €9

Notes
Les Arcs areas and La Plagne areas; family reductions; with 5+ passes one day in Three Valleys and Espace Killy, and reduced rate in Ste-Foy, La Rosière and La Thuile

kicker lines are in place for all levels. There is a good rail and box line, a big wall ride, a spine jump and a large gap jump – variety and fun for all.

There is a boardercross below Col de la Chal, the quality of which is a matter of dispute between two reporters, and two smaller parks above Plan-Peisey.

SNOW RELIABILITY ★★★★

Good – plenty of high runs

A high percentage of the runs are above 2000m, and when necessary you can stay high by using lifts that start around that altitude. Most of the slopes face roughly west, which is not ideal. Those from the Col de la Chal and the long runs down to Villaroger are north-facing, and the blacks on the Aiguille Rouge are shady enough to keep their snow well. The limited snowmaking is being gradually extended. Grooming is good.

FOR EXPERTS ★★★★★

Challenges on- and off-piste

Les Arcs has a lot to offer experts – at least when the high lifts are open (the Aiguille Rouge cable car, in particular, is often shut in bad weather).

Most black runs are now Natur' runs and become huge mogul fields – while some reporters welcome this, the lack of many groomed blacks means that the steeper groomed reds can get very busy. One of the quieter reds (and one of our favourites) is the lower part of the epic Aiguille Rouge-Villaroger run which has remarkably varying terrain – the start is a narrow black shelf which can be awkward (but this can be avoided by taking the Lanchettes chair from Arc 2000). There is also a great deal of off-piste potential. There are steep pitches on the front face of the Aiguille Rouge and secluded runs on the back side, towards Villaroger. A short climb to the Grand Col accesses several routes, including a quite serious couloir and an easier option. From Col de la Chal there is an easy route down towards Nancroix. The wooded slopes above 1600 are another attractive possibility and there are open slopes beside the pistes all over the place.

FOR INTERMEDIATES ★★★★

Plenty for all abilities

One strength of the area is that most main routes have easy and more difficult alternatives, making it good for mixed-ability groups. An exception is the solitary Comborcière black from Les Deux Têtes down to Pré-St-Esprit, which has no nearby alternatives. This long mogul-field justifies its classification and can be great fun for strong intermediates. Malgovert, from the same point towards Arc 1600, is a red Natur' piste and is tricky – it is narrow, as well as mogulled.

The woodland runs at either end of the domain, above Peisey-Vallandry and Villaroger, and the bumpy Cachette red down to 1600, also include some challenges. We especially like the Peisey-Vallandry area: its well groomed, tree-lined runs have a very friendly feel and are remarkably uncrowded much of the time, allowing great fast cruising. Good intermediates can enjoy the run to Villaroger.

The lower half of the mountainside above 1600/1800 is great for mixed-ability groups, with a choice of routes through the trees. The red runs from Arpette and Col des Frettes towards 1800 are quite steep but usually well groomed (except Clair Blanc).

Cautious intermediates have plenty of blue cruising terrain. Many of the runs around 2000 are rather bland and prone to overcrowding. Edelweiss is more interesting, with a short red alternative, and takes you to Arc 1950 from Col des Frettes. The blues above

ARC 1950

Arc 1950, just below Arc 2000, is a self-contained mini-resort that was built in the last decade. It is high and relatively snow-sure, traffic-free (you park under your apartment building) and laid out very conveniently, with genuinely ski-in/ski-out lodgings. It is attractively built, with wood and stone chalet-style buildings grouped around a central square and street.

The accommodation is in apartments, spacious and well furnished by French standards – a reporter notes the Radisson is 'particularly spacious, with saunas and outdoor pools'.

There are just enough restaurants to get you through a week, such as Hemingway's ('very good meat'), plus a reasonable choice of après-ski bars, a tiny but well-stocked supermarket, a bakery, a gift shop, a crêperie, ski school and ski and board equipment shops.

1800 are attractive but also crowded. A blue favourite of ours is Renard, high above Vallandry – usually with excellent snow.

And, of course, you have the whole of La Plagne's slopes to explore.

FOR BEGINNERS ★★★★★

No long greens, few free lifts

There are 'ski tranquille' beginner zones at each of the three main Arcs, and up the hill on the treeline above Vallandry and Plan-Peisey. The slopes in the three main Arcs are free to use at weekends, as is a chair serving a blue run at Plan-Peisey, but normally you pay via a points card. Bizarrely, a short lift at the bottom of 1800 and the first chairlift out of Villaroger are apparently always free, along with a couple of magic carpets at 1800 and 2000. Why can't they just make all the beginner lifts free? Sadly, the resort does not use the valuable green-run classification common to most other French resorts. In all sectors there are long, wide blue runs to move on to, and some are gentle enough to be green. An example is Forêt down to Vallandry.

FOR BOARDERS ★★★★★

A pioneering place

Ever since 1983 when Regis Rolland introduced the sport in the cult film Apocalypse Snow, Les Arcs has been a hot spot for snowboarders. It offers excellent freeriding, including steeps, gullies, trees, natural jibs and hits. And there are plenty of wide-open rolling slopes for intermediates and beginners too, especially at Vallandry and 1800. The terrain park is great and served by a snowboarder-friendly draglift. Most other lifts are chairs and gondolas. But beware of some long flat areas – especially at Arc 2000 and some linking blue runs (you may find it easier to take the wider reds).

FOR CROSS-COUNTRY ★★★★★

Very boring locally

Short trails, mostly on roads, is all you can expect, but the pretty Nancroix valley's 40km of pleasant trails are easily accessible by free bus.

MOUNTAIN RESTAURANTS ★★★★★

Not much choice high-up

They are mainly unremarkable.

Editors' choice Solliet (0668 960407) above Villaroger is a charming woody chalet with a warm ambience, table- or self-service and great views from the terrace. We had an excellent lunch here in 2010 after a change of owner.

Worth knowing about Chalets de l'Arc, just above Arc 2000, is a rustic place built in wood and stone. We were great fans in its early days, but on our last few visits (including 2011) we found the service rather slow, the welcome nominal and the food nothing special. However: a 2012 visitor finds it a 'winner' with the 'stiff staff softening up' and serving an 'excellent plat du jour – delicious chicken supreme with rice and veg'.

The busy Cordée, just above Plan-Peisey, has been repeatedly recommended for 'excellent food, first-class service'. The Crèche at Col de la Chal is tipped this year for 'friendly' service, 'perfect salmon' – even when busy. The little Blanche Murée is a pleasant, simple table-service in a chalet-style setting serving 'wild boar with gratin dauphinois – yum!'. The Arpette, above 1800, is a self-service that hits its target ('our favourite, friendly staff'). The Poudreuse above Vallandry has been 'tarted up' and become the 'sprightly' Enfants Terribles ('full marks for an excellent authentic potée Savoyarde', says a 2012 visitor). The tiny Bulle hut, near the Arcabulle chair above 2000, is fairly new – with 'excellent pizza at very reasonable prices', says a 2011 visitor.

The other good options are not very mountainous. At Pré-St-Esprit below Arc 2000, the 500-year-old Belliou la Fumée is set beside a car park; but it is charmingly rustic, and we've had good meals here. Over the years we and reporters have enjoyed excellent meals at the Ferme at Villaroger. If you want a top-notch meal and don't mind returning to 1600, go to Chalet d'Arcelle (see 'Eating out').

SCHOOLS AND GUIDES ★★★★★

Several, including a Brit school

British school New Generation is consistently recommended. A report last year is typical: 'Worth every cent – excellent instructor who suggested improvements that really made a difference.' 'Fourth year we have used them for private lessons, outstanding each time' was a response a couple of years ago. The ESF here is renowned for being the first in Europe to teach ski évolutif, where you start by learning parallel turns on short skis,

SCHOOLS

ESF Arc 1600
t 0479 074309

ESF Arc 1800
t 0479 074031

ESF Arc 2000
t 0479 074752

Arc Aventures 1800
t 0479 076002

Evolution 2 Arc 2000
t 0479 078553

New Generation
t 0479 010318
0844 770 4733 (UK)
www.skinewgen.com

Privilège Arc 1800
t 0479 072338

Spirit 1950
t 0479 042572

Classes (ESF prices)
6 5hr days €215

Private lessons
From €39 for 1hr

GUIDES

Bureau des Guides
t 0479 077119

gradually moving on to longer skis. Progress can be spectacular, but classes can be large. The Arc 2000 branch has had glowing comments in the past but we've had mixed reviews from 2012 visitors. Arc Aventures (International school) has been noted as 'good value' for an off-piste guide, while Spirit in 1950 has been tipped for 'friendly teachers and not too big groups'.

FOR FAMILIES ★★★★

Convenient choices

Les Arcs is a good choice for families wanting convenience. There is a children's area at 1800, complete with moving carpets, tobogganing and a climbing wall. There are also a couple of discovery pistes, at 1800 and 1600, for children to find out about flora and fauna of the Alps. The Pommes de Pin facilities in Arc 1800 have received favourable reports. Arc 1950 is particularly family friendly – Spirit 1950 there reportedly provides good care for smaller children, returning them well fed and rested. Comments on kids' ski classes have been positive. The Garderie in 2000 'impressed' this year – 'the two girls loved it'.

STAYING THERE

Most resort beds are in apartments. There is a long-established Club Med presence in Arc 2000 and there's a smarter one at Peisey-Vallandry.

Chalets There are lots of catered chalets in the Peisey-Vallandry area – covered at the end of this chapter. There are also lots of chalet-apartments in smart résidences with pools in Arc 2000 – operators include Skiworld, Ski Total, Inghams, Crystal and family specialist Esprit. Skiworld also has a couple of proper individual chalets above 1800.

Hotels The choice of hotels in Les Arcs is gradually widening.

***__Arcadien__ (1600) (0479 041600) 'Very reasonable, rooms relatively big.'

***__Cachette__ (1600) (0479 077050) Recommended, but expect lots of kids – 1600's childcare facilities are here. 'Spotlessly clean, helpful staff, very good food, dessert buffet to die for, themed evenings.'

***__Golf__ (1800) (0479 414343) A pricey 3-star, with sauna, gym, covered parking, kindergarten, spa, heated pool, steam, hot tub. Accepts weekend bookings.

***__Grand Paradiso__ (1800) (0479 076500) Locally judged to be worth four stars rather than its actual three ('very comfortable, good food').

**__Aiguille Rouge__ (2000) (0479 075707) 'Rooms clean but small.'

Apartments Beware – there are still plenty of unbearably cramped apartments in the older resort units. But there are now lots of good, modern apartments available, including the first units in the brand new Edenarc development above Arc 1800, and the several residences at Arc 1950. You'll find lots via companies such as Erna Low, Lagrange, Pierre & Vacances, Ski Collection, Ski Amis, Crystal, Ski Independence and Skitracer. In Arc 2000 the Chalet des Neiges, Chalet Altitude and Cimes des Arcs have above average apartments. The Alpages de Chantel above Arc 1800 (a Pierre & Vacances premium property) is attractive and comfortable, with pools, saunas and gyms. It is very convenient for skiing, but a bit isolated. The newish Roc Belle Face development in central Arc 1600, built in tiers down the hillside, is a Lagrange Prestige property. The Ruitor apartments, set between Charmettoger and Villards (in 1800), are 'excellent'.

CHILDCARE

La Cachette (1600)
t 0479 077050
Ages 4mnth to 12yr

Le Cariboo (1950)
t 0479 070557
Ages 9mnth to 13yr

Arc 2000
t 0479 076425
Ages 12mnth to 8yr

Ski school
Generally from age 3:
6 days €215 (ESF)

EATING OUT ★★★

Fair choice in Arc 1800

Arc 1800 has the best choice – about 15 restaurants; an ad-based (therefore not comprehensive) guide is given away locally. Reporters favour the Mountain Cafe, which has a varied menu ('good food, great buzz'), and San Diego ('consistently good, friendly service'). Tipped for tartiflette are the Laurus and Escale Gourmand.

Arc 1600's handful of restaurants include a couple of excellent ones. Chalet de L'Arcelle on the fringe of the village is a clear reporter favourite; it has a warm, quirky wood-and-stone interior and a mouth-watering carte – 'near Michelin one-star quality'. The Malouine with a 'largely Italian' menu has improved under new management. The Cairn is 'wood-panelled, with prompt, friendly service'; the Arquebuse serves traditional food in a cosy setting. For a quick snack, try the waffles at the Snack de l'Arbre.

In Arc 2000, Kilimandjaro has stood out in the past but a 2012 visitor finds the restaurant 'tired, with the once great wine list reduced to a rump'. Chez Eux is the latest 'go-to restaurant, warm woody interior, friendly staff, excellent roast pork'. The Savoy does a 'fantastic cheese board', and a 'delicate pannacotta with myrtilles', and has a 'superb wine list'.

Arc 1950 has a reasonable choice for a small place. They get very busy, and we are inclined to share the view of a reporter that the options are generally 'uninspiring'. But some receive positive reports. La Table des Lys ('excellent food, super wines') and Chalet de Luigi ('good selection of pastas') have been recommended.

APRES-SKI ★★

Arc 1800 is the place to be

Nightlife is not lively and mainly revolves around the bars. 1800 is the liveliest; some places have regular live music. The J.O. bar is open until the early hours and has a friendly atmosphere. Reporters like the friendly Red Hot Saloon for bar games, Chez Boubou at Charvet and the cosy Etranger.

ED COLEMAN

Arc 1950 is a high-density, conveniently laid out resort that also manages to look quite appealing →

ACTIVITIES

Indoor Squash (1800), saunas, solaria, multi-gym (1800), museums, cinemas, bowling (1800, 2000)

Outdoor Ice rinks (1800/ 2000), dog sledding, cleared paths, tobogganing, snowshoeing, paragliding, horse riding, skijoring, snowmobiling, ice grotto

GETTING THERE

Air Geneva 160km/ 100 miles (3hr); Lyon 215km/135 miles (3hr); Chambéry 130km/80 miles (2hr)

Rail Bourg-St-Maurice; frequent buses and direct funicular to resort

Although it's quieter, there are several options in 1600. The Abreuvoir, with live music and pool, is one reporter's 'favourite ski resort bar'. Stop by Chez Fernand for a friendly welcome, too. In Arc 2000 the Whistler's Dream, in the Chalet des Neiges could be worth a try. At 1950, several places operate as bars, such as the Belles Pintes. O'Chaud is open late, with live music or a DJ.

OFF THE SLOPES ★★★★★
Very limited

Les Arcs is not the place for an off-the-slopes holiday however, several of the newer apartment blocks have pools, and there are spa facilities at Arc 1950. There's bowling at 1800 and skating at 1800 and 2000. The cinemas have English films weekly. You can visit the Beaufort cheese dairy and go shopping in Bourg-St-Maurice, and there are walks.

LINKED RESORT – 1600m

PEISEY-VALLANDRY

Plan-Peisey and Vallandry are small, still-developing ski stations built in a traditional chalet style above the old village of Peisey, which has a bucket-lift up to Plan-Peisey. They sell themselves as Peisey-Vallandry, but the local cluster of villages, including one called Nancroix, is collectively known as Peisey-Nancroix. Got that?

Both resorts have good nursery slopes high up the hill on the tree-line, reached by chairlift. Of course, this means paying to get up there.

The cable car to La Plagne starts from **Plan-Peisey** – one hotel, a few shops, bars and restaurants but no real focus other than the lift station. A six-pack takes you to the local slopes.

UK operator Ski Amis has a 'premium service' chalet here with a hot tub (it also has several self-catered chalets here). Family specialist operator Esprit has six neat chalets, each with hot tub. Ski Beat has several chalets (some with sauna). The hotel Vanoise (0479 079219) has a good location, a pool and a fitness room: 'Staff were very friendly despite our appalling French, and the food was much better than expected,' says a 2011 visitor. The Arollaie is a smart, fairly new apartment development, with a small pool.

Of the restaurants, reporters like the Solan ('rustic style but sophisticated inside with reasonable prices'), the Vache and Chez Felix ('super food, popular with locals'). Après-ski is very quiet.

There is lodging down the hill in the characterful old village of Peisey, complete with fine baroque church. The other, mostly old, buildings include a few shops and a couple of bars and restaurants – a reader enjoyed the Ormelune. UK tour operator Mountain Heaven has a renovated old farm building run as a catered chalet with five en-suite rooms; there are three more in an annex, plus a sauna.

The Ancolie restaurant at Nancroix is worth the trip – a fabulous traditional auberge with welcoming

UK PACKAGES

Action Outdoors, Alpine Answers, Alpine Elements, BoardnLodge, Club Med, Crystal, Crystal Finest, Erna Low, Esprit, Independent Ski Links, Inghams, Interactive Resorts, Lagrange, Mountain Wave, Neilson, Pierre & Vacances, PowderBeds, Powder White, Ski Amis, Ski Beat, Ski Club Freshtracks, Ski Collection, Ski Expectations, Ski France, Ski Ici, Ski Independence, Ski Line, Ski Olympic, Ski Solutions, Ski Total, Skitracer, Ski Weekend, Skiworld, Snow Finders, Snowchateaux, SnowCrazy, Thomson
Peisey-Vallandry Club Med, Erna Low, Esprit, Lagrange, Mountain Heaven, Peak Retreats, PowderBeds, Ski Amis, Ski Beat, Ski Collection, Ski France, Ski Hiver, Ski Independence, Ski Line, Ski Olympic, Ski Solutions, Snow Finders, Snowchateaux
Bourg-St-Maurice Chill Chalet, Erna Low, Peak Retreats, Ski Collection

Phone numbers
From abroad use the prefix +33 and omit the initial '0' of the phone number

TOURIST OFFICES

Les Arcs
www.lesarcs.com

Peisey-Vallandry
www.peisey-vallandry.com

Bourg-St-Maurice
www.bourgsaint maurice.com

hosts and excellent food. (Be aware that taxis will rip you off for the short journey if you're not careful.)

Vallandry is a few hundred metres away from Plan-Peisey and linked by shuttle-bus. A fast quad takes you into the slopes. There are lots of chalets and a small pedestrian-only square at the foot of the slopes with a small supermarket and a ski shop.

Ski Olympic's big piste-side chalet hotel La Forêt has 'outstanding food, good rooms, fabulous views, friendly and helpful staff'. CGH has two smart apartment developments sharing a pool, sauna, steam and hot tub and great views – Orée des Cimes and Orée des Neiges, newly built for 2011/12. These apartments are available through Peak Retreats.

There are several restaurants. The Calèche does 'large portions of Savoyard classics'. The Mont Blanc bar is cool – 'friendly staff', and one of the cheaper options for lunch.

LINKED RESORT – 1200m

VILLAROGER

Villaroger is a charming, quiet, rustic little hamlet with three successive slow chairlifts going up to a point above Arc 2000; its slopes are not suitable for beginners. It has a couple of small bar-restaurants.

DOWN-VALLEY RESORT – 850m

BOURG-ST-MAURICE

With a funicular railway link to Arc 1600, Bourg-St-Maurice is marketed as part of Les Arcs, and does make a viable cheaper alternative to staying on the hill. But it is very different – not a ski resort, but a real valley town, with proper everyday shops and sizeable supermarkets. It is at the end of the TGV railway line, and therefore very appealing to rail travellers.

The funicular station is a walkable distance from the TGV platforms, but a drive or bus ride from most parts of Bourg. The advertised travel time is seven minutes, but that's for non-stop services, which in our experience are rare. In practice, staying in Bourg rather than Les Arcs costs you an hour a day in extra travelling time.

The plus side, of course, is that everything from accommodation to beer is cheaper. Depending on the time of the season and the exact comparison you make, you can rent an apartment for 30% to 60% less than the cost of a similar apartment on the hill. If you plan to ski Les Arcs (and La Plagne), you need to balance the cost savings against that lost hour a day.

But if you fancy a bit more variety, the appeal of Bourg-St-Maurice becomes clear. We spent a week here in 2010 and had a fab time skiing a different resort every day, from La Plagne to Val d'Isère. The more remote resorts are best accessed by car, though there are buses. But you can easily ski La Rosière (and linked La Thuile in Italy) by taking a bus to the chairlift above Séez which goes up into the slopes of La Rosière.

Built a few seasons ago, the CGH Coeur d'Or apartments are comfortable without being indulgent. Close to the two major supermarkets, they are a walk from the town but a drive (or free shuttle-bus ride) from the funicular.

A reporter reckons that the Angival (0479 072797), in a quiet back street, is 'the pick of the hotel crop'.

There are some good, unpretentious restaurants. Best in town (actually just outside the centre) is probably the delectable-sounding Arssiban. In the main pedestrian street, the Montagnole does a good job, too, while the Tsablo has become the Art des Mets.

SNOWPIX.COM / CHRIS GILL

Avoriaz 1800

The purpose-built ski-in/ski-out resort option on the French side of the big Portes du Soleil circuit

RATINGS

The mountains	
Extent	*****
Fast lifts	****
Queues	***
Terrain p'ks	*****
Snow	***
Expert	***
Intermediate	****
Beginner	****
Boarder	*****
X-country	***
Restaurants	****
Schools	***
Families	****
The resort	
Charm	**
Convenience	*****
Scenery	***
Eating out	***
Après-ski	***
Off-slope	*

RPI	95
lift pass	£180
ski hire	£110
lessons	£60
food & drink	£130
total	**£480**

KEY FACTS

Resort	1800m 5,910ft
Portes du Soleil	
Slopes	950-2275m 3,120-7,460ft
Lifts	198
Pistes	650km 404 miles
Green	13%
Blue	40%
Red	37%
Black	10%
Snowmaking	835 guns
Avoriaz only	
Slopes	1100-2275m 3,610-7,460ft
Lifts	36
Pistes	70km 45 miles
Snowmaking	126 guns

- + Good position on the main Portes du Soleil circuit, giving access to very extensive, quite varied runs
- + Very successful design – car-free, with ski-in/ski-out lodgings
- + Good children's facilities
- + Local slopes are among the best in the Portes du Soleil and generally have the best snow, but ...

- − Low altitudes and exposure to westerlies means some risk of poor snow lower down, and rain
- − Architecture doesn't suit everyone
- − Lacks a slick bag delivery system
- − Can get very crowded at weekends
- − Limited range of restaurants, very limited range of other amenities
- − Hardly any hotels

Of the many purpose-built resorts thrown up in France in the 1960s, Avoriaz is probably the best-designed – genuinely convenient in most respects, completely car-free and visually striking rather than offensive. And it is set in the highest, most snow-sure part of the relatively low (but very extensive) Portes du Soleil ski area. Avoriaz missed out on the new generation of smart apartment developments that have transformed self-catering in many French resorts, but it has now more than caught up, with some fabulous places opening last season and more due to open for 2012/13. Now how about a few more hotels?

THE RESORT

Avoriaz 1800 is a purpose-built resort perched on a sloping shelf above a dramatic, sheer rock face.

It is entirely free of wheeled traffic; cars are left in paid-for parks at the edge of the village – book a space underground to avoid a chaotic departure if it snows.

Avoriaz is on the main lift circuit of the Portes du Soleil – for an overview, look at our separate chapter. It has links to Châtel in one direction and to Champéry in Switzerland in the other – both covered in separate chapters.

It is above the valley resort of Morzine, to which it is linked by gondola (but not by piste). The slopes of Morzine and Les Gets, on the far side of Morzine, are covered by the Portes du Soleil lift pass; both get their own chapters.

There are two hamlets on the fringes of the Avoriaz ski area with lifts into it – Ardent and Les Prodains. Both are described at the end of this chapter. Car trips to Flaine and Chamonix are possible.

VILLAGE CHARM **

One of the best modern places

The village is all angular, dark, wood-clad, high-rise buildings – almost all apartments. It's not what you would call charming, but it is at least designed coherently. The snow-covered paths and pistes give the place quite a friendly Alpine feel, and both we and reporters have enjoyed the ambience, both day and night. Family-friendly events are laid on all season. A floodlit cliff behind the resort adds to its nocturnal charm. The lifties have been noted as friendly and helpful.

CONVENIENCE *****

It doesn't get much better

As our scale plan suggests, it's a compact place, with everything close to hand (turn to the Chamonix chapter, after this one, for a clear comparison). From the central reception area, you drag your luggage to your apartment on a borrowed sled, or fork out for a ride on a snowcat or horse-drawn sleigh. Wherever you stay, you should

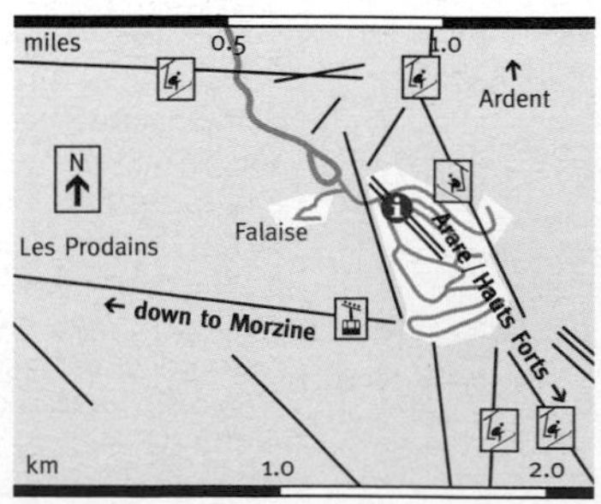

NEWS

2012/13: The Prodains cable car from Morzine is to be replaced by a gondola. A new aquatic centre – the Aquariaz – opened in July 2012, with water slides, river rapids, a climbing wall above a plunge pool and lots of tropical plants. The second phase of the luxury 5-star Amara apartments is due to open, as well as the 4-star Atria-Crozats residence.

2011/12: Two buildings opened in the first phase of the new 5-star Pierre & Vacances apartments Amara – with spa, pool, saunas etc – near the top of the resort. And a new ice rink opened near the centre. A pass that lets you ski for any five consecutive hours in a day replaced the half-day pass.

be able to ski from close to the door. The village is set on quite a slope; but elevators inside the buildings (and chairlifts outside, during the day) mean moving around is no problem – except when paths are icy.

SCENERY ★★★★★
Cliff-top panorama

The village is high and its position on a sunny balcony gives good views down across Morzine. From the high points there are great views of the Dents Blanches and the Dents du Midi.

THE MOUNTAINS

The slopes closest to Avoriaz are bleak and treeless, but fairly snow-sure.

Five runs – a blue, two reds and two blacks – are called 'snowcross' runs. We understand these are signed, patrolled and avalanche controlled but ungroomed. This is an appealing idea; but it hasn't been implemented properly. The concept of red and blue runs that are never groomed is unique to Avoriaz, and the maps distributed in other PdS resorts show these runs as ordinary pistes. We have reports of people expecting a defined, prepared piste, and finding themselves on a wide mogul field instead.

Another interesting innovation is that the Avoriaz slopes are divided into four sectors – beginner, family, forest and expert. With most of the snowcross runs falling in the family sector, we're not sure this works.

EXTENT OF THE SLOPES ★★★★★
360° choice

The village has lifts and pistes fanning out in all directions. Facing the village are the slopes of **Arare-Hauts Forts** and, when snow conditions allow, there are long, steep runs down to Les Prodains, way below the resort. To the left, lifts go off to the **Chavanette** sector on the Swiss border – a broad, undulating bowl. Beyond the border is the infamous Swiss Wall – a long, mogul slope with a tricky start, but not the terror it is cracked up to be unless it's icy. You can ride the chair down – lots of people do. At the bottom of the Wall is the open, gentle terrain of Planachaux, above Champéry, with links to the even bigger open area around Les Crosets and Champoussin.

Taking a lift up through the village of Avoriaz to the ridge behind it is the way to the prettily wooded **Lindarets-Brocheaux** valley, from where lifts go over to Châtel's Linga sector or up to Pointe de Mossettes, another way into Switzerland.

FAST LIFTS ★★★★★
Good system here and at Linga

In the Avoriaz sector the lifts are impressively modern – hence our rating. On the Linga slopes, on the way to Châtel, you'll again be mainly riding fast lifts. But be warned: beyond Châtel, and in the opposite direction towards Champéry, it's like stepping back 20 years. Maybe 30.

JOHN SCOTT

With the village set high up in the slopes, you can be reasonably confident of snow on the streets ➔

QUEUES ★★★
Main problems now gone
The main long-standing problem, the queue to get up from Les Prodains, when snow attracts visitors from Morzine, should be solved by the replacement of the old cable-car by a big gondola for 2012/13. Visitors report few other problems except returning from Les Lindarets in the afternoon, when you may wait 10 minutes. Peak-time crowds on the pistes (especially around the village) can be hazardous.

TERRAIN PARKS ★★★★★
Still leading the way
Avoriaz built the first terrain park in France, in 1993. It is still leading the way, and there are five parks and a super-pipe, all superbly maintained. Check www.snowparkavoriaz.com for details. Park lift passes are available. All are 'very well maintained'.

The expert park is at Arare and the kicker and rail lines are superbly shaped, designed and maintained. It also has an airbag jump – 'the most fun I had all trip', says a 2011 visitor.

Beginners and intermediates should head to La Chapelle – a 500m-long park littered with jumps of all sizes and fun little boxes, to suit all levels of skiers and boarders. Parkway, on the Trashers lift, is great for beginners and kids. It has mini-jumps and ride-on boxes, with green 'Go' lights to press before you drop, a smart safety-aware innovation.

The fourth park, The Stash in the Lindarets valley, is a great innovation imported from California – a wooded mountainside, with three different routes cut through the forest, and wooden and natural elements bringing all-mountain riding and freestyle together; great fun. The fifth park is the Lil'Stash – a mini version for younger kids. Just above the village is a good super-pipe. And there's a boardercross too.

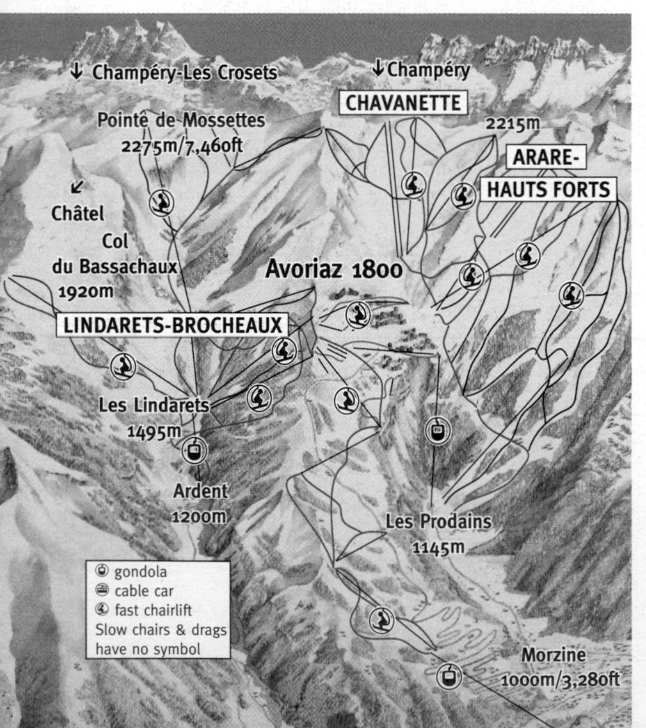

SNOW RELIABILITY ★★★
High resort, low slopes
Although Avoriaz itself is high, its slopes don't go much higher – and some parts of the Portes du Soleil circuit are much lower. Considering their altitude, the north-facing slopes below Hauts Forts hold snow well and the snow in Avoriaz is usually much better than over the border on the sunnier Swiss slopes. But when snow is sparse the smooth, grassy slopes of lower Morzine-Les Gets can be better than the rocky ones around Avoriaz, which need more snow. Grooming has impressed recent visitors.

FOR EXPERTS ★★★
Several challenging runs
Tough terrain is scattered about. The challenging runs down from Hauts Forts to Les Prodains (including a World Cup downhill) are excellent. There is a tough red and several long, truly black runs including one of the 'snowcross' runs we've talked about. Snow conditions on the lower runs can be poor, but there is snowmaking. The Swiss Wall at Chavanette will naturally be on your agenda (read the Champéry chapter, in the Switzerland section), and Châtel's Linga sector is well worth a trip. The black runs off

LIFT PASSES

Portes du Soleil

Prices in €

Age	1-day	6-day
under 16	33	164
16 to 19	40	197
20 to 63	44	219
64 plus	40	197

Free under 5

Beginner Special pass €23 a day

Notes family discounts; 5hr pass

Alternative passes Avoriaz only

SCHOOLS

ESF
t 0450 740565

Evolution 2
t 0450 740218

Alpine (AASS)
t 0450 383491

Classes
(ESF prices)
6 (4.75hr) days €180

Private lessons
From €40 for 1hr, for 1 or 2 people

CHILDCARE

Les P'tits Loups
t 0450 740038
3mnth to 5yr

Children's Village Annie Famose
t 0450 740446
From age 3

Ski schools
Ages 4 to 12 (6 days €180 – ESF)

the Swiss side of Mossettes and Pointe de l'Au are worth trying, and one reporter had a 'very good' day here exploring off-piste with a guide.

FOR INTERMEDIATES ★★★★

Virtually the whole area

Although some sections lack variety, the Portes du Soleil circuit through Châtel, Morgins and Champéry is excellent for all grades of intermediates, provided snow is in good supply on the lower slopes. Timid types not worried about pretty surroundings need not leave the Avoriaz sector: there are quiet and scenic blues to Les Prodains and the Arare and Chavanette sectors are gentle, spacious, above-the-treeline bowls. The Lindarets area is also easy, with pretty runs through the trees, but several reporters complain about long flat sections.

Further afield, Champoussin has a lot of easy runs, reached without too much difficulty via Les Crosets and Pointe de l'Au. Better intermediates have virtually the whole area at their disposal. The runs down to Pré-la-Joux and L'Essert on the way to Châtel, and those either side of Morgins, are particularly attractive – as are the long runs down to Grand-Paradis near Champéry when snow conditions allow. Pointe de Mossettes offers a less challenging route to Switzerland than the Swiss Wall itinéraire at Chavanette.

FOR BEGINNERS ★★★★

Convenient, but you pay

The nursery slopes seem small in relation to the size of the resort, but appear to cope. The slopes are sunny, yet good for snow, and link well to longer, easy runs. Our reservations are that the pistes can be busy, and that there are no free lifts. Why not?

FOR BOARDERS ★★★★★

Plenty to keep you busy all week

Avoriaz is great for expert riders. As well as state of the art 'conventional' parks, there's The Stash in the forest (see 'Terrain parks'). For safe freeriding after a dump, head for the ungroomed snowcross runs. For something more extreme, the long cliff-band accessed from the Arare lift is perfect for cliff drops of all sizes. It is well worth hiring a guide to exploit the off-piste riding. There are plenty of easy pistes (though some flat sections, especially in the Lindarets valley, on the descent from Mossettes), and very few draglifts, making this a good choice for beginners and intermediates too.

FOR CROSS-COUNTRY ★★★

Varied, with some blacks

There are 45km of trails, mainly between Avoriaz and Super-Morzine, with others around Lindarets and Montriond.

MOUNTAIN RESTAURANTS ★★★★

Good choice over the hill

Editors' choice The hamlet of Les Lindarets in the next valley consists of countless rustic restaurants – it is a popular tourist spot in summer. The jolly Crémaillière (0450 741168) has wonderful chanterelle mushrooms and great atmosphere. But on a good day it's difficult to beat the terrace of the, er, Terrasse (0450 741617) – a recent reporter agrees ('fine cooking, friendly efficient service').

Worth knowing about A 2012 reporter raves about Les Alpages, just above Les Lindarets – 'ate there at least three times – huge and tasty steak with pepper sauce; such friendly service; huge and hot hot chocolates'. And we have a 2012 report of 'a real find' on the Super-Morzine slopes, L'Passage – 'cosy, friendly, great service'.

SCHOOLS AND GUIDES ★★★

Positive reports

We lack new reports on group lessons, but a 2012 visitor has often booked the ESF for three days of 'great' private off-piste lessons. One visitor had 'inspirational' snowboard lessons with former pro Angelique Corrèze-Hubert through the Ecole de Glisse. The Avoriaz Alpine Ski School has British instructors and has been highly recommended, especially for 'quite excellent children's lessons'.

FOR FAMILIES ★★★★

'Annie Famose delivers'

With snow everywhere and not a wheeled vehicle to be seen, Avoriaz has obvious appeal. Then there's the Village des Enfants, which takes children from age three and is run by ex-downhill champ Annie Famose. Its facilities are excellent – a chalet full of activities and special slopes with fun things such as teepees. One reader warns, however, of 'noisy drunken revellers at night' and broken bottles in the snow.

GETTING THERE

Air Geneva 90km/ 55 miles (2hr); Lyon 215km/135 miles (3hr30)

Rail Cluses (42km/ 26 miles) or Thonon (45km/28 miles); bus and cable car to resort

UK PACKAGES

Alpine Answers, Club Med, Crystal, Erna Low, Independent Ski Links, Inghams, Interactive Resorts, Lagrange, Neilson, Pierre & Vacances, PowderBeds, Powder White, Rude Chalets, Ski Collection, Ski France, Ski Independence, Ski Total, Skitracer, Skiweekends.com, Thomson, White Roc, Zenith
Ardent Family Ski Company

ACTIVITIES

Indoor Health centre 'Altiform' (sauna, gym, hot tub), squash, cinema, bowling
Outdoor Ice rink, dog sledding, tobogganing, mountain biking on snow, ice diving, walking, snowshoeing, ski jöring, snowmobiling, sleigh rides, helicopter flights, 'yooner' tobogganing, caving

Phone numbers
From abroad use the prefix +33 and omit the initial '0' of the phone number

TOURIST OFFICE

www.avoriaz.com

STAYING THERE

Alternatives to apartments are few.
Chalets Inghams has a chalet for 12. Ski Total has four neighbouring chalets including Marie in its Platinum range. All are ski-in/ski-out.
Hotels There is not much choice.
*****Dromonts** (0450 740811) Owned by a celebrity chef and in the *Hip Hotels* guidebook. Reports welcome.
*****Lans** (0450 790090) Traditional family-run place 300m from Prodains lift up to Avoriaz – 'simple rooms, exceptional food, helpful patronne'.
Apartments Pierre & Vacances' new luxury Amara development is an exciting addition – a trusted observer rates these apartments 'among the very best I have seen'. There's a spacious lounge, a 'massive terrace with stunning views', underground parking, pool and every dining option you could want, including dinner in other resort restaurants. Ski Collection, PowderBeds, Inghams and Crystal offer this and other new residences, including P&V's Atria-Crozats.

EATING OUT ★★★

A few interesting options

There isn't much variety and the restaurants get very busy. The Table du Marché in hotel Dromonts (sister to similarly cool places in St Tropez and Marrakech) is the best in town, but of course pricey. We had an excellent meal in the cosy wood-panelled Salle à Manger at the Garde-Manger deli, serving three-course fixed-price menus changing daily. A couple of bars are worth noting: Chapka does 'great tapas' and Tavaillon 'the best burgers in town'. Earlier reporter tips include: Trappeurs ('perfect filet, huge portions and great choice'), the Bistro, Douchka and Intrêts for pizza, pasta and Savoyard fare, Au Briska for a cosy night out and Falaise for pizza.

APRES-SKI ★★★

The bars are fun

A few bars have a good atmosphere, particularly in happy hour. Top tips this year are Tavaillon ('very popular – shows sport from all over the world, spectacular cocktail of the day') and Shooters. Chapka is a hip bar with TV, live music and pool ('excellent service, toilets immaculate'). For late-night dance action, we're told the Place has bands.

OFF THE SLOPES ★

Not much at the resort

There's not a lot to keep non-skiers interested – few shops, and pedestrians are not allowed to ride the chairlifts. The Altiform Fitness Center has steam, saunas and hot tubs. A recent reporter enjoyed bowling. The smart new Aquariaz – a huge new water park and swimming pool facility – opened in summer 2012.

LINKED RESORT – 1200m

ARDENT

Ardent is a very quiet little place at the foot of the gondola up to Les Lindarets. It has the basics of life, including a bar and a ski shop. The Family Ski Company has eight chalets here, the most remote 150m from the gondola, the nearest only 30m from it.

LINKED RESORT – 1145m

LES PRODAINS

Les Prodains is at the foot of the cliffs on which Avoriaz sits. It has a cable car up to Avoriaz, due to be replaced for 2012/13 by a big gondola, meeting the needs of Morzine-based people to get to the Portes du Soleil circuit, and of Avoriaz-based people to return from the Hauts Forts runs or from Morzine. But there are also some chalets and small hotels – read our Hotels section.

OT CHAMONIX MONT-BLANC

Chamonix

HQ of French and arguably European mountaineering, with a magnetic attraction for tourists and off-piste thrill-seekers alike

RATINGS

The mountains	
Extent	***
Fast lifts	***
Queues	**
Terrain p'ks	***
Snow	****
Expert	*****
Intermediate	**
Beginner	**
Boarder	***
X-country	***
Restaurants	**
Schools	*****
Families	**
The resort	
Charm	****
Convenience	*
Scenery	*****
Eating out	*****
Après-ski	****
Off-slope	*****

RPI	100
lift pass	£180
ski hire	£100
lessons	£100
food & drink	£135
total	**£515**

NEWS

2012/13: The 4-star Mont-Blanc hotel is being refurbished and is due to reopen as a 5-star. A new mountain restaurant, Les Consorts, will open on Balme, we're assured.

2011/12: The Adret restaurant on Flégère was renovated, with new table-service and takeaway areas. And there's a new Big Air bag for freestyle fun on Brévent.

- \+ A lot of very tough terrain, especially off-piste
- \+ Amazing cable car to the Aiguille du Midi, for the famous Vallée Blanche
- \+ Stunning views wherever you are
- \+ Other resorts covered on extended lift pass, notably sunny Courmayeur
- \+ Town steeped in Alpine tradition
- \+ Lots of affordable hotels; an excellent short break destination

- − Several separate mountains, widely separated; mixed ability groups are likely to have to split up
- − Bad weather can shut the best runs
- − Still some old lifts, and queues in key spots
- − It's a busy town, with lots of road traffic; not a relaxing place
- − Shady and cold in midwinter
- − Few good mountain restaurants

Chamonix could not be more different from the archetypal high-altitude, purpose-built French resort. It hasn't been designed to deliver the smoothest possible experience to the widest possible market. It hasn't been designed.

You don't have to be an expert to enjoy the place – editor Gill once got away with taking his blue-run-skiing wife and novice kids for a week here. But it is the expert and the adventurous would-be expert who really must give Chamonix a permanent place on their shortlist. Be warned, though: there are those who try it and never go home – including lots of Brits.

THE RESORT

Chamonix is a long-established, year-round tourist town that spreads for miles along the valley in the shadow of Mont Blanc.

On either side of the centre, just within walking distance, are base stations of the cable car to the Aiguille du Midi, for the famous Vallée Blanche glacier run, and a gondola to Le Brévent. A third high-altitude area, La Flégère, is reached by cable car from the nearby village of Les Praz. There are then three other major ski areas.

At the top of the valley are the villages of Le Tour, at the foot of the Balme slopes (with an alternative base at Vallorcine), and Argentière, beneath the Grands Montets. These villages are described at the end of the chapter, but their slopes are taken in to the main part of the chapter.

Down the valley is Les Houches. This is entirely described at the end of the chapter; its lifts are not covered by the standard Chamonix lift pass.

Regular free ski-buses link all these points but can get crowded and aren't always reliable. There are also hourly trains (free with a guest card, and recommended by reporters) to Argentière, Vallorcine and Les Houches (where the lifts are a long walk from the station).

The Mont Blanc Unlimited lift pass covers not only Les Houches but also Verbier in Switzerland and Courmayeur in Italy. The first is a major expedition; the second is much more interesting, not least because the weather can be good in Italy when it is lousy in Chamonix. And there are free (with the Mont Blanc lift pass) buses through

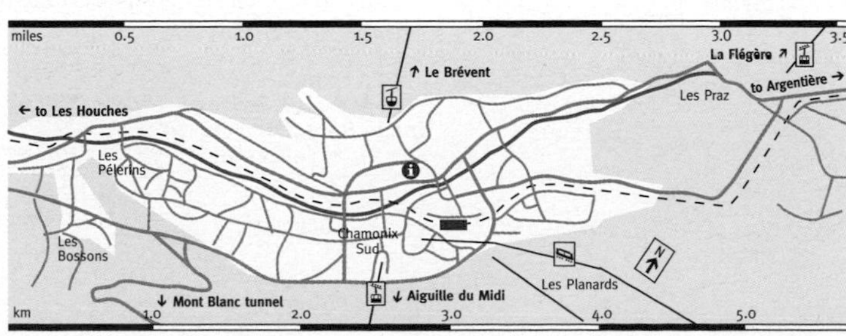

KEY FACTS	
Resort	1035m
	3,400ft
Slopes	1035-3840m
	3,400-12,600ft
Lifts	44
Pistes	155km
	96 miles
Green	16%
Blue	36%
Red	32%
Black	16%
Snowmaking	
	125 guns

the Mont-Blanc tunnel several times daily. Having a car is useful in lots of ways, and makes that outing to Verbier a practical proposition (though there is a weekly excursion bus too).

VILLAGE CHARM ★★★★★
Lots of atmosphere
It's a bustling place, with scores of hotels and restaurants and shops selling everything from tacky souvenirs to high-tech climbing gear. The car-free centre is full of atmosphere, with cobbled streets and squares, beautiful old buildings, a fast-running river and pavement cafes. Away from the centre, there are lots of apartment blocks. There are some disused buildings, and traffic clogs the streets at times.

CONVENIENCE ★★★★★
You don't come here for that
The obvious place to stay for the full experience is close to central Chamonix, where you can be a short walk from the gondola to Brévent. But most people just reconcile themselves to life on the buses or trains.

SCENERY ★★★★★
As dramatic as it gets
The mountains above Chamonix are not just high – the mighty Mont Blanc is the highest in Western Europe – they are also truly spectacular. The ride up to the Aiguille du Midi is breathtaking in every sense (we've known people need to lie down for a while at the top).

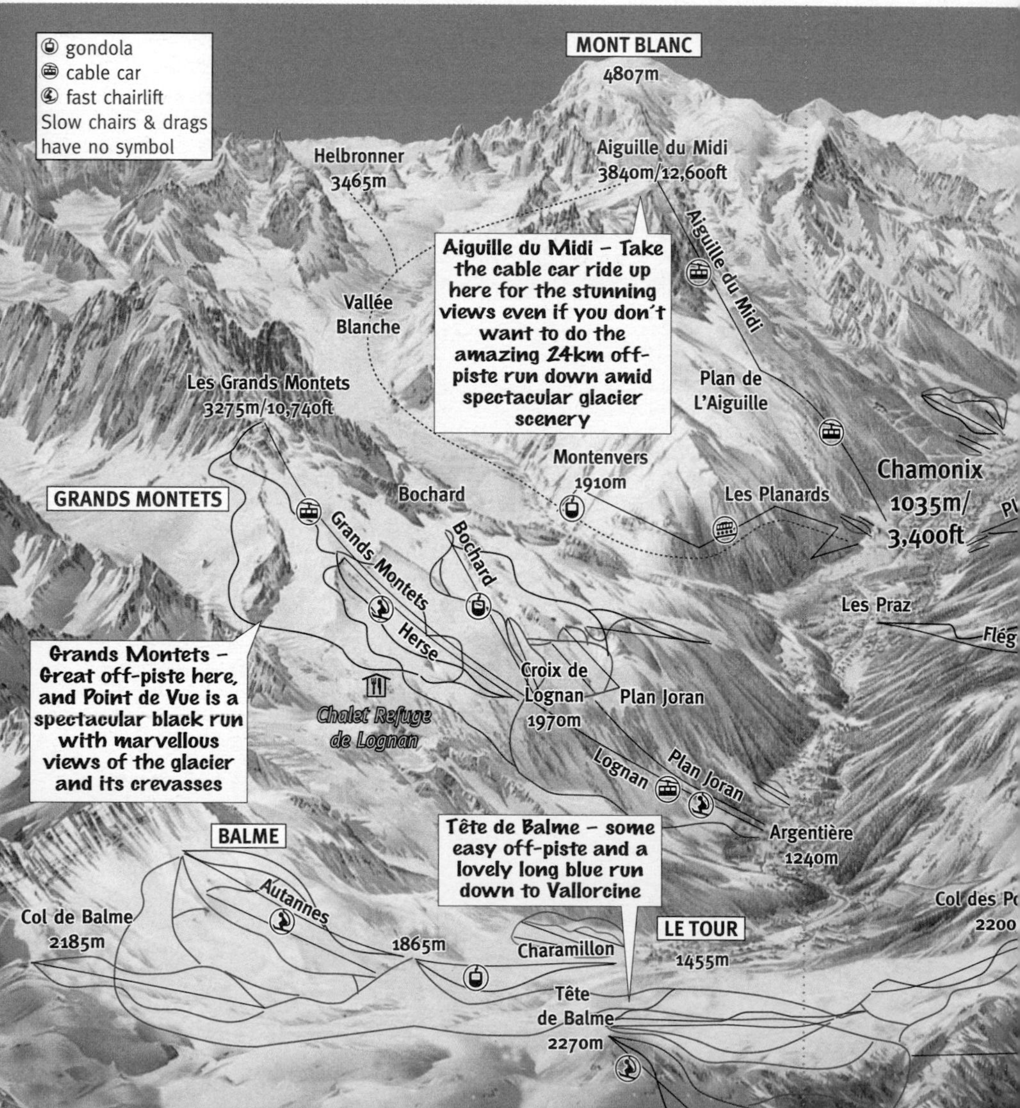

THE MOUNTAINS

Practically all the slopes – with the notable exception of Les Houches – are above the treeline; there are some runs through woods to the valley, but the black ones from Brévent and Flégère, in particular, are often closed and unpleasantly tricky if open.

There is a valley piste map that also shows the individual areas, but separate maps for each area would be better. We have had mixed reports on signposting and piste marking. In sectors other than Balme, the classification of runs often understates difficulty – in particular, some of the blues would be classified as red in other resorts.

EXTENT OF THE SLOPES ★★★
Very fragmented

The gondola for **Brévent** departs a short, steep walk or bus ride from the centre. There are runs on open slopes below the arrival point and a cable car goes on to the summit. There is a lift link to **Flégère**, also accessible via an inadequate old cable car from the village of Les Praz. These sunny areas give stunning views of Mont Blanc.

Up the valley at Argentière a cable car or chairlift take you up to **Les Grands Montets**. Chairs and a gondola serve open terrain above mid-mountain, but much of the best terrain is accessed by a further cable car of relatively low capacity, not covered by the standard lift pass (read 'Lift

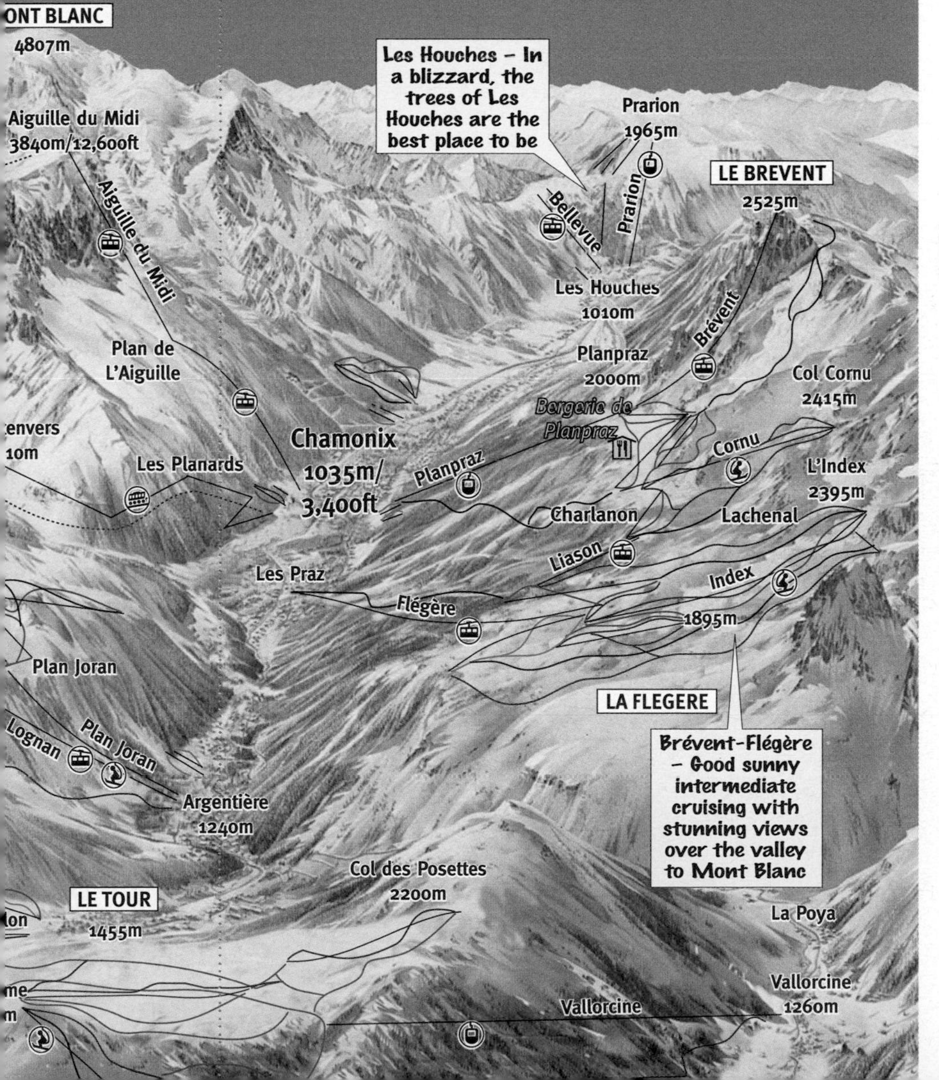

passes'). This shady area can be very cold in early season.

A little way further up the valley, the secluded village of Le Tour sits at the foot of the broad **Balme** area. A gondola goes up to mid-mountain, with a mix of drags and chairs above. There is also a lift up from Vallorcine.

Plus there are several low beginner areas dotted along the valley.

FAST LIFTS ★★★
Not enough

Cable cars and gondolas serve each sector, but many need upgrading. The handful of fast chairs are widely scattered. 'The lifts generally let the place down,' said a 2012 reporter.

QUEUES ★★
Ancient lifts, serious queues

Access to Brévent was transformed by the gondola upgrade a few years ago. But this was only one of the valley's problem lifts. The ancient Flégère cable car can generate queues of an hour or more – to go down as well as up. The lifts out of Argentière build queues, and the chairlift appears to be on its last legs – it no longer operates from the main station, but starts a short way up the slope. At mid-mountain, the top cable car is a famous bottleneck. You can book slots in advance (on the spot or online), preferably the day before, or join the 'standby' queue, which we've found to be an effective alternative; but one 2012 reporter found that bookings weren't honoured, which only added to the queues and the chaos. There may be queues for the lift up to Balme at La Tour, too; it can be quicker to take the train to Vallorcine. But we heard from one lucky January 2012 visitor who experienced no queues at all, even at the weekend.

Crowded pistes and skiers travelling too fast for the conditions can also be a problem in places – most notably on parts of the Grands Montets.

TERRAIN PARKS ★★★
A couple of options

The Snow Bowl park on Grands Montets incorporates features for all levels and includes kickers, rails, a step-up, step-down feature and a boardercross. The park is managed by the experienced HO5 crew, headed by ex-international pro Nico Watier. You can check the latest details at www.ho5park.com. At Brévent there are five rails and an airbag jump.

SNOW RELIABILITY ★★★★
Good high up; poor low down

The top runs on the north-facing Grands Montets slopes above Argentière generally have good snow, and the season normally lasts well into May. The risk of finding the top lift shut because of bad weather is more of a worry. There's snowmaking

SNOWPIX.COM / CHRIS GILL

The Grands Montets (in the centre, with Mont Blanc on the right) has lots of excellent steep, ungroomed slopes, usually with good snow ↓

THE BEST OFF-PISTE SKIING IN THE WORLD?

Chamonix is renowned as an extreme sports Mecca, with arguably some of the best off-piste skiing in the world. And while thrill seekers and off-piste specialists are spoiled for choice, there is plenty for those looking for their first powder experience, too.

__Les Houches__ and __Balme__, at opposite ends of the Chamonix Valley, are ideal for a first taste off the beaten track. The forested slopes of Les Houches are easy to navigate on bad-weather days, with gentle blue runs bringing you back to the valley. Balme's open slopes are perfect for a foray into deep snow in between the pistes, with firmer ground just a few reassuring metres away.

Snowboarders flock to __Flégère__ after a snowfall, its array of boulders and drop-offs turning it into a massive terrain park. The open bowl of Combe Lachenal is easily accessed from the top of the Index lift, and the south-facing slopes of this ski area provide excellent spring skiing.

From the top of __Les Grands Montets__ (3275m) skiing is mostly off-piste and on glacial terrain. The vast north-facing slope of the main face offers countless ways down, satisfyingly steep without being intimidating, with snow conditions that are often among the best in the valley. Off the back, there are several rewarding ways down to the Glacier d'Argentière. In the opposite direction you have access to the steep Pas de Chèvre run. Skiing under the colossal granite spire of Le Dru, with views of the Vallée Blanche, is an unforgettable experience. The Couloir du Dru and the Rectiligne are also on this face, reserved for the adventurous – with some slopes of 40/45°.

These are just some of the options, but the possibilities are endless. Together with heli-skiing on the Italian side of Mont Blanc and in neighbouring Switzerland, the wealth of off-piste on offer could keep you skiing for a lifetime. The Vallée Blanche is covered in a feature panel later in this chapter.

LIFT PASSES

Chamonix Le Pass

Prices in €

Age	1-day	6-day
under 16	32	181
16 to 64	43	213
65 plus	32	181

Free under 4

Beginner no deals

Senior 75 plus: 50% of adult price

Notes
Covers Brévent, Flégère, Balme, Grands Montets except top cable car plus four small beginner areas; family reductions

Alternative passes
Mont Blanc Unlimited (MBU) covers all the above plus Les Houches, Aiguille du Midi and Helbronner cable cars, Montenvers train, Lognan-Grands Montets cable car, and the Verbier (Switzerland) and Courmayeur (Italy) ski areas

on the busy Bochard piste and the run to the valley. Balme has a snowy location, a good late-season record and snowmaking on the run down to the valley at Le Tour. The largely south-facing slopes of Brévent and Flégère suffer in warm weather, and the steep black runs to the resort are often closed. Don't be tempted to try these unless you know they are in good condition – they can be very tricky. Snowmaking was increased at Flégère last year to improve the link to Brévent. Some of the low beginners' areas have snowmaking. Piste grooming is generally respectable.

FOR EXPERTS ★★★★★
One of the great resorts

Chamonix is renowned for its extensive steep terrain and deep snow. To get the best out of the area you really need to have a local guide. There is also lots of excellent terrain for ski-touring on skins. Read the feature panel for more off-piste possibilities.

The Grands Montets cable car offers stunning views from the observation platform above the top station – if you've got the legs and lungs to climb the 121 steep metal steps. (But beware: it's 200 more slippery steel steps down from the cable car before you hit the snow.) The ungroomed black pistes from here – Point de Vue and Pylones – are long and exhilarating. The former sails right by some dramatic sections of glacier, with marvellous views of the crevasses.

The Bochard gondola serves a challenging red back to Lognan and a black to either Plan Roujon or the chairlift below. Shortly after you have made a start down the black, you can head off-piste down the Combe de la Pendant bowl.

At Brévent there's more to test experts than the piste map suggests – there are a number of variations on the runs down from the summit. Some are very steep and prone to ice. The runs in Combe de la Charlanon are quiet and include one red piste and excellent off-piste if the snow is good.

At Flégère there are further challenging slopes – in the Combe Lachenal, crossed by the linking cable car, say – and a tough run back to the village when the snow permits. The short draglift above L'Index opens up a couple of good steep runs (a red and a black) plus a good area of off-piste.

Balme boasts little tough terrain on-piste but there are off-piste routes from the high points to Le Tour, towards Vallorcine or into Switzerland.

FOR INTERMEDIATES ★★★★★
Plenty of better resorts

Chamonix is far from ideal for intermediates unless they relish challenging slopes and trying off-piste.

SCHOOLS

ESF
t 0450 532257

BASS
t 0845 468 1003 (UK)

Evolution 2
t 0450 555357

Ski Sensations
t 0682 105922

Powderama
t 0616 871853

Summits
t 0450 535014

Classes
6 4hr days: €192

Private lessons
€120 for 2hr, for 1 or 2 people

GUIDES

Compagnie des Guides
t 0450 530088

Chamonix Experience
t 0977 485869

If what you want is mile after mile of lift-linked cruisey pistes, go elsewhere.

For less confident intermediates, the Balme area above Le Tour is good for cruising and usually free from crowds. There are excellent shady, steeper runs, wooded lower down, on the north side of Tête de Balme, served by a fast quad. A lovely blue run goes on down to Vallorcine but it is prone to closure.

The other areas have some blue and red runs. Even the Grands Montets has an area of blues at mid-mountain. The step up to the red terrain higher up is quite pronounced, however.

If the snow and weather are good, confident intermediates can join a guided group and do the Vallée Blanche (read our feature panel).

FOR BEGINNERS ★★★★★
Head for Balme

Chamonix is far from ideal for beginners too – there are countless better resorts in which to learn. There are limited but adequate nursery slopes either side of the town – Savoy, at the bottom of Brévent, and Les Planards on the opposite side (dark and cold in mid-winter). Moving on to longer runs means taking a lift up to Brévent or Flégère. La Vormaine, at Le Tour, is a much better bet: extensive, relatively high, sunny and connected to the slopes of the Balme area, where there are easy long runs to progress to. But it's 12km from Chamonix itself.

FOR BOARDERS ★★★★★
Leave it to the experts

The undisputed king of freeride resorts, Chamonix is a haven for advanced snowboarders who relish the steep and wild terrain, especially on the Grands Montets. This means, however, that in peak season it's crowded and fresh snow gets tracked out very quickly. The rough and rugged nature of the slopes means it is not best suited for beginners but for more experienced adventurous riders willing to try true all-mountain riding. The easiest terrain is at the Balme area, though there are quite a few difficult drags here (you can avoid these if you can hack the cat tracks to take you to other lifts, says a reporter). Most lifts elsewhere are cable cars, gondolas and chairs. If you do the Vallée Blanche, be warned: the usual route is flat in places. Check out former British champion Neil McNab's excellent extreme backcountry camps at: www.mcnabsnowboarding.com.

FOR CROSS-COUNTRY ★★★★★
A decent network of trails

Most of the 40km of prepared trails lie at valley level in and between Chamonix and Argentière. All the trails are shady and often icy in midwinter, and they fade fast in the spring sun. Catch the bus rather than ski between the Chamonix and Argentière areas, suggests a reporter, as the link is by 'steep and difficult trails'.

MOUNTAIN RESTAURANTS ★★★★★
Mainly dull, lacking choice

Editors' choice On Brévent the Bergerie de Planpraz (0450 530542) is a wood and stone building with self- and table-service sections and good food; but it gets very busy. On the Grands Montets the tiny, rustic Chalet-Refuge de Lognan (0688 560354), off the Variante Hôtel run to the valley, has marvellous views and simple but satisfying food.

Worth knowing about On Brévent the little Panoramic at the top enjoys amazing views over to Mont Blanc, and the food is fine. On Flégère the newly renovated table-service Adret is 'not outstanding, but definitely pretty good'. On the Grands Montets the Plan Joran has table- and self-service ('good soup and quiche') and a big terrace. There is a picnic room at Lognan by Le Spot snack bar. Tucked away in the woods to skier's right of the home run, the Crémerie du Glacier is a cosy spot for a croûte. At Balme, at the top of the gondola from Le Tour, there's an adequate self-service and a picnic area. For 2012/13 the new Les Consorts in a beautifully renovated farmhouse is due to open.

SCHOOLS AND GUIDES ★★★★★
The place to try something new

The schools here are particularly strong in specialist fields – off-piste, glacier and couloir skiing, ski touring, snowboarding and cross-country. English-speaking instructors and mountain guides are plentiful.

At the Maison de la Montagne is the main ESF office and the HQ of the Compagnie des Guides, which is highly rated (we and reporters have had very good guides from here) and has taken visitors to the mountains for 150 years. Both offer ready-made week-long 'tours' taking clients to a different

CHILDCARE

Panda Club (Evolution 2)
t 0450 555357
From age 3

Piou Piou (ESF)
0450 532257
From age 3

Babysitter list
At tourist office

Ski schools
Ages 3 to 12 (6 days from €286 – ESF)

mountain or resort each day.

Powderama is run by British instructor Simon Halliwell and offers five-day and weekend courses plus, at peak holiday times, specialized one-day clinics (off-piste, piste, moguls). For several years now there has been a branch of BASS here, with all British and Irish instructors. Evolution 2 was quick to rectify a beginner reporter's disappointing experience by providing an alternative instructor.

FOR FAMILIES ★★★★★
Very limited

Childcare is available from some of the ski schools. Evolution 2's Panda Club is used by quite a few British visitors; reports have been enthusiastic but the Argentière base can be inconvenient. Les Houches has better facilities, with a day care centre and children's club.

STAYING THERE

There is all sorts of accommodation, and lots of it.

Chalets Many chalets are run by small specialist operators. Quality tends to be high and value for money good. Inghams now runs the 60-bed Sapiniere, overlooking the nursery slope at the bottom of Brévent and not far from the centre, as a chalet hotel ('very high standard; glad to return to where we stayed when it was independent', said a 2012 reporter).

Hotels A wide choice, many modestly priced, the majority with no more than 30 rooms or so. Bookings for short stays are no problem – the peak season is summer. Momentum can fix whatever you want. Ski Weekends specialize in, er, weekends and offer Le Vert (see below) among others. Club Med has three linked buildings near the centre. Out at Le Lavancher is the 'hameau hôtelier' Les Chalets de Philippe (0607 231726) – a secluded cluster of lovingly furnished wooden chalets, most sleeping no more than three or four, with meals taken either in your own chalet on in a small central dining room.

*******Hameau Albert 1er** (0450 530509) Smart, 100-year-old chalet-style Relais et Châteaux hotel with farmhouse annexe, elevated to 5-star status in 2011. Restaurant with two Michelin stars. Pool.

******Auberge du Bois Prin** (0450 533351) A small modern chalet with a

SNOWPIX.COM / CHRIS GILL

The wooded slopes of Les Houches are the best place in the Chamonix valley to be in bad weather. In good weather they can be delightfully quiet ↓

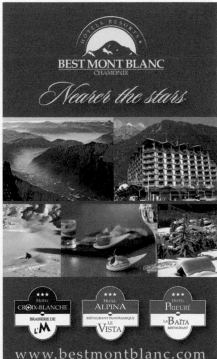

THE VALLEE BLANCHE

This is a trip you do for the stunning scenery. The views of the glacier and the spectacular rock spires beyond are simply mind-blowing. The standard run, although exceptionally long, is not steep – mostly gliding down gentle slopes (in places a bit too flat for snowboarders) with only the occasional steeper, choppy section to deal with. In the right conditions, it is well within the capability of a confident, fit intermediate. If snow is sparse, as it often is in early season, the run can be very tricky, with patches of sheet ice and exposed rocks, and narrow snow bridges over gaping crevasses. If fresh snow is abundant, different challenges may arise. Go in a guided group and check conditions before signing up at the Maison de la Montagne or other ski school offices. The trip is popular – on a busy day 2,500 people do it. To miss the crowds go very early on a weekday, or in the afternoon if you are a good skier and can get down quickly.

The cable car takes you to 3840m and the 3842 cafeteria (claimed to be Europe's highest restaurant) – check out the amazing view of Mont Blanc from here while you adjust to the dizzying altitude. Be prepared for extreme cold, too. A tunnel delivers you to the infamous ridge-walk down to the start of the run. Except at the start of the season, the walk is well prepared, with regular steps cut in the snow and fixed ropes to hang on to. If you have a backpack capable of carrying your skis, and crampons to give some grip, it's no problem; ask for them when you book your guide. Without those items, it can be tiring and worrying. Many parties rope up to their guides.

SNOWPIX.COM / CHRIS GILL

There are variants on the classic route, of varying difficulty and danger; on our last descent we did a mixture of the Petit Envers du Plan and the Vrai Vallée Blanche in 20cm of fresh snow under a blue sky with few other people around – it was absolutely magical, with hundreds of fresh-track turns among all that stunning scenery. Lack of snow often rules out the full 24km run down to Chamonix; a steep stairway (be warned: 311 steps) leading to a slow gondola links the glacier to the station at Montenvers, for the half-hour mountain railway ride down to the town.

GETTING THERE

Air Geneva 85km/ 55 miles (1hr15); Lyon 215km/ 135 miles (2hr45)

Rail Station in resort, on the St Gervais-Le Fayet/Vallorcine line. Direct TGV link from Paris on Friday evenings and at weekends

big reputation; great views; bit of a hike into town (closer to Brévent).
******Jeu de Paume** (Lavancher) (0450 540376) Alpine satellite of a chic Parisian hotel: a beautifully furnished modern chalet halfway to Argentière.
******Mont-Blanc** (0450 530564) Grand 19th-century place in a central location, due to re-open in October 2012 refurbished and upgraded to a 5-star.
******Morgane** (0450 535715) Cool modern style; excellent restaurant, Michelin-starred; good location near Aiguille de Midi cable car; pool, sauna.
*****Alpina** (0450 534777) Striking modern place just north of centre. Much the biggest in town – 138 rooms, most with balconies and mountain views. Sauna, hot tub.
*****Croix-Blanche** (0450 530011) Small, simple hotel and brasserie in centre.
*****Hermitage** (0450 531387) Near centre. Chalet style with lots of wood.
*****Lanchers** (0450 534719) Near Flégère. Classic little 2-star hotel revitalized and upgraded to 3-star status by British owner – recently refurbished and extended. Tipped again by reporter for quality food and friendly service.
*****Mercure** (0450 530756) Next to the station. 'Comfortable rooms, friendly service, nothing too much trouble.' Has its own ski hire facilities.
*****Oustalet** (0450 555499) In Chamonix Sud. 'Spacious, spotless, well-fitted rooms.'
*****Prieuré** (0450 532072) Mega-chalet on northern ring-road – handy for drivers, quite close to centre. Sauna, hot tub.
*****Vallée Blanche** (0450 530450) Smart, good-value B&B hotel, handy for centre and Aiguille du Midi.
****Arve** (0450 530231) Central, by the river; small rooms. Smart restaurant.
Clubhouse (0450 984220) Boutique hotel in an art deco mansion, with a wide choice of ultra-modern rooms.
Le Vert (0450 531358) In Le Gailland, a mile from Chamonix, with en suite

ACTIVITIES

Indoor Sports complex (swimming pool, sauna, steam room, tennis, squash, ice rink, fitness room, climbing wall), museums, library, cinemas

Outdoor Ice rink, snowshoeing, walking paths, tobogganing, dog sledding, paragliding

UK PACKAGES

Action Outdoors, Adventure Base, Alpine Answers, Alpine Elements, Alpine Weekends, Bigfoot Chamonix, BoardnLodge, Carrier, Chalet la Forêt, Chamonix.uk.com, Club Med, Collineige, Crystal, Crystal Finest, Elegant Resorts, Erna Low, Flexiski, High Mountain, Huski, Independent Ski Links, Inghams, Inspired to Ski, Interactive Resorts, Jeffersons, Lagrange, Luxury Chalet Collection, Marmotte Mountain, Momentum, Mountain Tracks, Mountain Wave, Neilson, Oxford Ski Co, Peak Retreats, Pierre & Vacances, PowderBeds, Powder White, Pure Powder, Rude Chalets, Ski Bespoke, Ski Club Freshtracks, Ski Collection, Ski Expectations, Ski France, Ski Independence, Ski Line, Ski Solutions, Skitracer, Ski Weekend, Skiweekends.com, Snow Finders, STC, Thomson, Tracks European Adventures, White Roc, Zenith

rooms for one to six people. Lively bar, top DJs, pool table, Sunday roast.
Apartments Many properties in UK package brochures are in convenient but cramped blocks in Chamonix Sud. The Ginabelle is different – a Pierre & Vacances Premium residence near the station, with pool and fitness facilities, also available through Peak Retreats and Skitracer.

EATING OUT ★★★★★
Plenty of quality places

The top hotels all have excellent restaurants and there are many other good places. One or two advertising-based local guides give useful information.

It's some years since we ate at the hotel Morgane's Bistrot; it was excellent then, and it has had a Michelin star since 2007. The Impossible is a favourite with us and with readers – a rustic chalet a short walk out of the centre with a varied menu; 'superb food, excellent value set menu, great wine list, friendly staff'. And we always enjoy the intimate Atmosphère, by the river, despite its two-sitting system. According to a regular reporter the Panier des 4 Saisons is 'very possibly the best restaurant in Chamonix' with its inventive modern regional French cuisine. The 'cosy' Monchu does good Savoyard food and service at reasonable prices. The Calèche gets booked up well ahead and is short on space but does 'excellent' traditional and more adventurous dishes.

Chamonix offers more variety than is normal in French resorts. Café de l'Arve is fairly new at the hotel de l'Arve, offering a modern, creative menu. Munchie offers a mix of French and Scandinavian cooking that makes a refreshing change.

Value-oriented reader tips include Pitz and Neopolis (both pizza), La Flambée ('good pizza, pasta, steak and local dishes') and the Poele ('no frills, good basic food, good value').

APRES-SKI ★★★★☆
You have to know where to go

Chamonix attracts a lot of young Brits and Scandis – blokes, mainly – wanting to après-ski hard after skiing hard. But it is not Austria, or even Méribel, where you can hear the top village bar as you ski home. It's a big town, and you have to know where to go. One exception is an obvious place at Flégère – the Rhododendrons, which has live music ('great atmosphere').

The tea-time après zone we hear most about is beside the train station. The Swedish-run Chambre Neuf gets 'packed, but not rowdy; live band from 5pm, dancing on the tables' but 'no hope of getting a table after about 3.30'. Elevation 1904, opposite, is a bit quieter.

Towards the river in Rue Whymper, the Lapin Agile is a relaxed wine bar doing Italian-style appetizers. Over the river is the central square with La Tarrasse ('spacious and pleasant'), to the left is Rue du Dr Paccard. The Pub gets packed with Brits ('on Burns night they piped in the haggis'). The Choucas opposite is equally popular for après and late night action. Or turn right for the key Rue des Moulins. Bar'dUp is a small, relaxed place with live music and DJs. Mix is a 'wicked' cool DJ bar. Top tip for grown-ups is Privilege, a relaxed, woody, rustic-chic place with table service and live acoustic music. Soul Food is 'cool, French'. In Chamonix Sud, Monkey Bar is frequented by 'those in the know'.

Just outside the centre, MBC is a micro-brewery; often has live bands.

There's a variety of nightclubs and discos. The Garage claims to be the biggest. The Cantina and the Choucas throb into the early hours, too. Real action enthusiasts may want to look at getting out of town to Le Vert ('hippest nightspot in town').

OFF THE SLOPES ★★★★★
An excellent choice

There's more off-slope activity here than in many resorts. Everyone other than those with medical issues should ride the Aiguille du Midi cable car. Excursion possibilities are endless. The Alpine Museum is 'very interesting but all in French', the library has some English language books and there's a good sports centre with a pool, ice skating and ice hockey matches.

OUTLYING VILLAGE – 1240m

ARGENTIERE

This old village is in an impressive setting towards the head of the valley, 9km from Chamonix – the Glacier d'Argentière towers above it and the Aiguille du Midi and Mont Blanc still dominate the skyline.

There's a fair bit of modern development, and the road through to

UK PACKAGES

Argentière Action Outdoors, Adventure Base, Alpine Answers, AmeriCan Ski, BoardnLodge, Collineige, Crystal, Crystal Finest, Erna Low, Lagrange, Peak Retreats, PowderBeds, Ski Club Freshtracks, Ski France, Ski Independence, Ski Weekend, White Roc
Les Houches Adventure Base, Alpine Answers, AmeriCan Ski, Bigfoot Chamonix, Erna Low, Lagrange, Peak Retreats, Pierre & Vacances, PowderBeds, Ski Collection, Ski Expectations, Ski France, Ski Independence, Zenith
Les Praz Chalet la Forêt
Vallorcine Erna Low, Peak Retreats, PowderBeds, Ski Independence

Phone numbers
From abroad use the prefix +33 and omit the initial '0' of the phone number

TOURIST OFFICES

Chamonix/Argentière
www.chamonix.com

Les Houches
www.leshouches.com

Le Tour, Vallorcine and Switzerland gets uncomfortably busy, but it still has a rustic appeal.

The lifts to the Grands Montets are about 600m from the slightly elevated centre of the village. It's a fair hike, but there are buses. Readers have enjoyed the two central 2-star hotels – the 'old fashioned, great value' Couronne (0450 540002) and the Dahu (0450 540155). But the two best hotels, both 3-star, are out near the lifts – the Grands-Montets (0450 540666), with pool, and the Montana (0450 541499).

Le Cristal d'Argentière is a smart Lagrange Prestige apartment development, between the centre and the lifts, with a decent pool (also available through Peak Retreats and Erna Low).

There's a reasonable choice of inexpensive, unpretentious restaurants and bars in the central area. Best known is the very popular Office, offering a traditional Brit-pub atmosphere and menu. Then there's the Grenier ('amazing food'), Dahu, Stone, Rusticana, Savoy, Rencard and Slalom. More reports, please.

OUTLYING VILLAGE – 1455m

LE TOUR

Le Tour is a charming, unspoiled little village 12km from Chamonix. The valley's best nursery slopes are next to the village, at La Vormaine. A gondola from the edge of the village serves the Balme slopes, an area of mainly easy runs also reachable from Vallorcine.

OUTLYING VILLAGE – 1260m

VALLORCINE

Vallorcine is a small, but developing, traditional mountain village over the Col des Montets, near the Swiss border and 16km from Chamonix. The village shares with Le Tour the main valley's Balme area.

A gondola and chairlift take you to Tête de Balme. A gentle blue run leads back to the village, but it is prone to closure. There's a separate small area of local slopes at La Poya.

Accommodation is mainly in apartments. The newish 4-star L'Ours Bleu, with pool and spa facilities, is featured by Peak Retreats and Erna Low. There's a limited choice of restaurants and bars. The Buvette at the station is a rustic restaurant with decent food and good for drinks while waiting for the train back to Chamonix (it takes 20 minutes).

OUTLYING VILLAGE – 1010m

LES HOUCHES

Les Houches is 6km down the valley from Chamonix. The wooded slopes are popular when bad weather closes other areas, but are not covered by the standard Chamonix pass. They give great views of the looming Mont Blanc massif.

It's a pleasant village, with an old core around a pretty church, but modern developments in chalet style have spread along the road at the foot of the slopes. Some of them are quite a way from the widely separated lifts going to opposite ends of the slopes – a gondola and a queue-prone cable car. On the mountain, all the lifts are slow. There are some awkward links in the network, and signing is poor.

There are nursery slopes and open, gentle runs at the top of the main lifts and long, worthwhile runs back towards the village – blue, red and a black that is Chamonix's World Cup Downhill course: a fine intermediate run, not deserving its black status. There a decent terrain park. But there are lots of draglifts and flat areas for boarders to avoid. The ESF gets good reports for children's classes – 'helpful, sensitive to needs; and flexible'.

Beyond the summit ridge is a very gentle area with cross-country loops and below that some pleasant, sunny woodland runs with views across to the slopes of Megève.

In good weather the slopes are quiet, and the views superb from the several attractive restaurants. The Vieilles Luges is 'like a step back in time; a great place'. Snow-cover on the lower slopes is not reliable, but there is a fair amount of snowmaking.

The village is quiet, but there are some pleasant bars and restaurants. Reporters have recommended the 3-star Hotel du Bois (0450 545035). Granges d'En Haut (0450 546536) is an exceptional development of luxury chalets where you could self-cater but there is also a smart restaurant; spa, small pool.

There are some good apartments with pools, including the 4-star Hameau de Pierre Blanche (available through Peak Retreats) and Pierre et Vacances' Hauts de Chavants.

Châtel

A distinctively French base in an ideal position for exploring the huge Portes du Soleil circuit which spans the French-Swiss border

RATINGS

The mountains

Extent	*****
Fast lifts	**
Queues	***
Terrain p'ks	***
Snow	**
Expert	***
Intermediate	****
Beginner	***
Boarder	**
X-country	***
Restaurants	***
Schools	***
Families	***

The resort

Charm	***
Convenience	**
Scenery	***
Eating out	***
Après-ski	***
Off-slope	**

RPI	95
lift pass	£180
ski hire	£100
lessons	£70
food & drink	£120
total	**£470**

NEWS

2012/13: Further snow-guns are planned.

2011/12: A six-pack replaced the Rochassons double chair from Plaine Dranse towards Avoriaz. Snowmaking was increased in the terrain park and in the Plaine Dranse area. A five-hour pass, which lets you ski for any five consecutive hours in a day, replaced the half-day pass.

+ Very extensive, pretty, intermediate terrain on Portes du Soleil circuit, with good local slopes
+ Wide range of cheap and cheerful, good-value accommodation
+ Pleasant, lively, French-dominated village, still quite rustic in parts

– Traffic congestion can be a problem at weekends and in peak season
– Low altitude and exposure to westerlies means some risk of rain and poor snow
– Some main lifts are a bus ride from the village centre
– Some drawbacks for beginners

Châtel offers an attractive blend of qualities much like that of Morzine – another established valley village in the Portes du Soleil area. Morzine is a bit more polished, Châtel (with a claimed 30 working farms) more rustic and down to earth. But its key advantage is that it is part of the main Portes du Soleil circuit. There is a gap in the circuit at Châtel, filled by buses; but this is more of an irritant to those passing through than for Châtel residents, for whom the excellent local bus services are part of the daily routine. On busy days it's worth trying the slopes of nearby La Chapelle-d'Abondance, which are pleasantly uncrowded.

THE RESORT

Châtel is a much expanded village near the head of the wooded Dranse valley, at the north-eastern limit of the huge French-Swiss Portes du Soleil ski circuit. It has two separate sectors of slopes, one linked to its French neighbour – high, purpose-built Avoriaz – and the other to two resorts in Switzerland: Morgins (on the Portes du Soleil circuit) and Torgon (not on the circuit).

A few kilometres down the valley is rustic La Chapelle-d'Abondance, with lifts into the Torgon slopes – covered at the end of this chapter.

VILLAGE CHARM ***
Rustic style, urban traffic

Châtel is still an attractive village, despite the inevitable expansion and reporters remark on the friendly locals. Modern, unpretentious chalet-style hotels and apartments rub shoulders with old farms where cattle still live in winter. But it is no rustic idyll: life revolves around two streets that are far from traffic-free: lots of visitors take cars, and they can clog the centre – especially at weekends.

CONVENIENCE **
No perfect position

Although there is a definite centre, the village sprawls along the road in from lake Geneva and the diverging roads up the hillside towards Morgins and along the valley towards the Linga and Pré-la-Joux lifts. There is an excellent, frequent though sometimes crowded free bus service linking the sectors. Staying centrally helps with catching the ski-bus to the outlying lifts before it gets very crowded, and simplifies après-ski outings – the night bus finishes at 8pm most nights. But there is accommodation near the Linga lift, if first tracks are the priority.

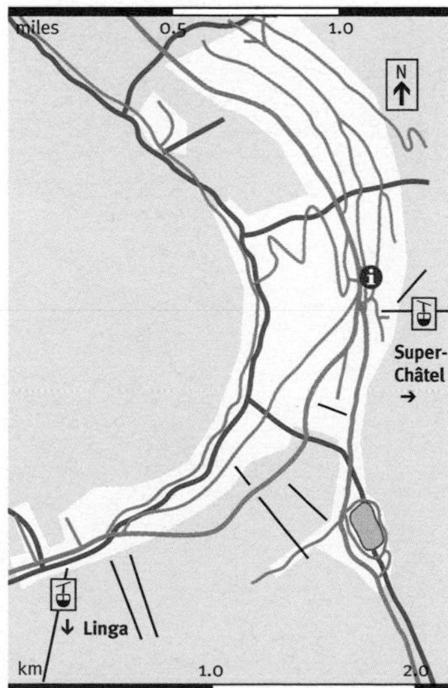

KEY FACTS	
Resort	1200m 3,940ft
Portes du Soleil	
Slopes	950-2275m 3,120-7,460ft
Lifts	198
Pistes	650km 404 miles
Green	13%
Blue	40%
Red	37%
Black	10%
Snowmaking	835 guns
Châtel only	
Slopes	1100-2205m 3,610-7,230ft
Lifts	45
Pistes	90km 60 miles
Snowmaking	175 guns

SCENERY ★★★
Lots of variety

Châtel's broad valley setting is very scenic, with Linga providing a splendid backdrop and pleasantly woody slopes curving in both directions. The lifts above Torgon give great views over Lake Geneva. As you travel around the Portes du Soleil circuit the dramatic Dents du Midi are constantly coming into view.

THE MOUNTAINS

Châtel sits between two sectors of the main Portes du Soleil circuit, each offering a mix of open and wooded slopes. For notes on the circuit read our special chapter on it.

EXTENT OF THE SLOPES ★★★★★
Two sectors to choose between

Directly above the village is **Super-Châtel** – an area of easy, open and lightly wooded slopes that is accessed by a gondola or a two-stage chair. From here you can embark on a clockwise Portes du Soleil circuit by heading to the Swiss resort of Morgins. Alternatively, you can head north for the slopes straddling a different bit of the Swiss border, above **Torgon** (where there are great views of Lake Geneva).

An anticlockwise circuit starts outside the village with a lift into the **Linga** sector – a gondola from Villapeyron followed by a newish six-pack to Tête du Linga or a choice of fast chairs from Pré-la-Joux. The faster way to Avoriaz is via Pré-la-Joux. There is night skiing at Linga on Thursdays.

FAST LIFTS ★★
Luxurious Linga

Linga and the Plaine Dranse area are well served now that the Rochassons double has been replaced by a six-pack – but in the Super-Châtel sector the lifts beyond the access gondola are almost entirely slow chairs and drags, whether you head for Morgins or for Torgon. Hence our rating.

QUEUES ★★★
Bottlenecks have been eased

In recent years queues have been eased throughout the Portes du Soleil by the installation of several fast new chairlifts. But queues form for the gondola to Super-Châtel when school parties gather there, and you can also face queues to get down again if the sunny home slope is shut by poor snow. The slow Morclan chair at Super-Châtel has queues too, if the gondola is coming up full. Reporters have also found lengthy queues at the Tour de Don and Chermeu draglifts at certain times of day, which have caused difficulties for skiers rushing back to Super-Châtel to pick up their children from ski school. A 2011 visitor had a gripe about the 'poor management' of queues which means that lifts often go up at much less than full capacity at peak times.

TERRAIN PARKS ★★★
One size suits all

The Smooth Park at Super-Châtel has lines to suit both beginners and experienced freestylers and include rails, kickers, boxes, hips and boardercross.

The resort is pleasantly rustic, and all in small-scale chalet style ➔

CHATEL TOURISME / JEAN-FRANCOIS VUARAND

LIFT PASSES

Portes du Soleil

Prices in €		
Age	**1-day**	**6-day**
under 16	33	164
16 to 19	40	197
20 to 63	44	219
64 plus	40	197

Free under 5

Beginner limited points card; lesson and lift deals

Notes family discounts; 5hr pass

Alternative pass Châtel only

SNOW RELIABILITY ★★★★★
The main drawback

The main drawback of the Portes du Soleil as a whole is that it is low, and exposed to mild weather from the west, so snow quality can suffer when it's warm. But a lot of snowmaking has been installed at Super-Châtel and on runs down to resort level. Linga and Pré-la-Joux are mainly north-facing and generally have the best local snow. The pistes to Morgins and towards Avoriaz get full sun.

FOR EXPERTS ★★★★★
Some challenges

The best steep runs – on- and off-piste – are in the Linga and Pré-la-Joux area. Beneath the Linga gondola and chair there's a pleasant mix of open and wooded ground, which follows the fall line fairly directly. And there's a serious mogul field between Cornebois and Plaine Dranse. Two pistes from the Rochassons ridge are steep and kept well groomed. On the way to Torgon from Super-Châtel, the Barbossine black run is long, steep and quite narrow and tricky at the top. There's plenty of good lift-served off-piste to be explored with a guide: on a recent visit we did a great run from Tête du Linga over into the next (deserted) valley of La Leiche – read the special off-piste feature panel in our Morzine chapter.

FOR INTERMEDIATES ★★★★★
Some great local terrain

When conditions are right the Portes du Soleil is an intermediates' paradise. Good intermediates need not go far from Châtel to find amusement; Linga and Plaine Dranse have some of the best red runs on the circuit. The moderately skilled can do the Portes du Soleil circuit without problem, and will particularly enjoy runs around Les Lindarets and Morgins. Even timid types can do the circuit, provided they take one or two short cuts and ride chairs down the trickier bits. But some blues are difficult when conditions are poor – in particular, one reporter witnessed skiers 'in tears' on the way down to Morgins from Châtel.

Visits to Avoriaz for the Hauts Forts runs and the ungroomed snowcross run are worthwhile for competent intermediates. And note that the runs back to Plaine Dranse are real reds, and the Rochassons piste especially can get extremely busy at the end of the day.

Don't overlook the Torgon sector, which has some excellent slopes, including challenging ones.

FOR BEGINNERS ★★★★★
Three possible options

There are good beginners' areas at Pré-la-Joux (a bus ride away) and at Super-Châtel (a gondola ride above the village). And there are nursery slopes at village level if there is snow there. Reporters have praised the Super-Châtel slopes and lifts, which 'allow the beginner to progress' and 'safely practise' on gentle gradients away from the main runs. Getting up to them is a bit of an effort, though. The home run from Super-Châtel can be tricky – narrow, busy, steep at the end and often icy. The Pré-la-Joux slopes are less varied, with some steeper draglifts.

SCHOOLS

ESF
t 0450 732264

ESI Pro Skiing
t 0450 733192

Henri Gonon
t 0450 732304

Sensations
t 0450 813251

BASS
t 020 3286 3661 (UK)

Ecole Ski Academy
t 0681 665280

Classes (ESF prices)
6 half-days (2½hr am)
€126

Private lessons
€38 for 1hr for 1 or 2 people

CHILDCARE

Mouflets Garderie
t 0450 813819
Ages 3mnth to 6yr

Piou Piou (Village des Marmottons)
t 0450 732264
Ages 3 to 6

Les Pitchounes
t 0450 813251
Ages 3 and 4

Ski schools
Generally from age 5 (ESF 6 half-days from €126)

FOR BOARDERS ★★

Best for beginners – beware drags

Avoriaz is the hard-core destination in the Portes du Soleil. Châtel is not a bad place to learn or to go to as a budget option. But many lifts in the Super-Châtel sector are drags and reporters warn they can be a 'painful experience'. The Linga area has good, varied slopes and off-piste possibilities and more boarder-friendly chairlifts.

FOR CROSS-COUNTRY ★★★

Pretty, if low, trails

There are pretty trails (9km) along the river and through the woods on the lower slopes of Linga, but snow-cover can be a problem. When combined with La Chapelle-d'Abondance's trails, the total is 40km. The tourist office produces good maps with suggested routes and trail times.

MOUNTAIN RESTAURANTS ★★★

Some quite good local huts

A cluster of atmospheric huts can be found at Plaine Dranse. The one that generates the reports from readers is Vieux Chalet, aka Chez Babeth – 'food is excellent but pricey, the interior camper than a field of pink bell-tents, and Babeth the owner is, as ever, absolutely barking'. In the Linga area the Ferme des Pistes is a cosy alpine barn, complete with stable-door. The chapter on Avoriaz has several recommendations at Les Lindarets, in the valley between the resorts.

There are picnic rooms at Plaine Dranse and the tops of the gondolas in the Super-Châtel and Linga sectors.

SCHOOLS AND GUIDES ★★★

Plenty of choice

There are seven schools in Châtel, including a branch of BASS (British Alpine Ski & Snowboard School), which we have no reports of – please send one if you use them. The International school has been recommended by reporters, including visitors who had a private lesson that was 'one of our best ever' and a recent visitor's grandson who had 'so much more fun' than in previous lessons with the ESF. But the ESF has also been praised, with comments such as 'very helpful and customer-focused'.

FOR FAMILIES ★★★

Some good facilities

The ESF-run Marmottons nursery has good facilities, including toboggans, painting, music and videos, and children (from three to six) are reportedly happy there. Ski Sensations has its own nursery area with a draglift and chalet at Linga.

STAYING THERE

This is emphatically a French resort. No big mainstream tour operators feature it.

Chalets A few catered chalets exist, including Chalet Le Dragon in La Chapelle-d'Abondance – see opposite.

Hotels Practically all the hotels are 2-stars, mostly friendly chalets, wooden or at least partly wood-clad. But there are some smarter places.

CHATEL TOURISME / JEAN-FRANCOIS VUARAND

Plaine Dranse offers countless lunch options ➔

UK PACKAGES

Connick, Interactive Resorts, Lagrange, Peak Retreats, PowderBeds, Ski Addiction, Ski France, Ski Line, Skialot, Snow Finders, Snowfocus, Susie Ward
La Chapelle-d'Abondance Chalet Le Dragon, Ski Addiction, Ski La Cote

ACTIVITIES

Indoor Spas in hotels, cinemas, library, bowling

Outdoor Ice rink, walks, cheese factory visits, ice diving, ice fishing, snowshoeing, paragliding, airboarding, 'snake-glisse', 'yooner' tobogganing

GETTING THERE

Air Geneva 80km/ 50 miles (2hr)

Rail Thonon les Bains (40km/25 miles)

Phone numbers
From abroad use the prefix +33 and omit the initial '0' of the phone number

TOURIST OFFICES

Châtel
www.chatel.com

La Chapelle-d'Abondance
www.lachapelle74.com

******Macchi** (0450 732412) Smart, modern chalet, spacious comfortable rooms, 'excellent food'; small pool, spa; central.
*****Fleur de Neige** (0450 732010) Woody chalet near centre; revamped 2010; spa, pool; Grive Gourmande restaurant is one of the best in town.
****Belalp** (0450 732439) Simple chalet, small rooms, but 'very good food'.
****Choucas** (0450 732257) Central location. 'Friendly owner.'
****Kandahar** (0450 733060) One for peace lovers: a Logis by the river, a walkable distance from the centre.
****Lion d'Or** (0450 813440) In centre, is fairly basic with a 'good atmosphere'.
****Roitelet** (0450 732479) 'Basic, good location, four-course dinner, made to feel part of the family.'
****Tremplin** (0450 732306) 'Excellent, good value. Owner cooks well but speaks no English.'
Apartments Peak Retreats offers two properties that set a new standard for Châtel, both with pools and various spa facilities – the MGM-built CGH-operated Chalets d'Angèle, and Grand Lodge. Châtel's supermarkets are reported to be small and overcrowded, but there is a large supermarket out in the direction of Chapelle-d'Abondance.

EATING OUT ★★★☆☆
Fair selection

There is an adequate number and range of restaurants. The Macchi and Fleur de Neige hotels both have ambitious restaurants. We've also enjoyed the Table d'Antoine restaurant of the hotel Chalet d'Alizée, though it's a few years ago. The rustic Vieux Four does ambitious dishes alongside Savoyard specialities and is approved by readers ('good value and the best food we had all week'). The Poya does 'a blend of traditional and contemporary cuisine'. The Pierrier and the Fiacre ('mains/pizzas good value') are more modest, everyday restaurants, good for families.

It's worth a trip to the hotel Cornettes in La Chapelle-d'Abondance (described on the right).

APRES-SKI ★★★☆☆
All down to bars

The Tunnel bar is very popular with the British and has a DJ or live music every night. The Avalanche is a very popular English-style pub with a 'good atmosphere and live music'. The Godille – close to the Super-Châtel gondola and crowded when everyone descends at close of play – has a more French feel. The 'small and cosy' Isba is the locals' choice, and shows extreme-sports videos. The bowling alley has a good bar.

OFF THE SLOPES ★★☆☆☆
Less than ideal

Those with a car can easily visit places such as Geneva, Thonon and Evian. There are some pleasant walks, sleigh rides, you can visit the cheese factory or the two cinemas, or join in daily events organized by the tourist office.

The Portes du Soleil as a whole is less than ideal for non-skiers who like to meet their more active friends for lunch: they are likely to be at some distant resort – maybe in another country – at lunchtime, and very few lifts are accessible to pedestrians.

DOWN-VALLEY VILLAGE – 1010m

LA CHAPELLE-D'ABONDANCE

This unspoiled, rustic farming community, complete with old church and friendly locals, is 5km down the valley from Châtel. It has its own quiet little north-facing area of easy wooded runs and a gondola on the outskirts links it to slopes between Torgon in Switzerland and Super-Châtel, and so the Portes du Soleil circuit. The Mousseron hut, near the Braitaz chairlift, is 'well worth a visit'.

Nightlife is virtually non-existent – just a few quiet bars, a cinema and torchlit descents. The Fer Rouge is a popular microbrewery, with live music.

The hotel Cornettes (0450 735024) is an amazing 2-star with 4-star facilities, including an indoor pool, a sauna, a steam room and hot tubs. It has been run by the Trincaz family since 1894 and has an atmospheric bar and an excellent restaurant with good-value menus. Look out for the showcases displaying puppets and dolls and for eccentric touches, such as ancient doors that unexpectedly open automatically.

Chalet Le Dragon is opposite the gondola into the main slopes and run as a catered chalet by its British owners. It has been fully renovated, with five bedrooms, new bathrooms and an outdoor hot tub. They run a minibus to and from other lifts too. A 2011 reporter was 'instantly wowed by the quality' and said it was 'the best chalet we have ever stayed in'.

SNOWPIX.COM / CHRIS GILL

Courchevel

Arguably the best of the half-dozen resorts that make up the famous Trois Vallées – with a choice of four different villages

RATINGS

The mountains	
Extent	*****
Fast lifts	****
Queues	****
Terrain p'ks	**
Snow	****
Expert	****
Intermediate	*****
Beginner	****
Boarder	****
X-country	****
Restaurants	***
Schools	****
Families	****
The resort	
Charm	**
Convenience	****
Scenery	***
Eating out	*****
Après-ski	****
Off-slope	***

RPI	120
lift pass	£200
ski hire	£135
lessons	£125
food & drink	£155
total	**£615**

KEY FACTS

Resort	1260-1850m 4,130-6,070ft
Trois Vallées	
Slopes	1260-3230m 4,130-10,600ft
Lifts	173
Pistes	600km 373 miles
Green	16%
Blue	40%
Red	34%
Black	10%
Snowmaking	2162 guns
Courchevel/ La Tania only	
Slopes	1260-2740m 4,130-8,990ft
Lifts	60
Pistes	150km 93 miles
Green	16%
Blue	38%
Red	37%
Black	9%
Snowmaking	44%

- ＋ Extensive, varied slopes
- ＋ Lots of slope-side accommodation
- ＋ Impressive snowmaking and piste grooming, and a decent lift system
- ＋ Partly wooded setting
- ＋ Choice of four very different villages
- ＋ Some great restaurants and top-notch hotels

- − 1850 and 1550 lacking in charm
- − Very high prices in 1850 and in mountain restaurants generally
- − The French feel has been lost, with half the visitors now from abroad
- − Not great for the indolent non-skier unless glitzy shops are your thing

Courchevel's ski area is the most compelling sector of the famous Trois Vallées, the biggest linked ski area in the world; if we're heading for the 3V, more often than not we'll head for Courchevel.

But it's not one destination, it's four. Swanky 1850 catches the headlines, with its airstrip, ritzy hotels and six Michelin-starred restaurants. The other villages have none of 1850's pretensions and high prices. There are plenty of affordable catered chalet holidays on sale here, even (thanks to the miracles worked by UK tour ops) in 1850. Sadly, there are few affordable lunches.

The resort quietly rebranded all the villages last year. You won't have noticed any difference last season but you should next – for more on that see below.

THE RESORT

The local council decided last autumn to rebrand its villages – see the feature panel opposite. But we have decided to stick with the old names for this edition until we can see how the name changes are put into practice on the ground and on the piste map next winter.

Courchevel 1850 (now simply Courchevel) was one of the first French resorts to be purpose-built in the years immediately after World War Two. The other villages were developed later, although they already existed as old hamlets.

The lowest village is Le Praz (aka 1300), then 1550 (now Courchevel Village), 1650 (now Moriond) and finally 1850.

1850 is big enough to have several distinguishable quarters. The main lift base and the central area around it is La Croisette; the resort spreads a long way up the hillside on the left through the chalet-filled suburbs of Cospillot and Nogentil to the Altiport, the resort's famously hazardous little airstrip. Part of these suburbs is the Jardin Alpin, a forested area with some of the swankiest hotels (and more modest chalets and apartments), served by its own gondola. On the opposite, right-hand side of La Croisette is another little 'downtown' area, with the suburbs of Chenus above it and Plantret below.

The other resort villages are smaller and simpler. The main part of 1650 has grown up along the road that links

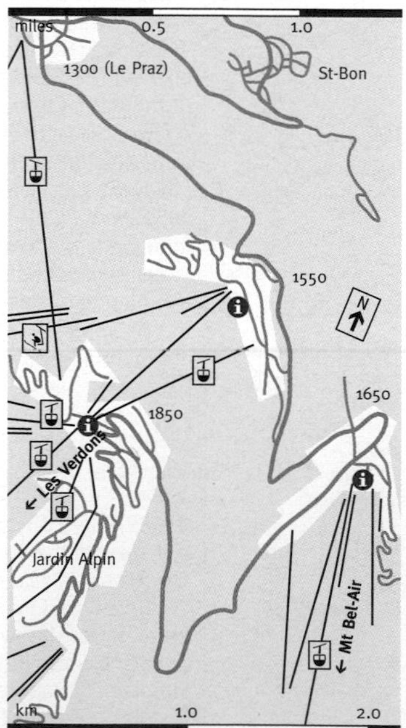

NEWS

2012/13: At 1850, the Biollay quad is due to be replaced by a six-pack, increasing capacity by around a third. It will finish higher up to access more runs. The popular Creux red from Saulire/ Vizelle to, er, Creux is due to have more snowmaking, as is the Cospillot blue back to base. At 1650, the 3 Vallées chair from near the top of the village has been removed, and a short gondola will take people to a spot from where they can ski or walk down to the main Ariondaz gondola. This is presumably in preparation for the main lifts out of 1650 being improved in future years.

2011/12: A six-pack replaced the Plantrey quad at 1850. There are two new family fun zones – one at 1650 with boarder-cross and one at 1550 with boxes and rails. The Magnestick system to hold chairlift safety bars down until near the end of the ride was installed. In 1850, two new 5-star hotels (K2 and Grandes Alpes) opened, while the Chabichou hotel opened a new restaurant and spa.

the resorts (though traffic is not intrusive); and the centre, around the lift base area, has been attractively developed and is lined with good local shops, restaurants and bars. Opposite the main gondola (reached by an escalator) individual chalets spread down the hill and are served by another (much longer) three-stage covered escalator. Then there is another area of chalet development spreading up the slopes to an area known as Belvedère. 1650 has its own distinct sector of slopes, connected to 1850. It also has a great Intersport rental shop right opposite the main gondola that has excellent demo skis.

1550 is a bit of a backwater, with a few blocks and many more individual properties, directly below 1850. Le Praz is an old village on a plateau at the bottom of wooded slopes.

La Tania, built for the 1992 Olympics and near Le Praz, gets its own chapter. With a car, Champagny is easily reached, linked to La Plagne.

VILLAGE CHARM ★★★★★
Not a strong point

Courchevel 1850 has most of the smart hotels and shops, and you would expect it to be a pretty smooth place in general. The reality is a let-down; when compared with other smart resorts, 1850 does not impress.

The approach is dreary, and at La Croisette you are confronted by the backside of the main lift station building, complete with garage entrances. Past this point, things improve: the streets are lined by smart shops and jolly restaurants. But the nearest thing to a central focus is where a hairpin bend on the busy road through the resort to the affluent suburbs touches the slopes. The areas above the centre are more pleasant – in places, peacefully rustic.

Central 1650 is more pleasant and has a friendly traditional feel and the traffic is not intrusive – we spent a very happy week there in 2012 on a well-earned holiday. 1550 is a pleasantly quiet, spacious mini-resort, bypassed by the road to 1850. Le Praz suffers from through-traffic, but away from the road is a low-key rustic place, with a friendly atmosphere, relatively unspoilt despite expansion for the 1992 Olympics – the ski jump is a prominent legacy.

CONVENIENCE ★★★★★
Varies – research your location

The villages all have lifts into the slopes, with much of the lodging close by, but in all cases you need to be careful about location if you want to avoid walks, sometimes with hills involved. 1850 has several pistes running through it, and a high proportion of ski-in/ski-out lodgings in all parts except the very centre, where you just plod to the lift base. Central 1650 lodging is a short walk to the lifts, with some ski-in/ski-out places up the hill and the handy covered escalator serving many places down the hill. 1550 is essentially arranged along the bottom of the slopes, with lifts immediately above most of the lodgings. Le Praz is in general the least convenient place: the lifts start a short walk outside the village. Frequent free buses link the villages.

SCENERY ★★★★★
Some good views

Most of the villages enjoy a pretty woodland setting and from parts of them and from the slopes above there are good views to Mont Blanc and over the valley to Champagny and Bellecôte (in the La Plagne ski area).

NAME CHANGES FOR THE COURCHEVEL VILLAGES

On the advice of a marketing agency, the local town council changed the names of its villages in autumn 2011. Its flagship Courchevel 1850 is now called just Courchevel. 1650 reverted to the name of the old village it is based on and is now Courchevel Moriond. 1550 becomes Courchevel Village. Le Praz (sometimes called 1300) is Courchevel Le Praz. But it was too late for them to change things in the resort literature and piste maps for last season because they were all printed.

Way back in Where to Ski and Snowboard 2000 we pointed out that the heights of the villages did not match the names: the ice rink in the centre of 1850m is at 1740m; the gondola station in 1650 is below 1600m; the middle of 1550 is at 1480m; the lake at 1300/Le Praz is at 1260m.

So we shouldn't be surprised that the names have changed; it has just taken them 13 years to respond to our remarks. But for this edition, we're sticking with the old names – until we see for ourselves next winter how the changes look on the ground and on the piste map.

Now that Signal is equipped with two fast chairs, it's a key feature of the skiing above 1650

Vizelle is a great hill, with testing red and black pistes all around it – and, of course, lots of off-piste

Méribel ↘
La Saulire 2740m/ 8,990ft
Creux Noirs 2705m
La Vizelle 2660m
Col de Chanrossa 2545m
CHANROSSA
Chanrossa
Signal
Marmottes
Suisses
Saulire
Vizelle
Creux
Aiguilles du Fruit
SAULIRE - CREUX
Biollay
Verdons
Chapelets
Bel Air
Signal
Altiport
Pralong
Praméruel 1825m
Jardin Alp.
Courchevel 185
Ariondaz
Grangettes
Courchevel 1650 (Moriond)
Courc
(Courch

Short new lift for 2012/13 gets you high enough to ski down to main gondola

Lots of easy skiing on the lower slopes above 1850, with plenty of fast lifts serving them

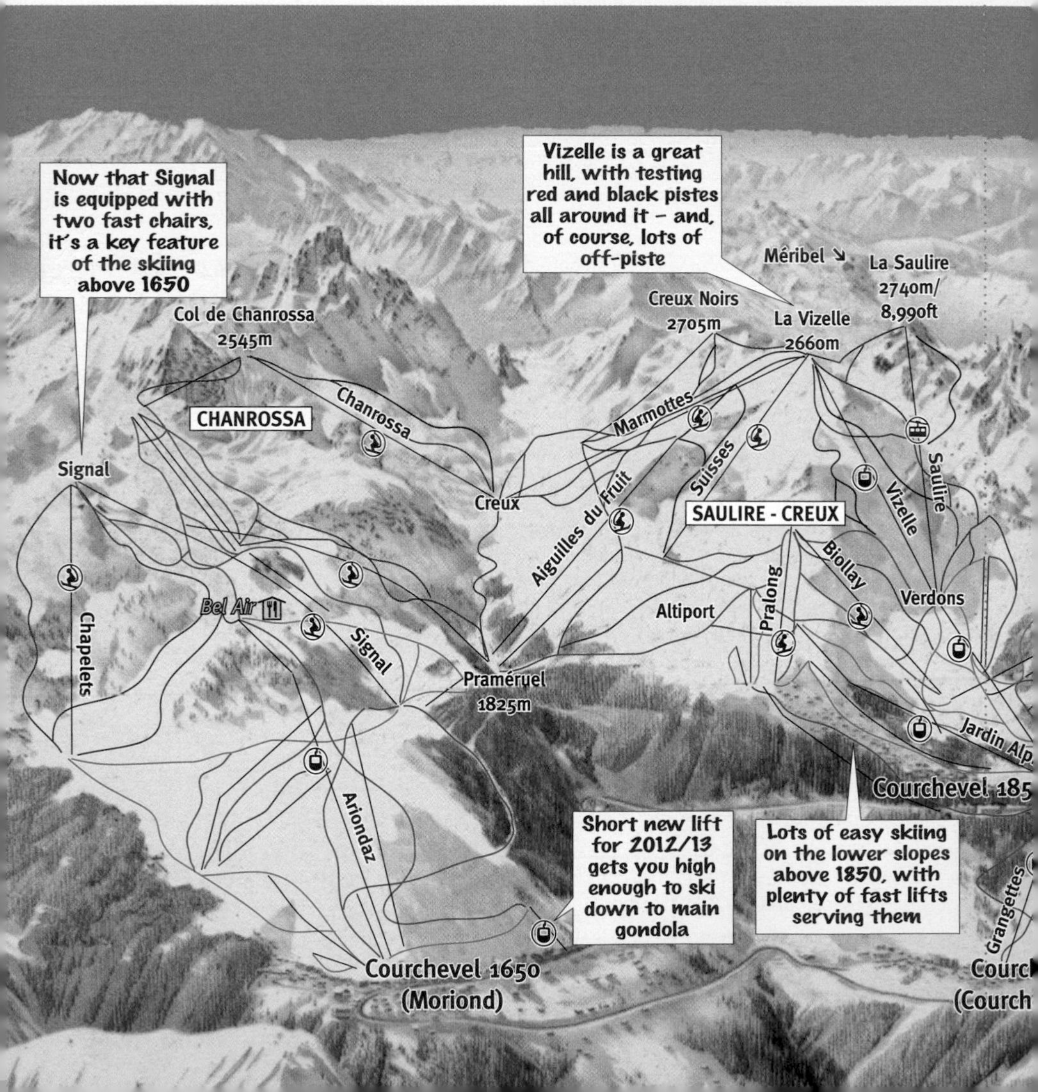

gondola
cable car
fast chairlift
Slow chairs & drags have no symbol

Méribel
Col de la Loze 2305m
Chenus 2245m
LOZE - PRAZ
Dou des Lanches
Excellent, testing runs in the woods, which really come into their own in bad weather
The long green home run made La Tania a much better place for beginners – see separate chapter
Coqs
Chenus
Plantrey
Praz-Juget
Jardin Alpin
hevel 1850
Grangettes
Touvets
Praz
Foret
La Tania
Courchevel 1550 (Courchevel Village)
Courchevel 1300 (Le Praz) 1260m/4,130ft
La Tania 1350m/4,430ft

LIFT PASSES

Trois Vallées

Prices in €

Age	1-day	6-day
under 13	37	184
13 to 64	49	244
65 plus	42	210

Free under 5, 75 plus

Beginner limited pass

Notes
Covers Courchevel, La Tania, Méribel, Val Thorens, Les Menuires and St-Martin; family reductions; pedestrian and half-day passes

Alternative passes
Courchevel/La Tania +3V extension; Courchevel 1650 only

OT COURCHEVEL / SEMAPHORE – PASCAL LEROY

They take grooming seriously here, but no longer hand out maps of which trails were groomed overnight ↓

THE MOUNTAINS

Although there are plenty of trees around the villages, most of the slopes are essentially open, with the notable exception of the runs down to 1550 and to 1300, and the valley between 1850 and 1650.

We have no complaints about the piste map or general signposting. But they need to improve information about which pistes have been groomed; it appears in small notices posted in lift stations but we found it inadequate on our 2012 visit (they used to hand out grooming maps – shame that has stopped).

EXTENT OF THE SLOPES ★★★★★
Huge variety to suit everyone

A network of lifts and pistes spreads out from 1850. The main axis is the **Verdons** gondola, leading to a second gondola to La Vizelle and a nearly parallel cable car up to La Saulire. These high points of the **Saulire-Creux** sector give access to a wide range of terrain above Courchevel (including a number of couloirs), to Méribel and thus the whole of the Trois Vallées. Next to the Verdons gondola is the Jardin Alpin gondola, which serves the higher hotels until 8pm but also links to lifts and pistes beyond.

To the right looking up, the Chenus gondola goes towards the **Loze-Praz** sector, which forms a second link with Méribel. Runs also go back from here to 1850, and through the woods to La Tania and 1300.

The main gondola from 1650 goes to Bel Air and further lifts on into the **Chanrossa** sector. This sector has links to Saulire-Creux at two points – Praméruel and Creux.

FAST LIFTS ★★★★
Plenty of them

You will occasionally find yourself on a slow chair, but there are only a couple of places where slow lifts are not avoidable. One is Col de la Loze; the other, more importantly, is the 1650 side of Chanrossa, where the best long, easy blues in the resort are served by drags. The piste map makes the distinction between slow and fast chairs, which helps. The Roc Mugnier six-pack has greatly improved access to 1650. A bit of history was made last year, with a six-pack replacing the Plantrey chair, said to be the world's first detachable quad, installed 29 years ago.

QUEUES ★★★★
Not a problem

The lift system is impressive, and even in peak season queues are minimal. But there can be a build-up at 1850 as the ski school gets going. The Biollay chair is very popular with the ski school and has been a problem in the past – but the new six-pack there should reduce queues. At 1650, the gondola may have peak-time queues; an upgrade is due for 2013/14. A 2012 visitor found 10-minute waits in mid-February at beginner drags in 1650.

ONE OF THE BEST FOR OFF-PISTE SKIING

Courchevel's image is of upmarket luxury and pampered piste skiing. But it is a great resort for off-piste too. Manu Gaidet is a Courchevel mountain guide and a ski instructor with the Courchevel ESF. He is also one of the world's top freeriders, and won the Freeride World Championship three years running. We asked him to pick out a few of the best runs. Always go with a guide.

For a first experience off-piste, the Tour du Rocher de l'Ombre is great. Access is easy from the left of the Combe de la Saulire piste, and you are never far from the piste. It is very quiet, the slope is very broad and easy and you get a real sense of adventure as you plan your way between the rocks. And the view of the Croix des Verdons is impressive. Keep to the left for the best snow.

The Chanrossa chairlift opens up several routes. Les Avals is one of my favourites, involving a short climb to the ridge to the south. This run is not technically difficult and is particularly beautiful in spring conditions. Another possibility is to traverse towards the Aiguille du Fruit, and pick your spot to start skiing down to Creux. And there is Plan Mugnier, a shady run with normally very good snow, but more difficult – for experienced off-piste skiers only – and starting with a 20-minute hike.

Le Curé is in the Saulire area: this narrow gully starts under a towering rock and offers a steady 35° slope; it is only for expert skiers who don't mind climbing to the Doigt du Curé starting point.

ACTIVITIES

Indoor Ice rink, bowling, climbing wall, exhibitions, concerts, cinemas, cookery courses, library; in hotels: health and fitness centres (swimming pools, saunas, steam room, hot tub, water therapy, weight training, massage)

Outdoor Hang-gliding, helicopter flights, paragliding, flying lessons, snowshoeing, snowmobile rides, ballooning, walking on cleared paths, tobogganing, ice climbing

TERRAIN PARKS ★★★★★

Freestyle for all the family

The Family Park below Verdons is now the main park and has lines to suit different levels, with a variety of jumps and obstacles including, at certain times, an airbag jump. Two smaller 'fun zones' were built for 2011/12, with boardercross above 1650 and the Bio Park with boxes and rails above 1550.

SNOW RELIABILITY ★★★★★

Very good

The combination of Courchevel's northerly orientation, its height, an abundance of snowmaking and excellent grooming usually guarantees good snow down to at least 1850 and 1650. The snow is usually much better than in Méribel, where the slopes get more sun. The runs to 1300 are prone to closure in warm weather.

FOR EXPERTS ★★★★★

Entertaining pistes, and ...

There is plenty to interest experts, even without considering the rest of the Trois Vallées. The most obvious expert runs are the shady couloirs you can see on the right near the top of the Saulire cable car. All three main couloirs were once black pistes (some of the steepest in Europe), but only the Grand Couloir remains a piste – the widest and easiest of the three, but reached by a narrow, bumpy, precipitous access ridge.

The shady slopes of La Vizelle and Creux Noirs are not seriously steep, but all the runs – tough reds and not-tough blacks – offer a worthwhile challenge. If you like groomed blacks in the early morning, keep an eye on the grooming notices at lift bases/ ticket offices to see when Suisses or M is groomed. Chanrossa often seems to have the most serious bumps. The blacks above Le Praz can be great fun, too – again, they are not seriously steep, but offer a vertical of almost 1000m.

There is a huge amount of off-piste terrain, including lots next to the pistes. The runs off Dou des Lanches through the trees down to La Tania and off the top of Creux Noir (via a little walk) down to join up with the Creux piste are recommended. The wooded areas in general are great for bad weather.

In good snow conditions you can ski all the way down (around 2000m vertical) from La Saulire to Bozel.

There is plenty of other off-piste terrain in this valley to try with a guide – see the feature panel above.

There's also an Avalanche Camp area under the Biolly chair near the terrain park with transceiver practice and avalanche rescue sessions.

FOR INTERMEDIATES ★★★★★

Paradise for red-run skiers

For confident intermediates, Courchevel's local slopes are simply fabulous. Every sector has long, testing red runs and easy blacks, and there is abundant easy off-piste to experiment in. There are too many excellent runs to list; every high-point – Signal, Chanrossa, Vizelle, Creux Noirs, Saulire, Chenus, Loze – offers one, two, three, four notable descents.

For timid intermediates, we're not

so enthusiastic. The red runs from Vizelle and Saulire can be quite testing, especially late in the day. But there are some excellent sectors to focus on. The long, narrow sector of blue slopes above 1650 is superb, and there is an array of excellent blue slopes above and below 1850 – the Biollay and Pralong fast chairs are the ones to head for here. On the ridge separating 1850 from La Tania, the Crêtes run and chair offer a great quiet area to build confidence on good snow. The runs on down to La Tania from here are long, rolling cruises, but how easy they are depends crucially on snow conditions.

OT COURCHEVEL / SEMAPHORE – PASCAL LEROY

1850 looks pretty from this carefully taken tourist office photo. It's not quite so charming from other viewpoints ↓

FOR BEGINNERS ★★★★
Great graduation runs
There are excellent nursery slopes above both 1650 and 1850. At 1650, there are short drags right above the village. At 1850 there is a small but good beginner area in the Jardin Alpin, reachable by the gondola, and an excellent bigger one at Pralong, near the airstrip. Absolute beginners have to get to this by road. Altogether there are eight free beginner lifts – an excellent arrangement. 1550 and 1300 have small nursery areas; but the former is quite steep. There are some excellent long runs to progress to.

FOR BOARDERS ★★★★
Upmarket all-rounder
Despite being an upmarket resort, Courchevel has always been popular with snowboarders. There are miles of well-groomed pistes, good freeride terrain and the lifts are in general very modern and quick, with few drags. The resort's freestyle facilities are not what you would call hard-core, though. The big snowboard hangout in 1850 is Prends ta Luge et Tire Toi.

FOR CROSS-COUNTRY ★★★★
Long wooded trails
Courchevel has a total of 65km of trails. Le Praz is the most suitable village, with trails through the woods towards 1550, 1850 and Méribel. Given enough snow, there are also loops around the village.

MOUNTAIN RESTAURANTS ★★★
Fine if you can afford them
Mountain restaurants are plentiful and pleasant, but uncomfortably pricey. Fortunately, the local lift pass permits lunch above La Tania; of course the 3V pass gets you to Les Menuires. The piste map does not name restaurants.
Editors' choice The Bel Air (0479 080093), above 1650, has always stood out for its warm welcome, efficient service, good food, splendid tiered terrace, nice woody interior and (by local standards) reasonable beer and cheap house wine (13 euros a bottle). But even here the food is unpleasantly pricey (25 euros for the plat du jour including a big salad). We had a bad report on it in 2011 but ate here ourselves twice in 2012 and thought it excellent. It and the cheaper Bouc Blanc (see the La Tania chapter) are our firm favourites in the area.

SCHOOLS
ESF in 1850 t 0479 080772
ESF in 1650 t 0479 082608
ESF in 1550 t 0479 082107
Supreme t 0479 082787 (UK: 01479 810800)
New Generation t 0479 010318 0844 770 4733 (UK) www.skinewgen.com
Magic t 0479 010181
Oxygène t 0479 419958
BASS t 0479 083387
RTM t 0615 485904
Classes (ESF 1850 prices) 6 5hr days €328
Private lessons From €100 for 1½hr

GUIDES
Guides de Courchevel t 0623 924612

Worth knowing about We had good table-service lunches at Verdons at the top of the gondola and at Pilatus, just below the Altiport; efficient table-service at both and huge portions at Pilatus; fun live music and dancing on the terrace at Verdons; both pricey though. The self-service Chenus is 'reasonably priced compared to other establishments'; 'good food and service'. The Courcheneige on the Bellecôte slope is tipped this year for 'excellent quality' and 'reasonable prices and large portions'.The Soucoupe at Loze is a traditional place and 'a real treat'. There are some very good places on the pistes running down to Croisette. The traditional Bergerie is tipped. Chalet de Pierres is famously pricey, but we confess to calling in for an occasional treat, and a repeat visitor confirms it is 'up to its usual standards of good food and service'. At 1550 the Oeil Boeuf on the Tovets run is a hit – 'steaks cooked on an open fire'.

SCHOOLS AND GUIDES ★★★★☆
Plenty of choice

Courchevel's branches of the ESF add up to the largest ski school in Europe, with over 700 instructors. We had mixed reports of children's classes this year. Three reporters who booked through Ski Esprit in 1850 were very satisfied. But one who booked independently in 1650 said his daughter was 'upset and demoralized' at the lack of feedback until the last day when she was told she had 'failed and should go back in the same class next year'.

Last season two of our editorial team were able to endorse the many positive reports we have received on New Generation (run by top British instructors): 'Absolutely brilliant. The instructor did just what we had hoped – building up our confidence so that we could then enjoy the ski area.'

Reporters also praise another Brit-based outfit, RTM Snowboarding: 'Excellent. My private lesson was the best ever.' BASS and Supreme are other Brit-run schools, but we lack reports on them.

Magic Snowsports Academy is run by an Anglo-French team and has native English-speaking instructors.

The Bureau des Guides runs all-day off-piste excursions.

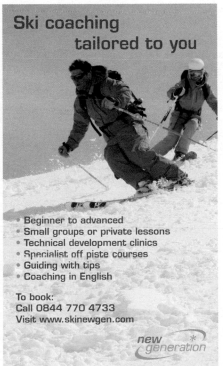

CHILDCARE

Village des Enfants (1850)
t 0479 080847
Ages 18mnth to 3yr

Les Petits Pralins de Moriond (1650)
t 0479 063472
Ages 6mnth to 6yr

Maison des Enfants (1550)
t 0479 082107
Ages from 18mnth

Ski schools
Most offer lessons from age 3 or 4 (ESF 1850 prices €335 for 6 days)

FOR FAMILIES ★★★★

Lots of suitable options

Courchevel is a good choice for families; there is lots of convenient lodging and gentle slopes. The 'Magnestick' system, to hold children securely on chairlifts, has been fitted to all fast lifts. The ESF Club des Piou-Piou at 1650, for kids aged three to five, is reportedly 'very well run and a good introduction to skiing for children'. Several UK chalet operators run nurseries. Family specialist Esprit operates in 1850 – read 'Chalets', next.

STAYING THERE

Chalets There are lots available – specialist agents list dozens of them.

1650 is UK chalet central. Le Ski, celebrating their 30th year there in 2013, now has 17 chalets in 1650 (more than any other operator has in the whole Courchevel valley), sleeping from two to 22. Thirteen of them have sauna, steam or hot tub. And their flagship Scalottas Lodge even has a pool with a current to swim against; they have five chalets in the Lodge, and we stayed in two of them last season, both with fabulous views, leather armchairs and sofas, solid wooden floors, a jacuzzi bath and hi-tech lights and heating. Bliss.

Ski Olympic is also a 1650 specialist, with the central Avals chalet hotel (complete with Rocky's bar) plus two large chalets. Skiworld has four chalets in 1650, including the traditional but smooth Estrella, with hot tub, and two in 1550.

Down in Le Praz, Mountain Heaven has a couple of chalets, including the very luxurious-looking Jardin d'Angele with sauna and outdoor hot tub. Crystal also has two down in 1300.

Inghams has three chalets and the very central 30-bedroomed chalet hotel Anémones in 1850 and two chalets with shared hot tub, sauna and steam room in 1650.

Ski Total has a chalet hotel bang in the centre of 1650 and three chalets (one very central) and a central 60-bed chalet hotel in 1850. Also in 1850, family specialist Esprit has a chalet hotel with a good pool right next to the lifts at Pralong. We had three glowing reports on its childcare and service in 2012.

There are some genuinely luxurious (and pricey) chalets in 1850 from operators like Consensio and Kaluma.

Hotels There are more than 40 hotels in Courchevel, mostly at 1850 and many of them very swanky. Two were awarded the new 'Palace' rating last year – the Cheval Blanc and the Airelles – to distinguish them from the 5-star standard invented only a few years back; 14 now hold 5-star status. The prices of the top places give new meaning to the word 'exorbitant' – it is possible to pay £1,000 per person per night without too much difficulty, though you can of course pay a lot less. In our listings we concentrate on more affordable places – and were pleased to have a 2-star recommendation last year.

COURCHEVEL 1850

*******Sivolière** (0479 080833) Chalet set among pines on the western edge of the village, with a reputation for friendly service despite the stars.

******Bellecôte** (0479 081019) A bit of Alpine atmosphere as well as luxury. Close to the Bellecôte piste.

******Chabichou** (0479 080055) Distinctive white building, right on the slopes; family-run, friendly and rustic, with very good food plus the option of a restaurant with two Michelin stars.

*****Courcheneige** (0479 080259) On the Bellecôte piste, with a rustic restaurant.

****Tovets** (0479 080333) Good value hotel right at La Croisette. 'Spacious rooms, plentiful food, delightful staff, perfect location – why pay more?' says a recent visitor.

COURCHEVEL 1650

*******Manali** (0479 080707) Smart and welcoming; slope-side, just above the gondola, with terrace; spa and pool (open to the public).

******Portetta** (0479 080147) Neat place at foot of slopes, with pool, spa, good restaurant – and the most civilized ski/boot room this side of the Atlantic.

*****Seizena** (0479 082636) Stylish and central (over road from the gondola).

UK PACKAGES

Alpine Answers, Alpine Elements, Alpine Weekends, Carrier, Consensio, Crystal, Crystal Finest, Elegant Resorts, Erna Low, Esprit, Family Friendly Skiing, Flexiski, Friendship Travel, Independent Ski Links, Inghams, Inspired to Ski, Interactive Resorts, Jeffersons, Kaluma, Lagrange, Le Ski, Luxury Chalet Collection, Mark Warner, Momentum, Mountain Wave, Neilson, Oxford Ski Co, Pierre & Vacances, PowderBeds, Powder White, Scott Dunn, Silver Ski, Ski Amis, Ski Bespoke, Ski Collection, Ski Expectations, Ski France, Ski Independence, Ski Line, Ski Olympic, Ski Power, Ski Solutions, Ski Total, Skitracer, Ski Weekend, Skiweekends.com, Skiworld, Snow Finders, Snoworks, STC, Supertravel, Ted Bentley, Thomson, White Roc

Le Praz Bigfoot Chamonix, Mountain Heaven, Ski Deep

GETTING THERE

Air Geneva 150km/ 95 miles (2hr15), Lyon 195km/ 120 miles (2hr30); Chambéry 110km/ 70 miles (1hr30)

Rail Moûtiers (24km/ 15 miles); transfer by bus or taxi

Phone numbers
From abroad use the prefix +33 and omit the initial '0' of the phone number

TOURIST OFFICE

www.courchevel.com

Courchevel 1550
*****Flocons** (0479 080270) Handsome chalet near the Tovets six-pack and the piste from 1850.
Courchevel 1300 (Le Praz)
*****Peupliers** (0479 084147) Traditional, smart, good restaurant.
Apartments Courchevel may not be apartment-dominated, but there is plenty of choice. If you want to self-cater in real style, take a look at the chalets in the resort literature. Ski Amis has privately owned apartments in several parts of the resort, and Skiworld has 'flexible catered chalets' where you can choose what catering (if any) you want. Mountain Heaven has a chalet in Le Praz. The best big residences are the Montagnettes Chalets de la Mouria in 1650 (apartments and semi-detached chalets), with sauna, steam and hot tub, and the renovated Chalets du Forum in central 1850 – a Pierres & Vacances Premium residence. Ski Collection features both these and the very attractive Portetta Mountain Lodges in 1650. Erna Low has a good range of properties, including the Lofts above Hotel Portetta. Skitracer is an apartment specialist.

EATING OUT ★★★★★
Pick your price

You can eat very well here, but you have more choice if you have a fat wallet. A non-comprehensive pocket guide is distributed. In 1850 there are no fewer than four places with two Michelin stars and two with one star. But we have no reports in 2012 of good meals in more affordable places – if you have one, please tell us.

In 1650 the Petit Savoyard (pizza as well as proper cooking) and the Schuss have had positive reports in the past. We ate at the tiny La Cabane and enjoyed it – though soy sauce seemed to be overdone on most of the dishes.

In Le Praz, the small and unpretentious Michelin-starred Azimut is much more affordable than equivalent places in 1650 (three-course menus from 28 euros), and we had a delicious meal there in 2012. The Table de Mon Grand-Père has 'superb food and atmosphere' but prices approaching 1850 levels. Bistrot du Praz is also expensive but worth it, say reporters. Cave de Lys is an atmospheric vaulted wine bar that serves tapas-style snacks.

APRES-SKI ★★★★
Take your pick

At close of play there is no great on-mountain scene, unless you count a final glass or two of champagne or lovely cakes at Cap Horn or Chalet de Pierres. In 1850 there are bars around Croisette that may come to life; but we get few reports on them these days. Later Kudeta's disco pumps until 4am, as does the Grange – a Moroccan-style place. There are some exclusive nightclubs, such as the Caves. The Mangeoire piano bar gets going late and is 'great fun' for live music. The Tremplin has karaoke. The Petit Drink specializes in wine and tapas. Oxygen is a cool lounge bar.

In 1650 there are several lively bars within a few yards of each other. The Bubble (refurbished for last season) and Rocky's are Brit-run, and the Bubble and the Boulotte fill up with chalet staff letting their hair down. We liked the Schuss for a quiet drink as the lifts closed (great views over 1550 from the windows of the rear tables) but were annoyed when a waiter tried to move us 30 minutes before the advertised time for turning the place into a restaurant. The lively Funky Fox has pool, live music or DJs, and the Club disco stays open late.

In 1550 there are a handful of bars that can develop a lively atmosphere – notably The Bar, and the bar of Ski Power's chalet hotel Chanrossa.

OFF THE SLOPES ★★★
Not ideal

There is quite a bit to do, but the emphasis is very much on physical activities. A non-skiers' guide to paths and itinéraires is distributed by the tourist office. A pedestrian lift pass for the gondolas and buses in Courchevel and Méribel makes it easy for non-skiers to get up the mountain to meet others for lunch. There is no public pool, and although some hotel pools are open to non-residents the prices are astronomical. Cinemas in 1850 and 1650 show English-speaking films. Snowshoeing among the trees and 'seriously awesome' tobogganing from 1850 to 1550 are popular. And you can take joyrides from the altiport. There is a pocket shopping guide listing fashion and jewellery shops in 1850. The prices in these shops are stratospheric, and most of the customers are Russian.

OT LES DEUX-ALPES

Les Deux-Alpes

Sprawling resort with a high, narrow ski area that will disappoint many intermediates; popular for summer skiing and boarding

RATINGS

The mountains	
Extent	***
Fast lifts	****
Queues	**
Terrain p'ks	*****
Snow	****
Expert	****
Intermediate	**
Beginner	***
Boarder	****
X-country	**
Restaurants	***
Schools	***
Families	****
The resort	
Charm	**
Convenience	***
Scenery	****
Eating out	****
Après-ski	****
Off-slope	**

RPI	90
lift pass	£170
ski hire	£95
lessons	£70
food & drink	£120
total	**£455**

NEWS

2012/13: The Diable gondola is to be replaced by a six-pack. A new blue run is being formed in the same area, down to the village – but it is unlikely to be completed this year. The Crêtes ski tow is to be replaced with a covered moving carpet.

2011/12: Snowmaking was introduced to the Demoiselles and Diable runs back to the resort.

+ High, snow-sure, varied slopes, including an extensive glacier area
+ Lots of good off-piste terrain
+ Stunning views of the Ecrins peaks
+ Wide choice of affordable hotels

− Piste network modest by big resort standards, and congested in places
− Home runs are either steep and icy or dangerously overcrowded
− Virtually no woodland runs
− Spread-out, rather messy resort

Les Deux-Alpes is a big resort, with a big mountain offering a splendid Alpine feel, and good snow on its high, shady runs. But it doesn't come from the standard major resort mould. It is not at all swanky – which means that smart apartments are hard to come by, but modest, good-value hotels are not. And its mountain is very unusual – tall and long, but narrow. Keen piste-bashing intermediates will find the pistes limited in extent.

We've been complaining since 1994 about the dangerous home runs here. We were told a year ago that they were planning a blue alternative to the icy blacks and hideously crowded green. It didn't materialize for 2011/12, and it's not likely to be there for next season. Shame.

THE RESORT

Les Deux-Alpes is a long, narrow village sitting on a high, remote col. It is modern, but seems to have grown haphazardly over the years without a coherent plan. Access is from the Grenoble-Briançon road to the north.

The six-day pass covers La Grave and gives two days in Alpe-d'Huez and days in Serre-Chevalier (an hour away over the Col du Lautaret) and other resorts. A car would be handy to make the most of these options, especially Serre-Che. There are buses twice a week to Alpe-d'Huez, but a better plan is to splash 65 euros on the splendid helicopter day-trip.

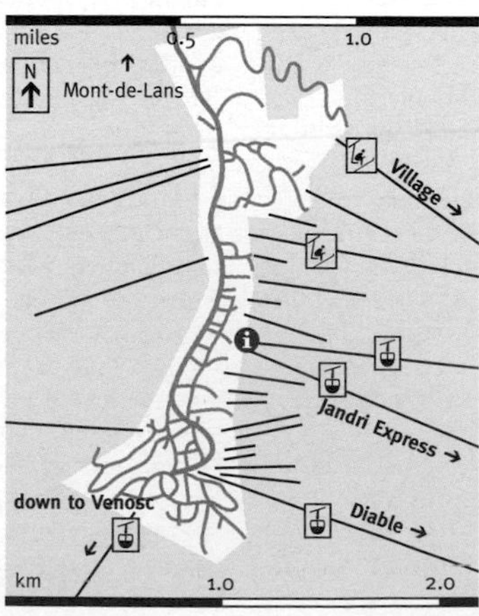

VILLAGE CHARM **

Lively, but that's all

The village is a long, sprawling collection of apartments, hotels, bars and shops, most lining the two streets that form the one-way traffic system. There is a wide range of building styles, from old chalets through 1960s blocks to more sympathetic recent buildings. It looks better as you leave than as you arrive – all the balconies face south. The place has quite a buzz, in the early evening at least.

CONVENIENCE ***

Three main parts

Lifts are spread fairly evenly along the village. There is no clear centre, but three sectors can be identified. As you enter the village from the north, roads go off left up the hill to Les 2 Alpes 1800 – inconvenient for shopping and nightlife. Go straight on instead and you come to the effective centre, with the major gondola stations, outdoor ice rink and lots of shops and restaurants. At the far end of the resort is Alpe de Venosc, with many of the bars and hotels, the most character and the best shops. The free shuttle-bus saves some long walks.

SCENERY ****

High southern peaks

The resort sits high among the southern Alps, with great views from the upper slopes of the Ecrins peaks.

KEY FACTS

Resort	1650m 5,410ft
Slopes	1300-3570m 4,270-11,710ft
Lifts	53
Pistes	205km 127 miles
Green	21%
Blue	45%
Red	22%
Black	12%
Snowmaking	211 guns

THE MOUNTAINS

The main slopes are all above the treeline, though there are trees directly above the village.

The piste map is much improved – it's very unusual for the Alps in that it breaks the slopes down in to several separate maps. But it is still very poor around mid-mountain.

At the same time, L2A has renamed all its runs, adopting a system that is supremely logical but bonkers (as well as boring). All runs leading to the Fée chair are now called Fée X, where X is a number from 1 to 7. So yes, it's easy to find a run down to the Fée lift. But will you be able to remember the runs you liked and the ones you didn't? No.

A few blue runs have short steep sections, and some runs are different colours on the map and the mountain.

EXTENT OF THE SLOPES ★★★

Surprisingly small

For a big resort, Les Deux-Alpes has a disappointingly small area of pistes. The main area goes high and stretches a long way – the top is almost 8km from the village – but it is very narrow. We are unconvinced by the claimed extent of 205km. (You'll see 225km claimed on the piste map, but amazingly it turns out 20km of this is cross-country loops.) One reporter last year who took the heli-trip to Alpe-d'Huez (claimed extent 250km) was 'surprised and delighted' by how much bigger that ski area was.

The western side of Les Deux-Alpes, now branded **Vallée Blanche**, is served by lifts from various parts of town. It is relatively low (the top is 2100m) and has only short pistes back to town, which get the morning sun.

On the broad, gentle slope east of the resort are about 10 beginner lifts, and above them a steep slope rising to the ridge of **Les Crêtes**. Lifts go up to the ridge from four points spread along the village. To get back to base you have a choice of one long, winding, narrow green run, often very crowded (and sometimes closed), or four short black runs. These are usually mogulled (one is never groomed), and often icy at the end of the day (they get the afternoon sun). Many visitors ride down. It's this mess that the resort is planning to sort out with a new blue run.

The ridge has lifts and gentle runs along it, and behind it lies the deep, steep Combe de Thuit. Lifts span the combe to the mid-mountain station at **Toura,** at the heart of the slopes. We seem to spend a lot of time on three key fast chairlifts in this area – Bellecombes, at the top of the Combe; Glaciers, carrying on towards the glacier; and Fée, on its own slightly separate hill.

The section of the mountain around and below Toura is very narrow – there is one main way down the mountain, and it gets crowded in the afternoon – but there are now three ways to avoid the worst of the crowds.

SNOWPIX.COM / CHRIS GILL

From Dôme de la Lauze you can embark on the world's biggest on-piste descent – 2270m vertical to Mont de Lans ↓

ACTIVITIES

Indoor Swimming pool, hot tub, sauna, sports centres (Club Forme, Acqua Center), squash, cinemas, games rooms, bowling, museums, library

Outdoor Ice rink, snowmobiling, paragliding, quad bikes, snowshoeing, ice climbing, sleigh rides, tobogganing

The top **Glacier du Mont de Lans** section has fine, easy runs with great views, served by an underground funicular and draglifts. There are steeper slopes off to the north, served by chairs. You can go from the top all the way down to Mont-de-Lans – a descent of 2270m that we believe is the world's biggest on-piste vertical.

A walk (or snowcat tow) takes you to the slopes of La Grave.

On Wednesdays, you can now sign up to make First Tracks up at glacier level after a 'snack' at 3200m.

FAST LIFTS ★★★★☆
Main lifts OK but ...

Les Deux-Alpes has some impressive lifts, with fast chair alternatives to the gondolas. But there are still a few draglifts and slow chairs around.

QUEUES ★★☆☆☆
Problems in the village

The village is large, and high-season queues for the gondolas in the morning can be serious. 2011 visitors reported waits of 45 minutes at the peak; one took to camping outside the lift station half an hour before it opened. The upgrade of the old Diable gondola to a six-pack, now planned for 2012/13, will help a bit. Up the mountain there are few problems, although the Crêtes area gets busy in peak season. The top lifts are prone to closure if it's windy, putting pressure on the lower lifts. There may be queues for the gondolas back to the village when snow is poor low down.

TERRAIN PARKS ★★★★★
Europe's biggest summer park

The heavyweight terrain park is located above Toura in the winter, then shifts up to the glacier in the summer. The winter park is maintained to an excellent standard, and features a slope-style line with three tables, rails, hips and boxes, a big air jump, half-pipe, kids-only mini park, beginner zone and rail zone, as well as a boardercross and a BBQ area. There's a 120m 4.5m-radius half-pipe.

SNOW RELIABILITY ★★★★☆
Excellent on higher slopes

The snow on the higher slopes is normally very good, even in a poor winter. On a tour in March 2012 that involved skiing crud in most resorts, we enjoyed packed powder most of the day here. Above 2200m most of the runs are north-facing, and the top glacier section guarantees good snow. More of a concern is bad weather shutting the lifts, or very low temperatures at the top. But the runs

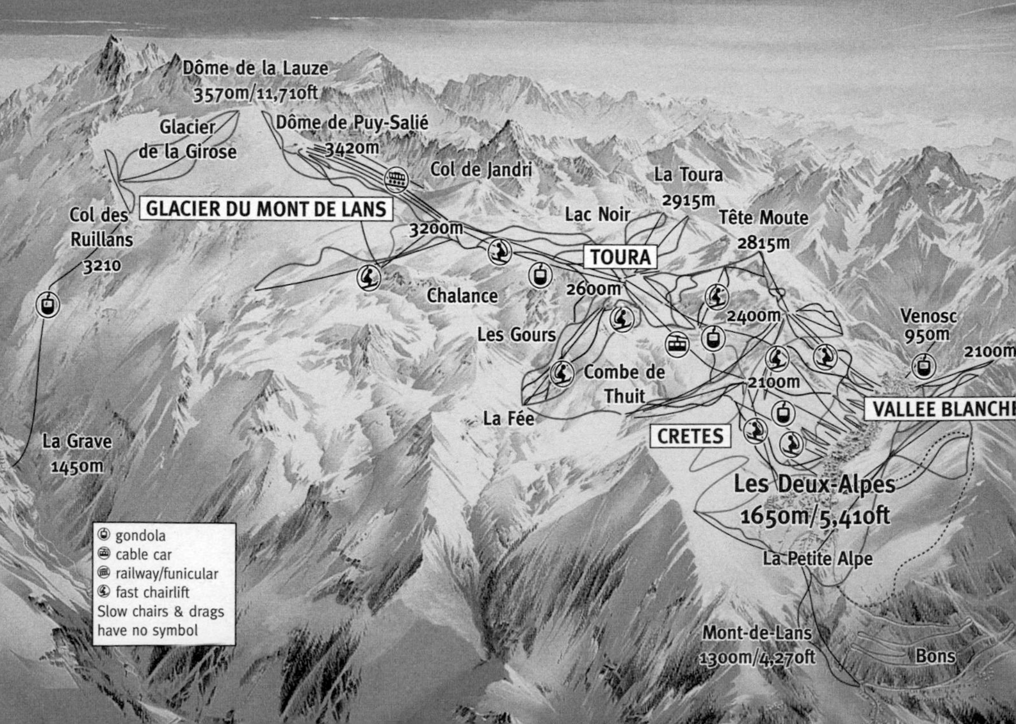

OFF-PISTE CHALLENGES FOR EVERYONE FROM NOVICE TO EXPERT

The off-piste routes in Les Deux-Alpes are numerous, and varied in difficulty. But never try them without the right equipment and a qualified guide.

*Both sides off the **Bellecombes** piste offer a wide range of varying terrain; it's important to take care here – there are several small cliff faces. For those keen to tackle couloirs this descent offers small ones that are ideal for your first attempts; they can be avoided, though.*

*Traversing across the top of the black Grand Couloir piste leads to the **North Rachas** area, with off-piste faces that normally offer good snow conditions all winter. The first large valley leads to three couloirs – one fairly broad and easy, the others much narrower and steeper. Traversing further leads to a much wider descent that avoids the three couloirs.*

*Strong skiers will enjoy the famous **Chalance** run (our favourite), which starts just below the glacier and descends 1000m to join the Fée 1 piste; there are several variations, mixing wide open slopes and rocky pitches. These faces are at times subject to quite a high avalanche risk.*

*Traversing above the north face of the Chalance leads to the couloir **Pylone Electrique** – a steep, narrow 200m-long couloir with the reward below it of an excellent wide powder field of moderate gradient. A rest on the Thuit chairlift is a must after this adrenalin-charged descent.*

*As well as these routes within the local lift network, there is a renowned descent to **St-Christophe** (you get a taxi back), and the famous **La Grave** terrain (see separate chapter) is easily accessed.*

LIFT PASSES

Super Ski

Prices in €

Age	1-day	6-day
under 13	33	164
13 to 64	41	205
65 plus	33	164

Free under 5, 72 plus

Beginner seven free lifts

Notes family rates; half-day and pedestrian passes; 6-day pass includes entry to swimming pool and ice rink and access to La Grave, and two days in Alpe-d'Huez and one day in Serre-Chevalier, Puy-St-Vincent, Montgenèvre and Sestriere

Alternative passes Ski Sympa – covers 21 lifts

GETTING THERE

Air Lyon 160km/ 100 miles (2hr45); Grenoble 110km/ 70 miles (2hr15); Chambéry 135km/ 85 miles (2hr15); Geneva 220km/ 135 miles (3hr30)

Rail Grenoble (70km/43 miles); four daily buses from station

just above the village from Les Crêtes face west, so they get a lot of afternoon sun and can be slushy or icy. Snowmaking covers some of the lower slopes – apparently including the home green run, at last.

When we visited, some runs were kept closed in the early morning because they were considered dangerously hard, and opened only once they had softened. This is an excellent scheme that should be copied elsewhere.

FOR EXPERTS ★★★★★
Off-piste is the main attraction

The area offers excellent off-piste – read the panel above. Until last season, five routes (including Chalance, described above) were identified as itinéraires, but they have now been removed from the map.

A free weekly Freeride Attitude event promotes off-piste safety (read 'Schools and guides').

There are a few black pistes. The run down the Bellecombes chair is a genuine black, with the best chance of good snow. Fée 6 from above Toura has one steep pitch at the end. Fée 5 isn't much more testing than the adjacent red. The runs down to the resort often have poor snow. The short black higher up served by the Super Diable chairlift is among the steepest.

Not one but two glaciers on p168.

FOR INTERMEDIATES ★★★★★
Limited cruising

Les Deux-Alpes can disappoint keen intermediates because of the limited extent of the pistes. Avid piste-bashers will cover the pistes in a couple of days. A lot of the runs are either rather tough – some of the blues could be reds – or boringly bland. The runs higher up generally have good snow, and there is some great fast cruising, especially from the glacier to Toura and on the mainly north-facing pistes served by the chairlifts off to the sides. You can often pick gentle or steeper terrain in these bowls as you wish. The chairlifts at the glacier serve great carving pistes. If it's open, the Vallée Blanche area apparently has quite testing red runs.

Less confident intermediates will love the quality of the snow and the gentleness of most of the runs on the upper mountain. Their problem might lie in finding the pistes too crowded.

FOR BEGINNERS ★★★★★
Good slopes

The nursery slopes beside the village are spacious and gentle and seven lifts are free. The run along the ridge above them is excellent, too, except when it's crowded at the end of the day. The glacier also has a fine array of very easy slopes. One visitor noted that his eight-year-old could 'ski from the glacier to the village on greens and blues – a real sense of achievement for a child'.

Diable au Coeur is an excellent restaurant and its umbrella bar enjoys fab views, but it's a bit out of the way for teatime après action →

SNOWPIX.COM / CHRIS GILL

SCHOOLS

ESF
t 0476 792121

International St-Christophe
t 0476 790421

European
t 0476 797455

Evolution2
t 0476 801798

Classes (ESF prices)
6 days €233

Private lessons
€42 for 1hr for 1 or 2 persons

GUIDES

Bureau des guides
t 0476 113629

FOR BOARDERS ★★★★

Big appeal

Les Deux-Alpes has become a snowboard Mecca over the past few years in summer when the pros descend en masse. Its cheap and cheerful atmosphere counts for a lot – while the limited pisted slopes aren't as off-putting to boarders as to skiers. In town there are good trampoline facilities and a huge airbag to get a feeling of what air-time is all about. Although the focus is on the terrain park, the freeriding is not to be underestimated, with plenty of steep challenging terrain. Beginners will find the narrow, flat crowded areas mid-mountain and the routes down to the village intimidating. Most of the lifts on the higher slopes are chairs.

FOR CROSS-COUNTRY ★★

Needs very low-altitude snow

There are small, widely dispersed areas. Given good snow, Venosc, reached by a gondola down, has the only worthwhile picturesque ones. Total trail length is 20km.

MOUNTAIN RESTAURANTS ★★★

A few good places

There are mountain restaurants at all the major lift junctions, but they are generally unremarkable.

Editors' choice Diable au Coeur (0476 799950) at the top of the Diable lift has excellent food (delicious confit de canard on our last visit) and service. Readers agree. The terrace gives good views, but sit as far as you can from the noisy adjacent chairlift machinery – instead be entertained by the 'enthusiastic people enjoying the hot tub'. The bigger but similarly excellent Chalet la Toura (0671 920768), in a fine position at Toura in the middle of the domain, is pleasantly woody, and serves good food.

Worth knowing about The Pano, at Toura, has 'a wide range of daily specials'. There is a small table-service restaurant attached to the big self-service Les Glaciers at 3200m. The Bergerie on the Pied Moutet slopes has been recommended for 'good local dishes and atmosphere'.

There are picnic rooms at the Toura lift junction, and at the glacier near the top of the cable car.

SCHOOLS AND GUIDES ★★★

Fair selection to choose from

There are plenty to choose between but we lack recent reports. Freeride Attitude is a free off-piste safety course (held Mondays between mid-January and mid-April) run by guides and patrollers who provide transceivers, shovels, probes etc and teach you how to use them.

FOR FAMILIES ★★★★

Fine facilities

The village nursery takes kids from six months to two years, the kindergarten from two to six years, and there are chalet-based alternatives run by UK tour operators. There are also seven

CHILDCARE

Crèche du Bonhomme de Neige
t 0476 790262
Ages 6mnth to 2yr

Garderie le Bonhomme de Neige
t 0476 790677
Ages 2 to 6

Ski schools
Snow gardens for ages 3 to 6; classes for ages 6 to 12 (6 days €233 with ESF)

UK PACKAGES

Action Outdoors, Alpine Answers, AmeriCan Ski, Club Med, Crystal, Erna Low, Friendship Travel, Independent Ski Links, Inghams, Interactive Resorts, Lagrange, Mark Warner, Mountain Wave, Neilson, Peak Retreats, Pierre & Vacances, Powder White, PowderBeds, Rocketski, Ski Club Freshtracks, Ski Collection, Ski Expectations, Ski France, Ski Independence, Ski Line, Ski Solutions, Skitracer, Ski Supreme, Skiworld, Snoworks, Thomson, Zenith

Phone numbers
From abroad use the prefix +33 and omit the initial '0' of the phone number

TOURIST OFFICE

www.les2alpes.com

free lifts at the village level and a kids' freestyle area. A past reporter found a lot going on for kids at the foot of the slopes: 'kids' quad bikes, ice rink, pool – good tobogganing terrain too'.

STAYING THERE

Les Deux-Alpes has that rarity in high-altitude French resorts, an abundance of affordable hotels.

Chalets Several UK tour operators run catered chalets or chalet hotels. Skiworld has four varied chalets including one with outdoor hot tub. Crystal has half a dozen, again one or two with hot tubs. Mark Warner runs a chalet hotel with pool in a slope-side position on the road up to 1800, tipped by a reporter this year.

Hotels There are about 30 hotels, of which the majority are 2-star or below.

******Chalet Mounier** (0476 805690) Smartly modernized. Good reputation for food. Pool, steam, sauna, hot tub. At the Venosc end of the resort.

******Farandole** (0476 805045) The other 4-star, also at the Venosc end.

*****Côte Brune** (0476 805489) Transformed in recent years, now a charming woody chalet. On the snow, near Jandri Express. We stayed here in 2012: comfortable rooms, good food.

*****Souleil'or** (0476 792469) No reports for a while, but pleasant and comfortable. Good central position at foot of slopes.

****Lutins** (0476 792152) Central, basic, convenient, clean and friendly.

Apartments There are plenty, but most are unremarkable, and some are about as simple as it gets these days. MGM-style residences with pools are notably absent. One of the better residences is Goléon / Val Ecrin, at the entrance to the resort – two linked chalet-style buildings, with sauna and steam room. All the main French apartment agents have properties. Peak Retreats has a bigger range than most, including self-catered chalets. Skitracer is an apartment specialist.

Out of resort Close to the foot of the final ascent to Les Deux-Alpes are two attractive small hotels, near ideal for anyone planning to visit Alpe-d'Huez, La Grave and Serre-Chevalier – the Cassini (0476 800410) at Le Freney and the Panoramique (0476 800625) at Mizoën.

An alternative is to stay in one of the hamlets close to the bottom of the gondola from the Venosc valley.

EATING OUT ★★★★
Plenty of choice

There are about 50 restaurants, including lots of simple places such as crêperies. The P'tit Polyte restaurant in the hotel Chalet Mounier has a high reputation. La Grange, L'Alisier, The Patate, Cloche and Crêpes à Gogo and Etable are reader recommendations. You can get a relatively cheap meal at Bleuets bar, and the Vetrata.

APRES-SKI ★★★★
Hit by exchange rate blues?

Les Deux-Alpes has long been one of the liveliest of French resorts, with plenty of jumping bars, several open until the early hours. But here, as in some other French resorts that have traditionally attracted a lot of young Brits and Scans on a budget, we detect a downturn in activity.

On the mountain, an attempt is being made to deliver Austrian-style afternoon après action, first at the Pano at Toura, and now at Diable au Coeur. Reports welcome.

There are still plenty of places to try in the village – the resort website lists about 25. Among the bars favoured by reporters are Pub le Windsor – a smaller, quieter place popular with locals; and the Polar Bear Pub – 'wood stove, serves Guinness'. Smokey Joes is a popular central sports bar and the Secret has live music and a wide choice of beers. The Red Frog has a big-screen TV and shows sports. The main bar at 1800 is O'Brians; the Tribeca pizzeria has 'a lovely ambience for grown-ups'.

The Avalanche is the main nightclub, at the Venosc end of town; up at 1800 is the other disco – Opéra.

OFF THE SLOPES ★★
Limited options

The pretty valley village of Venosc is worth a visit by gondola, and you can take a scenic helicopter flight to Alpe-d'Huez. There are lots of walks, a big outdoor pool and the Acqua Center has an indoor pool, sauna, steam and hot tub. There's an outdoor artificial ice rink. Several mountain restaurants are accessible to pedestrians. The White Cruise in a snowcat takes you across the glacier and provides wonderful views. There is now an ice cave in the glacier. The resort has a simulator that lets you experience what it's like to be caught in an avalanche.

OT FLAINE / PHOTOZOOM

Flaine

Uncompromisingly modern, high-altitude resort sharing a big, broad area of varied slopes with more rustic alternatives

RATINGS

The mountains	
Extent	****
Fast lifts	***
Queues	***
Terrain p'ks	***
Snow	****
Expert	****
Intermediate	*****
Beginner	*****
Boarder	***
X-country	**
Restaurants	**
Schools	***
Families	****
The resort	
Charm	*
Convenience	*****
Scenery	****
Eating out	**
Après-ski	*
Off-slope	*

RPI	95
lift pass	£180
ski hire	£100
lessons	£65
food & drink	£135
total	**£480**

NEWS

2012/13: The current four-seat Aup de Veran gondola is to be replaced by an eight-seater. A new MGM-built residence will open in the middle of Forum – Le Centaure. It will, of course, have to harmonize with Flaine's distinctive architectural style.

2011/12: A new six-pack, the Désert Blanc, replaced the old Perdrix and Platé chairs. More snowmaking was added to the bottom of the Faust, Almandine and Serpentine runs. And there was a new children's boardercross course.

- + Big, varied area of slopes
- + Reliable snow in the main bowl
- + Compact, convenient, mainly car-free village, plus traditional villages on the lower fringes of the area
- + Excellent facilities for children
- + Very close to Geneva airport

- − Some slow old chairlifts, though things are improving
- − Austere 1960s buildings
- − Bad weather can close main Flaine bowl and links to outer sectors
- − Nightlife not a highlight
- − Little to do off the slopes (in Flaine)

Flaine is best known as a convenient resort catering particularly well for families, but it has a much broader appeal than that. The Grand Massif is almost a match for Val d'Isère/Tignes in terms of extent, at least, and does not lack challenges. Apartments rule here. But you open up more lodging options by considering the outlying traditional villages – Samoëns (which has its own chapter) and Les Carroz and Morillon (covered here).

THE RESORT

Flaine was built from scratch in the 1960s at the foot of a big snowy bowl. It's high, but not super-high (it is set among trees); the road in from Les Carroz actually involves a final descent from a col some 250m higher. The architecture of the main village is distinctive and uncompromising; it has its admirers, not including us.

The road in passes two satellite mini-resorts: Hameau de Flaine – lots of small chalets and the newish residence Refuge du Golf – and Montsoleil, developed by Intrawest.

Flaine is linked with the lower, traditional villages mentioned above. A car gives you the option of visiting the Portes du Soleil, Megève or Chamonix.

VILLAGE CHARM *

Not to our taste

The concrete Bauhaus-style blocks that form the core of Flaine were supposed to exhibit 'the principle of shadow and light'. They look shocking from the approach road; from the slopes they are less obtrusive, blending into the rocky grey hillside. As a place to inhabit, Flaine has an austere feel, and some of the buildings are now looking tatty. For us, the outdoor sculptures by Picasso, Vasarely and Dubuffet do little. In contrast, the Hameau de Flaine is built in a traditional chalet style, as is Montsoleil. The resort is supposed to be traffic-free, and for most purposes it is, although roads do penetrate the village.

CONVENIENCE *****

A fine example

The main resort is tiny. There are two parts: Forum, centred on a square blending with the slopes, and Forêt up the hillside, linked by lift, with its own bars and shops, and most of the apartments. There are children all over the place; they are catered for with play areas. Hameau de Flaine is about 1km from the main village, and has one shop/bar/restaurant. Montsoleil is much nearer to the mother ship (a few hundred metres' walk) and it has linking pistes. The bus service to/from these areas is 'very efficient'; in the evening, we are told it is replaced by a free bookable taxi service.

SCENERY ****

Good all around the Massif

The scenery within the area is quite varied, with rocky ridges and partly wooded hillsides – the views from the dividing ridges across the Vernant and Molliets valleys are particularly lovely. To the south-west, the Aravis chain looks dramatic, while there are great views of the Mont Blanc massif from the high-points.

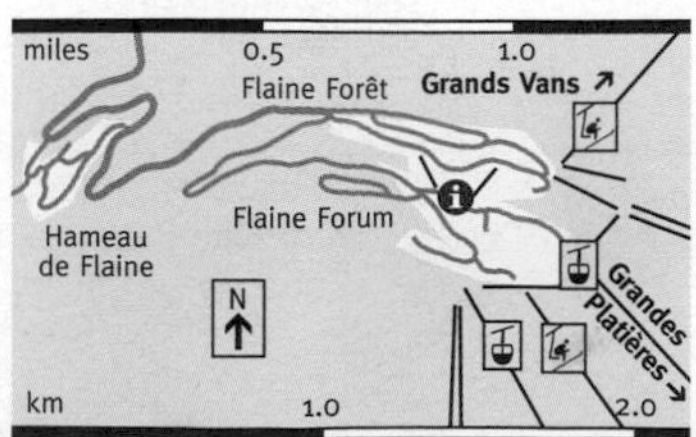

KEY FACTS

Resort	1600m 5,250ft
Grand Massif (Flaine, Les Carroz, Morillon, Samoëns, Sixt)	
Slopes	700-2480m 2,300-8,140ft
Lifts	69
Pistes	265km 165 miles
Green	11%
Blue	46%
Red	33%
Black	10%
Snowmaking	218 guns
For Flaine only	
Slopes	1600-2480m 5,250-8,140ft
Lifts	24
Pistes	140km 87 miles

SNOWPIX.COM / CHRIS GILL

The Blanchot restaurant enjoys a fine position high above the village ↓

THE MOUNTAINS

The slopes in the Flaine bowl are mainly open, but the lowest slopes are wooded. Outside the bowl, above the other villages, it's the opposite – most of the runs are below the treeline.

The latest piste map is a vast improvement on the previous version, with a better attempt to define the individual bowls; but it is still difficult to read, and sometimes misleading.

EXTENT OF THE SLOPES ★★★★☆
A big white playground

Grand Massif is an impressive area; but the greater part of the domain lies outside the main Flaine bowl and the links can be closed by bad weather.

The **Grandes Platières** jumbo gondola speeds you in a single stage up the north-west-facing Flaine bowl to the high-point of the Grand Massif. A six-pack offers an alternative, going part-way up. There are essentially four or five main ways down the treeless, rolling terrain back to Flaine, or to chairs in the middle of the wilderness. On skier's right, the Cascades blue run leads away from the lift system behind the Tête Pelouse down to the outskirts of Sixt, dropping over 1700m in its exceptional 14km length. The gentle/flat top half is hard work, especially for boarders, and the run is scenic rather than exciting. At the end you can get a bus (often crowded) to the lifts at Samoëns. Or spend some time exploring the slopes of Sixt – very quiet, with a non-trivial vertical.

On the near side of the Tête Pelouse, a broad catwalk leads to the experts-only **Gers** bowl. At the bottom, a flat trail links with the lower (more interesting) half of the Cascades run.

Back at Platières, an alternative is to head left down the lovely long red Méphisto to a quieter area of slopes beneath Tête des Lindars. This sector is also reachable by a second gondola from below the resort. The lower slopes are used as slalom courses.

The eight-seat Grand Vans chair, reached from Forum by means of a slow bucket-lift (or from Montsoleil via a short quad), gives access to the extensive slopes of **Les Carroz**, **Morillon** and **Samoëns** via the wide Vernant bowl, which is equipped with two fast chairlifts. There are two points on the road between Les Carroz and Flaine where lifts go up into the slopes – Les Molliets and Vernant. Both lift bases have car parks.

FAST LIFTS ★★★☆☆
Gradual progress

Flaine now gets an average rating for proportion of fast lifts. But there are still some frustrating lifts both inside and outside the Flaine bowl. All the chairs you need to get from Les Carroz to the Vernant valley, for Flaine, are slow. This year the old Aup de Veran gondola at Flaine is being modernized; it apparently died.

QUEUES ★★★☆☆
Still some problems

Many of the queue trouble spots are less acute than they once were, but the system can't cope with high-season crowds. A February 2011 visitor had 'horrendous queues of between five and 30 minutes at every lift'. At other times, things are bearable. But towards the end of the day expect delays at the Vernant chair to get back to the Flaine bowl. Also expect crowds on the blue piste leading down to it and on the run back to Flaine under the Grand Vans chair. An alternative is to go down Les Molliets or Vernant, and catch a bus.

Getting out of Flaine in the mornings should be greatly eased by the new eight-seat Aup de Veran gondola, though we wonder how the slow Diamant Noir chair up to Platières, which many people will head for, will handle the resulting pressure. Queues in the bowl can build up at weekends, when the lifts out of the bowl are shut by wind or when the lower resorts have poor snow.

TERRAIN PARKS ★★★★★
Cater for kids to experts

The main JamPark Pro (Jam = Jib and Air Maniacs) is in Flaine's Aujon area. It has a table, rails, kickers, a hip, a boardercross and a chill-out zone. Watch out for the draglifts round here, though. The park is in a rather isolated position on the edge of the ski area and reportedly closes early. There is a kids' park in Morillon.

SNOW RELIABILITY ★★★★★
Usually keeps its whiteness

Most of the main bowl faces north or north-west, and keeps snow well. There is snowmaking on the greater part of the Tête des Lindars area and on the nursery slopes, and more was installed at the bottom of the Faust, Almandine and Serpentine runs in 2011/12. The runs towards Samoëns 1600 and Morillon 1100 are north-facing too, and some lower parts have snowmaking, but below these mid-stations the runs can be tricky or closed. The Les Carroz runs are west-facing and low, and can suffer from strong afternoon sun as a result, but a few runs have snowmaking. Grooming is excellent.

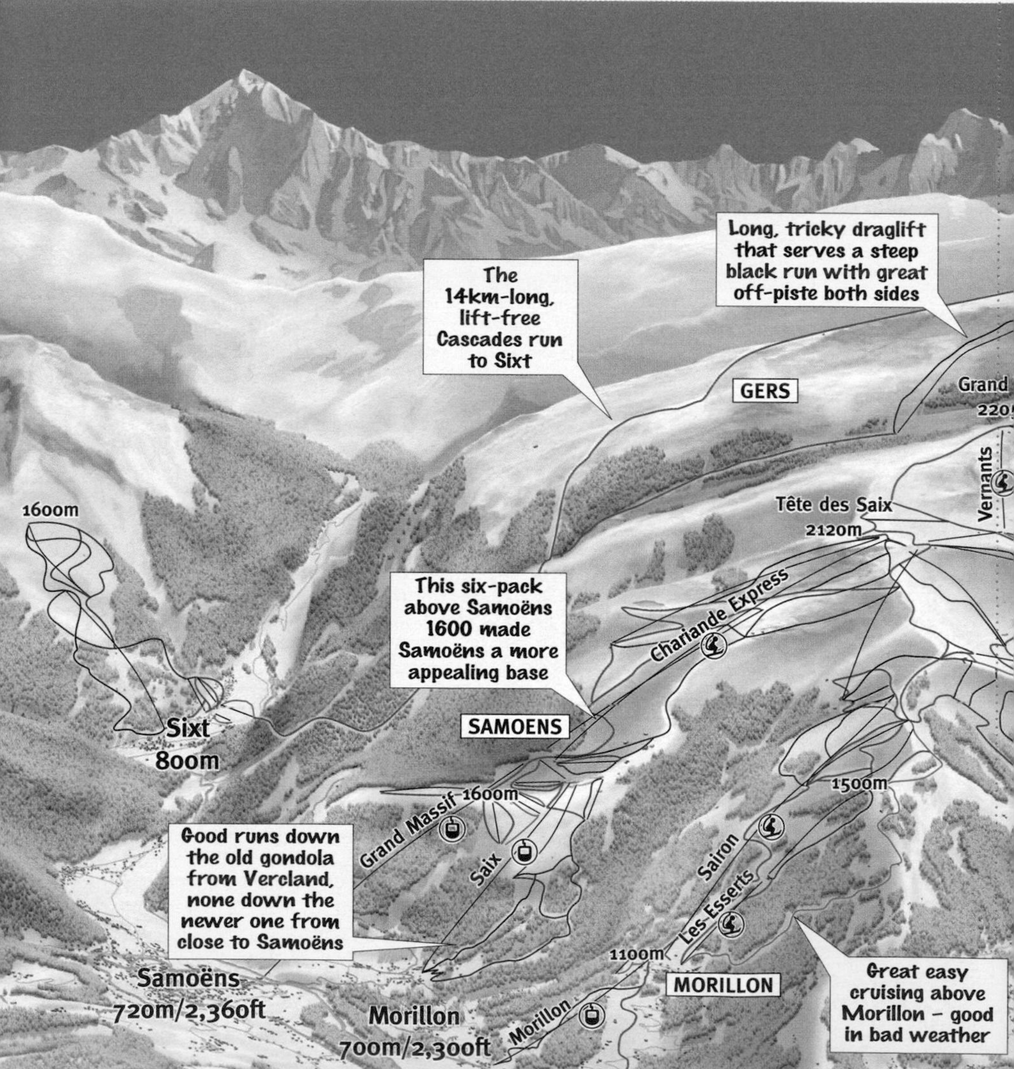

LIFT PASSES

Grand Massif

Prices in €

Age	1-day	6-day
under 16	32	161
16 to 63	41	213
64 plus	39	200

Free under 5, 75 plus

Beginner three free lifts

Notes family discounts

Alternative passes

Flaine area only

FOR EXPERTS ★★★★

Great fun with guidance

Flaine has some seriously challenging terrain. But much of it is off-piste and, although some looks like it can safely be explored without guidance, this impression is mistaken. The Flaine bowl is riddled with rock crevasses and potholes, and should be treated with glacier-style caution.

All the black pistes on the map deserve their classification. The Diamant Noir, down the line of the main gondola, is tricky because of moguls, narrowness and other people, rather than great steepness; the first pitch is the steepest. To skier's left of Diamant Noir are several short, steep off-piste routes through the crags.

Psst! Wanna see Austria's best-kept secret? Check out p168.

The Lindars Nord chair serves a shorter slope that often has the best snow in the area.

The Gers draglift, outside the main bowl, serves great on- and off-piste expert terrain in a north-facing bowl (of about 550m vertical) that normally has good snow top to bottom. The Onyx piste is a proper black and nearby off-piste slopes reach 45°. There are more adventurous ways in from the Grand Vans and Véret lifts. Further serious black pistes go down from Tête des Saix towards Samoëns. A reader recommends the Corbalanche

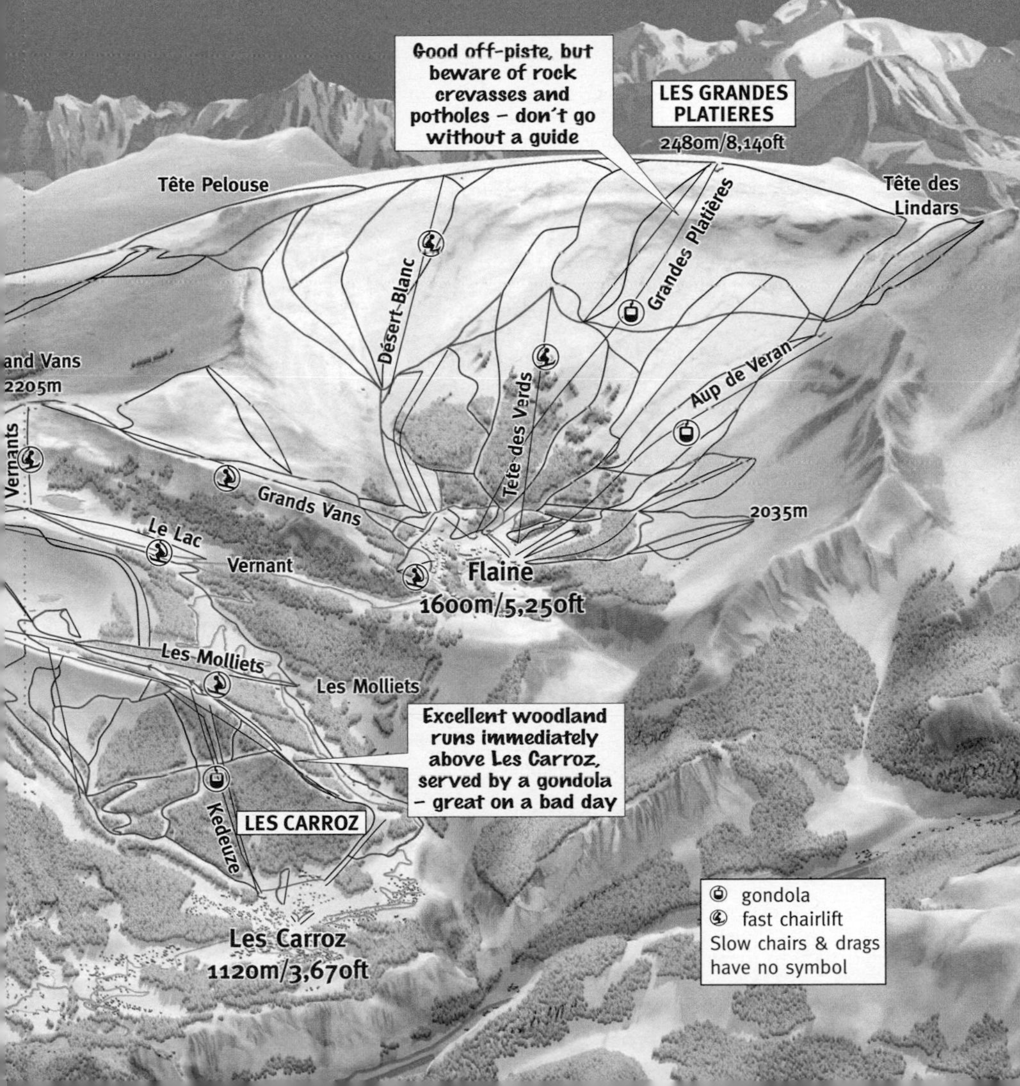

↑ Some of the runs can get busy, especially at weekends – Flaine is close to Geneva

SNOWPIX.COM / CHRIS GILL

GETTING THERE

Air Geneva 80km/ 50 miles (1hr30)

Rail Cluses (30km/ 19 miles); regular bus service

UK PACKAGES

Action Outdoors, Alpine Answers, Classic Ski, Crystal, Crystal Finest, Erna Low, Independent Ski Links, Inghams, Lagrange, Neilson, Pierre & Vacances, PowderBeds, Powder White, Ski Club Freshtracks, Ski Collection, Ski France, Ski Independence, Skitracer, Ski Weekend, Thomson, Zenith

TOURIST OFFICE

Flaine
www.flaine.com

piste and the off-piste bowl to skier's right, above the little Airon lake.

FOR INTERMEDIATES ★★★★★
Something for everyone

Flaine is ideal for confident intermediates, with a great variety of pistes (and usually the bonus of good snow, at least above Flaine itself). The diabolically named reds that dominate the Flaine bowl tend to gain their status from short steep sections rather than overall difficulty. The relatively direct Faust is great carving territory and Méphisto is popular with lots of reporters. There are gentler cruises from the top – Cristal, taking you to the newish Désert Blanc chair and Serpentine all the way home. The blues beneath Tête des Lindars are excellent for confidence building, but the drag serving them is not.

The connection with the slopes outside the main bowl is a blue run that can be tricky because of crowds, narrowness or poor snow. Once the connection has been made, however, all intermediates will enjoy the long tree-lined runs down to Les Carroz, as long as the snow is good. (The Perce-Neige run along the ridge to get to them is a bit narrow and exposed, though.) The long runs down to Morillon 1100 slopes are also excellent intermediate terrain – both the direct blue and lovely roundabout green.

FOR BEGINNERS ★★★★★
Fairly good

There are excellent nursery slopes right by the village, served by free lifts which make a pass unnecessary until you are ready to go higher up the mountain. There are some gentle blues to progress to on skier's right of the main bowl, beneath Tête Pelouse.

Progress to the gentle blues in the Tête des Lindars area is not easy due to several steep draglifts. An alternative is to get the bus to a gentle, quiet green at Vernant.

FOR BOARDERS ★★★
Beware the draglifts

Flaine suits boarders quite well – there's lots of varied terrain and plenty of off-piste with interesting nooks and crannies, including woods outside the main bowl. The key lifts are now chairs or gondolas (but beware the draglifts marked as difficult on the piste map plus the Aujon draglift). Black Side is the local specialist shop, with a cafe and bar in the central Forum.

FOR CROSS-COUNTRY ★★
Very fragmented

The Grand Massif claims 64km of tracks but only about 13km of that is around Flaine itself. Extensive tracks between Morillon and Les Carroz include some tough uphill sections.

MOUNTAIN RESTAURANTS ★★
Few options in the bowl

The piste map marks restaurants but does not name them. In the Flaine bowl, the rustic Blanchot, just above the treeline on skier's right, is the best bet – friendly, efficient service upstairs, and decent food. Busy, even when the resort is not. A reporter judges the self-service prices very high. The only other option above resort level is at the top of the main gondola. At Forum level, across the piste from the gondola, are two attractive, simple chalets – the Michet and the Eloge.

Outside the Flaine bowl, we have enjoyed the remote Gîte du Lac de Gers (0450 895514 – book in advance and ring for a snowcat to tow you up from the Cascades run) – simple, hearty food in splendid isolation. A 2012 reporter endorses it – 'really good, with excellent service'. Be aware that you have to ski on down to Sixt. Above Morillon the friendly and rustic Igloo has 'great food'; we've had an excellent plat du jour there. A 2012 reporter rates Chalet d'Clair – 'good vibe, cosy, wide menu, great burgers and desserts'. The woody Chalet les Molliets is generally well liked – 'atmospheric, cosy', 'copes with groups well', 'excellent plats'.

There are picnic rooms dotted around the Grand Massif, clearly marked on the piste map.

SCHOOLS

ESF
t 0450 908100

Internationale
t 0450 908441

Moniteurs indépendants
t 0450 937978

Super Ski
t 0681 061906

Ski Clinic
t 0666 139281

Freecimes
t 0664 118329

François Simond
t 0450 908097

Bruno Uyttenhove
t 0610 183082

Mountain Experience
t 0603 294486

Classes (ESF prices)
6 3hr days €149

Private lessons
From €42 for 1hr

GUIDES

Mountain guide
t 0450 900655

CHILDCARE

Les Petits Loups
t 0450 908782
6mnth to 3yr

Rabbit Club (ESF)
t 0450 908100
From 3yr

La Souris Verte (ESI)
t 0450 908441
3yr to 5yr

Hotel MMV Le Flaine
t 0492 126262
18mnth to 14yr

Ski school
Ages 3 to 11: €133 for 6 3hr days (ESF); English-speaking tuition: Catherine Pouppeville (0609 266008)

ACTIVITIES

Indoor Climbing wall, gym, bowling, cinema, cultural centre with art gallery and library

Outdoor Ice rink, snowshoeing, dog sledding, walking, snowmobiling, paragliding, helicopter rides, quad bikes, ice driving, snow kiting

SCHOOLS AND GUIDES ★★★

Mixed reports

A 2010 reporter who used the ESF got 'the best instructor we've ever had'. In the past we have had good reports on the International school, and on the racing-oriented Super Ski.

FOR FAMILIES ★★★★

Parents' paradise?

Flaine prides itself on being a family resort, and the number of English-speaking children around is a bonus. The schools offer classes for three- to five-year-olds.

STAYING THERE

Accommodation is overwhelmingly in self-catering apartments. For hotels, consider staying in Les Carroz.

Hotels The hotels now seem to be called 'club' hotels and are marketed by big French agencies – but also bookable through UK operators. B&B is available at the Cascade restaurant (0450 908766), up the hill.

Apartments Top option, underlined last year by the award of the new 5-star status, is the ski-in/ski-out Montsoleil/ Terrasses d'Eos residence – a Pierre & Vacances Premium property, outside the village: comfortable, good outdoor pool, sauna, steam, hot tub – but no restaurant or bar. But the new Centaure being built by MGM in Forum will doubtless be a close second. In Flaine Forêt, P&V also has the Forêt. Lagrange has several properties, including attractive chalets out at Hameau – also the location of the recently built Refuge du Golf, with pool. All these options are available through Ski Collection.

EATING OUT ★★

Limited choice

The choice is adequate, no more. We get most reports on the Brasserie les Cîmes in Forum – 'Great value, simple but well cooked food, good portions, caters extremely well for families.' What more could you ask? The Grain de Sel is 'very small, friendly, excellent value'. Other reader tips include the Grange, and the Ancolie in Hameau – 'first-class food', 'friendly staff and very comfortable bar'. They will ferry you to and from your residence.

APRES-SKI ★

Take your Kindle

You can eat and drink into the early hours here if you move around a bit – but you don't have much choice of venue. The White pub has a big-screen TV, rock music and punters trying to get pints in before the end of happy hour; live music some nights. The Perdrix Noire has an English pub atmosphere. The bar at the bowling alley is popular with families, and stays open until 3am. The Caves is a nightclub.

OFF THE SLOPES ★

Curse of the purpose-built

Flaine is not recommended for people who don't want to hit the slopes. But there is a great ice driving circuit where you can take a spin (literally) in your car or in theirs. Snowmobiling and dog sledding are popular, and there's a cinema and a gym. Shopping is extremely limited.

LINKED RESORT – 1120m

LES CARROZ

This is a sizeable, sprawling place (bigger than Flaine) – a sunny, traditional family resort in a lovely wooded setting. It has the lived-in feel of a real village where life revolves around the central square, with its cafes and restaurants. Traffic intrudes at peak times though.

It's not a convenient place – the

UK PACKAGES

Les Carroz 360 Sun and Ski, AmeriCan Ski, Crystal Finest, Erna Low, Peak Retreats, Pierre & Vacances, PowderBeds, Powder White, Ski France, Ski Independence, Skiology.co.uk, Zenith
Morillon Alps Accommodation, AmeriCan Ski, Erna Low, Lagrange, Peak Retreats, PowderBeds
Sixt AmeriCan Ski, Peak Retreats

Phone numbers
From abroad use the prefix +33 and omit the initial '0' of the phone number

TOURIST OFFICES

Les Carroz
www.lescarroz.com

Morillon
www.ot-morillon.fr

gondola starts a steep 300m walk up from the centre; the nursery drag is a help or you can use the free ski-bus which reporters say is very efficient. This lift serves some excellent slopes in the woods above the village, so this is a great place in bad weather. It's a good place for novices, with a beginner area at the top of the gondola, a wide green to progress to and a very gentle blue run back from Les Molliets. In high season the gondola may have 15-minute morning queues, and the runs back from Flaine get very crowded at the end of the day. There is regular praise for the ESF: one recent reporter had 'the best advanced class ever' while his young daughter 'wants to go back to her caring instructor'.

The ski school's torchlit descent is 'not to be missed' – ending with vin chaud and live jazz in the square.

There are half a dozen hotels, of which the pick are beside the Timalets red home run. The Servages d'Armelle (0450 900162) is a beautifully furnished little 4-star with seven rooms and three suites, housed in two old chalets, with a 'superb' (but pricey) restaurant. Milkhotel (0450 900618) is the new name for the renovated Bois de la Char, highly recommended this year – 'well managed, perfectly situated, excellent value; good set menu'.

Les Fermes du Soleil is a chalet-style Pierre & Vacances Premium residence with pool, hot tubs etc, close to the centre. Les Chalets de Jouvence is a similar CGH complex. Both available through Peak Retreats.

In 2012 we had excellent duck and steak at Aux Petits Ognions, a cosy place run by a charming couple. A visitor last year who tried several restaurants tips La Spatule – 'massive salads, good crêpes and steaks'. There are some tempting food shops in the central arcades.

There is more après-ski animation than in Flaine, but things are much quieter later on. The Marlow pub is popular at close of play; Pointe Noire, next door, is cheaper, we're told; and Carpe Diem gets busy when the other places close and 'has more character than the others'.

LINKED RESORT – 700m

MORILLON

Morillon is a small, quiet, traditional old village, with a few cafes, restaurants, bars, supermarket and shops spread out along the road through. Newer buildings are in chalet style and quite attractive. There's a 3-star hotel, the Morillon (0450 901032). A gondola goes up to the mid-mountain mini-resort of Morillon 1100 (aka Les Esserts), with slope-side apartments at the foot of wide, gentle and tree-lined slopes – popular with families and novices. A choice of red and blue runs go to the valley. These runs are low and good snow is not reliable, although the area as a whole is north-facing and keeps snow well.

Morillon 1100 has the essentials of life – two ski schools, three ski shops, a bakery, supermarket, a couple of restaurants and the Madison pub with 'live music and quizzes'. Recent reporters have been impressed by the ZigZag school.

OT LES GETS

Les Gets

Traditional-style village with a very French feel, providing serious competition for its more established linked neighbour, Morzine

TOP 10 RATINGS

Extent	*****
Fast lifts	***
Queues	***
Snow	**
Expert	***
Intermediate	****
Beginner	****
Charm	****
Convenience	***
Scenery	***

RPI	95
lift pass	£180
ski hire	£105
lessons	£65
food & drink	£120
total	**£470**

NEWS

2011/12: There is a new night shuttle-bus service, costing two euros per person. Snowmaking was increased, and 74 new apartments (La Fermes Emiguy) opened.

- + Good-sized, varied and lightly wooded slopes shared with Morzine
- + Attractive chalet-style village
- + Few queues or crowds locally unless good weekend weather attracts a weekend influx
- + Part of the vast Portes du Soleil ski pass region, but ...

- − It's quite a long way to the main Portes du Soleil circuit at Avoriaz
- − Low altitude and exposure to westerlies means some risk of rain and poor snow
- − Few challenging pistes
- − Slow, old chairs in some sectors
- − Weekend crowds

Les Gets is an attractive, small, family-friendly resort with a very French feel to it, partly because of appetizing food and wine shops lining the main street. The area of slopes that it shares with Morzine offers the most extensive local network in the Portes du Soleil, and in some respects Les Gets is the better base for that area. But if you intend to visit the main Portes du Soleil circuit repeatedly, it makes sense to stay closer to it, in Morzine.

THE RESORT

Les Gets is an attractive, sunny village of traditional chalet-style buildings, on the low pass leading to Morzine. The main road bypasses the village centre.

The local pass saves a fair bit on a Portes du Soleil pass, and makes a lot of sense for many visitors.

Village charm The village has a quiet ambiance that appeals to families, though it does liven-up at weekends. The main street is lined with attractive food and other shops and restaurants. The centre is fairly pedestrian-friendly too, and a popular outdoor ice rink adds to the charm.

Convenience Although the village has a scattered appearance, most facilities are close to the main lift station. There is a road-train shuttle that appeals mainly to families, but also free conventional buses around the village and buses to Morzine at 1.5 euros per journey. You can store skis and boots at the Perrières ski shop.

Scenery Good views from the high points – from Mont Chéry you get a great panorama of the village and slopes, with Mont Blanc beyond.

THE MOUNTAINS

Les Gets is not an ideal base for the Portes du Soleil circuit, but its local slopes are extensive.

Slopes The main local slopes – accessed by a gondola and fast chair-lift from the nursery slopes beside the village – are shared with Morzine, and are mainly described in that chapter. On the opposite side of Les Gets is Mont Chéry, accessed by a gondola followed by a chair or drag. The slopes here include some of the most challenging in the area, and are usually very quiet. Both sectors offer wooded and open slopes. Signage is considered 'very good'.

Fast lifts The village lifts are gondolas, but there are a lot of slow, old chairs both on Mont Chéry and in some sectors of the Morzine slopes.

Queues Read the Morzine chapter. Mont Chéry is crowd-free.

Snow reliability The nursery slopes benefit from a slightly higher elevation than Morzine, but otherwise our general reservations about the lack of altitude apply. You may get rain. The runs to the resort have snowmaking. The front slopes of Mont Chéry face south-east – bad news at this altitude (and in poor snow years they can be closed for much of the time); but the other two flanks are shadier. Grooming is good ('Pisteurs worked wonders; could ski back to resort in March in a poor snow year and warm temperatures,' says a 2011 visitor). The grassy slopes don't need much snow-cover and in a sparse snow year you may do better here than in higher, rockier resorts such as Avoriaz.

Terrain parks There's a boardercross on Chavannes plus a jib park with boxes and rails and the small Cross District park for beginners. On Mont Chéry there is a larger park and airbag.

Extent rating
This relates to the whole Portes du Soleil area.

Piste map
The whole local area is covered by the map in the Morzine chapter.

KEY FACTS

Resort	1170m
	3,840ft
Portes du Soleil	
Slopes	950-2275m
	3,120-7,460ft
Lifts	198
Pistes	650km
	404 miles
Green	13%
Blue	40%
Red	37%
Black	10%
Snowmaking	
	835 guns
Morzine-Les Gets only	
Slopes	1000-2010m
	3,280-6,590ft
Lifts	48
Pistes	120km
	75 miles
Snowmaking	70%

UK PACKAGES

Alpine Answers, Alpine Elements, Alpine Inspirations, AmeriCan Ski, ChaletBook, Crystal, Esprit, Ferme de Montagne, Independent Ski Links, Lagrange, Luxury Chalet Collection, Mountain Wave, Oxford Ski Co, Peak Retreats, PowderBeds, Reach4theAlps, Ski Expectations, Ski Famille, Ski France, Ski Independence, Ski Solutions, Ski Total, Skitracer, Ski Weekend, Snow Finders, VIP

Phone numbers
From abroad use the prefix +33 and omit the initial '0' of the phone number

TOURIST OFFICE

www.lesgets.com

Experts Black runs on the flank and back of Mont Chéry are quite steep and often bumped. In good snow there's plenty to do off-piste, including some excellent wooded areas.
Intermediates High-mileage piste-bashers might prefer direct access to the main Portes du Soleil circuit, but the local slopes have a lot to offer, with excellent reds on Mont Chéry.
Beginners The village nursery slopes are convenient. At Chavannes there is a bigger and more snow-sure area with four free lifts. There are lots of easy runs to progress to – including the Bleuets on Chavannes.
Snowboarding The local slopes are good for beginners and intermediates.
Cross-country There are 12km of good, varied loops locally.
Mountain restaurants See Morzine for places on the shared slopes. There are two restaurants on Mont Chéry giving great views. At the top is the Grande Ourse, run by an English family, offering snacks and table-service lunches rated 'very special' by a past reporter. We had a fab hot chocolate there in 2012, with welcoming service, but another report suggests service gets stretched in high season. At mid-mountain there's the Belvedère – and a picnic room.
Schools and guides You're spoilt for choice. BASS (the British Alpine Ski & Snowboard School) operates here. Les Gets Snowsports is also British-run and 'excellent'. And a reporter was impressed with the English-speaking instructors at Ecole de Ski 360 who got her six-year-old daughter cruising down the main slopes on day two.
Families This is a good resort for families. There are comprehensive facilities, including an American Indian-themed trail area on Chavannes with teepees, activities and a warpaint workshop – called the Grand Cry Territory – and major British family-specialist tour operators Esprit Ski and Ski Famille offer catered chalet holidays here.

STAYING THERE

There is a good selection of chalets and mid-range hotels.
Chalets Ski Famille has seven chalets here, including the 'very comfortable' Chalet Marjorie. Esprit Ski has four in one building (along with its own crèche). Ski Total also has three (two sharing an outdoor hot tub). There seems to be some uncertainty about which of these sister companies is offering chalet Monet. VIP's Altitude chalet is 'beautifully finished and furnished'. Private catered Chalet le Frene has been praised.
Hotels We greatly enjoyed our stay some years back at the Ferme de Montagne (0450 753679). It's a kind of cross between a small hotel and a chalet – a beautifully renovated farmhouse with eight luxury bedrooms, gourmet food, ski guiding, sauna, steam, outdoor hot tub, massage; right on the edge of town at La Turche. Of the 3-stars, the Crychar (0450 758050), at the foot of the slopes, is one of the best. The similarly convenient 4-star Marmotte (0450 758033) has added eight lovely wood-panelled rooms over its spa this year. In 2012 we stayed happily in the pleasant 2-star Stella (0450 758040).
Apartments Lagrange has two prestige properties – the central Sabaudia apartments and Les Fermes Emiguy (both with pool, hot tub, sauna etc). Peak Retreats offers these and other apartments and several self-catered chalets (some luxurious).
Eating out The Ferme de Montagne (see 'Hotels') serves excellent cuisine in lovely surroundings. The Tourbillon and Choucas ('fabulous house red') have been recommended. Try the Tyrol for pizza, the rustic Vieux Chêne for Savoyard specialities.
Après-ski Après-ski is quiet, especially on weekdays. But there are half a dozen bars; the obvious first target is the Irish Pub and the Black Bear above it. The Igloo disco is popular.
Off the slopes There's an outdoor ice rink and bowling. There are good shops, a cinema and an intriguing Mechanical Music Museum. Husky sleigh rides, snowshoeing and parapenting are possible. It's feasible to visit Geneva, Lausanne and Montreux from here, too.

SNOWPIX.COM / CHRIS GILL

La Grave

A world apart: an unspoiled mountain village beneath high, untamed off-piste slopes, some of them extreme and hazardous

TOP 10 RATINGS

Extent	*
Fast lifts	
Queues	****
Snow	***
Expert	*****
Intermediate	*
Beginner	*
Charm	***
Convenience	***
Scenery	****

RPI	90
lift pass	£170
ski hire	£90
lessons	£85
food & drink	£120
total	**£465**

NEWS

La Grave does not change much, and that is half the charm of the place.

- + Legendary off-piste mountain
- + Usually crowd-free
- + Usually good snow conditions
- + Link to Les Deux-Alpes
- + Easy access by car to other resorts

- − Poor weather means lift closures: on average, two days per week
- − Suitable for experts only
- − Through-traffic detracts from Alpine village atmosphere
- − Nothing to do off the slopes

La Grave enjoys cult status among experts. It has around 500 visitor beds and just one serious lift serving a high, wild and almost entirely off-piste mountainside. The result: an exciting, usually crowd-free area. Strictly, you ought to have a guide, but in good weather many people go it alone.

THE RESORT

La Grave is a small, unspoiled village built along the road up to the Col du Lautaret. A car is useful for access to Les Deux Alpes down the valley and Serre-Chevalier over the pass.

Village charm The centre has a rustic feel, some welcoming hotels and friendly inhabitants. But it is a bit plain, and traffic on the through-road can be intrusive.

Convenience The single serious lift starts a short walk below the centre.

Scenery La Grave is set on a steep hillside facing the impressive glaciers of majestic La Meije. Great views.

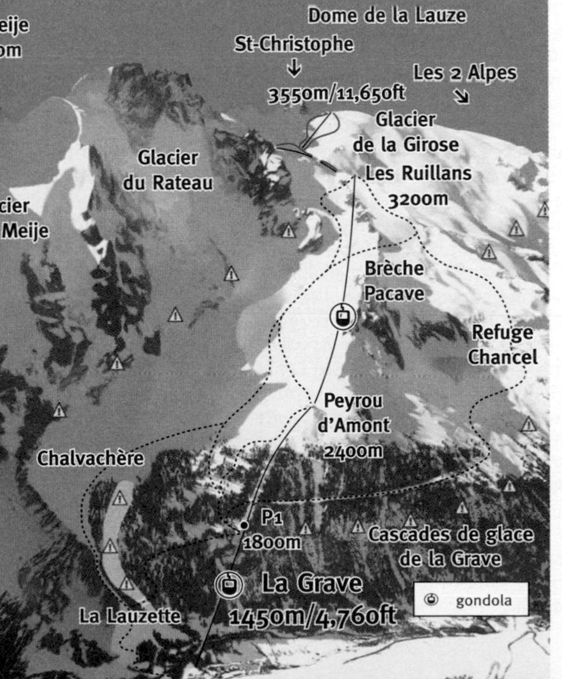

THE MOUNTAIN

A slow two-stage 'pulse' gondola (with an extra station at a pylon halfway up the lower stage) ascends into the slopes and finishes at 3200m. Above that, a short walk and a draglift give access to a second drag serving twin blue runs on a glacier slope of about 350m vertical – from here (after another walk) you can ski to Les Deux-Alpes. But the reason that people come here is to explore the legendary slopes back towards La Grave. These slopes offer no defined, patrolled, avalanche-protected pistes – but there are two marked itinéraires (with several variations usefully marked on the 'piste' map) of 1400m vertical down to the pylon lift station, or 1750m all the way down to the valley.

Slopes The Chancel route is mostly of red-run gradient; the Vallons de la Meije is more challenging but not too steep. People do take these routes without a guide or avalanche protection equipment, but we couldn't possibly recommend it.

There are many more demanding runs away from the itinéraires, including couloirs that range from the straightforward to the seriously hazardous, and long descents from the glacier to the valley road below the village, with return by taxi, bus, or strategically parked car. The dangers are considerable (people die here every year), and good guidance is essential. You can also descend a 'spectacular' valley southwards to St-Christophe, returning by bus and the lifts of Les Deux-Alpes.

Fast lifts There aren't any, and there's no need for any.

↑ Heading off to the steeps: don't be fooled by the gentle start: this guy's on his way to gnarly couloirs

OT LA GRAVE

KEY FACTS

Resort	1450m 4,760ft
Slopes	1450-3550m 4,760-11,650ft
Lifts	4
Pistes	5km 3 miles
Green/Blue	100%
The figures relate only to pistes; practically all the skiing – at least 90% – is off-piste	
Snowmaking	none

UK PACKAGES

Alpine Answers, Lagrange, Mountain Tracks, Peak Retreats, Pure Powder, Ski Club Freshtracks, Ski Weekend

Phone numbers
From abroad use the prefix +33 and omit the initial '0' of the phone number

TOURIST OFFICE

www.lagrave-lameije.com

Queues Normally, there are queues only at weekends. March is reportedly the busiest month, when queues can be serious. If snow conditions are poor, queues can build up for the gondola down from the lower stations.
Terrain parks There aren't any.
Snow reliability The chances of powder snow on the high, north-facing slopes are good, but if conditions are tricky, there are no pistes to fall back on apart from the three short blue runs at the top of the gondola.
Experts La Grave's uncrowded off-piste slopes have earned it cult status among hard-core skiers. Only experts should contemplate a stay here – and then only if prepared to deal with bad weather by sitting tight or struggling over the Col du Lautaret to the woods of Serre-Chevalier.
Intermediates The itinéraires get tracked into a piste-like state, and adventurous intermediates could tackle the Chancel. Most folk will soon tire of the three blue runs at the top of the gondola. The valley stations of Villar d'Arène and Lautaret, around 3km and 8km to the east respectively, and Le Chazelet, 3km to the north-west, offer very limited slopes with a handful of runs.
Beginners Novices tricked into coming here can go up the valley to the beginner slopes at Villar d'Arène, or to Le Chazelet, which has a fast quad and two snow-guns.
Snowboarding There are no special facilities for boarders, but advanced freeriders will be in their element on the open off-piste powder.
Cross-country There is a total of 20km of loops in the area.
Mountain restaurants Surprisingly, there are three. The excellent, tiny Refuge Chancel, where supplies and waste are backpacked in and out, is the pucka La Grave experience; call in during the morning to see what's cooking, and book.
Schools and guides There are claimed to be 30 or so guides, offering a wide range of services through their bureau. 'Excellent' is the usual verdict. See also 'Hotels' below.
Families Not really a family resort, but the tourist office knows of babysitters.

STAYING THERE

There are very few choices.
Hotels There are several simple options. The Brit-run 2-star Edelweiss (0476 799093) has quite basic rooms but does 'excellent' food and has a good wine list. The Skiers Lodge/Hotel des Alpes (0476 110318) offers all-inclusive week-long packages including guiding. A past reporter had an excellent week.
Apartments Bookable through the tourist office.
Eating out Most people eat in their hotels, though there are alternatives.
Après-ski The central Cafe des Glaciers, and the Castillan are the standard teatime venues. The bars of the Edelweiss and Skiers Lodge have live music. The Vieux Guide gets crowded later.
Off the slopes Anyone not using the slopes will find La Grave much too small and quiet.

Megève

One of the traditional old winter holiday towns; best for those who enjoy relaxed cruising and spectacular views

RATINGS

The mountains

Extent	*****
Fast lifts	**
Queues	****
Terrain p'ks	***
Snow	**
Expert	**
Intermediate	****
Beginner	***
Boarder	**
X-country	****
Restaurants	****
Schools	***
Families	***

The resort

Charm	****
Convenience	**
Scenery	*****
Eating out	****
Après-ski	**
Off-slope	****

RPI	95
lift pass	£160
ski hire	£110
lessons	£70
food & drink	£145
total	**£485**

NEWS

2012/13: A new bus service will run between Rochebrune and Le Jaillet; also horse-drawn sleighs between the end of the Calvaire blue and Le Jaillet.

2011/12: A six-pack replaced the old Mt Rosset chair on Mont d'Arbois, and a new quad, Ravine, opened at the top of Le Jaillet. The terrain park at Rochebrune was greatly developed.

- + Extensive easy slopes
- + Scenic setting, with splendid views
- + Charming old town centre
- + Some very smart hotels and shops
- + Great mountain restaurants
- + Good for weekends
- + Great when it snows – woodland runs with no one on them
- + Plenty to do off the slopes

- – Low altitude of slopes means a risk of poor snow, though the grassy terrain does not need deep cover
- – Lots of slow, old lifts remain
- – Three separate mountains, only two linked (by lift but not by piste)
- – Few challenging pistes, though good off-piste available
- – Very muted après-ski scene
- – Meals and drinks pricey

Megève has a medieval heart, but it was, in a way, the original purpose-built French ski resort – developed in the 1920s as an answer to Switzerland's irritatingly fashionable St Moritz. Although Courchevel long ago took over as France's swankiest resort, Megève's smart hotels still attract fur coats and fat wallets. Happily, you don't need either to enjoy the place. And make no mistake – it is highly enjoyable; just look at that list of plus points above.

This is one of our favourite places to be in falling snow, when Megève regulars take one look and retreat to their duvets. But when the sun's out and we want to zip around the 325km of pistes, we get very frustrated by the number of slow lifts. The area sits close to the bottom of our fast lifts league table. The resort still has a lot to learn from St Moritz (never mind Saalbach).

THE RESORT

Megève is in a lovely sunny setting and has a beautifully preserved, partly medieval centre. Visitors are mainly well-heeled French couples and families, who come here for an all-round holiday.

The skiing divides into three sectors. One is directly accessible by lifts from close to the centre and from the southern edge of town, another from an elevated suburb or from an out-of-town lift base. The third involves buses, for most people.

There are several alternative bases (which offer some good-value lodging) on the fringes of the area. St-Gervais and Le Bettex above it (described at the end of this chapter) have gondola access to the main sector. But beware slow access lifts from otherwise attractive spots. The slopes also link with La Giettaz; this has interesting local terrain, but is out on a limb and not a sensible base.

The Evasion Mont Blanc lift pass also covers Les Contamines. A car is handy for outings here, and perhaps for using the Princesse gondola.

VILLAGE CHARM ****
Old France at its best

Megève's charming old centre is pedestrianized and comes complete with open-air ice rink, horse-drawn sleighs, cobbled streets and a fine church. Lots of smart clothing, jewellery, antique, gift and food shops add to the chic atmosphere. The main Albertville road bypasses the centre, and there are expensive underground car parks. But the resort's clientele

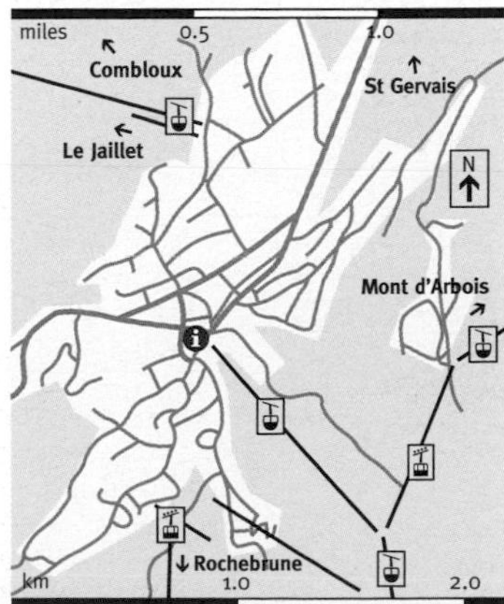

arrives mainly by car, and the resulting traffic jams and fumes can be a problem at times, particularly if you are based outside the very centre.

CONVENIENCE ★★

Stay close to a lift

Unless you have a car, staying close to one of the main lifts makes a lot of sense. Some of the best hotels are above the centre, close to the Mont d'Arbois gondola. But many lodgings depend on the free ski-buses, which are not super-frequent.

SCENERY ★★★★★

Beautiful town, beautiful views

The slopes are prettily wooded, but what earns Megève its five stars is the view of Mont Blanc from much of the ski area – especially l'Epaule.

THE MOUNTAINS

The slopes are largely below the treeline – this is a great resort in poor weather – though there are extensive open areas, particularly higher up in the Mont d'Arbois sector.

Piste classification often exaggerates difficulty. The piste map is badly designed and difficult to follow in places. Rochebrune and Mont d'Arbois are separate sectors; why not give them separate maps?

EXTENT OF THE SLOPES ★★★★★

More than enough for a week

Each of the three mountains has a worthwhile amount of terrain, and they add up to a great deal of skiing.

The town is most directly linked with the **Rochebrune** sector – a

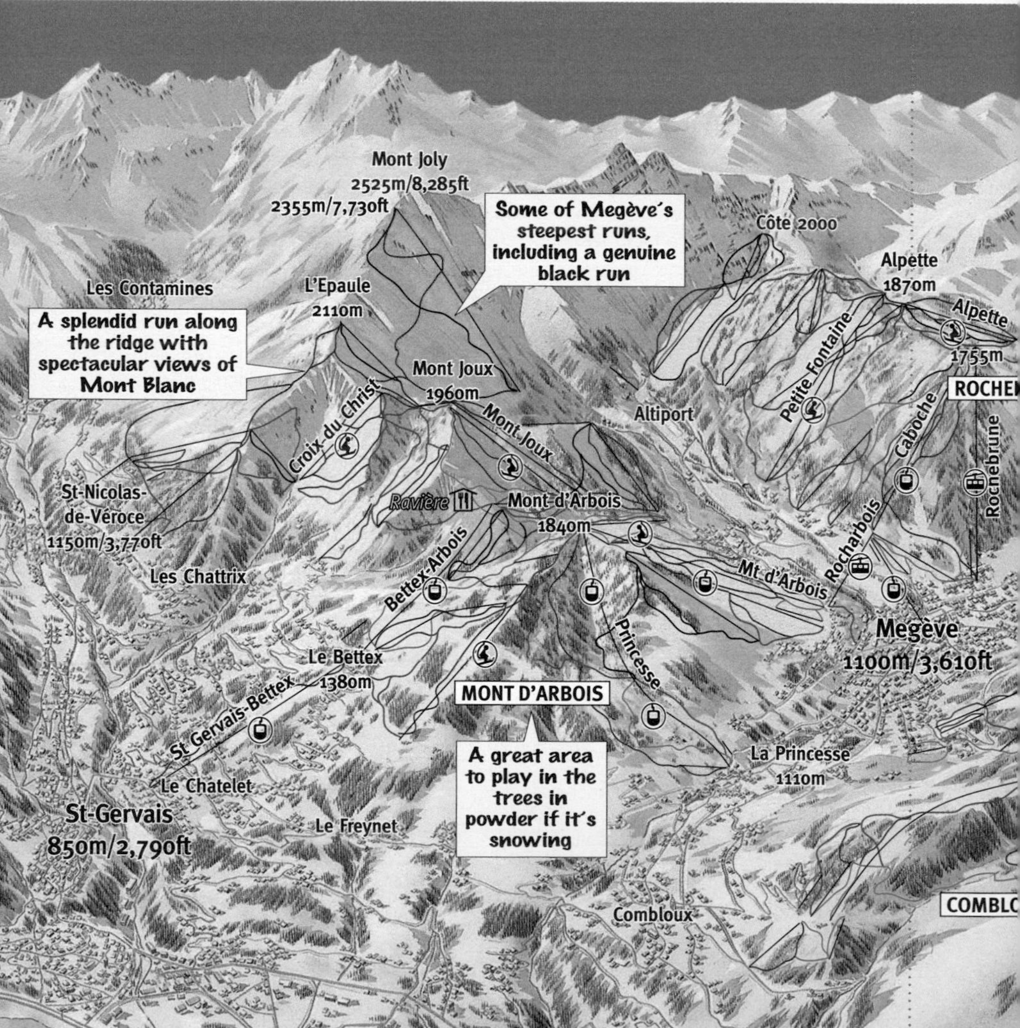

KEY FACTS	
Resort	1100m
	3,610ft
Slopes	850-2355m
	2,790-7,730ft
Lifts	84
Pistes	325km
	202 miles
Green	17%
Blue	30%
Red	40%
Black	13%
Snowmaking	
	485 guns

gondola goes up from the centre of town, and a cable car from the southern edge. A network of gentle, wooded, north-east-facing slopes, served by drags and mainly slow chairlifts, leads to the high point of Côte 2000, which often has the best snow. The minor peak of Alpette was the starting point for Megève's historic downhill course, now abandoned.

At just above resort level the Rocharbois cable car goes across the valley to link Rochebrune to the gondola for the bigger **Mont d'Arbois** sector, starting from an elevated suburb of the resort. The Princesse gondola starting a couple of miles north of the town (with extensive free car parking) offers another way up. A two-stage gondola comes up from St-Gervais via Le Bettex. You can work your way over to Mont Joux and up to the small Mont Joly area – Megève's highest slopes. And from there you can go to the backwater village of St-Nicolas-de-Véroce (there's a splendid red run along the ridge with wonderful views of Mont Blanc).

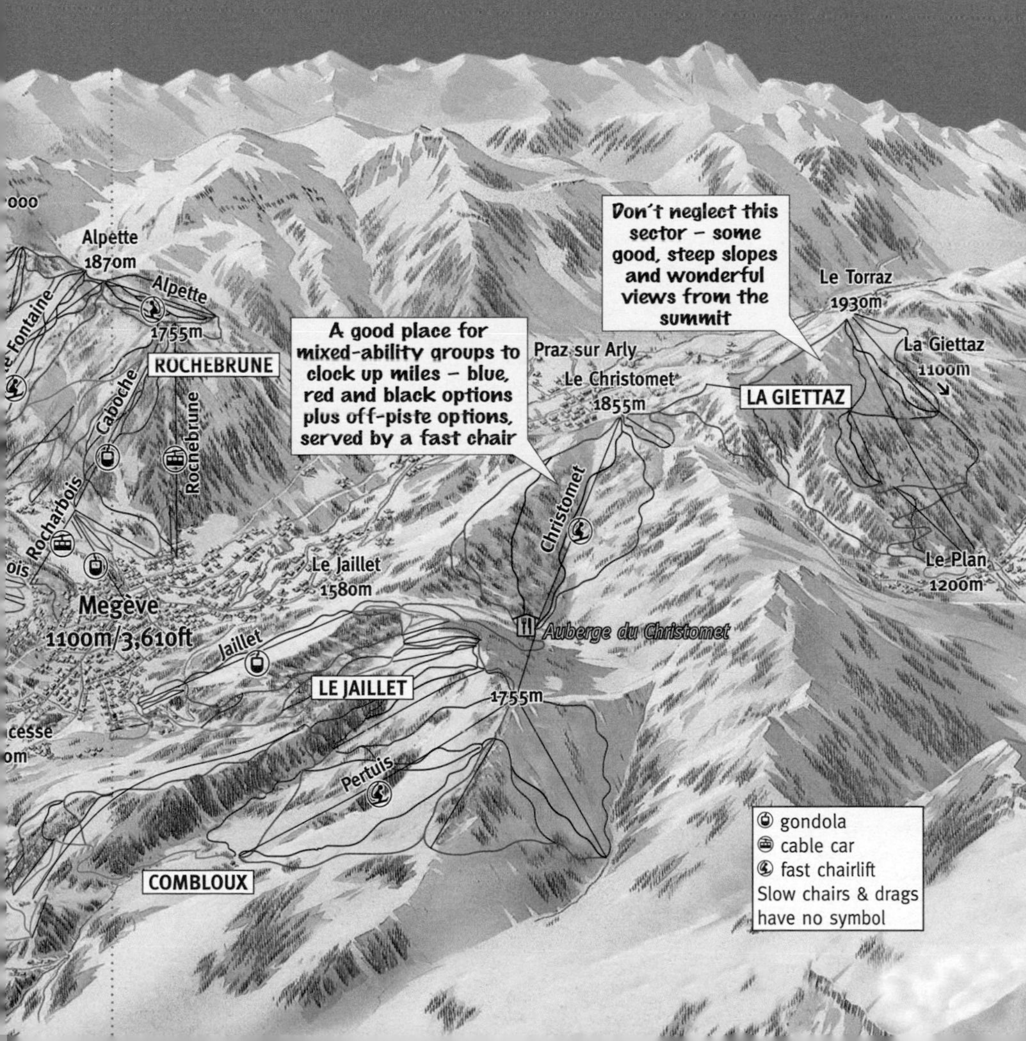

LIFT PASSES

Evasion Mont Blanc

Prices in €

Age	1-day	6-day
under 15	32	152
15 to 59	40	189
over 60	36	171

Free under 5, over 80

Beginner three free lifts; Rochebrune pass covers 6 lifts; three other limited passes, each covering one or two lifts

Notes
Megève pass resorts (list below) plus Les Contamines; family discounts

Alternative passes
Megève (Megève, La Giettaz, Combloux, St-Gervais and St-Nicolas); Jaillet-Combloux-Giettaz only pass; pedestrian pass

The third area is **Le Jaillet**, accessed by gondola from just outside the north-west edge of town, or much more slowly from the separate village of Combloux. The high point of Le Christomet is linked to the slopes of tiny **La Giettaz** – worth visiting, not least for the spectacular views from the summit.

FAST LIFTS ★★
Still too many slow ones

Megève continues to lag behind its rivals in the uplift business, and all reporters this year endorse our persistent criticism of this aspect. Gondolas and cable cars provide the main access, and fast chairs are dotted around – but overall three out of four lifts are slow. Last season one more slow lift was replaced, but the chair added on Le Jaillet is slow.

QUEUES ★★★★
Few weekday problems

Megève is relatively queue-free during the week, except at peak holiday time. But school holidays and sunny Sunday crowds can mean some delays. The long, steep Lanchettes and Roche Fort drags between Côte 2000 and the rest of the Rochebrune slopes can have 'ridiculously long waits' – as can the cable car linking the two mountains. Crowded pistes at Mont Joux and Mont d'Arbois can also be a problem. On a snowy day the slopes can be delightfully quiet as the pampered clientele stay in bed, leaving the fresh snow to you and us.

TERRAIN PARKS ★★★
Four, surprisingly

The park near the bottom of Rochebrune was apparently greatly developed last season, particularly for beginners. There is a 500m-long boardercross course and a freestyle airbag nearby. There is also a park on Mont d'Arbois, with a good line of jumps for all ability levels. Plus a host of rails and boxes and a boardercross. Combloux also has a park and La Giettaz a smaller park, albeit with a real multitude of jump sizes and a few rails. Both have boardercross.

SNOW RELIABILITY ★★
The area's main weakness

The slopes are low, with very few runs above 2000m, and quite sunny – the Megève side of Mont d'Arbois gets the afternoon sun. So in a poor snow year, or in a warm spell, snow on the lower slopes can suffer badly. Fortunately, the grassy slopes don't need much depth of snow. The resort has an extensive snowmaking network, but that can't work in warm weather.

FOR EXPERTS ★★
Off-piste is the main attraction

One of Megève's great advantages for expert skiers is that there is not much competition for the powder – many days after a fresh dump you can often make first tracks on good slopes.

The Mont Joly and Mont Joux sections offer the steepest slopes. The top chair here serves a genuinely black run, with some serious off-piste

SNOWPIX.COM / CHRIS GILL

Adequate view from Mont d'Arbois of Mont Blanc, Mont Joly (with the amazingly scenic Epaule run visible) and Mont Joux →

ACTIVITIES

Indoor Sports centre (tennis, ice rink, curling, climbing wall, swimming pool, sauna, solarium, gym), beauty treatments, health and fitness centres, museum, cinemas, casino, language courses, concerts and exhibitions, bridge, painting courses

Outdoor Cleared paths, snowshoeing, tobogganing, ice rink, horse-drawn carriage rides, ice climbing, adventure park, sightseeing flights, paragliding, ballooning

GETTING THERE

Air Geneva 90km/ 55 miles (1hr15); Lyon 180km/ 110 miles (2hr30)

Rail Sallanches (12km/7 miles); regular buses from station

off the back of the hill, and the slightly lower Epaule chair has some steep runs back down and also accesses some good off-piste, as well as pistes, down to St-Nicolas. The steep area beneath the second stage of the Princesse gondola can be a play area of powder runs among the trees. Cote 2000 has a small section of steep runs, including good off-piste.

The terrain under the Christomet chair can be a good spot to develop off-piste technique, given decent snow – and a reporter recommends the extensive woods at La Giettaz.

FOR INTERMEDIATES ★★★★☆
Superb if the snow is good

Good intermediates will enjoy the whole area – there is so much choice it's difficult to single out any particular sectors. Keen skiers are likely to want to focus on the fast lifts, and happily several of these serve excellent terrain – the Princesse and Bettex gondolas on Mont d'Arbois, the Fontaine and Alpette chairs on Rochebrune and the Christomet chair in the Le Jaillet sector. But don't confine yourself to those – there are lots of other interesting areas, including the shady north-east facing slopes on the back of Mont d'Arbois and Mont Joux and the front of Rochebrune, and the genuinely red/ black slopes of La Giettaz. The slopes above Combloux are well worth exploring, particularly the quiet reds and black served by the Jouty chairlift.

Megève is also a great area for the less confident. There are long, easy blue runs in all sectors. A number of gentle runs lead down to Le Bettex and La Princesse from Mont d'Arbois, while nearby Mont Joux accesses long, easy runs to St-Nicolas. Alpette and Cote 2000 are also suitable. As is most of Le Jaillet, especially the long easy runs down to Combloux.

FOR BEGINNERS ★★★☆☆
Good choice of nursery areas

There are beginner slopes at valley level, and more snow-sure ones at altitude on each of the main mountains. There are also plenty of very easy green runs to progress to.

FOR BOARDERS ★★☆☆☆
Beginner friendly

Boarding doesn't really fit with Megève's rather staid, upmarket image, and there are quite a few flat linking runs to deal with. But freeriders will love it after snowfalls. It's a good place to try snowboarding for the first time, with plenty of fairly wide, quiet, gentle runs and a lot of chairlifts and gondolas. The draglifts are generally avoidable. There are no specialist schools, but all the ski schools offer boarding lessons.

FOR CROSS-COUNTRY ★★★★☆
An excellent area

There are 75km of varied trails spread throughout the area. Some are at altitude, making meeting with Alpine skiers for lunch simple.

MOUNTAIN RESTAURANTS ★★★★☆
Something for all budgets

Megève has some chic, expensive, gourmet places, but plenty of cheaper options too. The Stanford Skiing website has an absolutely essential guide to download. The piste map marks restaurants but does not name them. The tourist office restaurant guide includes huts; it is not comprehensive.

Editors' choice The Auberge du Christomet (0450 211134) has a lovely setting at the foot of the Christomet chair on Le Jaillet with fabulous views and a cosy rustic interior. Endorsed this year by two experienced reporters, one rating it 'even better than last year'; 'wonderful fish', 'friendly, efficient service', 'good house wine'. It is accessible on foot and by car, and gets booked out well in advance. On Mont d'Arbois, La Ravière (0450 931571), tucked away in the woods near the Croix chair, is a tiny rustic hut that does a set meal; booking is essential.

Worth knowing about Mont d'Arbois is well endowed. The famously expensive Idéal 1850 is said to be excellent. There are several modest, small places worth seeking out. We liked Sous les Freddy's, near the Arbois chair; very good meat platter and home-made

SCHOOLS

ESF
t 0450 210097

Evolution 2
t 0450 555357

International
t 0450 587888

Freeride
t 0680 306898

Summits
t 0450 933521

Agence de Ski
t 0699 185200

BASS
t 0845 468 1003 (UK)

Revolution Glisse
t 0667 608964

Ski Pros
t 0681 610615

Powderama
t 0616 871853

Ski Technique
t 0616 766 948

Classes (ESF prices)
5 2.5hr days €149

Private lessons
€42 for 1hr

GUIDES

Bureau des Guides
t 0450 215511

desserts. Reports on the Gouet, on the Gouet piste, are good – 'friendly family service with great mountain fare'. The tiny Refuge de Porcherey above St-Nicolas offers 'lovely food and ambience'. The Espace at Mont Joux is 'friendly, reasonably priced'. At the bottom of the Communailles lift, O'Communailles has had good reports but has gone 'way upmarket'.

On Rochebrune/Cote 2000 the Alpette is the prestige place – 'good for a blowout'. We had a satisfying lunch in 2012 at Javen d'en Haut. Radaz has 'a sunny location, good value plats du jour'. Super Megève at the top of the cable car is 'pricey but good', with 'great atmosphere and attentive service'. On the back of the hill, Chalet le Forestier is an atmospheric hut with 'reliable plat du jour'. To economize, Petite Fontaine is a '4-star good-value snack bar'.

On Le Jaillet, Face au Mont Blanc does a great fixed-price buffet. A regular rates the Auberge Bonjournal towards La Giettaz – 'good menu, fair value, great views', 'friendly staff, nice ambience'. Two reporters rave about the tiny self-service Balcons de Lydie – 'fair prices', 'best view in Megève'.

SCHOOLS AND GUIDES ★★★
Good private lessons

The ESF is of course the major school. A reporter noted huge class sizes ('up to 20') even in January. Happily, it has lots of competition here, not only from the International school but also from smaller French schools and some British-run outfits. Powderama based in Chamonix will be offering private lessons here in 2012/13.

Expeditions to the Vallée Blanche (in Chamonix) and to heli-skiing (in Italy) can be arranged, and mountain guides are available (we've had a great morning powder skiing in the trees with Alex Périnet: 0685 428339).

FOR FAMILIES ★★★
Language problems

The kindergartens offer a wide range of activities. But lack of English-speaking staff could be a drawback. The slopes are family-friendly and the schools rated by reporters. There are snow gardens in the main sectors.

STAYING THERE

There is an impressive range of accommodation in the area.

Chalets Stanford is the Megève specialist; for a cheap and cheerful base, you won't do better than its Sylvana – a creaky old hotel, between the Rochebrune cable car and the centre. Right in the centre the Rond-Point – another old hotel – is restored to the programme. They also have a smarter 10-bed chalet, les Clochettes.

Hotels Megève offers a range of exceptionally stylish and welcoming hotels, mainly quite small and built in chalet style. The three lovely but very pricey 5-star places seem likely to be joined by a delectable fourth next season – Le Chalet.

******Chalet St Georges** (0450 930715) Central, close to the gondola. Warmly welcoming, with 24 rooms and suites.

******Fer à Cheval** (0450 213039) Rustic-chic at its best, with a lovely wood interior. Spa and pool.

******Flocons de Sel** (0450 214999) Food-oriented eight-room place in a cluster of chalets secluded a few km out. 'Pampering as good as it gets, amazing staff, best food ever,' says a reporter. Three Michelin stars. Spa.

*****Coeur de Megève** (0450 212530) Central, very close to the gondola.

*****Coin du Feu** (0450 210494) Mid-sized chalet between Rochebrune and Chamois lifts.

****Gai Soleil** (0450 210070) Simple Logis de France place – 'good location, excellent breakfast, wonderful staff', says a discriminating reporter.

Apartments Loges Blanches is central and smart, with pool and restaurant; bookable via Ski Collection. Pierre et Vacances and Lagrange each offer one or two properties. Stanford also has an apartment and an eight-bed self-catering chalet.

EATING OUT ★★★★
Very French

The tourist office produces a pocket guide with photos. There are lots of upmarket restaurants, many of them in

CHILDCARE

Meg'Accueil
t 0450 587784
From age 1

P'tites Frimrousses
t 0450 211869
Ages 1 to 3

Club Piou-Piou
t 0450 589765
Ages 3 to 5

Ski schools
From age 5; ESF prices: 5 mornings (2.5hr) €138

UK PACKAGES

Alpine Answers, Alpine Weekends, AmeriCan Ski, Carrier, Erna Low, Flexiski, Independent Ski Links, Inghams, Lagrange, Luxury Chalet Collection, Momentum, Oxford Ski Co, Peak Retreats, Pierre & Vacances, PowderBeds, Simon Butler Skiing, Ski Bespoke, Ski Collection, Ski Expectations, Ski France, Ski Independence, Ski Solutions, Ski Weekend, Snow Finders, Stanford Skiing, White Roc
St Gervais AmeriCan Ski, Erna Low, Holiday in Alps, Lagrange, Mountain Tracks, Peak Retreats, PowderBeds, Ski Club Freshtracks, Ski France, Ski Weekend, Snowcoach, Zenith
Combloux Erna Low, Peak Retreats

Phone numbers
From abroad use the prefix +33 and omit the initial '0' of the phone number

TOURIST OFFICES

Megève
www.megeve.com

St-Gervais
www.st-gervais.net

the better hotels. The gastro guide favourites – the Michelin-starred Roches Fleuries and the Flocons de Sel (read 'Hotels') – are a drive out of town. The Flocons has a more modest branch, Flocons Villages, that is popular with locals and gets two rave reports from readers this year – 'beautifully presented, outstanding value', 'miraculous lamb and veal, wonderful desserts, exceptional bread'.

The Brasserie Centrale does precisely what brasseries were invented to do – 'good entrecôte-frites and crème brulée'. The 'very French and friendly' Chamois is the place for a fondue and other regional specialities.

APRES-SKI ★★★★★

Strolling and jazz

Megève is a pleasant place to stroll around after the lifts close, but exciting it isn't. If there are lively bars for a post-piste beer, they have so far eluded us. And those looking for loud disco-bars later may be disappointed, too. Club de Jazz (aka the 5 Rues) is our choice – a very popular jazz club-cum-cocktail bar, that gets some big-name musicians and opens from tea-time to late. It's expensive, but a reporter notes helpfully that the cocktail measures are large, so 'you don't need more than one per hour'. The Cocoon is a Brit favourite, with live music and British sports TV. The casino is more slot machines than blackjack tables. Palo Alto has two discos.

OFF THE SLOPES ★★★★★

Lots to do

There is a 'fantastic' sports centre with a fitness room, pool and indoor ice rink, an outdoor ice rink, cinemas and a market on Fridays. Shopping is a serious business, aided by a tourist office pocket guide (combined with the restaurant guide). Trips to Annecy and Chamonix are possible. Walks are excellent, with 50km of marked classified paths, though a picky reporter tells us the marking is not super-clear. Meeting friends on the slopes for lunch is easy.

LINKED RESORT – 850m

ST-GERVAIS

St-Gervais is a handsome 19th-century spa town set in a narrow river gorge, with access to the slopes shared with Megève by a gondola from the fringes.

Although definitely a town, it's a pleasant place, with interesting food shops, cosy and sophisticated bars (we liked the trendy Pur bar for cocktails and posh nibbles), thermal baths and an Olympic ice rink. Prices are noticeably lower than in Megève. The resort has a train station and there are efficient bus services.

The lodgings are mostly modest – there are half a dozen 2-star hotels, and four 3-stars. Two hotels convenient for the gondola are the Liberty Mont Blanc (0450 934521), a pleasantly traditional 2-star with pool, and the 3-star Carlina (0450 934110), with a small pool and sauna. The unclassified Féline Blanche (0450 965870) is a hip boutique place with just ten rooms done out in black and white. The basic 2-star Val d'Este (0450 936591) has one of the best restaurants in town (Le Sérac).

Holiday in Alps has a large selection of self-catering lodgings to rent. Fermes de St Gervais is a smart Lagrange Prestige residence with a pool, a mile out of town. These and other properties are available through Peak Retreats and Zenith Holidays.

The gondola goes to Le Bettex, a mid-mountain area of restaurants, conveniently placed hotels and excellent nursery slopes. The gondola above Le Bettex serves a green run, making this an attractive base for beginners. We enjoyed staying recently at the 3-star Arbois-Bettex (0450 931222), with pool, spa and good restaurant; and dining at the lovely rustic Chalet Rémy – friendly service.

On the opposite side of St-Gervais is a rack-and-pinion railway, which in 1904 was intended to go to the top of Mont Blanc. It was never completed, and terminates at the top of the ski area of Les Houches (described in the Chamonix chapter); but sadly there are no lift pass sharing arrangements.

Les Menuires

AGENCE NUTS

The bargain base for the Trois Vallées – with increasing amounts of stylish accommodation as well as the original dreary blocks

RATINGS

The mountains	
Extent	*****
Fast lifts	****
Queues	****
Terrain p'ks	***
Snow	****
Expert	****
Intermediate	*****
Beginner	***
Boarder	****
X-country	***
Restaurants	***
Schools	***
Families	****
The resort	
Charm	**
Convenience	*****
Scenery	***
Eating out	***
Après-ski	***
Off-slope	*

RPI	100
lift pass	£200
ski hire	£110
lessons	£70
food & drink	£120
total	**£500**

NEWS

2012/13: A new six-seat chairlift is due to replace the old bucket-lift from the bottom of La Masse to Reberty.

2011/12: A moving carpet for beginners and pedestrians was installed at Les Bruyères. Two new 4-star residences opened in Reberty/ Les Bruyères. Walibi Gliss, a family-fun zone, with boardercross and slalom, was built at La Masse.

- + Speedy, mostly queue-free access to the huge Trois Vallées area
- + Lots of slope-side accommodation, with traffic well separated
- + Low prices by local standards
- + French atmosphere

- – Big, dreary blocks and gloomy indoor shopping malls in centre
- – Main intermediate and beginner slopes get a lot of sun
- – Some slopes can get very crowded

Les Menuires arguably has the best position in the Trois Vallées, and we've warmed to it as better (and better-looking) lodgings have continued to be built. With our RPI confirming it as the most affordable major resort in the area, we now view Les Menuires as a very attractive proposition – especially the traditional-style bits we've christened collectively 'Belles-Menuires'.

THE RESORT

Les Menuires is a purpose-built resort, dominated by large apartment blocks, with about 60% of the visitors French. It has excellent links to Val Thorens in the same valley and to the Méribel valley. The core of the resort is La Croisette, a horseshoe of 1960s- and 1970s-built apartment blocks plus a claustrophobic underground shopping mall right by a gondola and fast chairlift into the heart of the Trois Vallées slopes. Recent development has added various suburbs to the original core, and a second lift base across the mountainside at Les Bruyères.

VILLAGE CHARM ★★
Much improved

The original buildings that surround the main lift base are among the most brutal examples of the monolithic architecture of the 1960s and 1970s. They still dominate the centre of the resort; but more recent developments in the suburbs have been built in much more attractive chalet style in stone and wood, and many UK tour operators have their accommodation there. Read our Belles-Menuires feature later in the chapter.

A couple of the original buildings have been demolished (as we advised way back in the 1990s), and they have been replaced by attractive chalet-style

OT LES MENUIRES / P LEBEAU

Powering down La Masse, with the Croisette area of town on the left and Reberty and Les Bruyères on the right of the pic →

KEY FACTS

Resort	1800m 5,910ft
Three Valleys	
Slopes	1260-3230m 4,130-10,600ft
Lifts	173
Pistes	600km 373 miles
Green	16%
Blue	40%
Red	34%
Black	10%
Snowmaking	2162 guns
Les Menuires / St-Martin only	
Slopes	1400-2850m 4,590-9,350ft
Lifts	34
Pistes	160km 99 miles
Green	16%
Blue	46%
Red	30%
Black	8%
Snowmaking	418 guns

blocks. And the 'front de neige' has been smartened up.

So we are at last upping our charm rating from ★ to ★★ to reflect the improvements and the fact that you can stay somewhere pleasant (one 2012 visitor only went to the centre once in his week's stay in Bruyères).

CONVENIENCE ★★★★★
Easy to get around on skis

For most visitors, the resort is very conveniently arranged for skiing – a great deal of the accommodation is ski-in, and much of it ski-out.

If you stay in the central area, nothing is more than a short stroll away. 'It's the easiest resort to get around that I've ever stayed in,' said a 2012 reporter. If you stay in some of the outposts, it may be different. They have their own shops and bars, but if you want more choice, you are reliant on buses that are scheduled to run every 20 minutes until 8pm, less frequently after that. In the mornings, too, you may have some hiking to do if you want to start from a lift other than the nearest one.

SCENERY ★★★
Go up high

The scenery can be rather bleak, but there are grand views from the peaks of the ski area on both sides, especially from La Masse.

THE MOUNTAINS

Les Menuires is set on the treeline, with almost all the slopes above it. Piste map and signposting are good.

EXTENT OF THE SLOPES ★★★★★
Part of the huge Trois Vallées

Les Menuires is well positioned for exploring the whole of the huge Trois Vallées skiing area with its 600km of pistes. The major part of the local network of slopes spreads across the broad, west-facing mountainside between Les Menuires and St-Martin, with links to the Méribel valley at four points and to Val Thorens at the southern end.

A gondola and a fast chair go up from La Croisette, and the same from Les Bruyères. A gondola to the separate sector of La Masse, across the valley, starts below the village.

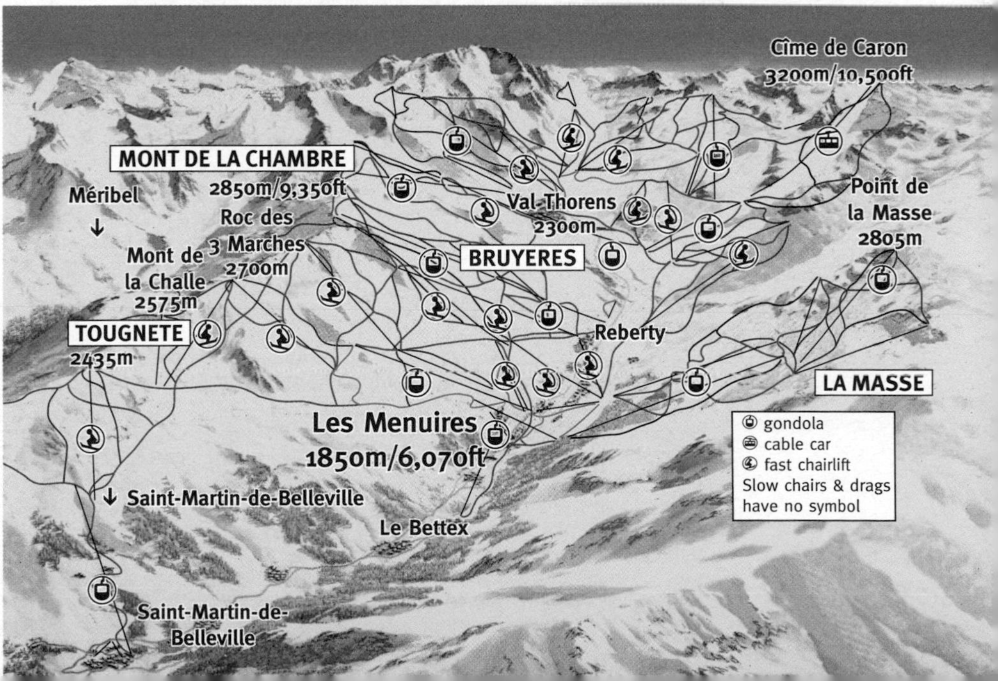

Les Belles-Menuires

La Plagne has its Belle-Plagne – why shouldn't Les Menuires have its Belles-Menuires? Or should it be Beaux-Menuires? Whatever ... We've made up this name to represent the attractive, chalet-style suburbs of Les Menuires – places where Méribel habitués might be happy.

These suburbs aren't simply built in chalet style – they also contain actual chalets. Most of them are operated by British tour operators that advertise on this spread, and are marked, approximately, on our map. They are concentrated up the slope in Reberty 2000, or down in Les Bruyères, a micro-resort complete with ice rink and swimming pool – and a major lift, the Bruyères gondola. The area shown also has the resort's best hotels, some smart apartment residences (read the margin panel), and an excellent slope-side restaurant, the Ferme.

Down the valley, on the opposite side of the resort centre, are further traditional-style, small-scale, relatively upmarket developments (read the left margin panel).

DOWN THE HILL

Below the main resort centre in Le Bettex, Ski Amis has a cluster of smart, independent chalets with outdoor hot tubs and saunas, 150m from the piste and the Bettex chairlift. A blue piste from the top of that takes you to the Tortollet chair to get up to Les Menuires and the Rocher Noir chair for La Masse. Absolutely Snow has two adjoining chalets in Le Bettex with in-house bar, sauna and outdoor hot tub.

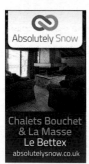

FAST LIFTS ★★★★
Good all over
All the major lifts out of the resort and up to the peaks are now fast chairs or powerful gondolas. The main slow ones left affect Le Bettex residents and beginners only.

QUEUES ★★★★
Very slight
Not usually a problem; most reporters comment on few queues. But the Bruyères gondola (for access to Val Thorens) is consistently mentioned by reporters ('15-minute queues at opening time'), and the Mont de la Chambre chair may get busy at peak times. Crowded slopes are more of a problem in general, particularly those leading down to the resort centre.

TERRAIN PARKS ★★★
Family-friendly
The BK park near the top of the Becca chair has blue and red lines of jumps and rails plus a boardercross. And there's the Acticross below it for kids. On La Masse there's the new Walibi Gliss slalom and boardercross area.

SNOW RELIABILITY ★★★★
Coverage good, quality variable
La Masse's height and northerly orientation ensure good snow for a long season. The main west-facing slopes obviously get lots of strong afternoon sun. They have lots of snowmaking, but the snow lower down is often icy in the morning and slushy later on. Of course, you're close to snow-sure Val Thorens.

APARTMENTS

In Reberty 2000, the Chalets du Soleil is an offshoot of the next-door 4-star hotel Kaya. Newly built up here for 2011/12 and in the same ownership is Chalet Julietta, with wellness facilities.

Slightly lower down, Alpages de Reberty is a Pierre & Vacances Premium residence with pool, sauna etc.

La Sapinière includes the Montagnettes residence Hameau de la Sapinière, with sauna, steam room and hot tub, a shop (including a bakery) and a restaurant.

Down in Les Bruyères, a new development for 2011/12 was Les Chalets du Mont Vallon, with pool, gym, sauna and a serious restaurant.

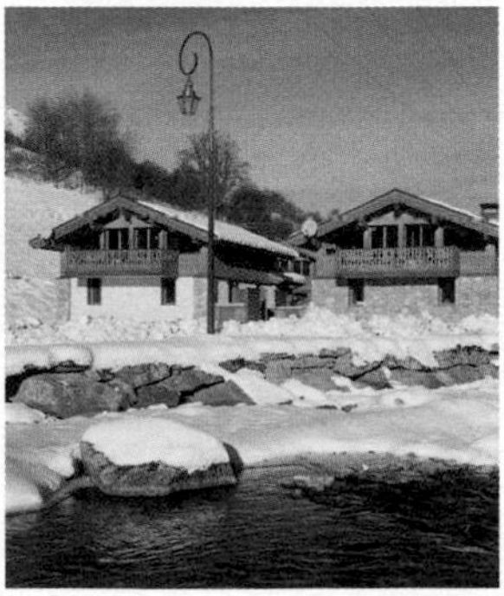

All the specialists in French apartments – Ski Collection, Lagrange, Erna Low – offer these and other residences.

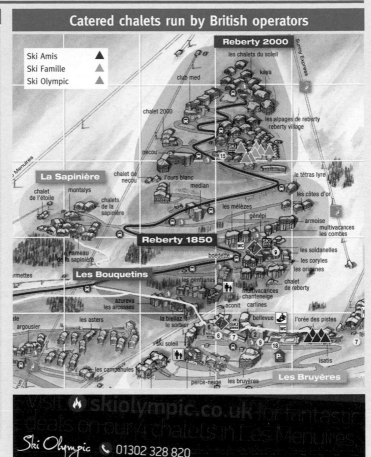

Catered chalets run by British operators

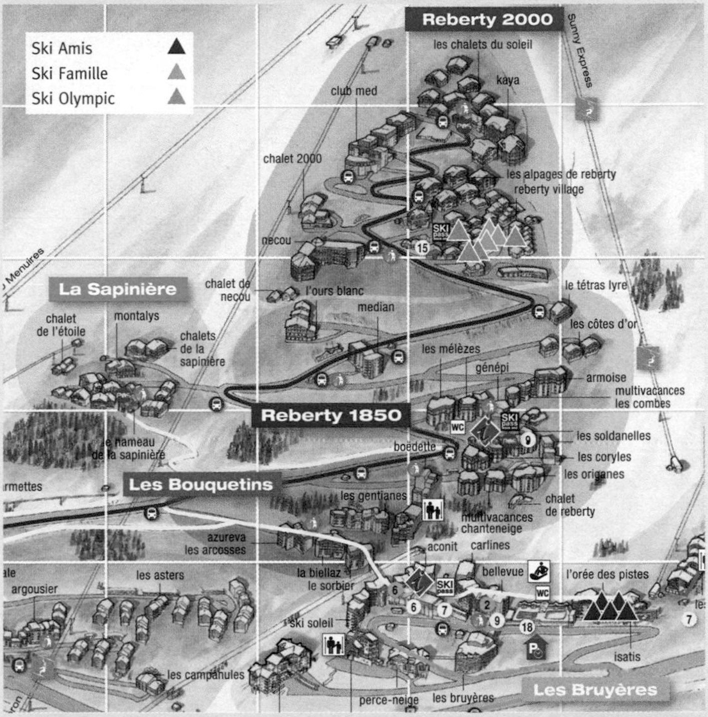

Ski Amis ▲
Ski Famille ▲
Ski Olympic ▲

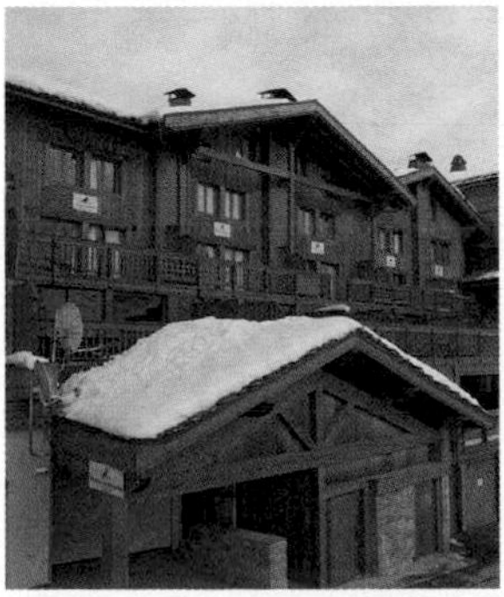

LIFT PASSES

Three Valleys

Prices in €

Age	1-day	6-day
under 13	37	184
13 to 64	49	244
65 plus	42	210

Free under 5, 75 plus

Beginner limited day pass €20

Notes
Covers Courchevel, La Tania, Méribel, Val Thorens, Les Menuires and St-Martin; family reductions; pedestrian and half-day passes

Alternative passes
Les Menuires/ St-Martin only; Vallée de Belleville only

CHILDCARE

Les Piou Piou
t 0479 006379
Ages 3mnth to 5yr

Ski school
From age 3 to 12: 6 days €260

ACTIVITIES

Indoor Centre sportif (swimming pool, sauna, steam, fitness, squash), library

Outdoor Tobogganing, outdoor pool (Bruyères), cleared paths, snowshoeing, paragliding

FOR EXPERTS ★★★★

Head for La Masse

The upper slopes of La Masse, served by the second stage of a fast jumbo gondola, are virtually all of stiff red or easy black steepness – great fast cruises when groomed, of almost 660m vertical, and with some of the best snow in the Trois Vallées. They are also usually very quiet compared with the rest of the slopes near here because La Masse is set off the busy Trois Vallées 'circuit', and most people from Méribel, Courchevel and Val Thorens don't make the detour.

There is also a huge amount of off-piste, including the wide, sweeping, not-too-steep Vallon du Lou off the back of La Masse towards Val Thorens (this used to be a marked itinéraire and was one of our favourite runs in the whole Trois Vallées). Other off-piste runs lead towards various villages from which you need transport back, but the Yvoses run takes you back into the Les Menuires lift system.

Read the other Trois Vallées resort chapters too.

FOR INTERMEDIATES ★★★★★

600km of pistes to choose from

With good snow, the slopes above the village on the west-facing side, virtually all blue and red, have a lot to offer. Don't miss La Masse as well – see 'For experts' above.

But the real attraction is the easy access to the rest of the Trois Vallées and its 600km of pistes, most of which are ideal intermediate terrain. There are lifts to four different points from which you can drop into the Méribel valley, and you can be at the far end of the Courchevel ski area in 1650 in around 90 minutes if you don't get distracted on the way. To get to Val Thorens, there's an easy blue run from the top of the Montaulever draglift that is quieter than the main runs down from the top of the Bruyères gondola. Read the other Trois Vallées resort chapters too.

FOR BEGINNERS ★★★

Snow quality a concern

The resort has improved its nursery areas – now with six moving carpets that are free – but snow quality here remains a concern because of the sunny aspect. A special lift pass is available for beginners, and there is a green run to the village from the Roc des 3 Marches gondola, and lots of easy blues to progress to, but they are prone to crowds.

FOR BOARDERS ★★★★

Beware flat parts

Slushy snow on the west-facing slopes won't worry boarders as it does skiers. But you'll still want to escape and

WENDY-JANE KING

Looking over Reberty to La Masse; most of its pistes are the other side of the ridge in the centre and right of this pic ➔

SCHOOLS

ESF
t 0479 006143

Ski School
t 0667 586777

Prosneige
t 0479 041835

Snowbow
t 0479 419403

Classes (ESF prices)
6 5hr days €190

Private lessons
€48 for 1hr

GETTING THERE

Air Geneva 150km/95 miles (2hr15); Lyon 190km/120 miles (2hr30); Chambéry 115km/70 miles (2hr)

Rail Moûtiers (25km/15 miles)

UK PACKAGES

Absolutely Snow, Alpine Elements, Carrier, Club Med, Crystal, Erna Low, Family Ski Company, Independent Ski Links, Lagrange, Neilson, Pierre & Vacances, PowderBeds, Powder N Shine, Powder White, Richmond Holidays, Ski Amis, Ski Collection, Ski Famille, Ski France, Ski Independence, Ski Olympic, Ski Supreme, Skitracer

Phone numbers
From abroad use the prefix +33 and omit the initial '0' of the phone number

TOURIST OFFICE

www.lesmenuires.com

explore the vast amount of terrain elsewhere in the Trois Vallées. The local terrain park is far from hard core, but the great DC Area 43 park above Méribel-Mottaret is easy to reach. Locally, there are few draglifts but some flattish sections of piste.

FOR CROSS-COUNTRY ★★★★★
Limited and low

The 28km of trails are along the valley between St-Martin and Les Menuires.

MOUNTAIN RESTAURANTS ★★★★★
Affordable fare

There are some excellent spots – good news for people based elsewhere in search of an affordable lunch.

Editors' choice The Grand Lac (0479 082578) is a big chalet in a fine spot at the bottom of the Granges chair where we've always had very good service and food – both plats du jour and other acceptable dishes (we had a huge omelette and excellent fries for 12.50 euros last season). Reporters agree (but one said service had deteriorated last season).

Worth knowing about Way across the hill, the Alpage is consistently praised and was a regular visitor's '2012 restaurant of the year'. The Sonnailles, off the valley-bottom Cumin run, is another favourite. In the almost-a-mountain-restaurant category, the Ferme, piste-side at Reberty 2000, is excellent. Consider the slope-side hotel terraces up here, too, particularly the Ours Blanc. On the La Masse side, Roches Blanches at the top of the first gondola has 'impressive food and service' and 'good, freshly prepared pizzas', says a 2012 visitor.

SCHOOLS AND GUIDES ★★★★★
Try the Ski School

The ESF gets mixed reviews; it seems to do a lot of off-piste stuff. A group of instructors operating here and in St-Martin under the startling name of Ski School offer only private lessons and are said to be 'really good'.

FOR FAMILIES ★★★★★
Lots of options

Good facilities. There are kids' 'villages' with indoor and outdoor facilities at both La Croisette and Les Bruyères. There are fun parks, tubing, kids' snow scooters and kids' quad bikes. Ski Famille is a family specialist with three chalets in Reberty and its own childcare arrangements.

STAYING THERE

La Croisette consists mainly of large apartment blocks. Reberty/Les Bruyères has hotels and chalets too.

Chalets See our Belles-Menuires feature earlier in the chapter.

Hotels There are good places on the slopes at Reberty/Les Bruyères.

******Kaya** (0479 414200) The resort's only 4-star – smart and modern.

*****Isatis** (0479 004545) In chalet style, right at the Bruyères gondola – 17 suites, all with hot tubs.

*****Ours Blanc** (0479 006166) Up the slope in Reberty.

Apartments There are lots of new developments in chalet style, most of them covered by our Belles-Menuires feature. In the suburb of Preyerand, just below the main resort centre, is the chalet-style 4-star residence Les Clarines, with spa and pool, and featured by Ski Collection. Ski Amis has units in all parts of the resort.

EATING OUT ★★★★★
Mix of gourmet and Savoyard

We had very good traditional and gourmet meals at the Cocon des Neiges (hotel Isatis). Up the slope in Reberty, the piste-side Ferme is very popular for its food (steaks etc), atmosphere and good-value menus. The K (hotel Kaya) is a good gourmet option. Other recent tips include the 'efficient, jolly' Chouette ('great crêpes'), the Marmite de Géant ('excellent Savoyard and more adventurous dishes') and the Vieux Grenier ('great atmosphere').

APRES-SKI ★★★★★
Not a lot of choice

It's pretty quiet in the evening. A reporter favourite for close-of-play beers is the Chouette at Les Bruyères. There is no shortage of bars in La Croisette, but those in the dreadfully claustrophobic mall are ruled out for us. The cabaret at Medz'é-ry is entertaining, we're told. There are discos at Croisette and Bruyères.

OFF THE SLOPES ★★★★★
Great sports centre

There is a big and seriously impressive sports/spa/pool/fitness centre, a 4km-long toboggan run down the Roc des 3 Marches gondola and paragliding. But this is basically a destination for skiers and boarders, and not very appealing for others.

Méribel

The enduring British favourite: a comfortable, upmarket chalet-style resort in the centre of the incomparable Trois Vallées

RATINGS

The mountains	
Extent	*****
Fast lifts	*****
Queues	****
Terrain p'ks	****
Snow	***
Expert	****
Intermediate	*****
Beginner	****
Boarder	****
X-country	***
Restaurants	***
Schools	****
Families	***
The resort	
Charm	***
Convenience	***
Scenery	***
Eating out	****
Après-ski	*****
Off-slope	***

RPI	110
lift pass	£200
ski hire	£115
lessons	£100
food & drink	£145
total	**£560**

KEY FACTS

Resort	1400-1700m 4,590-5,580ft
Trois Vallées	
Slopes	1260-3230m 4,130-10,600ft
Lifts	173
Pistes	600km 373 miles
Green	16%
Blue	40%
Red	34%
Black	10%
Snowmaking	2162 guns
Méribel only	
Slopes	1400-2950m 4,590-9,680ft
Lifts	42
Pistes	150km 93 miles
Green	11%
Blue	42%
Red	35%
Black	12%
Snowmaking	728 guns

- \+ Central to the Trois Vallées, the biggest lift network in the world
- \+ Pleasant chalet-style architecture
- \+ Impressive lift system
- \+ Very lively après-ski scene
- \+ Excellent piste maintenance and snowmaking; nevertheless ...

- − Snow on the west-facing side suffers from afternoon sun
- − Sprawling main village
- − Expensive, particularly for food and drink
- − Full of Brits
- − Some pistes can get crowded

A loyal band of regular visitors just love Méribel, and it's not difficult to see why. For keen piste-bashers who like to rack up the miles but dislike tacky post-war resorts, it's difficult to beat: unlike other modern purpose-built resorts, Méribel has always insisted on chalet-style architecture.

Other 3V resorts have the edge in some respects. For better snow opt for Courchevel or Val Thorens. For lower prices, Les Menuires. For a more compact village and a lower concentration of Brits, go virtually anywhere.

THE RESORT

Méribel was founded in 1938 by a Brit, Peter Lindsay, and has retained a strong British presence and influence ever since. It occupies the central valley of the Trois Vallées network and consists of two main resort villages.

The original resort is built on a steepish west-facing hillside with the home piste running down beside it to the main lift stations in the valley bottom, slightly below the village centre. The resort now spreads widely away from the centre and the piste; various quarters can be identified – among them Mussillon, beside the road in to the resort, where many individual chalets are located. A road winds up from the centre to the top of the main village. From there, one road goes on through woods to the outpost of Altiport (a snow-covered airstrip) while another goes under the home piste to a more recently developed area, Belvedere.

The satellite resort of Méribel-Mottaret, a mile or two up the valley, is centrally placed in the Trois Vallées ski area, offering quicker access to Val Thorens in particular. The hamlet of Méribel-Village, on the road from Méribel to Courchevel, has developed into a pleasant, quiet micro-resort. It is at the bottom of a blue run from Altiport, with a fast quad giving access to the other slopes.

You can stay in the valley below Méribel, in the spa town of Brides-les-Bains – see the end of this chapter – or in the village of Les Allues at a mid-station of the gondola from Brides.

A car is useful for outings to other resorts in the Tarentaise; you can access La Plagne via Champagny. But it can be useful around the village too.

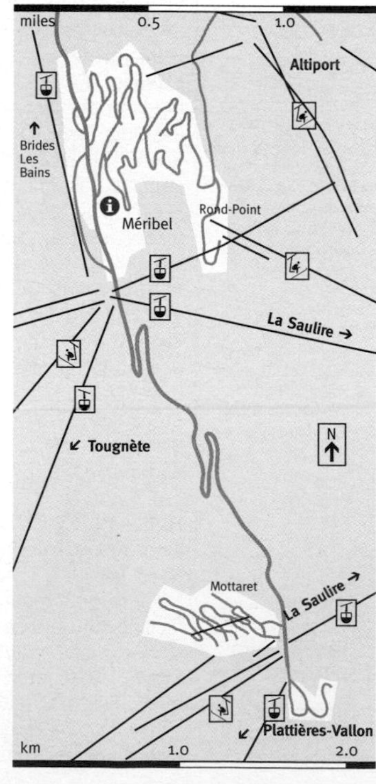

NEWS

2012/13: The first two sections of the Plattières gondola are due to be replaced by a 10-person gondola that will cut ride time from 22 minutes to nine minutes. The lower stage of the Saulire gondola is being replaced to match the upper stage installed for last season, cutting ride time to the top from 20 minutes to 12. The Choucas restaurant near the mid-station of this gondola will be redesigned to become a new Folie Douce (like those in Val d'Isère and Val Thorens). Two pistes will be remodelled to make them easier: the bottom part of the blue run to Mottaret by the Plattières gondola and the narrow-access blue to Chaudanne.

2011/12: The upper stage of the Saulire gondola from Méribel was replaced by a faster eight-seater. The Blanchot green run was remodelled to start at the gondola mid-station, creating a gentle run all the way to the resort.

VILLAGE CHARM ★★★

Built with style

Méribel is one of the most tastefully designed of French purpose-built resorts. The buildings are wood-clad, chalet-style and mainly low-rise, and they include a lot of individual chalets as well as big chalet-shaped blocks of apartments. Mottaret lacks these smaller chalets, and looks more block-like as a result, despite wood cladding on its apartment buildings. Even so, it's more attractive than many other resorts built for slope-side convenience. It has far fewer shops and bars and much less après-ski than Méribel itself, and nothing like the feel of a village.

CONVENIENCE ★★★

Shuttle to the slopes, usually

Although some lodgings are right on the piste beside the village, many depend on using free (and now 'excellent') public buses which run until midnight or private minibuses to and from the slopes. There are collections of shops and restaurants at a couple of points on the road through the resort – Altitude 1600 and Plateau de Morel.

Méribel-Village is a small place; it has some luxury chalets and apartments, but has very limited amenities – a bread shop, small supermarket, bar, pizzeria and a couple of restaurants.

Mottaret has spread up both steep sides of the valley, though most of the blocks are on the east-facing side. Many lodgings are ski-in/ski-out, but not all. Both sides are served by lifts for pedestrians – but the gondola up the east-facing slope stops at 7.30 and it's a long, tiring walk up.

SCENERY ★★★

Head for Vallon

The village is attractively set in woodland, below long craggy ridges – a satisfying although unspectacular scene. But there are wonderful glacial views from Mont du Vallon at the head of the valley.

THE MOUNTAINS

Most of the slopes are above the treeline, but there are some sheltered runs for bad-weather days. Piste classification is not always reliable – a problem compounded by exposure of many slopes to the sun. Signposting is now excellent. The piste map is adequate; but it could be so much better if it covered the two sides of the valley separately. Small notices are posted at various places telling you which runs have been groomed but we found it inadequate on our 2012 visit (they used to hand out grooming maps – shame that has stopped).

EXTENT OF THE SLOPES ★★★★★

Centre of a huge area

Leaving aside the rest of the Trois Vallées, this is a big area. Lifts go up to nine high-points on the ridges above the resort – two entry points to the Courchevel valley, no fewer than

MICHAEL MARLAIS

A good view of Saulire, with the run down from there to Mottaret in the distance that is badly affected by sun. In the foreground is the queue-prone chair to Tougnète →

six entry points to the Belleville valley shared by St-Martin, Les Menuires and Val Thorens, and Mont du Vallon, a very worthwhile cul-de-sac.

On the morning-sun side, chairs go up to the first two links with St-Martin, and some relatively quiet slopes back towards Méribel. To the left, a gondola and then a six-pack go from Méribel to **Tougnète**, for both Les Menuires or St-Martin. You can also head down to **Mottaret** from here. From there, a fast chair then a drag take you to Belleville entry point number four.

South of Mottaret are some of the best slopes in the valley, in the **Plattières-Vallon** sector at the head of the valley. The top stage of the old Plattières gondola (the first two stages are being replaced by a 10-seater for 2012/13), ends at the fifth entry point to the Belleville valley. To the east of this is the big stand-up gondola to the top of Mont du Vallon. The Côte Brune fast quad from near this area goes up to Mont de la Chambre, the sixth link with the next valley, and the only one giving direct access to Val Thorens.

On the afternoon-sun side, gondolas leave both Méribel and Mottaret for **Saulire,** the main link to Courchevel 1850. The other link is from Altiport, via a slow chairlift to Col de la Loze.

FAST LIFTS ★★★★★

Highly efficient system

Modern chairs and gondolas serve both sides of the valley, with good links into the rest of the Trois Vallées.

Great hill, both on- and off-piste: high, steep but not too steep, 750m vertical
Mont du Vallon 2950m/9,680ft
Mont Vallon
PLATTIÈRES - VALLON
Plan des Mains
Mures Rouge
Courchevel
SAULIRE
2740m
Excessive afternoon sun means the run down to Mottaret is often more difficult than you might wish
Better snow here than on most of the afternoon-sun side of the valley
Pas du Lac I & II
1750m
MOTTARET
BURGIN
Courchevel
Dent du Burgin
Col de la Loze
2305m
Adret
Saulire
Rhodos I & II
Chaudanne
Altiport
Méribel
1450m/4,760ft
A great area for beginners and near-beginners, with long green runs and a fast slow-loading chairlift
Olympic
Altiport
Méribel-Village
1400m/4,590ft
Brides-les-Bains

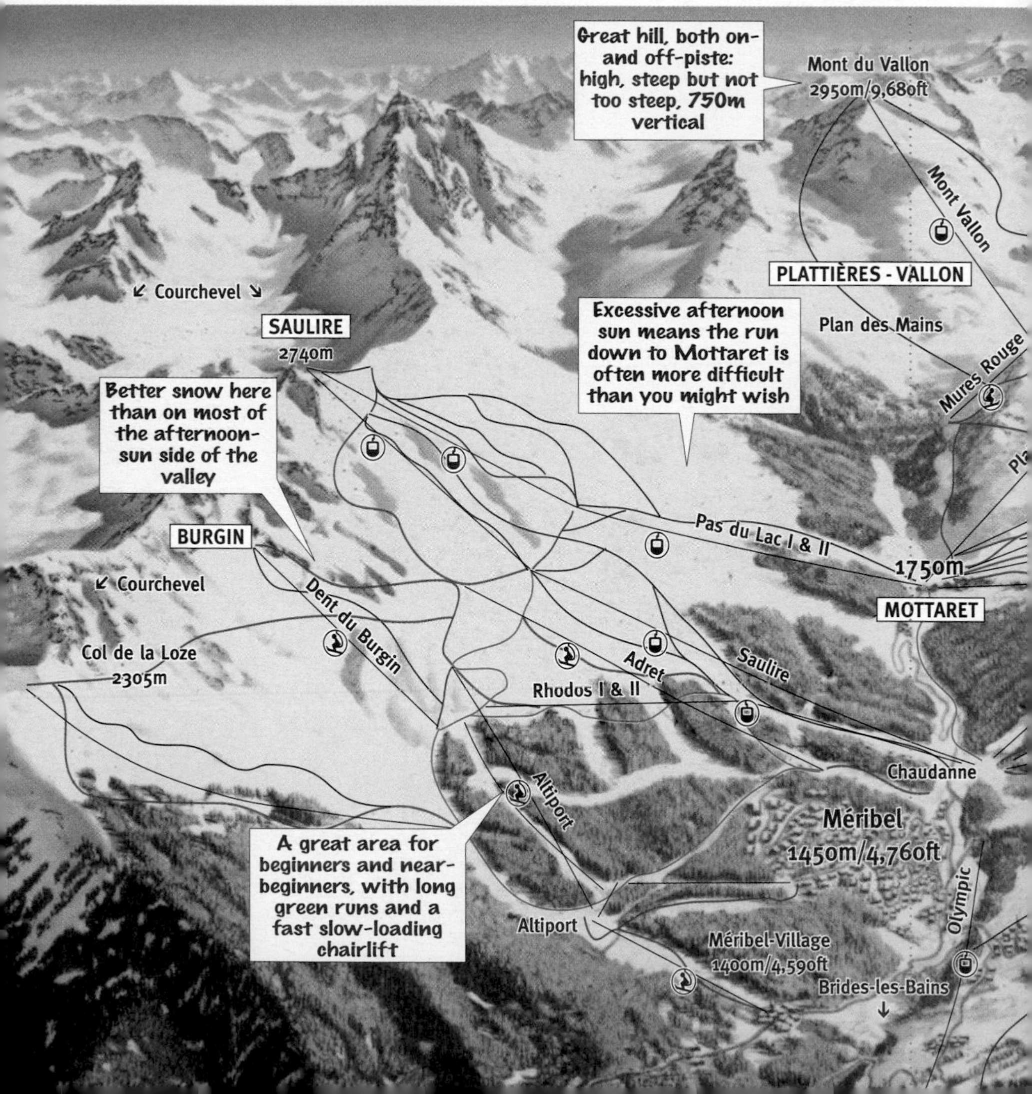

LIFT PASSES

Trois Vallées

Prices in €		
Age	**1-day**	**6-day**
under 13	37	184
13 to 64	49	244
65 plus	42	210

Free under 5, 75 plus

Beginner Mini pass

Notes
Covers Courchevel, La Tania, Méribel, Val Thorens, Les Menuires and St-Martin; family reductions; pedestrian and half-day passes

Alternative passes
Méribel and Méribel-Mottaret only with one-day Trois Vallées extension available

QUEUES ★★★★
3V traffic a persistent problem

The area is generally queue-free most of the time, but as more and more visitor beds are added to the Trois Vallées resorts, new bottlenecks emerge. The lift company could achieve a lot by employing lifties to usher people into half-empty cabins. If Les Arcs can do it ...

We and reporters alike have found that the six-pack above the Tougnète gondola is a serious bottleneck – it comes nowhere near coping with the combination of people coming up the gondola and people descending the four good pistes above.

The new Plattières gondola (which carries 40% more people than the old one) will cut queues there but put even more pressure on the old gondola third stage (which will remain in place) and the Côte Brune chair from people heading onward to Val Thorens. Both of the main gondolas for Courchevel from Méribel and Mottaret have been queue-prone; but the new one from Méribel should reduce problems there.

In this central valley the most serious problems result from the tidal flows of people passing through in the morning (when the tide coincides with the start of ski school) and in the late afternoon, when crowds on the runs to Mottaret can also be a problem.

Most people returning from Val Thorens form a queue for the Plan des Mains chair so as to avoid the flat start of the 'blue' Ours valley run.

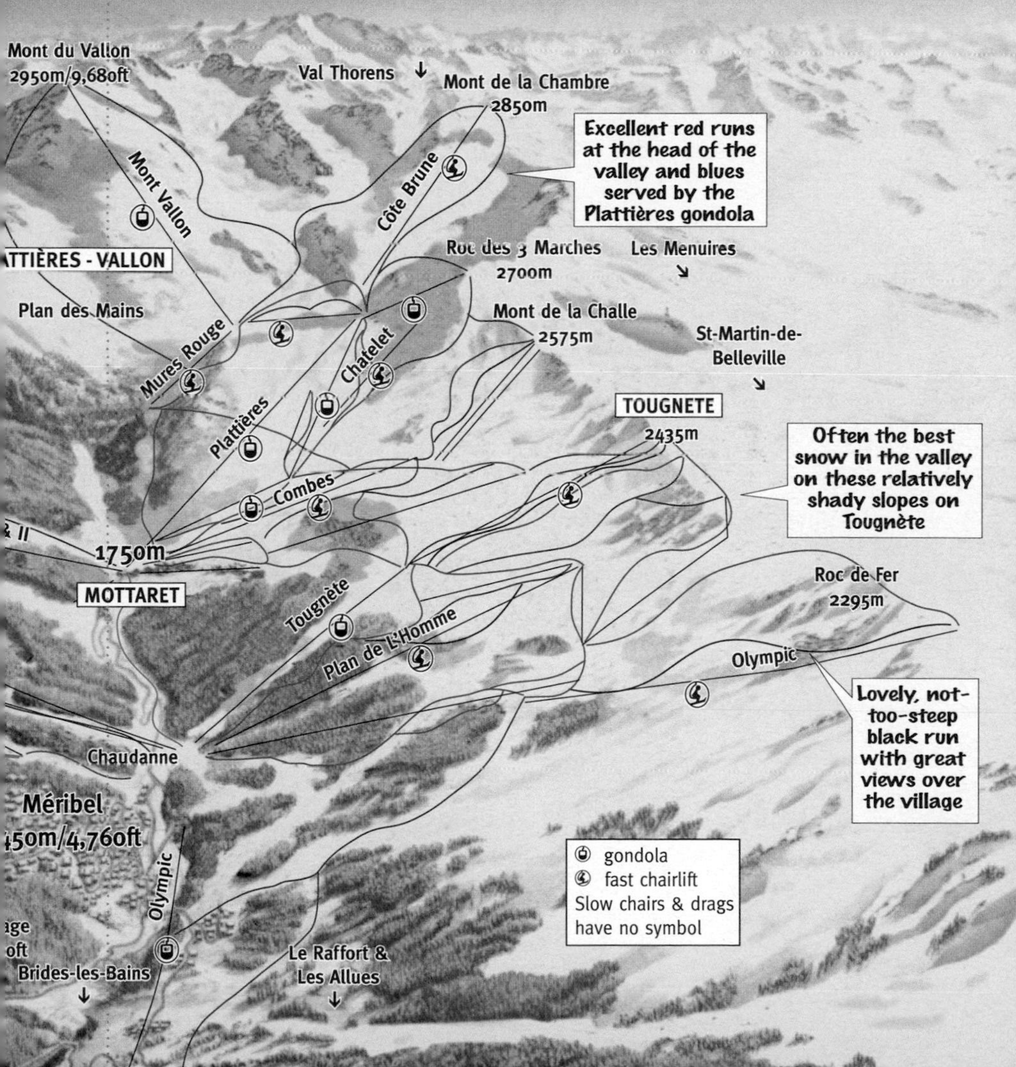

Confident skiers should use our trick instead: by-pass Plan des Mains by traversing above it, off-piste.

TERRAIN PARKS ★★★★
Two great areas
Méribel has two big parks. Moonpark at mid-mountain on Tougnète and served by the Arpasson draglift covers over 25 acres. In charge are the respected Ho5 crew. There are kickers, tables, rails and boxes and – new for 2011/12 – bio rails made of wood with beginner, intermediate and expert lines, a boardercross and a 'chill and grill' BBQ zone. You can be filmed and watch the results on a big screen.

Under the new Plattières gondola, the DC Area 43 park was massively expanded last season to be 1200m long with lots of features, lines for different abilities, 200m of rails, a half-pipe, boardercross and air bag jump. You can have your run recorded and play it back online.

Kids get their own mini-boardercross, P'tit Moon, on the west-facing slopes above the mid-station of the Rhodos gondola.

OT MERIBEL / JM GOUEDARD

The end of the almost flat green run from Mottaret to the main lifts out of Méribel at Chaudanne ↓

SNOW RELIABILITY ★★★
Not the best in the Trois Vallées
Méribel's slopes aren't the highest in the Trois Vallées, and they mainly face roughly east or west; the latter (the runs down from Courchevel) get the full force of the afternoon sun. In late season you soon get into the habit of avoiding this side in the morning, when it is still rock-hard having frozen overnight. Skiers coming over from Courchevel can get a real shock. The run down from Saulire to Mottaret is a particular problem – often like concrete for its whole 1000m vertical; in our countless visits over many years, we've only once found this run enjoyable. The slopes above Altiport get less direct sun and generally have decent snow. And the morning-sun side (the Tougnète side of the valley) can be excellent. At the southern end of the valley, a lot of runs are north-facing and keep their snow well, as do the runs on Mont du Vallon.

Snowmaking has been increased to the point where the lower runs have substantial cover. Lack of snow is rarely a problem. Grooming is said to be 'good'.

MERIBEL'S BEST OFF-PISTE RUNS

Méribel has a lot of very good off-piste to discover. Here, we pick out some of the best runs for skiers with at least some off-piste experience. Don't tackle them without guidance.

The run from near Roc de Fer to Le Raffort, a mid-station on the gondola from Brides-les-Bains, is an adventure with exceptional views. You ride the Olympic chairlift, go along the ridge, then ski a gentle bowl to finish among the trees.

The wide, west-facing slope above Altiport is enjoyable when the snow is fresh – varied terrain, from average to steep, some open some wooded, reached from the Tétras black run.

There are lots of runs suitable for more accomplished off-piste skiers. One is the Cairn, from the Mouflon piste at the top of the Plattières gondola; it starts in a fairly steep couloir and becomes wider, with a consistent pitch, until you reach the Sittelle piste.

The Roc de Tougne draglift accesses some challenging runs. To the right of the Lagopéde red piste is an area guides call the Spot – a rather technical and steep descent to the Sittelle piste. Alternatively, a 15-minute hike brings you to the Couloir du Serail, leading to the Mouflon red piste – a favourite because of the vertical, the constant pitch and the quality of snow.

Some of the best routes in the Méribel valley are accessed from the other valleys. The Col du Fruit is a classic, far away from the lifts and resorts. You ride the Creux Noirs chairlift in Courchevel, then walk along the ridge for 15 minutes before descending through the national park to Lac de Tueda and the cross-country tracks ... 800m of flat ground from the Mottaret lifts. Some of the best snow is accessed from the 3 Vallées 2 chairlift at Val Thorens. Ducking the rope at the top takes you into varied terrain mixing couloirs and gentle slopes, with exposures from north-east to north-west. Eventually you join the red Lac de la Chambre piste.

ACTIVITIES

Indoor Parc Olympique (ice rink, swimming pool, climbing wall), fitness centres, bowling, library, cinemas, museum, heritage tours

Outdoor Flying lessons, snowmobiles, dog sledding, snowshoeing, sleigh rides, cleared paths

FOR EXPERTS ★★★★☆
Exciting choices

The size of the Trois Vallées means experts are well catered for. In the Méribel valley, Mont du Vallon has lots to offer. The long, steep Combe Vallon run here is classified red; it's a wonderful, long, fast cruise when groomed (which it normally is), but presents plenty of challenge when mogulled. And there's a beautiful off-piste run in the next valley to the main pistes, leading back to the bottom of the gondola.

A good mogul run is down the side of the double Roc de Tougne draglift which leads up to Mont de la Challe. And there are steep, unrelenting runs from Tougnète back to Méribel – the upper Ecureuil piste is now a black while the adjacent Combe Tougnète is now a red. At the north end of the valley the Face run was created for the women's downhill race in the 1992 Olympics; served by a fast quad, it's a splendid cruise when freshly groomed (with great views over the village).

Nothing on the Saulire side is as steep as on the other side of the valley. The Mauduit red run is quite challenging, though – it used to be classified black. Throughout the area there are good off-piste opportunities – read our feature panel above, and the other Trois Vallées resort chapters.

FOR INTERMEDIATES ★★★★★
Paradise found

Méribel and the rest of the Trois Vallées form something close to paradise for intermediate skiers and riders; there are few other resorts where a keen piste-basher can cover so many miles so easily and with such satisfaction. Virtually every slope in the region has a good intermediate run down it, and to describe them all would take a book in itself.

For less adventurous intermediates, the Sittelle blue run from the top of the new Plattières gondola back down towards Mottaret is an ideal cruise – gentle and generally in good condition because of its north-facing aspect. But in the past, the last part (Martre) could get tricky, bumpy and very crowded later in the day; we are promised that this will be remodelled and made a lot easier for 2012/13. The red run into Mottaret on the other side of the valley gets dangerously icy and crowded; something should be done about this too.

Even early intermediates should find the runs over into the other valleys well within their capabilities, opening up further vast amounts of intermediate terrain. In Courchevel or Val Thorens you also get the bonus of better snow.

Virtually all the pistes on both

UK PACKAGES

Adventure Base, Alpine Action, Alpine Answers, Alpine Elements, Belvedere Travel, Carrier, Club Med, Consensio, Cooltip, Crystal, Crystal Finest, Elegant Resorts, Erna Low, Esprit, Flexiski, Friendship Travel, Independent Ski Links, Inghams, Interactive Resorts, Lagrange, Luxury Chalet Collection, Mark Warner, Meriski, Momentum, Mountain Wave, Neilson, Oxford Ski Co, Pierre & Vacances, PowderBeds, Powder White, Purple Ski, Scott Dunn, Silver Ski, Ski Amis, Ski Basics, Ski Beat, Ski Bespoke, Ski Blanc, Ski Club Freshtracks, Ski Collection, Ski Cuisine, Ski Expectations, Ski France, Ski Hame, Ski Independence, Ski Line, Ski Olympic, Ski Solutions, Ski Supreme, Ski Total, Skitracer, Ski Weekend, Skiweekends.com, Skiworld, Snow Finders, SnowCrazy, Snoworks, Sovereign Ski, Supertravel, Thomson, VIP, White Roc

Mottaret Alpine Answers, Crystal, Neilson, Pierre & Vacances, Ski France, Ski Independence, Ski Line, Thomson

Brides-les-Bains AmeriCan Ski, Crystal, Erna Low, Lagrange, Peak Retreats, Powder White, PowderBeds, Ramblers, Ski France, Skiweekends.com

sides of the Méribel valley will suit more advanced intermediates. Few of the reds are easy.

FOR BEGINNERS ★★★★

Strengths and weaknesses

Méribel continues to improve its appeal to beginners. At the core of this appeal is an excellent long green slope – gentle, wide, tree-lined – at Altiport (where one of the editors of this book learned to ski, [cough] years ago). This is a lift or bus-ride above the resort, which is not ideal. But the slope is served by a free draglift (and by a fast chair going higher which is not free). And there are green runs from the top and bottom of the drag back to Rond-Point, at the top of the village, where there is another free drag (beginners should take a lift or bus down from there as the blue run lower down is not easy). And now a green run goes from the mid-station of the Saulire gondola so that novices are able to ski from that point. The Mini lift pass gives access to a limited number of gentler slopes.

There is a small nursery slope at Rond-Point which is mainly used by the children's ski school.

At Mottaret, facilities are less impressive. There is an enclosed beginner area beside the village with a magic carpet; you can graduate from there to an almost flat green along the valley to the main Méribel lifts (though there may be speeding skiers racing past you).

FOR BOARDERS ★★★★

Loved by Brits

Méribel is a favourite for British snowboarders. The terrain is good and varied, with a worthwhile number of tree runs. Mont du Vallon has some very good steep freeriding that stays relatively untracked. There are lots of red runs here for intermediates and gentle blues and greens for beginners. Most lifts are chairs or gondolas, but beware of flat sections on the main routes to and from Val Thorens – and avoid the Ours blue run down to Mottaret from Mont du Vallon, which is very hard work. Specialist shops include Avalon Rider (which is in central Méribel).

FOR CROSS-COUNTRY ★★★

Scenic routes

There are about 33km in the Méribel valley. The main area is in the forest near Altiport and great for trying cross-country for the first time. There's also a loop around Lake Tueda, in the nature reserve at Mottaret, and for the more experienced an itinéraire from Altiport to Courchevel.

MOUNTAIN RESTAURANTS ★★★

A disappointing choice

There are few places worth singling out here, and there aren't enough restaurants to meet the demand, so many places get crowded. The self-service Folie Douce and table-service Fruitière will be welcome additions for 2012/13. Restaurants are not named on the piste map.

We've had a good lunch in the table-service part of Plan des Mains, and we're told the self-service has improved but would welcome more reports. The Chardonnet, mid-station of the Pas du Lac gondola, is 'a real find' and popular for its steak tartare prepared at the table, says a recent visitor. The Crêtes, on the Tougnète ridge has a 'genuine rustic interior, lovely food, but is pricey', says a 2012 visitor. The Coeur de Cristal, low down beside the Adret chair, does 'very nice, well presented food'. The Rhododendrons, at the top of the Altiport drag and Rhodos gondola, is a popular spot for its large terrace but gets mixed reviews.

SCHOOLS

ESF Méribel
t 0479 086031

ESF Méribel-Mottaret
t 0479 004949

Magic
t 0479 085336

New Generation
t 0479 010318
0844 770 4733 (UK)
www.skinewgen.com

Parallel Lines
t 0844 811 2779 (UK)

Snow Systems
t 0479 004022

BASS
t 0679 512405

Snow D'Light
t 0664 816010

Classes (ESF prices)
5 half-days (2.5hr per day): from €127

Private lessons
From €76 for 1.5hr for up to 4 people

GUIDES

Mountain guide office
t 0479 003038

This is one of the few resorts where we can be persuaded to descend to resort level for lunch on one of three slope-side hotel terraces – the Adray Télébar, the Allodis or the Altiport. All these are thoroughly excellent. Above Mottaret, the Grain de Sel gets a reader's vote for 'the best burger and chips – we went out of our way to visit twice'.

SCHOOLS AND GUIDES ★★★★

Some excellent options

The ESF is by far the biggest school, with over 450 instructors. It has an international section with instructors speaking good English. It offers useful options, such as off-piste groups, heli-skiing on the Italian border and Trois Vallées tours. Magic Snowsports Academy, the second largest school, is run by an Anglo-French team and has a number of native English-speaking instructors.

New Generation, a British school that operates in 10 resorts including Méribel and gets excellent reports – for example, 'progressed quickly', 'all excellent instructors', 'the perfect amount of jokes, drills, talks and brilliant skiing'.

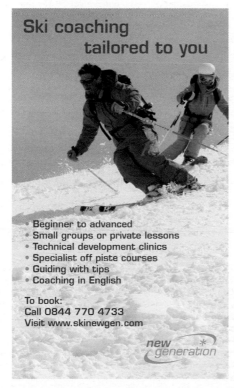

FOR FAMILIES ★★★

A popular chalet choice

Méribel is a sensible choice for families wanting a chalet holiday. What it lacks in convenience it gains in an impressive area, with gentle beginner slopes and a couple of fun family areas (Acticross with whoops, a tunnel, banked turns and slaloms and Moon Wild nature trail through the woods – both above Altiport). 'Magnestick' child safety systems have now been fitted to all fast chairlifts in the area to prevent them opening until near the end of the ride. But we rarely get reports on childcare facilities – no doubt many readers use the facilities of chalet operators. Family specialist Esprit operates here – see 'Chalets'.

STAYING THERE

Chalets Méribel has more chalets on the British market than any other resort. The specialist agents list scores of options. What really distinguishes Méribel is the range of recently built luxury chalets. Many have saunas, hot tubs or both. Some are well located, but many rely on minibus services.

The widest choice is from Ski Total, with 13 properties in the mid-to-large size range. Three deservedly get Total's top Platinum rating. Hot tubs, of course, and cinema and billiard room in the case of chalet Isba. Skiworld has 11 chalets of various sizes, including two swanky places with sauna and hot tub.

Purple Ski has five top-notch and highly individual chalets – in good positions, with lovely interiors, and outdoor hot tubs. Alpine Action has eight smart-looking chalets, most with sauna and/or hot tub and all with Freeview TV.

Ski Olympic has two properties at 1600: the smooth Parc Alpin with 12 luxurious rooms (all with plasma screen TVs), dinky swimming pool and sauna; and Charlotte with eight rooms (and no children allowed).

Family specialist Esprit has a 60-bed chalet hotel in a good slope-side position, up at Rond-Point – 'excellent; childcare beyond exemplary', says a recent guest.

Inghams has six chalets, plus a 60-bed chalet hotel in a prime spot near the lifts at Chaudanne. Crystal has four chalets.

Hotels Méribel doesn't compete with Courchevel in the fancy hotel stakes,

CHILDCARE

Les Saturnins
t 0479 086031
Ages 18mnth to 3yr

Les Piou Piou
t 0479 086031)
Ages 3 to 5

Childminder list
Available from the tourist office

Ski school
ESF runs classes for ages 5 to 13: 6 5hr days from €331

GETTING THERE

Air Geneva 140km/ 90 miles (2hr15); Lyon 190km/120 miles (2hr30); Chambéry 100km/ 60 miles (1hr30)

Rail Moûtiers (18km/11 miles); regular buses

but has some excellent places. Of course, they're not cheap.

****Grand Coeur** (0479 086003) Our favourite almost-affordable hotel in Méribel. Just above the village centre. Welcoming, mature building with plush lounge. Huge hot tub, sauna etc.

****Mont-Vallon** (0479 004400) The best hotel at Mottaret; good food, pool, sauna, squash, fitness room etc.

****Allodis** (0479 005600) Out of town at Belvedere, but ski-in/ski-out and excellent in every other way. Seriously good restaurant, superb service, pool, sauna, nice terrace and valley views.

****Altiport** (0479 005232) Smart and luxurious hotel, isolated at the foot of the Altiport lifts. Convenient for Courchevel, not for Val Thorens. Extensively refurbished for 2010/11.

***Arolles** (0479 004040) On the piste at the top of Mottaret, with the 'best ever staff, food from good to superb, lovely lounge'. Pool and sauna.

***Merilys** (0479 086900) At Rond-Point. B&B hotel plus apartments. Recommended this year by a regular reporter: 'very nice room, friendly staff, excellent breakfast'.

Adray Télébar (0479 086026) Welcoming piste-side chalet with pretty, rustic rooms, good food and popular lunch terrace. New spa, restaurant and lodges for 2010/11.

Apartments The two most impressive larger residences are Pierre & Vacances Premium properties – Les Fermes de Méribel is a classic tasteful MGM development of six large chalets with the usual good pool, gym, sauna, steam in Méribel-Village. Les Crêts is a big residence up at Mottaret. These properties are available through various agents including Ski Collection. Ski Amis and Skitracer have good ranges of apartments in various areas. Skiworld has a flexible catered chalet in Mottaret where you can choose what catering (if any) you want, plus apartments.

EATING OUT ★★★★

New places to try

There is a reasonable selection of restaurants, from ambitious French cuisine to pizza and pasta. For the best food, in plush surroundings, you won't beat the top hotels – we've had top-notch meals at the Grand Coeur and Allodis. The Zinc brasserie and Escale gourmet restaurant are at the highly regarded Altiport hotel. We've also enjoyed the Kouisena, with its very rustic, intimate interior and open-fire cooking of good meat. For the 'all French' experience and fine food, the Orée du Bois was suggested last year. In Mottaret, tucked away near the Plattières lift, Zig Zag is a good

↑ Chalet after chalet after chalet ... that's Méribel

OT MERIBEL / JM GOUEDARD

cheaper option (bar/traditional).

Just outside Méribel-Village, the Plantin is a lovely chalet doing a wide range of dishes. In the village, the unpretentious Brit-run Lodge du Village (pasta, Tuscany specials) serves 'some of the tastiest food in the Trois Vallées', and at prices that are modest by local standards.

APRES-SKI ★★★★★
Méribel rocks – loudly

Méribel's après-ski revolves around British-run places, and is far more animated than is usual in most French resorts. (Not that our readers have much time for this sort of thing, to judge by reports.) We're told the Arpasson hut (Tougnète) now has 'blaring music' in an attempt to create some on-mountain action.

At the top of the village, the 'legendary' Rond-Point is as lively as they come, packed from happy hour 4pm-5pm – live music, toffee vodka and crowd-surfing are the norm. It will no doubt be rivalled or outshadowed by the Folie Douce opening near the mid-station of the Saulire gondola for 2012/13 – expect wild parties as in the Val d'Isère and Val Thorens branches.

In town, try Jack's, not far from the main lift stations. The ring of bars on the main square do good business at teatime. The Doron attracts a younger crowd for videos, pool and 'good live bands' all evening. The Poste injects a bit of French cool into the scene ('good drinks, nice young crowd'). Later on, Dick's Tea Bar is the focus – now revamped and with a gastro-pub (The Den) next door. But they're away from the centre and slopes. Aviatic is a bar/club at the Altiport hotel.

In Mottaret the bars at the foot of the pistes get packed at teatime.

In Méribel-Village, the bar at Lodge du Village has live music at teatime a couple of nights a week.

OFF THE SLOPES ★★★★★
Quite a bit to do

The Olympic Centre has the ice rink where the Olympic events were held in 1992 and where you can watch regular hockey matches. It also has bowling, a climbing wall, a gym, a good public pool and a spa – these last two irritatingly separate, a reporter points out. You can take joyrides in the little planes that operate from the altiport. There are 25km of pleasant marked walks in several areas – eg between Méribel and the altiport area; down through hamlets to Les Allues (return by bus or gondola); and at Plan de Tueda, beyond Mottaret – 'gorgeous'. There's a good map of them, says a reporter. There is a pedestrian's lift pass, and accessible restaurants to meet friends for lunch. Both villages have a cinema. There are very few shops other than ski shops, even in Méribel itself.

Down-valley town – 600m

BRIDES-LES-BAINS

Brides-les-Bains is an old spa town way down in the valley. For the Méribel events in the 1992 Olympics the competitors were accommodated here and ferried up on a newly built gondola. It offers a quieter, cheaper alternative base, with some simple hotels, good-value apartments, adequate shops and restaurants. Skiweekends.com runs a chalet hotel here. The 3-star hotel Amelie (0479 553015) is near the spa and gondola ('spacious rooms, popular happy hour, but dinner hit and miss', says a 2012 visitor). There is a casino, but evenings are distinctly quiet. We have reports of one lively bar. The gondola ride to and from Méribel is supposed to take 25 minutes, but may take 40. It arrives at a point irritatingly short of the main lifts up the mountain. It also closes irritatingly early, at 5pm. But in good conditions you can ski off-piste to one or other of the mid-stations at the end of the day (or in exceptional conditions down to Brides itself). Given a car, Brides makes a viable base for visiting other resorts.

Phone numbers
From abroad use the prefix +33 and omit the initial '0' of the phone number

TOURIST OFFICE

www.meribel.net

SNOWPIX.COM / CHRIS GILL

Montgenèvre

The snowiest part of the Milky Way circuit reaching across to Sauze d'Oulx in Italy – now with through-traffic buried in a tunnel

RATINGS

The mountains

Extent	**
Fast lifts	**
Queues	****
Terrain p'ks	***
Snow	****
Expert	***
Intermediate	****
Beginner	*****
Boarder	***
X-country	***
Restaurants	**
Schools	***
Families	****

The resort

Charm	***
Convenience	***
Scenery	***
Eating out	**
Après-ski	**
Off-slope	*

RPI	85
lift pass	£160
ski hire	£85
lessons	£75
food & drink	£115
total	**£435**

NEWS

2012/13: There are plans to upgrade the Chalvet chair, presumably to a fast one.

2011/12: A fast quad replaced the Montquitaine chair from Claviere towards Montgenèvre. It serves a new blue run, equipped with snowmaking. A beginner snow park opened in the Chalvet sector. A short drag was installed to make Hameau de l'Obélisque ski-in/ski-out. A daily bus service from Briançon was introduced.

+ Good snow record means local snow is often the best in the Milky Way area
+ Plenty of intermediate cruising and good, convenient nursery slopes
+ A lot of accommodation close to the slopes, and some right on them
+ Great potential for car drivers to explore other nearby resorts, but ...

− Italian Milky Way resorts such as Sauze d'Oulx are not easy to explore without road transport
− Lots of slow lifts throughout the Montgenèvre slopes
− Local mountain restaurants poor
− Little to challenge experts on-piste
− Limited, mostly unsophisticated restaurants and après-ski places

Montgenèvre is set on a minor pass between France and Italy (hence the good snow record) at one end of the big cross-border Milky Way network. But it's a time-consuming trek from here to Italian Sestriere and Sauze d'Oulx at the far end. So unless you have a car it's best to focus on the local slopes shared with Claviere (also in Italy, but covered here – and an attractive alternative base).

The resort has made big strides in recent years, banishing through-traffic and developing modern upscale lodgings. But it now needs to prioritize investment in fast lifts – our day there last season was a distinctly slow-motion affair.

THE RESORT

Montgenèvre is a small village set on a high road pass only 2km from the Italian border. The village is set on the sunny slope above the main street (the through-road is now buried in a tunnel) looking over the nursery slopes at the foot of the north-facing slopes of Les Gondrans. Behind the village are the south-facing slopes of Le Chalvet. Both sectors have piste links with Claviere, right on the Italian border and gateway to the other Italian resorts of the Milky Way – Sansicario, Sestriere and Sauze d'Oulx. But it takes ages to get to those resorts on skis; best to drive or join a group going by private bus.

There are lift pass sharing arrangements with Serre-Chevalier, Puy-St-Vincent and Bardonecchia, easily reached by car, and with rather less easily reached Les Deux-Alpes and Alpe-d'Huez.

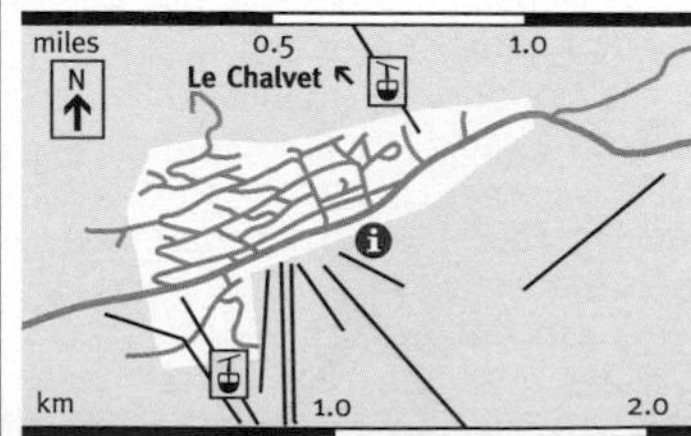

VILLAGE CHARM ***
Rustic and quiet

Cheap and cheerful cafes, bars and restaurants line the street running along the bottom of the nursery slopes, now carrying only local traffic. And a couple of narrow parallel streets with a few bars and restaurants and a church lie behind it. The old buildings give it a rustic and lived-in feel. Friendly natives and generally good snow add to the charm factor. The smart Hameau de l'Obélisque development at the eastern end of the village is wood-clad in chalet style and easy on the eye, too.

CONVENIENCE ***
Never far from a lift

It's a compact village – most of the lodgings are less than five minutes from a lift. But the main gondolas are at opposite ends of the village. Some of the newer lodgings in Hameau de l'Obélisque are right on the slopes and thanks to the new little draglift, ski-out as well as ski-in. The free bus service worked well for us in 2012.

SCENERY ***
Look north or south

The area is broken up by rocky outcrops and woods, with good views from the higher slopes on both sides of the pass.

KEY FACTS

Resort	1850m 6,070ft
Montgenèvre-Monts de la Lune (Claviere)	
Slopes	1760-2630m 5,770-8,630ft
Lifts	32
Pistes	110km 68 miles
Green	13%
Blue	34%
Red	36%
Black	17%
Snowmaking	55%
Milky Way	
Slopes	1390-2825m 4,560-9,270ft
Lifts	72
Pistes	400km 249 miles
Blue	25%
Red	55%
Black	20%
Snowmaking	60%

GETTING THERE

Air Turin 100km/ 60 miles (1hr30); Grenoble 170km/ 105 miles (3hr); Lyon 235km/145 miles (3hr)

Rail Briançon (12km/ 7 miles) or Oulx (15km/9 miles); buses available from both five times a day

THE MOUNTAINS

The slopes offer lots of variety – some high and open, some wooded lower down. Run classification on the local map, the Milky Way map and on the mountain are not reliably consistent. And many of the run classifications exaggerate difficulty; the black runs are not steep. Signposting is mainly adequate.

EXTENT OF THE SLOPES ★★☆☆☆
Nicely varied

Our stars are based on the local slopes; the Milky Way as a whole easily gets a ★★★★★ rating.

The north-facing slopes above Montgenèvre and Claviere divide into three sectors. The high, open slopes of **Les Gondrans** are reached by the Chalmettes chondola from the west end of the village; a green run brings you back. From the same gondola or by riding a chairlift to the lower, steeper wooded peak of Le Prarial you can access the sector of **l'Aigle**, which has links at valley level and at altitude via Colletto Verde to the **Monti della Luna** slopes of Claviere.

The sunny sector behind the village of Montgenèvre – **Le Chalvet** – has long been accessed by a gondola from the east end of the village. A more recently added alternative access is the Serre Thibaud chondola, starting halfway between Montgenèvre and Claviere. This chondola has opened up new blue and black runs into the main Chalvet bowl and into the valley beyond the Col de l'Alpet. The Chalvet runs are mainly on open slopes above the gondola; there are blue and green runs back to Montgenèvre, and a blue run to Claviere (it's a long slog across the village to get up the other side).

FAST LIFTS ★★☆☆☆
A persistent weakness

The main lifts out of the village are a chondola and a gondola. But slow chairs and drags predominate on the upper slopes. The piste map appears to identify fast chairlifts, but actually fails to do so reliably.

QUEUES ★★★★☆
Not a problem

Recent reporters have found the area pretty queue-free, even in peak season – a 2012 half-term visitor hit queues only at the weekend, and even then waited no more than five minutes.

TERRAIN PARKS ★★★☆☆
Various facilities

There's a half-pipe and a jump with an airbag to cushion landings on the lower slopes of the Gondrans sector and boardercross runs in both main sectors – 'super', says a reporter. A beginner snow park has opened in the Chalvet sector, and a regular park at Claviere – 'well maintained', but 'really needs its own short lift'.

SNOW RELIABILITY ★★★★☆
Excellent locally

Montgenèvre has a generally excellent snow record, receiving dumps from storms funnelling up the valleys to the east and west. The high north-facing

LIFT PASSES

Montgenèvre + Monts de la Lune

Prices in €

Age	1-day	6-day
under 15	29	155
15 to 59	37	195
60 plus	34	176

Free under 6; 75 plus

Beginner free lift in beginner area; lesson and lift deals

Notes
Montgenèvre and Claviere; 6-day-plus pass allows one day in the Milky Way, Alpe-d'Huez, Deux-Alpes, Serre-Che, Puy-St-Vincent and Bardonecchia; family reductions

Alternative passes
Montgenèvre only; Voie Lactée (Milky Way) area

SCHOOLS

ESF
t 0492 219046

A-Peak
t 0492 244997

Classes (ESF prices)
6 5hr days €235

Private lessons
From €40 for 1hr

CHILDCARE

Mini-club Les Marmottes (ESF)
t 0492 219046
Ages 6mnth to 5

Ski school
For ages 5 to 14 (6 days €335)

slopes naturally keep their snow better than the south-facing area. Snow-guns now cover 55% of the area, including most lower slopes; its use is 'intensive and very effective', says a reporter.

FOR EXPERTS ★★★

Some excellent off-piste

The local pistes offer few challenges – the Tetras piste on Le Chalvet is steep, but the other blacks are not. There is, however, ample off-piste terrain. On the Gondrans side, there's a small 'freeride zone' of ungroomed slopes that are avalanche controlled, but the real interest lies elsewhere. The Rocher de l'Aigle chair to Colletto Verde is a great starting point. In addition to off-piste variants on the red runs it serves, it accesses an excellent bowl leading down towards the Brousset chair. There are further good powder areas accessed from the top lifts on the Italian side. One reporter was taken on long off-piste runs off the back of Les Gondrans by ESF instructors. On the Chalvet side, the remote north-east-facing bowl beyond the Col de l'Alpet is superb in good snow and has black pistes, too. Heli-skiing can be arranged in Italy.

FOR INTERMEDIATES ★★★★

Plenty of cruising terrain

The overclassified blacks (mainly concentrated in the Chalvet sector) are just right for adventurous intermediates, and there are some excellent reds – such as the pleasantly narrow tree-lined runs to Claviere from Pian del Sole, and both the runs from Colletto Verde. Average intermediates can confidently explore the whole area – few of the reds are particularly challenging. Timid intermediates have some lovely long runs on which to build confidence on both the Gondrans and Chalvet sectors – the Phare is a particularly fine long blue on the latter. Getting around the area as a whole would be easier if the easiest reds were classified blue – key runs from Colle Bercia and from Pian del Sole, for example. The runs down to the village are easy cruises.

FOR BEGINNERS ★★★★★

One of the best

There is a near-perfect nursery slope area at the foot of the Gondrans sector – large, gentle, with a moving carpet and draglift, fenced off so that you don't get speeding skiers going through it. The moving carpet and a draglift outside the nursery area are free to use, so a full pass is not needed for complete beginners. Progression to longer runs could not be easier, with long, very easy green runs just up the hill at Les Gondrans. Le Chalvet also has the long, easy Phare blue run.

FOR BOARDERS ★★★

Something for everyone

There's plenty to attract boarders to Montgenèvre. There are good local beginner slopes and long runs on varied terrain for intermediates. The only real drawback is that a fair number of the lifts are drags and there are some flat sections (especially getting to and from Sestriere). There are some excellent off-piste areas with a few natural hits for more advanced boarders and a dedicated freeride area in the Gondrans sector. Snowbox is a specialist shop.

FOR CROSS-COUNTRY ★★★

Travel to the best of it

The 17km of local trails offer ample variety. But the best area is the 60km of trails in the unspoiled Clarée valley, starting an 8km drive away in Les Alberts at the bottom of the pass road's winding ascent from Briançon.

MOUNTAIN RESTAURANTS ★★

Head for Italy

In the Chalvet sector there's the table-service Bergerie, but most people eat in the village, or head for the Claviere sector where there are some pleasant simple huts; all agree that Baita La Coche is about the best – 'very friendly staff, rustic interior'.

SCHOOLS AND GUIDES ★★★

Encouraging reports

Reports on the ESF are generally positive: 'Our kids loved their classes,'

↑ The nursery slope is near-perfect – spacious, quiet, gentle, north-facing but not shaded, close to village facilities

EDDIE BAINES

UK PACKAGES

AmeriCan Ski, Carrier, Crystal, Crystal Finest, Erna Low, Go Montgenevre, Lagrange, Neilson, Peak Retreats, PowderBeds, Rocketski, Ski Bespoke, Ski Etoile, Ski France, Ski Independence, Ski Miquel, Skitopia, Skitracer, Thomson, Zenith

Claviere Crystal, Interactive Resorts, Rocketski, Skitopia, Skitracer

ACTIVITIES

Indoor Cinema, casino

Outdoor Natural ice rink, snowshoeing, snowmobiling, walking, tobogganing, tubing, 'yooner' tobogganing, ballooning

Phone numbers
From abroad use the prefix +33 and omit the initial '0' of the phone number

TOURIST OFFICE

Montgenèvre
www.montgenevre.com

Claviere
www.claviere.it

said a 2011 visitor. A 2012 reporter had real problems at first with his son's group lessons, but was very impressed by how it was sorted – the son is now keen to go back again. A skier who tried boarding with A-Peak in 2012 was 'very impressed'.

FOR FAMILIES ★★★★
Hugely improved

With the intrusive main road traffic removed, Montgenèvre is now a fine family resort. The beginner area has the Mini-club Les Marmottes and a snow garden for young children. There is also a childcare centre. Le Chalvet has a play area at the gondola top.

STAYING THERE

Development of Hameau de l'Obélisque, at the east end of the resort, has introduced a bit of class.

Chalets Zenith has two catered chalets here, one right by the Chalmettes lift. Crystal's 'economy' chalet Ourson is approved by a reader this year. Pot de Miel is a B&B run on chalet lines (with optional dinners) by an Australian and her ski instructor husband.

Hotels There are now two smart places in Hameau de l'Obélisque.

******Chalet Blanc** (0492 442702) Very comfortable, lovely soft duvets and pillows, smart bathrooms – we enjoyed our 2011 stay here. Spa.

Anova (0492 544804) New for 2011. Cool, relaxed, comfortable, good food. Pool, spa. We stayed happily in 2012.

Apartments There are some smart 4-star developments with pool and spa at Hameau de l'Obélisque – the Hameau des Airelles ('spacious apartments') and Chalet des Dolines are available through Peak Retreats.

EATING OUT ★★
Mainly no-frills

With about 10 no-frills places in the village, the choice is no more than adequate. For gourmets there is La Cloche – reports please. We and readers have enjoyed the Estable, a locals' favourite. Reader tips: Graal ('good basic food, free Wi-Fi'), Caesar ('superb', 'lively vibe') and Rafale ('nice food, great fire, really friendly').

APRES-SKI ★★
A few bars

The range is limited – it is a quiet village. The Refuge and the Jamy are popular cafe-bars at tea time. The Graal is a friendly, lively place with big TVs; the Ca del Sol is a cosy place with an open fire ('best chocolate'). The Chaberton has pool tables, and is 'lively later on'.

OFF THE SLOPES ★
Limited

The Monty Express 1400m-long two-seater monorail 'toboggan' run is said to be France's longest. A bus trip down to the beautiful old town of Briançon is possible.

LINKED RESORT – 1760m

CLAVIERE

Claviere is a small, traditional village just over the border in Italy. It is not chocolate-box pretty but, even more than Montgenèvre, it has been transformed by removal of through-traffic. Its single main street, lined by a few shops, restaurants and hotels, is now a positively charming place to wander about. The two main lifts – both slow quads – are conveniently close. Getting to the new Montquitaine chair is a slight uphill hike. The nursery slope is right next to the village, with a magic carpet. This year, as last year, we have glowing reports on the ski school's handling of kids – 'wonderful – could not have wished for a better start'.

Readers tip several restaurants: the Kilt ('excellent pizzas, sensible prices, very friendly'), Da Sandro and Gran Bouc ('good food and service, but a bit pricey'). Après-ski is very quiet; Baita La Coche mountain hut 'can do hot chocolates and crêpes in the evening and lay on snowcat transport'. The bar at the Roma hotel 'has good prices and Sky Sports'. Pub Gallo can be lively later on.

OT MORZINE / P JACQUES, FOC

Morzine

A large, lively, year-round resort with its own attractive slopes and linked by lift to the main Portes du Soleil circuit

RATINGS

The mountains

Extent	*****
Fast lifts	***
Queues	***
Terrain p'ks	**
Snow	**
Expert	***
Intermediate	****
Beginner	***
Boarder	****
X-country	****
Restaurants	***
Schools	***
Families	****

The resort

Charm	***
Convenience	**
Scenery	***
Eating out	***
Après-ski	****
Off-slope	***

RPI	95
lift pass	£180
ski hire	£90
lessons	£90
food & drink	£120
total	**£480**

NEWS

2012/13: The Troncs chairlift, useful for returning from Les Gets, will become a six-pack, and the Prodains cable car up to Avoriaz is to be replaced by a gondola.

2011/12: A new water sports centre opened, with a 25m pool, learner and paddling pools and a spa area. Nine more snow-guns were installed in the Pléney and Nyon sectors.

Extent rating
This relates to the whole Portes du Soleil area.

- + Good-sized, varied, lightly wooded slopes shared with Les Gets
- + Good nightlife by French standards
- + Quite attractive chalet-style town, popular in summer
- + Few queues or crowds locally unless good weekend weather attracts a weekend influx

- − Just off the Portes du Soleil circuit
- − Bus ride or long walk to lifts from much of the accommodation
- − Low altitude and exposure to westerlies means some risk of rain and poor snow
- − Few tough pistes for experts
- − Weekend crowds

Morzine is a long-established year-round resort, popular for its easy road access, traditional atmosphere and gentle wooded slopes; bad weather rarely causes problems (except that it rains here not infrequently). For keen piste-bashers wanting to ski the Portes du Soleil circuit regularly, the main drawback is that you're slightly off the main circuit. But there are ways to deal with that.

THE RESORT

Morzine is a well-established mountain resort, as popular in summer as in winter, sprawling along both sides of a river gorge – though with the centre emphatically on the west side, at the foot of the local slopes. These are shared with slightly higher Les Gets (covered in a separate chapter). Across town is a gondola forming the link with a chain of lifts leading to Avoriaz on the Portes du Soleil circuit.

Our view that the resort suits car drivers is widely shared. But the roads are busy and the one-way system takes some getting used to. Car trips to Flaine and Chamonix are feasible.

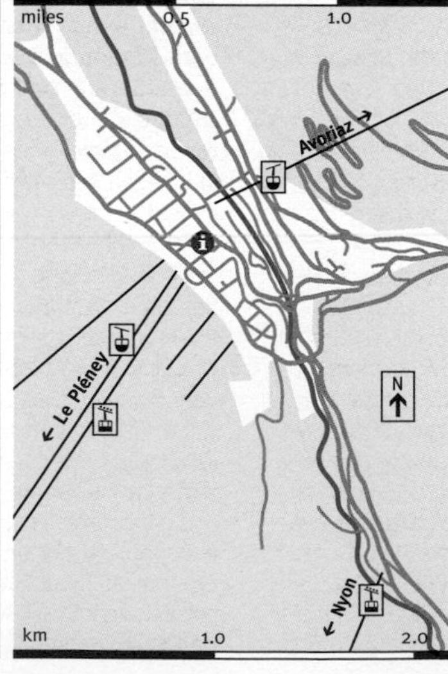

VILLAGE CHARM ***
Quietly attractive

The resort consists of chalet-style buildings, mostly small or mid-sized; they look cute under snow, and as that snow disappears towards spring the village quickly takes on a spruce appearance. Morzine is a family resort, and village ambience tends to be fairly subdued; but there is plenty of après-ski action.

CONVENIENCE **
It's a big resort ...

Morzine is a town where getting from A to B can be tricky. The best plan is to stay in or near the centre of town, a short walk from one or both of the gondolas. Restaurants and bars line the streets up to the lifts to Le Pléney, where a busy one-way street runs along the foot of the slopes. Accommodation is widely scattered; a multi-route bus service (including two electric buses) links all parts of the town to the lifts, including those for Avoriaz; but a reporter complains that the service is sporadic. There are also buses to Les Gets and to Ardent for a quick way into the Portes du Soleil circuit, missing out busy Avoriaz.

SCENERY ***
Quite good from the tops

Despite their modest top heights, the local peaks of Pointe de Nyon and Chamossière are not without drama (or impressive views, including Mont Blanc), and the slopes below them are attractively wooded.

There are acres and acres of lovely rollling intermediate terrain, lightly wooded ➔

LES GETS TOURIST OFFICE / NICOLAS JOLY

KEY FACTS

Resort	1000m 3,280ft
Portes du Soleil	
Slopes	950-2275m 3,120-7,460ft
Lifts	198
Pistes	650km 404 miles
Green	13%
Blue	40%
Red	37%
Black	10%
Snowmaking	835 guns
Morzine-Les Gets only	
Slopes	1000-2010m 3,280-6,590ft
Lifts	48
Pistes	120km 75 miles
Snowmaking	70%

LIFT PASSES

Portes du Soleil

Prices in €

Age	**1-day**	**6-day**
under 16	33	164
16 to 19	40	197
20 to 63	44	219
64 plus	40	197

Free under 5

Beginner lessons and lift pass packages

Notes family discounts; 5hr pass

Alternative passes Morzine-Les Gets only

ACTIVITIES

Indoor Swimming pool, ice rink, fitness centre (sauna, hot tub), library, cinemas

Outdoor Ice rink, snowshoeing, helicopter flights, snowmobiles, tobogganing, paragliding, ski joring, 'yooner' tobogganing, segway riding

THE MOUNTAINS

The local slopes are mainly wooded, with some open areas higher up. The piste map is fine, and signposting and classification are both 'good'.

EXTENT OF THE SLOPES ★★★★★
Good local area, plus the PdS

Our rating is for the whole Portes du Soleil linked area, the bulk of which is reached via Avoriaz. The local area – shared with Les Gets – is a fair size.

A gondola rises from the edge of central Morzine to **Le Pléney**. (The parallel cable car is normally not used.) Numerous routes return to the valley, including a run down to Les Fys – a quiet lift junction at the foot of the **Nyon-Chamossière** sector where the area's most challenging slopes are; Chamossière is served by a six-pack but Nyon still has a slow chair. This sector can also be accessed by a cable car starting a bus ride from Morzine. A slow chair from Les Fys along with a fast one from Le Grand Pré, further up the valley, connect with the sector of **Les Chavannes**, above Les Gets. At the far end of this sector, the bowl beneath Le Ranfoilly has no fewer than five radiating chairlifts together.

Beyond Les Gets, **Mont Chéry** is notably quiet, and well worth a visit.

Across town from the Le Pléney sector is a gondola leading (via another couple of lifts and runs) to Avoriaz and the main Portes du Soleil circuit. You take the gondola down at the end of the day – there's no piste. Alternatives are a bus ride or short drive to either Les Prodains, from where you can get a new gondola to Avoriaz or a chair into the **Hauts Forts** slopes above it, or to Ardent, where a gondola accesses Les Lindarets for lifts towards Châtel, Avoriaz or Champéry. There's floodlit skiing every Thursday and a torchlit descent every Tuesday.

FAST LIFTS ★★★
More fast chairs needed

The main access lifts are gondolas, cable cars or fast chairs, but higher up things are not so good: only Chamossière, Le Ranfoilly and La Rosta have a decent supply of fast chairs. Elsewhere, slow chairs and drags dominate.

QUEUES ★★★
Peak season problems

Queues aren't normally a problem except during peak holiday seasons and at weekends. Then queues can form for both the gondolas out of the resort. A 2012 high-season reporter staying in Avoriaz found 'long queues all day' to get up Pléney. The cable car from Les Prodains to Avoriaz has had queues in the past, but this is to be replaced by a gondola. Le Grand Pré has been an afternoon bottleneck, but this too should be relieved by this year's upgrade to a six-pack.

TERRAIN PARKS ★★
Lots to choose from

There is a park below Pointe de Nyon and parks and a boardercross in Les Gets (see Les Gets chapter). Or you can try one of the five excellent terrain parks in Avoriaz.

GETTING THERE

Air Geneva 95km/60 miles (1hr30); Lyon 215km/135 miles (3hr)

Rail Cluses or Thonon (30km/19 miles); regular bus connections to resort

SNOW RELIABILITY ★★★★★
A weakness at resort level

Morzine has a very low average height, and it can rain here when it is snowing higher up (almost every year some reporters mention days of rain). The grassy slopes don't need much snow-cover and in a sparse snow year you may do better here than in higher, rockier resorts such as Avoriaz. Snowmaking has been increased, most noticeably on the home runs. Reporters were not impressed by grooming last season.

FOR EXPERTS ★★★★★
A few possibilities

The runs from Pointe de Nyon and Chamossière are quite challenging, as are the black runs down the back of Mont Chéry and the Hauts Forts blacks at Avoriaz. In bad weather the medium-altitude, lightly wooded Ranfoilly bowl is a good place to head for. There is plenty of serious off-piste scope – see feature panel overleaf.

FOR INTERMEDIATES ★★★★★
Something for everyone

Good intermediates will enjoy the fine, challenging red and black down from Chamossière. Mont Chéry, on the other

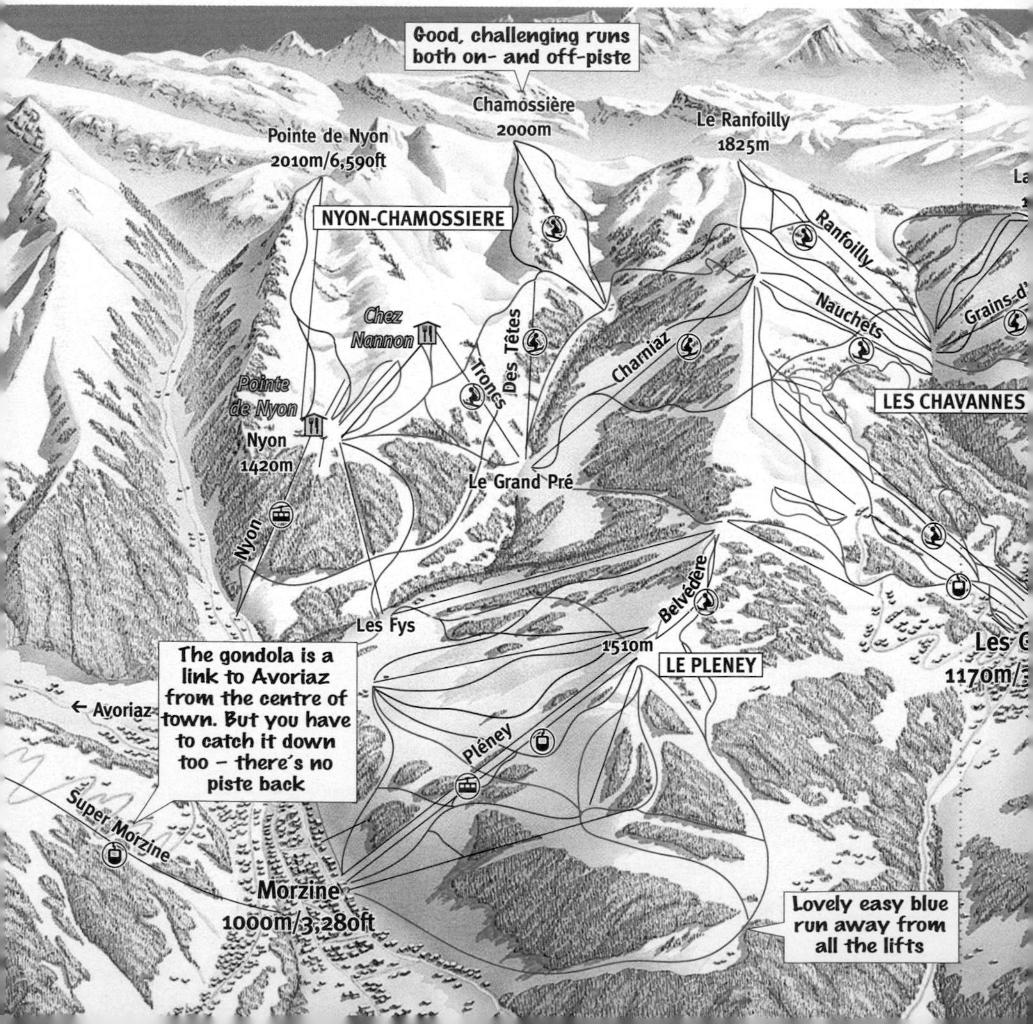

Good, challenging runs both on- and off-piste

Chamossière 2000m
Pointe de Nyon 2010m/6,590ft
Le Ranfoilly 1825m
NYON-CHAMOSSIERE
Ranfoilly
Nauchets
Grains-d'
Chez Nannon
Des Têtes
Charniaz
Tronc
Pointe de Nyon
Nyon 1420m
LES CHAVANNES
Le Grand Pré
Nyon
Belvédère
Les Fys
1510m
LE PLENEY
Les C
1170m/
← Avoriaz
Pléney
Super Morzine
Morzine 1000m/3,280ft

The gondola is a link to Avoriaz from the centre of town. But you have to catch it down too – there's no piste back

Lovely easy blue run away from all the lifts

side of Les Gets, has some fine steepish runs which are usually very quiet. Those looking for something less steep have a great choice. Le Pléney has a compact network of pistes that are ideal for groups with mixed abilities: there are blue and red options from every lift. One of the easiest cruises on Le Pléney is a great away-from-it-all, snow-gun-covered blue (Piste B) from the top to the valley lift station. Heading from Le Ranfoilly to Le Grand Pré on the blue is also a nice cruise. And the slopes down to Les Gets from Le Pléney are easy when conditions are right (the slopes face south). The Ranfoilly and Rosta sectors have easy blacks and cruisy reds served by fast chairs. And, of course, there is the whole of the extensive Portes du Soleil circuit to explore by going up the opposite side of the valley.

FOR BEGINNERS ★★★★★
Good for novices and improvers
The wide village nursery slopes are convenient, and benefit from snow-guns, though crowds are reported to be a problem ('insanely busy in French holiday weeks – 10-minute queues for the magic carpet'). There are excellent progression runs on Le Pléney, at Nyon, and at Super-Morzine.

FOR BOARDERS ★★★★★
Great for park and ride
Morzine is very popular with boarding seasonaires because of the extensive slopes, proximity to the excellent terrain parks in Avoriaz and the lower prices here. Former British champ Becci Malthouse is one of the people running the British Alpine Ski & Snowboard School. The slopes in Morzine are great for all abilities and have very few draglifts. But a reporter

SCHOOLS

ESF
t 0450 791313

Easy2Ride (E2SA)
t 0450 790516

Snow School
t 0486 688840

BASS
t 0871 780 1500 (UK)

Mint Snowboard
t 0450 841388

Classes (ESF prices)
6 5hr days €176

Private lessons
From €38 for 1hr for 1 to 2 people

GUIDES

Bureau des Guides
t 0450 759665

complained of irritating flat areas. Plenty of tree-lined runs make for scenic and interesting snowboarding and the more adventurous should hire a guide to explore off-piste.

FOR CROSS-COUNTRY ★★★★★
Good variety

There are around 70km of varied cross-country trails, not all at valley level. The best section is in the pretty Vallée de la Manche beside the Nyon mountain up to the Lac de Mines d'Or, where there is a good restaurant. The Pléney-Chavannes loop is pleasant and relatively snow-sure.

MOUNTAIN RESTAURANTS ★★★★★
Some excellent huts

There is no shortage of good places; restaurants are marked but not named on the piste map.

Editors' choice We have had several very enjoyable Savoyard lunches at the rustic Chez Nannon (0450 792115), between Nyon and Chamossière – cosy inside and a nice terrace. A regular visitor endorses this again in 2012: 'A real gem – the reblochon aux patates (much posher than tartiflette) is legendary.' The nearby Pointe de Nyon (0450 044564) is a lovely spacious place where we had excellent duck salad and ribs in 2012.

Worth knowing about La Païka, on the blue Vorosses run at the far end of Les Gets, is a 'rustic gem' doing wood-fired grills; serious wine list. The Wetzet at Ranfoilly 'is very welcoming' for a mid-morning chocolate. The Vaffieu above the Folliets chair 'can have slow service but the food is worth the wait'. A 2011 visitor raved about Lhottys at the top of the Nauchets chairlift for its 'peasant-style mountain soup – to die for'. Mouflon and Raverettes are also tipped.

SCHOOLS AND GUIDES ★★★★★
Good reports of most

Reporters praise the British Alpine Ski & Snowboard School (BASS) ('instructors very nice and helpful'), the Snow School ('taught my parents, who are in their mid-60s, and they're loving it') and Easy2Ride ('small group size and excellent, experienced instructor who spoke fluent English – despite being nervous, we all progressed well'). The ESF has been praised but a recent reporter noted groups as large as 18 at Christmas.

FOR FAMILIES ★★★★★
A fine family choice

Morzine caters well for families. On the mountain there are gentle, sheltered slopes and play areas. And there are plenty of other activities. Club des Piou-Piou is run by the ESF school and takes children from three years old. 'Excellent – my children, six and three, were happy,' says a 2010 visitor. Above Les Gets, at Chavannes, there is a big children's area. Day care is provided by several organizations.

OFF-PISTE RUNS IN THE PORTES DU SOLEIL AREA

The Portes du Soleil offers a lot of great lift-served off-piste. Here is a small selection. Like all serious off-piste runs, these should only be done with a guide.

Morzine – Nyon/Chamossière area

From the Chamossière chairlift, heading north brings you to two runs – one on the same north-west slope as the pistes, the other via a col down the north-east slope to the Nyon cable car in the Vallée de La Manche – a wild area, with a great view of Mont Blanc at first.

Avoriaz area – two suggestions

From the Fornet chairlift on the Swiss border, you head west to descend a beautiful, unspoiled bowl leading down to the village of L'Erigné. In powder snow you descend the west-facing slopes of the bowl; when there is spring snow, you traverse right to descend the south-facing slopes. Medium-pitch slopes, for skiers and snowboarders.

From the top of the Machon chairlift you traverse west, beneath the peaks of Les Hauts Forts, across Les Crozats de la Chaux – a steep, north-facing slope. You then turn north to descend through the forest to the cable car station at Les Prodains. Testing terrain, for very good skiers. And beware that the traverse can be dangerous following a snowfall.

Châtel area

From the top of the Linga chair, head north-west to cross the ridge on your right at a col and then head down the La Leiche slope to the draglift of the same name. It's a north-facing slope, starting in a white wilderness, taking you through trees back to civilization. Steep slopes – for good skiers only.

CHILDCARE

L'Outa nursery
t 0450 792600
Ages 3mnth to 5yr

Piou Piou (ESF)
t 0450 791313
From age 3

Cheeky Monkeys
t 0450 750548
From 3mnth

Jack Frost's
t 07817 138678 (UK)
From 3mnth

Ski school
From age 4: 6 days
€168 (ESF price)

UK PACKAGES

Absolutely Snow, Adventure Base, Alpine Answers, Alpine Elements, Alpine Weekends, AmeriCan Ski, Chalet Chocolat, Chalet Entre Deux Eaux, Chalet Famille, Chalet Gueret, ChaletBook, Challenge Activ, Classic Ski, Crystal, Erna Low, Host Savoie, Hugski, Independent Ski Links, Inghams, Inspired to Ski, Interactive Resorts, Lagrange, Momentum, Mountain Heaven, Mountain Tracks, Mountain Wave, Oxford Ski Co, Peak Retreats, Powder White, PowderBeds, Reach4theAlps, Ride & Slide, Rude Chalets, Ski Expectations, Ski France, Ski Independence, Ski Line, Ski Morzine, Ski Solutions, Ski Weekend, Skiology.co.uk, Skitracer, Skiweekends.com, Snow Finders, Star Ski Chalets, STC, Sugar Mountain, Thomson, Trail Alpine, VIP, White Roc, Zenith

Phone numbers
From abroad use the prefix +33 and omit the initial '0' of the phone number

TOURIST OFFICE

www.morzine-avoriaz.com

STAYING THERE

The tour operator market concentrates on hotels and chalets.

Chalets There's a wide choice. Be aware that chalets are widely spread around a large resort. Mountain Heaven has a premium chalet with outdoor hot tub close to the Nyon cable car. Inghams has three chalets in its programme. VIP has several.

Hotels Perhaps part of a general drift to more stars in France, about 10 hotels have moved up the scale in the last few years. There are now three 4-stars, and 3-star places dominate.

****Bergerie** (0450 791369) Recent upgrade to 4-star. Rustic B&B chalet, in centre. Friendly staff. Outdoor pool, sauna, massage.

****Dahu** (0450 759292) Long one of our favourites, and now a 4-star; over river from centre, but linked by footbridge; good restaurant; pool, hot tub etc. Shuttle to lifts.

***Airelles** (0450 747121) Central 3-star close to Pléney lifts. Good pool.

***Philibert** (0450 792518) Traditional, small chalet-style hotel, 1km from centre, free shuttle-bus.

***Champs Fleuris** (0450 791444) Good location near Pléney lifts. Pool.

***Côtes** (0450 790996) On the edge of town. Pool, sauna, gym, bowling.

***Tremplin** (0450 791231) At the foot of Pléney slopes. 'Comfortable, very friendly staff, free parking.'

***Equipe** (0450 791143) Long been a 2-star tip, now a 3-star; next to the Pléney lift with decent food and 'tiny' pool. Takes short-stay bookings.

Apartments. Aiglon de Morzine has 12 luxury units and is central – bookable through Erna Low. Peak Retreats has a self-catering chalet for 10. Also check out Inghams, Alpine Answers and Skitracer.

EATING OUT ★★★

A reasonable choice

There is a fair choice, including some fine hotel restaurants. Best in town is probably the Atelier in the hotel Samoyède, which offers traditional and modern cuisine. For value you will not beat the unpretentious Etale with its 'huge' pizzas and equally generous Savoyard dishes. The Flamme has been highly rated in the past. The Tyrolien 'serves hearty portions to groups of British skiers'. The Combe à Zorre does 'excellent lamb' but can get over-busy at weekends. Several 2011 visitors liked the Chamade – 'gourmet food at moderate prices'; 'food and service excellent'. Le Petit Coeur is a wine bar in the same ownership doing good tapas, pizza etc. The Matafan is also tipped.

L'Alpage is 'a new concept' – you arrive in a traditional kitchen and proceed to a dining room with communal tables (we think); the food sounds a bit cheesy.

APRES-SKI ★★★★

One of the livelier French resorts

Good by French resort standards. Several places around the base area get busy as the slopes empty – the Tremplin apparently has a 'super-trendy' DJ. The Crépu is pleasantly quiet early on but livens up late and has several screens to show sport. Other options include the long-established bar Robinson and the Dixie, with sport on TV, a cellar bar and some live music. Between the slopes and the centre, and all in the same building are: the Cavern, which is popular with seasonaires; the Coyote for arcade games and DJ; and the Tibetan (formerly the Boudha), with Asian decor and 'good, friendly atmosphere'. The Opéra and Laury's are late-night haunts.

OFF THE SLOPES ★★★

Quite good; excursions possible

There are two cinemas, an excellent ice rink, a new indoor pool and lots of pretty walks ('booklet available from tourist office, but some walks are difficult to find and some cross pistes, which can be dangerous'). Visitors have enjoyed visits to the cheese factory and watching ice hockey. Morzine has a reasonable range of shops, relatively glitz-free. Buses run to Thonon for more shopping, and car owners can drive to Geneva, Annecy or Montreux.

Paradiski

Les Arcs and La Plagne are pretty impressive resorts in their own right; the ability to explore both is just the icing on the cake

KEY FACTS	
Paradiski area	
Slopes	1200-3250m 3,940-10,660ft
Lifts	144
Pistes	425km 264 miles
Green	4%
Blue	52%
Red	28%
Black	16%

Nine years after its opening, the 200-person double-decker Vanoise Express cable car – which crosses a wooded valley to link Les Arcs and La Plagne, and thus form Paradiski – remains the world's biggest, as far as we know. When it opened, we were a bit sceptical. Sure, it was one of the biggest ski areas in the Alps, but weren't the two resorts quite big enough individually? Well, no. We're now quite used to staying in Arc 1950 and having lunch above Champagny. We might do it only once or twice in a week, but we always do it.

The Vanoise Express cable car spans the 2km-wide valley between Plan-Peisey (on the edge of the Les Arcs area) and a point 300m above Montchavin (on the edge of the La Plagne area).

The linking of these two major resorts is A Good Thing for the great British piste-basher who likes to cover as much ground as possible. For those who like a bit of a challenge, getting from your home base to both far-flung outposts of the area – Villaroger in Les Arcs and Champagny in La Plagne – would make quite a full day.

The link is also good for experts. Those based in either resort can more easily tackle the north face of La Plagne's Bellecôte, finishing the run in Nancroix. Those based in La Plagne who are finding the piste skiing a bit tame can easily get across to Les Arcs' excellent Aiguille Rouge.

If you want to make the most of the link it's sensible to stay near one of the cable car stations. But it's easily accessible from many other bases too.

On the Les Arcs side, **Plan-Peisey** and nearby **Vallandry** are in pole position. They are basically small, low-rise, modern developments, but built in a much more sympathetic style than the original Les Arcs resorts. They are quiet places to stay, but are expanding rapidly and a few UK operators have chalets there. You can also stay in the unspoiled old village of **Peisey**, 300m below and linked by bucket-lift to Plan-Peisey. These places are covered at the end of the Les Arcs chapter.

It's easy to get to the cable car station at Plan-Peisey from the main resort parts of Les Arcs. One lift and one run is all it takes to get there from **Arc 1800**, which is the biggest of the main resort units. From quieter **Arc 1600**, along the mountainside from 1800, it takes two lifts. **Arc 2000** and the stylish **Arc 1950** development seem further away, over the ridge that separates them from 1600 and 1800; but all it takes is one fast chair to the ridge and one long run down the other side. In the valley bottom beyond Arc

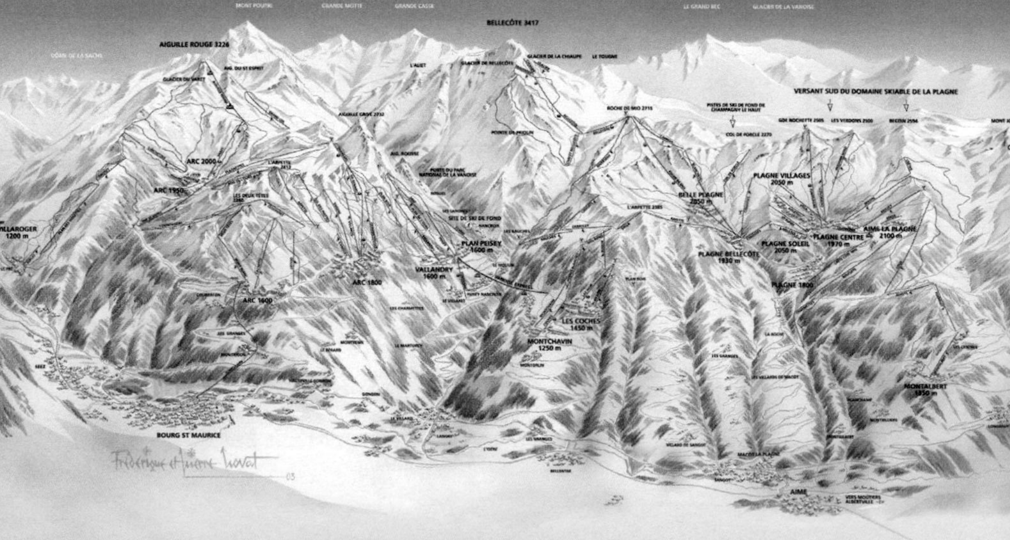

LIFT PASSES

Paradiski
Covers lifts in whole Paradiski area.
6-day pass €258
(65 plus and under 14 €193).

Paradiski Découverte
Covers lifts in Les Arcs area or La Plagne area plus one day Paradiski extension.
6-day pass €241
(65 plus and under 14 €181)

2000, the hamlet of Villaroger is not an ideal starting point.

On the La Plagne side, the obvious place to stay is **Montchavin**, which is below the Vanoise Express station. Montchavin is a carefully developed old village with modern additions built in traditional style. **Les Coches**, across the mountain from the station, is most easily reached with the help of a lift. It is entirely modern, but built in a traditional style. From either village, one lift brings you to the Vanoise Express cable car.

The other parts of La Plagne are some way from the cable car. But one long lift is all it takes to get from monolithic **Plagne-Bellecôte** up to L'Arpette, from which point it's a single long descent. The most attractive of the resort villages, **Belle-Plagne**, is only a short run above Plagne-Bellecôte. From the villages further across the bowl – **Plagne-Villages, Plagne-Soleil**, dreary **Plagne-Centre**, futuristic **Aime-la-Plagne** – you have to ride a lift to get to Plagne-Bellecôte. From **Plagne 1800**, below the bowl, add another lift. From the villages beyond the bowl – rustic, sunny **Champagny-en-Vanoise** and expanding **Montalbert** – it's going to be pretty hard work, but it's certainly possible.

RIDING THE VANOISE EXPRESS

The cable car ride from one resort to the other takes less than four minutes. The system is designed to be able to operate in high winds, so the risk of getting stranded miles from home is low. It can shift 2,000 people an hour, and although end-of-the-day crowds could be a snag in theory, they don't seem to be a problem in practice.

The lift company offers a six-day pass covering the whole Paradiski region, perhaps most likely to appeal to people based in the villages close to the lift. It's not cheap. But there is also a pass (Paradiski Découverte) that includes just one day in the other resort during the validity of the pass. Alternatively, you can buy a one-day extension to a Les Arcs or La Plagne six-day lift pass, as and when you fancy the outing.

SNOWPIX.COM / CHRIS GILL

The runs down to the cable car station near Montchavin, on the La Plagne side, give tantalizing views of the distant slopes of Les Arcs →

La Plagne

Villages from the rustic to the futuristic, spread over a vast area of intermediate terrain – mainly high and snow-sure

RATINGS

The mountains

Extent	****
Fast lifts	**
Queues	**
Terrain p'ks	****
Snow	****
Expert	****
Intermediate	*****
Beginner	****
Boarder	***
X-country	****
Restaurants	****
Schools	***
Families	****

The resort

Charm	**
Convenience	*****
Scenery	***
Eating out	***
Après-ski	***
Off-slope	*

RPI	105
lift pass	£200
ski hire	£105
lessons	£95
food & drink	£135
total	**£535**

KEY FACTS

Resort	1800-2100m 5,900-6,890ft
La Plagne only	
Slopes	1250-3250m 4,100-10,660ft
Lifts	107
Pistes	225km 140 miles
Green	8%
Blue	53%
Red	25%
Black	14%
Snowmaking	470 guns
Paradiski area	
Slopes	1200-3250m 3,940-10,660ft
Lifts	144
Pistes	425km 264 miles
Green	4%
Blue	52%
Red	28%
Black	16%
Snowmaking	791 guns

+ Extensive and varied intermediate pistes, plus excellent off-piste
+ Good nursery slopes
+ High and fairly snow-sure
+ Wide choice of resort villages: high or low, convenient or cute
+ Wooded runs of lower satellite resorts are great in poor weather
+ Cable car link to Les Arcs

− Few steep pistes
− Still lots of slow old chairlifts
− Serious high season queues
− Pistes get very crowded in places
− Lower villages can have poor snow, especially sunny Champagny
− Brutal architecture in some villages
− No long green runs
− Upscale accommodation still rare

With 225km of its own slopes, of which almost 80% are blue or red, La Plagne is an intermediate's paradise, even if you don't use the link to Les Arcs. For experts, it has the attraction that the huge area of off-piste doesn't get skied out too quickly. But the shortage of challenging pistes is a definite drawback, and it's sad to note that two of the most rewarding black pistes (dropping 800m vertical from the glacier) were wiped from the map three seasons ago.

Plagne-Bellecôte, effectively the hub of the lift and piste network, has had serious lift queues as long as we can remember; when snow is poor lower down, so has the Bellecôte gondola to (and from) the glacier. A solution to these problems is way overdue, but there is no sign of one. At least the resort is starting to sort the dire shopping malls of Plagne-Centre.

THE RESORT

La Plagne consists of no fewer than eleven separate 'villages'. Each is a self-sufficient mini-resort, though they vary widely in character. They divide basically into two groups: seven units purpose-built at altitude in a broad bowl, on or above the treeline; and four real villages, adapted and expanded for skiing, at lower altitude on the fringes of the area.

At the heart of the high-altitude area, Plagne-Centre is aptly named: it is the focal point for shops and après-ski. Directly below Centre is the chalet-filled suburb of Plagne 1800, spread across a steep hillside. A short lift ride away from Centre are the slightly higher units of Aime-la-Plagne, Plagne-Soleil and Plagne-Villages. Over a low ridge, beyond the last two, are Plagne-Bellecôte and Belle-Plagne above it.

Outside the main bowl, at the northern edge of the area, are Les Coches and Montchavin. At the southern edge is rustic Champagny. Beyond Aime-la-Plagne, at the western edge, is growing Montalbert. These are described later in the chapter.

A cable car from Montchavin links to Les Arcs via Peisey-Vallandry. Day trips by car to Val d'Isère-Tignes or the Trois Vallées resorts are possible. Staying in Champagny means quick access by car or taxi to Courchevel.

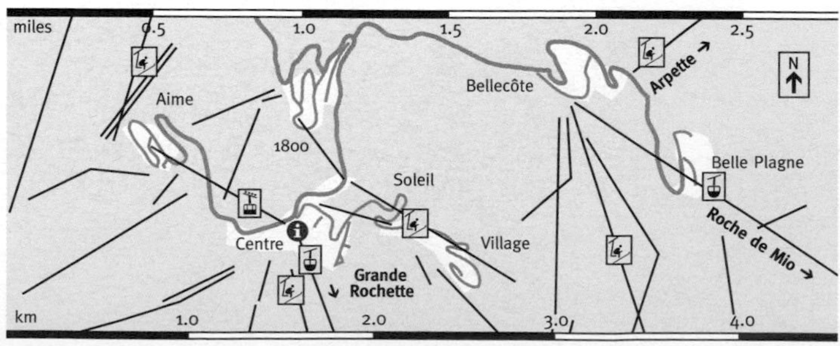

NEWS

2012/13: The Biolley sector is being revamped, with a six-pack replacing the Becoin chair, the Biolley chair and three drags. The pistes will be heavily modified, but details are not known. Phase two of the Plagne-Centre renovation project will be completed. And a new beginner zone is being built at the base.

2011/12: A six-pack replaced the slow Verdons Sud chair from Champagny to Les Verdons above Plagne-Centre.

A three-year project to renovate the shopping malls in Plagne-Centre began. A new swimming pool and spa complex opened in Montchavin.

VILLAGE CHARM ★★☆☆☆

Take your pick

The high-altitude villages vary quite a lot in character; our rating relates to Belle-Plagne and Plagne 1800, where most Brits go. The first unit to be built, in the 1960s, was Plagne-Centre. Typical of its time, it has ugly square blocks and dreary indoor 'malls' that house shops, bars and restaurants. At last, a three-year project is now underway to improve these malls, though we doubt they will manage to make them any less claustrophobic.

More recent developments are more stylish, but they can't compete with Centre in terms of facilities. Plagne 1800 is all in chalet style, so is visually inoffensive. Aime-la-Plagne, in stark contrast, is a group of monolithic blocks given a bold chalet-roof shape. Plagne-Soleil and Plagne-Villages mainly consist of small-scale apartment buildings finished in chalet style. The apartment buildings of Plagne-Bellecôte form a gigantic wall at the foot of the slopes leading down to it. By contrast, Belle-Plagne just above it is built in a pleasant chalet style, and has a mini-resort centre, though few shops.

CONVENIENCE ★★★★★

No worries at altitude

The high-altitude villages are mostly ski-in/ski-out – but much of Plagne 1800 presents challenges because of its steep setting, which has to be negotiated on foot. At Plagne Bellecôte you'll walk further inside your apartment building than outside. Belle-Plagne is now quite large, and spread over a steepish hillside that provokes the odd complaint from easily tired readers. Readers find Plagne-Soleil works well.

A free bus system between the core villages within the bowl runs until 1am, and readers seem happy with it.

SCENERY ★★★☆☆

Look to the horizon

The scenery makes an attractive and varied backdrop to the less attractive core villages. And Mont Blanc looms big on the horizon, especially from Montchavin and Les Coches.

THE MOUNTAINS

The majority of the slopes in the main bowl are above the treeline, though there are trees scattered around most of the resort centres. The slopes outside the bowl are open at the top but descend into woodland – and are the best place to be in bad weather. So there is something to be said for choosing a base outside the bowl.

Some runs are more difficult than their classification suggests, while others are easier – note our warning in 'For intermediates'. Piste names and classification seem to alter regularly. Signposting is fine though piste marking can be a bit vague in places. The piste map is quite difficult to follow in places.

OT LA PLAGNE / B KOUMANOV

Belle-Plagne looks across the main bowl, but is also handy for other good sectors ↓

EXTENT OF THE SLOPES ★★★★★

Multi-centred; can be confusing

Our rating relates to just the La Plagne area; the whole Paradiski area easily scores five stars.

La Plagne's pistes are spread over a wide area that can be broken down into seven sectors. From Plagne-Centre you can take a lift up to **Le Biolley**, from where you can head back to Centre, to Aime-la-Plagne or progress to **Montalbert**. But the main lift out of Plagne-Centre leads up to **La Grande Rochette**. From here there are good sweeping runs back down and an easier one over to Plagne-Bellecôte, or you can drop over into the sunny **Champagny** sector, for excellent long runs and great views of Courchevel.

From Plagne-Bellecôte and Belle-Plagne, you can head up to **Roche de Mio**, and have the choice of a gondola or two successive fast chairs (the first of which also accesses Champagny). From Roche de Mio, runs spread out in all directions – towards La Plagne, Champagny or **Montchavin/Les Coches**. This sector can also be reached by taking an eight-seat chair from Plagne-Bellecôte to L'Arpette.

From Roche de Mio you can also take a gondola down then up to the **Bellecôte glacier**. It is prone to closure by high winds or poor weather. The top chair is often shut in winter – but if open, it offers excellent snow and stunning views. The black piste below Col de la Chiaupe (new a couple of seasons ago) means that you can descend from the glacier on-piste to Les Bauches without riding the gondola back up to Roche de Mio; if you go all the way to Montchavin, it's 2000m vertical.

The piste map marks three draglifts (in the Biolley/Montalbert sectors) as 'difficult', and they are.

FAST LIFTS ★★★★★

Slow progress

Many key lifts are fast, and the Montchavin/Les Coches sector is pretty much sorted, but once you start to really explore other sectors of the slopes you find lots of old chairs and draglifts – Inversens at Roche de Mio, all three lifts above Les Bauches and the lifts from Montalbert towards Centre, for example. There is progress, even if it is slow. This year the Biolley sector is getting a major revamp, with a six-pack replacing no less than five slow lifts.

QUEUES ★★★★★

Serious bottlenecks remain

La Plagne's lift and piste network has some fundamental flaws. In particular, moving across the area often involves passing through Plagne-Bellecôte. This is now one of the worst bottlenecks in the Alps – long queues ('horrendous', 'worst in years') build in high season. The Roche de Mio gondola is especially bad ('20 minutes' in 2012, says a reporter), but the chairs from Bellecôte towards Centre and Montchavin are not queue-free. What's

LIFT PASSES

La Plagne

Prices in €

Age	1-day	6-day
under 14	34	163
14 to 64	45	217
65 plus	34	163

Free under 6

Beginner 17 free lifts

Senior 72 plus:1-15 days €6

Notes

La Plagne area; half-day passes; Paradiski extension

Alternative passes

Champagny only, Montchavin only, Montalbert only

Paradiski Découverte

Prices in €

Age	6-day
under 14	181
14 to 64	241
65 plus	181

Free under 6

Beginner no deals

Notes

La Plagne areas with one day in Paradiski

Paradiski

Prices in €

Age	1-day	6-day
under 14	38	193
14 to 64	51	258
65 plus	38	193

Free under 6

Beginner no deals

Senior 72 plus: 1-15 days €9

Notes

Les Arcs areas and La Plagne areas; family reductions; with 5+ passes one day in Three Valleys and Espace Killy, and reduced rate in Ste-Foy, La Rosière and La Thuile

needed is some lifts from Belle-Plagne, higher up.

Plagne-Centre also has problems; even the Bergerie six-pack builds queues (but they move quickly). The gondola to the glacier is queue-prone when snow is poor lower down – to get back up to Roche de Mio as well as to the glacier (we experienced horrendous queues to get back at the end of the day on our March 2011 visit).

In the Champagny sector, the upgrade of the Verdons Sud chair last year has of course relieved that bottleneck, but things have 'improved' now that it has been replaced by a six-pack for 2011/12.

Crowds on the pistes are now as much of a problem as lift queues. The worst-affected area is from Roche de Mio where a single blue piste takes all the pressure. In the afternoon, this run can be handling the traffic from four lifts – maybe 6,000 skiers an hour, or 100 a minute. The Trieuse and Arpette pistes into Bellecôte and some runs into Centre get badly crowded too. The slopes outside the main bowl are quieter, except runs to Montchavin late in the day.

TERRAIN PARKS ★★★★★
Lots of choices

With no fewer than five terrain zones, freestylers are well catered for. There is a 90m long, 3m high half-pipe at Plagne Bellecôte (plus an FIS-approved super-pipe, which hosts the World Cup but isn't open to the public). Belle-Plagne is home to the big park, split into three levels from beginner to more advanced zones, with a mix of jumps, boxes, rails, tables and other obstacles, plus an airbag. There's also a small park with beginner and progression obstacles. Then there are three boardercross courses dotted around.

SNOW RELIABILITY ★★★★★
Generally good except low down

Most of La Plagne's runs are snow-sure, being at altitudes between 2000m and 2700m on the largely north-facing open slopes above the purpose-built centres. The two sunny runs to Champagny are something else – one is often closed, the other (Les Bois) is kept open as much as possible with lots of artificial snow. Snowmaking on runs to all the villages is being improved. On our March 2011 visit we found most of the pistes in great condition, despite the lack of natural snowfall.

FOR EXPERTS ★★★★★
Few steep pistes; good off-piste

The two long, steep and bumpy black runs from Bellecôte to the Chalet chairlift below Col de la Chiaupe were returned to off-piste status in 2009/10 – not surprising, given that they were rarely open, but a shame all the same. The newish piste linking this area to Les Bauches and Montchavin doesn't really deserve its black status, but the Crozets black that meets it, from the bottom of the Inversens chair, is a good run.

Up on the glacier, Chiaupe merits its black status for a short stretch, but really the tough piste skiing is now confined to the Biolley sector. On the back of the hill, the Coqs and Morbleu blacks are seriously steep, Palsembleu less so. From the very top of this sector, Etroits owes its black status to a quite short pitch that is both steep and narrow, but is otherwise harmless. The long Emile Allais red down to the La Roche chair is north-facing, often quiet and great fun in good snow.

But experts will get the best out of La Plagne if they hire a guide and explore the vast off-piste potential – which takes longer to get tracked out than in more 'macho' resorts. The glacier and Biolley sectors have some excellent off-piste terrain. More serious undertakings include numerous runs from the glacier to Les Bauches (a drop of over 1400m). For the more experienced, the north face of Bellecôte presents a splendid challenge with usually excellent snow at the top. You can descend to Peisey-Nancroix (a drop of 2000m), enjoy a splendid lunch at the charming, rustic Ancolie (a real favourite of ours) and then catch a taxi or free bus to the Vanoise Express cable car. Another beautiful and out-of-the-way run starts with a climb and goes over the Cul du Nant glacier to Champagny-le-Haut.

FOR INTERMEDIATES ★★★★★
Great variety
Virtually the whole of La Plagne's area is a paradise for intermediates, with blue and red runs wherever you look. The main drawback is that many of them get overcrowded at times.

For early intermediates there are

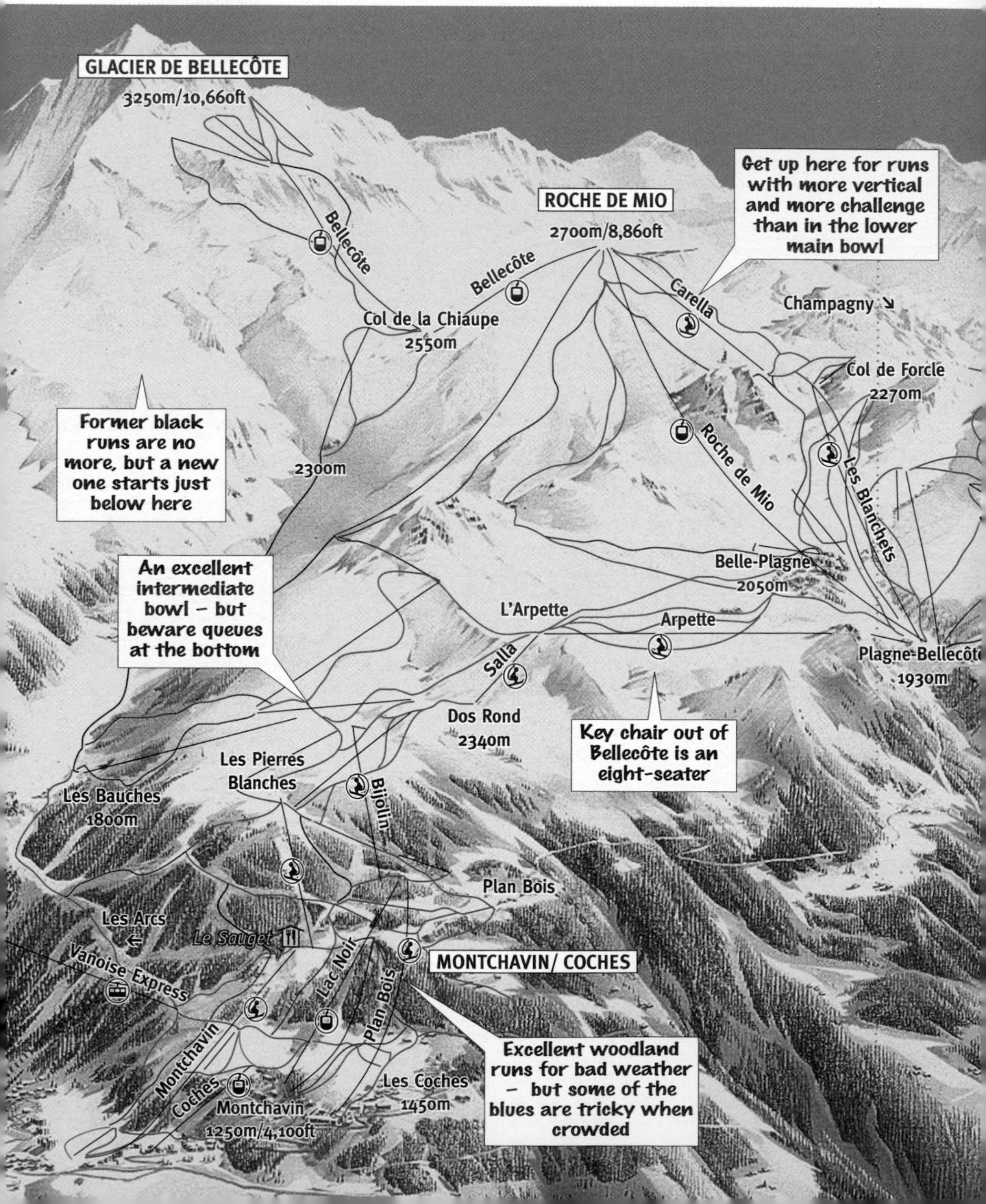

GLACIER DE BELLECÔTE
3250m/10,660ft
Bellecôte
Bellecôte
Col de la Chiaupe
2550m
ROCHE DE MIO
2700m/8,860ft
Get up here for runs with more vertical and more challenge than in the lower main bowl
Carella
Champagny ↘
Col de Forcle
2270m
Roche de Mio
Les Blanchets
Former black runs are no more, but a new one starts just below here
2300m
An excellent intermediate bowl – but beware queues at the bottom
Belle-Plagne
2050m
L'Arpette
Arpette
Salla
Plagne-Bellecôte
1930m
Dos Rond
2340m
Key chair out of Bellecôte is an eight-seater
Les Pierres Blanches
Les Bauches
1800m
Bijolin
Plan Bois
Les Arcs ←
Le Sauget
Vanoise Express
MONTCHAVIN/ COCHES
Lac Noir
Plan Bois
Montchavin
Coches
Excellent woodland runs for bad weather – but some of the blues are tricky when crowded
Les Coches
1450m
Montchavin
1250m/4,100ft

gondola
cable car
fast chairlift
Slow chairs & drags have no symbol

This area is being rejigged, with five slow lifts being replaced by one six-pack. We don't yet know what the pistes will look like.

The main bowl offers mainly easy runs of limited vertical

LA GRANDE ROCHETTE 2500m
Les Verdons 2500m
Champagny
Col de Forcle 2270m
Les Blanchets
Grande-Rochette
Colorado
2350m
LE BIOLLEY
Plagne-Villages 2050m
Plagne-Centre 1970m/ 6,460ft
Telemetro
Aime-la-Plagne 2100m
Plagne-Soleil 2050m
Plagne-Bellecôte 1930m
Plagne 1800
La Roche
Le Fornelet 1970m
MONTALBERT
Le Forperet
Montalbert
Plagne-Montalbert 1350m
Longefoy 1170m

Mira is uncomfortably steep for a blue run, and gets mogulled later in the day, but at least it is wide →

SNOWPIX.COM / CHRIS GILL

UK PACKAGES

Action Outdoors, Alpine Answers, Alpine Elements, Club Med, Crystal, Crystal Finest, Erna Low, Esprit, Ice and Fire, Independent Ski Links, Inghams, Interactive Resorts, Lagrange, Mark Warner, Mountain Heaven, Mountain Wave, Neilson, Oxford Ski Co, Pierre & Vacances, PowderBeds, Powder White, Silver Ski, Ski Amis, Ski Beat, Skibug, Ski Club Freshtracks, Ski Collection, Ski Expectations, Ski France, Ski Hiver, Ski Independence, Ski Line, Ski Olympic, Ski Soleil, Ski Solutions, Ski Supreme, Skitracer, Ski Weekend, Skiworld, Snowchateaux, SnowCrazy, Snow Finders, Thomson, VIP
Montchavin Chill Chalet, Lagrange, Peak Retreats, PowderBeds, Ski Hiver, Ski Soleil, Snowchateaux
Les Coches Erna Low, Family Ski Company, Ice and Fire, Lagrange, Mountainsun, Peak Retreats, Pierre & Vacances, PowderBeds, Ski France, Ski Independence, Ski Line, Snowchateaux
Montalbert Lagrange, Mountain Heaven, Ski Amis
Champagny Erna Low, Lagrange, Peak Retreats, PowderBeds, Ski France, Ski Independence

plenty of gentle blue motorway pistes in the main La Plagne bowl, and a long, interesting (but often very crowded) run from Roche de Mio to Belle Plagne, the Tunnel (going through, er, a tunnel). The blue runs either side of Arpette, on the Montchavin side of the main bowl, are glorious cruises – but beware, the blues further down towards Montchavin are quite challenging. The easiest way to and from Champagny is from the Roche de Mio-Col de Forcle area. Warning: the Mira piste from Grande Rochette and the Lanche Ronde up at Roche de Mio have steep pitches that will upset many blue-run skiers, although Mira has been widened at the top and you can avoid the moguls on the steepest section says a 2012 reporter. Verdons, nearby, is a great cruise too.

Better intermediates have lots of delightful long red runs to try. There are challenging red mogul pitches down from Roche de Mio to Les Bauches (a drop of 900m) – the first half is a fabulous varied run with lots of off-piste diversions possible; the second half, Les Crozats, is classified black, and can be tricky if snow is less than ideal. The Sources red to Belle Plagne is a good run, too.

The Champagny sector has a couple of tough reds – Kamikaze and Hara-Kiri – leading from Grande Rochette. And the long blue cruise Bozelet has one surprisingly steep section. The long Mont de la Guerre red, with 1250m vertical from Les Verdons to Champagny, is a fine away-from-all-lifts run with a decent red-gradient stretch half-way down, but long flattish tracks at the start and finish. There are further excellent red slopes in the other outlying areas – including the winding, tree-lined Les Coches.

FOR BEGINNERS ★★★★★
Comprehensive facilities

La Plagne is a good place to learn, with 18 free lifts in the whole area; each village has at least one. There are good facilities for beginners, provided you go to the right bits, and generally good snow. There are beginner areas in Centre, 1800, Aime and Bellecôte; and in Montchavin, Les Coches and Montalbert. But there are no long green runs to progress to from the nursery slopes. Although a lot of the blue slopes are easy, you can't count on that; some, as we note above, are quite testing.

FOR BOARDERS ★★★★★
Something for everyone

With such a huge amount of terrain, there is something for everyone – 'one of the best for boarding', says a 2012 visitor. Expert freeriders should hire a guide to explore the off-piste. Although this is a great place for beginners and intermediates, with huge wide-open rolling pistes, there are one or two flattish areas – for

example getting across Plagne-Centre, the middle of the Tunnel run and the blue run linking Les Bauches to Montchavin. Most draglifts have been replaced, and others can be avoided; the more difficult ones are marked on the piste map. The park caters for all levels and there are three boardercross runs – see 'Terrain parks'.

FOR CROSS-COUNTRY ★★★★
Open and wooded trails
There are 80km of prepared cross-country trails scattered around. The most beautiful of these are the 22km of winding track set out in the sunny valley around Champagny-le-Haut. The north-facing areas have more wooded trails that link the various centres.

MOUNTAIN RESTAURANTS ★★★★
An enormous choice
Mountain restaurants are an attraction of the area: numerous and varied – and crowded only in peak periods. But all our favourites are outside the main bowl, above the satellite villages.

Editors' choice We've had excellent meals at Chalet des Verdons Sud (0621 543924) above Champagny; reporters agree – appetizing food and good service, on a big terrace with a fine view or in the warmly woody interior. Above Montalbert, the Forperet (0479 555127) is an old farm, doing super 'very traditional, beautifully presented' home-made dishes. We had an excellent tartiflette there (as did a reporter). The rustic Sauget (0479 078351), above Montchavin, is a great place to hole up in poor weather for some highly traditional dishes.
Worth knowing about Readers' tips include the 'lovely' Plein Soleil at Plan Bois ('a bit cramped but excellent food'; 'nice clean loos'), Roc des Blanchets above Champagny ('stunning location, great food'), Borseliers above Champagny ('excellent variety of local dishes, reasonably priced plat du jour'), Bergerie above Plagne Village ('for the occasional free post lunch génépi'), Chalet des Glaciers on the, er, glacier ('tiny hut with hearty soup

TRY THE OLYMPIC BOBSLEIGH RUN – YOU CAN EVEN DO IT SOLO

If the thrills of a day on the slopes aren't enough, you can round it off by having a go on the bobsleigh run built for the 1992 Olympic Winter Games, based in Albertville. The floodlit 1.5km run has 19 bends, generating forces as high as 3g.

You can go in a driverless bob-raft (39 euros) reaching 50mph, which most people find quite exciting enough. Then there's the faster solo mono-bob (105 euros); we found this a great thrill – we had to close our eyes on the sharper bends. Fastest of all is the 'taxi-bob' (111 euros), where three of you are wedged in a real four-man bob behind the driver – advertised speed 68mph. Be sure your physical state is up to the ride; there are minimum age limits. The run is open on certain days only – book ahead. Additional insurance is available. One visitor loved the ride, but found the staff rude and impatient: 'They rushed us through, despite the fact that we were early.'

OT LA PLAGNE / J FAVRE

SCHOOLS

ESF (Belle)
t 0479 090668
Schools in all centres

Oxygène (Centre)
t 0479 090399

El Pro (Belle)
t 0479 091162

Reflex (1800)
t 0613 808056

Evolution 2
(Montchavin-Coches)
t 0479 078185

Classes (ESF prices)
6 days from €217

Private lessons
From €147 for 2.75hr for up to 5 people

in a bread bowl; outside seating only'). In Bellecôte, the takeaway kiosk McCoté does 10 euro meal deals for burger, frites and a drink – 'once we found this place we didn't eat anywhere else'. Above Montchavin, the Cristal des Neiges serves 'filling and tasty' food.

There's a picnic room ('sac hors sac') in Plagne Centre.

SCHOOLS AND GUIDES ★★★

Better alternatives to ESF

Each centre has its own ESF school, and we had a positive report in 2012 for Champagny: 'For the near beginner in our group, the lessons were fun, and the instructor built up a real sense of camaraderie among the diverse group.' Belle Plagne (arranged by Ski Esprit): 'My four-year-old had positive and encouraging instructors, and progressed well.' There are some very worthwhile alternatives too. The Oxygène school in Plagne-Centre is said to be 'great', 'my wife's snowboard instructor was excellent'. Reflex based in 1800 and Evolution 2 based in Montchavin have had good past reviews. Antenne Handicap offers private lessons for skiers with any kind of disability.

FOR FAMILIES ★★★★

Good facilities

Children are well catered for with facilities in each of the villages. In the past we've had good reports of the nursery at Belle-Plagne but not the one in Les Coches (see 'Les Coches').

CHILDCARE

P'tits Bonnets (Centre)
t 0479 090083

Marie-Christine (Centre)
t 0479 091181
18mnth to 6yr

ESF nurseries (from 18 mnth or 2yr):
Aime 0479 090475
Belle 0479 090668

Snow gardens run by ESF: ages from 3 to 5

Ski schools
3yr to 13yr or 16yr depending on village: 6 days €259 (ESF prices)

GETTING THERE

Air Geneva 200km/ 125 miles (3hr); Lyon 195km/120 miles (2hr45); Chambéry 120km/75 miles (1hr45)

Rail Aime (18km/ 11 miles) and Bourg-St-Maurice (35km/ 22 miles) (Eurostar service available); frequent buses from stations

Several UK chalet operators run childcare services – Esprit was particularly highly recommended by a 2012 reporter ('excellent from start to finish'). One or two reporters were concerned by the crowded pistes.

STAYING THERE

Chalets There are lots of catered chalets. Many are in apartments, but there are lots of proper little chalets in 1800 which is where most large UK tour operators have places. Crystal has about a dozen places, mostly in 1800. Inghams has half a dozen. Mountain Heaven has a mid-sized, all en suite place in a good location at 1800 – and a much larger chalet with sauna. Ski Beat has about a dozen chalets, mainly in 1800. Skiworld has nine chalets dotted around several parts of the resort. Family specialist Esprit has its flagship chalet hotel at Belle-Plagne, the exceptionally cool Deux Domaines – in a great position, with good pool and spa and 'excellent' childcare facilities that got a rave review from a 2011 reporter. In Centre, Ski Olympic has a ski-in chalet hotel ('great team, service and food'). Ice and Fire has a ski-in/out place at Plagne-Village, and a new bigger chalet with sauna in Centre. See also our descriptions of lower villages.

Hotels There are very few, and most are of 2-star or 3-star grading.

******Carlina** (0479 097846) Beside the piste below Belle-Plagne. Pleasant rooms, good restaurant, pool and spa centre. Family-friendly. We've enjoyed our stays here. Endorsed by a satisfied reader recently.

*****Araucaria** (0479 092020) Very modern 3-star at Plagne-Centre. Sauna, spa.

*****Balcons** (0479 557655) 3-star at Belle-Plagne. Pool.

Apartments There is a wide choice, including lots of smart new properties, most with pools, available through companies such as Ski Collection, Peak Retreats, Ski Amis, Pierre & Vacances, Ski Independence, Lagrange, Inghams, Crystal and Erna Low.

In Belle-Plagne there are two good Montagnettes residences, Le Vallon and Les Cîmes. In Plagne-Soleil the Granges du Soleil is a very comfortable CGH place with pool, spa and excellent views. Up at Aime is the Pierre & Vacances Premium residence Les Hauts Bois – 'spacious apartments, hotel standard spa facilities'. Lagrange has two Prestige residences: Aspen in Plagne-Villages and Chalets Edelweiss (seven chalet-style buildings sharing a pool) – right by the lift out of 1800.

EATING OUT ★★★★★

A reasonable choice

There is a decent range of casual restaurants including pizzerias and traditional Savoyard places. In Belle-Plagne, the Face Nord is recommended for 'excellent local cuisine and service'. The Matafan served up a hearty meal of grilled meats and good desserts on our recent visit and we enjoyed a very tasty three course meal at the hotel Carlina's restaurant 'C', which is also recommended for lunch. Down in Bellecôte, the Ferme does 'superb Savoyard food'.

Reader recommendations in Plagne-Centre include the Maison (steaks) and Scotty's for 'friendly service and good food'. The Refuge is charmingly rustic ('three-course skier's menu for 24 euros, helpful staff, space age loos').

In Plagne-Villages, the Casa de l'Ours does pizzas and steaks. In Plagne-Soleil, Monica's is 'excellent'.

In Plagne 1800, we had a good evening at Petit Chaperon Rouge – friendly, cosy atmosphere in a wooden chalet that serves local specialities at reasonable prices; the Loup Blanc is popular for 'fine steaks and pizza'.

At Aime-la-Plagne, the rustic old chalet Au Bon Vieux Temps on the slopes is open in the evening. The 'casual, family-friendly' Montana does pizza and the 'usual Savoyard suspects'. The Mont Blanc is also recommended.

APRES-SKI ★★★★★

Bars, bars, bars

Though fairly quiet during low season, La Plagne has plenty of bars, catering particularly for the younger crowd.

In Belle-Plagne, the Tête Inn and the Cheyenne are the main bars. In Plagne-Centre, the Igloo Igloo has an 'icy decor'. The PlanJA is popular and has English cider, apparently. Scotty's is 'lively', and the Luna is also tipped. The Mine is the focal point in Plagne 1800 – complete with old train and mining artefacts. Mama Mia's is a fun spot. Plagne Soleil has Monica's pub ('superb value drink'). Aime-la-Plagne is quiet. There are discos at Plagne-Centre, Belle-Plagne and at Plagne-Bellecôte.

ACTIVITIES

Indoor Sauna and solarium in most centres, squash (1800), fitness centres (Belle-Plagne, 1800, Centre, Bellecôte), library (Centre), climbing wall, bowling

Outdoor Heated swimming pool (Bellecôte), bobsleigh, marked walks, tobogganing, paragliding, helicopter rides, snowmobiles, ice climbing, ice rink, ice karting, snow quad bikes, snowshoeing, dog sledding, air boarding, zip slide

Phone numbers
From abroad use the prefix +33 and omit the initial '0' of the phone number

TOURIST OFFICES

La Plagne
www.la-plagne.com

Montchavin-Les Coches
www.montchavin-lescoches.com

Champagny
www.champagny.com

OFF THE SLOPES ★★★★★
OK for the active

As well as the sports and fitness facilities, there are plenty of winter walks along marked trails. It's also easy to get up the mountain on the gondolas, which both have restaurants at the top. There's an ice grotto on the glacier. Plagne 1800 has bowling and tubing. The Olympic bobsleigh run is a popular evening activity (see feature box). There are cinemas at Aime, Bellecôte and Plagne-Centre. Excursions are limited.

LINKED RESORT – 1250m

MONTCHAVIN

Montchavin is based on an old farming hamlet and has an attractive traffic-free centre. There are adequate shops, a kindergarten and a ski school. The local slopes have quite a bit to offer – pretty, sheltered runs, well endowed with snowmaking, with nursery slopes at village level, attractively surrounded by chalets and restaurants.

The main blue home runs from Dos Rond can be quite tricky (though you can take a more roundabout route via Les Bauches). Après-ski is quiet, but the village doesn't lack atmosphere and has a couple of nice bars, a nightclub, cinema, night skiing, ice rink, and a new swimming pool and the Espace Paradisio spa complex for 2011/12. Hotel Bellecôte (0479 078330) is convenient for the slopes, and we hear is being smartened up.

LINKED RESORT – 1450m

LES COCHES

Les Coches is a little way above Montchavin, across the hillside, and shares the same slopes. It is a sympathetically designed, quiet, modern mini-resort with a traffic-free centre. The hillside setting makes for some steep walks. There are nursery slopes across the mountainside, linked by bucket lift. It has a kindergarten. But Family Ski Company may be a better bet; it has two piste-side chalets close to the village centre. Ice and Fire has a smart-looking 24-bed chalet on the piste with a sauna. The Chalets de Wengen is a trio of comfortable chalet-style apartment buildings sharing a pool.

Dining out options approved by readers include the Poze (pizza), the Savoy'art, and Taverne du Monchu.

LINKED RESORT – 1350m

MONTALBERT

Montalbert is a traditional but much expanded village with a nice little front de neige area, with a choice of restaurant terraces. The lift out of the village is a fast one, but your progress to the main bowl depends on two further slow ones, so it takes quite a time to get to Centre. The local slopes are easy and wooded. Restaurant choice is adequate, Abreuvoir has 'reasonable prices in happy hour', Fiftys Legend has 'prompt service', Tourmente is a popular pub with a pool table and the Code is a 'racy but rocking' nightclub. The Aigle Rouge (0479 547843) is a simple hotel. Ski Amis has a central, all en suite, seven-room chalet with all the trimmings here, and various self-catering options. Mountain Heaven has self-catering apartments in several modern developments; the best of the apartments are notably spacious by French standards, and well furnished.

LINKED RESORT – 1250m

CHAMPAGNY

Champagny is a small, charming village in a pretty, wooded, sunny setting, with its modern expansion done sensitively. It has drawbacks: it is remote from the link to Les Arcs, its local slopes are exposed to full sun and the red run to the village that is most reliably open is rather steep and narrow for nervous intermediates (though you can ride the gondola down). It is well placed for an outing by taxi or car to Courchevel.

There is a beginner area with free lifts at the top of the gondola, and a boardercross higher up beside the Rossa chairlift.

The Glières (0479 550552) is a rustic old hotel with varied rooms, a friendly welcome and good food. The Ancolie (0479 550500) is smarter, with modern facilities. The Alpages de Champagny has 'generous-sized apartments', a pool and sauna. The Club Alpina apartments next to the gondola have been recommended.

The village is quiet in the evenings, but there is a 'good cinema' which opens in the afternoon in bad weather, and readers tip a few restaurants: Poya, Bouquetin ('uncomplicated ingredients expertly cooked') and Rochers, near the church.

SNOWPIX.COM / CHRIS GILL

Portes du Soleil

Low altitude, largely intermediate circuit of slopes straddling the French-Swiss border, with a variety of contrasting resorts

KEY FACTS	
Slopes	950-2275m
	3,120-7,460ft
Lifts	198
Pistes	650km
	404 miles
Green	13%
Blue	40%
Red	37%
Black	10%
Snowmaking	
	835 guns

The Portes du Soleil vies with the Trois Vallées for the title 'World's Largest Ski Area', but its slopes are very different from those of Méribel, Courchevel, Val Thorens and neighbours. The central attraction is an extensive circular tour, straddling the French-Swiss border, taking you through one or two French resorts and several small Swiss ones – great for keen intermediates who like a sensation of travel. You can travel the circuit in either direction, and longer or shorter variations are possible.

We have separate chapters on all the major Portes du Soleil resorts. On the French side, high, purpose-built **Avoriaz** usually has the best snow around. There's a break in the circuit at the traditional village of **Châtel** – you take a bus to bridge the gap.

On the Swiss side, **Champéry** is a classic, charming mountain village with a broad area of slopes spreading across the mountainside above the tiny, purpose-built satellite stations of Champoussin and Les Crosets. Then in a separate valley there is the larger, traditional village of Morgins. There's a short walk across the village here – less of an effort if you are travelling the circuit clockwise.

Back in France are two further traditional resorts, off the main circuit but linked by lift to Avoriaz – **Morzine** and **Les Gets**. They share the biggest area of local slopes in the region.

The lifts you ride doing the circuit vary widely. In the Avoriaz sector and in the Linga sector of Châtel the lifts are mainly modern and fast. On the far side of Châtel and on the Swiss side of the network, drags and old chairlifts dominate, and progress is slow.

The slopes are low by French standards, with top heights in the range 2000m to 2275m, and low points where snow may be particularly poor in Morgins and Châtel (1200m). In general, you can expect better snow on the north-facing French side of the circuit than on the sunnier Swiss side, particularly around Avoriaz/Champéry.

In the distant past there was a booklet-style map covering the whole of the Portes du Soleil. But now each resort has a map showing local lifts and pistes – you have to pick these up as you go. There's an overview map of the circuit on the back of each one.

Puy-St-Vincent

Underrated small modern resort with limited but varied slopes – good for young families who haven't been spoilt by mega-resorts

TOP 10 RATINGS	
Extent	**
Fast lifts	**
Queues	***
Snow	***
Expert	***
Intermediate	***
Beginner	***
Charm	**
Convenience	*****
Scenery	****

RPI	70
lift pass	£110
ski hire	£80
lessons	£65
food & drink	£110
total	**£365**

KEY FACTS	
Resort	1400-1600m 4,590-5,250ft
Slopes	1250-2700m 4,100-8,860ft
Lifts	12
Pistes	75km 47 miles
Green	18%
Blue	41%
Red	35%
Black	6%
Snowmaking	13%

- + Mostly convenient resort with friendly locals and great for families
- + Some great cross-country routes
- + Low prices overall

- – Slopes limited in extent
- – Few alternatives to apartments
- – Queues and crowds in peak season
- – Limited facilities and diversions

Puy-St-Vincent's ski area may be limited, but it offers a decent vertical and a lot of variety, including a bit of steep stuff. Provided you pick your spot with care, it makes an attractive choice for a family not hungry for piste miles.

THE RESORT

Puy-St-Vincent proper is an old mountain village, but most people stay in one of the purpose-built ski-stations. Station 1400 is a small development by the chairlift just along the mountainside from the old village; the major part, Station 1600, with long, white 1970s-style apartment blocks arranged across the hill, is a few hairpins further up. Spreading up the hillside from 1600 are newer chalet-style developments known as Station 1800. The three developments are linked by free buses till 8pm.

The six-day pass allows a day in Pelvoux, a short bus ride away (and in several more distant major resorts); this small area has quiet, very rewarding blue, red and black runs, and a vertical of over 1000m.

Village charm The main resort of 1600 is functional rather than charming. We and our reporters have found PSV a very friendly, welcoming resort.

Convenience 1600 is compact, with its few shops, bars and restaurants lining the foot of the slopes – ideal for families. Much of the lodging is ski-in/ ski-out; one main lift starts just below the village, which helps. 1800 is fine for the slopes but has no supermarket or bars, one restaurant and the bus stops at 8pm, so a night out in 1600 means an uphill slog home.

Scenery The resort has a lovely woody position above the valley; great views from the top to the Ecrins mountains.

THE MOUNTAINS

Within its small area, PSV packs in a lot of variety. A few reporters have judged some blue runs a bit tough. Piste map and signposting are 'clear'.

Slopes There are gentle slopes between 1600 and 1400, but most of the runs are above 1600. A fast quad goes up to the treeline at around 2000m. The top lift is a (slow) quad to La Pendine at 2700m, serving open slopes. More lifts serve further open

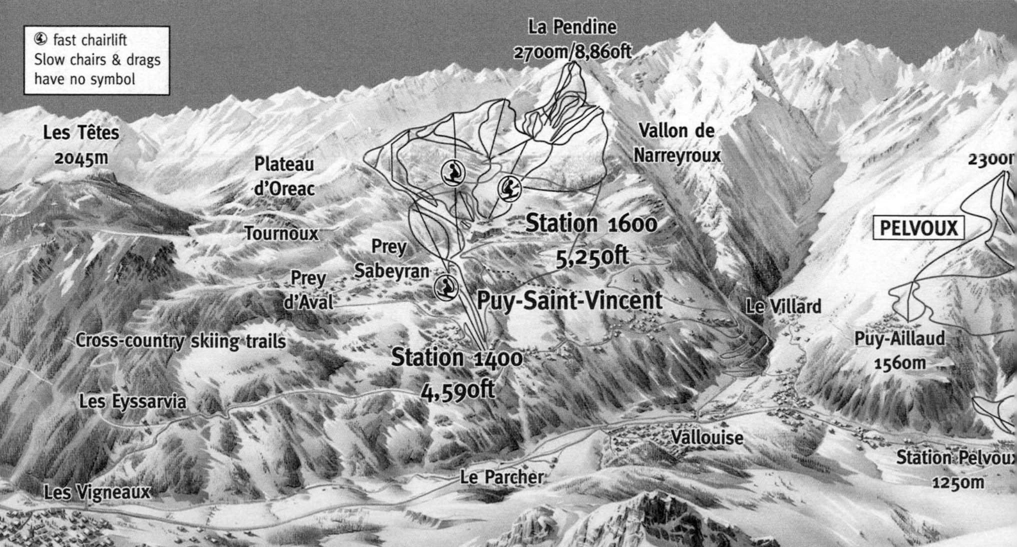

↑ The white buildings of 1600 are very convenient and blend in with the snow well. This pic is taken from 1800

SNOWBIZZ

UK PACKAGES

Erna Low, Lagrange, Ski Collection, Ski France, Snowbizz, Zenith

Phone numbers
From abroad use the prefix +33 and omit the initial '0' of the phone number

TOURIST OFFICE

www.paysdesecrins.com

runs here, and access splendid cruising runs that curl around the edges of the area into the woods.
Fast lifts The key lifts out of the resorts are fast chairs, some of the others are 'old and uncomfortable'.
Queues Reporters complain of crowds during French school holiday periods, but few problems at other times.
Terrain parks There is a park and boardercross on Pendine.
Snow reliability The slopes face north-east and are reasonably reliable for snow. Snowmaking covers much of the slopes at 1600 and runs to 1400.
Experts The two black runs are short but genuinely black, often with moguls. There are good off-piste opportunities in the high bowl and lower down in the trees, and longer routes to be tackled with guidance.
Intermediates Size apart, it's a good area for those who like a challenge – but there aren't many very easy runs.
Beginners A day pass is available for the drag on the small nursery area at 1400. Progression is not ideal: there is a long green from 2000m but it crosses several other pistes and is very busy as it approaches the resort.
Snowboarding There are slopes to suit all levels and not too many flat bits to deal with, but still some draglifts.
Cross-country The 30km of cross-country trails include some varied routes between 1400m and 1700m.
Mountain restaurants The woody, self-service Etoile des Neiges on the lower slopes has an open fire and is tipped for 'fantastic food and friendly staff'. The modern Bartavelles at the top of the chair from 1600 has great views and self- and table-service sections.
Schools and guides As well as the ESF there is a large International school run in partnership with tour operator Snowbizz. We have very positive reports: 'fun, friendly, knowledgeable'; 'excellent off-piste guiding'.
Families From all points of view the resort suits families well ('perfect', says a 2012 reporter). Snowbizz runs its own crèche ('large, light and airy, caring staff, lots of toys; our boys did not want to come home at night').

STAYING THERE

Most accommodation is in self-catering apartments at the foot of the slopes.
Hotels There are three hotels in 1400. We'd stay at the 3-star St-Roch: right by the lift, great views over the valley, good food, very friendly. The Pendine is just over the road, the Aigliere a bus ride away – both 2-stars.
Apartments Ski Collection features a couple of smart residences with pools and saunas at 1800. Snowbizz has very family-friendly places right by the shops and slopes at 1600.
Eating out There's a fair choice in 1600. Petit Chamois serves 'generous portions' and caters well for kids. The three hotel restaurants in 1400 have all been recommended.
Après-ski Après-ski is confined to a few bar-restaurants in 1600 and the hotel bars in 1400.
Off the slopes Village diversions are very limited, but there are 20km of walks, snowshoeing, parapenting, tobogganing and skating.

The Pyrenees

An underrated region with decent skiing and boarding at lower prices than the Alps and villages that remain distinctly French

RPI	85
lift pass	£150
ski hire	£110
lessons	£80
food & drink	£100
total	**£440**

UK PACKAGES

Les Angles Lagrange, Ski Collection, Ski France
Barèges Borderline
Cauterets AmeriCan Ski, Lagrange, Ski Collection
Font-Romeu Lagrange, Pierre & Vacances, Ski Collection, Ski France, Solo's, Zenith
La Mongie Lagrange, Pierre & Vacances, Ski Collection
St-Lary-Soulan AmeriCan Ski, Lagrange, Pierre & Vacances, Ski Collection, Ski France, Zenith

It is certainly true that ski areas in the French Pyrenees can't compete in terms of extent with the mega resorts of the Alps. But don't dismiss them: they have considerable attractions, including price – hotels and apartments can cost half as much as in the French Alps, and meals and drinks are cheaper. Provided the snow is good and you're not in search of steep mogul fields and wild après-ski, there is a surprising amount of variety packed into some of these smaller areas.

The Pyrenees are serious mountains, with dramatic, picturesque scenery, and are worth considering for beginners, intermediates and quiet family holidays at a lower cost. The resorts are attractively French, and many are old mountain villages which double up as spa towns. You'll also find charmless purpose-built satellites.

Access has improved, with low-cost airlines using Toulouse, Pau and Lourdes airports.

The locals (including lots of Spanish) like to visit at weekends, so the slopes can get busy. Queues are rare outside peak holidays though, and a lot of locals do cross-country rather than downhill. British visitors are still relatively few, so English is less widely spoken than in the Alps.

Cauterets

- ➕ Charming, old spa town
- ➕ Serious cross-country trails
- ➖ Downhill slopes very limited
- ➖ Long gondola ride to/from slopes

Cauterets is good for a short break; it's a relaxing old town, easy to reach, and its small downhill ski area suits a couple of days – try the cross-country too.

Many of Cauterets' buildings are well-preserved examples of the 19th century and the thermal spas are a popular attraction for visitors. British-run Mulcares in the Pyrenees offers central apartments and there is a wide choice of hotels. The town's position at the head of a wide, sunny valley means traffic is rarely a problem, despite its appeal as a large year-round tourist destination.

The skiing takes place in a high, open and treeless bowl, the Cirque du Lys, reached by a long gondola from town; you have to ride it down as well as up. There is parking up at Le Courbet (1360m), from where a short gondola departs for the slopes – though this was closed on our recent visit. The 36km of varied slopes radiate around the bowl, between 1730m and 2415m. The area just above the gondola top station is ideal for children and beginners, and was enlarged and a new moving carpet installed for 2012. There are some gentle blue runs for progression. But it does get busy at weekends, as does the main restaurant – a self-service.

Cauterets' jewel, though, is its 38km of cross-country, a short bus ride from town at Pont d'Espagne. It's one of the best areas we've seen, and amid beautiful scenery and waterfalls.

KEY FACTS

Resort	935m 3,070ft
Slopes	1730-2415m 5,680-7,920ft
Lifts	12
Pistes	36km
Snow-guns	Some

TOURIST OFFICE

www.cauterets.com

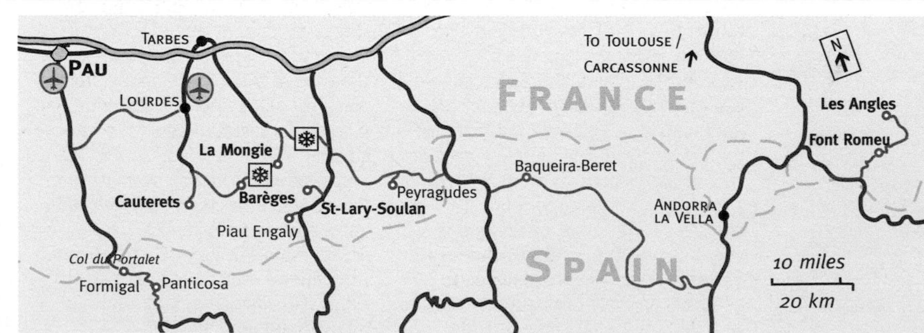

KEY FACTS

Resort	830m 2,720ft
Slopes	1700-2515m 5,580-8,250ft
Lifts	31
Pistes	100km
Snow-guns	270 guns

TOURIST OFFICE

www.saintlary.com

St-Lary-Soulan

- ➕ One of the biggest Pyrenean areas
- ➕ Attractive, traditional village
- ➖ Few challenges on-piste
- ➖ No runs back to the valley village

St-Lary combines an attractive, traditional village with one of the largest ski areas in the French Pyrenees – fine for intermediates wanting a sense of travel.

If you stay in the village, you ride a cable car or gondola both ways. Or you can stay up at purpose-built St-Lary 1700 (Pla-d'Adet).

Village charm St-Lary is pleasant with a narrow main street lined with wood and stone buildings.

Convenience Accommodation spreads from the centre along a river towards the hamlet of Soulan. Staying close to one of the two lifts is best.

Scenery The rocky ridges and open slopes give fine views including the Pyrenees National Park.

THE MOUNTAIN

The slopes cover three main sectors and most runs are above the treeline.

Slopes A cable car and gondola go up to an area of short slopes at St-Lary 1700. From there you can head for 1900 and a gondola towards a more extensive area of intermediate slopes.

Fast lifts Apart from the three above, there are three fast chairs; all other lifts are slow chairs and drags.

Queues 'No problem outside school holidays', says a 2012 visitor, who was told weekends can be busy.

Terrain parks There's a park, a boardercross and a pipe.

Snow reliability Reasonable; many slopes are north-east facing, almost half with snowmaking.

Experts The few black runs are not very challenging but there's off-piste at Courne Blanque and Soum de Matte.

Intermediates Most runs are gentle cruises, with a few more challenging red runs. Best for early intermediates.

Beginners Good nursery slopes, with two covered moving carpets at 1700, but there is no special lift pass.

Snowboarding There are good cruising runs, though still some old draglifts.

Cross-country Not the best choice.

Mountain restaurants L'Oule, by a lake, is an old refuge with decent self-service food. Rustic Les 3 Guides above 1900 ('excellent charcuterie, local wine by the pichet') and tiny La Cabane on the edge of 1700 do friendly table-service.

Schools and guides The four schools offer the usual options, though good spoken English cannot be guaranteed.

Families St-Lary is a good family resort, with kids' snow gardens, mini-terrain park and family fun area. The day care centre at 1700 takes children from 18 months to six years old.

STAYING THERE

Hotels The 4-star Mercure is linked to the spa and near the gondola; we enjoyed a 2012 stay there. The 3-star Pergola is charming with a good restaurant.

Apartments 4-stars with pool, sauna, steam, hot tub include l'Ardoisière (800m from the gondola), Cami Real (central) and Chalets de l'Adet (on the slopes). Pierre & Vacances has the 4-star Rives de l'Aure (near cable car). Ski Collection, Lagrange and Zenith have a good selection of places.

Eating out There's a fair choice, from pizzerias to grills. Our favourite is the Grange (local gourmet dishes). Other tips: the Gros Minet, Maison du

Cassoule, Pergola (in old village); Myrtilles, La Cabane (at 1700).
Après-ski Nightlife is quiet, but there are a few bars. Try the Fitzroy (Irish pub) or Balthazar (modern wine bar) or at 1700 Top Ski (music and tapas).
Off the slopes There's a big spa (with pools, sauna, steam and treatments), dog sledding, snowmobiling, snowshoeing, a cinema, a museum.

La Mongie / Barèges

- ⊞ One of the biggest Pyrenean areas
- ⊞ Contrasting villages but ...
- ⊟ Purpose-built La Mongie lacks charm
- ⊟ Lots of slow chairs and drags

Nicely varied slopes and good off-piste shared by two hugely contrasting resorts – one purpose-built, the other a centuries-old spa town.

La Mongie is a purpose-built, modern resort on one side of the high Col du Tourmalet pass (closed in winter). On the other side is Barèges, with which it shares the Grand Tourmalet ski area. The slopes span four valleys and are nicely varied with open bowls above La Mongie and a friendly tree-lined area above Barèges – all suitable for intermediates. The black runs are considered some of the toughest in the French Pyrenees and there is a lot of excellent off-piste including from the Pic du Midi Observatory (where you can stay the night), reached by cable car from La Mongie. There are few huts, but we loved the tiny wood-panelled Etape du Berger above La Mongie – where most food comes from the owner's farm and you choose your own meat – and the rustic Chez Louisette above Barèges.

La Mongie has little charm but is convenient, with lifts and pistes on its doorstep and good restaurant terraces from which to gaze at the scenery. On our 2012 visit we enjoyed our stay at a catered chalet in Barèges run by an English couple (see www.mountainbug.com); they also have the newly renovated 3-star Hotel du Tourmalet there. Barèges is a small, atmospheric old spa village (with a great modern addition to its traditional old spa building) with a narrow main street a free bus ride from the slopes.

KEY FACTS

Barèges-La Mongie	
Resort	1250-1800m 4,100-5,910ft
Slopes	1400-2500m 4,590-8,200ft
Lifts	36
Pistes	100km
Snow-guns	212 guns

TOURIST OFFICE

Domaine Tourmalet
uk.n-py.com
www.grand-tourmalet.com

Font-Romeu

- ⊞ High, fairly snow-sure slopes
- ⊞ Popular family resort
- ⊟ Limited in extent, with shortish runs
- ⊟ Weekend crowds

With Font-Romeu you can choose from a delightful old village or a purpose-built station at the foot of the woody, cruisey slopes. Beginners are well catered for.

The old village, complete with 12th century church and contrasting modern National Scientific Research Centre, is linked to the slopes by a gondola that you ride down as well as up. Alternatively, you can stay at Pyrenees 2000 – a purpose-built development at the foot of the lifts, and a short bus ride away.

The slopes span three partly wooded hills, with a good mix of runs and a new black run and boardercross built for 2012. There are a couple of free beginner lifts and good progression to gentle greens. There is a local lift pass, but the Neiges Catalan pass also covers Les Angles (see below) and six other resorts in the region. There are 111km of cross-country.

KEY FACTS

Resort	1775m 5,820ft
Slopes	1775-2215m 5,820-7,270ft
Lifts	23
Pistes	58km
Snow-guns	80%

TOURIST OFFICE

www.font-romeu.fr

Les Angles

- ⊞ Sheltered, tree-lined slopes
- ⊞ Good, gentle beginner terrain but ...
- ⊟ English less widely spoken here
- ⊟ Shortish runs that lack challenge

Les Angles is a small but charming stone village, complete with old church. The slopes are limited but relatively snow-sure and family-friendly.

Les Angles offers high but mainly wooded slopes that cover a broad hillside. Most runs are short and intermediate; over half are classified red, but there is a good proportion of gentler terrain. There are nursery slopes at village level and at 1800m – reached by free ski-bus. There is a decent terrain park and 42km of cross-country trails. Font-Romeu is 16km away. Off-slope diversions are few, but dog sledding is possible.

KEY FACTS

Resort	1650m 5,410ft
Slopes	1650-2375m 5,410-7,790ft
Lifts	19
Pistes	50km
Snow-guns	363 guns

TOURIST OFFICE

www.lesangles.com

SNOWPIX.COM / CHRIS GILL

La Rosière

A friendly, family-oriented little resort in a panoramic setting; the link to La Thuile in Italy adds much-needed interest to the skiing

TOP 10 RATINGS

Extent	***
Fast lifts	*
Queues	****
Snow	***
Expert	**
Intermediate	***
Beginner	*****
Charm	***
Convenience	***
Scenery	****

RPI 80

lift pass	£140
ski hire	£90
lessons	£65
food & drink	£115
total	**£410**

NEWS

2012/13: A six-pack is due to replace the slow Fort quad to Col de la Traversette, which will make access to La Thuile quicker. A new luxury apartment complex, the 4-star Lodge Hemera, with indoor pool, sauna, steam and hot tubs, is due to open in the village centre.

2011/12: The main Poletta terrain park has a new airbag.

KEY FACTS

Resort	1850m 6,070ft
Espace San Bernardo (La Rosière and La Thuile)	
Slopes	1175-2610m 3,850-8,560ft
Lifts	38
Pistes	160km 99 miles
Green	10%
Blue	31%
Red	40%
Black	19%
Snowmaking	25%

+ Pleasant, compact, friendly resort in a sunny setting: good for families
+ Good beginner slopes
+ Fair-sized area of slopes if you include linked La Thuile in Italy
+ Heli-skiing in Italy from the border
+ Fine panoramic views
+ Big dumps of snow when storms sock in from the west, but ...

− When storms do sock in, both local slopes and the Italian link can be bleak or closed

− Sunny slopes are affected by sun as the season progresses

− Mainly slow old lifts

− Local pistes rather limited and lacking variety

− Limited village diversions

La Rosière is very different from its famous neighbours such as Val d'Isère-Tignes and Les Arcs – much smaller, quieter, sunnier; more friendly, too, say reporters. Many reporters are also more impressed than we are by the skiing, which mainly consists of several short runs down a single open slope. And there are still far too many slow lifts. Happily, you can quite easily reach some of the slopes of La Thuile – more interesting, and served by better lifts.

THE RESORT

La Rosière has been developed in traditional chalet style high up on the road that climbs from Bourg-St-Maurice towards the Petit-St-Bernard pass to Italy. In winter the road ends at a car park below the main lifts in La Rosière. The resort has several identifiable parts, but the key distinction is between the main village and the developing satellite of Les Eucherts, a short bus ride – or a 'pleasant' floodlit forest walk – to the east. This is more or less self-sufficient, but offers less choice of everything than the main village.

Village charm The resort is attractively built in traditional styles; it is quiet, with a few shops and friendly locals; don't expect much lively nightlife. It is centred on the road through to the lift station car park; so although there is no real through-traffic, the centre is far from traffic-free.

Convenience It's a small place, where you may have only a short stroll to a lift, but big enough for many locations to require use of an 'efficient' free ski-bus. The satellite of Les Eucherts has its own fast chair into the slopes.

Scenery La Rosière's home slopes are south-facing, with great views over the Isère valley to Les Arcs and La Plagne.

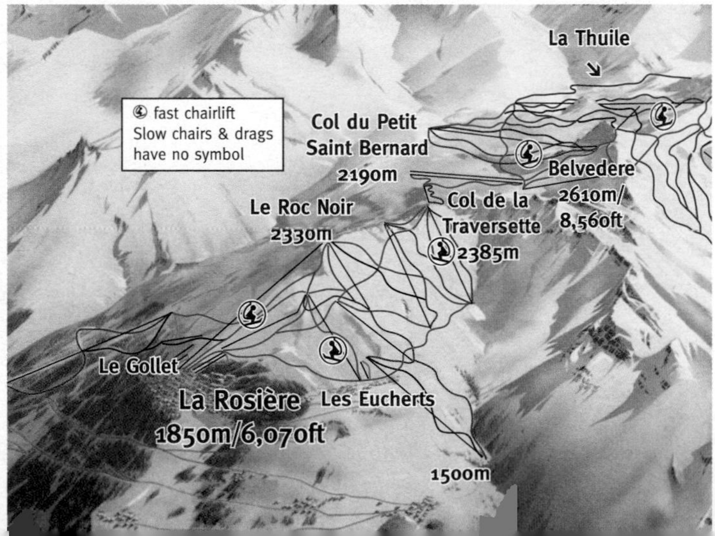

THE MOUNTAINS

La Rosière and La Thuile in Italy share a big area of slopes called Espace San Bernardo. The link with Italy's slopes is prone to closure because of high winds or heavy snow. There are few tree-lined runs.

Slopes Two fast chairs, one at the main village and one at Les Eucherts, take you into the slopes; then a series of parallel lifts allows progress across the mountain to Col de la Traversette, departure point for Italy (and due to be served by a new six-pack for 2012/13). West of the village is a separate sector with red and black runs descending through woods to the Ecudets chair – and a blue on down to the village of Seez (at about 900m) when snow is good. 'Grooming is superb,' says a 2012 visitor.

Fast lifts Only the two main village chairs and the planned new six-pack to Col de la Traversette are fast; all the others are slow. Some reporters have noted that these lift rides can be cold affairs if a wind is whistling over the pass.

Queues Reporters stress the lack of queues, even at peak times. If better weather on the Italian side sends crowds flocking over the border, expect some queues on the way back.

Terrain parks The main Poletta park is accessed by the drag of the same name and has green, blue, red and expert lines including a funbox, bumps, rails and – new this year – a big airbag. Just below this is the beginner Zouvino park accessed by the Lièvre Blanc drag from the village. There is also a boardercross at the far end of the slopes.

Snow reliability The slopes get a lot of snow from storms pushing up the valley, but conditions can be badly affected by sun or wind.

Experts There are a couple of short, easy but worthwhile black runs – we particularly like Ecudets, down the eponymous chairlift. And there are a couple of ungroomed, avalanche-controlled freeride zones (called 'Snowcross' areas) marked on the map. There is more serious, easily accessed off-piste terrain just outside the lift network. And there's heli-skiing from just over the Italian border.

Intermediates The main area is a broad open mountainside offering straightforward red pistes, mostly at the easy end of the spectrum and mostly short, with verticals in the range 300m to 450m. The exception is the Marmotte red, dropping over 800m to the chairlift below Les Eucherts. More interesting than anything on the main slope is the lovely wooded Fontaine Froide red, dropping 750m vertical to the Ecudets chair. Keen intermediates will want to make

SNOWPIX.COM / CHRIS GILL

Mountain huts are not a highlight (only two and both self-service) but the views are good ↓

UK PACKAGES

A Mountain Chalet, Alpine Answers, BoardnLodge, Crystal, Erna Low, Esprit, Independent Ski Links, Interactive Resorts, Lagrange, Mountain Heaven, Peak Retreats, Pierre & Vacances, PowderBeds, Ski Amis, Ski Beat, Ski Collection, Ski Expectations, Ski France, Ski Independence, Ski Olympic, Ski Solutions, Skitracer, Skiworld, Snow Finders, Snow Nation, SnowCrazy

multiple trips to the fast lifts and more varied terrain of La Thuile.

Blue-run skiers are effectively confined to the pistes near the village, served by the two fast lifts. Not surprisingly, they get quite busy. The longer blues running across the main slope are just tracks from A to B, so not of much interest. The outing to Italy involves a red run at the start; it is not especially tricky; but be aware that the two draglifts that follow total almost 3km in length.

Beginners There are good nursery slopes and short lifts near the main village (three are free to use) and near Les Eucherts. The blue runs above the village are excellent for progression.

Snowboarding Most lifts are chairs, making the place good for novices. And the sunny slopes are good for gentle freeriding in soft snow.

Cross-country There are 10km of trails.

Mountain restaurants There are only two, both self-service. Plan du Repos, in the heart of the slopes, is pleasant enough, with 'pretty good grub'.

Schools and guides We have had consistently good reports of the ESF – 'very good teachers', 'cater very well for English-speaking skiers', say recent visitors. Evolution 2 has had mixed reviews in the past; but a 2011 reporter praises her instructor for being 'knowledgeable and patient'. The Elite school offers clinics and private lessons.

Families The resort caters well for children – 'a great family resort', says a 2012 visitor. Family specialist Esprit has its own childcare facilities here and Crystal has its own private nanny service. There is a family lift pass that offers big savings to those with teenagers.

STAYING THERE

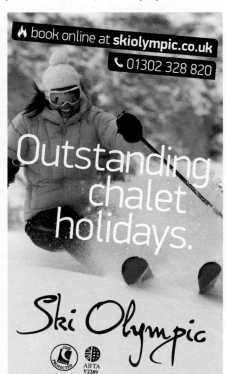

Chalets This is now a major chalet resort, with a surprising number of properties. Many are located in Les Eucherts. The biggest operator is family specialist Esprit, with 13 chalets varying from five to 30 beds, plus its usual comprehensive childcare ('staff were brilliant'). Mountain Heaven has a splendid-looking penthouse, with six en-suite rooms and an outdoor hot tub, and five other smart chalets. Ski Olympic has four chalets (including two with access to a pool, sauna, steam and hot tub) with from five to 20 rooms; 'this company was

There are pretty walks – some with great views over to Les Arcs and La Plagne →

OT LA ROSIERE / AURELIE CROUVISIER-DAUM

Phone numbers
From abroad use the prefix +33 and omit the initial '0' of the phone number

TOURIST OFFICE
www.larosiere.net

exceptional and gave us a wonderful holiday experience. And its female ski guide was quite simply superb, charming, enthusiastic company and very knowledgeable,' said a 2012 reporter. Skiworld has five smart mid-sized properties in the same area which it is planned will share a hot tub, steam and two saunas for this winter. Crystal has a cluster of four chalets in Les Eucherts, two of which are in their 'Finest' programme and have an outdoor hot tub.

Hotels There are a couple of 2-star hotels in the village, and more lower down the hill. Chalet Matsuzaka (0479 075313) is a Japanese-influenced 10-room 4-star at Les Eucherts.

Apartments Many of the best places are in Les Eucherts. Ski Amis has a range of properties from one to four bedrooms. Mountain Heaven has a few, including a smart-looking penthouse apartment. The major French self-catering operators have properties here. Lagrange and Skiworld feature the Cîmes Blanches residences – smart, with a 'lovely' pool, hot tub, sauna and steam room. Peak Retreats and Ski Collection also feature that plus the luxurious new Lodge Hemera (see 'News') and a couple of other places. Pierre & Vacances has the simpler Vanoise. For those who don't take self-catering too literally Montagne Saveurs is an outfit delivering 'fantastic food'.

Eating out Out of the dozen or so restaurants, readers' current favourites are the MacKinley ('charming with Savoie favourites and a log fire'), Genépi, the 'cosy' Ancolie in Les Eucherts and the 'atmospheric' Grange.

Après-ski Confined to a few bars in the village. The 'brilliant' Petit Danois has 'a fantastic band three days a week'. Bar Fusion is popular too, but quieter, say reporters. The Moobar at Les Eucherts is also tipped.

Off the slopes It's improving, but there's not a huge amount to amuse the non-skier – cleared walks, snowshoeing and paragliding, with ten-pin bowling and ice skating at Les Eucherts. There is a 'tiny' cinema. Lunch with skiing friends will have to be in the village; but keen skiers may want to visit La Thuile more than once – and when they do, they won't be tempted to come back for lunch.

SNOWPIX.COM / CHRIS GILL

Samoëns

Characterful but inconvenient base for the extensive and varied Grand Massif, shared with Flaine, Morillon and Les Carroz

TOP 10 RATINGS

Extent	****
Fast lifts	**
Queues	****
Snow	***
Expert	****
Intermediate	*****
Beginner	**
Charm	****
Convenience	*
Scenery	****

RPI	95
lift pass	£180
ski hire	£95
lessons	£60
food & drink	£135
total	**£470**

NEWS

2011/12: A new luxury five-bedroom chalet, Apassion, opened in the village.

PISTE MAP

Samoëns is covered on the Flaine map

SNOWPIX.COM / CHRIS GILL

Good views over the village from the home runs to Vercland ↓

- + Lovely historic village, with traffic-free centre and weekly market
- + Lifts into big, varied area shared with Flaine and Les Carroz
- + Glorious views from top heights
- + Very close to Geneva airport

- − Main access lift is way outside the village, and has no return piste
- − Not the best base for beginners
- − Limited choice of village bars, though decent range of restaurants

The impressive Grand Massif area is chiefly associated in Britain with high, purpose-built, apartment-dominated Flaine; but the network (described mainly in the Flaine chapter) can also be accessed from lower, traditional villages. And the cutest of these, if not the most convenient for skiing, is Samoëns.

THE RESORT

Samoëns is an attractive 'Monument Historique' – once a thriving centre for stonemasons, with their work much in evidence.

Village charm The resort has a small traffic-free centre of narrow streets lined by appealing food shops, and a pretty square (sadly not traffic-free) with a stone fountain, an ancient linden tree, a fine church and other medieval buildings. Also nearby is a nominally car-free area of modern development. The place as a whole retains the feel of 'real' rural France and makes a compelling base for families. There is a Wednesday market for your cheese supplies.

Convenience Slope access is by one of two gondolas, both a drive or 'reliable and frequent' ski-bus ride from the village: an old one across the valley and a newer one nearer to the village. You can ski down the old gondola, but only on red and black runs that can be tricky or closed; there are no runs to the new one. So it's a gondola then a bus at the end of the day. Not a problem, but not convenient.

Scenery The village has a pretty valley setting, with attractively woody ridges and glorious views from the tops.

THE MOUNTAINS

Most of the skiing directly above Samoëns is on open slopes beneath the peak of Tête des Saix.

Slopes The two gondolas from the valley arrive at separate points on the 'hilly plateau' of Samoëns 1600. This mini-resort is also reachable by road. A six-pack installed three seasons ago now whisks you up to Tête des Saix, from which point you can proceed towards Flaine via a narrow, crowded piste followed by a fast chair in the Vernant bowl. Or you can turn right to descend to Morillon or Les Carroz.

Fast lifts Mountain access is now respectably quick, but the area as a whole has many slow lifts still.

Queues The local lifts don't seem to present problems, but in high season you can expect delays on the way to Flaine. Thanks to the newish six-pack, the narrow piste towards Vernant is more crowded than ever.

Terrain parks The main park is in Flaine.

Snow reliability The slopes above Samoëns face due north, so above 1600 snow is fairly reliable. There is snowmaking around 1600, but one January visitor in 2011 was appalled by the state of the blue run from Tête des Saix, which lacked snowmaking and as a result was 'icy, with lots of stones'.

KEY FACTS

Resort	720-1600m 2,360-5,250ft

Grand Massif ski area (Samoëns and all linked resorts)

Slopes	700-2480m 2,300-8,140ft
Lifts	69
Pistes	265km 165 miles
Green	11%
Blue	46%
Red	33%
Black	10%
Snowmaking	218 guns

Massif ski area (excluding Flaine)

Slopes	700-2120m 2,300-6,700ft
Lifts	45
Pistes	125km 78 miles

UK PACKAGES

Alps Accommodation, AmeriCan Ski, BoardnLodge, Chalet Bezière, Chez Michelle, Erna Low, Lagrange, Peak Retreats, PowderBeds, Powder White, Ski Expectations, Ski France, Ski Independence, Ski Weekender, Zenith

Phone numbers
From abroad use the prefix +33 and omit the initial '0' of the phone number

TOURIST OFFICE

www.samoens.com

Experts The upper pistes on Tête des Saix are among the most testing in the Grand Massif, and there is lots of good off-piste in the region.
Intermediates Samoëns normally makes a satisfactory base for all but the most timid intermediates, who might be better off in Morillon. But note the comments above on snow conditions on Tête des Saix. From there you have a choice of good long runs in various directions. In good snow the valley runs to Vercland are highly enjoyable – the black is little steeper than the red, and used less.
Beginners Beginners buy a special pass and go up to 1600, where they will find gentle, snow-sure slopes – excellent when not crowded – but no long green runs to progress to. Morillon is a better bet. And the nursery slopes at Sixt are quiet.
Snowboarding Not a big boarding resort, partly perhaps because there are quite a few flat linking runs.
Cross-country There are trails on the flat valley floor around Samoëns, and more challenging ones up the valley beyond Sixt and up at Col de Joux Plane (1700m).
Mountain restaurants Several options at Samoëns 1600. We enjoyed friendly service and good food at Lou Caboëns, a small, woody place endorsed by a 2012 reporter. Mimy's is tipped for its 'massive burger in a lovely crusty roll'. The Pré d'Oscar is a handy spot for a drink at the end of the day. There's a picnic room at the bottom of the Marmotte piste at 1600, and several others in the Grand Massif marked on the piste map.
Schools and guides We've had good reports of the ZigZag school ('great attitude, patience, encouragement').
Families The Loupiots nursery takes kids from three months to five years old, and ski lessons are available. ZigZag does multi-activity courses.

STAYING THERE

Chalets We continue to get glowing reports of owner-run chalet Bezière ('outstanding', 'enormous bedrooms, food absolutely excellent').
Hotels There are several 2-star and 3-star places. We and readers have enjoyed the 3-star Neige et Roc (0450 344072), a walk from the centre – 'friendly staff, big spa area'. The Glaciers (0450 344006)offers 'great location, friendly staff'.
Apartments Self-catering is mostly in small-scale developments, and quite a lot of it in individual chalets. Alps Accommodation is a British-run Samoëns specialist with over 35 chalets and apartments available; we have an enthusiastic report this year on its 'cosy, well restored, traditional' Ancienne Fromagerie. Among many attractive options available through French specialist Peak Retreats are the Fermes de Samoëns, a smart Lagrange Prestige residence (with pool), the CGH residence Reine des Prés and the Ferme des Fontany.
Eating out A good selection of places. Table de Fifine, a short drive out, is a fine spot for a proper dinner, with a beautiful wooden interior – 'a favourite', says a 2012 reporter. Monde à l'Envers offers 'great atmosphere, food and service'. A 2012 reporter endorses the 'excellent' Bois de Lune. The Louisiane has 'great' pizzas.
Après-ski Nightlife is quiet and there is little choice of bars; Irish pub Covey's ('doubled in size and still the liveliest') and the 'more sophisticated and laid back' Savoie are the reader favourites.
Off the slopes Samoëns offers quite a range of activities. Snowmobiling up at Samoëns 1600 is wilder than is usual in the Alps. There's dog sledding and a reader recommends the snowshoeing. There is an outdoor, covered ice rink, and a sports and cultural centre.

SNOWPIX.COM / CHRIS GILL

Serre-Chevalier

One on its own, this – more character and less swank than you expect in a big French resort, and more woodland runs

RATINGS

The mountains	
Extent	★★★★
Fast lifts	★★
Queues	★★★
Terrain p'ks	★★★
Snow	★★★
Expert	★★★
Intermediate	★★★★
Beginner	★★★★
Boarder	★★★★
X-country	★★★
Restaurants	★★★★
Schools	★★★★
Families	★★★
The resort	
Charm	★★★
Convenience	★★★
Scenery	★★★
Eating out	★★★★
Après-ski	★★
Off-slope	★★★

RPI	90
lift pass	£170
ski hire	£95
lessons	£75
food & drink	£120
total	**£460**

NEWS

2012/13: In Le Monêtier, redevelopment of the base area will continue.

2011/12: A new self- and table-service restaurant, the Flocon, opened at Bachas above Le Monêtier. Also at Le Monêtier, a new two-storey restaurant was built at the base, plus a new building to house the crèche.

- ➕ Big, varied mountain offering a sense of travel as you ski
- ➕ Lots of good woodland runs
- ➕ One of the few big French areas based on old villages with character
- ➕ Good-value and atmospheric old hotels, restaurants and chalets
- ➕ Very friendly and welcoming locals

- ➖ Busy road runs through the resorts – through the heart of Le Monêtier
- ➖ A lot of indiscriminate new building took place in the 1960s and 70s
- ➖ Still too many drags and slow chairlifts at altitude
- ➖ Limited nightlife

This is one of our favourite places. It is one of the few French resorts offering the ambience you might look for in a summer holiday – a sort of Provence in the snow, with lots of small family-run hotels and restaurants in old stone buildings. And the slopes are equally distinctive, with the trees reaching appreciably higher altitudes than the Alpine norm. The minus points above shouldn't be ignored – it really is time Serre-Che merited more than ★★ for fast lifts – but we find they are far outweighed by the plus points.

THE RESORT

Serre-Chevalier is made up of a string of villages set on a valley floor, linked by a busy road.

The valley runs roughly north-west to south-east, below the north-east-facing slopes of the mountain range that gives the resort its name. From the north-west – coming over the Col du Lautaret from Grenoble – the three main villages are spread over a distance of 8km – Le Monêtier (or Serre-Che 1500), Villeneuve (1400) and Chantemerle (1350). Finally, at the extreme south-eastern end of the valley, is Briançon (1200) – not a village but a town (the highest in France). As well as the main villages there are nine smaller villages, some of which give their names to the communes: Villeneuve is in the commune of La Salle les Alpes, for example. Confusing? Yes.

The resort is not at all fashionable and there are no 4-star hotels. But there are more hotels here in the modestly priced Logis de France 'club' than in any other ski resort. This is a family resort, and it gets especially busy in the February/March French school holidays.

A six-day area pass (or rather your receipt for that pass) covers a day in each of Les Deux-Alpes, Alpe-d'Huez, Puy-St-Vincent, Montgenèvre/the Milky Way, Sestriere. All of these outings are possible by bus, but are easier by car. The road from Grenoble passes over the Col du Lautaret, which may require chains and is occasionally closed.

VILLAGE CHARM ★★★

Some quaint old parts

Each of the parts of Serre-Chevalier is based on a simple old village, with narrow cobbled streets lined by small shops, cosy bars, hotels and traditional restaurants that give each village a very French feel. Around these older parts there is a lot more modern development ranging in style from brutal to sympathetic. It is not a smart resort in any sense; even the older parts are roughly rustic rather than chocolate-box pretty. (A ban on

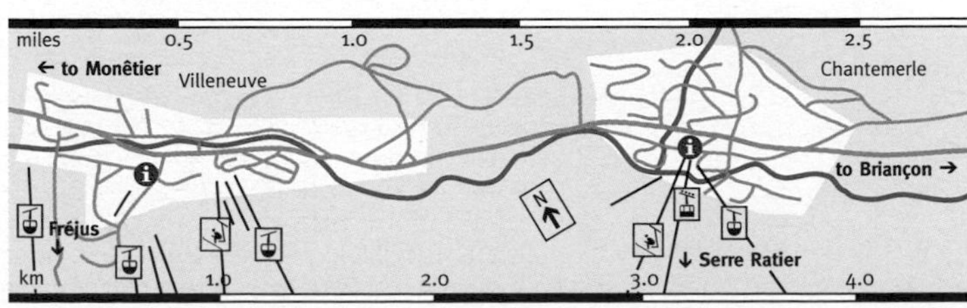

corrugated iron roofs would help.) But when blanketed by snow the older villages and hamlets do have an unpretentious charm, and we find the place as a whole easy to like.

Le Monêtier is the smallest, quietest and most unspoiled of the main villages, with new building which is mostly in sympathetic style. But it is the most seriously affected by traffic – it is bisected by the road to Grenoble, which skirts the other villages; pedestrians stroll about in the road, hoping the cars will avoid them.

Because the resort as a whole is so spread out, the impact of cars and buses is difficult to escape, even if you're able to manage without them yourself. But reporters seem happy to put up with the road and its traffic.

Briançon's 17th-century fortified upper quarter is a delight, with its traditional shops, auberges, pâtisseries and restaurants; it is a UNESCO World Heritage Site. By contrast, the modern functional area around the town's lift station, including good-value lodging and a casino, has little character.

Every year reporters stress how friendly and welcoming the locals are – hardly the norm in France.

CONVENIENCE ★★★★★

Good access but expect a walk

All four main resorts have lift access, either by gondola, cable car or fast chairs, to different parts of the ski area. Briançon has a gondola from the bottom of town; your hotel could be next to it, or miles from it. In Chantemerle the old village is not far from the lifts, but a lot of accommodation is further away across the main road. Villeneuve has quite a

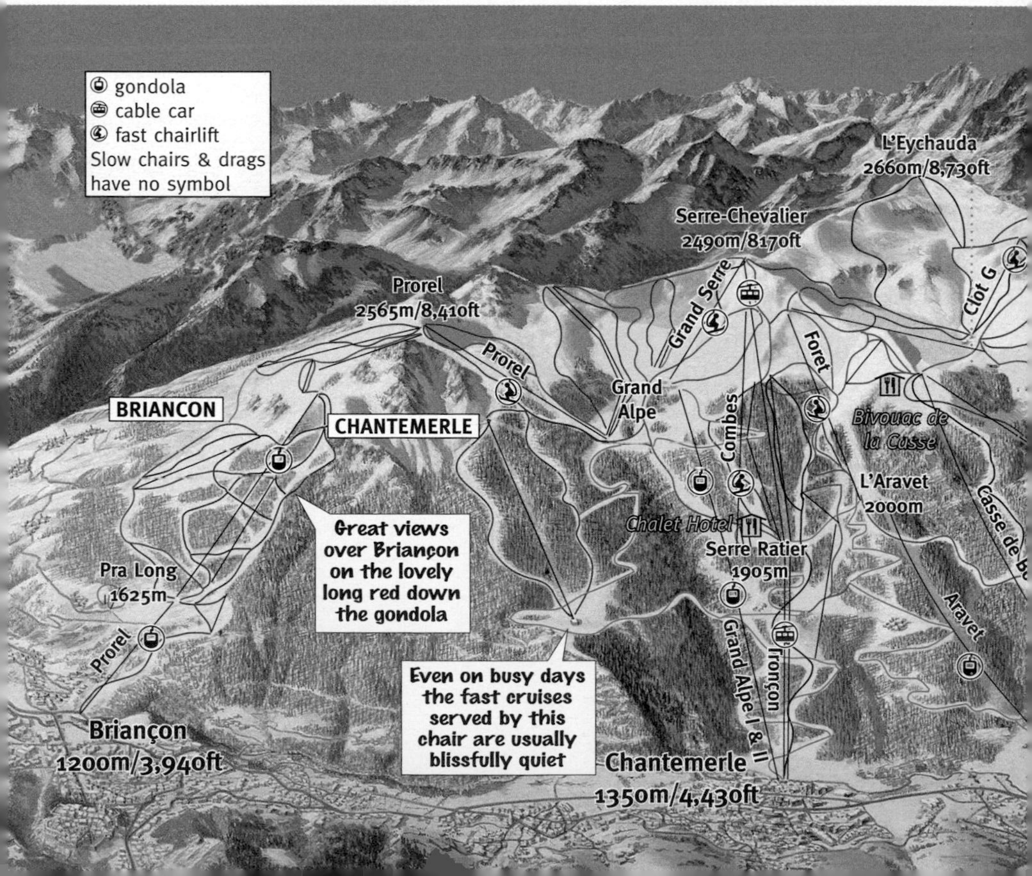

KEY FACTS	
Resort	1200-1500m 3,940-4,920ft
Slopes	1200-2735m 3,940-8,970ft
Lifts	62
Pistes	250km 155 miles
Green	22%
Blue	28%
Red	37%
Black	13%
Snowmaking	154 hectares

Ski a high altitude resort with low prices - see p168

few lodgings close to its multiple access lifts, but the old village is across the valley; if you want to combine character with convenience, consider the nearby hamlet of Le Bez – set between two gondolas. Le Monêtier has one main access lift, reached from the centre by bus or a 10-minute walk (downhill in the morning, uphill at the end of the day and tricky when ice is around). You can leave your gear at the lift base.

Local ski-buses circulate around the villages, and there are valley buses that link all the villages and lift bases (now until 11.30pm).

SCENERY ★★★★★

Great views from the tops

The Serre-Chevalier range is not notably dramatic seen from the valley, though there are great views from Briançon's old town. From the area's high points there are fine views of the rugged 4000m-high Ecrins massif.

THE MOUNTAINS

Trees cover almost two-thirds of the mountain, providing some of France's best bad-weather terrain (we once had a great day here when all the upper lifts were closed by high winds).

Reporters approve of the improved piste signposting – 'We barely looked at the piste map,' says a 2012 reporter. The map is reasonably clear. Piste classification tends to exaggerate difficulty. Many of our 2012 reporters view most blacks as over-rated, and many reds.

EXTENT OF THE SLOPES ★★★★★

Interestingly varied and pretty

Serre-Chevalier's 250km of pistes are spread across four main sectors above the four main villages, and you get a real feeling of travel as you move from one to another.

The sector above **Villeneuve** is the most extensive, reaching back a good way into the mountains and spreading over four or five identifiable bowls. The main mid-station is Fréjus. This sector is linked at altitude and mid-

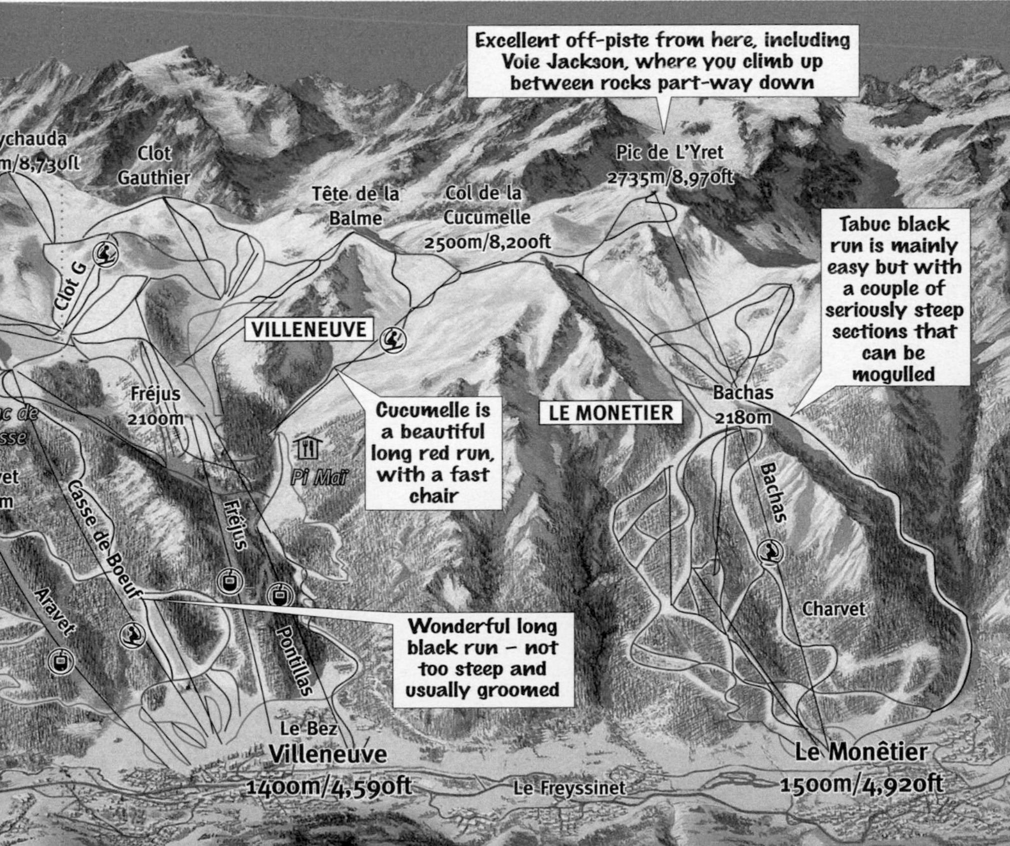
Excellent off-piste from here, including Voie Jackson, where you climb up between rocks part-way down
Clot Gauthier
Tête de la Balme
Col de la Cucumelle 2500m/8,200ft
Pic de L'Yret 2735m/8,970ft
Tabuc black run is mainly easy but with a couple of seriously steep sections that can be mogulled
Clot G
VILLENEUVE
Fréjus 2100m
Cucumelle is a beautiful long red run, with a fast chair
Pi Maï
LE MONETIER
Bachas 2180m
Bachas
Casse de Boeuf
Fréjus
Aravet
Pontillas
Charvet
Wonderful long black run – not too steep and usually groomed
Le Bez
Villeneuve 1400m/4,590ft
Le Freyssinet
Le Monêtier 1500m/4,920ft

↑ Above the Fréjus gondola at Villeneuve are beginner slopes and long green runs to progress to
SNOWPIX.COM / CHRIS GILL

Resort news and key links: www.wheretoskiandsnowboard.com

LIFT PASSES

Prices in €

Age	1-day	6-day
under 12	35	166
12 to 64	43	208
65 plus	33	187

Free under 6, over 75

Beginner limited pass in each area: eg Villeneuve €17

Notes
Briançon, Villeneuve, Chantemerle and Le Monêtier; 6+ days give one day in Les Deux-Alpes, Alpe-d'Huez, Puy-St-Vincent and Milky Way; reductions for families

Alternative passes
Individual areas of Serre-Chevalier

mountain to the slightly smaller **Chantemerle** sector. The onward link from Chantemerle to **Briançon** is over a high, exposed col via a six-pack. In the opposite direction, the link between Villeneuve and **Le Monêtier** was greatly improved in 2010 by the Vallons six-pack up the Cucumelle valley. Skiing from Le Monêtier to Villeneuve involves the red run down this valley, so timid skiers may prefer to use the bus service.

FAST LIFTS ★★★★★
Improvements, but slowly

A range of big lifts gets you out of the valley and progress has been made in upgrading some of the higher lifts. But there are still many old, slow lifts at altitude that hinder progress. In particular, the trio of slow chairs from Bachas at mid-mountain above Le Monêtier lead to complaints, though one view is that they keep the Villeneuve crowds away.

QUEUES ★★★★★
Still some bottlenecks

There are few problems getting out of the villages now, but there can be queues further up. Queues on the way to Le Monêtier have been relieved by the Vallons six-pack. Other bottlenecks include the Fréjus chair above the Pontillas gondola from Villeneuve, the Crêtes draglift it links with and the Côte Chevalier chair from the Villeneuve bowl to Chantemerle.

When the resort gets busy in the French school holidays, head for the slow Aiguillette chair at Chantemerle (see 'For intermediates'). And consider riding the gondolas down to avoid busy home runs.

TERRAIN PARKS ★★★★★
Fully featured

The main parks are easily reached from both Chantemerle and Villeneuve. Legendary ripper Guillaume Chastagnol and the Serre Che Brigade have been improving the parks for several years. The Serre Che snowpark is under the Forêt chair (but has a dedicated draglift). It incorporates about 30 different features (plus chill-out and BBQ area) – clearly marked out in three zones for all levels, including 23 tables, wall ride, rails, boxes and hip jump. A major focus has been placed on the great beginner area – 'My kids had a great time,' says a 2012 reporter. A boardercross accessible by the Grande Serre or Combes lifts is 'good, fast and flowing', says a reporter. The innovative Mélèzone, beside the Champcella draglift features various fun jibs built from larch wood in a wooded setting. There's also a small, fun boardercross near the Rocher Blanc chair.

SNOW RELIABILITY ★★★★★
Good – especially upper slopes

Most slopes face north or north-east and so hold the snow well, especially high up (there are lots of lifts starting at altitudes above 2000m). The slopes above Le Monêtier are high and shady, and often have the best snow. The weather is different from that of the northern Alps, and even that of Les Deux-Alpes or Alpe-d'Huez, over the col to the west. Some upper lifts may be prone to closure by high winds.

Snowmaking covers 75% of the pistes, including long runs down to each village. Piste grooming is generally excellent.

ACTIVITIES

Indoor Swimming pools, sauna, fitness centres, thermal baths, bowling, museums, cinemas, casino, libraries

Outdoor Ice rinks, cleared paths, dog sledding, snowshoeing, skijoring, ice driving, snowmobiling, snowkites, ballooning, paragliding

FOR EXPERTS ★★★★★

Deep, not notably steep

There is plenty to amuse experts – except those wanting extreme steeps. Half a dozen slopes – basically, black runs left ungroomed – are identified as 'brut de neige' areas.

The broad black runs down to Villeneuve (Casse du Boeuf – our favourite) and Chantemerle (Luc Alphand) are only just black in steepness. They are regularly groomed, and great fun for a fast blast, with their gradient sustained over an impressive vertical of around 800m. But one or the other may be closed for days on end for racing or training. The rather neglected Tabuc run, sweeping around the mountain away from the lifts to Le Monêtier, has a couple of genuinely steep pitches (which may be heavily mogulled) but is mainly a cruise. For other steepish runs, look higher up the mountain to slopes served by the two top lifts above Le Monêtier and the three above Villeneuve. The runs beside these lifts – on- and off-piste – form a great playground in good snow.

There are huge amounts of off-piste terrain throughout the area – both high-up and in the trees above Villeneuve and Chantemerle. We've enjoyed the La Voie Jackson run accessed from the Yret chair above Le Monêtier, which includes a short climb between rocks to a deserted open bowl. The Cucumelle valley at the western side of the Villeneuve sector offers plenty of gentle off-piste which is now much easier to exploit with the Vallons chairlift in place.

There are plenty of more serious off-piste expeditions, including: Tête de Grand Pré to Villeneuve or Le Monêtier and Couloir de Roche Corneille to Le Monêtier (both a climb from Cucumelle); off the back of L'Eychauda to Puy-St-André (isolated, beautiful, taxi ride home); l'Yret to Le Monêtier via Vallons de la Montagnolle; Tabuc also to Le Monêtier (steep at the start in a big bowl, very beautiful). The experts' Mecca of La Grave is nearby.

FOR INTERMEDIATES ★★★★★

Ski wherever you like

Serre-Chevalier's slopes ideally suit intermediates, who can buzz around without worrying about nasty surprises on the way. On the trail map red runs far outnumber blues – but most reds are at the easy end of the scale. The broad, open bowls above Grande Alpe and Fréjus offer lots of options. The runs on skier's right on the lower slopes of Le Monêtier are gentle, quiet and wind prettily through the woods.

There's plenty for more adventurous intermediates, though. Cucumelle on the edge of the Villeneuve sector is a beautiful long red that is served by a newish chairlift. The red runs off the little-used slow Aiguillette chair in the Chantemerle sector are worth seeking out – quiet, enjoyable fast cruises. Other favourites include Aya and Clos Galliard at Le Monêtier, and the wonderful long run from the top to the bottom of the gondola at Briançon (with great views of the town).

If the reds are starting to seem a bit tame, there is plenty more to progress to. Unless ice towards the bottom is a problem, the usually well-groomed blacks on the lower mountain should be on the agenda; try them early in the day when they are uncrowded and freshly groomed.

FOR BEGINNERS ★★★★★

All four areas OK

All four sectors have their own nursery areas, and cheap daily lift passes covering a handful of lifts, including access to mid-mountain where appropriate. At Chantemerle you generally go up to Serre Ratier – rated as good by a beginner reporter. At Villeneuve there are several slopes at valley level – all 'lovely' according to a skier having a first go this year at boarding – but also slopes up the Aravet gondola. At Le Monêtier the slopes are at the lift base – tipped by past reporters for 'better snow and fewer people' than elsewhere. There are also easy high runs to progress to in each sector – the best probably the green runs above the Fréjus gondola from Villeneuve. There are green paths from mid-mountain to Chantemerle and Villeneuve, though these may not be enjoyable late in the day when the runs become hard and others are speeding past.

FOR BOARDERS ★★★★
Plenty of scope for experts
The term 'natural playground' could have quite easily been coined in Serre-Chevalier. The slopes are littered with natural obstacles that seem made for confident snowboarders. Try the Cucumelle slope and the areas around the Rocher Blanc lift at Prorel for such terrain. For less expert boarders, the many draglifts can be a problem, as can the flat areas. There's a good terrain park for all abilities and ESI Generation in Chantemerle is a school that offers everything from beginners' lessons to freestyle courses.

FOR CROSS-COUNTRY ★★★
Excellent if the snow is good
There are 35km of tracks along the valley floor, mainly following the gurgling river between Le Monêtier and Villeneuve and going on up towards the Col du Lautaret.

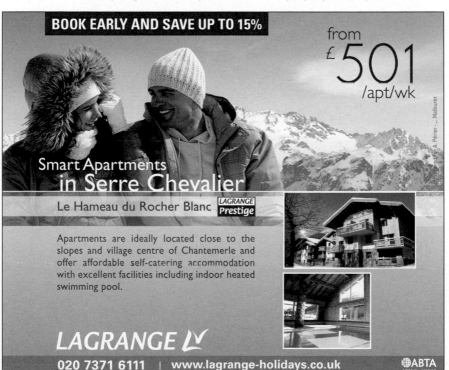

MOUNTAIN RESTAURANTS ★★★★
Some good places
Mountain restaurants are quite well distributed; they are marked on the piste map, but not reliably named.
Editors' choice At the top of the cable car and chair from Chantemerle, Chalet Hotel Serre Ratier (0492 205288) has a delightful large terrace and pretty dining room, good service and delicious food. Two other options are more expensive. Just above the Casse du Boeuf quad from Villeneuve, the Bivouac de la Casse (0492 248772) is an attractive chalet with both self- and table-service (inside and out). We were mightily impressed by both the food

SCHOOLS

ESF In all centres
t 0492 241741

ESI Generation
(Chantemerle)
t 0492 242151

Evasion (Chantemerle)
t 0492 240241

Buissonnière
(Villeneuve)
t 0492 247866

New Generation
t 0479 010318
0844 770 4733 (UK)
www.skinewgen.com

Insight
t 0679 068683

Experience
(Chantemerle)
t 0492 435871

Ski Connections
(Villeneuve)
t 0492 462832

Internationale
(Le Monêtier)
t 0683 670642

Classes (ESF prices)
6 days from €250

Private lessons
From €46 for 1hr

and service, and recent reporters endorse our view ('the owner comes round the tables to check everything is OK'). Shame about the plastic chairs on the terrace though. Pi Maï (0492 248363) in the hamlet of Fréjus is cosy on a bad day and charming on a sunny day, and it offers excellent food such as steaks and tartiflette and 'wholesome soup'.

Worth knowing about The Echaillon, just below the Bivouac, is a lofty chalet with open fire and a table-service section: 'quiche and salad just perfect'. The Bercail, near the top of the Aravet lift, is unusual – you order and pay self-service style, then your food is cooked and delivered to your table. The Aravet in the same area does 'deliciously thin and crispy pizzas – very, very good'. Above Chantemerle, we and a 2012 visitor loved the small table-service Troll – great, good-value food and very jolly service. The Grand Alpe self-service is spacious, and a bit cheaper than most places.

In the Briançon sector, the Pra Long chalet at the gondola mid-station has good views and food in both table- and self-service sections. The little Chalet de Serre Blanc, just down from the top of Prorel, has superb views but gets mixed reports – but 'it's cheap and you get a coffee thrown in', says a 2012 visitor.

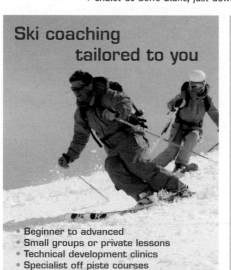

Above Le Monêtier the enlarged but still tiny Peyra Juana near the bottom is appealingly cosy. The self-service Chapka at mid-mountain does 'simple, tasty food' and has a 'welcoming central fire'. Both get packed on bad-weather days. But there's plenty of room at the new Flocons, near the Chapka. We had an excellent table-service lunch on the terrace last season; but despite 'lovely decor', a self-service meal inside was 'disappointing', says a reporter.

SCHOOLS AND GUIDES ★★★★

Choice of good outfits

For years we have been recommending British instructor Gavin Crosby, operating as EurekaSki. Last year he started a branch of another British outfit that is an established reader favourite in other resorts, New Generation. Gavin gets good reports time after time: 'terrific teaching, our Italian instructor helped us progress and built our confidence'; 'fantastic'. Classes with a maximum size of six

↑ In March 2012, with valley temperatures reaching summer heights, snowmaking kept the lower runs open and skiable

SNOWPIX.COM / CHRIS GILL

GUIDES

Montagne Aventure
(Villeneuve)
t 0492 247440

Bureau des Guides
t 0492 247590

Office des Guides
(Villeneuve)
t 0492 247320

Montagne et Ski
(Le Monêtier)
t 0492 244681

CHILDCARE

Les Schtroumpfs
t 0492 247095
9mnth to 5yr

Micro-crèche
t 0492 490086
3mnth to 5yr

Les Poussins
t 0492 240343
From 8mnth

Les Eterlous
t 0492 244575
6mnth to 6yr

EurekaSki
t 0679 462484
from 3mnth, private nannies

Ski school
Snow gardens for ages 3 to 5; from age 5, school classes (ESF 6 half-days €146)

(for adults and children) range from beginner to off-piste adventure. We've skied with Gavin a couple of times, and have been greatly impressed. Book well in advance to avoid disappointment. Meanwhile, Gavin's wife Mel offers a kind of concierge service for visitors under the EurekaSki name – see 'Staying there'.

Another British-run school, Ski Connections, also receives positive reports: 'Had the perfect combination of fun, challenge and learning, a great leap forward.' A 2011 reporter enthuses: 'Their all-inclusive bundle of ski hire, lift pass and lessons was very good value for beginners.'

We have received a number of reports on the Ecole de Ski Buissonnière over the years – most of them full of praise ('very good'). Two absolute beginners in one visitor's group were 'satisfied' with their snowboard lessons with ESI Generation.

A 2011 reporter enjoyed a private lesson with Brit Darren Turner of Insight: 'He was able to cope with a range of abilities and help us all.'

The ESF is improving. A 2011 visitor says, 'unrecognizable from the ESF of yore – English speaking instructors always available', while another found they'd take groups out with 'as few as two students'. And a recent reporter says three groups of kids 'had a great time' in their classes. Local chalet operator Hannibals has reported happy clients with the Chantemerle school. We've had positive feedback on the Internationale school. More reports please.

FOR FAMILIES ★★★
Facilities at each village

Serre Chevalier is popular with French families and there are good family-friendly events and activities. For childcare, Les Schtroumpfs in Villeneuve has been praised in the past. There is a micro-crèche (Les P'tits Loup) in Villeneuve too, taking children from three months to six years. EurekaSki can arrange childcare and private nannies.

STAYING THERE

There is a wide choice of lodging but very little of it has any claim to luxury.

Two resort-based operations EurekaSki (www.eurekaski.com) and Chez Serre Chevalier (www.chezserrechevalier.co.uk) are on hand to simplify life for visitors.

EurekaSki can arrange accommodation, passes, equipment rental, childcare, transfers etc. Chez Serre Chevalier is a tour operator offering accommodation and discounts when booked as a package including catering, transfers, passes, equipment hire, lessons, away days to nearby resorts and après activities.

Chalets Several operators offer catered chalets or chalet hotels. Hannibals has Marmottes, a well-renovated old farmhouse in old Chantemerle, five minutes from the lifts, with rooms all en suite. In Villeneuve, Zenith has two chalets, including the ski-in/ski-out Ridon, and Crystal has three. Inghams is introducing two mid-sized places in good positions here.

Hotels A feature of the resort is the range of attractive family-run hotels – many of them members of the generally reliable Logis de France consortium.

LE MONETIER

*****Auberge de Choucas** (0492 244273) Smart but small wood-clad rooms; serious restaurant. We have enjoyed a stay there.

****Alliey** (0492 244002) 'Excellent food and service.'

****Europe** (0492 244003) Simple well-run Logis in heart of old village, with pleasant bar, good food; rooms renovated in 2011.

VILLENEUVE

*****Christiania** (0492 247633) Civilized, family-run hotel on main road, crammed with ornaments.

****Vieille Ferme** (0492 249426) Stylish conversion on the edge of the village.

Resort news and key links: www.wheretoskiandsnowboard.com

GETTING THERE

Air Turin 120km/75 miles (1hr45); Grenoble 150km/95 miles (2hr45); Lyon 200km/125 miles (3hr15)

Rail Briançon (6km/4 miles); regular buses from station

UK PACKAGES

Action Outdoors, Alpine Answers, Alpsholiday, AmeriCan Ski, Chalet Chez Bear, Chez Serre Chevalier, Club Med, Crystal, Erna Low, Hannibals, Independent Ski Links, Inghams, Interactive Resorts, Lagrange, Neilson, Peak Retreats, Pierre & Vacances, PowderBeds, Rocketski, Ski Expectations, Ski France, Ski-in.co.uk, Ski Independence, Ski Miquel, Ski Solutions, Skitopia, Skitracer, Snow Finders, Snowed Inn Chalets, Thomson, Zenith

Briançon AmeriCan Ski, BoardnLodge, Peak Retreats

Phone numbers

From abroad use the prefix +33 and omit the initial '0' of the phone number

TOURIST OFFICE

www.serre-chevalier.com

***Chatelas** (0492 247474) Prettily decorated simple chalet by river in old part of town.

Maison du Bez (0492 248696) Ski-in/ski-out, traditional, 'quirky, with cosy lounge'. Sauna.

Chantemerle

****Boule de Neige** (0492 240016) In the old centre. Good past reports.

***Ricelle** (0492 240019) Charming, but across the valley from the slopes in Villard-Laté. Good food.

Apartments There is an increasing supply of high-quality residences. In the Lagrange Prestige range is Le Hameau du Rocher Blanc, by the slopes in Chantemerle (pool, gym, sauna, steam). This and L'Adret in Chantemerle (300m from the lifts, with spacious apartments, small indoor-outdoor pool and new two-person sauna) are bookable through Peak Retreats. Pierre & Vacances' well-placed residence Alpaga has been approved by reporters. In Le Monêtier the Arts et Vie is modern, right on the slopes and good value. EurekaSki has a selection of apartments in the Chalets de la Chamossière residence. The hotel Alliey has apartments too.

At altitude Two mountain restaurants have rooms: Pi Maï (0492 248363) and the Chalet Hotel Serre Ratier (0492 205288).

EATING OUT ★★★★☆

Unpretentious and traditional

In Le Monêtier, there are several good hotel-based options. At the upper end, the Maison Alliey (hotel Alliey) has a good reputation, and we've had an excellent dinner at the Auberge du Choucas. The Europe has reliable cooking at more modest prices. Reporter tips include the Brasera (for a pizza), the Kawa and the Belotte – 'good value'.

In Villeneuve, two 2011 reporters recommend the 'atmospheric' Refuge where the Alps Bell (cooking meat on a hot cast-iron bell) is popular. A recent visitor's favourite was the Petit Pont, with 'steaks to die for'. The Frog is Scottish-run. Other reader tips include the Marotte, a tiny stone building with classic French cuisine, the Manouille doing mountain dishes and more ambitious stuff, and the Bidule (seafood/fish) over in Le Bez.

In Chantemerle, we've had delicious dinners at the unpretentious Loup Blanc. Reporters approve, and also like the 'charming' Petit Chalet, 34 (fondue), Cabassa (pizza), Batchi, and the 'cool' Triptyque (traditional French dishes, 'fabulous burgers and crumble to die for').

In Briançon, the Péché Gourmand takes top slot; the location in the new part of town is ordinary, but the prices are accordingly modest. In the old town, tips are Lou Grand Caire (Nepalese specialities), Pied de la Gargouille (open-fire grills) and Valentin ('four courses for 26 euros').

APRES-SKI ★★☆☆☆

Quiet streets and few bars

Nightlife seems to revolve around bars, scattered through the various villages, and some reporters complain that the resort is too quiet.

In Le Monêtier the British-run Bar de l'Alpen has live music, sports TV, free nibbles and welcoming staff. In Villeneuve, head for the Grotte at the foot of the slopes (live music, happy hour and 'good bar food' – later on it 'doubles up as a nightclub'). Loco Loco in the old village is 'a funky little bar' that gets lively too. The Frog is popular with Brits, while the Cocoon has 'a good local atmosphere'. In Chantemerle the Station at the foot of the pistes is popular with Brits – Sky Sports and 'sells bottled real ale'; entertainment every evening; 'pub food is good'. The 'smart' Piano Bar on the main road gets a mention. In Briançon, there's a lively teatime scene (assisted by a happy hour) at the bar next to the gondola; the Eden has been mentioned, and Spirit and Duo are in the old town.

OFF THE SLOPES ★★★☆☆

Try the hot baths

The old town of Briançon is well worth a visit. There is a leisure complex with pools, sauna, hot tub and steam room. Briançon also has an ice hockey team – their games make 'a good night out'. In Le Monêtier there's a large thermal spa complex, Les Grands Bains ('superb tonic for tired limbs'), with indoor and outdoor pools, saunas, steam rooms, a 'chill-out' music grotto and a waterfall (some areas only for the over-18s). The hotel Alliey has a pool and spa. There is a public swimming pool in Villeneuve. Each of the villages has a cinema and an ice rink, and there is good walking on 25km of 'well-prepared trails'. You can learn to drive a piste-basher. Hot air ballooning is available.

Ste-Foy-Tarentaise

Tasteful, modern mini-resort appealing to families and experts – and to motorists as a base for expeditions to nearby mega-resorts

TOP 10 RATINGS

Extent	*
Fast lifts	**
Queues	*****
Snow	***
Expert	****
Intermediate	***
Beginner	**
Charm	***
Convenience	***
Scenery	***

RPI	75
lift pass	£90
ski hire	£90
lessons	£80
food & drink	£120
total	**£380**

NEWS

2011/12: Smart new 4-star apartments, the Etoile des Cîmes, opened, plus a new supermarket and ski hire shop next door.

KEY FACTS

Resort	1550m 5,090ft
Slopes	1550-2620m 5,090-8,600ft
Lifts	7
Pistes	32km 20 miles
Green	6%
Blue	24%
Red	47%
Black	23%
Snowmaking	10 guns

- + Safe untracked powder within the lift system, and epic runs outside it
- + Good base for visits to Val d'Isère/ Tignes, Les Arcs
- + Great value (and the cheapest lift pass of any resort in this book)
- + Quiet, even in peak periods, but ...

- − Too quiet for some visitors; very little après-ski action and very few restaurants
- − Very limited piste network
- − Mainly slow chairlifts with no covers; only one fast quad

Ste-Foy is a small, attractive, unpretentious resort built in the last 10 years, at the foot of what started life as a cult off-piste mountain. It remains excellent for experts but now attracts many others, including families. Keen piste-bashers will want to travel to big resorts nearby – easily done by car.

THE RESORT

Ste-Foy itself is a village straddling the busy road up from Bourg-St-Maurice to Val d'Isère. Its slopes start at Ste-Foy-Station (aka Bonconseil), which is set 4km off the main road. With a car you can visit some excellent restaurants close by and explore nearby resorts – Val d'Isère, Tignes, Les Arcs, La Plagne and La Rosière. Some tour ops organize excursions too. With a Ste-Foy lift pass for five days or more you can buy day passes for these resorts at substantially reduced rates.

Village charm Ste-Foy-Station is a complete resort in miniature, with a limited choice of bars and restaurants, a small supermarket and a newsagent; and these are surrounded by a cluster of chalets and chalet-style apartment blocks, all built in the traditional Savoyard style of wood and stone but without a real central focus. Lots of properties have been bought by Brits and Dutch: 'The atmosphere is very British,' says a recent reporter.

Convenience No accommodation is far from the lifts or nursery slope.

Scenery The Tarentaise mountains give a dramatic backdrop to Ste-Foy's pleasant setting among the trees.

THE MOUNTAIN

There is an attractive mix of wooded slopes above the village and open slopes higher up.

Slopes From the village three successive slow quad chairs take you to the top of the ski area. The first

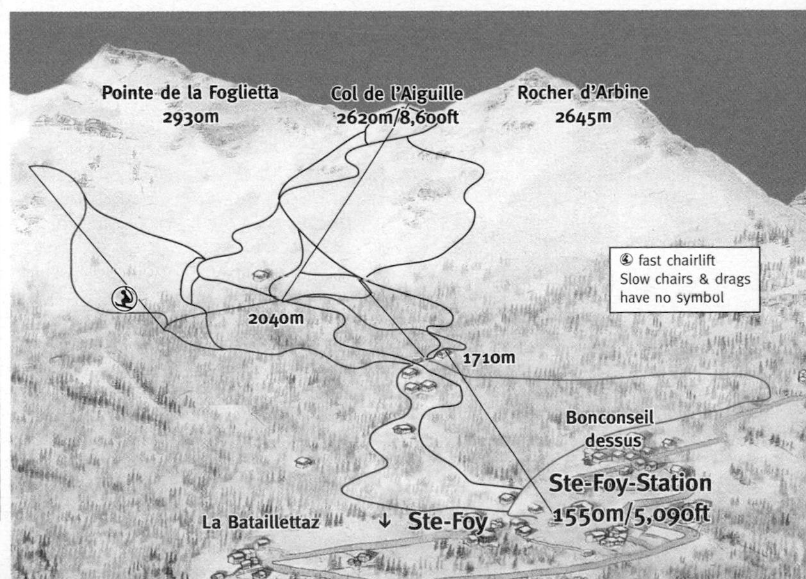

goes to a mid-mountain station with two small restaurants at Plan Bois. A second goes on to the treeline. And the third to the high point of Col de l'Aiguille at 2620m. From here there are slopes of almost 600m vertical above the treeline.

The two black runs here form the basis of two special off-piste zones that are marked but not explained on the piste map; we're told they are avalanche controlled and that the Crystal Dark/Off Tracks one is only open when the snow conditions and the weather are right. Slightly further down the hill is a less steep zone, Shaper's Paradise which has natural jumps and where people can build their own kickers.

The two lower chairs serve a few pleasant runs through trees and back to the base station. A six-pack serves a blue run to the east of the main area. The pistes are 'immaculately groomed', say 2012 visitors.

Fast lifts Just one fast chair.

Queues Despite all the new building and slow lifts, reporters hardly ever find queues at Ste-Foy ('hardly any, even in half-term week', says a 2012 reporter).

Terrain parks There isn't one. But in the Shaper's Paradise area you are encouraged to build kickers and other features.

Snow reliability The slopes face roughly north-west. Snow reliability can suffer on the sunnier bits, but the resort has 10 snowmaking guns that it uses on the blue and red runs down to the resort.

Experts Experts can have great fun on and between Ste-Foy's black and red runs, exploring lots of easily accessible off-piste and trees, including the special zones mentioned above. The lack of crowds means you can still make fresh tracks days after a storm.

There's more serious off-piste on offer too, for which you need a guide. There are wonderful runs from the top of the lifts down through deserted old villages, either to the road up to Val d'Isère or back to the base (via the deserted hamlet of Le Monal). And there's a splendid route down the north face of Foglietta in the next valley to the tiny village of Le Crot.

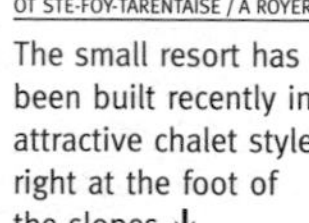
OT STE-FOY-TARENTAISE / A ROYER

The small resort has been built recently in attractive chalet style right at the foot of the slopes ↓

UK PACKAGES

Alpine Answers, Alpine Elements, Alpine Weekends, AmeriCan Ski, Chalet One, Erna Low, Inspired to Ski, Lagrange, Mountain Tracks, Oxford Ski Co, Peak Retreats, PowderBeds, Première Neige, Richmond Holidays, Ski Bespoke, Ski Club Freshtracks, Ski Collection, Ski France, Ski Independence, Ski Weekend, SnowCrazy

Phone numbers
From abroad use the prefix +33 and omit the initial '0' of the phone number

TOURIST OFFICE

www.saintefoy.net

The ESF runs group off-piste trips, with transport back to base and perhaps with lunch in the village of Le Miroir (see 'Eating out').

There's also a Bureau des Guides, which can arrange heli-skiing in Italy, including a route which also brings you back to near Le Miroir.

Intermediates The piste skiing is limited in extent, but you can enjoy 900m vertical of uncrowded reds and blues on the upper slopes above the top of the first chairlift. The red from the Col de l'Aiguille is a superb test for confident intermediates, who would also be up to the off-piste routes, especially the one back to base via Le Monal.

Beginners There are good fenced-off nursery slopes with free moving carpets in the village. You can progress to a long green run off the first chair, then to blues higher up – but they are not the easiest.

Snowboarding It's a great freeriding area, with lots of trees and powder between the pistes to play in, plus the Shaper's Paradise area for building kickers and other features.

Cross-country Go elsewhere. There are no prepared trails here.

Mountain restaurants There are two 'rustic and charming' restaurants near the top of the first chair. Tiny Les Brevettes is cosy but cramped – 'great if you can get in' – while Chez Léon is much more spacious. But many people head back to the base, where the Maison à Colonnes gets good reports.

Schools and guides A 2012 visitor found the ESF 'brilliant'. K Spirit is an alternative school. Mountain guides are 'totally great with huge knowledge of the area', says a 2012 reporter.

Families Les P'tits Trappeurs takes children from age three to 11. UK tour operator Première Neige also runs a nursery, the Cub Club ('nannies were lovely; our kids didn't want to leave'). They also lay on Party Nights such as kids' discos for four to 12 year olds from 6pm to 9pm.

STAYING THERE

Hotels Recommended places: the smartly refurbished Monal (0479 069007) down in Ste-Foy village; tiny, rustic Ferme du Baptieu (0479 069752) just above the village; Auberge sur la Montagne (0479 069583), near the bottom of the access road to Ste-Foy station.

Chalets and apartments Première Neige has a handful of luxurious-looking catered chalets (all with outdoor hot tubs) and lots of smart self-catered apartments and chalets. They also offer a mini-bus service to and from other resorts for a day's skiing there. Peak Retreats has apartments in the smart Etoile des Cîmes and Fermes de Ste-Foy (both with pool, hot tub, sauna, steam, fitness).

Eating out In Ste-Foy-Station the Bergerie does excellent food and Maison à Colonnes served 'one of the best pierrades I can remember', says a recent visitor. In the village of Le Miroir, Chez Merie is excellent (for lunch as well as dinner). In Ste-Foy village, La Grange is very highly rated by a regular reporter.

Après-ski Pretty quiet. Reporters have enjoyed the Iceberg piano bar. The Pitchouli is the place to go for a drink later on. The bar of the hotel Monal can get busy, too; tastings are held in the cellar wine bar there.

Off the slopes There's little to do off the slopes, but snowshoeing and dog sledding are available. The pool/spa at the Balcons de Ste-Foy apartments are open to non-residents for a fee.

SNOWPIX.COM / CHRIS GILL

St-Martin-de-Belleville

Explore the Trois Vallées from a traditional old village – and so avoid the Méribel crowds who descend on it for lunch

TOP 10 RATINGS

Extent	*****
Fast lifts	****
Queues	****
Snow	***
Expert	****
Intermediate	*****
Beginner	**
Charm	****
Convenience	***
Scenery	***

RPI 100

lift pass	£200
ski hire	£105
lessons	£70
food & drink	£120
total	**£495**

KEY FACTS

Resort	1400m 4,590ft
Trois Vallées	
Slopes	1260-3230m 4,130-10,600ft
Lifts	173
Pistes	600km 373 miles
Green	16%
Blue	40%
Red	34%
Black	10%
Snowmaking	2162 guns
Les Menuires / St-Martin only	
Slopes	1400-2850m 4,590-9,350ft
Lifts	34
Pistes	160km 99 miles
Green	16%
Blue	46%
Red	30%
Black	8%
Snowmaking	418 guns

+ Attractively developed traditional village with pretty church
+ Access to the whole Trois Vallées
+ Long, easy intermediate runs on rolling local slopes
+ Extensive snowmaking keeps runs open in poor conditions, but ...

– Snow on runs to the resort suffers from afternoon sun, and altitude
– No green runs for novices
– Some lodging a long trek from the lifts – transport needed
– Limited village facilities and diversions

St-Martin is a lived-in, unspoiled village with an old church (prettily lit at night), small square and buildings of wood and stone, a few miles down the valley from Les Menuires. As a quiet, relatively inexpensive, attractive base for exploration of the Trois Vallées it's unbeatable. But it is quiet.

THE RESORT

St-Martin was a backwater farming village until the 1980s, when chairlifts linked it to the slopes of Méribel and Les Menuires.

Village charm St-Martin is a pleasant old village, set on a steep slope, with its extensive modern developments all in traditional style. The main feature remains the lovely 16th-century church – prettily floodlit at night.

Convenience The village core is small, but some lodgings are quite a way from the lifts. The main lift is above the centre, but a draglift from the village square accesses it. There are some good local shops and a few 'touristy' ones.

Scenery St-Martin has one of the more attractive locations in the valley, set among quiet, lightly wooded slopes.

THE MOUNTAINS

The whole of the Trois Vallées can easily be explored from here. Our piste map in the Les Menuires chapter covers the local St-Martin slopes.

Slopes A gondola followed by a (very long) fast quad (a cold ride in the mornings) take you to a ridge from which you can access Méribel on one side and Les Menuires on the other.

Fast lifts Fast lifts get you into the slopes of Les Menuires or Méribel.

Queues Queues at the village gondola are not unknown.

Terrain parks None locally, but you can get to those above Les Menuires and Méribel relatively easily.

Snow reliability The local slopes get the full force of the afternoon sun, and the village is quite low. The home run is kept open by snowmaking to the

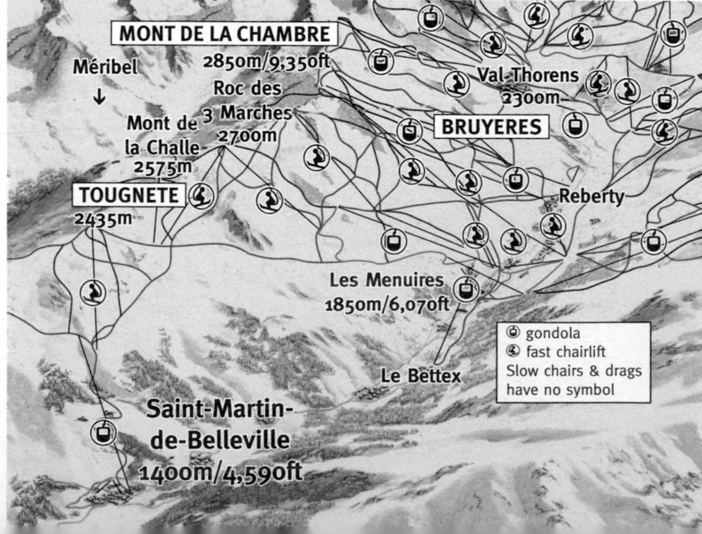

NEWS

2011/12: The home run was modified: an easier alternative now bypasses the tricky section just above the mid-station. The 3-star Alp hotel was refurbished. The 2-star Michelin restaurant La Bouitte expanded its dining area and added two more bedrooms.

bottom, but conditions are often poor.
Experts Locally there are large areas of gentle and often deserted off-piste. The descent from Roc de Fer to the village of Béranger is recommended. Head to La Masse for steep slopes.
Intermediates The local slopes are pleasant blues and reds, mainly of interest to intermediates. Things improved on the main blue home run for 2011/12 with the addition of an easier alternative section of piste above the mid-station to avoid the steep, narrow, often icy and congested section. Of course you can still take the alternative route of using the Méribel lifts to access the Verdet blue – an easy cruise, usually very quiet. One of our favourite runs is the rolling, wide Jerusalem red.
Beginners Not ideal – there's a small nursery slope but no long green runs to progress to. The blue run down the gondola is fairly gentle, though.
Snowboarding There is some great local off-piste freeriding available.
Cross-country There are 28km of trails in the Belleville valley.
Mountain restaurants Reporters love the Grand Lac (read the Les Menuires chapter). There are three atmospheric

old places to try lower on the home run: the reliable Loy ('friendly staff, good meals'), Chardon Bleu ('excellent plat du jour') and the small, woody Corbeleys. Just above the village is the Ferme de la Choumette (read 'Eating out').
Schools and guides Reports on ESF lessons are generally positive. A potential problem is that when demand is low you may have to go to Les Menuires to find a class of the right level. Instructors operating here and in Les Menuires under the startling name of Ski School offer private lessons only in English, and are reported to be 'really good'.

OT LES MENUIRES / R CASTEL

St-Martin is a pretty old village that has been expanded with buildings in traditional style ↓

UK PACKAGES

Alpine Answers, Alpine Club, Carrier, Crystal, Erna Low, Independent Ski Links, Kaluma, Oxford Ski Co, Peak Pursuits, Peak Retreats, PowderBeds, Ski Alpage, Ski Amis, Ski Bespoke, Ski France, Ski Independence, Skitracer, Snow Finders

Phone numbers
From abroad use the prefix +33 and omit the initial '0' of the phone number

TOURIST OFFICE

www.st-martin-belleville.com

British-run New Generation started operating here in 2011/12, and a regular reporter's husband was 'very satisfied' with his lesson.
Families One of our regular reporters on St-Martin has five children and seems to find it near-ideal, not least because it is so small and safe. Piou Piou club at the ESF takes children from 18 months to five years old. There are babysitters.

STAYING THERE

For a small village there's a good variety of accommodation.
Chalets The Brit-run Alpine Club (not really a club) has two luxurious chalets in the quiet hamlet of Villarabout, one newly built in traditional style with a double-height, open-plan living room and the other a beautifully converted, 100-year-old farmhouse with spectacular views. We've had good reports on food and service and there's a minibus service until 10pm daily. Peak Pursuits has a completely refurbished farmhouse a few minutes' drive from St-Martin that is family-friendly and has old beams, a vaulted dining room, open log fire and an outdoor hot tub. They run a minibus to and from the slopes.
Hotels There are several 3-stars, on which we lack recent reports. The Alp hotel (0479 089282), in pole position by the gondola, was refurbished by its new owners for 2011/12.
Apartments The stylish residence Chalets du Gypse is well placed beside the piste above the village, with a smart pool, hot tubs etc; available through Peak Retreats (which also has luxurious chalets in the next village of St-Marcel with hot tub and minibus transfers to and from the slopes). Ski Amis has an appetizing range of properties, mostly very central.
Eating out There is a good choice for a small village, no doubt due in part to the healthy lunchtime trade. The Montagnard, on the snow, is an atmospheric converted barn doing a good range of dishes. The Lachenal is a simple hotel that suffers from changing hands quite frequently (but does 'excellent lamb', says a reporter). The Voûte is still recommended for pizza and more serious dishes ('a faultless steak au poivre'). The Eterlou does 'great grills'. The Billig is a crêperie that also does 'a good-value plat du jour'. The Etna is a 'cheap and cheerful Italian', recommended in 2012 by a St Martin regular. The Ferme de la Choumette, slightly out of the village, is a working farm and cheesery – 'delicious food'. The Ferme Auberge Chantacoucou in Le Chatelard is similar, but we're told it's 'even better'. The Bouitte, up the road in St-Marcel, has two Michelin stars; we and a reporter had splendid meals there in 2011; yes, it is very expensive.
Après-ski Choice is limited. The Dahlia, at the bottom of the gondola, is popular for après-ski drinks. Pourquoi Pas? has live music; but for quiet evening drinks try Bar Joker or Billig.
Off the slopes Options are limited. The village has a sports hall, an 'excellent' museum with 'comprehensive audio guide in English' and free concerts in the church. And there's dog sledding, snowshoe trips, pleasant walks and a torchlit tour of the village. Pedestrians can ride lifts to and from Méribel.

JM GOUEDARD

La Tania

A well-placed budget base for the slopes of Courchevel and Méribel – and a pleasant place, with a good choice of catered chalets

TOP 10 RATINGS	
Extent	*****
Fast lifts	****
Queues	****
Snow	***
Expert	****
Intermediate	*****
Beginner	***
Charm	***
Convenience	****
Scenery	***

RPI	100
lift pass	£200
ski hire	£115
lessons	£85
food & drink	£120
total	**£520**

NEWS

2011/12: The new crèche and medical centre opened.

- ➕ Part of the Trois Vallées, with good access to Courchevel and Méribel
- ➕ Long runs through woods to the village: a great place in a storm
- ➕ Attractive, small, traffic-free village
- ➕ Much improved snowmaking but ...

- ➖ At this altitude, snowmaking is vital
- ➖ Limited village diversions
- ➖ Village nursery slope gets through-traffic (but higher one does not)
- ➖ Remote from the Trois Vallées' highest and most snow-sure slopes

La Tania is a good-value, family-friendly base from which to explore the slopes of its swanky neighbours, Courchevel and Méribel. Trips to the far end of the huge Trois Vallées are possible, but it is hardly the ideal starting point.

It is a purpose-built resort, and at 1350m about the lowest you'll find; its wood-clad buildings sit comfortably in a pretty woodland setting – quite a contrast to the bleakness of classic French ski stations.

THE RESORT

La Tania is set just off the minor road linking Le Praz (aka Courchevel 1300) to Méribel. Free buses go to Courchevel (but not Méribel). For evenings on the town, Méribel is slightly nearer than Courchevel 1850.

Village charm The village has grown into a quiet, attractive, car-free collection of mainly ski-in/ski-out chalets and apartments. There are a few lively bars and restaurants, but nightlife is still relatively low-key.

Convenience It's a small place – you can walk around the village in a couple of minutes – but big enough to have all the basic amenities (except a pharmacy). A gondola from one end of the village leads up into the slopes, and you should be able to ski back to a point close to your doorstep. And the lower nursery slope is central.

Scenery The resort is prettily set among the trees. But Col de la Loze makes a better viewpoint.

THE MOUNTAINS

The slopes immediately above La Tania and nearby Le Praz are wooded, and about the best place in the Trois Vallées to be in bad weather. Above mid-mountain, the slopes are open.

Slopes The gondola out of the village goes to Praz-Juget. From here draglifts go on up to Chenus or to Loze and the slopes above Courchevel 1850, and a fast quad goes to the link with Méribel via Col de la Loze. From all these points, varied, interesting intermediate runs take you back into the La Tania sector.

KEY FACTS

Resort	1350m 4,430ft
Trois Vallées	
Slopes	1260-3230m 4,130-10,600ft
Lifts	173
Pistes	600km 373 miles
Green	16%
Blue	40%
Red	34%
Black	10%
Snowmaking	2162 guns
Courchevel/ La Tania only	
Slopes	1260-2740m 4,130-8,990ft
Lifts	55
Pistes	150km 93 miles
Green	16%
Blue	38%
Red	37%
Black	9%
Snowmaking	44%

Fast lifts Our rating is for the whole Courchevel area lift system. The lifts above La Tania are not great – the gondola is not super-quick, and the alternatives are long draglifts that are labelled 'difficile'.

Queues The slopes above La Tania are relatively crowd-free, but there may be morning queues for the village gondola in peak season. The problem seems to be that it opens just in time for the ski school to pour on to it through their priority couloir, leaving everyone else waiting ('up to 30 minutes', said a February visitor).

Terrain parks There is no local terrain park or half-pipe, but you can get to Courchevel's 'Family Park' fairly easily.

Snow reliability Good snow-cover down to Praz-Juget is usual all season. Snowmaking covers the green run and the whole of the blue run back to the village; if, despite this, the runs are icy in the afternoon, you have the option of riding the gondola down.

Experts The mountainside above La Tania is steep enough to be interesting without being scary. The Dou des Lanches chairlift serves a lot of good off-piste terrain as well as an easy black piste. The Jean Blanc and Jockeys blacks from Loze to Le Praz are challenging more because of length than gradient.

Intermediates There are two lovely, long, undulating intermediate runs back through the trees to La Tania – though there's little difference in gradient between the blue and the red, and timid intermediates may want to use the Plan Fontaine green. On the higher slopes you have a choice of three or four pistes. Both the red Lanches and the black Dou des Lanches are excellent and challenging (the latter is often groomed). The Crêtes blue run and associated slow chair form an excellent, underused area for building confidence – high, sunny, with good snow.

Beginners There is a good beginner area and lift right in the village, and children are well catered for. But there's a lot of through-traffic on the

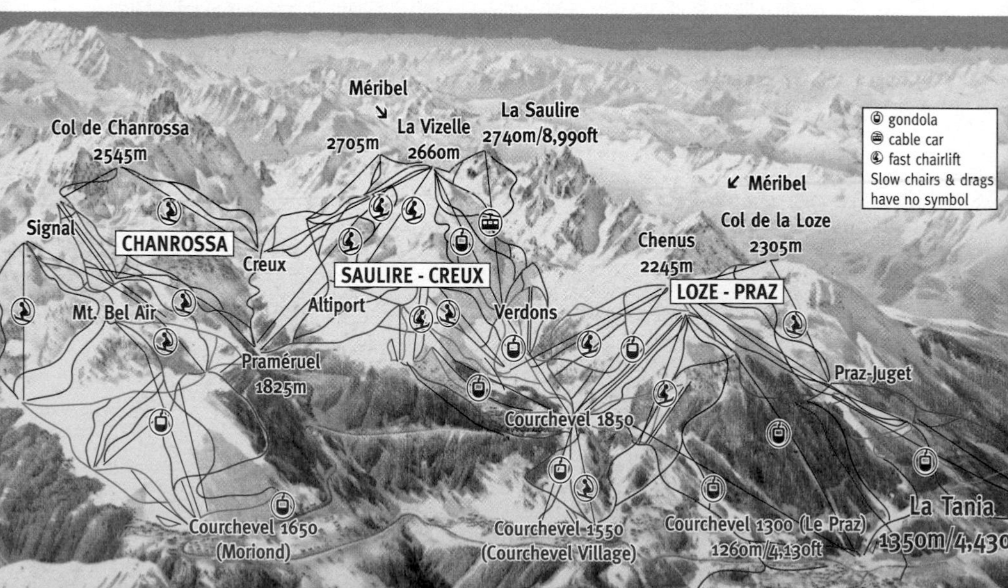

The shops, bars and restaurants are off to the left of this pic, and the gondola up to mid-mountain starts just under the bridge →

OT LA TANIA

main slope. There's now a more snow-sure area at the top of the gondola (Praz-Juget) with access to the Plan Fontaine green run to the village – a long, easy slope to progress to. This is an excellent arrangement; but the step up to the blue run back to the village is quite a big one.

Snowboarding It's easy to get around on boarder-friendly gondolas and chairlifts, avoiding drags.

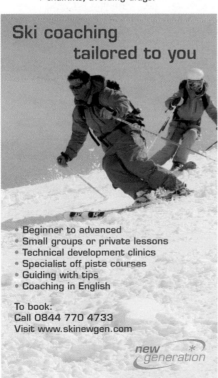

Cross-country There are 65km of trails in the Courchevel/La Tania area, many of them through the woods.

Mountain restaurants Bouc Blanc (0479 088026), near the top of the gondola out of La Tania, is a favourite – and much cheaper than Courchevel alternatives. It has friendly table-service in a wood-clad dining room, good food (reliable plat du jour) and wine (good-value pichets) and a big terrace. We've had our editorial team Christmas lunches there for the last two years, and editor Watts had two excellent meals there in March 2012. Reporters regularly endorse our view, but occasionally find service stretched. The tiny Roc Tania, up at Col de la Loze, is very pretty inside.

Schools and guides Reports of the ESF vary. Highly regarded British school New Generation gets excellent reports from its La Tania branch: '10/10: our instructor was the best I have come across. Attention to detail was superb – puts my experiences with ESF to shame,' enthuses a 2012 visitor. Another says: 'Absolutely fabulous – progressed from almost a beginner to lessons on a black.' Magic Snowsports delivered the goods for a family a couple of seasons ago: 'Kids loved the lessons, and they changed the groups over the first two days to make sure groups were of a similar standard.'

Families La Tania is popular with families looking for a quiet and convenient base, and a child-friendly atmosphere – 'excellent for our three-family group of 14, which included all ability levels'. Chez Nounours kindergarten takes both skiing and non-skiing children from three years

Resort news and key links: www.wheretoskiandsnowboard.com

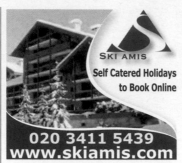

UK PACKAGES

Alpine Action, Alpine Answers, Crystal, Erna Low, Family Friendly Skiing, Independent Ski Links, Interactive Resorts, Lagrange, Le Ski, Nick Ski, Oxford Ski Co, Peak Retreats, Pierre & Vacances, PowderBeds, Silver Ski, Ski Amis, Ski Beat, Ski-Dazzle, Ski Deep, Ski Expectations, Ski France, Ski Hame, Ski Independence, Ski Line, Ski Magic, Ski Power, Ski Solutions, Skitracer, Ski Weekend, Skiweekends.com, Snoworks, Thomson

Phone numbers
From abroad use the prefix +33 and omit the initial '0' of the phone number

TOURIST OFFICE

www.latania.com

old. The Jardin des Neiges takes skiing children from the age of four. UK tour operators Le Ski and Ski Beat both operate nurseries. A list of babysitters (for children over six months old) is available from the tourist office.

STAYING THERE

Chalets There are lots of catered chalets here, mostly dotted around in the woods above the resort centre. Ski Amis has seven chalets sleeping from eight to 28 and all except one with outdoor hot tubs – we stayed in the premium service Chalets Elliot (East and West combined) last December and loved them. Major Courchevel operator Le Ski has three chalets here; a small one in a great piste-side location, and two largish ones that are particularly child-friendly, with family rooms – and they run a large crèche. Alpine Action has three smart chalets near the centre, two with outdoor hot tubs. Crystal has a 16-bed chalet.
Hotels The Montana (0479 088008) is a 'good value, comfortable and friendly' slope-side 3-star next to the gondola, with sauna and fitness club.
Apartments There are plenty of options from the major French specialist agencies – Peak Retreats, Lagrange, Erna Low. Ski Amis has a broad range of properties. Pierre & Vacances has three residences including the recently refurbished Christiania and Britania. There is a deli, bakery and small supermarket.
Eating out There's no doubt that the favourite among our reporters is the Taïga, over the road from the main village: 'popular, busy, very good'; 'fish soup outstanding'; 'friendly'; 'reasonably priced'; 'a serious chef'. The Ski Lodge does good-value fast food. The Marmottons is popular and 'reasonably priced'. We've had an excellent meal at the Michelin-starred Farçon, but the bill was a bit shocking. It feels a bit out of place here, frankly.
Après-ski It's quite lively at close of play, but again the choice is limited. The Ski Lodge has long been the focal après-ski place and has live bands – 'lively', 'friendly', 'cheapest for a beer'. The Chrome bar has regular live music. For a quieter time, the hotel Montana bar is worth trying.
Off the slopes The place is very small and limited. However, tobogganing, snowshoeing, dog sledding and paragliding are possibilities. The hotel Montana has a fitness club with a swimming pool. There are some cleared paths and snowshoe routes. Non-skiers can go up the gondola or take the bus to Courchevel to meet skiing friends for lunch.

SNOWPIX.COM / CHRIS GILL

Tignes

Stark apartment blocks and a bleak, treeless setting are the prices you pay for the high, snow-sure slopes and varied terrain

RATINGS

The mountains	
Extent	*****
Fast lifts	***
Queues	****
Terrain p'ks	***
Snow	*****
Expert	*****
Intermediate	*****
Beginner	**
Boarder	*****
X-country	***
Restaurants	***
Schools	****
Families	***
The resort	
Charm	*
Convenience	****
Scenery	***
Eating out	****
Après-ski	***
Off-slope	**

RPI	100
lift pass	£190
ski hire	£105
lessons	£80
food & drink	£135
total	**£510**

NEWS

2012/13: The old village of Tignes-les-Boisses is being redeveloped on a big scale and rebranded Tignes 1800. The first phase is due to open at the end of 2013.

Tignespace, a sports hall / conference centre / concert hall in Le Lac, is to be completely revamped.

2011/12: The Campanules hotel in Le Lac was upgraded from a 3-star to a 4-star. Le Jhana, a new 4-star residence, opened in Val Claret.

- + Good snow guaranteed for a long season – about the best Alpine bet
- + One of the best areas in the world for lift-served off-piste runs
- + Huge amount of varied terrain, with swift access to Val d'Isère
- + Lots of accommodation close to the slopes
- + Efforts to make the resort villages more welcoming are paying off

- − Resort architecture not to everyone's taste (including ours)
- − Bleak, treeless setting with many lifts prone to closure by storms
- − Still a few long, slow chairlifts
- − Beginners need an area pass to get to long green runs
- − Limited, but improving, après-ski

The appeal of Tignes is simple: good snow, spread over a wide area of varied terrain shared with Val d'Isère. The altitude of Tignes is crucial: a forecast of 'rain up to 2000m' means 'fresh snow down to village level in Tignes' (or at least to Tignes 2100, as they are now trying to rebrand the main resort).

We prefer to stay in Val, which is a more human place. But in many ways Tignes 2100 makes the better base: appreciably higher, more convenient, surrounded by intermediate terrain, with quick access to the Grande Motte glacier. And the case gets stronger as the resort tries to make the place more attractive and as more traditional chalet-style buildings appear.

The lift system has improved, too, with a burst of fast chairs on the western side of the Tignes bowl a few years ago. But investment has stalled since then, and there are still a few key links that need upgrading.

THE RESORT

Tignes was created before the French discovered the benefits of making purpose-built resorts look acceptable. But things are improving, and the villages are gradually acquiring a more traditional look and feel.

Tignes-le-Lac is the hub of the resort and is itself split into two sub-resorts: Le Rosset and Le Bec-Rouge. It's at the point where these two meet – a snowy pedestrian area, with valley traffic passing through a tunnel beneath – that the lifts are concentrated: a powerful gondola towards Tovière and Val d'Isère and a fast six-pack up the western slopes. There is also a suburb built on the lower slopes known as Les Almes. A nursery slope separates Le Rosset from the fourth component part, the group of apartment blocks called Le Lavachet, below which there are good fast lifts up both sides.

Val Claret is 2km up the valley, beyond the lake. From there, fast chairs head up to the western slopes, towards Val d'Isère and to the Grande Motte. An underground funicular also accesses the Grande Motte.

Beside the road along the valley to the lifts is a ribbon of development in traditional style, named Grande Motte (after the peak). Val Claret is built on two levels, which are linked by a couple of (unreliable) indoor elevators, stairs and hazardous paths.

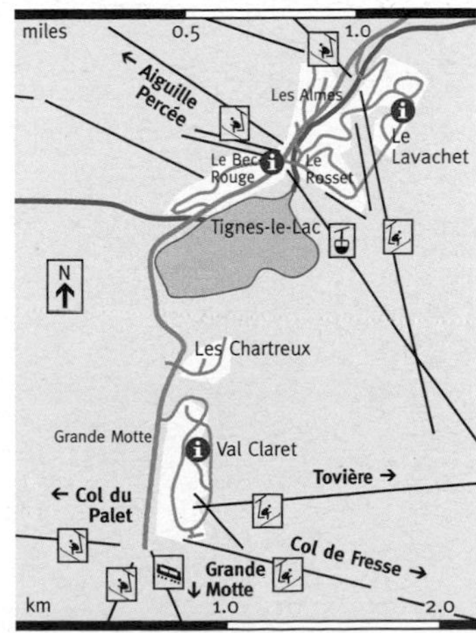

Down the valley from the main villages (which are becoming known as Tignes 2100) are two smaller places. Tignes-les-Boisses, quietly set in the trees beside the road up, is in the process of a 150-million euro redevelopment, with a new MGM eco-resort being built. It is being rebranded Tignes 1800 and is due to be complete by the end of 2014. Tignes-les-Brévières is a renovated old village at the lowest point of the slopes – a favourite lunch spot, and a friendly place to stay (but there's no bus service with the other Tignes 'villages').

VILLAGE CHARM ★★★★★
Functional, not fancy

Some of Tignes-le-Lac's smaller original eyesore buildings in the central part have been successfully revamped in chalet style. But the place as a whole is dreary, and the blocks overlooking the lake from Le Bec-Rouge will remain monstrous until the day they are demolished. A recent reporter described the architecture as 'absolutely hideous – in a way, it is so hideous that it is quite wonderful'. But some attractive new buildings have been added, both in the centre and on the fringes. The main part of Val

KEY FACTS

Resort	2100m 6,890ft
Espace Killy	
Slopes	1550-3455m 5,090-11,340ft
Lifts	79
Pistes	300km 186 miles
Green	15%
Blue	42%
Red	26%
Black	17%
Snowmaking	974 guns
Tignes only	
Slopes	1550-3455m 5,090-11,340ft
Lifts	47
Pistes	150km 93 miles

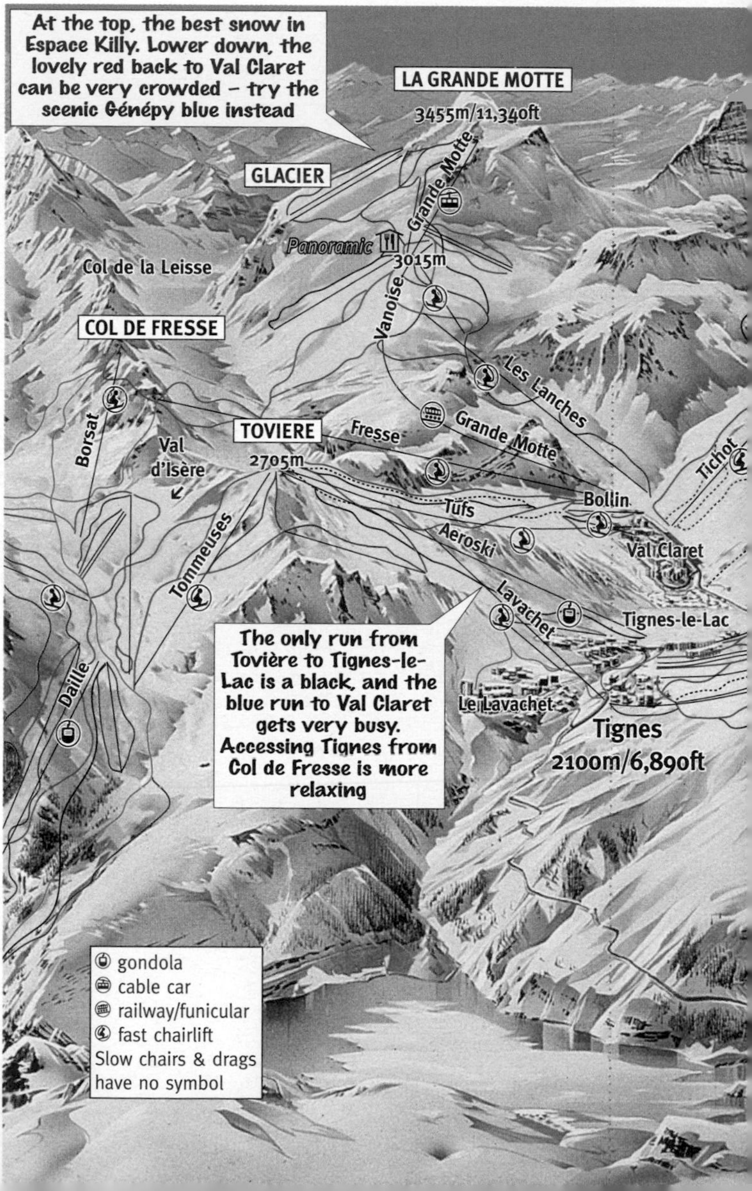

At the top, the best snow in Espace Killy. Lower down, the lovely red back to Val Claret can be very crowded – try the scenic Génépy blue instead

LA GRANDE MOTTE 3455m/11,340ft
GLACIER
Panoramic
3015m
Grande Motte
Col de la Leisse
Vanoise
COL DE FRESSE
Les Lanches
Grande Motte
Fresse
TOVIERE 2705m
Borsat
Val d'Isère
Tichot
Bollin
Tufs
Aeroski
Val Claret
Tommeuses
Lavachet
Tignes-le-Lac
Daille
Le Lavachet
Tignes 2100m/6,890ft

The only run from Tovière to Tignes-le-Lac is a black, and the blue run to Val Claret gets very busy. Accessing Tignes from Col de Fresse is more relaxing

gondola
cable car
railway/funicular
fast chairlift
Slow chairs & drags have no symbol

Claret, Centre, is an uncompromisingly 1960s-style development on a shelf above the valley floor.

So, if it's more charm you seek, stay in Les Brévières.

CONVENIENCE ★★★★
Good all rounder

Location isn't crucial, as a regular, free, 24-hour bus service (praised by reporters) connects all the villages except Les Brévières – but during the day the route runs along the bottom of Val Claret, leaving Val Claret Centre residents with a climb.

A lift or ski run is never more than a few minutes' walk away in Le Lac. 'Convenience was the main reason we chose to go to Tignes for our holiday this year, and we were not disappointed,' said a 2012 visitor.

SCENERY ★★★
Great from the glacier

Tignes is in a high, bleak, treeless bowl; when the sun shines, the rugged mountain terrain is splendid, especially from the glacial heights of the Grande Motte – feels like you're on 'top of the world'.

NDE MOTTE
n/11,340ft

Scenic, not very difficult off-piste runs to Champagny and Peisey-Nancroix start here (a guide is essential)

Col des Ves
2840m
COL DU PALET
2695m
Grattalu
L'AIGUILLE PERCÉE
2750m
Les Lanches
Grande Motte
Tichot
Merles
Bollin
Val Claret
Le Sol
Tignes-le-Lac
Lavachet
Palafour
Chaudannes
Le Lavachet
Tignes
2100m/6,890ft

The Sache is our favourite black run (so long as it's not top-to-bottom bumps): 1200m vertical down a secluded valley

Major new 'village' being developed here – completion due in 2014

Boisses
Sache
Les Boisses
1850m
Tignes 1800
Tignes-les-Brévières
1550m/5,090ft

LIFT PASSES

Espace Killy

Prices in €

Age	1-day	6-day
under 14	36	181
14 to 64	45	226
65 plus	36	181

Free under 5, over 75

Beginner five free lifts

Notes
Covers Tignes and Val d'Isère; half-day and pedestrian passes; family discounts; 5-day+ passes valid for a day in the Three Valleys and a day in Paradiski (La Plagne-Les Arcs); 2-day+ pass gives free access to pool and ice rink

Alternative passes
Tignes only

THE MOUNTAINS

The area's great weakness is that it can become unusable in bad weather. There are no woodland runs except immediately above Tignes 1800 and Tignes-les-Brévières. Heavy snow produces widespread avalanche risk, and wind closes the higher chairs.

Piste classification here isn't perfect, but it is more reliable than in Val d'Isère, and signposting is clear – 'extremely helpful during poor visibility'. But we've had complaints that lift and piste closing time information is unreliable (and sometimes different on the piste map and at the lift).

EXTENT OF THE SLOPES ★★★★★

High, snow-sure and varied

Tignes and Val d'Isère share a huge area of slopes known as L'Espace Killy. Locally, Tignes' biggest asset is the **Grande Motte** – and the runs from, as well as on, the glacier. An underground funicular from Val Claret whizzes you up to over 3000m in seven minutes. There are blue, red and black runs to play on up here, as well as beautiful long runs back to the resort.

The main lifts towards Val d'Isère are efficient: a high-capacity gondola from Le Lac to **Tovière**, and a fast chair from Val Claret to **Col de Fresse**. You can head back to Tignes from either: the return from Tovière to Tignes-le-Lac is via a steep black run, but there are easier blue runs to Val Claret.

Going up the opposite side of the valley takes you to a quieter area of predominantly east-facing slopes split into two main sectors, linked in both directions – **Col du Palet** and the **Aiguille Percée**. Several years ago, this whole mountainside was at last given some of the fast lifts it had needed for years – but investment has stalled and some chairs still need modernizing. These include the Col des Ves chair, at the south end of the Col du Palet sector, which serves one of the nine 'naturides' (see 'For experts'). You can descend from the Aiguille Percée to Tignes-les-Brévières or Tignes 1800 on blue, red or black runs. There are efficient gondolas back (including one built a couple of seasons ago from Tignes 1800), but the chairs above them are old and slow and much in need of upgrading.

FAST LIFTS ★★★

Improved but not good enough

Fast chairs and gondolas get you up the mountain from most parts of the resort. And there are some fast chairs higher up, too. But a few key slow ones remain that could do with being upgraded (including the chairs mentioned above and the one to the Aiguille Percée above Tignes-le-Lac).

QUEUES ★★★★

Very few

Even in February half-term, readers last season experienced very few queues. But if snow low down is poor, the Grande Motte funicular can generate queues; the fast chairs in parallel with it are often quicker, despite the longer ride time. These lifts jointly shift a lot of people, with the result that the red run down to Val Claret can be unpleasantly crowded (the roundabout Génépy blue is a much quieter option). The worst queues now are for the cable car on the glacier – half-hour waits are common. Of course, if higher lifts are closed by heavy snow or high winds, the lifts on the lower slopes have big queues. Otherwise there are usually very few problems; crowded pistes can be more of an issue.

↑ The scenery is pretty good when the sun is out; but the 'villages' aren't a pretty sight

OT TIGNES / MONICA DALMASSO

TERRAIN PARKS ★★★

X Games standard but...

Tignes was one of the first French resorts to build a terrain park and will be hosting its fourth successive European Winter X Games from 20 to 22 March 2013. The Swatch Snowpark is beneath the Grattalu chair on Col du Palet and has rails and kickers split into green, blue and red levels, plus a boardercross course and a free airbag jump. In the summer the park doubles in size and moves up to the Grande Motte for freestyle camps. The 120m long winter half-pipe is right at the bottom of the mountain in Val Claret, which means if it's open and you have the energy to hike, you can ride it for free. There is also a mini park at town level in Le Lac, so a day's freestyle for free is definitely an option.

Despite (or maybe because of) hosting the X Games, we've had reader criticism of facilities ('there weren't many rails open and it's not very big – the better park is in Val d'Isère').

SNOW RELIABILITY ★★★★★

Difficult to beat

Tignes has all-year-round runs (barring brief closures in spring or autumn) on its Grande Motte glacier. And the resort height of 2100m generally means good snow-cover right back to base for most of the long winter season – November to May. The west-facing runs down from Col de Fresse and Tovière to Val Claret suffer from the afternoon sun, although they have serious snowmaking. Some of the lower east-facing and south-east-facing slopes on the other side of the valley can suffer late in the season, too. Grooming is excellent – in 2011's challenging conditions 'a lot of wonderful work was done to keep pistes open and in good condition'; in 2012, we received only gushing comments about 'brilliant' conditions.

FOR EXPERTS ★★★★★

An excellent choice

Tignes has converted many of its black runs into 'naturides', which means they are never groomed (a neat way of saving money!) but they are marked, patrolled and avalanche protected. Many of them are not especially steep (eg the Ves run – promoted from red status and renamed after the local freeride hero Guerlain Chicherit). Perhaps the most serious challenge is the long black run from Tovière to Tignes-le-Lac, with steep, usually heavily mogulled sections (the top part, Pâquerettes, is now a naturide, but the bottom part, Trolles, is a normal black). Parts of this run get a lot of afternoon sun. Our favourite black run (still a 'normal' black) is the Sache, from the Aiguille Percée down a secluded valley to Tignes-les-Brévières. It can become very heavily mogulled, especially at the bottom – you can avoid this section by taking the red Arcosses piste option part-way down.

But it is the off-piste possibilities that make Tignes such a draw for experts, and the schools organize off-piste groups. See the feature box for a

GETTING THERE

Air Geneva 225km/140 miles (3hr30); Lyon 230km/145 miles (3hr15); Chambéry 145km/90 miles (2hr15)

Rail Bourg-St-Maurice (30km/19 miles); regular buses or taxi from station

few of the off-piste runs. The bizarre French form of heli-skiing is available here: mountaintop drops are forbidden, but from Tovière you can ski down towards the Lac du Chevril to be retrieved by chopper.

FOR INTERMEDIATES ★★★★★
One of the best
For keen intermediate piste-bashers who like varied terrain, the Espace Killy is one of the world's best areas.

Tignes' local slopes are ideal intermediate terrain. The runs on the Grande Motte glacier nearly always have superb snow. The runs from the top of the cable car are bizarrely classified red and black, but they are wide and mostly easy on usually fabulous snow, and could easily be blues. The Leisse run down to the chairlift of the same name is classified black and can get very mogulled, but usually has good snow. The red run all the way back to town is a delightful long cruise – though often crowded. The roundabout blue (Génépy) is much gentler and quieter.

From Tovière, the blue 'H' run to Val Claret is an enjoyable cruise and generally well groomed. But again, it can get very crowded.

There's lots to do on the other side of the valley, and the runs down from the Aiguille Percée to Tignes 1800 and Les Brévières are scenic and fun. There are red and blue options, and adventurous intermediates shouldn't miss the beautiful Sache black run. The runs from the Aiguille Percée to Le Lac are gentle, wide blues.

FOR BEGINNERS ★★★★★
Good nursery slopes, but ...
The nursery slopes of Tignes-le-Lac and Le Lavachet (which meet at the top) are excellent – convenient, snow-sure, gentle, free of through-traffic and served by a slow chair and a drag. The ones at Val Claret are less appealing: an unpleasantly steep slope within the village served by a drag, and a less convenient slope served by the fast Bollin chair. All of these lifts are free.

Although there are some fairly easy blues on the west side of Tignes, for long green runs you have to go over to the Val d'Isère sector. You need an Espace Killy pass to use them, and to get back to Tignes you have a choice between the blue run from Col de Fresse (which has a tricky start) or riding the gondola down from Tovière. And in poor weather, the high Tignes valley is an intimidatingly bleak place – enough to make any wavering beginner retreat to a bar with a book.

FOR BOARDERS ★★★★★
One of the best
Tignes has always been a popular destination for snowboarders. Lots of easily accessible off-piste and lower prices than Val d'Isère are the main attractions, and quite a few top UK snowboarders make this their winter home. There are a few flat areas (avoid Génépy and Myrtilles), but the lift system relies more on chairs and gondolas than drags. There are long, wide pistes to blast down, such as Grattalu, Carline and Piste H, with acres of powder between them to play in. And the backside of Col de Fresse in Val d'Isère is a natural playground. There are two specialist snowboard schools (Snocool and Alliance) and a Welsh-run snowboarder chalet (www.dragonlodge.com). Go to the Snowpark shop in Tignes-le-Lac for all your equipment needs.

FOR CROSS-COUNTRY ★★★★★
Interesting variety
The Espace Killy has 44km of cross-country trails, including 20km of tracks on the frozen Lac de Tignes, along the valley between Val Claret and Tignes-le-Lac, at Tignes 1800 and Les Brévières and up on the Grande Motte.

MOUNTAIN RESTAURANTS ★★★★★
A couple of good places
The mountain restaurants are not a highlight – a regular hazard of high, purpose-built resorts, where it's easy to go back to the village for lunch. The 'biggest rip-off' for a 2012 reporter was being charged 50c for the WC in almost all the restaurants.
Editors' choice Lo Soli (0479 069863) at the top of the Chaudannes chair is

A MECCA FOR OFF-PISTE SKIERS

Tignes is renowned for offering some of the best lift-served off-piste skiing in the world. There is a tremendous choice, with runs to suit all levels, from intermediate skiers to fearless freeriders and off-piste experts. Here's just a small selection. Don't go without a guide.

*For a first experience of off-piste, **Lognan** is ideal. These slopes – down the mountainside between the pistes to Le Lac and the pistes to Val Claret – are broad and not very difficult.*

*One of our favourite routes is the **Tour de Pramecou**. After a few minutes' walking at the bottom of the Grande Motte glacier, you pass around a big rock called Pramecou. There is then a multitude of possibilities, varying in difficulty – so routes can be found for skiers of different abilities.*

***Petite Balme** is a run for good skiers only – access is easy but leads to quite challenging north-facing slopes in real high-mountain terrain, far from the pistes.*

*To ski **Oreilles de Mickey** (Mickey's Ears) you start from Tovière and walk north along the ridge to the peak of Lavachet, where you get a great view of Tignes. The descent involves three long couloirs, narrow and pretty steep, which bring you back to Le Lavachet.*

*The best place to find good snow is the **Chardonnet** couloirs – they never get the sun. The route involves a 20-minute walk from the top of the Merles chairlift.*

*The **Vallons de la Sache** is one of the most famous routes – a descent of 1200m vertical down a breathtaking valley in the heart of the National Park, overlooked by the magnificent Sache glacier. Starting from the Aiguille Percée you enter a different world, high up in the mountains, far away from the ski lifts. You arrive down in Les Brévières, below the Tignes dam.*

*One of the big adventures is to go away from the Tignes ski area and all signs of civilization, starting from the Col du Palet. From there you can head for **Champagny** (linked to La Plagne's area) or **Peisey-Nancroix** (linked to Les Arcs' area) – both very beautiful runs, and not too difficult.*

SCHOOLS

ESF
t 0479 063028

Evolution 2
t 0479 083529

Snocool
t 0479 243094

333
t 0479 062088

Alliance
t 0645 120824
07753 219719 (UK)

New Generation
t 0479 010318
0844 770 4733 (UK)
www.skinewgen.com

BASS
t 0679 512405

Ultimate Snowsports
t 07772 690746 (UK)

Ali Ross Skiing Clinics
t 0479 064908

Classes (ESF prices)
6 days: €253

Private lessons
From €46 for 1hr

GUIDES

Bureau des Guides
t 0479 064276

a clear favourite. The terrace shares with the adjacent self-service Alpage a superb view of the Grande Motte; reporters endorse our opinion: 'excellent food, ambience and service'; 'did us proud, with epic hot chocolates and enjoyable tartiflette'. The table-service bit of the Panoramic (0479 066011) at the top of the funicular competes: 'wonderful views, very good spaghetti bolognese (enough to share), excellent puddings'.

Worth knowing about At the top of the Tichot chair from Val Claret, the Palet has a 'decent choice, big portions'. On the nursery slope above Val Claret, the Chalet du Bollin has been recommended as a pricier option. The big Panoramic self-service at the top of the funicular gets crowded, but has great views from its huge terrace and 'good portions'.

There are lots of easily accessible places for lunch in the resorts. One ski-to-the-door favourite of ours in Le Lac is the hotel Montana, on the left as you descend from the Aiguille Percée ('more competitively priced than others'). Others are the Ferme des 3 Capucines a short walk down from the bottom of the Chaudannes and Paquis chairs and the Arbina (see 'Eating out' for more on these two).

The Chalet du Pain is recommended for a 'quick cheap lunch', while the Jam Bar is a 'tiny cafe with brilliant, freshly made pasta sauces, great bruschetta and the best coffee'. In Val Claret the Taverne des Neiges is 'lively' with 'good food and service'; Pignatta serves 'best quality and value succulent pizzas'; the Aspen Cafe does 'big American-diner style portions for reasonable prices' and Carline is 'not fancy but convenient and quick'.

At the extremity of the lift system, Les Brévières makes an obvious lunch stop. A short walk round the corner into the village brings you to places much cheaper than the two by the piste. Sachette, for example, is crammed with artefacts from mountain life and offers 'lots of good cheese dishes'. The Armailly is recommended for its 'varied menu that didn't break the bank'. The Etoile des Neiges serves 'great, typical Savoyard food', but service can be 'poor'.

SCHOOLS AND GUIDES ★★★★

Plenty of choice

There are over half-a-dozen schools, including two specialist snowboard schools, plus various independent instructors. A reporter recommends Ali Ross Skiing Clinics (pre-booking

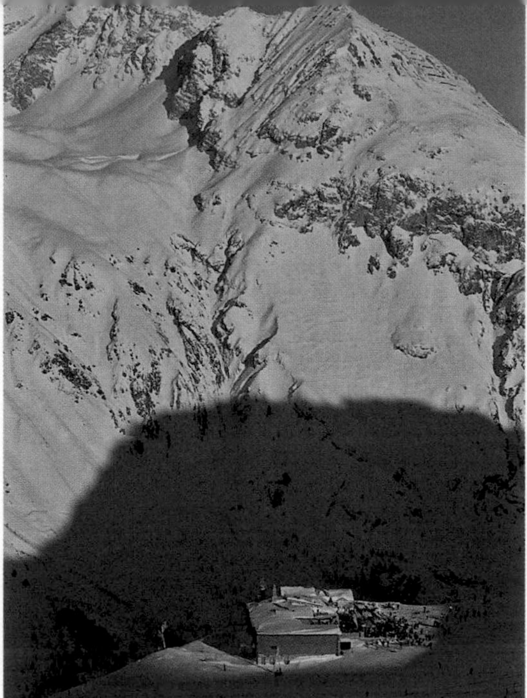

↑ The link to Val d'Isère is a big asset, but don't enjoy the Folie Douce après-ski so much that you miss the last lift home

SNOWPIX.COM / CHRIS GILL

CHILDCARE

Les Marmottons
t 0479 065167
From 30mnth

Piou Piou
t 0479 063028
Ages 3 to 5

Ski schools
From about age 4 (6 days €253 with ESF)

required) – 'a great character who achieved results'. Reporters advise that at busy times pre-booking is 'essential' for normal schools as well. ESF gets mixed reviews: one recent reporter's group abandoned their group lessons midway through the week because they were so bad; but another had a 'fantastic' day's guiding.

Another reporter had 'an excellent one-on-one private lesson' in which she 'improved her mogul and off-piste skills hugely and came away very happy' with New Generation, a British-run school with branches in several other resorts. We have had glowing reports of a British-run snowboarding outfit, Alliance: 'tuition was appropriate to our requirements, and very passionate and sincere – we improved our confidence and skills greatly'; 'excellent instruction'.

333 got a glowing report again this year ('best we've ever had, all gaining in confidence after a couple of hours'), backing up last year's comment that a lesson with 333 was the highlight of a reader's holiday. Ultimate Snowsports is also praised again, for 'making the lessons fun and challenging for the children in our group'.

Reports on Evolution 2 have been consistently positive: 'had a fantastic instructor who challenged everyone in the group. We all advanced our technique and she had us on reds by day three, blacks on day four'; 'very happy with the children's lessons booked through Ski Esprit'.

FOR FAMILIES ★★★★★

Good reports

We have had good reports on the Marmottons kindergarten – 'brilliant', said a father of a four year old – and the Spritelets ski classes arranged by Esprit Ski and Evolution 2: 'She loved her class and could snowplough by the end of the week.' British-run t4Nanny (www.t4nanny.com) was recommended – 'flexible and terrific'. Family specialist tour operator Esprit Ski runs chalets and comprehensive childcare here. With the cost of eating on the mountain so expensive, a family in 2012 appreciated the easy ski back to the apartment for lunch.

STAYING THERE

All three main styles of lodgings are available through tour operators. More luxury options are appearing.

Chalets UK tour operators' catered chalets are mainly in Le Lac. Ski Olympic has three, including the 40-bed chalet Rosset – recommended by reporters and with a top-floor living room overlooking the lake. Skiworld has 11 chalets (some with sauna and hot tub) and the swanky 40-bed Ski Lodge Aigle with pool and sauna. Ski Total has 14 chalets, including some very smart places, lots with sauna and outdoor hot tub, some with pool, and two in their top-of-the-market Platinum range. Their Chalet Anne-Marie was 'strongly recommended' by a reporter. Family specialist Esprit has seven chalets here, including the smart, modern 24-person Corniche with sauna, steam and hot tub. Crystal has eight places from smart to budget, including two in its 'Finest' range and a Riders' Lodge aimed at the younger end of the market that sleeps around 30. A regular reporter last year recommended Chalet Chardon run by small tour operator Snowstar: 'used to be Robert Maxwell's private apartment; lovely large lounge with floor-to-ceiling windows and a great view of the lake'.

Hotels The few hotels are small and concentrated in Le Lac.

******Campanules** (0479 063436) Smartly rustic chalet in upper Le Lac, with good restaurant. Upgraded from 3-star to 4-star last year.

UK PACKAGES

Action Outdoors, Alpine Answers, Alpine Elements, Carrier, Club Med, Crystal, Crystal Finest, Erna Low, Esprit, Flexiski, Friendship Travel, Independent Ski Links, Inghams, Inspired to Ski, Interactive Resorts, Lagrange, Mark Warner, Mountainsun, Mountain Wave, Neilson, Oxford Ski Co, Peak Retreats, Pierre & Vacances, PowderBeds, Powder White, Ski Amis, Ski Bespoke, Ski Club Freshtracks, Ski Collection, Ski Expectations, Ski France, Ski Ici, Ski Independence, Ski Line, Ski Olympic, Ski Solutions, Ski Supreme, Ski Total, Skitracer, Ski Weekend, Skiworld, Snowchateaux, Snow Finders, Snoworks, Snowpod, Snowstar, Thomson

ACTIVITIES

Indoor Wellness and fitness centres (pools, saunas, Turkish baths, hot tub, spa and beauty treatments, weight training), multi-sports hall, yoga, climbing wall, cinema, library, bowling, multimedia centre

Outdoor Dog sledding, mountaineering, ice climbing, ice driving, ice diving, ice rink, paragliding, snowmobiling, snowshoeing, ice karting, biking on snow, helicopter flights, horse riding on snow, snow kiting

Phone numbers
From abroad use the prefix +33 and omit the initial '0' of the phone number

TOURIST OFFICE

www.tignes.net

*****Diva** (0479 067000) Biggest in town (121 rooms). On lower level of Val Claret, a short walk from lifts. Comfortable rooms and excellent meals. Sauna.
*****Lévanna** (0479 063294) Central in Le Lac. Comfortable, with big hot tub.
*****Marais** (0479 064006) Prettily furnished, simple hotel in Tignes 1800.
*****Refuge** (0479 063664) Oldest hotel in Tignes (Le Lac). 'Well run.'
*****Village Montana** (0479 400144) Stylishly woody, on the east-facing slopes above Le Lac, with a 4-star suites section. Outdoor pool, sauna, steam, hot tub. 'Not cheap but first-class hotel with accommodating staff.'
****Arbina** (0479 063478) Well-run place close to the lifts in Le Lac, with lunchtime terrace, crowded après-ski bar and one of the best restaurants.
Génépy (0479 065711) Simple Dutch-run chalet in Les Brévières.
Apartments There are lots of apartments in all price ranges. Ski Collection, Ski Amis and Skitracer have a range of options. The growing number of smart places include Jhana, Ferme du Val Claret, Nevada and Pierre et Vacances' Ecrin des Neiges in Val Claret, and Télémark and Residence Village Montana in Le Lac. In Les Brévières, the Belvédère has very smart large apartments and chalets with three to six bedrooms. All the above have access to pool, sauna etc, but at extra cost in some cases. The Chalet Club in Val Claret is a collection of simple studios, but it has a free indoor pool, sauna and a restaurant and bar. Skiworld has 'flexible catered chalets' where you can choose what catering (if any) you want.

The supermarket at Le Lac is reported to be 'comprehensive but very expensive' – 'stock up in Bourg'.

EATING OUT ★★★★

Good places scattered about

The options in Le Lavachet are rather limited, though a recent reporter enjoyed the 'very reasonably priced' Ferme des 3 Capucines (we had a good lunch here on a recent visit, too). And we have very positive reports of the good-value, British-run Brasero. Finding anywhere with some atmosphere is difficult in Le Lac, though the food in some of the better hotels is good, particularly the Chaumière in the Village Montana. The upstairs restaurant at the Arbina is regularly recommended: 'very good service and excellent food; the three-course fixed menu is good value'. The 'atmospheric' Escale Blanche is popular with 'great food', but reporters disagree over its value. Repeated visitors have enjoyed 'traditional' food at the Eterlou, but service 'went downhill after we complained about the house wine'.

In Val Claret the Caveau is recommended for a special treat. Pepe 2000 has 'friendly staff' and 'lovely pizzas'. The Aspen Coffee Shop is 'cheap and cheerful' and does 'big portions at reasonable prices'.

APRES-SKI ★★★

Hidden away

Reporters agree that there is plenty going on if you know where to find it. Val Claret has some early-evening atmosphere and popular happy hours. The Drop Zone has live music, 'a good atmosphere and a dance floor that fills up pretty quickly'. Grizzly's is 'very cool' but pricey. The Couloir has a whisky lounge. A recent reporter 'always ended the night in the Melting Pot' and avoided the 'seedy' Blue Girl.

Le Lac is a natural focus for après-ski drinks. The lively Loop has live bands and a two for one happy hour from 4pm to 6pm, while the Embuscade is 'very friendly'. The bar of the hotel Arbina is our kind of spot – cosy with friendly service. It's a great place to sit outside and people-watch. The Alpaka Lodge bar is popular with Brits and 'a pleasant spot, especially if you manage to grab one of the sofas by the fire'. Bagus Bar is 'rocking'. Jack's is a popular late haunt.

Vincents in Les Brévières is 'lively, with lots of drinking, singing and sometimes live music'.

OFF THE SLOPES ★★

Good leisure centre

Tignes is not a resort for those who do not want to use the slopes. And some activities get booked up quickly – a reporter said it was impossible to find a free dog sledding slot in April. The ice skating on the lake includes a 500m circuit as well as a conventional rink. This and the pools of the Lagon leisure centre (various pools, slides, wellness and fitness facilities), which is praised by reporters, are free to use with a lift pass for two days or more. The museum in the Maison de Tignes is 'good'. A reporter's kids 'really enjoyed' the bowling at Tignes-le-Lac.

COURCHEVEL / J. KELAGOPIAN

Les Trois Vallées

With the swankiest resort in the Alps at one end, and the highest at the other: the biggest lift-linked ski area in the world

Despite competing claims, notably from the Portes du Soleil, in practical terms the Trois Vallées cannot be beaten for sheer quantity of lift-served terrain. There is nowhere like it for a keen skier or boarder who wants to cover as much mileage as possible while rarely taking the same run repeatedly. It has a lot to offer everyone, from beginner to expert. And its resorts offer a wide range of alternatives – from the big-name mega-resorts to much smaller places.

What's more, the area undersells itself. It should actually be known as the Quatre Vallées because it expanded south into the Maurienne before the first edition of this book was published almost 20 years ago.

The runs of the Trois Vallées and their resorts are dealt with in six chapters. The four major resorts are Courchevel, Méribel, Les Menuires and Val Thorens, but we also give chapters to St-Martin-de-Belleville, a village down the valley from Les Menuires, and La Tania, a modern development between Courchevel and Méribel.

None of the resorts is cheap, but of the major resorts **Les Menuires** is cheapest. The centre of the resort is an eyesore, but new developments have been built in chalet style, and two of the original buildings have been demolished to make way for new ones – something we suggested back in the 1990s. Les Menuires has an excellent position for exploration of the Trois Vallées as a whole.

Down the valley from Les Menuires is **St-Martin-de-Belleville**, a charming traditional village that has been expanded sympathetically. It has good-value accommodation and lift links towards Les Menuires and Méribel.

Up rather than down the Belleville valley from Les Menuires, at 2300m, **Val Thorens** is the highest resort in the Alps, and at 3230m the top of its

The Vallée de Belleville, with Les Menuires in the foreground and Val Thorens in the distance – just one of the, er, four valleys covered by the Trois Vallées →

OT LES MENUIRES / JP NOISILLIER / NUTSFR

slopes is the high point of the Trois Vallées. The snow in this area is almost always good, and it includes two glaciers where good snow is guaranteed. But the setting is bleak, and the lifts are vulnerable to closure in bad weather. It's a purpose-built resort and very convenient – and visually it is not comparable to Les Menuires, thanks to the smaller-scale buildings and more traditional styles.

Méribel is a multi-part resort. The highest component, **Méribel-Mottaret**, is about the best placed of all the resorts for getting to any part of the Trois Vallées system. **Méribel** itself, 200m lower, is a British favourite. It is the most attractive of the main Trois Vallées resorts, built in chalet style on a steep hillside. Parts of the resort are very convenient for the slopes and the village centre; parts are not. The growing hamlet of **Méribel-Village** has its own chairlift into the system. You can also stay down in the valley town of **Brides-les-Bains**.

Courchevel has four parts, which have recently been rebranded. Courchevel (the new name for what was formerly 1850) is among the most fashionable and expensive resorts in the Alps. The other parts – Le Praz (formerly 1300), Courchevel Village (formerly 1550) and Moriond (formerly 1650) – are much less expensive. Many people rate the slopes around here the best in the Three Valleys, with runs to suit all standards.

La Tania was built for the 1992 Olympics, just off the minor road linking Courchevel to Méribel. It has now grown into an attractive, car-free collection of chalets and apartment blocks set among the trees, and is popular with families. It has good nursery slopes and good intermediate runs in the woods above.

OT VAL D'ISERE / AGENCE NUTS

Val d'Isère

One of the great high mega-resorts, particularly (though not only) for experts – with an attractive town at the base

RATINGS

The mountains

Extent	*****
Fast lifts	****
Queues	****
Terrain p'ks	***
Snow	*****
Expert	*****
Intermediate	*****
Beginner	***
Boarder	****
X-country	*
Restaurants	***
Schools	*****
Families	****

The resort

Charm	***
Convenience	***
Scenery	***
Eating out	*****
Après-ski	****
Off-slope	**

RPI	100
lift pass	£190
ski hire	£110
lessons	£75
food & drink	£145
total	**£520**

NEWS

2012/13: The slow Fontaine Froide quad chairlift on Bellevarde is to be replaced by a six-pack that will start from the same place but finish at the top near the Olympique gondola. There are plans for a new jumbo gondola from the resort to Solaise, but it is not expected to open until 2014/15.
The L'Atelier d'Edmond restaurant at Le Fornet gained a Michelin star.

2011/12: Snowmaking was increased in the terrain park and the 'chill out' zone improved. Two hotels, the Christiania and Blizzard, were awarded 5-star status.

- ➕ Huge area shared with Tignes, with lots of runs for all abilities
- ➕ One of the great resorts for lift-served off-piste runs
- ➕ Once the snow has fallen, high altitude of slopes keeps it good
- ➕ Wide choice of schools, especially for off-piste lessons and guiding
- ➕ For a high Alpine resort, the town is attractive, very lively at night, and offers a good range of restaurants
- ➕ Wide range of package holidays – including some comfortable chalets

- ➖ Some green and blue runs are too challenging, and all runs back to the village are tricky
- ➖ You're quite likely to need buses at the start and end of the day (but they are very frequent and efficient)
- ➖ Many lifts and slopes are liable to close when the weather is bad
- ➖ At times seems more British than French – especially in low season
- ➖ Eating and drinking expensive – among the four priciest resorts in France for this

Val d'Isère is one of the world's best resorts for experts – attracted by the extent of lift-served off-piste – and for confident, mileage-hungry intermediates. You don't have to be particularly adventurous to enjoy the resort; but it would be much better for novices and timid intermediates if the piste classifications were more reliable.

The drawbacks listed above are mainly not serious complaints, whereas most of the plus-points weigh heavily in the balance. For a combination of seriously impressive skiing and very pleasant village ambience, there are few places we'd rather go.

THE RESORT

Val d'Isère spreads along a remote valley, which is a dead end in winter. The road in from Bourg-St-Maurice brings you dramatically through a rocky defile to La Daille – a convenient but hideous slope-side apartment complex and the base of lifts into the major Bellevarde sector of the slopes.

Carry on into the centre of town and turn right and you drive under the nursery slopes and major lifts up to both the Bellevarde and Solaise sectors to a lot of new development. Continue up the main valley instead, and you come first to Le Laisinant, a peaceful little outpost with a fast lift into the slopes, and then to Le Fornet, the fourth major lift station.

The developments up the side valley beyond the main lift station – in Le Châtelard and La Legettaz – are mainly attractive, and some offer ski-in/ski-out convenience. La Daille and Le Fornet have their (quite different) attractions for those less concerned about nightlife. A car is of no great value around the resort.

VILLAGE CHARM ***

Developing nicely

The outskirts of Val proper are dreary, but as you approach the centre the improvements put in place over the last 20 or so years become evident: wood- and stone-cladding, culminating in the tasteful pedestrian-only Val Village complex. Many first-time visitors find the resort much more

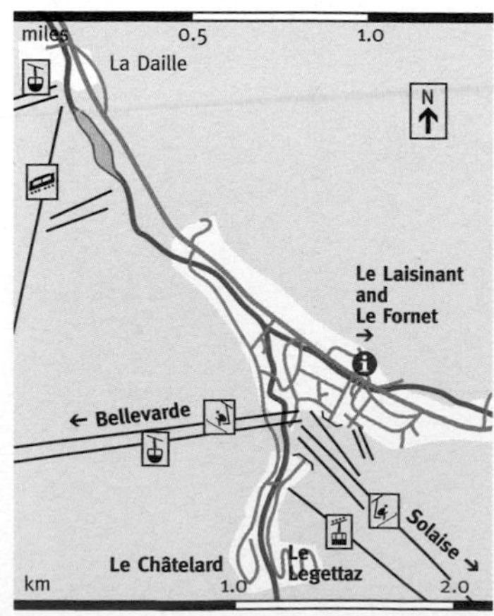

KEY FACTS

Resort	1850m 6,070ft
Espace Killy	
Slopes	1550-3455m 5,090-11,340ft
Lifts	79
Pistes	300km 186 miles
Green	15%
Blue	42%
Red	26%
Black	17%
Snowmaking	974 guns
Val d'Isère only	
Slopes	1785-3300m 5,860-10,830ft
Lifts	46
Pistes	150km 93 miles

SNOWPIX.COM / CHRIS GILL

There's no easy way down from Solaise, and many take the ski-anywhere route ↓

pleasant than they expected – 'Val has a lovely atmosphere and charm about it that surprised me,' said a 2012 first-timer.

CONVENIENCE ★★★★★
Mostly fine

There is a lot of traffic around, but the resort has worked hard to get cars under control and has made the centre more pedestrian-friendly. The location of your accommodation isn't crucial, unless you want to ski from the door or be close to a nursery slope. The main lift stations are served by very efficient and frequent free shuttle-buses; but in peak periods you may have to let a few full ones pass before there's space to board. But in the evening frequency plummets and dedicated après-skiers will want to be near the centre.

SCENERY ★★★★★
Valley deep, mountain high

The resort sprawls along a steep-sided river valley, beneath a series of high and partly-wooded mountain ridges. There are splendid views from the Pissaillas glacier.

THE MOUNTAINS

Although there are wooded slopes above the village on all sectors, in practice most of the runs here are on open slopes above the treeline, and a lot of lifts can close in bad weather. Several visitors confirm that piste grooming is good, and signposting was deemed 'excellent' by this year's reporters. But Val d'Isère vies with St Anton for the title of 'resort with most under-classified slopes'. Many blue and some green runs (including runs to the valley) are simply too steep, narrow and even bumpy; in other resorts they would be reds, or even blacks; we have a hefty file of complaints from readers (including nearly all our 2012 reporters) who agree with our judgement. The piste map has 'quiet skiing' zones marked on it. The local radio (96.1 FM) carries weather reports in English as well as in French.

EXTENT OF THE SLOPES ★★★★★
Vast and varied

Val d'Isère's slopes divide into three main sectors, two reachable from the village. Bellevarde is the mountain that is home to Val d'Isère's two famous downhill courses: the OK piste that is used for the World Cup every December and the Face piste that was used for the 1992 Winter Olympics and the 2009 World Championships. You can reach Bellevarde quickly by underground funicular from La Daille or the powerful Olympique gondola from near the centre of town. From the top you can descend to the valley, play on a variety of drags and chairs at altitude or take a choice of lifts to Tignes' slopes (see separate chapter).

Solaise is the other mountain accessible directly from the village. The Solaise fast quad takes you a few metres higher than the parallel cable car. Once up, a short drag or rope tow takes you over a plateau and down to a variety of chairs that serve this very sunny area of predominantly gentle pistes. From near the top of this area you can catch the fast Leissières chair (which climbs over a ridge and down the other side) to the third main area, in the valley running up to the Col de l'Iseran. This area can also be reached

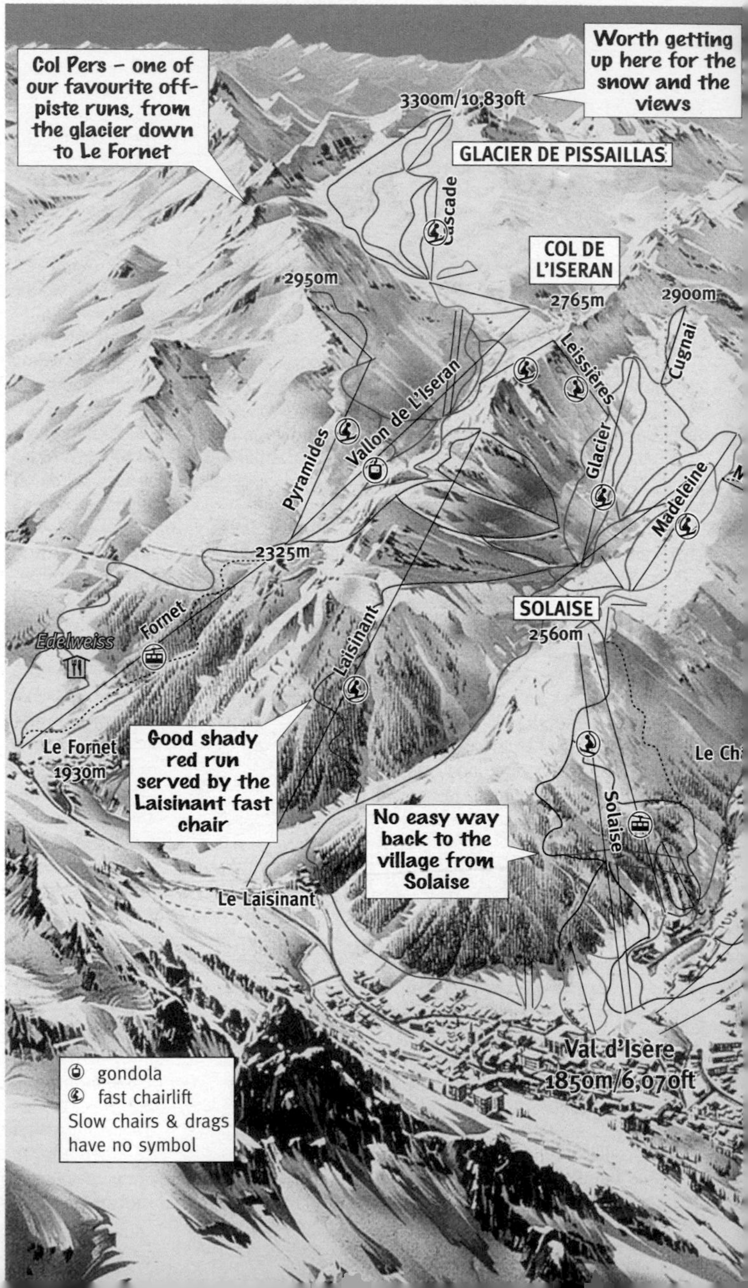

Col Pers – one of our favourite off-piste runs, from the glacier down to Le Fornet

3300m/10,830ft

Worth getting up here for the snow and the views

GLACIER DE PISSAILLAS

Cascade

COL DE L'ISERAN

2950m

2765m

2900m

Leissières

Cugnai

Vallon de L'Iseran

Pyramides

Glacier

Madeleine

2325m

SOLAISE

2560m

Fornet

Edelweiss

Laisinant

Le Fornet 1930m

Good shady red run served by the Laisinant fast chair

No easy way back to the village from Solaise

Solaise

Le Laisinant

Val d'Isère 1850m/6,070ft

gondola
fast chairlift
Slow chairs & drags have no symbol

AILLAS

Good area of varied intermediate runs at altitude, with a couple of fast chairs

2900m
Cugnai

Excellent runs down to the Manchet chair – though affected by sun later in the season

Lots of long, high easy runs – but also lots of slow old lifts

The blue from here is the easiest and least crowded intermediate route to Tignes

COL DE FRESSE
2770m

Glacier de la Grande Motte

Madeleine
Manchet
Le Manchet
1940m
Grand Pre
Borsat
Tignes
Fresse
TOVIERE
2705m

BELLEVARDE
Fontaine Froid 2705m
Marmottes
Tommeuses
Loyes
Le Châtelard
L'Olympique
Solaise
Funival
Bellevarde
Daille

The world's trickiest green run – narrow in parts and crowded and mogulled at the end of the day

The 1992 Winter Olympic men's downhill course is now a genuine black run and often mogulled from top to bottom

d'Isère
n/6,070ft

La Daille
1785m/5,860ft

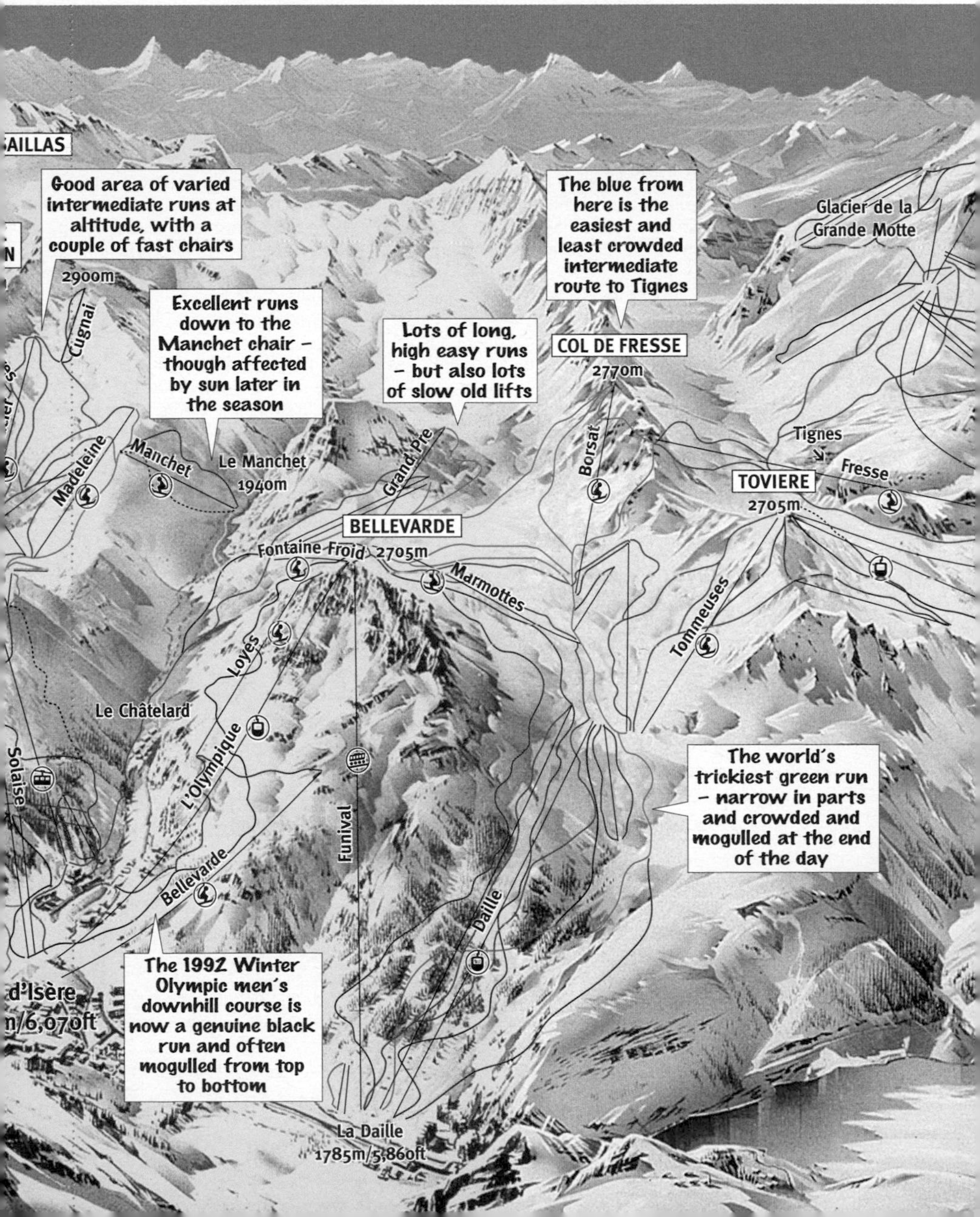

by the fast chair from Le Laisinant or by cable car from Le Fornet. At the top here is the **Glacier de Pissaillas**.

FAST LIFTS ★★★★
Access all areas
High capacity lifts provide good access from the valley and there are lots of fast chairs higher up. But there are still a few slow chairs and draglifts around.

QUEUES ★★★★
Few problems
Queues to get out of the resort have been kept in check by lift upgrades and additions – but occasionally the Olympique gondola up Bellevarde has a short wait. On Solaise the slow Lac chair back up to the Tête Solaise can generate queues, but a recent reporter praises 'the good queueing systems, with each chair filled to capacity'. Crowded pistes in high season is a more common complaint than queues.

TERRAIN PARKS ★★★
Beginners and experts welcome
Above the La Daille gondola and served by the Mont Blanc chairlift lies the DC Valpark (www.valdiserevalpark.com). Maintenance can be a bit hit or miss – but a recent April visitor said: 'My son really enjoyed messing about in the park which, all credit to those responsible, was kept open and maintained as well as possible in warm conditions.' There are 18 table jumps and 25 boxes and rails of all shapes and sizes. Plus a large hip, 3m wall ride and four kicker lines, with up to five jumps in a row ranging from 3m in the blue line to 20m in the pro line. Head to Tignes for a half-pipe.

SNOW RELIABILITY ★★★★★
One of the best
In years when lower resorts have suffered, Val d'Isère has rarely been short of snow. Even in a poor snow year like 2010/11, decent skiing was still available right until the end of the season. Once a big dump of snow has fallen, the resort's height means you can almost always get back to the village. But even more important is that in each sector there are lots of lifts and runs above mid-mountain, between about 2300m and 2900m. Many of the slopes face roughly north. And there is access to glaciers at Pissaillas or over in Tignes. There's snowmaking too.

FOR EXPERTS ★★★★★
One of the world's best
Val d'Isère is one of the top resorts in the world for experts. The main attraction is the huge range of beautiful off-piste possibilities – see the feature panel below.

THE BEST LIFT-SERVED OFF-PISTE IN THE WORLD?

Few resorts can rival the extent of lift-served off-piste skiing in Val d'Isère. Here is a selection of what's on offer. But don't try any of it without a guide and essential safety equipment.

Some runs are ideal for adventurous intermediates looking to try off-piste for the first time. The ***Tour du Charvet*** *goes through glorious scenery from the top of the Grand Pré chairlift on the back of Bellevarde. For most of the way it is very gentle, with only a few steeper pitches. It ends up at the bottom of the Manchet chair up to the Solaise area. The* ***Pays Désert*** *is an easy run with superb views on the Pissaillas glacier, high above Le Fornet and reached by traversing away from the pistes above cliffs from the top of the lift system. You end up at the Pays Désert draglift.*

For more experienced off-piste skiers, ***Col Pers*** *is one of our favourite runs. Again, it starts a traverse from the Pissaillas glacier. You go over a pass into a big, fairly gentle bowl with glorious views and endless ways down. If there is enough snow, you drop down into the Gorges de Malpasset and ski over the frozen Isère river back to the Fornet cable car. If not, you can take a higher route.*

Cugnai *is a wide, secluded bowl reached from the chair of the same name at the top of the Solaise sector. A steep (37 degree) slope at the far end descends beneath a sheer black rock wall and then narrows into a gully to the valley floor, leading to the Manchet chair.*

Banane *is reached via the Face de Bellevarde piste and is a long and impressive run (37 to 40 degrees) with spectacular views over the Manchet valley. For a real challenge intrepid experts should try the* ***Couloir des Pisteurs,*** *which requires a 20-minute climb from the Tour de Charvet. The view from the top is simply stunning. A very narrow steep couloir (44 degrees) bounded by rock faces brings you out on to a wide open slope above Le Grand Pré, right opposite Bellevarde.*

Then there's the whole of Tignes' extensive off-piste to explore of course.

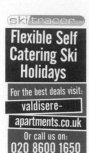

LIFT PASSES

Espace Killy

Prices in €

Age	1-day	6-day
under 14	36	181
14 to 64	45	226
over 65	36	181

Free under 5, over 75

Beginner five free lifts on nursery slopes; reduced price pass with ESF lessons

Notes
Covers Tignes and Val d'Isère; half-day and pedestrian passes; family discounts; 5-day-plus passes valid for a day in the Three Valleys and a day in Paradiski (La Plagne-Les Arcs)

Alternative pass
Val d'Isère only

ACTIVITIES

Indoor Sports centre (with pools, climbing wall, fitness, gym, sauna, steam, squash, climbing wall), fitness and health clubs, cinema

Outdoor Ice rink, walking, snowshoeing, ice climbing, dog sledding, ice driving, paragliding, microlight flights, helicopter flights

There may be better resorts for really steep pistes – there are certainly lots in North America – but there is plenty of on-piste action to amuse most experts, despite the small number of blacks on the piste map. And some of these have been converted to 'naturides', which means they are never groomed (a neat way of saving money!) but they are marked, patrolled and avalanche protected. Many reds and blues are also steep enough to get mogulled.

On Bellevarde the famous Face run is the main attraction – often mogulled from top to bottom, but not worryingly steep and a wonderful blast if it has been groomed. Epaule is the sector's other black run – where the moguls are hit by long exposure to sun and can be slushy or rock hard (it is prone to closure for these reasons too). Most of the blacks on Solaise and above Le Fornet are now 'naturides' (and the proper black from Solaise to the valley is no steeper than the alternative red).

Wayne Watson of off-piste school Alpine Expérience puts a daily diary of off-piste snow conditions and runs on the web at www.alpineexperience.com.

FOR INTERMEDIATES ★★★★★
Quantity and quality

Val d'Isère has just as much to offer intermediates as experts. There's enough here to keep you interested for several visits – though pistes can be crowded in high-season, and the less experienced should be aware that many runs are under-classified.

In the Solaise sector is a network of gentle blue runs, ideal for building confidence. And there are a couple of beautiful runs from here through the woods to Le Laisinant – ideal in bad weather, though prone to closure in times of avalanche danger.

Most of the runs in the Col de l'Iseran sector are even easier – ideal for early and hesitant intermediates. Those marked blue at the top of the glacier could really be classified green.

Bellevarde has a huge variety of runs ideally suited to intermediates of all levels. From Bellevarde itself there is a choice of green, blue and red runs of varying pitch. The World Cup downhill OK piste is a wonderful rolling cruise when groomed. The wide runs from Tovière normally offer the choice of groomed piste or moguls.

A snag for early intermediates is that runs back to the valley can be challenging. The easiest way is down to La Daille on a green run which would be classified blue or red in most resorts. It gets very crowded and mogulled by the end of the day. None of the runs from Bellevarde and Solaise back to Val itself is easy. Many early intermediates ride the lifts down.

FOR BEGINNERS ★★★
OK if you know where to go

The nursery slope right by the centre of town is 95% perfect; it's just a pity that the very top is unpleasantly steep. The lifts serving it are free.

Once off the nursery slopes, you have to know where to find easy runs; many of the greens should be blue, or even red. One local instructor admits: 'We have to have green runs on the map, even if we don't have so many green slopes – otherwise beginners wouldn't come to Val d'Isère.'

A good place for your first real runs off the nursery slopes is the Madeleine green run on Solaise (a 'quiet skiing' zone served by a six-pack). The Col de l'Iseran runs are also gentle and wide, and not overcrowded. There is good progression terrain (and a big 'quiet skiing' zone) on Bellevarde, too – though getting to it can be tricky. From all sectors, it's best to take a lift back down to the valley.

SCHOOLS

Alpine Experience
t 0479 062881

BASS
t 0679 512405

ESF
t 0479 060234

Evolution 2
t 0479 007729

Misty Fly
t 0479 073267

Mountain Masters
t 0479 060514

New Generation
t 0479 010318
0844 770 4733 (UK)
www.skinewgen.com

Oxygène
t 0479 419958

Progression
t 0621 939380

Ski Concept
t 0479 401919

Ski-lesson.com
t 0615 207108

Snow Fun
t 0479 061979

TDC
t 0615 553156

Top Ski
t 0479 061480

Classes (ESF prices)
6 days (3hr am, 2½hr pm) €397

Private lessons
From €44 for 1hr

FOR BOARDERS ★★★★

Watch out for flats

Val d'Isère's more upmarket profile attracts a different kind of holiday boarder from Tignes; the resort is, perhaps, seen as Tignes' less hard-core cousin. But the terrain here is great for freeriders. The easier slopes are suitable for beginners, and there are very few draglifts. But there are quite a few flat areas where you'll end up scooting or walking. Specialist snowboard shops are Misty Fly and Quiksilver Boardriders.

FOR CROSS-COUNTRY ★

Limited

There are a couple of loops in each of three areas – towards La Daille, on Solaise and out past Le Laisinant. More picturesque is the one going from Le Châtelard (on the road past the main cable car station) to the Manchet chair. But keen cross-country enthusiasts should go elsewhere.

MOUNTAIN RESTAURANTS ★★★

Acceptable – but expensive

For such an upmarket resort, there are surprisingly few enjoyable places to eat on the mountain. The major places are self-service and at the top of lifts. But everywhere gets busy and high-season service can be poor. And nearly every report we get remarks on how expensive they are ('hideously expensive', said one reporter). The one saving grace, says another, is that the portions are generally 'too large' so can be shared to cut the costs. Apart from prices, reporters' other major gripe is having to pay to use the loos in many mountain restaurants, even if you eat there.

Editors' choice The wood-and-stone Edelweiss (0610 287064), above Le Fornet, is our favourite for the best food and ambience. We've eaten there several times and had delicious lamb, duck and fish; reporters regularly send us rave reviews too ('Echo all you say; duck burger with foie gras is to die for,' says a recent visitor). It's a bit cramped inside, and if it's a nice day, we much prefer the sunny terrace.

Worth knowing about On Bellevarde, the Fruitière at the top of the La Daille gondola is kitted out with stuff from a dairy. Reporters used to rate it highly, and we had succulent duck there in 2012, but it crams in too many people and we've had some negative reports on it. More reports please. The busy table-service Trifollet halfway down the OK run 'always has a good plat du jour' which is 'very reasonable compared to others'. The Marmottes, near the base of the chair of the same name, is consistently recommended by readers and one of the cheapest places to eat – an efficient self-service with a big sunny terrace, helpful staff and good food ('decent goulash and spag bol without requiring a second mortgage'). And the Tanière (popular with locals) set between the two chairs going up Face de Bellevarde has been recommended.

← Not everyone likes the Leissières chair which links Solaise and Col d'Iseran and goes up over a ridge and down again; but it gives you great views over Solaise to the Grande Motte

SNOWPIX.COM / CHRIS GILL

GUIDES

Mountain guides
t 0687 528503

Tetra
t 0631 499275

On Solaise, reader tips include Tête de Solaise self-service at the top of the Solaise chair ('good choice and big portions'). The Datcha at the bottom of the Glacier Express has a small table-service section ('all the dishes were tasty and reasonably priced by Val d'Isère standards'; 'great range of fresh salads including tuna and salmon'). The Bar de L'Ouillette, at the base of the Madeleine chairlift, has a fun terrace with artificial palm trees and deck chairs, is 'friendly' and 'advertises its free loos!', but the queue at its tiny self-service counter may be slow-moving.

Above Le Fornet, the Signal at the top of the cable car has self- and table-service sections and a take-away snack bar – recent reporters recommend all three. You'll find us upstairs in the table-service section ('nice atmosphere, sensational food'; 'pricey but not bad value'). The snack bar served 'huge baguettes big enough to share'.

Of course there are lots of places in the resort villages. Arolay at Le Fornet is 'excellent for both lunch and dinner, with a lovely terrace', and the Michelin-starred Atelier d'Edmond

Wow! What's new in Austria? See p168.

(decorated like a carpenter's workshop and opposite the Fornet cable car) is 'serious (expensive) dining with impeccable service, good for a treat'. The terrace of hotel Brussel's in Val d'Isère, right by the nursery slopes, has 'good food and excellent service'. The Sun Bar at the base of the Olympique cable car is 'surprisingly good value', as is the Tartine, used by many ski instructors. In town, the Perdrix Blanche set menu is 'excellent', and the coffee shop in the Quiksilver store serves fresh smoothies and '17 different types of burger' – and gets packed on bad weather days.

SCHOOLS AND GUIDES ★★★★★

A very wide choice

There is a huge choice of schools, guides and private instructors – just look at the list in the margin opposite. But as they all get busy, at peak periods it's best to book in advance. Practically all the schools run off-piste groups as well as on-piste lessons.

New Generation, a British-run school that operates in 10 resorts, has a branch here that is consistently highly praised: 'Excellent progress made with my nervous beginner, er, intermediate wife. A week of group lessons with only five in the group – can't praise them enough!' said a 2012 reporter; 'The morning we had was one of the highlights of our holiday – lots of fun and we learned a lot too,' said another. The Development Centre (TDC) is a group of British instructors which offers intensive clinics for all levels and has been recommended this year: 'I fully appreciated the back to basics approach – it made a massive difference to my control on steeps.'

We've also heard in the past from satisfied pupils of BASS (British Alpine Ski & Snowboard School), Evolution 2 (for children's lessons arranged by Ski Esprit) and Oxygène. Misty Fly is a specialist snowboard school.

Alpine Expérience and Top Ski specialize in guided off-piste groups – an excellent way to get off-piste safely without the cost of hiring a guide as an individual. We have had great mornings out with both; reporters recommend both too. Heli-skiing trips can be arranged from over the border in Italy – heli-drops are banned in

CHILDCARE

Le Village des Enfants
t 0479 400981
Ages 18mnth to 13yr

Le Petit Poucet
t 0479 061397
Ages from 3

Babysitter list
Contact tourist office

Ski schools
Most offer classes for ages 5 up (ESF prices from €242 for 6 days)

GETTING THERE

Air Geneva 230km/ 145 miles (3hr30); Lyon 240km/ 150 miles (3hr15); Chambéry 145km/ 90 miles (2hr15)

Rail Bourg-St-Maurice (30km/19 miles); regular buses from station

France. Henry's Avalanche Talk at Dick's Tea Bar (every Tuesday last season – see www.henrysavalanchetalk.com for 2012/13) was 'very engaging and interesting', says a reporter.

FOR FAMILIES ★★★★
Good tour op possibilities

Many people prefer to use the facilities of UK tour operators such as family specialist Esprit Ski. But there's a 'children's village' for children from 18 months to 13 years, with supervised indoor and outdoor activities on the village nursery slopes. And Petit Poucet takes children from age three and will pick them up and take them home at any time during the day. However, a reporter who is a policeman says families need to be aware that the resort exudes a 'lager lout' feel at times.

STAYING THERE

More British tour operators go to Val (and Méribel) than anywhere else. Val d'Isère à la Carte specializes in arranging tailor-made holidays there.

Chalets This is Planet Chalet, with properties at every level of the market. Many of the most impressive are in the side valley running south from the village – some in the elevated enclave of Les Carats. YSE is a Val d'Isère specialist, with 20 varied chalets – from swanky apartments for four or six to proper big chalets. Le Ski has nine chalets, including six splendid all-en-suite places grouped together just up from the main street (with a big outdoor hot tub) and two luxurious chalets for eight nearby (which have huge living room windows and share another outdoor hot tub); all eight have a free pick-up and drop-off service. Skiworld has 12 varied chalets from smart to budget plus a smart 33-bedroomed chalet hotel with sauna, steam, hot tub. Ski Total has 15 smart places, including three very swanky ones in their Platinum range – one with outdoor hot tub, two with saunas – and a chalet hotel sleeping 80 at La Daille. Crystal has a handful of chalets, including three smart central ones with saunas in their Finest range. Inghams has two chalets (one right on the nursery slope) and a 24-bed chalet hotel in Le Fornet. Esprit, the family specialist, has a central chalet hotel.

There are some genuinely luxurious chalets in from operators like Consensio and Scott Dunn.

Hotels There are over 30, with increasing numbers at the luxury end: four 5-stars and five 4-stars.

*****__Barmes de L'Ours__ (0479 413700) The best in town. Close to slopes and centre. Rooms are in a different style on each floor. Excellent pool.

*****__Blizzard__ (0479 060207) Central. Comfortable. Indoor-outdoor pool and sauna. Good food and lively bar.

*****__Christiania__ (0479 060825) Big chalet. Chic but friendly. Pool, sauna.

****__Aigle des Neiges__ (0479 061888) Highly rated refurbished version of former Latitudes. Central. Sauna.

****__Auberge St Hubert__ (0479 060645) On main street. Two recent reporters praise it – 'very friendly family hotel'.

****__Avenue Lodge__ (0479 006767) Central and fairly new. 'Very modern decor, comfortable rooms.'

****__Tsanteleina__ (0479 061213) On the main road. Staff and bar area praised but not the food.

***__Kandahar__ (0479 060239) Smart, newish building above Taverne d'Alsace on main street.

***__Samovar__ (0479 061351) In La Daille. Traditional, with good food.

***__Sorbiers__ (0479 062377) Modern but cosy chalet, not far out.

**__Danival__ (0479 060065) B&B, piste-side location.

UK PACKAGES

Action Outdoors, Alpine Answers, Alpine Elements, Alpine Weekends, Carrier, Chardon Mountain Lodges, Club Med, Consensio, Crystal, Crystal Finest, Elegant Resorts, Erna Low, Esprit, Flexiski, Friendship Travel, Independent Ski Links, Inghams, Inspired to Ski, Interactive Resorts, Jeffersons, Lagrange, Le Ski, Luxury Chalet Collection, Mark Warner, Momentum, Mountain Wave, Neilson, Oxford Ski Co, Pierre & Vacances, PowderBeds, Powder White, Scott Dunn, Ski Amis, Ski Beat, Ski Bespoke, Ski Club Freshtracks, Ski Collection, Ski Expectations, Ski France, Ski Independence, Ski Line, Ski Olympic, Ski Power, Ski Solutions, Ski Supreme, Ski Total, Skitracer, Ski-Val, Ski Weekend, Skiweekends.com, Skiworld, Snow Finders, Snoworks, STC, Supertravel, Thomson, Val d'Isère A La Carte, VIP, White Roc, YSE

Phone numbers
From abroad use the prefix +33 and omit the initial '0' of the phone number

TOURIST OFFICE

www.valdisere.com

****Galise** (0479 060504) Central, family-run B&B. 'Comfortable, quiet.'
Forêt (0479 0600) Central, recently refurbished. 'Basic rooms, very friendly staff, outstanding food.'
Apartments There are thousands of apartments available. Among the best are Chalets du Jardin Alpin at the foot of Solaise, Chalets du Laisinant (at Le Laisinant) and Pierre & Vacances' Balcons de Bellevarde at La Daille and Chalets de Solaise (with outdoor pool) close to the centre. Ski Collection, Ski Amis, Ski Independence, Erna Low, Skitracer and local agency Val d'Isère Agence (0479 067350) have good selections. Skiworld has a central, flexible catered chalet where you can choose what catering (if any) you want, plus apartments. The supermarkets have been praised for 'enticing pre-cooked food'.

EATING OUT ★★★★★
Plenty of good places

The 70-odd restaurants offer a wide variety of cuisines; there's a free *Guide des Tables* booklet covering some, but many worthwhile places are missing.

At the top end, three places have a Michelin star: L'Atelier d'Edmond at Le Fornet (see 'Mountain restaurants'), La Becca at Le Laisinant (with a young chef from a local family) and La Table de l'Ours, in the Barmes de l'Ours hotel. The Grande Ourse, by the nursery slope, is another place to head for a top-of-the-range meal ('very good food, service and ambience'). The hotel Aigle des Neiges restaurants are rated highly by locals as is Arolay at Le Fornet (see 'Mountain restaurants').

There are plenty of pleasant mid-priced places. We always enjoy the unchanging Taverne d'Alsace. Bar Jacques is regularly recommended for its excellent food and set menu. Casserole and Pré d'Aval have both been recommended for their good-value set menus. Corniche has a 'lovely traditional ambience', 'good service and a range of well-cooked food'. A local says the Perdix Blanche is 'back on track with good service and a great menu; I went several times and it was always excellent'.

Other reporter tips: Chez Paolo is a 'good choice for family dining'; Casa Scara has 'good food'; Canyon caters to all pockets; but service at these last two has been criticized. The Grand Cocor has 'nice pizza'.

APRES-SKI ★★★★
Not as lively as it was?

A couple of reporters this year remarked that après-ski was quieter than they expected. But there are lots of bars, many with happy hours and then music and dancing later on.

The Folie Douce, at the top of the La Daille gondola, has become an Austrian-style tea-time rave, with music and dancing on tables; you can ride the gondola down. The Tipi bar on the Glacier run on Solaise is a 'nice place to stop for an afternoon drink – open air with rug-covered loungers'. At La Daille the bar at the Samovar hotel is a good spot for a quiet beer after skiing. In downtown Val, Blue Note (opposite the ESF) has a 'great low-key atmosphere' and 'offers free après-ski nibbles and a warm welcome'. Café Face is popular with loud music. The Moris pub (live music at tea time and later) and Saloon (under hotel Brussel's) fill up as the slopes close; Boubou and Bar Jacques are popular with locals. The Pacific Bar has sport on big-screen TVs. The basement Taverne d'Alsace is quiet and relaxing, as are Bar XV, the first-floor bar of the hotel Blizzard and Wine Not (with a 'great choice' of wines by the glass). The burger/coffee shop in the Quiksilver store serves fresh smoothies and attracts a 'cool young crowd'.

Later on, Dick's Tea Bar is the main disco (go early evening for Val's 'best value drinking', says a reporter). Doudoune is 'more expensive but nicer'. Graal is 'usually good'.

OFF THE SLOPES ★★
A reasonable amount to do

A new sports centre opened three seasons ago with two pools, sauna, steam, gym, climbing wall and is consistently praised by reporters; a lift pass for two days or more gets you one free swim. There's an outdoor ice rink and ice driving, and the range of shops is better than in most high French resorts. There are few mountain restaurants easy for pedestrians to get to. A reporter says the nature walk from Le Fornet to Pont St Charles in late season is fascinating.

Want to get the next edition free?
Send us a useful report on your holiday, and win one of 100 free copies. Find out more at:
www.wheretoskiandsnowboard.com

SNOWPIX.COM / CHRIS GILL

Val Thorens

Europe's highest resort, with guaranteed good snow – and other attractions, stylish lodgings and good restaurants among them

RATINGS

The mountains

Extent	*****
Fast lifts	*****
Queues	***
Terrain p'ks	****
Snow	*****
Expert	****
Intermediate	*****
Beginner	****
Boarder	****
X-country	*
Restaurants	****
Schools	***
Families	***

The resort

Charm	**
Convenience	*****
Scenery	***
Eating out	****
Après-ski	****
Off-slope	**

RPI	100
lift pass	£200
ski hire	£110
lessons	£75
food & drink	£135
total	**£520**

KEY FACTS

Resort	2300m 7,550ft
Trois Vallées	
Slopes	1260-3230m 4,130-10,600ft
Lifts	173
Pistes	600km 373 miles
Green	16%
Blue	40%
Red	34%
Black	10%
Snowmaking	2162 guns
Val Thorens-Orelle only	
Slopes	1800-3230m 5,900-10,600ft
Lifts	31
Pistes	150km 87 miles
Green	12%
Blue	38%
Red	39%
Black	11%

- ⊞ Extensive slopes for all abilities, locally and in the vast Trois Vallées
- ⊞ The highest resort in the Alps, and one of the most snow-sure
- ⊞ Compact, with ski-in/out lodgings
- ⊞ Convenient, gentle nursery slopes
- ⊞ Decent range of hotels for a high, purpose-built resort

- ⊟ Not a tree in sight
- ⊟ Away from the 'front de neige', not an attractive place to walk around
- ⊟ Not ideal for non-skiers
- ⊟ Some very crowded pistes and dangerous intersections
- ⊟ Queues for the justifiably popular Cîme de Caron cable car

For the enthusiast looking for the best snow available, it's difficult to beat Val Thorens. For a late trip, in particular, it's the best base in the wonderful Trois Vallées. But we normally prefer a cosier base lower down. That way, if a storm socks in, we can play in the woods; if the sun is scorching, we have the option of setting off for Val Thorens.

THE RESORT

Val Thorens is a classic purpose-built resort, high above the treeline at the head of the valley it shares with Les Menuires and St-Martin. Buses to/from Les Menuires are apparently not supposed to carry skiers and boarders (just pedestrians and cross-country skiers) – a crazy situation.

VILLAGE CHARM **

Functional but pleasantly so

Seen from the slopes, the resort is not as ugly as many of its rivals, and it has more of a lively ski resort buzz than most people expect. The buildings are mainly medium-rise and wood-clad; some are distinctly stylish. But many are designed with their smart 'fronts' facing the slopes, and look very dreary from the streets. And the place lacks a focus.

The streets are supposedly traffic-free; most visitors' cars are banished, except on Saturdays. Workers' cars still generate a fair amount of traffic, though, and Saturdays can be mayhem. You're advised to book parking in advance.

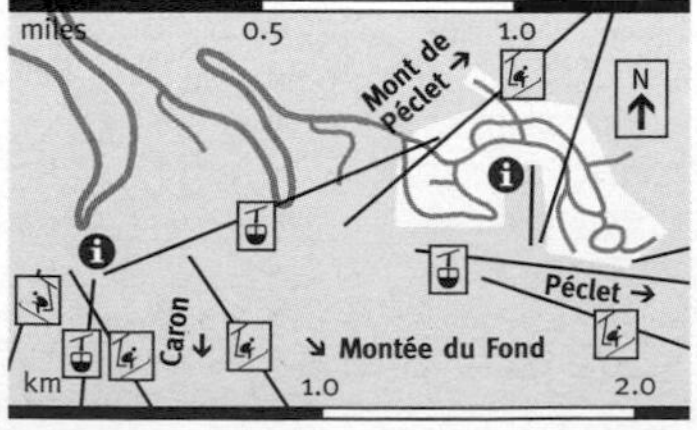

CONVENIENCE *****

Ski through the centre

It's a compact village with lots of ski-in/ski-out lodging. At its heart is the snowy Place de Caron, on the slope side rather than the street side of the central buildings, where pedestrians mix with skiers and boarders. Many of the shops and restaurants are here, along with some nice hotels; the sports and leisure centres are nearby.

The resort is basically divided in two by a little slope (with a moving carpet lift) that leads down from here to the broad main nursery slope running the length of the village. The upper half of the village is centred on the Place de Péclet, where there is one of two shopping malls. A road runs across the hillside from here to the chalet-style Plein Sud area, where many fairly recent apartments have been built and where many of the catered chalets run by UK tour operators are located. You can ski to and from some of these places, but it's often very tricky – reporters have complained of icy, uncleared paths.

The lower end of the village has some of the plushest lodgings, including the 5-star places in 'News'.

A free ski-bus runs every half hour on two separate routes.

SCENERY ***

Panoramas on high

The resort sits on a sunny, west-facing slope. The views are good from the village, fabulous from the high point at Cîme de Caron.

NEWS

2012/13: The Péclet gondola will be revamped with the addition of 10 cabins to increase capacity. The 4-star Hameau du Kashmir residence is due to open.

2011/12: The new Thorens jumbo gondola opened above the Portette chair, opening up two new runs – a red and a blue. A new red run on the slope down from the Méribel valley was built. Another 5km of snowmaking was added.

The new 5-star Altapura hotel opened, as did the resort's first 5-star apartment residence, Montana Plein Sud.

THE MOUNTAINS

The main disadvantage of Val Thorens is the lack of trees. Heavy snowfalls or high wind can shut practically all the lifts and slopes, and even if they don't close, poor visibility can be a problem. Some blue runs are pretty tough.

EXTENT OF THE SLOPES ★★★★★
High and snow-sure

The resort has a wide piste going right down the front of it, leading down to a number of different lifts. The big **Péclet** gondola heads more or less east from the resort and rises 700m to the Péclet glacier, with a choice of red runs or a blue down. Two of these link across to a wide area of runs beneath the ridge directly south of the resort, the high point of which is the **Pointe de Thorens**. Lifts go up to three points on the ridge. You can take very sunny red or blue runs into the 'fourth valley', the Maurienne, from the Col de Rosaël on the ridge, served by the Grand Fond jumbo gondola.

Above **Orelle** in the Maurienne valley two successive slow chairs go up to 3230m on the flanks of Pointe du Bouchet, the highest lift-served point in the Trois Vallées – stunning views. The former black run off the back here is now off-piste because of crevasse and avalanche danger.

The 150-person cable car to **Cîme de Caron** is one of the great lifts of the Alps, rising 900m in no time at all. It can be reached by skiing across from mid-mountain, or via the Caron gondola that starts below the village. From the top there is a choice of red and black pistes down the front, or a black into the Maurienne. Nearby, the relatively low **Boismint** sector is underused, but it is a very respectable hill with a total vertical of 860m.

Chairlifts heading north from the resort serve sunny slopes above the village and also lead to the link to the Méribel valley. Les Menuires can be reached via these lifts; the alternative Boulevard Cumin along the valley is nearly flat, and can be hard work.

FAST LIFTS ★★★★★
Very few slow ones

Recent investment means the lift system is impressive, with jumbo gondolas and fast chairs in most of the key places. It's quite surprising that none of the chairs has covers, though, considering the altitude and north-facing orientation of most slopes. Moving carpets have replaced old draglifts on the nursery slopes.

QUEUES ★★★
Persistent at the Cîme de Caron

Serious peak-time queues for the Cîme de Caron cable car are just a fact of life. You can plug in your iPod and accept the wait or get there early to avoid it. We think it's time a ticket system was operated here, so that you could ski while you wait. The chairlifts below the village are prone to queues – the Plein Sud chair (especially in the afternoon) and the Deux Lacs chair further down the slope. A reporter last year also fingered the Moutière chair, further down still. So the place is not

MICHAEL MARLAIS

Looking down over the Péclet gondola; up the hill to the right of the village is the Plein Sud area, which is where many of the catered chalets run by UK tour operators are located →

without its problems, though since the Rosaël chair back from the fourth valley was made a six-pack, the bottleneck there seems to have eased. Note that when snow is in short supply elsewhere, the pressure on the Val Thorens lifts can increase very markedly.

Crowded pistes, especially around the village, are a bigger problem than queues – compounded by people going too quickly. We have noticed this on recent visits, and lots of reporters have commented on it, too. We agree with a recent reporter who suggests that it is time the resort imposed slow skiing zones around the village – and policed them. Gendarmes on the slopes may not sound appealing, but the problem is serious.

TERRAIN PARKS ★★★★
Well designed
The terrain park on the 'Plateau' has been improving year-on-year. It is accessible via various chairlifts, served by a dedicated draglift and has a nice open layout. There are different areas that range from beginner to pro, with all sorts of tables, rails and box combinations. The hip/corner jump is excellent. The whole park is well maintained, and new obstacles are often built for local competitions. The park also has a giant airbag jump, to test your aerials before you put them to proper use on the snow. A separate boardercross lower down has some great banked turns, and lots for beginners. Neighbouring Les Menuires has a good park, too.

Aguille de Péclet
3560m
Glacier de Péclet
3100m
Glaci
Cha
PECLET
↙ Méribel
Col de la Chambre
2805m/9,200ft
A great lift for racking up the vertical – if it's working at full speed
Péclet
Bouquetin
Moraine
Portette
Chalet de la Marine
Cascades
Val Thorens
2300m/7,550ft
Plein Sud
Cairn
2 Lacs
Easy pistes around the village can get very crowded; and people go too fast here too, making collisions a hazard
Boismint
2660m
Caron
Boismint
BOISMINT
This sector is often quieter than those above the resort, and has a respectable 860m vertical
↙ Les Menuires
1800m/5,900ft
Lac du Lou

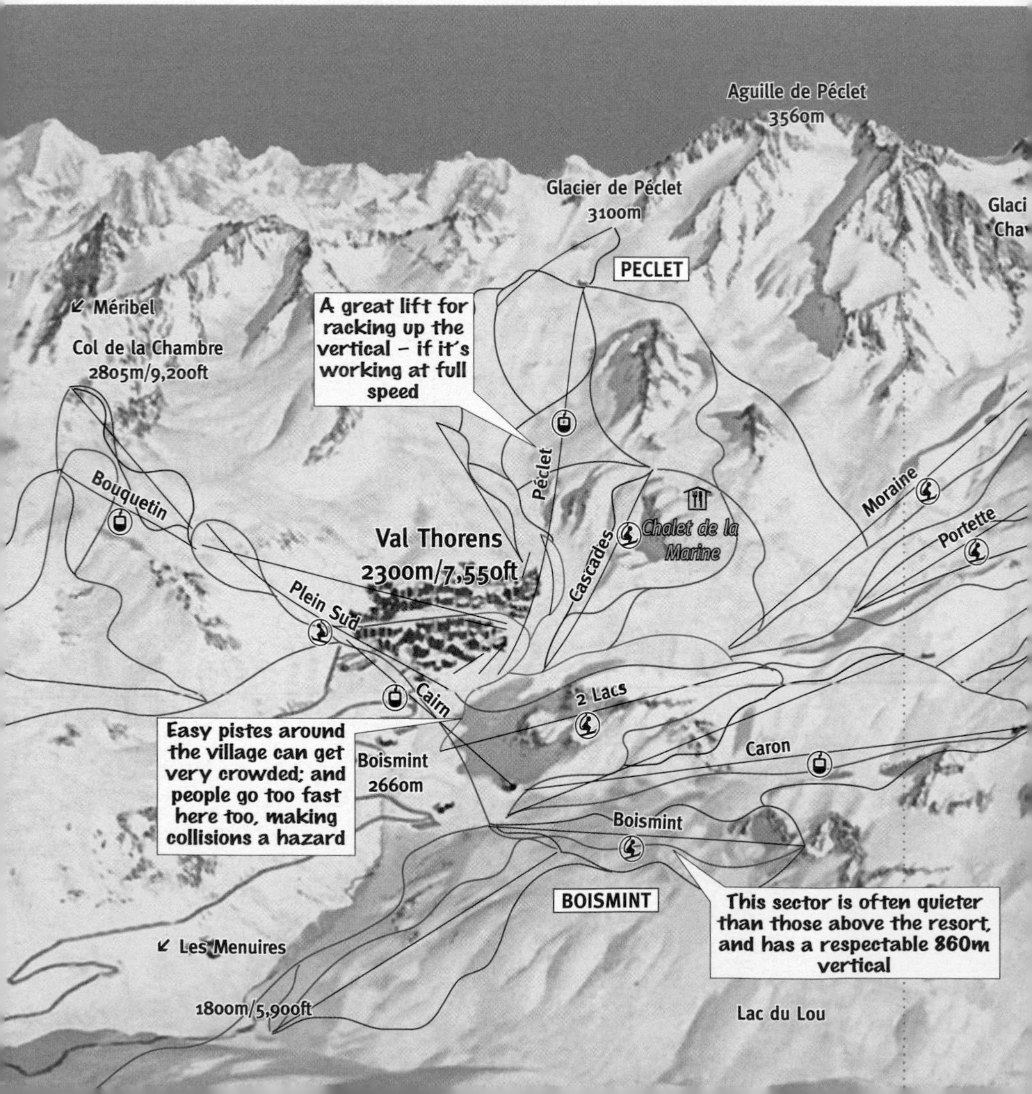

SNOW RELIABILITY ★★★★★
One of the best
Few resorts can rival Val Thorens for reliably good snow-cover, thanks to its altitude and generally north-facing slopes. Snowmaking covers a lot of the key pistes, including the crowded south- and west-facing runs on the way back from the Méribel valley and in the Orelle sector. But the terrain is rocky and needs a lot of snow for good coverage – we have found the higher runs patchy in some early season visits when snow throughout the Alps has been slow to arrive, and at times like that the off-piste terrain is obviously hazardous. The resort is offering a 'snow guarantee' that, between 24 November 2012 and 12 May 2013, no other European resort will have a higher number of connected runs open during your stay and you'll be able to ski to and from resort level; you'll be given a free skiing day on a future visit if either guarantee is not met; various conditions apply, of course.

FOR EXPERTS ★★★★
Lots to do off-piste
Val Thorens' local pistes are primarily intermediate terrain; many of the blacks could easily be classified red instead. The fast Cascades chair serves a short but steep black run that quickly gets mogulled. The pistes down from the Cîme de Caron cable car are challenging, but not seriously steep, and there's a good, sunny black run off the back into the fourth valley.

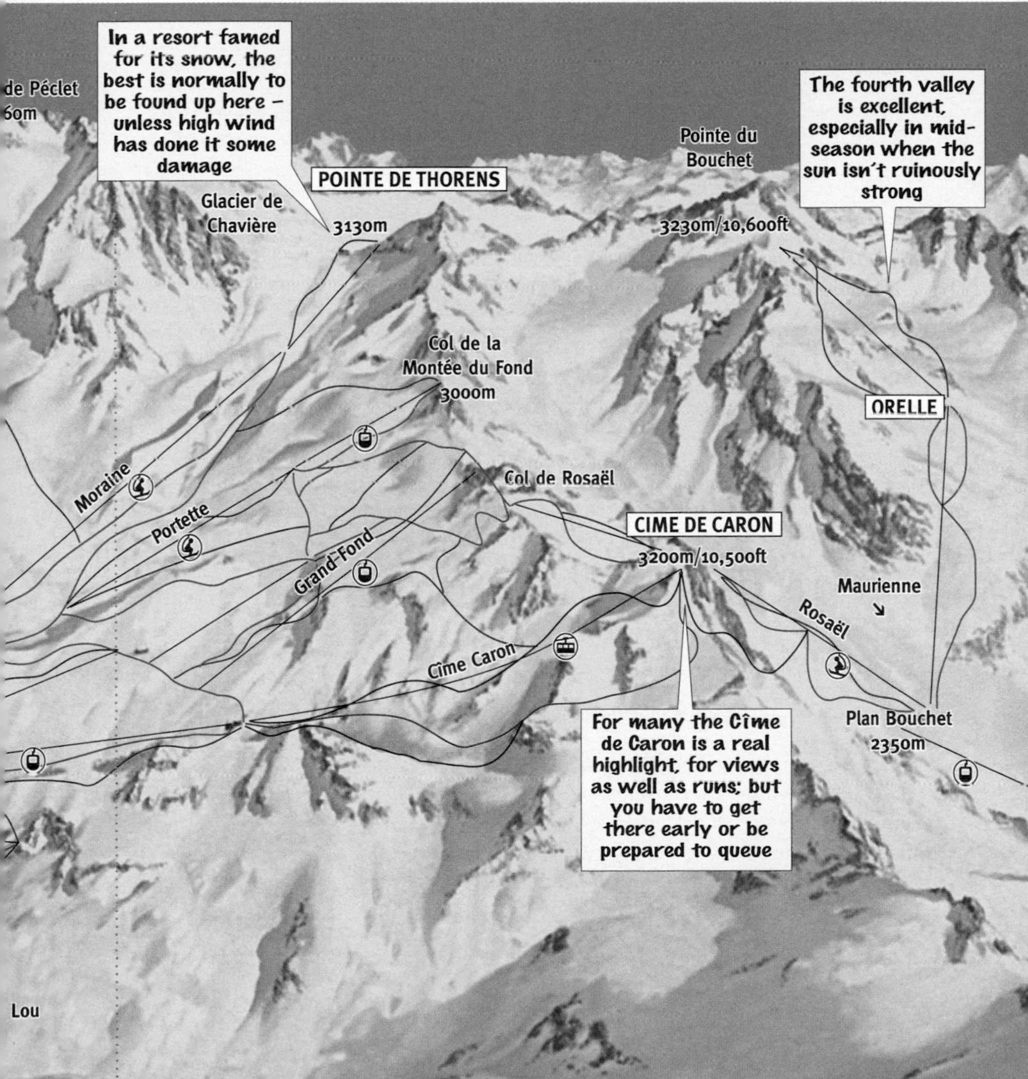

de Péclet
6om
In a resort famed for its snow, the best is normally to be found up here – unless high wind has done it some damage
POINTE DE THORENS
Glacier de Chavière
3130m
Pointe du Bouchet
3230m/10,600ft
The fourth valley is excellent, especially in mid-season when the sun isn't ruinously strong
Col de la Montée du Fond
3000m
ORELLE
Moraine
Portette
Col de Rosaël
CIME DE CARON
3200m/10,500ft
Grand-Fond
Maurienne
Rosaël
Cîme Caron
Plan Bouchet
2350m
For many the Cîme de Caron is a real highlight, for views as well as runs; but you have to get there early or be prepared to queue
Lou

LIFT PASSES

Trois Vallées

Prices in €

Age	1-day	6-day
under 13	37	184
13 to 64	49	244
65 plus	42	210

Free under 5, 75 plus

Beginner Nine lifts for 50% of Val Thorens day rate; free access to one draglift and four magic carpets

Notes
Covers Courchevel, La Tania, Méribel, Val Thorens, Les Menuires and St-Martin; family reductions; pedestrian and half-day passes

Alternative pass
Val Thorens-Orelle only; Vallée de Belleville only

The Falaise and Variante runs from the Grand Fond gondola can get heavily mogulled and be challenging. The sunny Goitshel run, one of the routes from the Méribel valley, is one of the easiest blacks we've seen, but it can be icy in the morning.

There is a huge amount of very good off-piste terrain to explore with a guide – read our feature panel below. But it does require good snowfall – note our remarks in 'Snow reliability'.

FOR INTERMEDIATES ★★★★★
Great in good weather

The scope for intermediates in the Trois Vallées is enormous. A keen intermediate can get to Courchevel 1650 at the far end in only 90 minutes or so, if not distracted on the way.

The local slopes in Val Thorens are some of the best intermediate terrain in the region. Most of the pistes are easy reds and blues (steeper on the top half of the mountain than the bottom) and made even more enjoyable by the excellent snow.

The snow on the red Col run is normally some of the best around. The blue Moraine below it is gentle and popular with the schools. The Grand Fond gondola serves a good variety of blue and red runs. The red and blue runs from the Péclet gondola are excellent. The Pluviomètre from the Trois Vallées chair is a glorious varied run, away from the lifts. Adventurous intermediates shouldn't miss the Cîme de Caron runs: the black here is very wide, usually has good snow, and is a wonderful fast cruise when freshly groomed (though reports suggest this is less likely than it was). Don't neglect the excellent, quiet Boismint area next door to Caron, either.

Blue-run skiers can now venture to the fourth valley, with the return run improved a few years back to become a blue (though not an easy one).

FOR BEGINNERS ★★★★
Good late-season choice

The slopes at the foot of the resort are very gentle and provide convenient, snow-sure nursery slopes, with moving carpet lifts and green runs. These are free, and there is a cheap pass for three serious lifts on the lower slopes – an excellent package. There are no long green runs to progress to, but the blues immediately above the village are easy. The resort's height and bleakness make it cold in midwinter, and intimidating in bad weather.

FABULOUS OFF-PISTE IN VAL THORENS

Val Thorens offers a huge choice of off-piste. And because of the high altitude, the snow stays powdery longer here than in lower parts of the Trois Vallées.

For those with little off-piste experience, the Pierre Lory Pass run is ideal. It is a very large and gentle slope, and you access the pass by doing an easy traverse on the Chavière glacier from the top of the Col chairlift. When you arrive at Pierre Lory Pass there are breathtaking views of the Aiguilles d'Arves in the Maurienne valley, and you will be just above the glacier du Bouchet, which you then ski down, rejoining the lift system at Plan Bouchet.

For those with more off-piste under their belt already, the Lac du Lou is a famous off-piste run of 1400m vertical. It is easily accessible from the Cîme de Caron. The many ways into this long, wide valley allow plenty of variety and opportunities for making first tracks; because many of the slopes face north or north-west it is not unusual to find good powder most of the ski season, even in late April. The views are stunning and you'll notice the quietness and vastness of the whole valley.

La Combe sans Nom in the fourth valley, also accessible from the Cîme de Caron cable car, usually offers superb skiing and snowboard conditions. There's a choice of south-, west- and, on the far side, some east-facing slopes, which makes for excellent spring skiing conditions.

For the more adventurous there are many options, including hiking up from the Col chairlift to a long run over the Gébroulaz glacier down to Méribel-Mottaret.

But don't even think about doing any off-piste runs without a fully qualified guide or instructor.

SCHOOLS

ESF
t 0479 000286

Ski Cool
t 0479 000492

Prosneige
t 0479 010700

Attitude
t 0479 065772

Classes (ESF prices)
6 days €214

Private lessons
from €41 for 1hr for 1-2 people

CHILDCARE

Nursery/mini-club (ESF)
t 0479 000286
Ages from 3mnth

Ski school
Ages 4 and over (ESF: 6 days €199)

GETTING THERE

Air Geneva 160km/ 100 miles (2hr30); Lyon 200km/ 125 miles (2hr45); Chambéry 120km/ 75 miles (2hr15)

Rail Moûtiers (37km/23 miles); regular buses from station

FOR BOARDERS ★★★★
Reliable all season

Val Thorens has always been popular with snowboarders; it is the highest and most snow-sure of the Trois Vallées resorts, and has a younger feel in comparison with Courchevel and Méribel – though it's almost as pricey. Being far above the treeline, the slopes are rather bleak; however, there are great steep runs, gullies and groomed pistes for all levels. The terrain park is worth a visit. The lifts are mainly chairs and gondolas.

FOR CROSS-COUNTRY ★
Go to Les Menuires

There are no cross-country trails in Val Thorens. Your best bet is the 28km link between Les Menuires and St-Martin-de-Belleville.

MOUNTAIN RESTAURANTS ★★★★
Lots of choice

For a high modern resort, the choice of restaurants is good, and improving. The piste map names the restaurants, unlike those of the other valleys. It's such a simple thing ...

Editors' choice We've had several good lunches in the rustic table-service section of the Chalet de la Marine (0479 000186), repeatedly endorsed by readers, including two this year. It has a big terrace with 'funky' music. The self-service section below has a wide choice. And the loos are 'the best on the piste'. The self-service Folie Douce and table-service Fruitière are modelled on the Val d'Isère originals, the latter with an interesting menu, well executed when we lunched there. Reporters in 2012 confirm that the après-lunch party is 'mental' – 'not to be missed'.

Worth knowing about The Chalet des 2 Ours is repeatedly recommended for food ('great homemade pasta'), service and views. The rustic Chalet des 2 Lacs is also a reader favourite; a regular visitor found service slack last year, but a 2012 reporter loved its 'homely feel, good food and log fire'.

The piste map shows picnic areas.

SCHOOLS AND GUIDES ★★★
Good reports

Prosneige is a small school that limits class sizes to 10 and gets very good reports. A 2012 reporter 'could not praise them enough – they really brought the children's skiing on across a wide range of ability'.

The ESF offers a wide choice of private and group classes, including freestyle and freeride courses. One reporter who was very pleased with their Club Med ESF teacher in 2011 had a bad experience in 2012 when put into an 'English-speaking ghetto' group where 'the instructor didn't do any teaching'. There are several guiding outfits.

FOR FAMILIES ★★★
Some facilities

There is a children's area, Espace Junior, beside the 2 Lacs chairlift and a good family toboggan run. The tourist office produces a handy family guide to weekly activities. We lack reports on the ESF nursery.

STAYING THERE

Accommodation is of a higher standard than in many purpose-built resorts – more comfortable and stylish.

Chalets Most catered chalets are apartments in quite big developments, mainly the relatively new ones above the resort centre. This has the advantage that you often have the use of a pool in the residence. There are no notably swanky places.

Skiworld has 16 units, Crystal eight (including a 'Riders Lodge' aimed at the younger end of the market) and Inghams seven, one new for 2012/13.

Ski Total has five that are more like actual chalets – two units in one chalet, three in another, all with shared saunas. And it added a standalone chalet to the programme last year with use of the pool and sauna at the nearby Chalet des Neiges residence. All look very smart.

Hotels Unusually for a high, purpose-built resort, there are plenty of hotels, and there's a Club Med, too.

*******Altapura** (0457 747474) This stylish new 5-star with indoor/outdoor pool etc opened last season. A reporter liked its 'unfussy atmosphere with tip-top food and service' but found it 'ferociously expensive'.

******Fitz Roy** (0479 000478) Smart, with good service and lovely rooms. Good restaurant with flexible half-board menu. Pool. Well placed at the heart of things.

*****Sherpa** (0479 000070) Highly recommended by past reporters. Cosy,

Where is Austria's Golden Gate? Answer on p168.

UK PACKAGES

Action Outdoors, Alpine Answers, Alpine Elements, Club Med, Crystal, Crystal Finest, Erna Low, Flexiski, Independent Ski Links, Inghams, Interactive Resorts, Lagrange, Momentum, Mountain Wave, Neilson, Pierre & Vacances, PowderBeds, Powder White, Ski Amis, Ski Bespoke, Ski Club Freshtracks, Ski Collection, Ski Expectations, Ski France, Ski Independence, Ski Line, Ski Solutions, Ski Supreme, Ski Total, Skitracer, Ski Weekend, Skiworld, Thomson
Orelle AmeriCan Ski, Peak Retreats, Zenith

ACTIVITIES

Indoor Sports centre (spa, sauna, fitness room, hot tub, tennis, squash, swimming pool, volleyball, table tennis, badminton, football), cinema, bowling, concerts

Outdoor Paragliding, microlight flights, snowmobiles, snowshoeing, walks, tobogganing, ice driving, bikes on snow, paintball, rolling bubble

Phone numbers
From abroad use the prefix +33 and omit the initial '0' of the phone number

TOURIST OFFICE

www.valthorens.com

lots of wood. Ski-in/ski-out.
*****Val Chavière** (0479 000033) 'Friendly, fab position, good set menu,' says a 2011 reporter.
*****Val Thorens** (0479 000433) Next door to Fitz Roy. Being renovated for 2012/13.
Apartments Val Thorens now has lots of smart chalet-style developments. These and many other residences are offered by UK operators and agents including Ski Collection, Ski Amis, Pierre & Vacances, Lagrange, Erna Low, Skiworld and Skitracer.

In the Plein Sud area, above the main village, there are several chalet-style residences. Among the best are Chalet Altitude and Chalet Val 2400, sharing a pool. The Balcons de Val Thorens has a 'fantastic' spa with pool. Many properties up here claim to be ski-in and possibly ski-out, but a couple of reporters have confirmed our own suspicion that access can be tricky in practice.

There are three Montagnettes residences, of which the clear leader is the hotel-style Oxalys, with pool, hot tubs, separate spa for those in the best apartments and a superb restaurant (see 'Eating out'); some of the units here are very impressive.

The 5-star Montana Plein Sud residence with pool etc opened last season. And the 4-star Hameau du Kashmir with three types of sauna and a pool is due to open for 2012/13.

EATING OUT ★★★★

Star quality

Val Thorens has something for most tastes and pockets. The resort's 'Holiday Guide' is very helpful, with photos and some idea of the cuisine.

Top of the range is the restaurant in the residence Oxalys, with two Michelin stars. We had a delicious and very inventive meal here; expensive, but worth it. The Fitz Roy and Val Thorens hotels also have serious restaurants. The Epicurien has gastro ambitions, too.

There are plenty of more modest places. The Galoubet was one reader's 'restaurant of the year' for choice, quality and service. For Savoyard stuff there's the Fondue ('friendly, intimate'), Auberge des Balcons ('nice food, attentive staff'), Chaumière ('good-quality steak and pasta') and the 'friendly' Cabane. The Vieux Chalet has a varied menu, including seafood and duck. The Steak Club found favour with a 2012 visitor: 'went three times – excellent pasta, steaks, burgers'. The Blanchot is a stylish wine bar with a simple but varied carte.

APRES-SKI ★★★★

Livelier than you might expect

Val Thorens is more lively than most high-altitude ski stations. The action now starts up the hill at the Folie Douce (see 'Mountain restaurants') or on the terrace of Club Med in the village. The Red Fox up at Balcons is crowded at close of play, with karaoke. The Frog and Roastbeef at the top of the village is a long-established British ghetto – though two reporters this year hated it ('sleazy', 'overrated'). The Saloon and the Downunder bar (formerly the Viking) are lively. Quieter bars include the cosy Rhum Box Cafe (aka Mitch's). Later on, the Malaysia cellar bar rocks from 11pm until the early hours with 'top quality' live bands and dancing.

OFF THE SLOPES ★★

Could be worse

Val Thorens is not ideal for non-skiers. But there's a sports centre with small pool, saunas, hot tubs, gym etc and a leisure centre with bowling (pricey) and pool tables. Free weekly concerts are held in the church (recommended by a reporter), and there are twice-weekly street markets, a small cinema and an ice-driving course. The toboggan run (longest in France) is 'great fun'. Pedestrians can get to some mountain restaurants, and the panorama from the Cîme de Caron is not to be missed. Buses to St-Martin and Les Menuires run four times a day except Saturdays. The Monday night welcome festivities are well done.

OUTLYING RESORT – 900m

ORELLE

Set at the foot of the gondola from the fourth valley (there's no piste down), Orelle isn't a recognizable resort, but offers good accommodation at a bargain price. A couple of hairpins up the hill from the lift base (there's a frequent ski-bus) is Hameau des Eaux, a smart complex of 200 apartments in eight chalet-style buildings, sharing a spa with decent pool – available through Peak Retreats and Zenith. It includes a small convenience store and a restaurant. The small town of St-Michel is 6km away.

Vars / Risoul

Two high, purpose-built resorts in an attractive setting, with a traditional French atmosphere and a big linked area of slopes

TOP 10 RATINGS

Extent	***
Fast lifts	*
Queues	****
Snow	***
Expert	**
Intermediate	****
Beginner	****
Charm	**
Convenience	****
Scenery	***

RPI	80
lift pass	£140
ski hire	£85
lessons	£75
food & drink	£105
total	**£405**

KEY FACTS

Resort	1850m 6,070ft
The entire Forêt Blanche ski area	
Slopes	1660-2750m 5,450-9,020ft
Lifts	50
Pistes	185km 115 miles
Green	17%
Blue	42%
Red	32%
Black	9%
Snowmaking	116 guns

+ Attractive, family-friendly resorts
+ Fair-sized, uncrowded area of slopes
+ High resorts, reasonably snow-sure, but with lots of treelined runs
+ Among the cheapest resorts in the French Alps

– Still mainly draglifts and slow old chairs, though a few fast ones
– Few on-piste challenges for expert skiers and boarders
– Little to do off the slopes
– Fairly remote location

Were they nearer Geneva, Vars and its linked neighbour Risoul might be as well known as Les Arcs and Flaine. The slopes of their shared Forêt Blanche area are equally extensive, and the villages are more attractive than either. We visited a couple of seasons ago and loved it, despite the seriously flawed lift system (it's probably the most antiquated in these pages). All a question of priorities ...

THE RESORT

Vars and Risoul are the most southerly French resorts to get a chapter in this book. Airport transfers can take some time. Vars includes several small, old villages on or near the approach road, chief among them Vars-Ste-Marie. There are lifts on the fringe of this village, but the focus for most visitors is higher, purpose-built Vars-les-Claux.

Village charm Vars-les-Claux has a lot of flat-roofed apartment blocks that look worse from up the mountain than in the village because in the village you can see the smaller chalet-style buildings as well. Reporters like the pleasant, relaxed atmosphere.

Convenience It's a small place, but spread along a winding, quite steep road, with two main clusters of shops, bars, restaurants and lodgings: the original focus at the base of the main gondola; and Point Show, 10 minutes' walk up the hill. Each has nursery slopes and fast lifts into the slopes. Buildings spread beyond these points, varying in convenience.

Scenery Pretty wooded slopes surround the village, and Pic de Chabrières has fine views.

THE MOUNTAINS

There are slopes on both sides of the valley, linked by pistes and by slow double chairlifts at the lower end of Vars-les-Claux.

Some reporters have found piste classification variable and the map unclear on the links between resorts.

Slopes The wooded, west-facing Peynier area is the smaller sector, and reaches only 2275m. The main slopes are in an east-facing bowl with links to the Risoul slopes at three points. There's also a speed-skiing course.

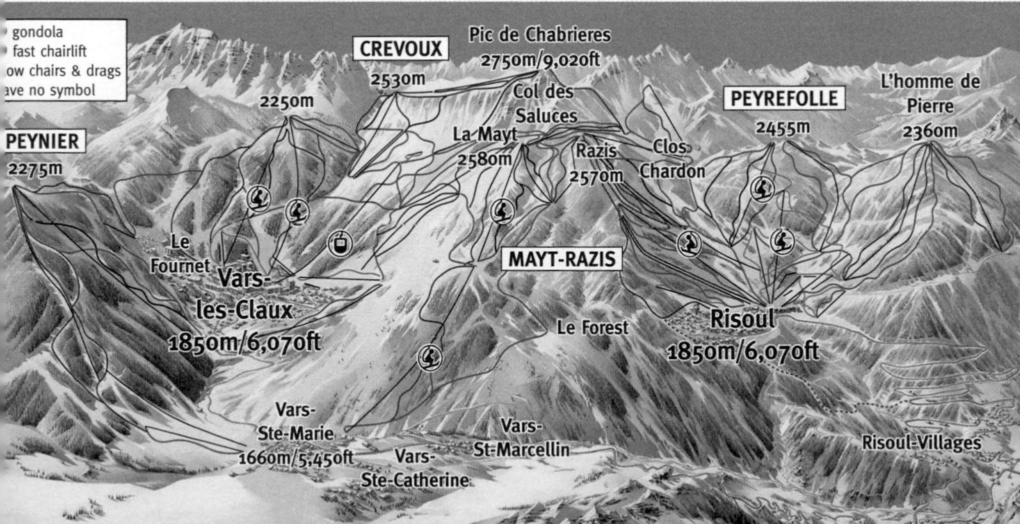

↑ Risoul's 'front de neige' is very pleasant and compact and safe for children

OT RISOUL

NEWS

2011/12: In Risoul, a quad replaced the triple Razis chair (which accesses the Vars sector), more snowmaking was installed, and a beginner terrain park and a four-seasons ice rink with a synthetic surface opened. In Vars, two new terrain parks were built: the Girly park with 13 obstacles all in pink and the Kid park for children from age three. And a new rail line was built in the Eyssina park.

Beneath it are easy runs, open at the top but dropping into trees.

Fast lifts After the three fast lifts out of the village it's draglifts and slow chairs unless you head down to Vars-Ste-Marie or over to Risoul.

Queues Queues are rare outside the French holidays, and even then Vars is not as busy as most family resorts. But a January 2012 visitor was concerned about crowding on the slopes, with lots of eastern Europeans and Russians about.

Terrain parks There are six freestyle areas, including two new ones – the Girly and Kid parks.

Snow reliability Not bad: the altitudes are quite high, the orientation mostly easterly, and snowmaking is plentiful.

Experts There is little to challenge experts on-piste, but there is plenty of off-piste terrain (and great off-piste tree skiing in Risoul, too).

Intermediates These are fine intermediate slopes, with a good mix of decent reds and easy blues. Jas du Boeuf from La Mayt is a gentle cruise. The Olympique red run from the top of La Mayt to Ste-Marie delights most reporters and is a very respectable 920m vertical. If you can face the slow chairlifts and tricky drags, there are good treelined runs in the separate Peynier sector.

Beginners There are three free lifts on good slopes in central Vars, with lots of progression runs throughout the area. Quick learners will be able to get over to Risoul by the end of the week.

Snowboarding There is good freeriding, but beginners might find the number of draglifts a problem.

Cross-country There are 10km of trails.

Mountain restaurants Most places are self-service. But the revamped Chal Heureux table-service place is 'good, with acceptable food and prices'.

Schools and guides A recent reporter had 'great' private lessons with ESF.

Families The ski school runs a nursery for children from two years old, and there is a ski kindergarten.

STAYING THERE

Hotels The Ecureuil (0492 465072) is an attractive, modern B&B chalet. Ste-Marie has a Logis de France – the Vallon (0492 465472).

Apartments Ski Collection features five apartment complexes. Pierre & Vacances has three, including the 4-star Albane – liked by a reporter.

Eating out There is a choice of simple, good-value places. The Après Ski at Point Show is worth a look, as is the Chaudron in Ste-Marie.

Après-ski Après-ski is animated at teatime. Later on, nightlife revolves around one or two bars.

Off the slopes There's tobogganing, ice skating, 34km of walking paths, cinema, leisure centre, snowmobiling, snowshoeing and dog sledding.

UK PACKAGES

Vars Crystal, Erna Low, Lagrange, Pierre & Vacances, PowderBeds, Ski Collection, Ski France
Risoul Crystal, Interactive Resorts, Lagrange, PowderBeds, Rocketski, Ski Collection, Ski France, Skitracer, Thomson, Zenith

Phone numbers
From abroad use the prefix +33 and omit the initial '0' of the phone number

TOURIST OFFICES

Vars
www.vars-ski.com
Risoul
www.risoul.com

Risoul 1850m

+ Uncrowded slopes
+ Some good off-piste terrain
− Still lots of difficult draglifts
− Limited mountain restaurants

Risoul 1850 is a modern ski station, purpose-built from the late 1970s onwards at the top of a winding road up from the original village of Risoul.

It is a quiet, apartment-based resort, popular with families – but not exclusively so.
Village charm Many of the original resort buildings are bulky eight- or nine-storey buildings, but wood-clad with some traditional style. Newer developments are attractive and chalet-style, made of wood and stone. The busy little main street, with a small range of shops, bars and restaurants, is far from traffic-free. But the locals offer a friendly and welcoming atmosphere.
Convenience The village meets the mountain in classic French purpose-built style, with sunny restaurant terraces facing the slopes and a compact centre. But some lodgings are a short but 'knackering' uphill walk away if you miss the last lift.
Scenery Risoul has a pleasantly woody setting beneath its slopes; reporters often comment on great views.

THE MOUNTAINS

The upper slopes are open, but those back to Risoul are prettily wooded, and good for bad-weather days.
Slopes The slopes, mainly north-facing, spread over several minor peaks and bowls, and connect with neighbouring Vars at two points.
Fast lifts There are three fast chairs accessing a good number of runs, but still lots of tricky 'difficile' draglifts.
Queues Queues are rare. But see the comment under Vars about crowds.
Terrain parks For 2012/13 there will only be the Zing beginner park with easy jumps and rails and a boardercross but no half-pipe.
Snow reliability Snow reliability is reasonably good; the slopes are all above 1850m and mostly north-facing. Snowmaking is fairly extensive.
Experts Risoul's main top stations access a couple of steepish descents. And there's some good off-piste terrain – including excellent, widely spaced tree skiing on not very steep slopes and areas accessed through gates that are closed when there's an avalanche risk (though these are not marked or explained on the piste map).
Intermediates There are decent reds and blues in all sectors. Almost all Risoul's runs return to the village, making it difficult to get lost.
Beginners Three free lifts serve good, convenient nursery slopes. There are lots of easy pistes to move on to.
Snowboarding There is a lot of good freeriding to be done throughout the area, although beginners might not like the large proportion of draglifts.
Cross-country There are 15km of trails.
Mountain restaurants Choice is limited. The Homme de Pierre 'brings you decent dishes cooked to order', says a 2012 visitor. And the self-service Tetras is a small, attractive hut, with 'good food, friendly staff', says a visitor who went there every day of his trip.
Schools and guides Reports on the ESF have been positive, and we had an excellent ESF guide on our visit.
Families Risoul is very much a family resort. Both ski schools operate ski kindergartens slightly above the village and reached by a child-friendly lift.

STAYING THERE

Most visitors stay in apartments.
Hotels The Chardon Bleu (0492 460727) is right on the slopes. You can also stay overnight up at the Tetras mountain refuge (0492 460983).
Apartments We enjoyed the 4-star Balcons de Sirius units – good pool, hot tub and sauna; Antarés is similar. Ski Collection has these and another property.
Eating out There's a decent choice offering fairly good value. Readers tips: Chérine (pizza, pasta), Marmite ('superb steaks and friendly staff') and Entre Pot ('very friendly, fantastic food'). We tried L'Extrad, which served huge portions (enough for two) of hearty mountain food.
Après-ski Nightlife is livelier than most people are expecting. There are several bars and the Relex club. Try the Babao and the Chalet or Eterlou for a quieter drink.
Off the slopes Limited. We enjoyed the guided night-time snowmobiling on adventurous and varied terrain. There's also tobogganing, snowshoeing and skating. Excursions to Briançon are possible.

Germany

Germany isn't a big destination for UK-based skiers. Over the page is a chapter on Garmisch-Partenkirchen, by far the most important downhill resort in Germany – famously the venue for the 1936 Olympics (when downhill racing was introduced, and Adolf Hitler got the facilities built on time). Seventy-five years later it hosted the 2011 World Championships. On this page is a non-comprehensive tour of the country's main skiing regions.

THE ALPS

Allgäu This region claims 300km of downhill runs and an amazing 800km of cross-country trails. The main lift systems operate under the regional name Das Hoechste. Highest of all is Nebelhorn (2225m) reached from the nice little town of **Oberstdorf** by a two-stage cable car to the main slopes (served by two chairs), with a third stage to the top for Germany's longest piste (7.5km). Oberstdorf is probably best known as the resort which kicks off the annual Four Hills ski jumping tournament held over each New Year period. The Post hotel has been praised for 'good, substantial, reasonably priced' meals. South of Oberstdorf you enter **Kleinwalsertal**, which belongs to Austria, strangely. The Kanzelwand slopes link with Fellhorn to form Germany's 'biggest and most modern' area, with three six-packs, two gondolas and nine other lifts. Walmendingerhorn, a little further up the valley, and Ifen are smaller areas and the Allgäu has lots of other resorts such as Oberjoch and Pfronten.
Bavarian Alps Garmisch-Partenkirchen is covered over the page. **Mittenwald** (915m) is a cute town in a spectacular setting. The cable car to Karwendel accesses an epic ski route dropping 1300m in 6km. Across the valley seven lifts serve modest slopes up to 1350m. The other resorts are on the fringes of the Alps, with less dramatic scenery. **Oberammergau** (835m and famous for its once-a-decade Passion Play) is another cute town, with a gondola to Laber (1685m) that accesses a long ski route and a direct black piste; across town a chairlift serves Kolbensattel (1270m). There are more extensive slopes on Brauneck above **Lenggries** (680m) – 34km of pistes with a top height of 1710m, and 18 lifts including a gondola.

There are other small resorts, some near the infamous Berchtesgaden.

THE REST

Black Forest In the south-west corner: a lot of cross-country, but downhill too. Feldberg reaches 1500m with 31 lifts and 55km of pistes.
Harz A low mountain range, south of Hanover. A handful of small resorts, the biggest being Braunlage.
Sauerland Low mountains east of Düsseldorf. Some 300km of cross-country. Winterberg has 21 lifts, Willingen a gondola and 11 drags.
Saxony On the border with the Czech Republic: a handful of low, small resorts, the most compelling at Fichtelberg above Oberwiesenthal.
Thüringer Wald North-east of Frankfurt: extensive cross-country, and a bit of easy downhill. The best-known resort is Oberhof.

BAYERISCHE ZUGSPITZBAHN BERGBAHN AG

← Germany has quite a few small ski resorts but Garmisch-Partenkirchen is by far the biggest and best known, and its glacier area (shown here) usually has excellent snow

WEBSITES

Allgäu
www.english.allgaeu.info
www.das-hoechste.de

Bavarian Alps
www.karwendelbahn.de
www.laber-bergbahn.de
www.brauneck-bergbahn.de

Black Forest
www.blackforest-tourism.com

Harz
www.harzinfo.de

Sauerland
www.wintersport-arena.de

Saxony
www.oberwiesenthal.com
www.fichtelberg-ski.de

Thüringer Wald
www.oberhof.de

MARKT GARMISCH-PARTENKIRCHEN

Garmisch-Partenkirchen

Twin resort towns sprawling at the foot of Germany's highest mountain, reaching glacial heights on the Austrian border

TOP 10 RATINGS

Extent	*
Fast lifts	***
Queues	***
Snow	***
Expert	****
Intermediate	***
Beginner	*
Charm	***
Convenience	**
Scenery	****

RPI	80
lift pass	£160
ski hire	£85
lessons	£70
food & drink	£95
total	**£410**

NEWS

2012/13: A six-pack is due to replace the Wetterwand T-bars on the glacier, starting lower down near the bottom of the Sonnenkar chair but ending at the same place as the T-bars did.

- + Weather-proof combo of fair-sized glacier and woods lower down
- + Some spectacular views
- + Some excellent, challenging runs
- + Good-value hotels, cheap for eating and drinking, good for short breaks
- − Except on glacier, very few long easy runs – beginners and timid intermediates beware
- − Many of the best runs descend to low altitude, where conditions are rarely good
- − Glacier access takes time

Garmisch is Germany's leading ski resort. It has two separate ski areas: one at low altitude with mainly tough runs, the other on a glacier with gentler terrain. It has plenty to amuse confident skiers for a couple of days, and with short transfers from Munich it makes a good short-break destination.

THE RESORT

Garmisch and Partenkirchen are separate towns that have merged as they have spread to fill the broad, flat valley bottom beneath the Zugspitze, while keeping their centres distinct.

There are smaller resorts on the Austrian side of the Zugspitze. These and the Garmisch ski areas are covered by the Top Snow Card.

Village charm Each half of the resort is a sizeable town – spacious and pleasant but not notably captivating.

Convenience You'll need to use trains, buses or cars at both ends of the day. The Zugspitze railway starts next to the main station, more or less between the two town centres; it goes to the glacier via the other lift bases.

Scenery The Wetterstein massif, of which the Zugspitze is the peak, is impressive, and there are great panoramic views from the top – plus some dramatic scenery lower down.

THE MOUNTAINS

The glacier is quite separate from the lower slopes, which the resort calls the 'Classic' area. In fact, that area also divides into two parts, awkwardly linked – a higher, almost treeless part (Alpspitz) and a lower, heavily wooded part (Hausberg-Kreuzeck). Piste marking is slack.

Slopes The **Hausberg-Kreuzeck** sector directly above the resort is accessed by two gondolas; these start a few km out of town and are served by the railway. These lower lifts have decent verticals and serve long runs; the lifts higher up are all much shorter. An inconspicuous narrow path and a rope tow form the link between this sector and the base of the higher **Alpspitz** sector, more directly reached via the Alpspitz cable car. Although the altitude is modest, this sector feels like high-mountain terrain, with dramatic scenery – Dolomite-like on the isolated Osterfelder and Bernadein runs, on skier's right.

There are two routes to the glacier: there's the railway from town that serves the 'Classic' area lift bases, which goes on to tunnel slowly through the mountain, emerging at the glacier; or there's the cable car from Eibsee that climbs 1950m to the Zugspitze – from there you have to ride another cable car down to the slopes. Although the Zugspitze is not notably high (2960m), its isolated position gives great views.

Above the main lift junction are typical blue glacier slopes served by multiple drags. Below it and spreading across the bowl is a range of good red runs and some good off-piste terrain served by two six-packs (one new for 2012/13) and two drags. None of these lifts rises more than 400m vertical, but in other respects it's a good area.

Fast lifts Access lifts are fast, but after that it's mainly drags and slow chairs.

Queues Fine weekends attract crowds from Munich; but at other times we don't expect problems.

Terrain parks On the glacier there is a 1km-long park (now served by the new six-pack) with expert and novice lines, with kickers, boxes and rails in each; plus another beginner park beside it.

Snow reliability The glacier area is small and remote, so conditions lower down are important. The lower main

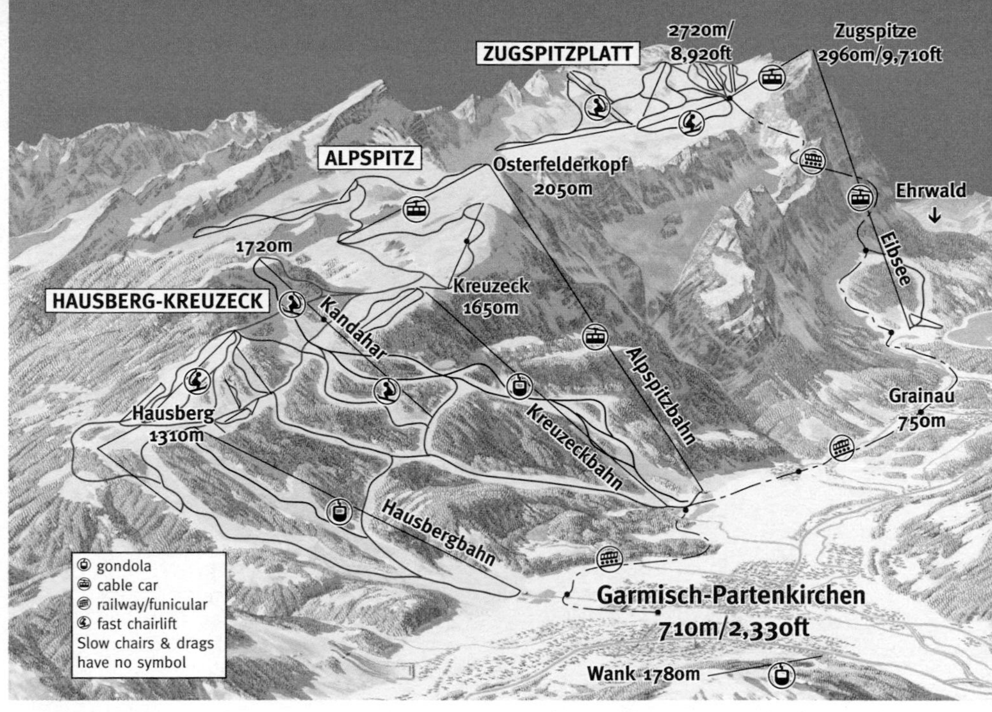

KEY FACTS

Resort	710m 2,330ft
Slopes	720-2720m 2,360-8,920ft
Lifts	30
Pistes	58km 36 miles
Blue	25%
Red	70%
Black	5%
Snowmaking	47%

UK PACKAGES

Momentum

Phone numbers
From elsewhere in Germany add the prefix 08821. From abroad use the prefix +49 and delete the initial '0'

TOURIST OFFICE

www.gapa.de

area is shady, but some of the best runs descend to valley level – ie to 720m. Despite comprehensive snowmaking, conditions at these altitudes can be poor even when there's great snow higher up, as we confirmed one January visit.
Experts The long runs to the valley are challenging enough to amuse most experts, particularly the excellent Kandahar downhill race course. The final pitch of this takes real bottle when icy at the end of the day. Higher up, there are off-piste opportunities in the Alpspitz sector and on the glacier.
Intermediates For confident skiers it's fine, but this is not a hill where timid intermediates can build confidence.
Beginners Learn elsewhere. The nursery slopes are fine, but they're up the mountain and there is no beginner pass. And the only easy runs to move on to are busy links between Kreuzeck and Hausberg (or on the glacier).
Snowboarding There are drags in all sectors, though many can be avoided.
Cross-country There are 28km of trails along the valleys, of varying difficulty.
Mountain restaurants The glass-sided Gletschergarten on the glacier has a roof that can open on sunny days. Hochalm below Alpspitz in the 'Classic' area does Bavarian fare. The Bayernhaus is worth a stop on the gentle blue run 6 from Hausberg.
Schools and guides There are several schools, but we lack reports.
Families The Kinderland centre at Hausberg looks good, with magic carpet and snow sculptures. There are family discounts on the lift pass.

STAYING THERE

Hotels There is one 5-star – Reindl's Partenkirchner Hof (943870), well placed for the rail stations – and lots of 4-stars and 3-stars. Tips are the 3-star Garmischer Hof (9110) and Atlas Post (7090), and the 4-star Zugspitze (9010). Rates are low in Alpine terms.
Apartments Can be booked via the tourist office.
Eating out Plenty of choice. Gasthof Fraundorfer and the upscale Alpenhof do hearty Bavarian food. Spago – in the Hotel Obermühle – is an Italian.
Après-ski There are bars at the lift bases where you can enjoy waiting for the next train home, and in town there are lots of cosy bars such as Zirbel Stube. Peaches is a lively bar.
Off the slopes There's lots to do, both outdoors and indoors. Walks include one through the Partnachklamm gorge and paths on the lift-served hill that is across town from the slopes – called Wank. There's an ice rink and toboggan runs – including a 5km run at Mount Hausberg that is floodlit twice a week.

tend to use it more effectively than other Alpine countries. We have skied in Courmayeur and in the Dolomites when little natural snow has fallen, and in each case there has been excellent cruising on pistes blanketed in man-made snow.

A lot of Italian runs seem flatteringly easy. This is partly because grooming is immaculate and partly because piste classification often seems to overstate difficulty. Nowhere is this clearer than in the linked slopes of La Thuile (in Italy) and La Rosière (in France), where a couple of lift rides take you from Italian motorways classified red to French mogul fields classified blue.

THIS HAS TO STOP

Italy seems to have been in the grip of 'legislation fever' for the last few years, with mixed results. Italian bars and restaurants are now smoke-free, a huge improvement. And it is now compulsory for children (under 14, we understand) to wear helmets on the slopes. But many areas have also made it illegal to go off-piste near their pistes, or to go off-piste at all, or to go off-piste outside defined routes or without a guide or without transceiver, shovel and probe. We've tried to get to the bottom of these developments; but a prompt, clear, accurate response to a slightly technical question such as this is not a speciality of Italian tourist bodies.

Some resorts tell us there are national laws; others, that it's a regional matter; others, that it's a local matter. Of course, there is then the matter of whether the law is applied and how it is policed. Where we have a clear view of the situation in a given resort, we've

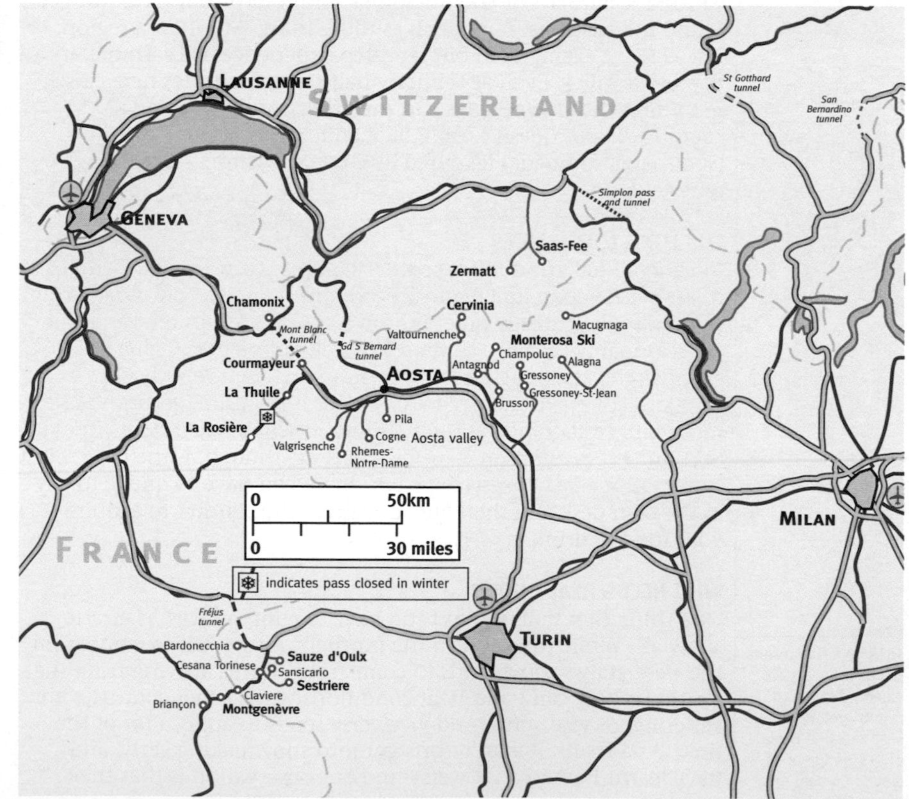

included that in the relevant chapter. We'll continue to investigate, and post the results on our website. Thankfully, we have no evidence of any interference in off-piste skiing in the Aosta valley, which is Italy's off-piste/heli-skiing HQ.

A bizarre twist last season was that Livigno overturned its blanket ban on off-piste skiing by designating half a dozen slopes in one sector of the area (Mottolino) as freeride zones, marking them on the piste map and constructing entry gates equipped with gadgets to check that your avalanche bleepers are working. This is a very welcome development, although we can't help thinking that a better scheme would have been to make these zones safe against avalanche risk. Some of them, after all, are between pistes, where the risk could easily be controlled. Still, at least there is now something for experts to do in Livigno, whereas two years ago there was essentially nothing.

DRIVING IN THE ITALIAN ALPS

There are four main geographical groupings of Italian resorts, widely separated. Getting to some of these resorts is a very long haul, and moving from one area to another can involve very long drives (though the extensive motorway network is a great help).

The handful of resorts to the west of Turin – Bardonecchia, Sauze d'Oulx, Sestriere and neighbours in the Milky Way region – are easily reached from France via the Fréjus tunnel, or via the good road over the pass that the French resort of Montgenèvre sits on.

Further north, and somewhat nearer to Turin than Milan, are the

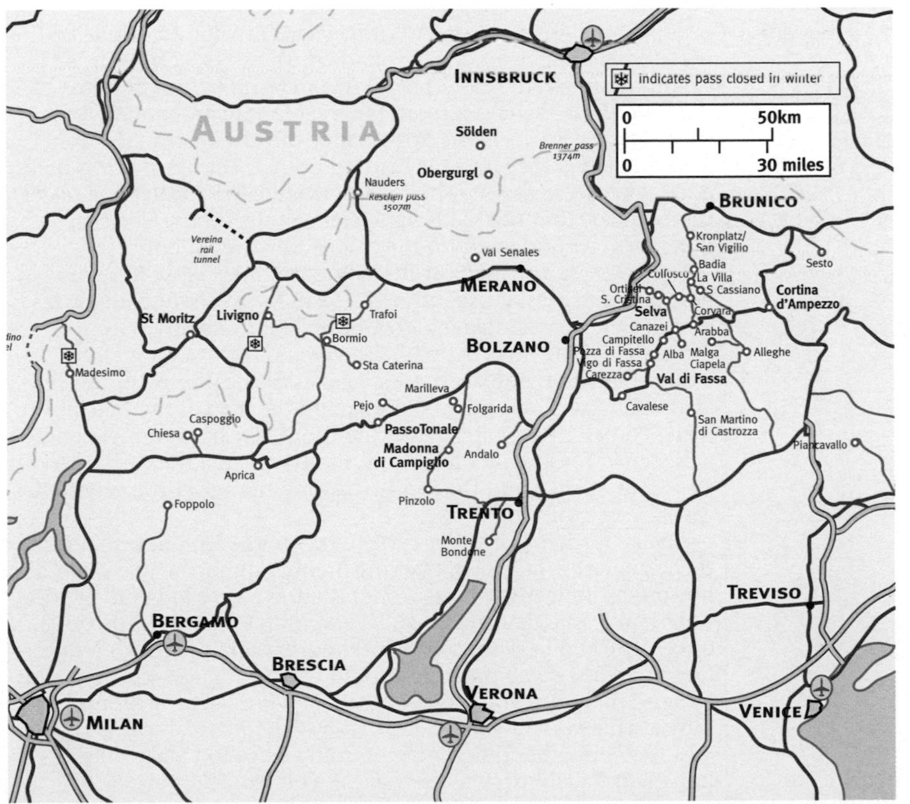

↑ Italy offers all sorts of resorts, from simple to swanky. Livigno is a pleasantly traditional village with a traffic-free core

SNOWPIX.COM / CHRIS GILL

resorts of the Aosta valley – Courmayeur, Cervinia, La Thuile and the Monterosa area are the best known. These (especially Courmayeur) are the easiest of all Italian resorts to reach from Britain or from Geneva airport (via the Mont Blanc tunnel from Chamonix in France). The Aosta valley can also be reached from Switzerland via the Grand St Bernard tunnel. The approach is high and may require chains. The road down the Aosta valley is a major thoroughfare, but the roads up to some of the other resorts are quite long, winding and (in the case of Cervinia) high.

To the east is a string of scattered resorts, most close to the Swiss border, many in isolated and remote valleys involving long drives up from the nearest Italian cities, or high-altitude drives from Switzerland. The links between Switzerland and Italy are more clearly shown on our larger-scale map at the beginning of the Switzerland section of the book than on the map of the Italian Alps included here. The major routes are the St Gotthard tunnel between Göschenen (near Andermatt) and Airolo – the main route between Basel and Milan – and the San Bernardino tunnel a little way to the east, reached via Chur.

Finally, further east still are the resorts of the Dolomites. Getting there from Austria is easy, over the Brenner motorway pass from Innsbruck. But getting there from Britain is a very long drive indeed – allow at least a day and a half. We wouldn't lightly choose to drive there and back for a week's skiing, except as part of a longer tour including some time in Austrian resorts. It's also worth bearing in mind that once you arrive in the Dolomites, getting around the intricate network of valleys on narrow, winding roads can be a slow business – it's often quicker to get from village to village on skis. Impatient Italian driving can make it a bit stressful, too.

SNOWPIX.COM / CHRIS GILL

Cervinia

One of a kind, this: for extensive, snow-sure, sunny, easy skiing, there is nowhere to match Cervinia. Good for late season holidays

RATINGS

The mountains

Extent	***
Fast lifts	****
Queues	****
Terrain p'ks	****
Snow	*****
Expert	*
Intermediate	****
Beginner	*****
Boarder	****
X-country	*
Restaurants	***
Schools	****
Families	**

The resort

Charm	**
Convenience	***
Scenery	****
Eating out	****
Après-ski	**
Off-slope	*

RPI	90
lift pass	£160
ski hire	£100
lessons	£80
food & drink	£105
total	**£445**

NEWS

2011/12: The Plateau Rosa cable car was renovated and now travels faster and has bigger windows and information about the slopes and weather inside. A new moving carpet was installed on the nursery slopes. And three new black runs above Salette in the Valtournenche sector apparently opened (they weren't on the piste map but we are told they will be for 2012/13).

- + Miles of long, consistently gentle runs; ideal for intermediates wary of steep slopes or bumps
- + Slopes are sunny, but high and pretty snow-sure
- + Impressive scenery
- + Excellent village nursery slope
- + The link with Zermatt in Switzerland provides more great runs, views and lunches but ...

- − Bad weather can close not only the Zermatt link but most of the higher lifts, severely limiting your options
- − Very little to interest those looking for challenges
- − Not a notably attractive village
- − Few off-slope amenities
- − Steep climb to the main gondola, although there is a chairlift alternative

If there is a better resort than Cervinia for those who like cruising on motorways in spring sunshine, we have yet to find it. And then there's the easiest of Zermatt's slopes just over the Swiss border.

And for the rest of us? Well, to be frank, the rest of us are better off elsewhere. In particular, those with an eye on bumps or powder over in Zermatt should probably think about residing there, not here. Despite major lift improvements in Zermatt, access to its best slopes is still a time-consuming business. And that's assuming the exposed, 3300m-high link is open.

The village was branded Cervinia when it was developed for skiing, but these days harks back to its mountaineering roots by prefixing that with its original name, Breuil. Ever heard of that? No, quite. So we'll stick with Cervinia.

THE RESORT

Cervinia is on the Italian side of the Matterhorn (or Monte Cervino in Italian), at the head of a long valley off the Aosta Valley. At weekends, the resort can fill up with visitors from Turin and Milan. At other times (in January especially), it can be full of Russians.

The slopes link to Valtournenche further down the valley (covered by the lift pass) and at high altitude to Zermatt in Switzerland (covered by a daily supplement, or a more expensive weekly pass – take your passport).

Day trips by car are possible to Courmayeur, La Thuile and the Monterosa Ski resorts of Champoluc and Gressoney. A six-day Cervinia Valtournenche pass covers two days in these other resorts. Or you can buy an Aosta Valley pass for the week and optionally add two days in Zermatt.

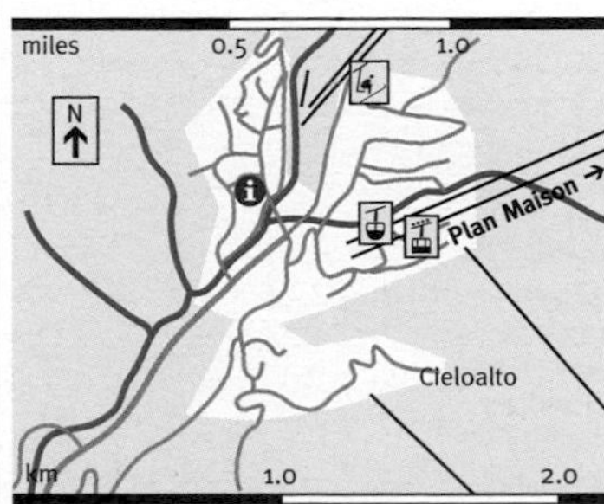

VILLAGE CHARM ★★

Somewhat lacking

The old climbing village grew into a ski resort (in the years before and after WW2) in a haphazard way, and the result is a bit of a mess – neither pleasing to the eye nor as offensive as the worst of the French purpose-built resorts. The centre is compact and traffic-free, and a pleasant enough place to walk around. But ugly apartment blocks and hotels spoil the views from the slopes.

CONVENIENCE ★★★

Up or down

As our plan makes clear, this is not a big place but location is still worth considering carefully. What used to be the main lift from the village, a gondola to Plan Maison, starts a hike up from the south end of the village –

irritating for some, 'truly awful' for others. But there is now a relatively recently built alternative of successive six-packs from the nursery slopes, next to the village centre, making this the obvious place to stay.

There are also developments above the main village, closer to the gondola. Some hotels run their own shuttle-bus and there's an efficient public bus from the Cieloalto complex, well to the south of the main village. We have had reports of poor maintenance meaning slippery and icy footpaths.

SCENERY ★★★★

Monte Cervino rules

The Matterhorn is less special from the Italian than from the Swiss side, but Cervinia's setting is impressive by normal standards, with the peak towering above the village, and fine views from the slopes.

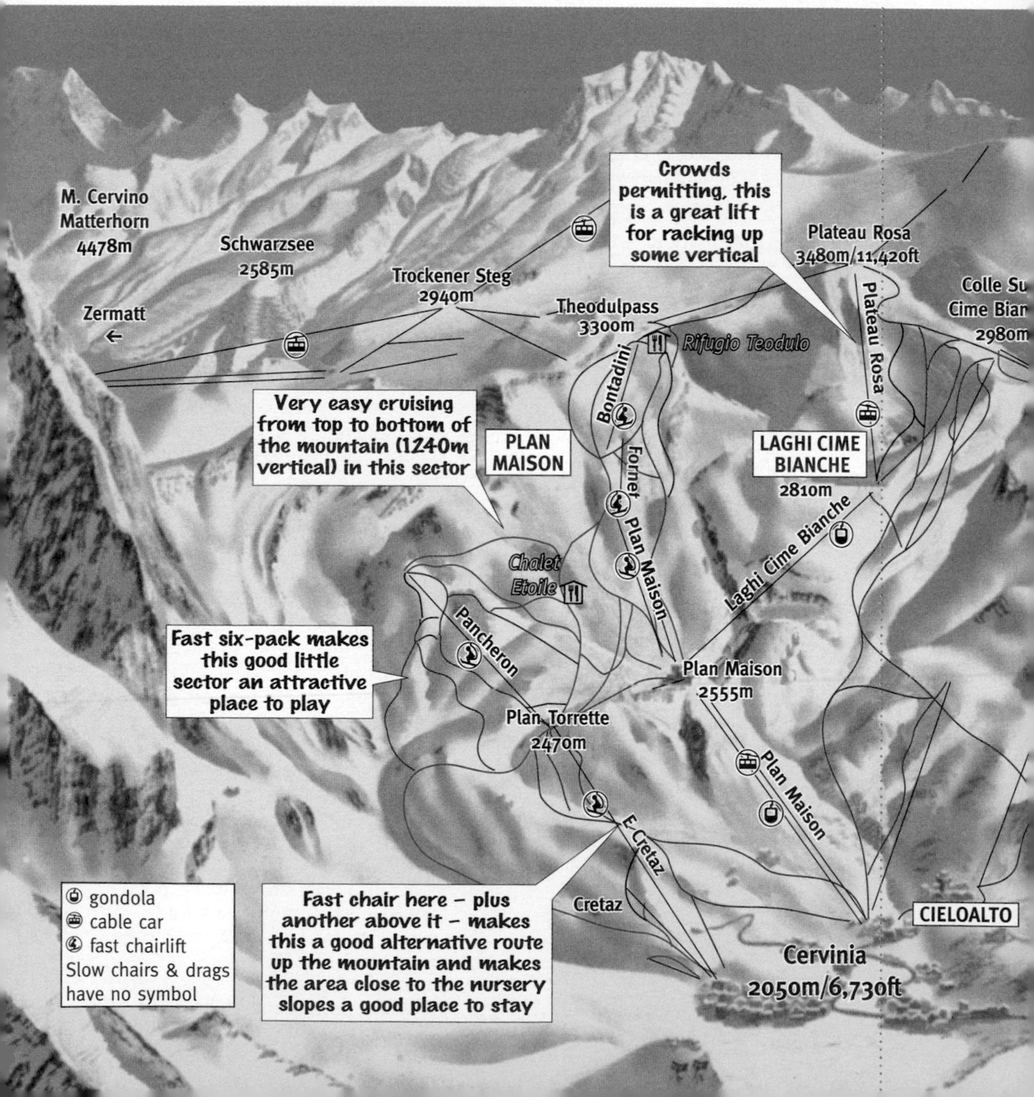

M. Cervino Matterhorn 4478m
Schwarzsee 2585m
Zermatt ←
Trockener Steg 2940m
Theodulpass 3300m
Rifugio Teodulo
Crowds permitting, this is a great lift for racking up some vertical
Plateau Rosa 3480m/11,420ft
Plateau Rosa
Colle Su Cime Bian 2980m
Bontadini
Very easy cruising from top to bottom of the mountain (1240m vertical) in this sector
PLAN MAISON
LAGHI CIME BIANCHE 2810m
Fornet
Plan Maison
Laghi Cime Bianche
Chalet Etoile
Pancheron
Fast six-pack makes this good little sector an attractive place to play
Plan Maison 2555m
Plan Torrette 2470m
Plan Maison
E Cretaz
Cretaz
CIELOALTO
Cervinia 2050m/6,730ft
Fast chair here – plus another above it – makes this a good alternative route up the mountain and makes the area close to the nursery slopes a good place to stay

gondola
cable car
fast chairlift
Slow chairs & drags have no symbol

GETTING THERE

Air Turin 120km/ 75 miles (2hr); Geneva 185km/ 115 miles (2hr45)

Rail Châtillon (27km/17 miles); regular buses from station

THE MOUNTAINS

Cervinia's main slopes are high, open, sunny and mostly west-facing. It's an unpleasant place when the weather is bad, and the top lifts forming the link with Zermatt are often closed because of high winds (sometimes for days), especially early in the season.

The piste map, which covers both Cervinia and Zermatt, and piste marking are praised by readers and piste grooming is generally good. The map shows planned cable cars to the Klein Matterhorn, from Plateau Rosa in Cervinia and Trockener Steg in Zermatt, but we're told these are not due until 2015/16. The high number of red runs on the map is misleading: most of them could be classified blue.

EXTENT OF THE SLOPES ★★★★★

High, wide and easy

Cervinia has the biggest, highest, most snow-sure area of easy, well-groomed pistes we've come across. The area has Italy's highest pistes and some of its longest. At the top you are 6km as well as 1400m vertical from the village.

A deep gorge splits the slopes into two main sectors. Looking up the hill, the lifts from the village take you into the left-hand sector at first.

A gondola takes you to the mid-mountain base of **Plan Maison**. We've rarely seen the parallel cable car working, but a regular visitor assures us it does move occasionally. A more convenient alternative for many is the six-pack from the village nursery slopes to Plan Torrette, where another

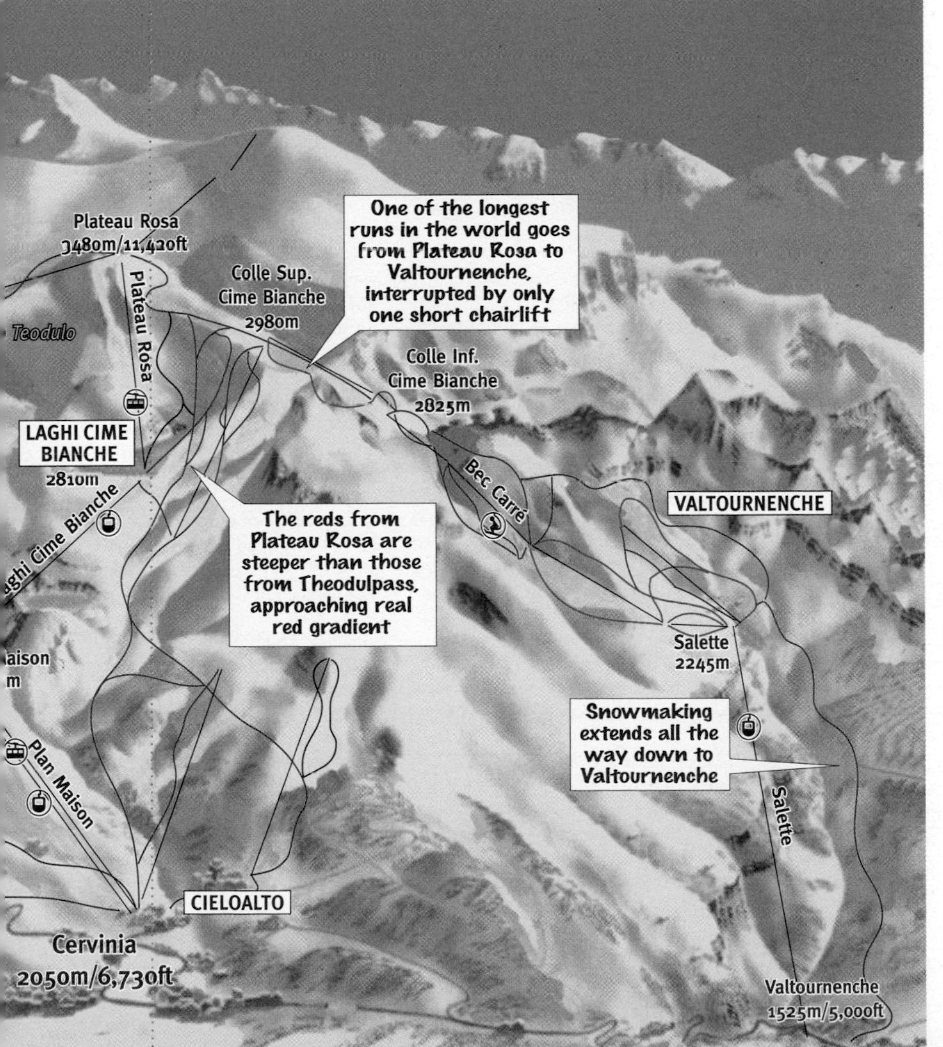

Plateau Rosa
3480m/11,420ft
Plateau Rosa
Teodulo
Colle Sup.
Cime Bianche
2980m
One of the longest runs in the world goes from Plateau Rosa to Valtournenche, interrupted by only one short chairlift
Colle Inf.
Cime Bianche
2825m
LAGHI CIME BIANCHE
2810m
Bec Carré
VALTOURNENCHE
The reds from Plateau Rosa are steeper than those from Theodulpass, approaching real red gradient
Salette
2245m
Snowmaking extends all the way down to Valtournenche
Salette
Plan Maison
CIELOALTO
Cervinia
2050m/6,730ft
Valtournenche
1525m/5,000ft

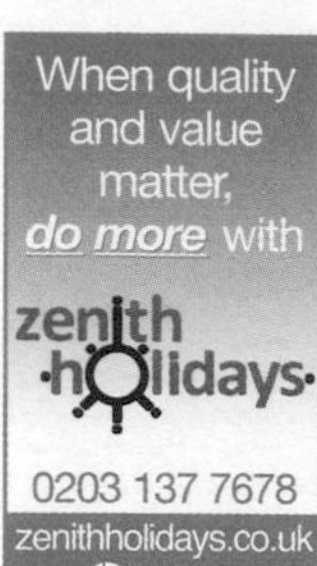

KEY FACTS

Resort	2050m 6,730ft
Cervinia/ Valt'nenche	
Slopes	1525-3480m 5,000-11,420ft
Lifts	24
Pistes	160km 100 miles
Blue	30%
Red	59%
Black	11%
Snowmaking	50%
Cervinia/ Valt'nenche/ Zermatt combined	
Slopes	1525-3820m 5,000-12,530ft
Lifts	57
Pistes	360km 225 miles
Blue	22%
Red	60%
Black	18%
Snowmaking	70%

THE ZERMATT CONNECTION

Getting to Zermatt's classic terrain on the Rothorn/Stockhorn sectors is much quicker than it once was. Thanks to the Furi to Riffelberg gondola, getting there and back by mid-afternoon is now no problem. But don't expect to spend very long on those Triftji moguls. On the way back there may be long queues for the Klein Matterhorn cable car and for the alternative long, slow T-bars. Allow plenty of time – and beware closure of the top lifts by high winds.

six-pack serves the good slopes under the Matterhorn – and gives pretty quick access to Plan Maison.

Above Plan Maison, a chain of three fast quads goes on up to Theodulpass, slightly the lower of two links with the slopes of Zermatt. From Plan Maison you can instead take a gondola across to **Laghi Cime Bianche**, and the right-hand sector. From there a big cable car goes up to Plateau Rosa, the other link with Zermatt. This is also the start of the splendid, wide Ventina run back to the cable car station (or on down to the village).

Part-way down you can branch off left for **Valtournenche**. The slopes here are served by three fast chairlifts, above a modern gondola from the village – but the final lift back to Cervinia is still a long draglift. From top to bottom the run down is not far short of 2000m vertical and a claimed 13km in length, interrupted only by a quad chairlift part-way.

There is also the very small, little-used **Cieloalto** area at the bottom of the Ventina run, served by a slow old chair to the south of the village. This has some of Cervinia's steeper pistes, and the only trees in the area.

FAST LIFTS ★★★★★
Few slow lifts left

Most of Cervinia's main lifts are fast and efficient. The few slow ones left are around the Valtournenche sector and at Cieloalto.

QUEUES ★★★★★
Very few problems

In general, neither we nor readers have complaints about queues in the main area of slopes. The gondola and six-pack out of the resort cope even at peak times, but the chair above Plan Maison does still get busy. Lifts at Valtournenche can be a 'problem' on peak weekends, says a recent visitor. Of course, the lower lifts may be busy when upper lifts are shut by wind.

TERRAIN PARKS ★★★★★
One of Italy's best

The 'Indian' terrain park by the fast Fornet chair is one of the best parks in Italy. Run by *Snowboard Italy*'s former editor, new creative obstacles are introduced every year. The park has been shaped so that riders can hit an easy line or an intermediate line. There is also an expert tabletop line, culminating in a 20m monster. The Italian flag down-rail is a good feature for intermediate and advanced riders, while the variety of bonk posts encourages you to try all the latest tricks. Helmets are compulsory. There is no half-pipe, but Zermatt's pipe is only just over the border.

SNOW RELIABILITY ★★★★★
A question of altitude

This is not a notably snowy corner of the Alps, and the slopes get the afternoon sun. But snow is usually good from early to late season thanks to altitude (these slopes are among the highest in the Alps), good grooming and snowmaking on most key runs from top to bottom – down to Valtournenche as well as Cervinia.

FOR EXPERTS ★★★★★
Forget it

This is not a resort for experts. There are a few black runs scattered here and there, but they are not reliably open and most of them would be classified red elsewhere; we have only one sighting of moguls, on the black above Plan Torrette. Three new black runs allegedly opened in the Valtournenche sector last season but were not marked on the piste map – we are assured they will be on the 2012/13 map. Accessible off-piste terrain is limited, and high winds can play havoc with fresh snow. But of course there is some off-piste potential – above Plan Torrette for example – and of course conditions are sometimes brilliant, and you then have the advantage that the snow can remain untracked for ages. Heli-skiing with guides can be arranged.

You can head over to Zermatt for more challenging slopes – look at the 'Zermatt connection' box in the margin.

FOR INTERMEDIATES ★★★★★
Miles of long, flattering runs

Virtually the whole area can be covered comfortably by average intermediates. From top to bottom there are wide, gentle, smooth runs. But strong intermediates will get bored quickly, and be itching to be off to Zermatt. The area on the right as you look at the mountain is best for more adventurous intermediates. The Ventina red is a particularly good fast cruise. You can use the cable car to do the top part repeatedly. The reds served by the Pancheron chair at Plan Torrette are also a bit more interesting

LIFT PASSES

Prices in €

Age	1-day	6-day
under 13	27	119
13 to 64	38	198
65 plus	31	159

Free under 8 and 80+

Beginner limited day pass €15

Notes
Covers all lifts on the Italian side, including Valtournenche; half-day passes; includes Aosta Valley extension from 3 days

Alternative passes
Valtournenche only; International (includes Zermatt)

than the norm, and tend to be attractively quiet. The runs towards Valtournenche are great cruises and very popular with reporters. The 13km run all the way down is very satisfying, through splendid rocky scenery.

FOR BEGINNERS ★★★★★
Gentle progress

A limited day pass covers the good village nursery slope, with its long moving carpet, and the adjacent chairlift. Complete beginners start there and graduate to the fine flat area around Plan Maison and the gentle blue runs above. Fast learners will be going from top to bottom of the mountain in a few days. But a 2012 visitor found many blues 'quite crowded', especially at weekends.

FOR BOARDERS ★★★★
Easy cruising

The wide, gentle and well-groomed slopes, generally good snow and lack of many draglifts make Cervinia pretty much ideal for beginner and early intermediate boarders. But there are some long, flat parts to beware of (notably around Plan Maison). Serious boarders will enjoy the terrain park, and there's a special pass (27 euros a day last season) which covers two chairlifts that access the park plus return trips on the Plan Maison gondola; there's also heli-boarding.

FOR CROSS-COUNTRY ★
Hardly any

There are only two short trails (both 3km or so).

MOUNTAIN RESTAURANTS ★★★
OK if you know where to go

There are some good places if you know where to go. Toilet facilities are a traditional cause of complaints from reporters, but several have now been improved. You can, of course, head over to Zermatt for lunch.

Editors' choice Chalet Etoile (0166 940220), on a blue run above Plan Maison is an old favourite, happily supported by a continuing flow of reader reports – 'sensational seafood pasta' says a 2012 reporter. There's an improved self-service section too. The much simpler Rifugio Teodulo (0166 949400) at Theodulpass is another good option – excellent pasta.

Worth knowing about Recent reporters tip Plan Torrette ('amazing food', 'old skiing artefacts on the wall') and the Bontadini ('free snacks on the bar', 'very good service'); both have self- and table-service sections. The Rifugio Guide de Cervino at Plateau Rosa is small and basic.

The restaurants are cheaper and less crowded in the Valtournenche sector. Tips above Salette include Motta ('basic decor, good value') and Lo Baracon dou Tene.

There's a picnic room at the Plan Maison cable car station – used regularly by a 2012 reporter.

SCHOOLS AND GUIDES ★★★★
Generally positive reports

Cervinia has three main schools. A 2010 snowboarder made 'good progress' in a private lesson with the Breuil school, and the Cervino school

SNOWPIX.COM / CHRIS GILL

The mid-mountain base of Plan Maison isn't pretty, but it does have good gentle runs above it served by high-speed chairlifts ↓

SCHOOLS

Cervino
t 0166 948744

Breuil
t 0166 940960

Matterhorn-Cervinia
t 0166 949523

Classes
(Cervino prices)
6 days (2hr 45min per day) €190

Private lessons
€38 for 1hr for 1 person

GUIDES

Guide del Cervino
t 0166 948169

CHILDCARE

Baby Club Biancaneve
t 0166 940201
Ages from 0 to 10

Ski school
Classes for children over 5

ACTIVITIES

Indoor Swimming pool, sauna, fitness centre, climbing wall, museum (at Plateau Rosa)

Outdoor Natural ice rink, hiking, tubing, snowmobiling, snow-biking, airboarding, mountaineering, snowshoeing, ice karting, kite skiing, paragliding

UK PACKAGES

Alpine Answers, Carrier, Club Med, Crystal, Crystal Finest, Elegant Resorts, Independent Ski Links, Inghams, Momentum, Mountain Wave, Ski Bespoke, Ski Club Freshtracks, Ski Line, Ski Solutions, Skitracer, Ski Weekend, STC, Thomson, Zenith

Phone numbers
From abroad use the prefix +39 (and do **not** omit the initial '0' of the phone number)

TOURIST OFFICE

www.cervinia.it

'seemed organized, instructors spoke decent English and worked hard on technique; my compatriot came on in leaps and bounds', says a 2012 report.

FOR FAMILIES ★★

No recent reports

The Cervino ski school runs a mini club. And there's a kindergarten area at Plan Maison.

STAYING THERE

Chalets Inghams opened the chalet-hotel Dragon last season, in a great position close to the nursery slope and with a popular après-ski bar.

Hotels There are almost 50 hotels, mostly 2- or 3-stars. Choose your location with care, or look for a place with its own shuttle-bus. The Club Med was highly praised by a 2012 reporter.

*****Hermitage** (0166 948998) Small, luxurious Relais et Châteaux just out of the village on the road to Cieloalto. Pool. Minibus to the lifts. Great views.

****Europa** (0166 948660) Well placed near nursery slope. Pool.

****Excelsior Planet** (0166 949426) Near the nursery slopes. Pool, spa and minibus to the lifts.

****Sertorelli Sport Hotel** (0166 949797) At south end of village. Saunas, steam and hot tub.

***Edelweiss** (0166 949078) At south end of village. Quirky and creaky place, but 'couldn't have better hosts'.

***Miravidi** (0166 948097) Central and recently updated hotel. 'Looked after us superbly,' says a recent visitor.

***Serenella** (0166 949041) Very Italian feel (and food), good location, friendly, good value.

Apartments There are many apartments, but few are available via UK tour ops.

At altitude Up at Plan Maison, Lo Stambecco (0166 949053) is a 3-star hotel ideal for early starts.

EATING OUT ★★★★

Plenty to choose from

Cervinia's 50 or so restaurants offer plenty of choice, but one reader notes that prices climb steeply once you leave pizza territory. 2012 reader tips include the Copa Pan bar's basement restaurant ('imaginative food, well presented, perfectly cooked'), Belle Epoque ('very good fish and seafood'), Falcone ('great pizzas', 'welcoming, informal, cosy') and Lino's ('good for pasta') which claims to serve 'probably the best pizzas in the world'. Previous tips include: Matterhorn (varied menu, including vegetarian), Grotta ('friendly, extensive menu, delicious food'), Jour et Nuit (restricted menu, good steaks). Dinner at Baita Cretaz, just above the village, makes a change.

APRES-SKI ★★

Disappoints many visitors

Plenty of people come here looking for action but find there isn't much to do except tour the bars. 'Take a good book,' said one reporter. At tea time you can do worse than to try the cakes at the Samovar. The hotel Grivola's bar is attractively woody, friendly and lively. The Copa Pan is lively (starting with a happy hour), with music. The Dragon Bar is popular with Brits and Scandinavians and has satellite TV and Wi-Fi; the Yeti is popular too (another happy hour) and serves 'great free nibbles with drinks'. Other recommendations include Hostellerie des Guides (with mementos of the owner's Himalayan trips). Discos liven up at weekends.

OFF THE SLOPES ★

Little attraction

There is little to do for those who don't plan to hit the slopes. Amenities include hotel pools, a fitness centre and a natural ice rink. There are few diverting shops. The walks are not great. Few mountain restaurants are reachable by gondola or cable car, and most of those are not special.

LINKED RESORT – 1525m

VALTOURNENCHE

Some 500m lower than Cervinia and 9km down the access road, Valtournenche offers lower prices and a rather more traditional style, and is worth considering as a base unless Zermatt is high on your agenda (getting there takes longer from here than from Cervinia). The village spreads along the busy, steep road up to Cervinia; it is reported to be 'not so much quiet as dead' in the evening.

A gondola leaves from the edge of the village, and fast lifts predominate above that. The epic run back from Plateau Rosa on the Swiss border is a great way to end the day.

There's a fair selection of simple hotels; some have shuttles to the lift. The 3-star Bijou (0166 92109) has been recommended in the past.

CORTINA TURISMO / DG BANDION

Cortina d'Ampezzo

The scenery will take your breath away even if the slopes don't; take your posh frocks to feel part of the high-season scene

RATINGS

The mountains	
Extent	***
Fast lifts	***
Queues	****
Terrain p'ks	**
Snow	***
Expert	**
Intermediate	***
Beginner	*****
Boarder	***
X-country	*****
Restaurants	****
Schools	***
Families	**
The resort	
Charm	****
Convenience	*
Scenery	*****
Eating out	*****
Après-ski	***
Off-slope	*****

RPI	105
lift pass	£200
ski hire	£110
lessons	£105
food & drink	£110
total	**£525**

NEWS

2012/13: A new red slope is due to open in the Faloria sector, served by an existing fast quad.

2011/12: In the Cinque Torri sector, a new double chairlift has replaced the ancient single-person chair and subsequent rope tow from mid-mountain to the Averau Refuge. In the Faloria sector, the Vitelli slope became a designated slow skiing zone with relax areas to soak up the views. A new 4-star hotel, the Rosapetra Spa Resort, opened – with wellness centre, gym and pool. And two 4-star hotels opened new spa areas – the Lajadira and the Bellevue.

- + Magnificent Dolomite scenery and a quite exceptional setting
- + Marvellous nursery slopes and good long cruising runs
- + Access to the vast area covered by the Dolomiti Superski pass
- + Attractive although rather towny resort, with lots of upmarket shops
- + Good off-slope facilities
- + No crowds or queues

- – Several separate areas of slopes, though well linked by buses
- – Erratic snow record
- – Expensive by Italian standards
- – Still quite a few slow lifts
- – Gets very crowded in town and in restaurants during Italian holidays
- – Few tough runs

If you like lazy days centred around indulgent lunches on sunny terraces, gazing at scenery that is just jaw-droppingly wonderful, this is the place. The town is ringed by dramatic, pink-tinged cliffs and peaks soaring above the slopes, giving picture-postcard views wherever you look. Every time we go back, the memory has faded and our jaws drop again.

Cortina is Italy's most fashionable resort, with all that entails – in high season, when the money is in town, a lot of strolling, people-watching, serious shopping and lengthy lunching goes on. The majority of Italian visitors don't go near the slopes except to drive up to a 'mountain restaurant' for lunch. Which is good for the rest of us because it means the slopes stay uncrowded.

Like most such swanky resorts, Cortina attracts more skiers driving Fords than driving Ferraris, even if few of the Fords are Cortinas. So it is not literally exclusive – and ordinary mortals will feel at home here. As an occasional change from serious ski resorts, we love it.

THE RESORT

Cortina is a sizeable town spread across a wide, impossibly scenic bowl. Although it runs World Cup races, and leapt to international prominence as host of the 1956 Winter Olympics, it relies for its appeal on other things – 70% of all Italian visitors don't step on to the slopes. People leave the slopes early, and by 5pm hardly anyone is still in ski gear. In the high season the streets are packed with people parading up and down the main street in their furs and baubles, shouting into their mobile phones and walking their tiny dogs.

Unlike most of the Dolomites, Cortina is pure Italy. The Veneto region has none of the Germanic traditions of the Südtirol, only a few miles away. And reporters have found the place friendly and welcoming.

San Cassiano is a short drive to the west, with links from there to Corvara and the other Sella Ronda resorts.

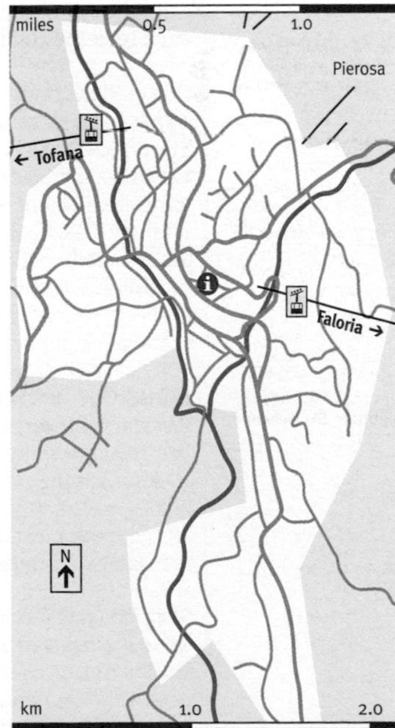

↑ Cortina has several separate smallish ski areas, but they are all well endowed with good mountain huts

SNOWPIX.COM / CHRIS GILL

KEY FACTS

Resort	1225m 4,020ft
Slopes	1225-2930m 4,020-9,610ft
Lifts	33
Pistes	115km 71 miles
Blue	50%
Red	35%
Black	15%
Snowmaking	95%

VILLAGE CHARM ★★★★☆
Bella Italia

The centre is the traffic-free Corso Italia, which is full of chic designer clothes shops, jewellery and antique shops, art galleries and furriers – finding a ski shop can be tricky. The picturesque church tower adds to the atmosphere.

Surrounding the centre is a busy one-way system, which struggles to cope with the traffic at weekends.

CONVENIENCE ★☆☆☆☆
Widely scattered

Staying centrally is best: the lifts to the two main areas of slopes are at opposite sides of town (and a fair way from the centre, though the distances are walkable). Other lifts are bus, car or taxi rides away. There are plenty of hotels in the centre but some are scattered around the outskirts. The top ones have their own shuttles, of course. The town bus service is efficient and 'very punctual' too; it is free to ski pass holders.

A car can be useful, especially for getting to the outlying ski areas and to make the most of other areas on the Dolomiti Superski pass.

SCENERY ★★★★★
Stand and admire

Cortina is surrounded by some of the most stunning mountain scenery in the skiing world – the Dolomite mountains are magnificent, with their pink-tinged cliffs and peaks rising up from pretty wooded valleys. They look particularly spectacular at sunset.

THE MOUNTAINS

There is a good mixture of slopes above and below the treeline.

EXTENT OF THE SLOPES ★★★☆☆
They add up ...

All Cortina's smallish, fragmented areas are a fair trek from the town centre. The highest is **Tofana**, accessed by successive cable cars starting from near the ice rink. The largest is **Pomedes**, accessed by the first cable car mentioned above followed by a blue piste, or by a tricky black piste from Tofana, or by chairlifts a bus ride away from the centre.

On the opposite side of the valley is the tiny **Mietres** area. A two-stage cable car from the east side of town leads to the **Faloria** area, from where you can head down to chairs that lead up into the limited but dramatic runs beneath **Cristallo**.

Other areas are reachable by road – in particular the road west over Passo Falzarego. First, there's the small but scenic **Cinque Torri** area. Excellent north-facing cruising runs are accessed by a fast quad, followed by a double chair that was new for last season (see 'News'). From the top, you can go

LIFT PASSES

Dolomiti Superski

Prices in €

Age	1-day	6-day
under 16	34	169
16 to 64	48	241
65 plus	43	217

Free under 8

Senior must be 65 before season starts

Beginner no deals

Notes

Covers 450 lifts and 1220km of pistes in the Dolomites, incl. all Cortina areas

Alternative passes

Cortina d'Ampezzo (Cortina, San Vito di Cadore, Auronzo and Misurina)

over the ridge to a sunny, panoramic red run on the back of the hill or to a chair which accesses another red run to the tiny – north-facing – **Col Gallina** area. From here you can take a blue back to Cinque Torri or a cable car from Passo Falzarego up to Lagazuoi that serves an excellent red/blue run back to the base station and accesses the famous 'hidden valley' run to the fringe of the Alta Badia area. (More on this in the Sella Ronda chapter.)

One way to tour the area is to use special ski itineraries (maps are available). 'Skitour Olympia' takes you on the 1956 Olympic courses.

FAST LIFTS ★★★★★
Some in each sector

The main access lifts are cable cars and there are fast chairs scattered throughout each sector, but a lot of slow old lifts remain too.

QUEUES ★★★★★
No problem

Most Italian visitors rise late, lunch at length and leave the slopes early. That means few lift queues and generally uncrowded pistes. One exception is the cable car from Passo Falzarego up to Lagazuol and the start of the famous 'hidden valley' run – not surprisingly, queues can form for this.

TERRAIN PARKS ★★★★★
Challenges for all

Socrepes has a 500m-long park for both beginners and intermediates, which has kickers, boxes, rails, and a wall ride. Helmets are compulsory. We're assured that the original park at Faloria will be built again for 2012/13.

SNOW RELIABILITY ★★★★★
Lots of artificial help

The snowfall record is erratic – it can be good here when it's poor on the north side of the Alps, and vice versa. But 95% of the pistes are covered by snowmaking, so cover is good if it is cold enough to make snow. As so often, it's the black runs that are most vulnerable when natural snow is short – several are south-facing, and liable to closure. Grooming is excellent.

FOR EXPERTS ★★★★★
Normally rather limited

Decent amounts of natural snow are the key factor – not only to provide plentiful off-piste (which will offer fresh tracks for days on end) but to ensure adequate snow cover on the few black runs that there are (some of which get a lot of sun). They include the excellent Forcella from Tofana to Pomedes: deservedly classified black, it goes through a gap in the rocks, and gives wonderful views of Cortina way down in the valley below. Cortina's most serious challenge is the Staunies run at the top of the Cristallo area – a south-facing couloir that we have never found open (tougher than it looks from below, warns a reporter). There are short but genuinely black runs below Pomedes and Duc d'Aosta.

There are some excellent red runs too, notably at Pomedes and Faloria.

FOR INTERMEDIATES ★★★★★
Fragmented and not extensive

To enjoy Cortina you must like cruising in beautiful scenery, and not mind doing runs repeatedly.

The runs at the top of Tofana are

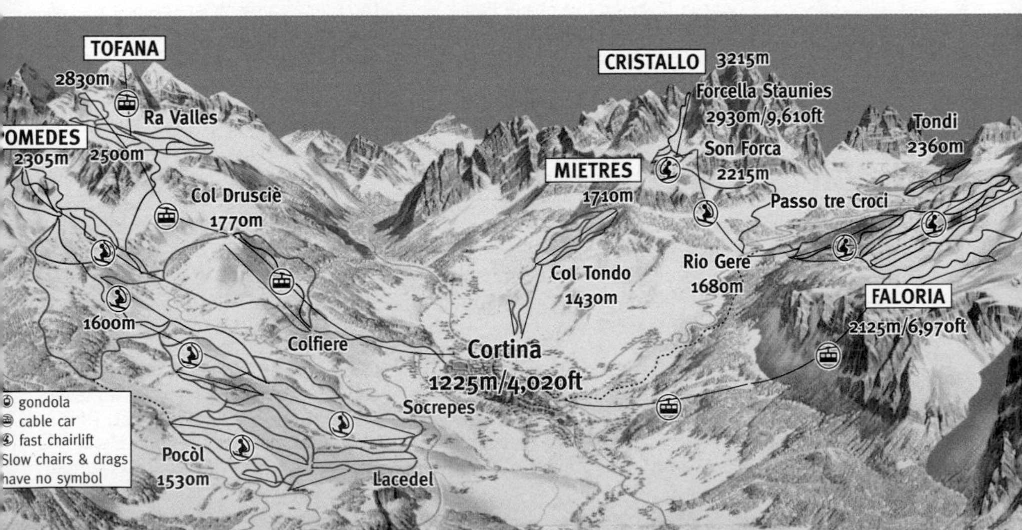

↑ The stunning scenery just makes you want to stand and stare (or stop at a rifugio to do so in comfort)

CORTINA TURISMO / DG BANDION

GETTING THERE

Air Venice 160km/ 100 miles (2hr15). Treviso 130km/ 80 miles (2hr). Sat and Sun transfers for hotel guests (advance booking required); 35-minute heli-transfers from Venice

Rail Calalzo (35km/ 22 miles) or Dobbiaco (32km/20 miles); frequent buses from station

UK PACKAGES

Alpine Answers, Crystal, Inghams, Momentum, Mountain Tracks, Oxford Ski Co, Ski Bespoke, Ski Club Freshtracks, Ski Solutions, Ski Weekend, Ski Yogi, Snow Finders, STC, Thomson, White Roc, Zenith

short but normally have the best snow. The highest are at over 2800m and mainly face north. But be warned: the only way back down is by the tricky black run described above or by cable car. The reds in the linked Pomedes area offer good cruising and some challenges.

Faloria has a string of fairly short north-facing runs – we loved the Vitelli red run, round the back away from the lifts. And the Cristallo area has a long, easy red run served by a fast quad.

It is well worth making the trip to Cinque Torri for fast cruising on usually excellent north-facing snow. And do not miss the wonderful 'hidden valley' red run from the top of the Passo Falzarego cable car (see the Sella Ronda chapter).

FOR BEGINNERS ★★★★★
Wonderful nursery slopes

While there are no special deals for beginners, the Socrepes area has some of the biggest nursery slopes and best progression runs we have seen. Points cards are issued by the day too. You'll find ideal gentle terrain on the main pistes but some of the blue forest paths can be icy and intimidating.

FOR BOARDERS ★★★★★
Wide slopes and plenty of chairs

Despite its upmarket chic, Cortina is a good resort for learning to board. The Socrepes nursery slopes are wide, gentle and served by a fast chairlift. And progress on to other easy slopes is simple because you can get around in all areas using just chairs and cable cars. Boarderline is a specialist snowboard shop that organizes instruction as well as equipment hire. In a normal snow year there is little off-piste, but there are some nice trees and hits under the top chairlift at Cinque Torri.

FOR CROSS-COUNTRY ★★★★★
One of the best

Cortina has around 70km of trails suitable for all standards, mainly in the Fiames area, where there's a cross-country centre and a school. Trails include a 30km itinerary following an old railway from Fiames to Cortina, and there is a beginner area equipped with snowmaking. Passo Tre Croci offers more challenging trails, covering 10km. A Nordic area pass is available.

MOUNTAIN RESTAURANTS ★★★★★
Good, but get in early

Many restaurants can be reached by road or lift, and fur coats arrive as early as 10am to sunbathe, admire the views and idle the time away on their mobile phones. In some places, skiers are decidedly in the minority. Although prices are high in the swishest establishments, we've found plenty of reasonably priced places, serving

SCHOOLS

Azzurra Cortina
t 0436 2694

Cristallo
t 0436 870073

Cortina
t 0436 2911

Dolomiti
t 0436 862264

Boarderline
t 0436 878261

Classes (Azzurra prices)
6 mornings (3hr) €425

Private lessons
€55 for 1hr; each additional person €18

GUIDES

Guide Alpine
t 0436 868505

CHILDCARE

Dolomiti Paradise
Play area for under 8s

Ski school
Classes from age 4

ACTIVITIES

Indoor Swimming pool, saunas, health spa, fitness centre, ice stadium, curling, museums, art gallery, cinema, concerts

Outdoor Olympic bobsleigh run, snowshoe tours, 6km of walking paths, tobogganing, ice climbing and trekking, snow kiting

Phone numbers
From abroad use the prefix +39 (and do **not** omit the initial '0' of the phone number)

TOURIST OFFICE

www.cortina.dolomiti.org

generally excellent food. Reporters stress the consistently high standard.

In the Socrepes area, the Rifugio Col Taron and the Rifugio Pomedes have received good reports. The Piè de Tofana and El Faral are also good. And Baita Son dei Prade above Pocol is 'never too crowded, wonderful lasagne', says a reporter.

There are good restaurants at Cinque Torri – the Scoiattoli, Rifugio Averau and Rifugio Fedare are all recommended. Rifugio Lagazuoi, a short hike up from the top of the Passo Falzarego cable car, also has great views.

SCHOOLS AND GUIDES ★★★★★
Mixed reports

Of the several ski schools, we've had mixed reports of the Cortina school over the years – though we lack recent reports. The Guide Alpine offers off-piste and touring.

FOR FAMILIES ★★★★★
Some good lift pass deals

Families will find a wide choice of lift pass deals and discounts for children and there are a couple of snow gardens. But don't count on good spoken English. And the fragmented slopes can make for stressful days with children.

STAYING THERE

Hotels dominate the market but there is some accommodation to rent.

Hotels There's a big choice, from 5-star luxury to 1-star and 2-star pensions.

*******Cristallo** (0436 881111) Top of the market. A hike from the town centre and Faloria lift, but there is a shuttle, of course. Pool, sauna, steam.

*******Miramonti Majestic** (0436 4201) Spectacularly grand hotel, 2km south of town. Pool, sauna, steam, hot tub.

******Ancora** (0436 3261) Elegant public rooms. On the traffic-free Corso Italia.

******Parc Victoria** (0436 3246) Rustic and family-run with small rooms but good food, at the Faloria end of town.

******Park Faloria** (0436 2959) Near ski jump, splendid pool, good food.

******Poste** (0436 4271) At the heart of the town, on the car-free Corso Italia. Large rooms, some with spa baths. An established reader favourite, though we lack recent reports.

*****Columbia** (0436 3607) B&B hotel a walk from Tofana lift but a bit of a hike from town.

*****Des Alpes** (0436 862021) On the edge of town. Hot tub, sauna, steam. Has been praised for service and friendly staff.

*****Menardi** (0436 2400) Welcoming roadside inn, a long walk from the town centre.

*****Olimpia** (0436 3256) Comfortable B&B hotel in centre, near Faloria lift.

****Montana** (0436 862126) Good value, central B&B.

Apartments There are some chalets and apartments – usually well outside the town centre – available for independent travellers.

EATING OUT ★★★★★
Huge choice

There's an enormous selection of restaurants, both in town and a little way out, doing mainly Italian food. The very smart and expensive El Toulà is in a beautiful old barn, just on the edge of town. Many of the best restaurants are even further out: the Michelin-starred Tivoli, the Meloncino al Camineto, the Leone e Anna, the Rio Gere (game dishes) and the Baita Fraina (pasta and meats).

APRES-SKI ★★★★★
Lively in high season

Cortina is a lively social whirl in high season, with lots of well-heeled Italians staying up very late.

The Lovat is one of several high-calorie teatime spots. There are many good wine bars: Enoteca has 700 wines and good cheese and meats and Villa Sandi and LP26 have been recommended. The liveliest bar is the Clipper, with a bobsleigh by the door. Discos liven up after 11pm.

OFF THE SLOPES ★★★★★
A classic resort

Cortina attracts lots of people who don't use the slopes, unless you count strolling across them – despite a lack of published information there are good and popular walks to be done in several sectors, particularly Pocol and Socrepes. There are lots of upmarket shops to flash the credit cards in. Many mountain restaurants are accessible by road. And there's plenty more to do, such as swimming and skating. There is a Planetarium near the ice rink and an observatory at Col Drusciè. There's polo on the snow occasionally. Excursions to Venice are easy. And you can visit the First World War tunnels at Lagazuoi.

Courmayeur

A seductive old village on the sunny side of spectacular Mont Blanc, best combined with visits to neighbouring resorts

RATINGS

The mountains

Extent	*
Fast lifts	***
Queues	****
Terrain p'ks	**
Snow	****
Expert	***
Intermediate	****
Beginner	*
Boarder	***
X-country	***
Restaurants	****
Schools	****
Families	**

The resort

Charm	****
Convenience	*
Scenery	****
Eating out	****
Après-ski	****
Off-slope	***

RPI	90
lift pass	£180
ski hire	£90
lessons	£80
food & drink	£105
total	**£455**

NEWS

2012/13: We are told a new terrain park and airbag are planned at 2000m. And a new two-stage cable car with rotating cabins to Punta Helbronner on Mont Blanc is under construction at a cost of 110 million euros. It is due to open by 2014/15. The first two sections of the existing cable car here are still working but the top section is now closed.

2011/12: Three new nightclubs opened. And area lift passes now give reductions on entrance to the thermal spa at Pré-Saint-Didier.

- + Charming old village; car-free centre with stylish shops and bars
- + Stunning views of Mont Blanc
- + Some good off-piste and heli-skiing
- + Comprehensive snowmaking
- + Some great mountain restaurants

- − Very small area of pistes; and lift-served off-piste limited while new cable car up Mont Blanc being built
- − Lots of drawbacks for beginners
- − No really tough pistes
- − No runs back to the village

Courmayeur is a great place for a short midweek break (or a day trip to escape bad weather in Chamonix), and we always look forward to a quick visit here. Excellent restaurants both on and off the mountain plus village bars among the most civilized in the skiing world are factors, we admit. The skiing is tricky to recommend, though. Its pistes best suit competent intermediates, who are likely to have an appetite for mileage that Courmayeur will arouse but not satisfy.

THE RESORT

Courmayeur is a traditional old mountaineering village that has retained much of its character despite becoming increasingly popular (especially at weekends) with the smart set from Milan and Turin.

La Thuile is an easy drive or bus ride away; Aosta/Pila and Chamonix are not far, and Cervinia and Monterosa are reachable; all are covered by various lift passes.

VILLAGE CHARM ****

Attractive and sophisticated

The village has a charming traffic-free core of cobbled streets and well-preserved old buildings. As the lifts close, the central Via Roma comes alive: people pile into the many bars, or browse the tempting delis and smart clothes shops (some now with doormen to stop celebrity spotters and some appointment-only at peak times, we're told); there's also a good bookshop. An Alpine museum and a statue of a long-dead mountain rescue hero add to the historical feel.

Away from the centre, there are pleasant woody suburbs but also a lot of conspicuous apartment blocks.

CONVENIENCE *

Buses to the lifts

A huge cable car on the southern edge of the village will take you to and from Plan Checrouit, at the heart of the slopes. You cannot ski back to the village, but you can ski to the base of the alternative gondola from Dolonne (across the valley); parking is much easier there, too. Buses serve both lift stations but readers have found services poor. Many hotels run shuttles that are welcomed by reporters.

Drivers can also go to Entrèves, up the valley, where there is a large car park at the cable car. Most people leave their gear in lockers up the mountain or at a lift base. Infrequent but timetabled buses go to La Palud, just beyond Entrèves, for the Monte Bianco cable car (though the top stage is currently closed – see 'News').

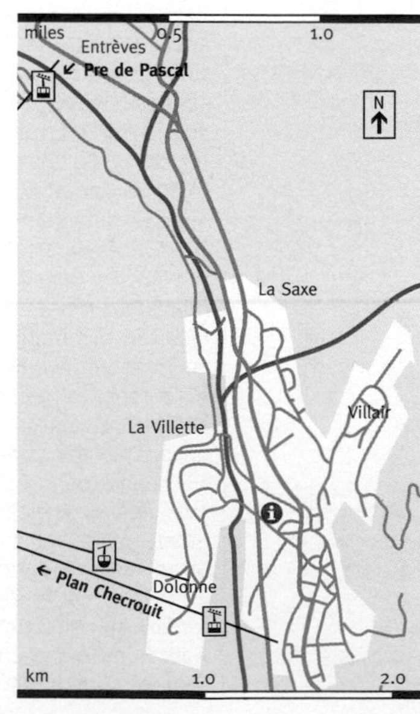

↑ This is a pretty good view of most of the ski area – Checrouit on the left, Val Veny on the right. Not much of it is there?

WENDY-JANE KING

KEY FACTS

Resort	1225m 4,020ft
Slopes	1210-2755m 3,970-9,040ft
Lifts	18
Pistes	36km 22 miles
Blue	27%
Red	59%
Black	14%
Snowmaking	70%

SCENERY ★★★★

Mont Blanc rules

The high glacial slopes of the Mont Blanc massif overlook Courmayeur's slopes. The views from the high points at Cresta d'Arp and Cresta Youla, especially, are stunning.

THE MOUNTAINS

The slopes above the focal point of Plan Checrouit are mainly wide open, but there are also wooded areas, particularly on the back side of the hill. The piste map was improved a few years ago and now shows lift names and direction but reporters criticize piste signposting and marking.

EXTENT OF THE SLOPES ★

Small but interestingly varied

Ever since this book started 18 years ago, the resort has claimed 100km of piste and we have been sceptical. Last season, at last, it changed its mountain statistics to reveal that it actually has 36km of pistes and 64km of off-piste (whatever that means); 36km is less than any other major resort in this book.

There are two distinct sectors, separated by a rocky ridge. The routes between the two can be a bit confusing at first. Above Plan Checrouit, the east-facing **Checrouit** area, accessed mainly by the Checrouit gondola, catches morning sun and has open, above-the-treeline slopes. The 25-person Youla cable car goes (infrequently) to the top of the pistes. A further tiny cable car to Cresta d'Arp serves only long off-piste runs.

Most people follow the sun over to the north-west-facing slopes of **Val Veny** in the afternoon. These are interesting, varied and treelined, with great views of Mont Blanc and its glaciers. The Val Veny slopes are also accessible by cable car from Entrèves, a few miles outside Courmayeur.

A little way beyond Entrèves a new cable car to Punta Helbronner, at the shoulder of **Mont Blanc** is being built. Until it opens (planned for 2014/15), only the first two stages of the old cable car remain open, so you cannot reach the famous Vallée Blanche run to Chamonix in France from the Italian side; and reaching the Toula glacier run on the Italian side is likely to involve skinning up.

FAST LIFTS ★★★

A mixed bag

The main access lifts are cable cars or a gondola. On the hill, there are fast lifts in most key spots, but the ancient Bertolini chair on the Val Veny side needs upgrading and a 2012 visitor says 'recent investment seems lacking and some lifts are a bit old and tatty'.

QUEUES ★★★★

Much improved

These days, queues are generally not a problem unless conditions trigger a weekend influx. There may still be queues to descend at the end of the day if the run to Dolonne lacks snow. On the back of the hill, Zerotta is a bottleneck – we waited 15 minutes in March 2011. The infrequent Youla cable car may require patience – it's worth it only for those heading off-piste.

LIFT PASSES

Prices in €

Age	1-day	6-day
under 14	30	128
14 to 64	43	213
65 plus	35	171

Free under 8

Beginner three free nursery lifts (but you have to pay for the gondola to reach them)

Notes
Covers Courmayeur and the Mont Blanc cable cars; 3- or 4-hour passes; weekly passes allow two days in another Aosta valley resort

Alternative passes
Non-skier; Mont Blanc Unlimited (includes Chamonix valley and Verbier); Valle d'Aosta (covers Aosta Valley ski areas, La Rosière and Alagna)

TERRAIN PARKS ★★★★★
New one planned

There has been a small park for beginners and intermediates at Dolonne but we are told a new one is planned at 2000m and that a boardercross is organized by the ski school for a few weeks a season.

SNOW RELIABILITY ★★★★★
Good for most of the season

Courmayeur's slopes are not high – mostly between 1700m and 2250m. Those above Val Veny face north or north-west, so they keep their snow well, but the Plan Checrouit side is too sunny for comfort in late season. There is snowmaking on most main runs, including the red run to the valley. So good coverage in early and mid-season is virtually assured – we've been there in a snow drought and enjoyed decent skiing entirely on man-made snow. Grooming is good.

FOR EXPERTS ★★★★★
Off-piste is the only challenge

Courmayeur has few challenging pistes. The black runs on the Val Veny side are not severe, but moguls are allowed to develop. If you're lucky enough to find fresh powder, you can have fantastic fun among the trees.

Classic off-piste runs go from Cresta d'Arp, at the top of the lift network, in three directions: a clockwise loop via Arp Vieille to Val Veny, with close-up views of the Miage glacier; east down a deserted valley to Dolonne or Pré-St-Didier; or south through the Youla gorge to La Balme, near La Thuile.

A day trip to Chamonix is appealing, especially as some classic runs on Mont Blanc can only be reached from there or by skinning until the new Italian cable car is opened.

There are also heli-drops, including a wonderful 20km run from the Ruitor glacier that ends near Ste-Foy in France – you take a taxi from there to La Rosière, ride the lifts back up from there and descend to La Thuile (then take another taxi back).

FOR INTERMEDIATES ★★★★★
Good reds, but limited extent

It's an intermediate's mountain, for sure, laced with interestingly varied, genuine red runs. But it is small; the avid piste-basher will ski it in a day. There are some good long runs – it's 700m vertical from Col Checrouit to

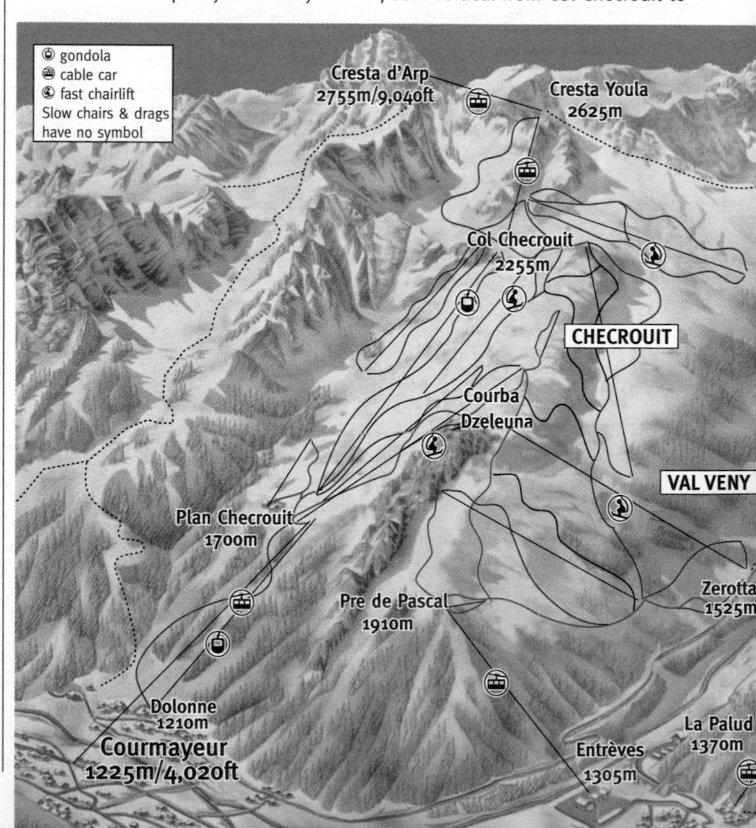

GETTING THERE

Air Geneva 100km/ 60 miles (1hr30); Turin 150km/95 miles (2hr)

Rail Pré-St-Didier (5km/3 miles); regular buses from station

SCHOOLS

Monte Bianco
t 0165 842477

Courmayeur
t 0165 848254

Classes
(Monte Bianco prices)
5 days (2hr per day) €187

Private lessons
From €41 for 1hr; additional person €13

GUIDES

Guides Courmayeur
t 0165 842064

CHILDCARE

Fun park Dolonne
9am-4.30

Mini club Biancaneve (Monte Bianco school)
Ages 0 to 10

Ski-tots (Mammolo) (Monte Bianco school)
For 3 and 4 year olds

Ski schools
From age 5

Zerotta, and 1400m vertical from Cresta Youla to Dolonne – but they are few. On the steeper Val Veny side of the ridge there are challenges to be found – while the reds and blues cut across the mountain, a row of easy blacks go down more directly.

For the timid intermediate, on the other hand, the area is short of confidence-building blue runs. There is basically one long blue on each side of the ridge, reached from Plan Checrouit via the six-seater Pra Neyron chair; that on the Val Veny side is better for the challenge-averse. Many of the reds, particularly up around Col Checrouit, and down to Plan Checrouit, do have the merit that they are generally wide, which helps a lot.

FOR BEGINNERS ★★★★★
Lots of drawbacks

Of course, you can learn to ski here, but you have obstacles in your path. There is a free lift on the beginner slope at Plan Checrouit, but you pay to get up to it, and it gets crowded. There is another up on the ridge, which again means paying for access. The best starting point for beginners is at the top of the Entrèves cable car, where there is a beginner slope with magic carpet, and easy longer runs on the Peindeint chair. As we explain under 'Intermediates', there are few other genuinely easy longer runs to progress to once off the nursery slope.

FOR BOARDERS ★★★★★
Mainly intermediate fun

Courmayeur's pistes suit intermediates well, and most areas are easily accessible by cable cars, chairs and gondolas (though the beginner slopes employ drags). For the more adventurous, there are off-piste routes. And a new terrain park is planned.

FOR CROSS-COUNTRY ★★★★★
Beautiful trails

There are 30km of trails. The best are the five covering 20km at Val Ferret, served by bus.

MOUNTAIN RESTAURANTS ★★★★★
A very good choice

The area is lavishly endowed with establishments ranging from rustic little huts that do table service of delicious pizza, pasta and other dishes to snack bars and a large self-service place – but strangely, they are not marked on the piste map.

Editors' choice On a recent visit we had splendid meals at Chiecco (338 7003035) at Plan Checrouit – a small hut with a welcoming host and a very varied menu, including fantastic chicken curry and wild boar stew. A 2012 reporter sends a rave review ('one of the best mountain huts I have eaten in') and there's a fine choice of local wines too. An old favourite of ours is Maison Vieille (337 230979), a cosy, rustic place with jolly service; we've always found the service and pasta excellent but one 2012 reporter complains of 'pasta adequate, service stressed' – more reports please.

Worth knowing about Another favourite at Plan Checrouit is the Christiania (book a table downstairs to escape the crowds). Nearby, the Chaumière pizzeria is family-run, serving 'a good choice of food' on a 'sunny terrace with superb views'. Alpetta serves homemade pastas and burgers and is 'great for families'. Reporters also like the Baita self-service for low prices and Bar du Soleil for more of those good views. At Col Checrouit, Chez Croux serves 'the best cakes and hot drinks on the mountain'. There is another clutch of worthwhile places in Val Veny: we enjoyed the smartly rustic Grolla for steaks and salads. The Petit Mont Blanc is also popular ('the roast suckling pig was fantastic') and in a 'fabulous position right under the face of Mont Blanc'.

SCHOOLS AND GUIDES ★★★★★
Good private lessons

Reports in 2011 and 2012 on private lessons with the Monte Bianco school are fairly enthusiastic, though the 2012 'instructor did not speak much English'. The Courmayeur school has 'a more snowboardy and young funky image'. There is a thriving guides' association ready to help you explore the area's off-piste; it has produced a helpful booklet showing the main possibilities. We had a super day in 2011 with solo guide Gianni Carbone (www.giannicarbone.com), who was patient and reassuring. A 2012 visitor's Vallée Blanche guides were 'excellent'.

FOR FAMILIES ★★★★★
Some facilities

There are children's playgrounds at Dolonne, Plan Checrouit and Val Veny, and a nursery at Plan Checrouit for children up to 10 years.

ACTIVITIES

Indoor Hotel swimming pools, sports centre (ice rink, climbing wall, fitness centre), tennis, museums, library

Outdoor Walking, snowshoeing, ice climbing

UK PACKAGES

Alpine Answers, Alpine Weekends, Crystal, Crystal Finest, Flexiski, Friendship Travel, Independent Ski Links, Inghams, Inspired to Ski, Interactive Resorts, Interski, Just Skiing, Mark Warner, Momentum, Ski Bespoke, Ski Club Freshtracks, Ski Expectations, Ski Line, Ski Solutions, Ski Weekend, Ski Yogi, Skitracer, Skiweekends.com, STC, Thomson, Tracks European Adventures, White Roc

Phone numbers
From abroad use the prefix +39 (and do **not** omit the initial '0' of the phone number)

TOURIST OFFICE

www.courmayeur.it
www.lovevda.it

STAYING THERE

There's a wide range of packages on offer (including some excellent weekend deals), mainly in hotels. Momentum Ski is an agent specializing in Courmayeur and can fix pretty much whatever you want here.

Chalets Some UK operators have catered chalets.

Hotels There are over 50 hotels, spanning the star ratings.

*****Royal e Golf** (0165 831611) Large, grand place in centre just off Via Roma. Outdoor pool, sauna, steam, hot tub, piano bar.

****Auberge de la Maison** (0165 869811) Small, atmospheric hotel in Entrèves; owned by the same family as Maison de Filippo (see 'Eating out').

****Cresta e Duc** (0165 842585) In centre. Praised by a past reporter. Steam, sauna, hot tub.

****Gran Baita** (0165 844040) Luxury place with antiques. Panoramic views. Pool, sauna, hot tub.

****Villa Novocento** (0165 843000) A short walk from the centre. Elegant lobby, good food and breakfasts. Sauna, steam, hot tub.

***Bouton d'Or** (0165 846729) Small, friendly B&B hotel near main square. Heartily endorsed: 'absolutely impossible to fault'; '3-star hotel with friendly 5-star service'.

***Courmayeur** (0165 846732) Near cable car. 'Very friendly, small rooms.'

***Maison Saint Jean** (0165 842880) Central, family-run, pool, steam, hot tub and sauna.

***Pilier d'Angle** (0165 869760) Friendly, cosy hotel in Entrèves; rooms and self-contained chalets. Good restaurant and wellness centre.

***Camosci** (0165 84238) 800m from centre, mini bus. 'Charming, traditionally decorated, plentiful food.'

Scoiattolo (0165 846721) Spacious rooms; near main square.

Apartments The 3-star Grand Chalet (0165 841448) is central with spacious apartments. Hot tub, steam and sauna are also available for non-residents.

At altitude Visiting Courmayeur and not staying in the charming village seems a bit perverse – if you're that keen to get going in the morning, this is probably not your ideal resort. But up the cable car at Plan Checrouit, the 1-star Christiania (0165 843572) has simple rooms; the 3-star Baita (0165 846542) is smarter.

EATING OUT ★★★★☆

Jolly Italian evenings

There is a great choice of places. A handy promotional booklet describes many of them (in English). We've been impressed by the traditional Italian cuisine of Cadran Solaire. La Terrazza serves classic and local cuisine plus pizzas and is highly recommended by a local. Reporters regularly recommend the Piazzetta ('nice food at a good price, extremely friendly'). Al Camin is a 'meat lover's paradise'. Mont-Fréty is a smart, modern place and 'a favourite of the Milan set'; but it failed to impress a 2011 visitor. 2012 reporters recommend Le Vieux Pommier ('a great atmosphere, serves a mixture of Italian and Savoyard fare') and Aria ('very friendly, an amazing wine list'). In Entrèves, the touristy but very jolly Maison de Filippo is rightly famous for its fixed-price, 36-dish feast. For a gourmet treat take a taxi to the Clotze in Val Ferret (same management as Chiecco – see 'Mountain restaurants').

APRES-SKI ★★★★☆

Stylish bar-hopping

Courmayeur has a lively evening scene – at weekends, at least – centred on stylish bars with comfy armchairs or sofas, often serving free canapés in the early evening. We like the Privé (great cocktails) and the back room of the Caffè della Posta with its 'laden plates of goodies that arrive with each round'. Bar Roma is an old favourite now under new management. A 2012 reporter enjoyed the 'cosy' Petit Bistro. The Cadran Solaire is where the big money from Milan and Turin hangs out. The American Bar has good live music. Three new nightclubs opened for 2011/12 – Courmaclub, Jset and Shatush. Or try the Covo in Entrèves (free shuttle-bus service).

OFF THE SLOPES ★★★☆☆

Lots on for non-slope users

The resort attracts many non-skiing Italians, who focus on showing off their togs and buying more of them. You can go by bus to Aosta, or up to Plan Checrouit where there are countless spots to meet friends for lunch. The huge sports centre is good (but has no pool). Don't miss a visit to the thermal baths at Pré-St-Didier – with over 40 spa 'experiences' including saunas and outdoor pools. The Parco Avventura (10km from town) has a 'great' ropes course.

APT LIVIGNO / L MARTINELLI

Livigno

Lowish prices and highish altitude – a tempting combination, especially when you add in a pleasant Alpine ambience

RATINGS

The mountains	
Extent	**
Fast lifts	****
Queues	****
Terrain p'ks	****
Snow	****
Expert	***
Intermediate	***
Beginner	****
Boarder	****
X-country	****
Restaurants	***
Schools	***
Families	**
The resort	
Charm	***
Convenience	**
Scenery	***
Eating out	***
Après-ski	***
Off-slope	**

RPI	80
lift pass	£160
ski hire	£75
lessons	£80
food & drink	£90
total	**£405**

NEWS

2011/12: A new children's area, with moving carpet lift, opened at the foot of the Costaccia gondola. New designated freeride zones were introduced on Mottolino, overturning the resort's previous blanket ban on off-piste skiing. The Cable Park opened near piste 20. The Larice hotel was renovated and upgraded to a four-star.

- + High altitude plus snowmaking means reliable snow
- + Large choice of beginners' slopes
- + Impressive modern lift system
- + Cheap by the standards of high, snow-sure resorts
- + Lively, friendly, quite smart village with a good Alpine atmosphere
- + Long, snow-sure cross-country trails

- − Few challenging pistes
- − Bleak setting, susceptible to white-outs and lift closures
- − Very long transfers; over five hours for some reporters
- − Village is very long and straggling, with no buses later in the evening
- − Nightlife can disappoint

Livigno's recipe of a fair-sized mountain, high altitude and fairly low prices is uncommon, and obviously attractive, and may be enough to get it on to your shortlist. But make sure the rest of the Livigno formula suits you – some of the drawbacks we list above are non-trivial.

We were amazed to find, when we visited in 2012, that the resort has ditched its previous ban on off-piste skiing in favour of six new freeride zones on Mottolino, with entry gates equipped with bleeper checkers. Poor snow conditions prevented exploration, but it looks like an excellent scheme.

THE RESORT

Livigno is set in a wide, remote valley near the Swiss border; the airport transfers are long and winding. The Alta Valtellina lift pass covers Bormio (about an hour's bus ride – free with the lift pass) and Santa Caterina (another 20 minutes). The Livigno pass gets you half-price on one day in St Moritz – an excursion not easily done from any other major resort.

VILLAGE CHARM ★★★

Pleasant enough

At the core of the resort is a single mainly pedestrian street, just over 1km long, lined by hotels, bars, specialist shops and supermarkets, with side streets linking to the parallel by-pass road. The buildings are small in scale and traditional in style, creating a pleasant atmosphere. Away from the central area, traffic can be intrusive.

CONVENIENCE ★★

Where you gonna stay?

It's a long, spread-out place – over 4km end to end. The pedestrian core is the most attractive all-round location, but the three major lifts are out at the extremities. Unless you opt to stay near one of these, you will make heavy use of the free bus services. The main lines run every 10 minutes, but get overcrowded at peak times and stop at 8pm. The complex route map requires serious study, but visitors have found the services 'regular' and 'efficient'. Taxis (including minibuses for groups) are affordable.

SCENERY ★★★

High and probably white

Livigno's high position and long ridges provide attractive views from both sides of the valley – but it can feel bleak and isolated.

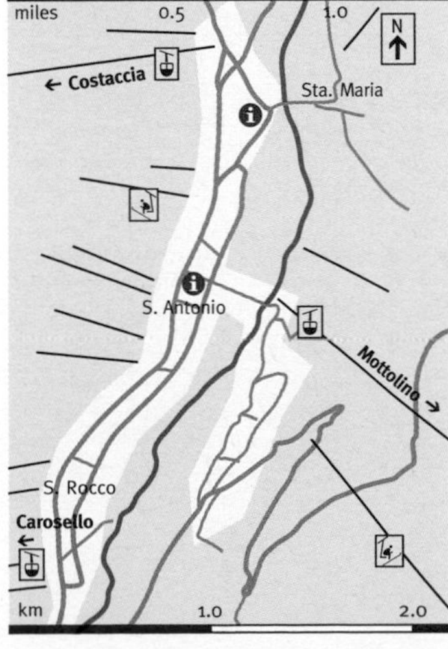

KEY FACTS

Resort	1815m 5,950ft
Slopes	1815-2795m 5,950-9,170ft
Lifts	30
Pistes	115km 71 miles
Blue	38%
Red	47%
Black	15%
Snowmaking	70%

LIFT PASSES

Prices in €

Age	**1-day**	**6-day**
under 15	33	138
15 to 64	41	199
65 plus	33	138

Free under 8

Beginner points card

Notes
Half-day passes and reduced Saturday passes; family reductions; 50% discount on day pass at St Moritz with a 3-day-plus pass

Alternative passes
Alta Valtellina pass covers Livigno, Bormio and Santa Caterina

THE MOUNTAINS

The slopes are on either side of the valley and are mainly above the treeline. It's not a good place in bad weather. Signposting is adequate, but the piste map does not identify runs. Night skiing is available on Thursdays.

EXTENT OF THE SLOPES ★★★★★
Widely spread

The slopes are more extensive than in many other budget destinations, but it's not a huge area and lots of the runs are very similar to one another.

A two-stage gondola at the north end of the village takes you up to **Costaccia**, where a long fast quad chairlift goes along the ridge towards the **Carosello** sector. The blue linking run back from Carosello to the top of Costaccia is flat in places and may involve energetic poling. Carosello is more usually accessed by the optimistically named Carosello 3000 gondola at the southern end of the village, which goes up, in two stages, to almost 2800m. Most runs return towards the village, but the Federia six-pack serves west-facing slopes on the back of the mountain.

The ridge of **Mottolino** is reached by a gondola or fast quad from Teola, across the valley from central Livigno. From the top, you can descend to fast quads on either side of the ridge, or take a very slow antique chair along the ridge.

We don't show on our map a link from the nursery drags at the bottom of Carosello to those below Costaccia; it's more of a walk than a run.

FAST LIFTS ★★★★★
A positive attraction

The lift system is impressively modern, with fast chairs and gondolas covering both sectors – though draglifts still serve the valley nursery slopes.

QUEUES ★★★★★
Few problems these days

Queues are generally not a problem. Delays can occur at the main gondolas at peak times, such as the Carosello 3000. A bigger problem is that winds can close the upper lifts, causing crowds lower down.

TERRAIN PARKS ★★★★★
Serious facilities

The main park behind Mottolino is an impressive freestyle zone for all levels. It also plays host to the World Rookie fest and River Jump contest – both on the Ticket to Ride calendar. It has kicker lines for all levels and is bordered by a big super-pipe, often used as a training ground by pros, and there are advanced rails in and around the jumps as well. There's also a huge airbag jump – perfect for trying out backflips and other advanced tricks.

Livigno's second park is at Carosello 3000. It also caters for all standards and includes another huge airbag jump. The two other parks – Amerikan, beside the Amerikan lift near Carosello, and the Del Sole area near the centre of town – are aimed at novices and juniors.

New in 2012 was the Cable Park in the middle of the village near lift 20. There are rails, boxes and jumps of varying difficulty, but the area is flat:

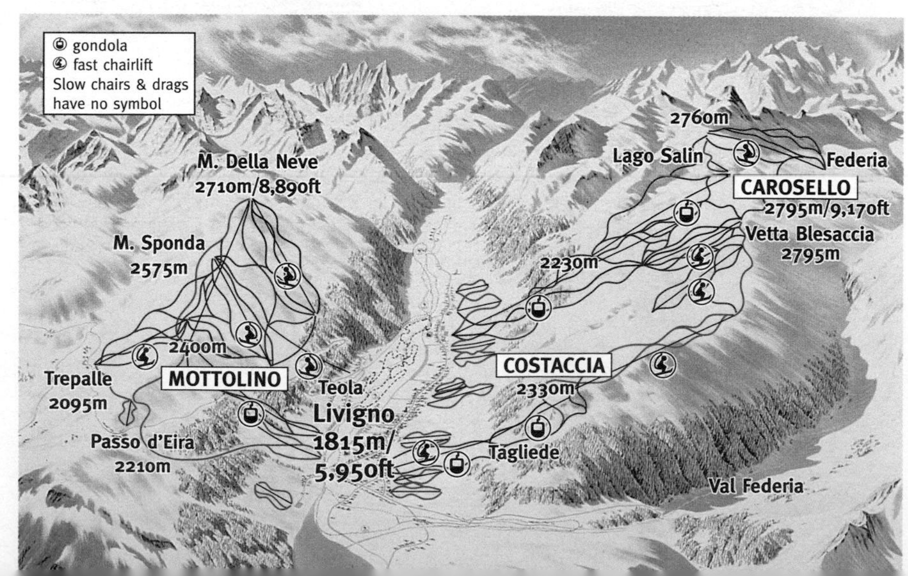

↑ Berghütte enjoys a good position near the bottom of Costaccia, with good views across the village to Mottolino

SNOWPIX.COM / CHRIS GILL

GETTING THERE

Air Bergamo 190km/120 miles (3hr45); Brescia 225km/140 miles (4hr45); Innsbruck 180km/110 miles (3hr15); Zürich 190km/120 miles (3hr30)

Rail Tirano (48km/ 30 miles); Zernez (Switzerland, 28km/ 17 miles); regular buses from station, weekends only

instead of using gravity, you are pulled along by a special cable system.

SNOW RELIABILITY ★★★★★
Very good, given precipitation

Livigno's slopes are high (you can spend most of your time around 2500m) and, with snow-guns on the lower slopes of Mottolino and Costaccia, the season is long.

FOR EXPERTS ★★★★★
Off-piste U-turn

There are several black runs on Mottolino, but they are of black steepness only in places, and regularly groomed. Having previously banned off-piste, the resort has now designated six slopes on Mottolino as freeride zones, and erected entry gates with safety warnings, avalanche risk information and gadgets to check the operation of your bleeper. This appears sensible and thoroughly organized, but a better idea would have been to make these areas avalanche-controlled. Some are between pistes, after all.

FOR INTERMEDIATES ★★★★★
Flattering slopes

Good intermediates will be able to have serious fun on the groomed blacks on Mottolino, as well as the wide choice of reds. The woodland black run from Carosello past Tea da Borch is narrow in places and can get mogulled and icy in the afternoon. Moderate intermediates have virtually the whole area at their disposal. The long run beneath the Mottolino gondola is one of the best, and there is also a long, varied, under-used blue going less directly to the valley. Leisurely types have several long cruises available; the blue beneath the fast chair at the top of Costaccia is a splendid slope.

FOR BEGINNERS ★★★★★
Excellent scattered slopes

A vast array of nursery slopes including those along the sunny lower flanks of Costaccia, are excellent for novices – although some of the slopes at the northern end are steep enough to cause difficulties. There are lots of longer blue runs to progress to.

FOR BOARDERS ★★★★★
Fun of all kinds

The pistes are in general big, wide, open and rolling motorways. The new freeride zones will be an obvious attraction for competent boarders. Beginners be warned: practically all the smaller lower slopes are serviced by drags. But the resort still attracts good numbers of beginners, and Madness is a specialist school.

FOR CROSS-COUNTRY ★★★★★
Good snow, bleak setting

Long snow-sure trails (30km in total) follow the valley floor, making Livigno a good choice, provided you don't mind the bleak scenery. There is a specialist school, Livigno 2000.

SCHOOLS

Centrale
t 0342 996276

Azzurra
t 0342 997683

Livigno Italy
t 0342 996767

Livigno Galli Fedele
t 0342 970300

Madness Snowboard
t 0342 997792

New
t 0342 997801

Classes
(Centrale prices)
6 days (2hr per day)
€112

Private lessons
€37 for 1hr; each additional person €10

CHILDCARE

Kinder Club (Centrale)
t 0342 996276
From age 3yr

M'eating Point
t 0342 997408
From age 3yr

'Pollicino'
t 366 262 6703
From age 3mnth

Ski school
Takes children from age 4 (6 2hr days €112)

ACTIVITIES

Indoor Aquagranda wellness park (swimming pool, sauna, fitness rooms), badminton, billiards

Outdoor Cleared paths, ice rink, snowshoeing, horse riding, tobogganing, dog sledding, go-karts on ice, snowmobiling, ice driving

UK PACKAGES

Inghams, Neilson, Skitracer

Phone numbers
From abroad use the prefix +39 (and do **not** omit the initial '0' of the phone number)

TOURIST OFFICE

www.livigno.eu

MOUNTAIN RESTAURANTS ★★★★★

No more than adequate

On Mottolino, the large M'eating Point refuge at the top of the gondola has a 'lively, overcrowded' self-service section that can be 'slow, resulting in cold food'. We've mixed reports of the small – and peaceful – table-service section: 'very average', says one; 'well-flavoured spaghetti', says another. Lower down there are rustic restaurants at Passo d'Eira and at Trepalle, on the back of the hill.

Carosello has a popular and 'acceptable' self-service place but more importantly a table-service wine bar and restaurant below doing 'outstanding' pasta dishes. Tea da Borch, in the trees lower down, has a Tirolean-style atmosphere. Along the hill in the Costaccia sector a reporter reckons the food at the Costaccia restaurant to be only average, while another remarks on the new and 'very clean' toilets. The Berghütte has an excellent position just above the nursery slopes in the Tagliede area and the food, although simple, is satisfying – and the service is efficient and friendly.

SCHOOLS AND GUIDES ★★★★★

Short but sweet classes

Past reports on the schools have generally been good, praising instruction and English. Classes are rated great value for money, but are mornings only (as is usual in Italy).

FOR FAMILIES ★★★★★

Not bad for Italy

The schools run classes for children from the age of four, and the Centrale school offers all-day non-skiing care for children from the age of three; the staff speak English. Beware the long, winding airport transfers.

STAYING THERE

Livigno has an enormous range of hotels and a number of apartments.

Hotels There is a wide choice.

******Bivio** (0342 996137) Welcoming chalet in centre with popular cellar bar. Good food à la carte. Pool and wellness area.

******Camana Veglia** (0342 996310) Charming old wooden chalet. Popular restaurant, well placed in Santa Maria.

******Intermonti** (0342 972100) Modern with pool and other mod cons; on the Mottolino side of the valley.

******Larice** (0342 996184) Stylish little B&B well placed for Costaccia lifts.

*****Champagne** (0342 996437) Pleasant B&B close to centre.

*****Loredana** (0342 996330) Modern chalet on the Mottolino side.

*****Montanina** (0342 996060) Very central, family run, 'friendly staff'.

*****Steinbock** (0342 970520) Nice little place, far from major lifts.

****Silvestri** (0342 996255) Comfortable place in the San Rocco area.

Apartments Available locally and from tour operators; a 2010 reporter was impressed with his 'massive' apartment from Neilson.

EATING OUT ★★★★★

Value for money

Livigno's restaurants are mainly traditional, unpretentious places, many hotel-based. Over the years we've had countless recommendations for where to eat. The latest recommendations include Paprika ('good flavour, good value') and Scala ('fish a speciality; flavour, service and ambiance excellent').

APRES-SKI ★★★★★

Lively, but disappoints some

The scene is quieter than some people expect – and the best places are scattered about, so the village lacks evening buzz. At tea time Tea del Vidal, at the bottom of Mottolino, is the place to be – 'après-ski is tame everywhere else', said one visitor – and it gets lively at the Stalet bar at the base of the Carosello gondola ('very friendly and warm') and at the central umbrella bar. Nightlife gets going after 10pm. The Kuhstall under the Bivio hotel is an excellent cellar bar with live music, as is the Helvetia, over the road. At the southern end of the village, Daphne's is 'one of the few lively bars in Livigno', Miky's is 'vibrant and very busy', and Marco's is popular. Kokodi is the main disco.

OFF THE SLOPES ★★★★★

New spa fails to impress

A 2011 visitor to the newish thermal spa/wellness centre rated it 'not a patch on Bad Gastein and twice the price' – but Bad Gastein does set the bar high. Other visitors have enjoyed the dog sledding, and tobogganing is also popular. And you can go bowling and ice-driving. Walks are uninspiring. There's duty-free shopping, of course – and trips to Bormio and St Moritz.

MADONNA TOURIST OFFICE

Madonna di Campiglio

A fashionable resort amid stunning scenery – a bit like Cortina, in other words, but with a more sensibly linked ski area

RATINGS

The mountains	
Extent	***
Fast lifts	****
Queues	***
Terrain p'ks	***
Snow	***
Expert	**
Intermediate	****
Beginner	***
Boarder	***
X-country	***
Restaurants	***
Schools	***
Families	***
The resort	
Charm	****
Convenience	***
Scenery	****
Eating out	***
Après-ski	***
Off-slope	**

RPI	90
lift pass	£160
ski hire	£95
lessons	£90
food & drink	£110
total	**£455**

KEY FACTS

Resort	1520m 4,990ft
Madonna, Folgarida, Marilleva, Pinzolo combined area	
Slopes	800-2505m 2,620-8,220ft
Lifts	62
Pistes	150km 93 miles
Blue	40%
Red	45%
Black	15%
Snowmaking	95%

- Splendid wooded setting in the dramatic Brenta Dolomites
- Pleasant, stylish village, bypassed by through-traffic, with car-free central zone
- Extensive, varied slopes, including the linked areas of Folgarida, Marilleva and now Pinzolo
- Lots of long, easy runs

- Although it has a compact core, the resort spreads along the valley
- Tough pistes are few, and widely separated around a big area – and off-piste is formally banned
- Quiet from dinner time onwards

Madonna di Campiglio may come second to Cortina d'Ampezzo for smart shops and bars, and for scenic drama, but by normal standards it is a very attractive resort. A return visit last winter confirmed it as one of our Italian favourites.

What triggered our visit was the new lift link to the slopes of Pinzolo, opened last season. The link involves no skiing, but there is no denying that jumping on a gondola for a 16-minute ride is slicker than waiting for buses, and we rate the new link highly. Pinzolo, like the other linked areas of Folgarida and Marilleva, adds considerably to the skiing, especially for confident skiers.

THE RESORT

Campiglio is a well established, quite fashionable resort, set near the head of a heavily wooded valley. Although the clientele is mainly Italian, the resort seems now to be attracting Russian visitors in considerable numbers. The regional lift pass covers not only the linked resorts but also others reachable by car or possibly bus, including Pejo and Passo Tonale.

VILLAGE CHARM ****

Smoothly traditional

Campiglio is mainly built in traditional Alpine style and has a polished air, at least around the central, car-free Piazza Righi and nearby streets, where there are quite a few diverting shops. The village is bypassed by through-traffic. Near the centre is a small park, and a lake, used for skating. The place doesn't go to sleep in the day, and is lively in the early evening.

SNOWPIX.COM / CHRIS GILL

March 2012: summer temperatures, and bare mountainsides. But good skiing here at Pinzolo, and in the distance at Campiglio – the white ribbon is the black Amazzonia run from Pradalago →

NEWS

2012/13: A new quad chair is due to open on the upper slopes of the Cinque Laghi sector, opening up some new pistes.

2011/12: The long-awaited gondola link with the Pinzolo slopes opened. On Monte Spinale a fast quad replaced the Boch chair. Pradalago gained a mini terrain park, and snowmaking was improved at Cinque Laghi and Grostè.

CONVENIENCE ★★★★★
Good links between sectors

The centre is fairly compact: the lifts to the Cinque Laghi and Pradalago sectors bracket most of the main hotels, and are a 5/10-minute walk apart. Five minutes from the centre is the gondola to the Spinale sector. Skiing links between these sectors and Grostè work well. But the resort spreads about 3km down the valley, while up the valley is the outlying suburb of Campo Carlo Magno, where there are further major lifts up to Grostè and Pradalago. The ski-bus is said to have improved of late; it may not be free in 2012/13. The better hotels run their own shuttles.

SCENERY ★★★★★
Splendid Dolomites

The resort has a splendid setting, with the dramatic cliffs of the Brenta group to the south-west.

THE MOUNTAINS

The upper slopes are open, the lower slopes attractively wooded. Many runs classified red could be blue.

EXTENT OF THE SLOPES ★★★★★
Plenty of variety

The Pradalago sector is linked via Monte Vigo to the slopes of Folgarida and Marilleva, and the new gondola from Cinque Laghi accesses the slopes

LIFT PASSES

Prices in €

Age	1-day	6-day
under 8	20	100
8 to 16	28	139
16 to 64	40	199
65 plus	36	179

Free under 8 if with family-paying adult

Notes
Madonna only; daily extensions for Pinzolo, Folgarida-Marilleva

Alternative passes
Pinzolo pass; Skirama Adamello Brenta covers Madonna, Pinzolo, Marilleva-Folgarida, Passo Tonale, Ponte di Legno, Andalo, Pejo, Monte Bondone and Folgaria-Lavarone

of Pinzolo. Reporters have been very impressed by immaculate grooming, as you expect in Italy these days.

FAST LIFTS ★★★★★
Some weaknesses

Most of the key lifts are fast chairs and gondolas, but moving around the area you will still meet some slow lifts. Examples include several lifts around Monte Spolverino and Monte Vigo, on Dos de la Pesa, on Monte Spinale and at Pinzolo. But at least the piste map clearly distinguishes fast chairs from slow ones, which can help a lot when planning your route or at least your timing – a rare thing in the Alps.

QUEUES ★★★★★
Not a big issue

Around Campiglio itself queues are rarely a problem except at ski school time in high season, when a 2012 report speaks of 10-minute waits. You may meet queues on the lifts around Monte Vigo and Monte Spolverino, and not only on the slow chairs.

TERRAIN PARKS ★★★★★
Serious efforts

The Ursus park, at Grostè, includes boardercross, quarter-pipe, rails, boxes and kickers. There's a special boarders' pass for the area. There is also a beginner park in the Pradalago sector.

SNOW RELIABILITY ★★★★★
Good snowmaking

Although many of the runs are sunny, they are at a fair altitude, and there has been hefty investment in snowmaking, which is now claimed to cover 95% of the runs. As a result, snow reliability is reasonable, despite an erratic snowfall record.

FOR EXPERTS ★★★★★
Relax and enjoy the view

As in many resorts in Italy, off-piste is formally banned, but the ban is often ignored. Finding ungroomed snow can be a bit of a challenge though – and this is not an area famed for reliable powder anyway. The trees around the Genziana chair at Pradalago are a good spot. There are black pistes dotted around – basically, one per sector – but they only just merit the classification. The lower part of Spinale Direttissima on the front of Monte Spinale is claimed to be 35°, which is a proper black. Few of the local reds present much challenge.

FOR INTERMEDIATES ★★★★★
Lots to do

Grostè and Pradalago have long, easy runs, and timid intermediates will love them, while confident skiers will need to seek out challenges. The long blue Pradalago Facile is a fabulous wide, scenic cruise. The nearby reds aren't a lot steeper, but the lovely, scenic black Amazzonia is quite testing. Grostè is both high and gentle, so has the feel of a glacier – but is entirely rock. All four runs at the very top are of blue gradient, although two are marked red. Lower down, Lame is a decent red. Next-door Monte Spinale has easy slopes on the back, linking to Grostè, but much tougher stuff on the front (read 'For experts'). Spinale Diretta (not to be confused with Spinale Direttissima) is an excellent genuine red. Cinque Laghi, Campiglio's racing mountain, has something for everyone. The long Cinque Laghi is tricky at the top, but is then a lovely genuine blue run ending prettily in woods; the famous 2 Tre is a good, varied red, quite steep towards the bottom.

Keen intermediates should not fail to explore the runs at Folgarida, Marilleva and Pinzolo. The Malghette red run on the way back from Monte Vigo is a favourite, with fabulous views across the valley; we'd be tempted to do laps on it if it were served by a faster lift.

FOR BEGINNERS ★★★★★
Get out of town

There are short drags near the village, but better nursery slopes up at Campo Carlo Magno, a bus ride out. The draglift here is not covered by the main lift pass, your expert friends should note. Progression to longer runs is easy – Pradalago is perfect.

FOR BOARDERS ★★★★★
Freeriders look elsewhere

The resort is popular with freestylers, and some major events have been held here.

FOR CROSS-COUNTRY ★★★★★
Respectable

There are 22km of pretty trails through the woods in a scenic setting up at Campo Carlo Magno.

MOUNTAIN RESTAURANTS ★★★★★
A fair selection

There are restaurants in all the obvious places, all named on the piste

↑ Great views of the Brenta massif from Doss del Sabion at the top of the Pinzolo slopes

SNOWPIX.COM / CHRIS GILL

map. Reports are all positive, though some reporters wish for more little rustic places. Some of the best are mountaineering refuges.

One of the most promising table-service places is at Chalet Fiat at Spinale; the self-service bit is stylishly done out, and has decent food, but finding a table can be a bit of a bunfight. Reader tips on Grostè: Boch, Stoppani ('elegant dining, fabulous views'), Graffer ('lovely position, very reasonable prices, efficient service') and Malga Montagnoli; on Pradalago: Viviani Pradalago ('characterful', 'traditional food, friendly service') and Cascina Zeledria ('cook your own on a hot rock before being towed back to the piste').

SCHOOLS AND GUIDES ★★★★★
Insist on English

There are several schools – Nazionale is the main one. Language has been a problem in the past, but we are assured that Nazionale and Rainalter have English-speaking instructors.

FOR FAMILIES ★★★★★
Do your own thing

The ski schools take children from four. The Rainalter Ski School offers non-ski activities for children between two and eight years. But we wonder if English is reliably spoken. The central park is an attractive feature.

STAYING THERE

There is a wide choice of hotels – dozens of 4-star and 3-star places – and some self-catering.

Hotels

****Lorenzetti** (0465 441404) At southern extremity of the resort, handy for the new gondola for Cinque Laghi and Pinzolo, and with shuttles to other lifts and the centre. Tipped by a regular visitor: 'Fabulous; excellent food and glorious views of the Brenta.'

****Maribel** (0465 443085) Stylish modern chalet out at Campo Carlo Magno – though not perfectly placed for the lift stations. Rooms and suites. Good wellness area.

****Oberosler** (0465 441136) 'Design' hotel (which in this case means bold modern decor) right next to the Spinale gondola and return piste. We enjoyed staying here in 2012 – good food, helpful staff.

***Italo** (0465 441392) Simple, quiet place 300m from Spinale lift – 'friendly, good food', says a 2012 reporter.

***Sportivo** (0465 441101) Small B&B in pole position metres from the Pradalago gondola station.

EATING OUT ★★★★★
Some good options

There are around 20 restaurants in the resort. Bear in mind that some of the bars also offer food. Reader tips include Antico Focolare ('spectacular ravioli in creamy nut sauce'), Le Roi ('crowded with happy people – great pizza and pasta') and, for a gourmet treat, the 'amazing' Da Alfiero in Piazza Palu at the south end of the park.

APRES-SKI ★★★★★
Early and late

As the slopes close, people pile in to several central places – Cafe Campiglio, Nardis Cafe and Bar Suisse – a very welcoming cafe-bar on the main square. Ober One at Oberosler hotel, at the bottom of Spinale, is more 'conveniently placed but not so popular', which may be because of the music it pumps out. As dinner time

SCHOOLS

Nazionale
t 0465 443243

Rainalter
t 0465 443300

Cinque Laghi
t 0465 441650

Classes
(Nazionale prices)
6 mornings €200

Private lessons
From €42 for 1hr

CHILDCARE

Baita del Bimbo (Rainalter school)
t 0465 443300
Age 2 to 8

Ski schools
From age 4; half-days or full days (10am to 4pm)

ACTIVITIES

Indoor Pools and spas in hotels

Outdoor Ice skating, snowshoeing, ice climbing, dog sledding

UK PACKAGES

Alpine Answers, Crystal, Crystal Finest, Flexiski, Momentum, Ski Club Freshtracks, Ski Expectations, Ski Solutions, Ski Yogi, Solo's, STC, Zenith
Folgarida Alpine Answers, Rocketski

GETTING THERE

Air Verona 150km/ 95 miles (3hr); Bergamo 160km/ 100 miles; Milan 200km/120 miles (3hr30)

Rail Trento (75km/ 45 miles)

TOURIST OFFICE

www.
campigliodolomiti.it

Phone numbers
From abroad use the prefix +39 (and do **not** omit the initial '0' of the phone number)

approaches, everyone disappears. Later in the evening Des Alpes, Cliffhanger and also Zangola (out of town) are possibilities. Cantina del Suisse (underneath Bar Suisse) has live music some evenings.

OFF THE SLOPES ★★★★★

Take your Kindle

There's not a huge amount to do. Skating on the lake and snowshoeing are popular, and the local Alpine guides offer ice climbing.

LINKED RESORT – 1400m

MARILLEVA

Marilleva is a modern resort consisting of several 1960s-style, ugly but functional, low-rise concrete buildings (most of them well screened by trees, thankfully) built on a mid-mountain shelf at 1400m and reached by road or gondola from the lower part of the resort at 900m, on the valley floor. There is cheap accommodation in the nearby valley village of Mezzana.

The slopes above Marilleva are excellent, steep, north-facing reds served by a gondola and a six-pack (with a few blues higher up the mountain), much better for adventurous intermediates than Campiglio's main Pradalago slopes. And the snow is usually the best in the area, because of the largely north-facing orientation. There's also a genuine black run on Dos de la Pesa served by a slow two-stage chairlift.

The Orti mountain restaurant directly above Marilleva offers 'fantastic views, good food and reasonable prices'.

LINKED RESORT – 1400m

FOLGARIDA

Folgarida is also purpose built and set above the floor of the Val di Sole, but it is beside the road over to Campiglio, and is much more traditional in style than Marilleva.

The resort spreads across the mountainside between two gondola stations, one right on the roadside at 1400m and the other some way off the road in a much more village-like area at 1300m. This part in particular feels more upmarket than Marilleva, with smart hotels and a few shops, but there are few other amenities. A 2011 reporter rates it excellent for families, with 'friendly, helpful locals'. You may encounter some fur-clad patrons, or in January families from Eastern Europe. One enthusiastic past reporter judged the 4-star hotel Caminetto (0463 986109) 'almost perfect'.

The slopes down to Folgarida are gentler than those above Marilleva, though they include an easy black, and one reader found some of the blues rather tricky.

Midway between Marilleva and Folgarida, an eight-person gondola runs from the valley village of Daolasa up to Val Mastellina, below Monte Vigo, the top section serving a long, sweeping red with lovely views of the Val di Sole below.

LINKED RESORT – 770m

PINZOLO

Pinzolo is the main town of the Val Rendena, south-west of Madonna di Campiglio, and a 20-minute drive (and a 750m descent) away. The long (and long-planned) gondola link between the slopes of Pinzolo and Campiglio opened in 2011.

From Pinzolo, a gondola followed by a fast chair take you via a lively mid-mountain congregation area with nursery slopes to the area's high point of Doss del Sabion (2100m), where there are great close-up views of the Brenta massif.

It's quite a challenging area, mainly consisting of genuine blacks (groomed when we have visited) and genuine reds, some of them at the steep end of the spectrum. Most of the runs are quite short, the conspicuous exception being the excellent black/red run of almost 900m vertical to the valley station of a second gondola at Tulot, just outside the town. Start at Doss del Sabion and you can extend this to 1300m. Many of the slopes are shady, so keep snow well.

The Rifugio Doss del Sabion at the top has a calm little table-service room as an alternative to the often hectic terrace and self-service. There is a restaurant a mid-mountain, too.

PInzolo sells itself as a family resort, and has good childcare facilities at mid-mountain, but we would expect language problems in a resort unknown in the UK.

There are plenty of guest houses and hotels, mainly 3-star but with some other options. One past reporter tipped the well-placed 4-star Quadrifoglio (0465 503600).

Monterosa Ski

One of Europe's best-kept secrets: three unspoiled villages, long easy pistes and excellent, uncrowded off-piste terrain

TOP 10 RATINGS

Extent	**
Fast lifts	*****
Queues	****
Snow	****
Expert	****
Intermediate	****
Beginner	**
Charm	***
Convenience	***
Scenery	****

RPI	80
lift pass	£160
ski hire	£90
lessons	£60
food & drink	£85
total	**£395**

NEWS

2011/12: At Gressoney, a new gondola replaced the existing one from Stafal to Gabiet.

The historic Rifugio Guglielmina above Alagna burnt down. It is not clear if it will be rebuilt.

KEY FACTS

Slopes	1200-3275m
	3,940-10,740ft
Lifts	23
Pistes	73km
	45 miles
Blue	17%
Red	71%
Black	12%
Snowmaking	97%

- + Fabulous off-piste and heli-skiing, for both intermediates and experts
- + Slopes usually quiet weekdays
- + Panoramic views
- + Good snow reliability and grooming
- + Quiet, unspoiled villages
- + Lovely long runs and a sensation of travel from place to place, but ...

- − Virtually no choice of route when touring the three valleys on-piste
- − Few challenges (or moguls) on-piste
- − High winds can close links
- − Few off-slope diversions
- − Can be very busy at weekends
- − Limited après-ski

Monterosa Ski's three resorts – Champoluc, Gressoney la Trinité and Alagna – are popular with weekenders from Milan and Turin. Internationally, the extensive off-piste terrain has long attracted experts; but the resorts are not household names, and they retain a friendly, small-scale, unspoiled Italian ambience that we (and a growing band of readers) like a lot.

The three-valley network of slopes is anything but small-scale: Alagna and Champoluc are an impressive 17km apart – slightly further apart than Courchevel and Val Thorens, to make the obvious comparison. But a glance at the piste map reveals that the Italian network is skeletal compared with the full-bodied Trois Vallées, and the lift company has now accepted our view that its piste figures were exaggerated. More about this later.

THE RESORT

There is one main village in each of the area's three valleys. Champoluc in the western Val d'Ayas and Gressoney in the central valley are both about an hour's drive up from the Aosta valley, to the south. Alagna is even more remote, and approached by a quite different route from the east. Like most Italian resorts, the villages really come to life only at weekends.

Down-valley from Gressoney la Trinité is Gressoney St Jean. Down-valley from Champoluc are Antagnod and Brusson. All have small slope areas covered by the Monterosa pass.

Day-trip outings are hard work, but Cervinia, La Thuile, Courmayeur and Pila are reachable by car. The Aosta Valley pass covers all of them.

Village charm All three villages are small-scale and pleasantly rustic, without being picture-postcard pretty.

Champoluc is strung out along the street running from the centre past various hotels to the gondola base, where a cluster of shops and bars forms a kind of distinct micro-resort.

Gressoney la Trinité is a quiet, neat little village, with cobbled streets, traditional wooden buildings and an old church – but also many disused buildings. But many people stay in skiers' satellites outside the village – read 'Convenience', below.

Alagna is a remote village with a solid church and some lovely old wooden farmhouses built in the distinctive Walser style.

Convenience In Champoluc you can get up the hill via the village gondola (you can store kit there overnight), or a funicular starting further up the valley at Frachey. There is a linking bus service, but we didn't find it effective.

Gressoney la Trinité is about 800m from the base station of a slow chairlift into the local slopes; there are a few hotels conveniently clustered around the lift base. The lifts for the other valleys go from the mini-resort of Stafal at the head of the valley. But its lodgings are quite widely spread away from the lifts. Buses are not frequent, or free.

Little Alagna is streets ahead of its neighbours in this respect: the gondola starts from the village square.

Scenery Some of the highest peaks in the Alps surround Monterosa Ski – a string of peaks over 4000m, and some over 4500m; the panoramic views from restaurant terraces are fabulous.

THE MOUNTAINS

The slopes offer an attractive mix of woodland runs lower down, particularly at Gressoney, and open slopes higher up; but open slopes dominate. As so often in Italy, run classification generally exaggerates difficulty. Signposting is adequate.

Slopes The slopes span vast distances, but don't add up to a huge amount of piste skiing. In earlier editions we suggested that the resort's piste kilometres were exaggerated, roughly by a factor of two – and now the lift company has quietly halved its claims for the linked area from a major 135km to a modest 73km. Amazing; but anyone can make mistakes.

The main three-valley network is very simple, with few variations. Starting from Frachey, up the valley from Champoluc, or from Alagna at the opposite end, you ride two or three lifts up to the first ridge, ski down to Stafal, ride two or three lifts up to the second ridge, ski down. All the descents are gloriously long; the run down to Alagna is 1760m vertical and 7km (previously 13.5km!). Champoluc and Gressoney have worthwhile local areas of slopes, but Alagna does not.

The gondola from Champoluc goes up to Crest, a mid-mountain nursery area with a further gondola and chairlift going on to Colle Sarezza. This area is linked to the runs above Frachey via a steep, narrow, bumpy red run; timid intermediates are better off starting at Frachey. At Gressoney, a pair of chairlifts go up from two points serving wooded runs of 400m/500m vertical, with piste links across the mountainside to Gabiet where you can join the three-valley system.

The main lift system is vulnerable to bad weather, so it is worth noting that both Champoluc and Gressoney have decent sheltered alternatives down-valley, at Antagnod and Bieltschocke. Both small areas offer some good off-piste.

Fast lifts The lifts are virtually all chairs and gondolas; most of the important chairs are fast, the ones out of Gressoney being exceptions.

Queues Problems arise mainly on sunny weekends and at peak periods, when the pistes can get busy. The Alpe Mandria chair above the Frachey funicular is a bottleneck. Also at Frachey there may be serious queues for the old double chair to Champoluc. The gondola and (particularly) the cable car at Alagna can build queues. The queue-prone gondola from Stafal to Gabiet has been upgraded, but the one above it gets busy at times.

Terrain parks Gressoney has a boardercross and there's now an 'excellent' park at Gabiet. Big air jumps are sometimes built near the top of the gondola from Champoluc.

Snow reliability Generally good, thanks to altitude and extensive snowmaking, which impresses reporters. Grooming is extremely thorough – bumps on the pistes don't last long. Alagna is relatively low, and sunny, and the home run suffers as a result.

Experts The attraction is the off-piste (the black pistes are not steep), with great runs from the high points of the lift system and some excellent heli-drops. Among the adventures we've enjoyed here was a heli-drop on Monte Rosa, skiing down to Zermatt and returning off-piste from Cervinia. But guides can take you to plenty of places lower down too, including the excellent Mandria forest area above Frachey. There is good, shady, easily accessible off-piste beside the long run from Passo Salati towards Alagna.
Intermediates There are excellent, long cruising runs from the ridges down into the valleys. Down towards Alagna, the black Olen piste (originally and rightly classified red) is a great blast, as is the tough red Alagna piste below it. Confident intermediates should take a guide and explore the gentler off-piste. The area is not ideal for timid intermediates, who should beware the run from Colle Sarezza mentioned under 'Slopes' above, and the red descent to Champoluc. Antagnod suits some people better.
Beginners The high nursery slopes at Crest above Champoluc, served by two moving carpets, are better than the lower ones at Gressoney. But neither has ideal gentle runs to progress to. Antagnod is better in this respect. Forget Alagna.
Snowboarding There's a boardercross at Gressoney and great freeriding. A reporter points out that a few important links involve flat trails.
Cross-country There are long trails: 25km around Gressoney St Jean, 17km in Champoluc; Brusson, down-valley from Champoluc, has the best trails in the area (38km) – 'fantastic', says a downhiller who gave it a go on a bad-weather day.
Mountain restaurants The mountain restaurants are generally simple, friendly, atmospheric and good value, and keep readers happy.

In the Val d'Ayas, there are three notably charming places serving excellent food in beautifully renovated old buildings – Rascard Frantze and l'Aroula above Champoluc and the 'really memorable' Stadel Soussun above Frachey. Other reader tips include: the 'atmospheric' Belvedere, the Ostafa ('excellent pasta'), the modern Campo Base ('the best hot chocolate'), and Lo Retsignon.

Tips in the Gressoney valley include, on the main runs, Sitten and Gabiet ('excellent pasta' and 'best bombardinos'), the friendly little Alpen Lys and Punta Jolanda; above Orsia, Morgenrot is regularly tipped.

In the Alagna valley, traditional favourite Rifugio Guglielmina burned down last season. Lower down, Alpen Stop at Pianalunga and the Baita just below it are recommended.
Schools and guides We have had mixed reports on the Italian ski schools – most recently, excellent private lessons both at Champoluc and Antagnod. We have had good reports of the ski school run by UK tour operator Ski 2 ('good, friendly instructors'). The Guide Monterosa guides in Gressoney are 'faultless', 'absolutely excellent'.
Families Facilities are limited. Talk to your tour operator.

STAYING THERE

A growing list of tour operators feature the area. We've had good reports of Monterosa specialists Ski 2 ('great from pick-up to drop-off').
Hotels For a small place, Champoluc has a good range of attractive hotels. Many readers have enjoyed the central, comfortable and friendly 4-star

↑ In the modern Italian way, grooming is very thorough – but you don't have to go far off-piste to find moguls, should you need them

SKI 2

UK PACKAGES

Champoluc Alpine Answers, Crystal, Inghams, Momentum, Mountain Wave, Ski 2, Ski Club Freshtracks, Ski Expectations, Ski Solutions, Ski Yogi, Snow Finders
Gressoney la Trinité Alpine Answers, Crystal, Crystal Finest, Inghams, Momentum, Mountain Tracks, Ski Club Freshtracks, Ski Yogi, Skitracer, Snoworks, STC
Alagna Alpine Answers, James Orr Heli-ski, Mountain Tracks, Ski Club Freshtracks, Ski Weekend, Ski-Monterosa

Phone numbers
From abroad use the prefix +39 (and do **not** omit the initial '0' of the phone number)

TOURIST OFFICE

www.monterosa-ski.com/en

Relais des Glaciers (0125 308182), not least for its in-house patisserie. We can report approval this year of the lovely 4-star Breithorn (0125 308734), despite some small rooms. In 2010 we enjoyed the friendly, woody 4-star La Rouja (0125 308767). Readers like the 3-star Champoluc (0125 308088) – 'very friendly, excellent position'. The central, creaky 3-star Castor (0125 307117) offers 'great atmosphere, good food, helpful, friendly staff'.

Comfortable lodgings up the hill are a local speciality. The new Hotellerie de Mascognaz (0125 308734), a satellite of the Breithorn, is a lovingly restored group of stone chalets in a very isolated spot reached by skidoo. Three mountain restaurants have charming rooms – Stadel Soussun (348 6527222), Rascard Frantze (0125 941065) and l'Aroula (347 0188095), where we had a wonderfully peaceful and comfortable stay last season.

At the Gressoney lift base, the 3-star Dufour (0125 366139) earns two glowing reports this year – 'charming owners, wonderful staff, excellent food', while the 'welcoming and friendly' Residence Valverde (0125 366148) is again approved. In the village, the Jolanda Sport (0125 366140) has had good reports. At the main lift base at Stafal, the modern Chalet du Lys (0125 366806) offers good rooms and 'excellent' food.

In Alagna, readers tip the Residence Mirella (0163 91286) – 50m from the lifts and above the village bakery ('superb' breakfasts, not surprisingly, and 'charming' hosts). Montagna di Luce (0163 922820) has rooms (read 'Eating out').

Eating out Most restaurants are in hotels, but there are a few stand-alone places. Reader recommendations include: in Champoluc, the Osteria Il Balivo ('terrific food and atmosphere') and the Grange up at Frachey; and in Alagna, the Unione ('good food but no written menu'), Dir und Don pizzeria/grill ('lively, excellent pizza') and (just outside Alagna) Montagna di Luce ('wonderful food and ambience').

Après-ski The evenings are generally quiet, at least during the week. In Champoluc, Atelier Gourmand is a 'cosy, rustic' reader favourite at the gondola base. The nearby Bistrot is popular too. And the Glaciers' patisserie is 'well worth the walk'. Golosone is a small, atmospheric, distinctly Italian wine bar; and the West Road pub in the hotel California has karaoke some nights. Pachamamas impressed one reader. At weekends, the Gram Parsons disco beneath the California gets going. Gressoney is even quieter; in Stafal the Giovanni is a 'great place for a decent beer at the end of the day'. In Alagna, the Mirella (read 'Hotels') and the Caffè della Guide in the hotel Monterosa have been recommended. The An Bacher Wi wine bar has had good reports.

Off the slopes There is an outdoor ice rink at Champoluc, and a sport hall plus big pool at Gressoney.

Passo Tonale

An excellent place to learn or to build confidence at moderate cost, with its appeal broadened by the link with Ponte di Legno

TOP 10 RATINGS

Extent	**
Fast lifts	****
Queues	****
Snow	****
Expert	*
Intermediate	***
Beginner	*****
Charm	**
Convenience	***
Scenery	***

RPI 70

lift pass	£150
ski hire	£65
lessons	£40
food & drink	£90
total	**£345**

NEWS

There are plans for new lifts on the Presena Glacier but no date for when they will be installed.

2011/12: A new mountain restaurant, Faita, opened on the Giuliana piste. In the resort a new ice cream bar opened, Bar Monticelli.

KEY FACTS

Resort	1885m 6,180ft

Passo Tonale and Ponte di Legno combined area

Slopes	1120-3015m 3,670-9,890ft
Lifts	30
Pistes	100km 62 miles
Blue	17%
Red	66%
Black	17%
Snowmaking	100%

- + Good-value mid-market lodgings
- + Sunny but snow-sure slopes
- + Plenty of uncrowded, easy runs, immediately above the village
- + Link to Ponte di Legno adds attractive, steeper, treelined runs
- − Not much locally for experts or keen intermediates
- − Local slopes are above the treeline and unpleasant in bad weather
- − Linear village strung along the pass road is no beauty

Passo Tonale's blend of attractions makes it a great place for beginners and timid intermediates. It's a more interesting destination for the more adventurous now that it is linked to the slopes above Ponte di Legno.

THE RESORT

Village charm The resort was developed mainly for skiing, along a road over a high pass; many of the buildings are in chalet style, but it lacks a focus, and traffic intrudes.

Convenience Tonale is fairly compact, with its hotels, shops, bars and restaurants spread along the bottom of the main slope area – so the nearest lift is generally not far away. The gondola to the glacier is well outside the village, but you can ski to it via the main slopes.

Scenery The setting can feel rather bleak, but the main slopes offer grand views of Presena, and Ponte di Legno's slopes also offer good views.

THE MOUNTAINS

The Tonale slopes are entirely above the treeline, and bad weather can mean white-outs and closures. The linked slopes of Ponte di Legno are almost entirely wooded – a great combination. Thirty minutes east is Marilleva (free bus daily, except Saturdays), linked to Madonna di Campiglio. Buy the right pass and you get a day there included, or more.

Slopes Tonale's home slopes are limited in extent; one reader 'skied every run in half a day'. The broad, gentle, sunny area north of the pass road, served by a row of chairs and drags, is much the larger of the two sectors, but it is not large; runs are short, with limited vertical. The north-facing sector is steeper, narrower and taller. An eight-seat gondola leads to a double chairlift, and above that is the small Presena glacier, with two drags.

A blue/red run through the trees (mostly easy but with a short steeper section) descends almost 600m to a slow chair into the Ponte di Legno slopes; this is followed by an easy black run – you must ride the gondola down to a different chair to avoid this.

Fast lifts The system is impressive – seven fast chairs on the Tonale slopes.

↑ The village runs across the bottom of the main area of slopes, with the peaks of Presena to the south

APT VAL DI SOLE / C BRIANI

UK PACKAGES

Crystal, Independent Ski Links, Neilson, Skitracer, STC, Thomson

Phone numbers
From abroad use the prefix +39 (and do **not** omit the initial '0' of the phone number)

TOURIST OFFICE

www.passotonale.it
www.adamelloski.com
www.valdisole.net

Queues In peak season, certain lifts get busy at ski school departure time, and the gondola back from Ponte di Legno can be oversubscribed. But generally there are no problems.
Terrain parks Directly above the village is a small park with jumps, boxes and jibs, and a beginners' area.
Snow reliability In a normal season, the altitude and setting ensure good conditions. The sunny main slopes can suffer in late season, while the glacial south side fares better. Strong wind can be a problem, but the wooded slopes of Ponte di Legno offer shelter. The snowmaking is impressive.
Experts There isn't much for experts within the lift system. But in good conditions there are epic off-piste runs from the glacier, including the impressive 16km Pisgana run towards Ponte di Legno (a vertical of 1650m).
Intermediates The gentle south-facing slopes – many labelled red but of blue gradient – are great for building confidence. We enjoyed the 4.5km Alpino piste down a deserted valley to the village. Adventurous intermediates will enjoy the Presena area. The glacier runs are short and not steep. The black run beneath the gondola is easy but rewarding. The red runs at Ponte di Legno are excellent, and correctly classified. The blacks are not steep.
Beginners Excellent: the sunny lifts on gentle slopes right by the village are ideal, with plenty of easy, wide blue runs to move on to, a couple of them quite long.
Snowboarding The gentle slopes and ability to get around mainly on chairlifts mean the area is good for beginner and intermediate boarders.
Cross-country Not ideal. There are 8km of trails at Passo Tonale and 44km at Vermiglio (10km east).

Mountain restaurants Readers have generally been happy, particularly with the modest prices. Most places have table- and self-service sections. Tips include the village-level Baracca ('the best – the ski-in terrace a bonus'), the new Rifugio Passo Paradiso ('good ambience') and the 'very friendly' Nigritella. At Ponte di Legno the rustic Valbione does excellent food.
Schools and guides A 2012 beginner reports good progress but confirms earlier reports of poor English.
Families The ski school takes kids from four, and it looks a good resort for skiing children. But there isn't much to do other than skiing.

STAYING THERE

Hotels There are around 30, most of them 3-stars, including the Sporting (0364 903781) where we had a pleasant short stay in 2012. Other 2012 visitors tip the 'great, friendly' Torretta (0364 903978) and the 'excellent' 4-star Miramonti (0364 900501) with pool and spa. Crystal's modern Paradiso (also with pool, spa) has repeatedly impressed reporters.
Apartments There are 1,400 beds in apartments, a few on the UK market.
Eating out Reporters seem content. Mainly hotel restaurants, including the 'good value' Torretta ('best in town with a genuine pizza oven').
Après-ski It's not wild, but there are a few spots to try. Reader tips include El Bait and La Botte (both with free après snacks), the Magic Pub, Nico's Bar, Heaven (in Sport Hotel Vittoria) and the disco in the Miramonti (now called the Up Fun Park & Disco Pub) and the Paradiso disco.
Off the slopes There's not a lot to do off the slopes – snowmobiling, snowshoeing, skating.

SAUZE D'OULX TOURIST OFFICE

Sauze d'Oulx

A lively village beneath an attractive area of slopes forming part of the extensive Milky Way; but non-trivial drawbacks persist

RATINGS

The mountains	
Extent	****
Fast lifts	***
Queues	***
Terrain p'ks	*
Snow	**
Expert	**
Intermediate	****
Beginner	*
Boarder	**
X-country	*
Restaurants	***
Schools	**
Families	**
The resort	
Charm	**
Convenience	**
Scenery	***
Eating out	***
Après-ski	****
Off-slope	*

RPI	80
lift pass	£150
ski hire	£95
lessons	£70
food & drink	£95
total	**£410**

NEWS

2012/13: A new easy piste from Rif Mollino to Sportinia is to open, completing the new alternative route to Sportinia.

2011/12: The two slow Rocce Nere chairs have been replaced by a fast quad, using the hardware of the Triplex lift. The top station of the Pian della Rocca fast chair has been moved to Rif Mollino above Sportinia and the lift renamed Lago Nero. A new beginner run opened in the Clotes area, and more snowmaking was provided for the Gran Pista down to Jouvenceaux.

- ➕ Extensive and uncrowded slopes – great intermediate cruising
- ➕ Mix of open and treelined runs is good for all weather conditions
- ➕ Entertaining nightlife
- ➕ Part of the Milky Way network, spreading across the border into France, but ...

- ➖ Full exploration of the Milky Way area really requires a car or taxis
- ➖ Erratic snow record and far from comprehensive snowmaking
- ➖ Lift system needs improvement
- ➖ Several drawbacks for beginners
- ➖ Steep walks around the village
- ➖ Crowds at weekends in season
- ➖ Few challenging pistes

Skiers with long memories are inclined to dismiss Sauze as lager-lout territory. In the 1980s and maybe 1990s the tabloid newspapers mined a rich vein of young Brits behaving badly here. There are still lots of lively bars and shops festooned in English signs, and lots of young Brits working in them, but it is a much more civilized place now, with the resort's Italian clientele more in evidence, especially at weekends (Sauze is Turin's closest decent-sized ski area). When we visit, we find we like the place more than we expect to.

But Sauze still has a problem: investment, lack of. With its acutely unreliable natural snow, it needs comprehensive snowmaking. And the rate of progress in upgrading lifts needs a serious boost, as well. What the resort seems to be doing instead is gradually reshuffling the lifts it already has, which doesn't quite do the trick – more on this later.

THE RESORT

Sauze d'Oulx sits on a sloping mountain shelf facing north-west to the mountains bordering France.

It is a mid-sized resort – a big village rather than a town – but it spreads quite widely. Out of the bustle of the centre, there are secluded apartment blocks in quiet, wooded areas and a number of good restaurants also tucked away.

The Via Lattea (Milky Way) lift pass covers not only next-door Sestriere and Sansicario, easily reached by lift and piste, but also the more remote slopes on the French border, above Claviere and Montgenèvre. These are much more easily reached by road.

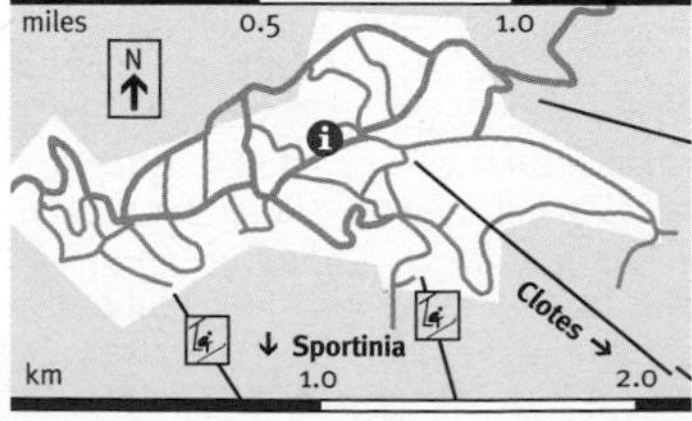

VILLAGE CHARM ★★
Falling behind?

The village has an attractive old core, with narrow, twisting streets and houses roofed with huge stone slabs. But most of the resort is modern and undistinguished, made up of block-like hotels relieved by the occasional chalet, spreading down the steep hillside from the slopes. There is little sign of investment in smart, woody hotels and apartments.

There is a central car-free zone, but at both ends of the day the rest of the village can be congested. The roads have few pavements and can be icy.

Despite the decline in lager sales, the centre is still lively at night; the late bars are usually quite full, and, in a good season, the handful of discos do brisk business – at the weekend, at least. Noise can be a problem in the early hours.

CONVENIENCE ★★
Uphill struggles

The Clotes chair, for the left-hand side of the network, is at the top of the village, up a short but steep hill. Some hotels are above this lift, and in good

KEY FACTS	
Resort	1510m 4,950ft
Milky Way	
Slopes	1390-2825m 4,560-9,270ft
Lifts	72
Pistes	400km 249 miles
Blue	25%
Red	55%
Black	20%
Snowmaking	60%
Sauze d'Oulx-Sestriere-Sansicario	
Slopes	1390-2825m 4,560-9,270ft
Lifts	41
Pistes	300km 186 miles
Snowmaking	38%

snow offer ski-in/ski-out convenience – but most are not. There is a moving carpet that cuts out part of the climb. The Sportinia chair, the most direct way to the heart of the slopes, is a strenuous and hazardous walk (often on slippery roads) further out. There is a free ski-bus service.

The smaller, lower village of Jouvenceaux is worth considering as a base, with a fast lift into the slopes and good red run back down.

SCENERY ★★★★★

Plenty of trees

The scenery is attractively woody, especially low down and along the Val di Susa. The sunny, open slopes higher up give wide panoramic views of the mountains bordering France.

THE MOUNTAINS

The higher slopes are open, the lower ones pleasantly wooded. Piste classifications change from year to year, and the signs on the ground don't always match the piste map. Pistes tend to be overclassified, with reds that should be blue and blacks that should be red. Piste marking may be absent. And signposting isn't great. Despite improvements, the Via Lattea piste map is still very difficult to follow – it is conceived as a marketing device rather than a skiing aid. Mad.

EXTENT OF THE SLOPES ★★★★★

Big and varied enough for most

Sauze's local slopes are spread across a broad wooded bowl above the resort, ranging from west- to north-facing. The main lifts are chairs, slow from the top of the village up to **Clotes** and fast from the western fringes to the heart of Sauze's slopes at **Sportinia,** a sunny mid-mountain clearing in the woods, with a ring of restaurants and hotels, and a small nursery area. You can now get from Clotes to Sportinia via a single fast chair (Lago Nero – in fact the existing Pian della Rocca chair realigned) and a new short blue run. Progress beyond Sportinia towards Sestriere and other resorts now goes via the fast Nuovo Rocce Nere chair, which has used the hardware of the Triplex chair to replace the two ancient Rocce Nere chairs.

The high point of the system is **Monte Fraiteve**. From here you can travel west on splendid broad, long runs to **Sansicario** – and on to a two-stage gondola near **Cesana Torinese** that links with **Claviere** and then **Montgenèvre**, in France, at the far end of the Milky Way (both are reached more quickly by car).

M Fraiteve is the main way to **Sestriere**. There is a red piste all the way down, but the slope faces south; the bottom section is rarely open – expect to ride the gondola down.

LIFT PASSES

Via Lattea

Prices in €

Age	1-day	6-day
over 8	34	180

Free under 8; 75 plus

Beginner Restricted day pass (€24)

Notes
Covers lifts in Sauze d'Oulx, Sestriere, Sansicario, Cesana and Claviere; half-day passes

Alternative passes
International (covers all the above plus Montgenèvre)

FAST LIFTS ★★★★★
Few and far between

Fast lifts are in a minority. There are still a lot of drags and old, slow chairlifts. Things are improving slowly but serious investment is needed to update the lift system.

QUEUES ★★★★★
Weekend problems

There can be queues on Saturdays when the hordes from Turin flock in. And crowds on the piste can be a problem then too ('dangerously overcrowded' and 'I was relieved to ski home in one piece', said a 2011 reporter). But during the week the slopes are usually quiet – though recent changes around M Fraiteve may have increased congestion there at peak times. The rearrangement of existing lifts that seems to be the lift company's way forward has solved some problems while creating others. Our regular reporter judges the net effect to be negative. Regulars will be glad to hear that the two ancient Rocce Nere chairs above Sportinia – which were painfully slow and prone to breakdown – have been replaced by a fast quad using the hardware of the Triplex lift. But this lift is now the only way to progress toward M Fraiteve, so of course it builds queues – major ones at the February peak, we hear. The quad from the village to Clotes has long generated queues. Part of the new arrangement (with the Pian della Rocca chair realigned to finish above Sportinia) is that this now forms a relatively quick route to Sportinia. So it will attract more customers. So ... what these guys need is some serious lift network modelling software. Oh, and some investment.

TERRAIN PARKS ★★★★★
Maybe

The location and size of the park did change from year to year – but for the last few years it has been at Sportinia. Don't count on it though: it may be closed with little explanation. There is a park at Sansicario too.

SNOW RELIABILITY ★★★★★
Can be poor, affecting the links

The area is notorious for erratic snowfalls, suffering droughts with worrying frequency – though recent seasons have been pretty good. Snowmaking has been increased throughout the area (including the Sportinia nursery slopes) but coverage is still far from complete. Great efforts are made to keep runs open in poor conditions. Grooming is in general 'immaculate'.

FOR EXPERTS ★★★★★
Head off-piste

There are black runs, but most of them do not deserve their classification. We're told the black Malafosse run is not fiercely steep, but is narrow and very isolated. There are quite a few off-piste opportunities within the lift network – between the pistes and down lift lines.

FOR INTERMEDIATES ★★★★★
Splendid cruising terrain

The whole area is ideal for confident intermediates who want to clock up the kilometres. The less confident are not helped by the silly classification of many easy runs as red.

The Moncrons sector at the east of the area is served only by drags but offers some wonderful, uncrowded cruising, some of it above the treeline. In the central part of the slopes there are some good long descents – red 11 is about 1000m vertical.

↑ From the slopes there are fine views over the village to the peaks on the French border

VIA LATTEA

SCHOOLS

Sauze Sportinia
t 0122 850218

Sauze d'Oulx
t 0122 858084

Sauze Project
t 0122 850654

Classes
(Sauze Sportinia prices)
6 3hr days: €180

Private lessons
€36 for 1hr

At the higher levels, where the slopes are above the treeline, the terrain often allows a choice of route. Lower down are pretty runs through the woods, where the main complication can be route-finding.

The long runs down to Jouvenceaux are splendid, flattering intermediate terrain, as are those below Sportinia.

The slopes above Sansicario are also excellent, including the amiable Olympic Women's Downhill and the particularly fine red run, away from the lifts, down to Pariol, the mid-station on the Cesana-Sansicario gondola. These runs are affected by the afternoon sun, though.

FOR BEGINNERS ★★★★★
Not a good choice

You might think a resort with cheap accommodation and gentle terrain would cater well for beginners, but you would be wrong. The main nursery area up at Sportinia has only a short moving carpet, and is reached by a chairlift. There is a day pass covering these plus two other lifts, but there is no suitable longer slope to progress to. There is a slope at village level with a free moving carpet, but the slope is too steep for complete beginners. The mornings-only classes (normal in Italy, of course) don't suit everyone. Once off the nursery slopes, the main problem is that so many easy runs are classified red.

FOR BOARDERS ★★★★★
Too many drags

A recent reporter found little to interest adventurous boarders and 'far too many drags' – which is a serious drawback for novice riders too. But competent intermediates will enjoy cruising on the well-groomed pistes. Don't count on finding a terrain park.

FOR CROSS-COUNTRY ★★★★★
You're on your own

There are no prepared loops in Sauze.

MOUNTAIN RESTAURANTS ★★★★★
Some pleasant possibilities

There are about 15 restaurants locally. They are generally pleasant, but can get very busy; few are remarkable. Stupidly, only some are marked on the piste map. There are several places at Sportinia; the Rocce Nere is repeatedly praised ('excellent food and service' confirms a regular reporter again this year). The 'cosy' Ciao Pais above Clotes does a 'tasty porcini mushroom pasta'. And the hotel Capricorno below it is the place for a serious table-service lunch; it is not cheap, and midweek in low season it can be deserted. Clot Bourget is recommended for 'fast service, best pizzas and good value'. The rustic Bar Clotes is 'a great end-of-day-bar'. The Bar Basset offers 'friendly service' and 'excellent views on a sunny day'. The Fontaine at Jouvenceaux is good for 'a quiet drink and snack' and the Bar Mavie at Sansicario is recommended for 'excellent food, views and sunbathing'.

SCHOOLS AND GUIDES ★★★★★
More reports, please

A 2011 visitor 'highly recommends' a private lesson with Roger Goodfellow of the Sauze d'Oulx school, who has been in Sauze for 30 years – 'we were of slightly different abilities but the lesson improved us all markedly'.

CHILDCARE

Ski school
6 half days €180 (Sportinia prices)

ACTIVITIES

Indoor Sauna, solarium, massage

Outdoor Ice rink, snowshoeing, walking, horse riding

UK PACKAGES

Crystal, Independent Ski Links, Inghams, Interactive Resorts, Mountain Wave, Neilson, Ski Line, Skitracer, Solo's, Thomson
Sansicario Crystal, Thomson

GETTING THERE

Air Turin 90km/ 55 miles (1hr30)

Rail Oulx (5km/ 3 miles); frequent buses

Phone numbers
From abroad use the prefix +39 (and do **not** omit the initial '0' of the phone number)

TOURIST OFFICE

Sauze d'Oulx, Cesana Torinese (Sansicario)
www.turismotorino.org
www.vialattea.it
www.comune.sauzedoulx.to.it

FOR FAMILIES ★★★★★

Tour operator alternatives

You might want to look at the nursery facilities offered by major UK tour operators in the chalets and chalet-hotels that they run here. All the schools take children from four years, and spoken English should be OK. The moving carpet on the village nursery slope is a great aid to sledging.

STAYING THERE

All the major mainstream operators offer hotel packages here.

Hotels Simple 2-star and 3-star hotels form the core, with a couple of 4-stars and some more basic places.

******Relais des Alpes** (0122 858585) 'Large rooms, food excellent with friendly restaurant staff.'

******Torre** (0122 859812) Cylindrical landmark 200m below the centre. Pool, spa, hot tub, sauna, steam.

*****Hermitage** (0122 850385) Neat chalet-style hotel beside the piste.

*****Stella Alpina** (0122 858731) Between main lifts. Well run by Anglo-Italian family: 'friendly'; 'quiet at night'; 'good Italian food'.

*****Terrazza** (0122 850173) In a quiet part of town, near the Clotes chair.

****Albergo Martin** (0122 858246) In Jouvenceaux. Basic, comfortable, with shuttle to the resort. 'Excellent value, helpful staff, good breakfast.'

****Biancaneve** (0122 850160) Pleasant, with smallish rooms. Near the centre.

****Villa Cary** (0122 850191) Continues to be praised by an annual visitor: 'ideal for people on a budget'.

Chalets Perhaps surprisingly, of the big tour operators only Neilson has a catered chalet here.

Apartments Plenty are available, some through UK operators.

At altitude The 4-star Capricorno (0122 850273), up at Clotes, is the most attractive and expensive hotel in Sauze – a charming little chalet beside the piste, with only 10 bedrooms. Not quite in the same league are the places up at Sportinia – though reporters have enjoyed them.

EATING OUT ★★★★★

Caters for all tastes and pockets

Sauze has over 30 restaurants. Typical Italian banquets of five or six courses can be had in places such as the Cantun. In the old town there are several cutely rustic places. Del Falco offers fine wines and fine food; Paddy McGinty's does steaks. Sugo's is a great place for pasta and has 'a good atmosphere', and the Pizza House 'serves excellent pizza, good value'.

APRES-SKI ★★★★★

Suzy does it with more dignity

If you're used to Austrian resorts you may be disappointed by the lack of open-air bars at the foot of the slopes, but in other respects Sauze's bars now impress most reporters, young and old. Choice is wide, with multiple happy hours, free antipasti in some places. The popular Assietta has lots of entertainments later on.

The Scotch bar in the hotel Stella Alpina is popular for English beer with a 'friendly welcome'. The Village Cafè, in a basement at the foot of the slopes, is 'big, friendly, fun' with a 'unique atmosphere'. And Bar Mira (formerly Miravallino) is a smart, lively bar offering live sport – 'happy hour is fantastic'. Max's ('happy hour lasts for four hours!') and Scatto Matto are both popular for 'excellent food, service and ski videos'. Try the Derby (below the hotel) for a bar with log fire and sofas, but also video screens. Il Lampione in the old town has a 'chilled out atmosphere and excellent beer'. Osteria dei Vagabondi is a live music venue (it starts late and prices are a bit higher here).

Other reader recommendations: the intimate, atmospheric bar Moncrons, the Club (formerly Schuss Bar) and the Cotton Club, a wood-clad late-night bar, good for jazz. Banditos is the one identifiable nightclub, but it wasn't open when a regular Sauze reporter visited in 2012.

OFF THE SLOPES ★★★★★

Go elsewhere

Shopping is limited, there are no gondolas or cable cars for pedestrians and there are few off-slope activities. Turin and Briançon are worth visiting.

LINKED RESORT – 1700m

SANSICARIO

Sansicario is ideally placed for exploration of the whole Milky Way. It is a modern, purpose-built, self-contained but rather soulless little resort, mainly consisting of apartments grouped around the small shopping precinct. The 46-room Rio Envers (0122 811937) is a comfortable, expensive 4-star hotel.

APT VAL DI FASSA / STEFANO ZARDINI

Sella Ronda

Endless intermediate slopes amid spectacular scenery, and a choice of attractive valley villages with a distinctive local culture

TOP 10 RATINGS

Extent	*****
Fast lifts	****
Queues	***
Snow	****
Expert	**
Intermediate	*****
Beginner	****
Charm	***
Convenience	***
Scenery	*****

RPI 95

lift pass	£200
ski hire	£90
lessons	£85
food & drink	£95
total	**£470**

NEWS

2012/13: In Arabba, a new chair, Carpazzo, is planned for the Porta Vescovo area, and more snowmaking is to be installed. In Corvara, the Boè cable car is to be upgraded. The Gran Risa piste is to be enlarged.

2011/12: The Bamby quad between San Cassiano and La Villa was upgraded to a six-pack. A new quad replaced one of the double chairs from Passo Campolongo to Monte Cherz, and a new snowpark opened in the Passo Campolongo area. The Costes da l'Ega lift at Corvara has been replaced by a quad.

TOURIST OFFICE

www.dolomitisuperski.com
www.sella-ronda.info

- + Vast network of connected slopes – suits intermediates particularly well
- + Stunning, unique Dolomite scenery
- + Lots of mountain huts with good food as well as fab views
- + Relatively low prices
- + Extensive snowmaking – one of Europe's best systems – but ...

- − They need it: natural snowfall is erratic in this southerly region
- − Few tough pistes, and off-piste is very limited – in general, banned
- − Mostly short runs with limited vertical (with notable exceptions)
- − Crowds on the Sella Ronda circuit
- − Still some old draglifts

The Sella Ronda is an amazing circular network of lifts and pistes taking you around the Gruppo del Sella – a mighty limestone massif with villages scattered around it. The spectacular Dolomite scenery is like something Disney might have conjured up for a movie or a theme park. But the geology that provides the visual drama also dictates the nature of the slopes. Sheer limestone cliffs rise out of gentle pasture land. The skiing is relaxing, not exciting.

The scale of it is some compensation; the distances you can cover on skis are huge – in overall dimensions, the network exceeds even the famed Three Valleys in France. In addition to the main Sella Ronda circuit, major lift systems lead off it at three main points along the way: Selva (covered in the chapter after this), Corvara and Arabba (both covered in this chapter). Another possible base is Canazei, at the south-west corner of the circuit, in the Val di Fassa; this gets its own chapter.

This is one of the few destinations where we pray for sun; snow would interfere with our scenery-gazing without bringing any real benefit – off-piste is off the agenda, and the snowmaking normally delivers reliably good piste conditions.

WENDY-JANE KING

Marmolada is a great side-trip, off the Sella Ronda circuit, from Arabba; the glacial red run from the top is superb carving territory →

CHOOSING A BASE

For good skiers, one of the best bases is Selva – covered in the next chapter along with Santa Cristina and Ortisei, slightly further down the Val Gardena. Another option for good skiers is Arabba.

Corvara is arguably the best all-round bet – well placed for access to Selva, Arabba, the Sella Ronda circuit, the Alta Badia area and excursions to Cortina (and the famous 'hidden valley' run – see feature panel). Colfosco is just next door. San Cassiano and La Villa are slightly off the Sella Ronda circuit.

Canazei and Campitello have their own modest ski areas, and reasonable access to Selva and Arabba (read the Val di Fassa chapter).

Your choice might be influenced by travel plans. There are countless possible arrival airports, and various transfer routes; some can take four or five hours, including interminable winding mountain roads, so it is well worth getting to grips with this angle.

The Dolomiti Superski pass covers not only the Sella Ronda resorts but dozens of others spread around this amazing region. The lift system logs your lift rides – so you can go online to check your distance and vertical.

The vast network of slopes requires a vast selection of piste maps – 12 Superski ones in all, plus locally produced ones for some resorts. Pick up local maps as you progress.

Arabba

- ⊞ Some of the best steep pistes in the area – shady too
- ⊞ Quick access to Marmolada glacier
- ⊟ Not a good base for novices, with more blacks than blues locally
- ⊟ Off-slope activities are limited

Arabba is a small, quiet but fast-growing village appealing particularly to people looking for more challenging terrain than this region normally offers – but also immediate access to the Sella Ronda and Alta Badia sectors.

Village charm The village is small and traditional in style. There are some shops, bars and restaurants, but this is not a place for lively nightlife.

Convenience It's a small place, but staying in the older part involves an uphill walk to reach the ski area, which provokes a few complaints from reporters. A newer area of hotels and chalets has developed higher up, better placed for the lifts and slopes.

Scenery Arabba is beautifully positioned between the stunning Gruppo del Sella and the glacial Marmolada massif, with great views at altitude.

THE MOUNTAIN

Arabba's local slopes are some of the highest in the region, and mainly above the trees.

Slopes The two-stage double-cable gondola and the cable car beside it rise from the top of the village almost 900m vertical to the high point at Porta Vescovo (2475m). From here a choice of runs return to the village or you can head off around the Sella Ronda circuit. From the mid-station of the gondola, chairs take you to Passo Padon and onwards to the Marmolada glacier. This is an excellent outing, despite the queues described later. The views from the top at 3270m are spectacular, and the 1500m vertical red run to Capanna Bill is splendid, with great snow on the top sections.

From the other side of the village, a fast quad gets you on the way to Burz, Passo di Campolongo and Corvara.

Fast lifts Access to and from the village is by fairly new fast lifts.

Queues The outing to Marmolada can be troublesome on a busy day, involving the bottleneck of the Sass de la Vegla double chair. Despite upgrades, there may be long waits for the Marmolada cable cars.

Terrain park A new park opened in the Passo Campolongo area in 2011/12.

Snow reliability Arabba offers some of the most snow-sure slopes in the Sella Ronda region. Good snow is far from assured, but snowmaking is extensive and the main runs are north-facing.

Experts Arabba has steep slopes to match those of Selva/Val Gardena. The north-facing blacks and reds from Porta Vescovo offer genuine challenges and there is some tempting off-piste terrain too – but look at the off-piste feature panel in the margin a few pages further on.

Intermediates The local slopes suit adventurous intermediates best. Most are quite challenging and those on the main circuit suffer from crowds. But the easy Alta Badia area is nearby.

KEY FACTS

Resort	1600m 5,250ft
Slopes	1600-2380m 5,250-7,810ft
Lifts	26
Pistes	62km

UK PACKAGES

Alpine Answers, Collett's, Inghams, Interactive Resorts, Momentum, Neilson, Ski Expectations, Ski Solutions, Ski Total, Ski Yogi, Skitracer, STC

Phone numbers
From abroad use the prefix +39 (and do **not** omit the initial '0' of the phone number)

TOURIST OFFICE

www.arabba.it

KEY FACTS

Sella Ronda
Linked network of Val Gardena, Alta Badia, Arabba, and of Canazei and Campitello in Val di Fassa

Slopes	1005-3250m
	3,300-10,660ft
Lifts	179
Pistes	433km
	269 miles
Blue	38%
Red	53%
Black	9%
Snowmaking	90%

LIFT PASSES

Dolomiti Superski

Prices in €

Age	1-day	6-day
under 16	34	169
16 to 64	48	241
65 plus	43	217

Free under 8

Beginner no deals

Notes
Includes all Sella Ronda resorts

Beginners It is not a good choice for beginners. There is a small nursery slope near the Burz chair, but access to longer easy runs for building confidence is tricky.

Snowboarding The slopes of Porta Vescovo offer some decent challenges. Most of the lifts are fast chairs or gondolas.

Cross-country There are no trails here – the terrain doesn't really suit them.

Mountain restaurants There's lots of choice, from rustic huts to larger places. Most are lively and many have great views – in this respect, Luigi Gorza at the top of the Porta Vescovo lifts takes some beating, but the food 'isn't great'. The smart new self-service Cesa da Fuoch at the mid-station has 'excellent and reasonable fresh-cooked pasta'; the Rifugio Plan Boè, between Arabba and Campolongo, has 'good food and service'. Below Marmolada, a 2011 visitor had a 'good value' meal at Passo Fedaia, and Capanna Bill lower down is a cosy spot. Rifugio Fodom just below Passo Pordoi is 'really busy but great fun' with 'good food but dire Europop'.

Schools The local Arabba school offers group and private classes. We have no recent reports.

Families The ski school takes children from three years.

STAYING THERE

New accommodation has been built at the top end of town, closer to the lifts.

Chalets Ski Total has the dinky six-bed chalet Heidi and three slightly larger places. Last season Inghams introduced three chalets sleeping 10 to 18 people.

Hotels There are about a dozen hotels. The favourite of one regular visitor is the 4-star Grifone (0436 780034) out at Passo Campolongo – 'remote, but food and service superb; excellent bar and health club/pool'. In the village, the 3-star Portavescovo (0436 79139) and the 4-star Sporthotel (0436 79321 are possibilities.

Apartments Self-catering accommodation is available.

Eating out Restaurant choice is limited. The central hotels all have busy restaurants. Reporters consistently praise Miky's Grill in the hotel Mesdì

THE SELLA RONDA CIRCUIT

You can ski around the huge Sella massif in either direction by following very clear coloured signs; it's easily managed in a day by even an early intermediate. The clockwise route is slightly quicker and offers more interesting slopes, but is much busier – so many reporters prefer the anticlockwise route, despite a tedious series of five lifts from Corvara. Some resort piste maps include a Sella Ronda map; most take something close to a bird's eye topographical view. (Bizarrely, at least one puts south at the top.) A very detailed topo map is available from the tourist offices (and some lift stations).

The runs total around 23km and the lifts around 14km. There is one bit where no skiing is possible: you ride the Borest chair at Corvara in both directions. The lifts take a total of about two hours (plus any queuing). We've done the circuit in just three and a half hours excluding diversions and hut stops; five or six hours is a realistic time when things are crowded.

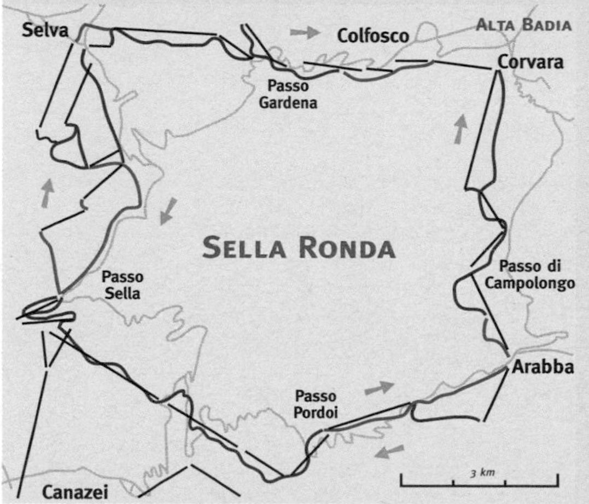

If you set out early and make good time, you can divert from the circuit, notably at Selva and Arabba. Less confident intermediates could explore the Alta Badia area, east of Corvara.

Not everyone likes it. You may find that 'it's a bit of a slog', 'too busy and crowded', 'over-hyped, and over-regimented' and 'not a relaxing business when it's busy'. And boarders should be aware that there are quite a few flat bits.

If you pick your time – low season or a Saturday, in good weather – and start early, we reckon it's worth doing.

ALDIAVOLO
ZUM TEUFEL

The scenery of the Sella Ronda area is stunning, as these pictures show.

All of these shots were taken in March 2012 by Wendy King, for some years a key member of our editorial team and editor of our associated website. Wendy died of cancer in April at the age of 44; there is more about her at the front of the book.

When she went to the Sella Ronda, Wendy didn't know that it would be her last skiing trip, although she might have feared it would be. When we came to prepare this chapter in May, we found that she had filed an unusually rich set of photos from the trip – so we have devoted a bit of extra space to a selection of them. Wendy would have been fiercely proud to see these pictures published, and rightly so.

('good value'; 'very good quality steaks and meat; mixed grill a speciality'). And reporters rate again Al Table as 'friendly and good value', serving everything from 'simple pasta and great pizzas to well-cooked steak'. The Alpenrose hotel will send its horse-drawn sleigh to pick you up if you book a table in its Stube Ladina. For something a bit different, you can go up to Rifugio Plan Boè by snowmobile for dinner and dancing.

Après-ski The après-ski is limited. There are three bars and, according to recent reports, the central Bar Peter seems to be the focus – 'very lively but quieter later on', says a 2011 visitor. Reporters also mention the Stube in the Portavescovo hotel ('the closest thing in Arabba to a focal village bar, although it clears out at 8pm') and the Treina. Cosy hotel bars are other options in the village. The atmospheric Rifugio Plan Boè up the mountain is good for a last drink on the piste.

Off the slopes Off-slope diversions are few. There are some shops and cafes, and there's an ice rink. Snowmobiling and snowshoeing are available.

Corvara

- ⊞ One of the best locations, where Alta Badia meets the Sella Ronda
- ⊞ Pleasant, lively village
- ⊞ Local slopes suit novices, but ...
- ⊟ Few challenges locally
- ⊟ Alta Badia still has plenty of drags and slow chairlifts

Corvara rivals Selva from most points of view, the main exception being that of experts, who have to travel in search of challenges; for families and novices it takes some beating – though nearby Colfosco merits consideration too.

KEY FACTS

Resort	1570m 5,150ft
Slopes	1330-2530m 4,360-8,300ft
Lifts	52
Pistes	130km
Snow-guns	392 guns

UK PACKAGES

Collett's, Inghams, Momentum, Ski Yogi

Phone numbers
From abroad use the prefix +39 (and do **not** omit the initial '0' of the phone number)

TOURIST OFFICE

www.altabadia.org

Village charm The place is lively and family-friendly, with a pleasant centre that is bypassed by through traffic.

Convenience The main shops and some hotels cluster around a small piazza at the top end of the village, and if you are based here nothing is more than a stroll away; but the rest of Corvara sprawls along the valley floor, so you may have some walking to do.

Scenery The setting is superb: there are impressive rock faces and spires all around the village, notably the distinctive Sassongher.

THE MOUNTAIN

Corvara is well positioned, with village lifts heading off to reasonably equidistant Selva, Arabba and San Cassiano. The local slopes are gentle and confidence-boosting.

Slopes Lifts go off in three directions. A long gondola heads south towards Boè and Arabba for the clockwise Sella Ronda circuit. Two successive fast quads head west towards Colfosco and the anticlockwise route around the circuit. The area around both lifts can get congested at peak times. A slow chair or a gondola takes you into the slopes shared with San Cassiano and La Villa.

Fast lifts New fast lifts are gradually improving the area.

Queues We regularly have reports about long waits for the Borest chair between Corvara and Colfosco (which forms an inescapable part of the Sella Ronda circuit in both directions), but otherwise there are few problems.

Terrain park There is a terrain park above San Cassiano, easily reached from Corvara.

Snow reliability As in the rest of the Sella Ronda area, natural snowfall is erratic, but snowmaking and grooming are excellent.

Experts Very few of Corvara's slopes offer any real challenges. The short black above Boè is really no more than a red in gradient. The much longer wooded runs down to La Villa include a just-about-genuine black. Otherwise, you're off to Selva or Arabba. Look at the feature panel in the margin over the page for off-piste runs.

Intermediates There's a vast network of slopes ideal for cruising and confidence-boosting. On one side is the network of rolling hills shared with San Cassiano; on the other, above Colfosco, the more dramatically set Val Stella Alpina, off the Sella Ronda circuit, plus the long, gentle runs from Passo Gardena – essentially one long nursery slope. The red back to the village underneath the Boè cable car that goes off towards Arabba is usually uncrowded and retains good snow. The adventurous can head for the steeper, wooded pistes going down to La Villa.

GOURMET SKIING

The Alta Badia – the area around La Villa, including Badia, San Cassiano, Corvara and Colfosco – has gradually built up a culture of top-flight cooking, and is now starting to capitalize on its success in doing so. For many years, its top hotels have run excellent gourmet restaurants, but now the tourist office has developed an excellent scheme to encourage serious cooking in mountain restaurants, too. This involves pairing up mountain restaurant chefs with 'starred' chefs from resort restaurants in the area, plus their chums from around Europe.

There are three local 'starred' restaurants. The chef from the Rosa Alpina hotel in San Cassiano is teamed up with Ütia Bioch up at 2080m. The chef from the Ciasa Salares hotel partners Ütia Bamby. The guy from the restaurant at La Perla in Corvara works with Ütia I Tablà. Chefs from Milan, Slovenia, Lugano, St Moritz, Munich etc are paired with eight other mountain restaurants.

The deal is that each restaurant offers a single dish created by its partner chef, costing little or nothing more than other dishes on the menu but offering something special – certainly something you wouldn't expect to find in a rustic mountain restaurant. When we visited in 2011, we ate at I Tablà, where we had superb knuckle of pork in honey with thyme-scented polenta and chanterelles.

TOURIST BOARD ALTA BADIA

A wine from Südtirol is suggested for each dish. The tourist office produces a handsome pocket-sized brochure listing the restaurants and the special dishes. It sponsors other foodie schemes too – for example, a series of mountain restaurants between La Villa and Santa Croce, above Badia, form a 'gourmet skitour', detailed in another little brochure.

These schemes encourage variety and quality in mountain nosh; we approve.

Beginners There's a decent nursery area and lots of easy runs to progress to on both sides of the village, making this one of the best bases in the Sella Ronda area for beginners.

Snowboarding Novices can make rapid progress on gentle slopes. A few awkward draglifts remain, but most can be avoided.

Cross-country One of the better bases in the area. The Alta Badia area offers 38km of trails, including a 10km valley loop on the way to Colfosco.

Mountain restaurants Lots of choice in the area. Look at our gourmet feature panel, above, and at the San Cassiano section, where we cover places between the two resorts.

Schools There's a local branch of the Alta Badia school – reports welcome.

Families A 2012 visitor found the school instructors 'very good' with the children in his party. The ski school's Kinderland takes children from the age of three.

STAYING THERE

Stay near the main square at the top end of the village to be near the lifts and home pistes.

Hotels There are some deeply comfortable 4-star hotels here. La Perla (0471 831000) is one of our all-time favourites, offering superb food and service in a relaxed atmosphere and perfect position at the top of the village. The similarly well-placed Col Alto (0471 831100) continues to receive praise: 'superb spa', 'huge bedrooms in the new annex', 'welcoming, friendly staff' and 'well situated' are 2012 comments. The Posta Zirm (0471 836175) also has a large spa; but we lack recent reports.

Eating out A reasonable choice. Most of the hotels have à la carte restaurants – the Stüa de Michil in La Perla hotel has a Michelin star, and greatly impressed us – superb food and a warm atmosphere. See also San Cassiano.

Après-ski The fashionable place to go at close of play these days seems to be L'Murin, a rustic outbuilding of La Perla. We've no recent reports on the famous tea-dance scene in the basement of the Posta Zirm.

Off the slopes There's a covered ice rink, indoor tennis courts, an outdoor climbing wall and snowshoeing.

KEY FACTS	
Resort	1540m 5,050ft
Slopes	1330-2530m 4,360-8,300ft
Lifts	52
Pistes	130km
Snow-guns	392 guns

UK PACKAGES

Alpine Answers, Carrier, Momentum, Mountainsun, Powder Byrne, Scott Dunn, Ski Bespoke

Phone numbers
From abroad use the prefix +39 (and do **not** omit the initial '0' of the phone number)

TOURIST OFFICE

www.altabadia.org

San Cassiano

- ⊞ Local Alta Badia slopes are friendly, extensive and scenic
- ⊞ Small, quiet village with some notably good hotels
- ⊟ Lifts and pistes are outside village
- ⊟ Slightly off the Sella Ronda circuit
- ⊟ Alta Badia still has plenty of drags and slow chairlifts

If you prefer San Cassiano to Corvara it's likely to be because you particularly like one of its excellent hotels – or because you want a quiet time. In every other respect, Corvara has the edge.

San Cassiano is a pleasant little village with some good hotels, sharing slopes with Corvara and La Villa.

Village charm It's a quiet, civilized resort, without much animation. It is bypassed by the road to Cortina.

Convenience Most hotels are close to the village centre – around a five-minute walk from the gondola and slopes (but most of the better hotels have their own shuttle-buses).

Scenery The village is set in an attractive, tree-filled valley. The views from the slopes are superb.

THE MOUNTAIN

The local slopes adjoin the main Sella Ronda circuit.

Slopes A gondola starting just outside the village rises to Piz Sorega. From the top, fast chairs form the links with Corvara and La Villa, or you can head for Pralongia and the long runs home. Most of the area has very gentle slopes, ideal for easy cruising.

Fast lifts Essentially well-connected, but some old chairs and drags remain.

Queues Few problems, thanks to continual lift upgrades.

Terrain park You'll find boardercross, jumps, rails and humps.

Snow reliability The Dolomites have an erratic snowfall record, but snowmaking and grooming are excellent.

Experts Experts would be wise to stay elsewhere. There are steeper runs at La Villa, but it's a bit of a trek to Selva or Arabba. Read the feature panel in the margin on the facing page.

Intermediates Pretty much ideal if you love easy cruising on flattering, well-groomed runs. The red option back to the valley is a serious red though. There's relatively quick access to the famous 'hidden valley' run (described in our feature panel).

Beginners There are nursery slopes a short bus ride away at Armentarola, and at the top of the gondola – not ideal. But there are plenty of long, easy slopes to progress to.

Snowboarding Endless carving on quiet pistes and there's a terrain park.

Cross-country There are 25km of trails.

Mountain restaurants Look at our gourmet feature panel. There are countless options on the slopes

THE 'HIDDEN VALLEY'

If you like runs in spectacular scenery well away from all signs of civilization, don't miss the easy red run from Lagazuoi, reached by cable car from Passo Falzarego. The pass is easily accessible from Armentarola, close to San Cassiano – shared taxis run a shuttle service (5 euros each) to the pass from here. There's also a bus from San Cassiano (but it is reported to be crowded and slow).

The run is one of the most beautiful we've come across, and delights most reporters. Views from the top of the cable car are splendid, and the run passes beneath sheer, pink-tinged Dolomite peaks and frozen waterfalls. Because the cable car has low capacity, the run is never crowded. Make time to stop at the atmospheric Rifugio Scotoni near the end ('thoroughly enjoyable').

At the bottom, it's a long skate to a horse-drawn sled with ropes attached, which tows you back to Armentarola (for a couple of euros). This is more of a challenge than the run, and the risk of a pile-up if someone falls has concerned some reporters. We're told there is a bus alternative. At Armentarola there is a draglift up to a run back to San Cassiano.

ALAN LIPTROT

OFF-PISTE

Off-piste skiing is generally prohibited in the Sella Ronda area – as in many Italian areas. This doesn't stop people doing it where the temptation arises. And it doesn't rule out some spectacular routes, away from the pistes, where it's accepted you can safely go with guidance.

There are some well-known routes on the Sella massif, reached via the cable car from Passo Pordoi. There are fairly direct descents back to the pass (the very sunny Forcella) or down the Val Lasties towards Canazei. But the classic run is the Val Mesdì, a long, shady couloir down to Colfosco, reached by hiking across the massif. Marmolada, the highest peak of the Dolomites, is the other obvious launching point. It offers a range of big descents on and off the glacier.

There is a mountain guides office in the centre of Corvara (www.altabadiaguides.com).

UK PACKAGES

Colfosco Inghams
Badia Collett's, Crystal, Thomson

TOURIST OFFICE

Colfosco, La Villa, Badia
www.altabadia.org

between San Cassiano and Corvara. Most are woody and cosy in traditional style, but Las Vegas is a wild exception – cool, minimalist, with huge windows to make the most of the views. A 2012 lunch visitor says: 'Loved it! Food excellent, especially the pasta.' We haven't had lunch here, but we have enjoyed a superb dinner. I Tablà is quite a plain little place but does excellent food – and a reader notes that it offers 'outstanding value'. Piz Arlara, another participant of the Taste for Skiing Initiative (see panel), is recommended by a 2012 visitor: 'excellent crispy suckling piglet'. Punta Trieste is recommended for 'excellent pasta' but is 'so, so busy'. Other reader tips include Club Moritzino above La Villa ('fine wines, delicious cheeses, charming host'), Col Alt ('excellent venison') and Bioch ('superb meal'). Pralongià is 'better than most'.

Schools A snowboarder in a reporter's party 'had private lessons and the instructor was excellent' and a beginner 'progressed very quickly' – more reports welcome.

Families The school offers the usual arrangements for children and there are several kids' parks.

STAYING THERE

Hotels The Rosa Alpina (0471 849500) is a splendid place – genuine comfort, great food, good spa. Its three restaurants include the St Hubertus, which has two Michelin stars ('equal to some of the best in London, but also at least as expensive!' says a 2012 visitor). The Fanes (0471 849470) is a smart chalet-style place with indoor-outdoor pool and a spa. You can stay up the mountain at the modern, trendy Las Vegas restaurant (0471 840138).

Eating out As well as the Rosa Alpina's St Hubertus, two restaurants in the area have one Michelin star; one, the Siriola in the hotel Ciasa Salares, is in Armentarola, just up the road; for the other see Corvara. Las Vegas will take you up the mountain in a snowcat for dinner (you can ride back down or ski in front of the cat's headlights).

Après-ski It starts up the mountain with loud music at Las Vegas. A reporter confirms that you can still stay late at La Utia on the home run and ski down after dark. Nightlife is very limited.

Off the slopes There are some lovely walks amid the stunning scenery.

Other resorts

LINKED RESORT – 1645m

COLFOSCO

Colfosco is a smaller, quieter satellite of Corvara, 2km away. It has a fairly compact centre with a group of large hotels spread along the road from Corvara towards Passo Gardena and Selva, enjoying splendid views of the Gruppa del Sella. On the snow it's connected to Corvara and the clockwise Sella Ronda circuit by the two-way Borest chairlift. In the opposite direction, a gondola goes towards Passo Gardena. There are excellent nursery slopes and the runs back from Passo Gardena are easy, long cruises, making this a great base for novices. Check out our Corvara entry too.

LINKED RESORT – 1435m

LA VILLA

Like San Cassiano, La Villa is a bit detached from the Sella Ronda circuit. It's a much busier place, with the road from Brunico and Bolzano running through it. On the other hand it is much more conveniently arranged, with lifts and pistes on both sides of the village, and nursery slopes dotted around. A 2011 visitor complains of inadequate rental shops, and poor spoken English both there and in the ski school. We've had repeated glowing reports on the hotel Antines (0471 844234) – 'one of the best, with an outstanding restaurant'; 'very friendly staff'.

LINKED RESORT – 1325m

BADIA

This small roadside village (formerly known as Pedraces) is out on a limb beyond La Villa, so is difficult to recommend as a base for the region as a whole. But some will find it more interesting now that there is a free bus link with Piccolino (20 minutes), where a gondola goes into the Plan de Corones/Kronplatz ski area. The village has its own one-run ski area with a fast quad and a slow double chair to Santa Croce (2045m) where there is a famous old rifugio with 'fabulous views' (and a tiny church).

VAL GARDENA TOURIST OFFICE

Selva / Val Gardena

Pleasant village amid spectacular Dolomite scenery, well placed for skiing on and off the vast Sella Ronda lift network

RATINGS

The mountains	
Extent	*****
Fast lifts	****
Queues	***
Terrain p'ks	***
Snow	****
Expert	***
Intermediate	*****
Beginner	***
Boarder	***
X-country	*****
Restaurants	*****
Schools	***
Families	**
The resort	
Charm	***
Convenience	***
Scenery	*****
Eating out	***
Après-ski	***
Off-slope	***

RPI 95

lift pass	£200
ski hire	£90
lessons	£85
food & drink	£95
total	**£470**

NEWS

2011/12: A six-pack replaced the Sasso Levante triple chair at Passo Sella.

+ A key resort of the Sella Ronda region, with all the usual plus points: extent, snowmaking, scenery, mountain huts
+ Excellent local slopes, with big verticals by Sella Ronda standards
+ Mix of open and wooded slopes
+ Excellent nursery slopes
+ Attractive but strung-out village in a lovely wooded setting

− Some of the minus points of the Sella Ronda region too, notably: erratic natural snowfall, crowds on the main Sella Ronda circuit

− No easy long runs immediately above Selva; buses or taxis are needed for access to them up at Plan de Gralba

− Busy road through the village

Selva is one of three sizeable resorts near the head of Val Gardena (a name well known to 'Ski Sunday' viewers) and one of the main bases to consider for a visit to the unique Sella Ronda region described in the chapter before this one. Selva remains one of our favourite bases in the area, essentially because of the local slopes, including two race courses through woods to the valley that are among the most satisfying runs in the area – not least because they offer decent verticals. Beginners and timid intermediates, though, are probably better off staying in Corvara or Colfosco, described in the Sella Ronda chapter.

THE RESORT

Selva is a long roadside village at the head of the Val Gardena.

For many years this area was part of Austria, and it retains a Tirolean charm. German is more widely spoken than Italian, and many visitors are German, too. Most places have two names: Selva is also known as Wolkenstein and the Gardena valley as Gröden. We do our bit for Italian unity by using the Italian place names. The local language, Ladin, also survives – giving a third name to some places. Not surprisingly, visitors find all this confusing. The valley is famed for wood carvings, which are on display (and sale) wherever you look.

At the end of this chapter we describe two other bases. Santa Cristina is the next village down-valley, almost merging with Selva; lifts from both villages meet on the steep racing hill of Ciampinoi. Further down-valley is Ortisei, the main town of Val Gardena, beneath the distinct Alpe di Siusi area. Both have lifts to another distinct area, Seceda. Another possible base is the village of Siusi (1005m) with a gondola up to Alpe di Siusi.

VILLAGE CHARM ***
Pity about the traffic

The village has traditional Tirolean-style architecture and an attractive church, but is a sprawling place and suffers from through-traffic (and a lack of parking facilities). Despite the World Cup fame of Val Gardena, Selva is a good-value, civilized, low-key resort – relaxed and family-friendly in many respects, once you get away from the intrusive through-road.

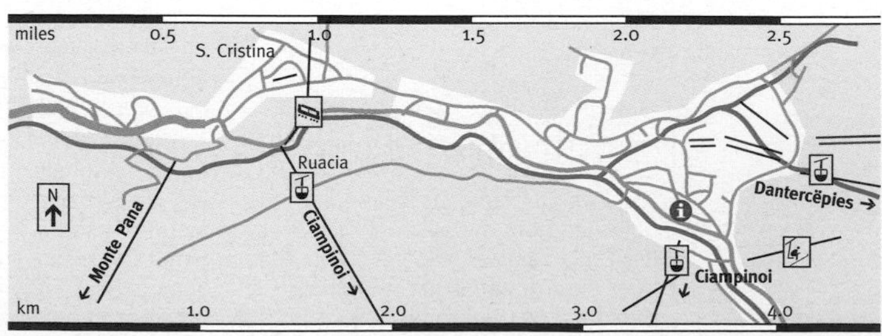

CONVENIENCE ★★★★★
Choose your spot with care
From the village, gondolas rise in two directions. The Ciampinoi gondola goes south from near the centre of the village to start the anticlockwise Sella Ronda route. The Dantercëpies gondola, for the clockwise Sella Ronda route, starts above the village at the top of the nursery slopes (but accessible via a central chairlift and a short run down). The most convenient position to stay is near this chair or one of the gondolas.

There are local buses until early evening – €7 for a weekly card. They generate all sorts of complaints from reporters: lack of buses; not running to time; confusion between the public and the skiers' bus. There's a night bus between Selva and Ortisei. All the 4-star hotels run their own free shuttle-buses.

SCENERY ★★★★★
Pretty in pink
The village enjoys a lovely setting under the impressive pink-tinged walls of Sassolungo immediately above Ciampinio and the Gruppo del Sella – a fortress-like massif 6km across that lies at the hub of the Sella Ronda circuit (described in the separate chapter before this one).

THE MOUNTAINS

Selva's own slopes cover both sides of the valley. The lower slopes are wooded, with open slopes higher up.

The local piste map exists in several variations, which reporters find confusing. The maps show neither names nor numbers for the runs. Piste signing provokes some criticism.

The Dolomiti Superski pass covers not only Selva and the Sella Ronda resorts but dozens of others. It's an easy road trip to Cortina.

EXTENT OF THE SLOPES ★★★★★
High-mileage excursions
The **Dantercëpies** gondola goes off eastwards to start the clockwise Sella Ronda circuit and serves lovely red runs back to Selva. On the other side of the valley, the **Ciampinoi** gondola goes south for the anticlockwise circuit via **Plan de Gralba** and accesses several shady pistes, leading back down to Selva and Santa Cristina, including the famous World Cup Downhill run.

In S Cristina, another gondola accesses Ciampinoi, and an underground train links the lift base to a gondola on the outskirts for the sunny **Seceda** area. In this sector, runs descend to Santa Cristina or to Ortisei

WENDY-JANE KING

Although there are plenty of quiet backwaters, the village spreads along the road up to Passo Sella and Canazei ↓

– a red run of about 7km. And from Ortisei a gondola on the other side of the valley takes you to and from **Alpe di Siusi** – a gentle elevated area of quiet, easy runs, cross-country tracks and walks. You can proceed from here to the backwater **Monte Pana** (which is connected to Ciampinoi) by bus, but it's a slow affair.

FAST LIFTS ★★★★☆
Getting better

The main access lifts are gondolas, and there are lots of fast chairs above them, so progress can be quick. But the area only just scrapes into our 4-star category; there are still a few slow chairs and drags – an irritant on Alpe di Siusi, for example.

QUEUES ★★★☆☆
Still some problems

New lifts have greatly improved the area as a whole. The gondolas out of the village are naturally busy at the morning peak, and the drags up to the Dantercëpies gondola may hold you up, too. Other problems may arise on lifts that are part of the Sella Ronda circuit. The gondola out of Ortisei that takes you half-way to Seceda ensures that the cable car above it is over-busy in the mornings.

TERRAIN PARKS ★★★☆☆
Facilities spread around

There are parks at Passo Sella, Piz Sella ('excellent', says a 2010 reporter) and at Alpe di Siusi.

SNOW RELIABILITY ★★★★★
Excellent when it's cold
The slopes are not high – there are few above 2200m and most are between 1500m and 2000m. Natural snowfalls are erratic, but the snowmaking is exceptionally good. During severe droughts we have enjoyed excellent pistes here, and our reporters are regularly impressed – 'wonderful', 'stunning', 'unbelievable' are typical comments. Problems arise only if it is too warm to make snow.

FOR EXPERTS ★★★★★
A few good runs
There are few challenges, essentially no moguls (the blacks all get groomed) and a low likelihood of powder. There are few major off-piste routes because of the nature of the terrain and off-piste is prohibited in places; see the off-piste panel in the Sella Ronda chapter.

The Val Gardena World Cup piste, the Saslong, is one of several steepish runs between Ciampinoi and both Selva and Santa Cristina. It is kept in racing condition, but it is open to the public much of the time and makes a wonderful fast cruise – it's one of our favourite runs. The long red runs from Dantercëpies are entertaining, too.

FOR INTERMEDIATES ★★★★★
Fast cruising on easy slopes
There is a huge amount of skiing to do, in several areas.

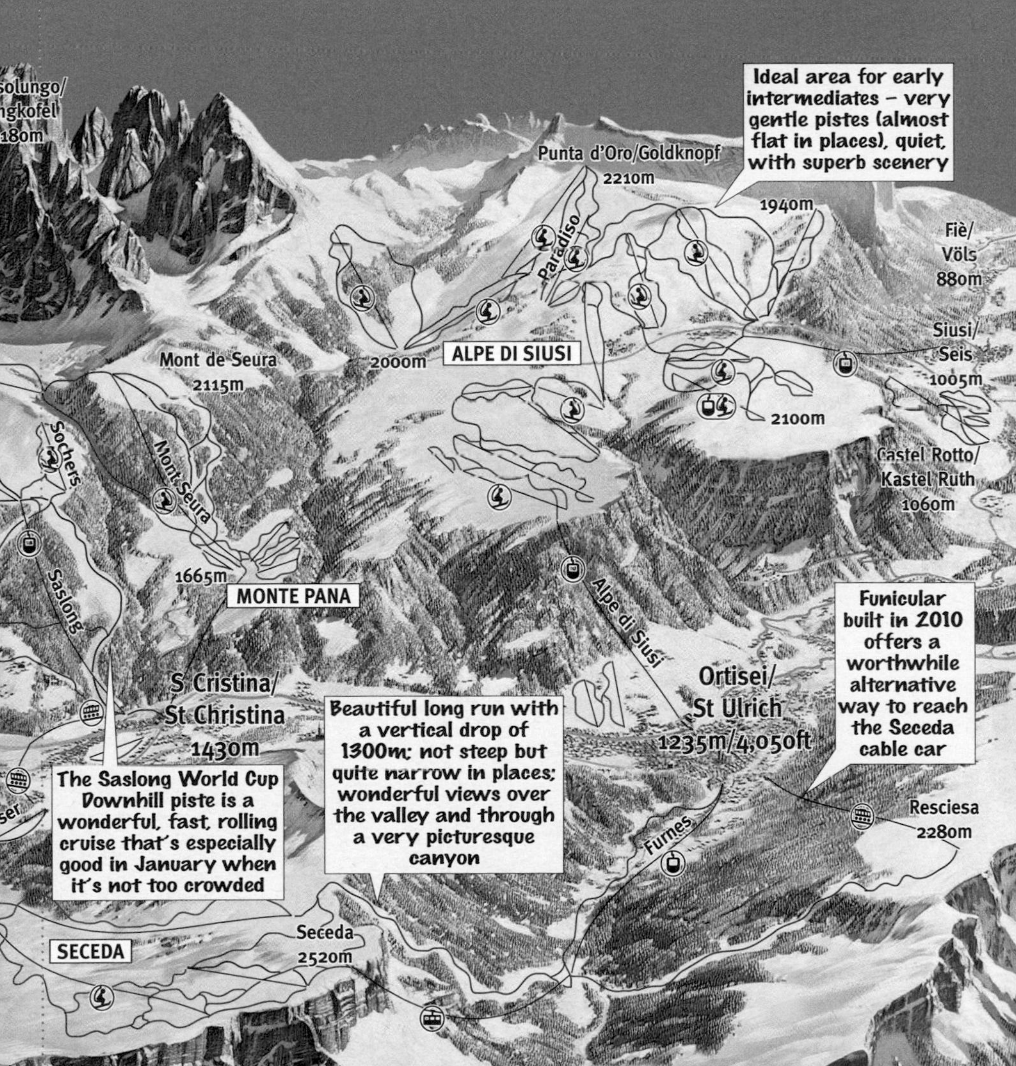

Ideal area for early intermediates – very gentle pistes (almost flat in places), quiet, with superb scenery
Punta d'Oro/Goldknopf 2210m
1940m
Fiè/ Völs 880m
Paradiso
Mont de Seura 2115m
2000m
ALPE DI SIUSI
Siusi/ Seis 1005m
2100m
Sochers
Mont Seura
Castel Rotto/ Kastel Ruth 1060m
1665m
MONTE PANA
Saslong
Alpe di Siusi
Funicular built in 2010 offers a worthwhile alternative way to reach the Seceda cable car
S Cristina/ St Christina 1430m
Ortisei/ St Ulrich 1235m/4,050ft
Beautiful long run with a vertical drop of 1300m; not steep but quite narrow in places; wonderful views over the valley and through a very picturesque canyon
The Saslong World Cup Downhill piste is a wonderful, fast, rolling cruise that's especially good in January when it's not too crowded
Resciesa 2280m
Furnes
Seceda 2520m
SECEDA

KEY FACTS

Resort	1565m 5,130ft
Sella Ronda linked network: Val Gardena, Alta Badia, Arabba, and Canazei and Campitello in Val di Fassa	
Slopes	1005-2520m 3,300-10,660ft
Lifts	179
Pistes	433km 269 miles
Blue	38%
Red	53%
Black	9%
Snowmaking	90%
Val Gardena-Alpe di Siusi only	
Slopes	1005-2520m 3,300-8,270ft
Lifts	79
Pistes	175km 109 miles
Blue	30%
Red	60%
Black	10%
Snowmaking	95%

LIFT PASSES

Dolomiti Superski

Prices in €

Age	1-day	6-day
under 16	34	169
16 to 64	48	241
65 plus	43	217

Free under 8

Beginner Points card

Senior must be 65 before season starts

Notes

Covers 1220km of piste and 450 lifts in the Dolomites, including all Sella Ronda resorts

Alternative pass

Val Gardena-Alpe di Siusi

Competent intermediates will love the red and black descents from Dantercëpies and Ciampinoi to Selva (but more timid intermediates may find them too steep and/or crowded).

The blue runs in the Plan de Gralba area are gentle, great for building confidence; the red run to get there from Ciampinoi is a real obstacle – it's steep and crowded and can be icy – so you might want to go by road.

The quiet red and black runs at Mont de Seura, above Monte Pana, are worth exploring.

The broad Alpe di Siusi above Ortisei is ideal for confidence-building. The red runs that dominate the map are rarely red in practice, and they are crowd-free (and impossibly scenic). Runs are mostly of limited vertical, the main exception being the red from Punta d'Oro – 500m vertical.

The Seceda sector has good red and blue runs at altitude, and splendid runs to the valley – an easy blue/red to Santa Cristina and the beautiful red Cucasattel, passing through a natural gorge to Ortisei.

FOR BEGINNERS ★★★★★
Great slopes, but ...

The village nursery slopes below the Dantercëpies gondola are excellent – spacious, convenient, and kept in good condition. There are lots of gentle, long runs to progress to, but they are at Plan de Gralba and Alpe di Siusi, and reached by road.

FOR BOARDERS ★★★★★
Limited options

Selva attracts few boarders. There's little to challenge experts, and off-piste opportunities are limited, but the nursery slopes are good and there are lots of gentle runs to progress to. The main valley lifts are all gondolas or chairs. There are three terrain parks and a couple of half-pipes.

FOR CROSS-COUNTRY ★★★★★
Beautiful trails

There are 115km of trails, all enjoying wonderful scenery. The 12km trail up the Vallunga valley is particularly attractive, with neck-craning views all around. Almost half the trails have the advantage of being at altitude (so better snow as well as better views), running between Monte Pana and across Alpe di Siusi.

MOUNTAIN RESTAURANTS ★★★★★
A real highlight

There are countless lively, characterful huts, with helpful staff, good food and modest prices. 'Not a bad one all week' is a typical reporter's comment. They are not identified on the resort piste map.

In the Dantercëpies sector, readers have tipped the Panorama – a cosy, rustic suntrap at the foot of the drag near the top – the Pastura and the Ciampac down in the Vallunga.

In the Plan de Gralba area the Rif Emilio Comici set beneath the massive Sassolungo (arrive early if you want the sun) gets repeated recommendations – 'fantastic but always crowded'. Nearby Piz Sella is recommended for pizza. Vallongia offers good food and service and has a cool ice bar. Piz Seteur offers 'great food' at least in its table-service section. Baita Sole is a cute but simple place with fine food, although service was a little stretched when we were

ALAN LIPTROT

Alpenglow on Sassolungo and Sassopiatto, towering over Ciampinoi and Alpe di Siusi, seen from Mont Seuc →

SCHOOLS

Selva Gardena – Ski Academy Peter Runggaldier (Ski Factory)
t 0471 795156

2000
t 0471 773125

Top School Val Gardena
t 0471 794099

Classes (Selva prices)
6 half days €187

Private lessons
From €40 for 1hr

GUIDES

Val Gardena Mountain Guide Association
t 0471 794133

CHILDCARE

Selvi mini club
0471 795156
Ages 0 to 4yr

Casa Bimbo (at S Cristina)
0471 793013
From 0 to 3yr

Ski school
For age 4 to 12:
6 days from €323
(Selva price)

there last season. At Passo Sella, Rif Friedrich August has Highland cattle strolling around outside, and closely related steaks on sale inside.

In the Seceda sector there are countless options. Daniel Hütte is 'very cosy in a storm'. On the run back to S Cristina, a regular visitor recommends Baita Pramulin. Near the top of the long Cucasattel run to Ortisei, the small Curona is a favourite of two repeat visitors ('friendly; best strudel'); lower down, Val d'Anna is another reader favourite for pastries.

Alpe di Siusi is said to have over 40 places to choose from. Our specialist reporter picks out Laurinhütte ('welcoming, excellent food, great views'), Zallinger Hütte ('charming – a great find'), Sanon Hütte ('fantastic views, cheerful service') and Mont Seuc, at the top of the gondola – 'perfect for watching the cliffs turn red over a last drink'.

SCHOOLS AND GUIDES ★★★★★
No worries

1990s racing star Peter Runggaldier has merged his Ski Academy with the resort's main Selva Gardena school, which has been recommended by several readers. A 2012 visitor recommends the ski safari, although unhappy with the large group size and range of ability on some days.

FOR FAMILIES ★★★★★
It's all down to the detail

At first sight, in general, the village does not seem ideal for families. It's a sprawling place requiring use of not entirely efficient buses, with a busy through-road. But make the right arrangements and pick your location with care, and you can have very successful family holidays here. An obvious first step is to look at UK tour operators with their own nursery facilities, of which Esprit is the clear leader. A 2012 visitor praised her son's Selva Gardena instructor arranged through Esprit: 'good English, took his responsibilities with his pupils very seriously'.

STAYING THERE

Chalets There is a fair choice of catered chalets, including some good ones with en suite bathrooms, and some with childcare – specialist Esprit has one large property and three smaller ones.

Hotels There are about 20 4-star hotels in Selva, about 40 3-stars and numerous lesser hotels. It is not a small place. Few of the best are well positioned – though they generally operate shuttle-buses.

******Aaritz** (0471 795011) Best-placed 4-star, opposite the gondola.

******Gran Baita** (0471 795210) Large, luxurious sporthotel, with lots of mod cons including pool. A few minutes' walk from centre and lifts.

******Granvara** (0471 795250) Just out of town but free shuttle, great views, pool and a spa.

******Mignon** (0471 795092) Good value, close to lifts – 'comfortable, with fantastic dinners, friendly staff'.

******Oswald** (0471 795151) One Californian reader's top choice in Europe. 'Good rooms, fantastic food, very helpful staff.' Near a ski-bus stop and with its own shuttle.

******Savoy** (0471 795343) Next to the 'slow but quiet' Ciampinoi chairlift. One reader's regular favourite – 'amazing food, comfortable rooms plus great indoor/outdoor swimming pool'.

*****Gardena** (0471 793313) in Santa Cristina: 'Excellent food, very well appointed rooms.'

*****Linder** (0471 795242) An established reader favourite in a central location: 'very welcoming family'. Pool and spa.

*****Miara** (0471 794627) Next to the Ciampinoi gondola. 'Modern, quiet, with friendly helpful owners.'

*****Solaia** (0471 795104) Superbly positioned for lifts and slopes.

*****Stella** (0471 795162) Good location at the Sella Ronda lifts; 'very good food'.

Villa Seceda (0471 795297) A 'friendly' B&B near the nursery slopes.

Apartments We have had excellent reports of the Villa Gardena and Isabell apartments.

At altitude We have a report this year of a 'fabulous' stay at the hotel Sochers (0471 792101), up at 2000m next to the Saslong downhill run from Ciampinoi.

EATING OUT ★★★★★
Adequate choice

The better restaurants are mainly based in hotels or, ironically, B&B guest houses. Reader tips include: Armin's Grillstube ('inexpensive and cosy cellar restaurant'), the Sal Fëur in the Garni Broi ('relaxed atmosphere, generous portions'), the Bula

GETTING THERE

Air Verona 215km/ 135 miles (2hr45); Bolzano 55km/ 35 miles (1hr); Treviso 200km/ 125 miles (3hr30); Brescia 240km/150 miles (3hr30); Milan 340km/210 miles (4hr30); Innsbruck 120km/75 miles (1hr45)

Rail Chiusa (27km/ 17 miles); Bressanone (35km/22 miles); Bolzano (40km/ 25 miles); frequent buses from station

UK PACKAGES

Alpine Answers, Crystal, Crystal Finest, Esprit, Independent Ski Links, Interactive Resorts, Momentum, Mountain Wave, Neilson, Ski Solutions, Ski Total, Skitracer, Ski Yogi, Snow Finders, STC, Thomson
Ortisei Crystal, Inghams, Ski Expectations, Thomson
S Cristina Ski Club Freshtracks

ACTIVITIES

In Val Gardena:

Indoor Swimming pool, sauna, bowling, ice rink, climbing wall, fitness centre, tennis, museum, chess

Outdoor Sleigh rides, snowshoeing, tobogganing, ice climbing, ice rink, paragliding, extensive cleared paths

Phone numbers
From abroad use the prefix +39 (and do **not** omit the initial '0' of the phone number)

TOURIST OFFICE

www.valgardena.it

('fabulous pasta and pizza, staff genuinely seem to care'), the Rino and the Bellavista for pizza, and the Costabella for grills.

APRES-SKI ★★★★★
Not without action

At close of play some of the mountain restaurants offer distractions. Piz Seteur was as lively and fun as ever when we visited last season. The hotel Sochers is said to be good for a quiet drink. At the base, the Stua is a popular last stop (and if you settle in for the evening, live music may arrive mid-evening; 'fairly-priced drinks') and Kronestube has been recommended ('good atmosphere'). Café Mozart on the main street is 'a convivial place for a relaxed coffee'. Later on the village streets are fairly quiet, but there are places to go. The Goalies Irish pub offers 'the best rock classics' but we're told it has a smoking area near the bar. There are several places with DJs open until about 1am – notably the Laurinkeller, the 'very busy' Luislkeller – 'Oompah Euro pop all the way and well priced beer' – and Yello's, a basement bar on the main street: 'busy and very loud'. The serious nightclub is the Dali, open until 3am, busy and with dance music for 'a younger clientele'.

OFF THE SLOPES ★★★★★
Good variety

There are many spectacular walks to be done on Alpe di Siusi and Rasciesa, in particular. There's a sports centre, snowshoeing, tobogganing and sleigh rides. In 2012 a reporter's family enjoyed watching a tense ice hockey match – quite a big deal in these parts. There are buses to nearby Ortisei and more distant Bolzano, with a museum featuring 5,000-year-old Oetzi the Ice Man, among many attractions. And there are coach excursions to Cortina and Verona. A group of hotels has formed Val Gardena Active, offering free excursions. Pedestrians can reach many good mountain restaurants.

LINKED RESORT – 1430m

S CRISTINA

A few km downvalley from Selva, at the bottom of the race course from Ciampinoi, S Cristina is a pleasant village well worth considering as an alternative base. It has gondolas towards Ciampinoi and Seceda (their base stations linked by an underground railway), and a slow chairlift up to a ring of nursery slopes at Monte Pana (but no piste back). There is accommodation up here, too. There's a good range of hotels in the village from 5-star down, and countless B&Bs.

LINKED RESORT – 1235m

ORTISEI

Ortisei is an attractive, prosperous market town with a life of its own apart from tourism. It's full of lovely buildings, pretty churches, smart shops and tempting cafes, and has an interesting museum, a large hot-spring swimming pool and an ice rink. The valley road follows the river, bypassing the centre. The local slopes offer an astonishing six toboggan runs – one from Rasciesa 6km long and accessed by funicular – as well as vast amounts of easy skiing. If you plan to spend time on the Sella Ronda circuit beyond Selva, plan on using the ski-buses.

The gondola to the Seceda slopes is easily reached from the centre by a 300m-long series of moving walkways and escalators. Alternatively, you can reach the top of that gondola, and the start of the Seceda cable car, by riding the Rasciesa funicular and descending a red piste. The gondola for Alpe di Siusi is a similar distance out, across the river – a footbridge from the centre is the best approach, going over the valley road too. Note that to move from one area to another involves quite a walk.

The nursery area, school and kindergarten are also over the river, along with a fair range of accommodation. The fine public indoor pool and ice rink are also here.

There are hotels and self-catering accommodation to suit all tastes and pockets and many good restaurants, mainly specializing in local dishes. The 3-star hotel Dolomiti Madonna (0471 796207) was recommended in 2011 despite its location at the very end of the town – 'delightful evening meals'. The 5-star Adler (0471 775001) is tipped this year for its 'excellent food and outstanding staff'; another visitor prefers the 5-star Gardena (0471 796315): 'outstanding food, nicer guest rooms, unbeatable ski guide and fewer people'. Après-ski is quite jolly, and many bars keep going till late.

SESTRIERE TOURIST OFFICE

Sestriere

Altitude is the main attraction of this, Europe's first purpose-built resort; some would say it's the only attraction

TOP 10 RATINGS

Extent	****
Fast lifts	***
Queues	***
Snow	****
Expert	***
Intermediate	****
Beginner	***
Charm	*
Convenience	***
Scenery	***

RPI	85
lift pass	£150
ski hire	£95
lessons	£85
food & drink	£95
total	**£425**

NEWS

2012/13: Two new easy pistes are to open: from Anfiteatro to Pragelato to access the Pattemouche area and from Anfiteatro to Borgata. A Club Med is due to open in Pragelato in December 2012.

- + Local slopes suitable for most levels, with some tougher runs than in most neighbouring resorts
- + Part of the extensive Milky Way area, with Sauze d'Oulx and Sansicario only one lift away
- + Snowmaking covers all but one or two marginal slopes, but ...

- – It needs to, given the very erratic local snowfall record
- – The village is a bit of an eyesore
- – For a purpose-built resort, not conveniently arranged
- – Weekend and peak-period queues
- – Little après-ski during the week

Sestriere was built for snow – high, with north-west-facing slopes – and it has very extensive snowmaking, too. So even if you are let down by the notoriously erratic snowfalls in this corner of Italy, you should be fairly safe here – certainly safer than in Sauze d'Oulx, over the hill. All of which makes Sestriere a great weekend away for the residents of Turin. As a holiday destination for residents of Tunbridge Wells, it doesn't have such a strong case.

THE RESORT

Sestriere was the first purpose-built resort in the Alps, developed by Fiat's Giovanni Agnelli in the 1930s.

Village charm The resort sits on a broad, sunny and windy col. Neither the site nor the village, with its rows of apartment blocks, looks very hospitable – despite improvements for the 2006 Winter Olympics.

Convenience The village is not huge, and some accommodation is close to the snow – it depends where you stay; but basically the buildings are on one side of the col and the skiing is on the other, and some of the walks between the two are non-trivial. The slightly lower satellite of Borgata is less convenient for nightlife and shops. The valley town of Pragelato is a viable base, with its cable car link up to the Motta slopes.

Scenery The Motta slopes are high and rolling, with extensive views across the Milky Way and its part-wooded slopes to the mountains on the French border.

THE MOUNTAINS

The local skiing is on shady slopes, mainly open with some woodland, facing the village. Sestriere is at one extreme of the big Franco-Italian Milky Way area – though the slopes around the border are best reached by road.

PISTE MAP

Sestriere is covered on the Sauze d'Oulx map

VIA LATTEA

Fine snow-sure slopes rise on M Sises from the bottom of the village →

KEY FACTS

Resort	2035m 6,680ft
Milky Way	
Slopes	1390-2825m 4,560-9,270ft
Lifts	72
Pistes	400km 249 miles
Blue	25%
Red	55%
Black	20%
Snowmaking	60%
Sestriere-Sauze d'Oulx-Sansicario	
Slopes	1390-2825m 4,560-9,270ft
Lifts	41
Pistes	300km 186 miles
Snowmaking	38%

UK PACKAGES

Alpine Answers, Club Med, Crystal, Inghams, Interactive Resorts, Momentum, Neilson, Ski Line, Skitracer, Thomson, White Roc

Phone numbers
From abroad use the prefix +39 (and do **not** omit the initial '0' of the phone number)

TOURIST OFFICE

www.turismotorino.org
www.vialattea.it
www.comune.sestriere.to.it

Slopes The local slopes, served by drags and chairs, are in two main sectors: Sises, directly in front of the village, and Motta, above Borgata; Motta is more varied and bigger, with more vertical. Across the valley, a gondola goes up from a car park west of the village to M Fraiteve, for access to Sauze d'Oulx, Sansicario and the rest of the Milky Way. There are blue and red runs back from M Fraiteve – but both are sunny, and you usually have to ride the gondola down. Signposting and piste marking are poor and the piste map covering the whole Via Lattea is difficult to follow.
Fast lifts The lifts are mainly modern, though there are still some inadequate, slow, old ones, both here and over in Sauze.
Queues The main lifts can have queues on sunny weekends when people flock up from Turin. Now that all the lifts out of Sestriere, Sauze and Sansicario meet at M Fraiteve the summit area is 'very congested' at peak times, says a repeat visitor, and there may be serious queues for the gondola down.
Terrain parks A terrain park was built by the Baby lift last season – and there are parks in Sauze d'Oulx and Sansicario.
Snow reliability The Italian part of the Milky Way gets notoriously unreliable snowfalls, but Sestriere has comprehensive snowmaking. When combined with its altitude and orientation, this means you can count on good cover on the pistes. Don't expect powder, though.
Experts There is a fair amount to amuse – steep pistes served by the drags at the top of both sectors, three now designated as mogul fields. Given good snow, there is some decent off-piste. Don't count on it, though.
Intermediates Both sectors also offer plenty for confident intermediates, who can also explore practically all of the Milky Way areas, conditions permitting. The runs in the Motta sector offer more of a challenge than elsewhere.
Beginners The terrain is good for beginners, with several nursery areas and the gentlest of easy blue runs down to Borgata. A special day pass covers use of five lifts. But there is a lack of easy runs to progress to.
Snowboarding Competent boarders will enjoy cruising the pistes and the draglifts are largely avoidable.

Cross-country There are three loops covering about 12km.
Mountain restaurants The woody Raggio di Sole at Anfiteatro offers 'good local food, and good music'. Despite its valley-bottom location, Il Capret at Borgata is popular with readers – 'very friendly staff, reasonable prices, clean toilets'.
Schools and guides There are four schools: the main ones are the Nazionale and Vialattea, and there are two smaller schools: the Olimpionica and a school in Borgata.
Families There are no special facilities for children. The two main schools have mini-clubs for children aged three and four and offer lessons for children from the age of five.

STAYING THERE

Most accommodation is in apartments.
Hotels There are a dozen hotels, mostly 3-star or 4-star. The 4-star Cristallo (0122 750707) is central. The hotel du Col offers 'an ideal location', 'good food', 'excellent staff'. The 3-star Biancaneve (0122 755177) has 'great food, good service'. The Shackleton Mountain Resort (0122 750773) is a smart, modern complex with pool and wellness centre. Just out of the village is the luxurious Roseo (0122 7941), formerly the Principi di Piemonte. The Village Resort Spa in Pragelato will reopen as a Club Med in 2012.
Apartments The Villagio Olimpico apartments built for the 2006 Olympics are reasonably central.
Eating out There are plenty of options. The rustic Antica Spelonca in Borgata has been recommended for 'great local dishes'. Other reader tips include Pinky ('renowned for pizza and pasta but steak to die for'), Last Tango and Ritrovo.
Après-ski The quietness of the place during the week, when the Italians are absent, disappoints some visitors. Pinky (see 'Eating out') has a popular bar with low sofas in the classic Italian casual-chic style. Other reader tips for a good atmosphere include Brahms, Pub Black Pepper and the Tabata disco.
Off the slopes There's more to do than most visitors realize. There are some smart shops, a fitness centre, an ice rink, a sports centre and pool, and other diversions such as dog sledding. Outings are possible to nearby Pragelato and also to Turin – only 100km away by road.

CONSORZIO OPERATORI TURISTICI LA THUILE

La Thuile

A spread-out resort with a mix of ancient and modern parts and extensive, easy, snow-sure slopes linked with La Rosière in France

TOP 10 RATINGS

Extent	***
Fast lifts	***
Queues	****
Snow	****
Expert	**
Intermediate	****
Beginner	****
Charm	***
Convenience	***
Scenery	***

RPI	85
lift pass	£140
ski hire	£90
lessons	£85
food & drink	£105
total	**£420**

NEWS

2011/12: The terrain park moved to beside the Piloni blue run in the Les Suches area. A new snow kiting area opened at altitude on the Petit St Bernard Pass; a special school offers lessons. The San Bernardo red was widened at the start. Snowmaking was increased, and 25% of pistes are now covered.

- + Fair-sized area linked to La Rosière in France
- + Strikingly crowd-free slopes
- + Excellent beginner and easy intermediate slopes
- − The tough runs are low down, and most low, woodland runs are tough
- − The French link is exposed to bad weather, and the return is slow
- − Not the place for lively après-ski

La Thuile has a lot going for it. If you are limited to school holidays and have had enough of the peak-season crowds over the hill in France, it could be just the job – provided a quiet village appeals to you as much as quiet slopes.

THE RESORT

La Thuile is based on an old mining village which has been expanded and restored. The attractive centre with shops, bars and restaurants is at the entrance with newer developments fairly widely spread. The modern Planibel complex, at the base of the lifts, looks a bit like a French purpose-built resort. The pass includes two days in other Val d'Aosta resorts, and free buses run to nearby Courmayeur, making this an easy outing.

Village charm The village centre is attractive but many people find the Planibel complex rather soulless.

Convenience The main village is separated from the ski area by a river and most accommodation is served by a regular free bus. The Planibel complex is right by the main lift, with a few other hotels nearby.

Scenery The scenery is varied, with open bowls and lower wooded slopes overlooked by the nearby Mont Blanc massif. Good views into France.

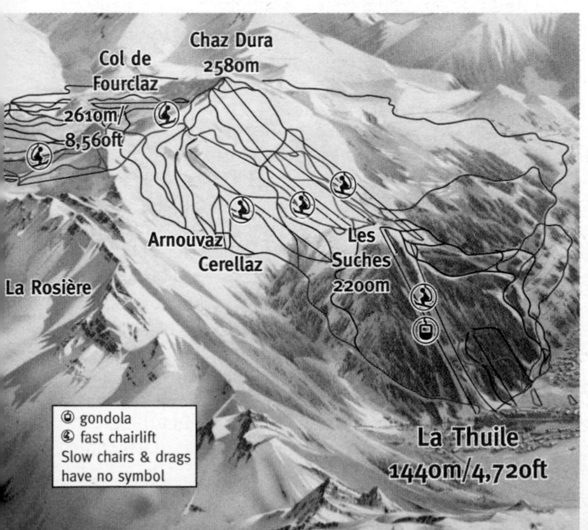

THE MOUNTAINS

La Thuile has quite extensive slopes linked to those of La Rosière via slopes above the Petit St Bernard pass (a good area which is poorly covered on the over-compressed piste map). Many runs marked red deserve no more than a blue rating. Strong winds can close high lifts, including the link. A 2012 visitor says the signposting is 'easy to follow, especially to and from France'.

Slopes A gondola out of the village takes you to Les Suches and an alternative chair to 100m below it. Shady black runs go back down directly to the village through the trees, and a couple of reds take more roundabout routes. Chairs take you up to Chaz Dura for access to a variety of gentle bowls and slightly more testing slopes on the back of the ridge. From there two chairs go up to the link with La Rosière. Immediately above the lift base is the small Maison Blanche area.

Fast lifts The key lifts are fast chairs and a gondola.

Queues Short queues may form at the gondola first thing, but not at the chair. There are no problems once you are up the hill. Reporters regularly comment on the lack of queues, and a 2012 comment is typical: 'Not a single queue all week. Yippee.'

Terrain parks The park moved to Les Suches area this year.

Snow reliability Most of La Thuile's slopes are north- or east-facing and above 2000m, so the snow keeps well. There's also a decent amount of snowmaking; grooming is 'excellent'. The snow was in fine condition when we were there in hot April 2012 sunshine and experienced ice and slush elsewhere on the same trip.

KEY FACTS

Resort	1440m 4,720ft
Espace San Bernardo (La Rosière and La Thuile)	
Slopes	1175-2610m 3,850-8,560ft
Lifts	38
Pistes	160km 99 miles
Green	10%
Blue	31%
Red	40%
Black	19%
Snowmaking	25%

UK PACKAGES

Alpine Answers, Crystal, Inghams, Interski, Just Skiing, Momentum, Neilson, Ski Bespoke, Ski Club Freshtracks, Ski Solutions, Skitracer, Thomson, Tracks European Adventures

Phone numbers
From abroad use the prefix +39 (and do **not** omit the initial '0' of the phone number)

TOURIST OFFICE

www.lathuile.it

Experts The black pistes down through the trees from Les Suches are serious stuff, as well as two steepish blacks at Maison Blanche. The black slopes down to the pass are easier – only just genuine, but there is also plenty of good off-piste here; fast quads mean you can do quick circuits in this area. Don't hope for moguls on-piste.

Heli-lifts are available. The Ruitor glacier offers a 20km run to Ste-Foy in France, a short taxi ride from La Rosière for the lifts for La Thuile.

Intermediates The slopes above Les Suches consist almost entirely of gentle blue and red runs, ideal for cruising and carving but free of challenges. There are also long reds through the trees back to the resort – easy but pleasant. The red runs on the back side of the top ridge, down towards the Petit St Bernard pass, are less gentle. The pass road forms the roundabout San Bernardo red to the village taking 11km to drop only 600m; avoid in fresh snow.

The skiing in La Rosière is more testing – mostly genuine red runs, sometimes with moguls, and with snow more affected by sun. The route back starts with a genuine red, and involves long, exposed draglifts.

Beginners There are no free lifts, but a day pass (5 euros) allows use of the moving carpet on the village nursery slope. There is also a nursery area up at Les Suches and long easy blues above there, ideal for progression. You ride the gondola down.

Snowboarding These are great slopes for learning. You need ride only chairlifts and the gondola, and most of the slopes are easy. For the more experienced there are great tree runs, good freeriding and some good carving runs. But there are some frustratingly flat sections too.

Cross-country La Thuile has four loops of varying difficulty on the valley floor, adding up to 16km of track.

Mountain restaurants Sadly, nowhere near as good as many other Italian resorts. We liked the ambience of the Off Shore, above Arnouvaz, a small hut with an eclectic mix of 1960s/70s memorabilia and music and nautical/ Asian/African themes – simple food such as panini, pasta and pizza which you order at the bar. Maison Carrel off run 30 is a table-service place with floor to ceiling windows that gets good reviews from readers; we've had both good and bad experiences there. Other reader tips: Chalet de Cantamont on run 16, the self-service Mélèze at the top of the gondola, Riondet on run 7.

Schools and guides A 2012 visitor found the 'teaching was effective, but there were some language issues'.

Families There is a nursery area, with mini-club and snow garden. The village kindergarten and the Planibel hotel club both take children from four to 12. Over fives can join ski school.

STAYING THERE

Hotels The 4-star Planibel (0165 884541) is large and characterless, but readers like its ideal location, pools, sauna, steam room and gym. The B&B hotel du Glacier (0165 884137), a short walk above the lifts, gets repeated rave reviews, mainly thanks to its energetic owner Susanna. The Miramonti (0165 883084), in the old village (shuttle on demand), recently refurbished in traditional style, offers 'excellent food and service'. Chalet Eden (0165 885050), a short walk from the lifts, is an eco-hotel with a big spa and highly recommended by a 2012 reporter ('very large room, gourmet four-course meals, lots of open fires').

Apartments Reporters say that the furniture and fittings in the Planibel apartments are in need of upgrading, but that they are spacious and good value – 'perfectly adequate'.

Eating out Reader tips include the Grotta ('friendly, good pizza, pasta, fondue'), Pizzeria Dahü ('good value'), Coppapan ('steaks to die for') and Coq Maf ('best steak in 37 years of skiing').

Après-ski Nightlife is quiet. The Konver is open until late and has a regular DJ.

Off the slopes There are few shops; the Planibel has a pool; there are walks, dog sledding and a climbing wall. Pedestrians can ride the gondola, but can't reach the best lunch spots.

SNOWPIX.COM / CHRIS GILL

La Thuile has remarkably quiet pistes; but mountain restaurants are not one of its strong points ↓

TRENTINO TOURIST OFFICE

Trentino

Not a resort, but a region with a few big resorts and a lot of smaller ones that deserve to be better known on the UK market

Trentino is a fabulously scenic region that is rather neglected by the British. The resorts best known in the UK, Madonna di Campiglio and Passo Tonale, are covered in detail in their own chapters. Canazei and Campitello, linked to the huge and increasingly well known Sella Ronda network, are covered in the chapter on Val di Fassa. That leaves a lot of small ski areas that you may not have heard of, most of which are covered here.

WESTERN TRENTINO

Madonna di Campiglio is Trentino's biggest and best-known resort – a chic place with mainly easy slopes that attracts an affluent, almost exclusively Italian clientele. Its ski area has long been linked to those of Marilleva and Folgarida, in the Val di Sole to the north, and since last season has had a gondola link in the opposite direction to Pinzolo, to the south. The separate chapter on Madonna di Campiglio, a few pages back, covers all three of these satellite resorts.

Marilleva is a functional modern resort set in woods at 1400m and reached by road or gondola from a lower part of the resort at 900m, on the valley floor. It has some of the most challenging skiing in the region.

Although also modern, **Folgarida** is built in a more traditional style. It spreads along the road leading from the Val di Sole towards Madonna di Campiglio, with lift bases at 1400m and 1300m. There is a black descent to the latter base, but generally the slopes down to Folgarida are gentler than those above Marilleva.

Midway between Marilleva and Folgarida, an eight-seat gondola runs from the village of **Daolasa** up to Val Mastellina where there are links to both neighbouring areas.

Pinzolo (770m) is the main town of the Val Rendena, south-west of Madonna di Campiglio. A long and long-planned link with the slopes of Campiglio opened in 2011. The area has mainly genuinely challenging red runs and some easy groomed blacks.

Passo Tonale is a short drive west of Marilleva – a high, snow-sure resort on the border of Lombardia. It has its own chapter.

Just a few km along the Val di Sole west of Marilleva, up a side valley, is **Pejo** or Peio (1400m), a spa village with a modest mid-mountain area of slopes at about 2000m, but also with a slick state-of-the-art cable car from

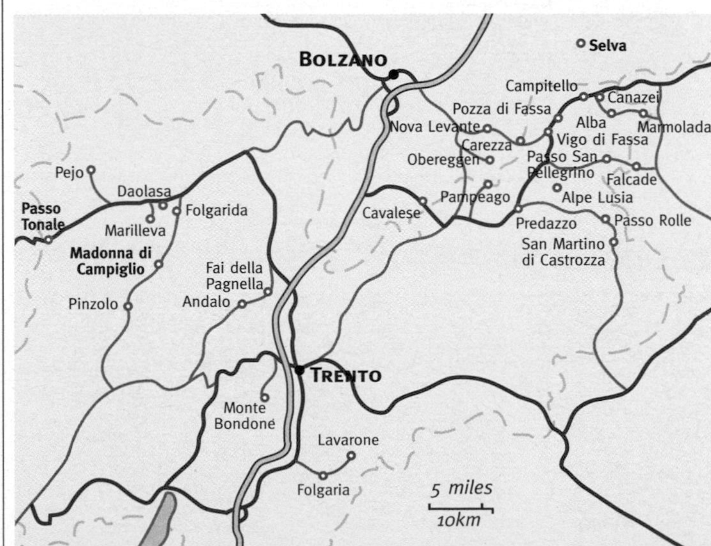

Your next ski holiday
starts at home
Photos Trentino Marketing S.p.A. - S. Angelani, Orienimages.com, A. Trovati, G. Zotta

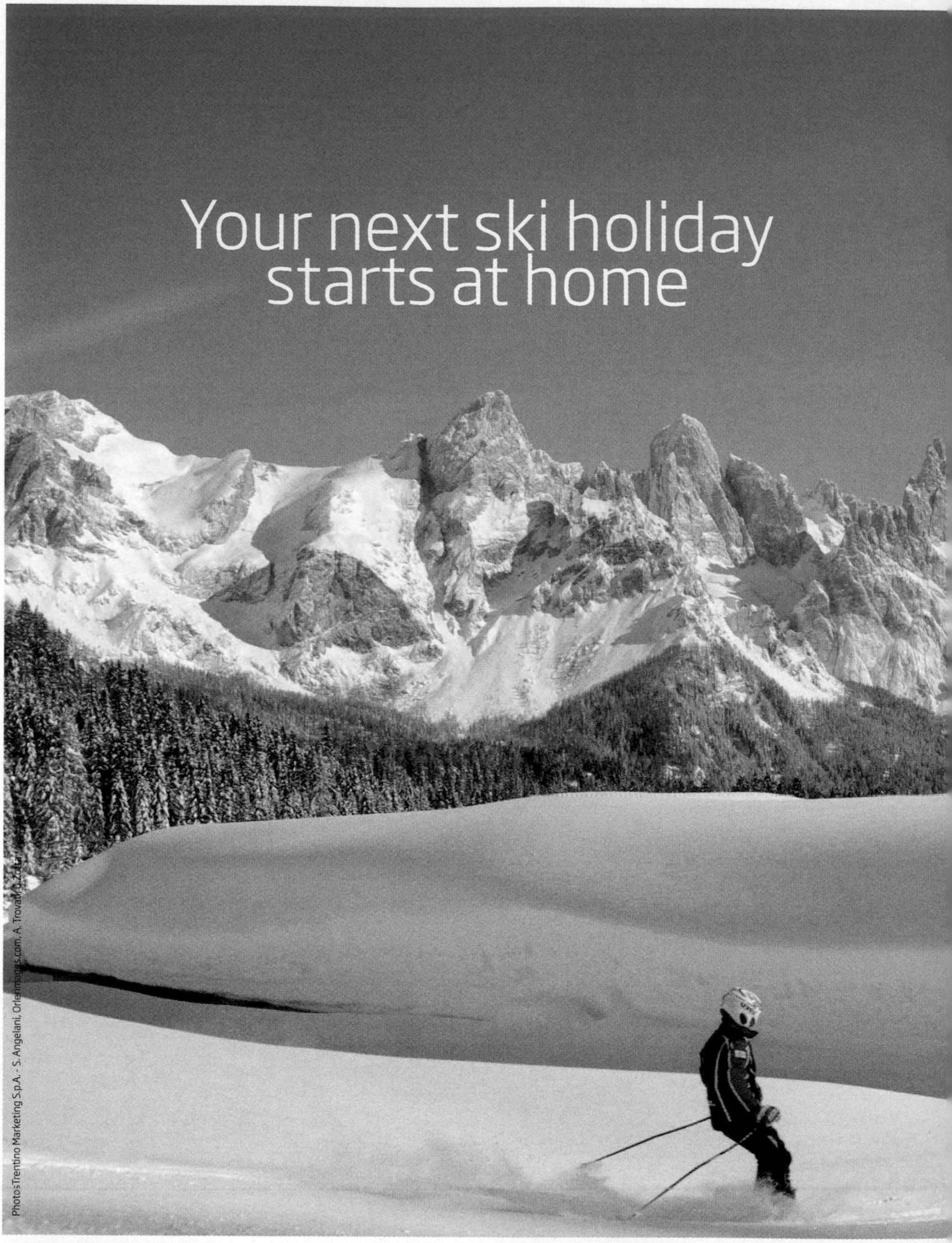

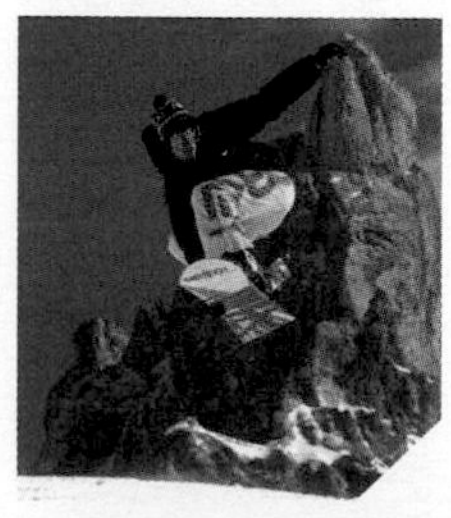

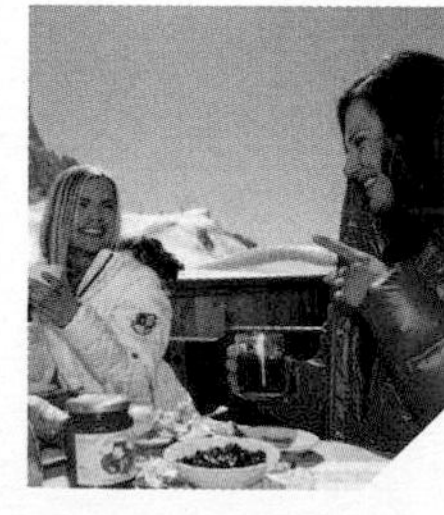

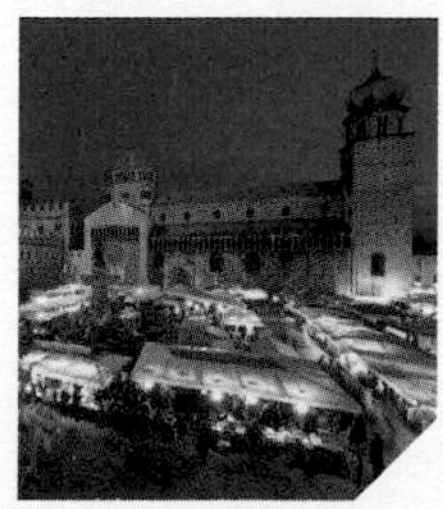

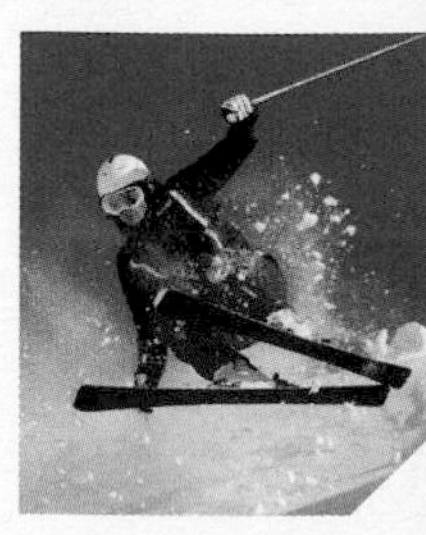

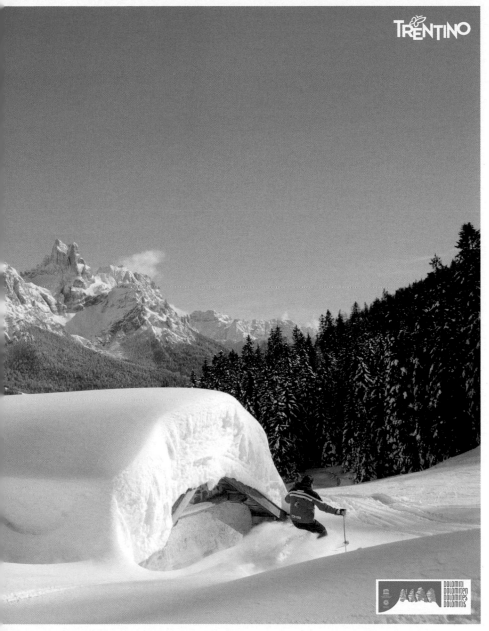

UK PACKAGES

Folgaria *Solo's, STC*

there, opened in 2010, serving a long red run from about 3000m (2990m, we believe). Red and black runs go on down from mid-mountain to the village, giving an impressive total descent of almost 1600m vertical. The access lift is a modern gondola.

We skied the main slopes of Pejo last season; sadly, we encountered a somewhat challenging combination of slushy snow and dense cloud, so didn't learn a lot about the mountain. We can recommend the food in the warmly woody table-service section of Lo Scoiattolo, the main mid-mountain restaurant, and the home-made arolla-pine liqueur at the Rif Doss dei Cembri, higher up.

All these areas (and the resorts described in the 'Around Trento' section below) are covered by the Superskirama Adamello-Brenta ski pass. With a car, it would be perfectly possible (and very entertaining) to explore all these areas in a week.

AROUND TRENTO

Trento is the main town of Trentino, and its local hill is **Monte Bondone.** Five roadside chairlifts serve partly wooded slopes here on Palon (2090m), with a longest run of 4km dropping 800m and served by a fast quad. The whole area is covered by snowmaking. There's a terrain park – and great Dolomite views.

South-east of Trento are the small resorts of **Folgaria** (1165m) – not to be confused with Folgarida – and **Lavarone.** Lavarone has a handful of lifts; Folgaria has over 20, serving 60km of runs with 100% snowmaking.

To the north-west are the slopes on Paganella (2125m) shared by **Fai della Paganella** (1000m) and **Andalo** (1050m). Andalo is a sizeable resort with a small local town feel. One eight-seat gondola goes up from near the centre of Andalo, and another leaves from a big car park nearby. Five of the other 16 lifts are fast chairs. The runs are mainly genuinely challenging reds and can be long (a maximum vertical of almost 1100m); most are northish-facing and so keep their snow in good condition. We especially enjoyed the Dosa Larici and La Rocca reds down to Santel (the nearest lift base to Fai). There's a beginner area near the Andalo base but only a few short blue runs (all at the top), so we don't recommend it for novices or timid intermediates.

OTHER TRENTINO RESORTS

The biggest linked ski area in the world, the Sella Ronda circuit plus offshoots, is partly in Trentino. The Sella Ronda chapter a few pages back mainly covers the parts of the area in the Sud Tirol. **Canazei** and **Campitello,** at the south-west corner of the circuit, are in Trentino but covered in our chapter on Val di Fassa.

At the bottom of the Val di Fassa is the small town of Moena. About 2km east of the town is the lift system of **Alpe Lusia**. Further east are more extensive slopes at **Passo San Pellegrino**, linked with **Falcade** in Veneto. To the west is another lift network at **Carezza**, linked with **Nova Levante** in Alto Adige.

Continuing downstream from the Val di Fassa, you are now in the Val di Fiemme. Near **Predazzo** there is a lift up to the slopes shared with **Pampeago** and **Obereggen**, across the border in Alto Adige. Finally, the town of **Cavalese** has lifts up to the Alpe Cermis slopes.

To the south of the Val di Fassa/Val di Fiemme axis, a steep road leads over the high **Passo Rolle** – where there is a small network of drags and chairs serving easy slopes on either side of the road.

Over the pass, the road leads down to the resort of **San Martino di Castrozza** (1470m). San Martino has a fabulous setting beneath a soaring wall of Dolomite cliffs and peaks – the Pale di San Martino. The village is not notably cute – there are some large, block-like buildings – but it is pleasant enough. The slopes – which are entirely intermediate in difficulty – are split into three sectors, only two of them linked (at altitude).

PHOTO ARCHIVE VAL DI FASSA

Val di Fassa

Two resorts linked in to the Sella Ronda circuit, and several much smaller separate areas well worth exploring for a day or two

NEWS

2011/12: In Canazei a new snowpark and a new aquatic centre opened.

UK PACKAGES

Canazei *Crystal, Independent Ski Links, Interactive Resorts, STC, Thomson*
Campitello *Crystal, Thomson*

TOURIST OFFICE

www.fassa.com

The Val di Fassa runs from the town of Moena to an abrupt end at the massive twin obstacles of the Gruppo Sella and glacial Marmolada. The valley's biggest resort, Canazei, is at the south-west corner of the famous Sella Ronda circuit (which has its own chapter). Campitello, 2km down the valley, also has a lift into the circuit. A separate network links Alba (up the valley) to Pozza di Fassa (down the valley). And there are separate areas at Vigo di Fassa and Carezza.

Canazei is a sizeable, bustling, pretty, roadside village of narrow streets, rustic buildings, traditional-style hotels and little shops, set at 1465m beneath a heavily wooded mountainside.

The village itself is slightly off the main Sella Ronda circuit, but its main slopes form part of it. A 12-person gondola (powerful, but queue-prone) rises 470m to Pecol, at the foot of the slopes of Belvedere. These are linked in one direction to the slopes of Passo Pordoi and Arabba, and in the other to Passo Sella and Col Rodella (above Campitello), and then on to Selva. A red run returns to Canazei, but it gets the afternoon sun and is often closed.

The Belvedere slopes are open and sunny, with modest verticals of about 450m. Almost all are graded red; this exaggerates their difficulty, but rules the resort out for timid intermediates and beginners – and the nursery slope is across the valley from the village.

The grand 4-star Schloss Hotel Dolomiti (0462 601106) in the centre is one of the oldest hotels: 'very Italian, good food and lots of choice, stylish and historic', says a 2012 visitor. The 4-star Perla (0462 602453), also central, is praised by a 2011 visitor for 'great food and value, amazing spa'.

There are numerous restaurants, and the après-ski is surprisingly animated. The Rose Garden and Osteria, at the bottom of the home run, and the Paradis (a converted barn – 'great fun') are popular at close of play. The 'friendly' International bar and ice cream parlour is quieter. La Stua di Ladins serves local wines.

Off-slope entertainment consists of beautiful walks and shopping. There's also a pool, sauna and Turkish baths.

Neighbouring **Campitello** (1445m) is a pleasant, unremarkable village, smaller, quieter and cheaper than Canazei, and still unspoiled. There are no pistes back to the resort but a cable car rises 1000m up to Col Rodella and the slopes above Passo Sella. At the start of the day this lift can build queues even in January, and in high season they can be 'massive' – get the bus up to Canazei's gondola. There is no nursery slope.

The 2-star Fiorenza (0462 750095) is recommended for its 'good bedrooms and friendly owners'; the stylish 3-star Gran Paradis (0462 750135) has a pool and spa. Après-ski is quite lively – the White Rabbit pub (formerly Da Giulio) gets packed.

About 2km up the valley from Canazei, a cable car just beyond **Alba** goes up to a small area of slopes (six lifts, 15km of runs) above Ciampac, which is linked around the back of the low peak of Crepa Negra to another small area of slopes (seven lifts, 17km of runs and 'excellent' mountain huts) above **Pozza di Fassa**, which is down-valley from Canazei and Campitello.

Over the road from Pozza another small area of slopes (six lifts, 16km of runs) links Pera to **Vigo di Fassa.** A road from there leads west to **Carezza** (aka Passo Costalunga) where yet another area of slopes (16 lifts, 40km of runs, 18 huts!) links with Nova Levante, in Alto Adige.

Switzerland

SWISS FRANC

Back in the winter of 2007 we were getting SF2.4 for £1. When we went to press for this edition the rate was SF1.44, which makes everything 66% more pricey in terms of £s than five years ago. Things were even worse late last summer when the rate hit around SF1.2 to £1; the Swiss authorities got so worried about the franc's strength that they decided to peg the Swiss franc to the euro so that it would not continue to rise.

Switzerland is home to some of our favourite resorts. Only two resorts in this book are awarded *** for both resort charm and spectacular scenery – the essentially traffic-free Swiss villages of Mürren and Wengen. Many other Swiss resorts are not far behind in the charm and scenery stakes. Many resorts have impressive slopes, too – including some of the biggest, highest and toughest runs in the Alps – as well as a lot of good intermediate terrain. For fast, queue-free lift networks, Swiss resorts are not known as pacesetters – too many historic cable cars and mountain railways for that. But the real bottlenecks are steadily disappearing. And there are compensations – the world's best mountain restaurants, for one, and pretty reliable accommodation, too.**

Until recently, one of the drawbacks of Switzerland was that smoking was allowed in public areas. But now nearly every canton that matters has banned smoking except in dedicated smoking rooms, and all hotels, restaurants and bars have smoke-free areas.

There's no doubt that Switzerland is expensive. That is largely because of the strength of the Swiss franc – see the panel in the margin. Our price survey shows that food and drink now costs more in the cheapest Swiss resort than in the most expensive French resort, Courchevel. Overall holiday costs are less unreasonable: when you add in the cost of lifts, ski hire and lessons, a couple of Swiss resorts work out close to the European average. But most are way, way above it, and Swiss resorts dominate the above-average category in our price index results. Until the exchange rate improves further, most people will simply go elsewhere.

Many Swiss resorts have a special relationship with the British, who invented downhill skiing in its modern form in Wengen and Mürren by persuading the locals to run their mountain railways in winter, to act as ski lifts, and by organizing the first downhill races. An indication of the continuing strength of the British presence in these resorts is that Wengen has an English church.

TRADITIONAL YEAR-ROUND RESORTS

While France is the home of the purpose-built resort, Switzerland is the home of the mountain village that has transformed itself from traditional farming community (or health retreat) into year-round holiday resort. Many of Switzerland's most famous mountain resorts are as popular in the summer as in the winter, or more so. This creates places with a more lived-in feel to them and a much more stable local community.

Many villages are still dominated by a handful of families lucky or shrewd enough to get involved in the early development of the area. This has its downside as well as advantages. The ruling families have been able to stifle competition and bar newcomers from taking a slice of their action. Alternative ski schools – to compete with the traditional, nationally organized school, resulting in continuing pressure to raise standards – were slower to come in than in other Alpine countries, for example. But this grip has at last started to weaken.

ENGADIN ST MORITZ /SWISS-IMAGE.CH / MAX WEISS

← Not all Swiss resorts are chocolate box pretty but most have a lot going for them. This is St Moritz with its high snow-sure setting and race course on its frozen, snow-covered lake

SWISS RAIL PASSES

These are the main options – there are others. On any of the passes listed, children under 16 accompanied by at least one parent travel free.

Swiss Pass *Covers unrestricted travel on most of the Swiss railway network, buses and postal buses during the period of validity – 4, 8, 15 or 22 days; or one month. Prices: 4 days from £185; 8 days from £265*

* *Includes panoramic rail routes as well as trams and buses in 38 towns*
* *50% discount on the price of using most of the mountain railways*
* *Free entrance to about 400 museums*
* *15% discount for two and more adults travelling together*

Swiss Transfer Ticket *Permits travel between the Swiss border or airport and your destination, out and back, by the most direct route. Valid for one month. You can use two different airports. Prices: from £90*

SWISS-IMAGE.CH / CHRISTOF SONDEREGGER

Swiss Flexi Pass *Permits unrestricted travel across Switzerland, like the Swiss Pass, on 3, 4, 5 or 6 days of your choice during a one-month period of validity. On days when you choose to use the card, you just write the date on the card. On days when you choose not to use up one of the 3, 4, 5 or 6 days, the pass gets you a discount of 50%. There's 15% discount for two and more adults travelling together. Prices: 3 days from £176; 6 days from £280*

Swiss Card *An extension of the Transfer Ticket. As well as travel to and from your destination, you get a 50% discount on all rail, bus and boat fares during the one-month period of validity – and on some cable car fares. Prices: from £128*

The quality of service throughout Switzerland is generally high. The food is almost universally of good quality and much less stodgy than in neighbouring Austria. Even the standard rustic dish of rösti is haute cuisine compared to Austrian sausages. And in Switzerland you get what you pay for: the cheapest wine, for example, is not cheap, but it is reliable.

Perhaps surprisingly for such a traditional, rather staid skiing nation, Switzerland has gone out of its way to attract snowboarders. Davos may hit the headlines mainly when it hosts huge economic conferences, but yards from the conference hall there are dudes getting big air on the Bolgen slope's training kickers. Little-known Laax claims one of Europe's best terrain parks.

Switzerland, like Italy, doesn't have much time for tree-huggers who object to the impact of helicopters on wildlife. Heli-skiing is not unrestricted, but it is available, whereas in Austria it is confined to Lech-Zürs and in France it is confined to the retrieval of clients from valley bottoms – you can't be deposited on a peak.

GETTING AROUND BY TRAIN

The Swiss railway network is famously extensive and reliable. The trains run like clockwork to the advertised timetable – if you think a Swiss train is late, make sure your watch is right before you complain. (There is, however, some truth in the cynical view that the trains are able to run on time because the timetables incorporate long stops at stations.)

The rail network is a perfectly viable means of reaching many resorts. There are often linking services that run to the top of the mountain, doubling as ski lifts, too. We did a week-long tour of Valais resorts two seasons ago to see how it worked in practice. Our feature panel explains the main rail passes you might use.

Our tour took us first from Geneva to Crans-Montana, then on to the Aletsch Arena area at the far eastern end of the Valais – look for the resorts of Riederalp and Bettmeralp on our map. Next, we backtracked to Zermatt, and before returning to Geneva we left the rail network to try the post bus services to and from Saas-Fee – a resort inexplicably not served by a railway.

Things went pretty smoothly, but not perfectly. At Sierre, where we were to change to the funicular for Crans, we failed to detect the shuttle-bus and had quite a walk from one station to the other. We were surprised to find that our tickets were not valid for the cable car up to Riederalp. And we were repeatedly disappointed by the inadequate luggage space, even in first-class carriages. We would use the railways again if visiting resorts like Riederalp and Zermatt where you can't take cars. And our post bus adventure went to plan, too, with the most satisfactory luggage space of the trip.

GETTING AROUND BY CAR

Access to practically all Swiss resorts is fairly straightforward when approaching from the north – just pick your motorway. But many of the high passes that are perfectly sensible ways to get around the country in summer are closed in winter, which can be inconvenient if you are moving around from one area to another.

There are very useful car-carrying trains in various places; they can cut out huge amounts of driving. One key link is between the Valais (Crans-Montana, Zermatt etc) and Andermatt via the Furka tunnel, and another is from Andermatt to the Grisons (Laax, Davos etc) via the Oberalp pass – closed to road traffic in winter but open to trains except after very heavy snowfalls. Another rail tunnel that's very handy is the Lötschberg, linking Kandersteg in the Bernese Oberland with Brig in the Valais. The recently opened Lötschberg Base Tunnel is lower, longer and faster, but it takes only passenger and freight trains.

St Moritz is more awkward to get to than other major resorts. The main road route is over the Julier pass. This is normally kept open, but at 2285m it is naturally prone to heavy snowfalls that can shut it for a time. Fallbacks are car-carrying rail tunnels under the Albula pass and the Vereina tunnel from near Klosters.

SWISS TOBOGGAN RUNS

SWISS-IMAGE.CH / CHRISTIAN PERRET

The Austrians might dispute it, but Switzerland seems to do tobogganing on an unmatched scale. It isn't just the famous Cresta run at St Moritz (check out that chapter for more information); it's that so many resorts have epic runs. The longest in the world, they say, is at Grindelwald – 15km from the Faulhorn via Bussalp to the resort; it's fantastically scenic, being surrounded by famous peaks, but it does involve a 2hr30 hike from the top of the First gondola.

There are plenty of other extraordinary runs, without the hiking penalty. Fiesch in the little-known Aletsch Arena area has a 13km run, Saas-Grund below Saas-Fee has one of 11km. Even macho Verbier has a 10km run from Savoleyres, dropping 850m.

These car-carrying rail services are generally painless. Often you can just turn up and drive on. But carrying capacities are obviously limited. Some services (eg Oberalp) carry only a handful of cars, and booking is vital. Others (eg Furka, Lötschberg, Vereina) are much bigger operations with much greater capacity – but that's a reflection of demand, and at peak times there may be long queues – particularly for the Furka tunnel from Andermatt, which Zürich

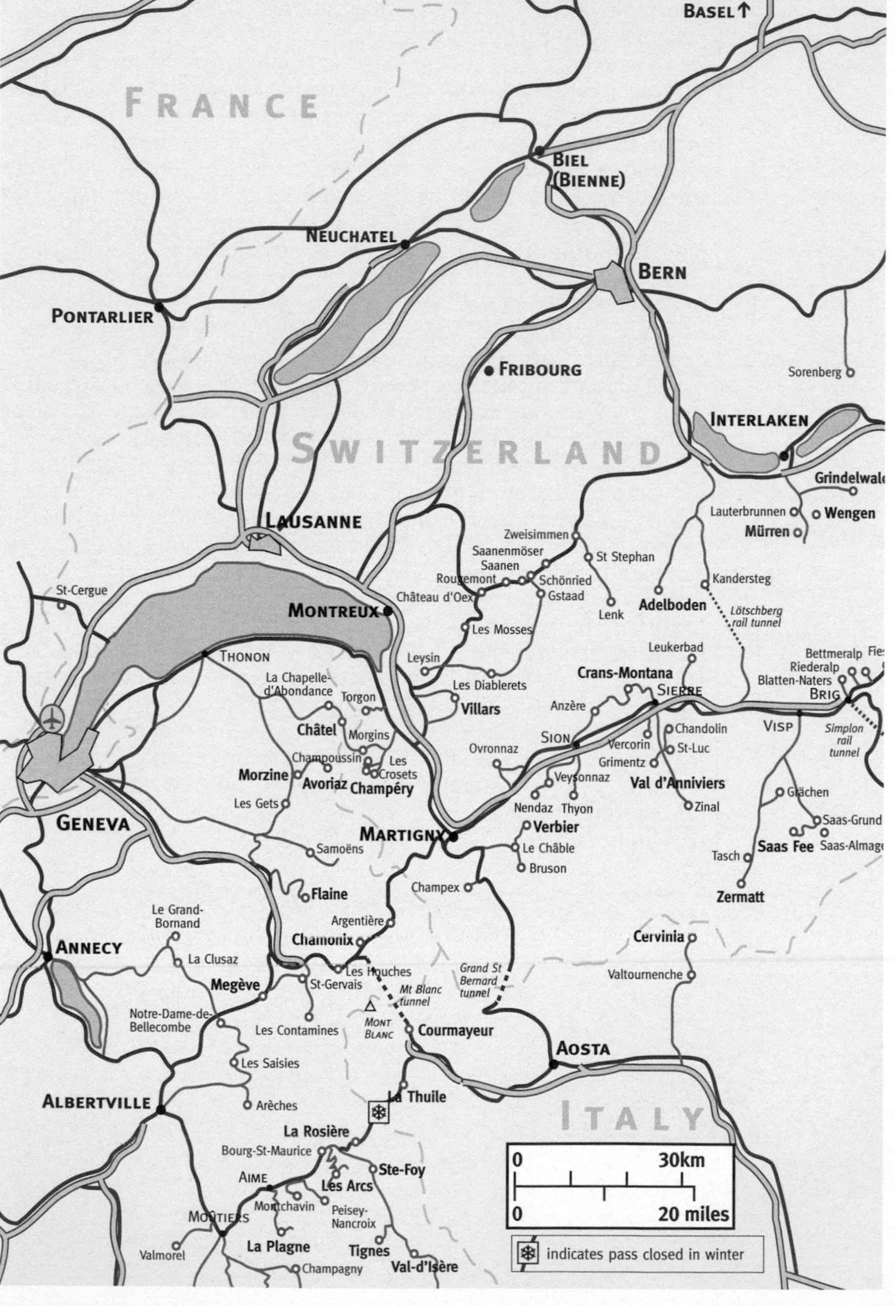

residents use to get to the big Valais resorts. There is a car-carrying rail tunnel linking Switzerland with Italy – the Simplon. But most routes to Italy are kept open by means of road tunnels. Read the Italy introduction for more information.

To use Swiss motorways you have to buy an annual permit to stick on your windscreen. These cost SF40, are sold at the border and are valid for 14 months – from 1 December to 31 January.

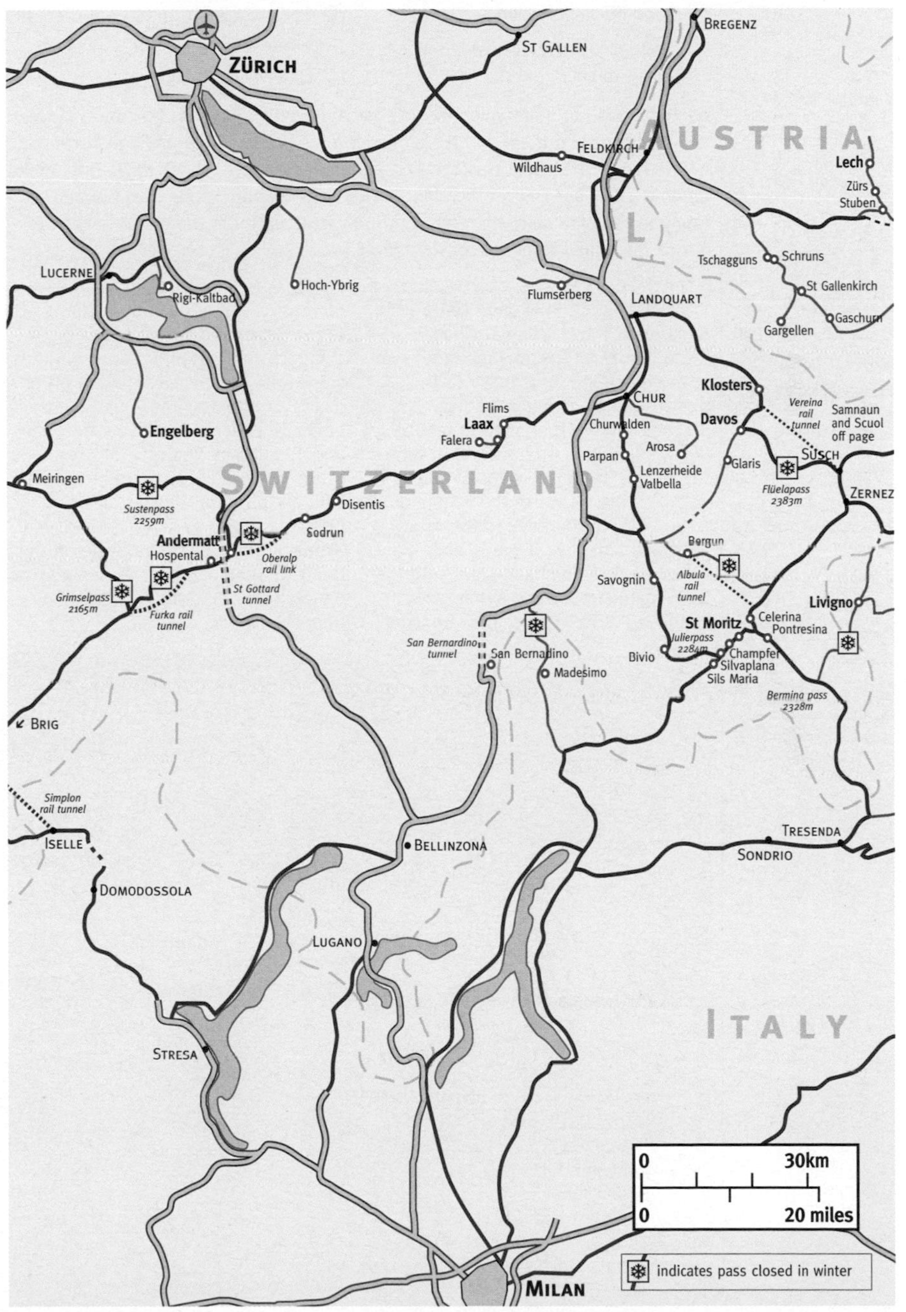

Adelboden

Traditional village with plenty to do off the snow – but also with extensive, varied and scenic slopes, some also accessible from Lenk

TOP 10 RATINGS

Extent	***
Fast lifts	***
Queues	***
Snow	***
Expert	**
Intermediate	***
Beginner	****
Charm	****
Convenience	**
Scenery	****

RPI 120

lift pass	£190
ski hire	£130
lessons	£95
food & drink	£190
total	**£605**

NEWS

2012/13: A blue run from Sillerenbühl to Aebi is due to open.

KEY FACTS

Resort	1355m 4,450ft
Slopes	1070-2360m 3,510-7,740ft
Lifts	57
Pistes	185km 115 miles
Blue	44%
Red	45%
Black	11%
Snowmaking	60%

- ➕ Chalet-style mountain village in a splendid setting
- ➕ Good off-slope facilities
- ➕ Some pleasantly uncrowded slopes linked to Lenk, but ...

- ➖ The slopes are fragmented and widely spread; access can be slow
- ➖ Not a place for bumps but there are plenty of off-piste opportunities
- ➖ Quiet, limited nightlife

Adelboden is not quite your classic postcard-pretty village, but it comes close, and offers a good blend of attractions. 100 years ago it had an English church, and they say the priest was the first ski instructor here. These days, Brits make up only a few per cent of the visitors (we have found our primitive German brought into play more than is usual in Switzerland). But the resort is keen to attract more, and it merits consideration.

THE RESORT

Adelboden is a traditional village tucked away on a sunny mountainside at the head of a long valley to the west of the much better known Jungfrau region. The Jungfrau resorts (Wengen, Mürren etc) are within day-trip range. Its major sector of slopes is linked to the slopes in the village of Lenk, in the next valley to the west.

Village charm The village is built more or less entirely in chalet style, and the long, main street (not car-free, but nearly so) is lined by chalets housing shops. It's a pity many of them have racks of cheap goods out in front.

Convenience The village is fairly compact, but getting to and from the slopes usually involves quite a bit of hassle or at least time. There is no perfect location, unless you are clear about which lift you plan to use. Buses to Engstligenalp are included with the lift pass; those to Elsigen-Metsch are not.

Scenery The 3000-metre peaks of the Bernese Oberland make an impressive panorama both from the village and from the slopes.

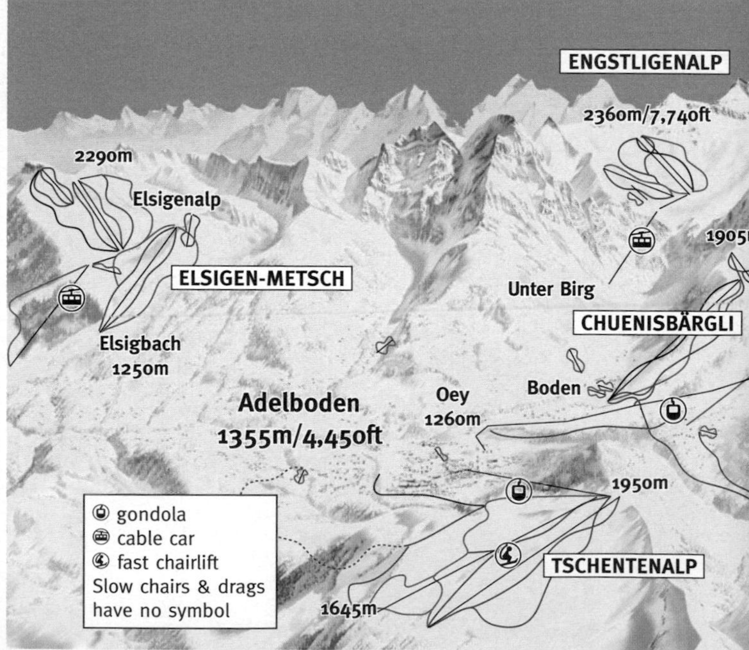

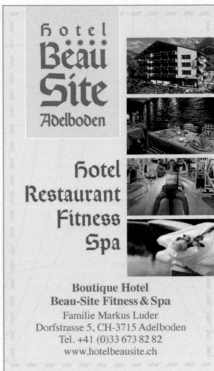

← The high, snowy bowl of Engstligenalp looks tempting from Tschentenalp, and is worth an outing

SNOWPIX.COM / CHRIS GILL

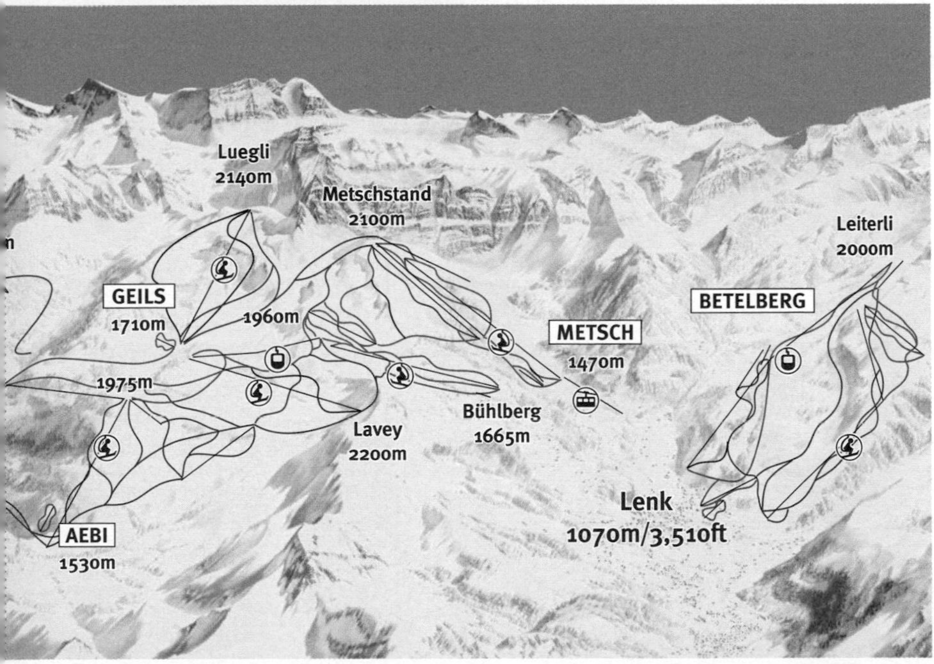

UK PACKAGES

Crystal, PowderBeds, Solo's

Phone numbers
From elsewhere in Switzerland add the prefix 033; from abroad use the prefix +41 33

TOURIST OFFICE

www.adelboden.ch

ADELBODEN TOURIST OFFICE

Occasional patches of trees add to the attractions of the main Geils bowl ↓

THE MOUNTAINS

Adelboden's slopes are split into five varied sectors, widely spread. The main sector stretches across to Lenk, where a sixth area is reached by bus.

Slopes Village lifts access three of the sectors. A small cable car/gondola hybrid goes up to Tschentenalp, with an itinerary back to the village. An even smaller lift goes down to Oey, where a proper gondola goes up to Chuenisbärgli and then on to the major sector (taking 15 minutes in total) which has three sub-sectors – Geils, Aebi and Metsch (above Lenk). There is a pretty run home to Oey.

Engstligenalp, a flat-bottomed high-altitude bowl, is reached by a cable car 4km south of the resort; Elsigen-Metsch is 5km away to the north-east.

Fast lifts The main lifts are fast, but there are still a fair few slow lifts.

Queues The main access gondolas get busy at peak times, and the two main lifts out of Geils can develop queues. A January 2011 visitor found queues at the Bühlberg chair at Metsch. The little lift linking Oey to the centre is a real bottleneck; public and hotel buses offer a way round it.

Terrain parks The Gran Masta Park has jumps, big air, rails, snack bar and chill-out zone. There's a boardercross run, and skiercross out at Elsigen.

Snow reliability Most slopes are above 1500m, so reliability is reasonable, especially at north-facing Tschentenalp and Luegli. Snowmaking is extensive, and grooming is good.

Experts The black pistes generally merit the rating, at least in parts, and are great fun unless you crave bumps – they are groomed regularly. Off-piste possibilities are good and don't get tracked out quickly; the Lavey and Luegli chairs in the Geils bowl access routes to Adelboden and Lenk. Engstligenalp has off-piste potential.

Intermediates All five areas deserve exploration. There is a lot of ground to be covered in the main sector; at Geils and Aebi the runs are mainly excellent wide reds, but on the sunny Metsch side there is great blue cruising. Quiet Tschentenalp is worth a visit.

Beginners There are good nursery slopes in the village and at the foot of nearby sectors. But progress to longer runs requires a bit of planning.

Snowboarding There are still lots of draglifts. There are two specialist schools, and a freeride zone at Engstligenalp.

Cross-country There are trails along the valley to Engstligenalp where there is a high-altitude, snow-sure circuit.

Mountain restaurants There are plenty of pleasant spots.

Schools and guides We lack recent reports.

Families Lots of facilities including several toboggan runs. Several hotels offer childcare.

STAYING THERE

There is locally bookable self-catering, and some 30 pensions and hotels.

Hotels The central 4-star Beau-Site (673 2222) offers 'excellent breakfast, helpful staff; worth paying for a better room upstairs'; the Cambrian (673 8383) has also had good reports.

Eating out The Bären has 'good prices, excellent food'; the Kreuz does 'delicious pizza and meringue'.

Après-ski There are several tea rooms and bars to head for at close of play, including some in central hotels. The village seems pretty quiet later on.

Off the slopes The leisure arena offers various diversions. Some hotel pools are open to the public. There are several toboggan runs of up to 5km. Some mountain huts are reachable on foot and there are well-marked hiking paths. Special lift passes are available for walkers.

ANDERMATT TOURIST OFFICE

Andermatt

A slow-paced, old-fashioned resort with some great steep, high terrain on- and off-piste (and the snowfall to go with it)

TOP 10 RATINGS

Extent	**
Fast lifts	**
Queues	**
Snow	****
Expert	****
Intermediate	**
Beginner	*
Charm	****
Convenience	***
Scenery	***

RPI	115
lift pass	£180
ski hire	£95
lessons	£120
food & drink	£190
total	**£585**

NEWS

Work has started on a huge luxury development on the outskirts of the village, with the first properties expected to open in 2013. The plan is to build new lift and piste links to Sedrun, too.

- ➕ Attractive, traditional village
- ➕ Excellent snow record
- ➕ Some good steep pistes, off-piste terrain and ski-touring opportunities
- ➕ Good access from Zürich

- ➖ Not a resort for beginners, or mileage-hungry intermediates
- ➖ Limited off-slope diversions
- ➖ English not universally spoken
- ➖ Busy at weekends

Little old Andermatt seems about to be overwhelmed by the construction of what amounts to a new village on the outskirts of the original, with countless luxury hotels and apartments. For the moment, at least, the appeal of the tall, steep, snowy, largely off-piste Gemsstock is undiminished, and unthreatened. How quickly the quiet, traditional village will alter remains to be seen.

THE RESORT

Andermatt gets a lot of weekend business, but at other times can seem deserted. East–west links with the Grisons and the Valais rely on car-carrying trains. The lift pass also covers the slopes of Sedrun – 20 minutes away and a popular excursion (see the Directory) – and linking trains. The small Winterhorn area has closed.

Village charm The town is quietly attractive. Charming wooden houses and handsome churches line the main street that runs from the central river bridge to the cable car.

Convenience The centre is compact, but the lifts are on opposite sides of the town; take your choice. A minibus shuttle runs half-hourly in the main season, but at the extremes of the season may run at weekends only.

Scenery The local Gemsstock peak is well defined and higher than its neighbours, with rugged steep terrain.

THE MOUNTAINS

Andermatt's local skiing is split over two unlinked mountains, both limited in extent. Most slopes are above the trees and piste marking is slack – bad news in a resort prone to white-outs.

Slopes A two-stage cable car from the edge of the village serves the open, steep, north-facing and usually empty slopes of Gemsstock. Across town is the gentler, sunny Nätschen area.

Fast lifts The Gemsstock cable car and the chair to Gutsch in the Natschen sector are the only fast lifts.

Queues The Gemsstock cable car can generate queues, even in low season.

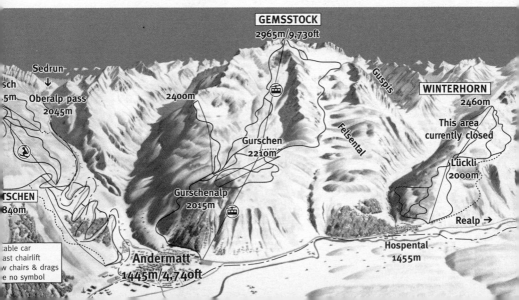

GEMSSTOCK
2965m/9,730ft
Sedrun
Oberalp pass
2045m
2400m
Guspis
WINTERHORN
2460m
This area currently closed
Felsental
Gurschen
2210m
Lückli
2000m
Gurschenalp
2015m
Realp →
Hospental
1455m
Andermatt
1445m/4,740ft
able car
ast chairlift
w chairs & drags
e no symbol

KEY FACTS

Resort	1445m
	4,740ft
Slopes	1445-2965m
	4,740-9,730ft
Lifts	20
Pistes	125km
	78 miles
Blue	22%
Red	46%
Black	32%
Snowmaking	36%

UK PACKAGES

Alpine Answers, Mountain Tracks, PowderBeds, Ski Club Freshtracks, Ski Solutions, Ski Weekend

Phone numbers
From elsewhere in Switzerland add the prefix 041; from abroad use the prefix +41 41

TOURIST OFFICE

www.andermatt.ch

Terrain parks Gemsstock has one.
Snow reliability The area has a justified reputation for reliable snow. Nätschen gets a lot of sun. Piste grooming is generally good.
Experts It is most definitely a resort for experts. The north-facing bowl beneath the top Gemsstock cable car is a glorious, long, steep slope (about 900m vertical), usually with excellent snow, down which there are countless off-piste routes, an itinerary and a piste. Outside the bowl, the Sonnenpiste is a fine, open red run curling away from the lifts to the mid-station, with more off-piste opportunities. From Gurschen to the village there is a black run, not steep but often tricky. Routes outside the bowl go down the Felsental or Guspis valleys towards Hospental, or steeply into the deserted Untertal, to the east (ending in a bit of a walk). Nätschen has black pistes, and off-piste terrain, including worthwhile itinerary routes.
Intermediates Intermediates needn't be put off Gemsstock: the Sonnenpiste can be tackled, and at mid-mountain there are some short blues and an easy but longer black run (the latter served by a tricky draglift). Nätschen's sunny mountain is well worth a visit, as are the red runs of Sedrun.
Beginners Not ideal; but the lower half of Nätschen has a long, easy blue run.
Snowboarding The cable car accesses some great freeride terrain.
Cross-country There are 28km of loops along the valley.
Mountain restaurants Inadequate. On Gemsstock, Gadäbar by the Lutersee T-bar is a quieter, simple alternative to the Gurschen hut, which has a table-service section but struggles to meet demand. You can picnic at Gurschen and at Nätschen hut.
Schools and guides The Swiss ski school, Andermatt Xperience and Bergschule Uri/Mountain Reality are the options, and Snowlimit is a specialist snowboard school.
Families There are friendly slopes at Nätschen; the Swiss school does classes. Family passes are available.

STAYING THERE

Andermatt's accommodation is mostly in cosy 2- and 3-star hotels.
Hotels River House (887 0025) is a stylish, upmarket B&B in a 250-year-old building, with eight individually designed rooms. And see 'Eating out'. Gasthaus Sternen (887 1130) is an attractive central chalet. The 3-star Sonne (887 1226), towards the Gemsstock lift, is a lovely old place.
Apartments The hotel Monopol (887 1575) has apartments.
Eating out The restaurant at the River House has been well supported (meat and fish dishes with a 'modern twist'). Café Toutoune (cafe, restaurant and lounge bar) is smart, with a Mediterranean/veggie bias. Gasthaus Sonne is a more traditional alternative.
Après-ski We like the cosy bar Alt Apothek at River House for tea and cake (live music later on). Other possibilities include the Curva at the hotel Monopol and the Spycher. The Picadilly pub and Dancing Gotthard liven up at weekends.
Off the slopes There's a toboggan run at Nätschen. The fitness centre at the hotel Drei König is open to the public. There are 20km of maintained footpaths.

SIMON MEDLEY

← The Gemsstock cable car accesses fabulous black and red pistes and off-piste routes, and not surprisingly builds queues even in January

CHAMPERY TOURIST OFFICE

Champéry

Picture-postcard village that few UK tour operators feature these days, with access to the Portes du Soleil circuit

TOP 10 RATINGS

Extent	★★★★★
Fast lifts	★
Queues	★★★★
Snow	★★
Expert	★★★
Intermediate	★★★★
Beginner	★★
Charm	★★★★
Convenience	★
Scenery	★★★★

RPI	120
lift pass	£190
ski hire	£130
lessons	£100
food & drink	£190
total	**£610**

NEWS

2011/12: At Les Crosets, a six-pack replaced the slow Grand Conche chair and the draglift of the same name. This makes another welcome speedy route to Avoriaz.

- + Charmingly rustic mountain village
- + Access to Portes du Soleil circuit
- + Quiet, relaxed – yet plenty to do off the slopes

- − Local slopes suffer from the sun
- − No runs back to the village
- − Lift system is antiquated
- − Not good for beginners

Champéry is great for intermediate skiers looking for a quiet time in a lovely place. Access to the Portes du Soleil circuit is not bad; Avoriaz is fairly easy to get to – and there may be better snow there. With exchange rates as they are, readers are not flocking here; if you do go, a report would be welcome.

THE RESORT

Champéry is on the Swiss side of the Portes du Soleil region, with fairly quick links to Avoriaz in France, and to the Lindarets valley separating Avoriaz from Châtel.

Village charm The village is friendly and relaxed, with classic old wooden chalets and a charming atmosphere.

Convenience Champéry's slopes are mainly high above the village, reached by a cable car which starts at the railway station, down a steepish hill, away from the main street. The village spreads over quite an area, but there is a free shuttle-bus.

Scenery The resort sits beneath the dramatic Dents du Midi – impressive both from the village and the slopes.

THE MOUNTAINS

Once you get up to them, the local slopes are open, friendly and relaxing.

Slopes Champéry's sunny slopes are part of the big Portes du Soleil circuit, which links resorts in Switzerland and France. There's a special chapter on the Portes du Soleil in the France section. The village cable car or a fast six-seat chairlift from Grand Paradis, a short free bus ride from Champéry, go up to the edge of the bowl of Planachaux. If snow is good, there are a couple of pistes back to Grand Paradis – one curling well away from the lift system – but no pistes back to Champéry. With a couple of lift rides you can end up at the French border.

Fast lifts A real drawback for the Swiss side of the Portes du Soleil is that there are very few fast lifts, especially above Champoussin and Morgins – where ancient draglifts and slow chairs prevail. There are plans to modernize the system but hold-ups in getting the necessary permission.

Queues If snow is poor, expect end-of-day queues for the cable car down to the village. Few other problems.

Terrain parks The Superpark is a good terrain park at Les Crosets. Its features include kickers, rails, jibs, spines, boxes and a chill-out area. There are

CHAMPERY TOURISME / PAT SHARPLES

Gentle, sunny slopes below, much tougher stuff higher up ↓

There is the occasional exception, but mainly it's chalets, chalets, chalets ... →

CHAMPERY TOURISME

KEY FACTS

Resort	1050m 3,440ft
Portes du Soleil	
Slopes	950-2275m 3,120-7,460ft
Lifts	196
Pistes	650km 404 miles
Green	13%
Blue	40%
Red	37%
Black	10%
Snowmaking	800 guns
Swiss side only	
Slopes	1050-2275m 3,440-7,460ft
Lifts	34
Pistes	100km 62 miles

other (excellent) parks in Avoriaz.

Snow reliability The snow on the north-facing French side of the link with Avoriaz is usually better than on the Swiss side, which basically faces east but includes some south-facing slopes. The Champéry area would benefit from more snowmaking.

Experts The Swiss Wall, on the Champéry side of Pas de Chavanette, these days an itinéraire, has an unjustified reputation for great steepness; but it is long and bumpy, and provides great amusement when riding the chairlift that rises over it. The other blacks from the border ridge are worthwhile, too, and there are broad off-piste slopes you can traverse to. There's also good terrain across the border at Pas de Chavanette where the slopes are less sunny and snow is often better.

Intermediates Confident intermediates have the whole Portes du Soleil at their disposal. Locally, the runs home to Grand Paradis are good when the snow conditions allow. Les Crosets is a junction of several fine runs. There are slightly tougher pistes from Mossettes and Pointe de l'Au, leisurely cruising above Champoussin, and delightful tree-lined meanders from La Foilleuse to Morgins. From Col des Portes du Soleil a long blue run goes down a quiet, wooded valley to Morgins; but after a good descent to the rustic Tovassière restaurant the run is a path dropping only 200m in 4km.

Beginners Far from ideal. The Planachaux runs, where lessons are held, are steepish and small (as well as remote from the village) and some of the local blue runs are verging on red steepness.

Snowboarding Not ideal for beginners (see above) and there are several draglifts (some quite steep). Good terrain parks in Les Crosets and Avoriaz for intermediates and experts though, and some good powder areas.

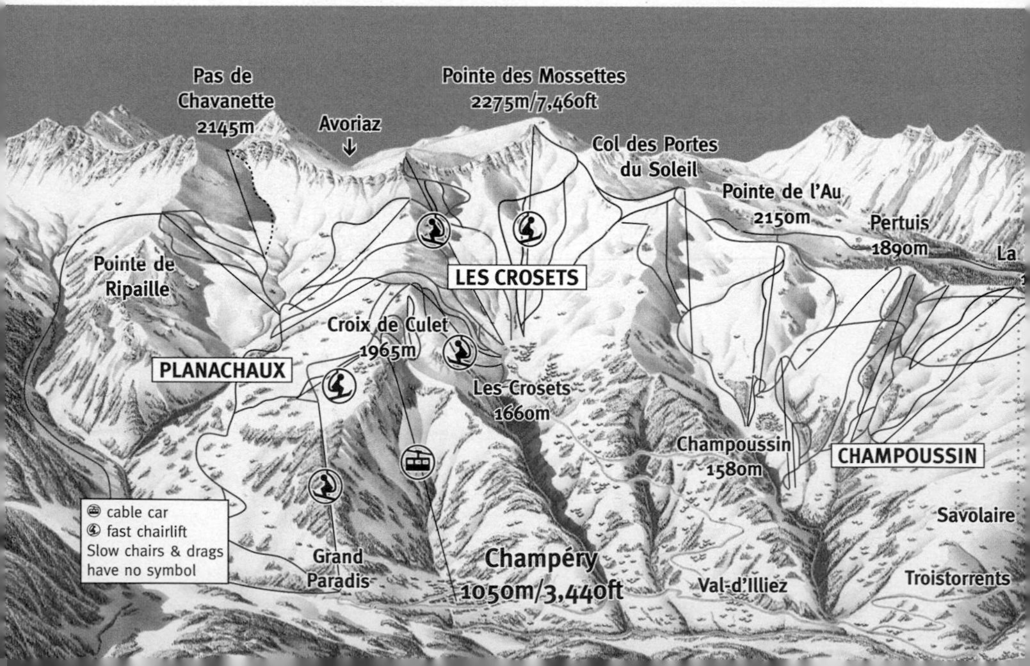

UK PACKAGES

Alpine Answers, Erna Low, Independent Ski Links, Momentum, PowderBeds, Scott Dunn, Ski Freedom, Ski Independence, Ski Weekend, White Roc
Les Crosets Mountain Lodge
Morgins Ski Morgins, Ski Rosie

Phone numbers
From elsewhere in Switzerland add the prefix 024; from abroad use the prefix +41 24

TOURIST OFFICES

Champéry
www.champery.ch
Les Crosets / Champoussin / Val-d'Illiez
www.valdilliez.ch
Morgins
www.morgins.ch

Cross-country It's advertised as 10km – not a lot – with 4km floodlit every night, but the snow is unreliable.
Mountain restaurants There are about 15 in this sector of the Portes du Soleil, between Champéry and Morgins, marked but not named on the piste map. Chez Coquoz near the Planachaux chair offers a warm welcome, excellent food and a knockout Valais wine list. The tiny Lapisa on the way to Grand Paradis is delightfully rustic – they make cheese and smoke meat on the spot.
Schools and guides We get few reports. At least the Swiss school faces healthy competition from the Freeride Co and Redcarpet Snowsport School.
Families Champéry wouldn't be high on our shortlist for a family trip, given the lack of slopes at village level.

STAYING THERE

A few UK tour operators offer packages here.
Hotels There's a handful of 3-star and 2-star hotels, and more than the usual number outside the star system. We lack recent reports, but past reporters have recommended the 3-star Beau Séjour (479 5858) and National (479 1130); and the rustic Auberge Le Paradis (479 1167).
Apartments Erna Low and Ski Independence have some smart, modern, spacious apartments with good views in The Lodge.
Eating out Mitchell's is stylish and modern, and we had a good meal there on our last visit a few years back. You can eat tapas-sized dishes in the Centre wine bar and other reader tips are the bistro in the hotel National, the Farinet and Le Pub.
Après-ski Mitchell's, with big sofas and a fireplace, is popular at teatime. There are a few bars, and the Crevasse and Farinet are nightclubs.
Off the slopes Walks are pleasant and the railway allows lots of excursions. There's ice climbing and snowshoeing. The Palladium at the bottom of the village incorporates the Swiss national ice sports centre with various other facilities including pool and tennis.

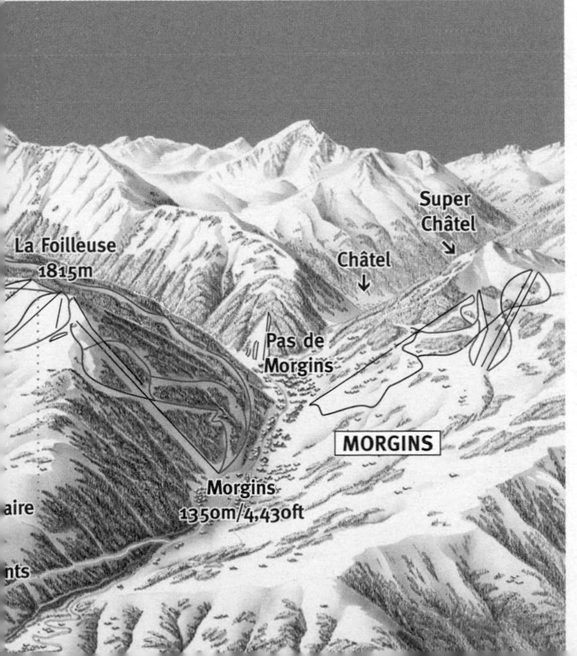

LINKED RESORT – 1660m

LES CROSETS

A good base for a quiet time and slopes on the doorstep. The 3-star Télécabine hotel (479 0300) has 'basic rooms but extremely helpful staff, and the five-course dinner is delicious'.

LINKED RESORT – 1580m

CHAMPOUSSIN

A good family choice – no through traffic, on the slopes – is the 3-star Alpadze Lou Kra (pool, gym, two restaurants – 476 8300).

LINKED RESORT – 1350m

MORGINS

Over the hill from the other resorts covered here and close to Châtel in France, Morgins is a fairly scattered, but attractive, quiet resort with a gentle nursery slope right in the village. The hotel Reine des Alpes (477 1143) is well thought of.

DOWN-VALLEY VILLAGE – 950m

VAL-D'ILLIEZ

About 4km down the valley from Champéry, and in a similar position facing the Dents du Midi, Val-d'Illiez has no lifts or slopes, but makes a viable base – there are buses and trains up to Champéry. The road up to Les Crosets and Champoussin branches off here. Down in the valley bottom is the Thermes Parc thermal spa. The hotel du Repos (477 1414) is comfortable, woody and British-run; in the centre, opposite the station, with a piano bar, a bar/bistro and a trattoria as well as a dining room.

Crans-Montana

An increasingly stylish big-town base with a fabulous panoramic view and sun-soaked slopes

TOP 10 RATINGS

Extent	***
Fast lifts	****
Queues	***
Snow	**
Expert	**
Intermediate	****
Beginner	***
Charm	**
Convenience	**
Scenery	****

RPI	135
lift pass	£220
ski hire	£145
lessons	£110
food & drink	£215
total	**£690**

NEWS

2012/13: The Chetzeron mountain restaurant plans to open smart lodging above the restaurant for December 2012.

The Momentum Ski Festival and City Ski Champs will be held here again – from 14 to 17 March 2013.

KEY FACTS

Resort	1500m 4,920ft
Slopes	1500-3000m 4,920-9,840ft
Lifts	28
Pistes	140km 87 miles
Blue	39%
Red	50%
Black	11%
Snowmaking	21%

UK PACKAGES

Alpine Answers, Carrier, Momentum, Oxford Ski Co, PowderBeds, Ski Line, Ski Safari, Ski Solutions, Skitracer, Ski Weekend
Aminona Lagrange

+ Large, varied piste area
+ Splendid setting and views
+ Excellent, gentle nursery slopes
+ Decent cross-country trails
+ Very sunny slopes, but ...

− Snow is badly affected by the sun
− Large, busy, urban resort
− For many people, life revolves around driving or buses
− Few challenges except off-piste

We love the views, the local scenery and some of the mountain restaurants and smart lodgings in Crans-Montana. It's just a shame that the place is more like a city than a rustic village and that the slopes face south – the strong sunshine that's so lovely in dark December days can spoil the snow from mid-season on.

THE RESORT

Set on a broad shelf facing south across the Rhône valley, Crans-Montana is really two towns, their centres a mile apart and their fringes merging. The resort is reached by road or by a funicular railway from Sierre. There are also places to stay at the other base stations, a mile east at Les Barzettes (aka Les Violettes, strictly the name of the hill above) and further out at Aminona. Outings to Zermatt, Saas-Fee and Verbier are possible.

Village charm Both Crans and Montana are emphatically towns rather than villages, with little traditional Alpine character and a lot of traffic. But the wooded setting softens the urban feel a bit. Crans is the more upmarket part, with fancy shops, an increasing number of 5-star hotels and an improved pedestrian-friendly centre.

Convenience The towns spread widely away from their respective gondola stations and many visitors need to use cars or the free half-hourly shuttle-bus.

Scenery The panoramic views over the Rhône valley to the peaks bordering Italy are breathtaking.

THE MOUNTAINS

There's a pleasant mix of open and wooded runs offering few challenges. Pistes are not named or numbered on the piste map and only occasionally on the ground. Weird. Virtually all the runs are red, but many are gentle and wide enough to be blue.

Slopes The slopes are spread over a broad mountainside, with lifts from four valley bases. Gondolas from Crans

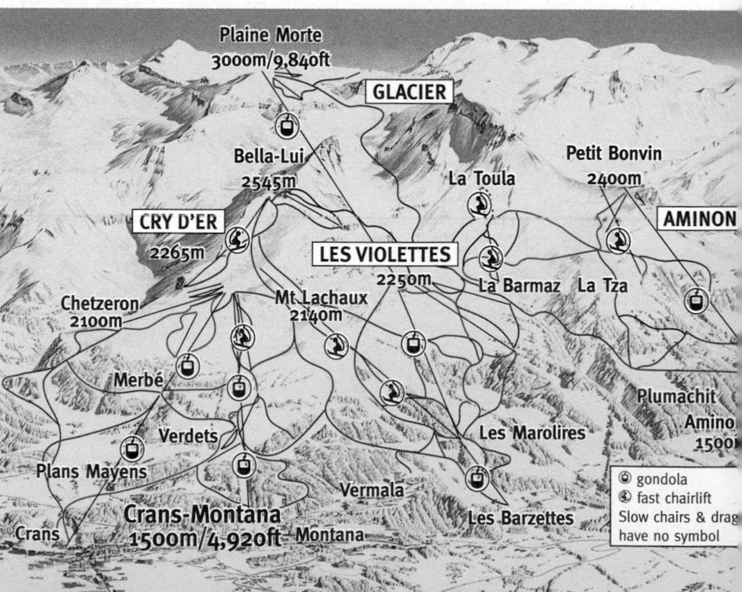

↑ The sun: Crans-Montana's south-facing aspect makes for a good suntan but it also spoils the snow much of the time
CRANS-MONTANA TOURISME

Phone numbers
From elsewhere in Switzerland add the prefix 027; from abroad use the prefix +41 27

TOURIST OFFICE
www.crans-montana.ch

and Montana meet at Cry d'Er – an open bowl descending into patchy forest. A third gondola accesses the next sector, Les Violettes. A six-pack from the mid-station here links with Cry d'Er. Above Les Violettes, a jumbo gondola goes up to the Plaine Morte glacier. The fourth sector is served by a gondola from Aminona. Some runs down to the valley are narrow paths.
Fast lifts A few slow lifts remain; the slow chair up from La Barmaz to Les Violettes is a particularly weak point.
Queues None on our recent visits.
Terrain parks The 100,000-square-metre main park, with features for all levels, plus a beginner park, half-pipe and boardercross are all at Cry d'Er.
Snow reliability The runs on the Plaine Morte glacier are very limited, and nearly all the other slopes get a lot of direct sun. There is snowmaking on the main runs but the condition of the snow depends heavily on the weather. Some runs to resort level have often been closed on our visits.
Experts There are few steep pistes and the only decent moguls are on the short slopes at La Toula. There's plenty of off-piste, particularly beneath La Toula, La Tza and Chetzeron – the best place to go in a storm. There are more adventurous routes outside the lift network – Les Faverges is a beautiful, easy valley bringing you to Aminona.
Intermediates There's a lot to do, including some notably long runs. The 12km run from Plaine Morte to Les Barzettes starts with top-of-the-world views and powder, and finishes among pretty woods. The Piste Nationale downhill course is a good fast cruise.
Beginners There are excellent nursery areas at resort level (on the golf course) and at mid-mountain but no special beginner passes.
Snowboarding Despite the resort's mature image, boarding is popular. Avalanche Pro is a specialist shop and school. There are few draglifts.
Cross-country There are 17km of trails, plus a glacier trail (limited opening).
Mountain restaurants A special section of the piste map marks 25 huts (although some are just bars). Our traditional favourite is Merbé, but we have lately fallen for the smart, cool Chetzeron – all steel, glass, wood and stone, and good food at prices no higher than elsewhere. At Violettes, the cute Cabane CAS is another favourite, serving traditional meals with great views over the valley. A local recommends Pépinet which he says is Roger Moore's favourite.
Schools and guides We have no recent reports of the Swiss schools, but past reports have been mainly positive.
Families This doesn't strike us as a natural family resort.

STAYING THERE

Hotels and apartments are plentiful. Crans Luxury Lodges (480 3508) are five nearly new slope-side chalets above Les Barzettes, combining chalet-style privacy with deep comfort and hotel service. We loved them.
Hotels There are some very swanky lodgings. We love two dinky little places – 5-star LeCrans (486 6060), way above the town, with chalet-style suites, and Relais & Châteaux Pas de l'Ours (485 9333) – chic but welcoming, on the edge of town.
Eating out There is a big variety of places, from French to Lebanese to Thai. Among the best is the Bistrot in the Pas de l'Ours hotel. Senso has been tipped by a regular visitor.
Après-ski At close of play, Dutch-run bar/restaurant Zérodix at the Crans lift base is the happening place. After that, New Haven and Monk'is (also a club) have been recommended.
Off the slopes There are swimming pools in hotels, two ice rinks, dog sledding, tubing, tobogganing, snowshoeing, 63km of walks, a cinema, casino and model train museum. Sierre and Sion are close.

Davos

A grey urban sprawl at the centre of a glorious Alpine playground (for skaters and langlaufers as well as downhillers)

RATINGS

The mountains

Extent	****
Fast lifts	****
Queues	***
Terrain p'ks	****
Snow	****
Expert	****
Intermediate	*****
Beginner	**
Boarder	*****
X-country	*****
Restaurants	***
Schools	***
Families	**

The resort

Charm	**
Convenience	**
Scenery	****
Eating out	***
Après-ski	***
Off-slope	*****

RPI	130
lift pass	£220
ski hire	£120
lessons	£120
food & drink	£210
total	**£670**

- + Very extensive slopes
- + Some superb, long, and mostly easy pistes away from the lifts, with trains to bring you back to base
- + Lots of accessible off-piste terrain, with several marked itineraries
- + Good cross-country trails
- + Plenty to do off the slopes

- − Davos is a huge, busy place with dreary block-style buildings, lacking ski-resort atmosphere
- − Five separate areas of slopes
- − Lots of T-bars on outlying mountains
- − The only piste back to town from the main Parsenn area is a black

One of your editors learned to ski in Davos, so it has a special place in our affections. Many return visits have confirmed the appeal of its slopes, which are both distinctive and extensive, and have revealed its considerable off-piste potential. But the town/city (it could never be called a village) does not get any easier to like. Davos may be the more convenient base for access to most of the mountains it shares with Klosters, but Klosters has the welcoming, intimate feel of a ski resort, and Davos does not.

THE RESORT

Davos is set in a high, broad, flat-bottomed valley, with its lifts and slopes either side. Arguably it was the very first place in the Alps to develop its slopes. The railway up the Parsenn was one of the first built for skiers (in 1931), and the first draglift was built on the Bolgen nursery slopes in 1934. You can reach the resort by train, but the trip from Zürich airport involves two changes. The Davos Express coach transfer service is a recommended alternative.

Davos shares its slopes with the famously royal resort of Klosters, which gets its own chapter. Trips are possible by car or rail to St Moritz (via the Vereina rail tunnel) and Arosa, and by road to Laax-Flims and Lenzerheide.

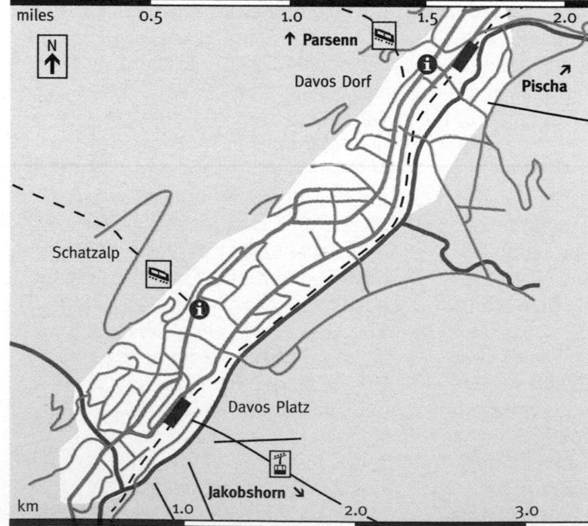

VILLAGE CHARM **

City in the mountains

The resort is more like a city than a village, and plagued by traffic. It started life as a health resort and many of its massive luxury hotels were built as sanatoriums. Sadly, that's just what they look like and ski resort ambience is notably lacking. It is now well known for its conference and sporting facilities too.

CONVENIENCE **

Take the train

The resort has two main centres, Dorf and Platz, about 2km apart. Transport is good, with an 'excellent' bus service around the town as well as the railway linking Dorf and Platz to Klosters and other villages. It's a good idea to arm yourself with timetables. Easiest access to the main Parsenn area is from Dorf, via the funicular railway; Platz is better placed for Jakobshorn, the sports facilities, smarter shopping and the evening action.

SCENERY ****

Pick your viewpoint

It's an area of grand, wide views across the broad, deep, wooded valleys from one sector of the slopes to another, and to high peaks beyond.

NEWS

2012/13: More snowmaking is planned for Parsenn and Rinerhorn.
2011/12: On Jakobshorn, a fast quad replaced the Brämabüel draglift up from Jschalp. A new room-only designer hotel – Fiftyone – opened.

KEY FACTS

Resort	1550m 5,090ft
Slopes	810-2845m 2,660-9,330ft
Lifts	53
Pistes	320km 199 miles
Blue	23%
Red	42%
Black	35%
Snowmaking	40%

THE MOUNTAINS

Most of the pistes are above the treeline – there are few in the woods and most are genuine blacks. Piste classification is questionable; many blue and red runs are of similar pitch. The piste map generally looks clear, but tries to cover too much ground in a small space – at some points it is simply misleading and distances are unclear. Signposting is generally fine, but reporters have complained that the long runs to Küblis and Serneus are poorly marked.

EXTENT OF THE SLOPES ★★★★☆

Vast and varied

You could hit a different mountain around Davos nearly every day for a week. The out-of-town areas tend to be much quieter than the ones directly accessible from the resort.

The Parsennbahn funicular from Davos Dorf takes you to mid-mountain, where a choice of a six-pack or a further, newly renovated funicular take you on up to the major lift junction of Weissfluhjoch, at one end of the **Parsenn**. The only run back to town is a sunny black that can have poor snow (the alternative runs to Klosters are shadier). At the other end of the wide, open Parsenn bowl is Gotschnagrat, reached by cable car from the centre of Klosters. There are exceptionally long intermediate runs down to Klosters and other villages (see feature panel later in chapter).

Across the valley, **Jakobshorn** is reached by cable car or chairlift from Davos Platz; this is popular with snowboarders but good for skiers too. **Rinerhorn** and **Pischa** are reached by bus or (in the case of Rinerhorn) train.

Pischa is now a designated freeride area, with half the runs left ungroomed and just three main lifts. Several of the runs here are now marked as unpatrolled as well as ungroomed – a very unusual arrangement for runs going down beside a lift, and one we don't like. But reporters tell us that these runs are sometimes groomed, and then have blue markers, not yellow.

In 2010/11 the little **Schatzalp-Strela** area above Platz – which had been closed for several years – partly reopened; however, it is not covered by the main lift pass.

Beyond the main part of Klosters, a gondola goes up from Klosters Dorf to the sunny, scenic **Madrisa** area.

FAST LIFTS ★★★★☆

Key ones are fine but ...

The main lifts from the valley are mostly gondolas or cable cars. Higher up, Jakobshorn is very well served for fast chairs and Parsenn reasonably so (hence the 4-star rating). But the upper lifts on Madrisa, Rinerhorn and Pischa are entirely T-bars except for one slow double chair on Madrisa.

QUEUES ★★★☆☆

Few problems

Davos has improved its key lifts and generates relatively few complaints. But there can still be lengthy queues at the cable car out of Klosters and the Totalp chair on the mountain at Parsenn at peak times and weekends. Crowded pistes have raised concern – in the Parsenn sector around Weissfluhjoch especially. In contrast, the Jakobshorn is said to be quiet.

DESTINATION DAVOS KLOSTERS / SWISS-IMAGE.CH / CHRISTOF SONDEREGGER

We guess the place looks OK if you like your roofs flat; lovely setting, anyway ↓

TERRAIN PARKS ★★★★☆
Entry level to Olympic standard
Two of the mountains have parks, but Jakobshorn is the focus of the action with the big Jatz Park. At 2300m, with snowmaking to be sure, it's open from mid-November to the very end of the season, and looked after by a small dedicated team. Three lines (including kickers from 2m to 18m, rainbow rail, down rails and a spine feature with wall ride and tyre bonk) provide something for everyone, although it's clear the better features are geared towards higher end riders. Jakobshorn is also home to a super-pipe – one of Europe's largest; it is floodlit four evenings a week. For smaller crowds, head to Pischa – next to the Mitteltäli lift you'll find an array of rails and kickers. There are boardercross courses on Parsenn, Pischa and Madrisa. There is also a mini-park for children on Rinerhorn.

SNOW RELIABILITY ★★★★☆
Good, but not the best
Davos is high by Swiss standards. Its mountains go respectably high, too. Not many of the slopes face directly south, but Pischa does suffer from excessive sun. Snow reliability is generally good higher up. Snow-guns cover a few of the upper runs on the Parsenn, several on the Jakobshorn, and the home runs from the Parsenn to Davos Dorf and Klosters. Piste grooming is generally good; but the super-long runs to the valley can become a bit neglected.

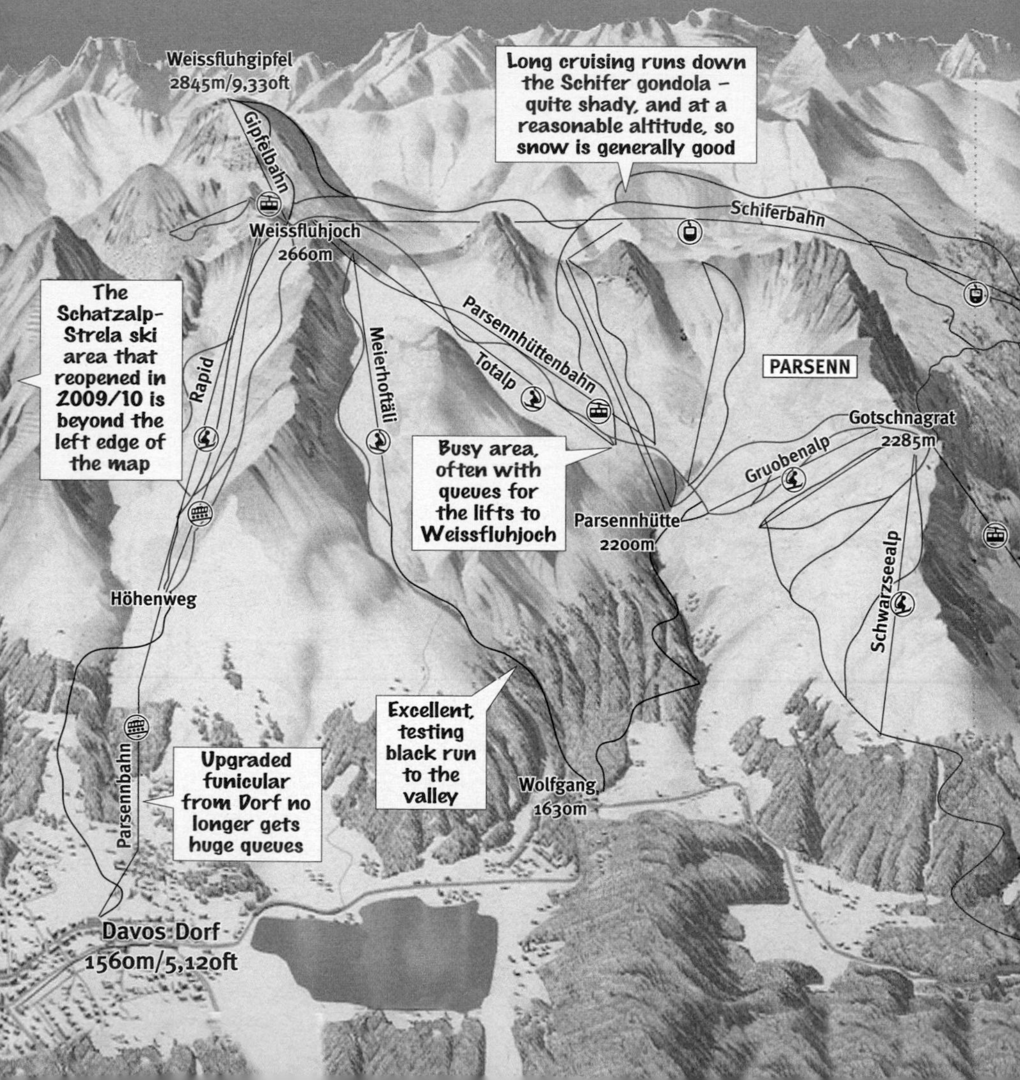

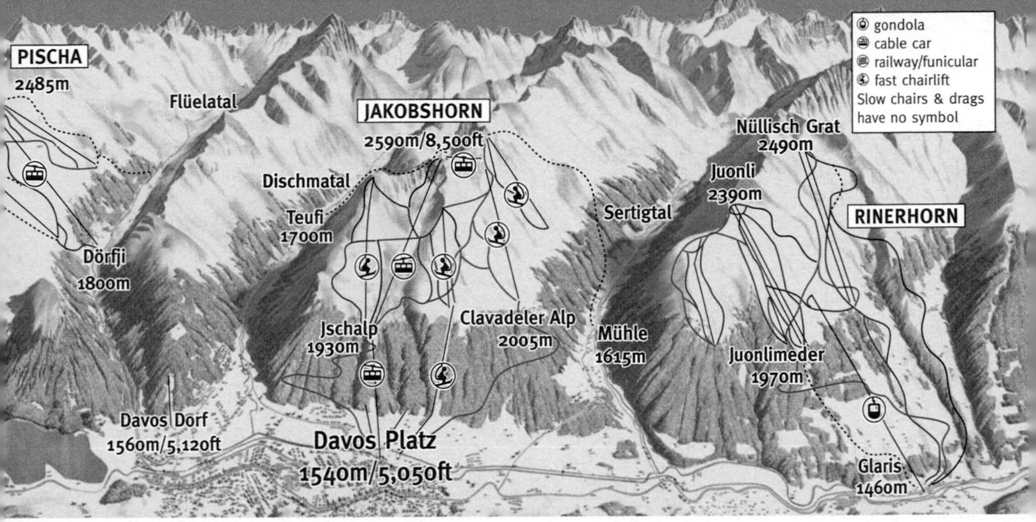

- gondola
- cable car
- railway/funicular
- fast chairlift

Slow chairs & drags have no symbol

PISCHA
2485m

Flüelatal

JAKOBSHORN
2590m/8,500ft

Dischmatal

Teufi
1700m

Dörfji
1800m

Sertigtal

Nüllisch Grat
2490m

Juonli
2390m

RINERHORN

Jschalp
1930m

Clavadeler Alp
2005m

Mühle
1615m

Juonlimeder
1970m

Davos Dorf
1560m/5,120ft

Davos Platz
1540m/5,050ft

Glaris
1460m

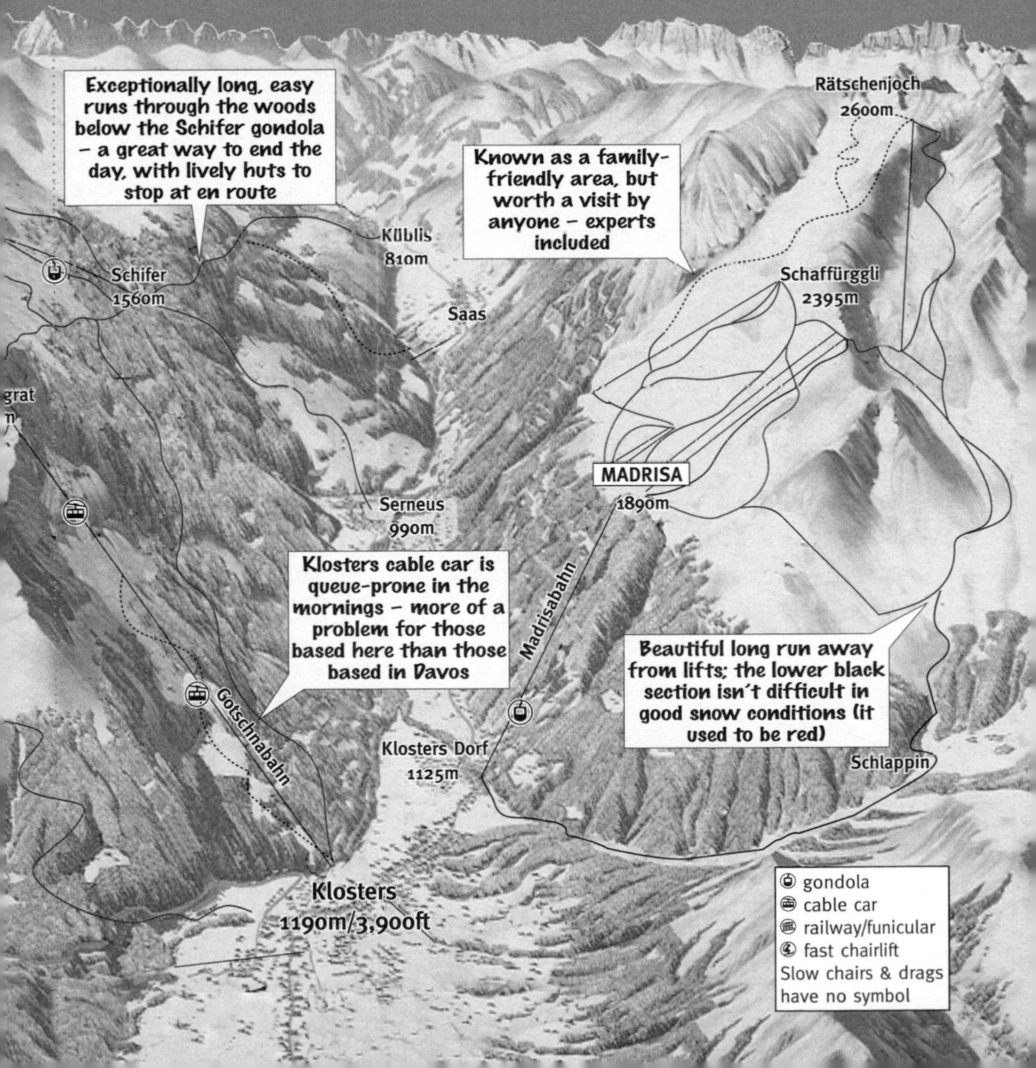

Exceptionally long, easy runs through the woods below the Schifer gondola – a great way to end the day, with lively huts to stop at en route

Known as a family-friendly area, but worth a visit by anyone – experts included

Rätschenjoch
2600m

Küblis
810m

Schifer
1560m

Saas

Schaffürggli
2395m

MADRISA
1890m

Serneus
990m

Klosters cable car is queue-prone in the mornings – more of a problem for those based here than those based in Davos

Madrisabahn

Gotschnabahn

Beautiful long run away from lifts; the lower black section isn't difficult in good snow conditions (it used to be red)

Klosters Dorf
1125m

Schlappin

Klosters
1190m/3,900ft

- gondola
- cable car
- railway/funicular
- fast chairlift

Slow chairs & drags have no symbol

↑ The perfect way to enjoy a very tempting-looking strudel

DAVID ASHMORE

LIFT PASSES

Davos/Klosters

Prices in SF

Age	1-day	6-day
under 13	28	127
13-17	48	223
18 plus	69	318

Free under 6

Senior if 65+ (women 64+), 10% reduction on regional passes of 3+ days

Beginner no deals

Notes Does not cover Schatzalp

Alternative passes Individual areas; pedestrian single tickets

FOR EXPERTS ★★★★

Plenty to do, given snow

The appeal of this area for experts depends to a considerable degree on the snow conditions. Although there are challenges to be found at altitude, most of the rewarding runs descend through the woods to valley level, and are not reliable for snow. The black pistes include some distinctive, satisfying descents. The Meierhoftälli run to Wolfgang is a favourite – quite steep and narrow. The run from Parsennhütte to Wolfgang is less challenging; it probably owes its black status due to one short tricky section.

There are also some off-piste itineraries – runs that are supposedly marked but not patrolled. At one time, these runs were a key attraction for adventurous skiers not wanting to pay for guidance, but over the decade to 2005 no fewer than 10 of them disappeared from the map, including the infamous Gotschnawang run down the top stage of the Klosters cable car and its less fearsome neighbours, Drostobel and Chalbersäss. Many of these abandoned runs have had piste status at some time in the past, and are not difficult to follow if you know what you are doing. Two of the most satisfying itineraries that remain are long ones from the top of Jakobshorn, both with decent restaurants at the end. The start of the run to Mühle is not obvious, which has led more than one reporter into difficulty; once found, the run is reportedly nowhere steeper than a tough red. The run to Teufi is more often closed: it goes first down a steep 200m gully, but thereafter is easier.

There is also excellent 'proper' off-piste terrain, for which guidance is more clearly needed. Reporters have enjoyed heading away from the pistes above Serneus and Küblis. The long descent from Madrisa to St Antönien, north of Küblis, is popular, not least for the views along the way. And there are some short tours to be done. Arosa can be reached with a bit of help from a train or taxi, and from there you can go on to Lenzerheide, but you'll need a train back. From Madrisa you can make easy circular tours to Gargellen in Austria.

FOR INTERMEDIATES ★★★★★

A splendid variety of runs

For intermediates this is a great area. There are good cruising runs on all five mountains, so you would never get bored in a week. This variety of different slopes, taken together with the wonderful long runs to the Klosters valley, makes it a compelling area with a unique character.

As well as the epic runs described in the feature panel there is a beautiful away-from-the-lifts run to the valley from the top of Madrisa back to Klosters Dorf via the Schlappin valley (it's an easy black – classified red until the mid-1990s).

The Jakobshorn has some genuine challenges, notably by the Brämabüel drag. Rinerhorn is more of a cruise. Pischa is the gentlest of the Davos mountains but now branded as freeride territory; in good snow it should be a decent spot for first attempts at skiing ungroomed stuff.

FOR BEGINNERS ★★

Platz is the more convenient

There are no free lifts but each sector offers day or half-day passes. The Bolgen nursery slope beneath the Jakobshorn is adequately spacious and gentle, and a bearable walk from the centre of Platz. Dorf-based beginners face more of a trek out to Bünda though – unless staying at the hotel of the same name. There are easy runs to progress to, spread around all the sectors. The Parsenn sector probably has the edge, with long, easy intermediate runs in the main Parsenn bowl, as well as in the valleys down from Weissfluhjoch. And there is a dedicated slow skiing piste alongside the Parsennbahn too – though a reporter says that people still speed through it.

ACTIVITIES

Indoor Swimming pools, solarium, climbing wall, tennis, squash, badminton, wellness centre, sauna, massage, ice rink, horse-riding school, golf driving range, cinema, casino, galleries, museums, libraries

Outdoor Over 111km of cleared paths, ice climbing, ice rinks, curling, snowshoeing, tobogganing, hang-gliding, paragliding

GETTING THERE

Air Zürich 165km/ 105 miles (2hr30); Friedrichshafen 150km/95 miles (2hr30)

Rail Stations in Davos Dorf and Platz

FOR BOARDERS ★★★★★

Epic

Davos is a Mecca for keen snowboarders. And Jakobshorn is the favoured mountain for many of them, with its top-notch park and super-pipe. It's also a great area to learn on. Rinerhorn has trees galore and pistes like roller coaster rides. Pischa is the freeride hill with huge marked off-piste areas. Parsenn has a boardercross, night riding and is host to international freeride competitions on the face beneath the Weissfluhgipfel, but watch out for the flats on the runs down to the Schifer gondola. And if you have a family in tow, the kids can stay out of trouble in the beginners' park at Rinerhorn. Synergy Snowsports is a specialist school and Top Secret Davos is a specialist shop and school. There are several cheap hotels geared to boarders, notably the Bolgenhof near the Jakobshorn, the Snowboardhotel Bolgenschanze and the Snowboarders Palace.

FOR CROSS-COUNTRY ★★★★★

Long, scenic valley trails

Davos is a popular spot for langlauf, and it's not difficult to see why. It has a total of 123km trails, classic and skating, running along the flat main valley and reaching well up into the side valleys of Sertigtal, Dischmatal and Flüelatal that lead away south-east. There is a cross-country ski centre on the outskirts of the town. Trails are free.

MOUNTAIN RESTAURANTS ★★★

Stay high or go low

Most high-altitude restaurants are dreary self-service affairs – but there are good table-service exceptions. Overall, reader reports are mixed.

Our favourite, Bruhin's, has changed hands and is called Weissfluhgipfel – a 2011 reporter says the cooking is still 'at the same excellent level'. The prices remain high, too. The Weissflujoch is 'friendly' but 'crowded', while the Gruobenalp at Gotschnagrat is 'welcoming, with perfect sausage dishes and strudel', says a repeat visitor. Above it, the Gotschnagrat is 'friendly, with decent mountain fare'. The Totalp bar is recommended 'for a marginally cheaper meal'. There are compelling places lower down in the Parsenn sector. Readers enjoy the Höhenweg at the Parsennbahn mid-station for 'excellent pizzas' and 'quick service, even when busy'; there's also table-service. There are several rustic 'schwendis' in the woods on the way down to the Klosters valley: the cosy Chesetta is one that's been recommended in the past. You may find darkness falls – some sell wax torches to light your way.

On Jakobshorn the Jatzhütte is unusual, with changing decor such as mock palm trees, parrots and pirates – and serves 'delicious soups'. Châlet Güggel is also tipped: 'excellent'; 'rustic charm and efficient service'.

On Pischa, the Mäderbeiz at Flüelamäder is an 'extremely pleasant'

THE PARSENN'S SUPER-RUNS

The runs from Weissfluhjoch that head north, on the back of the mountain, make this area special for many visitors. The pistes that go down to Schifer and then on to Küblis and Serneus, and the one that curls around to Klosters, are a fabulous way to end the day, given good conditions. The run to Saas used to be a red piste but is now marked as an ungroomed and unpatrolled route.

The runs are classified red. They are not steep, but the latter parts can be challenging because of the snow conditions – they get heavily skied, they are not reliably groomed, and by the end you are at low altitudes. Signposting is not always good, either. What marks these runs out is their sheer length (10-12km) and the resulting sensation of travel they offer – plus a choice of huts in the woods at Schifer and lower down on the way to Klosters. You can descend the 1100m vertical to Schifer and take the gondola back up. Once past there, you're committed to finishing the descent.

If you are based in Davos, the return journey is by train (included in the lift pass).

ALAN SHEPHERD

SCHOOLS

Swiss Davos
t 416 2454

Top Secret
t 413 7374

Pat. Skilehrer Rageth
t 416 3901

Snow & You
t 079 636 7030

Synergy Snowsports
t UK 0141 416 3525

Classes
(Swiss prices)
6 4hr days SF375

Private lessons
Half day SF220 for 1-2 persons

CHILDCARE

Kinderland Pischa
t (0)79 660 3168
Age from 3

TOPSI kindergarten
t 413 4043
Age from 30mnth

Babysitter list
At tourist office

Ski school
From age 4 (6 days SF375)

UK PACKAGES

Alpine Answers, Alpine Weekends, Carrier, Crystal, Crystal Finest, Flexiski, Headwater, Inghams, Luxury Chalet Collection, Momentum, Neilson, Oxford Ski Co, PowderBeds, Ski Bespoke, Ski Club Freshtracks, Ski Safari, Ski Solutions, Skitracer, Ski Weekend, Switzerland Travel Centre, White Roc

Phone numbers
From elsewhere in Switzerland add the prefix 081; from abroad use the prefix +41 81

TOURIST OFFICE

www.davos.ch

and spacious woody hut. And on Rinerhorn, try the Hubelhütte.

There are two picnic rooms: at the Weissfluhjoch on Parsenn and at the Jatzmeder on Rinerhorn.

SCHOOLS AND GUIDES ★★★★★

Decent choice

There are several options but we lack recent reports – more welcome. Top Secret offers small groups (maximum of eight). Guiding outfit Swissfreeride specializes in all-inclusive off-piste weeks. Synergy Snowsports provides enthusiastic guiding and instruction by Brits.

FOR FAMILIES ★★★★★

Not ideal

There are plenty of amusements, but Davos is a rather spread-out place in which to handle a family. The kids' ski schools operate a Disney-themed slope at Bolgen. Kinderland Pischa offers childcare, and there is a snow garden on Rinerhorn. But Madrisa Land at Klosters is a more comprehensive facility.

STAYING THERE

Although most beds are in apartments, hotels dominate the UK market.

Hotels A dozen 4-stars and about 30 3-stars form the core. The tourist office runs a central booking service.

*******Flüela** (410 1717) The more atmospheric of the 5-star hotels, in central Dorf. Pool.

******National** (415 1010) Five minutes from centre of Davos Platz. 'Good service and five-course dinners.'

****** Sheraton Waldhuus** (417 9333) Convenient for langlaufers. Quiet, modern, tasteful. Pool and spa facility. 'Bucolic setting, ideal for families.'

******Sunstar Park** (413 1414) At far end of Davos Platz. Pool, sauna, spa.

******Waldhotel** (415 1515) In Platz. 'Looked after really well; beautiful pool,' says a 2012 visitor. Undergoing a facelift over the summer of 2012.

*****Davoserhof** (417 6777) Our favourite. Small, old, beautifully furnished, excellent food; in Platz.

*****Ochsen** (417 6777) Good-value; near the train station in Platz.

*****Panorama** (413 2373) In central Platz. Pool, sauna.

****Alte Post** (417 6777) Traditional place in central Platz.

Fiftyone Designer hotel. Room only; internet bookings only.

EATING OUT ★★★★★

Wide choice, mostly in hotels

In a town this size, you need to know where to go. For a start, get the tourist office's pocket guidebook. The more ambitious restaurants are mostly in hotels. There are two good Chinese places, in the hotels Europe and Grischa. Go to the Carretta in Platz for pizza and pasta, and the small and cosy Gentiana for fondues and gamey dishes (with an upstairs stübli). Excursions out of town are popular. The Höhenweg (at the mid-station of the funicular) is open some evenings, but you pay to ride the funicular.

APRES-SKI ★★★★★

Generally quiet

At tea time, mega-calories are consumed at the Weber and the Schneider. The Scala (hotel Europe) has a popular outside terrace. Nightlife is generally quiet. The rustic little Chämi bar is lively and popular with locals. The smart Ex Bar attracts a mixed age group. Nightclubs tend to be sophisticated, expensive and lacking atmosphere during the week. The pick are the Cabanna, Cava Davos and Rotliechtli. Bolgenschanze and Bolgen-Plaza attract lots of boarders. There's a casino.

OFF THE SLOPES ★★★★★

Great, apart from the buildings

Looks aside, Davos has lots to offer the non-skier/rider. The towny resort has shops and other diversions, and transport along the valley and up on to the slopes is good – though the best of the mountain restaurants are well out of range.

The sports facilities are excellent. Europe's biggest natural ice rink is supplemented by artificial rinks, indoor and outdoor. Spectator events include speed skating as well as ice hockey. The Eau-là-là leisure centre incorporates pools and wellness facilities. There are lots of walks on the slopes, around the lake and along the valleys (special map available). There's tobogganing on Rinerhorn and Schatzalp (both floodlit), but the best in the area is the longer run on Madrisa. A 2011 reporter recommends the 'extraordinarily scenic, cheap and easy' day trips by train to St Moritz, Scuol (for the spa) and Preda-Bergün for the 6km toboggan run. Another reader recommends the local museums and galleries.

Engelberg

A high, distinctive mountain with some classic off-piste runs, above a solid valley town dominated by an ancient monastery

TOP 10 RATINGS

Extent	**
Fast lifts	***
Queues	**
Snow	***
Expert	****
Intermediate	***
Beginner	**
Charm	**
Convenience	*
Scenery	****

RPI	110
lift pass	£190
ski hire	£95
lessons	£115
food & drink	£170
total	**£570**

NEWS

2011/12: A tubing/ activity slope opened at Trübsee. Two snowshoe trails and a children's area opened at Brunni.

KEY FACTS

Resort	1050m 3,440ft
Slopes	1050-3030m 3,440-9,940ft
Lifts	24
Pistes	82km 51 miles
Blue	33%
Red	57%
Black	10%
Snowmaking	70%

- ➕ Easily reached from Zürich airport
- ➕ Reliable snow on the high, shady slopes of Titlis
- ➕ Some classic off-piste runs
- ➖ Fragmented slopes, some poor links
- ➖ Ski-bus needed from most lodgings
- ➖ Limited piste area, mostly above the trees

Quick access and abundant lodgings make Engelberg great for short breaks. And Titlis is a compelling mountain, particularly for experts. When you're after a quick weekend fix of powder, the towny nature of the resort is not a problem.

THE RESORT

The resort was named after the 12th-century Benedictine monastery (Engelberg means the mountain of the angel) that dominates the town as you look down from the lifts. It was very popular with Brits in the early 1900s.

Village charm The place is more of a town than a village. Its grand Victorian hotels, some recently renovated, have been joined by chalet-style buildings and concrete blocks. There is one traffic-free cobbled street.

Convenience It's a free shuttle-bus, sometimes over-busy, or longish walks to the lifts from most hotels.

Scenery There's lots of visual drama from the high, glacial slopes.

THE MOUNTAINS

The mainly treeless, shady slopes of Titlis rise almost 2000m above the town. The separate slopes of Brunni are sunnier and gently wooded.

Slopes The pistes in the main area are limited and fragmented by the glaciers and rugged terrain.

There are two main sectors: Titlis-Stand and Jochpass. A gondola goes up to Trübsee, whence two successive cable cars go up to Stand and then Klein Titlis – the latter rotating 360° on the way (worth the trip for the view alone). From Trübsee, you can also head for Jochpass via a two-way chairlift to Alpstübli. At Jochpass the top is served by a fast six-pack, with another couple of chairs lower down. The much smaller Brunni area is reached by a cable car from the other side of town.

Fast lifts High-capacity cable cars and gondolas provide the main access.

Queues Big queues form for the gondola out of town at weekends and in peak season (half-hour waits are reported). Pistes can get uncomfortably busy too.

Terrain parks The park is at Jochpass, with jumps, kickers and rails.

Snow reliability The high, north-facing slopes of Titlis and Jochpass keep their snow well and have a long season. The resort says 70% of the resort is snow-sure, including glacial runs and

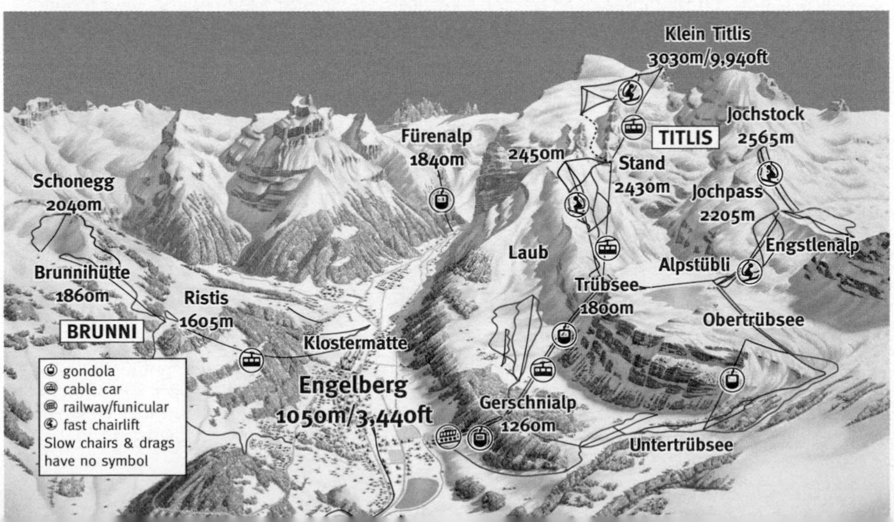

UK PACKAGES

Alpine Answers, Chalet Espen, Crystal, Inntravel, Momentum, Mountain Tracks, PowderBeds, Ski Club Freshtracks, Ski Independence, Ski Safari, Ski Solutions, Ski Weekend, Ski-Monterosa, Skitracer, STC, White Roc

Phone numbers
From elsewhere in Switzerland add the prefix 041; from abroad use the prefix +41 41

TOURIST OFFICE

www.engelberg.ch

ENGELBERG-TITLIS / CHRISTIAN PERRET

The monastery is a prominent feature of the towny resort ↓

those with snowmaking.

Experts There is lots of superb off-piste. The classic Laub run is 1000m vertical down a hugely wide, consistently steep face with great views of town. We enjoyed even more the less popular 2000m vertical Galtiberg run from the top, which ends among streams and trees, with a bus back to town. The off-piste at the top of Titlis looks great but is not without danger. There are few black pistes; the itinerary from Titlis to Stand is steep and often mogulled.

Intermediates Most runs are steep reds, and there are few easy cruises. The reds at the top naturally offer good snow. The Jochpass area is often quieter than Titlis, with enjoyable blue and red runs, including lovely long ones down to the valley station.

Beginners There's a good isolated beginner area at Gerschnialp, served by draglifts, and smaller areas at Trübsee and Untertrübsee. You have to use lifts to and from these slopes (limited passes are available); and there are few longer easy runs to progress to – all far from ideal.

Snowboarding The beginner area is served by draglifts, so it's not ideal. But there is excellent freeriding if you hire a guide. Beware of the flat start to the runs down from Jochpass.

Cross-country There are 40km in total with valley trails and loops at altitude.

Mountain restaurants An impressive choice. Our favourite, and that of reporters, is Skihütte Stand, a woody table-service place beside the cable car to Titlis: 'good main courses, friendly service'. Jochpass is another recommendation. Try Untertrübsee for 'perfect' rösti with bacon and eggs. The Trübsee hotel has table-service ('food and service excellent, quiet even on a busy day') and self-service.

There are picnic rooms at Stand, Toporama at Titlis and at Klostermatte in the Brunni area.

Schools and guides There is a choice of schools: Swiss ski and snowboard, Prime, Boardlocal and Active Snow Team. The local guiding outfit is Outventure.

Families Globi's Winterland at Brunni is best for families, with play areas and lifts. Special passes are available. The Swiss ski school takes children from age three, and the kindergarten from two. Some hotels offer childcare, and the tourist office has details of babysitters.

STAYING THERE

There are lots of hotels, B&Bs and apartments.

Hotels The 3-star Edelweiss (639 7878) is 'excellent for families with young children'. The Schweizerhof (637 1105) is centrally located with 'good food and service, spacious rooms'. The Ski Lodge (637 3500) is popular and has 'friendly staff' (avoid rooms above the bar, say reporters), and The Alpenclub (637 1243) is a central guest house.

Eating out There is a huge variety of restaurants – more than 50 – from traditional Swiss to Tex-Mex (at the Yucatan In the Hotel Bellevue-Terminus), Chinese (Moonrise), and Indian (Chandra at the Terrace hotel). We had splendid chicken/veal dishes at the hotel Central; large portions, very well presented. The Ski Lodge is 'one of the best' (gourmet duck, salmon).

Après-ski The liveliest venues are the Yucatan (main square) and the Chalet (bottom of the gondola); both have popular happy hours. But a recent visitor found the Yucatan 'quiet mid-week, with slow service'. The Ski Lodge bar is 'pleasant'. For dancing, try Eden or the Spindle nightclub.

Off the slopes The 12th-century monastery and its cheese-making factory and shop are worth a visit. And there's a fair collection of shops. It's worth taking a trip up the cable cars for the views and a tour of the ice grotto. There are many walking and snowshoeing trails, an igloo bar at Trübsee (you can stay the night there), tubing, sledging and a good sports centre. Up the valley, a gondola goes up to Fürenalp, where there is walking, tobogganing and snowshoeing. Lucerne is a possible train trip.

GRINDELWALD TOURIST OFFICE

Grindelwald

Traditional mountain village set beneath the towering Eiger and with an old cog railway still the main way up to the slopes

RATINGS

The mountains	
Extent	***
Fast lifts	****
Queues	**
Terrain p'ks	***
Snow	**
Expert	**
Intermediate	****
Beginner	***
Boarder	***
X-country	**
Restaurants	***
Schools	***
Families	**
The resort	
Charm	****
Convenience	**
Scenery	*****
Eating out	***
Après-ski	***
Off-slope	****

RPI	125
lift pass	£220
ski hire	£105
lessons	£105
food & drink	£200
total	**£630**

NEWS

2012/13: The Wixi chair will be replaced by a six-pack.

2011/12: Snowmaking was increased. The First Flyer zip wire was included in the lift pass.

- + Dramatically set, beneath the north face of the Eiger
- + Lots of long intermediate runs
- + Pleasant old village with long mountaineering history
- + Fair amount to do off the slopes, including splendid walks

- − Slow, queue-prone trains and gondolas to access the main slopes
- − Few challenging pistes for experts
- − A fair trek to visit Mürren
- − Natural snow-cover unreliable (but substantial snowmaking now)
- − Village gets little midwinter sun

For stunning views from the resort and the slopes, there are few places to rival Grindelwald. The village is nowhere near as special as Mürren or Wengen, just over the hill, but it does provide direct access to Grindelwald's own First slopes.

The main access lifts are appalling, taking half an hour to ride even if you don't have to queue (for the gondola) or wait (for the train). Grindelwald regulars accept all this as part of the scene. We're not Grindelwald regulars.

THE RESORT

Grindelwald is a long village set along a road that runs across a hillside facing the towering north wall of the Eiger, which means that the resort gets very little sun in January. Its main slopes are shared with Wengen; and there is a separate area of sunny slopes on First. Getting to the tougher, higher slopes of Mürren on snow and lifts is a lengthy business (around three hours to the top). Trips to other resorts are not very easy.

VILLAGE CHARM ****
Not quite in the Wengen league

The central buildings are mainly in traditional chalet style, in keeping with its long mountaineering history. And the station and cog railway add to the olde-worlde charm. The village can feel very jolly at times (eg during the snow carving festival in January, when huge sculptures are created). Although the road through goes nowhere, traffic on it can be intrusive.

CONVENIENCE **
Not a strong point

The most convenient places to stay are in the centre near the main station or at Grund, departure point of the main access lifts and arrival point of the main home piste, about 80m vertical lower. If you stay in the centre, you can also take the train up, but you need to catch it back up from Grund on the way home too. Staying near the centre means the gondola up the First area is a walkable distance. At the foot of First are nursery slopes, ski school and kindergarten. Buses link the lift stations – 'very efficient and regular, even when the roads are covered in snow', says a 2012 visitor.

SCENERY *****
Unrivalled

The mountains in these parts are legendary among climbers – from all over the slopes there are superb views, not only of the Eiger but also of the Wetterhorn and other peaks.

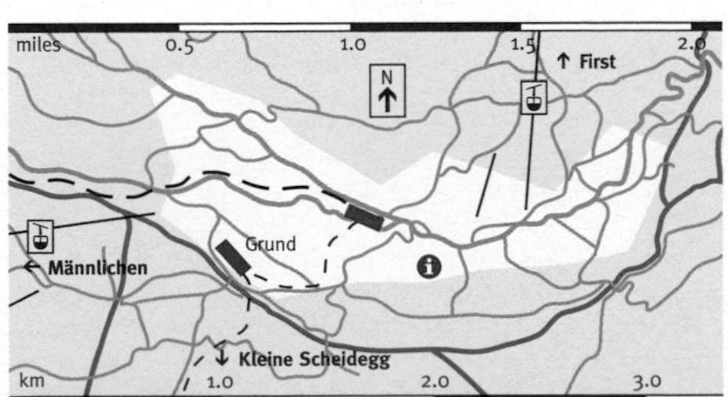

THE MOUNTAINS

The major area of slopes is shared with Wengen and offers a mix of a few wooded runs and much more extensive open slopes higher up. The smaller First area is mainly open. There are several areas designated as wildlife reserves, where you may well spot chamois.

Piste marking and piste map are poor; reporters find the Männlichen slopes, in particular, confusing.

KEY FACTS

Resort	1035m 3,400ft
Jungfrau region	
Slopes	945-2970m 3,100-9,740ft
Lifts	44
Pistes	213km 132 miles
Blue	33%
Red	49%
Black	18%
Snowmaking	40%
First-Männlichen-Kleine-Scheidegg	
Slopes	945-2500m 3,100-8,200ft
Lifts	32
Pistes	161km 100 miles
Snowmaking	65%

GETTING THERE

Air Zürich 160km/100 miles (2hr45); Bern 70km/45 miles (1hr30); Basel 165km/105 miles (2hr30)

Rail Station in resort

EXTENT OF THE SLOPES ★★★☆☆
Broad and mainly gentle

The area shared with Wengen spreads broadly beneath the Eiger. From Grund, near the western end of town, you can get to **Männlichen** by an appallingly slow two-stage gondola or to **Kleine Scheidegg** by an equally slow cog railway (with some trains starting in the centre of town). The slopes of the separate south-facing **First** area are reached by a long, slow gondola starting a walk or short bus ride east of the centre.

FAST LIFTS ★★★★☆
Better high up

Getting up into the main area from the village is seriously slow, but new fast chairlifts continue to improve the area higher up – most recently, the six-pack to Eigergletscher and the Wixi six-pack (due for 2012/13).

QUEUES ★★☆☆☆
Can be dreadful at the bottom

These days visitors generally find few problems once they are on the mountain, but the train and the Männlichen gondola at Grund can be crowded at peak periods. Queues for the gondola can be very bad in high season, especially on Saturdays – this is the obvious entry point for residents of Bern attracted by the special family pass deals on Saturdays. And the gondola goes very slowly, too. The increased capacity on the First gondola should have eased congestion there.

TERRAIN PARKS ★★★☆☆
First things first

The White Elements Pro Park on First next to the Bärgelegg lift offers rails, boxes, kickers and jumps for different abilities, plus a separate 100m super-pipe. In 2011/12 there was also a warm-up park on Oberjoch.

SNOW RELIABILITY ★★☆☆☆
Improved snowmaking helps

Grindelwald's low altitude means that natural snow is often in short supply or in poor condition. First is a bit higher than the Männlichen area, and may have better snow in midwinter; but it is sunny, and less snow-sure as spring approaches. A lot of snowmaking has been added recently too, and the resort claims that more than 65% of its slopes are now covered. When we were there in 2009, it had not snowed for a few weeks and a warm Föhn wind had melted a lot of snow, but most slopes were in good condition. Piste maintenance gets mixed reviews.

FOR EXPERTS ★★☆☆☆
Few on-piste challenges

The area is quite limited for experts, but there is some fine off-piste if the snow is good. Heli-trips are organized. We and readers have enjoyed the splendid Bort Direct black run on First. This turns into a downhill route between Bort and town and is quite tough, especially when the snow has suffered from the sun.

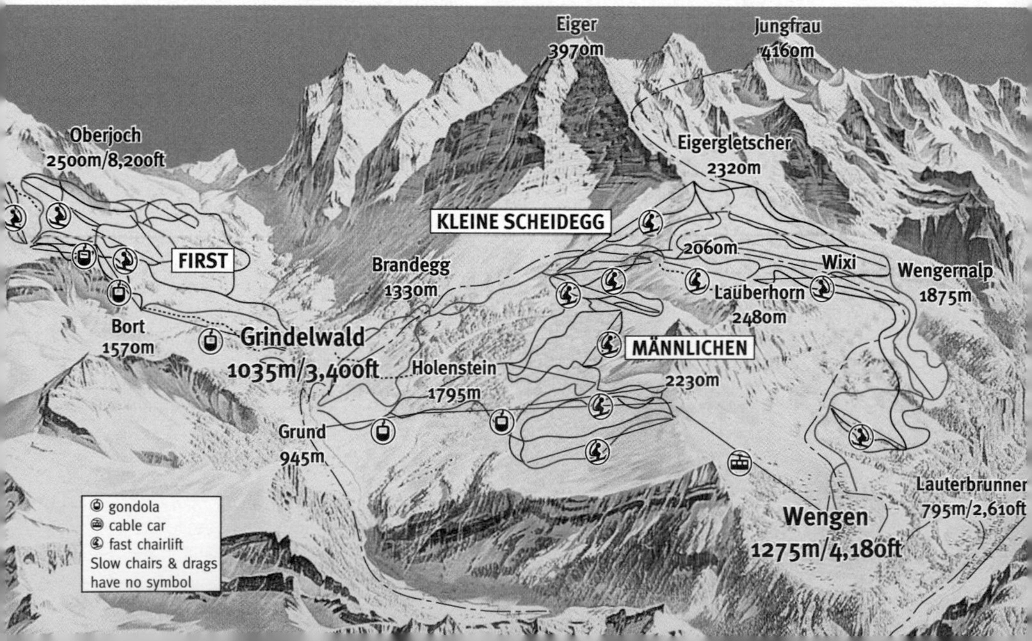

The major junction of Kleine Scheidegg, with one of the Alps' most spectacular backdrops →

JUNGFRAU REGION MARKETING AG

LIFT PASSES

Jungfrau

Prices in SF

Age	1-day	6-day
under 16	31	157
16 to 19	50	251
20 to 61	62	314
62 plus	56	283

Free under 6 (if with parent)

Beginner points card

Notes Covers trains between villages and Grindelwald ski-bus; day pass is First-Kleine Scheidegg-Männlichen area only; 6-day-plus pass allows one day in Zermatt

Alternative passes Grindelwald and Wengen only; Mürren only; non-skier pass

SCHOOLS

Swiss
t 854 1290

Buri Sport
t 853 3353

Swiss Kleine Scheidegg
t (0)79 311 1474

Felix Ski Paradies
t 853 1288

Privat-ski.ch
t 853 0473

Altitude
t 853 0040

Reeves
t (0)79 843 5679

Classes (Swiss prices)
5 (4hr) days SF415

Private lessons
From SF85 for 1hr for 1 or 2 persons

FOR INTERMEDIATES ★★★★

Ideal intermediate terrain

In good snow, First makes a splendid intermediate playground, though the general lack of trees makes the area less friendly than the larger Kleine Scheidegg-Männlichen area. Nearly all the runs from Kleine Scheidegg are long blues or gentle reds – great cruising terrain. On the Männlichen there's a choice of gentle runs down to the mid-station of the gondola – and in good snow, down to the bottom. For tougher pistes, head for the top of the Lauberhorn lift and the runs to Kleine Scheidegg, or to Wixi (following the World Cup downhill course). The north-facing run from Eigergletscher served by the Eigernordwand six-pack often has the best snow late in the season.

FOR BEGINNERS ★★★

Depends where you go

The Bodmi nursery slope at the bottom of First is scenic but not particularly convenient. Snow quality can also suffer from the sun and the low altitude, and fast skiers and tobogganers racing through are off-putting. Kleine Scheidegg has a better, higher beginner area and splendid long runs to progress to, served by the railway. There are no free lifts, but a points card is available.

FOR BOARDERS ★★★

Best for intermediates

Intermediates will enjoy the area most, while experts will hanker for Mürren's steep, off-piste slopes. First is the main boarders' mountain, not only because of the terrain park and big pipe but also because of the open freeride terrain near the top. There are still a few drags dotted around.

FOR CROSS-COUNTRY ★★

Okay but shady

There are 15km of prepared tracks. Almost all of this is on the valley floor, so it's shady in midwinter and may have poor snow later on.

MOUNTAIN RESTAURANTS ★★★

Wide choice

There are lots, all clearly marked on the piste map. Read the Wengen chapter for additional options. Brandegg, on the railway, is regularly recommended ('still very good', 'legendary doughnuts'). Other reader tips include: the Genepi on First; and Berghaus Aspen just above Grund ('best-ever rösti'). On First we enjoyed Bort, where the old building houses a restaurant built in contemporary style. One reader loved the tiny Alpweg, not for the food but for a welcoming, local atmosphere – 'where the locals break out into song and yodelling'.

There are three picnic rooms: at the middle-station Schreckfeld on First; at the Männlichen top station; and at the Brandegg.

SCHOOLS AND GUIDES ★★★

Good reports

A 2012 visitor says of the Swiss school: 'I've always had good experiences with this school and its various instructors at all levels.' The Privat school offers off-piste guiding.

FOR FAMILIES ★★

Lacks convenience but ...

It's not a convenient place for families (see 'For beginners'). Snowli Children's Club based at Bodmi (First) takes kids from three years old and operates a bus from the village. Snowli Club Sunshine is a nursery and play area at the top of Männlichen.

CHILDCARE

Snowli Club Sunshine
t 854 1280
From 6mnth

Snowli Club Bodmi
t 854 1280
From age 3

Felix Ski Paradies
t 853 1288
From age 3

Ski schools
From age 3 or 4 (5 half days SF193)

ACTIVITIES

Indoor Sports centre (pool, sauna, steam, fitness), ice rink, curling, museum

Outdoor 80km of cleared paths, ice rink, tobogganing, snowshoeing, ice climbing

UK PACKAGES

Alpine Answers, Crystal, Elegant Resorts, Inghams, Momentum, Neilson, Powder Byrne, PowderBeds, Ski Club Freshtracks, Skitracer, Switzerland Travel Centre, Thomson, White Roc

Phone numbers
From elsewhere in Switzerland add 033. From abroad use the prefix +41 33.

TOURIST OFFICE

www.grindelwald.com

STAYING THERE

The hotels UK tour operators offer are mainly at the upper end of the market.

Hotels There's a 5-star, seven 4-stars and plenty of more modest places.

*****Grand Regina** (854 8600) Big and imposing; right next to the station. Pool and spa.

****Belvedere** (888 9999) Over 100 years old, comfortable, family-run, friendly, close to the station. Pool, steam, sauna, hot tub.

****Schweizerhof** (854 5858) Close to the station. Pool.

***Derby** (854 5461) Modern; next to station.

***Eiger** (854 3131) 'Spacious rooms, superb friendly service, great wellness facilities.'

***Gletschergarten** (853 1721) Out past First gondola. 'Friendly, good English spoken, four-course meals.'

***Hirschen** (854 8484) Family-run; by nursery slopes. Good food.

***Wetterhorn** (853 1218) Cosy, simple chalet way beyond the village, with great views of the glacier.

Apartments The Eiger hotel has apartments.

At altitude Berghaus Bort (853 1762), at the First gondola mid-station, has proper rooms and dormitories.

EATING OUT ★★★

Hotel based

There's a wide choice of good hotel restaurants such as the Hirschen, Challistübli in the Kreuz & Post, Schmitte in the Schweizerhof, and the Alte Post. Hotel Spinne has the candlelit Rôtisserie, and Onkel Tom's Hütte is an Italian. A 2011 reporter recommends the Steinbock ('good food, reasonable prices, pizza cooked in wood oven, busiest place in town').

APRES-SKI ★★★

Getting livelier

Tipirama (a wigwam at Kleine Scheidegg) is a fun place immediately after skiing (but 'becoming a bit tatty'), sometimes with DJs and live bands. There are various (mainly open air) bars to stop in on the way down to Grund. The liveliest are the Rancher (on run 22), attracting a young crowd; Holzerbar (on run 21) and the Aspen hotel (just below). In town, the terrace of the C&M Café und Mehr is good for coffee and cake. Later on, there's live music in several bars and hotels, such as the Challibar (hotel Kreuz & Post); but it isn't a place for bopping until dawn. The Espresso bar in the Spinne hotel seems to be the liveliest and the renovated Gepsi Bar in the hotel is 'a continual favourite'. Later on, people head for the Mescalero (in the Spinne) and Plaza (in the Sunstar) clubs.

OFF THE SLOPES ★★★★

Plenty to do, easy to get around

There are many cleared paths with magnificent views and a special (but pricey) pedestrian lift pass. Many of the mountain huts are accessible to pedestrians. A trip to Jungfraujoch is spectacular (read the feature panel), and train trips are easy to Interlaken and Bern. Tobogganing is big here; there are over 50km of runs, including what is claimed to be the world's longest (15km); but it starts a 2hr30 walk from the top of the First gondola. First also has the First Flyer – a zip-wire affair – free if you have a ski pass. There's ice hockey and curling to watch, an indoor rope park and an excellent sports centre with pool. Scenic flights around the spectacular peaks from Männlichen are popular – read the Wengen chapter.

THE JOURNEY TO THE TOP OF EUROPE

From Kleine Scheidegg you can take a train through the Eiger to the highest railway station in Europe – Jungfraujoch at 3450m. The journey is a bit tedious – you're in a tunnel except when you stop to look out at magnificent views from two galleries carved into the sheer north face of the Eiger. At the top is a big restaurant complex, an 'ice palace' carved out of the glacier and fabulous views of the Aletsch glacier (a UNESCO World Heritage Site). The cost in 2011/12 was SF58 with a Jungfrau lift pass for three days or more.

JUNGFRAU REGION MARKETING AG

Klosters

Ski the extensive slopes of Davos from a traditional village base – with Davos traffic happily banished to a bypass some years ago

TOP 10 RATINGS

Extent	****
Fast lifts	****
Queues	**
Snow	****
Expert	****
Intermediate	*****
Beginner	***
Charm	****
Convenience	**
Scenery	****

RPI	125
lift pass	£220
ski hire	£95
lessons	£115
food & drink	£210
total	**£640**

NEWS

2011/12: On Jakobshorn, a fast quad replaced the Brämabüel draglift up from Jschalp.

- + Extensive slopes shared with Davos
- + Some lovely long intermediate runs
- + Lots of accessible off-piste terrain
- + Some cute mountain restaurants
- + Pleasant traditional village, these days bypassed by the valley traffic

- − The slopes are spread over six widely separated areas
- − Preponderance of T-bars is a problem for some visitors
- − Queue-prone cable car
- − May be too quiet for some visitors

In a word association game, 'Klosters' might trigger 'Prince of Wales'. The resort has even named its queue-prone cable car after him. Don't be put off: Klosters is not particularly exclusive, and makes an attractive alternative to towny Davos, with which it shares its slopes.

THE RESORT

Klosters is a sizeable village with a relaxed Alpine atmosphere.

Village charm Klosters Platz is the main focus – a collection of upmarket, traditional-style hotels around the railway station. Traffic for Davos and the Vereina rail tunnel takes a bypass – an improvement still much appreciated by old hands like us.

Convenience The cable car up the wooded slopes of Gotschna starts in the heart of the Platz. The village spreads along the valley road, fading into the countryside; then you come to the even quieter village of Klosters Dorf, and the gondola to Madrisa. Local train and bus services are good.

Scenery The contrast between steeply wooded valleys and high, craggy peaks is impressive.

THE MOUNTAINS

Most of the runs are on open slopes above steeper woodland.

Slopes A cable car from the railway station in Platz takes you to the Gotschnagrat end of the Parsenn area shared with Davos. These slopes are dealt with in the Davos chapter. A gondola from Dorf takes you up to the scenic Madrisa area, which we deal with here. There's also a little slope at Selfranga (floodlit some evenings), a suburb of Platz.

Fast lifts Apart from the gondola, Madrisa is poorly served.

Queues Queues for the Gotschna cable car can be a problem at weekends and peak times, but visitors report that they found no queues elsewhere.

Terrain parks Madrisa has a boardercross course.

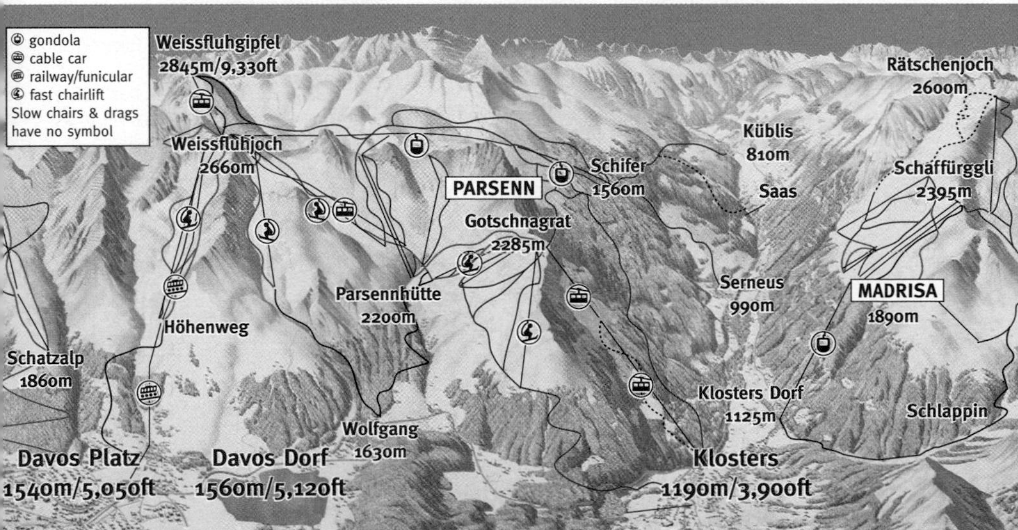

↑ Madrisa has something for everybody – and the off-piste doesn't get tracked out quickly

DESTINATION DAVOS KLOSTERS

KEY FACTS

Resort	1190m 3,900ft
Slopes	810-2845m 2,660-9,330ft
Lifts	53
Pistes	320km 199 miles
Blue	23%
Red	42%
Black	35%
Snowmaking	40%

UK PACKAGES

Alpine Answers, Carrier, Crystal Finest, Flexiski, Independent Ski Links, Inghams, Luxury Chalet Collection, Momentum, Neilson, Oxford Ski Co, PowderBeds, Powder Byrne, PT Ski, Pure Powder, Ski Bespoke, Ski Club Freshtracks, Ski Expectations, Ski Independence, Ski Safari, Ski Solutions, Skitracer, Ski Weekend, Snow Finders, STC, Supertravel, Switzerland Travel Centre, White Roc

Phone numbers
From elsewhere in Switzerland add 081; from abroad use the prefix +41 81

TOURIST OFFICE

www.klosters.ch

Snow reliability It's usually good higher up. The home runs are quite low, but now have snowmaking, and piste grooming in general remains 'excellent', says a 2012 visitor.

Experts The lift-served off-piste possibilities are the main appeal, on Madrisa as elsewhere in the region – and on 'family-friendly' Madrisa it doesn't get skied out so quickly.

Intermediates Madrisa is not huge, but it is all excellent intermediate terrain. The black run to the valley is not difficult unless conditions make it so.

Beginners There is a slope between Dorf and Platz, plus Selfranga; but Madrisa's higher slopes are more appealing. Be aware that Madrisa closes before the area as a whole. No special lift-pass deals.

Snowboarding Local slopes are good, but more boarders stay in Davos.

Cross-country There are 35km of free trails and lots more up at Davos; a Nordic ski school offers lessons.

Mountain restaurants For the Parsenn read the Davos chapter. On Madrisa the woody Erika at Schlappin, halfway down the black run to the valley, offers 'excellent atmosphere and food'.

Schools and guides There is a choice. Both Swiss and Saas are well regarded for good, English-speaking instructors: 'helpful, perceptive and encouraging' says a 2012 visitor of Saas. Adventure Skiing has been praised for private guiding: 'the guides knew the area well and were safety conscious'.

Families Madrisa Land adventure park has lots to offer children, and access is free to kids under six years old. The kindergarten there takes children from birth to six years. There is also an indoor playroom and the Saaseralp restaurant has a special play area. The ski schools offer classes to children from the age of three.

STAYING THERE

Hotels For most people, central Platz is the best location. There's the smart Chesa Grischuna (422 2222), and in 2009 we stayed at the comfortable and welcoming 3-star Rustico (410 2288) – see 'Eating out'. The readers' favourite is the 4-star Alpina (410 2424) – again recommended this year for 'good food and location'. Other possibilities are the woody old Wynegg (422 1340), a perennial British favourite, and the 4-star Silvretta Park Hotel (423 3435). In Dorf the Sunstar Albeina (423 2100) has a 'lovely location, is very comfortable'.

Apartments Apartments are available through local agencies.

Eating out Good restaurants abound, but there are few cheap and cheerful places. Top of the range is the Walserhof, with a Michelin star ('outstanding'). We enjoyed Asian fusion at the Rustico hotel (the owner's wife is Asian). Other possibilities: Casanna at Platz, Chesa Grischuna (varied menu and good wines), Al Berto and Fellini (pizza). And the dear old Wynegg.

Après-ski Gaudy's umbrella bar at the foot of the slopes is 'a welcome place for a drink in lively surroundings'. In the village, the Chesa Grischuna has a pianist. The bars at the Alpina and at the Wynegg are popular too. The Casa Antica is a small disco.

Off the slopes Klosters is an attractive base for walking (there's a special map available) and cross-country skiing. Tobogganing is popular – there is an exceptional 8.5km run from Madrisa to Saas. There is an ice rink, and some hotel pools are open. A new gramophone and radio museum opened in 2012. Read the Davos chapter for ideas for train outings.

SWISS-IMAGE / MOUNTAIN MARKETING AG

Laax

Contrasting villages beneath high, wide, sunny slopes – well known to Swiss weekenders, and becoming known more widely

TOP 10 RATINGS

Extent	★★★★
Fast lifts	★★★★★
Queues	★★★★
Snow	★★★
Expert	★★★
Intermediate	★★★★★
Beginner	★★★★
Charm	★★★
Convenience	★★★
Scenery	★★★

RPI	125
lift pass	£230
ski hire	£95
lessons	£125
food & drink	£180
total	**£630**

NEWS

2012/13: Two six-packs are planned. One will start from Lavadinas and replace an old double that started a bit lower down at Alp Ruschein. The other will go from Treis Palas to Crap Masegn. Both will be served by some new runs too.

2011/12: A six-pack replaced two draglifts from Alp Dado to the ridge above Crap Sogn Gion. It serves new blue runs and a new freestyle area.

- ➕ Extensive, varied slopes ideal for intermediates, shared with Flims
- ➕ Generally efficient lift system, but with some long ride times
- ➕ One of Europe's best terrain parks

- ➖ Sunny orientation can spoil snow
- ➖ Bus rides or long walks from some lodgings to the lifts
- ➖ Most convenient lodgings are in 'villages' we find difficult to like

Laax and neighbouring Flims share a ski area that is, in terms of piste km, one of Switzerland's biggest. It used to be marketed as Flims (and still is in the summer) but now likes to be known as Laax in the winter – maybe because it's trying to change its image to appeal to the youth, snowboard and freestyle markets as well as its traditional well-heeled family clientele. It has invested heavily in terrain parks, half-pipes, indoor freestyle facilities and organizing high-profile events such as the Brits Snow and Music Festival. Most of our reporters like the skiing but not the slope-side resorts.

THE RESORT

Laax is a resort of parts. Laax Dorf is the original rustic village; just outside it is a much newer big, busy lift base/hotel/parking complex, now known as Laax, of which the recently completed Rocksresort development is a part. The slopes spread across to other lift bases at Flims Dorf and Falera.

Village charm Laax Dorf is pleasantly traditional, with quiet suburbs set around a lake. Laax is modern and more youth-oriented, and is 'all grey rock with flat roofs and lacks any alpine charm', as a 2012 reporter put it. Flims Dorf is traditional but unremarkable, spread along the road through it (though a bypass now takes the through-traffic). Flims Waldhaus is a more appealing leafy suburb with upscale secluded hotels, most of which run their own mini-buses to and from the slopes. Falera, once a quiet hamlet, has been much expanded in traditional style.

Convenience It depends where you stay. The smart hotels in Waldhaus run courtesy buses and there are 'quick and efficient' free ski-buses.

Scenery There are grand panoramic views to the peaks on the Italian border from the upper slopes.

WENDY-JANE KING

One of our favourite runs starts from the top of the glacier and goes down a deserted valley to Lavadinas – where there'll be a new six-pack ➔

KEY FACTS

Resort	1100m 3,610ft
Altitude	1100-3020m 3,610-9,910ft
Lifts	29
Pistes	220km 137 miles
Blue	29%
Red	32%
Black	39%
Snowmaking	16%

THE MOUNTAINS

The slopes are mostly open but there are also some quite long woodland runs. The piste map shows unexplained 'freeride runs' (dotted on our map); we hear they are avalanche-protected, but not all are patrolled. It also marks a run from La Siala all the way down to Flims as an 'insider tip' – a run which a 2012 reporter found 'superb'. A regular visitor complains of poor lift/run status info at the base and sparse info about lift closing times. Many of the black runs could really be classified red.

Slopes There are long gondolas into the slopes from both Flims Dorf and Laax (plus a cable car of exceptional length from Laax). Above mid-mountain, there is a complex web of lifts and runs. The glacier is limited; but it accesses a superb long run to Lavadinas.

Fast lifts The system is impressive with most lifts being fast chairs, gondolas and cable cars. Two new six-packs for 2012/13 move Laax firmly into our ***** category.

Queues There may be queues for the village lifts at peak times and for the glacier drags. The new six-pack at Lavadinas should cut queues there. High winds can close the upper lifts and put pressure on the lower ones.

Terrain parks Laax is one of the top resorts in Europe for freestylers and has four parks in the Crap Sogn Gion area, catering for every standard from beginner to pro-rider, where many high-profile competitions are held (including the British freestyle championships). Between them, they have 56 obstacles, 14 kickers, an airbag and two pipes (super- and mini-) plus an 'excellent' freestyle slope to Curnius. The glacier has an early season park, too. An indoor Freestyle Academy at the base in Laax offers tuition.

Snow reliability Upper runs are fairly snow-sure. The lower ones can suffer from sun, even early in the season, and some can close (the runs from Cassons and the glacier are also prone to closure); key ones have snowmaking but more is needed.

Experts The black pistes present few challenges, but the freeride runs add a lot of excellent terrain – timing your descents can be crucial, though, to avoid rock-hard moguls. There is a huge amount of good off-piste terrain, notably from La Siala and Cassons.

Intermediates A superb area. Reporters are often surprised by the extent, length and variety of the slopes. The bowl below La Siala is huge and gentle. For the more confident, there are plenty of reds and some easy

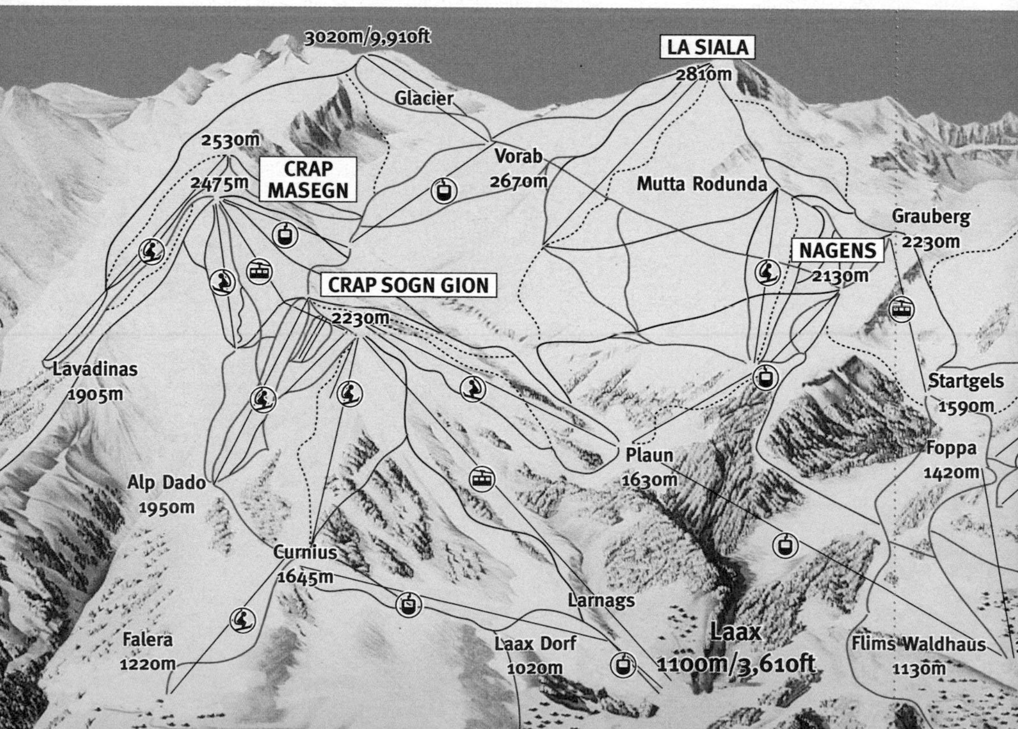

UK PACKAGES

Alpine Answers, Crystal, Crystal Finest, Erna Low, Momentum, PowderBeds, Powder Byrne, Ski Club Freshtracks, Ski Expectations, Ski Safari, Ski Weekend, Skitracer, Snow Finders, Switzerland Travel Centre, Zenith

Flims Alpine Answers, Crystal, Crystal Finest, Independent Ski Links, Momentum, PowderBeds, Powder Byrne, Ski Solutions, Ski Weekend, Skitracer, Switzerland Travel Centre, White Roc

Phone numbers

From elsewhere in Switzerland add the prefix 081; from abroad use the prefix +41 81

TOURIST OFFICE

Flims, Laax and Falera

www.laax.com

blacks. The sheltered Grauberg valley is a good area for long and fast runs. The long black run from the glacier is one of our favourites and is steep only at the top. The Downhill piste from Crap Sogn Gion is also excellent. Some of the freeride runs are great for trying off-piste, but some are steep.

Beginners There are beginner areas at village level (which can suffer from the sun) and at Crap Sogn Gion and good easy runs to progress to. There were various beginner lift passes last season.

Snowboarding Hugely popular. Apart from the top terrain parks, there's good freeriding. Many linking pistes have flat/uphill stretches though – plan carefully.

Cross-country There are 55km of trails.

Mountain restaurants The piste map describes the main ones – helpfully identifying the more ambitious places. In this category are the two we hear most about – Startgels (aka Alpenrose) for its views, fine grills and Italian specials, and Tegia Larnags, a 'charming' farmhouse with typically Swiss dishes. Tegia Curnius is a popular self-service ('excellent rösti'). Also tipped: Tegia Miez ('simple, rustic, excellent meats'), Foppa ('excellent schnitzel and ravioli') – both table-service – and Nagens (self-service but 'fantastic pasta').

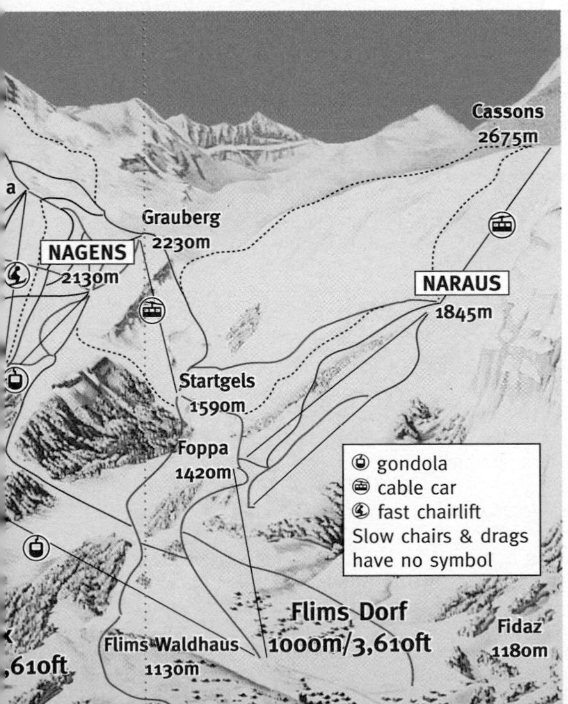

You can eat a picnic inside at Cafe NoName (Crap Sogn Gion) on the lower floor only and on the terrace there (great views of the terrain park) and at Vorab.

Schools and guides The school is run by the lift company, USA-style. We've had glowing reports of children's instruction, and a 2012 reporter says they kept 'an eye on things very effectively' after his grandson had a few problems. Another reporter had 'excellent private instruction with an extremely friendly instructor with excellent English'.

Families There are 'Wonderlands' at all three bases.

STAYING THERE

Hotels At Laax the 'design hotel' Signina (927 9000) at Rocksresort has 'excellent staff, good breakfasts, pool, wonderful indoor tennis courts'. The 4-star Laaxerhof (920 8200) is almost ski-out/in and has good-sized rooms and its stubli has been praised. Laax Dorf offers the charming little Posta Veglia (921 4466).

In Flims Dorf the cheap and cheerful Arena (911 2400) – with 'cool rooms, friendly and helpful staff, good restaurant and the best bar in town' – suits boys' trips (see 'Après-ski').

In Flims Waldhaus the Cresta (911 3535) has 'excellent food, service and top spa facilities'. The Adula (928 2828) is similarly praised by a regular visitor.

Apartments The tourist office has a long list of available apartments.

Eating out In Laax, Rocksresort places include Nooba ('excellent Asian food, friendly staff'), and the smart Grandis (fine wines and BBQ specialities). In Laax Dorf the Posta Veglia has a lovely old stube, with a plainer room behind. In Flims, a regular visitor recommends the two à la carte restaurants of the hotel Adula.

Après-ski There are busy bars at the lift bases at close of play. Later on, clubs at the hotel Arena and the Riders Palace at Laax throb until late.

Off the slopes There's a big sports centre on the edge of Flims, with ice rink and a pool, and 100km of 'really excellent' marked walks. Shopping is limited. Outings to historic Chur are easy.

SNOWPIX.COM / CHRIS GILL

Mürren

The dinky, car-free mountain village where the British invented downhill ski racing; stupendous views from one epic run

RATINGS

The mountains	
Extent	*
Fast lifts	*****
Queues	***
Terrain p'ks	**
Snow	***
Expert	***
Intermediate	***
Beginner	***
Boarder	**
X-country	*
Restaurants	**
Schools	***
Families	***
The resort	
Charm	*****
Convenience	***
Scenery	*****
Eating out	**
Après-ski	**
Off-slope	***

RPI	125
lift pass	£220
ski hire	£120
lessons	£95
food & drink	£200
total	**£635**

NEWS

2012/13: The sports centre is being renovated and a wellness centre added.

2011/12: The Birg mountain restaurant was revamped.

- \+ Tiny, charming, traditional village, with 'traffic-free' snowy paths
- \+ Stupendous scenery, best enjoyed descending from the Schilthorn
- \+ Good sports centre
- \+ Good snow high up, even when the rest of the region is suffering

- − Extent of local pistes very limited, no matter what your level of expertise
- − Lower slopes can be in poor condition
- − Quiet, limited nightlife

Mürren is one of our favourite resorts. There may be other mountain villages that are equally pretty, but none of them enjoys views like those from Mürren across the deep valley to the rock faces and glaciers of the Eiger, Mönch and Jungfrau: simply breathtaking. Then there's the Schilthorn run – 1300m vertical with an unrivalled combination of varied terrain and glorious views.

But our visits are normally one-day affairs; those staying for a week are likely to want to explore the extensive intermediate slopes of Wengen and Grindelwald, across the valley. And that takes time.

It was in Mürren that the British more or less invented modern skiing. Sir Arnold Lunn organized the first ever slalom race here in 1922. Some 12 years earlier his father, Sir Henry, had persuaded the locals to open the railway in winter so that he could bring the first winter package tour here. Sir Arnold's son Peter was a regular visitor for 95 years, until his death in November 2011.

THE RESORT

Mürren is one of a trio of resorts set amid the fabulous scenery of the Jungfrau group. It has an amazing position, set on a shelf high above the valley floor, across from Wengen, and can be reached only by cable car from Stechelberg or from Lauterbrunnen (via Grütschalp, where you change to a train). To get to Wengen, you go down to Lauterbrunnen by lift or piste, and catch the cog railway up. You can then ski to Grindelwald, but getting to the First area on the far side of Grindelwald is a long trek.

VILLAGE CHARM *****
Picturesque and peaceful

You can't fail to be struck by Mürren's beauty and tranquillity. Paths and narrow lanes weave between little wooden chalets and a handful of bigger hotel buildings – all normally blanketed by snow.

Mürren's traffic-free status is being somewhat eroded; there are now a few delivery vehicles. But it still isn't plagued by electric carts and taxis in the way that many other traditional 'traffic-free' resorts are. Even Wengen seems busy by comparison.

CONVENIENCE ***
Small enough not to matter

The village is tiny by general resort standards. But it's 1km from end to end, and there is no transport, so it pays to plan your end-of-day return to the village with a bit of care.

SCENERY *****
Glorious panorama

The views from the village and from the Schilthorn are magnificent. The grandeur of the Eiger, Mönch and Jungfrau across the valley as you descend the slopes is outstanding.

THE MOUNTAINS

Despite its small size, Mürren's ski area is interestingly varied. The lower slopes are below the treeline, but in practice it is an inhospitable area when the weather is bad.

EXTENT OF THE SLOPES *
Small but interesting

Mürren's slopes aren't extensive. But there is something for everyone, including a vertical of some 1300m to the village. There are three connected areas. The biggest is **Schiltgrat**, served by a fast quad chair at the south end

KEY FACTS	
Resort	1650m 5,410ft
Jungfrau region	
Altitude	945-2970m 3,100-9,740ft
Lifts	44
Pistes	213km 132 miles
Blue	33%
Red	49%
Black	18%
Snowmaking	40%
Mürren-Schilthorn only	
Slopes	1650-2970m 5,410-9,740ft
Lifts	12
Pistes	54km 34 miles

GETTING THERE

Air Zürich 155km/95 miles (3hr); Bern 65km/40 miles (2hr); Basel 160km/100 miles (2hr45)

Rail Lauterbrunnen; transfer by mountain railway and cable car

of the village. A short funicular goes from the middle of the village to the nursery slope at **Allmendhubel** – linked by red run and now by return chairlift to the slightly higher **Maulerhubel**. Runs go down from here to Winteregg and a newish fast quad.

Then there are the higher slopes reached by cable car to **Birg**. Below Birg, the fast Riggli chair serves a shady slope, and lower down two more chairs serve sunnier slopes. A further cable car goes up to the Schilthorn and its revolving restaurant – check out the feature panel. In good snow you can ski from here (via a short chairlift) right down to Lauterbrunnen – almost 16km and 2175m vertical; below Winteregg, it's mostly narrow paths. Every January the Inferno race for amateurs is run over this route (without using the chairlift).

FAST LIFTS ★★★★★
Only one weakness
It's only skiing at mid-mountain, below Obere Hubel, that you're forced to use slow chairs – and they are short.

QUEUES ★★★
Generally not a problem
Mürren doesn't get as crowded as Wengen and Grindelwald, except on sunny Sundays. But there can be queues for the cable cars to Birg and Schilthorn; the top stage has only one cabin, so capacity is limited.

TERRAIN PARKS ★★
Affirmative
There is a terrain park on the lower slopes of Schiltgrat, with jumps, a couple of pipes and chill-out bar area.

SNOW RELIABILITY ★★★
Good on the upper slopes
The Jungfrau region does not have a good snow record – but we've always found Mürren has the best snow in the area. When Wengen-Grindelwald (and Mürren's lower slopes) have problems, the slopes up at Birg often have packed powder snow. The runs from below Engetal to Allmendhubel and parts of the lower slopes have snowmaking, as does the woodland path on down to Lauterbrunnen.

FOR EXPERTS ★★★
An attractive cocktail
The run from the top of the Schilthorn starts with a steep but not terrifying slope, in the past generally mogulled but now more often groomed. It flattens into a schuss to Engetal, below Birg. Then there's a wonderful,

LIFT PASSES

Jungfrau

Prices in SF

Age	1-day	6-day
under 16	31	157
16 to 19	50	251
20 to 61	62	314
over 62	56	283

Free under 6 (if with parent)

Beginner points card

Notes Covers trains between villages and Grindelwald ski-bus; day pass is for Mürren-Schilthorn area only; 6-day-plus pass allows one day in Zermatt

Alternative passes Grindelwald and Wengen only; Mürren only; non-skier pass

ACTIVITIES

Indoor Alpine Sports Centre: swimming pool, sauna, solarium, steam bath, massage, fitness room

Outdoor Ice rink, curling, tobogganing, cleared paths, snowshoeing, paragliding

JUNGFRAU REGION MARKETING AG

Practically every part of the resort gives a fabulous view across to the famous Jungfrau and co; this is Allmendhubel ↓

wide run with stunning views over the valley. Below the Engetal lifts you hit the Kanonenrohr (gun barrel). This is a shelf with solid rock on one side and a steep drop on the other – protected by nets; it is wider than it once was, and is now not seriously scary. After an open slope and scrappy zigzag path, you arrive at the 'hog's back' and can descend towards the village on either side of Allmendhubel.

There are steep, grooming-free mogul runs at Birg and from Schiltgrat towards the village. There is quite a lot of off-piste potential, notably runs into the Blumental – from Schiltgrat (the north-facing Blumenlucke) and from Birg (sunnier Tschingelchrachen). And there are more adventurous runs from the Schilthorn top station.

FOR INTERMEDIATES ★★★

Limited, but Wengen nearby

Keen piste-bashers will want to make a few trips to the long cruising runs of Wengen-Grindelwald. The best easy cruising run in Mürren is the north-facing blue down to Winteregg. The reds on the other low slopes can get mogulled, and snow conditions can be poor. The runs up at Engetal, below Birg, normally have good snow.

Competent, confident intermediates can consider tackling the Schilthorn.

FOR BEGINNERS ★★★

Not ideal, but adequate

The main nursery slopes at Allmendhubel, up the funicular, are a little on the steep side, but secluded and quiet. You pay via points cards. From there, you have easy blue runs to graduate to in each of the sectors; since construction of the chairlift link from Maulerhubel to Allmendhubel, getting back from Maulerhubel to the village poses no difficulty.

FOR BOARDERS ★★

Tough going for intermediates

The major lifts are snowboard-friendly cable cars and chairlifts. The terrain above Mürren is suitable mainly for good freeriders – it's steep, with a lot of off-piste. Intermediates will find the area tough and limited; nearby Wengen is gentler and larger.

FOR CROSS-COUNTRY ★

Forget it

There's a 12km loop along the Lauterbrunnen valley. But snow is unreliable at valley height.

MOUNTAIN RESTAURANTS ★★

Nothing outstanding

You'll want to visit the Schilthorn even if it's only for a drink – check out the feature panel. Other reader tips include the cosy Schilthornhütte, at Obere Hubel, and the rustic, secluded Suppenalp lower down in the Blumental – but it gets no sun in January. Gimmelen is famous for its apple cake, but is self-service (and slow service, says a 2012 visitor). The Schiltgrathüsi, near blue run 23, offers 'good value' lunches; 'lovely coffee stop' says another 2012 visitor. The refurbished restaurant at Birg offers table-service. Winteregg is 'good and not expensive'.

SCHILTHORN – SPECTACULAR REVOLVING RESTAURANT AND AN EPIC DESCENT

Piz Gloria revolves once an hour, displaying a fabulous 360° panorama of peaks and lakes. We don't find the ambience very tempting, but reporters have enjoyed the 'amazingly tasty' and 'surprisingly good value' meals. You can enjoy the views from the terrace, and can also take in a 15-minute film show including clips from the famous Bond movie featuring the place. What you must not miss, if you are half-competent on skis or board, is the fabulous black run from here, more or less to village level, described under 'For Experts'.

JUNGFRAU MARKETING AG

SCHOOLS

Swiss
t 855 1247

Classes
5 half-days (2hr) SF170

Private lessons
SF140 for 2hr for 1-2 persons

CHILDCARE

Kinder Paradis
t 856 8686
Ages 3 to 8yr

Babysitter list
Available from tourist office

Ski school
From age 3 (5 2hr days SF170)

UK PACKAGES

Inghams, Momentum, PowderBeds, Ski Line, Ski Solutions, Switzerland Travel Centre
Lauterbrunnen Ski Miquel

Phone numbers
From elsewhere in Switzerland add the prefix 033; from abroad use the prefix +41 33

TOURIST OFFICE

www.mymuerren.ch
www.muerren.ch

SCHOOLS AND GUIDES ★★★

No recent reports

We lack recent reports. But the school has a long tradition of teaching Brits.

FOR FAMILIES ★★★

Attractive

Mürren is attractive for a quiet family holiday, not least because of the relaxed, safe and snowy village, and the free facilities (read 'Off the slopes'). There is a nursery slope with a rope tow. Children as young as three can now have lessons.

STAYING THERE

Hotels There are fewer than a dozen.
****Eiger** (856 5454) Chalet style; next to station. Widely recommended for good blend of efficiency and charm. Good food; pool.
***Alpenruh** (856 8800) Attractively renovated chalet next to the cable car.
***Jungfrau** (856 6464) Perfectly placed for families, in front of the baby slope and close to the funicular.
Alpenblick (855 1327) Simple, small, modern chalet near the station.
Apartments There are plenty of chalets and apartments in the village for independent travellers to rent.
At altitude We have a good report of a stay at Suppenalp (855 1726) – 'good atmosphere, friendly host, excellent dinner, basic facilities, incredibly creaky – they issue earplugs'. You can borrow toboggans.

EATING OUT ★★

Mainly in hotels

The main alternative to hotels is the rustic Stägerstübli – a bar as well as a restaurant, and popular with locals, serving regional dishes. The Jägerstubli in the hotel Bellevue is recommended for 'amazing' veal stew. The Edelweiss, and Alpenruh have been recommended in the past.

APRES-SKI ★★

Not entirely devoid of life

The tiny Stägerstübli is cosy, and the place to meet locals. The Bliemlichäller disco in the Blumental hotel caters for kids, the bar in the Eiger for a more mixed crowd.

OFF THE SLOPES ★★★

Tranquillity plus diversions

There is a very good sports centre – being renovated for 2012/13, with new spa facilities. The pool and ice rink are free to those staying in Mürren. The toboggan run from Allmendhubel to the village is 'great'. There are lots of prepared walking trails. 2012 visitors report that paragliding seems to have become very popular. Excursions to Bern and Interlaken are easy. Skiers can easily return to the village to meet non-skiers for lunch, and non-skiers can ascend the cable cars to the Schilthorn – though at a price.

DOWN-VALLEY VILLAGE – 795m

LAUTERBRUNNEN

This is a good budget base, with a bit of resort atmosphere and access to both Wengen (until late) and Mürren. We've happily stayed at two hotels – the 3-star Schützen (855 3026) and 2-star Oberland (855 1241), also recommended for its food; the 3-star Silberhorn (856 2210) is once again highly recommended by a repeat visitor for its 'great value' five-course dinners. There are bars in the hotels Horner, Steinbock and Silberhorn. Ski Miquel's chalet hotel is said to be of an 'excellent standard'.

Saas-Fee

For practical purposes, the highest skiing in the Alps, plus a cute old village at the base; great for an early/late break

RATINGS

The mountains

Extent	**
Fast lifts	****
Queues	***
Terrain p'ks	*****
Snow	*****
Expert	**
Intermediate	****
Beginner	*****
Boarder	****
X-country	***
Restaurants	***
Schools	****
Families	****

The resort

Charm	*****
Convenience	**
Scenery	****
Eating out	****
Après-ski	****
Off-slope	****

RPI	130
lift pass	£240
ski hire	£95
lessons	£125
food & drink	£200
total	**£660**

NEWS

2013/14: A new eight-person gondola is planned from the car park at the edge of the village via the nursery slope area to Spielboden. It will eventually go on to Längfluh and maybe to the top of the mountain.

2012/13: More snowmaking is planned in the Längfluh area.

2011/12: The Spielboden mountain restaurant is now owned by the Michelin-starred Fletschorn hotel and has been refurbished. The revolving restaurant at Allalin has been refurbished and renamed Threes!xty.

- + Most runs are at exceptionally high altitude, and snow-sure; great for early or late-season trips
- + Traditional, car-free village, with clear attractions for families
- + Dramatic setting amid high peaks and glaciers
- + Good off-slope facilities

- − Small area of slopes
- − Mainly easy runs, with little to amuse experts (glacier limits off-piste exploration)
- − Many visitors face some long walks around the village
- − Shady and cold for much of winter
- − Bad weather can shut the slopes

Saas-Fee is one of our favourite places – a sort of miniature Zermatt without the conspicuous consumption. As well as the charm factor there's the super-reliable snow: you spend most of your days here at an altitude – between 2500m and 3500m – that is unrivalled in the Alps. It's a compelling combination.

We tend to drop in here for a day or two at a time, so the limited extent and challenge of the slopes is not a worry; if we were here for a week, we'd soon be taking trips to Saas-Grund and even Zermatt. But if you don't mind skiing the same flattering slopes every day, Saas-Fee takes some beating.

THE RESORT

Saas-Fee is a traditional mountain village of narrow streets, lined by old chalets and free of cars, which made a 2012 visitor feel 'safe allowing the children to wander through the streets'. It's not completely free of traffic, though: electric taxis and trucks are not the nuisance that they are in Zermatt, but do provoke complaints.

The worthwhile slopes of Saas-Almagell and Saas-Grund are not far away, and you can buy a lift pass that covers them and the linking buses. Trips to Zermatt are time-consuming but possible, and with a six-day pass the day pass for Zermatt costs just SF30. Some tour ops arrange trips.

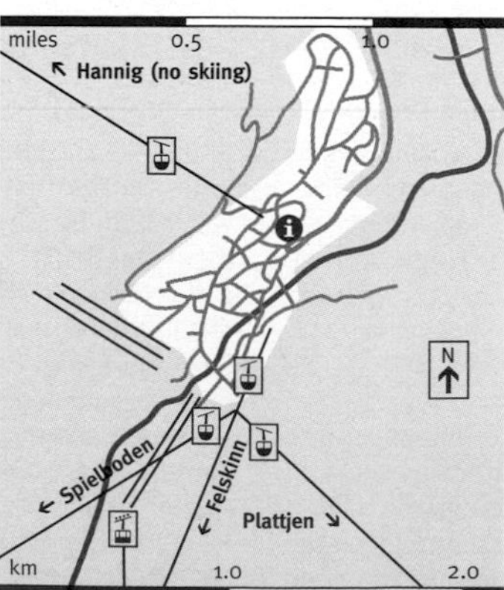

VILLAGE CHARM *****
Unpretentious rural idyll

Despite expansion, Saas-Fee still feels like a village, with cow sheds still in evidence. It doesn't have much of a central focus, but we'll forgive that; it's a charming place just to stroll around and relax in – at least when the spring sun is beating down (it's a chilly place in midwinter). There are some smart hotels (plus many more modest ones) and good bars and restaurants.

CONVENIENCE **
A hike maybe

Although it's a small village, it's about 2km long, and the slopes and most of the lifts are at one end. There are free but limited public mini-buses and a road-train, and the bigger hotels run their own taxis. But most people, most of the time, just walk everywhere. The biggest lift – the Alpin Express gondola – starts from a more central location (that you can ski back to). And you can store your gear near the lifts, which helps.

SCENERY ****
The Pearl of the Alps

Saas-Fee has stunning views up to a ring of 4000-metre peaks – on a sunny day the restaurant terraces by the nursery slopes at the south end of the village are a magnet. Higher up, the views are even better.

KEY FACTS

Resort	1800m 5,910ft
Slopes	1800-3500m 5,910-11,480ft
Lifts	21
Pistes	100km 62 miles
Blue	25%
Red	50%
Black	25%
Snowmaking	22%

LIFT PASSES

Saas-Fee

Prices in SF

Age	1-day	6-day
under 16	37	190
17 to 18	58	294
19 to 64	68	346
65 plus	63	318

Free under 10

Beginner pass for village lifts only

Notes

Covers Saas-Fee only; single and return tickets on main lifts; also afternoon passes

Alternative passes

Whole valley pass; passes for each of the other Saastal ski areas (Saas-Grund, Saas-Almagell, Saas-Balen)

THE MOUNTAINS

The upper slopes are largely gentle, while the lower mountain, below the glacier, is steeper and rockier, needing good snow-cover. There is very little shelter in bad weather: during and after heavy snowfalls you may find yourself limited to the nursery area.

Take it easy when climbing out of the top lift station at 3500m: some people can't handle the thin air.

Some of the red runs on the glacier would be better classified as blue.

Saas-Fee is one of the leading resorts for ski touring; the extended Haute Route from Chamonix via Zermatt ends here.

EXTENT OF THE SLOPES ★★★★★

A glacier runs through it

There are two routes up to the main **Felskinn** area. The 30-person Alpin Express gondola, starting across the river from the centre of the village, takes you there via a mid-station at Morenia. The alternative is a short drag across the nursery slope at the south end of the village, and then the Felskinn cable car.

From Felskinn, the Metro Alpin underground funicular hurtles up to **Allalin**. From below here, two draglifts access the high point of the area.

Also from the south end of the village, a gondola leaves for Spielboden. This is met by a cable car that takes you up to **Längfluh**.

Between Felskinn and Längfluh is an off-limits glacier area with huge crevasses. A very long draglift from Längfluh takes you to a point where you can get down to the Felskinn area. These two sectors are served mainly by draglifts, and you can get down to the village from both.

Another gondola from the south end of the village goes up to the separate, small area of **Plattjen**.

FAST LIFTS ★★★★★

Too many T-bars

The area is a strange mixture of powerful fast lifts and a lot of 'ghastly long and cold T-bars', as a recent reporter put it; there are only two chairlifts. Blame the glaciers, on which it's tricky to build chairlifts. Our rating may look mysterious, but over half the lifts are fast, which puts Saas-Fee comfortably into the 4-star range.

QUEUES ★★★★★

Still peak season problems

We had no problems with queues in February and March 2011 visits, and have no reports from readers of particular problems. But at peak holiday periods, you may meet long queues for the Felskinn cable car ('an hour to reach Felskinn'). There may also be queues up at Längfluh and for

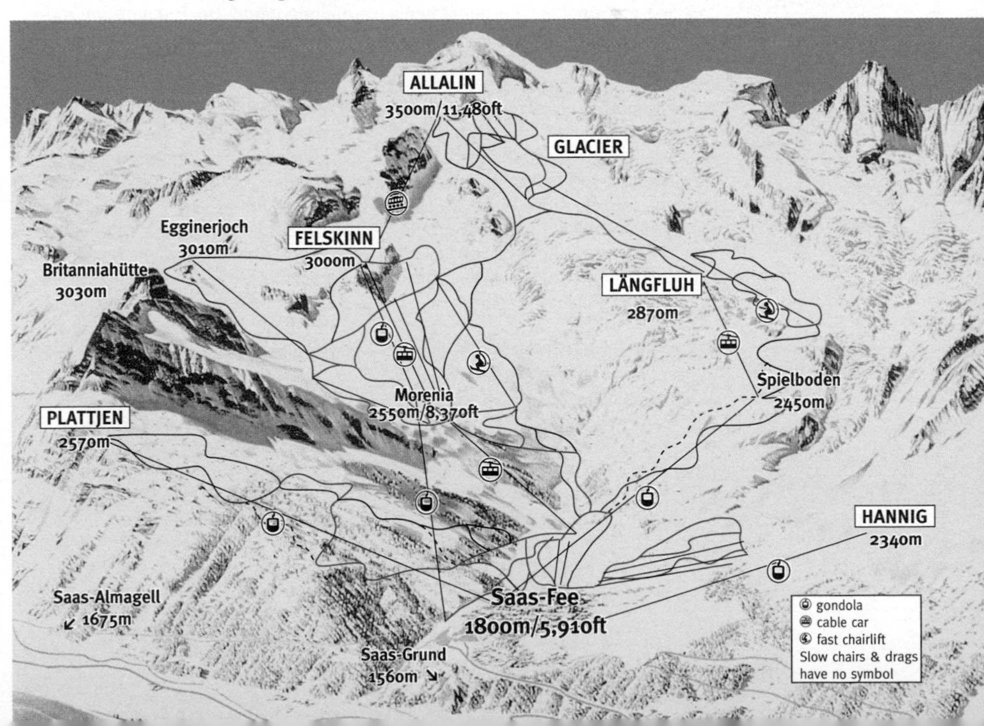

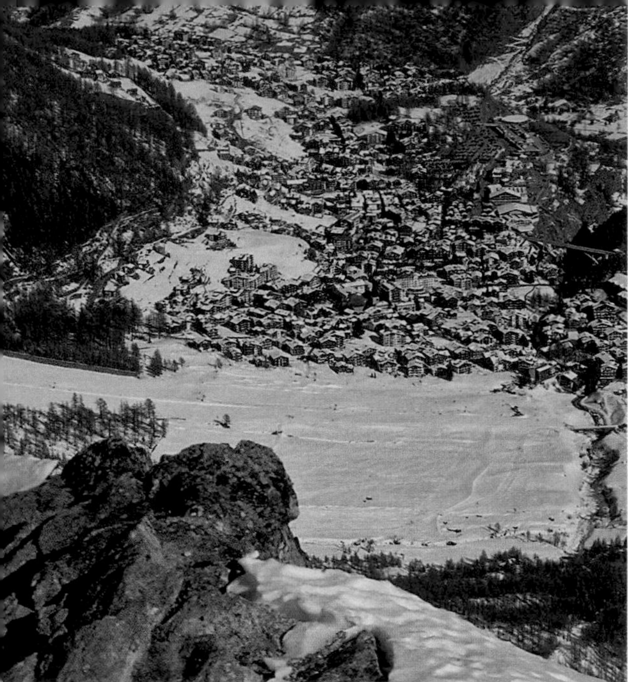

↑ Although Saas-Fee is quite spread out it's still basically a small traditional mountain village and a very pleasant place to stroll around

SNOWPIX.COM / CHRIS GILL

Resort news and key links: **www.wheretoskiandsnowboard.com**

GETTING THERE

Air Sion 75km/ 45 miles (1hr45); Geneva 225km/ 140 miles (3hr30); Zürich 250km/ 155 miles (4hr); Milan 200km/ 125 miles (3hr30)

Rail Brig (38km/ 24 miles) or Visp; regular buses from station

the highest draglifts. Crowds on the home run from Morenia can be a problem at the end of the day, and when bad weather closes higher lifts.

TERRAIN PARKS ★★★★★
Well developed
The 42 Crew (www.42crew.ch) who run the show here are renowned for building great parks. The big Morenia park has a plethora of kickers, rails and boxes, and a world-class half-pipe. Shapers are constantly changing the rail and box lines to keep the park creative as well as adding interesting obstacles. There's a park for beginner freestylers at the foot of the mountain near the nursery slopes; you'll find plenty of entry-level jumps and rails here. In summer, the park moves up to the glacier and you will often see pro riders honing their skills there.

SNOW RELIABILITY ★★★★★
A question of altitudes
Most of Saas-Fee's slopes face north and many are above 2500m, making this one of the most reliable resorts for snow in the Alps. The glacier is open most of the year. Lower down, on the runs back to the resort, snow quality and cover can be more patchy, but snowmaking seems adequate. Grooming is also adequate.

FOR EXPERTS ★★
Not a lot to keep your interest
There is not much steep stuff – the handful of short, sharp pitches dotted around the area just merit their black classification. The slopes around the top of Längfluh can provide good powder, and there are usually moguls above Spielboden. There is excellent tree skiing on Plattjen but it requires serious depths of snow to cover the very rocky terrain. On the main sector, the glacier puts limits on the off-piste even with a guide – crevasse danger is extreme. But there are extensive touring possibilities.

FOR INTERMEDIATES ★★★★
Great for gentle cruising
For early intermediates and those not looking for much of a challenge, Saas-Fee is ideal. For long cruises, head for Allalin. The top of the mountain, down as far as Längfluh in one direction and Morenia in the other, is ideal, with gentle reds leading to even gentler blues, and usually excellent snow.

The reds around mid-mountain are a bit more challenging, notably at Längfluh. The descents from Allalin to the village offer a leg-testing 1700m vertical. The lower runs have steepish, tricky sections and can have poor snow, and the blues here are mainly narrow paths – timid intermediates might prefer to take a lift down from mid-mountain. Don't ignore the rather neglected Plattjen, which is basically of red-run gradient.

FOR BEGINNERS ★★★★★
A great place to start
There's a superb, large, out-of-the-way nursery area at the edge of the village, as snow-sure as any you will find. Those ready to progress can head for the gentle blues between Felskinn and Morenia and the red runs (which are of only blue gradient) on the glacier. A useful beginners' pass covers all the short village lifts.

FOR BOARDERS ★★★★
Backed from the beginning
Saas-Fee has backed snowboarding from its inception and provides year-round riding. The terrain suits intermediates and beginners best; there's little to satisfy experts and the glacier limits freeriding, but carvers will find wide, well-groomed pistes to shred down. The main access lifts are gondolas, cable cars and a funicular,

SCHOOLS

Swiss
t 957 2348

Eskimos
t 957 4904

Optimum Snowsports
t 957 2039

Classes
5 3hr days SF193 (no full day lessons)

Private lessons
SF80 for 1hr

CHILDCARE

Gästekindergarten Murmeli
t 957 4057
Ages 18mnth to 6yr

Swiss
t 957 2348
Ages from 3

Ski school
From age 5 (5 3hr days SF193)

ACTIVITIES

Indoor Bielen leisure centre: swimming, hot tub, steam bath, solarium, sauna, tennis, badminton; museums

Outdoor 30km of cleared paths, ice rink (skating, curling, snow bowling), tubing, tobogganing, snow-shoeing, 'Feeblitz' bobsleigh

but nearly all the rest are T-bars. The high altitude and the glacier mean the resort is a favourite for early-season and summer riding.

FOR CROSS-COUNTRY ★★★

Good local trail and lots nearby

There is a nice short (6km) trail at the edge of the village and 26km down in the Saas valley.

MOUNTAIN RESTAURANTS ★★★

Huge improvements

Saas Fee's mountain restaurants used to be mediocre at best. But in the last few years two have been taken over by the resort's two top hotels and improved beyond recognition. The piste map gives details and phone numbers for these and several others.

Editors' choice The Vernissage Berghaus Plattjen (just down from the top of Plattjen), in the Ferienart hotel stable, has great Alpine atmosphere, delicious hearty food, excellent service and wonderful glacier views from a tiny terrace. We look forward to trying the Spielboden hut which was taken over and refurbished last season by the Fletschorn hotel (where the food has a Michelin star). Reporters say it is 'superb' and 'very good quality if expensive'; a local says 'it is the best mountain restaurant with Berghaus Plattjen closely following; you can have a bowl of a really fantastic soup, or you could have a wonderful three course lunch'.

Worth knowing about Before the two above appeared, our favourite was the cosy Gletschergrotte, slightly off the run from Spielboden (watch for signs on the left) – 'amazing views and food' says a 2012 reporter but 'be prepared for a wait'. Of the self-service restaurants, the one at Längfluh has a great view of the glacier and its crevasses from its large terrace and at Morenia the food is 'cooked fresh while you wait'. For something different, a 15-minute trek from the pistes at Felskinn brings you to Britanniahütte, a real climbing refuge with great views; understandably, food is simple.

There's a room in the Morenia where you can eat your own packed lunch.

SCHOOLS AND GUIDES ★★★★

Good reports

Optimum Snowsports, Saas Fee's first British-run school, opened a couple of years ago and in 2011 we had a glowing report on both kids' classes and adult private lessons: 'a truly inspiring and talented instructor'. A 2012 visitor also found it 'excellent'. A recent visitor said of the Swiss school: 'efficient and fun for kids'. Eskimos has a good reputation too and a 2012 reporter says 'there can be few schools better'.

FOR FAMILIES ★★★★

Safely suitable

The village and its gentle nursery slopes form a great environment for families. The kids' fun park proved a 'great introduction' for one toddler. Several hotels have an in-house kindergarten. There's a day care centre for children from 18 months to six years and there's also a babysitting service. Child-friendly operators Esprit and Family Ski Company both have chalet hotels here.

WORLD'S HIGHEST REVOLVING LUNCH?

If you fancy 360° views during lunch, head up to Threes!xty, the world's highest revolving restaurant at Allalin, which was refurbished last season and where you can get a different vista with starters, mains and pud. Only the bit of floor with the tables on it revolves; the stairs stay put (along with the windows – watch your gloves). The other two revolving cafes in the Alps are also in Switzerland – at Mürren and Leysin – and we rate the views there better. But it's an amusing novelty that most visitors enjoy. To reserve a table next to the windows phone 957 1771.

SAAS-FEE TOURISM / SWISS-IMAGE.CH

UK PACKAGES

Alpine Answers, Alpine Life, Crystal, Crystal Finest, Erna Low, Esprit, Family Ski Company, Independent Ski Links, Inghams, Interactive Resorts, Momentum, Neilson, Oxford Ski Co, PowderBeds, Ski Bespoke, Ski Expectations, Ski Independence, Ski Line, Ski Safari, Ski Solutions, Ski Total, Skitracer, Skiweekends.com, Snow Finders, Switzerland Travel Centre, Thomson

Phone numbers
From elsewhere in Switzerland add the prefix 027; from abroad use the prefix +41 27

TOURIST OFFICE

www.saas-fee.ch

STAYING THERE

Chalets We have had excellent reports on Haus Jessica run by Alpine Life ('the best catered chalet in the village by some margin', says a 2012 reporter; 'wonderful, fantastic staff, excellent food' was an earlier opinion); hot tub, sauna/steam room. Ski Total has a 50-bed chalet hotel in a prime spot, over the street from the nursery slopes. See also 'For families', above.
Hotels There are over 50.
*****Ferienart** (958 1900) Central top hotel. Superb blend of comfort, service and relaxed style. Half-board food about the best we've had.
****Saaserhof** (958 9898) Near lifts. Reputation for good service and food.
****Allalin** (958 1000) 'Large rooms, outstanding food, fantastic staff.'
***Bristol** (958 1212) Good location right by the nursery slopes. 'Spotless rooms,' says a recent visitor.
***Europa** (958 9600) Near the Hannig gondola. 'Clean, comfortable'; 'good food'; 'gorgeous wellness facilities'.
***Waldesruh** (958 6464) Close to the Alpin Express and 'family friendly'.
Fletschhorn (957 2131) Upmarket, elegant chalet in the woods. A trek from the village and lifts, but they'll drive you, of course; great food.
Hohnegg (957 2268) Small, more rustic alternative to the Fletschhorn, in a similarly remote spot.
Apartments Two 2012 reporters recommend Chalet Feekatz, which has six bedrooms ('beautiful, a 10-minute walk from centre'). Perla apartments were a previous recommendation.

EATING OUT ★★★★

Good variety

Gastronomes will want to head for the Michelin-starred and expensive Fletschhorn – endorsed by a 2012 reporter. We like the woody Bodmen, which has great food and a varied menu. The hotel Ferienart operates several good restaurants including the serious Vernissage, the Mandarin (Asian) and Del Ponte (Italian). Don Ciccio's is 'child-friendly' and does 'great pizza and pasta'. The Vieux Chalet (for fondue) and the hotel Tenne have been recommended.

APRES-SKI ★★★★

Lively bars and clubs

At close of play, the SnowPoint umbrella bar at the foot of the slopes and the terraces of Zur Mühle and the Black Bull in the main street are always buzzing. Later on, Nesti's and the Fee Pub are lively. The popular Popcorn has now moved to near the tourist office. Where it was is now the Dom Bar with live music every night. Metropol, Poison and Night-Life are other popular clubs.

OFF THE SLOPES ★★★★

A mountain for pedestrians

The Hannig mountain is dedicated to walking, snowshoeing, paragliding and tobogganing. The leisure centre has a 25m pool, indoor tennis and a sunbed area. The Feeblitz 'roller-coaster-style' ride is good fun. The museums are interesting and if you like ice caves, don't miss the world's largest. The tourist office organizes daily walks.

St Moritz

One of a kind: a panoramic high-altitude playground with as much happening off the slopes as on them

RATINGS

The mountains	
Extent	*****
Fast lifts	****
Queues	***
Terrain p'ks	****
Snow	****
Expert	****
Intermediate	****
Beginner	**
Boarder	****
X-country	*****
Restaurants	***
Schools	***
Families	**
The resort	
Charm	**
Convenience	*
Scenery	****
Eating out	****
Après-ski	***
Off-slope	*****

RPI	150
lift pass	£250
ski hire	£130
lessons	£140
food & drink	£235
total	**£755**

NEWS

2012/13: Visitors will be able to obtain lift passes for SF25 a day if they stay at least two nights in one of the 100 hotels in St Moritz that are participating in the scheme.

2011/12: New panoramic cabins with windows to floor level were fitted to the Diavolezza cable car. The former Chesa Guardalej hotel in Champfèr was completely renovated and became the 5-star Giardino Mountain.

- + Wonderful panoramic scenery
- + Extensive intermediate slopes
- + High, and fairly snow-sure
- + Off-slope activities second to none (and a whole mountain dedicated to non-skiing activities)
- + Some good mountain restaurants, some with magnificent views

- − A sizeable town, with little traditional Alpine character and some big block buildings
- − Several unlinked mountains
- − Runs on home mountain mostly fairly easy and lacking variety
- − Can be pricey, as you'd expect from such a fashionable resort

St Moritz is Switzerland's definitive 'exclusive' winter resort: glitzy, fashionable and, above all, the place to be seen – a place for an all-round winter holiday, with an unrivalled array of wacky diversions such as cricket on snow, and countless festivals. It has long been popular with upper-crust Brits, who come for the sledging. Well, OK: for the world-famous Cresta Run. But, like all such self-consciously smart resorts, it makes a perfectly good destination for anyone. We were there in 2012 and loved the place, as usual.

The town of St Moritz is a bit of a blot on the landscape; but that landscape is truly spectacular. Our skiing here is regularly interrupted by the need to stand and gaze, and once installed on a terrace we take some shifting.

THE RESORT

St Moritz is at the heart of the upper Engadin – the remote, high valley of the En, which becomes the Austrian Inn (as in Innsbruck). The valley bottom is filled by a chain of lakes, one of which separates the two parts of St Moritz. On a steep hillside above the lake, St Moritz Dorf is the fashionable main town. Beside the lake is the more ordinary spa resort, St Moritz Bad. The skiing is in several separate sectors; only one, Corviglia, is reachable directly from the resort.

In winter the lake is used for eccentric activities including horse and greyhound racing, show jumping, polo, golf and even cricket. And there's a whole mountain (Muottas Muragl) set aside for not skiing – see 'Off the slopes'. The upper Engadin is superb for walking and cross-country skiing, which is very big here; the Engadin Ski Marathon attracts over 12,000 entries.

The home slopes are shared with Celerina, down the valley (see end of chapter). And there are other possible bases along the valleys.

There is a fabulously scenic railway from Zürich, but it's quicker to drive. A car is handy around the resort, too: the bus service is covered by the lift pass; but it gets crowded at peak times. A car greatly speeds up visits to the more distant mountains. Trips are possible to Davos and other resorts, including Austrian and Italian ones; you get a half-price pass in Livigno, for example. There is a strong Italian flavour to the area – lots of Italian visitors, workers, food and wine.

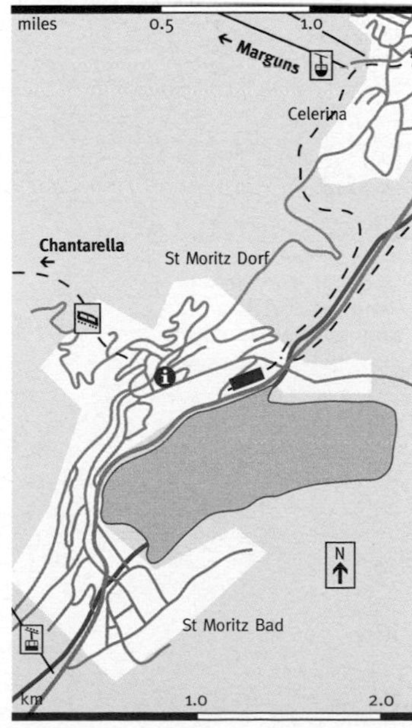

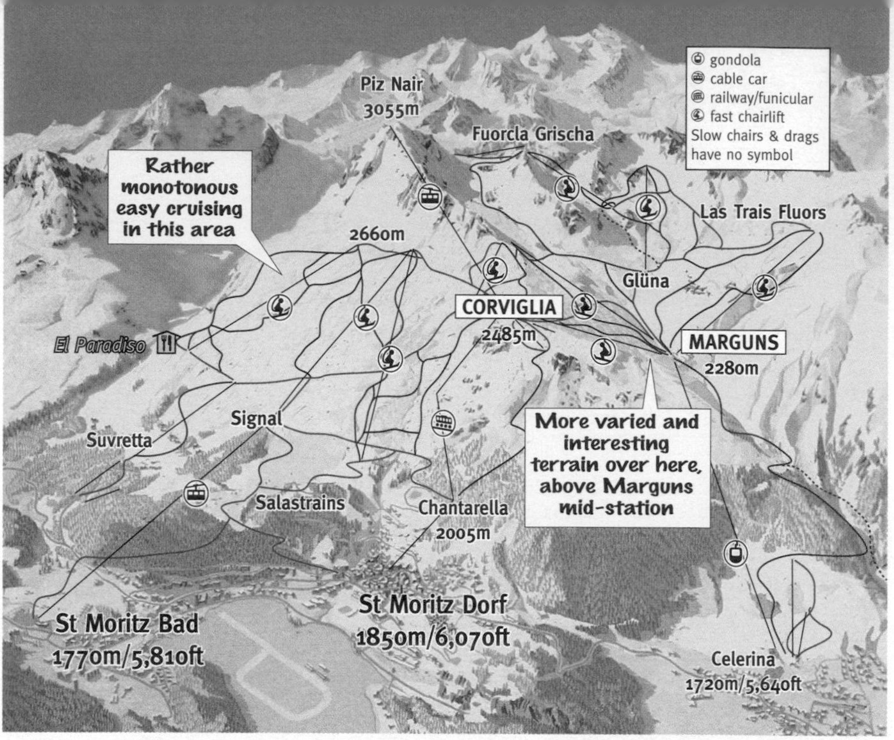

gondola
cable car
railway/funicular
fast chairlift
Slow chairs & drags have no symbol

Piz Nair
3055m

Fuorcla Grischa

Rather monotonous easy cruising in this area

2660m

Las Trais Fluors

Glüna

CORVIGLIA
2485m

MARGUNS
2280m

El Paradiso

Signal

Suvretta

More varied and interesting terrain over here, above Marguns mid-station

Salastrains

Chantarella
2005m

St Moritz Dorf
1850m/6,070ft

St Moritz Bad
1770m/5,810ft

Celerina
1720m/5,640ft

cable car
fast chairlift
Slow chairs & drags have no symbol

PIZ CORVATSCH
3305m/10,840ft

Good red runs starting on the glacier, with fabulous views of Piz Bernina

Murtèl-Corvatsch

Fuorcla Surlej

Murtèl
2700m

Curtinella

A lovely, easy black – a great way to end the day, with a pit stop part-way down

Giand'Alva
2645m

2495m

Alp Surlej

Surlej-Murtèl

Rabgiu

Alp Margun
2270m

Hahnensee
2155m

St. Moritz Bad
1770m/5,810ft

Surlej
1870m

KEY FACTS	
Resort	1770m 5,810ft
Slopes	1730-3305m 5,680-10,840ft
Lifts	56
Pistes	350km 217 miles
Blue	20%
Red	70%
Black	10%
Snowmaking	30%
For Corviglia only	
Slopes	1730-3055m 5,680-10,020ft
Lifts	22
Pistes	100km 62 miles

VILLAGE CHARM ★★★★★
Urban glitz instead

In the main resort towns there is little traditional Alpine character; St Moritz is very much a glitzy town rather than a cute village. St Moritz Dorf has two main streets – lined with boutiques selling Rolex, Cartier, Hermes – a few side lanes and a small main square. St Moritz Bad is less urban, and less prestigious. Many of the buildings in both parts of the resort are block-like.

CONVENIENCE ★★★★★
Bad is good – or better, at least

It's a perfectly convenient resort if you are content to ski Corviglia, stay in central Dorf and ride the funicular, or stay on the edge of Bad and use the Signal cable car. But both parts of the resort spread widely away from these lifts, and to ski other mountains transport is needed. For keen skiers, Bad is the better base – you can ski back to it from both local sectors. If this is all too much for you, the local heli-skiing outfits will drop you at the top of the lifts. It's that kind of place.

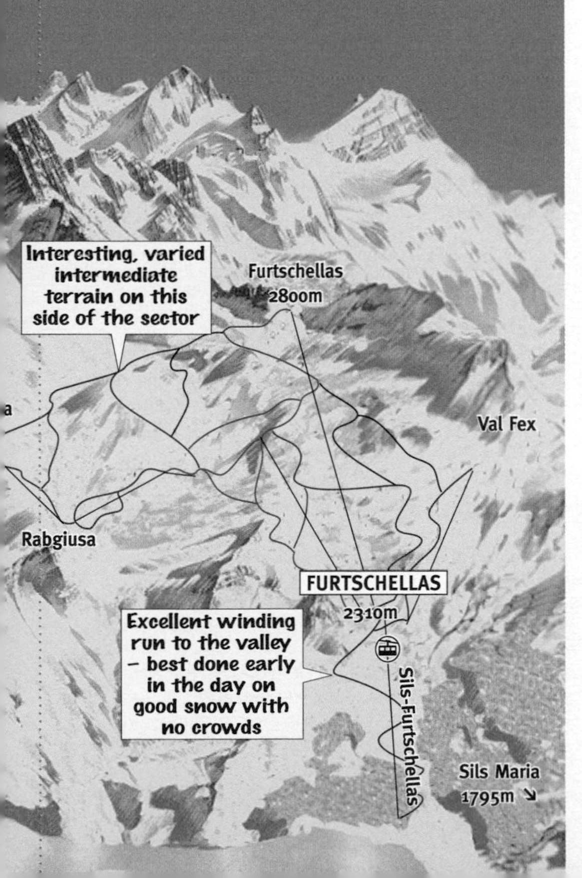

Interesting, varied intermediate terrain on this side of the sector
Furtschellas
2800m
Val Fex
Rabgiusa
FURTSCHELLAS
2310m
Excellent winding run to the valley – best done early in the day on good snow with no crowds
Sils-Furtschellas
Sils Maria
1795m

SCENERY ★★★★★
Fabulous panoramas

The lake-filled valley, with 4000m peaks forming the Italian border to the south, provides mesmerizing views from Corviglia, and the close-up views of Piz Bernina from Corvatsch are stunning. Should we award five stars?

THE MOUNTAINS

There are lots of long, wide, well-groomed runs with varied terrain – practically all on open slopes above the trees. The 350km of pistes are in three separate areas, covered on three very clear piste maps; our maps show only the two main areas (Corviglia and Corvatsch) close to St Moritz. Every Friday, from 7pm to 2am, the 4.2km piste down from the middle station on Corvatsch is floodlit.

EXTENT OF THE SLOPES ★★★★★
Big but broken up

From St Moritz Dorf a two-stage railway goes up to **Corviglia**, a lift junction at the eastern end of a sunny and rather monotonous area of slopes facing east and south over the main valley. The peak of Piz Nair, reached from here by cable car, separates these slopes from the less sunny and more varied ones in the wide bowl above **Marguns** – and gives fabulous views across the valley to Piz Bernina. From Corviglia you can (snow permitting) head down easy paths to Dorf and Bad; you'll probably pass through Salastrains – just above Dorf, with nursery slopes, restaurants and two hotels. There is a red run from Marguns to Celerina.

From Surlej, a few miles from St Moritz, a two-stage cable car takes you to the north-facing slopes of **Corvatsch**, which reach glacial heights. From the mid-station at Murtèl you have a choice of reds to Stüvetta Giand'Alva and Alp Margun. From the latter you can work your way to **Furtschellas**, also reached by cable car from Sils Maria. If you're lucky with the snow, you can end the day with the splendid Hahnensee run, from the northern limit of the Corvatsch lift system at Giand'Alva down to St Moritz Bad – a black-classified run that is of red difficulty for 95% of its 6km length. It often opens around noon, when the snow softens. It's a five-minute walk from the end of the run to the cable car to Corviglia.

The third area consists of two peaks on opposite sides of the Bernina pass road to Italy, about 20km away (50 minutes by bus). **Diavolezza** (2980m) has excellent north-facing pistes of 900m vertical, down its cable car. **Lagalb** (2960m) is a smaller area with quite challenging slopes – west-facing, 850m vertical – served by a smaller cable car. From late February these cable cars run until 5pm.

FAST LIFTS ★★★★
Plenty of options
St Moritz has invested heavily in upgrading lifts, especially on Corviglia and Marguns, where there are fast chairs all over the place. Corvatsch still has some T-bars, though. The area as a whole has a lot of modest-sized cable cars – both for getting out of the resort and for access to peaks.

QUEUES ★★★
Not much of a problem
Queues for the cable cars are not unknown, and we had a high-season report of a one-hour queue to get out of Bad in 2010. But reporters have generally had good experiences lately and say that the slopes tend to be quiet early and late in the day.

TERRAIN PARKS ★★★★
World class facilities
The Crowland Park on Corviglia is easily reached from Celerina as well as St Moritz. The park was designed with female pro skiers and snowboarders and advanced riders in mind, and is home to some of the biggest contests for women. There are three lines, the hardest including a big 12m tabletop jump, plus a brilliant 400m easy line. There are many rails and boxes of all sizes, and a boardercross course. The Engadinsnow Park on Corvatsch has a bagjump, half-pipe and boardercross and uses natural terrain features.

SNOW RELIABILITY ★★★★
Improved by good snowmaking
This corner of the Alps has a rather dry climate, but the altitude means that any precipitation is likely to be snowy. The top runs at Corvatsch are glacial and require good snow depths to be safe. There is snowmaking in each sector, and grooming is excellent.

FOR EXPERTS ★★★★
Dispersed challenges
Few of the black runs are genuinely steep; those at Lagalb and Diavolezza are the most challenging. But there is good off-piste terrain, and it doesn't get tracked out. There is an excellent north-facing slope immediately above Marguns, for example. There are tough routes from Piz Nair and the Corvatsch summit. More serious expeditions can be undertaken – eg the Roseg valley from Corvatsch.

Out at Diavolezza, a very popular and spectacular off-piste glacier route goes off the back beneath Piz Bernina to Morteratsch. There's a 30-minute plod at first, then it's downhill, with splendid views. It is not difficult, but may take you close to crevasses; we wouldn't do it without a guide. On the front of the mountain, the Gletscher chair accesses an excellent shady run down Val d'Arlas. And across at Lagalb, a route goes steeply off the back down towards La Rosa.

There are a couple of firms offering heli-drops on Fuorcla Chamuotsch, for runs back to the Engadin valley.

FOR INTERMEDIATES ★★★★
Good but flattering
St Moritz is great for intermediates. Most pistes on Corviglia are very well groomed, easyish reds that could well have been classified blue – ideal

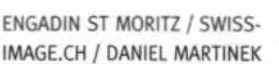
ENGADIN ST MORITZ / SWISS-IMAGE.CH / DANIEL MARTINEK

If you have a need to spend on stuff you don't need, St Moritz has the necessary retail opportunities ↓

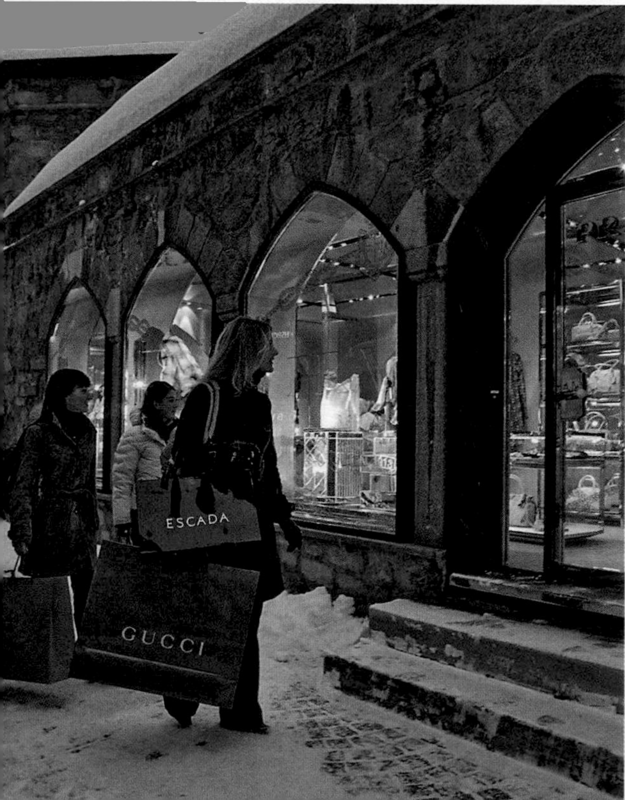

LIFT PASSES

Upper Engadin

Prices in SF

Age	1-day	6-day
under 13	24	122
13 to 17	49	243
18 plus	73	365

Free under 6

Senior no deals

Beginner no deals

Notes
Covers Corviglia, Corvatsch, Diavolezza-Lagalb and Zuoz, the Engadin bus services and stretches of the Rhätische Bahn railway; family discounts; 1-day price is for Corviglia only

Alternative passes
Half-day and day passes for individual areas

GETTING THERE

Air Zürich 220km/135 miles (3hr15); Friedrichshafen 210km/130 miles (2hr45); Upper Engadine airport 5km/3 miles

Rail Mainline station in resort

SCHOOLS

Swiss
t 830 0101

Suvretta
t 836 6161

Classes (Swiss prices)
3 3hr days SF280

Private lessons
From SF100 for 1hr

cruising terrain, or monotonous, depending on your view. The Marguns bowl is more interesting, including some easy blacks and the pleasant Val Schattain run away from the lifts.

The Corvatsch-Furtschellas area is altogether more varied, interesting and challenging, as well as higher and wider. In a word, wilder. There are excellent red runs in both parts of the area, including the runs from the Corvatsch glacier, which give fabulous views, and descents to the two valley stations – particularly the Furtschellas one. Do these in the morning, and at the end of the day return to St Moritz Bad via the lovely Hahnensee run – an easy black. There isn't much easy skiing at Corvatsch; some of the blues (eg the lower bit of 19) should be red.

Diavolezza is mostly intermediate stuff, too. There is an easy open slope at the top, served by a fast quad, and a splendid long intermediate run back down under the lift. The link to Lagalb requires use of parts of a black run, but it is of red gradient. (Plans to improve this link seem to have stalled.) Lagalb has more challenging pistes – two reds and a genuine black.

FOR BEGINNERS ★★

Not ideal

Beginners start up at Salastrains or Corviglia, or slightly out of town at Suvretta. Celerina has good, broad nursery slopes at village level and a child-friendly lift. But progression from the nursery slopes to longer runs is rather awkward – there are few blue runs without a difficult section. Nor are there any free lifts, or particularly helpful special passes.

FOR BOARDERS ★★★★

Very welcoming

The terrain in St Moritz is boarder-friendly. Freeride tours are available through the ski schools and the best freeride terrain is on Diavolezza and Corvatsch, but there are several draglifts on Corvatsch. Apart from those, most of St Moritz's lifts are chairs, gondolas, cable cars and trains; beginners will enjoy the rolling blue runs, and intermediates will relish the red runs. The great thing for freeriders is that terrain can stay untracked for days after a snowfall. There's a very good and varied park on Corviglia. The World Snowboard Tour stops off at the Engadinsnow Park. Playground in Paradise is a specialist board shop.

FOR CROSS-COUNTRY ★★★★★

Excellent

This is one of the premier regions in the Alps, with 200km of trails, some floodlit, amid splendid scenery and with fairly reliable snow. A reporter recommends lessons at the Langlauf Centre near the hotel Kempinski. But the best bases are outside St Moritz, along the valleys.

MOUNTAIN RESTAURANTS ★★★

Some special places

Mountain restaurants are plentiful, and include some of the most glamorous in Europe. Not surprisingly, prices can be high. The piste maps have pictures and phone numbers of the restaurants.
Editors' choice El Paradiso (833 4002), secluded at the extreme southern end of Corviglia, has it all: breathtaking views from the big terrace, a tastefully renovated, slightly trendy interior, great service and top-notch food. Fuorcla Surlej (842 6303, though we doubt they'll take a reservation), on the Fuorcla run from the Corvatsch glacier, could not be more different: a remote refuge serving basic food, sometimes very slowly. But the view of Piz Bernina and Piz Roseg from the snowy ramshackle 'terrace' is among our top three in the world.
Worth knowing about On Corviglia, the top lift station houses several restaurants run under the umbrella title of Mathis Food Affairs, including the famously swanky Marmite. Not our cup of tea, but a trusted reporter this year records his 'best ever skiing lunch' here. The more atmospheric Chasellas is also recommended, particularly for strudel. Lej da la Pêsch, behind Piz Nair, is a cosy spot, better for a snowy day than a sunny one. On the Corvatsch side, the cosy, rustic Alpetta has been tipped in the past, and the varied menu looked good to us on a recent visit. Hahnensee, on the run of that name to Bad, is a splendid place to pause in the sun.

There are two picnic rooms: at the Diavolezza cable-car base and in the Marguns restaurant building.

SCHOOLS AND GUIDES ★★★

Internal competition

There are two main schools, the 'very good' Swiss school (St Moritz) and the 'excellent' Suvretta attached to the eponymous hotel. Some other hotels have private instructors, too. The St Moritz Experience runs heli-trips.

CHILDCARE

Salastrains
t 830 0101
Run by Swiss school

Schweizerhof hotel
t 837 0707
From age 3

Palazzino – in Badrutt's Palace Hotel
t 837 1000
Ages 3 to 12

Kempinski Hotel
t 838 3838

Ski school
Ages from 5; 5 days SF330

ACTIVITIES

Indoor Golf range, tennis, squash, health spa, casino, cinema, museums

Outdoor 150km of cleared paths, ice rink, curling, ice climbing, snowshoeing, sleigh rides, tobogganing, paragliding, bobsleigh rides, Cresta Run, snow kiting, horse riding

FOR FAMILIES ★★★★★

Choose a hotel with a nursery

There's a kindergarten and children's restaurant at Salastrains, and we'd be inclined to stay up there if you can afford it. Some hotel nurseries are open to non-residents.

STAYING THERE

There is a Club Med, which has its own restaurants on the main slope sectors. The tourist office can provide a list of apartments.

Hotels From Switzerland's highest concentration of 5-stars, we allow ourselves one.

*******Kempinski** (818 383838) Unfashionable but spacious location in Bad. 'The only 5-star where I felt vaguely relaxed,' says a young but widely experienced reporter.

******Bären** (830 8400) Heartily recommended in the past. 'More welcoming than the glitzier places, top-notch staff and very good food.'

******Crystal** (818 362627) Austere-looking central place with contrasting traditional rooms, and interesting art in public areas.

******Monopol** (837 0404) Good value (for St Moritz); in centre of Dorf. Repeatedly approved by readers. Good spa facilities.

******Nira Alpina** (818 386970) Brand new 'design' hotel right by the Corvatsch cable-car station in Surlej. 'Great food, fab bar; faultless.'

******Schweizerhof** (837 0707) 'Relaxed' hotel in central Dorf, five minutes from the Corviglia lift. Après-ski hub.

*****Laudinella** (836 0000) In Bad. Cool decor; seven varied restaurants. 'Comfortable rooms, helpful staff.' Fitness facilities limited and not free.

*****Nolda** (833 0575) One of the few chalet-style buildings, close to the cable car in Bad.

*****Sonne** (838 5959) 'Very comfortable and generous rooms' in Bad, not far from the lake.

Landhotel Meierei (838 7000) Relaxing traditional country hotel in a quiet setting across the lake.

At altitude The 3-star chalet-style Salastrains (830 0707) is on the lower slopes of Corviglia and has great views. Muottas Muragl (842 8232), at over 2500m on the non-skiing mountain, was fully renovated for last season and has even better views.

EATING OUT ★★★★★

Mostly chic and expensive

A lot of restaurants here are very pricey. We liked the three smooth, expensive restaurants in the Chesa Veglia (an ancient 'rustic' outpost of Badrutt's hotel) – 'excellent food, service and ambience', confirms a reporter. A top, world-class restaurant is Bumanns Chesa Pirani, a fine old house out of town in La Punt. We had an excellent dinner in 2012 at the charming, polished hotel Bellavista in Surlej. Of course you can eat more cheaply, and that often means eating basic Italian. The hotels Laudinella and Sonne, in Bad, both have wood-fired pizza ovens, approved of by a reader. The Laudinella has six other restaurants too. For something completely different ... La Baracca is a big shed in the car park of the Signal cable car doing simple but thoroughly good food in a canteen-like setting.

An evening up at Muottas Muragl, between Celerina and Pontresina, offers spectacular views, a splendid sunset and dinner.

THE CRESTA RUN

No trip to St Moritz is really complete without a visit to the Cresta Run. It's the last bastion of Britishness (until recently, payment had to be made in sterling) and male chauvinism (women need an invitation from a club member). Any adult male can pay around £350 for five rides (helmet and lunch at the Kulm hotel included). You lie on a toboggan (called a 'skeleton') and hurtle head-first down a sheet ice gully from St Moritz to Celerina. Watch out for Shuttlecock corner – that's where most of the accidents happen.

ENGADIN ST MORITZ / SWISS-IMAGE.CH / JR LARRAMAN

UK PACKAGES

Alpine Answers, Alpine Weekends, Carrier, Club Med, Crystal, Crystal Finest, Elegant Resorts, Flexiski, Inghams, Jeffersons, Luxury Chalet Collection, Momentum, Neilson, Oxford Ski Co, PowderBeds, Powder Byrne, Scott Dunn, Ski Bespoke, Ski Independence, Ski Line, Ski Safari, Ski Solutions, Skitracer, Supertravel, Switzerland Travel Centre

Phone numbers
From elsewhere in Switzerland add the prefix 081; from abroad use the prefix +41 81

TOURIST OFFICES

St Moritz
www.stmoritz.ch

Celerina
www.engadin.stmoritz.ch/celerina/

APRES-SKI ★★★★★

Caters for all ages

There's a big variety of après-skiing age groups here. The fur coat count is high – people come to St Moritz to be seen. For tea and good cakes head for Hanselmann's. The Roo bar terrace outside the hotel Hauser is 'definitely the focal après drinking spot'.

Bobby's Pub attracts a young crowd, as does the loud music of the Stübli, one of the bars in the hotel Schweizerhof: the others are the Mulibar, with a trendy chill-out setting and dancing, and the chic Piano Bar. The Cresta, at the Steffani, is popular with the British, while the Cava below it is louder, livelier and younger. We don't get many reports on the late-night scene, but the Diamond Club has been mentioned. The two most popular discos are Vivai (expensive), and King's at Badrutt's Palace (even more expensive; jackets and ties required). If you need to liberate even more cash, try the casino.

OFF THE SLOPES ★★★★★

Excellent variety of pastimes

Even if you lack the bravado for the Cresta Run, there is lots to do. In midwinter the snow-covered lake provides a playground for events such as polo, horse racing and cricket, but then activities are limited as the lake starts to thaw. There's an annual 'gourmet festival', with chefs from all over the world. The Engadin museum is said to be 'very interesting'. And the shopping is simply 'incredible' if your plastic remains flexible.

There are extensive well-marked walking trails, which a reporter loved (a map is available). Muottas Muragl is a mountain set aside for not skiing – with funicular access to snowshoeing, tobogganing and an igloo village – all with stunning panoramic views.

Some hotels run special activities, such as a curling week. Other options are hang-gliding and indoor tennis. Several reporters rave about the views from the Bernina Express train to Italy, with 'amazing bends and scenery'. Another visitor highly recommends a trip by train to Scuol for the 'fabulous spa with great facilities; a combi pass covers travel plus spa'. There's an 'excellent' public pool in Pontresina.

LINKED RESORT – 1730m

CELERINA

At the bottom end of the famous Cresta Run, Celerina is an appealing base if you want a quiet time – it is unpretentious and villagey, but lacks a central focus (and has very few shops). It has good access to the Corviglia/Marguns sector – a gondola to Marguns. It spreads quite widely, with a lot of second homes, many owned by Italians (the upper part is known as Piccolo Milano). There are some appealing small hotels – reporters like Chesa Rosatsch (837 0101) – and a couple of bigger 4-stars. The modern Inn Lodge (834 4795) has rooms and dormitories for the budget-conscious. The food at the Chesa Rosatsch attracts non-resident diners and has been recommended. The Freestyle School (opened in 2010) focuses on park practice.

SNOWPIX.COM / CHRIS GILL

A favourite corner of Corviglia – the sunny red run from Fuorcla Grischa to Lej da la Pêsch, beneath Piz Nair ↓

Val d'Anniviers

Exceptionally cute, unspoiled villages beneath high, snow-sure slopes. Sounds perfect? Well, there are some drawbacks ...

TOP 10 RATINGS

Extent	**
Fast lifts	*
Queues	****
Snow	****
Expert	****
Intermediate	***
Beginner	***
Charm	*****
Convenience	**
Scenery	****

RPI	100
lift pass	£170
ski hire	£95
lessons	£60
food & drink	£190
total	**£515**

NEWS

2012/13: Grimentz: the capacity of the gondola from the base to Bendolla is due to be increased. Vercorin: there are plans to revamp the gondola, and 2km more snowmaking is due to be installed.

2011/12: Work on a new gondola from Grimentz to the Zinal ski area began in spring 2012, but it will not open until November 2013. Another 1km of snowmaking was installed at Grimentz.

KEY FACTS

Resorts	1340-2000m
	4,400-6,560ft
Slopes	1340-3000m
	4,400-9,840ft
Lifts	45
Pistes	220km
	137 miles
Blue	36%
Red	52%
Black	12%
Snowmaking	13%

- + Charming unspoiled villages
- + Excellent, extensive off-piste
- + Reliable snow-cover
- + No crowds, few queues
- + Four varied ski areas offering good intermediate cruising, but ...

- − Each area has very limited pistes
- − Lots of slow chairs and draglifts
- − Very quiet villages; dead, even
- − Almost entirely open slopes
- − Timetabled buses or ideally a car needed to get between the areas; and the roads are not the best.

In some ways, Val d'Anniviers is in a bit of a time warp. There is plenty of modern accommodation and some modern lifts in key spots. But most of the villages have unspoilt rustic cores with old wooden houses and narrow lanes; and you spend a lot of time on the slopes riding draglifts and not much riding fast chairs (there are only four in the whole valley). Approach the area with the right attitude and you'll probably find it all quite a refreshing change from high-pressure resorts with high-speed everything.

The Val d'Anniviers runs almost due south from the huge trench of the Valais at Sierre. The resort villages are all at least 1000m above Sierre, and the road up has in places been carved out of sheer rock faces. This may help to explain why the valley has been rather neglected by the international travel trade.

The main villages present plenty of chocolate-box photo opportunities, with lots of old wooden houses and barns, narrow paths and lanes and few shops. Most of the lodging is in more modern, less photogenic areas spreading around these old village cores, but the development is generally tasteful and low-rise, and the atmosphere relaxed.

There are five resort villages. On the morning-sun side of the valley, the slopes of Zinal are linked to those of Grimentz by a long, isolated black run. A new gondola will make the return journey from the 2013/14 season but for 2012/13 you'll still have to return by bus. On the afternoon-sun side, the slopes of Chandolin and St-Luc are properly linked at high and low altitude, and are marketed as one. Vercorin is a smaller separate area, with cable car access from Chalais, just outside Sierre, in the Rhône valley.

Except at Vercorin, nearly all the slopes are above the treeline and there's a lot of skiing above 2400m, which usually means good snow. All of the individual areas are small, but they add up to a decent amount.

Buses (free with a lift pass) link the villages and lift bases – the little town of Vissoie is the hub, where you change services. You need to plan times carefully, but a 2011 reporter happily used them to get around.

1650m / 2000m

ST-LUC / CHANDOLIN

These are the sunniest of the main ski resort villages and their slopes are well linked to form the biggest ski area. St-Luc also has the attraction of a fabulous, characterful old hotel.

A funicular goes up from the edge of St-Luc and a high-speed chair from the edge of Chandolin. Both are served by the free ski-buses. The 65km of slopes face west to south-west, so the snow suffers from the sun. Apart from Chandolin's fast quad, there is only one other chair – the other 11 lifts are all drags.

The pistes suit beginners and intermediates best; though there are two black runs (one very short, the other back to the foot of the funicular), five short itinerary routes (including one that we reckon is the steepest marked run in the Alps) and a gnarly freeride area where competitions are held. There are some testing reds, but in general the slopes are gentle, easy cruising territory. A highlight is the long, easy red run from Bella Tola at 3000m away from all the lifts at the extreme skier's left edge of the ski area down to the Tipi

UK PACKAGES

St-Luc Alpine Answers, Inntravel, Ski Bespoke, Ski Safari
Zinal Alpine Answers, Mountain Tracks, Ski Freedom, SkiZinal
Grimentz Alpine Answers, Erna Low, Mountain Heaven, Mountain Tracks, Ski Club Freshtracks, Ski Safari

bar and ski-bus stop – a great way to end the day. There's a good beginner area and a terrain park near the top of the St-Luc funicular.

There are some good mountain restaurants with fine views. Above Chandolin the tiny Illhorn has a limited menu but a cosy panelled room (and fab pear tart); the Tsapé is a smart, stark place, high-up, with good local cuisine; above St-Luc, the Bella Tola is a traditional, table-service hut.

Both Chandolin and St-Luc are fairly spread out. But St-Luc has a cute, compact old centre with a small outdoor après-ski bar. The 4-star hotel Bella Tola (475 1444) is just a few strides from here. Built in 1859, it has been beautifully renovated by its current owners, with a fine spa, great sunny terrace, and good restaurant serving notably 'excellent fish dishes'. We enjoyed staying there enormously.

1670m

ZINAL

This small village near the head of the valley doesn't have the charm of the other villages. It has a small area of slopes with stunning views of high peaks including the Matterhorn.

A modern cable car goes to Sorebois at 2440m, the hub of the ski area. Most of the slopes face roughly east and keep their snow well.

The runs are mainly short (some only 200m or 300m vertical) but include some good reds – our favourites are those from Combe Durand at the edge of the ski area, served by a steepish draglift that also accesses a freeride area. The one fast chairlift serves wide and gentle blue runs, ideal for novices. The two short black runs are really of red steepness. There is a longer red run (with a black variant on the lower part) back to the village. And there's great off-piste in bowls between the pistes. From the top of the area, Piste du Chamois is a real highlight – a long, easy black run down a shady deserted bowl with lots of accessible off-piste, ending with a woodland path to Grimentz (or to Mottec to catch the bus).

Zinal is popular with families and there's a good beginner area and children's snow garden.

There are only two huts. On weekends and holidays the Sorebois self-service ('decent, reasonable value food') offers an 'all you can eat' buffet in a revamped area downstairs.

Zinal has a handful of hotels. The central 2-star Pointe de Zinal (475 1164) does excellent food and the 2-star Le Trift (475 1466) is 'comfortable with adequate but small rooms and good food'.

1570m

GRIMENTZ

Grimentz has a richly deserved reputation for its extensive off-piste. And it has a small area of varied pistes above its very cute old village.

The village is spread out on quite a steep slope and a lot of new building has been going on. Here (more than in the other villages) there is a

Combe Durand
Corne de Sorebois
2895m
2440m
ZINAL
Zinal
1670m/5,480ft
Piste du Chamois
288
Bella Tola
3000m/
9,840ft
Mottec
GRIMENTZ
Grimentz
1570m/5,150ft
2130m
Roc d'Orzi
2855m
2770m
St-Jean
Tignousa
2180m
St-Luc
1650m/5,410ft
2470m
ST LUC-CHANDOLIN
Vissoie
Mt Major
2375m
Illhorn
2600m
Chandolin
2000m/6,560ft
VERCORIN
Vercorin
1340m/4,400ft
gondola
cable car
railway/funicular
fast chairlift
Slow chairs & drags
have no symbol
Chalais
Sierre
560m/1,840ft
To
Geneva
→

↑ Grimentz has a small area of varied snow-sure pistes, but its real attraction for experts is excellent off-piste; and by 2013/14 it should be linked by a new gondola to Zinal

WENDY-JANE KING

Phone numbers
From elsewhere in Switzerland add the prefix 0848 (for Coeur du Valais) and 027 (for everywhere else); from abroad use the prefix +41 and omit the initial '0'

TOURIST OFFICES

Val d'Anniviers
www.sierre-anniviers.ch

Grimentz
www.grimentz.ch

St-Luc
www.saint-luc.ch

Vercorin
www.vercorin.ch

Zinal
www.zinal.ch

Chandolin
www.chandolin.ch

separation between the cute old centre – lots of tiny old barns and narrow paths – and the skiers' accommodation. Much of this is conveniently close to the gondola up to Bendolla at 2130m – but some is less conveniently placed on the opposite side of the old village.

Bendolla has a good, roped-off beginner area and snowgarden for kids, and above it are two main sectors. On the right as you look up are easy blue and red runs. On the left are steeper and quieter runs, including two blacks, one of which goes from the top to almost the bottom of the mountain (1300m vertical) and is interestingly varied. The main run to the village is quite steep, but you can ride the gondola.

The real attraction for experts is the extensive off-piste. We did a great run with a guide off the back of Roc d'Orzival: a huge, ski-anywhere bowl that goes on for hundreds of turns before dropping into an area of widely spaced trees and a long run-out.

We lack recent reports, but both the Swiss and the International ski schools have received positive past reports – especially for teaching kids.

The functional main Bendolla restaurant is mainly self-service ('lengthy wait, poor food', said a 2012 reporter), with a small table-service section where we had an enjoyable meal. Reporters favour the more rustic Etable du Marais below Grands Plans ('fantastic, huge rösti'). We've had good pasta at the self-service Orzival.

As the lifts close, Chez Florioz on the piste just above the village is the place for a drink – very welcoming host. The best restaurants are probably those in the main hotels. But we have also enjoyed an excellent meal at Arlequin (a pizzeria). Bar le Country is a lively sports bar.

We have had comfortable stays and good food at the two 3-star hotels – the Alpina (476 1616) almost opposite the gondola and the less convenient Cristal (475 3291). The 'comfortable' 2-star Bec de Bosson is recommended by a 2012 visitor.

UK tour operator Mountain Heaven's Cole Ridge catered chalet is right on the slopes, with an outdoor hot tub, a sauna and stunning views. Mountain Heaven also has some smart, central self-catered chalet-apartments.

1340m

VERCORIN

The smallest area of slopes, and not so easily reached from other resorts.
The pretty village of Vercorin, perched on a shelf overlooking the Rhône valley, is reached by a winding road or by a cable car from Chalais, just outside Sierre. This is followed by a free ski-bus to a two-stage gondola. The slopes suit intermediates best.

VERBIER TOURIST OFFICE

Verbier

Big, chalet-style resort that attracts powder hounds from all over the world – and big-spending night owls from Geneva

RATINGS

The mountains

Extent	*****
Fast lifts	****
Queues	***
Terrain p'ks	***
Snow	***
Expert	*****
Intermediate	***
Beginner	**
Boarder	***
X-country	*
Restaurants	***
Schools	*****
Families	***

The resort

Charm	***
Convenience	**
Scenery	****
Eating out	****
Après-ski	*****
Off-slope	***

RPI	140
lift pass	£240
ski hire	£130
lessons	£115
food & drink	£215
total	**£700**

NEWS

2012/13: A new gondola linking Bruson to Le Châble is planned, but we have no details. A new 4-star hotel, the Cordée des Alpes, is due to open. The planned new lift from Les Esserts to Savoleyres has been postponed again, now to 2013/14.

2011/12: A six-pack (Mayentzet) replaced the two successive slow chairs from just above the nursery slopes to Les Ruinettes. Snowmaking has also been improved in this area. A new mountain restaurant, Le Dahu, opened at the bottom of the Chaux Express chair. A new snow garden opened at La Tzoumaz.

- + Extensive, challenging slopes with a lot of off-piste and long bump runs
- + Upper slopes offer a real high-mountain feel, plus great views
- + Sizeable, animated village in a sunny, panoramic setting
- + Lively, varied nightlife
- + Much improved lift system, piste grooming and signposting, but ...

- − Piste map and piste naming still have a long way to go
- − Some overcrowded pistes and areas
- − The 4 Valleys network is much less wonderful than it looks on paper
- − Sunny lower slopes will always be a problem, even with snowmaking
- − Some long walks/rides to lifts
- − Expensive bars and restaurants

For serious off-piste routes and for mogul fields, Verbier is one of the world's cult resorts. For vibrant nightlife, too, it is difficult to beat. At first, with its claimed 410km of pistes, Verbier also seems to rank alongside the French mega-networks as a dream resort for keen piste skiers who like to ski for a week without doing the same run twice. But if the French 3 Vallées floats your boat, you may be sorely disappointed by the Swiss 4 Vallées. The network is an inconveniently sprawling affair, with lots of tedious links.

Verbier's local pistes leave a lot to be desired, too: in comparison with the slopes of somewhere like Courchevel, they are distinctly limited. A good intermediate skier could cover them in a day. This is partly because many of the runs that could and should be black pistes are classified as unpatrolled itinéraires – something that we have been moaning about for years.

THE RESORT

Verbier enjoys an impressive setting on a wide, sunny balcony facing spectacular peaks. It's a fashionable, informal, very lively place that teems with cosmopolitan visitors. Most are younger than visitors to other big Swiss resorts.

The resort is at one end of a long, strung-out series of interconnected slopes, optimistically branded the 4 Valleys and linking Verbier to Nendaz, Veysonnaz, Thyon and other resorts. These other resorts have their own pros and cons. All are much less lively in the evening than Verbier, appreciably cheaper places to stay, and some are more sensible bases for those who plan to stick to pistes rather than venture off-piste – the Veysonnaz-Thyon sector, in particular, is much more intermediate-friendly than Verbier. As bases for exploration of the whole 4 Valleys, only tiny Siviez is much of an advance on Verbier. You can also stay down in the valley village of Le Châble, which has a gondola up to Verbier and on into the slopes. Across the valley, Bruson is more attractive as a place to visit for a day than to stay in. There is more on these places at the end of the chapter.

Chamonix and Champéry are within reach by car. But a car can be a bit of a nuisance in Verbier itself. Parking is tightly controlled; your chalet or hotel may not have enough space for all guests' cars, which means a hike from the free parking at the sports centre or paying for garage space.

Danni Sports was praised by a 2011 reporter: 'Extremely helpful and friendly, good choice of equipment for hire, and they do a half-price ski-service happy hour mid-week.'

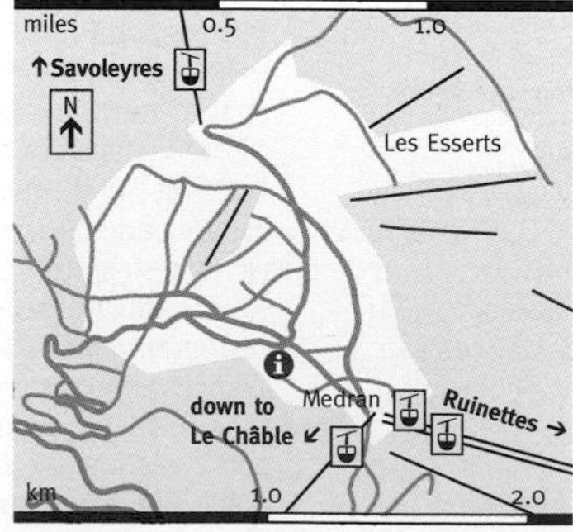

↑ Verbier is Switzerland's Chalet Central. This shot shows the lower slopes of the rather neglected Savoleyres sector

VERBIER-ST-BERNARD

KEY FACTS

Resort	1500m 4,920ft
4 Valleys area	
Slopes	1500-3330m 4,920-10,930ft
Lifts	89
Pistes	410km 255 miles
Blue	39%
Red	44%
Black	17%
Snowmaking	13%
Verbier, Bruson and Tzoumaz/Savoleyres sectors only (covered by Verbier pass)	
Slopes	1500-3025m 4,920-9,920ft
Lifts	39
Pistes	203km 126 miles
Blue	49%
Red	27%
Black	24%
Snowmaking	120 guns

VILLAGE CHARM ★★★☆☆
Busy upmarket chalet town

The resort is an amorphous sprawl of chalet-style buildings. Most of the shops and hotels (but not chalets) are set around the Place Centrale and along the sloping streets stretching both down the hill and up it to the main lift station at Médran, 500m away. At close of play this street, in particular, is buzzing with après-ski activity. These central areas get unpleasantly packed with cars at busy times, especially weekends when lots of people are coming and going, which rather detracts from the ambience.

CONVENIENCE ★★☆☆☆
Pick your spot

It's a sprawling resort where most people suffer some inconvenience. But most people just get used to using the free buses, which run on several routes until 8pm. They're generally efficient, but some areas have quite an infrequent service.

The Médran lift station is a walkable distance from the Place Centrale, so staying between the two has attractions. If nightlife is not a priority, staying somewhere near the upper (north-east) fringes of the village may mean that you can almost ski to your door – plus there is a piste linking the upper nursery slopes to the one in the middle of the village. Skiing from the door is less likely. More chalets are built each year, with many newer properties inconveniently situated along the road to the lift base for the secondary Savoleyres area, about 1.5km from Médran.

SCENERY ★★★★☆
A circle of Alpine peaks

Verbier is surrounded by stunning Alpine scenery; from the top of Mont-Fort there are impressive views in all directions, including Mont Blanc to the west and the Matterhorn to the east.

THE MOUNTAINS

Essentially this is high-mountain terrain. There are wooded slopes directly above the village, but the runs here are basically just a way home at the end of the day. There is more sheltered woodland skiing in other sectors of the 4 Valleys – particularly above Veysonnaz.

The piste signposting has been improved and the piste map now has some (but not all) runs named – but in type too small to read. What's more, the piste names are still not posted on the mountain. So it's less of a shambles than it was, but still a shambles. And readers still complain: 'spent ages looking at the map with print too small to read', 'need more big maps at top of runs' and 'map fails to adequately show up and down' are recent reports.

EXTENT OF THE SLOPES ★★★★★
Very spread out

Savoleyres is a small area effectively isolated from the major network, reached by a gondola from the north-west end of the village. This area is underrated and generally underused. A new access gondola from the central nursery slopes is planned, but has been repeatedly delayed. It has open, sunny slopes on the front side, and long, pleasantly wooded, shadier runs on the back. You can take a catwalk across from Savoleyres to the foot of Verbier's main slopes.

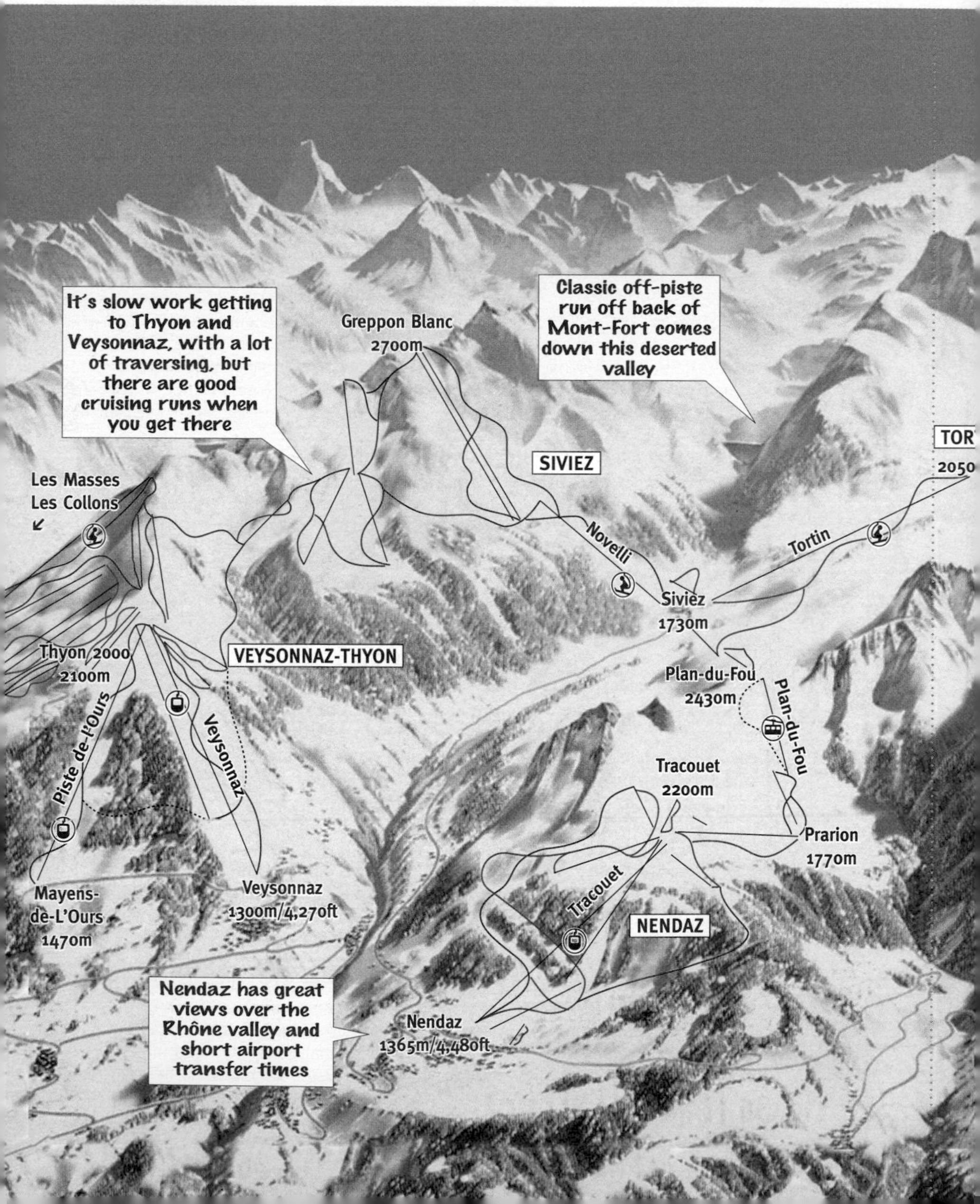

These are served by lifts from Médran, at the opposite end of the village. Two gondolas rise to Les Ruinettes and then a gondola and chairlift continue on to **Les Attelas**. From Les Attelas a small cable car goes up to Mont-Gelé, for steep off-piste runs only. Heading down instead, you can go back westwards to Les Ruinettes, south to La Chaux or north to Lac des Vaux. From Lac des Vaux

It's slow work getting to Thyon and Veysonnaz, with a lot of traversing, but there are good cruising runs when you get there
Greppon Blanc 2700m
Classic off-piste run off back of Mont-Fort comes down this deserted valley
SIVIEZ
TOR
2050
Les Masses
Les Collons
Novelli
Tortin
Siviez 1730m
Thyon 2000
2100m
VEYSONNAZ-THYON
Plan-du-Fou 2430m
Plan-du-Fou
Piste de-l'Ours
Veysonnaz
Tracouet 2200m
Prarion 1770m
Mayens-de-L'Ours 1470m
Veysonnaz 1300m/4,270ft
Tracouet
NENDAZ
Nendaz has great views over the Rhône valley and short airport transfer times
Nendaz 1365m/4,480ft

chairs go to Les Attelas and to Chassoure, the top of a wide, steep and shady off-piste mogul field going down to **Tortin**, with a gondola back.

You can also ride a chondola from Les Ruinettes to the sunny, easy slopes of La Chaux. At the bottom of these slopes a jumbo cable car goes up to **Col des Gentianes** and the glacier area. The lovely, often quiet, red run back down to La Chaux is one of our favourites. A second, much smaller cable car (now with new panoramic cabins) goes up from Gentianes to the **Mont-Fort** glacier. From the top, there's only a long, steep black run back down. From Gentianes you can head down on another off-piste route to Tortin; the whole north-facing run from the top to Tortin is almost 1300m vertical. A cable car returns to Col des Gentianes.

Below Tortin is the gateway to the rest of the 4 Valleys, **Siviez**. From here, a ridiculously outdated chair goes off into the long, thin **Nendaz** sector. A

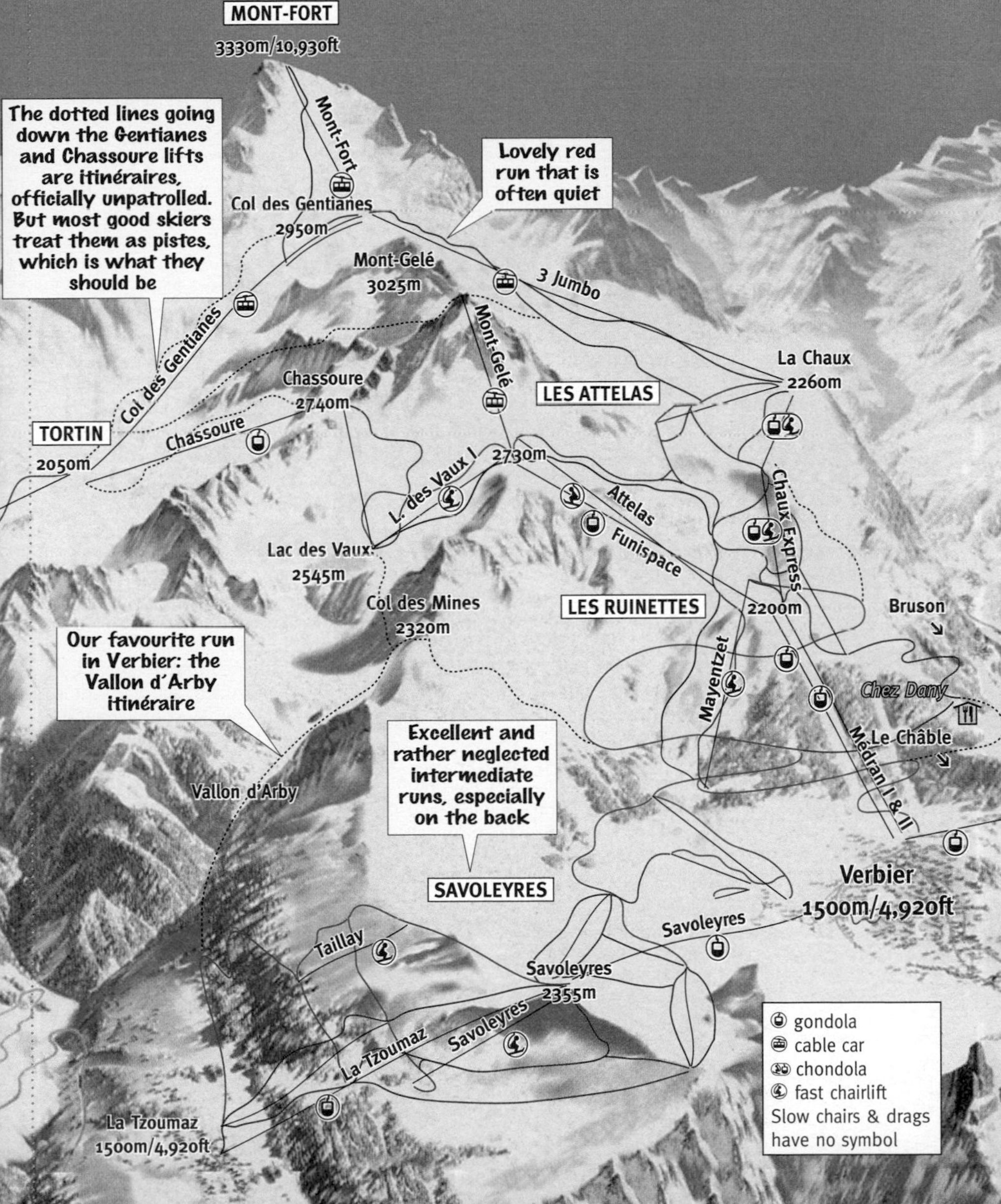

OFF-PISTE FOR ALL

Verbier has some of the best, most extensive and most varied off-piste in the world, and major freeride competitions are held there every year. Here, we pick out just a few of the off-piste runs on offer. See 'For experts' for the status of itinéraires; for the other runs here you should hire a guide.

The Col des Mines and Vallon d'Arby itinéraires, accessible from Lac des Vaux, are relatively easy, though there may be some unnerving moments on the traverse to the point where they split. The first is a long, open slope back to Verbier and the latter a very beautiful run in a steep-sided valley down to La Tzoumaz and the Savoleyres lifts. Further afield, the long Eteygeon itinéraire from Greppon Blanc above Siviez is 'wonderfully varied and should not be missed', says a reporter; it ends up on the road and you catch a bus back to Les Masses (see end of chapter).

Stairway to Heaven is usually quiet (we were the only people on it on a March visit) and its snow is kept in good condition by the lack of crowds and its shady orientation. It starts a short ski, pole and steep climb from Col des Gentianes. Then you drop over the ridge into a deserted valley, and it's a long, relatively easy ski down to Tortin, pretty much parallel to the Gentianes itinéraire.

The Mont-Gelé cable car offers some of the most amazing terrain accessible anywhere by lift, with long runs down to Siviez on steep but open slopes, before a scenic traverse and schuss along the valley. Or go down the opposite side of the mountain through the steep rock face towards Lac des Vaux (not a route for the faint hearted). The many couloirs accessible from Attelas can also be fantastic. There are serious adventures to be had off the back of Mont-Fort – we loved it (except for the long walk out past Lac de Cleuson); it's a vast bowl and we found fresh powder, even though it hadn't snowed for days; you end up at Siviez.

fast quad heads the other way towards **Veysonnaz-Thyon**, via a couple of drags and a lot of catwalks.

Allow plenty of time to get to and from these remote corners – the taxi-rides home are expensive.

The slopes of **Bruson,** across the valley from Verbier, are described briefly at the end of this chapter.

FAST LIFTS ★★★★
Locally fine

The main access lifts are gondolas and chairs. Further afield, more upgrades are needed to improve links throughout the 4 Valleys (especially between Siviez and Veysonnaz-Thyon, where draglifts are the norm).

QUEUES ★★★
Not the problem they were

Queues have been greatly eased by investment in powerful new lifts and have barely been a problem for reporters over the past few years. There may be queues at Médran if Sunday visitors fill the gondola from Le Châble, but they shift quickly.

Queues still occur for outdated lifts in the outlying 4 Valleys resorts, and the quad at Siviez gets busy at peak times and if the weather is poor.

The quiet Savoleyres is generally queue-free.

TERRAIN PARKS ★★★
Expert and beginner options

The Swatch Snowpark, Verbier's main freestyle area, is at La Chaux. It has separate lines for varying levels: blue, red and black. Features are varied, with kickers, boxes and rails of all types and a giant airbag. Freestyle coaching (check www.snowschool.ch) is available.

SNOW RELIABILITY ★★★
Improved snowmaking

The slopes of the Mont-Fort glacier always have good snow, naturally. The runs to Tortin are normally snow-sure, too. But nearly all of this terrain is steep and mogulled, and much of it is formally off-piste. Most of Verbier's main local slopes face south or west and are below 2500m – so they can be in poor condition at times. Snowmaking covers the whole main run down from Les Attelas to Médran at the top of the village. The slopes of La Chaux, the nursery slopes and some of the Savoleyres sector are also well-served. At Veysonnaz-Thyon snowmaking now covers 80% of the area. We have been very impressed with its use on the runs down to Mayens-de-L'Ours and to Veysonnaz. Piste grooming is good throughout the 4 Valleys.

LIFT PASSES

4 Valleys/Mont-Fort

Prices in SF

Age	1-day	6-day
under 14	34	176
14 to 19	54	281
20 to 64	68	351
65 plus	54	281

Free under 6; over 77

Beginner limited pass SF29

Notes

Covers Verbier, Mont-Fort, Bruson, La Tzoumaz, Nendaz, Veysonnaz and Thyon including ski-buses; part-day passes; family reductions

Alternative passes

Verbier only; La Tzoumaz/Savoleyres only; Bruson only

FOR EXPERTS ★★★★★

The main attraction

Verbier has some superb tough slopes, many of them off-piste and needing a guide – see feature panel. There are few conventional black pistes; most of the runs that might have this designation are now defined as itinéraires – which means they are 'marked, not maintained, not controlled'. They are said to be closed if unsafe but this information is not made public – and if they are not patrolled you should not ski them alone. We'd like to see these runs given black piste status, so you know clearly where you stand. The black pistes that do exist are mostly indistinguishable from nearby reds. The front face of Mont-Fort is an exception: a long mogul field, with a choice of gradient from steep to intimidatingly steep. The World Cup run (Piste de l'Ours) at Veysonnaz is a steepish, often icy red, ideal for really speeding down when in good nick. The two most popular itinéraires to Tortin are both excellent in their different ways. The one from Chassoure starts with a rocky traverse at the top and is then normally one huge, steep, wide mogul field. The north-facing one from Gentianes is longer, less steep, but feels much more of an adventure (keep left for shallower slopes and better snow).

FOR INTERMEDIATES ★★★★★

Hit Savoleyres – or Veysonnaz

Many mileage-hungry intermediates find Verbier disappointing. The intermediate slopes in the main area are concentrated between Les Attelas and the village, above and below Les Ruinettes, plus the little bowl at Lac des Vaux and the sunny slopes at La Chaux. This is all excellent and varied intermediate territory, but there isn't much of it; to put it in perspective, this whole area is no bigger than the tiny slopes of Alpbach, and it is used by the bulk of the visitors staying in one of Switzerland's largest resorts. So it is often crowded, especially the otherwise wonderful sweeping red from Les Attelas to Les Ruinettes. There is excellent easy blue run skiing at La Chaux, including a 'slow skiing' piste. Getting back from La Chaux to Les Ruinettes is easy: as well as the chondola, there is a short piste from the top of the lift avoiding the steepest section down.

The under-used Savoleyres area has good intermediate pistes, usually better snow and fewer people. It is also a good hill for mixed abilities, with variations of many runs. There is a blue run linking this sector to the Médran lift base, but the way down to that link from the top is not easy.

The Veysonnaz-Thyon and Nendaz sectors are worth exploring (those not willing to take on the itinéraires can ride the lifts down).

FOR BEGINNERS ★★★★★

OK but not ideal

There are sunny nursery slopes close to the middle of the village and at Les Esserts, at the top of it. These are fine provided they have snow, and they are well-equipped with snowmaking. Day passes covering these two areas cost SF29 in 2011/12 (free for children). For progression, a local Verbier pass is

SCHOOLS

Swiss
t 775 3363

Fantastique
t 771 4141

Adrenaline
t 771 7459

Altitude
t 771 6006

New Generation
t 771 1181 /
+33 479 010318
0844 770 4733 (UK)
www.skinewgen.com

European Snowsport
t 771 6222

Powder Extreme
t 076 479 8771
020 8123 9483 (UK)

Warren Smith Ski Academy
t 01525 374757 (UK)

Classes
(Swiss prices)
6 half days SF280

Private lessons
From SF175 for 2hr for 1 or 2 people

GUIDES

Bureau des guides
t 775 3370

Olivier Roduit
t 771 5317

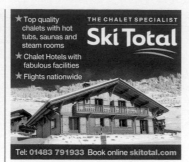

available. Progression to longer runs is not straightforward, but there are easy blues at La Chaux and on the back of Savoleyres.

FOR BOARDERS ★★★
Extreme freeride heaven

Verbier has become synonymous with extreme snowboarding and is generally seen as a freeriders' resort, with powder, cliffs, natural hits and trees all easily accessible. Not surprisingly, it is on the Freeride world tour (see www.freerideworldtour.com). For years the Bec des Rosses has been home to Verbier Extreme – the most high-profile event of its kind. There is a lot of steep and challenging terrain to be explored with a guide, but the pistes and itinéraires will provide most riders with plenty to think about. Chairlifts and gondolas serve the main area, with no drags. The area is far from ideal for beginners and timid intermediates, who should stick to the lower blue runs and the Savoleyres area, but there are several draglifts there. There is a good terrain park.

FOR CROSS-COUNTRY ★
Little on offer

There's a 4km loop in Verbier, 10km at Les Ruinettes-La Chaux and 8km down the valley in Champsec and Lourtier.

MOUNTAIN RESTAURANTS ★★★
Surprisingly uninspiring

It's not difficult to get an enjoyable lunch, but it's easy to go wrong. There are too few huts, so they get too crowded. The standards of food and service get mixed reviews.

Editors' choice In the main area, the rustic Chez Dany (771 2524) is a classic old chalet on the itinéraire on the southern fringe of the area: 'great atmosphere, beautiful forest setting', is the endorsement of a 2012 visitor.

Worth knowing about Some reader favourites are far-flung. Among the most frequently recommended are the Chottes between Siviez and Veysonnaz-Thyon ('large terrace; potage paysanne a favourite') and the Caboulis on the run down to Veysonnaz is recommended for 'very good soup'. At Les Collons the Cambuse has 'excellent food and is not too expensive'. At Siviez, Chez Odette has changed hands but it is 'essentially unchanged with good food and big helpings', says a 2012 visitor.

Closer to home, there are some nice places on Savoleyres, though most rarely generate reports. The Croix de Coeur at the top is an attractive 15-sided building with great views from the terrace and 'very pleasant' table-service of good food. Don't overlook the rustic Marmotte and the Namasté lower down, or the Sonalon, on the fringe of the village.

Back in the main sector, the restaurants at Les Ruinettes were smartened up a few years ago: the Cristal offers fine dining under the former chef of Chalet d'Adrien but visitors say the self-service restaurant is 'poor' and 'uninspiring'. The Olympique at Les Attelas includes a good table-service restaurant. The Cabane Mont-Fort is a proper mountain refuge off the run to La Chaux from Col des Gentianes: 'one of the best for atmosphere' but gets packed. A new restaurant, the Dahu, opened at the bottom of the La Chaux chair last season; reports, please. Chalet Carlsberg has a good position at La Combe and has impressed us with fast and efficient service. Carrefour, near the top of the nursery slopes, does 'great food, worth a visit'. Mayen, accessible from both the main Verbier slopes and the Col des Mines, has 'great views' and 'very good table service'.

There are two picnic rooms: at Les Ruinettes and at the Savoleyres restaurant.

SCHOOLS AND GUIDES ★★★★★
Good reports

There's no shortage of schools to choose between. New Generation, well established and a reader favourite in several top French resorts, has its first Swiss branch in Verbier. We were very impressed with our mountain guide from Adrenaline. We have had good reports of Altitude: 'booked five 3hr off-piste lessons and were the only

CHILDCARE

Schtroumpfs
t 771 6585
Ages 3mnth to 3yr

Chalet Services
t 079 519 2925
Childcare in your own chalet

Kids Club
t 775 3363
Age 3 to 6

Babysitter list
At tourist office

Ski school (Swiss)
From age 4 (6 half days SF290)

Wow! What's new in Austria? See p168.

two in the group'. European Snowsports is praised this year for competitive pricing of private lessons and for providing a native English speaking instructor. British instructor Warren Smith runs his Ski Academy here and Powder Extreme specializes in off-piste. We have skied with both outfits and thought them good. A 2011 customer on Warren Smith's course felt misled by the pre-course marketing but found her skiing 'more relaxed and fluent' after the course.

FOR FAMILIES ★★★

Good for childcare

The nursery slopes are central, and the Swiss school's facilities are good. A new snow garden opened at La Tzoumaz in 2011/12. There are considerable reductions on the lift pass price for families too. The possibility of leaving very young babies at the Schtroumpfs nursery is valuable. Nanny services are offered by Chalet Services Verbier.

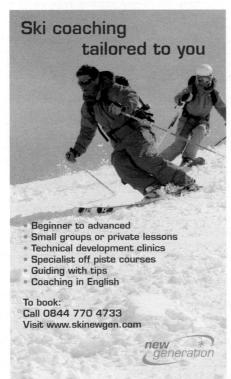

STAYING THERE

There are surprisingly few apartments and B&Bs, though there are inexpensive B&Bs in Le Châble. Hotels are pricey for their gradings.

Chalets Verbier is the chalet-party capital of Switzerland, with some very luxurious places. Ski Verbier has an impressive portfolio at the top of the market. Ski Total has a chalet hotel (the Montpelier – 'well run, good food, fantastic staff', says a 2012 visitor) and three chalets – all very smart and with facilities such as pool, sauna, steam. Skiworld has a large central chalet with jacuzzi and sauna. Inghams has two chalets, and a chalet-hotel in the main square. Crystal Finest has two smart chalet-apartments in a new building near Médran.

Hotels There is a 5-star, four 4-stars, ten 3-stars and a few simpler places.

*******Chalet d'Adrien** (771 6200) Relais & Chateaux. A beautifully furnished low-rise 29-room chalet, with top-notch cooking. In a peaceful setting next to the Savoleyres lift, with great views. Neat spa/gym/pool.

******Nevaï** (775 4000) Modern, minimalist, trendy, next to Farm Club (same ownership). Après-ski bar.

******Vanessa** (775 2800) Central, with spacious apartments as well as rooms.

*****Farinet** (771 6626) Central, British-owned, with a focal après-ski bar.

*****Poste** (771 6681) Midway between centre and Médran; pool. Some rooms small. 'Pleasant atmosphere.'

*****Rotonde** (771 6525) Much cheaper; well positioned between centre and Médran; some budget rooms.

Apartments There are surprisingly few on the UK market. Ski Expectations has a conveniently located, Swiss-owned four-bedroom chalet and studio apartment. Ski Verbier has some nice-looking places.

EATING OUT ★★★★

Plenty of choice

There is a wide range of restaurants; many are listed in a free pocket guide.

The 5-star Chalet d'Adrien is one of the best gourmet places in town (one Michelin star). We had an excellent meal in the Nevaï hotel. King's (under the same ownership) is another of our favourites – innovative food in a stylish, club-like setting. We've also had good meals in the stylish, 'quiet and sophisticated' Millénium. The small Ecurie in hotel

ACTIVITIES

Indoor Sports centre (swimming pool, ice rink, curling, squash, sauna, solarium, steam bath, hot tub), museums, galleries

Outdoor Cleared walking paths, paragliding, snowshoeing, ice climbing, dog sledding, tobogganing

GETTING THERE

Air Geneva 160km/100 miles (2hr15)

Rail Le Châble (7km/4 miles); regular buses to resort or gondola

UK PACKAGES

Alpine Answers, Alpine Weekends, Belvedere Travel, Bramble Ski, Chalets Unlimited, Crystal, Crystal Finest, Elegant Resorts, Erna Low, Flexiski, Independent Ski Links, Inghams, Interactive Resorts, Jeffersons, Kaluma, Luxury Chalet Collection, Momentum, Mountain Beds, Mountain Tracks, Oxford Ski Co, PowderBeds, Powder White, Ski Bespoke, Ski Expectations, Ski Freedom, Ski Independence, Ski Line, Ski Safari, Ski Solutions, Ski Total, Skitracer, Ski Verbier, Ski Weekend, Skiweekends.com, Skiworld, Snow Finders, Snoworks, STC, Supertravel, V-Ski, VIP, White Roc
Nendaz Alpine Answers, Crystal, Erna Low, Lagrange, Ski Club Freshtracks, Ski Independence, Skiworld, Ted Bentley
Veysonnaz Crystal, Erna Low, Luxury Chalet Collection, Oxford Ski Co

Ermitage has a 'traditional atmosphere' and does 'very good' food. The Rouge Restaurant and Club offers a wide-ranging menu ('lovely pumpkin soup').

For Swiss specialities, try the Relais des Neiges ('quieter than many; excellent food'), the Caveau, Vieux Verbier by the Médran lifts or Esserts by the nursery slopes. The ever-popular Fer à Cheval is known for its pizzas but other dishes are also very good ('superb steak tartare'). Downstairs in the Pub Mont Fort you can get good value gastropub food. The 'hanging meat' has to be tried at Al Capone, out near the Savoleyres gondola – also known for its pizzas; we had excellent pizzas at Borsalino, near the centre of town.

You can be ferried by snowmobile up to Chez Dany or the Marmotte for a meal, followed by a torchlit descent.

APRES-SKI ★★★★★
Throbbing but expensive

On the slopes, popular stops include the Rocks bar at Ruinettes, either of the tents of 1936 or the Chalet Carlsberg. In town, the Offshore Coffee Bar at Médran is ever-popular for people-watching, milk shakes and cakes. The Big Ben pub is lively. The Nevaï hotel has live music on its terraces and the Rouge at the bottom of the golf course has a popular sun deck.

Then if you're young, loud and British, it's on to the Pub Mont-Fort – there's a widescreen TV for live sport. The Nelson and Fer à Cheval ('great atmosphere from après through to the small hours') are popular with locals. The absolutely central Farinet has won awards for its après-ski and rocks to live bands regularly ('packed with people dancing on the tables and bar – an iconic après-ski place'). Or you can sip cocktails in its lounge bar next door.

After dinner the Pub Mont Fort is again popular (the shots bar in the cellar is worth a visit). Crock No Name is a cool cocktail bar often with a blues band or a DJ. T-Bar is 'packed' for live rugby and football, and 'best on live music nights'. King's is a quiet cellar bar with 60s decor. The Farm Club is seriously expensive – on Friday and Saturday packed with rich Swiss paying SF220 for bottles of spirits.

The Public Club (formerly Coco), Casbah (in hotel Farinet) and Coup d'Etat are nightclubs.

OFF THE SLOPES ★★★
A few things to do

Verbier has an excellent sports centre (with pool, saunas, hot tubs), dog sledding between Les Ruinettes and La Chaux and some nice walks. Montreux is an enjoyable train excursion from Le Châble, and Martigny is worth a visit for the Roman remains and art gallery. Reporters have recommended the spa complex at Lavey-les-Bains. Various mountain restaurants are accessible to pedestrians – a walkers' pass covers most of the local lifts. There are popular long toboggan runs on Savoleyres.

LINKED RESORT – 1365m

NENDAZ

Nendaz is little known in Britain but is a major resort, with over 17,000 beds (practically all in apartments). Most of the resort is modern, built in traditional chalet style and has great views across the Rhône valley.

It's a sizeable and sprawling place and the centre is busy with traffic. The local bus services are reliable, but get oversubscribed at peak times. There are 100km of walks, an ice rink, fitness centre, climbing wall, squash courts.

A 12-person gondola takes you to the top of the local slopes at Tracouet. This is a splendid, sunny little shelf with gentle slopes and long, shady red and blue runs back down to Nendaz. But getting to and from the rest of the 4 Valleys can be a slow business and key links on the way have no snow-making and can be closed. Getting back involves taking an itinéraire (or riding a cable car down) followed by a black run – too tricky for many intermediates. Many people prefer to drive/bus to Siviez, and start/finish skiing there.

UK chalet company Ted Bentley has two chalets, with outdoor hot tubs. There are a couple of small 3-star hotels – the 'basic but pleasant' Mont-Fort (288 2616) is 150m from the lifts: 'friendly'; 'cool urban' bar. There's also a plentiful supply of apartments (Skiworld has a new three-bed one right opposite the gondola).

There's quite a wide choice of restaurants including Tex-Mex, pizzas, Thai and sushi, as well as steaks and local mountain food. Chez Edith, a tiny restaurant on the way to Siviez has been recommended.

There are some excellent woodland pistes in the outlying Thyon-Veysonnaz sector →

OFFICE DE TOURISME VEYSONNAZ

LINKED RESORT – 1730m

SIVIEZ

Siviez, a small huddle of buildings in an isolated spot, is effectively a junction of the slopes of Verbier, Nendaz and Veysonnaz-Thyon. It is the best base from which to explore the whole 4 Valleys lift network, though lodging is limited almost entirely to apartments. There are daytime buses to/from Nendaz. The long and gentle blue run through the sheltered valley from Tortin is super beginner progression territory. It is also an excellent base for doing the tough skiing of Verbier – you can end the day with a descent of 1600m vertical from Mont-Fort; no noise in the evenings; perfect.

LINKED RESORT – 1300m

VEYSONNAZ

Veysonnaz is a small, family resort, sunny in the afternoon, at the foot of an excellent, long red slope from the ridge above Thyon. A second excellent (though often icy) red, regularly used for major races, descends to the isolated lift base of Mayens-de-L'Ours.

The resort is spread widely across and down the hillside, with extensive views across the Rhône valley. The original attractive old village, complete with church, is two hairpin bends below Veysonnaz Station, the lift base and the main focus of the place for the visitor. The link up to Thyon is an eight-seat gondola, but progress from there towards Verbier is a slow business. Taking a car means you can drive to Siviez for much quicker access to the Verbier slopes. Shuttle-buses serve the lifts, but they are not super-frequent and do not run on Saturdays.

Veysonnaz Station has the essential facilities – half a dozen bars and cafes, four restaurants, a disco or two and a wellness centre with swimming pool and spa facilities (closed Saturdays). There are adequate shops, including a butcher and baker.

Accommodation is mainly in apartments – substantial chalet-style buildings dotted along the road the lift base is on. There are plenty of smaller chalets, too. There are two 3-star hotels next to the gondola station: the Chalet Royal (208 5644) has 'stunning views', though not from all rooms, and 'generally good' food. The Magrappé (208 5700) has 'a bit of atmosphere' and is more the focus of lively après-ski. There are some B&Bs.

There are two schools: Swiss and Neige Aventure. And there is a children's day care centre on the mountain. There is a 5km cross-country trail along the mountainside, with grand views.

LINKED RESORT – 2100m

THYON 2000

Thyon 2000 is a purpose-built collection of plain, medium-rise apartment blocks just above the treeline at the hub of the Veysonnaz-Thyon sector of the 4 Valleys. The apartments are a bit of a blot on the landscape, but some of them at least are of a high standard, according to a reporter this year. It has the basics of resort life – supermarket, newsagent, a couple of restaurants (the Luge pizzeria is rated 'excellent, with friendly atmosphere and reasonable prices' by a 2012 visitor), an indoor pool, a disco. A free shuttle-bus runs to Les Collons. There's a fair-sized terrain park and boardercross, children's snow-garden and a kindergarten, as well as a ski school. The slopes are ideal for families and beginners, with two nursery lifts close to the accommodation. The lift network shared with Les Collons and Les Masses is elderly and slow (though gradually being improved). Snowmaking is extensive.

LINKED RESORT – 1800m

LES COLLONS

Some 300m below Thyon, at the foot of a broad, east-facing slope, Les Collons is nothing more than a couple of strings of chalet-style buildings spread along two roads following the hillside, 50m vertical apart; a lot of building has been going on here recently, but the place remains 'a ghost town'.

Three draglifts go up towards Thyon from the upper level of the resort, and a chairlift from the lower level takes you above Thyon. There's 6km of cross-country. A free shuttle-bus runs to Thyon.

Most accommodation is in apartments, but there are also a couple of modest hotels – including the 3-star Cambuse (281 1883) just below one of the lift bases. There's a wider range of bars, restaurants and other diversions than in Thyon, plus a 1km toboggan run through the woods above the village. Prepared walking trails add up to a modest 8km.

LINKED RESORT – 1515m

LES MASSES

Half-a-dozen hairpins down the mountainside from Les Collons, Les Masses is no more than a hamlet at the base of the double chairlifts that form the southern limit of the Thyon-Veysonnaz slopes. The home run is a red. Accommodation is in apartments. There is a grocery and a bar/restaurant.

LINKED RESORT – 1500m

LA TZOUMAZ

This tiny hamlet sits in a quiet valley on the shady, wooded side of Verbier's Savoleyres slope sector. There are a handful of small hotels, shops and restaurants, forming a very quiet place to stay and ski this underrated sector. A free bus serves the lifts. A newish gondola and a couple of fast chairs serve most of the slopes here. The 10km toboggan run back to the base area is one of the longest in the region; we're told by the tourist office that it is 'a professional run, not suitable for children under seven and helmets are recommended'.

LINKED RESORT – 820m

LE CHÂBLE

Le Châble is a busy roadside village in the valley, at the bottom of the hairpin road up to Verbier. It is linked to Verbier by a queue-free gondola that goes on (without changing cabins) to Les Ruinettes, which means access to the slopes can be just as quick as from Verbier. Buses run late too. Le Châble is on the rail network, and is also convenient for drivers who want to visit other resorts. And it is handy for Bruson. There are several modest hotels, of which the 2-star Giétroz (776 1184) is the pick.

OUTLYING RESORT – 1000m

BRUSON

Bruson is a small village on a shelf just above Le Châble, across the valley from Verbier, and reached by a short free bus ride. Its lifts are covered by the Verbier pass. From the village a slow chair goes up over gentle east-facing slopes to Bruson les Forêts (1600m). The open slopes above here are served by a quad chair up to a ridge, on the far side of which is a short draglift serving a tight little bowl. In addition to the intermediate pistes served by these lifts there are large areas of underused off-piste terrain, notably through woods on the front side accessed by the drag on the back. The off-piste down the back towards Orsières is good; you return by train. It is a great place to escape the crowds for a day – and maybe find powder when Verbier is skied out. There are rather vague plans to build a lift link from Le Châble.

Phone numbers
From elsewhere in Switzerland add the prefix 027; from abroad use the prefix +41 27

TOURIST OFFICES

Verbier / Le Châble (Bruson) / La Tzoumaz
www.verbier-st-bernard.ch

Nendaz / Siviez
www.nendaz.ch

Veysonnaz
www.veysonnaz.ch

Thyon 2000 / Les Collons / Les Masses
www.thyon-region.ch

Villars

Traditional year-round resort with local low-altitude slopes, a cog railway and a much needed but far-flung glacier

TOP 10 RATINGS

Extent	***
Fast lifts	**
Queues	***
Snow	**
Expert	**
Intermediate	***
Beginner	****
Charm	***
Convenience	**
Scenery	***

RPI	115
lift pass	£200
ski hire	£100
lessons	£105
food & drink	£190
total	**£595**

NEWS

2011/12: A six-pack replaced the double chair to Petit Chamossaire. Two runs were dedicated to slow skiing, one at Bretaye and the other on Les Chaux. A skiercross course was built on the Grand Chamossaire slope. And the Alpe Fleurie restaurant in the resort reopened after refurbishment.

- + Pleasant, year-round resort
- + Fairly extensive intermediate slopes
- + Close to Geneva airport

- − Unreliable snow-cover
- − Short runs on the upper slopes
- − Little to amuse experts on piste

Villars is popular with second-home owners because of its closeness to Geneva airport. For many keen skiers, its low altitude and far from snow-sure slopes will rule it out. But for a varied family holiday it has its attractions.

THE RESORT

Villars sits on a sunny hillside looking across the Rhône valley to the Portes du Soleil. Its home slopes link to those of Les Chaux, above the delightfully rustic village of Gryon. You can get a whole area pass covering Les Diablerets (linked by lifts and pistes) and also Leysin and Les Mosses, both of which are easy outings by rail or road. It also covers Glacier 3000, the small glacier area beyond Les Diablerets, halfway to Gstaad. Getting to and from the glacier is a long, slow business though – from Les Diablerets you need to catch a bus to the glacier lift or walk 10 minutes to the Isenau area to ski down to it. Outings to Verbier are easily possible.

Village charm Villars is more like a town than a village, with sprawling suburbs of smart chalets and several international schools. The focus is a longish, traffic-filled but pleasant high street lined with a variety of shops.

Convenience A slow cog railway goes from the main street up to the slopes around Bretaye. A gondola at the other end of town is quicker. It's best to stay near to one of these or at a hotel with its own shuttle-bus, though ski-buses run every 20 minutes or so most of the ski day.

Scenery The scenery is more dramatic than you might expect.

THE MOUNTAINS

There's a good mix of wooded and open slopes. But the piste map and signing could be improved.

Slopes The cog railway goes up to the col of Bretaye, which has intermediate slopes on either side. To the east, open slopes go to La Rasse and the link to Les Chaux. There used to be another piste to La Rasse down from Chaux Ronde, but this is now an itinerary; it has a tricky section at the top that is often closed. There's an

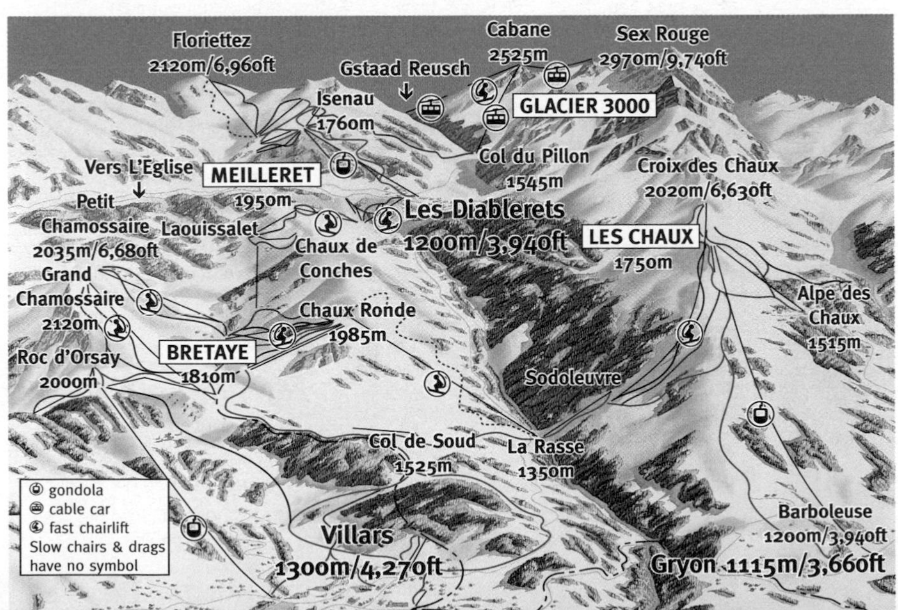

← Villars is a big place, more like a town than a village. But it's prettily set with views over the Rhône valley to the Portes du Soleil

VILLARS TOURISM

KEY FACTS

Resort	1300m 4,270ft
Villars, Gryon and Les Diablerets (excludes Glacier 3000)	
Slopes	1115-2120m 3,660-6,960ft
Lifts	34
Pistes	100km 62 miles
Blue	37%
Red	53%
Black	10%
Snowmaking	20%

Phone numbers
From elsewhere in Switzerland add the prefix 024; from abroad use the prefix +41 24

TOURIST OFFICE

www.villars.ch

alternative blue run from Bretaye. From Les Chaux there are runs to Barboleuse above Gryon, with a gondola back up. The gondola from Villars takes you to Roc d'Orsay, from where you can head for Bretaye or back to Villars. A long, slow, two-way chairlift links to Les Diablerets. The glacier area has very gentle slopes at the top, but there is a splendid run down the Combe d'Audon (red whenever we've skied it, but now undeservedly classified black on the piste map) with a dramatic cliff face rising up on the right. You can descend to the valley or part way down catch a fast chair which serves another splendid run that's still a red.
Fast lifts Fast lifts exist, but so do old chairs and drags.
Queues The lifts at Bretaye get busy mainly at peak times, but the new six-pack to Petit Chamossaire should mean no queues there. The buses and train can get overcrowded.
Terrain parks There's one at Chaux Ronde and a smaller one at Diablerets.
Snow reliability Low altitude and sunny slopes mean snow reliability isn't good – though on such gentle, grassy terrain, deep snow-cover isn't needed. Recent snowmaking on the runs back to town and at La Rasse is a welcome improvement.
Experts Little on-piste challenge but some good off-piste with a guide.
Intermediates The local slopes offer a good variety. Les Chaux has some steeper slopes and a lovely long cruisy blue to Barboleuse. The run from Meilleret to Les Diablerets is a delightful long cruise that can be deserted first thing in the morning.

Beginners The nursery slope behind the station is free to use. There is another at Gryon. There are gentle but often crowded runs at Bretaye.
Snowboarding There are a few tricky draglifts but good intermediate slopes.
Cross-country There are 50km of trails; those up the valley past La Rasse are long and pretty. There are more in the depression beyond Bretaye.
Mountain restaurants They are often oversubscribed. We hear most about Lac des Chavonnes (a short walk below Petit Chamossaire) and the Col de Soud for 'very good food, a real sun trap'. The Golf Club does 'delicious tartiflette'. Above Gryon, we like the relatively quiet Des Chaux at Les Chaux and Refuge Frience (it's a walk back to the T-bar though). The Etable is a converted farmhouse at Sodoleuvre above La Rasse. There are picnic rooms at the top of the Roc d'Orsay gondola and at Les Chaux.
Schools and guides Past reports have been positive.
Families La Trottinette non-ski nursery takes children up to six.

STAYING THERE

Hotels We enjoyed staying at the 4-star central Golf (496 3838) – big rooms, spa facilities. Nearby is the 3-star Alpe Fleurie (496 3070). The 4-star Eurotel Victoria (495 3131) is near the gondola and 'almost ski-in'.
Eating out Cookie, out past Barboleuse, does traditional and Asian-fusion food (with Indian food in a tent in the garden). Francis does 'good pizza' and the Sporting serves traditional dishes/grills.
Après-ski The rustic Buvette d'Arrivée on the home run above the top of town is popular at close of play, as is the Sporting. Try the Moon Boot Lounge for cocktails.
Off the slopes Activities include paragliding, snowshoeing, skating, tobogganing and swimming. There are 'excellent' walks and rail trips.

UK PACKAGES

Alpine Answers, Alpine Weekends, Carrier, Club Med, Crystal, Crystal Finest, Independent Ski Links, Lagrange, Momentum, Neilson, PowderBeds, Ski Bespoke, Ski Expectations, Ski Independence, Ski Line, Ski Safari, Ski Solutions, Ski Weekend, Skitracer, Switzerland Travel Centre, Thomson, Tracks European Adventures

SNOWPIX.COM / CHRIS GILL

Wengen

A charming old village, stunning scenery, an old cog railway and gentle intermediate slopes make for a relaxing and leisurely holiday

RATINGS

The mountains

Extent	***
Fast lifts	****
Queues	***
Terrain p'ks	*
Snow	**
Expert	**
Intermediate	****
Beginner	***
Boarder	**
X-country	*
Restaurants	****
Schools	***
Families	****

The resort

Charm	*****
Convenience	***
Scenery	*****
Eating out	**
Après-ski	**
Off-slope	****

RPI	125
lift pass	£220
ski hire	£105
lessons	£105
food & drink	£200
total	**£630**

NEWS

2012/13: The Wixi double chair is to be upgraded to a covered six-pack.

2011/12: Snowmaking was improved in the Eigergletscher and Männlichen areas.

- + Some of the most spectacular scenery in the Alps
- + Small, traditional, nearly traffic-free Alpine village
- + Lots of long, gentle runs, ideal for leisurely intermediates
- + Nursery slopes in heart of village
- + Calm, unhurried atmosphere
- + Good resort for families and groups that include non-skiers. It's easy to get around on mountain railways

- − Limited terrain for experts and adventurous intermediates
- − Natural snow unreliable (but substantial snowmaking now)
- − Trains to slopes are slow and there are still a few old lifts
- − Getting to/from Grindelwald's First area can take hours
- − Subdued in the evening, with little variety of nightlife

Given the charm of the village, the friendliness of the locals and the drama of the scenery, it's easy to see why many people love Wengen – including large numbers of Brits who have been going for decades. It's great for a relaxing time, for those who don't take their skiing too seriously, for families and for mixed groups of intermediates and non-skiers.

Keen piste-bashers should not underestimate the drawbacks. If you're used to modern mega-resorts, you'll find Wengen a huge contrast, and may have difficulty adjusting. But the spectacularly scenic Jungfrau region is one that every keen skier should experience; and to experience all of it Wengen, centrally placed between Mürren and Grindelwald, is the best base.

THE RESORT

Wengen is one of three resorts close together in the Jungfrau region. It is set on a sloping shelf above the Lauterbrunnen valley, opposite Mürren, and reached only by a cog railway, which carries on up to Kleine Scheidegg and the slopes shared with Grindelwald. Access to Mürren involves a train down to Lauterbrunnen, a cable car up and then another train (or a bus from Lauterbrunnen to a different two-stage cable car to Mürren). Access to the First area of Grindelwald is an even longer process, including skiing down to Grindelwald and crossing town. The Jungfrau lift pass covers all of this. Outings further afield aren't really worth the effort.

VILLAGE CHARM *****

Almost traffic-free

The village was a farming community long before skiing arrived; it is still tiny, but dominated by sizeable hotels, mostly of Victorian origin. So it is not exactly chocolate-box pretty, but it is charming and relaxed, and almost traffic-free. There are electric hotel taxi-trucks and a few ordinary, engine-driven taxis. (Why, we wonder?)

The short main street is the hub. Lined with chalet-style shops and hotels, it also has the ice rink and village nursery slopes right next to it.

CONVENIENCE ***

Compact, but hilly in parts

Wengen is small, so location isn't as crucial as in many resorts. But those who don't fancy a steepish morning climb should avoid places down the hill, below the station. The ridge where the slopes of Wengen meet those of Grindelwald is reached either by train or by cable car – much quicker. Both stations are central. There are hotels on the home piste, convenient for the slopes.

SCENERY *****

Three of the best are here

The views across the valley are stunning. They get even better higher up, when the famous trio of peaks comes fully into view – the Mönch (Monk) in the centre protecting the Jungfrau (Maiden) on the right from the Eiger (Ogre) on the left.

KEY FACTS

Resort	1275m 4,180ft
Jungfrau region	
Slopes	945-2970m 3,100-9,740ft
Lifts	44
Pistes	213km 132 miles
Blue	33%
Red	49%
Black	18%
Snowmaking	40%
First-Männlichen-Kleine Scheidegg only	
Slopes	945-2500m 3,100-8,200ft
Lifts	32
Pistes	161km 100 miles

LIFT PASSES

Jungfrau

Prices in SF

Age	1-day	6-day
under 16	31	157
16 to 19	50	251
20 to 61	62	314
over 62	56	283

Free under 6 (if with parent)

Beginner points ticket

Notes Covers trains between villages and Grindelwald ski-bus; day pass is for First-Kleine Scheidegg-Männlichen area only; 6-day-plus pass allows one day in Zermatt

Alternative passes Grindelwald and Wengen only; Mürren only; non-skier pass

THE MOUNTAINS

Although Wengen is famous for the fearsome Lauberhorn Downhill course – the longest and one of the toughest on the World Cup circuit – its slopes are best suited to early intermediates. Most of the Downhill course is now open to the public and the steepest section (the Hundschopf jump) can be avoided by an alternative red route. Most of Wengen's runs are gentle blues and reds, ideal for cruising.

Piste marking and piste map are poor; reporters find the Männlichen slopes, in particular, confusing. And following heavy snowfalls in 2009, one visitor found piste markers had disappeared under the deep snow – 'a potentially dangerous, not to mention avoidable, problem'.

EXTENT OF THE SLOPES ★★★★★
Picturesque playground

Most of the slopes are on the Grindelwald side of the mountain. From the railway station at Kleine Scheidegg you can head straight down to Grindelwald or work your way across to the top of the Männlichen. This area is served by a drag and several chairlifts, and can be reached directly from Wengen by the cable car. There are a few runs back down towards Wengen from the top of the Lauberhorn, but there's really only one below Wengernalp.

FAST LIFTS ★★★★★
OK except for the train

The fast cable car and slow train are the main access lifts; new fast chairs replacing old lifts have improved things higher up; the most recent was the Eigernordwand six-pack from below Kleine Scheidegg (on the Grindelwald side) to Eigergletscher, and the Wixi double chair is due to be replaced by a six-pack for 2012/13.

QUEUES ★★★★★
Village crowds, better higher up

Both the train and the cable car can be crowded at peak periods. It is best to avoid travelling up at the same time as the ski school. Queues up the mountain have been alleviated a lot in the last few years by the installation of fast chairs, and reporters have experienced few problems in midweek. But weekends can be busy, especially on the Grindelwald side of the hill – the obvious entry point for residents of Bern attracted by the special family pass deals on Saturdays.

TERRAIN PARKS ★★★★★
A fair trek

There isn't one. The nearest parks are at First and Mürren – each a fair trek.

SNOW RELIABILITY ★★★★★
Improved snowmaking helps

Most slopes are below 2000m, and the few runs on the Wengen side of the ridge are sunny; the long blue run back to the village is particularly vulnerable. But a lot of snowmaking has been added recently, and some 60% of the slopes in the Kleine Scheidegg-Männlichen area are now covered. When we were there in 2009, it had not snowed for a few weeks and a warm Föhn wind had melted a lot of snow, but most slopes were in good condition. Piste maintenance gets mixed reviews.

FOR EXPERTS ★★★★★
Few challenges

Wengen is quite limited for experts. The only genuine black runs in the area are parts of the Lauberhorn World Cup Downhill and a couple of pistes from Eigergletscher towards Wixi including Oh God (which used to be off-piste). There are some decent off-piste runs from under the north face of the Eiger and the Eigernordwand lift helps with access to these. More adventurous runs from the Jungfraujoch become possible later in the season (see the Grindelwald chapter for more about going to the Jungfraujoch). For more challenges it's well worth going to nearby Mürren, around an hour away. Heli-trips are organized if there are enough takers.

FOR INTERMEDIATES ★★★★★
Wonderful if the snow is good

Wengen and Grindelwald share superb easy-intermediate slopes. Nearly all are long blue or gentle red runs (though there are genuine reds too); read the Grindelwald chapter. The run back to Wengen is a relaxing end to the day, although it can be crowded and the snow can be patchy.

For tougher pistes, head for the top of the Lauberhorn chair and then the runs to Kleine Scheidegg, or to Wixi (following the start of the Downhill course). You could also try the shady run from Eigergletscher, which often has the best snow late in the season.

FOR BEGINNERS ★★★★★
Not ideal

There's a nursery slope in the centre of the village – convenient and gentle, but it gets afternoon sun and at this modest altitude the snow can suffer. There's a beginners' area at Wengernalp and some short beginner lifts up at Kleine Scheidegg, but of course to use these you have to take the train down as well as up, or tackle the blue run down to the village, which can be tricky, with some flat sections. None of these areas offers free lifts, but there are alternatives to buying a full lift pass (there is a points card). There are plenty of good, long, gentle runs to progress to on the slopes above Grindelwald, reached either by train to Kleine Scheidegg or cable car to Männlichen.

FOR BOARDERS ★★★★★
Best for beginners

Wengen is not a bad place for gentle boarding – the nursery area is not ideal, but beginners have plenty of slopes to progress to, with lots of long blue and red runs served by the train and chairlifts. Getting from Kleine Scheidegg to Männlichen means an unavoidable draglift, though. And the slope back to Wengen is narrow and almost flat in places, so you may have to scoot. For the steepest slopes and best freeriding, experts will want to head for Mürren.

FOR CROSS-COUNTRY ★★★★★
There is none

There's no cross-country in Wengen itself, which seems a shame given the nature of the resort. There are 12km of tracks down in the Lauterbrunnen valley, where the snow is unreliable.

MOUNTAIN RESTAURANTS ★★★★★
Plenty of variety

Editors' choice The Jungfrau hotel at Wengernalp (855 1622) is an old favourite of ours – and of reporters: 'beautiful' views from the terrace; the menu is limited, but the rösti is excellent. You also get magnificent views from the narrow balcony of Wengen's highest restaurant, Eigergletscher.

Worth knowing about The station buffet at Kleine Scheidegg receives repeated endorsements ('good food', 'efficient, friendly service'). A 2012 reporter enjoyed a 'great' lunch at the busy Eigernordwand restaurant ('really good goulash soup'). The Allmend, near the top of the Innerwengen chair and the train stop, has wonderful views but 'no atmosphere – even at the end of the day', says a 2012 visitor. Far better, in the opinion of two reporters this year, is Mary's Cafe at the bottom of the Lauberhorn: 'really good lunch'; 'best snack of the week'. There is a picnic room at the Männlichen top station. For restaurants above Grindelwald, read that chapter.

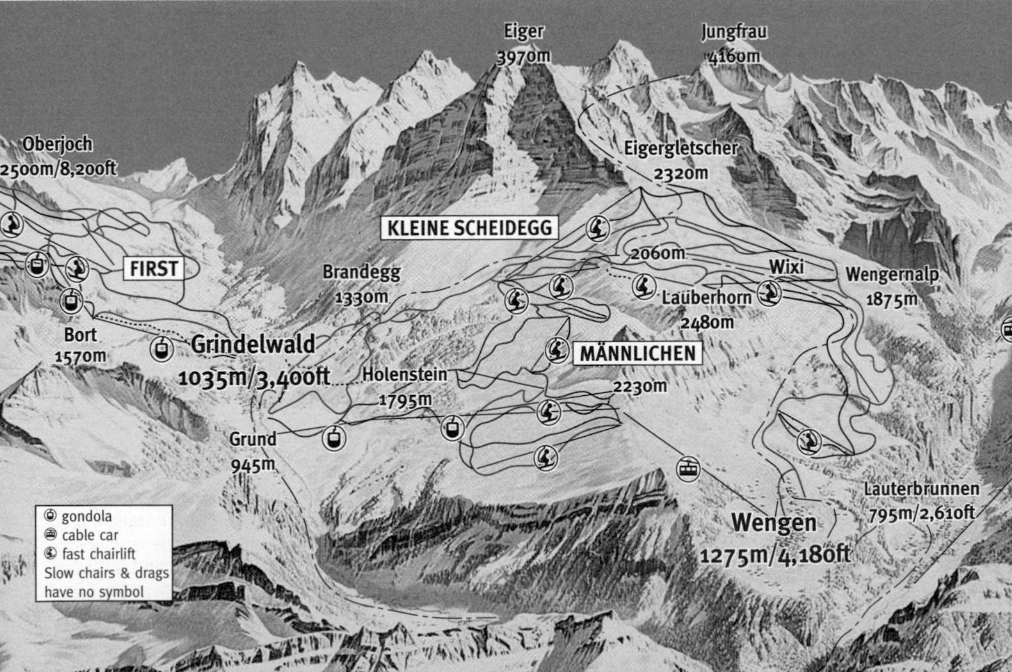

THE BRITISH IN WENGEN

There's a very strong British presence in Wengen. Many Brits have been returning for years to the same rooms in the same hotels in the same week, and treat the resort as a sort of second home. There is an English church with weekly services, and a British-run ski club, the DHO (Downhill Only) – so named when the Brits who colonized the resort persuaded the locals to keep the summer railway running up the mountain in winter, so that they would no longer have to climb up in order to ski down again. That greatly amused the locals, who until then had regarded skiing in winter as a way to get around on snow rather than a pastime to be done for fun. The DHO is still going strong.

JUNGFRAU REGION MARKETING AG

SCHOOLS

Swiss
t 855 2022

Privat
t 855 5005

Altitude
t 853 0040

Classes
(Swiss prices)
6 3hr days SF275

Private lessons
From SF149 for 2hr

CHILDCARE

Playhouse
t 856 8585
From 18mnth

Snowli Club Sunshine
t 854 1280
From 6mnth

Ski school
The Swiss school takes ages 3 up (6 3hr days SF275)

ACTIVITIES

Indoor Swimming pools (in hotels), sauna, solarium, whirlpool, massage (in hotels)

Outdoor Ice rink,curling, 50km of cleared paths, tobogganing, ice climbing, paragliding, snowshoeing

SCHOOLS AND GUIDES ★★★☆☆
Reports please

We have no reports again this year. Guides are available for heli-trips and off-piste.

FOR FAMILIES ★★★★☆
Conveniently placed

It is an attractive and reassuring village for families. The nursery slope is in the centre and there are two kindergartens. There is a list of babysitters available at the tourist office. The train gives easy access to higher slopes.

STAYING THERE

Most accommodation is in hotels. There is only a handful of catered chalets (none especially luxurious). Self-catering apartments are few, too.

Staying down in Lauterbrunnen will halve your accommodation costs and give faster access to Mürren.

Hotels There are about two dozen hotels, mostly 4-star and 3-star, with a handful of simpler places.

******Beausite Park** (856 5161) The best in town reputedly: 'very well run with charming staff, good food'. Good pool, steam, sauna, massage. Situated at top of nursery slopes

******Caprice** (856 0606) Small, smartly furnished, chalet-style, just above the railway. Sauna and massage.

******Regina** (856 5858) Grand Victorian hotel with piano bar, sun terrace, spa and fitness room – 'tremendous food and service though drinks are expensive', says a 2011 visitor.

******Silberhorn** (856 5131) Comfortable, modern and central. 'Great views, quality five-course meals, and attractive spa.'

******Sunstar** (856 5200) Family-friendly, modern, on main street right opposite the cable car. 'Extremely welcoming, good rooms, pool a bit cool' is the verdict of a 2012 visitor.

******Wengener Hof** (856 6969) No prizes for style or convenience, but recommended for peace, helpful staff, spacious rooms with good views. 'A truly warm welcome, excellent food.'

*****Alpenrose** (855 3216) Long-standing British favourite; eight minutes' climb to the station.

*****Belvédère** (856 6868) Some way out, buffet-style meals, family-friendly, spacious rooms and grand art nouveau public rooms. 'Highly recommended.'

*****Falken** (856 5121) Further up the hill. Another British favourite.

Apartments The hotel Bernerhof's decent Résidence apartments are well positioned just off the main street, and the hotel facilities are available for guests to use.

At altitude You can stay at two points up the mountain reached by the railway: the expensive Jungfrau hotel (855 1622) at Wengernalp – with fabulous views – and at Kleine Scheidegg, where there are rooms in the big Bellevue des Alpes (855 1212) and dormitory space above the Grindelwaldblick restaurant (855 1374) and the station buffet.

EATING OUT ★★☆☆☆
Mainly hotel-based

Most restaurants are in hotels and offer good food and service. The Silberhorn offers varied and 'excellent' five-course meals. The Bernerhof has

GETTING THERE

Air Zürich 155km/ 95 miles (3hr); Bern 65km/40 miles (2hr); Basel 160km/100 miles (2hr45)

Rail Station in resort

UK PACKAGES

Alpine Answers, Club Med, Crystal, Inghams, Momentum, Neilson, PowderBeds, Ski Club Freshtracks, Ski Line, Ski Solutions, Skitracer, STC, Switzerland Travel Centre, Thomson

Phone numbers
From elsewhere in Switzerland add the prefix 033; from abroad use the prefix +41 33

TOURIST OFFICE

www.wengen.ch

good-value traditional dishes. The little hotel Hirschen offers speciality steaks. The hotel Regina's food is 'excellent but they won't serve tap water'. There's no shortage of fondues in the village, and several bars do casual food. Da Sina is a steakhouse and pizzeria. Cafe Gruebi is the place for cakes.

APRES-SKI ★★☆☆☆
It depends on what you want

People's reactions to the Wengen après-ski scene vary widely, according to their expectations and their appetites.

If you're used to raving in Kitzbühel or Les Deux-Alpes, you'll rate Wengen dead, especially for young people. If you've heard it's dead, you may be pleasantly surprised to find that there is a handful of small bars that do good business both early and late in the evening.

On the mountain, the outdoor Läger Bar, next to the Männlichen chair, is good for 'sitting in a deckchair in the sun'. Tipirama (a wigwam at Kleine Scheidegg) is a fun place immediately after skiing, sometimes with DJs and live bands ('becoming a bit tatty' though). We've had mixed reviews of the Start Bar on the Lauberhorn ('fantastic views', 'live music at weekends', 'tasty pancakes' but 'very unfriendly service' and 'expensive'). The Wäsch bar at the Bumps section of the home run is a popular final-run stop-off.

In the village the tiny, 'pleasant' Pickel Bar is popular at the end of the day. The small, traditional Tanne is also recommended for 'more sophisticated fare'. Sina's, a little way out of the centre, next to the Club Med, has 'realistic pricing', big-screen TV, live music and karaoke. Rocks Bar, with its plasma screens showing Sky Sports, has 'the best Guinness'. There are discos and live music in some hotels.

OFF THE SLOPES ★★★★☆
Good for a relaxing time

With its unbeatable scenery and pedestrian-friendly trains and cable car (there's a special – but pricey – pass for pedestrians), Wengen is a superb resort for those who want a relaxing holiday. It's easy for mixed parties of skiers and non-skiers to meet up for lunch on the mountain. There are some lovely walks, and ice skating, tobogganing and curling ('great fun – an instructor can be provided') are popular. Several hotels have health spas. The cinema often shows English-language films.

Excursions to Interlaken and Bern are possible by train, as is the trip up to the Jungfraujoch (see the Grindelwald chapter). From Männlichen there are scenic flights giving splendid close-up views of the mountains and glaciers, either by helicopter or much cheaper small plane.

SNOWPIX.COM / CHRIS GILL

The heart of the village is the little square next to the station, with the main street leading away to the cable car ↓

Zermatt

A magical combination of nearly everything you could want from a ski resort, both on and off the slopes

RATINGS

The mountains	
Extent	★★★★
Fast lifts	★★★★★
Queues	★★★
Terrain p'ks	★★★
Snow	★★★★
Expert	★★★★
Intermediate	★★★★
Beginner	★★
Boarder	★★★
X-country	★
Restaurants	★★★★★
Schools	★★★
Families	★★
The resort	
Charm	★★★★
Convenience	★★
Scenery	★★★★★
Eating out	★★★★★
Après-ski	★★★★★
Off-slope	★★★★

RPI	140
lift pass	£260
ski hire	£130
lessons	£115
food & drink	£210
total	**£715**

NEWS

2012/13: More snowmaking is planned from Furi to town. Work is due to start on creating a new run back to town from Sunnegga to replace the existing narrow path low down.

2011/12: A new red piste from Grunsee to the mid-station of the Findeln chair opened. A new toboggan run opened at Furi, with special evenings managed by the hotel Silvana. And the Papperla Pub reopened following a refit.

- + Wonderful, high and extensive slopes in four varied areas
- + Spectacular high mountain scenery
- + Charming, if rather sprawling, old mountain village, largely traffic-free
- + Reliable snow at altitude
- + World's best mountain restaurants
- + Nightlife to suit most tastes
- + Smart shops
- + Linked to sunny Cervinia in Italy
- + Extensive helicopter operation

- − Main lifts may be a long walk, or a crowded bus or taxi ride from home
- − Far from ideal for novices, despite recent efforts to improve matters
- − High prices for everything, including lift pass (one of Europe's priciest)
- − Slow train up to Gornergrat
- − Some lift queues at peak periods
- − Annoying electric taxis in 'car-free' streets detract from ambience
- − Few options to ski in bad weather; can be really windy or cold too

Our verdict is short and simple: you must try Zermatt before you die. There is nowhere else to match it. Its drawbacks are non-trivial but, for us and for virtually all our reporters, these pale into insignificance compared with its attractions. Editor Watts regularly takes his holiday here. Enough said.

THE RESORT

Zermatt started life as a simple farming village, developed as a mountaineering centre in the 19th century, then became a winter resort. Summer is still as big as winter here.

The village is car-free, but not traffic-free – electric buggies operating either as hotel shuttles or as public taxis zip around the streets. Residents can drive up to Zermatt, but the rest of us must park at Täsch (or more distant Visp) and arrive by train. At Täsch there's a big car park (SF14.50 a day) and you can wheel luggage trolleys on and off the trains.

Zermatt mainly attracts a well heeled international clientele; the clientele is also relatively, er, mature for what is quite a sporty resort.

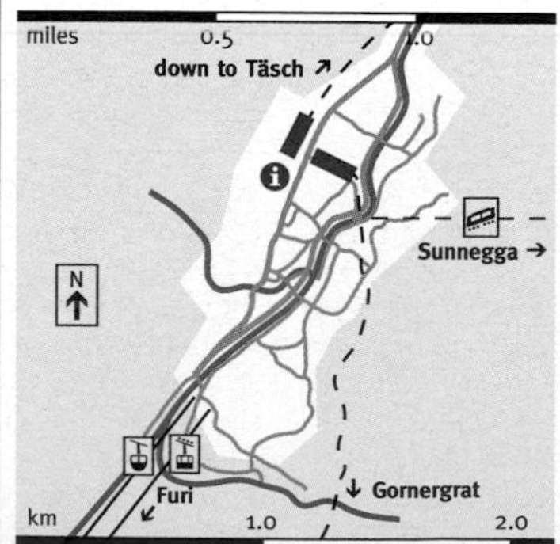

VILLAGE CHARM ★★★★

Old and new in harmony

The resort is a mixture of ancient chalets and barns, grand 19th-century hotels and modern buildings, most in traditional style but some decidedly funky. The oldest, most charming part of the village has narrow lanes and old wooden barns with slate roofs, many of them supported on stone 'legs'. But modern-day Zermatt sprawls along both sides of the river with a lot of new building at both ends and up the sides of the mountains that rise steeply on each side.

Arriving at the station, it all seems very towny, especially if there is no snow on the ground. The centre doesn't have the relaxed, rustic feel of other car-free resorts, such as Wengen and Saas-Fee. The main street running away from the station is lined with luxury hotels, restaurants, banks and glitzy shops. The electric taxis are intrusive, especially at busy times.

CONVENIENCE ★★

Lifts at opposite ends

The village is small enough to get around on foot in the evenings, but not in ski boots and carrying skis. There is a free ski-bus; but it is inadequate at peak times, especially returning from the Matterhorn area.

You arrive at a fair-sized square at the north end of the resort, where you

↑ You can see the Matterhorn from pretty much everywhere on the slopes. This T-bar takes you close to the Italian border

SNOWPIX.COM / CHRIS GILL

KEY FACTS

Resort	1620m
	5,310ft
Zermatt only	
Slopes	1620-3820m
	5,310-12,530ft
Lifts	33
Pistes	200km
	124 miles
Blue	16%
Red	61%
Black	23%
Snowmaking	39%
Zermatt-Cervinia-Valtournenche combined	
Slopes	1525-3820m
	5,000-12,530ft
Lifts	57
Pistes	360km
	225 miles
Blue	22%
Red	60%
Black	18%
Snowmaking	70%

find ranks of electric taxis and hotel shuttles and horse-drawn sleighs.

The cog railway to the Gornergrat sector starts from near the main station. The Sunnegga underground funicular for the Rothorn sector is a few minutes' walk away, but the lifts to Furi and the other sectors (and the link to Cervinia) are over 1km away.

Staying near the lifts to Furi gives swift access to three of the four sectors. But a more central location can combine proximity to the Gornergrat and Sunnegga railways, and to most of the resort's shops, bars and restaurants.

Some accommodation is up the steep hill across the river in Winkelmatten, which has its own reliable bus service.

SCENERY ★★★★★
On a grand scale

Zermatt's emblematic, unmistakable Matterhorn is not visible from central parts of the village – if you want the famous view from your balcony, stay on the east side of the village, or at the south end – but once you are on the slopes its unreal profile dominates the views from just about everywhere. And the cable car trip up to the Klein Matterhorn opens up vast panoramas, as well as close-up glacier views.

THE MOUNTAINS

Practically all of the slopes are above the treeline – a run served by the Sunnegga funicular is the main exception, and once you pass below the Patrullarve chair this is mainly a path to the village.

A single piste map covers both Cervinia and Zermatt fairly clearly, and lists recommended 'ski safari' routes of either 10,500m or 12,500m vertical; but if you want lift names you'll have to get hold of the Cervinia version. The map shows planned cable cars to the Klein Matterhorn, from Trockener Steg in Zermatt and Plateau Rosa in Cervinia but we're told these are not due until 2015/16. It also shows three other planned lifts for which no timescale has been fixed.

In each sector there are runs marked in yellow on the resort map and dotted on ours, called 'itinéraires' on the piste map or 'freeride' runs on the Cervinia one. We'll call them itineraries. The terms are not explained on the maps – a ridiculous and dangerous state of affairs. They are probably not patrolled (we saw a sign at the top of one saying 'No control at end of day') – if skiing them alone, take care.

On Thursdays, you can get first tracks from Trockener Steg. For SF30, you can take the lift at 7.40am, about an hour ahead of the herd, ski deserted pistes for a while, then have a buffet breakfast at the Ice Pizzeria. We prefer our normal routine of the 8am train to Gornergrat, followed by deserted pistes before the hordes get out of bed.

Once a month there are moonlight descents from Rothorn with the ski patrol, including a fondue at the restaurant at the top, for SF70.50.

We have been impressed by service improvements over the years: polite and helpful lift staff; big boards at the bottom of each sector indicating which lifts and pistes are open in all sectors (though a 2012 visitor found that after a snowfall some runs were closed half-way down with no prior warning that he had seen); useful announcements in English on the train and some cable cars; and free tissues at most lift stations.

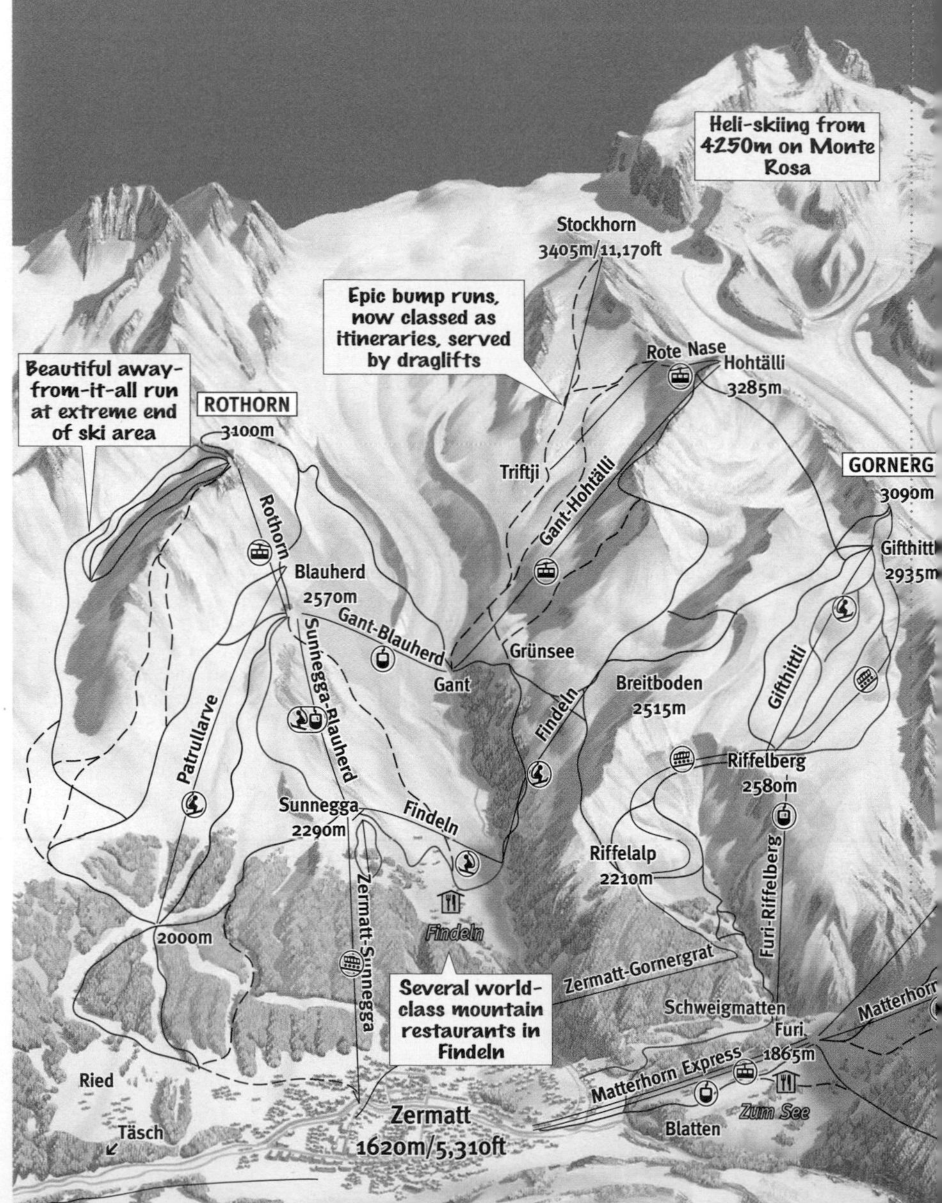

EXTENT OF THE SLOPES ★★★★★
Beautiful and varied

Zermatt's slopes divide naturally into four main sectors. The resort likes to identify more sectors on its maps. But at least it has now given up branding most of them as various forms of 'paradise', leaving only the Matterhorn Glacier Paradise.

The **Rothorn** sector is reached by an underground funicular to Sunnegga starting by the river, not far from the centre of the village. The main nursery area is just below Sunnegga, reached by a miniature funicular. A hybrid chondola goes from Sunnegga to Blauherd, where a cable car goes up to Rothorn.

The second main area, **Gornergrat,** is reached from Zermatt by cog railway trains that take 30 or 40 minutes to the top – arrive at the station early to get a seat (best on the right-hand side to enjoy the fabulous views). We love getting the 8am train with the lifties and restaurant staff. It arrives at the

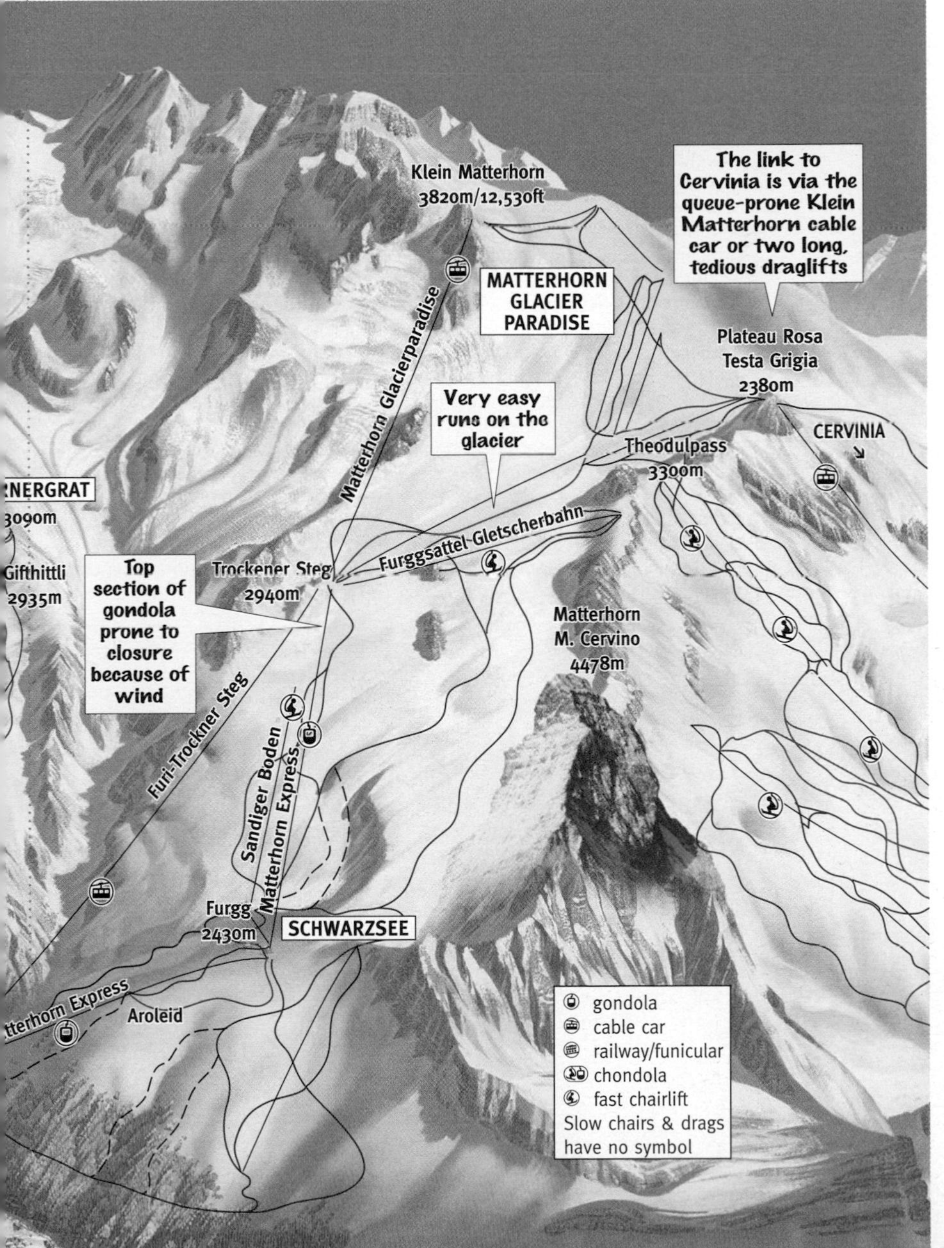

top just as they drop the rope to open the pistes, and you have the slopes to yourself for an hour or two.

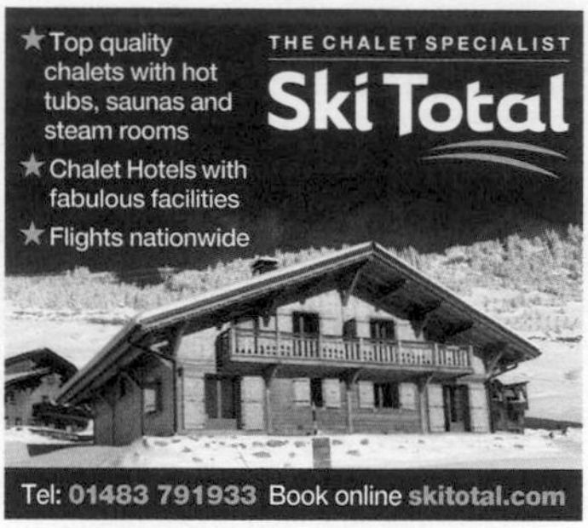

The Rothorn and Gornergrat sectors, separated by the Findel valley, are linked by pistes and itineraries descending to two lift stations.

The Matterhorn Express gondola from the south end of the village goes first to Furi (where you can change to another gondola to go to Riffelberg, for Gornergrat) and on to the small but worthwhile **Schwarzsee** area.

The same gondola goes on up to Trockener Steg, focal point of the third major sector, the super-high **Matterhorn Glacier Paradise**. This can also be reached by a jumbo cable car from Furi – quicker if you time it right, and less liable to closure by wind. Above Trockener Steg another cable car makes a spectacular ascent to Klein Matterhorn. When you arrive, you walk through a long tunnel, to emerge on top of the world for the highest piste in Europe; there's a self-service restaurant and you can stay up here too. This area links to Cervinia – you peal off left from the glacier at one of two points.

There are pistes back to the village from all sectors – though some can be closed or tricky due to poor snow conditions. They can be hazardous at the end of the day, due to crowds and speeding skiers – note our remarks under 'For intermediates'.

FAST LIFTS ★★★★★

Now top notch

All Zermatt's four sectors are well-connected by fast chairs, gondolas, big cable cars or mountain railways. There are of course slow lifts in places, but most can be avoided. A few reporters complain about the Gornergrat train being slow.

QUEUES ★★★★★

Main problems being solved

Zermatt has improved its lift system hugely in recent years, eliminating major bottlenecks. Again, all this year's reporters are generally positive, but a couple of problems remain.

The Klein Matterhorn cable car has queues much of the time (up to an hour mid-morning; quieter in the afternoon) – one regular reporter recommends jumping this queue occasionally by splashing out 200 francs a head for a 20-minute heli-lift to Plateau Rosa incorporating a close-up tour of the Matterhorn – 'fantastic;

SNOWPIX.COM / CHRIS GILL

The ice rink in the centre of the village gets a lot of sun – good for mid-winter but it has often been out of action on our March visits ↓

OFF-PISTE RUNS FROM THE ACCESSIBLE TO THE EPIC

Zermatt offers a wide variety of off-piste runs for all abilities, from off-piste beginner to expert. And if the runs reached from the lift system aren't enough, heli-skiing is available (and popular).

Zermatt's 'itineraries' (explained, as far as possible, under 'The mountains') open up a lot of ungroomed terrain. If you love long mogul pitches, those in the Gornergrat sector served by the Stockhorn and Triftji draglifts are the stuff of dreams. Being north-facing and high, this area keeps good snow long after a new snowfall (but it needs deep snow, and does not normally open until February, or even March). The itineraries carry on down from the Triftji T-bar to Gant, but snow quality can deteriorate on this lower part. There are two wonderful itineraries from Rothorn, with spectacular views (though again they need good snow-cover to be really enjoyable). At Schwarzsee there are a couple of steep north-facing gullies through the woods.

Away from the marked runs, there are marvellous off-piste possibilities from the top lifts in each sector, but they are dangerous, because of rocky and glacial terrain; guidance is essential. Stockhorn is a great starting point; descending towards Gant, one special run goes down 'the lost valley'; going in the other direction, there is an excellent descent to the Gornergletscher, ending at Furi. Be warned: getting off the end of the glacier can be tricky – it may involve walking along narrow rocky paths above long drops or side-stepping down steep slopes, depending on snow levels (we've encountered both). In the Schwarzsee sector there are many good slopes, including 'innru waldieni', right underneath the Matterhorn, reached from the Hörnli T-bar.

Zermatt is the Alps' biggest heli-skiing centre; at times the helipad has choppers taking off every few minutes. There are only a few drop points. The classic run is from over 4250m on Monte Rosa and descends over 2300m vertical through wonderful glacier scenery to Furi; note our warning above.

LIFT PASSES

Zermatt

Prices in SF

Age	1-day	6-day
under 16	38	186
16 to 19	64	315
20 to 64	75	371
65 plus	71	349

Free under 9

Beginner Wolli Ski Pass covering nursery area at Sunnegga

Notes
Covers Swiss side of the border; half-day passes and single-ascent tickets on some lifts

Alternative passes
International for Zermatt and Cervinia; International-Aosta for Zermatt and Cervinia plus 2 days in Val d'Aosta; Peak Pass for pedestrians

one of the highlights of my life'.

The gondola to Trockener Steg is prone to closure in high winds, putting pressure on the alternative cable-car in these conditions.

A real bottleneck is Gant in the Findel valley – notably the old, slow gondola to Blauherd. Half-hour waits are common here in high season. There are plans to construct a piste from Gant down the valley to the Findeln chairlift so that the gondola can be retired, but that is not due until 2014.

The top section of piste from Hohtälli can get dangerously busy ('awful crowds on a narrow red that was bumped by mid-morning').

TERRAIN PARKS ★★★★★
Things are getting better

The reporter who last year described Gravity Park, next to the Furggsattel six-seat chair, as 'pants' was delighted to find a huge improvement in 2012: 'just brilliant, 100 times better than before, with lots of big jumps, little jumps, rails, half-pipe, big rollers – now just get some music and it will really rock'. In the summer, the park moves up to Plateau Rosa where a six-man crew shape the 600m park daily. A nicely integrated 120m-long super-pipe sits next to an array of kickers, rails, a quarter-pipe, wall ride, mail box and tree jib.

SNOW RELIABILITY ★★★★★
Generally good

Zermatt has rocky terrain and a relatively dry climate. But it also has some of the highest slopes in Europe, and quite a lot of snowmaking. Three of the four sectors go up to over 3000m, the Matterhorn Glacier Paradise area has summer skiing and there are loads of runs above 2500m, many of which are north-facing.

There is snowmaking, in all four sectors, on at least some pistes from above 3000m right down to resort level and coverage is still being increased. On repeated March visits we have been impressed with its use on the runs to resort level. Piste grooming is generally excellent.

FOR EXPERTS ★★★★★
Head off-piste

There is some great off-piste when conditions are right – see our feature panel – but Zermatt doesn't get huge snowfall, so you can't always count on it, particularly early in the season. There are few challenging pistes. That's one of the consequences of designating their toughest regularly skied runs as itineraries (see under 'The mountains'). The handful of black runs marked on the piste map are not worthy of their classification; the one with the steepest pitches (Blauherd-Patrullarve) is also very wide.

FOR INTERMEDIATES ★★★★★

Mile after mile of beautiful runs

Zermatt is ideal for adventurous intermediates. Many of the blue runs tend to be at the difficult end of their classification. Reds vary unhelpfully: some are quite tough; some ought to be blue. Few are really what you might call 'cruising' runs.

Among our favourites in the Gornergrat sector are the very beautiful reds down lift-free valleys from both Gornergrat (Kelle) and Hohtälli (White Hare) to Breitboden – we love these first thing in the morning, before anyone else is on them. The steepest part of Kelle is classified black, but an easier red variant bypasses it. From Breitboden you can go on down to Gant, or to the mid-station of the Findeln chairlift, or to Riffelalp on a run that includes a narrow wooded path with a sheer cliff and magnificent views to the right.

On the Rothorn sector, the 5km Kumme/Tufternkumme run – from Rothorn itself to the bottom of the Patrullarve chair – also gets away from the lift system and has an interesting mix of straight-running and mogul pitches (but it gets a lot of sun and lacks snowmaking).

In the Matterhorn Glacier Paradise sector the reds served by the fast quad chair from Furgg are gloriously set at the foot of the Matterhorn. The Furggsattel chair from Trockener Steg serves more pistes with stunning views, notably the Matterhorn piste – blue in gradient for most of its great length, but classified red because of a short, steep pitch near the end which causes problems for many skiers.

For timid intermediates, the best

THE WORLD'S BEST MOUNTAIN RESTAURANTS ★★★★★

The choice of restaurants is enormous, the standard high. We list here only a selection. It is best to book. The tourist office restaurant directory has photos but does not indicate prices. Beware: some places don't take cards.

Below Sunnegga, down at Findeln, are several attractive, expensive, rustic restaurants sharing a great Matterhorn view. Chez Vrony (967 2552) has long been one of our (and readers') favourites; service can be stretched but is reliably friendly, and the food excellent. We hope Vrony's flirtation with a two sitting system is over. We regularly get enthusiastic reports on the Adler (967 1058), with its outdoor BBQ – 'delicious food', 'impeccable service' – and Findlerhof (967 2588) – 'wonderful pasta with mussels'. The Paradies (967 3451) is also recommended. Further up the Findel valley, in a beautiful, isolated situation off the run from Rothorn, Fluhalp (967 2597) is another favourite – excellent food and service, often with live music on the huge terrace. Up at Blauherd, the old self-service place has become Blue Lounge – a cool modern bar serving tapas to jazz and other music. Lower down, Tuftern famously does 'slabs of bread and cheese on a terrace with a great view'. On Gornergrat, the Alphitta (967 2114) below Riffelalp is 'a lovely spot'.

In sharp contrast to all the rustic huts, at Trockener Steg we recommend highly the Ice Pizzeria (967 1812) – a smart, modern table-service place with great views. Higher up, the secluded Gandegghütte (079 607 8868) has stunning views and good, simple food; no milk, so no hot choc though. Over at Schwarzsee, the Stafelalp (967 3062) is a reader favourite – glorious position, 'excellent food; friendly, prompt service', though a 2012 reader found it too 'upmarket'.

At Furi, restaurant Furri (966 2777) serves 'simple good food with a smile' and Simi (967 2695), tucked away, does 'great grills on its open fire'. Just above Furi, Aroleid (967 2658) is a reader favourite – 'tops for rösti' – and hotel Silvana (966 2800) is 'spacious, good food, decent value'. Below Furi, are countless places to pause on the way home, though they are not ideally placed for lunch (unless you are calling it a day). Zum See (967 2045) is a charming old hut, reputedly the best restaurant on the mountain – we've certainly eaten well there. Below it, Blatten (967 2096) serves 'one of the best strudels'. And Marmottes (967 8282) is a little hut with a serious menu; 'delicious tuna and salmon carpaccio' says a recent visitor.

SNOWPIX.COM / CHRIS GILL

↑ At 3100m the Kulmhotel Gornergrat is the highest hotel in Switzerland. And it has amazing views, including, of course, the Matterhorn

ZERMATT TOURISM

SCHOOLS

Swiss
t 966 2466

Stoked
t 967 7020

Summit
t 967 0001

European Snowsport
t 967 6787

Adventure
t 967 5020

Almrausch
t 967 0808

AER
t 967 7067

Prato Borni
t 967 5115

Classes (Swiss prices)
5 days (10am to 3.30 with lunch break)
SF350

Private lessons
SF170 for 2hr for 1 or 2 people

GUIDES

Alpin Center
t 966 2460

runs are the blues from Blauherd on Rothorn, and above Riffelberg on Gornergrat, and in good weather the super-high runs between Klein Matterhorn and Trockener Steg. Of these, the Riffelberg area often has the best combination of good snow and easy cruising, and is understandably popular with the ski schools.

In the Matterhorn Glacier Paradise sector most of the runs, though marked red on the piste map, are very flat and include the easiest slopes Zermatt has to offer, as well as the best snow. Even an early intermediate can make the trip to Cervinia, via Theodulpass rather than the more challenging run from Plateau Rosa.

Beware the black run from Furgg to Furi at the end of the day. It is not steep, but gets chopped up, mogulled in places and very crowded. A much more relaxed alternative is the scenic Weisse Perle run from Schwarzsee (the Stafelalp variant is even more scenic but has a short uphill section).

FOR BEGINNERS ★★★★★
Still far from ideal

These days the resort makes an effort to cater for beginners – there are beginner areas dotted around on all four sectors, and a main one has been developed (with three moving carpets and two rope tows) at Leisee and reached by a short funicular from Sunnegga. There is now a half-price pass to get you to and from that area, which is a step forward. But we have had reports from readers who judge this small area inadequate. And progression to longer runs is awkward – the Zermatt slopes as a whole are very challenging for near-beginners, which includes fast learners who are ready to quit the nursery slopes after a couple of days. Of course you can learn to ski here, but given a choice we would go elsewhere.

FOR BOARDERS ★★★★★
Some good angles

The slopes are best for experienced freeriders and there's a terrain park above Trockener Steg. There are adequate beginner areas, complete with moving carpet lifts, which we've seen many beginner snowboarders having lessons on. The main lifts are boarder-friendly: train, funicular, gondolas, cable cars and fast chairs, and there aren't too many flat bits. Stoked is a specialist school.

FOR CROSS-COUNTRY ★★★★★
Down the valley

There are 17km trails from Täsch to Randa (don't count on good snow).

SCHOOLS AND GUIDES ★★★★★
Competition paying off

The main Swiss school seems to have improved since competing schools were permitted, and our most recent reports have been positive. Of the other schools, Summit and European Snowsport are staffed mainly by Brits. We've had mixed reports on Summit recently – some criticisms of beginner lessons, but enthusiasm for an intermediate class. Stoked snowboard school is made up of young

CHILDCARE

Kinderparadies
t 967 7252
Ages from 3mnth

Kidactive
t 077 405 3957

Kinderclub Pumuckel (Hotel Ginabelle)
t 966 5000
Ages from 30mnth

Schwarzsee (Stoked)
t 967 7020
Ages from 30mnth

Nico Kids Club (Schweizerhof hotel)
t 966 0000
Ages from 2 to 8

Snowli Village (Swiss)
t 966 2466
Ages 4 to 5

Private babysitters
List at tourist office

Ski school
From age 6; 5 full days incl. lunch SF395 (Swiss prices)

instructors, some of whom are British and all of whom speak good English. Again, we have had mixed reports. Our one reporter on Prato Borni last year was very happy.

FOR FAMILIES ★★★★★
Good hotel nurseries
The prices, the general inconvenience of the place and the challenges facing beginners and near-beginners work against families. But, as our margin panel shows, there are plenty of facilities for children and we don't doubt that they are thoroughly well run. The tourist office has a list of babysitters. And families do have successful holidays here, some repeatedly. Choose your location with care, says one reader. Another notes that the number of hotels offering family suites is a plus-point.

STAYING THERE

Chalets Several operators have places here; many of the most comfortable are in apartment blocks. Ski Total has a remarkable 18 properties – mostly with six or eight beds, a couple with more and some with sauna, steam room or hot tub. Skiworld has four chalet-apartments, including three very smart modern ones in the same building. Inghams has four chalets sleeping from six to 16 plus a chalet hotel. Crystal has two chalets for six.
Hotels There are over 100 hotels, mostly comfortable and traditional-style 3-stars and 4-stars, but taking in the whole range. What distinguishes Zermatt is the number of 'hip' places, many of which are listed below.
*******Mont Cervin** (966 8888) Biggest in town. Elegantly traditional. Pool etc.
*******Omnia** (966 7171) Designer hotel, minimalist, central, reached by a lift in a rock, smart fitness centre.
*******Zermatterhof** (966 6600) Traditional 'grand hotel' style, with piano bar. Pool, sauna.
******Alex** (966 7070) Close to train stations. An old favourite, though few recent reports. Large pool, sauna.
******Beau Site** (966 6868) Grand place over the river with Matterhorn views. 'Simply the best we've stayed at.'
******Cervo** (968 1212) Hip place with rooms, suites, chalets for up to 10. At the end of the piste from Sunnegga.
******Coeur des Alpes** (966 4080) Smart, modern B&B place at south end of town; relaxed, friendly feel.
******Europe** (966 2700) Superb place over the river from the church, with fab modern rooms in new extension. We stayed here in 2011.
******Julen** (966 7600) Charming, modern-rustic chalet over the river.
******Matterhorn Focus** (966 2424) Super-stylish B&B designed by Heinz Julen, right by the Matterhorn lifts.
******Mirabeau** (966 2660) Heartily tipped by two reporters in 2011 – 'outstanding food, friendly staff, excellent spa – made our holiday'.
******Monte Rosa** (966 0333) Well-modernized original Zermatt hotel in centre; full of climbing mementos. 'Wonderful,' says a 2011 report.
******Sonne** (966 2066) In quiet setting; 'superb' wellness centre. 'The staff couldn't do enough and took us to the lifts every morning.'
*****Alpenroyal** (966 6066) 'Good value, comfortable, staff friendly, good food.'
Apartments There are lots. We have repeatedly enjoyed staying in the amazingly cheap apartments of the hotel Ambassador (966 2611), with free use of pool and sauna, but they are overdue for a refurb.
At altitude There are several hotels on the hill, of which the pick is the 5-star Riffelalp Resort (966 0555), at the first stop on the Gornergrat railway, with pool, spa and its own evening trains. Highly recommended – luxurious, but 'not at all stuffy'. We fancy staying a couple of nights at the Kulmhotel Gornergrat (966 6400) at the top of the mountain and the highest hotel in Switzerland.

EATING OUT ★★★★★
Huge choice
There are over 100 restaurants to choose from: top-quality haute cuisine, through traditional Swiss food, Chinese, Japanese and Thai to egg and chips. There is even a McDonald's. The tourist office produces a directory, with photos. One reader reckons that you pay a lot less in restaurants at the south end of the village, well away from the centre.

At the top end of the market, a regular visitor tips the cool hotel Cervo ('excellent food, very smart, nice small dining rooms'), Heimberg ('continues to be fab'), Omnia ('wonderful decor, interesting food and wine') and Chez Gaby ('great grilled food, prawns, etc').

At more modest prices, we've enjoyed the Schwyzer Stübli (local specialities and live Swiss music and

UK PACKAGES

Alpine Answers, Alpine Weekends, Carrier, Crystal, Crystal Finest, Elegant Resorts, Elysian Collection, Flexiski, Independent Ski Links, Inghams, Interactive Resorts, Lagrange, Luxury Chalet Collection, Momentum, Mountain Tracks, Neilson, Oxford Ski Co, PowderBeds, Powder Byrne, Pure Powder, Scott Dunn, Ski Club Freshtracks, Ski Expectations, Ski Independence, Ski Line, Ski-Monterosa, Ski Safari, Ski Solutions, Ski Total, Skitracer, Skiweekends.com, Skiworld, Snow Finders, STC, Supertravel, Switzerland Travel Centre, Thomson, VIP, White Roc, Zenith

GETTING THERE

Air Geneva 240km/150 miles (4hr); Zürich 265km/165 miles (4hr30); Sion 80km/50 miles (2hr)

Rail Station in resort

ACTIVITIES

Indoor Hotel saunas and swimming pools (some open to public), climbing wall, museums, cinema

Outdoor Ice rinks, curling, 50km cleared paths, snowshoeing, tobogganing, helicopter flights, ice climbing, paragliding

Phone numbers
From elsewhere in Switzerland add the prefix 027; from abroad use the prefix +41 27

TOURIST OFFICE

www.zermatt.ch

dancing), good value Mexican and Swiss dishes at the Weisshorn and decent Thai food at Rua Thai. Sparky's pub/restaurant is praised for its 'basic but nourishing food', which includes vegetarian options, stews and curries. The Pipe serves interesting Asian/African fusion dishes but we lack reports since it relocated in 2010. 'Absolutely rammed' Grampi's is tipped again this year, for 'very good simple food, good service'. Other reader tips include: Casa Rustica ('good Swiss food'); Klein Matterhorn for fish/pasta ('superb food'); Schäferstube ('some of the best lamb dishes in the village'); Stockhorn ('simple food done well'); and the dear old Whymper-Stube ('great food, very friendly service, reasonable prices').

APRES-SKI ★★★★★
Something for everybody

There's a good mix of sophisticated and informal fun, though it helps if you have deep pockets. Promenading the main street checking out expensive clothes and watches is a popular early-evening activity.

There are lively places to pause on your final descent. On the way back from Rothorn, Othmar's Skihütte and Olympia Stübli have great views, and the funky Cervo where the piste ends has a popular outdoor bar with live music. Caffè Snowboat (near the Sunnegga funicular) is a small, modern place that looks like a, er, boat with a deck and lounge bar. On the way back from Furi there are lots of options, some described under 'Mountain restaurants'. Very near the end of the run, Hennu Stall blasts out loud music and attracts huge crowds – live bands play most days.

For a lively bar through the evening you won't beat the revamped Papperla Pub. The long-established North Wall doesn't get many mentions in reports but still seems to be the season-worker favourite. Potters Bar (geddit?) is a relaxed British pub.

There are plenty of quieter places. The Vernissage is our favourite – unusual, stylish and modern, with the projection room for the cinema built into the upstairs bar and displays of art elsewhere; 'great ambience and decor'. Elsie's famous bar is wood-panelled and atmospheric; it attracts an older crowd, but gets seriously busy early and late. Reader tips include Brit-run Sparky's ('best priced beer in town'), the Little Bar (crowded if there are 10 people in) and the cosy/cramped Hexen. Of the hotel bars, the Alex has comfy sofas, good service and a pool table but doesn't like taking credit cards for modest bar bills and the Pollux is 'reliably good'.

Later on, the hotel Post complex has something for everyone, from a quiet, comfortable bar (Papa Caesar's) to a lively disco (Broken), live music (Pink) and various restaurants. The T-Bar draws a young crowd for dancing and live bands. At Grampi's ('very lively later in the evening'), there is a disco below. The Schneewittchen nightclub (Papperla) is very popular.

OFF THE SLOPES ★★★★
Considerable attractions

Zermatt is an attractive place to spend time. As well as expensive jewellery and clothes shops, there are interesting places selling food, wine, books and art. It is easy (but costly) for pedestrians to get around on the lifts and meet others for lunch, and there are some nice walks (70km) – a special map is available. If the weather is good, the Klein Matterhorn cable car is an experience not to be missed: there is a small self-service restaurant at the top as well as a viewing platform and an ice cave, with 'incredible carvings'. Be aware that the air is thin up there, though. The Matterhorn Museum in the village is worth seeing. You can take a helicopter trip around the Matterhorn (see 'Queues'). There is a cinema, and free village guided tours. For an icy experience, visit (or stay at) the Igloo above Riffelberg.

DOWN-VALLEY VILLAGE – 1450m

TÄSCH

Täsch, where visitors must leave their cars, is just a 12-minute train ride from Zermatt, so makes a viable base. There are several 3-star hotels charging half the Zermatt price. The Täscherhof (966 6262) and Walliserhof (966 3966) ('nice and friendly, very good chef') have been recommended by reporters. Täsch is very quiet in the evening, but it's no problem to spend evenings in Zermatt – trains run until 12.30am Monday to Wednesday, and hourly all night from Thursday to Sunday. And taxis can operate up to the edge of Zermatt.

NTURE

USA

Most people who give it a try find America is pretty seductive, despite the relatively small sizes of its ski areas. What got the US started in the UK market was its (generally) reliable snow, and that remains a key factor. Other factors are the relatively deserted pistes, the high quality of accommodation, the excellent and varied resort restaurants, the high standards of service and courtesy, and the immaculate piste grooming. Depending on the resort, you may also be struck by the cute Wild West ambience and the superb quality of the snow. Of course, US skiing does have disadvantages, too. Not least of which is the cost – long-haul air fares have risen and local prices are high (all US resorts fall into our red category – the most expensive – for their RPI and the five priciest resorts in the entire book are American).

We have organized our US chapters in regional sections – California, Colorado, Utah, Rest of the West and New England.

Most American resorts receive serious amounts of snow – typically in the region of 6m to 12m (or 250 to 500 inches, as they measure it there) in a season; that's around double the 3m to 6m that resorts like Chamonix, St Anton and Val d'Isère in Europe average. It tends to arrive in more frequent falls than in Europe too, so your chances of hitting fresh snow are appreciably higher. And most resorts have serious snowmaking facilities that are used well – laying down a base of snow early in the season rather than patching up shortages later. There are wide differences in quantity and quality of snowfall, both between individual resorts and between regions.

The classification of pistes (or trails, to use the local term) is different from that in Europe. Red runs don't exist. The colours used are combined with shapes. Green circles correspond fairly closely to greens in France and easy blues in the rest of Europe. American blue squares correspond to blues and easy reds in Europe; the tougher ones are sometimes labelled as double squares, or as blue-black squares. Then there are black diamond runs, which is where things get interesting. Single diamonds correspond fairly closely to European blacks and really tough reds. But then there are

PATROLLED AND AVALANCHE-CONTROLLED OFF-PISTE

One of the great attractions of North American resorts to us is that they have patrolled and avalanche-controlled ungroomed terrain that would be classified as off-piste in Europe. Each resort has a 'ski area boundary'; this may be marked by signs on the trees bordering the trails or there may be a rope running right round the ski area boundary. The 'boundary' may be moved depending on snow conditions, and anywhere within the boundary is known as 'in-bounds' and is patrolled and avalanche controlled. In-bounds terrain includes areas between marked and groomed trails and often big areas of ski-anywhere bowls or steep couloirs (or chutes, to use the local term). In Europe such terrain is normally off-piste, and we recommend you ski it only with a qualified local guide; in North America it is safe to ski it without that expense. North America also has what it calls backcountry, which is the area outside the ski area boundary (and which you are often forbidden to access except through gates placed at various points on the boundary). This is not controlled or patrolled and should be treated like European off-piste and skied only with a guide.

ASPEN / DANIEL BAYER

← You couldn't go this far off-piste in the Alps without risking avalanche danger. But you can in the US – see feature panel on the right

multiple diamonds. Double diamond runs are seriously steep – usually steeper than the steepest pistes in the Alps. A few resorts have wildly steep 'extreme' double diamonds, or triple diamonds.

The most obvious drawback to the US is that many resorts have slopes that are very modest in extent compared with major Alpine areas. But usually there are other resorts nearby – so if you are prepared to travel a bit, you won't get bored. Roads are good, and car hire is cheap (watch out for extra insurance charges, though). But if snow is expected, you will need a 4WD or snow chains (you'll have to buy them – we've yet to find a US rental company that will provide them). It's also true that in many resorts the mountains are slightly monotonous, with countless similar trails cut through the forest. You don't usually get the spectacular mountain scenery and the distinctive high-mountain runs of the Alps. But the forest runs do offer good visibility in bad weather, and unlike in Europe, it's normal to be able to ski in among the trees themselves (or glades as they call them) – great fun in fresh snow.

GREAT GROOMING AND DESERTED SLOPES

Piste grooming is taken very seriously – most US resorts set standards that only the best Alpine resorts seem to be able to match. Every morning you can expect to step out on to perfect 'corduroy' pistes. But this doesn't mean that there aren't moguls – far from it. It's just that you get moguls where the resort says you can expect moguls, not everywhere.

The slopes of most US resorts are blissfully free of crowds – a key advantage that becomes more important as the pistes of Europe become ever more congested. If you want to ski quickly and safely with less fear of collisions, head for the States.

Ski schools offer consistently high standards but, unlike in Europe, people don't sign up for a week, only for one or two lessons as they feel the need. Most resorts offer free guided tours of the ski area once or twice a day (usually carried out by volunteers who get a free lift pass in return); and many have 'mountain hosts' on hand to help you find your way. Piste maps are freely available at lift stations, and signposting is generally exemplary.

Lifts are generally efficient, and queues are orderly and short, partly because spare seats are religiously filled with the aid of cheerful, conscientious attendants who ask 'How are you today?' or urge you to 'Have a nice day' every time you get on a lift. You'll also find that Americans on chairlifts with you will be keen to talk to you on the way – weird to Europeans, but we like it. First-time visitors are surprised that some chairlifts in the States do not have safety bars; even on a chair that has a bar, you will find Americans curiously reluctant to use it, and eager to raise it as soon as the top station is in view. They worry about being trapped, not falling off. The lifts close irritatingly early – as early as 3pm in some cases (and some upper lifts might start closing as early as 1.30pm). That may explain another drawback of America – the dearth of decent mountain restaurants. The norm is a monster self-service refuelling station – designed to minimize time off the slopes.

US resort towns vary widely in style and convenience, from cute restored mining towns to purpose-built monstrosities. Two important things the resorts have in common are high quality, spacious accommodation and restaurants that are reliably good and varied in cuisine. Young people should be aware that the rigorously

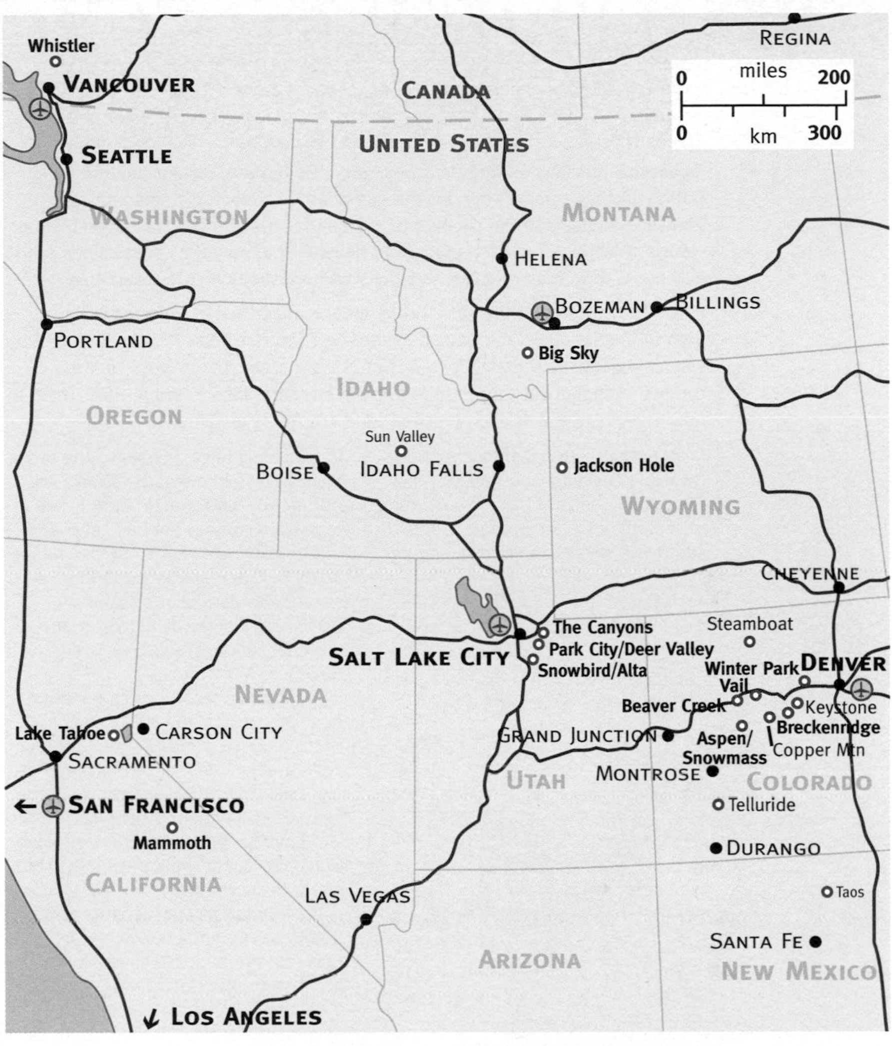

enforced legal age for drinking alcohol is 21; even if you are older, carry evidence of age, especially if you look younger than you are.

Crossing the pond is no longer cheap and neither are extras such as lift passes, ski hire and ski school – all these are generally much more expensive than in Europe. And eating and drinking is no longer the bargain it once was. Take a look at our price panels for each resort for an idea of what to budget for. With lift passes, in many resorts you can save huge amounts by buying in advance through tour operators or websites. Part of the reason for increased costs is the change in the exchange rate (local prices have risen by 35% in the last five years in terms of £s just because of that); and maybe increased costs is one reason why we are now receiving fewer reader reports on US resorts than we used to.

In the end, your reaction to skiing and snowboarding in America may depend on your reaction to America. If repeated exhortations to have a nice day wind you up – or if you like to ride chairlifts in silence – you'd better stick to the Alps. We love skiing there.

California/Nevada

California? It means surfing, beaches, wine, Hollywood, Disneyland and San Francisco cable cars. Nevada means gambling. But this region also has the highest mountains in the continental USA and some of America's biggest winter resorts, usually reliable for snow from November to May (last season was an exception, with unusually low snowfalls and unusually high temperatures).

Most visitors head for the Lake Tahoe area, mapped below. Spectacularly set high in the Sierra Nevada 320km east of San Francisco, Lake Tahoe is ringed by skiable mountains containing 14 downhill resorts and seven cross-country centres – the highest concentration of winter sports resorts in the USA. Then, a long way south (more often reached from LA), there is Mammoth.

Each of the three major 'destination' resorts – Heavenly and Squaw Valley, at opposite ends of Lake Tahoe, and Mammoth, way off our map to the south – is covered in its own chapter immediately after this page. The other main Lake Tahoe resorts (shown on our map) each have an entry in the resort directory at the back of the book. Many are well worth visiting for a day or two, especially the four second-division resorts – Alpine Meadows, Kirkwood, Northstar and Sierra-at-Tahoe. We also enjoyed Sugar Bowl and Mount Rose.

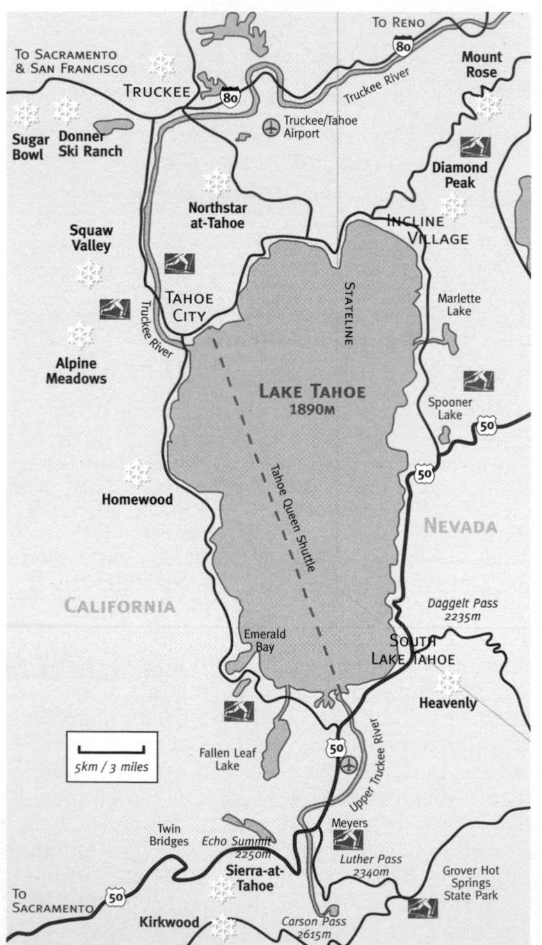

Californian resorts often have the deepest accumulations of snow in North America, which Rockies powder connoisseurs are inclined to brand as wet 'Sierra Cement'. The snow can be heavy. But mostly the snow is fine, at least by Alpine standards – we've had truly fabulous powder days in all the major resorts here.

Californian resorts don't have the traditional mountain-town ambience that can add an extra dimension to holidays in other parts of the States, particularly Colorado. The recently developed car-free plaza in South Lake Tahoe called Heavenly Village and the pedestrian Village at Mammoth – both linked to the slopes by gondola – haven't achieved a great deal in this respect. But Squaw Valley and Northstar have both developed attractive base villages.

You could visit all these resorts by car (best to have a 4WD) from a single base at Heavenly or somewhere thereabouts; but a two-centre holiday also including some time at the north end of the lake would be better. A lift pass covering seven resorts around the lake and another valid at seven northern resorts are both available through tour operators (also see www.skilaketahoe.co.uk and www.gotahoenorth.com).

HEAVENLY SKI RESORT / SCOTT MARKEWITZ

Heavenly

Heavenly is unique: one of America's biggest mountains, with fabulous lake and 'desert' views, above a tacky casino town

RATINGS

The mountains	
Extent	***
Fast lifts	****
Queues	****
Terrain p'ks	*****
Snow	****
Expert	***
Intermediate	****
Beginner	****
Boarder	****
X-country	**
Restaurants	*
Schools	****
Families	**
The resort	
Charm	*
Convenience	*
Scenery	****
Eating out	****
Après-ski	***
Off-slope	***

RPI	160
lift pass	£360
ski hire	£120
lessons	£190
food & drink	£135
total	**£805**

TANYA BOOTH

The views over Lake Tahoe are way out of the ski resort norm ↓

- ➕ Spectacular views of Lake Tahoe and Nevada from slopes
- ➕ Fair-sized mountain that offers a sensation of travelling around
- ➕ Large areas of widely spaced trees – fabulous in fresh powder
- ➕ Some serious challenges for experts
- ➕ Numerous other worthwhile resorts within an hour's drive
- ➕ Good snow record plus impressive snowmaking facilities
- ➕ Unique nightlife in town at base

- ➖ Town at base, South Lake Tahoe, is a messy, traffic-ridden place
- ➖ No trail back to Heavenly Village at the base of the gondola
- ➖ Lifts vulnerable to wind closure
- ➖ Pronounced step from easy groomed blues to mogulled blacks
- ➖ If natural snow is poor, most of the challenging terrain may be closed
- ➖ Mountain restaurants dire (though new one in 2011 an improvement)
- ➖ Very little traditional après-ski

With a top height of 3060m and vertical of 1060m, Heavenly is the highest and biggest of the resorts around famously deep, pure and beautiful Lake Tahoe. It has the best lake views, too. But anyone drawn by the scenic setting is likely to be dismayed by the barren base town of South Lake Tahoe, straddling busy US Highway 50. You could stay out of town, close to one of the other lift bases.

And the skiing? If your taste is for easy Alpine blacks or tough reds, just be sure you are ready to step up to ungroomed stuff – you'll find the blues tame.

THE RESORT

South Lake Tahoe, on the shore of the lake, is primarily a summer resort. It straddles the California-Nevada border, and its economy is based on gambling, which Nevada permits. The central Stateline area is dominated by a handful of high-rise hotel-casinos built on the Nevada side of the line.

These brash but comfortable hotels offer good-value rooms (subsidized by the gambling), swanky restaurants and various entertainments. Picking your way between the slot machines in ski gear, carrying skis or board, is weird.

NEWS

2011/12: Many of the upper runs on the California side were substantially widened, and three new intermediate trails were built on the Nevada side. A new ski school building for children and a new kids' adventure zone opened at Adventure Peak. The terrain parks have been revamped and a new half-pipe introduced.

KEY FACTS

Resort	1900m 6,230ft
Slopes	2000-3060m 6,570-10,040ft
Lifts	30
Pistes	4,800 acres
Green	20%
Blue	45%
Black	35%
Snowmaking	73%

Near the casino area is the small Heavenly Village, purpose-built around the main lift base. There are other lift base areas (with lodgings) on both the California and Nevada sides of the hill.

Other resorts around the lake are easily visited from a base here, and lift passes that cover several areas are available. A car is handy to explore them (although buses, some free, are available) and to get to many of the best restaurants, but parking can be expensive.

The obvious gateway airport is San Francisco, but Reno is much closer, and the road up less likely to be affected by snow.

VILLAGE CHARM ★☆☆☆☆
The highway rules

From a distance the casinos look like a classic American downtown area, which you'd expect to be full of shops and bars. But there's hardly any of that – just the seriously busy and pedestrian-hostile Highway 50. The rest of the town spreads for miles along the road – dozens of low-rise hotels and motels (some quite shabby), stores, wedding chapels and so on. The general effect is less dire than it might be, thanks to the camouflage of tall trees. Heavenly Village provides a downtown après-ski focus (basically just one bar), but is otherwise not a great success.

CONVENIENCE ★☆☆☆☆
Gamble on the gondola?

The central area close to Heavenly Village and the gondola looks the obvious place to stay, despite the lack of trails down to it. Some of the casino-hotels are within five minutes' walk of the gondola, but others are a hike away. There are lodgings close to the other lift bases – California Lodge, up a heavily wooded slope 2km out of South Lake Tahoe, and the more remote Nevada bases, Boulder Lodge and Stagecoach Lodge. And there are cheaper places literally miles from a lift, and used largely by people with cars. There are free shuttle-buses. You can ski down at the end of the day to all these other bases.

SCENERY ★★★★☆
Splendid panoramas

The views over Lake Tahoe, ringed by snow-capped mountains, are spectacular. The casinos are a conspicuous part of those views from the lower slopes, though not from above mid-mountain; the long Ridge Run, across the top, is good for lake views. In the other direction the slopes overlook wild and arid Nevada – sufficiently arid to be classified as desert, though the Sahara it ain't.

THE MOUNTAIN

Practically all of Heavenly's slopes are cut through forest, but in many areas the forest is not dense and there is excellent tree skiing. The trail map gives a good indication of the density of trees. As elsewhere in the US, this 'off-piste' terrain is 'patrolled', but only by hollering – ineffective if you are unconscious; don't ski the trees alone.

Two days a week, am and pm, there are free and 'excellent' mountain tours led by forest rangers.

EXTENT OF THE SLOPES ★★★☆☆
Interestingly complex

The mountain is complicated, and getting from A to B requires more careful navigation than is usual on American mountains. Quite a few of the links between different sectors involve long, flat tracks.

There is a clear division between the California side of the mountain (above South Lake Tahoe) and the Nevada side. If lift closures leave you on the wrong side, it's not a big deal – the bus rides don't take long.

The gondola from South Lake Tahoe goes to one end of the California side. There is no skiing back to the town. At the other end of this side, the steep lower slopes are served by the Aerial Tramway (cable car) and Gunbarrel fast chair from California Lodge. The much more extensive upper slopes are served by four fast chairs, one going up to the Skyline trail to the Nevada side.

The Nevada side is more fragmented, but the central focus is East Peak Lodge. Above it is an excellent intermediate area, served by two fast quad chairs, with a downhill extension served by the Galaxy chair. From the fast Dipper chair back up, you can access the open terrain of Milky Way Bowl, leading to the seriously steep chutes of Mott and Killebrew Canyons, served by the Mott Canyon chair. Below East Peak Lodge are runs down to Nevada's two bases, Stagecoach and Boulder – the latter often quiet because its chairs are slow.

LIFT PASSES

Heavenly

Prices in US$

Age	1-day	6-day
under 13	50	180
13 to 18	79	348
19 to 64	88	474
65 plus	79	348

Free under 5

Beginner combined lesson/limited lift pass/equipment deals

Notes
These are the online prices booked at least a week in advance; reduced prices to international visitors who pre-book through a UK tour operator; ticket window prices are much higher

FAST LIFTS ★★★★

California does it better

Most people can spend practically all their time on fast chairs. The Mott Canyon chair is slow, but that's a niche market. The main weaknesses are the slow chairs up from Boulder Lodge.

QUEUES ★★★★

Gondola up and down

The gondola can have queues to go up and particularly to go down – and because of this you'll see signs advising you to get back to the gondola ridiculously early. Pay no attention – have a beer or two at the top while waiting for the queue to dissipate. Or forget the gondola and head for one of the other bases, and jump on a shuttle. A couple of recent visitors have found queues for the slow Groove chair and the Sky Express at the end of the day when people are returning to base. Another reported crowds around the lifts from East Peak Lodge on the Nevada side. Some lifts, including the gondola, also seem prone to closure because of wind. Most reporters have had few other problems, often commenting on uncrowded slopes.

TERRAIN PARKS ★★★★★

Splendid for all abilities

Heavenly has something for everyone – all sensibly located on the California slopes. The Progression Park, at Adventure Peak near the top of the gondola, is the smallest of Heavenly's parks and part of the new kids' adventure zone; it has small rails, gentle jumps and boxes designed to help youngsters explore.

The Groove Park, at the top of the lifts up from California Lodge, has beginner/intermediate features such as small jumps and boxes for riders wanting to move to the next level. Intermediates should head to Player's Park off the Canyon chair; this is a great progression area, with three lines, a collection of intermediate rails, boxes, wall rides, recycled features, jibs and bonks. High Roller Park, near the top of the Canyon chair, serves expert riders; there is a large double-jump line – with jumps exceeding 20m in length – as well as large boxes, rails, wall rides and recycled features that often elevate 1m–3m off the snow. Ante Up Park under the Tamarack chair is intended for advanced and intermediates; all its features use recycled materials.

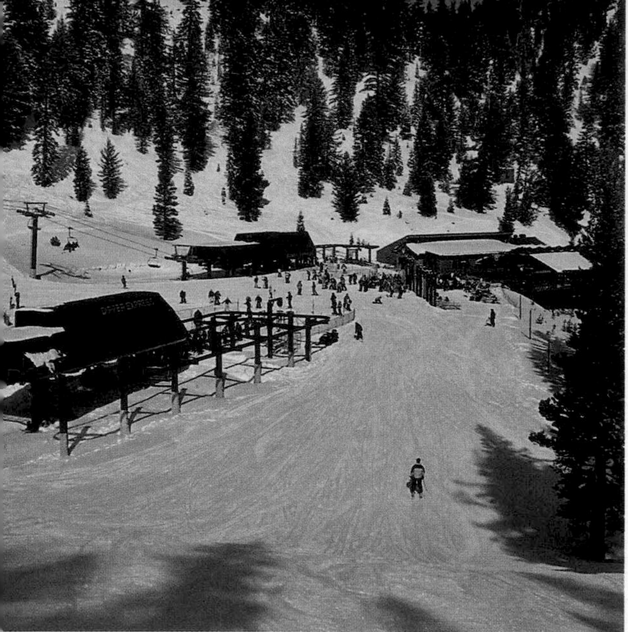

↑ East Peak Lodge is the central focus on the Nevada side

TANYA BOOTH

Resort news and key links: www.wheretoskiandsnowboard.com

GETTING THERE

Air San Francisco 320km/200 miles (3hr45); Reno 90km/55 miles (1hr30); South Lake Tahoe, 15min

UK PACKAGES

Alpine Answers, AmeriCan Ski, American Ski Classics, Crystal, Crystal Finest, Erna Low, Independent Ski Links, Interactive Resorts, Momentum, Ski Independence, Ski Line, Ski Safari, Ski Solutions, Skitracer, Skiworld, Supertravel, Virgin Snow

SNOW RELIABILITY ★★★★☆

Fewer worries for intermediates

Heavenly averages an impressive 360 inches per year, but the weather here is much less consistent than further inland, and last season was an especially poor year for snow. When snow is poor and temperatures are cold enough, intermediates can still have a good time thanks to impressive snowmaking and grooming. But much of the challenging ungroomed terrain can be closed when snow is poor. A useful TV programme, *Another Heavenly Morning*, covers snow conditions each day.

FOR EXPERTS ★★★☆☆

Some specific challenges

The black runs under the California base lifts – including the Face and Gunbarrel (often used for mogul competitions) – are seriously steep. We've seen lots of people struggling on the top-to-bottom icy bumps. Many of the single diamonds higher up are at the easy end of the range. Ellie's, at the top of the mountain, may offer continuous moguls too, but was groomed and a great fast cruise when we last skied it. Skiways Glades and the Pinnacles, to skier's right of that, offer friendly, widely spaced trees. Lower down, a trusted reader raves about Maggie's Canyon.

On the Nevada side there are some excellent single-diamond glade areas too – notably to skier's left of the slow North Bowl chair. And there is some really steep stuff. Milky Way Bowl provides a gentle single-diamond introduction to the double-diamond terrain beyond it: the chutes in the otherwise densely wooded Mott and Killebrew Canyons are seriously steep and narrow. They are accessed through roped gateways, and are not to be underestimated. The Mott Canyon chair is slow, but you may not mind. Good natural snow is needed for the Canyons to be enjoyable (or open).

FOR INTERMEDIATES ★★★★☆

Lots to do

The California side offers a progression from the relaxed cruising of the long Ridge Run, starting right at the top of the mountain, to more challenging blues dropping off the ridge towards Sky Deck. More confident intermediates will want to spend time on the Nevada side, where there is more variety of terrain, more carving space and some great longer cruises down to the lift bases. But really strong intermediates looking for challenges need to be prepared to step up to the tree runs – maybe starting with Powderbowl Woods or The Pines – or to the blacks, which are often mogulled.

FOR BEGINNERS ★★★★☆

An excellent place to learn

There are excellent beginner areas at the top of the gondola, at California Lodge and at Boulder Lodge. On the California side there are gentle green runs to progress to at the top of the cable car. Package deals of tuition and lift ticket are worth looking into.

FOR BOARDERS ★★★★☆

Perfect playground – nearly

Heavenly has several terrain parks, and the resort's naturally varied terrain makes a perfect playground for advanced freeriders. Intermediates will have fun too, especially if there's powder in the trees. And there are good areas for beginners. But beware: there are many flat spots where you'll have to scoot. Boardinghouse at Heavenly Village is the local snowboard-only shop.

FOR CROSS-COUNTRY ★★☆☆☆

A separate world

The serious stuff is around the lake – notably at the Spooner Lake: over 80km of prepared trails.

SCHOOLS

Heavenly
t 775 586 7000

Classes
Half-day learn-to-ski package (includes equipment and pass) from $142

Private lessons
From $425 for 3hr

CHILDCARE

Day Care Center
t 775 586 7000
Ages 6wk to 6yr

Ski school
Ages 4 to 13 (boarding 5 to 13)

ACTIVITIES

Indoor Casinos, spas, galleries, cinema, museums

Outdoor Lake cruises, snowmobiling, gondola rides, helicopter tours, tubing, ski biking, sleigh rides, dog sledding, hot springs, small ice rink, ballooning, snowshoeing

Phone numbers
Different area codes are used on the two sides of the stateline; for this chapter, therefore, the area code is included with each number

From distant parts of the US, add the prefix 1. From abroad, add the prefix +1

TOURIST OFFICE

www.skiheavenly.com

MOUNTAIN RESTAURANTS ★☆☆☆☆
Dire – but new one helps

The on-mountain catering is grossly inadequate, especially in bad weather. However, a new restaurant, Tamarack Lodge, opened at the top of the gondola in 2011, and reporters are united in welcoming it: 'a great improvement', 'fairly standard food but quality fine, and the place is large and comfortable'. Gunbarrel Grill in Lakeview Lodge at the top of the tram gets a mention for its 'excellent' buffet. The other options are outdoor decks serving BBQs and pizzas (hugely unenjoyable in a blizzard, as we can testify) and grossly overcrowded cafeterias. East Peak Lodge offered a reporter 'as bad an example of piste food as I ever hope to encounter'.

SCHOOLS AND GUIDES ★★★★☆
Small groups if you're lucky

A recent reporter sums up the general view well: 'Excellent tuition for all levels, with everyone progressing well; the beginners were skiing black-diamond tree runs by the end of the week.' Groups are generally small.

FOR FAMILIES ★★☆☆☆
Head for Adventure Peak

Heavenly offers various children's programmes and facilities. A new kids' ski school building and adventure zone opened at Adventure Peak for 2011/12, and Adventure Peak is home to family activities such as tubing too.

STAYING THERE

Accommodation in the South Lake Tahoe area is abundant and ranges from the huge casinos to quite small motels.

Hotels Of the main casino hotels, Harrah's (775 588 6611) and Harveys (775 588 2411) are the closest to the gondola. Rooms booked on the spot are expensive; packages are cheaper.

******Embassy Suites** (530 544 5400) Luxury suites close to the gondola. Breakfast and après cocktails included.

******MontBleu Resort** (775 588 3515) 'Cheap rooms; can be noisy at night.'

*****Inn by the Lake** (530 542 0330) 'Posh motel', less convenient but 'big rooms, nice view'. Hot tub, pool.

*****Lakeland Village** (530 544 1685) Wide range of 'very comfortable' lodgings. A 2011 reporter rated his townhouse there 'very large and comfortable'.

*****Station House Inn** (530 542 1101) A Best Western; 'comfortable and well maintained'; 'excellent choice of full cooked breakfasts'.

*****3 Peaks Resort** (530 544 4131) Convenient, with large rooms. Pool.

*****Timber Cove Lodge** (530 541 6722) Bland but well run, with lake views from some rooms.

Apartments Plenty of choice.

EATING OUT ★★★★☆
Good value and choice

There's a huge variety, at least if you are prepared to drive (and not drink). The casino hotels' all-you-can-eat buffets offer fantastic value and variety, and there are 'gourmet' choices too – try 19 Kitchen and Bar on the 19th at Harveys. LewMarNel's at the Station House Inn serves good fish, pasta, steak and veal ('delicious filet mignon'). Evan's American Gourmet Cafe does 'wonderful fresh food' and has an extensive wine list. The Stateline Brewery does 'excellent pub fare'. MacDuff's Public House, near the Inn by the Lake, is billed as a Scottish pub and has a wood-fired pizza oven and pub grub. Other reporter tips include Hunan Garden for Chinese, Fresh Ketch at Tahoe Keys Marina ('good fish; went twice and loved it') and Zephyr Cove Resort. Heidi's serves a 'vast' breakfast, or try Nikki's Chaat (Indian), the Blue Angel or the Driftwood Cafe.

APRES-SKI ★★★☆☆
From bars to baccarat

An Austrian-style umbrella bar near the top of the gondola and Fire+Ice at the foot of it (with an outdoor seating area with open fires and heaters) both get busy. Whiskey Dick's, on the main highway, has regular live music. Later on, the casinos have shows, occasionally with top-name entertainers, as well as endless opportunities for throwing your money away gambling.

OFF THE SLOPES ★★★☆☆
Quite a bit to entertain

If you want to get away from the bright lights, try a boat trip or a hot-air balloon ride. Pedestrians can use the cable car or the gondola to share the lake views. Adventure Peak, at the top of the gondola, has tubing, snow biking, tobogganing and a zip-line. There are lots of snowshoe trails and a public swimming pool.

Mammoth Mountain

A big, sprawling mountain above a car-oriented, sprawling but pleasantly woody resort, a six-hour drive from Los Angeles

RATINGS

The mountains

Extent	***
Fast lifts	****
Queues	****
Terrain p'ks	*****
Snow	****
Expert	****
Intermediate	****
Beginner	****
Boarder	*****
X-country	****
Restaurants	**
Schools	****
Families	****

The resort

Charm	**
Convenience	**
Scenery	***
Eating out	*****
Après-ski	***
Off-slope	*

RPI	155
lift pass	£340
ski hire	£130
lessons	£215
food & drink	£115
total	**£800**

NEWS

2012/13: June Mountain, under the same ownership as Mammoth and a scenic 30 minute drive away, was covered by the Mammoth lift pass. Sadly, June will not open this winter. We're not surprised because the last time we skied June there were only six skiers on the mountain they were almost outnumbered by lifties.

2011/12: The High-Five Express quad replaced the slow triple Chair 5. A new half-pipe opened, as did a tubing park.

+ One of North America's bigger ski hills, with something for everyone
+ Mix of open Alpine-style bowls and classic American wooded slopes
+ Impressive snowfall record
+ Uncrowded slopes most of the time
+ Mightily impressive terrain parks
+ Good views by US standards

− Mammoth Lakes is a rather straggling place with no focus, where life revolves around cars

− Most, though not all, lodgings are miles from the slopes

− Weekend crowds in high season

− Wind can be a problem

Mammoth may not be mammoth in Alpine terms – from end to end, it's less than one-third of the size of Val d'Isère/Tignes, in area more like one-sixth – but it is big enough to amuse many people for a week.

These days there is something resembling a village to stay in – The Village, a typically careful Intrawest confection of lodgings, restaurants and shops that has a gondola up to the slopes and a very easy green piste back. But most people stay elsewhere – in hotels, condos and houses spread around the vast wooded area of Mammoth Lakes – and never go near it. Pick your location carefully, and you can walk to a lift; get a car, and you open up lots of options.

THE RESORT

The mountain is set above Mammoth Lakes, a small year-round resort that spreads over a wide area of woodland and is close to Yosemite National Park (local entrance road closed in winter). The drive up from Los Angeles takes around five hours (more in poor conditions). You pass through the Santa Monica mountains close to Beverly Hills, then the San Gabriel mountains and Mojave Desert (with the world's biggest jet-plane parking lot) before reaching the Sierra Nevada.

VILLAGE CHARM **

Good first impressions

The place is entirely geared to driving, with no discernible centre – hotels, restaurants and little shopping centres are scattered along the four-lane highway called Main Street and Old Mammoth Road, which crosses it.

The resort buildings are generally timber-clad in traditional style – even the local McDonald's has been tastefully designed – and are set among trees. So although it may be short on village ambience, the place has a pleasant enough appearance – particularly when under several feet of snow, which it often is. The Village is car-free, and neatly designed.

CONVENIENCE **

Canyon Lodge is closest

Two lift bases are both a mile or two from most of the hotels and condos. The major one is Canyon Lodge, with a big day lodge and hotels and condos in the area below it. The Village is linked to Canyon Lodge by a gondola, so is a fairly convenient base. You can ski back on a green run too – though it is very flat in parts. The minor base is Eagle Lodge (aka Juniper Springs, which is strictly the name of the adjacent condos).

A road skirts the mountain to two other major base areas: Mill Cafe, and Main Lodge, a mini-resort with a big day lodge. You can stay here, in the Mammoth Mountain Inn; but you are then four miles from the 50+ restaurants in Mammoth Lakes.

'Fantastic, reliable, frequent and free' shuttle-buses run on several colour-coded routes serving the lift bases. Night buses run until midnight. But a car is useful.

SCENERY ***

Hint of the Alpine

The resort has a wooded setting below open Alpine style ridges. From the top there are great views north-east into Nevada, and of the jagged Minarets to the west ('wow, wow and wow again', says a 2012 reporter).

Mammoth has a huge variety of terrain, and during the week its trails are usually blissfully quiet →

MAMMOTH MOUNTAIN

KEY FACTS

Resort	2425m 7,950ft
Slopes	2425-3370m 7,950-11,050ft
Lifts	28
Pistes	3,500 acres
Green	25%
Blue	40%
Black	35%
Snowmaking	33%

THE MOUNTAIN

The 28 lifts access an impressive area, suitable for all abilities. The highest runs are open, the lower ones sheltered by trees, with lightly wooded slopes at mid-mountain that are great on a stormy day.

Finding your way around is not easy at first. All the chairlifts are numbered (the traditional practice), and some are also named (a relatively new practice), but the trails are rather ill defined, and signposting on the mountain is sporadic. However, our 2012 reporters had no problems (and liked the piste maps on the chairlift safety bars). The free tours by mountain hosts are 'excellent'.

EXTENT OF THE SLOPES ★★★★★
Lots for everyone

As you can see from our star ratings, Mammoth is good for every ability of skier and boarder. A trusted reporter who visited in both 2011 and 2012 remarks on the 'fantastic variety of runs; it has everything you could possibly want'. From **Main Lodge** the two-stage Panorama gondola goes via McCoy Station right to the top. From here, there are countless ways down the front of the mountain that range from steep to very steep – or vertical if the wind has created a cornice, as it often does. Or you can go off the back of the hill, down to **Outpost 14**, whence Chair 14 or Chair 13 brings you back to lower points on the ridge. The third option is to follow the ridge, which curls around and eventually brings you down to the Main Lodge area – though you might not realize that without careful study of the trail map. This route brings you past an easy area served by a double chair, and a very easy area served by the Discovery fast quad.

McCoy Station can also be reached using the Stump Alley fast chair from **Mill Cafe**, on the road up from town. The fast Gold Rush quad, also from Mill Cafe, takes you into the more heavily wooded eastern half of the area. This has long, gentle runs served by lifts up from **Canyon Lodge** and **Eagle Lodge** and seriously steep stuff as well as some intermediate terrain served by lifts 25 and 22 and some excellent tree skiing.

FAST LIFTS ★★★★★
Where it counts

The main access lifts from every base are fast chairs or gondolas. But there are still several slow old lifts. The Outpost area is the least well served for fast lifts. Usefully, the trail map lists the ride time of every lift.

QUEUES ★★★★★
Normally quiet slopes

Mammoth's lifts and slopes are usually very quiet, with very few queues: 'Queues? What queues?' says a 2012 visitor. But on fine peak-season weekends hordes of people may arrive from Los Angeles, and the lifts can struggle to cope.

One 2012 reporter was sad to discover the 'Black Pass': by paying a premium you can jump any queues – 'no more equality on the slopes'.

LIFT PASSES		
Mammoth Mountain		
Prices in US$		
Age	**1-day**	**6-day**
under 13	30	180
13 to 18	75	398
19 to 64	96	510
65 plus	76	435
Free under 7, over 80		
Beginner fixed price pass of $59 for four chairs		
Notes Discounts for online advanced booking; afternoon pass		

TERRAIN PARKS ★★★★★
Difficult to beat

Mammoth's world-class Unbound Terrain Parks areas are made up of no fewer than 10 parks, all looked after with 'artistic proficiency'. There are over 50 jumps, 65 jibs and three half-pipes in 90 acres of freestyle territory. Easiest are the Eagle Park at Eagle Lodge (with easy rollers), Disco Park at Main Lodge (with small low-to-the-snow rails and boxes) and the Wonderland Park by Chair 7 (with a mini-pipe and micro-scale rails, boxes and mini-jumps). For intermediate to advanced riders South Park, Jibs Galore (Chair 4) and Forest Trail (Chair 6) Park are playgrounds offering a bewildering choice of rails and kickers. Alternatively, take on the X-Course boardercross (Chair 4). Finally Main Park, situated off Chair 6 above Main Lodge, is huge; everything here is up to pro standard. Kickers range from 18m to 24m long and border the famous super-duper pipe (183m long, with 7m walls) that looms over the car park and dwarfs the super-pipe beside it; it is cut daily. Main Park is serviced by a fast chairlift, allowing for a full lap time of only eight minutes. The Art Park near Canyon Lodge has custom-painted features. The parks can get very crowded at weekends.

SNOW RELIABILITY ★★★★
A long season

Mammoth has an impressive snow record – an annual average of 385 inches, which puts it ahead of major Colorado resorts and about on a par with Jackson Hole. Its slopes are appreciably higher than those of the Tahoe resorts, and it has an ever-expanding array of snow-guns, so it enjoys a long season – it sometimes has slopes open on 4 July, and even with last season's poor snow, skiing was possible till late May. The mountain faces roughly north-east; the relatively low and slightly sunny slopes down to Eagle Lodge are affected by warm weather before others. Strong winds are not uncommon on the upper mountain, and the snow quality can be affected. But you may find powder is just shifted down the hill. Visitors in 2012 reported excellent grooming.

FOR EXPERTS ★★★★
Some very challenging terrain

The steep double-diamond chutes strung across the width of the mountain top provide wonderful opportunities for experts. Fortunately for the rest of us there are three or four broad single-diamond slopes, requiring rather less bottle.

There is lots of challenging terrain lower down, too, much of it lightly wooded and therefore good to ski in bad conditions; Chair 5, Chair 22 (the top of which is higher than the very top of Heavenly) and Broadway are often open in bad weather when the top is firmly shut, and their more sheltered slopes may in any case have the best snow. There are plenty of good slopes over the back towards Outpost 14, too.

Many of the steeper trails are short

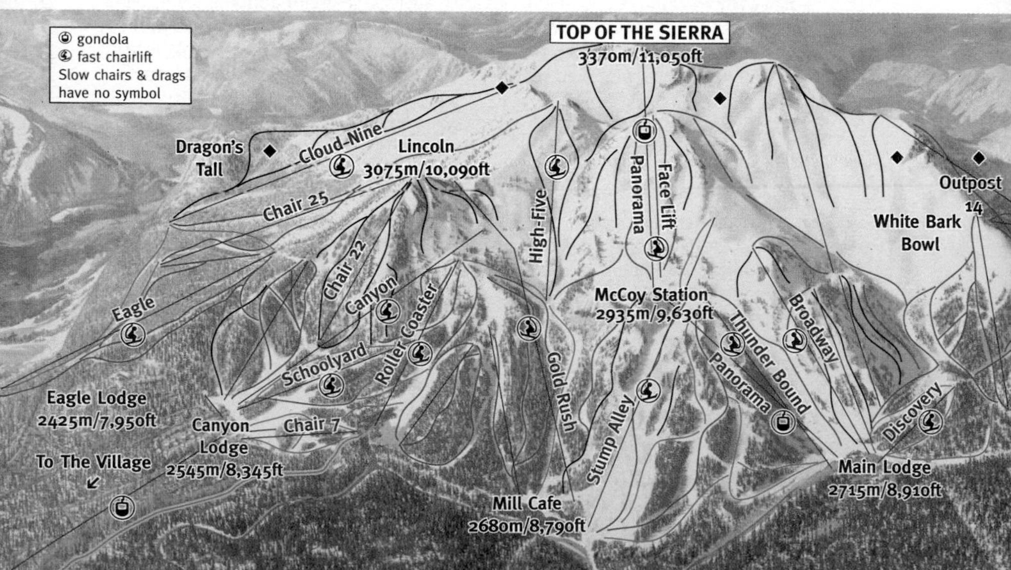

Mammoth's Unbound Terrain Parks include no fewer than 10 parks and three pipes, in 90 acres of freestyle territory. Amazing! →

MAMMOTH MOUNTAIN / PEATROSS

by Alpine standards (typically under 400m vertical), but despite this we've had some great powder days here.

FOR INTERMEDIATES ★★★★
Lots of great cruising
Although there are exceptions, most of the lower mountain, below the treeline, is intermediate cruising territory and generally flattering.

Some of the mountain's longest runs – blue-blacks served by the Cloud Nine Express and Chair 25 – are ideal for good intermediates. There are also some excellent, fairly steep woodland trails down to Mill Cafe. Most of the long runs above Eagle Lodge, and some of the shorter ones above Canyon Lodge, are easy cruises. There is a variety of terrain, including lots of gentle stuff, on the right hand side of the trail map.

FOR BEGINNERS ★★★★
Good, gentle slopes
Chair 7 and the Schoolyard Express chair (at the Canyon Lodge base) and Discovery Chair (at Main Lodge) serve quiet, gentle green runs – perfect terrain for novices. These lifts, plus two others, are included in a beginner lift pass. Excellent instruction and top-notch piste maintenance usually make progress speedy, delighting reporters.

FOR BOARDERS ★★★★★
Great parks and terrain
Regularly voted one of the best snowboard resorts in the USA by *Transworld Snowboarding* magazine readers, Mammoth has encouraged snowboarding since its early days: 'We felt like we were being welcomed home here!' said a 2012 reporter. A huge amount has been spent on the terrain parks, and this tends to overshadow just how good the mountain's natural terrain really is. Largely serviced by hassle-free fast chairs and gondolas, this is a snowboarder's heaven with terrain to suit every ability level. Wave Rave snowboard shop on Main Street has a big selection of gear.

FOR CROSS-COUNTRY ★★★★
Very popular
Two specialist centres, Tamarack (31km) and Sierra Meadows (ungroomed), provide lessons and tours. A recent reporter enjoyed 'gorgeous vistas gliding through the forest around mountain lakes'. And there are lots of ungroomed tracks, including some through the pretty Lakes Basin area.

MOUNTAIN RESTAURANTS ★★
Back to base ...
There are really only two or three lunch options on the hill. 'Food is OK or even quite good ... ambience isn't,' says a 2012 reporter. 'At least the prices aren't excessive,' adds another. Top of the Sierra Cafe and Market is small and 'very functional' but has 'views to die for'. McCoy Station at mid-mountain offers a wide choice, and the table-service Parallax next door is pleasant, with a splendid view from its picture windows. A fair-weather option is the primitive

SCHOOLS

Mammoth Mountain
934 0685

Classes
Half-day (2.5hr) $140

Private lessons
From $114 for 1hr

CHILDCARE

Small World
t 934 0646
Newborn to 6yr

Ski school
Ages 3 to 13

GETTING THERE

Air Los Angeles 494km/307 miles (5hr); Reno 275km/175 miles (4hr15)

ACTIVITIES

Indoor Spa, art gallery, art centre, cinema, theatre

Outdoor Ice rink, gondola rides, snowmobiling, tubing, snowshoeing

UK PACKAGES

AmeriCan Ski, American Ski Classics, Independent Ski Links, Momentum, Ski Independence, Ski Line, Ski Safari, Ski Solutions, Skitracer, Skiworld, Snow Finders, Supertravel, Virgin Snow

Phone numbers
From distant parts of the US, add the prefix 1 760; from abroad, add the prefix +1 760

TOURIST OFFICE

www.mammothmountain.com

outdoor BBQ at Outpost 14, and 2011 saw the introduction of the Roving Mammoth, a snowcat that drives around the mountain selling burritos and stuff.

Mammoth does not designate picnic rooms as such; rather, all seating is open to all guests, whether they purchase their lunch on-site or bring it with them.

SCHOOLS AND GUIDES ★★★★
More reports needed

We have no recent reports. But there are 'workshops' with a maximum of four guests and three-day 'camps' (eg park and pipe, moguls and over-50s).

FOR FAMILIES ★★★★
Family favourite

Mammoth is keen to attract families. The focal points are the Woolly's Forest childcare centres at the Mammoth Mountain Inn at the Main Lodge area and at the Village, with comprehensive facilities for children up to six years old. Kids from age three can have ski lessons, and there are four Kids Adventure zones with fun features for skiers and boarders, two non-skiing Play Zones and a new tubing park with its own lift.

STAYING THERE

There's a good choice of hotels (none very luxurious or expensive) and condos. The condos tend to be out of town, either near the lifts or on the road to them.

****Westin Monache Resort** (934 0400) Condo hotel near The Village gondola: restaurant, hot tubs, pool.

***Alpenhof Lodge** (934 6330) Comfortable and central, Shuttle-bus stop and plenty of restaurants nearby.

***Mammoth Mountain Inn** (934 2581) Good value, but way out of town at Main Lodge.

***Sierra Nevada Lodge** (934 2515) Central; recently renovated. Spa. 'Charming, old-fashioned hotel with retro decor, but modern facilities,' says a 2012 reporter.

Apartments The Village Lodge is close to many restaurants and shops; Juniper Springs Resort is near the Eagle base; both are of high quality. Other comfortable options are the Seasons 4 condos (close to the Village), the 1849 Condos (Canyon Lodge area) and the nearby Mammoth Ski and Racquet Club.

EATING OUT ★★★★★
Outstanding choice

Mammoth has 50+ restaurants offering a wide choice from typical American to Japanese. There's a local menu guide covering many but not all.

The chalet-style Lakefront in the Tamarack Lodge is one of the best, with great views and excellent food with a French theme (not cheap though). Rafters and the Red Lantern Chinese in the Sierra Nevada Lodge both have 'excellent cuisine and are good value for money, especially in happy hour when prices are reduced', says a 2012 reporter. We've had excellent dinners at Skadi (fine dining) and Whiskey Creek (also a saloon). Giovanni's is good for pizza and pasta. Slocums is a popular steakhouse. Angels has typical American family food – burgers, steaks, ribs. Chart House is part of a chain and specializes in seafood and steaks. For 'good home cooking' try the meat loaf or prime rib at the Stove.

Other possibilities include Shogun for Japanese or Gomez's for Tex-Mex. For a hearty breakfast, try the, er, Breakfast Club. The Side Door cafe is an appealing eatery in The Village. The Parallax at McCoy Station opens for snowcat dinners up the mountain.

APRES-SKI ★★★
Lively at weekends

At the close of play, the Yodler at Main Lodge is the liveliest spot – an old chalet (brought from Switzerland, they claim). Tusks at Main Lodge and the Dry Creek bar in the Mammoth Mountain Inn across the road are other choices. Lakanuki is a 'Hawaiian-style bar in the Village that attracts a younger crowd'. Nightlife revolves around a handful of bars which liven up at weekends: Whiskey Creek (stays open late), Grumpy's sports bar and quieter Slocums. An après-ski bus runs from Main Lodge to The Village, connecting with the town buses.

OFF THE SLOPES ★
Mainly sightseeing

Outdoor activities include skating, tubing, snowmobiling, snowshoeing, thermal hot springs and pleasant drives. Mono Lake and the WW2 centre at Manzanar on the road to Los Angeles have been recommended. There is factory shopping nearby, too. But overall, Mammoth isn't a great place for non-skiers.

SQUAW VALLEY SKI CORP / NATHAN KENDALL

Squaw Valley

The site of the 1960 Olympics has a lot to offer novices and experts, and the little purpose-built village is worth a few days' stay

TOP 10 RATINGS

Extent	***
Fast lifts	***
Queues	****
Snow	****
Expert	****
Intermediate	**
Beginner	****
Charm	***
Convenience	****
Scenery	***

RPI	145
lift pass	£330
ski hire	£110
lessons	£170
food & drink	£115
total	**£725**

KEY FACTS

Resort	1890m 6,200ft
Slopes	1890-2760m 6,200-9,050ft
Lifts	33
Pistes	4,000 acres
Green	25%
Blue	45%
Black	30%
Snowmaking	15%

- \+ Lots of challenging terrain
- \+ Impressive snow record
- \+ Superb beginner slopes
- \+ Convenient, pleasant, purpose-built village at the base

- − Not for mile-hungry intermediates
- − Lifts prone to closure by wind
- − Limited range of village amenities
- − Best to have a car if you want to explore several other ski areas too

When Intrawest built a neat little base village a decade ago, Squaw became a more attractive place to stay. But the village is small, and the ski area won't suit everyone – in particular, keen piste-bashers who like cruising groomed runs will find it limited. We would always combine it with a stay at the other end of the lake to ski Heavenly and the resorts south of the lake. A few years ago, Squaw's founder and owner died; the resort is now under dynamic new ownership and major changes are afoot. Last season, it at last marked runs and classified them for difficulty – on both the mountain and the piste map. Before that, finding your way around and runs that suited you was a real challenge.

THE RESORT

Squaw is the major resort at the north end of Lake Tahoe. Since construction of the car-free Village, staying here has become more attractive; but it is still also popular as a day trip from South Lake Tahoe and Heavenly. There are shuttle-buses. There are other lodgings around the valley, and at Tahoe City. The lift pass also covers neighbouring Alpine Meadows (a 10-minute ride by half-hourly free shuttle-buses).

Village charm The Village is very small but works well, and older buildings next to it are not unpleasant. Empty retail units were reported in 2011, but we have no more recent reports.

Convenience The Village is at the base of the main lifts. The self-contained, luxurious, conference-oriented Resort at Squaw Creek hotel has its own chairlift into one end of the network.

Scenery There are fabulous views of Lake Tahoe from Squaw Peak.

THE MOUNTAINS

One of the attractions of the area is that the slopes are lightly wooded. The resort has, until recently, been stupidly unhelpful about navigation. Only from last season have trails been shown on the trail map and signposted on the ground.

Slopes A gondola and a big cable car rise 600m to the twin stations of Gold Coast and High Camp (linked by the Pulse gondola). Above them is a wide area of beginner slopes, and beyond that the three highest peaks of the area, with lifts of modest vertical; much the biggest is Squaw Peak's Headwall six-pack: 535m.

From High Camp you can descend into a steep-sided valley from which the Silverado chair is the return.

Two other peaks are accessed directly from the village. A fast quad serves steep KT-22; a slow triple goes to rather neglected Snow King.

SQUAW VALLEY / TOM O'NEILL

Squaw's slopes are lightly wooded right to the top and offer lots of great ungroomed terrain ↓

NEWS

2012/13: A triple chair at High Camp is to be replaced by a six-pack called the Big Blue Express for quicker access to the terrain parks and the Granite Chief and Silverado areas. A rope tow is also to be installed for easier access to the parks.

2011/12: All trails were given names, classified for difficulty and shown on the piste map; and signposting was installed. A new Activity Zone for kids opened at the base area, with tubing and snowmobiles. The lift pass now covers Alpine Meadows (a 10-minute shuttle-bus ride).

UK PACKAGES

AmeriCan Ski, American Ski Classics, Crystal, Independent Ski Links, Interactive Resorts, Momentum, Ski Independence, Ski Safari, Skitracer, Supertravel, Virgin Snow

Phone numbers
From distant parts of the US, add the prefix 1 530; from abroad, add the prefix +1 530

TOURIST OFFICE

www.squaw.com

Squaw's cable car runs in the evenings to serve the floodlit slopes (including a 5km run to the base area), and terrain parks and the dining facilities at High Camp.

Fast lifts There are fast lifts in each sector, but also slow old chairs.

Queues There are few problems usually, but the weather and weekend invasions are key factors.

Terrain parks Riviera Park offers intermediate and expert jump lines, a night-accessible pipe with 5.5m walls, and big jib features. The Gold Coast Park is constantly updated with innovative features. There are other parks when conditions permit, and parks designed for kids and novices.

Snow reliability An impressive 450 inches on average, plus snowmaking.

Experts The possibilities for experts on KT-22, Squaw Peak, Granite Chief and the Silverado valley are huge, with lots of steep chutes and big mogul fields; many extreme skiing and boarding movies are made here. Now that the runs are marked on the map and on the mountain, it should be easier to find your way around – reports please.

Intermediates Blue-run skiers have a choice of some lovely cruises in the Emigrant and Snow King sectors and a 5km top-to-bottom run. But there is not much more groomed cruising, so keen piste-bashers will find the area limited. There is, however, lots of steep blue and easy black terrain to test your deep-snow or mogul skills.

Beginners The Papoose nursery area has a gentle slope served by a double chairlift – a special beginner package, with lift pass, is available. There's a superb choice of easy runs to progress to at altitude, notably at High Camp.

Snowboarding This is one of the most snowboarder friendly resorts around. The higher areas are full of steep and deep gullies, cliff drops, kicker building spots and tree runs, and the parks are kept in excellent shape.

Cross-country There are 18km of groomed trails at Squaw Creek.

Mountain restaurants Uninspiring, except in terms of views.

Schools and guides As well as group lessons, the school runs specialist workshops – eg Chutes and Hikes, Over 55s – on certain dates.

Families Squaw offers slope-side convenience and a children's on-slope play area at the Papoose base. Squaw Kids takes children from three years.

STAYING THERE

Hotels The PlumpJack Inn (583 1576) is our favourite – comfortable, stylish, central. The Resort at Squaw Creek (583 6300) offers luxury rooms, an outdoor pool and hot tubs, and 'fantastic buffet breakfasts'.

Apartments The Village has well-appointed ski-in/ski-out condos.

Eating out The PlumpJack Inn has an excellent restaurant. More routine places include the Auld Dubliner pub ('good Guinness stew'), Fireside (pizza/pasta) and Mamasake (sushi). You can eat up at High Camp.

Après-ski The Olympic House has several venues. In the Village, the places above mostly function as bars, too: Auld Dubliner has live music on a Friday, but is 'dead during the week'. Uncorked at Squaw Valley is a wine bar with live music and wine tastings.

Off the slopes High Camp has an ice rink and other activities. The Trilogy Spa offers a range of treatments.

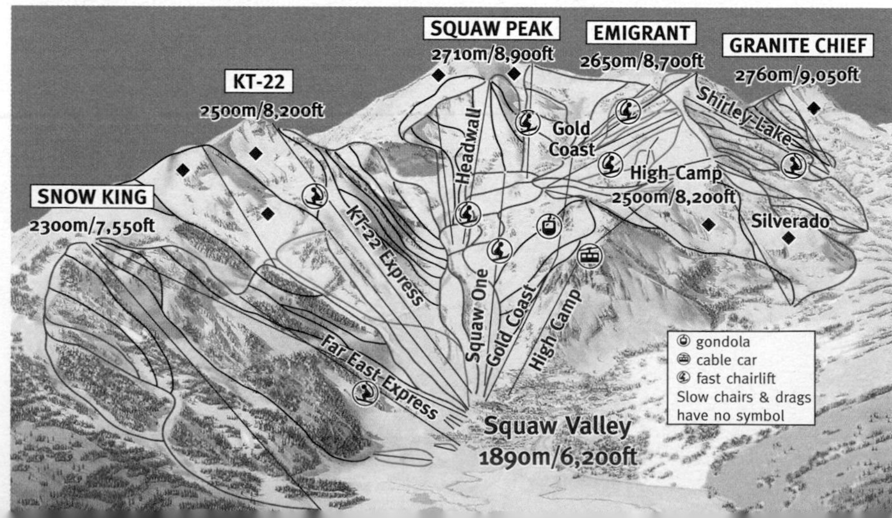

VAIL RESORTS / BOB WINSETT

Colorado

Colorado is the most popular American destination for UK visitors, and justifiably so: it has the most alluring combination of attractive resorts, slopes to suit all abilities and excellent, reliable snow – dry enough to justify its 'champagne powder' label. It also has direct scheduled BA flights to Denver, an easy drive from most of the resorts (unless it's snowing).

Colorado has amazingly dry snow. Even when the snow melts and refreezes, the moisture seems to be magically whisked away, leaving it soft and powdery. Even the artificial snow is of a quality you'll rarely find in Europe. And like most North American rivals, Colorado resorts generally have excellent, steep, ungroomed areas that you can ski safely without a guide.

The resorts vary enormously. If you want cute restored buildings from the mining boom days of the late 1800s, try the dinky old towns of Telluride or Crested Butte or the much bigger Aspen. Other resorts (such as Aspen's modern satellite, Snowmass) major on convenience. Some (such as Vail and Beaver Creek) deliberately pitch themselves upmarket, with lots of glitzy, expensive hotels, while others (such as Breckenridge and Winter Park) are much more down to earth.

You could consider renting a car and touring several resorts – maybe cutting costs by staying in valley towns rather than resorts.

Six major resorts get write-ups in this section. The others with blue circles on the map below have entries in the resort directory at the back of the book – of these Steamboat, Copper Mountain, Keystone, Crested Butte and Telluride have proper resort villages, while the others cater mainly for day visitors.

Many Colorado resorts are extremely high. As a result, most visitors are at risk of altitude sickness, which can spoil your trip. We always start in one of the lower resorts – or do a night in Denver to acclimatize.

SNOWPIX.COM / CHRIS GILL

Our favourite American resort, Aspen, combines a captivating town, great mountains, good snow and quiet slopes ↓

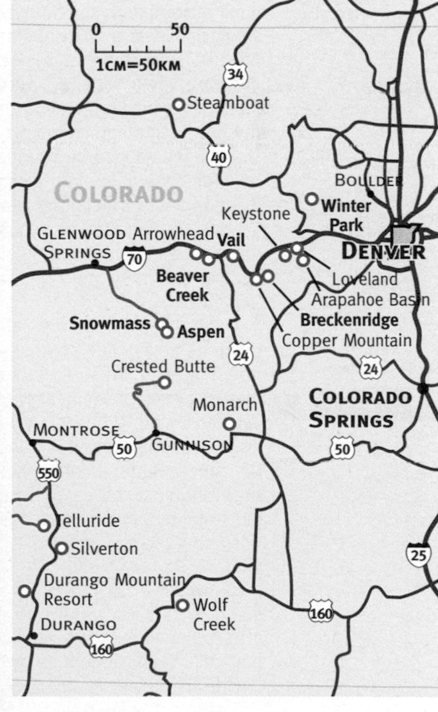

ASPEN / DOUG CHILD

Aspen

Don't be put off by the ritzy image – with a fun, historic town and quiet, extensive slopes, this is America's best resort

RATINGS

The mountains	
Extent	****
Fast lifts	****
Queues	****
Terrain p'ks	*****
Snow	*****
Expert	*****
Intermediate	*****
Beginner	*****
Boarder	****
X-country	****
Restaurants	***
Schools	*****
Families	**
The resort	
Charm	****
Convenience	**
Scenery	***
Eating out	*****
Après-ski	****
Off-slope	****

Our extent rating relates to the whole Aspen-Snowmass area. Aspen alone would rate **

RPI	185
lift pass	£370
ski hire	£200
lessons	£230
food & drink	£135
total	**£935**

NEWS

2011/12: At Tiehack on Buttermilk, a new fast quad replaced the existing slow lifts, cutting ride time by 60%. The gladed terrain it serves has been extended. The Merry-Go-Round restaurant at mid-mountain on Aspen Highlands reopened after a $6m makeover.

- ＋ Notably uncrowded slopes
- ＋ Attractive, characterful old mining town, with lots of smart shops
- ＋ Great range of restaurants
- ＋ Excellent Aspen Highlands and Snowmass just up the road
- ＋ Extensive slopes to suit every standard, but ...
- − Slopes split over four separate mountains (including Snowmass), served by efficient, free buses
- − Expensive, and tending to become more so as cheap places disappear
- − A bit isolated from the rest of Colorado if you're set on a two-centre trip

A 2011 editorial visit confirmed that Aspen is still our favourite American resort. It has everything we look for – well, everything except convenience. Our affection depends heavily on the presence of Aspen Highlands, a little way down the valley, and on Snowmass, considerably further down the valley (covered in a separate chapter). So most days you have to ride a bus; that doesn't worry us, and doesn't seem to worry readers who report on the place – most people who try it are captivated, and can't wait to go back.

Many rich and some famous guests jet in here, and for connoisseurs of cosmetic surgery the bars of the top hotels can be fascinating places. And the place does seem to be drifting even further upmarket, with ever fewer funky bars and ever more international-brand shops. But, like all other 'glamorous' ski resorts, Aspen is actually filled by ordinary holidaymakers. Don't be put off.

THE RESORT

In 1892 Aspen was a booming silver-mining town, with 12,000 inhabitants, six newspapers and an opera house. But the town's fortunes took a nosedive when the silver price plummeted in 1893, and by the 1930s the population had shrunk to 700 or so, and the handsome Victorian buildings had fallen into disrepair. Development of the skiing started on a small scale in the late 1930s. The first lift was opened shortly after the Second World War, and Aspen hasn't looked back.

Aspen Mountain is right above the town, its access lifts starting yards from the main street. And there are three other ski areas nearby (all covered by the ski pass). Around 3km from Aspen are Buttermilk and Aspen Highlands. Buttermilk has the Inn at Aspen hotel at the base. Highlands has a limited amount of lodgings (including the very smart Ritz Carlton Club).

Snowmass, 14km away, is a proper resort in its own right – with great attractions as a base for families, in particular – and it gets its own chapter.

VILLAGE CHARM ****

Smart old town

Aspen's historic centre – with a typical American grid of streets – has been preserved to form the core of the most fashionable ski town in the Rockies, and one of the most charming. There's a huge variety of restaurants, bars, swanky shops and galleries.

A mixture of developments spreads out from the centre, ranging from the homes of the super-rich through surprisingly modest hotels and motels to mobile homes for the workers. Though the town is busy with traffic, it moves slowly, and pedestrians effectively have priority in much of the central area.

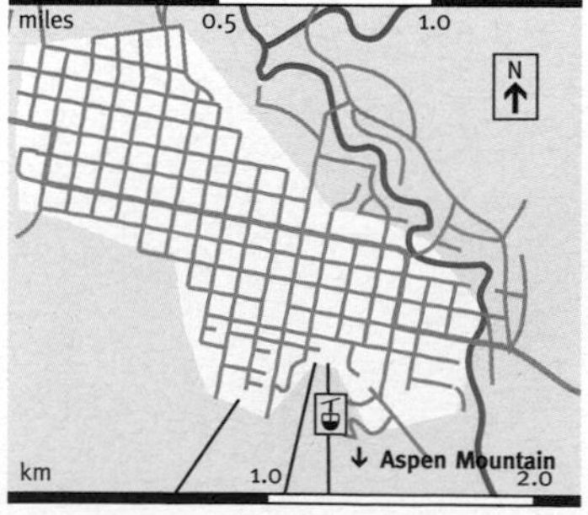

LIFT PASSES

Four Mountain Pass

Prices in US$

Age	1-day	6-day
under 13	66	348
13 to 17	91	498
18 to 64	100	552
65 plus	91	498

Free under 7

Senior over 70: $399 for unlimited period

Beginner included in price of lessons

Notes

Includes shuttle-bus between the areas. Prices given are prices online 7 days in advance (window prices are higher). Savings if you purchase in advance through certain UK tour operators

ASPEN / DANIEL BAYER

Ridge of Bell on Aspen Mountain gets double-diamond steep at this point, but you have easier options to left and right ↓

CONVENIENCE ★★★★★
Better by bus

Aspen is very unusual in being a cute old town with a major lift close to the centre: the gondola to the top of Aspen Mountain is only yards from some of the top hotels. Downtown Aspen is quite compact by American resort standards, but it spreads far enough to make the free ski-bus a necessity for many visitors staying less centrally. You also need buses to get to the other mountains, of course. Generally, they work well. But they can get crowded, and you may need to keep an eye on the timetables.

SCENERY ★★★★★
Beautiful Bells

The views from the upper part of Highlands are the best – the famous and distinctive Maroon Bells that appear on countless postcards. Buttermilk enjoys great views too.

THE MOUNTAINS

Most of the slopes are in the trees. All the mountains have free guided tours at 10.30, given by excellent volunteer ambassadors. At Highlands there is a special Highland Bowl tour on Wednesdays at noon. The ratio of acres to visitor beds is high, and the slopes are usually blissfully uncrowded. Signposting could be better where runs merge.

EXTENT OF THE SLOPES ★★★★★
Widely dispersed

Each of the four mountains is worth a visit. Much the most extensive mountain in the area is at Snowmass – see separate chapter. Note that our extent rating includes Snowmass.

Once you are up the gondola, a series of chairs serves the ridges of **Aspen Mountain**. In general, there are long cruising blue runs along the valley floors and short, steep blacks down from the ridges.

Buttermilk is the smallest, lowest and least challenging mountain, accessed by a fast quad from the fairly primitive main base lodge. The runs fan out from the top in three directions – back to the base, down to Tiehack and down to West Buttermilk (with fast quads back from all three).

Aspen Highlands consists essentially of a single ridge served by three fast quad chairs, with easy and intermediate slopes along the ridge itself and steep black runs on the flanks – very steep ones at the top. And beyond the lift network, a free snowcat ride leads to Highland Bowl, where gates access a splendid open bowl of entirely double-black gradient.

FAST LIFTS ★★★★★
Serving bottom to top

Each mountain has a few key fast chairs or a gondola up to the top stations; the other lifts are slow chairs.

GET THE BEST OF THE SNOW, ON- AND OFF-PISTE

Aspen offers special experiences for small numbers of skiers or riders.

First Tracks *The first skiers to sign up each day get to ride the gondola up Aspen Mountain at 8am the next morning and get first tracks on perfect corduroy or fresh powder. Well worth doing. Free but numbers are limited! When we did it, we took our time over the descent, to let the start-of-day queue at the bottom dissipate, but we're told you now ski in a guided group at a set pace.*

Powder Tours *Spend the day finding untracked snow in 1,500 acres of backcountry beyond Aspen Mountain, with a 12-passenger heated snowcat as your personal lift. You're likely to squeeze in about 10 runs in all. You break for lunch at an old mountain cabin. Costs $410 per person.*

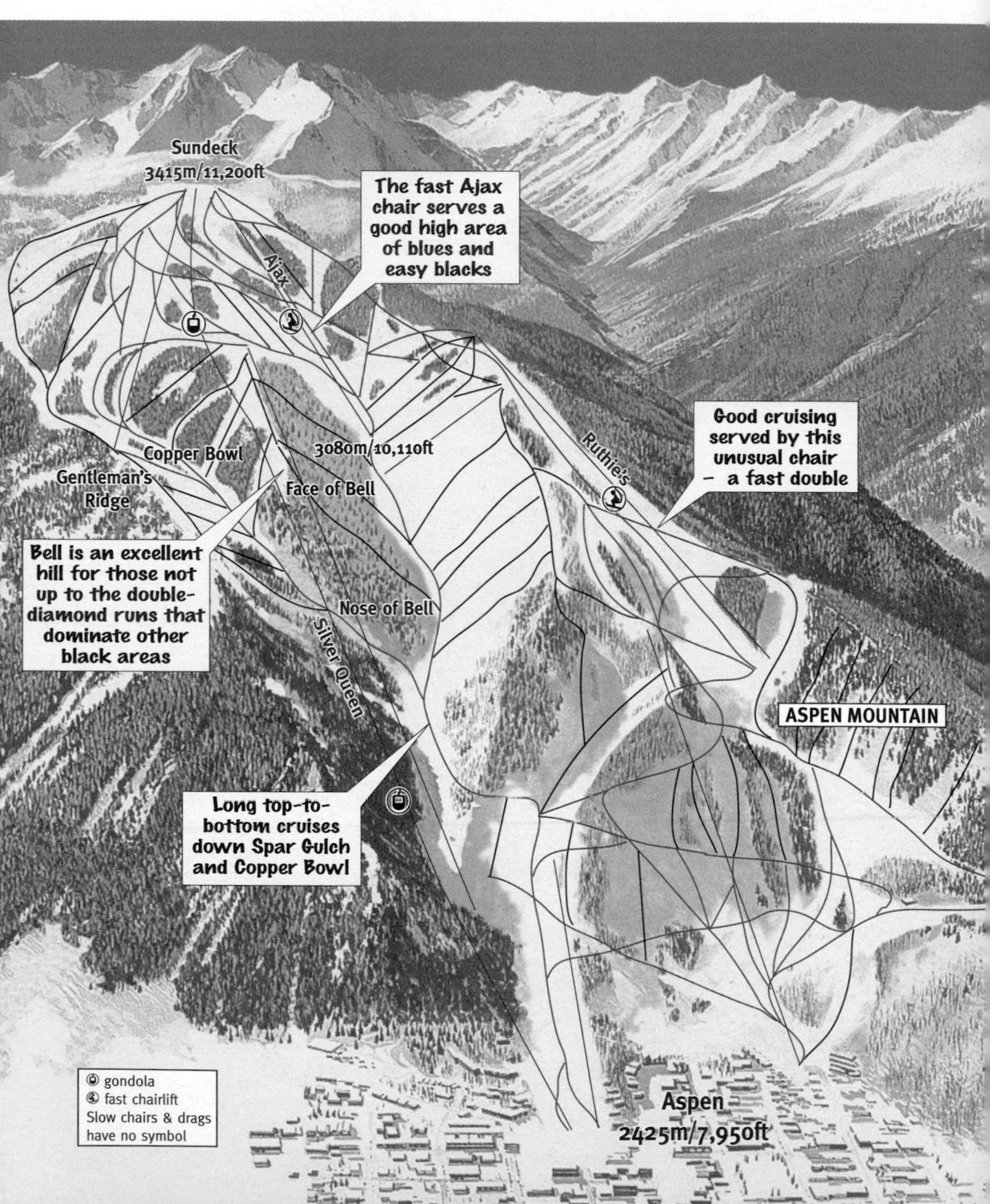
Sundeck
3415m/11,200ft
The fast Ajax chair serves a good high area of blues and easy blacks
Ajax
Ruthie's
Good cruising served by this unusual chair – a fast double
Copper Bowl
3080m/10,110ft
Gentleman's Ridge
Face of Bell
Bell is an excellent hill for those not up to the double-diamond runs that dominate other black areas
Nose of Bell
Silver Queen
ASPEN MOUNTAIN
Long top-to-bottom cruises down Spar Gulch and Copper Bowl
gondola
fast chairlift
Slow chairs & drags have no symbol
Aspen
2425m/7,950ft

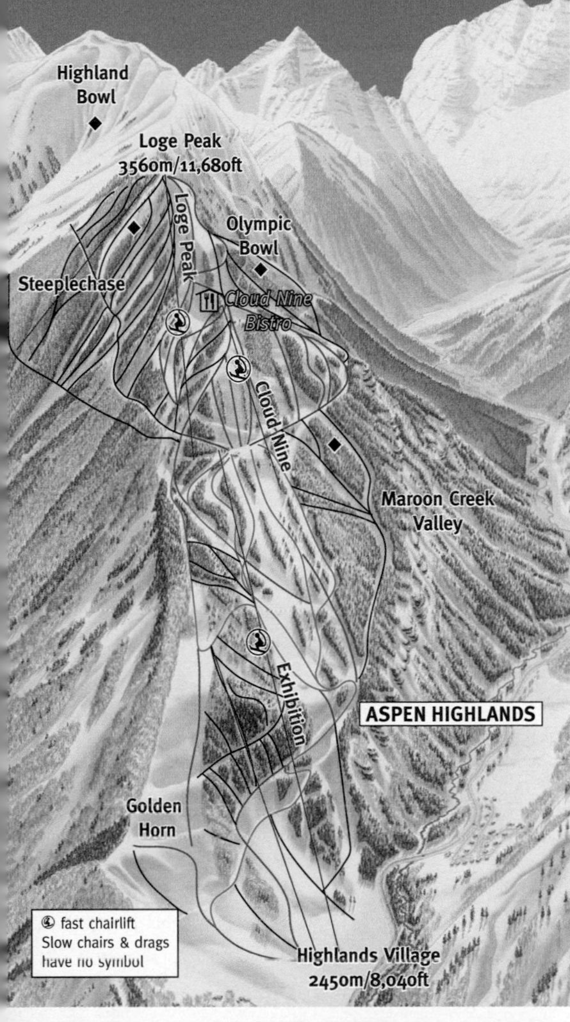

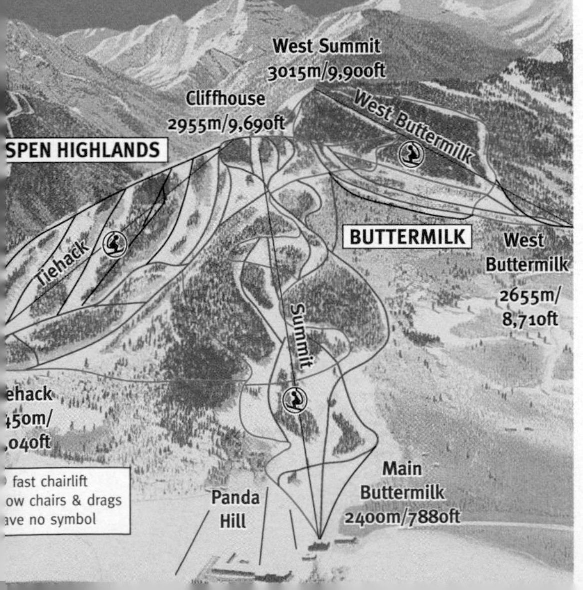

QUEUES ★★★★
Few problems
Major queues are rare on any of the mountains – you may hit a few during the college spring break in March. At Aspen Mountain, the gondola can still have delays at peak times. You can use the slow Shadow Mountain chair, instead, with a short uphill walk to reach it. Aspen Highlands is almost always queue-free, even at peak times. The lift out of Main Buttermilk sometimes gets congested.

TERRAIN PARKS ★★★★★
X Games standard
Aspen has two pipe and park mountains – Snowmass (see separate chapter) and Buttermilk. Buttermilk Park is famous as the home of the Winter X Games, and stretches over 3km from the top to the bottom of the mountain – it is said to be the longest in the world. It has over 100 features, the X Games slope-style course and a world-class super-pipe that's over 150m long with 6.7m walls.

SNOW RELIABILITY ★★★★★
Rarely a problem
Aspen's mountains get an annual average of 300 inches of snow – not in the front rank, but not far behind. In addition, all areas have substantial snowmaking. Immaculate grooming adds to the quality of the pistes, and the light traffic can only help.

FOR EXPERTS ★★★★★
Buttermilk is the only soft stuff
There's plenty to choose from – all the mountains except Buttermilk offer lots of challenges, and it is relatively easy to find untouched powder in the many gladed areas.

Aspen Mountain has a formidable array of double black diamond runs. From the top of the gondola, Walsh's, Hyrup's and Kristi are on a lightly wooded slope and link up with Gentleman's Ridge and Jackpot to form the longest black run on the mountain. A series of steep glades drops down from Gentleman's Ridge. The central Bell ridge has less extreme single diamonds on both its flanks, including some delightful lightly wooded areas. On the opposite side of Spar Gulch is another row of double blacks, collectively called the Dumps, because mining waste was dumped here.

At Highlands there are challenging runs from top to bottom of the

KEY FACTS	
Resort	2425m 7,950ft
Aspen Mountain	
Slopes	2425-3415m 7,950-11,210ft
Lifts	8
Pistes	675 acres
Green	0%
Blue	48%
Black	52%
Snowmaking	31%
Aspen Highlands	
Slopes	2450-3560m 8,040-11,680ft
Lifts	5
Pistes	1,028 acres
Green	18%
Blue	30%
Black	52%
Snowmaking	11%
Buttermilk	
Slopes	2400-3015m 7,880-9,900ft
Lifts	8
Pistes	470 acres
Green	35%
Blue	39%
Black	26%
Snowmaking	23%
Total with Snowmass	
Slopes	2400-3815m 7,880-12,510ft
Lifts	42
Pistes	5,305 acres
Green	10%
Blue	45%
Black	45%
Snowmaking	12%

mountain. Consider joining a guided group as an introduction to the best of them. Highland Bowl, beyond the top lift, is superb in the right conditions: a big open bowl with access gates reached by hiking (but there are usually free snowcat rides to cut out the first 20-minute walk). The trail map usefully gives key facts for each run – orientation and average and steepest pitch, from a serious 38° to a terrifying 48°.

Left of the bowl, the Steeplechase area consists of a number of parallel natural avalanche chutes, and their elevation means the snow stays light and dry. The Olympic Bowl area on the opposite flank of the mountain has great views of the Maroon Bells and some serious moguls. The Thunderbowl chair from the base serves a nice varied area that's often underused.

FOR INTERMEDIATES ★★★★★

Grooming to die for

Most intermediate runs on Highlands are concentrated above the mid-mountain Merry-Go-Round restaurant, many served by the Cloud Nine fast quad chair. But there are other good slopes – don't miss the vast, neglected expanses of Golden Horn, on the eastern limit of the area.

Aspen Mountain has its fair share of intermediate slopes, but they tend to be tougher than on the other mountains. Copper Bowl and Spar Gulch, running between the ridges, are great cruises but can get crowded. Upper Aspen Mountain, at the top of the gondola, has a dense network of well-groomed blues served by the Ajax fast chair. The unusual Ruthie's chair – a fast double, apparently installed to rekindle the romance that quads have destroyed – serves more cruising runs.

Buttermilk offers good, easy slopes to practise on, and can be extraordinarily quiet. And good intermediates should be able to handle the relatively easy black runs – when groomed, these are a real blast. Buttermilk is also a great place for early experiments off-piste.

Read the Snowmass chapter too.

FOR BEGINNERS ★★★★★

Can be a great place to learn

Buttermilk is superb. West Buttermilk has beautifully groomed, gentle, often deserted runs, served by a quad. The easiest slopes of all, though, are at the base of the Main Buttermilk sector – on Panda Hill. Despite its macho image and serious double-diamond terrain, Highlands boasts the highest concentration of green runs in Aspen, served by the fast Exhibition chair.

FOR BOARDERS ★★★★

Loads of scope

There is a huge amount of terrain to explore, which will satisfy all levels of boarder – especially when you include Snowmass (see our separate chapter). The hills are free of draglifts and have few flat sections. Buttermilk is the least testing of the mountains, with gentle carving runs and freeriding – but it's also home to the most serious terrain park.

ASPEN / HAL WILLIAMS

Aspen is America's most diverting resort town, with countless shops and galleries as well as restaurants ➔

SCHOOLS

Aspen
t 923 1227

Classes
Full day (5hr) $139

Private lessons
$655 for full day for up to 5 people

CHILDCARE

Snow Cubs
t 923 1227
Ages 8wk to 4yr

Cubs on Skis, Bears, Pandas and Grizzlies
t 923 1227
Various different groups for ages 30mnth to 4yr, 3 to 4 and 5 to 6

Babysitting services
Several

Ski school
Ages 7 to 12, $107 per day (incl. lunch)

GETTING THERE

Air Aspen 6km/4 miles (15min); Eagle 110km/70 miles (1hr45); Denver 360km/225 miles (4hr45)

Rail Glenwood Springs (63km/39 miles)

UK PACKAGES

Alpine Answers, AmeriCan Ski, American Ski Classics, Carrier, Crystal, Crystal Finest, Elegant Resorts, Erna Low, Flexiski, Frontier, Independent Ski Links, Interactive Resorts, Momentum, Oxford Ski Co, PowderBeds, Scott Dunn, Ski Bespoke, Ski Expectations, Ski Independence, Ski Line, Ski Safari, Ski Solutions, Skitracer, Skiworld, Snow Finders, Supertravel

FOR CROSS-COUNTRY ★★★★

Backcountry bonanza

There are 90km of groomed trails between Aspen and Snowmass in the Roaring Fork valley – the most extensive cross-country network in the US. And the Ashcroft Ski Touring Center maintains around 35km of trails around Ashcroft, a mining ghost town. The Pine Creek Cookhouse (925 1044) does excellent food and is accessible only by ski, snowshoe or horse-drawn sleigh. Aspen is at one end of the famous Tenth Mountain Division Trail, heading 370km north-east almost to Vail, with 12 huts for overnight stops.

MOUNTAIN RESTAURANTS ★★★

Good by American standards

Surprisingly, Highlands and Snowmass (see separate chapter) have good table-service places and Aspen Mountain doesn't.

Editors' choice At Highlands, Cloud Nine bistro (544 3063) is the nearest thing in the States to a cosy Alpine hut, with excellent food – thanks to an Austrian chef. Not wildly expensive, either – $34 for two courses (daily changing set menu). We had a delicious elk stew here in 2011.

Worth knowing about On Aspen Mountain there's the Sundeck self-service – about as good as an American self-service restaurant gets – light and airy with great views across to Highland Bowl. Bonnie's self-service is another option: 'fantastic white chilli bean soup', 'hearty stews and burgers'. On Highlands, the newly refurbished mid-mountain Merry-Go-Round self-service has 'a comfortable bar area', where one 2012 reporter enjoyed 'one of the best pastas ever'.

On Buttermilk the mountaintop Cliffhouse specializes in a Mongolian barbecue stir-fry, and Bumps (self-service) offers a 'good range'. You can picnic at The Cafe West, Top of West warming hut, Bottom of Tiehack warming hut and No Problem Cabin.

SCHOOLS AND GUIDES ★★★★★

One of the best?

Aspen's school is highly regarded, and group classes are usually small and of a high standard: 'Maximum of three people in each lesson and the same instructor for the three days,' says a 2011 visitor. A 2012 reporter praises the free 'Inside Tracks' programme being run by the school in conjunction with one hotel – and which they are hoping to extend to others. You get a day skiing with a pro, who will act as a guide as well as give you pointers on your technique.

FOR FAMILIES ★★

Choice of nurseries

Aspen caters well for families, with Buttermilk the focus for lessons. Children are bussed to and from the mountain's impressive Fort Frog, and the kids' trail map is a great idea. But Snowmass has clear advantages for young families.

STAYING THERE

Hotels There are places for all budgets, including very grand places such as the Hyatt and St Regis on which we never get reports. Most smaller hotels provide a good free après-ski cheese and wine buffet.

*******Jerome** (920 1000) Step back a century: Victorian authenticity combined with modern-day luxury. Several blocks from the gondola.

*******Little Nell** (920 4600) Stylish, modern hotel right by the gondola, with popular bar. Fireplaces in every room, outdoor pool, hot tub, sauna. Smart condos too.

******Lenado** (925 6246) Smart modern B&B place with open-fire lounge, individually designed rooms.

*****Aspen** (925 3441) Spacious, basic rooms; pool, hot tub; 10 minutes' walk to gondola. Near bus stop.

*****Aspen Mountain Lodge** (925 7650) Small, friendly, in a quiet location. 'Very friendly, helpful staff.'

*****Limelight Lodge** (925 3025) Recently rebuilt in modern style, central. Pool, tubs. Recommended by a 2012 visitor 'on just about every count': 'great rooms, good breakfasts, pretty good location'.

*****Molly Gibson Lodge** (925 3434) Pool, hot tub. Opposite hotel Aspen. 'Excellent value for money,' says a 2012 visitor. 'Modern and comfortable with extensive breakfasts.'

*****The Sky** (925 6760) Hip, swanky New York-style hotel in great location by gondola.

****Mountain Chalet** (925 7797) Cosy lodge five minutes from gondola. Pool, sauna, steam and games room.

****St Moritz Lodge** (925 3220) Aspen's youth hostel. A 2012 visitor remarks: 'Not many hostels have a heated pool and complimentary happy hour! Super-friendly guests and staff.'

ACTIVITIES

Indoor Recreation Center (pool, ice rink, climbing wall), Club & Spa (spa, fitness), galleries, cinemas, theatre, museum

Outdoor Snowshoeing, ice skating, snowmobiling, ballooning

Phone numbers
From distant parts of the US, add the prefix 1 970; from abroad, add the prefix +1 970

TOURIST OFFICE

www.aspensnowmass.com

ASPEN SNOWMASS / DANIEL BAYER

The jewel in the Aspen Highlands crown – Highland Bowl (top left) and the Temerity/ Steeplechase area ↓

Apartments The standards here are high, even in US terms. Many of the smarter developments have their own free shuttle-buses. The Gant, Aspen Square and Aspen Meadows Resort have been recommended.

EATING OUT ★★★★★
Dining dilemma

Aspen has an excellent blend of upmarket places and cheaper options. Some giveaway magazines include menu guides, and there are basic listings at www.eataspen.com. Every year brings a raft of closures and new ventures; we welcome your reports.

Top of the range places include: Il Mulino (an outpost of a classy Italian restaurant in New York) in the Little Nell residences; Syzygy, Piñons and the Montagna (in the Little Nell hotel) – all with innovative American cooking; Matsuhisa (Japanese fusion); and the Rustique Bistro, Brexi Brasserie ('lovely food, but a bit dark') and Cache Cache (all French). New for 2011/12 was Steakhouse 316, a small 'boutique' steakhouse in 1920s style: 'Pricey, but fantastic steaks! Great service.' The tiny Wild Fig has 'a varied, Mediterranean-influenced menu'. The underground Zocalito offers Latin American cuisine: 'absolutely delicious' was one 2012 visitor's verdict.

You can eat more cheaply at a lot of the smart places by eating at the bar – basically, you get smaller portions and can't book, which of course may suit you. We did this very happily on our 2011 visit at Jimmy's (American), L'Hostaria and Campo de Fiori (both Italian).

Mid-market and cheaper choices include: Little Annie's ('massive portions', 'a meat feast'), Asie (Asian fusion – 'astonishingly good' dumplings); Hickory House Ribs ('an Aspen institution – very busy and generous helpings'); Brunelleschi's ('good Italian food', 'excellent service', 'very family friendly'); Cantina ('friendly service and good Tex Mex'); Red Onion (refurbished saloon/grill – 'large portions'); Su Casa (Mexican – 'central; good value'); Ute City (American style bistro – 'varied menu, great value').

APRES-SKI ★★★★
Lots of options

In the late afternoon, we've known Cloud Nine on Highlands to turn into a very un-American Austrian-style après-ski venue – booze-fuelled dancing on the tables in ski boots. A few bars at the bases get busy – notably Out of Bounds at Highlands and Ajax Tavern ('very lively upmarket crowd') in Aspen. The Terrace Bar at the Little Nell is a great place for gazing at facelifts; 39 Degrees at the Sky hotel has a chic atmosphere.

Later on, wine connoisseurs could try Victoria's Espresso & Wine Bar. Many of the restaurants are also bars – Jimmy's (spectacular stock of tequila), for example. The J-bar of the Jerome hotel dates back to 1889 and has a traditional feel ('great place to stop for a pre-dinner drink or two'). Aspen Billiards adjoining the fashionable Cigar Bar is an upscale venue for playing pool. The Aspen Brewing Company, the local micro-brewery, is now in the centre of Aspen.

For music and dancing, head for Belly Up ('good selection of live music') or the Regal Watering Hole. Or you can get a week's membership of the famous Caribou club.

OFF THE SLOPES ★★★★
Silver service

Aspen has lots to offer, especially if your credit card is in good shape. There are literally dozens of art galleries, as well as the predictable clothes and jewellery shops. There are plenty of shops selling affordable stuff. Glenwood Springs is worth a visit for its hot-spring outdoor pool. The Aspen Recreation Center at Highlands has a huge swimming complex and an indoor ice rink. Hot-air ballooning is possible too. Some mountain restaurants are accessible to pedestrians.

JACK AFFLECK

Beaver Creek

Exclusive and very pricey modern resort with quiet, varied slopes. Good for a pampered stay or a day trip from Vail

TOP 10 RATINGS

Extent	**
Fast lifts	*****
Queues	*****
Snow	*****
Expert	****
Intermediate	****
Beginner	*****
Charm	**
Convenience	****
Scenery	***

RPI	170
lift pass	£320
ski hire	£170
lessons	£230
food & drink	£135
total	**£855**

NEWS

2012/13: A new women's race course is being built in the Birds of Prey area, which will add a small amount of new terrain and extend the snowmaking.

2011/12: A fast quad replaced the Rose Bowl triple chairlift.

- + Slopes generally quiet on weekdays
- + Mountain has it all, from superb novice runs to daunting moguls
- + Fast chairlifts all over the place
- + Compact, traffic-free village centre

- − Lacks any Wild West atmosphere
- − Very expensive
- − Disappointing mountain restaurants
- − Not much going on at night

'Not exactly roughing it' is the strangely coy slogan of Vail's kid sister resort, discreetly underlining its status as about the smoothest resort in the US. We don't find the exclusive resort village particularly appealing, but the mountain certainly is. We wouldn't dream of visiting Vail without spending a day or two here. A pity that it's impossible to get a decent lunch on the hill.

THE RESORT

Beaver Creek, 16km to the west of Vail, was developed in the 1980s and is unashamedly exclusive. The lift system spreads across the mountains to Bachelor Gulch, a small collection of relatively new condos and houses and a Ritz-Carlton hotel, and to Arrowhead, a slope-side hamlet that is less pricey than Beaver Creek. Below here is the valley town of Avon, where there are free car parks for day visitors (parking in the resort itself is expensive and limited); you can take a free shuttle to the village or a fast chair up to Bachelor Gulch. A gondola links the Riverfront area of Avon to this chair.

Day trips to Vail, Breckenridge and Keystone (all covered by the lift pass) and Copper Mountain are possible.

Village charm The village centres on a small, smart, modern pedestrian area with upmarket shops, open-air ice rink and heated pavements.

Convenience There are top-quality hotels and condos right by the slopes, and escalators up from the centre.

Scenery The scenery is pleasantly woody rather than dramatic.

VAIL RESORTS, INC

The resort village is a compact, dense affair, a bit too urban for our taste ↓

THE MOUNTAINS

All the slopes are below the treeline, though there are some more open areas. Free two-hour mountain tours are operated every day at 10am. At the top of most main lifts is a big piste map board (and lights showing which runs have been groomed – a great idea that we haven't seen before). They take their 'slow skiing zones' seriously here too – with big banners across the piste warning that skier speed is monitored.

Slopes The slopes immediately above Beaver Creek divide into two sectors, each accessed by a fast quad chair – one centred on Spruce Saddle, the other on Bachelor Gulch (which links to Arrowhead). Between these are Grouse Mountain and Larkspur Bowl, again with fast quads. Off to the left is another varied sector, which is now served by a fast quad.

Fast lifts Nearly all key lifts are now fast chairs, and beginners get their own gondola.

Queues Queues aren't normally a problem, but improved lift access from the valley may be attracting more visitors. A reporter found it 'busier than Vail at Spring Break'. But on all our visits (including February 2011) the slopes have been blissfully deserted, and a Sunday visitor in 2012 reports 'no queues to speak of' anywhere.

Terrain parks Park 101 is a small beginners' park, Zoom Room has intermediate-level features, and Rodeo has big hits for advanced riders.

KEY FACTS	
Resort	2470m 8,100ft
Slopes	2255-3485m 7,400-11,440ft
Lifts	25
Pistes	1815 acres
Green	19%
Blue	43%
Black	38%
Snowmaking	39%

UK PACKAGES

Alpine Answers, AmeriCan Ski, American Ski Classics, Crystal, Crystal Finest, Elegant Resorts, Frontier, Independent Ski Links, Momentum, Oxford Ski Co, PowderBeds, Ski Bespoke, Ski Independence, Ski Line, Ski Safari, Skitracer, Skiworld, STC, Supertravel

Central reservations phone number
496 4900

Phone numbers
From distant parts of the US, add the prefix 1 970; from abroad, add the prefix +1 970

TOURIST OFFICE

www.beavercreek.com

There's a 110m-long half-pipe, off Barrel Stave. Parkology is a park and pipe programme for kids.
Snow reliability An impressive snow record (average 325 inches) and snowmaking mean you can relax. But Grouse Mountain can have thin cover (some call it Gravel Mountain).
Experts There is plenty of satisfying steep terrain. In the Birds of Prey and Grouse Mountain areas most runs are long, steep and mogulled, but the new women's race course and the existing men's course are groomed periodically, making great fast cruises. Grouse and Stone Creek Chutes have great steep glades.
Intermediates There are marvellous long, quiet, cruising blues everywhere you look, including top-to-bottom runs with a vertical of 1000m.
Beginners There are excellent nursery slopes at resort level – served by a short gondola – and, unusually, a further large area at altitude. And there are plenty of easy long runs to progress to in several areas.
Snowboarding Good riders will love the excellent gladed runs and perfect carving slopes. The resort is great for beginners, too.
Cross-country There's a splendid, mountain-top network of tracks at McCoy Park (over 32km), reached via the Strawberry Park lift.
Mountain restaurants Spruce Saddle at mid-mountain is the main place – a food court in an airy log building; but it can get very busy. Red Tail Camp offers the 'usual American food' and also gets busy. Spago at the Ritz-Carlton down at Bachelor Gulch is the best bet for table service.
Schools and guides We lack recent reports, but don't doubt that the school is excellent.
Families Small World Play School looks after non-skiing kids from two months to six years from 8.30 to 4pm. At the top of the Buckaroo gondola are adventure trails and a tubing park.

STAYING THERE

Hotels Lots of upmarket places, such as the Ritz-Carlton and Park Hyatt. The Osprey, Charter and Pines Lodge combine hotel facilities with luxury condo convenience.
Apartments Elkhorn Lodge, Oxford Court, St James Place and SaddleRidge are slope-side condos. For cheaper luxury, consider staying in Arrowhead.
Eating out SaddleRidge is plush and packed with photos and Wild West artefacts. Toscanini, the Golden Eagle Inn, Dusty Boot (in St James Place), and Beaver Creek Chophouse have been recommended. Spago (at the Ritz-Carlton) offers fine dining at Bachelor Gulch. You can take a sleigh ride to dine at a swanky Beano's cabin on the slopes. Or try the valley towns; a reader recommends Outback in Avon for 'excellent steaks'. The resort runs shuttle-buses between Beaver Creek and Avon daily from 8am to 10pm.
Après-ski Try the Coyote Cafe and McCoy's (live bands) and the 8100 Mountainside Bar at Park Hyatt.
Off the slopes Smart shops and galleries, an ice rink, ballooning, dog sledding, snowshoeing and concerts.

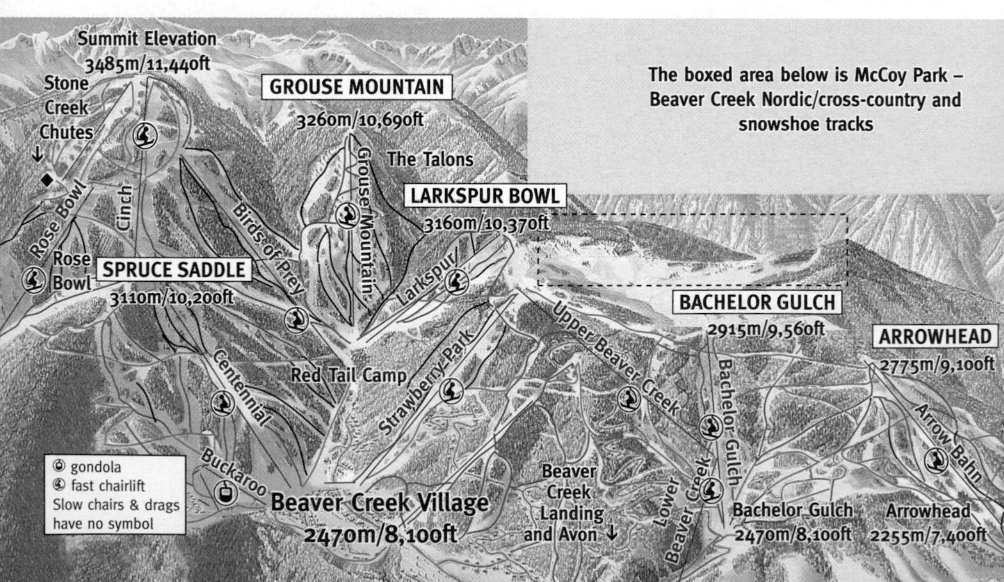

VAIL RESORTS INC / BOB WINSETT

Breckenridge

A sprawling resort with a cute 'Wild West' core, beneath a wide, varied mountain; increasing amounts of slope-side accommodation

RATINGS

The mountains

Extent	**
Fast lifts	****
Queues	****
Terrain p'ks	*****
Snow	*****
Expert	****
Intermediate	****
Beginner	*****
X-country	****
Boarder	*****
Restaurants	**
Schools	*****
Families	****

The resort

Charm	***
Convenience	***
Scenery	***
Eating out	*****
Après-ski	***
Off-slope	***

RPI	150
lift pass	£310
ski hire	£150
lessons	£205
food & drink	£100
total	**£765**

NEWS

2011/12: The former Great Divide Lodge was fully renovated and reopened as the DoubleTree by Hilton, with pool, spa and fitness facilities.

KEY FACTS

Resort	2925m 9,600ft
Slopes	2925-3915m 9,600-12,840ft
Lifts	31
Pistes	2,358 acres
Green	14%
Blue	31%
Black	55%
Snowmaking	24%

- + Slopes have something for all abilities – good for mixed groups
- + Cute Victorian Main Street, with mainly sympathetic new buildings
- + Plenty of lively bars and restaurants
- + Shared lift pass with four other worthwhile resorts nearby
- + Efficient lifts mean few queues
- + Some slope-side accommodation
- + Short transfer from Denver, but ...

- − At 2925m the village poses a risk of altitude sickness if you go there directly from the UK
- − Very prone to high winds, affecting mainly the high, advanced slopes
- − On-piste terrain not very extensive, with few long runs
- − Lack of good, central hotels
- − Main Street is a thoroughfare – always busy with traffic

A repeat visit in 2011 confirmed that we like Breckenridge a lot. The town is attractive and lively, with Wild West roots and lots of places to eat and drink. The slopes are fabulous for beginners. And for experts too, provided the ungroomed top slopes are open – as they were on our most recent visit, when we whooped it up in fresh powder in the bowls above Peak 7. Sadly, they are too often closed by wind – as we've found many times. Intermediates mainly interested in mileage should plan to explore other resorts (covered by the lift pass) by car or bus too; they'll find Breck limited for a week.

Heed our warning about altitude sickness. At almost 3000m this is the highest resort to get a full chapter in this book – and the altitude you sleep at is a key factor. Like many readers, editor Gill has been affected by altitude sickness here, and now always spends time in a lower resort before hitting Breckenridge; a couple of nights in Denver is an alternative way to cut the risk.

THE RESORT

Breckenridge was founded in 1859 and became a booming gold-mining town. Old clapboard buildings line much of Main Street, and the streets nearby have been well renovated. Small shopping malls and other buildings have been added in similar style. But there are some (rather out-of-place) modern buildings too.

The resort is in the same ownership as Vail, Beaver Creek and Keystone. A multi-day lift ticket covers all these plus Arapahoe Basin. All of them plus Copper Mountain can be reached by bus (free except for the trips to Vail or Beaver Creek).

VILLAGE CHARM ***
A festive treat

The town centre is lively in the evening – particularly at weekends – with lots of people strolling around the shops on their way to or from the 100-plus restaurants and bars in and around the busy main street. Christmas lights and decorations remain throughout the season, giving the town a festive air. This is enhanced by a number of festivals such as Ullr Fest – honouring the Norse God of Winter – and snow sculpture championships.

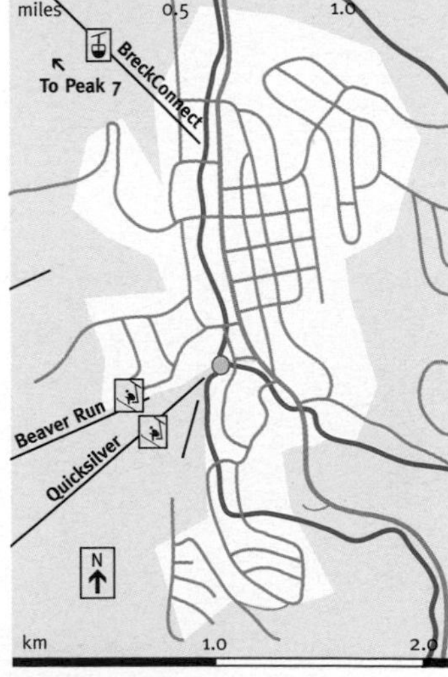

CONVENIENCE ★★★

Slope life or nightlife

There is a lot of slope-side lodgings, including smart recent developments at the bases of Peaks 7 and 8. But there is also some inconveniently distant from both Main Street and the lift base stations. Hotels and condos are spread over a wide area and linked by regular, free shuttle-buses (less frequent in the evening – worth staying centrally if you plan to spend much time in Main Street). There are a couple of supermarkets – one just behind Main Street, the other on the outskirts and a long walk if you don't have a car.

SCENERY ★★★

Peak after peak

This is high country; on a clear day above the treeline there are extensive views of Colorado's highest summits – many of which reach over 4000m.

THE MOUNTAINS

The slopes are mainly cut through the forest, but there is quite a lot of steeper skiing above the treeline (and prone to closure by high winds).

The resort used to have some runs classified as blue-black. They have now scrapped these and made them single black diamond – a real backward step because the old blue-blacks (mainly on Peak 10) are still great intermediate cruises and the new black classification may put people off trying them.

EXTENT OF THE SLOPES ★★

Small but fragmented

There are four sectors, linked by lift and piste. Two fast chairlifts go from one end of the town up to **Peak 9**, one accessing mainly green runs on the lower half of the hill, the other mainly blue runs higher up. From there you can get to **Peak 10**, with black runs (including former blue-blacks) served by one fast quad.

The **Peak 8** area – tough stuff at the top, easier lower down – can be reached by a fast quad from Peak 9. The base lifts of Peak 8 at the Bergenhof can also be reached by the slow Snowflake lift from the suburbs, or by gondola from the fringes of town – where there's ample parking. The six-pack serving the lower slopes of **Peak 7** can be accessed from Peak 8 and from the gondola's mid-station.

The higher open slopes on Peaks 7 and 8 are accessed by a T-bar – a rarity in these parts – reachable from either base, and by the Imperial fast quad at the top of the Peak 8 lift network. The resort claims a top height of 3960m, but that involves a hike of 45m vertical at the very top.

FAST LIFTS ★★★★

Good coverage

Breckenridge's gondola and nine fast chairlifts cover all four sectors and provide good access from either end of town – the slow Snowflake chair to Peak 8 in between is an obvious exception, which will be an irritant if you are based nearby.

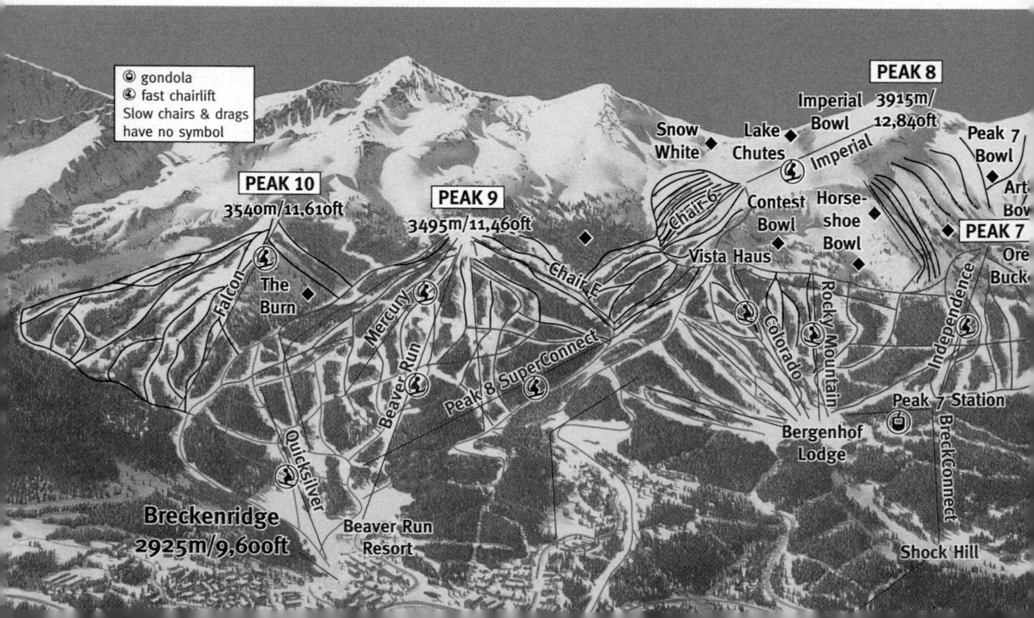

↑ The top slopes of Peaks 8 and 7 are treeless, and are often badly affected by high winds

JONATHAN CLARK

LIFT PASSES

Prices in US$

Age	1-day	6-day
under 13	54	234
13 to 64	93	432
65 plus	82	372

Free under 5

Beginner included in price of lessons

Notes

Covers Breckenridge, Keystone and Arapahoe Basin, plus 3 days (on a 6-day pass) at Vail and Beaver Creek; prices are online rates for early Feb purchased 14 days in advance of trip; window rates in resort are considerably higher; best prices for international visitors if pre-book through a UK tour operator (it is not necessary to buy a complete holiday package to obtain these prices)

QUEUES ★★★★

Peak times possibly

You do get queues at peak times, but the fast chairs (and the lifties making sure they are filled) make light work of peak-time crowds. There may be queues for the old Chair 6 on a powder day and the slow Snowflake chair that gives access to Peak 8 for thousands of condo-dwellers. But recent reporters have had no complaints.

TERRAIN PARKS ★★★★★

Something for everyone

The main focus is Peak 8, with three parks for different ability levels. Freeway is one of the best parks in North America and the largest of Breck's park, featuring a series of big jumps, obstacles and a super-pipe. Next to it, Park Lane offers a variety of challenging features. And Trygves has gentle jumps and rollers for beginner freestylers. On Peak 9 are two more parks: Bonanza is a beginner progression park, and Gold King bridges the gap between Bonanza and Park Lane. See www.breck1080.com.

SNOW RELIABILITY ★★★★★

Ample quantities

With its high altitude, Breckenridge boasts a great natural snow record – annual average 300 inches. That is supplemented by substantial snowmaking (used mainly early in the season to form a good base). There are a lot of east- and north-east-facing slopes, which hold snow well. But high winds can remove or spoil the snow, notably on exposed upper runs.

FOR EXPERTS ★★★★

Lots of short but tough runs

A remarkable 55% of the runs are classified black – that's a higher proportion than famous 'macho' resorts such as Jackson Hole, Taos and Snowbird. And a good proportion are classified as 'expert' (double-diamond) or 'extreme' terrain. But most runs are short – most of the key lifts offer verticals of around 300m.

Peak 8 is at the core of the tough skiing. The lightly wooded slopes served by Chair 6 are a good place to start – picturesque and not too steep. Below, steeper runs lead further down to the junction with Peak 9. Above, the Imperial quad accesses huge amounts of above-the-treeline terrain and longer runs. You can hike up to the double-diamond Imperial Bowl, and the 'extreme' Lake Chutes and Snow White areas. Or you can traverse round the back towards Peak 7 and double-diamond runs in the bowl (we had a great time in fresh snow there on our 2011 visit); the T-bar on Peak 8 accesses the lower parts of these runs (single diamonds) and the double-diamond Horseshoe and Contest bowls. On the lower, wooded part of Peak 8 is a worthwhile area of single diamonds.

Peak 9's wooded North Slope under Chair E is excellent – shady, sheltered and steep – we've had great runs down Devil's Crotch, Hades and Inferno. Peak 10 has easy black runs (former blue-blacks) down the central ridge, but more challenging stuff on both flanks. To skier's left is a lovely, lightly wooded area called The Burn.

ACTIVITIES

Indoor Recreation centre on outskirts (accessible by bus): pool, gym, tennis, climbing wall; spas, ice rink, theatre, cinema, museums, galleries

Outdoor Horse-drawn sleigh rides, dog sledding, snowmobiles, ice rink, snowshoeing, tobogganing

SCHOOLS

Breckenridge
t 496 4700

Classes
Day (4.5hr) $150

Private lessons
$475 for 3hr for up to 3 people

GETTING THERE

Air Denver 165km/ 105 miles (2hr15)

FOR INTERMEDIATES ★★★★
Nice cruising, limited extent

Breckenridge has some good blue cruising runs for all intermediates. But dedicated piste-bashers are likely to find the runs short and limited in variety. Peak 9 has the easiest slopes. It is nearly all gentle, wide, blue runs at the top and almost flat, wide, green runs at the bottom. And the ski patrol is supposed to enforce slow-speed skiing in certain areas.

Peak 10 has a number of easy, normally groomed, black runs that used to be classified blue-black, such as Crystal and Centennial, which make for good fast cruising. Peaks 7 and 8 both have a choice of blues on trails cut close together in the trees. Adventurous intermediates can also try some of the high bowl runs and more gentle gladed runs such as Ore Bucket glades on the fringe of Peak 7 and the runs beneath Chair 6 on Peak 8.

FOR BEGINNERS ★★★★★
Excellent

The bottom of Peak 9 has a big, virtually flat area and some good, gentle nursery slopes. There's then a good choice of green runs to move on to. Beginners can try Peak 8 too, with another selection of green runs and a choice of trails back to town. There is a special beginner package available (see 'Schools and guides').

FOR BOARDERS ★★★★★
One of the best

Breckenridge is pretty much ideal for all standards of boarder and hosts several major US snowboarding events. Beginners have ideal nursery slopes and greens to progress to. Intermediates have great cruising runs, all served by chairs. The powder bowls at the top of Peaks 7 and 8 make great riding and can be accessed via the Imperial quad, so avoiding the awkward T-bar. Boarders of all levels will enjoy the choice of excellent terrain parks. Nearby Arapahoe Basin is another area for hardcore boarding in steep bowls and chutes.

FOR CROSS-COUNTRY ★★★★
Specialist centre in woods

Breckenridge's Nordic Center is prettily set in the woods between the town and Peak 8 (served by the shuttle-bus). It has 32km of trails and 16km of snowshoeing trails. A further 22km of cross-country is on the golf course.

MOUNTAIN RESTAURANTS ★★
Improved by more base options

Of the self-service places above base level, Peak 9 restaurant is the 'best' of a mediocre bunch, serving 'reasonable' food. Both Ten Mile Station, where Peak 9 meets 10, and the dreary Vista Haus on Peak 8 are food-court operations. But they get nightmarishly busy at weekends. Sevens is a smart table-service restaurant at the Peak 7 base; there's a quick service window too: Sevens Express. The Ski Hill Grill at the base of Peak 8 has a smart decor with lots of stone and a 'good variety' of self-service food (including Asian fusion).

SCHOOLS AND GUIDES ★★★★★
Excellent reports

Reporters have praised the small classes. The beginner package includes lessons, equipment rental and lift pass, and the school's special

VAIL RESORTS, INC

Expansion of Breck's downtown area has consistently been done in the original mining-town style, and the result is easy on the eye ↓

CHILDCARE

Child Care Centers
t +1 888 576 2754
Age 8wk to 3yr

Summit Sitters
t 513 4445

Mountain Sitters
t 512 261 5053

Ski school
Ages 3 to 13 (from $158 per day inc lift pass)

UK PACKAGES

Alpine Answers, AmeriCan Ski, American Ski Classics, Crystal, Crystal Finest, Erna Low, Flexiski, Frontier, Independent Ski Links, Inghams, Interactive Resorts, Momentum, Oxford Ski Co, PowderBeds, Ski Bespoke, Ski Expectations, Ski Independence, Ski Line, Ski Safari, Ski Solutions, Skitracer, Skiworld, Snow Finders, STC, Supertravel, Thomson, Virgin Snow

Phone numbers
From distant parts of the US, add the prefix 1 970; from abroad, add the prefix +1 970

TOURIST OFFICE

www.breckenridge.com

clinics include women's and telemark. The school's full-day Adventure Sessions offer guided instruction for intermediates and experts.

FOR FAMILIES ★★★★

Excellent facilities

Past reports on the children's school and nursery have been full of praise. The Mountains of Discovery Program aims to combine teaching and fun on the slopes (for kids aged three to 13 years).

STAYING THERE

Chalets Several tour operators have very comfortable chalets. Skiworld has three smart places, all with outdoor hot tubs, and Crystal Finest features a swanky privately-run place with hot tub near Peak 8.

Hotels There's a noticeable lack of good places close to Main Street.

******DoubleTree by Hilton** (547 5550) (Formerly Great Divide, renovated in 2012.) A short walk to the slopes and a bearable walk to Main Street.

******Lodge & Spa at Breckenridge** (453 9300) Stylish luxury spa resort set out of town among 32 acres, with great views. Private shuttle-bus. Pool, tub, steam, sauna and massage.

******Beaver Run** (453 6000) Huge, slope-side resort complex with 520 spacious rooms. Pools, hot tubs.

******Barn on the River** (453 2975) B&B on Main St. Hot tub.

Apartments There is a huge choice. Mountain Thunder Lodge (near the gondola and the supermarket), Hyatt Main Street Station (near the Quicksilver lift) and One Ski Hill Place at Peak 8 are recommended at the luxury end. A regular visitor also recommends the Village at Breckenridge for location, quality and value ('cavernous and very comfortable'), Trails End, Corral, One Breckenridge Place and Saddlewood. A cheaper option is Der Steiermark (Peak 9 base). River Mountain Lodge is praised for 'quality, cost and location'.

EATING OUT ★★★★★

Over 100 restaurants

There's a wide range, from typical US food to fine dining. At peak times they get busy, and many don't take bookings. The Breckenridge Dining Guide (available online) lists the full menu of most places.

Recent visitors confirmed the attractions of the Hearthstone (modern American cuisine in a beautiful 100-year-old house): 'excellent; attentive service'. For no-nonsense grills-and-fries in a pub ambience, we've enjoyed both the Brewery (famous for mega 'appetizers', such as buffalo wings, and splendid beers) and the Kenosha steakhouse. Reader tips: Whale's Tail (mainly, but not only seafood), Mi Casa ('lively' Mexican), South Ridge (predominantly fish – 'good atmosphere'), Downstairs at Eric's (burgers and pizzas), Michael's (Italian), Steak & Rib ('bit of an institution; stacks of photos and memorabilia') and Spencer's, at Beaver Run resort (steaks and seafood). The Blue Moose does the usual killer breakfasts.

APRES-SKI ★★★

The best in the area ...

There's not much tea-time animation at the lift bases. The Maggie, at the base of Peak 9, 'has music on the terrace but doesn't stay open much beyond 5pm'. Park Avenue Pub, just off Main Street, and the Brewery were lively on our recent visits. Later on we've enjoyed the Gold Pan saloon (reputedly the oldest bar west of the Mississippi); reader tips include the Liquid Lounge and Fatty's. Cecilia's serves good cocktails; Burke and Riley's is an Irish bar; Downstairs at Eric's is a disco sports bar, and Three20South has live bands.

OFF THE SLOPES ★★★

Pleasant enough

Breckenridge is a pleasant place to wander around, with plenty of souvenir and gift shops plus a free museum. Silverthorne (about 30 minutes away by free bus) has bargain factory outlet stores.

NEARBY TOWN – 2765m

FRISCO

Staying in Frisco makes sense for those touring or on a tight budget. It's a pleasant small town with bars, restaurants and good-value lodgings. Hotel Frisco (668 5009) is on Main Street. The Lake Dillon Lodge (668 5094) is handy for the bus. Restaurants include Backcountry Brewery, Tuscato (Italian), Blue Spruce Inn (steaks), the Boatyard (pizzas) and Food Hedz World Cafe ('good duck and steak').

ASPEN/SNOWMASS PICTURE LIBRARY

Snowmass

Aspen's modern satellite – with impressively varied and extensive slopes, and a smart new fledgling Base Village

TOP 10 RATINGS

Extent	****
Fast lifts	*****
Queues	****
Snow	*****
Expert	*****
Intermediate	*****
Beginner	*****
Charm	**
Convenience	****
Scenery	****

RPI	180
lift pass	£370
ski hire	£200
lessons	£230
food & drink	£125
total	**£925**

NEWS

2012/13: The former Silvertree Hotel is being transformed into the Westin Snowmass Resort, due to open in December 2012. At the top of the Elk Camp gondola a new, much bigger restaurant is due to open to replace Café Suzanne.

- \+ Varied mountain, with the biggest vertical in the US – 1340m
- \+ Aspen accessible by free bus
- \+ Uncrowded slopes
- \+ Lots of slope-side lodgings

- − Limited dining, shopping and nightlife
- − Diversions of Aspen town are a bus ride away

The slopes of Snowmass are a key part of the attraction of nearby Aspen as a destination. As a base, Snowmass has obvious appeal for families wanting easy cruising on their doorstep; its appeal is starting to broaden as more shops and restaurants open at the new Base Village – but progress is slow.

THE RESORT

Snowmass is a modern, purpose-built resort, with low-rise buildings set alongside the gentle home slope. Within these buildings is Snowmass Village Mall. Further down the hill is a new Base Village, the development of which has been slowed by the current recession.

Village charm The new Base Village has added a bit of style to what is a rather plain modern resort.

Convenience Much of the lodging is ski-in/ski-out, and Snowmass Village Mall has a small cluster of shops and restaurants. Efficient free bus services (crowded at times) link Snowmass with Aspen's mountains and town – the one to Aspen runs to 2am.

Scenery The views from the high-points are long but not dramatic.

THE MOUNTAIN

Most of the slopes are in the forest; higher ones are only lightly wooded.

Slopes Snowmass is big by US standards – almost 8km across, with the biggest vertical in the US. Chairlifts and a gondola diverge from the base to go up to two high-points at either end of the ski area – Elk Camp and Sam's Knob. Links higher up go to the two sectors in the middle, High Alpine and Big Burn, where a draglift goes to the high-point on The Cirque. The Two Creeks base is nearer Aspen.

Fast lifts Most key lifts are fast. But there are still a couple of long, slow chairs that can be cold in midwinter.

Queues Any problems can usually be avoided. The home slope gets busy.

Terrain parks Snowmass has a 6.7m super-pipe and three parks: Lowdown

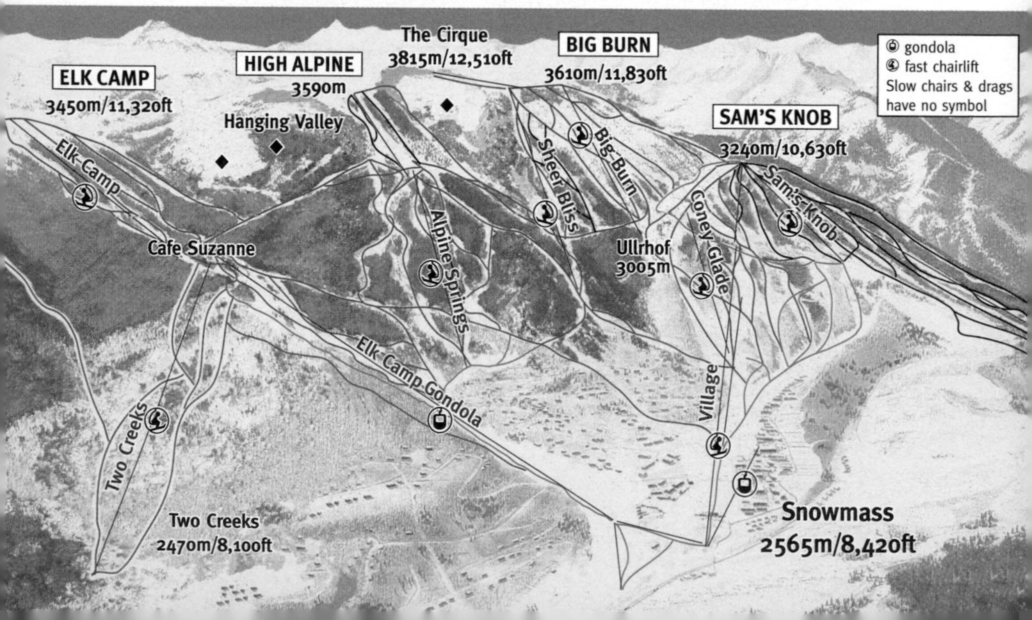

ELK CAMP 3450m/11,320ft
HIGH ALPINE 3590m
The Cirque 3815m/12,510ft
BIG BURN 3610m/11,830ft
SAM'S KNOB 3240m/10,630ft
Hanging Valley
Elk Camp
Cafe Suzanne
Alpine Springs
Sheer Bliss
Big Burn
Sam's Knob
Coney Glade
Ullrhof 3005m
Elk Camp Gondola
Village
Two Creeks
Two Creeks 2470m/8,100ft
Snowmass 2565m/8,420ft
gondola
fast chairlift
Slow chairs & drags have no symbol

Out at the extremity of the area, on skier's left, you may find you have runs all to yourself ➔

SNOWPIX.COM / CHRIS GILL

KEY FACTS

Resort	2565m 8,420ft
Snowmass only	
Slopes	2470-3815m 8,100-12,510ft
Lifts	21
Pistes	3,132 acres
Green	6%
Blue	50%
Black	44%
Snowmaking	7%

See Aspen chapter for statistics on other mountains – star rating for extent includes them all

UK PACKAGES

Alpine Answers, AmeriCan Ski, American Ski Classics, Crystal, Ski Independence, Ski Safari, Supertravel

Phone numbers
From distant parts of the US, add the prefix 1 970; from abroad, add the prefix +1 970

TOURIST OFFICE

www.aspen snowmass.com

(beginner), Little Makaha (intermediate) and Snowmass (expert), with about 90 features in total including jibs, rails and jumps.

Snow reliability With 300 inches a year plus snowmaking, it's good.

Experts There's great terrain, although the steep runs tend to be short. Consider joining a guided group as an introduction. Our favourite area is around the Hanging Valley Wall and Glades – beautiful scenery and steep wooded slopes. The other seriously steep area is The Cirque, reached by draglift from Big Burn to the area's highest point. From here, the Headwall is not terrifyingly steep, but there are also narrow, often rocky, chutes – Gowdy's is one of the steepest.

Intermediates Excellent – the best mountain in the Aspen area for intermediates (and by far the biggest). All four sectors have lots to offer. Highlights include: the top slopes on Big Burn – a huge, varied, lightly wooded area, including the Powerline Glades for the adventurous; long, top-to-bottom cruises from Elk Camp and High Alpine; regularly groomed single-black runs from Sam's Knob. Long Shot is a glorious 5km run, normally ungroomed, lost in the forest, ending at Two Creeks, and well worth the short hike from the top of Elk Camp.

Beginners In the heart of the resort is a broad, gentle beginners' run. An even easier slope (and less busy) is the wide Assay Hill, at the bottom of Elk Camp. There's also a beginner area served by three lifts at Elk Camp Meadows, at the top of the Elk Camp gondola. From Sam's Knob there are long, gentle cruises back to the resort.

Snowboarding A great mountain, whatever your boarding style.

Cross-country Excellent trails between here and Aspen – see Aspen chapter.

Mountain restaurants There are three table-service places: Gwyn's High Alpine (established over 30 years), Lynn Britt Cabin (old log cabin, elegant table settings) and Sam's Smokehouse (newish, big windows, great views) – all do good food. And Up 4 Pizza has 'excellent facilities', says a 2012 visitor. You can picnic at the Wapiti Wildlife Center at the top of Elk Camp and in the warming huts at the top of Sam's Knob, Big Burn and High Alpine.

Schools and guides We've had mixed reports. A 2011 visitor had two different teachers with 'no real enthusiasm or feedback', but his son had the same teacher throughout: 'very enthusiastic, good feedback'.

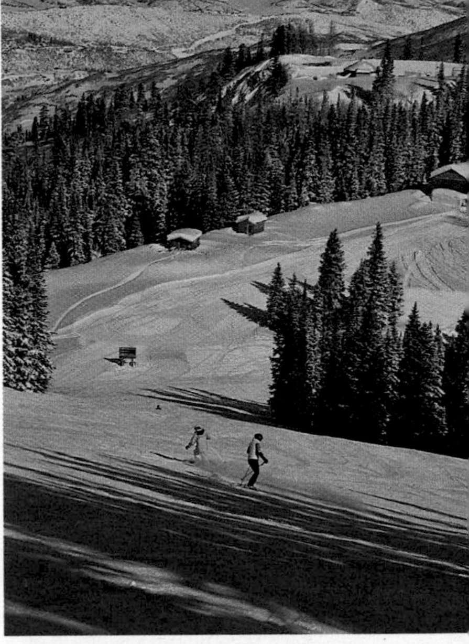

Families Snowmass is a family-friendly resort. The Treehouse adventure centre at Base Village is a very impressive facility and there are special trails and trail maps for children.

STAYING THERE

Most accommodation is self-catering.

Hotels The focal hotel, the Silvertree, is being transformed into the Westin Snowmass Resort (923 8200). A 2011 visitor raves about the Stonebridge Inn (923 2420): 'excellent bar and restaurant; awesome outdoor pool and hot tubs'. The luxury Viceroy (923 8000) is at Base Village.

Apartments Capitol Peak and Hayden Lodge are luxury condos at Base Village. Tamarack Townhouses and Crestwood Condos are popular. A 2012 visitor found the Timberline condos 'OK', with 'good attentive staff'.

Eating out The Eight K restaurant in the Viceroy is very highly recommended by a 2012 visitor, especially the 'chef's tables' where the atmosphere is 'more laid back'. Il Poggio is recommended for Italian. Base Camp has reasonable prices and Buchi is a Japanese restaurant.

Après-ski Try Base Camp (live music) or, at Base Village, Sneaky's Tavern ('great guitarist/singer playing' says a 2012 visitor). Venga Venga Cantina & Tequila Bar was new for 2012.

Off the slopes There's snowshoe trails, snowcat rides and dog sledding.

Vail

A vast, swanky resort with some very swanky hotels at the foot of one of the biggest (but also busiest) ski areas in the States

RATINGS

The mountains	
Extent	****
Fast lifts	*****
Queues	**
Terrain p'ks	*****
Snow	*****
Expert	****
Intermediate	*****
Beginner	***
Boarder	***
X-country	***
Restaurants	**
Schools	*****
Families	****
The resort	
Charm	***
Convenience	***
Scenery	***
Eating out	*****
Après-ski	***
Off-slope	***

RPI	165
lift pass	£320
ski hire	£170
lessons	£230
food & drink	£120
total	**£840**

NEWS

2012/13: A new gondola is to replace the Vista Bahn chair from Vail Village to mid-mountain, increasing capacity by 40%.

2011/12: The 10th, a much-needed new table-service mountain restaurant, opened at Mid-Vail.

- + One of the biggest areas in the US – great for confident intermediates, especially
- + The Back Bowls are big areas of treeless terrain – unusual in the US
- + Fabulous area of ungroomed, wooded slopes at Blue Sky Basin
- + Largely traffic-free resort centres, very pleasant in parts – but ...

- − Resort is a vast sprawl
- − Slopes can be crowded by American standards, with serious lift queues
- − Inadequate mountain restaurants
- − Blue Sky Basin and the Back Bowls may not be open in early season; warm weather can close the Bowls
- − Expensive, with lots of luxury lodgings but few budget options

We always enjoy skiing Vail; it's a big mountain with a decent vertical, and Blue Sky Basin's 'adventure' skiing is a key attraction. But it is far from being our favourite American mountain. In an American resort you expect the runs to be pretty much crowd-free – and in any resort, these days, you expect 20-minute lift queues to be a thing of the past. In these respects, Vail disappoints.

A repeat visit in 2011 confirms that when the budget runs to a swanky billet in Vail Village or the new Lionshead area, we're happy enough with the resort, too; it is a pleasant place to wander around. But we're not enthusiastic about Vail Village's pseudo-Tirolean style, and the rest of the huge resort lacks character. In the end, we reckon Vail can't compete with more distinctively American resorts based on old mining or cowboy towns.

THE RESORT

Vail is an enormous resort, stretching almost four miles along the I-70 freeway running west from Denver. Beaver Creek, 16km away, is covered by the lift pass and is easily reached by bus. Breckenridge and Keystone – both owned by Vail Resorts and covered by the lift pass – and Copper Mountain are possible excursions.

VILLAGE CHARM ***
No real identity

Standing in the centre of Vail Village, surrounded by chalets and bierkellers, you could be forgiven for thinking you were in the Tirol – which is what Vail's founder, Pete Seibert, intended back in the 1950s. But this is now just one part of a huge resort, built mostly in anonymous (but smart) modern style.

CONVENIENCE ***
There's always the bus

The vast village has a free and efficient bus service ('always on time'), which makes choice of location less than crucial. But the most convenient – and expensive – places to stay are in the mock-Tirolean Vail Village, near the Vista Bahn fast chair, or at Lionshead, near the gondola – a recently redeveloped area that now has some very smart lodgings to match Vail Village. There is a lot of accommodation further out – some on the far side of the I-70.

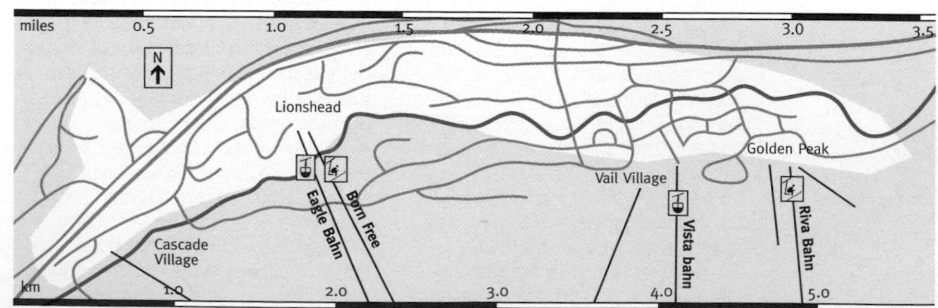

KEY FACTS	
Resort	2500m 8,200ft
Slopes	2475-3525m 8,120-11,570ft
Lifts	31
Pistes	5,289 acres
Green	18%
Blue	29%
Black	53%
Snowmaking	9%

SNOWPIX.COM / CHRIS GILL

Vail's front side is laced with good blue and black runs – some easy, some quite challenging; this one descends to the focal point of Mid-Vail ↓

SCENERY ★★★★★
Rolling Colorado

Like most Colorado resorts, Vail is set among rather softly contoured mountains with forest reaching to the top of the slopes.

THE MOUNTAINS

You get a real sense of travelling around Vail's mountains – something missing in many smaller American resorts. Run classification exaggerates the difficulty of some runs – some of the blacks, in particular. Some runs are partly classified blue, partly black, which means fewer surprises if you pay close attention to the map. There are free mountain tours at 10.30 and separate tours of Blue Sky Basin at 11am every day. The slopes have yellow-jacketed patrollers who stop people speeding recklessly.

EXTENT OF THE SLOPES ★★★★★
Something for everyone

Vail has the second biggest area of slopes in the US (Big Sky/Moonlight Basin has 223 acres more), and they can be accessed via three main lifts. From Vail Village, the Vista Bahn gondola goes up to the major mid-mountain focal point, Mid-Vail; from Lionshead, the Eagle Bahn gondola goes up to the Eagle's Nest complex; and from the Golden Peak base area just to the east of Vail Village, the Riva Bahn fast chair goes up towards the Two Elk area.

The front face of the mountain is largely north-facing, with well-groomed trails cut through the trees. At altitude the mountainside divides into three bowls – Mid-Vail in the centre, with Game Creek to the south-west and Northeast Bowl to the, er, north-east. Lifts reach the ridge at three points, all giving access to the **Back Bowls** (mostly ungroomed and treeless) and through them to **Blue Sky Basin** (mostly ungroomed and wooded, with a 'backcountry' feel).

FAST LIFTS ★★★★★
Plenty of them

There are lots of fast lifts on both sides of the mountain. All three of Blue Sky Basin's lifts are fast chairs.

QUEUES ★★★★★
Can be bad

The front side of Vail has some of the longest lift lines we've hit in the US, especially at weekends because of the influx from nearby Denver. Even on a mid-December visit we hit big queues. Mid-Vail is a bottleneck that is difficult to avoid; 20-minute waits are common (and 45 minutes is not unheard of). The Northwoods chair and the Eagle Bahn gondola are other hot spots. And a 2012 reporter found large queues at Mountaintop Express, too. But other reporters have been luckier: 'rarely major lift queues'.

TERRAIN PARKS ★★★★★
Three to choose between

There are three parks. Beginner and intermediate freestylers will want to explore the Bwana and Pride parks, located under the Eagle Bahn gondola on Bwana run. Here, a selection of small to medium-sized jumps and boxes gradually become more challenging as you progress through each park. More advanced riders will be best served at the Golden Peak Terrain Park. Located halfway down the Riva Bahn chairlift, the park is home to various high-profile events and is often in the top ten in terrain

Two Elk Lodge
3420m/11,220ft
Sourdough
Patrol
Headquarters
3430m/11,250ft
The major bottleneck that gives Vail its reputation for serious queues
Wildwoo
3345m/10,9
Northeast Bowl
Northwoods
Mountaintop
Wildwood
Highline
Mid-Vail
3125m/10,250ft
Avanti
Vail's most challenging terrain, served by two fast lifts
Riva Bahn
Vista Bahn
FRONT SIDE
Golden Peak
gondola
fast chairlift
Slow chairs & drags have no symbol
Vail Village
2500m/8,200ft
Lionshead
2475m/8,120
Patrol Headquarters
3430m/11,250ft
Game Creek Bowl
Two Elk Lodge
3420m/11,220ft
China Bowl
Sun Down Bowl
Sun Up Bowl
Siberia Bowl
Outer Mongolia Bowl
Inner Mongolia Bowl
High Noon
Tea Cup Bowl
Tea Cup
Orient Express
BACK BOWLS
3000m/9,840ft
Pete's
fast chairlift
Slow chairs & drags have no symbol
2865m/9,400ft
2915m/9,560ft
Skyline
Blue Sky Basin

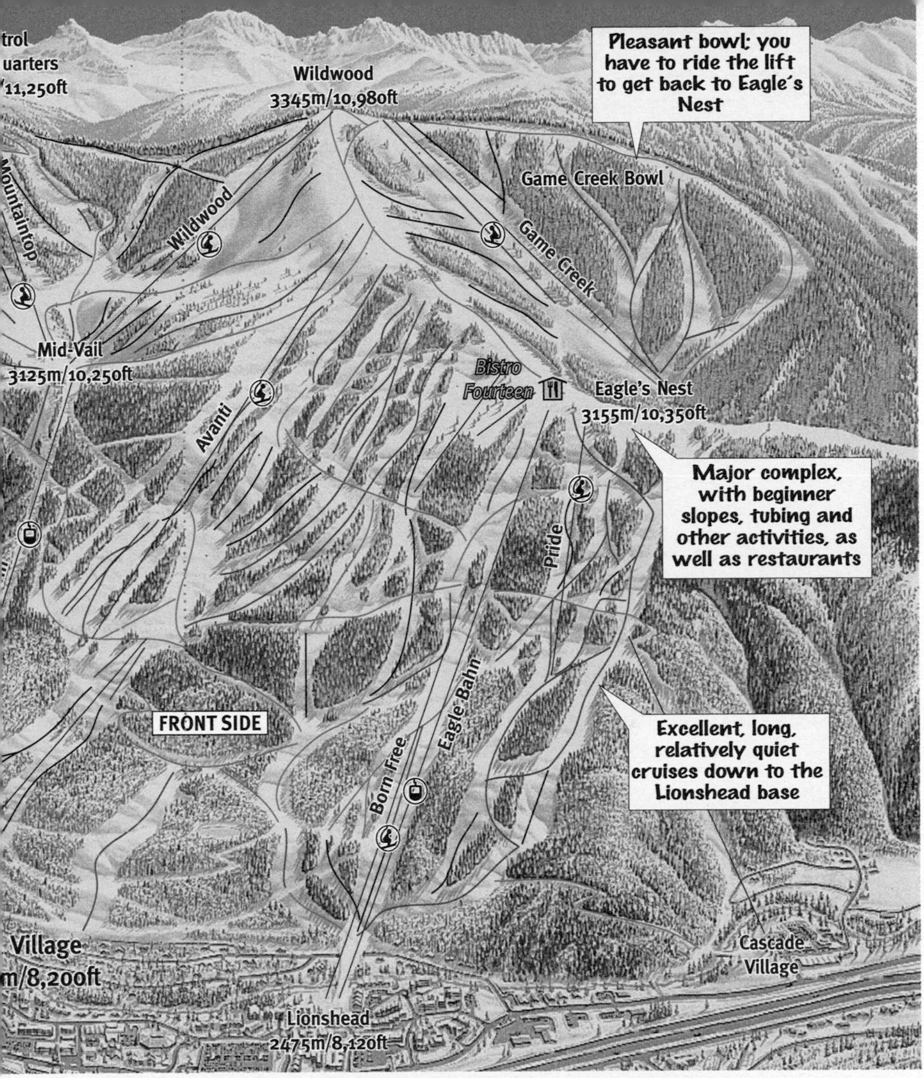

trol
uarters
'11,250ft
Wildwood
3345m/10,980ft
Pleasant bowl; you have to ride the lift to get back to Eagle's Nest
Game Creek Bowl
Mountaintop
Wildwood
Game Creek
Mid-Vail
3125m/10,250ft
Bistro Fourteen
Eagle's Nest
3155m/10,350ft
Avanti
Major complex, with beginner slopes, tubing and other activities, as well as restaurants
Pride
FRONT SIDE
Eagle Bahn
Born Free
Excellent, long, relatively quiet cruises down to the Lionshead base
Village
m/8,200ft
Cascade Village
Lionshead
2475m/8,120ft

3525m/11,570ft
Belle's Camp
3500m/11,480ft
fast chairlift
Slow chairs & drags have no symbol
Pete's Bowl
Earl's Bowl
Earl's
Pete's
Skyline
BLUE SKY BASIN
Orient Express
3000m/9,840ft
2915m/9,560ft

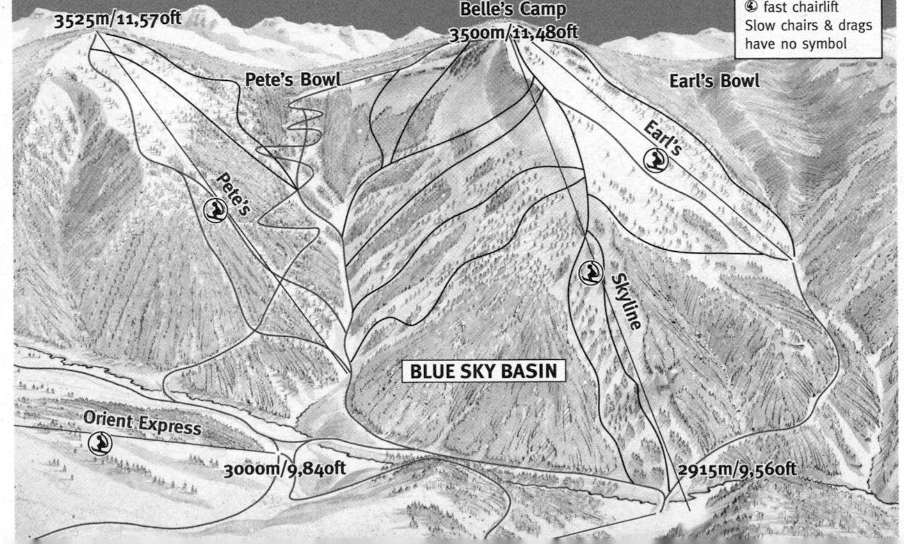

LIFT PASSES

Colorado

Prices in US$		
Age	**1-day**	**6-day**
under 13	69	324
13 to 64	102	480
65 plus	92	420

Free under 5

Beginner included in price of lessons

Notes

Covers Vail, Beaver Creek, Breckenridge, Keystone and Arapahoe Basin; prices are online rates for early February purchased 14 days in advance of trip; window rates in resort are considerably higher; best prices for international visitors if pre-book through a UK tour operator (it is not necessary to buy a complete holiday package to obtain these prices)

park lists and polls. Last season there were nine jumps ranging up to 15m in length, and 30 jibs, boxes and rails.

SNOW RELIABILITY ★★★★★
Excellent, except in the Bowls

As well as an exceptional natural snow record (average 348 inches), Vail has extensive snowmaking, normally needed only in early season. Grooming is excellent. Both the Back Bowls and Blue Sky Basin usually open later in the season than the front mountain. Blue Sky is largely north-facing (and wooded) and keeps its snow well. But the Bowls are sunny, and in warm weather snow can deteriorate to the point where they are closed or only a traverse is kept open to allow access to Blue Sky Basin; for the best snow, head skier's right from the top of the Game Creek chair, where the sun has least effect because the runs are east-facing.

FOR EXPERTS ★★★★
Lots of variety

Vail's Back Bowls are vast areas, served by four chairlifts and a short draglift. You can go virtually anywhere you like in the half-dozen identifiable bowls, trying the gradient and terrain of your choice. There are interesting, lightly wooded areas, as well as the open slopes that dominate the area. Some 87% of the runs in the Back Bowls are classified black but are not particularly steep, and they have disappointed some expert reporters, who seek more challenge and variety.

Blue Sky Basin has much better snow than the Back Bowls and some great adventure runs in the trees – some widely spaced, some very tight, some on relatively gentle terrain, some quite steep. All the runs funnel into the same run-out so you can't get lost.

On the front face there are some genuinely steep double black diamond runs, which usually have great snow; they are often mogulled, but they are sometimes groomed to make wonderful fast cruising. The fast Highline lift – on the extreme east of the area – serves three black runs. Prima Cornice, served by the Northwoods Express, is one of the steepest runs on the front of the hill.

If the snow is good, try the backcountry Minturn Mile – you leave the ski area through a gate in the Game Creek area to descend a powder bowl and finish on a path by a river – ending up at the atmospheric Saloon. Go with a local guide.

FOR INTERMEDIATES ★★★★★
Ideal territory

The majority of Vail's front face is great intermediate terrain, with easy cruising runs. Above Lionshead, especially, there are excellent, long, relatively quiet blues – Bwana, Born Free and Simba all go from top to bottom. Game Creek Bowl, nearby, is excellent, too. Avanti, underneath the chair of the same name, is a nice cruise.

As well as tackling some of the easier front-face blacks, intermediates will find plenty of interest in the Back

VAIL RESORTS, INC

Blue Sky Basin is an excellent area of black and blue runs, shady and wooded. This photo is probably taken from the top of China Bowl ↓

SCHOOLS

Vail
t 496 4800

Classes
Full day $140

Private lessons
From $745 for 1 day for up to 6 people

CHILDCARE

Child Care Centers
t 754 3285
Ages 2mnth to 6yr

Ski school
Ages 3 to 15; full day including lunch from US$160 per day

ACTIVITIES

Indoor Athletic clubs and spas

Outdoor Tubing, ski biking, snowmobiling, snowshoe excursions, bungee trampolining, dog sledding

UK PACKAGES

Alpine Answers, AmeriCan Ski, American Ski Classics, Carrier, Crystal, Crystal Finest, Elegant Resorts, Erna Low, Flexiski, Frontier, Independent Ski Links, Interactive Resorts, Momentum, Oxford Ski Co, PowderBeds, Scott Dunn, Ski Bespoke, Ski Expectations, Ski Independence, Ski Line, Ski Safari, Ski Solutions, Skitracer, Skiworld, Snow Finders, STC, Supertravel, Thomson

Bowls. Some of the runs are groomed and several are blue, including Silk Road, which loops around the eastern edge, with wonderful views. Some of the unpisted slopes are ideal for learning to ski powder. Confident intermediates will also enjoy Blue Sky Basin's clearly marked blue runs and the easier ungroomed runs there (Cloud 9 is a lovely gentle area of groomed glades; In the Wuides is a bit steeper but still lovely).

FOR BEGINNERS ★★★★★

Good but can be crowded

There are fine nursery slopes at resort level and at altitude, and easy longer runs to progress to. But they can be rather crowded.

FOR BOARDERS ★★★★★

Big isn't always best

The terrain is about as big as it comes in America. Beginners will enjoy the front side's gentle groomed pistes (but not the crowds), good for honing skills and serviced by fast chairlifts. But beware of flat areas, especially at the top of the Wildwood and Northwoods lifts, and cat tracks. The back bowls will keep most expert and intermediate riders busy for days. Blue Sky Basin is definitely worth checking out, with its acres of natural trails, gladed trees and cornices. There are three terrain parks too.

FOR CROSS-COUNTRY ★★★★★

Go for Golden

Vail's cross-country areas (17km) are at the foot of Golden Peak and at the Nordic Center on the golf course. There are 10km of snowshoe trails too.

MOUNTAIN RESTAURANTS ★★★★★

Surprisingly poor

Vail's mountain restaurants are disappointing for such a big, upscale resort. The major self-service restaurants can be unpleasantly crowded from 11am to 2pm.

Editors' choice The table-service Bistro Fourteen (754 4530) at Eagle's Nest is in an airy room and does good food at not exorbitant prices. The 10th (754 1010) sounds like good news: a new table-service place at Mid-Vail – reports, please.

Worth knowing about There are self-service places at several major lift junctions. Two Elk is a huge, airy place that many visitors find satisfactory, but it can get unpleasantly crowded. Try

Wildwood for BBQs, Buffalo's for soup and sandwiches. You can take your own food and cook it on free BBQs at Belle's Camp at the top of Blue Sky Basin (take your own booze too) – which is just as well, because there is no other catering in that sector.

SCHOOLS AND GUIDES ★★★★★

Among the best in the world

The school has an excellent reputation and we have a glowing report again this year: 'Probably the best I've ever experienced; knowledgeable and encouraging instructors who want to make sure your trip is fun.' You can sign up for lessons on the mountain. The school's full day Adventure Sessions offer guided instruction for intermediates and experts.

FOR FAMILIES ★★★★★

Good all round

The main children's centre is at Golden Peak and takes kids aged three to 15; the nursery takes kids from two months to six years. There are splendid areas with adventure trails and themed play zones, such as the Magic Forest and Chaos Canyon. There's even a special kids' cafe area at Mid Vail. There are kids' snowmobiles and trampolines at Adventure Ridge.

STAYING THERE

There's a big choice of packages to Vail and it's easy to organize your own visit too, with regular airport shuttle services.

Chalets Ski Independence has a smart chalet across the I-70 from Vail with some big bedrooms (and a couple of smaller ones with shared bathrooms) and an outdoor hot tub. 'Excellent food and hosts,' says a 2012 visitor. Skiworld has a couple of smart chalets with outdoor tubs in East Vail.

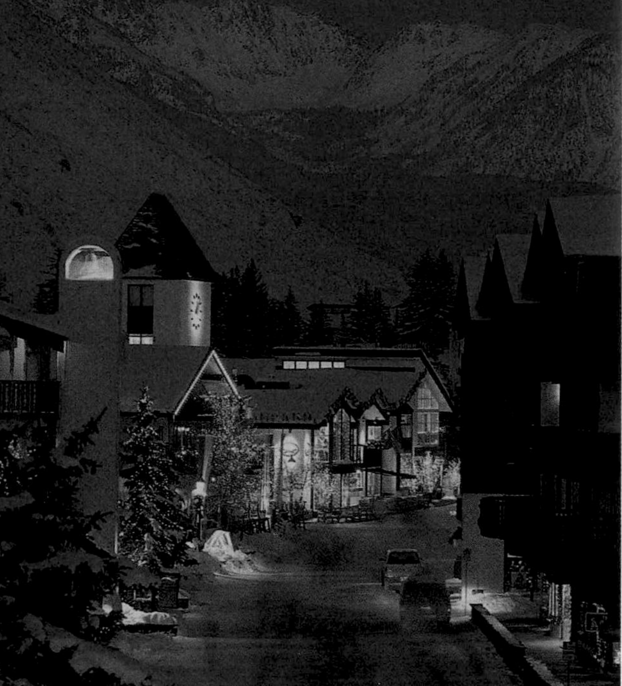

↑ Vail is a purpose-built resort dating from the 1960s, but the heart of Vail Village was built in Tyrolean style

VAIL RESORTS, INC

Resort news and key links: **www.wheretoskiandsnowboard.com**

GETTING THERE

Air Eagle 55km/ 35 miles (45min); Denver 195km/ 120 miles (2hr15)

Central reservations phone number
t 496 4500

Phone numbers
From distant parts of the US, add the prefix 1 970; from abroad, add the prefix +1 970

TOURIST OFFICE

www.vail.com

Hotels Vail's hotels are nearly all upmarket and expensive (becoming even more so with the opening in recent years of the luxurious Ritz-Carlton, Four Seasons and Solaris hotels). Other top-rank places include the Vail Cascade (with its own lift into the slopes), the plushly Bavarian Sonnenalp and the brilliantly convenient Lodge at Vail (right by the Vista Bahn). Other slightly more affordable places include:
****__Manor Vail Resort__ At Golden Peak. Suites with sitting area, fireplace, kitchen, terrace. Hot tub and pools.
****__Marriot Mountain Resort__ At Golden Peak. Spa, pool, hot tub.
***__Evergreen Lodge__ Between village and Lionshead. More affordable than others. Outdoor pool, sauna and hot tub. Sports bar.
Apartments There's a wide range of apartments, from standard to luxury. The Racquet Club at East Vail has lots of amenities. At Vail Village, Mountain Haus is central and high quality. Vail Cascade Resort and Spa is good value, including breakfast and use of the hotel's leisure facilities. And Manor Vail might be a preferred family choice – it's beside the children's ski school. Good value places at Lionshead include Village Inn Plaza, Vantage Point, the Antlers, Enzian, Westwind and Vail 21.

EATING OUT ★★★★★
Endless choice

Whatever kind of food you want, Vail has it – but most of it is expensive.

Fine-dining options include Elway's (which replaced the Wildflower in the Lodge in 2011/12), Centre V (French-inspired; in the Arrabelle), the Tour (modern French) and Ludwig's (in the Sonnenalp). For Alpine ambience try Pepi's in the hotel Gramshammer or the Alpenrose. You can take the gondola up to Eagle's Nest and be driven by snowcat to the Game Creek Club for dinner (it's a private members' club at lunchtimes).

For more moderate prices, we've found Blu's 'contemporary American' food satisfactory; Billy's Island Grill does steaks and seafood ('good service and menu'); and Campo de Fiori is an excellent Italian. The Chophouse at Lionshead serves seafood and steaks. Reader recommendations include: Sweet Basil ('modern American cuisine') and Lancelot (steaks), both at Vail Village; May Palace (Chinese) and Nozawa (Asian) in West Vail; also Sapphire (seafood, with oyster bar), Montauk (seafood), Los Amigos (Mexican), Russell's (steak), Vendetta's (Italian) and Pazzo's (pizzas). There's a new restaurant in the Solaris hotel: Matsuhisa (Asian cuisine)

APRES-SKI ★★★★★
Fairly lively

Lionshead is quiet in the evenings; but Garfinkel's has a DJ, sun deck and happy hour. The Red Lion in Vail Village has live music, big-screen TVs and huge portions of food. The George models itself on an English-style pub. Pepi's is popular, and Los Amigos is lively at four o'clock. The Tap Room in the Vista Bahn building is a relaxed woody bar.

You can have a good night out at Adventure Ridge at the top of the gondola. As well as restaurants and bars, there's lots to do on the snow.

OFF THE SLOPES ★★★★★
A lot to do

Getting around on the free bus is easy, and there are lots of activities. The factory outlets at Silverthorne are a must if you can't resist a bargain. Pedestrians can get to Eagle's Nest for lunch by gondola.

WINTER PARK / BYRON HETZLER PHOTOGRAPHY

Winter Park

A radical alternative to the run of Colorado resorts, for those more interested in snow and space than in après-ski amusements

RATINGS

The mountains	
Extent	***
Fast lifts	****
Queues	****
Terrain p'ks	*****
Snow	*****
Expert	****
Intermediate	****
Beginner	*****
Boarder	***
X-country	****
Restaurants	***
Schools	*****
Families	****
The resort	
Charm	**
Convenience	***
Scenery	***
Eating out	**
Après-ski	*
Off-slope	*

RPI	150
lift pass	£310
ski hire	£160
lessons	£175
food & drink	£105
total	**£750**

- + The best snowfall record of all Colorado's major resorts
- + Good terrain for all abilities
- + Quiet on weekdays
- + Leading resort for teaching people with disabilities to ski and ride
- + Largely free of inflated prices and ski-resort glitz

- − 'Village' at the lift base is still very limited and dead in the evening
- − Town is a bus ride away and lacks the usual shops and restaurants
- − Trails tend to be either easy cruises or stiff mogul fields
- − Some tough terrain liable to closure by bad weather

Winter Park's ski area – developed for the recreation of the citizens of nearby Denver, and still owned by the city – is world class. When Intrawest (developers of resorts such as Whistler) got involved a few years ago, there was the prospect of a world-class resort being developed at the base, too. But things have stalled, and expansion plans now seem to have been put on hold.

For the present, there's only a small, very quiet 'village' at the base, and most lodging, shops and restaurants are a bus ride away.

THE RESORT

Winter Park started life in the 19th century: when the Rio Grande railway was built, workers climbed the slopes to ski down. One of its mountains, Mary Jane, is named after a legendary 'lady of pleasure' who is said to have received the land as payment for her favours. The resort (at 2745m) is one of the highest to get a chapter in this book (only Breckenridge is higher) so there is a risk of altitude sickness if you go straight there from the UK. And the approach road from Denver is seriously high – crossing the Continental Divide at Berthoud Pass (3450m) – and Alpine in character, with very un-American hairpin bends. Don't plan on driving over in the dark. Having a car makes day trips to Denver and to resorts such as Copper Mountain, Breckenridge (see separate chapter) and Keystone possible.

You can stay at The Village at the base of the slopes or in the town of Winter Park, linked by shuttle-bus.

VILLAGE CHARM **

Old or new?

Most accommodation is in spacious condos scattered around either side of US highway 40, the road through the town of Winter Park. Drive into the town at night, and the neon lights make it seem like a real ski resort town – but in the cold light of day it's clear that the place doesn't amount to much. It even lacks a proper supermarket – the nearest is a drive or free bus ride away at Fraser.

WINTER PARK RESORT

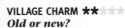

← Proximity to the Continental Divide, in the distance, is said to account for Winter Park's top-notch snow record

NEWS

2012/13: A new tubing hill is to open.

2011/12: The Village Way Trail was improved to make it easier for beginners to return to base. The Burton Experience Snowboarding Lounge was introduced so that beginners can meet instructors and learn about the sport prior to taking a lesson.

KEY FACTS

Resort	2745m 9,000ft
Slopes	2745-3675m 9,000-12,060ft
Lifts	25
Pistes	3,081 acres
Green	8%
Blue	36%
Black	56%
Snowmaking	10%

Stylish lodgings have been developed at or near the foot of the slopes, to form a very small car-free mini-resort known as The Village at Winter Park. Confusingly, an area between the mountain and the town is known as Old Town.

CONVENIENCE ★★★

Walk or ride

If you stay in The Village, you are right by the slopes. Shuttle-buses run between town and the lift base, and hotels and condos also have shuttles.

SCENERY ★★★

See the Continental Divide

You are almost on the Continental Divide here, with views of the rolling hills in the other direction from the top of Parsenn Bowl.

THE MOUNTAINS

There's a good mix of terrain that suits all abilities – when it's all open. There are guided tours at 10am and 1pm ('The guide was knowledgeable and friendly,' says a 2011 reporter). Route finding can be tricky in places.

EXTENT OF THE SLOPES ★★★

Interestingly divided

Winter Park's ski area is big by US standards. There are five distinct, but well-linked, sectors. From the main base, a fast quad takes you to the peak of the original **Winter Park** mountain. From there, you can descend in all directions.

Some runs lead back towards the main base and over to the **Vasquez Ridge** area on skier's left, served by the Pioneer fast quad.

To skier's right you can descend to the base of **Mary Jane** mountain, where four chairs up the front face serve tough runs; other chairs serve easier terrain on the flanks. Going down the back of Mary Jane you can head for the **Parsenn Bowl**, riding the Panoramic Express chair for intermediate terrain above and in the trees. From Parsenn, conditions permitting, you can hike for up to half an hour to access advanced and extreme terrain at **Vasquez Cirque**. You can return to Parsenn Bowl using the Eagle Wind chair, saving a long run-out to the base of the Vasquez Ridge area and the Pioneer lift.

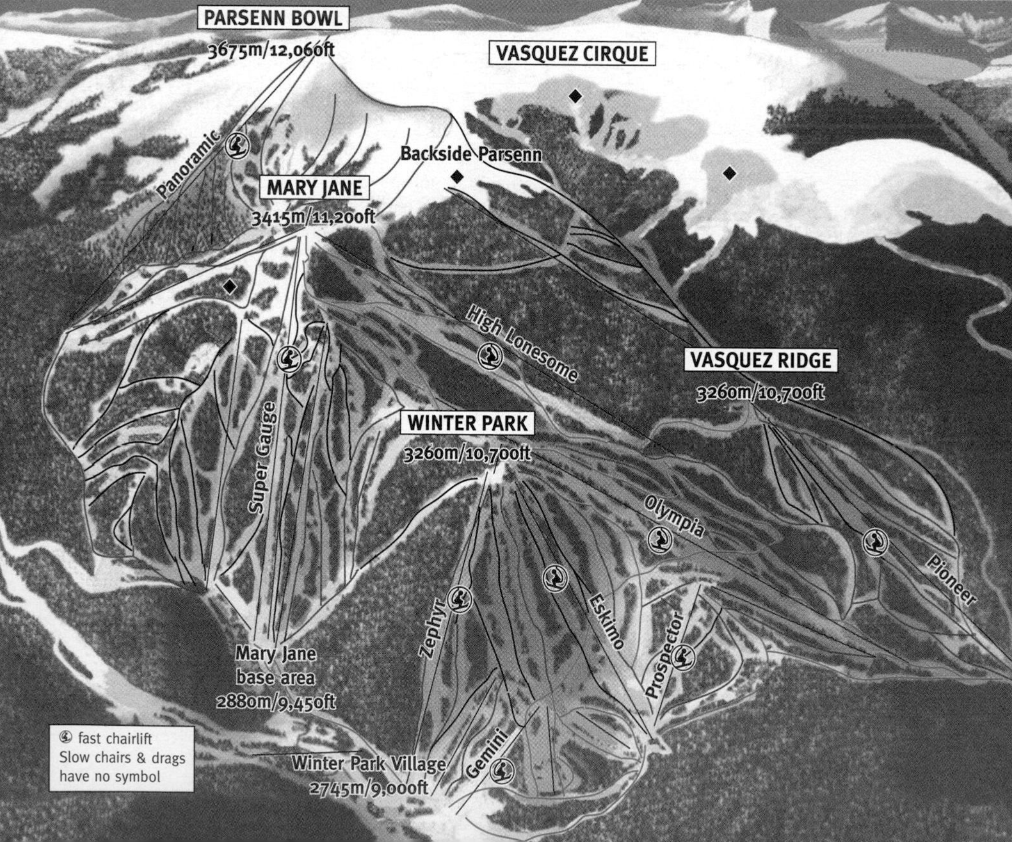

SKIING AND BOARDING FOR THE DISABLED

Winter Park is home to the US National Sports Center for the Disabled (NSCD) – the world's leading centre for teaching skiing and snowboarding to people with disabilities. If you are disabled and want to learn to ski or snowboard, there's no better place to go. It's important to book ahead so that a suitably trained instructor is available. The NSCD can help with travel and accommodation arrangements. See www.nscd.org.

LIFT PASSES

Prices in US$

Age	1-day	6-day
under 13	52	234
13 to 64	90	456
65 to 69	80	426

Free under 6

Seniors Age 70+, daily ticket is $52

Beginner included in price of lessons

Notes
These are advance-purchase prices; special deals for disabled skiers

UK PACKAGES

Alpine Answers, AmeriCan Ski, American Ski Classics, Crystal, Erna Low, Independent Ski Links, Interactive Resorts, Momentum, PowderBeds, Ski Independence, Ski Safari, Ski Solutions, Skitracer, Skiworld, Snow Finders, Supertravel, Thomson, Virgin Snow

FAST LIFTS ★★★★

Adequately covered

Fast chairs have gradually replaced old lifts, though a few slow ones remain.

QUEUES ★★★★

Quiet during the week

During the week the mountain is generally quiet; however, the Zephyr Express can get busy at peak times, and there can be weekend crowds and queues (including at Discovery Park, says a 2011 visitor).

TERRAIN PARKS ★★★★★

Parks for all standards

All six parks were upgraded a couple of seasons ago and 15 further rails were installed in 2011/12. The flagship Rail Yard park – with 30 features including big jumps, jibs, boxes, a host of variously shaped rails and quarter-, half- and super-pipes – is enough to challenge most experts. It runs down much of the front of Winter Park mountain for 1.3km. Halfway down it crosses a bridge so that those on the Village Way green run can cross the park safely. At the bottom are the huge features of Dark Territory, open to special pass holders only (you need to pay $20, sign a waiver and watch a safety video to get the pass). For those who prefer smaller hits, there are the Re-Railer and Gangway parks for intermediates nearby. There's also the beginner-intermediate Ash Cat on the Jack Kendrick green run plus the Starter park under Prospector Express and the Bouncer park in The Village – both for beginners. Check them out at www.rlyrd.com.

SNOW RELIABILITY ★★★★★

Among Colorado's best

Winter Park's position, close to the Continental Divide, gives it an average yearly snowfall of 330 inches – higher than most major Colorado resorts. Snowmaking covers a lot of Winter Park mountain's runs.

FOR EXPERTS ★★★★

Some hair-raising challenges

Mary Jane has some of the steepest mogul fields, chutes and hair-raising challenges in the US. On the front side is a row of long black mogul fields that are quite steep enough for most of us. There are some good genuine blacks on Winter Park mountain, too.

Some of the best terrain is open only when there is good snow and/or weather – so it's especially unreliable early in the season. The fearsome chutes of Mary Jane's back side – all steep, narrow and bordered by rocks – need a lot of snow and are accessed by a control gate. Parsenn Bowl has superb blue/black gladed runs and black diamond gladed runs on the back side down to the Eagle Wind chair. Vasquez Cirque, the least reliably open area, has excellent ungroomed expert terrain but not much vertical before you hit the forest.

FOR INTERMEDIATES ★★★★

Choose your challenge

From pretty much wherever you are on Winter Park mountain and Vasquez Ridge you can choose a run to suit your ability. Most blue runs are well groomed every night, giving you perfect early morning cruising on the famous Colorado 'corduroy' pistes. Black runs, however, tend not to be groomed, and huge moguls form. If bumps are for you, try Mary Jane's front side. If you're learning to love them, the blue/black Sleeper enables you to dip in and out.

Parsenn Bowl has grand views and several gentle cruising pistes as well as more challenging ungroomed terrain. There are blue and blue-black runs and glades here, offering a nice range of gradients. It's also an ideal place to try powder for the first time. But when it's actually snowing you are better off riding lower lifts, sticking to the powdery edges of treelined runs for better visibility. The blue-black Hughes is a great thrash home at close of play.

FOR BEGINNERS ★★★★★

About the best we've seen

Discovery Park is a 25-acre dedicated area for beginners, reached by a high-speed quad and served by two more chairs. As well as a nursery area and longer green runs, it has an adventure trail through trees. Sorensen Park learning zone at the base area is good too. There are lots of long green runs, but some are perilously close to flat.

FOR BOARDERS ★★★

Beware the moguls and flats

There is some great advanced and extreme boarding terrain and a high probability of fresh powder to ride. And the terrain parks are great. The resort is also good for beginners and intermediates, with excellent terrain

SCHOOLS

Winter Park
t 1 800 729 7907

National Sports Center for the Disabled
t 726 5514
Special programme for disabled skiers and snowboarders

Classes
Day (5.5hr) from $99

Private lessons
$389 for 3hr for 1 to 3 people

CHILDCARE

Wee Willie's
t 1 800 420 8093
Ages 2mnth to 6yr

Ski school
Takes ages 3 to 14 ($149 per day including lift ticket, and GPS tracking)

GETTING THERE

Air Denver 165km/ 105 miles (2hr15)

Rail Denver, Sat and Sun only

ACTIVITIES

Indoor Fitness clubs, hot tubs (in hotels), museum

Outdoor Ice rink, snowshoeing, ski bikes, snowcat tours, tubing (at Fraser)

Central reservations
toll-free number (from within the US)
1 800 979 0332

Phone numbers
From distant parts of the US, add the prefix 1 970; from abroad, add the prefix +1 970

TOURIST OFFICE

www.skiwinterpark.com

for learning. But there are quite a few flat spots to beware of, and a lot of the steep runs have huge moguls, which many boarders find tricky. In 2011/12 the Burton Experience Snowboarding Lounge opened at the Winter Park Resort Rentals, West Portal. Here beginners can meet their instructors and learn about the sport prior to taking a lesson.

FOR CROSS-COUNTRY ★★★★

Lots of it nearby

There are several areas nearby (none actually in the resort) with over 200km of groomed trails plus backcountry tours and generally excellent snow.

MOUNTAIN RESTAURANTS ★★★

Some good facilities

The highlight is the Lodge at Sunspot, at the top of Winter Park mountain. This wood and glass building has a welcoming bar with a roaring log fire and table- and self-service sections – but it gets very busy. Lunch Rock Cafe at the top of Mary Jane has 'excellent views', does quick snacks and has a deli counter. And there is a self-service ('reasonable prices' but 'overcrowded') at Snoasis, by the beginner area. Otherwise, it's down to the bases. The Club Car at the base of Mary Jane offers table service and a varied menu. You can eat your own 'sack' (packed) lunch at Moffat Market (at the base) and Mary Jane Market (at The Village).

SCHOOLS AND GUIDES ★★★★★

Varied reports

'Good choice of instructors' and 'need to limit class size' are recent comments on the school. Two new variations on standard classes in 2011/12 were 'Kids and Adults Max Four PM' Lessons – which have a relaxed start at 11.45 and a guaranteed maximum of four guests per instructor – and 'Adult Full Day Lessons' (for all levels) – group lessons that include a complimentary on-mountain lunch. There are also themed lessons such as bumps, women-only, telemark clinics and three-day steep and deep camps.

FOR FAMILIES ★★★★

Some of the best

Wee Willie's Child Care at the base area houses day-care facilities, taking kids from two months to six years, and is the meeting point for children's classes, which have their own areas.

STAYING THERE

Chalets Skiworld has a lovely log-cabin chalet with outdoor hot tub: 'The best we've ever stayed in – very spacious, Wi-Fi, bus stop outside,' says a visitor.

Hotels There are a couple of hotel/ condo complexes with restaurants and pools near, but not in, the new Village.

*****Iron Horse Resort** Outdoor pool and hot tubs, steam room.

*****Vintage Hotel** Linked by the car park bucket lift to The Village. 'Amazing value', 'comfortable and convenient' say reporters, but another comments that the bar closed at 9pm. Outdoor pool and tub.

Apartments The Zephyr Mountain Lodge, Fraser Crossing and Founders Pointe are swish places in The Village. There are a lot of comfortable condos in or on the way to town. Reader tips: Beaver Village, Sawmill Station, Red Quill, Meadowridge, Crestview Place.

EATING OUT ★★

A real weakness

There isn't the range of places you get in most 'destination' resorts. For 'fine dining' you have to drive 13km to Devil's Thumb Ranch. Get hold of the giveaway Grand County menu guide. In town, reporters are keen on Deno's (seafood, steaks etc), New Hong Kong (Chinese), Gasthaus Eichler (German-influenced food), Carlos and Maria's (Tex-Mex), Fontenot's (seafood and Cajun), Hernando's (pizza/pasta) and Lime ('good Mexican food').

APRES-SKI ★

If you know where to go ...

At close of play, there's action in The Village at the Derailer Bar and Doc's Roadhouse ('great atmosphere'), and at the Club Car at the base of Mary Jane. The Cheeky Monk serves an 'amazing' selection of Belgian beers. Later on, Deno's and the Winter Park Pub in town are the main hot spots. Moffat Station micro brewery has good beer.

OFF THE SLOPES ★

Mainly the great outdoors

Reporters enjoy the floodlit tubing at Fraser – and a new tubing hill is to open at the base for 2012/13. There's also skating at the base area rink and snowmobiling to the Continental Divide. The Silverthorne factory outlet stores are 90 minutes away.

Utah

'The Greatest Snow on Earth' is Utah's marketing slogan. And it's not far from the truth: some Utah resorts do get huge amounts of snow – usually light, dry powder. If you like the steep and deep, you should at some point make the pilgrimage here. And if you like a beer or two après-ski, don't be put off by the image of a 'dry' Mormon state – getting alcohol has never been a problem (and the laws were greatly relaxed in 2009, anyway). But boarders beware: two of its top resorts don't allow snowboarding.

The biggest dumps fall at Alta (which bans boarding) and Snowbird. Their average of 500 inches of snow a year (twice as much as some Colorado resorts) has made them the powder capitals of the world. Park City, 45 minutes' drive away, is the main 'destination' resort of the area and a sensible holiday base; upmarket Deer Valley (which also bans boarding) is next door; and Canyons is only a short drive away. Although only a few miles from Snowbird/Alta as the crow flies, these resorts get 'only' 300 to 350 inches of snow. We have separate chapters on these five resorts.

Of course, you're not guaranteed fresh powder. Last season was a poor one, for example, with Alta and Snowbird getting less than 300 inches (but there was still plenty of good groomed and ungroomed skiing on our February 2012 visit). And the season before was a near-record, with over 700 inches. In 2008, we spent a week in Park City when it virtually never stopped snowing. Every day we had fresh, knee-high powder. We never made it to Alta or Snowbird: the access road to them was often closed by avalanche danger – but in any case the snow on the three local mountains was awesome.

Other resorts worth visiting (covered in the resort directory at the end of the book) include **Brighton** and **Solitude**, in the valley next to Alta/Snowbird and blessed with similar amounts of snow. The snow gets tracked out less quickly because the resorts attract far fewer experts. The main claim to fame of **Sundance** is that it's owned by Robert Redford; it averages 320 inches of snow. It was unknown **Snowbasin** (400 inches), well to the north, that hosted the Olympic downhill events in 2002. **Powder Mountain** (500 inches), a bit further north, is aptly named. As well as 2,700 acres of lift-served slopes there are 3,000 acres of guided snowcat skiing.

Until 2009 the sale and consumption of alcohol was tightly controlled in Utah, the Mormon state. Until then, to get a drink in bars and clubs you had to pay a fee to become a member or be the guest of a member. At some places you had to order food in order to get a drink. These rules have now been scrapped. There are still differences between bars and restaurants, but effectively you don't need to worry about them, and as long as you are over 21 (and have ID to prove it) you should have no problem getting alcoholic drinks between 10am and midnight or 1am. The amount of spirits allowed in a drink has been increased too.

TOURIST OFFICE

Ski Utah
www.skiutah.com

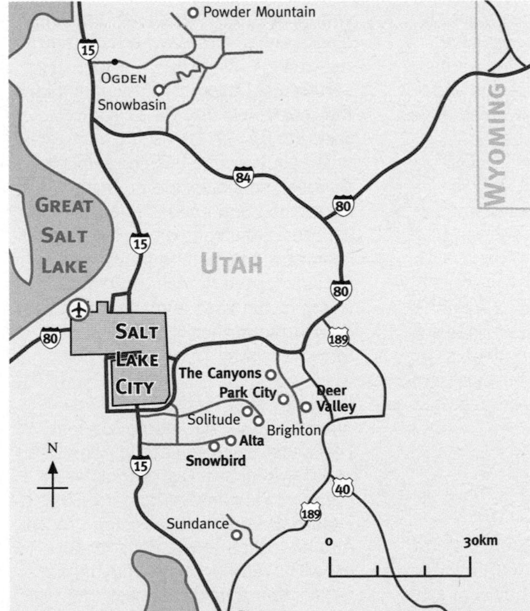

ALTA / SUNSPOT

Alta

Cult powder resort linked to Snowbird but with less brutal architecture and a friendlier, old-fashioned feel

TOP 10 RATINGS

Extent	***
Fast lifts	****
Queues	***
Snow	*****
Expert	*****
Intermediate	***
Beginner	***
Charm	**
Convenience	****
Scenery	***

RPI	150
lift pass	£300
ski hire	£190
lessons	£155
food & drink	£115
total	**£760**

NEWS

2012/13: There are plans for a new eco-friendly building at Wildcat Base, including ticket office, admin offices and toilets.

- + Phenomenal snow and steep terrain mean cult status among experts (there's great beginner terrain, too)
- + Linked to Snowbird, making it one of the largest ski areas in the US
- + Ski-almost-to-the-door convenience

- − 'Resort' is no more than a scattering of lodges, so not much après-ski atmosphere, and few off-slope diversions
- − Limited groomed runs for intermediates

Alta and Snowbird are the powder capitals of the world (the snow here is as plentiful, frequent and light as it comes), and add up to a great area for adventurous skiers (much less so for boarders, who are banned from Alta). Of the two, Alta is our preferred base – it has a friendlier, small-scale feel.

THE RESORT

Alta sits at the craggy head of Little Cottonwood Canyon, 2km beyond Snowbird and less than an hour's drive from downtown Salt Lake City. Both the resort and the approach road are prone to avalanches and closure: visitors can be confined indoors for safety.

Village charm Where once there was a bustling and bawdy mining town, there is now just a strung-out handful of lodges and parking areas.

Convenience Life revolves around the two separate lift base areas – Albion and Wildcat – linked by a bi-directional rope tow along the flat valley floor. There are about a dozen places to stay, all convenient for the lifts.

Scenery Alta is recognized for its impressively rugged scenery and challenging, sparsely wooded ridges.

ALTA SKI AREA

Alta's lightly-wooded slopes have long had cult status among local experts ↓

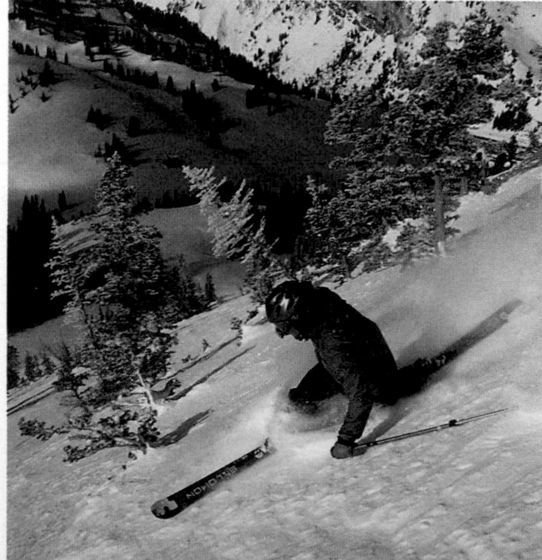

THE MOUNTAINS

Check out the separate chapter for the linked Snowbird slopes. Unlike most US resorts, Alta does not differentiate between single and double black diamond trails – regrettable, we think.

Slopes Most of Alta's slopes are lightly wooded. The dominant feature of the terrain is the steep end of a ridge that separates the area's two basins. To the left, above Albion Base, the slopes stretch away over easy green terrain towards the blue and black runs from Point Supreme and from the top of the Sugarloaf quad (also the access lift for Snowbird). To the right, above Wildcat Base, is a more concentrated bowl with blue runs down the middle and blacks either side, served by the fast two-stage Collins chair. The two sectors are linked at altitude, and by a flat rope tow along the valley floor.

Fast lifts Fast chairs depart from each base; another one links to Snowbird.

Queues The slopes are normally uncrowded and queues rare. But it is said to be difficult to board the Collins chair at the mid-station at times because of the number of people skiing to the base and boarding there.

Terrain parks There isn't one.

Snow reliability The quantity and quality of snow – an average 500 inches a year – and the northerly orientation put Alta in the top rank. Last season was unusually poor, with 'only' 390 inches. But 2010/11 was a near-record, with over 700 inches.

Experts Even before the Snowbird link Alta had cult status among local experts, who flocked to the high ridges after a fresh snowfall. There are dozens of steep slopes and chutes.

KEY FACTS

Resort	2600m 8,530ft
See Snowbird for Alta/Snowbird area	
Alta only	
Slopes	2600-3215m 8,530-10,550ft
Lifts	11
Pistes	2,200 acres
Green	25%
Blue	40%
Black	35%
Snowmaking	Some

UK PACKAGES

American Ski Classics, Momentum, Skitracer

Phone numbers
From distant parts of the US, add the prefix 1 801; from abroad, add the prefix +1 801

TOURIST OFFICE

www.alta.com

But finding the best spots is tricky without local guidance and quite a lot of traversing is involved.
Intermediates There isn't a lot of groomed terrain (more in Snowbird). But adventurous intermediates happy to try ungroomed slopes and learn to love powder can have a good time.
Beginners Albion has a nursery area and gentle lower slopes, with a beginner lift pass covering three lifts. But it's hard to recommend such a narrowly focused resort to beginners.
Snowboarding Boarding is banned, but it's allowed in Snowbird, and guided snowcat boarding is available nearby.
Cross-country 5km of groomed track.
Mountain restaurants There's one in each sector. Watson Shelter on the Wildcat side is light and airy with big windows, self- and table-service sections and a small coffee bar; we enjoyed the table-service Collins Grill here – they supply slippers and have an unusual menu (eg creole soup, snails and prawns en croûte, as well as more standard fare). Alf's on the Albion side is a standard self-service. Or you can head back to base.
Schools and guides The ski school specializes in powder lessons – though there are regular classes, too.
Families Day care for children from six weeks to nine years is available at the Children's Center at Albion Base.

STAYING THERE

None of the hotels is luxurious in US terms, but most fill up with repeat visitors and, unusually for the US, offer half-board (ie dinner included).
Hotels We enjoyed our 2012 stay at the venerable Alta Lodge (742 3500): comfortable rooms, an atmospheric bar. It has developed a cult following by operating a bit like a catered chalet, serving dinner at shared or private tables. Saunas, indoor hot tubs. Rustler Lodge (742 2200) is more luxurious, with a big outdoor pool, but impersonal. The comfortable, modern and conveniently located Goldminer's Daughter (742 2300) and the basic Peruvian Lodge (742 3000) are cheaper. The Snowpine Lodge (742 2000) was the first lodge to be built in the Canyon (in 1938), is convenient and has a sauna and outdoor hot tub.
Eating out It is possible, but eating in is the normal routine.
Après-ski This rarely goes beyond a few drinks in one of the hotel bars. The Goldminer's Daughter Saloon is the main après-ski bar for day visitors; the upstairs lounge has sofas, an open fire and huge floor-to-ceiling windows.
Off the slopes There are few options other than snowshoeing, the Cliff Lodge spa down the road at Snowbird or a sightseeing trip to Salt Lake City.

CANYONS / HUGHES MARTIN

Canyons

One of the five biggest ski areas in the US, with a small purpose-built resort at the base of the slopes on the edge of Park City

TOP 10 RATINGS	
Extent	***
Fast lifts	***
Queues	****
Snow	****
Expert	****
Intermediate	****
Beginner	**
Charm	**
Convenience	****
Scenery	***

RPI	160
lift pass	£320
ski hire	£190
lessons	£175
food & drink	£115
total	**£800**

NEWS

2011/12: $1 million was invested in improving the snowmaking, which more than doubled. Zipline tours were introduced at mid-mountain. A new children's activity area opened, including ice forts and ice bowling. Bistro at Canyons in the Silverado Lodge opened, serving kosher food.

- + Relatively extensive area of slopes
- + Modern lift system with few queues
- + Easy access to Park City and Deer Valley ski areas
- + Can stay at the base, but ...

- − Village is limited
- − Snow on the many south-facing slopes is affected by sun
- − Many runs are short
- − Few green runs

Canyons has the potential to become the most extensive ski area in the US (and already claims it is among the five biggest), with nine linked mountains. Anyone having a holiday in adjacent Park City should plan to visit.

THE RESORT

Canyons has been transformed over the past decade or so. The area of the slopes has more than doubled, and a small car-free village built at the base.
Village charm The village has lodgings and a few shops, restaurants and bars. But it doesn't add up to much – you can stroll round it in 10 minutes or so.
Convenience Staying at the base is convenient for Canyons ski area. There are buses from the base of the access lift direct to Park City and its ski area; Deer Valley requires one change.
Scenery A series of broad, long ridges are separated by valleys and most of the area is fairly densely wooded.

THE MOUNTAINS

Canyons gets its name from the valleys between the nine mountains that make up the ski area.

Free daily mountain tours start at 10.30, and a First Tracks programme runs three times a week; former Olympic medallists guide you around the slopes before they officially open.
Slopes Red Pine Lodge, at the heart of the slopes, is reached by an eight-seat gondola from the village. A fast quad reaches a higher point. From the top of both lifts you can move in either direction across a series of ridges and valleys. Runs come off both sides of each ridge and generally face north or south. Most runs are quite short (less than 500m vertical), with some long, quite flat run-outs. If you return to the resort from the Sun Lodge area, you need to take a rope tow, which some people find awkward.
Fast lifts The core of the lift system either side of Red Pine Lodge consists of fast quads, but the Dream Peak sector has no fast lifts.
Queues We found no queues on our February 2012 visit.
Terrain parks A new terrain park for all abilities, served by the Saddleback chair, was built in 2011; it's a mile long and includes 50 features and nine

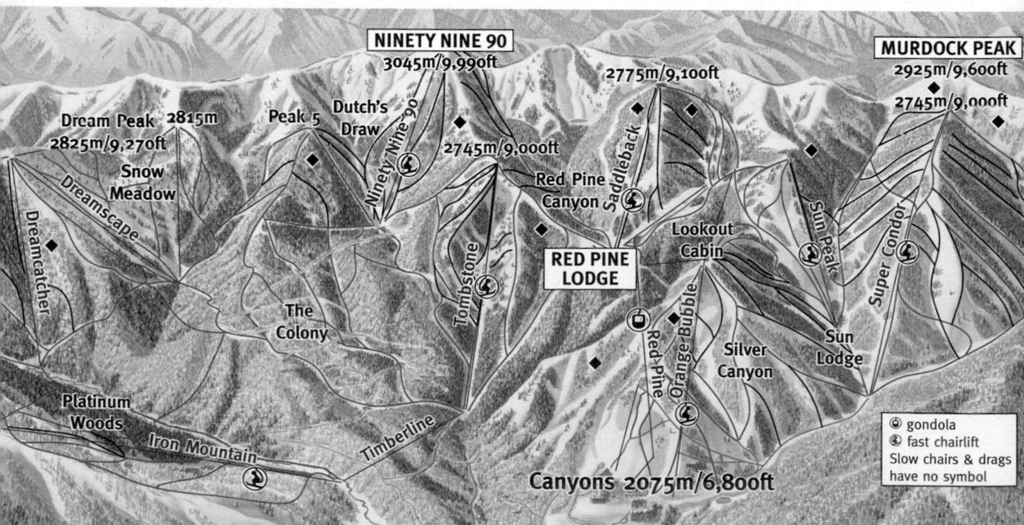

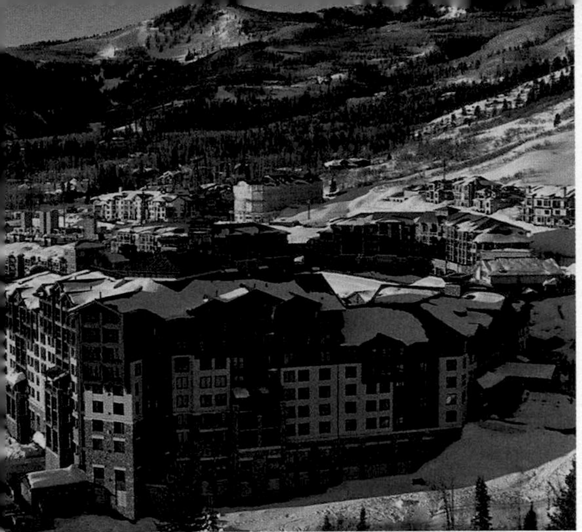

↑ The small resort at the foot of the slopes has been built in the last decade or so

CANYONS RESORT / MIKE STONER

KEY FACTS

Resort	2075m
	6,800ft
Slopes	2075-3045m
	6,800-9,990ft
Lifts	19
Pistes	4,000 acres
Green	10%
Blue	44%
Black	46%
Snowmaking	6%

UK PACKAGES

AmeriCan Ski, American Ski Classics, Independent Ski Links, Ski Safari, Skitracer

Central reservations
Call 1 866 604 4171 (toll-free from within the US)

Phone numbers
From distant parts of the US, add the prefix 1 435; from abroad, add the prefix +1 435

TOURIST OFFICE

www.canyonsresort.com

jumps. There are six natural half-pipes (marked on the trail map).

Snow reliability Snow here is not the best in Utah. It gets as much on average as Park City (350 inches) and more than Deer Valley. But the south-facing slopes suffer in late-season sun. Snowmaking doubled last season.

Experts There is steep terrain all over the mountain. We particularly liked the north-facing runs off Ninety Nine 90, with steep double black diamond runs plunging down through the trees. We had a great time here on our last visit, after fresh snow. A short hike from the top accesses some fine powder runs even days after a snowfall. There is also lots of double-diamond terrain on Murdock Peak (a 20-minute hike from the Super Condor lift). Runs off the Peak 5 chair are more sheltered. And there's heli-skiing too.

Intermediates There are groomed blue runs for intermediates on all the main sectors except Ninety Nine 90. Some are quite short, but you can switch from valley to valley for added interest. From the Super Condor and Tombstone fast chairs there are excellent double blue square runs. The Dreamscape area can be quiet, and is great for early experiments in off-piste powder. Getting back from here you ski through The Colony – an area of huge homes for the super-rich.

Beginners There are good areas with moving carpets up at Red Pine Lodge. But the run you progress to is rather short and gets very busy.

Snowboarding Except for the flat run-outs from many runs, it's a great area, with lots of natural hits. Canis Lupus is a mile-long natural half-pipe.

Cross-country None in resort. The Park City golf course has 20km and Soldier Hollow near Homestead Resort 26km.

Mountain restaurants Red Pine Lodge is a large, attractive building with a busy cafeteria, table-service restaurant and big deck. Reporters have found the Sun Lodge quieter. The smart table-service Lookout Cabin has wonderful views from huge windows, and we had excellent game stew there in 2012. Cloud Dine specializes in salads and sandwiches. The Dreamscape and Tombstone Grill snack huts offer simple food outdoors. People can bring their own lunch into any of the self-service places.

Schools and guides No recent reports; but as well as the usual classes, there are special clinics. Children's classes are for ages four to 14.

Families There's day care in the Grand Summit Hotel for children from six weeks to six years, and at the school for ages two and three years.

STAYING THERE

Hotels The Waldorf Astoria is the best, set below the village and served (till 5.30pm) by its own gondola. We stayed at the Grand Summit in 2012, but our standard King room was disappointing – small, no chair, no glasses in room or bathroom. Silverado Lodge is the other main hotel. All have pools and hot tubs.

Apartments The Hyatt Escala Lodge (with pool and hot tubs) and Westgate Resort and Spa are pricey and luxurious. Of the cheaper places Timberwolf condos have been praised; other options include Bear Hollow, Hidden Creek, Red Pine and Sundial.

Eating out We had a great meal at The Farm (excellent fillet steak and buffalo osso bucco) – the best place in town. Red Tail Grill does Tex-Mex, Bistro offers 'modern American' kosher food, and the tiny Alpine House serves a tapas menu and has an impressive wine list. Red Pine Lodge at the top of the gondola does a BBQ on Saturdays, with a C&W band and dancing.

Après-ski It's generally pretty quiet. The Umbrella Bar is the main focus as the lifts close.

Off the slopes There's a great zipline tour that we enjoyed (two short training wires followed by a minute-long whizz above a deep canyon), snowshoeing, snowmobiling, dog sledding, and a factory outlet mall and Salt Lake City and Park City nearby.

DEER VALLEY RESORT

Deer Valley

Top of the Ivy League of US ski resorts: it promises, and delivers, the best ski and gastronomic experience – we love it

TOP 10 RATINGS

Extent	**
Fast lifts	****
Queues	****
Snow	****
Expert	***
Intermediate	****
Beginner	****
Charm	***
Convenience	****
Scenery	***

RPI 165

lift pass	£320
ski hire	£190
lessons	£210
food & drink	£120
total	**£840**

NEWS

2012/13: A high-speed quad called Mountaineer Express is planned to replace the slow Deer Crest chair on Little Baldy Peak. The deck paving at Empire Canyon Lodge will be heated.

2011/12: Four moving carpets were installed in the beginner areas.

KEY FACTS

Resort	2195m 7,200ft
Slopes	2000-2915m 6,570-9,570ft
Lifts	21
Pistes	2,026 acres
Green	24%
Blue	43%
Black	33%
Snowmaking	33%

UK PACKAGES

AmeriCan Ski, Momentum, Oxford Ski Co, Ski Independence, Ski Safari, Skitracer

+ Immaculate piste grooming, good snow record and lots of snow-guns
+ Good tree skiing
+ Brilliant free black-diamond tours
+ Many fast lifts and no queues
+ Good restaurants and lodgings

− Relatively expensive
− Small area of slopes
− Mostly short runs of less than 400m vertical
− Quiet at night, though Park City is right next door

Deer Valley prides itself on pampering its guests, with valets to unload your skis, gourmet dining, immaculately groomed slopes, limited numbers on the mountain – and no snowboarding. Park City ski area is right next door – nothing more than a fence separates the two – and any skier visiting the area should try both. For most people, Park City town is the obvious base; but there are some seductive hotels here at mid-mountain Silver Lake.

THE RESORT

Just a mile from the end of Park City's Main Street, Deer Valley is overtly upmarket – famed for the care and attention lavished on the slopes and the guests. But it is unpretentious.

Village charm The Silver Lake area is something of a mid-mountain focus.

Convenience Most lodgings are right on the slopes.

Scenery From Bald Mountain there are extensive views to Park City and the Jordanelle reservoir. And the views of the reservoir on the run down to the Jordanelle gondola are spectacular.

THE MOUNTAINS

The slopes are varied and interesting. Deer Valley's reputation for immaculate grooming is justified, but there is also a lot of exciting tree skiing – and some steep bump runs, too. There are free mountain tours for different standards. We have been on two three-hour black-diamond tours, and they were both brilliant, taking us through fresh powder in the trees that we would never have found on our own. Reporters praise these tours, too.

Slopes Two chairs take you up Bald Eagle Mountain, just beyond which is the mid-mountain focus of Silver Lake Lodge. You can ski from here to the isolated Little Baldy Peak, served by a gondola and a new fast quad chairlift, with mainly easy runs to serve property developments there (though a local loves skiing these first thing because they are immaculately groomed and deserted with great views). But the main skiing is on three linked peaks beyond Silver Lake Lodge – Bald Mountain, Flagstaff Mountain and Empire Canyon. The top of Empire is just a few metres from the runs of the Park City ski area but crossing the fence that divides the two is banned.

Fast lifts Fast quads rule; the three main peaks have nine.

Queues Waiting in lift lines is not something that Deer Valley wants its guests to experience, so it limits the number of lift tickets sold. But it has built four lifts ending at the same place at the top of Flagstaff – resulting in hordes of people trying to go in different directions (insane – and not what you'd expect in Deer Valley).

Terrain parks There isn't one.

Snow reliability Excellent, and there's plenty of snowmaking too.

Experts Despite the image of pampered luxury there is excellent expert terrain on all three main mountains, including fabulous glades, bumps, chutes and bowls. And the snow doesn't get skied out quickly. The Ski Utah Interconnect Tour to Alta starts here (see the Park City chapter).

Intermediates There are lots of superbly groomed blue runs.

Beginners There are nursery slopes at Silver Lake Lodge as well as the base, and gentle green runs to progress to.

Snowboarding Boarding is banned.

Cross-country There are 20km of trails on the Park City golf course and 26km at Soldier Hollow near Homestead Resort plus lots of backcountry scope.

Mountain restaurants The best in Utah, with attractive wood-and-glass self-

↑ Deer Valley is famous for its immaculate grooming; but there's plenty of great ungroomed terrain and bumps too

DEER VALLEY

Central reservations
Call 645 6538

Phone numbers
From distant parts of the US, add 1 435; from abroad, add the prefix +1 435

TOURIST OFFICE

www.deervalley.com

service places at Silver Lake (we had delicious lamb stew and turkey chilli), Empire Canyon and the base lodge. You can eat your own packed lunches at all three. For table-service try the Stein Eriksen Lodge, Goldener Hirsch or Royal Street Cafe at Silver Lake.

Schools and guides The ski school is doubtless excellent; book in advance.

Families The Children's Center accepts children from two months to 12 years.

STAYING THERE

A car is useful for visiting other nearby Utah resorts, though Deer Valley, Park City and Canyons are all linked by efficient shuttle-buses.

Hotels The St Regis Resort, Montage Deer Valley, Stein Eriksen Lodge and Goldener Hirsch are some of the plushest hotels in any ski resort.

Apartments There are many luxury apartments and houses to rent. Reader tips include Ridgepoint, Royal Plaza and The Woods at Silver Lake – and Aspenwood and Boulder Creek at Snow Park (cheaper).

Eating out Of the gourmet restaurants, Mariposa is the best. We enjoyed the all-you-can-eat Seafood Buffet (it's not just seafood) and a 'Fireside Dining' evening at Empire Canyon Lodge: four courses, each one served at a different fireplace. It's held four nights a week.

Après-ski Edgar's Beers & Spirits Lounge at the base area is the main après-ski venue, with live music at weekends. For more choice, it's not far to Main Street in Park City.

Off the slopes Park City has lots of shops and galleries etc. Salt Lake City has concerts, sights and shopping. Balloon rides, snowmobiling and snowshoeing are popular.

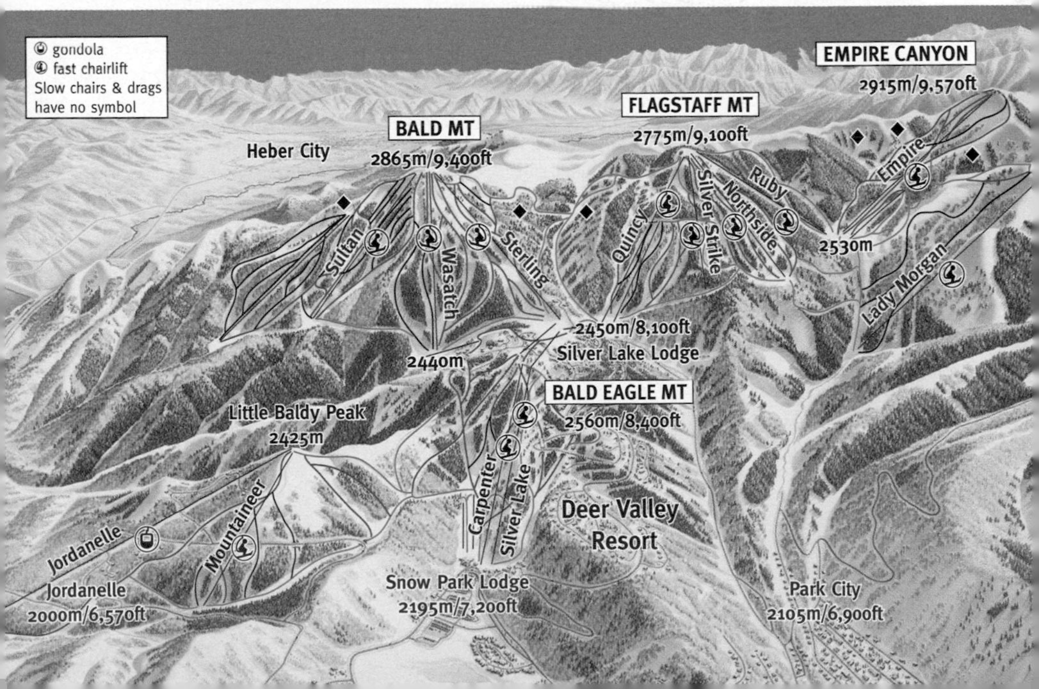

SNOWPIX.COM / CHRIS GILL

Park City

Stay near the cute and lively old Main Street and visit the three local mountains plus some further afield for a varied holiday

RATINGS

The mountains	
Extent	***
Fast lifts	***
Queues	****
Terrain p'ks	*****
Snow	****
Expert	****
Intermediate	****
Beginner	****
Boarder	****
X-country	***
Restaurants	**
Schools	****
Families	**
The resort	
Charm	***
Convenience	**
Scenery	***
Eating out	*****
Après-ski	***
Off-slope	***

RPI	160
lift pass	£320
ski hire	£190
lessons	£180
food & drink	£115
total	**£805**

NEWS

2012/13: There are plans to upgrade the capacity and energy efficiency of the snow-guns.

2011/12: At Resort Base a triple chair replaced the Three Kings double that serves the terrain park and super-pipe. A new beginner area was also built here, served by two moving carpets. Three-day 'I Ride Park City' freestyle camps were introduced for youngsters aged nine to 15. A two-person zipline was also installed.

- + Entertaining, historic Main Street, convenient for the slopes
- + Lots of bars and restaurants make nonsense of Utah's Mormon image
- + Easy to visit several resorts; and three are right in town

- − Town is an enormous, charmless sprawl, with most lodgings a drive from Main Street and the slopes
- − Runs tend to be rather short, with limited vertical
- − Still too many slow chairlifts

Staying in Park City has clear attractions, particularly if you are based near the centre to make the most of lively Main Street. It makes an excellent base for touring all of Utah's main resorts.

The Park City Mountain Resort ski area (covered in this chapter) is just one of three local ski areas covered by the Three Resort Pass (available through some UK tour operators but not locally – buy before you go) and easily reached by frequent and free buses. The other two are Deer Valley ski area (separated from the Park City slopes only by a fence between two pistes, and by separate ownership with different objectives – all very strange, to European eyes) and Canyons, which is a little further away. Then there are the famously powdery resorts of Snowbird and Alta, less than an hour away; you need a separate lift pass for them. These four resorts each have their own chapter.

THE RESORT

Park City is about 45 minutes by road from Salt Lake City. It was a silver-mining boom town, and at the turn of the 19th century it boasted a population of 10,000, a red-light area, a Chinese quarter and 27 saloons.

VILLAGE CHARM ***
A colourful past

Careful restoration has left the town with a splendid historic centrepiece in Main Street, now lined by a colourful selection of bars, restaurants, galleries and shops, many quite smart, but there are touristy souvenir places too. New buildings have been tastefully designed to blend in smoothly. But most lodging is in the sprawling and characterless suburbs, a drive or bus ride from Main Street. Traffic levels can be bad, especially at weekends.

CONVENIENCE **
Depends on your base

The slow Town chairlift goes up to the slopes from Main Street, but the main lifts are on the fringes at Resort Base; there are lodgings out there but most are a bus ride away.

Deer Valley, Canyons and Park City are linked by free shuttle-buses that reporters praise, which also go around

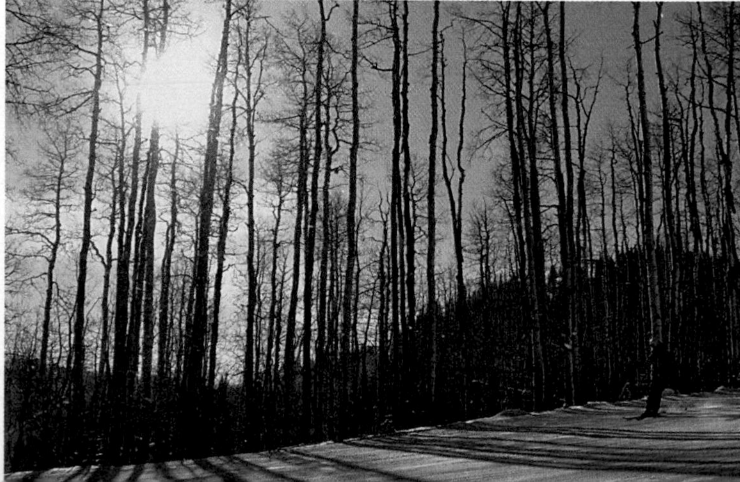

PARK CITY MOUNTAIN RESORT

Most of the easy trails run along ridges or in the valley bottoms →

KEY FACTS	
Resort	2105m 6,900ft
Slopes	2105-3050m 6,900-10,000ft
Lifts	16
Pistes	3,300 acres
Green	17%
Blue	52%
Black	31%
Snowmaking	15%

UK PACKAGES

Alpine Answers, AmeriCan Ski, American Ski Classics, Crystal, Crystal Finest, Independent Ski Links, Momentum, PowderBeds, Ski Independence, Ski Line, Ski Safari, Ski Solutions, Skitracer, Skiworld, Thomson, Virgin Snow

town and run until fairly late, but we found it a pain waiting for buses in the evenings on our recent visits. A car is useful (especially for visiting ski areas outside Park City).

If you're not hiring a car, pick a location that's handy for Main Street and the Town chair or the free bus.

SCENERY ★★★

Gently undulating ridges

In contrast to Park City's sprawling mass, the rounded mountain ridges have a modest and gentle presence.

THE MOUNTAIN

Park City Mountain Resort consists mostly of blue and black trails cut through the trees, with easier runs running along the ridges and the valleys between. The more interesting terrain is in the lightly wooded bowls and ridges at the top. The trail map marks several black 'Signature Runs' that are groomed every night ('A great blast first thing,' says a 2012 reporter) – and a few 'Adventure Alley' blue runs among the trees ('great fun').

Reporters have enjoyed the free mountain history tours of the slopes that look at the area's silver mining heritage and take place at 1.30. There are also free intermediate and advanced tours of the slopes at 10am. A long intermediate run, a beginner run and the Three Kings terrain park are floodlit for night skiing till 9pm.

It is much cheaper to buy lift passes in advance than on the spot. Signposting is clear.

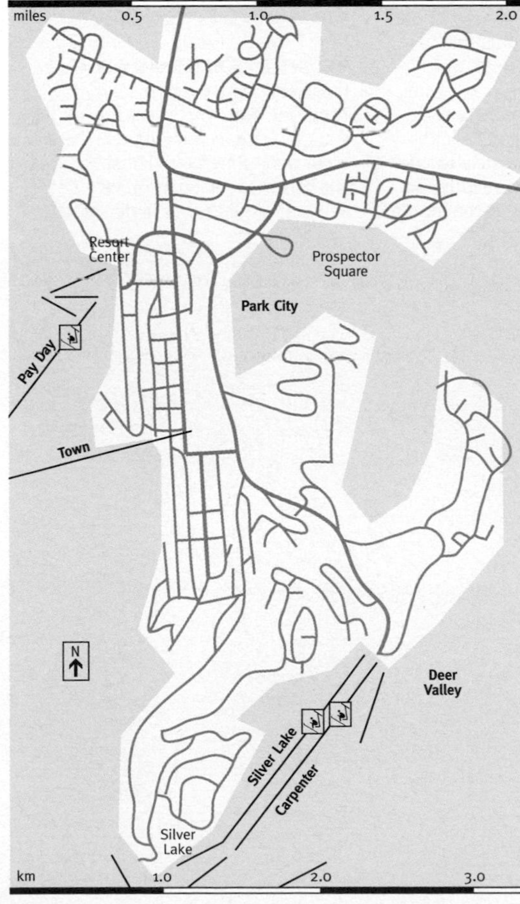

EXTENT OF THE SLOPES ★★★

Bowls above the woods

The ski area is bigger than Deer Valley but smaller than Canyons. Most of the easy and intermediate runs lie between Summit House and the base area, and are spread along the sides of a series of interconnecting ridges. Virtually all the steep terrain is above Summit House in a series of ungroomed bowls, and accessed by the McConkey's six-pack and the old, slow Jupiter double chair.

FAST LIFTS ★★★

Not up to usual US standards

Two fast chairlifts whisk you up from Resort Base and others beyond take you to Summit House. But there are still too many slow lifts serving the upper mountain and some of the best steep slopes.

QUEUES ★★★★

Peak period crowds

It can get pretty crowded (on some trails as well as the lifts) at weekends and in high season. You can pay extra for a Fast Tracks pass to jump queues on six main lifts.

TERRAIN PARKS ★★★★★

Among the best in the world

There are three terrain parks here to suit all levels. The vast number of kickers, rails and pipes are maintained daily, and rank among the best in the world. See www.pcride.com. The Ridge is a great entry-level park, Three Kings is for all abilities and floodlit for night riding till 9pm, and King's Crown is the park for pros, with the biggest jumps and features. The Eagle super-pipe was used for the 2002 Winter Olympics and today is consistently one of the best pipes in the world.

LIFT PASSES

Prices in US$

Age	1-day	6-day
under 13	60	312
13 to 64	96	528
65 plus	64	336

Free under 7

Beginner half-day 'Never Ever' lesson includes First Time lift

Notes
Includes ski-bus; day passes are window rates; 6-day prices are advance-purchase prices; additional discounts if purchased in advance with lodging

Alternative passes
Three Resort (Park City, Canyons, Deer Valley) International Pass available only to international visitors and in advance of holiday departure

Intermediate level kids aged nine to 15 can join three-day 'I Ride Park City' freestyle camps to learn park and all-mountain skills.

SNOW RELIABILITY ★★★★
Not quite the greatest on Earth

Utah is famous for the quality and quantity of its snow. Park City's record doesn't match those of Snowbird and Alta, but an annual average of 360 inches is still impressive, and ahead of most Colorado figures. Snowmaking covers about 15% of the terrain.

FOR EXPERTS ★★★★
Lots of variety

There is a lot of excellent advanced and expert terrain at the top of the lift system. It is all marked as double diamond on the trail map, but there are many runs that deserve only a single-diamond rating.

McConkey's Bowl is served by a six-pack and offers a range of open pitches and gladed terrain; we've had some great runs here on each of our visits. The slow, old Jupiter lift accesses the highest bowls, which include some serious terrain – with narrow couloirs, cliffs and cornices – as well as easier wide-open slopes. We had some enjoyable runs through fresh snow in lightly wooded terrain by heading to the right at the top of the lift, then skiing down without hiking. But if you are prepared to hike, you can find fresh powder most of the time – turn left for West Face, Pioneer Ridge and Puma Bowl, right for Scott's Bowl and the vast expanse of Pinecone Ridge, stretching for miles down the side of Thaynes Canyon.

Lower down, the side of Summit House ridge, serviced by the slow Thaynes and Motherlode chairs, has some little-used black runs, plus a few satisfying trails in the trees. There's a zone of steep runs towards town from further round the ridge. And don't miss Blueslip Bowl near Summit House – so called because in the past when it was out of bounds, ski company employees caught skiing it were fired, and given their notice on a blue slip.

Skiers (no snowboarders, due to some long flat run-outs) should consider doing the Ski Utah Interconnect Tour – see the feature panel opposite. Park City Powder Cats offers snowcat skiing and Wasatch Powderbird Guides heli-skiing.

FOR INTERMEDIATES ★★★★
OK for a day or two

There are blue runs served by all the main lifts, apart from Jupiter. The areas around the King Con high-speed quad and Silverlode six-pack have a dense network of great (but fairly short)

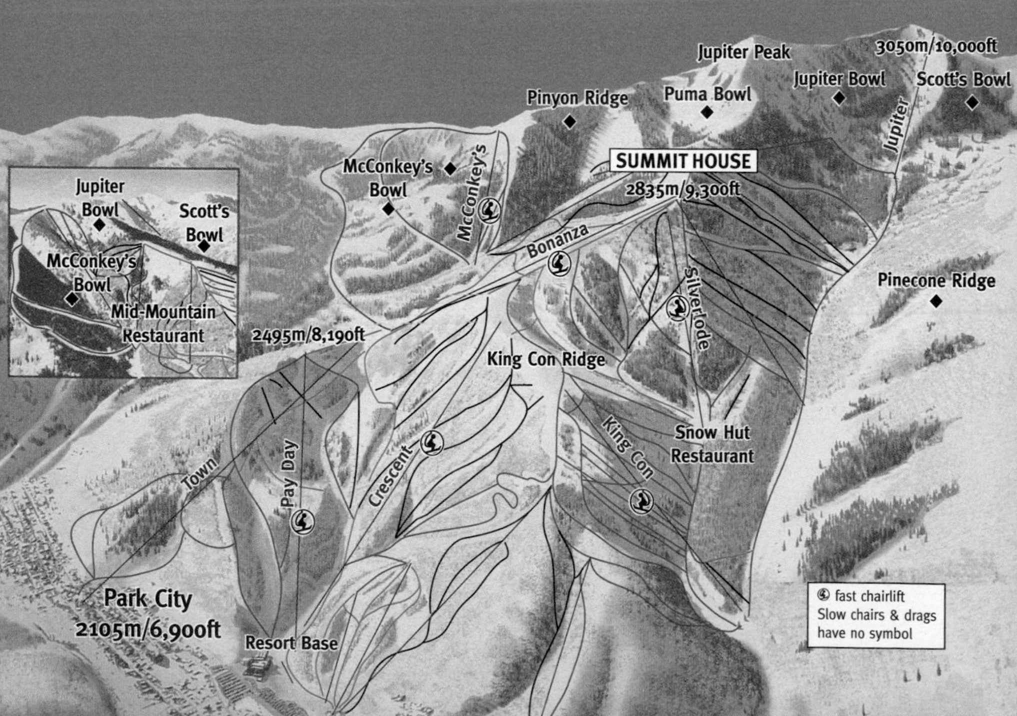

SCHOOLS

Park City
t 1 800 227 2754

Classes
1 3hr lesson $99

Private lessons
From $130 for 1hr

CHILDCARE

Signature Programs
(run by ski school)
t 1 800 227 2754
Ages 3½ to 5

Guardian Angel
Babysitting service

Ski Town Sitters
Babysitter finder service

Ski school
Ages 6 to 14, 9am-3pm, $220 per day including lunch

GETTING THERE

Air Salt Lake City 55km/35 miles (1hr)

cruising runs. There are also more difficult trails close by, for those looking for a challenge. The 'Signature Runs' and 'Adventure Alleys' (see first para under 'The Mountain' above) are good ideas and worth trying.

But there are few long, fast cruising runs – most trails are around 1–2km, and many have long, flat run-outs. The Pioneer and McConkey's chairlifts are off the main drag and serve some very pleasant, often quiet runs. The runs under the Town lift have great views of the town. Mileage-hungry intermediates should explore other nearby resorts, too.

FOR BEGINNERS ★★★★

A good chance for fast progress

The 'Never Ever' deal offers first-timers a half-day taster lesson including a lift pass and equipment rental. In the new beginner area, novices will start on moving carpets; classes graduate up the hill quite quickly, and there's a good, gentle and wide 'easiest way down' – the three-and-a-half-mile Home Run – all the way from Summit House. It's easy enough for most to manage after only a few lessons. The Town chair can be ridden down.

FOR BOARDERS ★★★★

Plenty of scope

It was not until 1996, when Park City won its Olympic bid, that the resort lifted its ban on snowboarding. Since then it has steamrollered ahead to attract boards by building some of the best terrain parks in the world. And there's some great ungroomed terrain as well: the higher bowls offer treelined powder runs and great kicker-building spots. Beginners will have no trouble on the lower slopes.

FOR CROSS-COUNTRY ★★★

Some trails; lots of backcountry

There are prepared trails on the Park City golf course (20km), next to the downhill area, and at Soldier Hollow near Homestead Resort (25km), just out of town. There is lots of scope for backcountry trips.

MOUNTAIN RESTAURANTS ★★

Standard self-service stuff

The Mid-Mountain Lodge is a picturesque 19th-century mine building that was heaved up the mountain to its present location near the bottom of Pioneer chair. The food is standard self-service fare, but most reporters prefer it to the alternatives. The Summit House has chilli, pizza, soup and good views from a big deck; Snow Hut is a log building that often has an outdoor grill; Viking Yurt is a coffee house in a tent halfway down the Bonanza chairlift. There are more options down at Resort Base.

SCHOOLS AND GUIDES ★★★★

Good past reports

We lack recent reports, but past reviews have been very positive.

FOR FAMILIES ★★

Well organized

There are a number of licensed carers. The ski school takes children from age three and a half. Book in advance.

THE SKI UTAH INTERCONNECT TOUR

Good skiers prepared to do some hiking should consider this excellent guided backcountry tour that runs four days a week from Deer Valley to Snowbird. (Three days a week it runs from Snowbird, but only as far as Solitude.) When we did it (a few years back, starting from Park City) we got fresh tracks in knee-deep powder practically all day. After a warm-up run to weed out weak skiers, we went up the top chair, through a 'closed' gate in the area boundary and skied down a deserted, prettily wooded valley to Solitude. After taking the lifts to the top of Solitude we did a short traverse/walk, then down more virgin powder towards Brighton. After more powder runs and lunch back in Solitude, it was up the lifts and a 30-minute hike up the Highway to Heaven to north-facing, treelined slopes and a great little gully down into Alta. How much of Alta and Snowbird you get to ski depends on how much time is left. The price ($295) includes two guides, lunch, lift tickets and transport home.

SNOWPIX.COM / CHRIS GILL

↑ Historic Main Street is the focal point and a pleasant place to wander round, even in bad weather

PARK CITY CHAMBER & VISITORS BUREAU / TYLER GOURLEY

ACTIVITIES

Indoor Silver Mountain Sports Club and Spa (pools, hot tubs, sauna, steam room, gym); other fitness clubs, spa treatments, bowling, museum, galleries

Outdoor Ice skating, snowmobiles, sleigh rides, hot-air ballooning, dog sledding, tubing, snowshoeing, winter fly fishing, zipline, alpine coaster

Phone numbers
From distant parts of the US, add the prefix 1 435; from abroad, add the prefix +1 435

TOURIST OFFICE

www.parkcitymountain.com
www.visitparkcity.com

STAYING THERE

We prefer to stay near Main Street and its bars and restaurants, but most accommodation is in the sprawling suburbs. These, such as Kimball Junction, are relatively cheap (but soulless) and convenient if you have a car and want to try different resorts.

Hotels There's a wide variety, from typical chains to individual little B&Bs.

*****Park City** (200 2000) Swanky all-suite place on outskirts. Pool, sauna, hot tub.

****Silver King** (649 5500) De luxe hotel/condo complex at base of the slopes, with indoor-outdoor pool.

****Washington School House** (649 3800) Historic old inn, recently renovated, in a great location near Main Street.

***Best Western Landmark Inn** (649 7300) At Kimball Junction. Pool.

***Park City Peaks** (649 5000) 'Large, dated rooms, great value, friendly staff, good breakfast', indoor-outdoor pool and 'outdoor hot tub you could boil a lobster in', but out of town. We stayed here and thought it adequate.

***Yarrow** (649 7000) Adequate charmless base, a 15-minute walk from Main Street. Pool, hot tub.

Apartments There's a big range. The Town Lift condos near Main Street and Park Avenue condos are both modern and comfortable, the latter with a pool and hot tubs. Silver Cliff Village is adjacent to the slopes and has spacious units and access to the facilities of the Silver King Hotel. Other ski-in/ski-out recommendations from reporters are Silver Star and Snow Flower. Blue Church Lodge is a well-converted 19th-century Mormon church with luxury condos and rooms.

EATING OUT ★★★★★
Lots of choice

There are over 100 restaurants. Our favourites are Wahso (Asian fusion; excellent food but slow service on our 2012 visit), 350 Main (new American) and Riverhorse (in a grand, high-ceilinged first-floor room with live music). Zoom is the old Union Pacific train depot, now a trendy restaurant owned by Robert Redford (past reports have been mixed though). Chez Betty (American/French) is small with excellent food – expensive though.

For more basic food we like atmospheric No Name Saloon and enjoyed their signature buffalo burgers and draft beers on our 2012 visit. Squatters is a good micro brewery a bit out of town. Other reporter tips include Fuego Bistro & Pizzeria, Cisero's and Grappa (Italian), Chimayo (South-western), Bangkok Thai, Wasatch Brew Pub (for steaks), Bandit's Grill ('great cowboy food'), the Eating Establishment (fish), and Butcher's Chop House. See Deer Valley for other options.

APRES-SKI ★★★
Plenty around

As the slopes close, Legends is the place to head for at Resort Base. After that, go to Main Street. The Wasatch Brew Pub makes its own ale. O'Shuck's and No Name Saloon are lively, and there's usually live music and dancing at weekends. The Bar Boheme is newish (at the hip hotel Sky Lodge).

For clubs, try the Ten Pin at the bowling alley and Cisero's.

OFF THE SLOPES ★★★
Some things of interest

At the resort there's a roller coaster style toboggan ride on rails, tubing and a new zipline. Backcountry snowmobiling, balloon flights and trips to Nevada for gambling are popular. There is a bowling alley. You can learn to ski jump or try the Olympic bob track at the Olympic Park down the road – 'worth the effort'. Robert Redford's Sundance Film Festival is held each January. There are lots of shops and galleries. There's discount shopping at a factory outlet mall at Kimball Junction. Salt Lake City is easily reached and has some good concerts, shopping and Mormon heritage sites.

SNOWBIRD / DEREK SMITH

Snowbird

A powder-pig paradise linked to neighbouring Alta; with big concrete and glass base buildings that remind us of Flaine

TOP 10 RATINGS

Extent	***
Fast lifts	****
Queues	***
Snow	*****
Expert	*****
Intermediate	***
Beginner	**
Charm	*
Convenience	*****
Scenery	***

RPI	155
lift pass	£300
ski hire	£190
lessons	£195
food & drink	£115
total	**£800**

NEWS

2012/13: The Little Cloud double is due to be replaced by a high-speed quad.

2011/12: A new expert bowl, Zone 5, opened near the top of the Peruvian chair with some of the most challenging steeps around.

SNOWBIRD

Why they built a monstrosity like the Cliff Lodge at the foot of such wonderfully powdery slopes sure beats us ↓

- + Unrivalled quantity and quality of powder snow, combined with fabulous ungroomed slopes
- + Link to Alta makes it one of the largest ski areas in the US
- + Slopes-at-the-door convenience

- − Limited groomed intermediate runs – but more than at Alta
- − Tiny, claustrophobic resort 'village'
- − Stark concrete Bauhaus architecture
- − Very quiet at night

There can be few places where nature has combined the steep with the deep better than at Snowbird and next-door Alta. The resorts' combined area is one of the top powder-pig paradises in the world (at least for skiers – boarders are banned from Alta). So it is a shame that Snowbird's concrete, purpose-built 'base village' is so lacking in ski resort ambience.

THE RESORT

Snowbird lies 40km from Salt Lake City in Little Cottonwood Canyon – just before Alta. Both the resort and (particularly) the approach road are prone to avalanches and closure: visitors are sometimes confined indoors for safety.

Village charm The resort buildings are mainly block-like and lack any semblance of charm.

Convenience The resort area and the slopes are spread along the road on the south side of the narrow canyon. The focal Snowbird Center (lift base/ shops/restaurants) is towards the eastern, up canyon end. All lodgings are within walking distance, and most are ski-in/ski-out. There are shuttle-buses, with a service to Alta.

Scenery Snowbird's setting is rugged and rather Alpine. Hidden Peak's lofty heights give impressive views.

THE MOUNTAINS

Snowbird's link with Alta (see separate chapter) forms one of the largest ski areas in the US. The stats show Snowbird and Alta's ski areas to be of fairly similar size, but Snowbird's feels much bigger to us. There are free mountain tours at 9.30 and 10.30 each day. The nursery slopes are floodlit three evenings a week.

Slopes The north-facing slopes rear up from the edge of the resort. Six access lifts are ranged along the valley floor, the main ones being the 125-person cable car (the Aerial Tram) to Hidden Peak, the Peruvian Express quad and the Gadzoom fast quad. To the west, in Gad Valley, there are runs ranging from very tough to very easy. Mineral Basin, behind Hidden Peak, has 500 acres of terrain for all abilities, but can be badly affected by sun.

Fast lifts The key lifts are fast. Baldy Express, one of two fast quads in Mineral Basin, forms the link with Alta.

Queues The big problem has always been the cable car, with queues of up to an hour at times. But the Peruvian Express chair provides an alternative way to the top (via a long tunnel at the top with a moving carpet that leads to Mineral Basin and then the Mineral Basin Express chair).

Terrain parks There is one for all levels, containing rails, hits and a box.

Snow reliability Snowbird and Alta average 500 inches of snowfall a year – twice as much as some Colorado resorts and around 50% more than the nearby Park City area. Last season was an unusually poor one, with 'only' 380 inches. But two seasons ago they

KEY FACTS

Resort	2470m 8,100ft
For Snowbird and Alta combined area	
Slopes	2365-3350m 7,760-11,000ft
Lifts	24
Pistes	4,700 acres
Green	25%
Blue	37%
Black	38%
Snowmaking	12%
Snowbird only	
Slopes	2365-3350m 7,760-11,000ft
Lifts	13
Pistes	2,500 acres
Green	27%
Blue	38%
Black	35%
Snowmaking	21%

UK PACKAGES

Alpine Answers, AmeriCan Ski, American Ski Classics, Independent Ski Links, Momentum, Ski Independence, Ski Safari, Skitracer, Skiworld

Phone numbers
From distant parts of the US, add the prefix 1 801; from abroad, add the prefix +1 801

TOURIST OFFICE

www.snowbird.com

smashed all records with over 700 inches. There's snowmaking in busy areas too.

Experts The trail map is liberally sprinkled with double black diamonds, and some of the gullies off the Cirque ridge – Silver Fox and Great Scott, for example – are exceptionally steep and frequently neck-deep in powder. Lower down lurk the bump runs, including Mach Schnell – a great run straight down the fall line through trees. There is wonderful ski-anywhere terrain in the bowl beneath the high Little Cloud chair, and the Gad 2 lift opens up attractive tree runs (and is the best place to be in a white-out). Fantastic go-anywhere terrain under the High Baldy traverse is controlled by gates. Mineral Basin has more expert terrain. Backcountry tours and heli-skiing are also offered.

Intermediates The winding Chip's Run provides the only comfortable route from the top back to town. There's good cruising in Mineral Basin – take the narrow Path to Paradise traverse for a wide blue-black and head up the Baldy Express lift for the easiest cruises. For adventurous intermediates wanting to try powder skiing, the bowl below the Little Cloud lift is a must. There are some challenging runs through the trees off the Gad 2 lift. The groomed runs don't add up to a lot but there's more than in Alta.

Beginners There is a nursery slope next to Cliff Lodge and the Mountain Learning area part-way up the hill. And a special lift pass is available ($20). But progression to longer runs is not easy. Go and learn elsewhere.

Snowboarding Competent freeriders will have a wild time in Snowbird's powder, though there are some flat spots to beware of. And Alta bans boarders.

Cross-country No prepared trails (though there are in next-door Alta).

Mountain restaurants It's the Mid-Gad Lodge self-service or back to one of the bases – try the table-service Forklift and Rendezvous.

Schools and guides The school has a good reputation though we lack recent reports.

Families Camp Snowbird takes children aged 12 and under. The 'kids ski free' programme allows children (six and under) to ski for free with an adult ($15 a day in 2011/12 for the Tram). Baby Thunder is a gentle family area.

STAYING THERE

Hotels There are several lodges and smaller condo blocks. Cliff Lodge (a huge concrete building) and The Lodge at Snowbird are both convenient and have pools and hot tubs, but they lack charm – and we lack recent reports.

Eating out Cliff Lodge and Snowbird Center are the focal points, with various options, including the 'fine dining' Aerie in the Cliff Lodge.

Après-ski Après-ski is a bit muted. The Tram Club and El Chanate Cantina are lively as the slopes close, but don't expect them to be later on.

Off the slopes There's not much to do apart from snowshoeing, snowmobiling and visiting Salt Lake City and the spas in various lodges.

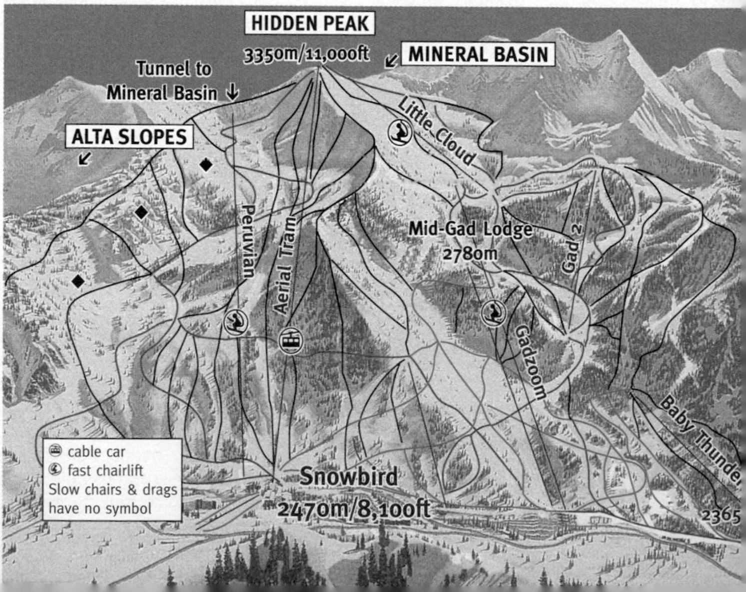

JACKSON HOLE / GORAN ASSNER

Rest of the West

This section contains detailed chapters on just two resorts – Jackson Hole in Wyoming and Big Sky in Montana. Below are notes on these and various other resorts in different parts of the great chain of mountains that stretches from Washington in the north to New Mexico in the south.

The resorts of Washington state and Oregon are covered in our resort directory at the end of this book. We visited Oregon a couple of seasons back; our exploration was hampered by poor early-season snow, but if you want to try somewhere largely undiscovered by fellow Brits, it is worth considering. The major resorts are **Mt Hood** (which has three separate areas of slopes: Mt Hood Meadows, Mt Hood Skibowl and Timberline) and **Mt Bachelor.** These get extended entries in the resort directory.

Sun Valley, Idaho, was America's first purpose-built resort, developed in the 1930s by the president of the Union Pacific Railway. It quickly became popular with the Hollywood movie set and has managed to retain its stylish image and ambience; it has one of our favourite luxury hotels. Also in Idaho is the USA's newest purpose-built resort – **Tamarack**, two hours north of Boise. The company developing the resort went bankrupt in 2009, but it has operated four days a week for the past couple of seasons, and season passes for 2012/13 were on sale when we went to press.

Jackson Hole in Wyoming is a resort with an impressive snow record and equally impressive steep slopes. Jackson town has a touristy Wild West cowboy atmosphere. Check out the separate chapter. A 90-minute drive from Jackson over the Teton pass (slower if you go by excursion bus) brings you to **Grand Targhee**, which gets even more snow. The slopes are usually blissfully empty, and are much easier than at Jackson. The main Fred's Mountain offers 1,500 acres and 610m vertical accessed from a central fast quad. One-third of smaller Peaked Mountain is accessed by a fast quad, while the rest – around 500 acres – is used for guided snowcat skiing.

About four hours north of Jackson, just inside Montana, is **Big Sky**, which has one of the biggest verticals in the US and together with neighbouring **Moonlight Basin**'s linked terrain is the biggest ski area in the US. When we visited, we were very impressed – particularly by the lack of crowds. Check out the Big Sky chapter. From Big Sky you might also visit **Bridger Bowl**, a 90-minute drive away. It boasts broad, steep, lightly wooded slopes that offer wonderful powder descents after a fresh snowfall.

A long way south of all these resorts, **Taos** in New Mexico is the most southerly major resort in America, and because of its isolated location it is largely unknown on the international market. There's a small chalet-style base village with a handful of lodges; the adobe town of Taos, home to many famous artists and writers over the years, is 30km down the road. There's some good terrain for all standards, but the ski area is best known for steep, challenging terrain, some of which you hike to.

UK PACKAGES

Sun Valley AmeriCan Ski
Grand Targhee Ski Safari
Taos AmeriCan Ski, American Ski Classics, Skiworld

WADE MCKOY / FPI

Jackson Hole after a snowfall is a dream come true for experts and adventurous intermediates ↓

Big Sky

America's biggest linked ski area, with extraordinarily quiet slopes; unappealing modern resort village, though

RATINGS

The mountains	
Extent	****
Fast lifts	**
Queues	*****
Terrain p'ks	****
Snow	*****
Expert	****
Intermediate	****
Beginner	*****
Boarder	****
X-country	****
Restaurants	*
Schools	****
Families	****
The resort	
Charm	**
Convenience	****
Scenery	***
Eating out	***
Après-ski	*
Off-slope	**

RPI	140
lift pass	£320
ski hire	£130
lessons	£180
food & drink	£90
total	**£720**

NEWS

2011/12: Five new trails opened on Andesite Mountain, accessed from the Ramcharger chair. New digital information signs on lift/run status were installed. A newly extended Solace Spa and Salon also opened.

- + Linked ski area bigger than Vail, with a big vertical by US standards
- + By far the quietest slopes you will find in a major resort, anywhere
- + Among the cheapest resorts in the US for food and drink
- + Excellent snow record
- + Some comfortable slope-side accommodation, but ...

- − Many condos are spread widely away from the lift base
- − Base area lacks charm, though things are improving, slowly
- − Resort amenities are limited, with little choice of nightlife
- − Tiny top lift accessing the most testing terrain is prone to queues
- − Remote location

Big Sky is renowned for its powder, steeps and big vertical. Since the resort buried the hatchet with next-door Moonlight Basin and agreed a joint lift pass, they have been able to boast the biggest linked ski area in the US.

They should also be boasting the world's least crowded slopes – we and our reporters have been astonished by the lack of people. Big Sky gets an average of 2,000 people on its slopes – that's about two acres each. We have no idea how they make this arrangement work financially. We're happy to take advantage of it while it lasts. But if ambling around in the evening soaking up the mountain village atmosphere is part of your holiday, forget it.

THE RESORT

Big Sky is set amid the wide open spaces of Montana, one hour from the airport town of Bozeman. The resort has been purpose-built at the foot of the slopes on Lone Mountain and Andesite Mountain. The main focus of development is Mountain Village, at the lift base. Bridger Bowl ski area is an easy day trip by car.

VILLAGE CHARM **

Some way to go

Mountain Village is a hotchpotch of buildings in different styles set vaguely around a traffic-free central plaza and bordered by car parks and service roads. There are a few hotels, a handful of bars and restaurants, a variety of shops and some slope-side condos. The French-style underground Mountain Mall has shops and access to many of the bars and restaurants and some of the lodging.

CONVENIENCE ****

Generally fine

There is quite a bit of lodging at or close to the lift base. Some outlying condos and houses are served by lifts to the slopes, but most rely on the 'comparatively poor' free bus services; a car is a better idea.

SCENERY ***

The lone ranger

Lone Mountain is Big Sky's signature peak, its distinctive summit rising over 1000m above the village and Andesite Mountain's wooded slopes. From the top, there are panoramic views of Montana and Yellowstone.

THE MOUNTAINS

Taking Big Sky and Moonlight Basin's slopes together, they cover a big area (5,512 acres), with long runs for all abilities. There are free mountain tours at both Big Sky and Moonlight. Despite the marketing hype about the linked area, for many people it makes sense to decide which area to ski when, and buy tickets accordingly, rather than buy a joint pass for the duration of your stay. The piste maps are separate. A 2011 visitor complained of 'the general lack of decent piste markings'.

EXTENT OF THE SLOPES ****

The most extensive in the US

Lone Mountain provides the resort's poster shot, with some seriously steep, open upper slopes. From Mountain Village a fast quad goes to mid-mountain. From there you can get to the Lone Peak triple chair, which

The Mountain Village doesn't amount to much more than what you see here, photographed from lower Andesite →

TANYA BOOTH

KEY FACTS

Resort	2285m 7,500ft
Big Sky only	
Slopes	2070-3400m 6,800-11,160ft
Lifts	21
Pistes	3,832 acres
Green	14%
Blue	26%
Black	60%
Snowmaking	10%
Big Sky and Moonlight Basin combined	
Slopes	2070-3400m 6,800-11,160ft
Lifts	28
Pistes	5,512 acres

takes you up to the Lone Peak Tram – two 15-person gondola cabins, operated as if they were a cable car. This leads to the top and fabulous 360° views. The Dakota triple chairlift serves Lone's south face and its steep bowls and glades. But a couple of reporters have found the area prone to closure due to avalanche risk. Lone Mountain's lower slopes are wooded and varied, as are those of **Andesite Mountain**, which has less vertical but three of the five fast lifts, including one from Mountain Village. From various points on Lone Mountain you can head down to the **Moonlight Basin** slopes, which start with a slow chair from Moonlight Lodge. Runs from the top of that lead to the Six Shooter fast chair, which, together with the slow Lone Tree quad, serves nearly all Moonlight's wooded, largely easy intermediate terrain. The Headwaters lift at the top serves expert-only runs.

FAST LIFTS ★★☆☆☆
Needs some more

There are five fast quad chairs, but many of the chairs are still old triples and doubles.

QUEUES ★★★★★
Only for the Tram

The tiny Tram continues to attract queues on powder days and in peak season. Queues are rare otherwise: 'Even on a Saturday morning powder day, the most we stood in line was two minutes,' says a 2012 visitor. But there are still a lot of slow lifts.

TERRAIN PARKS ★★★★☆
Plenty of choice

Swifty Park on Lone Peak has large jumps, rails and boxes for advanced riders. There is a natural half-pipe near the Lone Peak triple chair and an intermediate park, Swifty 2.0, near the village. There is a beginner park by the Explorer chair. Moonlight has the Zero Gravity park, with boxes, rails, jumps, jibs and hits under the Six Shooter chair, and a beginner park near the base.

SNOW RELIABILITY ★★★★★
No worries here

Snowfall averages 400+ inches – more than most resorts in Colorado. Grooming is good, too.

FOR EXPERTS ★★★★☆
Enough to keep you amused

All of the terrain accessed from the Tram is single or double black diamond. The steepest runs are the Big Couloir on the Big Sky side and the North Summit Snowfield on the Moonlight side. For both, you are required to have a partner to ski with, an avalanche transceiver and a shovel. We'd recommend a guide, too. There are easier ways down, though – Liberty Bowl is easiest. Marx and Lenin are a little steeper. The Dakota Territory has 212 acres of black-diamond glades, chutes and high bowls, to skier's right of Liberty Bowl – served by a triple chairlift. Lower down, the Lone Peak Triple, Challenger and Shedhorn chairs also serve good steep terrain. There are some excellent gladed runs, especially on Andesite. In the Moonlight sector the Headwaters is the biggest challenge – but it gets windblown and you may have to pick your way through rocks at the top. The further you hike to skier's left the steeper the couloirs. There are some good gladed runs lower down.

LIFT PASSES

Big Sky only

Prices in US$ inc tax

Age	1-day	6-day
under 18	64	384
18 to 69	84	474
70 plus	74	444

Free under 11

Beginner first half-day lesson includes a base area pass

Notes

Discounts for online purchase and purchase with lodging

Alternative pass

Big Sky-Moonlight Basin Interconnect covers Moonlight Basin too

FOR INTERMEDIATES ★★★★

Great deserted cruising

The bulk of the terrain on both mountains is of intermediate difficulty (including lots of easy blacks). The main complaint we have is that they don't seem to groom any blacks – with no people, they would be fabulous when groomed. But there is lots of excellent blue run cruising served by fast chairs and with few others on the runs – Ramcharger, Southern Comfort and Thunder Wolf on Andesite, Swift Current on Lone Mountain and Six Shooter in the Moonlight sector. Several wide, gentle bowls offer a good introduction to off-piste. And there are some good easy glade runs such as Singlejack on Moonlight and The Congo on Andesite. In general the groomed blues at Moonlight are easier than those at Big Sky, especially the ones served by the Lone Tree chair. Adventurous intermediates could try Liberty Bowl from the top of the Tram; but be prepared for a rocky, windswept traverse between wooden barriers at the top to access the run.

FOR BEGINNERS ★★★★★

Ideal – lots of lovely greens

Go to Big Sky rather than Moonlight. There's a good, well-developed nursery area at the base of the Explorer chair with a separate Explorer pass. There is a Learn to Ski taster half or full day including lesson, equipment rental and Explorer pass. There are long, deserted greens to progress to from those lifts and on Andesite.

fast chairlift
Slow chairs & drags have no symbol
LONE MTN
3400m/11,160ft
North Summit Snowfield
Headwaters
Deepwater Bowl
Lone Tree
BIG SKY RESORT
Six Shooter
Iron Horse
Pony Express
Moonlight Basin
2135m/7,000ft
Madison Lodge
Derringer

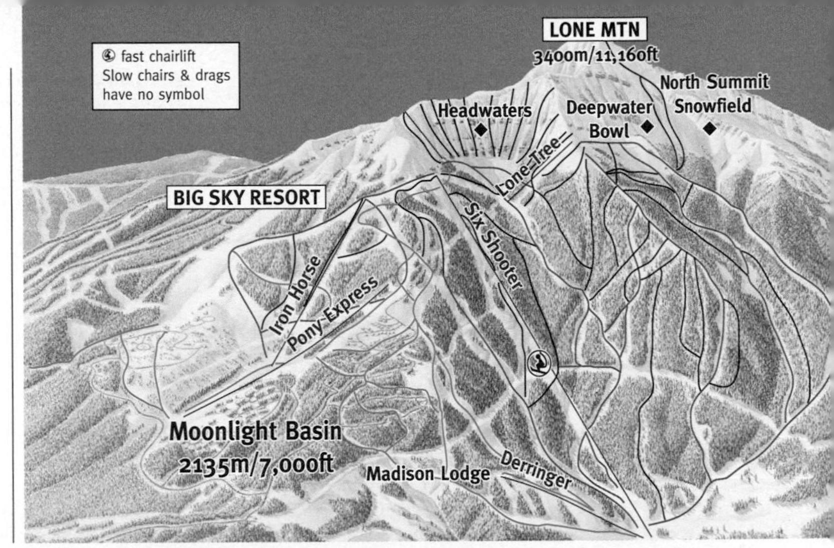

LONE MTN
3400m/11,160ft
Expert slopes on the south face are now more accessible thanks to a triple chairlift back here
Tiny cable car to the peak builds serious queues when conditions are good
South Face
Dakota Territory
Liberty Bowl
Big Couloir
North Summit Snowfield
The Bowl
The slopes over here are even quieter than those in the main Big Sky area
Headwaters
MOONLIGHT BASIN
Six-Shooter
Good, testing but not extreme slopes on this sector, served by slow chairs
Swift Current
Moonlight Basin
2135m/7,000ft
Mountain Village
2285m/
7,500ft
cable car
fast chairlift
Slow chairs & drags have no symbol

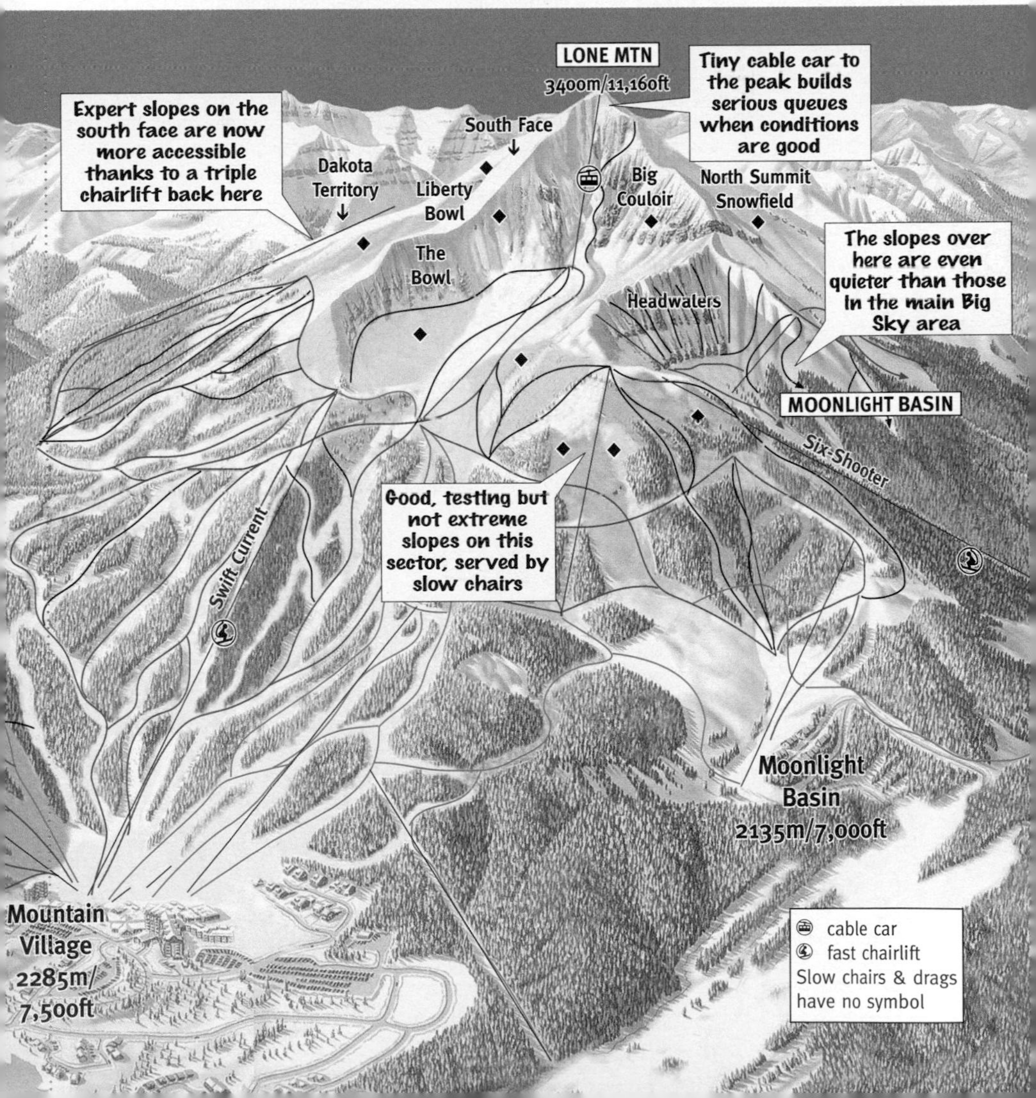

SCHOOLS

Big Sky
t 995 5743

Classes
Half day (2.5hr) $72

Private lessons
From $247 for 2hr

CHILDCARE

Lone Peak Playhouse
t 993 2220
Ages 6mnth to 8yr

Ski school
Ages 4 to 14; 9.45 to 3.15; $152 per day

ACTIVITIES

Indoor Solace Spa (massage, beauty treatments), fitness centres in hotels

Outdoor Snowmobiles, snowshoeing, sleigh rides, tubing, fly fishing, ziplines, visiting Yellowstone National Park

GETTING THERE

Air Bozeman 70km/ 45 miles (1hr15)

UK PACKAGES

AmeriCan Ski, American Ski Classics, Ski Bespoke, Ski Independence, Ski Safari

Central reservations
Call 995 5000; toll-free number (from within the US) 1 800 548 4486

Phone numbers
From distant parts of the US, add the prefix 1 406; from abroad, add the prefix +1 406

TOURIST OFFICE

Big Sky
www.bigskyresort.com

Moonlight Basin
www.moonlightbasin.com

FOR BOARDERS ★★★★

Something for everyone

The terrain has lots of variety, with few flats. Experts will enjoy the steeps and the glades, freestylers the good terrain parks, and novices the easy cruising runs served by chairlifts. Instruction is 'excellent'.

FOR CROSS-COUNTRY ★★★★

Head for the Ranch

There are 85km of 'excellent' trails at Lone Mountain Ranch ('helpful staff'), and more at West Yellowstone.

MOUNTAIN RESTAURANTS ★

Back to base for lunch?

The Shedhorn Grill is a yurt (tent) on the south side of Lone Mountain, doing simple meals. Then there's the newish Black Kettle on the front of Lone Mountain – soup and snacks.

SCHOOLS AND GUIDES ★★★★

Good reputation

The Big Sky school has a good reputation. One reporter's private lesson was 'a good mix of technical and guiding'. And visitors regularly praise the beginner snowboard classes: 'exceptionally happy with the quality of the instruction'.

FOR FAMILIES ★★★★

Usual high US standard

Lone Peak Playhouse in the slope-side Snowcrest Lodge will take kids to and from ski school ('perfect', says a reporter). Children 10 years and under ski free with an adult. There's a Kids' Club in the Huntley Lodge and snow garden at the base.

STAYING THERE

Hotels There's not much choice.
****Summit** (548 4486) Best in town; central, slope-side, good rooms, outdoor hot pool with good views.
*****Huntley Lodge** (548 4486) Big Sky's original hotel; central, part of Mountain Mall, outdoor pool, hot tubs, saunas. 'Unacceptable inter-room noise; ask for an upper floor,' complains a 2012 reporter.
*****The Lodge at Big Sky** (995 7858) Five minutes' walk to slopes; a shuttle at peak times. Indoor pool, indoor/outdoor hot tubs. 'Large rooms, friendly staff, but basic food.'
*****Rainbow Ranch** (995 4132) Five miles south of resort. Luxury riverside rooms and cabins. Recommended.

Apartments The good-value Stillwater condos have been recommended, along with Village Center, Arrowhead, Snowcrest, Big Horn, Black Eagle and, way out of town, Powder Ridge and Lone Moose. Check location carefully.

EATING OUT ★★★

A fair choice for a small place

A 2011 reporter recommends the Lone Peak Brewery ('excellent eatery'). Tips from earlier years include: M.R. Hummers ('varied menu, good value'), The Cabin (seafood, 'good elk' and steaks), Andiamo ('stylish, fresh pasta in big portions') and Whiskey Jack's (burgers, beers, Tex-Mex). Down in the valley, Rainbow Ranch is good for 'fine dining', and a 2011 reporter enjoyed 'good steaks and burgers' at the Corral. Moonlight dinners and live music are held at a backcountry yurt.

APRES-SKI ★

Limited but entertaining

Nightlife is generally quiet ('revolves around a few functional bars – not particularly exciting'). But there are a few places to try, most with regular live music. Chet's bar is 'entertaining' and also has pool. The Carabiner in the Summit and Whiskey Jack's are popular. The Black Bear can be lively, says a reporter.

OFF THE SLOPES ★★

Mainly the great outdoors

There's snowmobiling, snowshoeing, sleigh rides, a floodlit tubing hill, ziplines, visiting Yellowstone National Park (highly recommended by reporters), treatments at the revamped Solace Spa; the Huntley Lodge pool and spa is open to all for a fee.

LINKED RESORT – 2135m

MOONLIGHT BASIN

There's not much at Moonlight base except a few condos and cabins and the impressive Moonlight Lodge – spacious and log-built, with high ceilings and beams. The bar at the Lodge is lively as the slopes close, and the Timbers restaurant there gets good reviews. But we have been disappointed by the spa, and our nearby condo was poorly maintained. Maybe the Cowboy Heaven Cabins (995 6600) spread up the hillside are better. We had an enjoyable dinner a drive away at the Headwaters Grille, at Madison base area.

Jackson Hole

Touristy 'Wild West' town 12 miles from big, exciting slopes, and a small, modern base village with a famous après-ski saloon

RATINGS

The mountains	
Extent	***
Fast lifts	****
Queues	***
Terrain p'ks	***
Snow	****
Expert	*****
Intermediate	**
Beginner	***
Boarder	***
X-country	****
Restaurants	**
Schools	****
Families	****
The resort	
Charm	***
Convenience	****
Scenery	***
Eating out	*****
Après-ski	****
Off-slope	***

RPI	155
lift pass	£370
ski hire	£145
lessons	£185
food & drink	£100
total	**£800**

- + Tough expert-only terrain and one of the US's biggest verticals
- + Jackson town has an entertaining Wild West ambience
- + Unspoiled, remote location
- + Excellent snow record
- + Some unique off-slope diversions
- + The airport is only minutes away

- − The town is 30 minutes by bus from the slopes, though the lift base has attractive places to stay
- − Low altitude and sunny orientation mean snow can deteriorate quickly
- − Groomed cruising is in relatively short supply
- − Getting there from the UK involves at least one stop and plane change

Our 2011 editorial visit confirmed that Jackson Hole's metamorphosis is almost complete. When we first visited in the early 1990s, you went for its gnarly mountain, shedloads of snow and big vertical – simple as that. It had few facilities at the base or on the mountain and an antiquated lift system. The place attracted hardcore expert skiers, many of them regulars or locals.

But ownership changed and there was a new vision. Now there's a modern (though still inadequate) cable car, a gondola, several fast chairs serving easy terrain, a bunch of upscale hotels at the base, a table-service restaurant on the mountain – and many more beginners, intermediates and families around as a result. Some old stagers hate the change; we love it.

THE RESORT

The town of Jackson, with its wooden sidewalks, cowboy saloons and pool halls, sits on the edge of Jackson Hole – a high, flat valley surrounded by mountain ranges in Wyoming. Jackson gets many more visitors in summer than in winter, thanks to the nearby national parks. The slopes are a short drive away. At the base is Teton Village, which has developed a lot over the past few years, with an increased choice of bars, restaurants and hotels – some notably upscale.

A popular excursion by car or daily bus is over the Teton pass to the smaller resort of Grand Targhee, which gets even more snow. Read the Rest of the West intro.

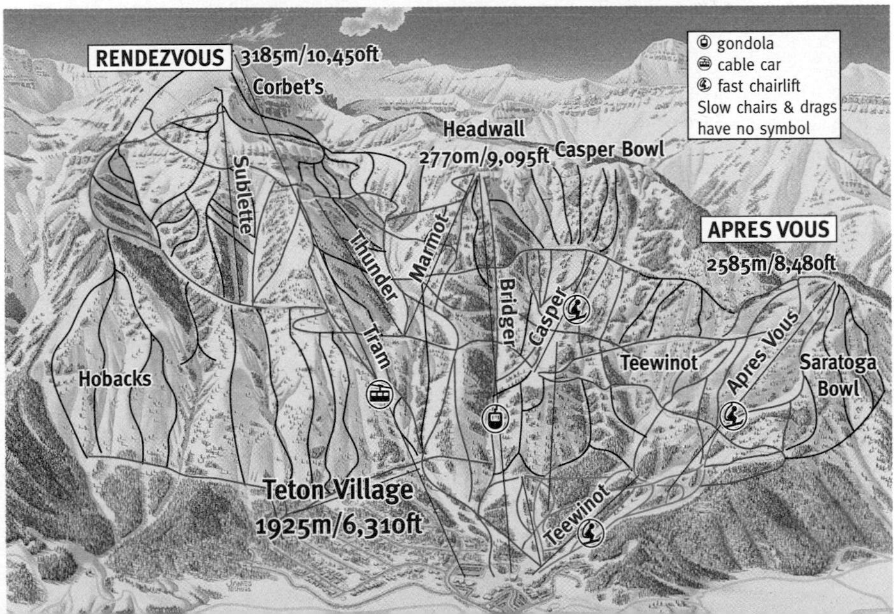

↑ Corbet's Couloir looks a doddle from below, once you have managed to overcome the slight hurdle of jumping in to it. Is it really 50°?

JHMR / KEN REDDING

NEWS

2012/13: A new fast quad is planned to replace the Casper triple chairlift.

2011/12: A new double chair, the Marmot, was installed from the base of the Thunder quad to the top of the Bridger gondola, simplifying movement from Rendezvous towards the Apres Vous sector.

VILLAGE CHARM ★★★★★
Cowboy or convenient

To amuse summer tourists Jackson town strives to maintain its Wild West flavour – and succeeds. It has lots of clothing and souvenir shops, plus upmarket galleries aimed at second-home owners. In winter it's all a bit quiet, but still quite amusing and pleasant. The efficient town bus and friendly and helpful locals are praised by reporters. Teton Village is modern and quite pleasant, but it doesn't really resemble a village.

CONVENIENCE ★★★★★
Stay at the slopes

From Jackson, getting to the slopes means a $3 30-minute bus ride or a slightly quicker drive followed by payment of $15 to park. Our preferred option is to stay at the base and take the bus into town for the occasional night out.

SCENERY ★★★★★
You can see forever

You get great long views across the wide plain of Jackson Hole from the slopes, which rise abruptly from the valley floor.

THE MOUNTAINS

Most of the slopes are below the treeline, but most of the forest is not dense. The piste map identifies only a handful of chutes as double-diamond experts-only runs, and we'd say the classification is pretty accurate; but some visitors reckon the toughest single diamonds would be double diamonds elsewhere.

EXTENT OF THE SLOPES ★★★★★
One big mountain, one small

The main lifts out of Teton Village are the Bridger gondola and the Tram (US-speak for cable car). The Tram takes you up 1260m to the summit of **Rendezvous** mountain – an exceptional vertical for the US. It can be very cold and windy at the top, even when it's warm and calm below. To the right looking up, fast quads access **Apres Vous** mountain, with half the vertical of Rendezvous and mostly much gentler runs. Between these two, the Bridger gondola goes up over a broad mountainside split by gullies, and gives speedy access to the Thunder and Sublette chairs – serving some of the steepest terrain on Rendezvous – and the Casper Bowl chair, from which you can traverse over to the Apres Vous area. The new Marmot double chair – see 'News' – makes moving across the mountain without returning to the bottom easier.

Snow King is a separate area right by Jackson town. Locals use it at lunchtime and in the evenings (it's partly floodlit).

FAST LIFTS ★★★★★
Few at mid-mountain

Fast lifts access both mountains; slow chairs rule on the upper mountain, but a reader points out that they rise steeply, and permit a lot of vertical in a day.

QUEUES ★★★★★
Only for the Tram

The new Tram (which opened in 2008) has double the hourly capacity of the old one. But it still holds only 100 people, and many locals do laps on it all day long. So it still generates queues – we waited 20 minutes on our 2011 visit, and a February 2012 visitor waited 30 minutes. Queues elsewhere on Rendezvous are rare, but if wind closes the Tram, the result is '20-minute queues all over Apres

KEY FACTS

Resort	1925m 6,310ft
Slopes	1925-3185m 6,310-10,450ft
Lifts	12
Pistes	2,500 acres
Green	10%
Blue	40%
Black	50%
Snowmaking	8%

LIFT PASSES

Prices in US$

Age	**1-day**	**6-day**
under 15	57	330
15 to 64	95	546
65 plus	71	408

Free under 6 (Eagle's Rest and Teewinot lifts only)

Beginner ticket for Eagle's Rest and Teewinot lifts ($25)

Notes Afternoon ticket available

Alternative passes Grand Targhee; Snow King Mountain

Vous'. One reader's tip to avoid queuing on powder days is to head for Apres Vous and 'great first tracks in the Saratoga Bowl' (though the Teewinot chair you need to get there can be busy these days).

TERRAIN PARKS ★★★

Six plus a pipe

Two seasons ago, four all-natural Burton Stash parks opened. In addition, there are two terrain parks on the lower mountain with features from beginner through to advanced plus music playing and a 137m-long super-pipe; Dick's Ditch is a 450m-long natural half-pipe.

SNOW RELIABILITY ★★★★

Deep snow, strong sun

The claimed average of 460 inches of snow is much more than the average for most Colorado (and some Utah) resorts. But the base elevation is low for the Rockies, and the slopes are fairly sunny – they basically face south-east (Apres Vous more south). The steep lower slopes, like the Hobacks, may be in poor shape, or even shut, and the higher slopes can be affected too – on our 2011 visit they were frozen solid because of very low temperatures after a melt. The flanks of some ridges have a more northerly orientation, and a reporter says that Saratoga Bowl keeps its snow well. Locals claim that you can expect powder roughly half the time. Don't assume early-season conditions will be good.

FOR EXPERTS ★★★★★

Best for the brave

For the good skier or boarder who wants challenges without the expense of off-piste guides, Jackson is one of the world's best resorts. Rendezvous mountain offers virtually nothing but black slopes. The routes down the main Rendezvous Bowl are not particularly fearsome; but some of the alternatives are. Go down the East Ridge at least once to stare over the edge of the notorious Corbet's Couloir. It's the jump in that's special; the slope you land on is a mere 50°, they say.

Below Rendezvous Bowl, the wooded flanks of Cheyenne Bowl offer serious challenges, at the steep end of the single black diamond spectrum. If instead you take the ridge run that skirts this bowl to the right, you get to the Hobacks – a huge area of open and lightly wooded slopes, gentler than those higher up, but still black and usually with big moguls; check snow conditions before embarking on these – there's no turning back.

Corbet's aside, most of the steepest slopes are more easily reached from the slightly lower quad chairs. From the Sublette chair, you have direct access to the short but seriously steep Alta chutes, and to the less severe Laramie Bowl beside them. Or you can track over to Tensleep Bowl – pausing to inspect Corbet's from below – and on to the less extreme (and less chute-like) Expert Chutes, and the single-black Cirque and Headwall areas. Casper Bowl often has good powder, and the Crags is an area of bowls, chutes and glades reached by hiking – both are accessed through gates. Thunder chair serves steep, narrow, fairly shady chutes. Again, the lower part of the mountain here offers lightly wooded single diamond slopes.

The gondola serves some good, underused expert terrain, particularly to skier's left of the lift, including the glades of Woolsey and Moran Woods. Even Apres Vous has serious, usually quiet, single blacks in Saratoga Bowl.

The gates into the backcountry access over 3,000 acres of amazing terrain, which should be explored only with guidance. You can stay out overnight at a backcountry yurt (tent). There are some helicopter operations.

FOR INTERMEDIATES ★★

Exciting for some

They have tried hard to improve the intermediate terrain, with fast lifts and much more grooming than in the old days. There are good cruising runs on the front face of Apres Vous, and top-to-bottom quite gentle blues from the gondola. But they don't add up to a great deal of mileage, and you shouldn't consider Jackson unless you want to tackle ungroomed runs. It's then important to get guidance on steepness and snow conditions. A good number of blues are identified on the trail map as more difficult, and many of these are less frequently groomed too – these are the places to get the hang of powder. The steepest single blacks are steep, intimidating when mogulled and fearsome when hard. The daily grooming map is worth consulting, but falling snow will mean moguls form.

SCHOOLS

Jackson Hole
t 1 800 450 0477

Classes
Full day $120

Private lessons
Half day (3hr) from $400

CHILDCARE

Kids' Ranch
t 1 800 450 0477
ages 6mnth to 6yr

Ski school
Explorers: ages 7 to 14; $155 per day

TANYA BOOTH

The base village has grown hugely in recent years. The Teewinot chair serves excellent beginner slopes ↓

FOR BEGINNERS ★★★★★
Fine, up to a point

There are good broad, gentle beginner slopes and a lift pass covering the two chairs that serve them. The progression to the blue Werner run off the Apres Vous chair is gradual enough and the mid-mountain blues on the Casper Bowl chair are reached via the chairs from the beginner area. But few other runs will help build confidence.

FOR BOARDERS ★★★★★
Steep and deep thrills

Jackson Hole is a cult resort for expert snowboarders, as for skiers. It's not bad for novices either. But intermediates not wishing to venture off the groomed runs will find the resort limited. Six terrain parks and a super-pipe provide the freestyle thrills. There are some good snowboard shops, including the Hole-in-the-Wall at Teton Village.

FOR CROSS-COUNTRY ★★★★★
Plenty of scenic choices

The Saddlehorn Activity Center at Teton has 17km of trails and organizes trips into the National Parks. And there are lots of groomed trails in the surrounding National Parks.

MOUNTAIN RESTAURANTS ★★★★★
Bridger blossoms

The complex at the top of the Bridger gondola has a coffee shop and fast food pizza area downstairs and a light and airy self-service with good views upstairs serving fresh stir-fry Asian dishes as well as standard fare; and there's also the Couloir table-service restaurant. We enjoyed the Couloir – sit near the entrance for great views over the valley and town through floor-to-ceiling windows and further in for views of the Headwall and Corbet's through smaller windows. The food is good but not gourmet – burgers, salads, upmarket sandwiches, pasta. Corbet's Cabin has 'great waffles', and the restaurant at the base of the Casper chairlift does a wide range of self-service food. There are simple snack bars at four other points on the mountain. There are some excellent places at the base.

SCHOOLS AND GUIDES ★★★★★
Learn to tackle the steeps

The school is highly regarded and has generated favourable reports from readers. As well as the usual lessons, there are also special types on certain dates. The four-day Steep and Deep Camp (pre-booking required) was 'carefully matched to ability, good value and a maximum five in each group'.

Rendezvous Backcountry Tours has been recommended for exploring the backcountry from Teton Pass.

FOR FAMILIES ★★★★★
Adventures on the Ranch

There were lots of kids around having fun on our 2011 visit. The redesigned 'Kids' Ranch' facilities are good, including regular pizza parties in the evenings. There's a fun kids' version of the trail map.

STAYING THERE

Teton Village is our preferred option now that there are comfortable hotels there. You can catch the bus to town for a night out – the last one back is around 11pm. Some town hotels are far from central.

Hotels Because winter is low season, town hotel prices are low.

TETON VILLAGE

*****__Four Seasons Resort__ (732 5000) Stylish luxury, with art on the walls, superb skier services, health club, an exceptional outdoor pool; perfect position just above the base.

****__Snake River Lodge & Spa__ (732 6000) Smartly welcoming and comfortable, with fine spa facilities.

****__Terra__ (739 4000) Smart, boutique

GETTING THERE

Air Jackson 20km/ 15 miles (45mins)

UK PACKAGES

Alpine Answers, AmeriCan Ski, American Ski Classics, Crystal, Elegant Resorts, Independent Ski Links, Inghams, Momentum, Scott Dunn, Ski Bespoke, Ski Independence, Ski Line, Ski Safari, Ski Solutions, Skitracer, Skiworld, Supertravel

ACTIVITIES

Indoor Fitness centres, spas (in hotels), concerts, wildlife art and other museums

Outdoor Snowmobiles, snowshoeing, sleigh rides, dog sledding, paragliding, snow kite boarding

Phone numbers
From distant parts of the US, add the prefix 1 307; from abroad, add the prefix +1 307

TOURIST OFFICE

www.jacksonhole.com

'eco' hotel, rooftop 'infinity' hot tub, pool. Spa. Nice breakfast cafe. No bar.
****Teton Mountain Lodge & Spa** (734 7111) Very comfortable. Good indoor and outdoor pool and fitness centre.
*****Alpenhof** (733 3242) Tirolean-style, with varied rooms. Good food, lively bar. Pool, sauna, hot tub.
***Hostel** (733 3415) Basic, good value. Recommended by a 2011 reporter.

JACKSON TOWN

******Rusty Parrot Lodge** (733 2000) Stylish, small, with a rustic feel. Hot tub, spa. 'Food, service as good as ever.'
******Wort** (733 2190) Central, above Silver Dollar Bar. Hot tub. Comfortable.
*****Lodge at Jackson Hole** (739 9703) Western-style on outskirts. Big rooms. Free breakfast. Pool, sauna, hot tubs. Shuttle to the slopes.
*****Parkway Inn** (733 3143) Central. 'Decent sized rooms. Friendly. Highly recommended.' Free breakfast. Pool, sauna, hot tubs. Shuttle to the slopes.
****49'er Inn and Suites** (733 7550) Central, good value.
****The Lexington** (733 2648) Fairly central. Pool, hot tubs.

BETWEEN THE TWO

*******Amangani Resort** (734 7333) Hedonistic luxury in isolated position way above the valley.
******Spring Creek Ranch** (733 8833) Exclusive retreat; cross-country on hand. Hot tub, spa.
Apartments There is lots of choice at Teton Village and better value places a mile or two away. Surprisingly little in and around Jackson town. Love Ridge and Snow King are 'good value'.

EATING OUT ★★★★★

A wide range of options

Jackson offers a range of excellent dining options. To check out menus, get hold of the local dining guide.

At Teton Village Il Villaggio Osteria at the hotel Terra has a good choice of Italian and seafood dishes. The Couloir at the top of the gondola opens on Thursday and Friday nights with a four-course gourmet menu for $89 – we had great foie gras and bison.

In Jackson town there is a big choice. We loved the Asian/Japanese-fusion dishes to share at The Kitchen. The Cadillac Grill (steaks, burgers, seafood) is 'great for families'. Blue Lion is small, with 'intimate dining areas, traditional menu and friendly service'. The Million Dollar Cowboy Bar's basement steakhouse has had good reports. The Snake River brew-pub – not to be confused with the expensive Snake River Grill – has a 'great, happy atmosphere' and has 'inventive toppings' on its pizzas plus a great range of beers. Sweetwater used to serve good elk and buffalo, but a 2012 visitor found 'everything was sweetened, even the steak and chicken'. Other suggestions: the Merry Piglets (Mexican), Bubba's BBQ, Thai Me Up and Bon Appe Thai ('This is the real thing – real Thai chefs, authentic herbs and flavours; the pad Thai noodles are great.'

APRES-SKI ★★★★☆

Amusing saloons

The renowned Mangy Moose is the focus of après-ski activity at Teton Village – a big, happy place, often with live music – though it closed at 10pm mid-week during our stay.

In town, the Silver Dollar Bar (with 2032 silver dollars inlaid in the counter) was packed with locals dancing to live country music at 8pm on the Saturday night of our 2011 visit. Round the corner the big Million Dollar Cowboy Bar, featuring saddles as bar stools, gets lively later and also has live music and dancing. The Rancher is an upstairs bar with pool and live music and attracts a younger crowd. Town Square Tavern also has pool and often live music. Out of town, the Stagecoach Inn at Wilson is famously lively on Sunday nights.

OFF THE SLOPES ★★★☆☆

'Great' outdoor diversions

Yellowstone National Park is 100km to the north. You can tour the park by snowcat or snowmobile with a guide; numbers are now restricted to reduce pollution. Some visitors really enjoy the park; we were underwhelmed – largely because of the noise and fumes from the snowmobiles and driving everywhere in convoy. You can go by coach, though. The National Elk Refuge, with the largest elk herd in the US, is next to Jackson and across the road from the National Museum of Wildlife Art. Reporters recommend both – and walks beside the Snake river, spotting eagles and moose. In town there are some 40 galleries and museums and various shops, including a number of outlets for Western arts and crafts. Shopping and restaurant discounts can be gained by joining the Jackson Hole Ski Club ($30).

AMERICAN SKIING COMPANY / NATHAN BILOW

New England

You go to Utah for the deepest snow, to Colorado for the lightest powder and swankiest resorts, to California for big mountains and relatively low prices. You go to New England for ... well, for what? Extreme cold? Rock-hard artificial snow? Mountains too limited to be of interest beyond New Jersey? Yes and no: all of these preconceptions have some basis, and in the end the East can't compete with the West. But they don't give the full picture.

Yes, it can be cold: one of our reporters recorded –27°C, with wind chill producing a perceived –73°C. Early in the season, people routinely wear face masks to prevent frostbite. It can also be warm – another reporter had a whole week of rain that washed away the early-season snow. The thing about New England's weather is that it varies – rather like old England's. The locals' favourite saying is: 'If you don't like the weather, wait two minutes.'

Many of the resorts get impressive amounts of natural snow over the season – in some years. But New England doesn't usually get much deep powder to play in. And snowmaking plays a big part in the resorts' operations. They have big snow-gun installations, designed to ensure a long season and to help the slopes to 'recover' after a thaw. They were the pioneers of snowmaking technology; and 'farming' snow, as they put it, is something they do superbly well.

The mountains are not huge in terms of trail mileage. But several have verticals of over 800m (on a par with Colorado resorts such as Keystone), and most have over 600m (matching Breckenridge), and are worth considering for a short stay, or even for a week if you like familiar runs. For more novelty, a two- or three-centre trip is the obvious solution. Consider renting a car and doing a tour.

Most resorts suit snowboarders well, and many have serious terrain parks.

You won't lack challenge – most of the double black diamond runs are seriously steep. And you won't lack space: most Americans visit over weekends, which means deserted slopes on weekdays – except at peak holiday periods.

It also means the resorts are keen to attract long-stay visitors, so UK package prices are low. But the big weekend and day trip trade also means few New England resorts have developed atmospheric resort villages – just a few condos and a hotel, maybe, with places to stay further out geared to visitors with cars.

New England is easy to get to from Britain – a flight to Boston, then perhaps a three- or four-hour drive to your resort. And there are some pretty towns to visit, with their clapboard houses and big churches. You might also like to consider spending a day or two in Boston – one of America's most charming cities. Or have a shopping spree at the factory outlet stores that abound in New England.

We cover two of the most popular resorts on the UK market, Killington and Stowe, briefly on the opposite page. But there are many other small areas, too, shown on the map and covered in our directory at the back of the book.

PACKAGES

Killington American Ski Classics, Crystal, Independent Ski Links, Ski Independence, Ski Line, Ski Safari, Ski Solutions, Skitracer, Skiworld, Thomson, Virgin Snow

Stowe American Ski Classics, Crystal, Crystal Finest, Elegant Resorts, Independent Ski Links, Ski Independence, Ski Line, Ski Safari, Skitracer, Virgin Snow

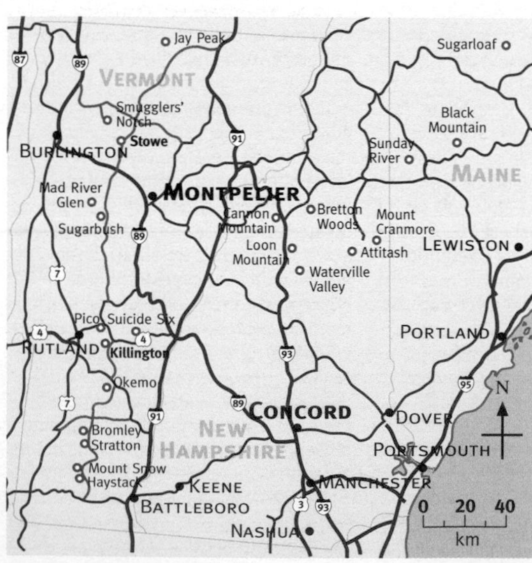

Killington

- New England's biggest ski area
- Excellent nursery slopes
- Lively après-ski and nightlife

- Widely spread lodgings, with no proper resort village
- Terminally tedious for non-skiers

Killington caters mainly for weekend visitors who drive in from the east-coast cities. There is no resort village in the usual sense.

Most of Killington's hotels and restaurants are spread along a five-mile approach road; the car is king. But there's also a free day-time shuttle-bus service around the base areas and lodgings. Beyond this it costs $2. The lift pass covers Pico – a separate little mountain next door.

The ski area spreads over a series of wooded peaks, with an impressive number of lifts and runs crammed into a modest area. Killington Base is the main focus, with chairlifts radiating to three of the peaks. Queues and crowded slopes can be a problem at weekends. It's a complex mountain, but the map and signing are fine. It has a good snow record (average 250 inches) and lots of snowmaking.

There are a handful of genuine double diamond fall-line runs to suit experts, steepest on Bear Peak. There are also lots of easy cruising blue and green runs all over the slopes. The resort is excellent for complete beginners too: the Snowshed base home slope is really one vast nursery slope. There are good facilities for children at Ramshead, where there is a well-equipped Family Center. Freestyle areas abound on Bear Mountain, on the back of Skye Peak. The Snowshed base lodge has several eating options.

Most hotels are a drive or bus ride away, but there is a wide choice of places to stay and dine. The Grand Resort at Snowshed is a swanky 4-star. Try the Santa Fe Steakhouse ('good seafood too'), Grist Mill (steaks) or Peppino's for Italian. Killington has a well-deserved reputation for a vibrant après-ski scene too, led by the famous Wobbly Barn – with live music.

Off the slopes? There's a new tubing park plus dog sledding and snowmobiling, but do take a car.

KEY FACTS

Resort	670m 2,200ft
Slopes	355-1285m 1,170-4,220ft
Lifts	22
Pistes	752 acres
Snow-guns	80%

TOURIST OFFICE

www.killington.com

Stowe

- Classic, cute Vermont town
- Queue-free except at weekends
- Great children's facilities

- Slopes a bus ride from town
- Slow chairlifts in main area
- Lacks après-ski animation

Stowe is one of New England's cutest towns, its main streets lined with dinky clapboard shops and restaurants. The slopes have something for everyone.

The small slopes of Mount Mansfield, Vermont's mainly wooded highest peak, are a 15-minute drive away. There's a good, free, day-time shuttle-bus service, but a car is useful.

The slopes span two main sectors, Mansfield and Spruce Peak, linked by gondola at base level. Up the mountain the Four Runner chair has been replaced by a fast quad. The area is largely queue-free during the week. Snowmaking is extensive, with a big investment planned for 2012/13.

The main slopes are dominated by the famous Front Four – a row of double black diamond runs, with genuine challenges for experts. But there is plenty of easier stuff, too. The nursery slopes at Spruce Peak are excellent, and there are splendid long green runs to progress to. There are three terrain parks, and the resort is popular with snowboarders. Children's facilities are excellent, too. There are a couple of decent huts. The Cliff House, at the top of the gondola, has table-service.

Much of the lodging is along the road between the town and the slopes – though you can now stay at the swanky Stowe Mountain Lodge, right by the lifts. Elsewhere, the Green Mountain Inn is a reader favourite. There are restaurants of every kind in the town; the Whip (Green Mountain Inn), Trattoria La Festa and the Solstice (Stowe Mountain Inn) are good choices. Nightlife is fairly muted but the Matterhorn and the Rusty Nail (live music, dancing) on the access road from the town are popular.

Stowe is a pleasant place to spend time off the slopes – at least if you like shopping. There is snowmobiling and dog sledding too. Ben & Jerry's ice cream factory is just down the road.

KEY FACTS

Resort	475m 1,560ft
Slopes	390-1135m 1,280-3,720ft
Lifts	13
Pistes	485 acres
Snow-guns	90%

TOURIST OFFICE

www.stowe.com

Canada

In many ways Canada combines the best that the US has to offer – good service, a warm welcome, relatively quiet slopes, good lift systems with lots of fast lifts, frequent dumps of snow, great grooming and a high standard of accommodation – with more spectacular scenery. It also has the advantage that you can get direct flights to its main airports without having to change planes and go through customs part-way through your journey. But it is no longer cheap – long-haul air fares have risen and local prices are high (all Canadian resorts fall into our red category – the most expensive – for their RPI).

If Canada – well, western Canada at least – has one central attraction, it is snow. In an average year, you can expect frequent and abundant falls to provide the powder you dream of. And, as in the US, there is lots of steep terrain within resort area boundaries, which is therefore avalanche protected and safely skiable without guidance. If you really want untracked powder and are feeling flush, there is nothing to beat western Canada's amazing heli-skiing and snowcat skiing operations. The east is different: expect snow and extremes of weather much like New England's. The main attraction of Québec for us is the French culture and ambience, plus the advantage of a shorter flight time. In both east and west, lifts close much earlier than in Europe – as early as 3pm in some cases (and some upper lifts might start closing as early as 1.30pm).

The Canadian people are another attraction. They share the American service culture but have a sincerity in putting it into practice that we (and our reporters) appreciate. In the west you'll also find spectacular scenery quite unlike what you generally find in the US. You may also see an impressive range of wildlife, especially in the Rockies and the interior of British Columbia.

Canada is not as cheap as it was (local prices have risen by 45% in terms of £s in the last five years just because of exchange rate changes), and lift pass prices are high compared with the Alps. Reporters now remark on the cost – and the number of reports we're getting on Canadian resorts has fallen.

Note that the legal age for buying and consuming alcohol is 18 in Alberta and Québec and 19 in British Columbia. The law is strictly enforced, so carrying your passport as evidence of age is a good idea even if you are well over the required age.

SNOWPIX.COM / CHRIS GILL

Canada has several worthwhile smaller resorts as well as the big names of Whistler and Banff. This is Fernie, one of our favourites ↓

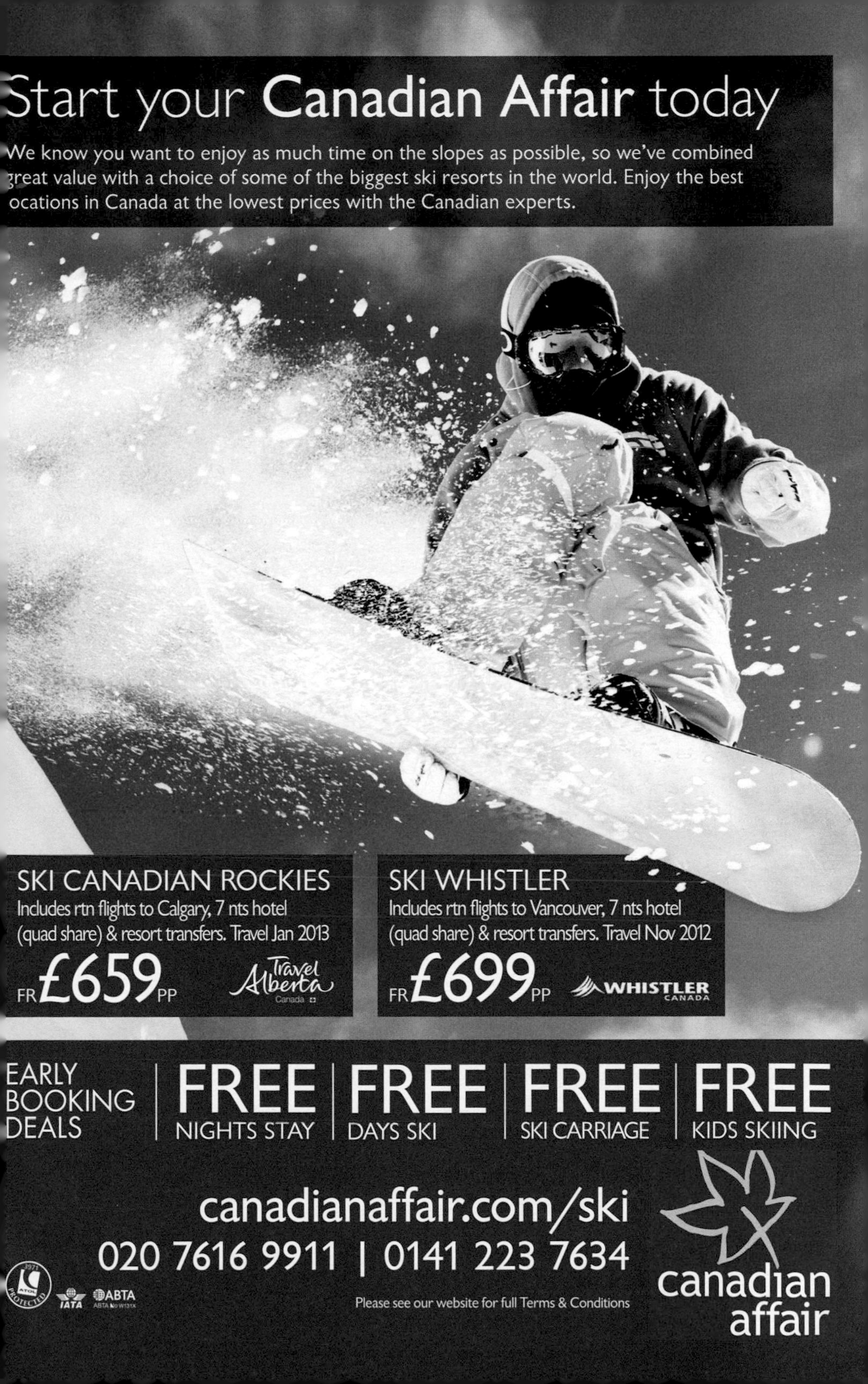

Start your Canadian Affair today
We know you want to enjoy as much time on the slopes as possible, so we've combined great value with a choice of some of the biggest ski resorts in the world. Enjoy the best ocations in Canada at the lowest prices with the Canadian experts.
SKI CANADIAN ROCKIES
Includes rtn flights to Calgary, 7 nts hotel (quad share) & resort transfers. Travel Jan 2013
FR £659 PP
Travel Alberta Canada
SKI WHISTLER
Includes rtn flights to Vancouver, 7 nts hotel (quad share) & resort transfers. Travel Nov 2012
FR £699 PP
WHISTLER CANADA
EARLY BOOKING DEALS
FREE NIGHTS STAY
FREE DAYS SKI
FREE SKI CARRIAGE
FREE KIDS SKIING
canadianaffair.com/ski
020 7616 9911 | 0141 223 7634
ATOL PROTECTED 3971
IATA
ABTA
Please see our website for full Terms & Conditions
canadian affair

Western Canada

For international visitors to Canada, the main draw is the west. It has fabulous scenery, good snow and a wonderful sense of the great outdoors. The big names of Whistler, Banff and Lake Louise capture most of the British market, but there are lots of good smaller resorts that the more intrepid visitors are now exploring. You can have a great trip by renting a car and combining two or more of these, perhaps with a couple of days on virgin powder served by helicopters or snowcats as well.

The three big resorts mentioned above and six of the smaller ones get their own write-ups in this section.

Whistler is plenty big enough to amuse you for a whole holiday. Most visitors to Banff or Lake Louise, a half-hour drive apart, will spend time at both (and could also fit in day trips to Kicking Horse and Panorama).

But none of the others has enough terrain to keep a keen piste-basher amused for a week or ten days without skiing the same runs several times. So we'd suggest that if you want variety, you combine two or more on one holiday. Even if you don't want to drive, it is easy to combine, say, Sun Peaks with Whistler, Big White or Silver Star (and the latter two with each other) using regular buses between them.

Places that don't get a full chapter that you might also consider for a longer tour include Jasper (which you can reach via the spectacular Icefields Parkway drive from Lake Louise), Apex, Red Mountain, Panorama and Kimberley – these all have entries in the resort directory.

We once spent two weeks driving from Whistler to Banff, calling in at lots of smaller resorts on the way. It was a fantastic trip; for eight days in the middle it did not stop snowing, and the variety of slopes and resorts made for great contrasts throughout the trip.

If you fancy a day or two snowcat-skiing, there are lots of possibilities, including great operations near Fernie (see chapter). Revelstoke has both cat- and heli-skiing right from the resort.

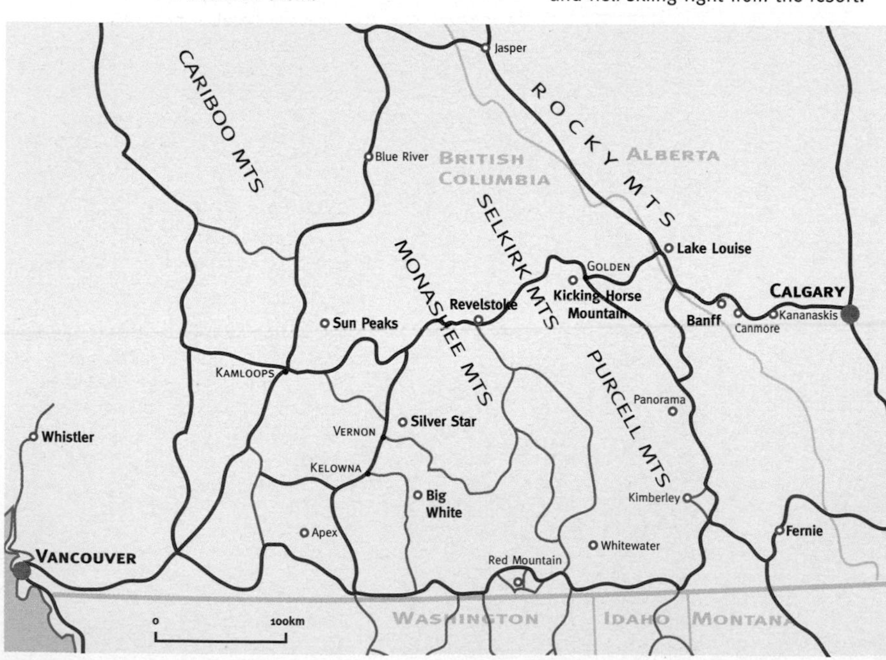

Banff

A major summer resort amid spectacular National Park scenery, with varied ski areas – including Lake Louise – a bus ride from town

RATINGS

The mountains

Extent	***
Fast lifts	****
Queues	****
Terrain p'ks	****
Snow	****
Expert	****
Intermediate	****
Beginner	***
Boarder	****
X-country	****
Restaurants	***
Schools	****
Families	****

The resort

Charm	***
Convenience	*
Scenery	****
Eating out	*****
Après-ski	***
Off-slope	*****

RPI	150
lift pass	£350
ski hire	£125
lessons	£175
food & drink	£115
total	**£765**

NEWS

2011/12: The shuttle-bus service to the ski areas was improved, with more buses and pick-up points – much needed, judging by the complaints we've received about previous seasons' bus services. Mt Norquay's historic teahouse reopened at the top of the mountain, and the tubing park was extended.

+ Spectacular high-mountain scenery – quite unlike the Colorado Rockies
+ Lots of touristy shops, restaurants and bars
+ Good-value lodging because winter is the area's low season
+ Excellent snow at main local area, Sunshine Village, but ...

− It's a 20-minute bus ride then a long gondola ride away
− You'll probably want to ski Lake Louise too, 45 minutes away
− Most lifts/runs are of limited vertical
− Can be very cold (–30°C or less)
− Banff lacks ski resort atmosphere, though it's not an unattractive town

Banff is nothing like your typical ski resort. We enjoy its restaurants and bars, but not the daily commuting to Sunshine Village or Lake Louise (which gets its own chapter). Even the small local hill, Norquay, is a bus ride out of town.

The alternative is to stay a few nights mid-mountain at Sunshine Village and a few at Lake Louise. Lake Louise also has the advantage of being much closer to Kicking Horse, which makes a great day trip for powderhounds.

THE RESORT

Banff is a big summer tourist town, with two ski areas nearby. Mt Norquay is a tiny area of slopes overlooking the town. Sunshine Village, whose base station 20 minutes' drive from Banff, is a much bigger mountain; despite the name, it's not a village (it has just one hotel at mid-mountain) nor is it notably sunny (sitting on the Continental Divide, it has an excellent snow record).

Most visitors buy a three-area pass that also covers the resort of Lake Louise, 45 minutes' drive away – dealt with in a separate chapter. Bus excursions are available to the more distant resorts of Panorama and Kicking Horse (the latter especially worthwhile) and the smaller (and closer) resort of Nakiska, and day trips for heli-skiing are offered locally.

VILLAGE CHARM ***

Pleasantly touristy

Banff consists basically of a long main street connecting the 'downtown' area – a small network of side roads built in grid fashion, lined with clothing and souvenir shops aimed at summer visitors – with a large area of hotel and condo lodgings. The buildings are low-rise, and some are wood-clad. The town is pleasant enough, but it's essentially a modern tourist town, without the character of the classic American cowboy or mining towns.

CONVENIENCE *

Sprawling town, outlying slopes

Banff is a sprawling place, and many of the lodgings (even on the main Banff Avenue) can be quite a way from the downtown area. A car can be helpful here, especially in cold weather. But there are plentiful taxis.

To get to the slopes bus services for each mountain (free with the Tri-area lift pass) pick up from many of the main hotels – but getting from your hotel to the lift base can take much longer than the advertised time because of the number of stops. For Sunshine this is 20 minutes; when you arrive, there is a long access gondola to ride.

SCENERY ****

Distinctive and dramatic

Banff National Park offers spectacular scenery – that's what brings the millions of summer visitors – and the town's setting is dramatic. Sunshine's Lookout mountain, right on the Continental Divide, gives panoramic views into British Columbia.

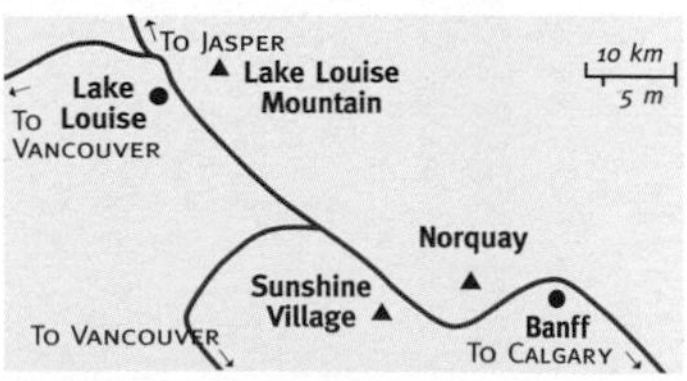

LIFT PASSES

Tri-area lift pass

Prices in C$

Age	1-day	6-day
under 13	31	176
13 to 17	63	474
18 to 64	84	533
65 plus	63	474

Free under 6

Beginner lift, lesson and rental package

Notes

Day pass is for Sunshine only; 3-day-plus pass covers all lifts and transport between Banff, Lake Louise, Norquay and Sunshine Village; prices include 5% tax

THE MOUNTAINS

The Sunshine Village slopes are mostly above the treeline, although there is a wooded sector – served by the second section of the gondola – and some lightly wooded slopes higher up.

Mt Norquay is a much smaller area of quiet, wooded slopes. But it's worth a visit, especially in bad weather or as a first-day warm-up.

Each area (and Lake Louise) has its own trail map, and there's one that shows all three areas too. The signposting at the top of each lift is praised, but at Sunshine it is difficult to follow some trails after that ('Signs are small and difficult to spot,' says a recent reporter).

There are good, free mountain tours led by friendly volunteer hosts.

EXTENT OF THE SLOPES ★★★★★
Lots of variety

The main slopes of **Sunshine Village** are not visible from the base station: you ride a gondola to Sunshine Village itself, with a mid-station at the base of Goat's Eye Mountain.

Goat's Eye is served by a fast quad rising 580m – much the most serious lift on the mountain. Although there are some blue runs, this is basically a black mountain, with some genuine double diamonds (including the extreme terrain of the Wild West area – see 'For experts').

Further up at Sunshine Village, lifts fan out in all directions, with short runs back from Mount Standish and longer ones from Lookout Mountain. From the top here you can access the more extreme terrain of Delirium Dive – see 'For experts'.

The 2.5km green run to the gondola base is a pretty cruise. Go down while the lifts are still running, and you can take the Jackrabbit chair to cut out a flat section. Delay your descent and you'll avoid the close-of-play crowds. The Canyon trail is a fun alternative for more advanced skiers and riders. The lower part is marked black; it's just a bit narrow and twisty in places. The final option is to ride the gondola down; many people do.

The slopes at **Norquay** are served by a row of five parallel lifts and have floodlit trails twice a week.

FAST LIFTS ★★★★★
New one for Sunshine

At Sunshine, most sectors of the slopes have fast chairs. The main weakness is the stoppage-prone Wawa chair; and a 2012 reporter saw three different chairs break down over two days, one for 20 minutes ('not what you want when it's cold and snowing', she pointed out). Norquay is so small that lift speed is hardly an issue, but it does have one fast chair.

QUEUES ★★★★★
Sunshine can get busy

Many visitors are day-trippers from cities such as Calgary – so the slopes are fairly quiet during the week. Public holidays and weekends at Sunshine have provoked past complaints of long queues; it can get busy. But even when busy, queues generally move quickly, and there are effective singles lines you can use if in a hurry. On busy weekends, we're told the trick is to arrive at the gondola by 9am.

TERRAIN PARKS ★★★★★
Park – and ride ...

At Sunshine, the Rogers terrain park on Lookout Mountain covers an impressive 12 acres of terrain with obstacles geared towards beginners and intermediates. The park is divided

↑ Sunshine Village has spectacular scenery; this is the Continental Divide chairlift on Lookout Mountain

SKI BANFF-LAKE LOUISE-SUNSHINE / SEAN HANNAH

KEY FACTS

Resort	1380m 4,530ft
Norquay, Sunshine and Lake Louise	
Slopes	1630-2730m 5,350-8,950ft
Lifts	26
Pistes	7,748 acres
Green	23%
Blue	39%
Black	38%
Snowmaking	24%
Norquay only	
Slopes	1630-2135m 5,350-7,000ft
Lifts	5
Pistes	190 acres
Green	20%
Blue	36%
Black	44%
Snowmaking	85%
Sunshine only	
Slopes	1660-2730m 5,440-8,950ft
Lifts	12
Pistes	3,358 acres
Green	20%
Blue	55%
Black	25%
Snowmaking	none

into two; the larger Lower Divide has a wide selection of obstacles and jumps; Grizzly is more jib-oriented. Experts should not miss the Norquay park, designed by Jeff Patterson, head park designer for Triple Crown events. Gap jumps, tabletops, rails and boxes litter the park, which also boasts a boardercross. The park is floodlit twice a week from January to March. You can lap the park in less than five minutes, with a great view from the chair.

SNOW RELIABILITY ★★★★
Excellent

Sunshine Village claims '100% natural snow', a neat reversal of the usual snowmaking hype. In a poor snow season, some black runs can remain rocky (especially those on Goat's Eye), but the blues are usually fine. 'Three times the snow' is another Sunshine slogan – a sly comparison between the impressive average snowfall here (360 to 400 inches, depending on the source) and the modest 180 inches at Lake Louise and 120 inches on Norquay. But we're told the Sunshine figures relate to Lookout, and that Goat's Eye gets less snow than this. At Norquay there is snowmaking on all green and blue pistes. Late-season snow on Sunshine is usually good (we've had great April snow there).

FOR EXPERTS ★★★★
Pure pleasure

Sunshine has plenty of open runs of genuine black steepness above the treeline on Lookout, but Goat's Eye is much more compelling. It has a great area of expert double black diamond trails and chutes, both above and below the treeline. But the slopes are rocky and need good cover, and the top can be windswept. The double diamond runs at skier's left reportedly hold their snow better than the rest of the mountain.

There are short, not-too-steep black runs on Mount Standish. One more challenging novelty here is a pitch known as the Waterfall run – because you do actually ski down over a snow-covered frozen waterfall. But a lot of snow is needed to cover the waterfall and prevent it reverting to ice. Also try the Shoulder on Lookout Mountain; it is sheltered, tends to accumulate powder and has been deserted whenever we've been there (probably because access to it involves a long traverse that can be tricky and is poorly marked).

A popular backcountry route follows the back of the Wawa ridge, through a river valley ('great fun – tight turns in the trees of the river bed'); a guide is essential, of course.

Real experts will want to get to grips with Delirium Dive on Lookout Mountain's north face and the Wild West area on Goat's Eye (with some narrow chutes and rock bands). For both you must have a companion, an avalanche transceiver, a probe and a shovel – and a guide is recommended. It is best to book in advance and rent your transceiver and shovel in Banff (you can't in Sunshine). We tried

Delirium in a group with the ski patrol, who provided equipment, and the scariest part was the walk in, along a narrow, icy path with a sheer drop (protected by a flimsy-looking net).

Norquay's two main lifts give only 400m vertical, but both serve black slopes, and the North American chair accesses a couple of serious double diamond runs.

Heli-skiing is available from bases outside the National Park in British Columbia – roughly two hours' drive.

FOR INTERMEDIATES ★★★★

Ideal runs

Half the runs on Sunshine are classified as intermediate. Wherever you look there are blues and greens – and some of the greens are as enjoyable (and pretty much as steep) as the blues.

We particularly like the World Cup Downhill run, from the top of Lookout to the Village. All three chairs on Mount Standish are excellent for building confidence, provided you choose a sensible route down. The slow Wawa chair gives access to the Wawa Bowl and Tincan Alley ('great first blues'). This area also offers some shelter from bad weather.

There's a delightful wooded area under the second stage of the gondola

Goat's Eye has some great steep terrain – single and double black diamond runs and an extreme zone. But it's very rocky and windswept and needs a lot of snow to be enjoyable

GOAT'S EYE
2600m/8,530ft
Goat's Eye
Wild West ◆◆
Wolverine
1660m/5,440ft
2020m/6,630ft

If it's snowing hard, visibility is usually best on the easy runs in the trees around here and on the long run down to the bottom of the gondola

gondola
fast chairlift
Slow chairs & drags have no symbol

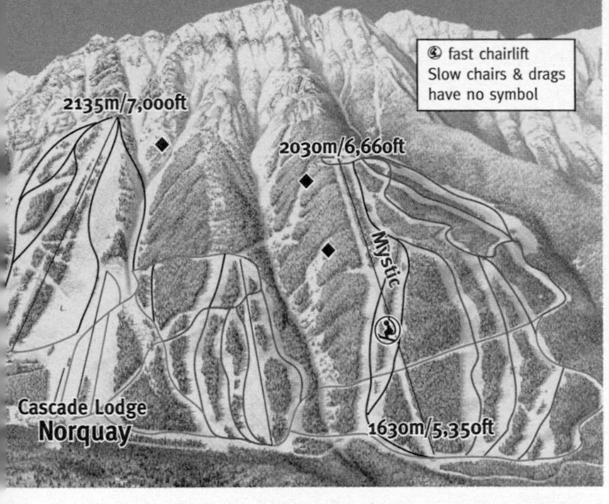

fast chairlift
Slow chairs & drags have no symbol
2135m/7,000ft
2030m/6,660ft
Mystic
Cascade Lodge
Norquay
1630m/5,350ft

served by the Jackrabbit and Wolverine chairs. The blue runs down Goat's Eye are good cruises too, some of them with space to indulge in fast carving.

The Mystic Express at Norquay serves a handful of quite challenging treelined blues and a couple of blacks that are sometimes groomed.

FOR BEGINNERS ★★★
Pretty good terrain
Most beginners start with a package that includes a lift pass and tuition. Sunshine has a good nursery area at the Village, served by a moving carpet. And there are great long green runs to progress to, served by the fast Strawberry Express chair.

Norquay has a good small nursery area with a moving carpet and gentle greens to progress to, served by the Cascade chair.

Banff is not the ideal destination for a mixed party of beginners and more experienced friends. The beginners are likely to want familiar surroundings, while the more experienced will want to travel.

ne of the extreme zones for which you need a mpanion, an avalanche ransceiver and a shovel to be allowed to enter the other is Wild West on Goat's Eye)
LOOKOUT
2730m/8,950ft
Easy cruising along the Continental Divide – which helps to account for Sunshine's impressive snowfall record
Delirium Dive
Continental Divide
Angel
MOUNT STANDISH
2400m/7,870ft
Strawberry Express
Mount Standish
Sunshine Village 2160m/7,080ft
Gondola
Wawa
2330m/7,640ft
The Sunshine Mountain Lodge is great for a couple of nights' stay. It's right on the slopes with a big outdoor hot-pool, a sauna and a good restaurant

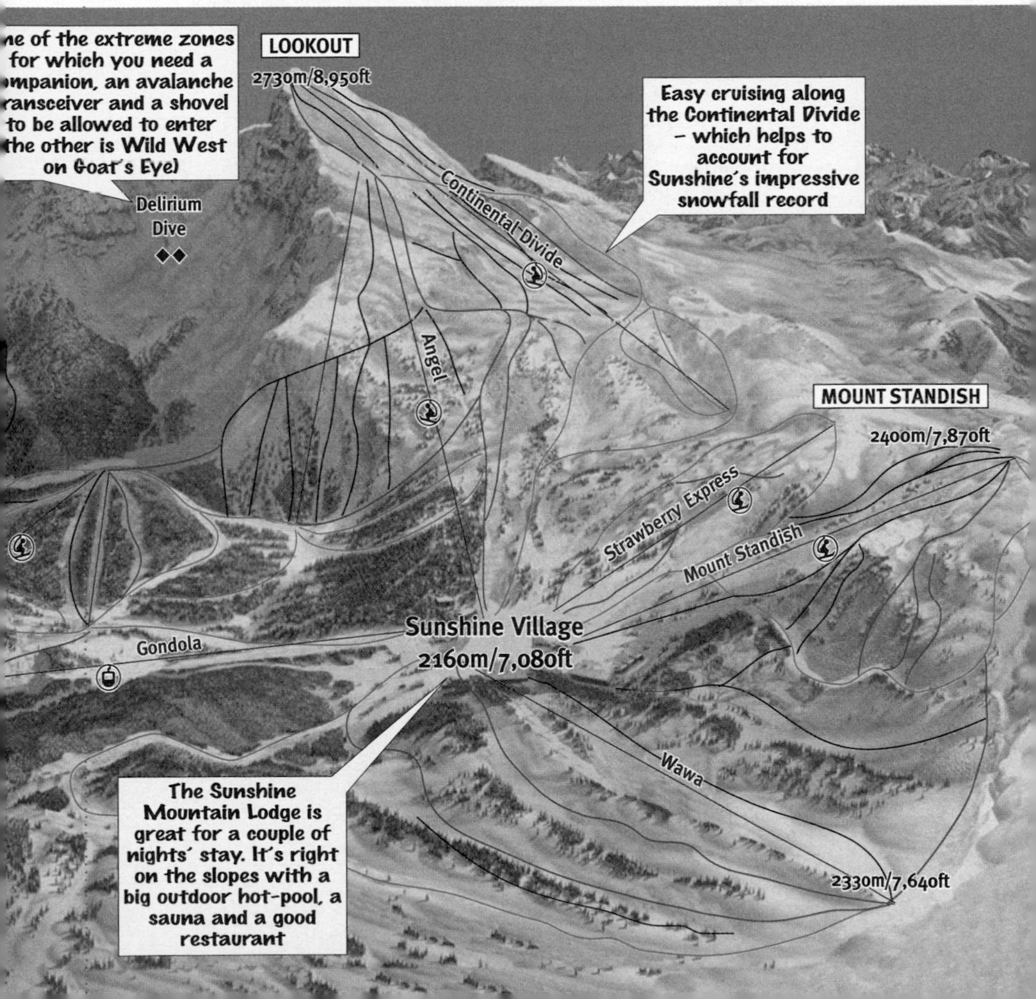

SCHOOLS

Ski Big 3
t 760 7731

Banff-Norquay
t 762 4421

Sunshine Village
t 1 877 542 2633

Classes (Big 3 prices)
3 days' guided tuition of the three areas C$314 incl. tax

Private lessons
Half day (3hr) C$398, incl. tax, for up to 5 people

CHILDCARE

Tiny Tigers (Sunshine)
t 762 6563
Ages 19mnth to 6yr

Kid's Place (Norquay)
t 760 7709
Ages 19mnth to 6yr

Childcare Connection
t 760 4443
Childminding in guest accommodation

Ski school
Takes ages 6 to 12 (3 days C$314, incl. tax)

SKI BANFF-LAKE LOUISE-SUNSHINE

You get great views over Banff and to Mt Rundle from the top of Norquay ↓

FOR BOARDERS ★★★★★
A good base

Boarders will feel at home in Banff, and there is some excellent freeriding terrain. Natural features are part of the appeal, with ledges, jumps and tree gaps aplenty. But Sunshine has some flat areas to beware of (such as the green run to the base – see 'Extent of the slopes' for tips on avoiding the worst of this), and the blue traverse on Goat's Eye is tedious. A trip to Lake Louise's Powder Bowls is a must for freeriders.

There are specialist snowboard shops in Banff: Rude Boys, Rude Girls and Unlimited Skate & Snow.

FOR CROSS-COUNTRY ★★★★★
High in quality and quantity

It's a good area for cross-country. There are trails near Banff, around the Bow River, and on the Banff Springs golf course. But the best area is around Lake Louise. Altogether, there are around 80km of groomed trails within Banff National Park.

MOUNTAIN RESTAURANTS ★★★★★
Quite good

With a mini-resort at mid-mountain, Sunshine offers better options than usual in North America. Our favourite is the welcoming Chimney Corner Lounge in the Sunshine Mountain Lodge with a big open fire – endorsed by reporters ('tasty and good value', said a 2012 visitor). The Day Lodge offers different styles of catering on three floors – the table service Lookout Lounge has great views and does a buffet.

At Norquay, the big, stylish, timber-framed Cascade Lodge is excellent – it has table- and self-service restaurants.

SCHOOLS AND GUIDES ★★★★★
Some great ideas

Each mountain has its own school. But recognizing that visitors wanting lessons won't want to be confined to just one mountain, the resorts have organized an excellent Club Ski Program – three-day courses starting on Sundays and Thursdays that take you to Sunshine, Norquay and Lake Louise on different days, offering a mixture of guiding, instruction and fun social events. Reporters are generally full of praise for these.

FOR FAMILIES ★★★★★
Excellent choices

There are various school and activity programmes for all ages. Some lodges have family lounges, with games and TVs. We've had good reports of the schools: 'kind and friendly instructors' and 'very accommodating – my boy is now a tremendous skier'. All three resorts offer childcare. The Tiny Tigers Ski and Play Program introduces youngsters to the slopes.

GETTING THERE

Air Calgary 140km/ 85 miles (1hr45)

UK PACKAGES

Alpine Answers, AmeriCan Ski, American Ski Classics, Canadian Affair, Crystal, Crystal Finest, Elegant Resorts, Frontier, Independent Ski Links, Inghams, Interactive Resorts, Momentum, Mountain Wave, Neilson, Oxford Ski Co, PowderBeds, Ski Bespoke, Ski Independence, Ski Line, Ski Safari, Ski Solutions, Skitracer, Skiworld, Snow Finders, Supertravel, Thomson, Virgin Snow

ACTIVITIES

Indoor Film theatre, museums, galleries, swimming pools (one with water slides), gym, squash, weight training, bowling, hot tub, sauna, climbing wall

Outdoor Swimming in hot springs, ice rink, sleigh rides, dog sledding, ice climbing, snowmobiles, ice walks, ice fishing, helicopter tours, snowshoeing, tobogganing, tubing

Phone numbers
From distant parts of Canada, add the prefix 1 403; from abroad, add the prefix +1 403

TOURIST OFFICE

www.skibanff.com
www.banffnorquay.com
www.SkiBig3.com

STAYING THERE

A huge amount of accommodation is on offer, with lots of varied hotels.

Hotels Summer is peak season here, with generally lower prices in winter. Frontier offers several good hotels.

*******Fairmont Banff Springs** (762 2211) A late-19th-century, castle-style property outside town (no shuttle-bus – you have to use taxis). It's a town in itself – 2,000 beds, 40 shops, several restaurants and bars, a nightclub and a superb spa (which costs extra).

******Banff Caribou Lodge** (762 5887) On the main street, slightly out of town. Wood-clad, individually designed rooms (some small). Very good Red Earth Spa, good restaurant and bar. Repeatedly recommended by reporters.

******Banff Park Lodge** (762 4433) Best-quality, central hotel, with hot tub, steam room and indoor pool.

******Fox** (760 8500) On the main street. Hotel rooms and suites, with a restaurant, fitness area and an unusual 'cavern' style hot pool.

******Rimrock** (762 3356) Spectacularly set out of town, with great views and a smart health club. Luxurious.

*****Buffalo Mountain Lodge** (762 2400) Slightly out of town but in a beautiful location. Good food. Hot tub.

*****Irwin's Mountain Inn** (762 4566) On Banff Avenue: 'good location and excellent value'.

****Homestead Inn** (762 4471) Central, with cheap, good-sized rooms.

Apartments Don't expect luxury – but there are some decent options. The Banff Rocky Mountain Resort is set in the woods on the edge of town, with indoor pool and hot tubs. The Douglas Fir resort is a bit out of town but has a free shuttle and is popular with families; it has lots of facilities such as adults' and kids' swimming pools and a giant indoor playground.

At altitude The Sunshine Mountain Lodge (705 4000) makes a very welcoming, comfortable base at Sunshine Village. Luggage is transported while you ski. Rooms vary in size, with 30 luxury ones. Big outdoor hot pool. Sauna. Good restaurant. Guests can get on the slopes half an hour early.

EATING OUT ★★★★★
Lots of choice

Banff boasts over 100 restaurants, from McDonald's to the fine dining restaurant in the Banff Springs hotel. The award-winning Maple Leaf Grille offers fine seafood and steak dishes, and over 600 different wines. We've enjoyed the designer-cool Saltlik – good game, steak and fish.

Of the dozens of places that readers recommend, popular spots are Melissa's (central, 'varied menu and good ambience'), Athena ('excellent large pizzas – good value for money'), Giorgio's (beef, fish, Italian) and Magpie & Stump (Tex-Mex, with Wild West decor). Old Spaghetti Factory is a good family choice. Try Bison for steaks, fish and live music. And for traditional burgers and ribs try Keg, Bumper's, Wild Bill's or Tony Roma's.

APRES-SKI ★★★
Night on the town is best

There's little teatime après-ski because the town is a drive from the slopes. Mad Trapper's Saloon at the top of the Sunshine gondola is the best bet during the close-of-play happy hour, but it gets crowded.

In town later, the two main live music venues are the Rose & Crown and Wild Bill's – country and western style, perhaps with line dancing. The Banff Avenue Brewing Company is the local micro-brewery. The Elk and Oarsman has a lively sports bar. The St James's Gate Olde Irish pub claims to be 'one of the premier Irish pubs in the world'. There are a couple of good nightclubs.

OFF THE SLOPES ★★★★★
Lots to do

Banff has lots to do off the slopes. Outdoor activities include skating, snowshoeing, dog sledding and snowmobiling. Ice canyon walks are popular – notably Johnson Canyon – and there's wildlife to see.

Shopping and soaking in the spas and hot springs are popular – the Red Earth Spa at the Caribou Lodge has the works and is open until 8pm. There are sightseeing tours and several museums. Some reporters have enjoyed evenings in Calgary watching the ice hockey. A recent reporter enjoyed a good day out in Canmore.

BIG WHITE SKI RESORT / KLAUS GRETZMACHER

Big White

It's not big by Euro-resort standards, but it's certainly white. There are few places to match it for learning to ski powder

TOP 10 RATINGS	
Extent	★★★
Fast lifts	★★★★
Queues	★★★★★
Snow	★★★★★
Expert	★★★
Intermediate	★★★★
Beginner	★★★★
Charm	★★
Convenience	★★★★
Scenery	★★★

RPI	135
lift pass	£300
ski hire	£130
lessons	£135
food & drink	£120
total	**£685**

KEY FACTS	
Resort	1755m 5,760ft
Slopes	1510-2320m 4,950-7,610ft
Lifts	16
Pistes	2,765 acres
Green	18%
Blue	54%
Black	28%
Snowmaking	In terrain park

- + Great for learning to ski powder
- + Slopes quiet except at weekends
- + Convenient, purpose-built village with high-quality condos and a traffic-free centre; good for families
- + Lots of non-skiing snow-based activities at Happy Valley

- − Visibility can be poor, especially on the upper mountain, because of snow, cloud or freezing fog
- − Few off-slope diversions, and it's isolated without a car
- − Limited après-ski

'It's the snow' says the Big White slogan. And as slogans go, it's spot on. If you want a good chance of skiing powder on reasonably easy slopes, put Big White high on the shortlist. If you want a suntan (or lively après-ski, or extensive steep terrain), look elsewhere; but if you are an intermediate looking to learn to ski powder or try gladed skiing, there can be few better places. Consider combining it with another BC resort such as Silver Star or Sun Peaks for variety.

THE RESORT

Big White is a still growing, purpose-built resort less than an hour from Kelowna airport. Silver Star (see separate chapter) is around two and a half hours away and under the same ownership; twice-a-week direct transfers make a two-centre holiday easy, and you can also just go for the day twice a week.

Village charm It is rather spread out but attractive in wood and stone, with a family-friendly traffic-free centre.

Convenience Much of the place is ski-in/ski-out of smart modern condos.

Scenery Trees fill the views wherever you look; and near the top of the mountain the trees usually stay white all winter and are known as 'snow ghosts'; they make visibility tricky in a white-out but are great fun to ski between on clear days.

THE MOUNTAINS

Much of the terrain is heavily wooded. But the trees thin out towards the summits, leading to almost open slopes in the bowls at the top. There's at least one green option from the top of each lift, but the one from Gem Lake is narrow and can be tricky and busy. In general, the easiest slopes are on the right as you look at the mountain (including some very easy glade skiing) and get steeper the further left you go.

Slopes Chairs run from points below

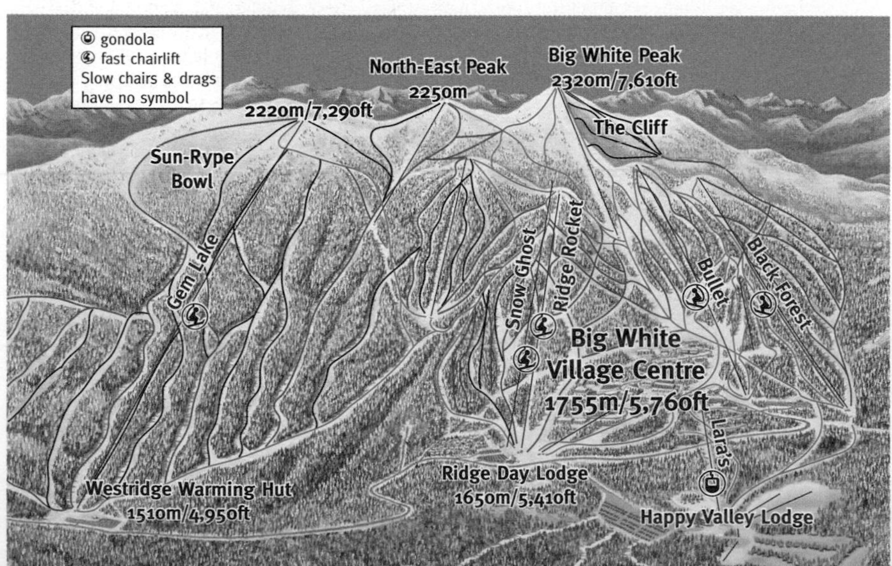

↑ The resort centre is small, attractive, traffic-free and family-friendly

BIG WHITE SKI RESORT

NEWS

2012/13: Some 5km of new cross-country trails are planned. A kids' ski clothing shop is due to open along with an après-ski sleigh ride to a warming hut for pizza and hot chocolate (aimed at families). Climbing clinics on the ice tower and snowshoe courses are planned for all ages and abilities.

2011/12: New large-diameter tube rails were installed in the terrain park, and an 18m ice climbing tower was built. A new family restaurant, the BullWheel, opened.

village level to above mid-mountain, serving the main area of wooded beginner and intermediate runs above and beside the village. A T-bar and four chairs serve the higher slopes. Quite some way across the mountainside is the Gem Lake fast chair, serving a range of long top-to-bottom runs; with its 710m vertical, this lift is in a different league from the others. 'Snow hosts' (highly praised by reporters) run free guided ski tours every day (at 9.30 and 1.30). The signposting and piste map and classification are good ('excellent', says a recent visitor). There is night skiing Tuesday to Saturday evenings on four slopes.

Fast lifts The lifts from the village and the Gem Lake lift are all fast. But the other upper lifts are tediously slow.

Queues Queues are very rare.

Terrain parks Served by a double chair and snowmaking, the excellent Telus park includes three 9m jumps, rails and hits for all levels, large-diameter tube rails (new last season), a half-pipe and a boardercross, and is highly praised by reporters. The park is open for night riding Thursday to Saturday.

Snow reliability Big White has a reputation for great powder; average snowfall is about 300 inches, which is similar to many Colorado resorts. One reporter points out that most slopes face south-west to south-east and the snow can suffer in periods of sunshine; but on each of our three visits it snowed practically non-stop, and we hardly saw the sun.

Experts The Cliff area at the top right of the ski area is of serious double black diamond pitch; the runs are short, but you can ski them repeatedly using the Cliff chair. Sun-Rype bowl at the opposite edge of the ski area is more forgiving ('Excellent place to ski deep powder,' says a 2011 reporter). There are some long blacks off the Gem Lake chair and several shorter ones off the Powder and Falcon chairs. There are glades to explore – and bump runs too.

Intermediates The resort is excellent for cruisers and families, with long blues and greens all over the hill. Good intermediates will enjoy the easier blacks and some of the gladed runs too. There is marvellous easy skiing among the trees in the Black Forest area (which we loved when it was snowing) and among the snow ghosts (see 'Scenery'), which we loved when it was clear. Some of the blues off the Gem Lake chair are quite steep, narrow and challenging.

Beginners There's a good dedicated beginner learning area at Happy Valley and lots of long easy runs to progress to. Every day three slopes are designated slow zones, gated and patrolled.

Snowboarding There's some excellent beginner and freeriding terrain with boarder-friendly chairlifts and few flat areas to worry about.

Cross-country A reporter enjoyed the 25km of 'great open spaces and wooded routes'. She found trail maps good but some of the signage poor.

UK PACKAGES

Alpine Answers, AmeriCan Ski, American Ski Classics, Canadian Affair, Frontier, Neilson, Ski Independence, Ski Line, Ski Safari, Ski Solutions, Skiworld

Central reservations
Call 765 8888; toll-free (within Canada) 1 800 663 2772

Phone numbers
From distant parts of Canada, add the prefix 1 250; from abroad, add +1 250

TOURIST OFFICE

www.bigwhite.com

BIG WHITE SKI RESORT

The trees near the top usually remain snow covered all winter; the resulting 'snow ghosts' are great fun to ski between ↘

Mountain restaurants There aren't any – it's back to the bottom for lunch. You can eat a packed lunch at any of the day lodges or at the warming hut.
School and guides We receive rave reviews from reporters for both adults' and children's lessons. A reporter had 'great-value' snowboard lessons booked through a tour op, and his six-year-old 'made rapid progress on black moguls and in the trees (with only one other in his group lessons)'.
Families The excellent day care centre takes children from 18 months to five years; it organizes evening events too.

STAYING THERE

A good range of accommodation is featured by specialist tour operators Frontier Ski and Ski Independence. A 2011 visitor found the supermarket 'ludicrously expensive'.
Hotels Chateau Big White is our reporters' favourite: 'excellent location', 'room was huge', 'cosy fires'; ask for a room facing away from the village to avoid late-night noise. The White Crystal Inn receives better reviews than the Inn at Big White.
Apartments Condo standards are high. Stonebridge and Towering Pines are both central, ski-in/ski-out, with big, well-furnished rooms and private hot tubs on the balconies. Other reporter tips include Black Bear and (a bit less luxurious) Eagles and Whitefoot Lodge.
Eating out We had a superb meal at the 6 Degrees bistro, sharing delicious dishes (tapas-style); endorsed by a 2012 reporter; not cheap. We've also had good meals in the Swiss Bear in the Chateau Big White (endorsed by a 2012 reporter) and the Kettle Valley Steakhouse at Happy Valley ('steaks perfectly cooked'). Reporters also recommend the 'charming' upstairs restaurant at Snowshoe Sam's and Carvers in the Inn at Big White ('very friendly service, mix of Canadian and Asian cuisine, excellent beef vindaloo'). The BullWheel is a new family place with handmade burgers.
Après-ski In general, après-ski is fairly quiet. The ground floor of Snowshoe Sam's has a DJ and live entertainment.
Off the slopes Happy Valley is a great area for families, with ice skating, snowmobiling, snow biking, tubing, dog sledding, sleigh rides, snowshoeing and an 18m ice climbing tower. There are two spas and a shopping shuttle to Kelowna.

SNOWPIX.COM / CHRIS GILL

Fernie

Lots of snow and lots of steeps – one of our favourites, with a choice of convenient base lodging or a valley town

RATINGS

The mountains	
Extent	***
Fast lifts	**
Queues	****
Terrain p'ks	**
Snow	****
Expert	*****
Intermediate	**
Beginner	****
Boarder	***
X-country	***
Restaurants	*
Schools	****
Families	****
The resort	
Charm	**
Convenience	****
Scenery	***
Eating out	***
Après-ski	***
Off-slope	**

RPI	145
lift pass	£320
ski hire	£155
lessons	£130
food & drink	£120
total	**£725**

NEWS

2011/12: A new triple chairlift to the top of Polar Peak was installed. It starts from above Currie Bowl and goes to the summit ridge, opening up terrain which is entirely above the treeline and includes 22 new runs (16 of them double black, four single black, two blue) and giving Fernie a vertical of over 1000m. A new box feature was added to the rail park.

+ Good snow record, with less chance of rain than at Whistler (and less chance of Arctic temperatures than at resorts further north)
+ Great terrain for those who like it steep and deep; good for confident intermediates too
+ Snowcat operations nearby
+ Some good on-slope accommodation available, but ...

– Mountain resort is very limited
– Access to many excellent runs is via slow lifts and long traverses
– After a dump it can take time to make the bowls safe
– Limited groomed cruising
– On-mountain signposting needs further improvement
– One basic mountain restaurant

Fernie has long had cult status among Alberta and British Columbia skiers. It now attracts quite a few British visitors, and the reports we get are almost all positive. Like us, reporters are impressed by the adventurous nature of the skiing – it's mostly ungroomed, and much of it is steep, with a lot of lightly wooded slopes (not common in Europe). Curiously, it's now quite a good resort for novices, too. Cautious intermediates unhappy about giving the ungroomed terrain a go are the ones who need to look elsewhere.

Fernie town, a couple of miles from the lift base, has few of the usual tourist trappings, but makes an amusing change from the ski resort norm.

THE RESORT

Fernie Alpine Resort is set a little way up the mountainside from the flat Elk Valley floor and a couple of miles from the little town of Fernie. Outings to Kimberley are possible; a coach goes weekly, taking about 90 minutes.

VILLAGE CHARM **

Unpretentious small town

A slope-side resort has grown from very little in recent years, but there's still not much there except convenient lodging and a few restaurants, bars and small shops. It is quiet at night. There's much more going on in the town of Fernie, named after William Fernie – a prospector who discovered coal here and triggered a boom in the early 1900s. Much of the town was destroyed by fire in 1908, but some buildings survived.

Fernie is primarily a place for locals, not tourists. There are some lively bars, decent places to eat and good outdoors equipment shops. It is down to earth rather than charming, and reporters' reactions to it vary: some like staying in a 'real' town while others are unhappy about the highway that runs through it. Most stress the friendliness of the locals.

CONVENIENCE ****

Base lodging or bus ride

There is accommodation at the resort and in town. Buses between town and mountain run hourly and cost C$3 one way, stopping at some of the bigger hotels on the way. They run until 2am on Friday and Saturday nights. A reporter found drivers 'happy to be flagged down'.

SCENERY ***

The rocky ridges are impressive

Fernie's two main peaks, Grizzly and Polar, are part of the steep-sided Lizard Range. They provide an impressively rocky backdrop. There are good views across the Elk Valley too.

THE MOUNTAINS

Fernie's 2,500 acres pack in a lot of variety, from superb green terrain at the bottom to ungroomed chutes, open bowls and huge numbers of steep runs in the trees. Quite a few runs go directly down the fall line.

EXTENT OF THE SLOPES ***

Bowl after bowl

What you see when you arrive at the lift base is a trio of impressive mogul slopes towering above you. These

NEW PISTE MAP, NEW ON-MOUNTAIN SIGNPOSTING – BUT YOU STILL NEED A GUIDE

On our most recent visit we were delighted to find, after years of complaining about the dreadful piste map and inadequate on-mountain signposting, that both had at last been improved. The new map is bigger, with the different bowls clearly marked. Big new signs clearly mark each bowl at the top of the access lifts. And there are new signs to mark the runs – but only at the start of each run. You're likely to miss some of them because they are set ludicrously high in trees and almost hidden.

DAVE WATTS

So things have improved, but more signs are needed to mark key traverses (especially through the trees) and directions once you have embarked on a run. Finding some of the runs marked on the map is still very difficult, and you can easily end up in tight trees on slopes of triple-diamond steepness – as we did on an earlier visit.

For the moment, at least, to explore the best of Fernie's steep terrain you need guidance. Guides have taken us to runs that we'd never have found on our own. One solution is to join a two-day Steep and Deep camp early in your stay (read 'Schools and guides').

KEY FACTS

Resort	1065m 3,490ft
Slopes	1065-2135m 3,490-7,000ft
Lifts	10
Pistes	2,504 acres
Green	30%
Blue	40%
Black	30%
Snowmaking	15%

excellent black runs exemplify one of the weaknesses of Fernie's lift system: to get to them you must ride lifts way off to the left or right, and then make long traverses to get to the start of the runs proper – a slow business.

The slow Deer chair approaches the foot of black slopes, but goes no further. It serves the main green-run novices' zone.

On the right, riding the slow Elk quad followed by the fast Great Bear quad takes you to the junction where **Lizard Bowl** meets **Cedar Bowl.** You can traverse across both of these and drop down into the bowls pretty much wherever you like. Both have trails marked on the piste map but are ski-anywhere terrain among open snowfields and lightly wooded slopes. At the far side of Cedar Bowl are steeper runs among tighter trees from Snake Ridge. The Haul Back T-bar brings you out of Cedar to ride the Boomerang chair. This serves a mini-bowl between Lizard and Cedar.

Off to the left, the Timber Bowl fast quad chair gives access to **Siberia Bowl** and the lower part of **Timber Bowl**. But for access to the higher slopes of Timber Bowl and to **Currie Bowl** you must take the slow White Pass quad. A long traverse from the top gets you to the steeper slopes on the flanks of Currie (our favourite area). On the way, you pass the new slow triple chair which accesses the open and mainly steep runs from **Polar**

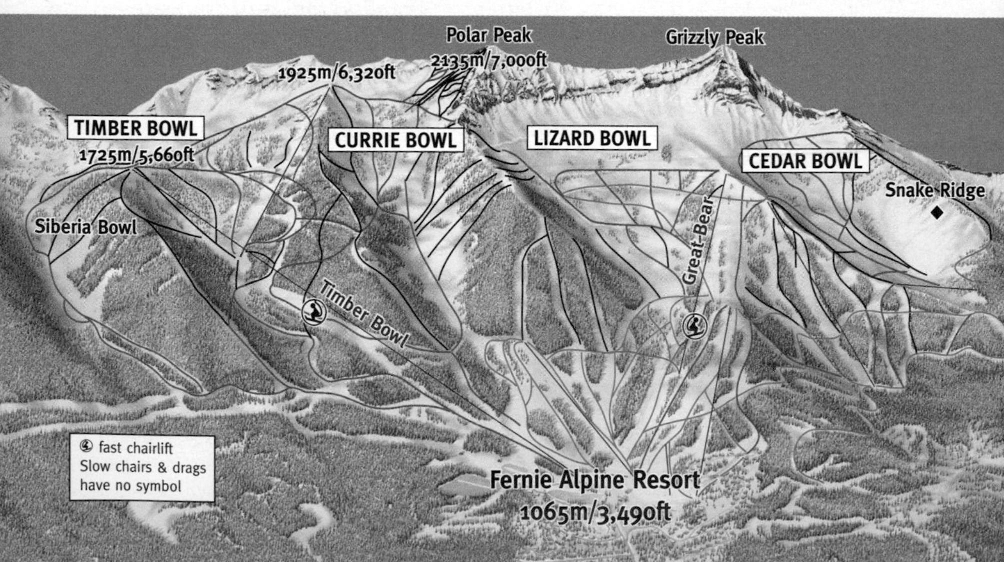

LIFT PASSES

Prices in C$

Age	1-day	6-day
under 13	26	157
13 to 17	57	340
18 to 64	81	485
65 plus	65	390

Free under 6

Beginner rental, limited pass and tuition deals

Notes

Prices include taxes; half-day pass available

GETTING THERE

Air Calgary 340km/210 miles (4hr15)

Peak, the highest runs in the ski area. If you descend Currie Bowl you have to go right to the lift base, and it takes quite a while to get back up, but the run from Polar Peak to the base is over 1000m.

Free mountain tours are available twice a day, but they only scratch the surface (read the final paragraph of the feature panel opposite).

FAST LIFTS ★★

A poor show

There are only two fast chairs, serving opposite ends of the mountain. And only one of them goes up from the resort base area. Slow chairs and a draglift elsewhere make getting around a slow process. Even so, you may spend more time traversing through forest than riding lifts.

QUEUES ★★★★

Not usually a problem

Queues are generally rare unless there are weekend crowds from Calgary or heavy snow keeps part of the mountain closed. But people complain about the slow chairlifts, and about breakdowns on one or two.

TERRAIN PARKS ★★

Just a rail park

Fernie no longer builds a traditional park. Instead, there is a patrolled rail park beside the Great Bear Express – you'll need a special pass (C$5 per day) and must sign a waiver to use it.

SNOW RELIABILITY ★★★★

A key part of the appeal

Fernie has an excellent snow record – with an average of 350 inches per year, it's better than practically anywhere in Colorado. But the altitude is modest: rain is not unknown, and in warmer weather the lower slopes can suffer. Too much snow can be a problem, with the high bowls prone to closure – we've had reports of them being shut all week. Snowmaking has been increased over recent years and now covers most of the base area. Piste grooming has also been increased; we have been impressed with it on our most recent visits.

FOR EXPERTS ★★★★★

Wonderful with guidance

The combination of heavy snowfalls and abundant steep terrain with the shelter of trees makes this a superb mountain for good skiers, so long as you know where you are going. Read the feature panel opposite. It has taken us half a dozen visits to get to know the mountain reasonably well.

There are about a dozen identifiable faces offering genuine black or double black slopes, each of them with several alternative ways down and all worth exploring. Pay attention to the diamonds: the singles are usually pretty tough, and the doubles are serious. Even where the trail map shows trees to be sparse, expect them to be close together, and where there aren't any, expect alder bushes to be protruding unless there's lots of snow.

There are a few areas where you can do laps fairly efficiently, but mostly you have to put up with a cycle of long traverse–descent–run-out–lift–lift on each lap (with an extra lift to get to the new Polar Peak area).

There are backcountry routes you can take with guidance (some include an overnight camp) and snowcat operations in other nearby mountains – read the feature panel overleaf. A regular reporter especially enjoyed exploring Fish Bowl, a short hike outside the resort boundary from Cedar Bowl.

FOR INTERMEDIATES ★★

Getting better

When we first visited, only the green and blue runs on the lower mountain were groomed. But things have moved on, as the resort tries to cater for a wider clientele. On our more recent visits a few runs from the top were groomed, including some great blue cruisers down Lizard Bowl – easily reached using the fast Great Bear quad. But it doesn't add up to much, and if you are not happy to try some of the easier ungroomed terrain in the bowls and glades, we'd recommend that you go elsewhere. For the adventurous willing to give the powder a go, though, Fernie should be on your shortlist.

FOR BEGINNERS ★★★★

Surprisingly, pretty good

There's a good nursery area served by two lifts (a moving carpet and a drag), and the lower mountain served by the Deer and Elk chairs has lots of wide, smooth trails to gain confidence on. But the green runs from the upper lifts are usually cat-tracks, which nonetheless have tough parts to them.

SCHOOLS

Fernie Telus
t 423 2406

Classes
C$125 per day (incl. taxes)

Private lessons
From C$131 (incl. taxes) for 1.5hr

CHILDCARE

Resort Kids
t 423 2430
Age 18mnth to 6yr

Ski school
Ages 6 to 12 (C$99 per day, incl. taxes)

SNOWPIX.COM / CHRIS GILL

Fernie's ungroomed terrain is a good mixture of open bowls and tree skiing. To make the most of it, get a guide early in your holiday ↓

FOR BOARDERS ★★★★★
Fine if you're good

Fernie is a fine place for good boarders (and there are a lot of local experts here). Lots of natural gullies, hits and endless off-piste opportunities – including some adrenalin-pumping tree runs and knee-deep powder bowls – will keep freeriders of all abilities grinning from ear to ear. But there's a lot of traversing involved to get to many of the best runs – hard work in fresh snow and bumpy later. The main board shops, Board Stiff and Edge of the World, are in downtown Fernie. It's not a brilliant place for freestylers – the terrain park has gone and been replaced by a smaller rail park, for which you'll need a special pass.

FOR CROSS-COUNTRY ★★★★★
Some possibilities

There are 10km of trails in the forest adjacent to the resort. In the Fernie area as a whole there are around 50km of tracks.

MOUNTAIN RESTAURANTS ★★★★★
One tiny sit-down place

Lost Boys Cafe is a tiny self-service place in a fine position at the top of Timber Bowl with a basic, limited menu but 'excellent chilli' as well as 'breathtaking views'. Bear's Den at the top of the Elk chair is an open-air fast-food kiosk.

Naturally, most people eat at the base area. The ancient no-frills Day Lodge serves soups, burgers and daily specials. Snow Creek Cafe is handy for the nursery slopes. Look at 'Eating out' to see other options – we usually head for the Corner Pocket.

SCHOOLS AND GUIDES ★★★★★
Highly praised

Reporters praise the school, which seems to achieve rapid progress – no doubt partly because groups are often very small. A recent visitor was very happy with his 'really brilliant' private lessons, but also noted that class sizes are often very small, making group lessons very good value.

There are several programmes to help you get the best out of the mountain. The Steep and Deep camp has had good feedback; it is a two-day programme (C$299) where you get technique tips while exploring steep terrain – a great way to get to know at least some of the mountain. We've had good sessions being guided by some of their instructor-guides. 'First Tracks' (C$269 for three people) is a two-hour private lesson that gets you up the mountain at 8am, before the lifts are open to others.

FOR FAMILIES ★★★★★
Good day care centre

There's a day care centre in the Cornerstone Lodge. Once a week there's a craft night for children aged six to 12. And there's a Wilderness Adventure Park with cut-outs of bears and wolves. The ski school offers a 'family' private lesson option.

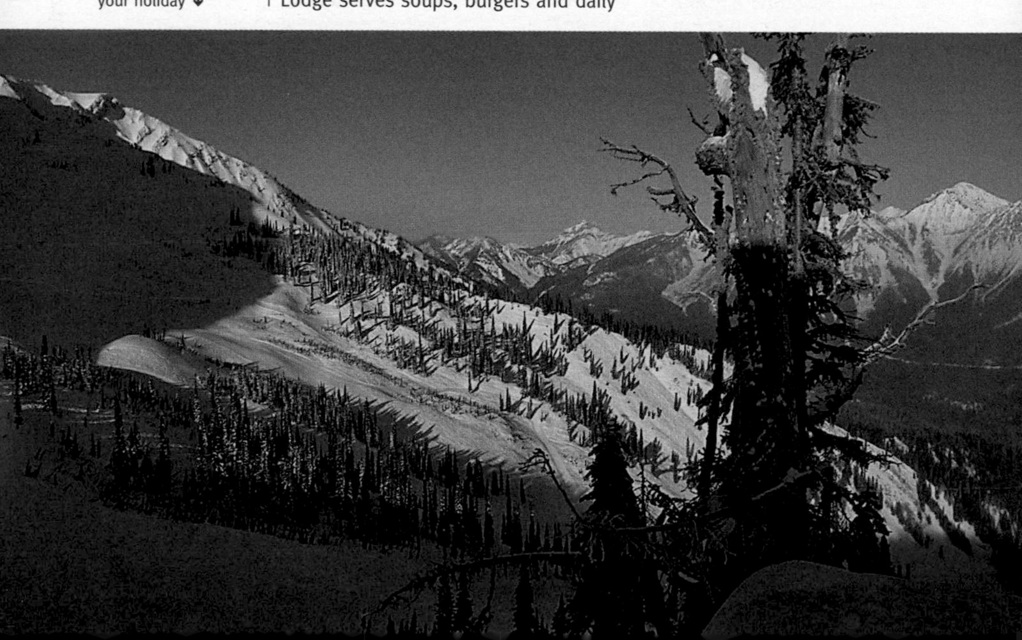

RIDE THE SNOWCATS – HELI-SKIING AT AN AFFORDABLE PRICE

Good skiers who relish off-piste should consider treating themselves to some cat skiing, where you ride snowcats instead of lifts; there are several operations in this area. On our most recent visit, we had two fabulous days at Island Lake Lodge (423 3700), which does all-inclusive packages in a luxury lodge (spacious rooms, big lounge, three hot tubs, bar, excellent food) 10km from Fernie, reached only by snowcat, amid 7,000 acres of spectacular bowls and ridges. It has 26 rooms and three cats. In a day you might do 10 to 14 powder runs averaging 500m vertical, taking in all kinds of terrain from gentle open slopes to some very Alpine adventures. You can do single days on a standby basis. Fernie Wilderness Adventures (877 423 6704) has three cats accessing 3,000 acres.

SNOWPIX.COM / CHRIS GILL

UK PACKAGES

Alpine Answers, AmeriCan Ski, American Ski Classics, Canadian Affair, Canadian Powder Tours, Crystal, Frontier, Independent Ski Links, Inghams, Interactive Resorts, Momentum, Neilson, Ski Independence, Ski Safari, Ski Solutions, Skitracer, Skiworld, Snow Finders

ACTIVITIES

Indoor Aquatic Centre (pool, hot tub, steam), fitness centre, climbing wall, spas, cinema, museum, gallery, library, brewery tour

Outdoor Walking, snowmobiling, ice rink, curling, dog sledding, sleigh rides, hi-tech treasure hunt, snowshoe excursions

Central reservations phone number
Call 1 877 333 2339 (toll-free from within Canada)

Phone numbers
From distant parts of Canada, add the prefix 1 250; from abroad, add the prefix +1 250

TOURIST OFFICE

www.skifernie.com

STAYING THERE

Chalets Canadian Powder Tours has one with an outdoor hot tub in town.
Hotels There's a wide choice.
******Best Western Fernie Mountain Lodge** Next to the golf course near town. Pool, hot tub, fitness room. But a 30-minute bus ride to the slopes.
******Lizard Creek Lodge** Best ski-in/ski-out condo hotel: spa, outdoor pool and hot tub. We've enjoyed staying here a couple of times.
******Snow Creek Lodge** Similar to the Lizard Creek Lodge.
*****Alpine Lodge** B&B on edge of resort. 'Homely and welcoming.'
*****Griz Inn Sport Hotel** Condo hotel at foot of slopes. Pool.
*****Park Place Lodge** On highway; easy walk to centre of town, lively pub; pool and hot tub in main lobby.
*****Timberline Lodges** Very comfortable condos a shuttle-ride from the lifts.
*****Wolf's Den Lodge** At base of slope. Basic but convenient. Hot tub.
Apartments The Cornerstone Lodge is a modern condo hotel.

EATING OUT ★★★
Better choice in town

At the base, there isn't a huge choice. The restaurant of Lizard Creek Lodge offers 'generous portions – lamb shank particularly good'. Yamagoya in the Alpine Lodge does Japanese ('good to eat some lighter food for a change', 'wonderful ice cream'); there's another branch in town. Kelsey's (part of a chain) serves standard and reliable steaks, burgers, pasta and pizza. The Corner Pocket at the Griz Inn has a wide-ranging menu ('superb steaks').

In the town of Fernie, there are quite a few options. On our last visit we had two excellent (though pricey) meals at the Picnic – innovative 'fine dining', including dishes to share, and cool surroundings (stone walls, wooden floors, waiters in black). We also enjoyed a simpler meal at the Brick House (burgers, grills) and various Asian cuisines at Curry Bowl. A 2011 visitor recommends the Indian food at the out-of-town Stanford hotel. The Old Elevator is a converted grain store with 'a sophisticated menu, friendly service'). Mezzaluna is Italian; the Pub at Park Place Lodge offers good pub grub.

APRES-SKI ★★★
Have a beer

When the lifts close head for the Griz Bar above the Day Lodge. During the week, the mountain resort bars are pretty quiet later on. In town, the bars of the Royal hotel are popular with locals, as is the Park Place Lodge Pub, which is usually busy, friendly and welcoming (with pool and table-football tables and big-screen TV).

OFF THE SLOPES ★★
Get out and about

The Arts Station has two galleries, a theatre and craft studios, and there is a walking tour of historic Fernie – you buy a C$5 self-guided booklet from the visitor information centre or retailers. Watching the local ice hockey team, the Ghostriders, is 'well worth doing – good fun', says a reporter. There's a pool at the Aquatic Centre in town. But the main diversion is the great outdoors.

Kicking Horse

One of Canada's newest resorts: only a few lifts, but great powder at the top, and a small village at the base

TOP 10 RATINGS

Extent	***
Fast lifts	***
Queues	****
Snow	****
Expert	****
Intermediate	***
Beginner	***
Charm	**
Convenience	****
Scenery	***

RPI	145
lift pass	£300
ski hire	£135
lessons	£175
food & drink	£120
total	**£730**

- + Great terrain for experts and some for adventurous intermediates
- + Big vertical served by a gondola
- + Splendid mountain-top restaurant

- − Resort village still small and quiet
- − Gondola needs a mid-station to make the most of the mountain
- − Few groomed intermediate runs

Kicking Horse was developed from a small local hill in 2000, when a long gondola was built to two high, powder-filled bowls – previously heli-skiing country. There were great ambitions to turn it into a major resort. But things moved much more slowly than was planned, and the original owner eventually sold out in December 2011 to a company that owns five other Canadian resorts including Fernie. Let's hope they can make a go of things because the mountain has huge potential, and both the lift system and the small resort village at the base need to be expanded to make the place worth a week's stay. Meanwhile, it's best for a short stay, or a day trip if you're staying in Banff or Lake Louise.

THE RESORT

Eight miles from the logging town of Golden, Kicking Horse still has only two main lifts and a tiny base village. Daily Powder Express buses run from Banff and Lake Louise – the 2011/12 cost was C$110, including a lift pass.

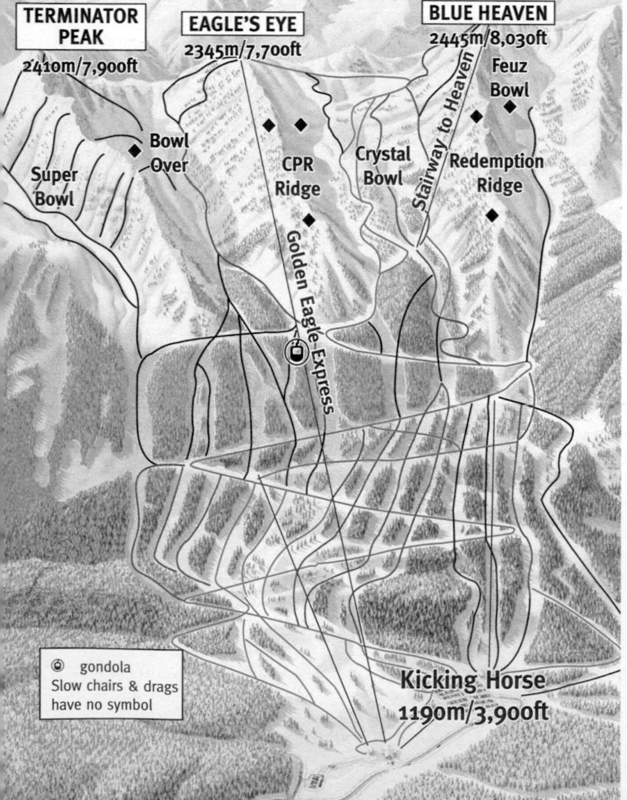

Village charm The small resort village at the lift base has several lodges, a few restaurants and bars, a ski shop and a general store. The town of Golden has no real appeal.
Convenience Fine if you stay at the mountain, and why not?
Scenery The scenery is not without drama – especially from the top.

THE MOUNTAINS

The lower two-thirds of the hill is wooded, with trails cut in the usual style. The upper third is a mix of open and lightly wooded slopes spread over four separate bowls, with scores of ways down for experts through the open terrain, chutes and trees.
Slopes The eight-seat gondola to Eagle's Eye takes you to the top in one stage of 1150m vertical. It serves three bowls and CPR Ridge. To the left as you ride the gondola is Bowl Over. Or take the narrow Milly Goat Traverse along a ridge towards Super Bowl, which opened two seasons ago – but the last part of this 'traverse' is a hike up to Terminator Peak or around the back. To the right of the gondola is Crystal Bowl; you can do laps here on the slow chair to the slightly higher peak of Blue Heaven, which also accesses Feuz Bowl. From Bowl Over, Super Bowl and Feuz Bowl – and also from below the chair in Crystal Bowl – you have to make the full descent to the base as there is no mid-station on the gondola. Two chairlifts near the base serve the lower runs that formed the original ski area here. There are

Kicking Horse has some seriously hairy terrain for experts →

KICKING HORSE RESORT / WALLY RANDALL

NEWS

2012/13: The resort hopes to build more groomed trails for intermediates from the top of the Stairway to Heaven chair and Redemption Ridge. The tubing park will move to the new beginner area.

2011/12: The resort was sold to Resorts of the Canadian Rockies, which owns five other Canadian resorts including Fernie. A new beginner area was built at the base and is served by a moving carpet. And a new groomed trail along Redemption Ridge and into Feuz Bowl was built.

KEY FACTS

Resort	1190m 3,900ft
Slopes	1190-2445m 3,900-8,030ft
Lifts	5
Pistes	2,825 acres
Green	20%
Blue	20%
Black	60%
Snowmaking	Some

UK PACKAGES

Alpine Answers, AmeriCan Ski, American Ski Classics, Canadian Affair, Crystal, Frontier, Independent Ski Links, Momentum, Neilson, Ski Independence, Ski Safari, Ski Solutions, Skitracer, Skiworld

Central reservations
Call 439 5425

Phone numbers
From distant parts of Canada, add the prefix 1 250; from abroad, add the prefix +1 250

TOURIST OFFICE

www.kickinghorseresort.com

free mountain tours twice a day.

Fast lifts Just the gondola.

Queues We've had reports of serious weekend queues for the gondola. During the week, though, it's quiet.

Terrain park There's a small park on the lower slopes.

Snow reliability An average of 275 inches of snow a year is not enough to put the resort in the top flight, but it's not far off. The top slopes usually have light, dry powder, but the lower ones may have crud and thin cover; and with most of the runs, you have to descend the lower slopes every time – a real drawback.

Experts From the top, you can go right into the gentle Crystal Bowl via an easy piste, or via serious chutes from CPR Ridge; or go left down pleasantly wooded single diamond slopes into Bowl Over; or head to Super Bowl. The Stairway to Heaven chair serves further single diamond wooded slopes. Feuz Bowl offers various challenges, not all of genuine double diamond steepness, and gets tracked out less quickly. The lower half of the mountain has short black runs cut through the woods, some with big moguls. There is heli-skiing nearby.

Intermediates Adventurous types will have a fine time learning to play in the powder from Blue Heaven down to Crystal Bowl. Most of it is open, but you can head off into trees if you want to. There is very little groomed cruising, other than a top-to-bottom 10km winding green run. The new owners hope to create more groomed intermediate terrain, but for now timid intermediates should go elsewhere.

Beginners The (new) beginner area is fine, with easy slopes on the lower mountain for progression.

Snowboarding Freeriders will love this powder paradise.

Cross-country Dawn Mountain has loops of 30km, plus skating trails.

Mountain restaurants The Eagle's Eye at the top of the gondola is Canada's best mountain restaurant – excellent food and service in stylish log-cabin surroundings with splendid views. The Heaven's Door yurt (tent) in Crystal Bowl serves snacks; many people lunch at one of the lodges at the base.

Schools and guides A reporter took a group lesson which 'was worth every cent – a lot of fun and we learned a lot'; she also enjoyed the free tours.

Families The school teaches children from the age of three.

STAYING THERE

There are smart, quite large condo-style lodges on the slopes. But we'd choose to stay in one of three much more captivating family-run places (each with about 10 rooms and outdoor hot tubs) a short walk away – described below.

Hotels The log-built Vagabond Lodge features a fabulous first-floor living room and comfortable, traditional-style rooms ('combines the atmosphere of a European mountain refuge with the luxury of a North American 5-star resort'). Copper Horse Lodge has spacious but more austere rooms in modern styles. Winston Lodge (formerly Highland Lodge; now under new ownership) has handmade wooden furniture, a welcoming sitting room and a cosy, woody bar. In Golden, a reader has enjoyed staying at the Auberge Kicking Horse B&B.

Apartments The Whispering Pines and the Selkirk Townhomes have been recommended.

Eating out Eagle's Eye at the top of the gondola opens on Friday and Saturday evenings ('excellent food but prices to match'). The Pub in Winston Lodge does burgers, steaks, pizzas etc. Corks in Copper Horse Lodge does 'excellent food and friendly service'. Kuma is a sushi bar. In Golden, Kicking Horse Grill, Eleven22 ('fusion dining') and the out-of-town Cedar House are rated.

Après-ski Quiet. As the slopes close, the Pub at Winston Lodge has a deck, blazing fireplaces indoors and out and music. In Golden the Mad Trapper and Golden Taps are lively bars.

Off the slopes There is snowmobiling, snowshoeing, tubing and an ice rink; plus a wolf centre near Golden.

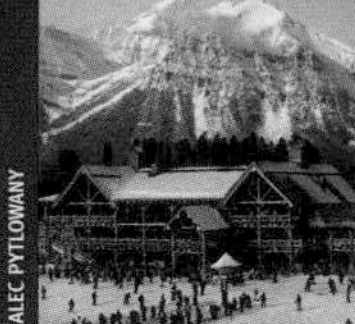
SKI BANFF / LAKE LOUISE / ALEC PYTLOWANY

Lake Louise

Stunning views and the biggest ski area in the Banff region, with some good places to stay but no real village

RATINGS

The mountains	
Extent	★★★
Fast lifts	★★★★
Queues	★★★★
Terrain p'ks	★★★★
Snow	★★★
Expert	★★★★
Intermediate	★★★★
Beginner	★★★
Boarder	★★★
X-country	★★★★★
Restaurants	★★
Schools	★★★★
Families	★★★★
The resort	
Charm	★★★
Convenience	★
Scenery	★★★★
Eating out	★★
Après-ski	★★
Off-slope	★★★★

RPI	155
lift pass	£350
ski hire	£125
lessons	£175
food & drink	£125
total	**£775**

NEWS

2011/12: The shuttle-bus service from Banff was improved.

- [+] Spectacular high-mountain scenery, in a largely unspoilt wilderness
- [+] Large ski area by local standards
- [+] Snowy slopes of Sunshine Village within reach (see Banff chapter)
- [+] Excellent very scenic cross-country

- [–] 'Village' is just a few hotels and shops, quiet in the evening
- [–] Slopes a drive or bus ride away
- [–] Snowfall record modest
- [–] Can be very cold, and the chairlifts have no covers

If you care more for scenery than for après-ski action, Lake Louise is worth considering for a holiday. We've seen a few spectacular mountain views, and the view from the Fairmont Chateau Lake Louise hotel of the Victoria Glacier across frozen Lake Louise is as spectacular as they come: simply stunning.

Even if you prefer the more animated base of Banff, you'll want to make expeditions to Lake Louise during your holiday. It can't compete with Sunshine Village for quantity of snow, but it's an interesting mountain. And from the slopes you get a distant version of that stunning view.

THE RESORT

Lake Louise is small, but it's a resort of three distinct parts. First, there's the splendid lake itself overlooked by the huge Fairmont Chateau Lake Louise hotel. Then there's Lake Louise 'village' – a spacious collection of hotels, condos, petrol station, liquor store and a few shops a couple of miles away in the valley bottom. Finally, a mile or two across the valley, there's the lift base station.

Sunshine Village and Norquay ski areas (covered in our Banff chapter) are 45 minutes away by road. Buses (covered by the Tri-area lift pass) run only two days a week to each (on the days the ski school Club Ski program goes there). So having a car helps. Bus trips also run to the more distant resorts of Kicking Horse and Panorama, subject to demand, and there are heli-skiing day trips.

VILLAGE CHARM ★★★
Low key and relaxed

The 'village' has no focus other than a small shopping mall, but it's a quiet and relaxing place. Up at the lake, it's all about the setting: the scenery provides the charm, and somehow the scale of the giant hotel seems perfectly appropriate.

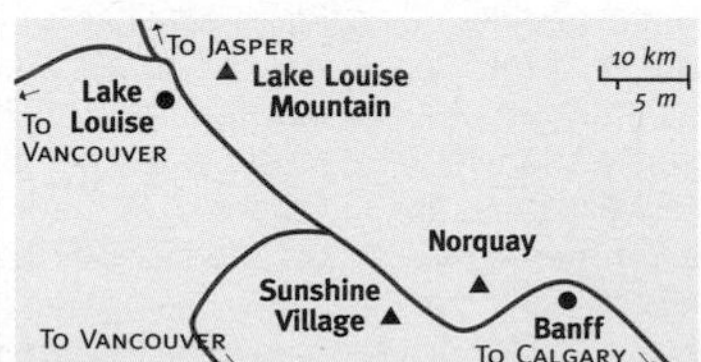

CONVENIENCE ★
Lake or village, not slopes

Most lodging is around the 'village'. Buses run every half hour to the ski area. Staying up at the Chateau, or near it, just means a slightly longer bus ride. Taxis are said to be 'ridiculously expensive'.

SCENERY ★★★★
Splendid lakes and mountains

Lake Louise itself is in a spectacular setting beneath the Victoria Glacier. Tom Wilson, who discovered it in 1882, declared: 'As God is my judge, I never in all my exploration have seen such a matchless scene.' Neither have we. It can be appreciated from many of the rooms of the Fairmont Chateau Lake Louise hotel on the lake shore, and there are grand views from the ski area of other peaks and glaciers, including Canada's Matterhorn lookalike, Mount Assiniboine.

THE MOUNTAINS

There's an attractive mixture of high, open slopes, low trails cut through forest and gladed slopes between the two. There are good, free guided tours at 10am and 1.15. Louise is known for fiercely low temperatures; we've luckily escaped them on recent visits.

KEY FACTS

Resort	1645m 5,400ft
Sunshine, Norquay and Lake Louise	
Slopes	1630-2730m 5,350-8,950ft
Lifts	26
Pistes	7,748 acres
Green	23%
Blue	39%
Black	38%
Snowmaking	24%
Lake Louise only	
Slopes	1645-2635m 5,400-8,650ft
Lifts	9
Pistes	4,200 acres
Green	25%
Blue	45%
Black	30%
Snowmaking	40%

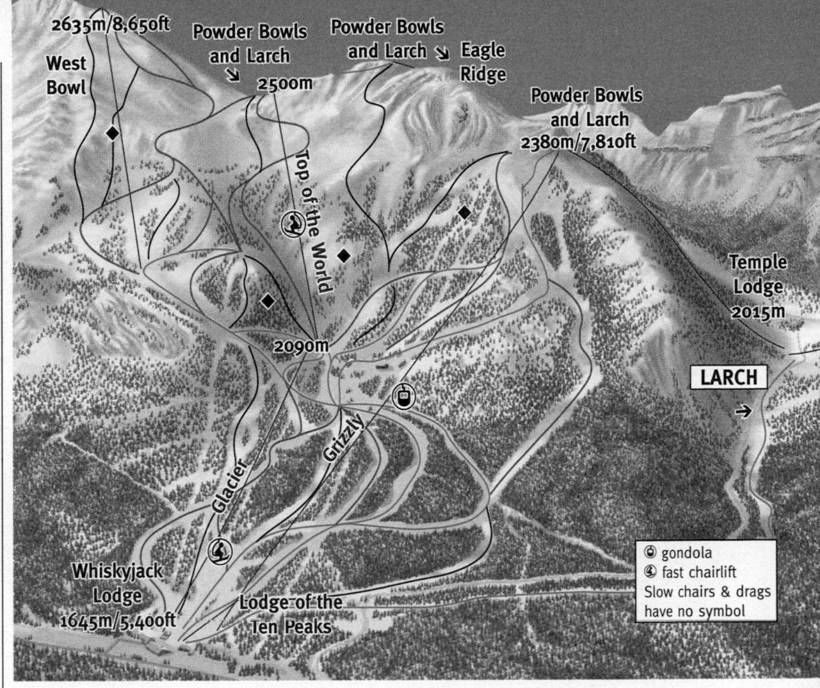

EXTENT OF THE SLOPES ★★★★★

A wide variety

The Lake Louise ski area is a fair size by North American standards – it ranks sixth in skiable area – but is quite modest by Alpine standards; a good intermediate could ski the groomed trails in a day or two. A 2012 reporter complains of the terrain park taking up too much of the lower mountain and 'limiting the options for regular skiers'.

From the base area (see the map above) you have a choice of a fast quad to mid-mountain, followed by a six-pack to the top centre of the **Front Side** (or South Face), or a gondola direct to a slightly lower point off to the right side. From both, as elsewhere, there's a choice of green, blue or black runs (good for a group of mixed abilities who want to keep meeting up). In poor visibility, the gondola is a better option, as the treeline goes almost to the top there. Or you can stay on the lower part of the mountain using the chairs. From mid-mountain on the left, the long Summit draglift takes you to the high point of the area.

From here or the top chair you can go over the ridge and into the **Powder Bowls** – almost treeless, shady and mainly steep (though there are easy ways round the steep parts). From the top of the gondola, the Ptarmigan area is more wooded. From below the bowls you can take the Paradise lift back to the top again or go on down to Temple Lodge, base station of the Ptarmigan chair to the main mountain and a fast chair to the separate **Larch**

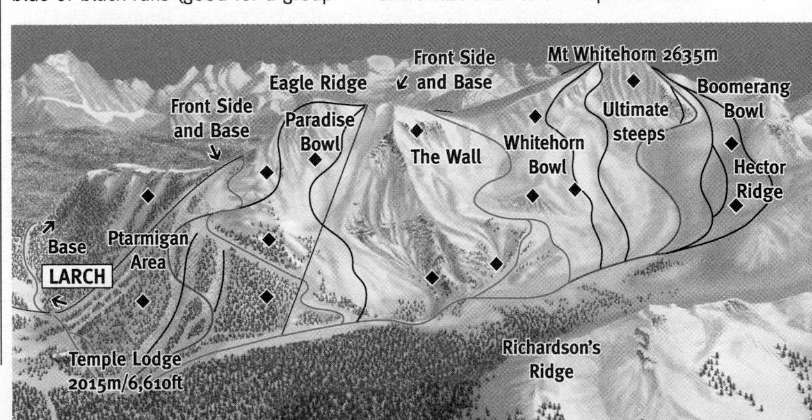

LIFT PASSES

Tri-area lift pass

Prices in C$

Age	1-day	6-day
under 13	26	176
13 to 17	63	474
18 to 64	84	533
over 65	63	474

Free under 6

Beginner lift, lesson and rental package

Notes

Day pass is for Lake Louise only; 3-day-plus pass covers all lifts and transport between Banff, Lake Louise, Norquay and Sunshine Village; prices include 5% tax

ACTIVITIES

Indoor Hotel-based pools, saunas and hot tubs

Outdoor Ice skating, walking, swimming in hot springs, sleigh rides, dog sledding, snowmobiling

area (just off our map). Its lift-served vertical is a modest 375m, but the sector has pretty wooded runs for all abilities. From Temple Lodge there's a long green path back to the base area.

FAST LIFTS ★★★★☆
Beware the cold rides

There is gondola and fast chair access to most of the slopes on the Front Side, and to Larch. The few slow lifts serve steep slopes where your descent may take some time, so the lift ride time is bearable. This is a famously cold resort, and reporters regularly complain of extremely cold rides.

QUEUES ★★★★☆
Not during the week

Queues are rarely a problem midweek. But half of the area's visitors come for the day from nearby cities, such as Calgary, so there can be queues for some lifts at weekends and public holidays ('up to 45 minutes for the gondola on the Saturday', says a 2012 visitor). Busy pistes and lift breakdowns can be a problem too.

TERRAIN PARKS ★★★★☆
Better every year

After a brief absence in 2008, the terrain park is improving year on year. The 2012 park featured 27 features set out in clearly defined areas including progression and XL jumps, plus a skier/boardercross.

SNOW RELIABILITY ★★★☆☆
Usually OK

Lake Louise gets around 180 inches a year on the Front Side, which is not a lot, and nowhere near as much as Sunshine Village down the road (see the Banff chapter). The Front Side faces south-west, which is not good; but the Powder Bowls face north-east, and Larch north. Snowmaking covers 40% of the pistes. Grooming is fine.

FOR EXPERTS ★★★★☆
Widespread pleasure

There are plenty of steep slopes – but bear in mind that powder is less likely here than in many other Canadian resorts. On the Front Side, as well as a score of marked black diamond trails in and above the trees, there is the alluring West Bowl, reached from the Summit drag – a wide, open expanse of snow outside the area boundary to be explored with a guide.

Inside the boundary, the Powder Bowls (aka The Ultimate Steeps) area on the Back Side offers countless black mogul/powder runs, though there is no great variation in character. From the Summit drag, you can drop into Whitehorn 2 if it is open, directly behind the peak – a row of exceptional chutes almost 1km long. Starting from the blue Boomerang trail, you can also access much tamer, wide, open slopes in Boomerang Bowl.

The Top of the World six-pack takes you to the very popular Paradise Bowl/Eagle Ridge area, also served by its own triple chair on the Back Side – there are endless variants here, ranging from comfortably steep single diamonds to very challenging double diamonds. The seriously steep slope served by the Ptarmigan quad chair has great gladed terrain and is a good place to escape the crowds and find good snow.

The Larch area has some steep double diamond stuff in the trees. And with good snow-cover, the open snowfields at the top are great for those with the energy to hike up.

Heli-skiing day trips are available to bases outside the National Park in British Columbia.

FOR INTERMEDIATES ★★★★☆
Some good cruising

Almost half the runs are classified as intermediate. But from the top of the Front Side the blue runs down are little more than paths in places, and there are very few blues or greens in the Powder Bowls. Once you get part-way down the Front Side the blues are much more interesting. And when groomed, the Men's and Ladies' Downhill black runs are great fast cruises on the lower half of the mountain. Juniper, in the same area, is a varied cruise. Meadowlark is a beautiful treelined single black run to the base area, curling away from the lifts – to find it from the Grizzly Express gondola, first follow the Eagle Meadows green. The Larch area has some short but ideal intermediate runs – and reporters have enjoyed the natural lumps and bumps of the aptly named blue, Rock Garden ('never had so much fun; really away from it all').

The adventurous should try the blue Boomerang run – which starts with a short side-step up from the top of the Summit drag – and also some of the ungroomed terrain in the Powder Bowls reachable from that run.

↑ The views from the ski area are impressive by North American standards

THE LAKE LOUISE SKI AREA LTD / HENRY GEORGI

SCHOOLS

Ski Big 3
t 760 7731

Lake Louise
t 522 1333

Classes (Big 3 prices)
3 days guided tuition of the three areas C$314 incl. tax

Private lessons
Half day (3hr) C$398, incl. tax, for up to 5 people

CHILDCARE

Lake Louise Daycare
t 522 3555
Ages 18 days to 6yr

Ski school
Takes ages 6 to 12 (3 days C$314, incl. tax)

FOR BEGINNERS ★★★☆☆
Some long greens

Lake Louise offers first-timers a 'discover skiing or boarding' package that includes a lift pass with a day's or half-day's tuition. There is a decent nursery area near the base served by a short T-bar. You progress to the gentle, wide Wiwaxy (a designated and policed 'slow ski zone'), Pinecone Way and the slightly more difficult Deer Run or Eagle Meadows. The greens in the Powder Bowls and in the Larch area are worth trying for the views, though some do contain slightly steep pitches and can get busy ('Our beginner was very nervous trying the Saddleback Bowl,' said one past reporter).

FOR BOARDERS ★★★☆☆
Something for everyone

Lake Louise is a great mountain for freeriders, with plenty of challenging terrain in the bowls and glades. Beginners will have fun on the Front Side's blue and green runs. But there's a T-bar at the base area, and beware of the vicious Summit button lift (top left looking at the trail map). Also avoid the long, very gentle green run through the woods from Larch back to base. This is flat in places and a nightmare for boarders. Freestylers will enjoy the varied terrain park.

FOR CROSS-COUNTRY ★★★★★
High in quality and quantity

It's a very good area for cross-country, with around 80km of groomed trails in the National Park – plenty of scenic stops needed. There are 20km of excellent trails in the local area and at Lake Louise itself. An alternative is the secluded Emerald Lake Lodge, 40km away and with some lovely trails.

MOUNTAIN RESTAURANTS ★★☆☆☆
Good base facilities

There is only one proper mountain hut in winter. The Temple Lodge near the bottom of Larch and the Ptarmigan chair is a rustic style building with 'very good' table- and 'reasonable' self-service restaurants, but can get unpleasantly crowded.

Most people eat at the base, where there are big-scale but 'soulless' facilities. The World Cup Alpine Room in the Whiskyjack Lodge offers fixed-price, 'high quality' buffet lunches and 'good value' breakfasts. The Lodge of the Ten Peaks is a hugely impressive log-built affair with various 'fairly efficient' eating, drinking and lounging options.

SCHOOLS AND GUIDES ★★★★☆
All reports positive

We lack recent reports, but all past reports we have on file are positive, for both adults' and children's classes: 'excellent private lessons'; 'great instructor who worked hard to make sure everyone in our mixed-ability group learnt new stuff'; 'the children made good progress and enjoyed themselves'. Be aware, though, that your instructor may change from day to day – a common arrangement in North America. See the Banff chapter for details of the excellent three-day, three-mountain Club Ski and Club Snowboard Program.

FOR FAMILIES ★★★★☆
Good facilities

The resort is keen to attract families and has good school and childcare facilities: 'Really well run; my son enjoyed the good mix of lessons and playtime,' says a recent visitor. Parents are lent free pagers too. The Minute Maid Wilderness Adventure Park is a kids' learning area at the base. The school gets good reviews and offers a fun programme for teenagers.

The terrain park takes up a lot of the lower mountain ➔

THE LAKE LOUISE SKI AREA LTD / HENRY GEORGI

UK PACKAGES

Alpine Answers, AmeriCan Ski, American Ski Classics, Canadian Affair, Crystal, Crystal Finest, Elegant Resorts, Frontier, Independent Ski Links, Inghams, Momentum, Mountain Wave, Neilson, Oxford Ski Co, PowderBeds, Ski Bespoke, Ski Independence, Ski Line, Ski Safari, Skitracer, Skiworld, Snow Finders, Supertravel, Thomson, Virgin Snow

GETTING THERE

Air Calgary 195km/ 120 miles (2hr30)

Phone numbers
From distant parts of Canada, add the prefix 1 403; from abroad, add the prefix +1 403

TOURIST OFFICE

www.skilouise.com
www.SkiBig3.com

STAYING THERE

You might like to consider a two-centre holiday, combining Lake Louise with, say, Banff or Kicking Horse.
Hotels Summer is the peak season here. Prices are much lower in winter.
*****Fairmont Chateau Lake Louise** (522 3511) Grand monster with 500 rooms and seven restaurants in a fantastic setting with stunning views over frozen Lake Louise to the glacier beyond; shops, pool, hot tub, sauna.
****Post** (522 3989) Small, relaxed, comfortable Relais & Châteaux place in the village, with excellent restaurant (huge wine list), pool, hot tub, steam room. Avoid rooms on railway side. 'Beautifully furnished; friendly, helpful.'
***Deer Lodge** (522 3991) Charming old hotel next to the Chateau. Small rooms, but helpful staff and good food. Roof-top hot tub.
***Lake Louise Inn** (522 3791) Cheaper option in the village, with pool, hot tub and sauna. One recent reporter has stayed there nine times.
Apartments Some are available but local shopping is limited. The Baker Creek Chalets (522 3761) are a popular retreat for a traditional 'log cabin, log fire, isolation and wildlife' experience.
At altitude Skoki Lodge (522 1347) is a charming log cabin, 11km on skis from Temple Lodge. Built in the 1930s.

EATING OUT ★★★★★

Limited choice

The Post hotel's restaurant has repeatedly impressed us and reporters with its ambitious food and excellent service – 'exceptional, if expensive'. The Chateau has the top-notch Fairview Dining Room and the 'really good' Glacier Saloon ('sea chowder soup and bison pie both excellent'). Readers also like the Timberwolf Cafe (Italian) at the Lake Louise Inn, the Mountain restaurant (Thai curry, burgers) and Village Grill (Western/ Chinese menu) for cheaper options.

APRES-SKI ★★★★★

Lively at teatime, quiet later

At close of play there is some action in the main base lodge, but the hub is the Kokanee Kabin, which has live music most weekends, a terrace and an outdoor fire. Later on, things are fairly quiet. Try the Glacier Saloon, in Chateau Lake Louise, the Explorer's Lounge in the Lake Louise Inn or the Outpost Pub in the Post hotel.

OFF THE SLOPES ★★★★★

Beautiful scenery

Lake Louise makes a lovely, peaceful place to stay for someone who does not intend to hit the slopes but enjoys the great outdoors. The lake itself makes a stunning setting for walks, snowshoeing, cross-country skiing and ice skating. Reporters highly recommend the dog sledding and the Wilson Icefield discovery tour – a helicopter flight, snowshoe walk and lunch ('BBQ with superb steaks'). There are lots of attractions around the Banff area too (see Banff chapter).

Lake Louise is near one end of the Columbia Icefields Parkway, a three-hour drive to Jasper through national parks – one of the world's most beautiful drives.

Revelstoke

New resort rapidly acquiring cult status for its steep terrain; shame it's so remote and without a proper village yet

TOP 10 RATINGS

Extent	***
Fast lifts	*****
Queues	*****
Snow	****
Expert	*****
Intermediate	**
Beginner	*
Charm	**
Convenience	***
Scenery	****

RPI	140
lift pass	£310
ski hire	£150
lessons	£135
food & drink	£115
total	**£710**

KEY FACTS

Resort	510m 1,680ft
Slopes	510-2225m 1,680-7,300ft
Lifts	5
Pistes	3,121 acres
Green	7%
Blue	45%
Black	48%
Snowmaking	at base

- + Fabulous, steep, ungroomed terrain
- + Great cat- and heli-skiing
- + Stunning views over frozen Columbia river
- + Good-value lodging in town

- − Not much intermediate terrain
- − No snowmaking on main slopes
- − Very remote location
- − Resort base village still tiny; Revelstoke town unremarkable

Until five years ago Revelstoke was a small hill for locals served by one short lift. But a gondola and two fast chairs have transformed it into a resort with the biggest vertical in North America and around 3,000 acres of slopes, more than many Canadian rivals. Its terrain is mostly ungroomed and steep; if you enjoy adventure skiing, put it on your shortlist. Consider combining it with other resorts as a two- or three-centre holiday. There's a fledgling resort village at the base, but for now the best place to stay is Revelstoke town.

THE RESORT

Revelstoke is remote. Getting there from the UK involves two flights to get to Kelowna or Kamloops followed by a three-hour drive. Or it's a drive of five hours from Calgary, or six hours from Vancouver; and that's in good weather. The new Village at the base of the gondola is still tiny, and there's a lot more building planned. Better to stay in Revelstoke town for more choice of lodging and restaurants.

Village charm The town is in the North American grid pattern with a mix of unremarkable old and new buildings. It's a working town rather than a resort. The new Village at the base is still at an early stage of development.
Convenience The mountain is a five-minute drive from town. Shuttle-buses are 'regular and reliable'.
Scenery The views over the partly frozen Columbia river are stunning, as are the towering peaks rising up around the slopes.

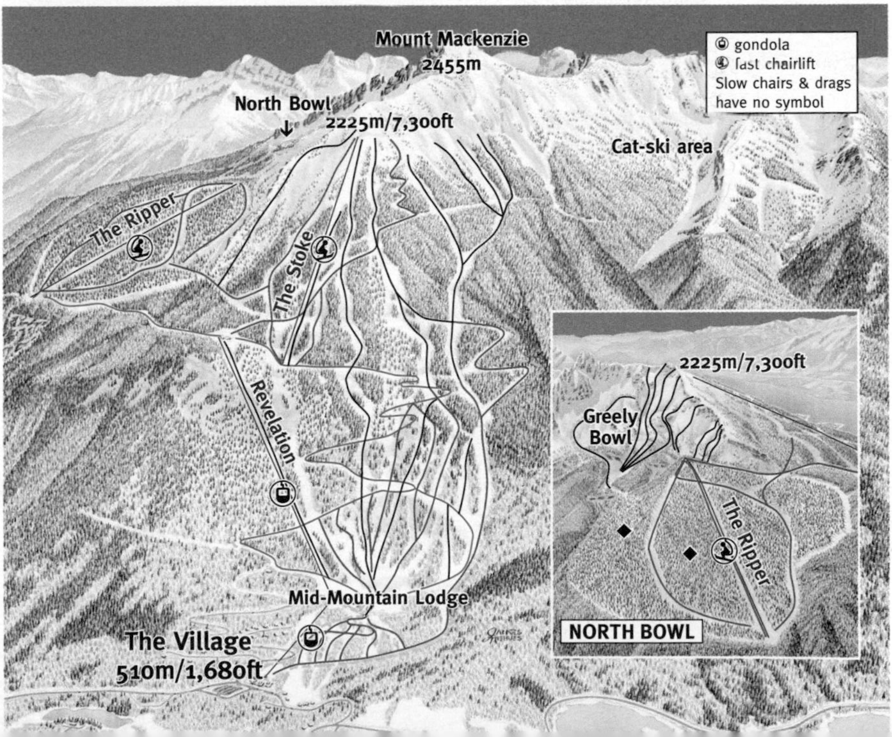

The new Village at the base of the gondola exists, but it is still tiny ➔

REVELSTOKE / PURE STUDIOS

NEWS

2011/12: The new Turtle Creek beginner area and floodlit tubing park opened at the base area, served by a moving carpet and equipped with snowmaking. Nelsen Lodge at the base was rebranded Sutton Place Hotel, and the final phase opened, including 107 new rooms and suites, a new outdoor heated pool, hot tubs, fitness facilities, wine bar and children's day care centre.

UK PACKAGES

AmeriCan Ski, American Ski Classics, Canadian Affair, Consensio, Crystal, Frontier, Momentum, Neilson, Oxford Ski Co, Pure Powder, Ski Bespoke, Ski Safari, Ski Solutions, Skiworld

Phone numbers
From distant parts of Canada add the prefix 1 250; from abroad use the prefix +1 250

TOURIST OFFICE

www.revelstoke mountainresort.com

THE MOUNTAINS

A two-stage gondola takes you from the Village to mid-mountain, from which you can reach both the fast quads. The trail map marks black runs, but there's no single/double diamond differentiation. And reporters remark that lots of the runs are much longer than they appear from the map. Be prepared for extreme cold (–41°C with wind chill on our December visit).
Slopes Its 3,121 acres make it bigger than most Canadian resorts; plus it has 5,000 acres of cat- and heli-skiing.
Fast lifts All three main lifts are fast.
Queues We have no reports of queues, and several readers have said they had the trails all to themselves.
Terrain parks There isn't one.
Snow reliability They claim an average of 360 to 540 inches a year – up there with the best. But there's snowmaking only on the new beginner area at the base, and the lower slopes can suffer (and may be closed).
Experts Experts are flocking to Revelstoke. On skier's left, there are long top-to-bottom black runs; many are often groomed. On skier's right, North Bowl (reached by a long traverse and, to some of the runs, a hike) is a huge area of ungroomed steep terrain. In between are several big areas of glades with nicely spaced trees. Then there's cat- and heli-skiing.
Intermediates Most blues are steepish and suit adventurous intermediates best. The Ripper chair accesses the easiest blues. And there's a 15km-long blue/green run from top to bottom. But the intermediate terrain doesn't add up to much (the claimed 45% gives a misleading impression).
Beginners Go elsewhere. Although a new beginner area opened in 2011, the only easy run from the top of the gondola is long, narrow and winding.
Snowboarding There's fabulous freeriding but lots of flats, especially getting to and from North Bowl.
Cross-country 26km of groomed trails.
Mountain restaurants The Mid Mountain Lodge serves decent food but gets packed. Reporters like the 'stylish' Rockford Asian-fusion restaurant at the base. You can eat your own food at Mid Mountain Lodge.
Schools and guides The ski school aims to help people progress from groomed runs to the backcountry.

STAYING THERE

Hotels The final stage of the first lodging at the base village opened last season. Revelstoke has several motels and a few more charming B&Bs and hotels. We stayed at the Courthouse Inn (837 3369), which was friendly and did a great breakfast. Reporters have enjoyed the Inn on the River (837 3262) with great views over the river, the central Regent Inn (837 2107), which dates from the 1920s, and the Hillcrest Hotel (837 3322) and new Best Western Plus (837 2043) – both on the edge of town.
Eating out There are a few good coffee shops. For dinner, try Woolsey Creek and, in the Regent Inn, 112 (both 'fine dining'), Zala's ('nice halibut, pizzas'), Bad Paul's ('family-friendly, huge portions'), the Village Idiot ('popular, live music, burgers, pizzas, steaks, wraps'), and Kawakubo ('great sushi').
Après-ski 'Very quiet', but try the Village Idiot (see above), the Rockford (at the lift base), Last Drop (comfy sofas, log fire; in Powder Springs Inn), River City (music, pool; in Regent Inn).
Off the slopes The Aquatic Centre is 'excellent': pools, hot tubs, saunas.

SILVER STAR RESORT / DON WEIXL PHOTOGRAPHY

Silver Star

Car-free, purpose-built village designed to resemble a Victorian-era mining town, with slopes for all standards

TOP 10 RATINGS	
Extent	***
Fast lifts	****
Queues	*****
Snow	****
Expert	****
Intermediate	***
Beginner	****
Charm	***
Convenience	*****
Scenery	***

RPI	135
lift pass	£300
ski hire	£130
lessons	£135
food & drink	£120
total	**£685**

- Cute, colourful village
- Very family-friendly
- Some good runs for all abilities
- Excellent cross-country skiing

- Tiny village; very quiet at night
- Limited choice of accommodation (but some high-quality condos)
- Ski area not huge

This quiet, family-friendly resort has a tiny traffic-free centre resembling a 19th-century mining town. There are slopes to suit everyone, and it's easy to combine a stay here with one at Big White, which has the same owners.

THE RESORT

Silver Star is a small, purpose-built resort right on the slopes. Big White (see separate chapter) is around two and a half hours away.

Village charm The village has brightly painted Victorian-style buildings with wooden sidewalks and faux gas lights. It's a bit Disneyesque but works well.

Convenience The centre is compact and car-free. Ski-in/ski-out chalets are dotted in the trees too.

Scenery The views from Silver Star's summit are over gently rolling hills.

THE MOUNTAINS

The mountain has trees going right to the top and four main linked sectors.

Slopes The Vance Creek area has mainly easy intermediate runs served by the Comet six-pack, which starts below the village. From there you can reach the Silver Woods area of mainly intermediate slopes and glades, served by a high-speed quad. The top of the Comet chair links to the Attridge area which has a mix of easy runs and short steep blacks served by its own slow chairs too. It also links to the

SILVER STAR MOUNTAIN RESORT

This pic makes Silver Star look quite spread out. But the centre is very small and compact ↓

NEWS

2012/13: A new four-lane bowling alley – Pinheads – is due to be built underneath the Firelight Lodge.

2011/12: Heli-skiing is now possible direct from the resort – expect six to eight runs in a day.

KEY FACTS

Resort	1610m 5,280ft
Slopes	1155-1915m 3,790-6,280ft
Lifts	12
Pistes	3,065 acres
Green	15%
Blue	40%
Black	45%
Snowmaking	none

UK PACKAGES

AmeriCan Ski, Canadian Affair, Frontier, Neilson, PowderBeds, Ski Independence, Ski Line, Ski Safari, Skiworld

Central reservations Call 558 6083; toll-free (within Canada) 1 800 663 4431

Phone numbers From distant parts of Canada, add the prefix 1 250; from abroad, add +1 250

TOURIST OFFICE

www.skisilverstar.com

Putnam Creek sector on the back side, which has lots of steep blacks and easier blues, all served by a fast quad.
Fast lifts There's one for each sector.
Queues 'No queues,' says a recent visitor. We skied here on a busy Saturday and waited a few minutes for the Comet chair at peak times but the trails were still delightfully deserted.
Terrain parks The 16-acre Telus park on Vance Creek is excellent for experts and intermediates, and the Kiddie park for beginners is beside it. There's a boardercross in the Silver Woods area.
Snow reliability Silver Star gets an average of 276 inches a year – not in the top flight but not far off.
Experts Putnam Creek has a dense network of single and double black diamond runs plunging through the trees, many of them mogul runs. The runs to the left as you ride up the chair are north-facing and keep their snow well. There are some good short blacks in the Attridge area, too. Heli-skiing was new for 2011/12.
Intermediates Vance Creek has mainly easy cruising runs. Silver Woods has lovely runs cut through the trees and easy blues amid the trees themselves. Putnam Creek also has excellent blue cruising. Good intermediates will appreciate the groomed black runs (they groom at least two each night – look on the boards for which ones).
Beginners There's a nursery area by the village with a moving carpet and long easy green runs to move on to.
Snowboarding Intermediates will enjoy the blue runs and glades. But the steep bump runs in Putnam Creek are tough. And there are some flat areas (including the way to Putnam Creek).
Cross-country They claim 'The Best Nordic Skiing in North America' and have over 100km of trails.
Mountain restaurants The small atmospheric table-service Paradise Camp on Putnam Creek is popular and serves good stews and soups.
Schools and guides We've had good reports of adults' and kids' lessons.
Families Star Kids takes children aged 18 months to six years; reporters have sent us glowing reports.

STAYING THERE

It is mainly specialist North American operators who come here, such as Frontier Ski and Ski Independence.
Hotels A recent reporter liked the Bulldog Hotel ('fairly basic rooms, fun bulldog pictures on the wall'). The Vance Creek, Lord Aberdeen and Pinnacles are the other main options. The Samesun Backpackers Hostel has both normal and dorm rooms.
Apartments We stayed in a huge, luxurious condo with private hot tub in the Snowbird Lodge and loved it – as did a 2012 visitor. Snowbird and Firelight Lodge (ask for a condo overlooking the skating pond and tubing hill) are the best in town – both ski-in/ski-out. Other recommendations include Chilcoot Lodge, Creekside, Grandview and Pinnacles.
Eating out Reporters' favourite is the Bulldog Grand Cafe (Asian-influenced food and 'ribs that melt in your mouth'). Other tips: the Silver Grill Steak & Chop House for fine dining ('good food, friendly service'), Long John's Pub with silver mining theme decor, Isidore's ('Swiss with a twist'), Bugaboos for breakfast.
Après-ski It's very quiet. But the Saloon, Den and Lord John's Pub may be lively and have live entertainment.
Off the slopes There's a natural ice rink on a lake, tubing, snowshoeing, snowmobiling and sleigh rides.

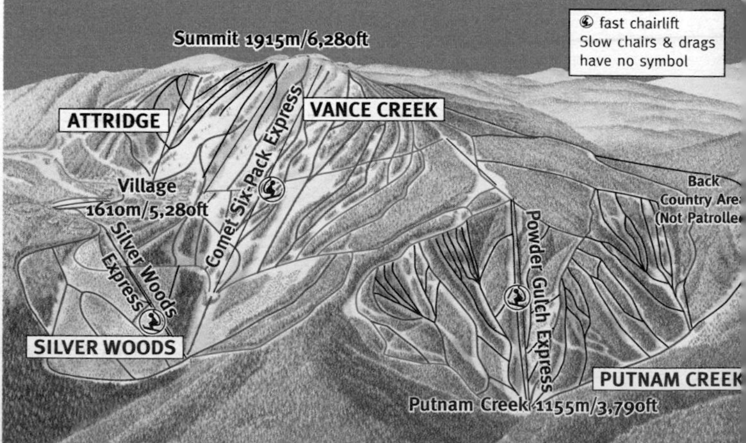

Sun Peaks

Attractive car-free village at the foot of three linked mountains with varied slopes including some unusual easy groomed glade runs

TOP 10 RATINGS

Extent	***
Fast lifts	**
Queues	*****
Snow	****
Expert	***
Intermediate	****
Beginner	****
Charm	***
Convenience	****
Scenery	***

RPI	140
lift pass	£310
ski hire	£130
lessons	£150
food & drink	£120
total	**£710**

NEWS

2011/12: The resort celebrated the 50th anniversary of skiing on Tod Mountain. A couple of new restaurants opened and several lodges were renovated.

- + Great terrain for early intermediates
- + Excellent glades
- + Slopes very quiet during the week
- + Good for families

- – Village may be too small and quiet for some tastes
- – Ski area modest by Alpine standards

Sun Peaks has sprung from the drawing board since the mid-1990s. It has a friendly, attractive small village and a fair amount of varied terrain – enough for three or four days, say. We suggest combining it with resorts such as Whistler, Silver Star or Big White on a two- or three-centre trip.

THE RESORT

Until 1993 Sun Peaks was Tod Mountain, a local hill for the residents of nearby Kamloops. Since then the ski area has been expanded, and a small (smaller than many reporters expect), attractive resort village has developed. There are regular transfers to other resorts such as Whistler – making a two-centre trip easy. Day trips to Revelstoke are organized.

Village charm The low-rise pastel-coloured buildings have a vaguely Tirolean feeling to them. It's a pleasant place to stroll around and very family-friendly. The traffic-free main street is lined with lodgings, restaurants and shops, including a smart art gallery, a chocolate shop and a few coffee bars.

Convenience Much of the accommodation is ski-in/ski-out.

Scenery The slopes are pleasantly wooded and Mt Tod's modest summit gives views over gently rolling terrain.

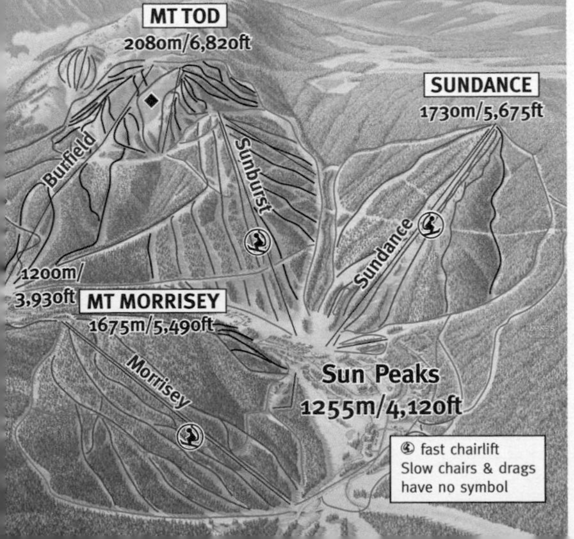

THE MOUNTAINS

There are three linked mountains, but the links to and from Mt Morrisey from the other two are roundabout and flattish. Free guided tours are run twice a day (9.15 and 1pm), and you can ski for free with Nancy Greene (former Olympic champion, Canada's Female Athlete of the 20th Century and a Canadian senator) when she's in town. Don't miss it – she's great fun. At the top of each main lift there is a board showing which pistes in that area have been groomed. Each day at least one single black diamond piste is groomed.

Slopes With almost 3,700 acres of skiable terrain, Sun Peaks is the second biggest ski area in British Columbia (Whistler is the biggest) – but it's not big by Alpine standards.

One lift goes from the centre of the village to mid-mountain on the resort's original ski hill, Mt Tod. This has mainly black runs, but there are easier blues and greens, too. Many of Mt Tod's steepest runs are served only by the slow Burfield quad, which takes over 20 minutes to get to the top and is frequently the subject of complaint by reporters (there's a mid-station that allows you to ski the top runs only). The Sundance area – also reached from the village centre – has mainly blue and green cruising runs. Both Sundance and Tod have some great gladed areas to play in (12 of them marked on the trail map).

Mt Morrisey is reached by a long green run from the top of Sundance and has a delightful network of easy blue runs with trees left uncut in the trails, effectively making them groomed glade runs that even early intermediates can try.

The Delta Sun Peaks Resort has a great outdoor pool and hot tub right by the slopes ➔

SUN PEAKS RESORT / ADAM STEIN

KEY FACTS

Resort	1255m 4,120ft
Slopes	1200-2080m 3,930-6,820ft
Lifts	11
Pistes	3,678 acres
Green	10%
Blue	58%
Black	32%
Snowmaking	3%

UK PACKAGES

AmeriCan Ski, American Ski Classics, Canadian Affair, Erna Low, Frontier, Independent Ski Links, Momentum, Neilson, Ski Bespoke, Ski Independence, Ski Line, Ski Safari, Ski Solutions, Skitracer, Skiworld, Snow Finders, Virgin Snow

Phone numbers
From distant parts of Canada, add the prefix 1 250; from abroad, add the prefix +1 250

TOURIST OFFICE

www.sunpeaksresort.com

Fast lifts The three distinct sectors are each served by a high-speed quad. The other lifts are painfully slow.
Queues Weekdays are usually very quiet; it's only at peak weekends that you might find short queues.
Terrain parks The park has advanced, intermediate and beginner areas, served by snowmaking. But there is no half-pipe.
Snow reliability Sun Peaks gets an average snowfall of 220 inches a year: not in the top league but better than some. The snow can suffer on the lower part of Mt Tod's south-facing slopes, especially later in the season.
Experts Mt Tod has most of the steep terrain, and you can ski some good (but short) steep and gladed runs without descending to the bottom by riding the Burfield quad from its mid-station and the Crystal and Elevation chairs. Some of the blacks on Mt Morrisey (such as Static Cling) have steep mogul sections, too.
Intermediates This is great terrain for early intermediates: there are the easy and charming groomed glades of Mt Morrisey, lovely swooping blues on Sundance and the long 5 Mile run from Mt Tod. More adventurous intermediates can also tackle the easier glades (such as Cahilty) and blacks (such as Peek-A-Boo).
Beginners There are nursery slopes right in the village centre, with long easy greens to progress to.
Snowboarding Boarders can explore the whole mountain. But there are flat greens to and from Mt Morrisey.
Cross-country 30km of groomed trails and 14km of backcountry trails.
Mountain restaurants The Sunburst Lodge is the only option and gets busy; its cinnamon buns are highly recommended. The Umbrella Cafe at the Morrisey base serves hot soup and sandwiches. And it's easy to return to a village restaurant for lunch – Mountain High Pizza is 'great value'; Bento's Day Lodge has basic hot food and drinks. You can eat your own packed lunch there – and also downstairs at Sunburst Lodge.
Schools and guides Past reports have been good, but we lack recent ones. As well as standard lessons, there are Super Groups (maximum of three people), women-only lessons and freestyle coaching.
Families The play school takes children from 18 months to five years and the ski school children from three years.

STAYING THERE

Hotels Nancy Greene's Cahilty Lodge is a comfortable ski-in/ski-out base, and you get the chance to ski with her and husband Al Raine (former Canadian ski team coach). The ski-in/ski-out Delta Sun Peaks Resort (outdoor pool and hot tub) in the village centre is regularly recommended. We've enjoyed staying at both. Fireside Lodge and the family run Heffley Boutique Inn have been recommended too.
Apartments Delta Residences are 'luxurious, ski-in/ski-out and central'. Crystal Forest and McGillivray Creek condos have been tipped – some have private hot tubs. Other well-positioned condos include Forest Trails, Snow Creek Village and Timberline Village.
Eating out For a small resort, there's a good choice of restaurants. Reader tips include Powder Hounds ('great value', 'varied menu'), Steakhouse, Servus (more sophisticated food), Chopstixx (Japanese and Thai), Bella Italia, and Mantles in the Delta Sun Peaks ('quality dining'). Cahilty Creek Bar and Grill and Black Garlic Bistro (Asian fusion) were new last season.
Après-ski It's quiet. Bottom's and Masa's are the main après-ski bars. Morrisey's in the Delta is supposed to be like a British pub. At weekends MackDaddy's nightclub in the Delta can get lively. There are fondue evenings with torchlit descents.
Off the slopes There's skating, tubing, tobogganing, snowmobiling, bungee trampolining, dog sledding, sleigh rides, snowshoeing and swimming.

WHISTLER RESORT ASSOCIATION/ PAUL MORRISON

Whistler

North America's biggest mountain, with terrain to suit every standard and a big, purpose-built, largely car-free village

RATINGS

The mountains	
Extent	****
Fast lifts	*****
Queues	**
Terrain p'ks	*****
Snow	****
Expert	*****
Intermediate	*****
Beginner	***
Boarder	*****
X-country	***
Restaurants	**
Schools	*****
Families	****
The resort	
Charm	***
Convenience	****
Scenery	***
Eating out	*****
Après-ski	****
Off-slope	***

RPI	160
lift pass	£360
ski hire	£155
lessons	£170
food & drink	£120
total	**£805**

NEWS

2011/12: A piloted four-person bobsled ride, gaining speeds of more than 135km/hr, is now on offer at the Whistler Sliding Center. You can also try the skeleton (on your own). The ski school launched the Max 4 Program, limiting adult groups to a maximum of four people.

+ North America's biggest, both in area and vertical (1610m)
+ Excellent combination of high open bowls and woodland trails
+ Good snow record
+ Almost Alpine scenery
+ Attractive modern village, purpose-built with car-free central areas
+ Good range of village restaurants and lively après-ski

- Proximity to Pacific Ocean means a lot of cloudy weather, and rain at resort level is not unusual
- Inadequate lift system; queues can be a big problem at peak times
- Overcrowded runs also a problem
- Mountain restaurants are mostly no more than functional (and all are overcrowded)
- Resort restaurants over-busy, too

Whistler is unlike any other resort in North America. In some respects – the scale, the high bowls and glaciers, the scenery, the crowds – it is more like an Alpine resort. But like most resorts on the western side of North America, it offers the advantages of excellent snow and a lot of woodland runs as well.

All things considered, the mountain is about the best that North America has to offer, and for us a visit here is always a highlight of the season. But we'll admit that we are generally lucky with the weather, and haven't had to put up with much rain at resort level – a real hazard. And we time our visits to avoid peak periods and weekends, and therefore the worst of the crowds.

THE RESORT

Whistler Village sits at the foot of its two mountains, Whistler and Blackcomb, a scenic 113km drive from Vancouver on Canada's west coast.

Whistler started as a locals' ski area in 1966 at Creekside. Whistler Village, a 10-minute bus ride away, was developed in the late 1970s; Upper Village – around the base of Blackcomb Mountain and a 10-minute walk from Whistler Village – was started in the 1980s.

VILLAGE CHARM ***

High rise but tasteful

The three main centres are all traffic-free. The architecture is varied and, for a purpose-built resort, quite tasteful – but it is all a bit urban, with lots of blocks approaching 10 storeys high. There are also many chalet-style apartments on the hillsides. Some reporters find the central Village Square area noisy in the early hours.

CONVENIENCE ****

Peak 2 Peak makes a difference

With the Peak 2 Peak gondola in place, Whistler Village, Upper Village and Creekside are all equally convenient – you can easily access both mountains by taking a maximum of three lifts.

Whistler Village has most of the bars, restaurants and shops, and two gondolas (one to each mountain). A pedestrian bridge over an access road links the main centre to newer Whistler Village North (further from the lifts), making a huge car-free area of streets lined with shops, condos and restaurants.

Upper Village is much smaller and quieter. So is Creekside, which was revamped and expanded in preparation for its role as the Alpine finish area in the 2010 Olympics.

There is a free bus between central

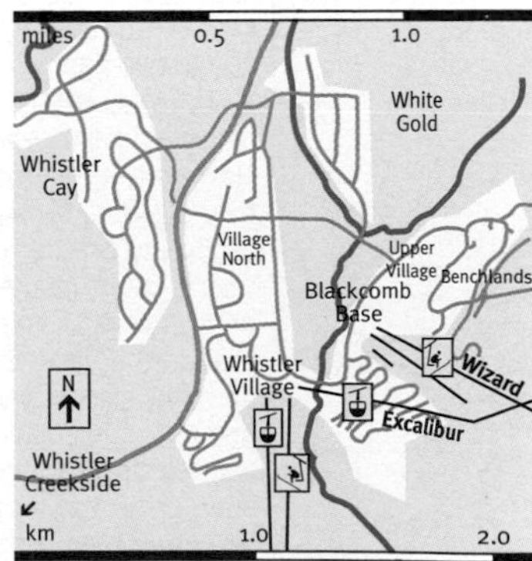

↑ Whistler has lots of fast quad chairlifts. But it really needs to replace some key ones with modern six- and eight-seaters

TOURISM WHISTLER / STEVE ROGERS

KEY FACTS

Resort	675m 2,210ft
Altitude	650-2285m 2,140-7,490ft
Lifts	37
Pistes	8,171 acres
Green	18%
Blue	55%
Black	27%
Snowmaking	7%

Whistler and Upper Village, but it can be just as quick to walk. Some lodging is a long way from the centre and means taking buses (not free) or taxis. Some hotels have free buses, which will pick you up as well as take you to restaurants and nightlife.

SCENERY ★★★★★
Almost Alpine

There are splendid views of the deep Fitzsimmons Creek valley from both mountains, and especially from the Peak 2 Peak gondola, which goes right across it – the views from the two cabins with glass floors are particularly spectacular. The upper slopes give good views to coastal sounds, high open bowls, glaciers and ridges.

THE MOUNTAINS

The mountains offer an excellent combination of high, open bowls and sheltered forest runs.

Many reporters enthuse about the mountain host service and the 'go slow' patrol – some find the latter over-zealous, but crowded slopes, especially on the runs home, mean they're often needed; we approve.

Signposting is excellent. But every year some reporters complain about inaccuracies on the trail map (in 2012 one noted missing pistes and pistes marked one colour on the map and another on the ground); most seem to be happy with it though.

EXTENT OF THE SLOPES ★★★★★
The biggest in North America

Whistler and Blackcomb together form the biggest area of slopes, with the longest runs, in North America.

Whistler Mountain is accessed from Whistler Village by a two-stage, 10-person gondola that rises over 1100m to Roundhouse Lodge at mid-mountain. Or you can use two fast quads – if they are running (see feature panel opposite).

Runs down through the trees fan out from the gondola: cruises to the Emerald and Big Red chairs and longer runs to the gondola mid-station.

From Roundhouse you can see the jewel in Whistler's crown – magnificent open bowls, served by the fast Peak and Harmony quads. The bowl beyond Harmony is served by the Symphony quad. The bowls are mostly go-anywhere terrain for experts, but there are groomed trails, so anyone can appreciate the views. Roundhouse is the departure point of the Peak 2 Peak gondola to Blackcomb.

A six-seat gondola from Creekside also accesses Whistler Mountain.

Access to **Blackcomb** from Whistler Village is by an eight-seat gondola, followed by a fast quad. From the base of Blackcomb you take two consecutive fast quads up to the main Rendezvous restaurant – departure point of the Peak 2 Peak gondola. From Rendezvous you can also go left for great cruising terrain and the

LIFT PASSES

Prices in C$

Age	1-day	6-day
under 13	48	261
13 to 18	86	443
19 to 64	101	523
65 plus	86	443

Free under 7

Beginner lift and lesson deal

Notes
Prices include sales tax. 1-day price is window price; 6-day price is online advance purchase price

Glacier Express quad up to the Horstman Glacier area, or right for steeper slopes, the terrain park or the 7th Heaven chair. The 1610m vertical from the top of 7th Heaven to the base is the biggest in North America. A T-bar from the Horstman Glacier brings you (with a short hike) to the Blackcomb Glacier in the next valley – away from all lifts.

Fresh Tracks is a deal that allows you to ride up Whistler Mountain (at extra cost) from 7.30, have a buffet breakfast and get to the slopes as they open – very popular with many reporters. Free guided tours of each mountain are offered at 11.30.

FAST LIFTS ★★★★★
Can't cope with the crowds

The resort has more fast lifts than any other in North America. Gondolas provide the main access, with lots of fast chairs after that. But the chairs are all quads – none is a six-pack or eight-seater as is now common in the Alps – and they can't handle the crowds (see 'Queues').

QUEUES ★★★★★
An ever-increasing problem

Whistler has become a victim of Its own success. At peak periods (eg Christmas and New Year) and weekends when people pour in from Vancouver, queues can be 'horrendous'. There are displays of waiting times at different lifts, which readers generally find useful.

Some reporters have signed up with the ski school just to get lift priority. Others have visited Vancouver at the weekend to avoid the crowds.

The routes out of Whistler Village in the morning can be busy (we once had a report of a queue of more than 200 metres for the gondola to Blackcomb). Creekside is less of a problem, but gets long queues at weekends. Some of the chairs higher up also produce long queues: the Harmony quad, especially, is no longer up to the job even when the resort as a whole is quiet (even the singles line can take ages); and the Emerald and Peak chairs are bottlenecks too – one reporter noted a 45-minute wait for the Peak chair on a Sunday in January. We have reports of lift closures too: a reader says that the Peak chair was open 'only once during our 11-day stay', and another visitor adds that 'on powder days, it wouldn't open until 11.30'. A reader found the Fitzsimmons and Garbanzo quads 'rarely open', despite queues for the gondola. Crowds on the slopes, especially the runs home, can be annoying, too.

TERRAIN PARKS ★★★★★
World class for all abilities

While both mountains have parks, freestylers tend to head to Blackcomb, which is home to the Olympic-standard Global Pipe (with walls almost 7m high and shaped daily), the Mini Pipe with 4.5m high walls, a revamped boardercross course ('a good laugh with friends') and three terrain parks. There's a clear rating system in place, based on size (S, M, L, XL). On Blackcomb, novices should begin in the Terrain Garden. It features small rails and rollers to help you get a feel for airtime and improve your control. The M-L Nintendo Park is vast, but is usually the busiest. With many step-up jumps, hips, tabletops, rails and

HOW WHISTLER NEEDS TO IMPROVE

Whistler is one of our favourite North American resorts. But it has serious drawbacks that need to be addressed – many of them to do with overcrowding. This isn't just our view but that of many of our recent reporters too. The number of reports we had last year dropped to just one; this year it is four. Ten years ago we got over 20. Of course, this is partly to do with exchange rates and higher air fares making a holiday here pricier than it used to be. But we think it is partly because people are fed up with the resort's failure to get its act together. Our priorities would be:

- *Replace outdated fast quads with six-packs and eight-seaters to cut the appalling peak-period queues (see 'Queues')*
- *Restrict the number of day tickets sold (as Lech and Deer Valley do) to prevent serious overcrowding (on pistes as well as lifts)*
- *Keep the lifts open until later; closing at 3pm or 3.30pm in late February is ridiculous*
- *Open lifts that could relieve the pressure on others at busy times – eg the Fitzsimmons chair from the base of Whistler*
- *Groom more runs more of the time*
- *Build a new lift designed to serve Lower Peak to Creek and nearby runs in bad weather*
- *Encourage more restaurants to open, both on and off the mountain*

boxes, this park will suit intermediate to advanced riders. Very confident freestylers should hit the L-XL Highest Level Park (part of the Nintendo Park); the fact that you need to sign a waiver, wear a helmet and buy a special pass indicates the size of the obstacles here. On Whistler mountain, the Habitat Park by the Emerald chair has something for everyone, from beginner boxes to medium jumps and jibs and 15m+ XL tabletops. There's the Couger beginners' park too.

SNOW RELIABILITY ★★★★
Excellent at altitude
Snow conditions at the top are usually excellent – the snowfall averages over 400 inches a year (that's way more than most Colorado resorts). And the last three seasons have been among the snowiest ever for the resort, with well over 500 inches recorded each year. But because the resort is low and close to the Pacific, the bottom slopes can have poor snow or slush – leading people to 'download' from the mid-

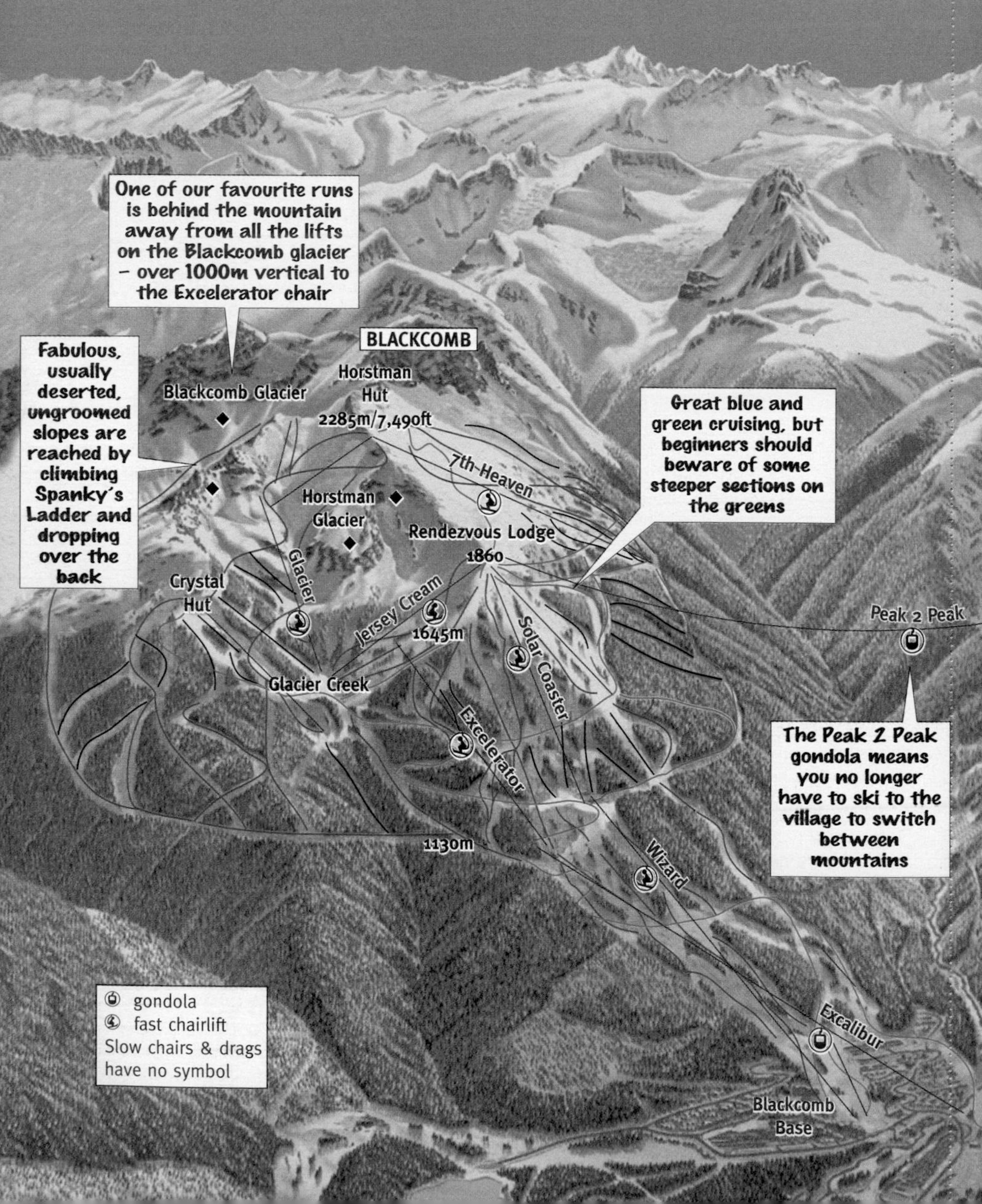
One of our favourite runs is behind the mountain away from all the lifts on the Blackcomb glacier – over 1000m vertical to the Excelerator chair
Fabulous, usually deserted, ungroomed slopes are reached by climbing Spanky's Ladder and dropping over the back
BLACKCOMB
Horstman Hut 2285m/7,490ft
Blackcomb Glacier
7th Heaven
Horstman Glacier
Rendezvous Lodge 1860
Great blue and green cruising, but beginners should beware of some steeper sections on the greens
Crystal Hut
Glacier
Jersey Cream
1645m
Solar Coaster
Peak 2 Peak
Glacier Creek
Excelerator
The Peak 2 Peak gondola means you no longer have to ski to the village to switch between mountains
1130m
Wizard
gondola
fast chairlift
Slow chairs & drags have no symbol
Excalibur
Blackcomb Base

stations, especially in late season Some reporters complain of poor piste maintenance ('some runs said to have been groomed were clearly not').

FOR EXPERTS *****

Few can rival it

Whistler Mountain's bowls are enough to keep experts happy for weeks. Each has endless variations, with chutes and gullies of varied steepness and width. The biggest challenges are around Flute, Glacier, Whistler and West Bowls – you can go anywhere in these high, wide areas.

Blackcomb's steep slopes are not as extensive as Whistler's, but some are more challenging. From the top of the 7th Heaven lift, traverse to Xhiggy's Meadow for sunny bowl runs. If you're feeling brave, go in the opposite direction and drop into the extremely steep chutes down towards Glacier Creek, including the infamous 41° Couloir Extreme (which can have massive moguls at the top), Secret

There's more terrain out here at the edge of the area than this map suggests – blue runs and easy glades as well as tougher stuff in Flute Bowl
WHISTLER MOUNTAIN
2180m/7,160ft
The classic high bowls that first gave Whistler cult status among expert skiers in the 1980s and 1990s
Rhapsody Bowl
Piccolo
Flute Bowl
Symphony
Symphony Bowl
Glacier Bowl
The Peak
Whistler Bowl
West Bowl
Bagel Bowl
Roundhouse Lodge
1850m
Harmony
2 Peak
1595m
Emerald
Big Red
The 1530m vertical Peak to Creek runs are excellent in good snow
1425m
Whistler Village
Garbanzo
Raven's Nest
1300m
Take the gondola from 7.30 for uncrowded fresh tracks skiing and a buffet breakfast
1005m
These Creekside runs were the 2010 Olympic downhill and Super G courses
Creekside
Fitzsimmons
Creekside
650m/2,140ft
Whistler Village
675m/2,210ft

ACTIVITIES

Indoor Sports arena (ice rink, pool, gym, squash), tennis, spa and health clubs, climbing wall, art galleries, museums, library, cinema

Outdoor Flightseeing, snowshoeing, snowmobiling, sno-limo (chauffeur-driven motorized sled), walking, snowcat tours, dog sledding, tubing, sleigh rides, bungee jumping, ziplining

Bowl and the very steep Pakalolo couloir. Our favourite runs are the less frequented but also seriously steep bowls reached by a short hike up Spanky's Ladder, after taking the Glacier Express lift. You emerge after the hike at the top of a huge deserted area with several ways down; best to have a guide.

Both mountains have challenging trails through trees. The Peak to Creek area offers 400 acres below Whistler's West Bowl to Creekside.

There's also backcountry guiding, cat-skiing and heli-skiing available by the day. A recent reporter had 'two incredible days' with Powder Mountain cat-skiing. Other reporters used Coast Range mountain guides ('top-quality guides and superb skiing') and found the heli-skiing 'expensive but a great experience'. We recommend the two-day Extremely Canadian clinic (see 'Schools and guides') for getting the most out of the in-bounds steeps.

FOR INTERMEDIATES ★★★★★

Ideal and extensive terrain

Both mountains are an intermediate's paradise. In good weather, good intermediates will enjoy the easier slopes in the high bowls. One of our favourite intermediate runs (though we concede the latter part is a bit tedious) is down the Blackcomb Glacier, from the top of the mountain to the Excelerator chair over 1000m below. This 5km run, away from all lifts, starts with a two-minute walk up from the top of the Showcase T-bar. Don't be put off by the 'Experts only' sign. You drop over the ridge into a wide bowl and traverse the slope to get to gentler gradients – descend too soon and you'll get a shock in the very steep double diamond Blowhole.

The blue runs served by the 7th Heaven chair are 'heavenly on a sunny day' – Hugh's Heaven is 'relatively empty' on weekdays and 'great for getting speed up'. Lower down there are lots of perfect cruising runs through the trees – ideal when the weather is bad.

On Whistler Mountain, the ridges and bowls served by the Harmony and Symphony quads have lots to offer – not only groomers but also excellent terrain for experiments off-piste. Jeff's Ode to Joy provided a snowboarding reporter with 'lots of variety from Alpine to glade'. The Saddle run from

Whistler Village and Village North merge together to form a huge pedestrian-only area lined with shops, condos and restaurants ➔

WHISTLER BLACKCOMB / PAUL MORRISON

the top of the Harmony Express lift is a favourite with many of our reporters, though it can get busy. The blue Highway 86 path, which skirts West Bowl from the Peak to Creek trail, has beautiful views over a steep valley and across to the rather phallic Black Tusk mountain. The 7km-long Peak to Creek blue run itself is good too, especially when groomed – check before setting off. The green Burnt Stew Trail also has great views, and accesses lots of easy off-piste terrain.

Lower down the mountain there is a vast choice of groomed blue runs, with a series of fast chairs to bring you back up to the top of the gondola. It's a cruiser's paradise – especially the aptly named Ego Bowl. A great long run is the fabulous Dave Murray Downhill all the way from mid-mountain to the finish at Creekside – used as the 2010 Olympic men's downhill course. Although it is classed black, it's a wonderful fast and varied cruise when it has been groomed.

FOR BEGINNERS ★★★★★

OK if the sun shines

Whistler has excellent nursery slopes by the mid-station of the gondola, as does Blackcomb at the base. Both have facilities higher up too. There is a lift pass and lesson deal on certain dates (see 'Schools and guides'), but no free lifts. The map has easy runs and slow zones marked.

On Whistler, there are some gentle runs from the top of the gondola. Their downside is other people speeding past. On Blackcomb, there are green runs from top to bottom. The top parts are very gentle, with some steeper pitches lower down.

In general, greens can be trickier than in many North American resorts – steeper, busier and, on the lower mountain, in less good condition.

Another serious reservation is the weather. Beginners don't get a lot out of heavy snowfalls, and might be put off by rain.

FOR BOARDERS ★★★★★

Epic – winter and summer

Whistler has world-class terrain parks as well as epic terrain for freeriders: bowls with great powder and awesome steeps, steep gullies, tree runs, and shedloads of natural hits, wind lips and cliffs. There are mellow groomed runs ideal for beginners and intermediates, too, and the lifts are generally snowboard-friendly; there are T-bars on the glacier, but they're not vicious. The resort has as high a reputation for summer snowboarding and camps on the glacier as for its winter boarding, and the summer Camp of Champions is hugely popular. Specialist snowboard shops include Showcase and Katmandu Boards.

FOR CROSS-COUNTRY ★★★★★

Picturesque but low

There are over 28km of cross-country tracks around Lost Lake, starting by the river on the path between Whistler and Blackcomb. But it is low altitude, so conditions can be unreliable. A specialist school, Cross-Country Connection (905 0071) offers lessons, tours and rental. Keen cross-country merchants can go to the Whistler Olympic Park and its 90km of trails (around 20 minutes away by car).

SCHOOLS

Whistler/Blackcomb
t 967 8950

Classes
Full day from C$188 (max 4 in class)

Private lessons
Half day (3hr) C$461

Extremely Canadian
t 1 800 938 9656

GUIDES

Whistler Guides
t 938 9242

CHILDCARE

Whistler Kids
t 1 800 766 0449
Ages 18mnth to 4yr

Ski school
Ages 3 to 12 (C$629 for 5 days)

MOUNTAIN RESTAURANTS ★★★★★
Overcrowded

The main restaurants sell decent, good-value food but are charmless self-service stops with long queues; most get incredibly crowded. They're huge, but not huge enough. 'Seat-seekers' are employed to find you space, but success is not guaranteed. The piste map advises eating before 11.30 (sorry?) or after 1pm. Blackcomb has the Rendezvous, mainly a big (850-seat) self-service place but also home to Christine's, a table-service place that is the best on either mountain. Glacier Creek is a huge (1,496-seat) but better self-service place. Whistler has the gigantic (1,740-seat) Roundhouse, which a recent visitor thought 'offered a good selection but was pricey, and food quality was hit and miss'; Steep's Grill is its unremarkable table-service refuge from the crowds.

There are smaller places, but they're still packed at normal times, and may be closed in early and late season. On Blackcomb are two tiny huts with great views – Crystal Hut ('amazing waffles') and Horstman Hut ('excellent goulash and mulled wine'). On Whistler, Raven's Nest is small and friendly, and does soups, sandwiches and BBQs; the Chic Pea ('cinnamon rolls to die for') and Harmony Hut are other options.

You can eat your own picnic at any of the main self-service places.

SCHOOLS AND GUIDES ★★★★★
A great formula

The new Max 4 Program limits the number in an adult group to a maximum of four. And they now run Discover Whistler Days at some periods outside high season when you get a discount (up to 30% in 2011/12) of the normal cost of lessons and rentals. A 2012 reporter who took private lessons says, 'In a day we progressed from doing greens and occasional blues to taking on blacks.' The school also runs special programmes such as Ski Esprit groups, which last for three to five days and combine instruction with guiding – with the same instructor daily (unusual for North America); many of our reporters have enjoyed these groups. The three-day Dave Murray Camps, which include race training, are 'superb for strong intermediates to experts', says a 2012 reporter. The Extremely Canadian two-day camps run three times a week and are for those who want guiding (maybe with a bit of coaching) in Whistler's steep and deep terrain and are a great way of finding the best steep terrain. We have been with them several times and have been impressed. A recent reporter said, 'A well spent C$400, whether you want to increase your skills/confidence or just ski some great terrain.'

Backcountry day trips or overnight touring are available with the Whistler Alpine Guides Bureau.

FOR FAMILIES ★★★★★
Impressive

Blackcomb's base area has the slow-moving Magic chair to get children part-way up the mountain. Whistler's gondola mid-station has a splendid kids-only area. A reporter found the staff 'friendly, instilling confidence'. The school now uses the Flaik GPS real-time tracking system so that each child's exact location is known at all times. There's a Magic Castle on Blackcomb and a Family Zone and Tree Fort on Whistler. One reporter enthused about 'climb and dine': kids combine dinner with a few hours' climbing at The Core.

STAYING THERE

Whistler has every kind of lodging you might want. Ski Independence, Frontier Ski and Whistler specialists Cold Comforts all offer an impressive range of hotels and apartments in and around the resort.

Chalets Skiworld has a six-bedroom chalet with an outdoor hot tub.

Hotels There is a wide range, including a lot of top-end places.

*******Fairmont Chateau Whistler** (938 8000) Well run, luxurious, at the foot of Blackcomb. We and reporters love it. Excellent spa with pools and tubs.

GETTING THERE

Air Vancouver 135km/85 miles (2hr15)

UK PACKAGES

Alpine Answers, AmeriCan Ski, American Ski Classics, Canadian Affair, Carrier, Cold Comforts Lodging, Crystal, Crystal Finest, Elegant Resorts, Erna Low, Flexiski, Frontier, Independent Ski Links, Inghams, Interactive Resorts, Kaluma, Momentum, Mountain Wave, Neilson, Oxford Ski Co, PowderBeds, Scott Dunn, Ski Bespoke, Ski Club Freshtracks, Ski Expectations, Ski Independence, Ski Line, Ski Safari, Ski Solutions, Skitracer, Skiworld, Snow Finders, Solo's, STC, Supertravel, Thomson, Virgin Snow

Phone numbers
From distant parts of Canada, add the prefix 1 604; from abroad, add the prefix +1 604

TOURIST OFFICE

www.whistler blackcomb.com
www.tourismwhistler.com

*****Four Seasons** (935 3400) Luxury hotel five minutes' walk from Blackcomb base, but with ski valet service at the base. Unremarkable public areas but good food. Good fitness/spa facilities.
*****Westin Resort & Spa** (905 5000) Luxury all-suite hotel at the foot of Whistler mountain next to the lifts, with pools and hot tubs ('overcrowded though', says a reporter).
****Crystal Lodge** (932 2221) In Whistler Village. Pool/sauna/hot tub. Discounts in several restaurants and shops in building.
****Glacier Lodge** (905 4607) In Upper Village. Large rooms, 'good value'.
****Pan Pacific Mountainside** (905 2999) Luxury, all-suite, at Whistler Village base. Pool/steam/hot tub. Recommended by a recent reporter.
****Sundial Boutique** (932 2321) In Whistler Village; one- and two-bedroom suites. Rooftop hot tubs.
***Lost Lake Lodge** (580 6647) Out by the golf course; studios and suites. Pool/hot tub.
***Tantalus Resort Lodge** (932 4146) In Whistler Village; targets families and groups. Hot tub/sauna.
***Whistler Village Inn & Suites** (932 4004) Central, side-by-side buildings. Good value. Hot tub/sauna/pool.
Apartments There are plenty of spacious, comfortable condominiums. Price tends to be dictated by location – ski-in/ski-out condos are pricier than those a shuttle-ride from the lifts.

EATING OUT ★★★★★
Good but crowded

Reporters are enthusiastic about the range, quality and value of places to eat, but there aren't enough restaurant seats to meet demand. You have to book well ahead (which may mean months ahead in some cases). Or resign yourself to queuing for one of the places that doesn't take bookings.

At the top of the market, the Rimrock Cafe near Whistler Creek specializes in seafood and game and has several different small areas which makes it feel more intimate than many Whistler restaurants; we have eaten very well there.

In Whistler Village, we've also enjoyed Araxi ('top quality for a special occasion; recommend the scallops and chorizo and the venison', says a recent reporter) and Il Caminetto di Umberto (a classy Italian). The pricey Ric's Grill and cheaper Keg are both part of chains but do good seafood and steak. Mid-market places include: Quattro and Old Spaghetti Factory ('real value', says a 2012 reporter) for Italian, Bocca ('casual, good bar food, excellent service'), 21 Steps ('excellent varied menu'), Three Below ('reasonably priced; great banana in puff pastry with caramel'), and Earl's ('burgers, ribs, good micro-beers'). Others to try are Sushi Village ('great sashimi, generous portions'), Mongolie (Asian), Teppan (Japanese) and Kypriaki Norte (Greek). In Village North, Hy's Steakhouse and the lively Brewhouse are good for steaks and ribs. There are plenty of budget places, including the après-ski bars below. You can also take a snowcat to the Crystal Hut for fondue, music and the history of Whistler.

APRES-SKI ★★★★
Something for most tastes

Whistler is very lively. We get most reviews on the Garibaldi Lift Company, which a 2012 visitor confirms is still 'buzzing from 4pm onwards, with good live music'. Other tips are the Brewhouse ('impressive model train runs all the way round the interior'), Longhorn (with a terrace), Dubh Linn Gate Irish pub ('good food, live entertainment') and Tapley's. Merlin's is the focus at Blackcomb base, with sports TV, beer 'by the pitcher' and 'good bar food'. Dusty's is the place at Creekside – good beer, loud music.

Later on, Buffalo Bill's is lively. Tommy Africa's, Maxx Fish, Moe Joe's and Garfinkel's are the main clubs.

OFF THE SLOPES ★★★
Quite a lot to do

Meadow Park Sports Centre has a full range of fitness facilities. There are several luxurious spas and an eight-screen cinema. Reporters recommend walks around the lake and the climbing wall at The Core. Ziptrek Ecotours offers tours on ziplines and suspension bridges through the forest between Whistler and Blackcomb mountains – 'great fun' says a reporter. You can also do ATV/snowmobile trips and dog sledding. A 2012 reporter enjoyed the Fire & Ice show (held every Sunday evening). Excursions to Squamish (for eagle watching) and to Vancouver are easy. And non-slope users can get around the mountain easily (don't miss the Peak 2 Peak gondola for great views).

Eastern Canada

For us the main attraction of skiing or riding in eastern Canada is the French culture and language that are predominant in the province of Québec. It really feels like a different country from the rest of Canada. And the resorts are only a six-hour flight from the UK, compared with a 10-hour flight for western Canada.

Be prepared for variable snow conditions, including rock-hard pistes and ice; and be prepared for extreme cold in early and midwinter too; you might be lucky but you might not. But cold weather means the extensive snowmaking systems, common to all the resorts, can be effective for a long season. Don't go expecting light, dry powder – if that's what you want, go west.

UK PACKAGES

Tremblant Alpine Answers, American Ski Classics, Crystal, Crystal Finest, Erna Low, Frontier, Independent Ski Links, Inghams, Neilson, Ski Bespoke, Ski Independence, Ski Safari, Ski Solutions, Skitracer, Skiworld, STC, Thomson, Virgin Snow

For people heading on holiday for a week or more, eastern Canada really means the province of Québec, its capital, Québec City, and the main destination resort Tremblant (covered below) nearer Montreal. French culture and language dominate the region. Notices, menus, trail maps and so on are usually printed in both French and English. Many ski area workers are bilingual or only French-speaking. And French cuisine abounds.

Slopes in all resorts are small, both in extent and vertical. The weather is very variable, so the snow – though pretty much guaranteed by snowmaking – varies greatly in quality.

Québec City makes a good base for access to several ski areas. Old Québec, at the city's heart, is North America's only walled city and is a World Heritage site. Within the city walls are narrow, winding streets and 17th- and 18th-century houses. It is situated right on the banks of the St Lawrence river. In January/February there is a famous two-week carnival, with an ice castle, snow sculptures, dog-sled and canoe races, parades and balls. But most of the winter is low season, with good-value rooms available in big hotels.

Stoneham is the closest ski area to Québec City, around 20 minutes away. The biggest and most varied resort is Mont-Ste-Anne 30 minutes away. Le Massif is around an hour away – a cult area with locals. These three resorts have extended entries in the resort directory at the back of the book.

KEY FACTS

Resort	265m 870ft
Slopes	230-875m 750-2,870ft
Lifts	14
Pistes	654 acres
Snow-guns	1066 guns

TOURIST OFFICE

www.tremblant.ca

Tremblant

- ＋ Charming, purpose-built core village
- ＋ Some good runs for all abilities
- − Very limited in extent
- − Weekend queues and crowds

Tremblant is eastern Canada's leading destination ski resort, about 90 minutes' drive from Montreal.

The Intrawest core village is purpose-built in the cute style of old Québec, with buildings in vibrant colours and narrow, cobbled, traffic-free streets; it feels very French. There is a regular, free ski-bus and a local town service.

The slopes are pleasantly wooded. A heated gondola from the village takes you to the top of the so-called South Side. From here you can drop over the back onto the North Side. Most lifts are fast chairs. At weekends there can be queues, but they tend to move quickly. Half the runs are blacks; most are at the easier end of their grading, but there are bump runs and glades. There is good intermediate cruising and an excellent nursery area with long, easy greens to progress to. One terrain park is aimed at advanced freestylers, one at intermediates and another at beginners; there's also a children's adventure area. There's over 80km of cross-country.

Many people return to town for lunch, but the Grand Manitou at the top of the gondola has good views and decent food. Of the hotels, the Fairmont Tremblant is the most luxurious. There are ample condos. Restaurants and bars are plentiful. Try the Forge Grill or Ya'ooo Pizza Bar. The Shack brews its own beer. Off the slopes there is an 'expensive' pool complex, snowshoeing, skating, tubing etc. Reporters enjoy visiting Montreal.

Spain

RPI	95
lift pass	£180
ski hire	£120
lessons	£85
food & drink	£95
total	**£480**

UK PACKAGES

Baqueira-Beret Crystal Finest, Neilson, Scott Dunn, Ski Miquel
Formigal Crystal, Skitracer, Thomson, White Roc, Zenith
Sierra Nevada Crystal, Thomson

- ➕ Vibrant Spanish culture gives a different experience from the Alps
- ➕ Low prices for food and drink
- ➕ Few crowds outside peak times
- ➖ Access can be difficult, with lengthy drives to reach Pyrenean resorts
- ➖ Still lots of old lifts, but improving

Spanish resorts vary enormously, so it's difficult to generalize. Nearly all the main ones, though, are benefitting from recent investment. The three we feature here have respectably sized and varied terrain that compares favourably with many smaller Alpine resorts. And at an appreciably lower cost, too.

The relatively low cost and the relaxed ambience of eating, partying and posing are key parts of the appeal of Spanish skiing. The majority of resorts are in the Pyrenees, and the villages are built more for convenience than charm. But they do offer a wide range of lodging set in some of the Pyrenees' most stunning scenery.

There is a group of worthwhile resorts in the west, between Pau and Huesca. Formigal is now the largest, and making a steady comeback on the wider market. Candanchu and Astún nearby are popular on the Spanish market. The downside is access, which can be tricky from France if snowfall closes key mountain passes. There are long drives up from Spanish airports, too, but weekly charter flights to Huesca have cut some transfer times.

In the south of Spain is the high resort of Sierra Nevada, a quite different experience and close to the coast – a two-centre trip is possible.

The other main group of resorts is just east of Andorra and includes La Molina and Masella (Alp 2500). These have brief descriptions in the resort directory at the back of the book.

KEY FACTS

Resort	1500m 4,920ft
Slopes	1500-2510m 4,920-8,240ft
Lifts	33
Pistes	120km
Snow-guns	608 guns

TOURIST OFFICE

www.baqueira.es

Baqueira-Beret

- ➕ Compact modern resort
- ➕ Lots of good intermediate slopes
- ➖ Main village lacks atmosphere
- ➖ Still some old, slow lifts

Baqueira's village is not inspiring, but the resort has a well-linked and developing ski area that appeals to intermediates. Fine for beginners too.

Baqueira was purpose-built in the 1960s and has its fair share of drab high-rise blocks. The central area is clustered below the road that runs through to the high pass of Port de la Bonaigua, while the main lift base is just above it. The village is small enough for location not to be too much of an issue. And there are big car parks with shuttles to the lift base.

The slopes are split into three distinct but well-connected areas – Baqueira, Beret and Bonaigua – with long, intermediate runs, practically all of them on open, treeless slopes. Most are above 1800m, with extensive snowmaking and more this year, but afternoon sun is a problem in spring. There are fast chairs dotted around, including a long six-pack.

Experts will find few on-piste challenges, but there is extensive off-piste and four ungroomed itinerary runs (including Escornacrabes, which both our 2012 reporters said was not for the faint hearted). There are good nursery slopes with moving carpets at Beret, and at the top of the gondola – the blues there are on the tough side though. Queues are rarely of major concern. The Brit-run BB Ski School is praised, including for off-piste guiding. The huts disappoint and lack variety, but Pla de Beret and Bonaigua ('good pizza') have table-service, and a 2012 reporter tips the San Miguel tapas bar at Bonaigua and the small bar at Tanau 1700 for 'hearty mountain soups and stews'.

There are good-quality hotels: the 5-star AC Baqueira (a Marriott) is 'the best'. The Escornacrabes does 'good hamburgers', but the best restaurants and bars are down the valley. Some hotels have pools and spas, but there is little else to amuse non-skiers.

Formigal

KEY FACTS	
Resort	1550m 5,090ft
Slopes	1500-2250m 5,090-7,380ft
Lifts	21
Pistes	137km
Snow-guns	22%

TOURIST OFFICE

www.aramon.co.uk
www.formigal.com

- ➕ Sizeable, varied area for all abilities
- ➕ Linked valleys give sense of travel
- ➖ Traffic congestion in resort
- ➖ Wind-prone slopes, lacking trees

Formigal has the largest ski area in the Spanish Pyrenees, and varied terrain. Recent investment is slowly attracting more British visitors – reports welcome.

The resort is on the Spanish-French border at the Col de Portalet, which can be closed in heavy snowfall and prevent direct access from France.

The village – of purpose-built apartment blocks and smart hotels – is on the east side of the Tena valley. The central street is pleasant enough, with an attractive clocktower and replica church as its focus, but it is spoiled by heavy traffic.

There are excellent free shuttles to and from the slopes, which span the west side of the valley and spread over four side-valleys. Most are north- and south-facing treeless slopes, prone to wind. Grooming is good and snowmaking extensive. Queues are rare outside holiday periods. Sextas is the nearest of the four bases to the village, with an eight-seat chair. All four have big car parks and US-style day lodges including big self-service cafeterias. There are fast chairs linking the lower parts of each valley, and runs for all standards from the tops.

Experts have four freeride areas, plus heli-skiing. Many of the black runs could be red, though. The nursery slopes are excellent. There are good intermediate runs; the gentle blue Rio from Cantal to Sextas is ideal for the more timid. The only tree-lined run is a remote lovely cruise, quiet because access is by a long, slow chair.

Confident skiers can ride a snowcat above Portalet, which accesses remote runs and freeride terrain to Anayet. The huge terrain park is one of the best we've seen, and there's a kids' mini-park and newish boardercross. We enjoyed good Italian food at the Cantal Trattoria, and the huts at Gemsbock and Sarrios were revamped last year, with new menus. The school has a good reputation. Families are well catered for with 'slow ski zones', family zones and an Indian 'village'.

There is a choice of 3- and 4-star hotels (the Aragon Hills and Abba Formigal have pools and spas), lots of apartments and over 30 restaurants, from Spanish to pizzerias. We had good gourmet food at the Vidocq. Après-ski is low-key, but the Marchica bar at Sextas is lively at close of play. Later on, the Cueva is a popular disco, and Keeper is fairly new.

Off-slope activities include dog sledding, floodlit tobogganing and snowmobile outings up to a mountain hut. Thermal baths are nearby.

Sierra Nevada

KEY FACTS	
Resort	2100m 6,890ft
Slopes	2100-3300 6,890-10,830ft
Lifts	29
Pistes	102km
Snow-guns	350 guns

TOURIST OFFICE

www.sierranevada.es

- ➕ Reasonably good snow record
- ➕ Fine beginner slopes
- ➖ Exposed, and prone to wind
- ➖ Crowds at weekends

Despite its southerly position near Granada, Sierra Nevada is a high, modern resort with a modest area of slopes. It gets its own weather, of course.

Pradollano is the hub, a stylish modern base with shops, restaurants and bars set around traffic-free open spaces. Most of the accommodation is in older, less smart buildings along a steeply winding road. From town, two gondolas go up to the mid-station at Borreguiles, and a two-stage fast quad goes up above there. There are four identifiable sectors, well linked, with a good range of intermediate and easy runs but not a lot for experts. There are excellent nursery slopes at mid-mountain – expanded for 2011/12 – and a terrain park with an FIS standard half-pipe. There are also good views from the mountain of the plains and towns – and on a clear day across the Med to Africa. Weekends can be busy, and queues may develop for some of the older lifts, especially the chair up the village slope. The home run can get crowded too. Sierra Nevada can have good snow years when the Alps has bad, and vice versa. Most slopes face north-west, but some get the afternoon sun. And when the wind blows, as it does, the slopes close; there are no trees. The Sol y Nieve hotel – with spa and good kids' facilities – was recommended by a 2012 reporter.

Finland

- ✚ Good for families and beginners
- ✚ Ideal terrain for cross-country
- ✚ Reliable snow well into spring
- ✚ Chance of seeing Northern Lights

- ▬ Can be bitterly cold (and dark in the early season)
- ▬ Small ski areas lacking challenge
- ▬ Draglifts are the norm

For skiers with no appetite for the hustle and hassle of Alpine resorts in high season – especially families, perhaps – escaping to the white silence of Lapland can be an attractive alternative. Finland has the lion's share of Lapland, and we started getting more reports on it – but they've more or less dried up. The resorts are small but rapidly developing both their ski areas and their facilities.

The Arctic landscape of flat and gently rolling forest, countless lakes and the occasional treeless hill is a paradise for cross-country skiing.

It also offers good beginner and intermediate downhilling, albeit on a small scale. None of the areas has significant vertical by alpine standards, and in some cases it is seriously limited. The resorts usually open a few runs in late November. For two months in midwinter the sun does not rise – at least, not at sea level. Most areas have floodlit runs. The mountains do not open fully until mid-February, when a normal skiing day is possible and Finnish schools have holidays that usually coincide with ours – making it a busy time. Finland comes into its own at the end of the season, with friendlier temperatures and long daylight hours. Easter is extremely popular, and the slopes are crowded. If you're lucky, you may see the Northern Lights – one March visitor saw them three times ('a great sight').

Conditions are usually hard-packed powder or fresh snow from the start of the season to the end (early May).

The temperature can be extremely variable, yo-yoing between 0°C and –30°C several times in a week. Fine days are the coldest, but the best for skiing: it may be 10 to 15 degrees warmer on the slopes than at valley level. 'Mild' days of cloud and wind are worse, and face masks are sold.

The staple Finnish lift is the T-bar; chairs and gondolas are rare. Pistes are wide and well maintained, as are nursery slopes. The Finns are great boarders and consider their terrain parks far superior to those in the Alps; super-pipes are increasingly common.

There are few mountain restaurants – but you are never far from the base, with its self-service restaurants. The ski areas also have shelters or 'kotas' – log-built teepees with an open fire and a smoke hole – where you can warm up and cook your own food.

Ski school is good, with English widely spoken. All ski areas have indoor playrooms for small children, but they may be closed at weekends.

Excursions are common and generally very popular – husky sledding, snowmobile safaris, a reindeer sleigh ride and tea with the Lapp drivers in their tent. Reporters are generally very enthusiastic about these off-slope adventures.

Hotels are self-contained resorts, large and practical rather than stylish, typically with a shop, a cafe, a bar with dance floor, and a pool and sauna with outdoor cooling-off area. Hotel supper is typically served no later than seven, sometimes followed by a children's disco or dancing to a live band. Finns usually prefer to stay in cabins, and tour operators offer the compromise of staying in a cabin but taking half-board at a nearby hotel. Cabins vary, but are mostly well equipped, with a sauna and drying cupboard as standard.

The main resorts are Levi and Ylläs, respectively 17km north and 50km west of Kittilä, which has charter flights from Britain. They are described here. Three other resorts worth considering are: Ruka, 80km south of the Arctic Circle, close to Kuusamo airport and the Russian border; Pyhä, 150km north-east of Rovaniemi; and Iso-Syöte, Finland's southernmost fell region. These are covered in our resort directory at the back of the book.

UK PACKAGES

Ylläs Inghams, Inntravel, Skiworld
Levi Crystal Finest, Inghams, Skiworld

Phone numbers
From abroad use the prefix +358 and omit the initial '0' of the phone number

Ylläs

KEY FACTS	
Resort	255m
	840ft
Slopes	255-715m
	840-2,350ft
Lifts	29
Pistes	53km
Snow-guns	40 guns

TOURIST OFFICE

www.yllas.fi

- ⊞ Best for novices and nordic fans
- ⊞ Few queues and reliable late snow
- ⊟ Slopes a bus ride from the villages
- ⊟ Bars and restaurants not a highlight

Ylläs is Finland's largest resort; it's a quiet family area with an increasing choice of accommodation dotted around its two villages.

Ylläs mountain has two main bases, both 4km from the mountain. The minor one is Ylläsjärvi near the Sport Resort Ylläs base, the major one Äkäslompolo near the Ylläs-Ski base. Development is taking place at both, and closer to the slopes too.

It is Finland's largest downhill ski area – but still has only 53km of pistes on two broad flanks with runs that suit novices best. Second- and third-week skiers will rapidly conquer the benign black runs. Past reports of the ski school have been positive. And there's a mountain-top restaurant.

The area has 330km of cross-country trails, 38km of which are floodlit, transforming it from awkward sprawl to doorstep ski resort of limitless scope. There are also 15 cafes along the tracks. From the lift base trails fan out around the mountain, across the frozen lake and away through the endless forest.

The Äkäs cabins at Äkäslompolo have been recommended. Dining out is slowly improving, with five newish restaurants at the Taiga base (Sport Resort Ylläs) opening a couple of seasons ago. These include a pizzeria. Established favourites in town include more upmarket Poro for traditional fish and roast dishes. Julie's suits families better (pizza and burgers).

Off-slope activities include snowmobiling (410km of tracks), dog sledding, reindeer safaris, snowshoeing and ice fishing.

Levi

KEY FACTS	
Resort	205m
	670ft
Slopes	205-530m
	670-1,740ft
Lifts	26
Pistes	44km
Snow-guns	20%

TOURIST OFFICE

www.levi.fi

- ⊞ Lodging convenient for slopes
- ⊞ Airport transfer only 15 to 20 mins
- ⊟ Not ideal for beginners
- ⊟ Can be very windy

Levi's convenience is its key appeal for visitors. There are good hotels and plentiful off-slope diversions too. Midwinter can be bleak on the hill though.

Levi is a small, purpose-built village of hotels, apartments and cabins at the foot of its slopes.

The runs are mostly intermediate (only one green and three black). A gondola and a six-pack take you up from the village base, but apart from another gondola serving the World Cup slope, the other lifts are drags. They can be bleak and exposed in bad weather, but the area usually has a long season. A third of the slopes have snowmaking, and 17 are floodlit. The main terrain park is 'excellent' with boxes, rails, a spine, plus big and small lines; half-pipe and super-pipe. There are several mountain restaurants (including the Okta in the Panorama hotel). Cross-country trails total 230km. Vilpuri Kids' Land has lifts and tobogganing areas, plus day care.

Levi's biggest hotel is the Spa Levitunturi (016 646301), with a bowling alley and huge spa facility – including 17 pools and nine saunas. The hotel Levi Panorama (336 3000) is at the top of the mountain, reached by gondola. The Sokos hotel (016 3215 500) and the Levilehto apartments (403 120200) have been recommended (though the latter are 'a 10-minute walk to the slopes').

There are dozens of places to eat. The Hullu Poro (Crazy Reindeer) complex has impressed reporters and has several restaurants including fine dining, traditional Finnish, Asian and a steakhouse. Of the handful of bars, Oliver's Corner is supposedly lively. Off-slope activities include snowmobiling, reindeer and husky safaris, snowshoeing, ice fishing and skating on the frozen lake. You can also visit a reindeer and a husky park.

Norway

- ➕ One of the best places in Europe for serious cross-country skiing
- ➕ The home of telemark – plenty of opportunities to learn and practise
- ➕ Freedom from the glitz and ill-mannered lift queues of the Alps
- ➕ Impressive terrain parks
- ➕ Usually reliable snow conditions throughout a long season

- ➖ Very limited downhill areas
- ➖ Very basic mountain restaurants
- ➖ Booze is prohibitively taxed
- ➖ Scenery more Pennine than Alpine
- ➖ Après-ski that is either deadly dull or irritatingly rowdy
- ➖ Short daylight hours in midwinter
- ➖ Highly changeable weather
- ➖ Limited off-slope activities

For downhillers who fancy a change from the usual ski-resort glitz, Norway could be just the place. For families with young children, in particular, it can make sense; you'll have no trouble finding junk food to please the kids – the mountain restaurants serve little else. Speaking for ourselves, any one of our first three ➖ points is enough to make us pause. Add together all the negatives, and you can count us out. One reporter ticked us off for this 'narrow-minded view'. He makes great play of the fact that he can be in Lillehammer four hours after taking off from Edinburgh. Four hours after taking off from Gatwick, we can be in Megève or Chamonix. Hmmm, tricky call ...

There is a traditional friendship between Norway and Britain, and English is widely spoken.

For the Norwegians and Swedes, skiing is a weekend rather than a special holiday activity, and not an occasion for extravagance. So at lunchtime they haul sandwiches out of their backpacks as we might while walking the Pennine Way, and in the evening they cook in their apartments. Don't expect a tempting choice of restaurants.

The Norwegians have a problem with alcohol. Walk into an après-ski bar at 5pm on a Saturday and you may find young men already inebriated – not merry, but incoherent. And this is despite – or, some say, because of – incredibly high taxes on booze. Restaurant prices for wine are ludicrous, and shop prices may be irrelevant – Hemsedal has no liquor store. Our one attempt at self-catering there was an unusually sober affair as a result. Other prices are generally not high by Alpine standards.

Cross-country skiing comes as naturally to Norwegians as walking; and even if you're not very keen, the fact that cross-country is normal, and not a wimp's alternative to 'real' skiing, gives Norway a special appeal. Here, cross-country is both a way of getting about the valleys and a way of exploring the hills. What distinguishes Norway for the keen cross-country skier is the network of long trails across the gentle uplands, with refuges along the way where backpackers can pause for refreshment or stay overnight. More and more Norwegians are taking to telemarking, and snowboarding is very popular – local youths fill the impressive terrain parks at weekends. For downhill skiing, the country isn't nearly so attractive. Despite the fact that it is able to hold downhill races, Norway's Alpine areas are of limited appeal. The most rewarding resort is Hemsedal, covered on the next page.

Norway's other widely known resorts are Geilo and Voss, on the railway line from Bergen to Oslo. Tryvann is just 20 minutes from the centre of Oslo, on a spur of the underground system, and popular with the locals. Lillehammer is well known too, of course – site of the 1994 Olympics; but it's a lakeside town not a downhill ski resort (the Alpine races were held some distance away). Other main resorts are Trysil, on the border with Sweden, Beitostølen in the Jotunheimen National Park, and Oppdal. All are covered in the directory at the back of the book.

KEY FACTS

Resort	640m 2,100ft
Slopes	670-1450m 2,200-4,760ft
Lifts	24
Pistes	47km
Snow-guns	45%

Phone numbers
From abroad use the prefix +47

TOURIST OFFICE

www.hemsedal.com
www.skistar.com/hemsedal

Hemsedal

- + Convenient slope-side lodging
- + Some quite challenging slopes
- + Excellent children's nursery slopes
- − Not much of a village
- − Weekend queues
- − Exposed upper mountain

Hemsedal is both an unspoiled valley and a village, the latter also referred to as Trøym and Sentrum ('Centre') – but you can also stay at the lift base or higher up in the slopes, a mile or so away.

Hemsedal is a three-hour drive from Oslo and geared mainly to weekenders arriving by car or coach. But there is a ski-bus linking all parts and floodlit paths to/from the centre. The lift pass also covers smaller Solheisen, up the valley. Geilo is an hour away.

Sentrum is a bus ride from the slopes and little more than a small area of low-rise apartments/hotels, shops, a garage, a bank and a couple of cashpoints. There's a developing area of lodgings close to the base. You can also stay further up the hill where there are several areas of more or less ski-in/ski-out lodgings.

Hemsedal's slopes pack a lot of variety into a small space. Fast lifts serve a high proportion of the slopes, though a few awkward drags remain. There can be weekend crowds and queues for the main access lifts. Otherwise it is quiet. There are four good parks and a mini park for kids; plus boardercross. Snowmaking covers 45% of the slopes, with more installed in 2011/12. There is quite a bit to amuse experts: several black pistes and wide areas of gentler off-piste terrain served by drags. Mileage-hungry piste-bashers will find Hemsedal's runs very limited. There are quite a few red and blue runs to play on, and splendid long green runs – but they get a lot of traffic. Beginners have a separate, gentle nursery area. The resort caters well for families, and the kids' nursery slopes at the lift base are now very well developed with more activities planned for 2012/13.

There are 120km of prepared cross-country trails in the valley and forest, and (in late season) 90km at altitude.

There is one functional self-service mountain restaurant.

The best hotel is the Skogstad (320 55000) in Sentrum – comfortable, with a spa; but its bar and nightclub may be noisy at weekends. The hotel Skarsnuten (320 61700), on the hill, is stylishly modern. But apartments dominate. The chalet-style Alpin Lodge by the nursery slopes includes 30 apartments, restaurants and shops.

The dining choices are OK; the Big Horn at Fjellandsby is a popular steakhouse, and there's the Lodgen bar and restaurant (Italian) at the Alpin Lodge; plus more places in town.

Après-ski starts at the Skistua (Skisenter), which also has live music at the weekends. The bars and clubs get rowdy at weekends and holidays, but can be very quiet midweek.

Off-slope diversions include tobogganing, dog sledding, bowling and snowmobiling.

HEMSEDAL TOURIST OFFICE

Hemsedal offers a good range of slopes and just a hint of Alpine-style scenic drama ↓

Sweden

- Snow-sure from December to May
- Unspoiled, beautiful landscape
- Uncrowded pistes and lifts
- Super nordic and off-slope activities

- Limited challenging downhill terrain
- Small areas by Alpine standards
- Lacks dramatic Alpine scenery
- Short days during the early season

Sweden appeals most to those who want an all-round winter holiday in a different environment and culture. Standards of accommodation, food and service are good, and the people are welcoming, lively and friendly, but most of the downhill areas are limited in size and challenge.

Holidaying in Sweden is a completely different experience from a holiday in the Alps. Although virtually everyone speaks good English, menus and signs are often written only in Swedish. The food is delightful, especially if you like fish and venison. And resorts are very family-friendly. It is significantly cheaper than neighbouring Norway, but reporters still complain that eating and drinking is very expensive.

Days are very short in early-season. But from early February the lifts usually work from 9am to 4.30pm and by March it is light until 8.30pm. Most resorts have some floodlit pistes.

On the downside, downhill slopes are limited in both challenge and extent, and the lift systems are dominated by T-bars. There's lots of cross-country and backcountry skiing.

Après-ski is taken very seriously – with live bands from mid- to late afternoon. There is plenty to do off the slopes: snowmobile safaris, ice fishing, dog sled rides, ice climbing, saunas galore and visiting local Sami villages.

The main resort is Åre, described below. Others include Sälen, the largest, and Vemdalen. These two, plus Riksgränsen, Björkliden (both above the Arctic Circle) and tiny Ramundberget are covered in our directory at the back of the book.

Åre

- Good for intermediates and novices
- Excellent children's facilities

- High winds can affect snow and lifts
- Few expert challenges

Sweden's biggest ski area, with lots to do off the slopes as well as on. Not great for keen skiers but good for families wanting a change from the Alps.

The centre of this small lakeside town has old, pretty, coloured wooden buildings and some larger modern additions. Lodgings are spread out along the valley.

There are two separate areas of slopes linked by a ski-bus. The main area has fast lifts to the top (including a gondola, chondola, cable car, funicular and fast chair), and a fast chair accesses the separate Duved area. But nearly all other lifts are drags. Queues are rare (but a 2012 reporter told of 15- to 20-minute waits at New Year for a key T-bar).

The slopes offer mainly beginner and intermediate tree-lined terrain, with two windswept bowls above that are prone to closure. Experts will find the slopes limited, especially if the high bowls are closed. But there is a lot of off-piste. For intermediates there are steep, sometimes icy, black and red runs back to town, and lots of pretty blue runs through the trees. You get a real sense of travelling around on the main area. Beginners have good facilities in both sectors. There are three terrain parks and 58km of groomed cross-country trails. The ski school has a good reputation, and children have special areas. Kids under seven get free lift passes if wearing helmets. Mountain huts are good.

The best central hotel is the charming old Diplomat Åregården. There are ample apartments and cabins and lots of restaurants, from pizza to Japanese. Après-ski is lively, with the Fjällgården, Tott and Åregården packed from 3pm. Off-slope diversions are plentiful.

KEY FACTS

Resort	380m 1,250ft
Slopes	380-1275m 1,250-4,180ft
Lifts	46
Pistes	100km
Snow-guns	70%

UK PACKAGES

Neilson

TOURIST OFFICE

www.skistar.com

Bulgaria

RPI	45
lift pass	£100
ski hire	£40
lessons	£40
food & drink	£50
total	**£230**

- + Costs very low by Alpine standards
- + Good ski schools
- + Lively bars and nightlife

- − Poor snow record, though snowmaking has been improved
- − Small ski areas
- − Cheap booze attracts 18-30 crowds

Bulgaria best suits novices and early intermediates looking for a jolly time at bargain basement prices. Bansko's arrival on the scene in 2004 raised the bar for the country's other main resorts, which are now starting to catch up.

Bulgaria has traditionally been a place for a cheap and cheerful holiday. It is well worth considering if you are a beginner or early intermediate on a budget and want a lively time, fuelled by cheap booze. Don't expect sophistication or big ski areas. A keen piste-basher could ski all the runs in even the biggest resort in a day.

But the ski schools have an excellent reputation. And Bansko has some good hotels and a modern lift system. Even Pamporovo now has a six-pack. The scenery and culture provide a very different holiday experience to the Alps.

Borovets

KEY FACTS	
Resort	1300m 4,270ft
Slopes	1300-2560m 4,270-8,400ft
Lifts	13
Pistes	58km
Snow-guns	75 guns

TOURIST OFFICE

www.borovets-bg.com

- + Lively, convenient village
- + Some good intermediate slopes

- − Not ideal for beginners
- − Nightlife can be tacky

Borovets is a mixture of large, modern hotels and small bars, clubs and restaurants. The slopes suit intermediates best.

Most people come here on packages and stay in big hotels with their own bars, restaurants and shops within them. There is also a large selection of quirkier and lively small bars, shops and eating places lining 'The Strip' as a 2012 reporter describes the 300m long street in which he 'counted at least 26 – there must be over 40 if you include the back streets. Borovets is now the Benidorm of skiing with touts outside most bars trying to get you in; it's a shanty-town mix of wooden huts plus big hotels'. And a 2011 reporter complained of 'dogs roaming the streets'. Nevertheless, the resort's beautiful woodland setting gives a degree of Alpine-style charm.

A long, slow gondola rises over 1000m in 25 minutes to reach both the short, easy slopes of Markoudjika and the longer, steepish Yastrebets pistes. The runs are best for good intermediates, and include some longish reds. The resort is not ideal for novices: nursery slopes are crowded, and the step from easy blues to testing reds is a big one. There is night skiing and 35km of cross-country.

Queues form for the gondola at peak times ('45 minutes', says a recent reporter) and for the nursery draglifts. The gondola is also said to be prone to closure by wind. Grooming is erratic. The ski school is consistently praised: this year a reader said that he 'progressed from complete beginner to red runs in a week' and that his instructor 'regularly spent more than the allotted time with the group'.

Most reporters stay at the Samokov or the Rila. Noise can be a problem at the latter, say reporters; and a 2012 guest found it 'a good basic hotel but a bit tired; the self-service buffet meals were always cold'. Recent visitors found the Lion 'clean, tidy, with friendly staff' and thought the villas at the Iglika Palace were 'basic, but quiet and comfortable'. Food shopping is limited.

The Black Cat restaurant has 'good food, service and a lovely open fire'. There are plenty of lively bars with 'dancing girls and live music'. Buzz is said to be one of the liveliest, and No Limits is a newish bar/disco in the Rila hotel. 'Black Tiger is a noisy karaoke bar packed with drunken Brits,' said a 2012 reporter who preferred Katy's Pub 'with a guitarist in the attic' and Mamacita's Mexican restaurant and bar.

UK PACKAGES

Borovets Balkan Holidays, BoardnLodge, Crystal, Mountain Wave, Neilson, Skitracer, Thomson
Bansko Balkan Holidays, Crystal, Independent Ski Links, Neilson, Skitracer, Thomson
Pamporovo Balkan Holidays, Crystal, Independent Ski Links, Mountain Wave, Skitracer, Thomson

There are also 'adult' bars, but they are away from the main streets, and advertising is now said to be banned, though there are plenty of 'touts'.

Tour operator reps organize pub crawls, folklore evenings etc. Excursions to the Rila monastery or to Sofia by coach are interesting.

KEY FACTS

Resort	990m 3,250ft
Slopes	990-2600m 3,250-8,530ft
Lifts	13
Pistes	70km
Snow-guns	160 guns

TOURIST OFFICE

www.banskoski.com

Bansko

- ➕ Lots of fast lifts on the mountain
- ➕ Atmospheric town centre
- ➕ Friendly, helpful locals
- ➖ Long, queue-prone access gondola
- ➖ Few off-slope diversions
- ➖ Some unfinished buildings evident

Bansko is an old town, set on a flat valley floor in the scenic Pirin National Park, that has been catapulted into the 21st century by the installation of modern lifts that opened in 2004 and the construction of a lot of lodgings.

The area near the base of the access gondola to the slopes has been developed hugely in the last ten years or so and has a lot of modern hotels, apartments, bars and restaurants. Many hotels run shuttle-buses to/from the lift. Reporters like what they find, and many go back repeatedly.

The older part of town is a fair distance from the gondola and looks no great beauty on the outskirts, but the central square reveals a quiet and charming heart, and there are few outward signs of commercial tourism.

The slopes are reached by an eight-seat gondola to Bunderishka, for which there are long queues in the morning ('can be over an hour'). To avoid them, a reporter advises getting there at 8.15 before the lift officially opens. A planned additional gondola is now on the back burner. Queues further up the mountain are rare.

There is an easy blue piste back to the town, with snowmaking and floodlighting. Most lifts are fast chairs, and successive ones take you up mainly north-facing slopes to the high point of the area. You can ski down reds or blues to Shiligarnika, or a red followed by the Tomba black to Bunderishka. Some of these are quite long and challenging.

The resort map shows a chair going

BANSKO SKI AREA

Cheap booze is one of Bulgaria's key attractions; good ski schools are another ↓

The Bansko gondola has long morning queues. But once you are up the mountain, fast chairs transport the crowds effectively →

BANSKO SKI AREA

up to the right of Bunderishka; this has not worked for several years. The nursery slopes near the top of the gondola are good, with little through-traffic. There is a terrain park. Past reports of the ski schools have been good. Children have a snow garden, and the kindergarten takes kids from four to seven years old.

Reporters find the runs reasonably well groomed, but a 2012 visitor complains about lack of piste marker poles. Snow is more reliable than the Bulgarian norm.

Mountain huts are mostly self-service, and the food 'rather basic'. A recent reporter enjoyed lunch at the Goat. A 2012 reporter advises: 'The lift company runs all the on-piste places, but a short stroll through the woods will take you to independent hotels with good-value fresh food'.

Hotels near the gondola station include the swanky Florimont with its own casino and the 5-star Kempinski Grand Arena, with good facilities and 'extensive breakfasts'. The Emerald is 'convenient for the gondola, with superb rooms, friendly staff and tasty, hot food'. The Lion has 'spacious, spotlessly clean rooms and a pool, steam and sauna'.

Reporters enthuse about the town's many mehanas (traditional inns) with roaring fires, real Bulgarian food and good wine. And there are lots of lively bars – readers' tips include the Lion pub in the Lion hotel, the Flora in the Emerald hotel ('happy hour from noon till midnight with two-for-one drinks; open till 5am'), Diamonds and Amigos.

Off-slope activities include skating, paragliding, snowmobiling and ten-pin bowling. Many hotels have spas.

Pamporovo

- ➕ Pretty, tree-lined slopes
- ➕ Good, low-cost choice for novices
- ➖ Limited extent and short runs
- ➖ Poor piste maintenance

Pamporovo is a purpose-built village, in a pretty woodland area a short shuttle-bus ride from its easy slopes that suit beginners best.

The resort is strictly for beginners and near-beginners, with mostly easy and short runs. Others will find the limited area rather inadequate. The 37km of slopes are pretty and sheltered, with pistes cutting through pine forest. Some beginners find the runs rather too narrow, and our most recent reporter complained of grooming 'only one day in the week, which made it difficult for beginners'. There's a half-pipe. Snow reliability is poor, but snowmaking covers 90% of the slopes. There are plenty of mountain huts.

The ski schools are repeatedly praised – instructors are patient, enthusiastic and speak good English, and class sizes are usually quite small. There are 40km of cross-country trails.

A reporter recommends the hotel Finlandia ('comfortable; friendly staff; plentiful but plain food').

KEY FACTS

Resort	1650m 5,410ft
Slopes	1450-1935m 4,760-6,350ft
Lifts	15
Pistes	37km
Snow-guns	90%

TOURIST OFFICE

www.
pamporovoresort.com

Romania

RPI	35
lift pass	£60
ski hire	£40
lessons	£40
food & drink	£35
total	**£175**

UK PACKAGES

Poiana Brasov Balkan Holidays

Phone numbers
From abroad use the prefix +40 and omit the initial '0' of the phone number

TOURIST OFFICE

www.poiana-brasov.com

- + Cheap packages, and very low prices on the spot
- + Interesting excursions and friendly local people
- + Good tuition from keen instructors

- − Primitive facilities, especially mountain restaurants and toilets
- − Uninspiring food
- − Very limited slopes

Romania sells mainly on price. On-the-spot prices, in particular, are very low. Provided you don't have unreasonably high expectations, you'll probably come back from Poiana Brasov content. It allows complete beginners to try a ski holiday at the minimum budget, and to have a jolly time in the evenings without adding substantially to that cost.

Romania's main resort – and the only one featuring in any UK package programme – is **Poiana Brasov** (1030m). It is a short drive above the city of Brasov in the Carpathian mountains, about 120km (on alarmingly rough, slow roads) north-west of the capital and arrival airport, Bucharest.

The resort is purpose-built, and has the air of a spacious, pleasant holiday camp. But it is not designed for the convenience of skiers: some serious-sized hotels are right by the lifts, but most are scattered about a pretty, wooded plateau, served by regular buses and cheap taxis.

The slopes are extremely limited – 20km of pistes in total. They consist of decent intermediate tree-lined runs of about 750m vertical, roughly following the line of the main cable car and gondola, plus an open nursery area at the top. In 2011/12 four new slopes (two blues and two reds) opened, accessed by a new quad and a six-pack. There are some nursery lifts at village level, which are used when snow permits. Night skiing is also available. The resort gets weekend crowds from Brasov and Bucharest, and queues can result, but during the week there are few problems.

A key part of the resort's appeal is the friendly and effective teaching.

Hotel standards are higher than you might expect. The linked 3-star Bradul (0268 417 866) and 4-star Sport (0268 407330) hotels are handy for the lower nursery slopes and for one of the cable cars. Guests in both have use of the Sport's spa facilities. A swanky Radisson hotel with over 180 rooms and smart spa facility is due to open in 2014.

Après-ski revolves around the hotel bars and nightclubs – plus outings to rustic barns for barbies with gypsy music and to the bars and restaurants of Brasov. With cheap beer and very cheap spirits on tap, things can be quite lively. Off-slope facilities are limited; there are two good-sized pools (in hotels) and bowling. An excursion to nearby Bran Castle (Count Dracula's lair) is also popular.

Slovenia

RPI	70
lift pass	£145
ski hire	£50
lessons	£70
food & drink	£90
total	**£355**

UK PACKAGES

Kranjska Gora Balkan Holidays, Crystal, Mountain Tracks, Thomson
Kanin-Bovec BoardnLodge, Mountain Wave
Bled (for Vogel) Balkan Holidays, Crystal, Thomson

TOURIST OFFICES

www.slovenia.info

Bled
www.bled.si

- ➕ Low prices
- ➕ Beautiful, varied scenery
- ➕ Good beginner slopes and lessons

- ➖ Limited, mostly easy slopes
- ➖ Still lots of slow, antiquated lifts
- ➖ Mountain huts not a highlight

Slovenia offers lower prices and fewer crowds than the Alps, attracting economy-minded visitors from neighbouring Italy and Austria as well as Britain and the Netherlands. The ski areas are limited and still a bit antiquated, though making obvious investments. Most suit novices well.

Slovenia – which is bordered by Italy, Austria and Croatia – has 30 or so ski areas, the main ones concentrated in the Julian Alps in the west, dominated by its highest mountain, Mt Triglav; all are small and some are tiny. None is likely to keep the adventurous piste-basher amused for a week; but you can have an enjoyable trip touring by car or by combining several resorts from one base. EasyJet (from Stansted) and Adria (from Gatwick) fly to Ljubljana.

The season is shorter than in the Alps (except at Kanin) and the resorts low. Most slopes are below 2000m.

Prices are low, and there is a positive feel – and a warm and hospitable welcome. Standards of service and accommodation have improved – the hotels may not be particularly attractive, but many are new or modernized, complete with pools, spas and often free Wi-Fi.

Getting around is relatively easy, and most ski areas are within a 40-minute drive of each other on good roads. And the main resorts are within a two-hour bus ride of Ljubljana. Bled, with its beautiful lake and fairly lively nightlife, is an attractive base. It has just one steepish slope. But other resorts nearby include Kranjska Gora and lesser known Krvavec, Kanin, Vogel and Kobla (the only ski area in Slovenia reachable by train).

The other main group of resorts centres on Maribor to the east, a quite different area of low-slung wooded ridges. But it has the biggest ski area in the country at 43km.

The Ski Pass Slovenia covers all resorts in Slovenia.

Most resorts fit best into the intermediate category but differ on their suitability for novices. Experts will find few black runs, but there is good off-piste when conditions permit. Lift systems are improving and queues rare. Most Slovenians visit at weekends; midweek the slopes can be deserted. A common feature of many areas is an access lift with no runs back to valley level. One drawback for us is the lack of quality lunches: snacks and picnics are the norm, so hearty menus and cute huts are rare. Ski schools are of a high quality and cheap, with good spoken English. Other winter activities are big in Slovenia, too, so there is plenty to do off the slopes.

KEY FACTS

Resort	1450m 4,760ft
Slopes	1450-1970m 4,760-6,460ft
Lifts	11
Pistes	30km
Snow-guns	95%

TOURIST OFFICE

www.rtc-krvavec.si

Krvavec

- ⊞ Convenient for short breaks
- ⊞ Quiet slopes midweek
- ⊞ Jolly, family atmosphere
- ⊟ Lacks proper resort base
- ⊟ Short, mainly south-facing runs
- ⊟ Not ideal for novices

Krvavec has been voted Slovenia's best ski area and is just 8km from Ljubljana airport. There's no central village, but then most visitors are locals on day trips from the city.

Krvavec has some of the country's steepest slopes, including five black runs. It is a lively place, especially at weekends. Most visitors are families on day trips. Bled is 40 minutes by daily bus (free with the lift pass). There is no resort, but there is one hotel on the slopes and some lodging in nearby Cerklje. The local lift pass also covers Rogla, near Maribor.

A gondola goes up to the slopes, which span three partly wooded hills from a high point of 1970m. The lifts include a six-pack and a quad; queues are rare. The pistes get a lot of sun, though snowmaking is extensive and grooming good. There is a terrain park and a good nursery slope and children's area, complete with moving carpet, but few easy blues to progress to. The mid-mountain Plaza has picnic spots and snack bars. Kriska Planina is an Alpine-style hut. Snowshoeing is popular, and on Friday and Saturday evenings you can try tobogganing, air boarding and zorbing.

KEY FACTS

Resort	810m 2,660ft
Slopes	810-1295m 2,660-4,250ft
Lifts	18
Pistes	20km
Snow-guns	Some

TOURIST OFFICE

www.kr-gora.si

Kranjska Gora

- ⊞ Good for novices and families
- ⊞ Convenient, good, slope-side hotels
- ⊟ Slopes limited in extent, variety, length and vertical
- ⊟ Still some old lifts, and gets busy

Despite limited slopes (most other areas are bigger), Kranjska Gora is offered by more UK tour operators than any other Slovenian resort. It's a good-value, pretty and compact resort that is popular with families. Since the centre is fairly small, most facilities are near the slopes, too.

Kranjska Gora is close to the Austrian and Italian borders. Day trips to ski in resorts over the borders are possible.

The 20km of wide, tree-lined pistes rise to 1295m and best suit very unadventurous intermediates and novices – though there is a World Cup slalom black run. The slopes above Podkoren are quiet and gentle. There are four quads, but still lots of draglifts. And getting around involves tedious traversing. Queues are rare despite busier slopes here. Snow reliability is poor, but snowmaking covers most pistes. There is a terrain park and a children's area with a moving carpet. Cross-country trails total 40km. It is back to base for lunch, but Bedancu is a good self-service beside chair 7.

Hotels are plentiful and to a high standard, most with pools and spas. For slope-side convenience, the Lek, Prisank and Larix are best. The Alpina and adjacent aqua park are popular with families. We liked the Kompas, with excellent breakfast buffet and good pool. For eating out try the Kotnik and Via Napoli (hotel Prisank) pizzerias, and the Ostarija for finer dining. Ice skating, night tobogganing and snowshoeing are popular.

KEY FACTS	
Resort	460m 1,510ft
Slopes	1140-2290m 3,740-7,510ft
Lifts	9
Pistes	30km
Snow-guns	Some

TOURIST OFFICE

www.boveckanin.si

Kanin

- ✚ Splendid Dolomite-like scenery
- ✚ High, reliably snow-sure slopes
- ✚ Long runs down Italian side
- ▬ More remote than the other areas
- ▬ Upper mountain bleak and exposed
- ▬ Bovec quiet at night

Adventure capital Bovec has an isolated position in the splendid Soca Valley; its ski area Kanin is a cross-border resort with uncrowded intermediate slopes.

Kanin, linked to Sella Nevea in Italy, is Slovenia's highest ski area, with the biggest vertical (1150m). The link is by a red piste and a jumbo cable car to return. There are 30km of largely intermediate terrain, and a shared lift pass that also covers the Arnoldstein area in Austria. The resort enjoys a long season and reliable snow.

Bovec has an attractive centre, with a few shops, hotels and restaurants. The Kanin hotel is comfortable with a super pool and spa centre. The smaller Mangart is a modern place, with suites and dormitories. There are free ski-buses to the lift station.

A long gondola from the edge of town rises to 2200m, from where chairs (including two quads) and a draglift serve two short, easy blues up top and longer red runs back to the gondola mid-station or towards Italy. Kanin is not ideal for beginners though; the blues are high and exposed. Intermediates have a choice of genuine red runs – the two down to Sella Nevea are north-facing and sheltered, and interrupted only by one chairlift. There are off-piste routes to be explored, though much of the limestone terrain is pitted with hollows and holes that make it hazardous.

Mountain huts are limited. Bovec Sports offers lots of activities, and the Triglav National Park centre (Slovenia's only National Park) is worth a visit.

KEY FACTS	
Resort	570m 1,870ft
Slopes	1535-1800m 5,040-5,910ft
Lifts	7
Pistes	18km
Snow-guns	None

TOURIST OFFICES

www.vogel.si
www.bohinj.si/kobla

Vogel

- ✚ Beautiful lake setting, pretty runs
- ✚ Good choice of huts
- ▬ Bus ride from most lodging
- ▬ Limited in extent and challenge

Vogel overlooks stunning Lake Bohinj, part of the Triglav National Park. It's tiny, but is the main ski area within commuting distance of Bled.

Vogel has the best conditions and prettiest slopes in the area. Buses arrive daily from Bled; but there are small hotels and restaurants near the base and in villages along the lakeside (served by free ski-bus).

The 18km of partly wooded slopes are reached by a cable car up from the valley. A fast quad serves a mid-mountain area, with a single-seat chair to the high point at 1800m (great views). Pistes served by another chair and three drags include a lovely gentle blue. There is a separate nursery slope, a children's area and a terrain park. When conditions permit, a long red run returns to the bottom cable car station via a quiet, pretty valley. Several of the huts are nicer than the Slovenian norm.

For a change of scene Kobla, with 24km of wide, wooded runs, is a short bus ride away at Bohinjska Bistrica – the railway terminus. The 5-star Bohinj Park hotel is eco-friendly, with pool, cinema and bowling. Next door is a huge aqua park. Near Vogel, the 3-star Zlatarog is comfortable.

KEY FACTS	
Resort	325m 1,070ft
Slopes	325-1330m 1,070-4,360ft
Lifts	21
Pistes	43km
Snow-guns	95%

TOURIST OFFICE

www.maribor-pohorje.si

Maribor-Pohorje

- ✚ Good access, close to the city
- ✚ Gentle, sheltered slopes for novices
- ▬ Mostly short runs
- ▬ Few challenges except the FIS run

Slovenia's second city, Maribor, is 6km from its local slopes – where there's also limited lodging. There's little vertical to be achieved, but some varied terrain.

This is the country's biggest ski area, and continues to develop.

The lifts include a six-pack and a gondola to Pohorje summit. There's night skiing, and snowmaking covers 95% of the area. There are 27km of cross-country trails. The area lift pass also covers Kranjska Gora. The Pohorje school offers a wide range of classes. There are several atmospheric old inns serving good, Hungarian-influenced food. The 4-star Arena and 3-star Videc hotels are slope-side.

Scotland

- ➕ Easy to get to from northern Britain
- ➕ It is possible to experience perfect snow and very satisfying skiing
- ➕ Decent, cheap accommodation and good-value packages
- ➕ Midweek it's rarely crowded
- ➕ Lots to do off the slopes

- ➖ Weather is extremely changeable and sometimes vicious
- ➖ Snowfall is erratic
- ➖ Slopes limited; runs mainly short
- ➖ Queueing can be a problem
- ➖ Little ski resort ambience and few memorable mountain restaurants

Scottish skiing conditions are unpredictable, to say the least. If you live nearby and can go at short notice when things look good, the several ski areas are a tremendous asset. But booking a holiday here as a replacement for your usual week in the Alps is just too risky.

Most of the slopes in most of the areas suit intermediates best. But all apart from The Lecht also offer one or two tough or very tough slopes.

For novices who are really keen to learn, Scotland could make sense, especially if you live nearby. You can book instruction via one of the excellent outdoor centres, many of which also provide accommodation. The ski schools at the resorts themselves are also very good.

Snowboarding is popular, and most of the resorts have some special terrain features, but maintaining these facilities in good nick is problematic. When the conditions are right, the natural terrain is good for freeriding.

Cairngorm is the best-known resort, with 11 lifts and 37km of runs. Aviemore is the main centre (with a shuttle-bus to the slopes), but you can stay in other villages in the Spey valley. The slopes are accessed by a funicular from the main car park up to Ptarmigan at 1100m.

Nevis Range is the highest Scottish resort, with slopes reaching 1190m. It has 11 lifts plus a long six-seat gondola which accesses the slopes. The 35km of runs are on the north-facing slopes of Aonach Mor. A new base cafe and bigger hire shop opened in 2011. There are many B&Bs and hotels in and around Fort William, 10 minutes away by bus.

Glenshee is the largest ski area, with 40km of runs spread out over three minor parallel valleys served by 22 lifts. It includes some natural quarter-pipes. In 2011/12 a new double chairlift opened to access the Cairnwell cafe and the slopes in that area. Glenshee is primarily a venue for day-trippers, though there are hotels, hostels and B&Bs in the area.

Glencoe's seven lifts and 20km of runs lie east of moody Glen Coe itself. A double chairlift and a drag go up to the main slopes, including the nursery area. There are freeriding opportunities and a challenging descent on Flypaper, the resort's steepest run. 'Great-value, cosy' cafe at the base. The isolated Kings House Hotel is 2km away.

The Lecht is largely a novices' area, with 13 lifts and 20km of runs on the gentle slopes beside a high pass, with a series of parallel lifts and runs above the car parks. With a maximum vertical of only 200m, runs are short. There's extensive snowmaking, a terrain park, and a day lodge at the base. The village of Tomintoul is 10km away.

FURTHER INFORMATION

The VisitScotland organization runs an excellent website at: ski.visitscotland.com

Japan

- Reliable deep powder snow in Hokkaido resorts, lift-served
- Exotic atmosphere, fabulous food
- Polite and gracious locals
- Night skiing is the norm, allowing a long ski day if you want one

- The language barrier
- Pricey and lengthy trip; 6,000 miles, with a change of plane
- Lack of off-slope diversions
- Snowfall can go on for weeks in Hokkaido resorts

Although it is roughly the same size as the British Isles, Japan has hundreds of ski resorts. A surprising number of UK tour operators now feature Japanese resorts, going to places on the northern island of Hokkaido that have developed something like cult status with keen skiers and riders from Australia. The reason is simple: humongous, frequent and reliable falls of powder snow.

In these remote parts of Japan, hardly anything is written in English, and no English-language media are available (except websites). Going independently sounds like hard work; but presumably going with a tour operator is not.

UK PACKAGES

Niseko Crystal, Crystal Finest, Independent Ski Links, James Orr Heli-ski, Mountain Tracks, Mountain Wave, Ski Independence, Ski Safari, Skitracer, Skiworld
Rusutsu Crystal, Independent Ski Links, Ski Independence, Ski Safari, Skitracer
Furano Mountain Tracks, Mountain Wave, Ski Independence, Ski Safari, Skiworld
Hakuba Mountain Wave, Ski Safari, Skiworld

You fly in to Sapporo (about two hours by bus to Rusutsu and a bit longer to Niseko or Furano), via Tokyo or Osaka. As you are travelling such a great distance you might want to combine your skiing with a stay in Tokyo or (preferably) Kyoto.

Niseko is made up of three areas of slopes – Grand Hirafu (Hirafu and Hanazono), Annupuri and Niseko Village – with a total of 30 lifts covered by a single pass. The three are linked, but not as efficiently as you might wish. There are modern lifts, but also some old single chairs on upper slopes.

The most popular and most easily accessible area, Grand Hirafu, is open from 8.30am to 8.30pm, thanks to one of the world's largest – and most heavily used – night skiing operations. A new eight-seat gondola (replacing the old four-seat version), a day lodge, restaurants and a children's area opened in 2011/12 in celebration of the resort's 50th anniversary. For 2012/13 a new centre is due to open for lift passes, equipment hire and ski school.

Niseko has a well-deserved reputation for powder snow, which falls almost constantly from December to the end of February. Skiing waist-deep powder is an everyday occurrence. Clearly, this will suit some holiday skiers and not others. Niseko does offer groomed runs, but you can get those closer to home, and get a tan while you ski them. The snow does stop sometimes, and when it does the powder gets tracked out quickly. But it's usually not too long before another snowstorm marches in across the Sea of Japan from Siberia, and the powder returns. The terrain is not steep, disappointing some hard-core experts.

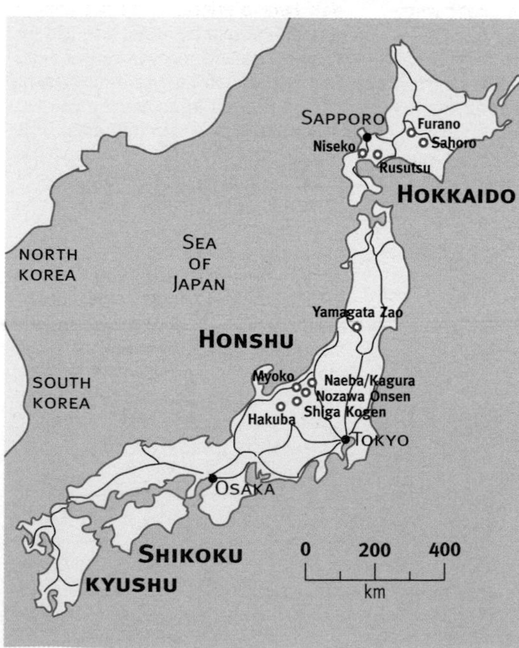

← There are lots of resorts on the main island of Honshu; only the better-known ones are shown on our map. But the best snow is on Hokkaido

Fresh powder and lots of it: that's the reason to head for Japan ➔

SKI INDEPENDENCE

KEY FACTS

Niseko	
Slopes	235-1210m 770-4,180ft
Lifts	30
Pistes	48km
Blue	30%
Red	40%
Black	30%

Rusutsu	
Lifts	19
Pistes	42km
Blue	30%
Red	40%
Black	30%

Furano	
Slopes	235-1210m 770-4,180ft
Lifts	11
Pistes	25km
Blue	40%
Red	40%
Black	20%

More information

To really get to grips with the resorts on offer in Japan, spend some time delving into this site: www.snowjapan.com

TOURIST OFFICES

Niseko
www.nisekotourism.com
www.niseko.ne.jp/en/index.html

Hirafu
www.grand-hirafu.jp/winter/en/

Niseko Village
www.niseko-village.com

Annupuri
www.cks.chuo-bus.co.jp/annupuri/english.php

Rusutsu
www.rusutsu.co.jp

Furano
www.skifurano.com

The lack of sun has not proved a deterrent to Australians, who now come in their thousands. For them, guaranteed powder and reasonable costs have been an unbeatable combination. For UK-based travellers, the cost is higher: from around £2,300 for a week in Niseko and a two-night stopover in Tokyo on the way home, says tour operator Ski Independence.

There are several modern ski-in/ski-out hotels (but little else) at the bases. The Hilton Niseko Village at the foot of the slopes is among the best, with spectacular views from most of the rooms and its own spa and onsen (see below). Or you can stay in the atmospheric little town of Hirafu where there are now some impressive modern apartments alongside traditional pensions and lodges, raising accommodation standards well above the norm for the simple country town. The lift bases are well serviced by free shuttle-buses.

While there isn't a lot to do except ski (and snowshoe), eat and drink in Hirafu, the Australian influx means that the little town makes up for its lack of sophistication with a vibrant nightlife and plenty of variety in the way of bars, restaurants and tiny underground-style clubs. There are now a few very upmarket restaurants in town and several chic bars. And an igloo-style Ice Bar is dug out of a snowdrift each year, complete with icicles on the roof and a real bar selling all manner of cocktails.

Rusutsu is about an hour from Niseko, and makes a viable day trip; or you could combine the two in a two-centre holiday. The slopes, over three interlinked mountains, are more limited, but offer slightly more challenge. The snow here can be as good as in Niseko (though it doesn't fall in quite the same quantity), and it doesn't get tracked out so quickly. There's also a good terrain park, kids' park and half-pipe. The pivotal, self-contained Rusutsu Resort Hotel complex offers a wide choice of good restaurants plus bars, a shopping mall, swimming pool, wave pool and onsen.

One of the main alternatives to these two on Hokkaido is **Furano** – one of the more famous resorts within Japan, capable of hosting World Cup events and offering a tad more vertical than Niseko, at 950m over two linked sectors. It is five to six hours from Niseko and Rusutsu, so not within day-trip range. This is a resort where you can either stick to the relatively easy trails or join a guided group to explore off-piste. You can also go with a guided group to the lift-served but ungroomed Asahidake mountain (a live volcano, around an hour away). One of the most comfortable hotels is the New Furano Prince, a free five-minute ride on the resort shuttle from the main base and a 10-minute bus ride from town; again it has great views and its own onsen.

The largest ski area in Japan is on the main island of Honshu: **Shiga Kogen**, comprising 21 interlinked resorts and a huge diversity of terrain covered by one lift ticket. It was the site of several major events in the 1998 Winter Olympics.

Hakuba is also handy to reach by train if you find yourself in Tokyo and don't have time for the trip to Hokkaido. It is a group of 10 resorts accessing more than 200 runs amid the rugged peaks of Japan's 'Alps'.

THE ONSEN EXPERIENCE

Onsen are complexes of hot baths to soak in, showers and communal volcanic thermal pools; they are a key part of Japanese culture and a major part of après-ski. All onsen are basically set up in the same way: men and women shower and bathe in their separate areas. Then, if they wish, they can congregate to soak and have a drink in a communal thermal pool, which more often than not will be outside and surrounded by snow.

REFERENCE SECTION

SKI BUSINESSES

This is a list of ski businesses including all the holiday operators and ski travel agents we know about.

247 Recruit
Ski jobs and training directory
Tel 08452 247 450

360 Sun and Ski
Family holidays in Les Carroz, French Alps
Tel +33 450 903180

Absolutely Snow
Holidays to France, Andorra and Norway
Tel 01244 439801

Action Outdoor Holidays
All-inclusive holidays in the French Alps
Tel 0845 890 0362

ActivityBreaks.com
Flexible breaks and group specials
Tel 028 9094 1671

Adventure Base Ltd
Flexible catered/self-catered chalets/apartments in Morzine and Chamonix
Tel 0845 527 5612

Alpine Inspirations
Self-catered chalets in Les Gets
Tel 0845 4747901

Alpine Action
Catered chalets in Méribel and La Tania
Tel 01273 466535

Alpine Answers
Ski travel agent + tailor-made holidays
Tel 020 7801 1080

Alpine Club
Chalets in St-Martin-de-Belleville
Tel +33 7784 5710

Alpine Elements
Holidays in France and Austria
Tel 0844 273 5205

Alpine Life
Catered chalet in Saas-Fee
Tel 07801 982645

Alpine Weekends Ltd
Weekends in the Alps
Tel 020 8944 9762

Alps Accommodation
Accommodation in Samoëns and Morillon
Tel +33 (0) 450 985056

Alpsholiday
Apartments in Serre-Chevalier
Tel +33 492 204426

Altitude Holidays
Ski travel agent
Tel 0870 870 7669

AmeriCan Ski
North America specialist plus undiscovered gems in France
Tel 01892 779900

American Ski Classics
Holidays in major North American resorts
Tel 020 8607 9988

Ardmore Educational Travel
Group and school trips
Tel 01628 826699

Balkan Holidays
Bulgaria, Slovenia and Romania holidays
Tel 0845 130 1114

Bassingbourn Snowsports Centre
Dry snowsports centre in Royston, Hertfordshire
Tel 0845 072 8293

Belvedere Travel
Luxury self-catered chalets/ apartments in Méribel and Verbier
Tel 01264 738 257

Bigfoot Chamonix
Holidays in the Chamonix Valley
Tel +33 450 530063

BoardnLodge.com Ltd
Catered and self-catered holidays in Europe
Tel 020 3239 1349

Borderline
Apartments, chalets and hotels in Barèges
Tel +33 562 926895

Bramble Ski
Chalets in Verbier and St Anton
Tel 020 7060 0824

Canadian Affair
Flights and holidays in Canada
Tel 0141 248 6777 / 020 7616 9999

Canadian Powder Tours Chalet Holidays
Chalet holidays in Western Canada
Tel +1 250 423 3019

Carrier
Upmarket chalets and hotels in the Alps, the USA and Canada
Tel 0161 491 7670

Catered Ski Chalets
Ski travel agent
Tel 020 3080 0202

Chalet Bezière
Chalet in Samoëns
Tel +33 450 905181

ChaletBook Limited
Chalet accommodation agency in the Portes du Soleil
Tel 0845 680 6802

Chalet Chez Bear
Chalet in Serre-Chevalier
Tel 00 33 492 211170

Chalet Chocolat
Self-catered chalet in Morzine
Tel 01872 580814

Chalet Le Dragon
Chalet in La Chapelle d'Abondance
Tel +33 450 172913

Chalet Entre Deux Eaux
Chalet in Morzine
Tel +33 450 37 47 55

Chalet Espen
Chalet in Engelberg
Tel +41 41 637 2220

Chalet Famille
Chalet in Morzine
Tel 0870 068 3456

Chaletfinder.co.uk
Ski travel agent
Tel 01453 766094

Chalet la Forêt
Self-catered chalet in Chamonix
Tel 07545 575277

The Chalet Group
Promotes owner-run chalets in Europe

Chalet Gueret
Luxury chalet near Morzine
Tel 01884 255437

Chalet Kiana
Self-catered chalet in Les Contamines
Tel 07968 123470

Chalet One
Catered chalet in Ste-Foy
Tel +44 (0) 7899 911855

Chalets Unlimited
Chalets in Verbier
Tel 01442 832629

Chalet de Valmorel
Chalet in Valmorel
Tel +33 479 245229

Challenge Activ
Chalets and apartments in Morzine
Tel +33 633737971 / +33 450 790307

Chamonix.uk.com
Apartment holidays in central Chamonix
Tel 01224 641559

Le Chardon Mountain Lodges Val d'Isère
Luxury chalets in a private hamlet in Val d'Isère
Tel 0131 209 7969

Chez Michelle
Self-catering apartment in Samoëns
Tel 01372 456463

Chez Serre Chevalier
Flexible trips to Serre-Chevalier
Tel 020 8144 1351

Chill Chalet
Accommodation in Paradiski
Tel 01273 725622

Classic Ski Limited
Holidays for 'mature' skiers/ beginners
Tel 01590 623400

Club Europe Schools Skiing
Schools trips to Europe
Tel 0800 496 4996

Club Med
All-inclusive holidays in 'ski villages'
Tel 08453 670670

Cold Comforts Lodging
Whistler specialist
Tel 0800 881 8429

Collett's Mountain Holidays
Holidays in the Dolomites
Tel 01799 513331

Collineige
Chamonix valley specialist
Tel 01483 579242

Connick Ski
Chalet with in-house ski school in Châtel
Tel +33 450 732212 / +33 607 131537

Consensio Holidays
Luxury chalets in The Three Valleys, Val d'Isère and Revelstoke
Tel 0203 393 0833

Contiki Holidays
Holidays for 18-35s
Tel 0845 075 0990

Cooltip Mountain Holidays
Chalet in Méribel
Tel 01964 563563

The Corporate Ski Company
Event management company
Tel 020 8542 8100

Crystal Ski
Major mainstream operator
Tel 0871 231 2256

Crystal Finest
Ski holidays to Europe and North America
Tel 0871 971 0364

Directski.com
Holidays in Europe and North America
Tel 0800 201 205

Elegant Resorts
Luxury ski holidays
Tel 01244 897333

Elevation Holidays
Holidays in the Austrian Alps
Tel 01622 370570

Elysian Collection
Luxury chalets in Zermatt
Tel +353 1 288 6634

Erna Low
Self-drive holidays and accommodation in the Alps; tailormade packages to North America
Tel 0845 863 0525

Esprit Ski
Families specialist in Europe
Tel 01483 791900

Exodus
Cross-country skiing holidays
Tel 0845 287 4217

Family Friendly Skiing
Family specialist in the Three Valleys – in-house nannies
Tel +33 450 327121

Family Ski Company
Family skiing holidays in France and Switzerland
Tel 01684 540333

Ferme de Montagne
Luxury boutique chalet hotel in Les Gets
Tel 0844 669 8652 / +33 450 753679

Flexiski
Weekends and corporate events in Europe
Tel 020 8939 0864

Friendship Travel
Holidays for singles 25 to 60
Tel 0871 200 2035

Frontier Ski
Holidays in Canada and the USA
Tel 020 8776 8709

Go Montgenevre
Holidays in Montgenèvre
Tel +33 (0)688 358473

Hannibals
Holidays in Serre-Chevalier
Tel 01233 813105

Headwater Holidays
Cross-country skiing holidays
Tel 0845 527 7061

High Mountain Holidays
Holidays in Chamonix
Tel 01993 775540

Holiday in Alps
Self-catered chalets and apartments in St Gervais and Les Contamines
Tel 01327 828239

Host Savoie
Catered chalets and apartments in Morzine
Tel 07714 508395

Hugski Holidays
Catered chalet in Morzine
Tel 07738 550151

Huski
Catered and self-catered chalet holidays in Chamonix
Tel 0800 520 0935

Ice and Fire
Catered chalets in La Plagne (Paradiski)
Tel 07855 717997

Ifyouski.com
Ski travel agent
Tel 0844 338 0060

Iglu.com
Ski travel agent
Tel 020 8542 6658

Independent Ski Links
Ski travel agent
Tel 01964 533905

I Need Snow
Ski travel agent
Tel 020 8123 7817

Inghams
Major mainstream operator
Tel 01483 791111

Inntravel
Holidays in the snow
Tel 01653 617920

Inspired to Ski
Holidays with tuition in France and Italy
Tel 020 8133 4131

Interactive Resorts
Agent specializing in catered chalets worldwide
Tel 020 3080 0202

Interhome
Self-catered apartment and chalet rentals in Europe
Tel 020 8877 6370

Interski
Family/group holidays with tuition in the Aosta valley
Tel 01623 456333

Jagged Horizons
Corporate trips to the Alps
Tel 020 8123 7817

James Orr Heli-ski
Heli-skiing packages in Canada
Tel 01799 516964

Jeffersons Private Jet Holidays
Luxury holidays by private jet
Tel 020 8746 2496

Just Skiing
Courmayeur specialist plus La Thuile
Tel 01202 479988

Kaluma Ski
Tailor made private and corporate holidays in the Alps
Tel 01730 260 263

Kwik Ski
Ski travel agent
Tel 0800 655 6300

Lagrange Holidays
Ski holidays in Europe
Tel 020 7371 6111

Le Ski
Chalets in Courchevel, Val d'Isère and La Tania
Tel 01484 548996

Live the Season
Seasonal accommodation and long-term holiday specialists in Europe and Canada
Tel 0203 286 5959

Luxury Chalet Collection
Luxury chalets in the Alps
Tel 01993 899420

Mark Warner
Chalet hotel holidays in big-name resorts
Tel 0844 273 6777

Marmotte Mountain Adventure
Chalets in Chamonix Valley
Tel +33 682 891523

Meriski
Chalet specialist in Méribel
Tel 01285 648518

MGS Ski Limited
Hotel and apartments in Val Cenis
Tel 01603 742842

Momentum Ski
Specialists in ski weekends and tailor-made holidays
Tel 020 7371 9111

Mountain Beds
Accommodation agents and Verbier specialists
Tel 01502 471960

A Mountain Chalet
Catered chalet in La Rosière
Tel 01704 879554 / +33 479 065738

Mountain Heaven
Catered and self-catered accommodation in France and Switzerland
Tel 0151 625 1921

Mountain Lodge
Chalet hotel in Les Crosets, Portes du Soleil
Tel 0845 127 1750

Mountainsun Ltd
Chalets in Europe – short breaks and week-long trips
Tel 01273 257008

Mountain Tracks
Off-piste, hut-to-hut touring and avalanche awareness
Tel 020 8123 2978

Mountain Wave Travel
Accommodation in Europe
Tel 01430 471943

Neilson
Major mainstream operator
Tel 0845 070 3460

Nick Ski
Catered chalet in La Tania
Tel +33 673 436769

The Oxford Ski Company
Ski travel agency
Tel 01993 899420

Peak Pursuits
Catered chalet in St Martin de Belleville
Tel 01322 866726

Peak Retreats
Holidays to traditional French Alps resorts
Tel 0844 576 0170

PGL Ski
School group specialist and holidays for teenagers
Tel 0844 371 0101

Pierre & Vacances
8,000+ ski apartments in France
Tel 0870 0267 145

Pilaski
Holidays in Pila, Aosta Valley
Tel 01478 613561

PowderBeds
Hotels and apartments in Europe and North America
Tel 0131 243 8097

Powder Byrne
Luxury holidays in European resorts
Tel 020 8246 5300

Powder N Shine
Luxury chalets in Reberty (Les Menuires)
Tel 0845 163 7596

Powder White
Holidays in big-name resorts
Tel 020 8877 8888

Première Neige
Catered/self-catered holidays in Ste-Foy; nanny service
Tel 0870 383 1000

PT Ski
Holidays in Klosters
41 Napier Avenue, London
Tel 020 7736 5557

Pure Powder
Powder skiing in Canada, Alaska, Chile and Europe
Tel 020 7736 8191

Purple Ski
Chalet holidays in Méribel
Tel 01885 488799

Ramblers Holidays
Mostly cross-country skiing holidays
Tel 01707 331133

Reach4theAlps
Holidays in the French Alps
Tel 0845 680 1947

Richmond World Holidays
Christian holidays
Tel 020 3004 2661

Ride & Slide
Chalets in Morzine
Tel +33 450 388 962

Rocketski.com
Club hotels and chalets in France and Italy
Tel 01273 810777

Rude Chalets
Holidays in Morzine, Avoriaz and Chamonix
Tel 0870 068 7030

Scott Dunn Ski
Luxury chalets and hotels in the Alps and N America
Tel 020 8682 5050

Select Chalets
Chalets in Hochkönig
Tel 01273 645666

Silver Ski
Chalet holidays in France
Tel 01622 735544

Simon Swaffer
Apartment in La Plagne
Tel 07919 170227

Simon Butler Skiing
Holidays in Megève with ski instruction included
Tel 0870 873 0001 / 01483 212726

Simply Alpine
Agent for accommodation in Europe and N America
Tel 023 9279 8901

Ski Ici
Low carbon holidays to French resorts
Tel 07779 006689

Ski 2
Specialists in Champoluc (Monterosa)
Tel 01962 713330

Ski Addiction
Chalets/hotels in the Portes du Soleil
Tel +33 607 979736

Skialot
Chalet in Châtel
Tel 0780 156 9264

Ski Alpage
Chalet in St-Martin-de-Belleville
Tel +33 479 089228

Ski Amis
Catered chalet and self-catered holidays in the French Alps
Tel 020 3411 5439

Ski Basics
Catered chalets in Méribel
Tel 0845 123 6064

Ski Beat
Catered chalets in the French Alps
Tel 01243 780405

Ski Bespoke
Tailor-made holidays in the Alps and N America
Tel 01243 200202

Ski Blanc
Chalet holidays in Méribel
Tel 020 8502 9082 / +33 622 056416

SkiBound
School trips
Tel 01273 244570

Skibug
Catered chalets in La Plagne
Tel 0845 260 7573

Ski Club Freshtracks
Group holidays for Ski Club of Great Britain members
Tel 020 8410 2022

Ski Collection
French 3- and 4-star self-catering apartment specialist
Tel 0844 576 0175

Ski Cuisine
Chalets in Méribel
Tel 01702 589543

Ski-Dazzle
Chalet holidays in Les Trois Vallées
Tel +33 479 001725

Ski Deep
Chalets in La Tania and Le Praz
Tel +33 479 081905

Ski-direct.co.uk
Ski travel agent
Tel 0844 553 3501

Ski Etoile
Hotels and self-catered apartments in Montgenèvre
Tel 01952 253252

Ski Europe
Ski travel agent
Tel 01350 728869

Ski Expectations
Small travel agency specializing in ski holidays
Tel 01799 531888

Ski Famille
Family properties in the Alps
Tel 0845 644 3764

Ski France
Packaged and tailor-made holidays in France
Tel 01273 358538

Ski Freedom
Catered and self-catered chalets in Verbier, Champéry and Zinal
Tel +41 (0)7888 10978

Ski Hame
Catered chalets in Méribel and La Tania
Tel 01875 320157

Ski Hiver
Chalets in Paradiski
Tel 020 8144 4160

Ski-in.co.uk
Self-catered apartment and chalet in Serre-Chevalier
Tel 01630 672540

Ski Independence
USA, Canada, Japan, France, Switzerland and Austria
Tel 0131 243 8097

Skiing Austria
Agent for accommodation in Austria
Tel 020 8123 7817

Ski La Cote
Self-catered chalet in the Portes du Soleil
Tel 01482 668357

Ski Line
Ski travel agent + chalets in Europe and North America
Tel 020 8313 3999

Ski Magic
Chalet holidays in La Tania
Tel 0844 993 3686

Ski McNeill
Ski travel agent
Tel 028 9066 6699

Ski Miquel Holidays
Small but eclectic programme
Tel 01457 821200

Ski-Monterosa Ltd
Monterosa (Alagna) specialist
Tel 020 7361 0086

Ski Morgins Holidays
Self-catered and B&B holidays in Morgins
Tel +41 24 477 3451

Ski Morzine
Accommodation in Morzine
Tel 0845 370 1104

Skiology.co.uk
Catered chalets in Les Carroz and Morzine
Tel 07894 758535

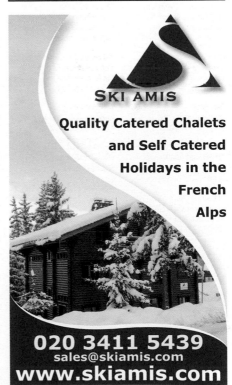

Ski Olympic
Chalet holidays in France
Tel 01302 328820

Ski Peak
Specialist in Vaujany
Tel 01428 608070

SkiPlan Travel Service
Schools programme
Tel 0871 222 6565

Ski Power
Chalets in La Tania, Courchevel and Val d'Isère
Tel 01737 306029

Ski Safari
Multi-resort safaris
Tel 01273 224060

Ski Soleil
Chalet and apartments in La Plagne
Tel 020 3239 3454

Ski Solutions
Ski travel agent + tailor-made holidays
Tel 020 7471 7700

Ski Supreme
Holidays to France and to Pila (Italy)
Tel 0845 194 7541

Ski Surf
Ski travel agent
Tel 020 8731 2111

Skitopia
Hotels and self-catering in the French Alps
Tel 0844 412 9919

Ski Total
Chalet holidays in Europe
Tel 01483 791933

Skitracer.com
Ski travel agent
Tel 020 8600 1650

Ski Travel Centre
Ski travel agent
Tel 0845 118 0092

Ski-Val
Catered chalets in Val d'Isère and St Anton
Tel 01822 611200

Ski Verbier
Specialists in Verbier chalets
Tel 020 7401 1101

Ski Weekend
Tailor-made short breaks
Tel 01392 878353

Ski Weekender
Ski weekend specialist in La Clusaz
Tel 0845 557 5983

Skiweekends.com
Weekends and short breaks to the Alps
Tel 08444 060600

Skiworld
Catered chalets, hotels and self-catering apartments in Europe, USA and Canada
Tel 08444 930 430

Ski Yogi
Hotels and catered chalets agent in Italy
Tel 01799 531886

SkiZinal
Catered/self-catering chalets in Zinal (Val d'Anniviers)
Tel 0208 144 7575

Sloping Off
Schools holidays
Tel 01273 648200

Snowbizz
Family ski specialist in Puy-St-Vincent
Tel 01778 341455

Snowcard Insurance Services
Winter sports insurance
Tel 01295 660836

Snowchateaux
Catered chalet holidays in Paradiski and Tignes
Tel 0800 066 4996

Snowcoach
Holidays to France
Tel 01727 866177

SnowCrazy
Chalets in the French Alps
Tel 0845 260 2910

Snowed Inn Chalets
Catered chalets in Serre-Chevalier
Tel 07527 162098

Snow Finders
Travel agent + tour operator to Europe and N America
Tel 01858 466888

Snowfocus
Catered chalet with childcare in Châtel
Tel 01392 479555

Snow Hounds
Ski travel agent
Tel 01243 788487

Snowlife
Catered chalet in La Clusaz
Tel 01534 863630

Snow Nation
Fully-catered hotel in La Rosière
Tel 0845 230 1754

Snoworks Ski Courses
Performance ski courses and adventure skiing
Tel 0844 543 0503

Snowpod
Hosted apartments with a twist in Tignes
Tel 07881 725062

Snowscape
Weekly and flexible trips to Austria
Tel 08453 708570

Snowslippers
Trips to Austria for groups
Tel 07837 093989

Snowstar Holidays
Catered chalets in Tignes
Tel 020 8133 8411

Snowy Pockets
Chalet/apartment holidays in France and Switzerland
Tel +41 (0) 813 565257

Solo's
Singles' holidays
Tel 0844 815 0005

La Source
Accommodation in Villard-Reculas (Alpe-d'Huez)
Tel 01707 655988

Sovereign Ski
Luxury chalets in Méribel
Tel 0751 858 2147

Stanford Skiing
Megève specialist
Tel 01603 477471

Star Ski Chalets
Chalets in Morzine
Tel +33 679 181401

STC Ski
Europe and North America, specializing in Austria
Tel 01483 771222

Sugar Mountain
Chalet in Morzine
Tel +33 450 749033

Supertravel
Upmarket European and North American holidays
Tel 020 7962 9933

Susie Ward Alpine Holidays
Upmarket accommodation in Châtel
Tel +33 450 734087

Switzerland Travel Centre
Specialists in Swiss resorts
Tel 020 7420 4934

Ted Bentley Chalet Holidays
Luxury catered and self-catered chalet holidays in Courchevel and Nendaz
Tel 01934 820854

Teletext Holidays
Travel agency
Tel 0844 767 6395

Thomson Ski
Major mainstream operator
Tel 0871 971 0578

Tracks European Adventures
Customized tours in the Alps
Tel 024 498 1347

Trail Alpine
Chalet in Morzine
Tel 01745 570106

TravelSAC
Ski travel agent
Tel 01323 842599

V-Ski
Self-catered chalets in Verbier
Tel +41 (0)79 431 9228

Val d'Isère A La Carte
Specialists in Val d'Isère hotel/self-catering holidays
Tel +33 629 894457

VIP
Chalets in the Alps
Tel 0844 557 3119

Virgin Snow
Holidays to America and Canada
Tel 0844 557 4321

White Roc
Tailor-made hotel/self-catering holidays
Tel 020 7792 1188

YSE
Chalet holidays in Val d'Isère
Tel 0845 122 1414

Zenith Holidays
Holidays in the Alps and Pyrenees
Tel 020 3137 7678

SKI RETAILERS

Here we list ski equipment shops – all these shops stock this guidebook.

SOUTH-WEST ENGLAND

Chelstondirect.com
Unit 6 Monument View, Chelston Business Park, Wellington TA21 9ND
Tel 0844 351 1078

Devon Ski Centre
Oak Place, Newton Abbot, Devon TQ12 2EX
Tel 01626 351278

Snow & Rock
Units 1-3 Shield Retail Centre, Link Road, Filton, Bristol BS34 7BQ
Tel 0117 914 3000

Snow & Rock
Unit 2 Bishops Retail Park, Sidmouth Rd, Exeter EX2 7JH
Tel 01392 357600

SOUTH-EAST ENGLAND

Snow & Rock
54-55 Market Street, Brighton, Sussex BN1 1HH
Tel 01273 827660

Snow & Rock
99 Fordwater Road, Chertsey, Surrey KT16 8HH
Tel 01932 566886

Snow & Rock
Unit 4, 230-250 Purley Way, Croydon CR0 4XG
Tel 0208 253 0180

Snow & Rock
188 Kensington High Street, London W8 7RG
Tel 020 7937 0872

Snow & Rock
4 Mercer Street, Covent Garden, London WC2H 9QA
Tel 020 7420 1444

Snow & Rock
4 Gray's Inn Road, Holborn, London WC1X 8HG
Tel 020 7831 6900

Snow & Rock
Sporting Club, 38-42 King's Road, Chelsea, London SW3 4UD
Tel 020 7589 5418

Snow & Rock
47-51 William Street, London EC4R 9AF
Tel 020 7256 3940

Snow & Rock
5th floor Harrods, 87-135 Brompton Road, London SW1X 7XL
Tel 020 7173 6476

Snow & Rock
North Face, 28 Palace St, Victoria, London SW1E 5JD
Tel 020 7630 4969

Snow & Rock
The Boardwalk, Port Solent, Portsmouth, Hampshire PO6 4TP
Tel 023 9220 5388

Snow & Rock
Unit 1 Davidson Way, Rom Valley Way, Romford, Essex RM7 0AZ
Tel 01708 436400

Wipeout
Southfield, Woodside Hill, Chalfont St Peter, Bucks SL9 9TB
Tel 0208 133 8240

MIDDLE ENGLAND

Snow & Rock
14 Priory Queensway, Birmingham B4 6BS
Tel 0121 236 8280

EASTERN ENGLAND

Alpine Room
71-73 Main Road, Danbury, Essex CM3 4DJ
Tel 01245 223563

Snow & Rock
Hemel Ski Centre, St Albans Hill, Hemel Hempstead, Hertfordshire HP3 9NH
Tel 01422 235305

SnowFit/Revolutionz
Yarefield Park, Old Hall Road, Norwich NR4 6FF
Tel 01603 716655

NORTHERN ENGLAND

Freetime Climb + Ski
1-2 Market Street, Carlisle, Cumbria CA3 8QJ
Tel 01228 598210

Glide & Slide
5/7 Station Road, Otley, West Yorkshire LS21 3HX
Tel 01943 461136

Snow & Rock
Metro Park West, Gibside Way, Gateshead NE11 9XS
Tel 0191 493 3680

Snow & Rock
Princess Parkway, Princess Park, Didsbury, Manchester M20 8ZE
Tel 0161 448 4444

Snow & Rock
Unit 6, Chill Factore Centre, Trafford Way, Trafford Quays, Manchester M41 7JA
Tel 0161 746 1010

Snow & Rock
Unit 1 Eastham Point, New Chester Road, Eastham, Wirral CH62 8HJ
Tel 0151 328 5500

NORTHERN IRELAND

Macski
140 Lisburn Road, Belfast BT9 6AJ
Tel 028 9066 5525

REPUBLIC OF IRELAND

Snow & Rock
Unit 3.2 Dundrum Town Centre, Dundrum, Dublin 14
Tel 00 353 (0) 1 2924700

RESORT DIRECTORY / INDEX

This is an index to the resort chapters in the book; you'll find page references for about 400 resorts that are described in those chapters (note that if the resort you are looking up is covered in a chapter devoted to a bigger resort, the page reference will be to the start of the chapter, not to the exact page on which the minor resort is described). You'll also find here brief descriptions of around 1,000 other resorts, most of them smaller than those we've covered in full.

Key

Lifts
Pistes
UK tour operators

49 Degrees North USA
Inland area with best snow in Washington State, including 120-acre bowl reserved for powder weekends.
1195m; slopes 1195–1760m
5 780 acres

Abetone Italy
Resort in the exposed Apennines, less than two hours from Florence and Pisa.
1400m; slopes 1200–1940m
25 70km

Abtenau Austria
Sizeable village in Dachstein-West region near Salzburg, on large plain ideal for cross-country.
710m; slopes 710–1190m
7 12km

Achenkirch Austria
Unspoiled, low-altitude Tirolean village close to Niederau and Alpbach. Beautiful setting overlooking a lake.
930m; slopes 930–1800m
30 50km Ramblers

Adelboden 454

Les Aillons-Margériaz France
Traditional village near Chambéry. Nicely sheltered slopes.
1000m; slopes 1000–1900m
21 40km

Alagna 412
Small resort on the east fringe of the Monterosa Ski area.

Alba 447
Pretty village in Val di Fassa.

Alberschwende 192
Village in Bregenzerwald.
720m 8 18km

Albiez-Montrond France
Authentic old French village in Maurienne valley with good views. Own easy slopes; close to other ski areas.
1500m; slopes 1500–2200m
13 67 hectares

Alleghe Italy
Dolomite village near Cortina in a pretty lakeside setting close to numerous areas.
1000m 24 80km

Les Allues 282
Rustic village on the road up to Méribel.

Alpbach 107

Alpe-d'Huez 202

Alpe-du-Grand-Serre France
Tiny resort near Alpe-d'Huez and Les Deux-Alpes. Good for bad-weather days.
1370m; slopes 1370–2185m
14 55km

Alpendorf Austria
Outpost of St Johann im Pongau, at one end of an extensive three-valley lift network linking via Wagrain to Flachau – all part of the Salzburger Sportwelt area. Good intermediate runs.
850m; slopes 800–2185m
64 200km
Crystal, Snowslippers

Alpenglow USA
Alaskan ski resort.
762m; slopes 2500–3900m
4 320 acres

Alpenregion Bludenz 195

Alpine Meadows USA
Squaw Valley's neighbour, with similar, lightly wooded terrain, an impressive snow record and runs of all classifications, but a modest total vertical; excellent beginner slopes and mostly uncrowded. The resort boundary is open – expeditions require guidance. There's no resort in the European sense, but there's lots of lodgings close by in lakeside Tahoe City.
2085m; slopes 2085–2635m
13 2400 acres
Virgin Snow

Alps Resort South Korea
Korea's most northerly snow-reliable resort, about five hours from Seoul. 5

Alta 576

Alta Badia 423
Part of the Sella Ronda circuit.

Radstadt-Altenmarkt Austria
Unspoiled village, well placed just off the Salzburg-Villach autobahn for numerous resorts including snow-sure Obertauern and those in the Salzburger Sportwelt.
855m; slopes 855–1570m
8 20km

Alto Campoo Spain
Barren, desolate place near Santander; undistinguished slopes but magnificent wilderness views. *1650m; slopes 1650–2130m* 13

Alt St Johann Switzerland
Old cross-country village with Alpine slopes connecting into Unterwasser area near Liechtenstein.
900m; slopes 900–2260m
17 60km

Alyeska USA
Alaskan area 60km from Anchorage, with luxury hotel.
75m; slopes 75–1200m
9 785 acres
Frontier, Skiworld

Aminona 462
Purpose-built resort in the Crans-Montana network.

Andalo 443
Trentino village not far from Madonna.

Andelsbuch 192
Village in Bregenzerwald.
615m 8 15km

Andermatt 457

Andorra la Vella 88
Andorra's capital.

Angel Fire USA
Intermediate area near Taos, New Mexico. Height usually ensures good snow.
2620m; slopes 2620–3255m
5 455 acres

Les Angles 318

Ankogel Austria
Limited but varied area in the Hohe Tauern region in Carinthia; close to the Molltal Glacier and Slovenia. Mostly red and black runs; longest is 7km. Lift station a short drive from Mallnitz village.
1300m; slopes 1300–2635m
7 35km

Annaberg-Lungötz Austria
Peaceful village near Filzmoos in a pretty setting, sharing a sizeable area with Gosau.
775m; slopes 775–1620m
33 65km

Annupuri 658
Interlinked area in Niseko, Japan.

Antagnod Italy
Day-trip area near Champoluc, above Aosta valley. Great views to Monte Rosa. No village, but family oriented with quiet nursery slopes and handful of runs.
1710m; slopes 1710–2305m
4 14km

Anthony Lakes USA
Small area in Oregon with one chair and two beginner lifts.
2165m; slopes 2165–2435m
3 21 trails

Anzère Switzerland
Sympathetically designed modern resort on a sunny balcony near Crans-Montana, with uncrowded slopes suited to leisurely intermediates. Lots of old, slow lifts but the area is very much a family resort, with village nursery slopes and spa centre. Little to challenge experts except the 5km Pas de Maimbre black run, an itinerary and some gentle off-piste. There's a terrain park. For a small place there is a reasonable choice of restaurants and bars. Lots of marked walks and a 3km toboggan run.
1500m; slopes 1500–2420m
11 52km Lagrange

Aosta Italy
Historic valley town with a long gondola ride up to mountain resort of Pila. Aosta is a real working town with people in suits rather than skiwear. It has good-value accommodation, a lot more bars and restaurants than Pila, and a lovely traffic-free centre. Other resorts in the Aosta valley are within day-trip distance and are covered by the lift pass.
1800m; slopes 1550–2750m
14 70km

Aosta valley Italy
Region north of Turin with Italy's highest skiing and dominated by Monte Bianco (Mont Blanc). Lots of resorts covered by the Valley pass.

Apex Canada
Small, friendly, rather isolated modern village. Well worth stopping off here for a night or two on a tour of western BC resorts. Varied terrain that suits confident intermediates best, but also excellent beginner slopes.
1575m; slopes 1575–2180m
4 1112 acres
Frontier, Ski Safari

Aprica Italy
Ugly, straggling village between Lake Como and the Brenta Dolomites, with bland slopes and limited facilities.
1180m; slopes 1180–2300m
18 50km

Arabba 423

Aragnouet-Piau France
Purpose-built mid-mountain satellite with lifts up from the old valley town too. Best suited to families, beginners and early intermediates.
1850m; slopes 1420–2500m
12 65km

Arapahoe Basin USA
Developing, exceptionally high day-skiing area near Keystone. Excellent snowfall record and very long season. Good mix of open and wooded runs of every standard, plus serious steeps.
3285m; slopes 3285–3800m
7 900 acres

Araucarias Chile
Exotic area in central Chile, around and below a mildly active volcano in the Conguillio National Park.
1500m 4 350 hectares

Arcalis 88
Isolated ski area in Andorra.
1940m; slopes 1940–2625m
13 28.5km

Les Arcs 212

Ardent 222
Quiet hamlet with quick access to Avoriaz.

Åre 649

Arêches-Beaufort France
Secluded little village 25km from Albertville, with mostly intermediate terrain on two areas 3km apart. The slopes of both Les Saisies and Les Contamines are less than 25km away.
1080m; slopes 1080–2300m
12 55km

Argentière 227
Village beneath Chamonix's Grands Montets.

Arinsal 90

Arizona Snowbowl USA
Small but interesting ski area just outside the pleasant town of Flagstaff. Worth a visit if en route to the nearby Grand Canyon in winter..
slopes 2690–3290m 4

Arnoldstein / Dreiländereck Austria
One of several little areas overlooking Villach.
680m; slopes 680–1455m
7 17km

Arolla Switzerland
Tiny village in pretty riverside setting south of Sion in the Val d'Hérens. Main attraction is heli-skiing. Wonderful descents from 3800m.
2000m; slopes 2000–2890m
6 47km

Arosa Switzerland
A classic all-round winter resort, near Chur. High and remote, in a sheltered basin at the head of a beautiful wooded valley. The centre is not particularly pretty, though its lakeside setting adds charm. It is a quiet family place, where people stroll in fur coats, take sleigh rides, or skate across the frozen lake. A hill separates this area from the older, prettier Inner-Arosa up the valley. Lodging spreads widely, but there is an excellent free shuttle-bus. The slopes cover two main sectors mostly above the treeline; mainly enjoyable cruises. The shadier Hörnli area holds its snow well. The runs are not particularly challenging, though there are off-piste opportunities. Beginners have easy slopes at mid-mountain, but they can get crowded, though queues are rare.
1740-1830m; slopes 1800–2655m 13 70km
Alpine Answers, Crystal, Crystal Finest, Momentum, PowderBeds, Powder Byrne, Ski Bespoke, Ski Safari, Ski Solutions, Ski Weekend, Snow Finders, Snowy Pockets, Switzerland Travel Centre, White Roc

Arrowhead 555
Slope-side hamlet next to Beaver Creek.

Artesina Italy
Purpose-built Piedmont resort south of Turin, lacking character and atmosphere. Part of Mondolé ski area with Prato Nevoso.
1300m; slopes 1320–2100m
23 130km

Ascutney Mountain USA
Family resort in Vermont 60km from Killington, 200km from Boston.
6 200 acres

Asiago Italy
Sizeable resort close to Verona, but at low altitude and with limited vertical.
1000m; slopes 1000–1380m
8 12 pistes

Aspen 548

Attitash USA
One of the biggest ski areas in eastern US. Uncrowded slopes. Lodging in nearby North Conway, and other New Hampshire areas close by.
slopes 180–715m
12 280 acres

Au 192
Village in Bregenzerwald.
800m; slopes 800–2060m
8 44km

Auffach 107
Small village in Ski Juwel (Alpbachtal-Wildschönau).

Auris-en-Oisans 202
Quiet hamlet linked to Alpe-d'Huez.

Auron France
Pleasant, family-oriented resort with varied, sheltered, intermediate slopes; a stark contrast to nearby Isola 2000.
1600m; slopes 1150–2450m
20 135km
Ski France

Auronzo di Cadore Italy
Sizeable village that's a cheaper base for visiting Cortina. Its own slopes are of negligible interest.
865m; slopes 865–1585m
5 7km

Aussois France
Charming rustic working village near Modane in the Maurienne valley. Small but interesting south-facing ski area, good for intermediates and families.
1500m; slopes 1500–2750m
10 55km
AmeriCan Ski, Peak Retreats

Autrans France
Major cross-country village, close to Grenoble. Two limited areas of downhill slopes.
1050m; slopes 1050–1650m
12 20km

Avon USA
Small town only a couple of miles from Beaver Creek. Inexpensive base from which to ski Beaver Creek, Vail and Breckenridge.
AmeriCan Ski, Ski Line

Avoriaz 1800 222

Axamer Lizum Austria
Mountain outpost of the Inn-side village of Axams. A simple ski station and nothing more, but it does have some good slopes and reliable snow conditions. Covered by standard Innsbruck pass.
1580m; slopes 830–2340m
10 40km Crystal

Axams Austria
Quiet village in Innsbruck area, at bottom of the Axamer Lizum ski area.
880m; slopes 830–2340m
10 40km

Ax-les-Thermes France
Sizeable spa village near Font-Romeu and Andorra. Gondola access to the ski area above Bonascre. Mostly fast chairlifts, serving a modest area of intermediate slopes.
1400m; slopes 1400–2400m
17 75km Zenith

Bad Gastein 111

Badger Pass USA
Base for 350 miles of superb backcountry touring in Yosemite National Park. Spectacular views.
2195m; slopes 2195–2435m
5 90 acres

Badia (Pedraces) 423
Roadside village linked via La Villa to the Sella Ronda.

Bad Kleinkirchheim Austria
Spacious, quiet spa village in south-east Austria spread out along a valley near the Italian and Slovenian borders. Virtually all the slopes are ideal for intermediates; BKK has little to keep experts interested apart from the beautiful, long Franz Klammer downhill run, which goes from top to bottom away from all the lifts. For beginners there are nursery slopes at BKK and there are easy blue runs to progress to. There are 23 mountain restaurants in the two main sectors. BKK takes cross-country seriously, with 50km of tracks. Most of the hotels are comfortable 4-stars and there are lots of gasthofs and self-catering apartments. There are plenty of places for eating out, too. Après-ski is relatively quiet, but there's plenty to do off the slopes – spa facilities are excellent.
1090m; slopes 1090–2055m
25 100km
BoardnLodge, STC

Banff 605

Bansko 650

Baqueira-Beret 643

Barboleuse 513
Quiet base for skiing the Villars slopes.

Bardonecchia Italy
Sizeable railway town set in an attractive valley near the entrance to the Fréjus road tunnel; overlooked until the 2006 Turin Winter Olympics brought investment and raised its profile as a good-value intermediate destination. What it lacks in classic mountain charm, it gains in a fairly extensive area of slopes on two separate mountains linked by free bus. There are plenty of hotels, and the former Olympic village residence has spacious apartment accommodation. The resort's easy road and rail links mean it is popular with weekenders from Turin, but otherwise fairly quiet during the week with plenty of leisurely cruising on uncrowded pistes – worth considering as a base for touring other nearby French and Italian resorts too. Snow reliability isn't particularly great though and, coupled with the large number of awkward draglifts, may deter some visitors.
1310m; slopes 1290–2695m
23 100km
Alpine Answers, Crystal, Erna Low, Neilson, Thomson

Barèges 318

Bariloche (Catedral) Argentina
The place to stay when skiing Cerro Catedral, this was once a quaint lakeside town, but is now a substantial resort – including the Llao Llao Resort and Spa. The slopes at Cathedral are 20 minutes by shuttle-bus.
slopes 1030–2180m
39 103km

Les Barzettes 462
Smaller base along the road from Crans-Montana.

Bayrischzell Germany
Bavarian resort south of Munich and close to Austrian border.
800m; slopes 1090–1563m
25 40km

Bear Mountain USA
Southern California's main area, in the beautiful San Bernardino National Forest region. Full snowmaking.
slopes 2170–2685m
12 195 acres

Bears Town South Korea
Modern resort with runs cut out of thick forest. Biggest resort near Seoul (only an hour's drive), so it can get very crowded. English-language website at www.bearstown.com. 9

Bear Valley USA
Resort in northern California, between Lake Tahoe and Yosemite.
2010m; slopes 2010–2590m
10 1280 acres

Beaulard Italy
Little place just off the road between Sauze d'Oulx and Bardonecchia.
1215m; slopes 1215–2120m
6 20km

Beaver Creek 555

Beaver Mountain USA
Small Utah area north of Salt Lake City, too far from Park City for a day trip.
2195m; slopes 2195–2680m
3 525 acres

Beitostølen Norway
Small family resort in southern Norway (east of Bergen), with lots of cross-country in the region.
900m 9 25km

Belleayre Mountain USA
State-owned resort near Albany, New York State. Cheap but old lifts and short runs.
775m; slopes 775–1015m
7 170 acres

Bellwald Switzerland
Traditional Rhône valley resort near Fiesch, Riederalp and Bettmeralp. Part of the Goms Valley region.
1600m; slopes 1600–2560m
5 30km

Ben Lomond Australia
Small intermediate/beginner area in Ben Lomond National Park, Tasmania, 260km from Hobart.
1450m; slopes 1460–1570m
6 14 hectares

Berchtesgaden Germany
Pleasant old town close to Salzburg, known for its Nordic skiing but with several little Alpine areas nearby. *550m*

Bergün Switzerland
Traditional, quiet, unspoiled, virtually traffic-free little family resort on the rail route between Davos and St Moritz. 5km toboggan run.
1375m; slopes 1400–2550m
3 23km

Berkshire East USA
Resort in Massachusetts, southern New England, near the Mohawk Trail.
slopes 165–525m
5 200 acres

Berwang Austria
Quiet village in a spacious valley close to Lermoos. It claims the most skiing of the region too (36km) – though many runs are short and easy. The Zugspitz Arena lift pass, to which our figures relate, covers these and the other resorts of the valley. The village enjoys a splendid winter-wonderland setting, with lifts rising on two sides. There is a good mix of sunny and shady slopes, shared with Bichlbach; some of these give over 500m vertical to the lift station. There are good cross-country loops at altitude, plenty of huts and a long toboggan run.
1340m; slopes 990–2960m
52 147km
Ski Bespoke

Bessans France
Old cross-country village near Modane well placed for touring Maurienne valley resorts.
1710m; slopes 1740–2200m
2 3km

Besse France
Charming old village built out of lava, with purpose-built slope-side satellite Super-Besse. Beautiful extinct-volcano scenery.
1050m; slopes 1300–1850m
23 43km Lagrange

Bethel USA
Pleasant, historic town very close to Sunday River, Maine. Attractive alternative to staying in the resort.

Le Bettex 269
Small base above St-Gervais, with links to Megève.

Bettmeralp Switzerland
Central village of the sizeable Aletsch area near Brig, high above the Rhône valley, amid spectacular glacial scenery. Reached by cable cars from the valley.
1950m; slopes 1925–2870m
35 100km

Beuil-les-Launes France
Alpes-Maritimes resort closest to Nice. Medieval village which shares area with Valberg.
1460m; slopes 1400–2011m
26 90km

Bezau 192
Bregenzerwald village.
620m 8 15km

Biberwier Austria
Village near Lermoos, with mainly shady local slopes more or less spilt equally into red and blue runs. Makes a quiet base from which to access the rest of the Zugspitz Arena (to which our figures relate). The main lift from the valley is a six-pack, and there are quiet nursery slopes at the base – with a very long moving carpet. There is a terrain park, half-pipe and boardercross course. There are a couple of pleasant restaurants and bars. Like Lermoos, the village benefits from a tunnel to remove traffic from the centre.
990m; slopes 990–2960m
52 147km

Bichlbach Austria
Smallest of the Zugspitz Arena villages, sharing slopes with Berwang. Austria's first chondola lift starts here. An unspoiled base for visiting the rest of the area.
1080m; slopes 990–2960m
52 147km

Bielmonte Italy
Popular with day trippers from Milan. Worthwhile on a bad-weather day.
1200m; slopes 1200–1620m
9 20km

Big Powderhorn USA
Area with the most 'resort' facilities in south Lake Superior region – and the highest lift capacity too. The area suffers from winds.
370m; slopes 370–560m
10 250 acres

Big Sky 590

Big White 612

Bischofshofen Austria
Working town and mountain resort near St Johann im Pongau, with very limited local runs and the main slopes starting nearby at Mühlbach (Hochkönig area).
545m; slopes 545–1000m
1 2km

Bivio Switzerland
Quiet village near St Moritz and Savognin, with easy slopes.
1770m; slopes 1780–2560m
4 40km

Björkliden Sweden
538m vertical. Feb-to-May Arctic Circle area. Ultra snow-reliable. You can even ski in caves – beautiful ice formations. Magnificent Lapland views.
5 15km

Björnrike Sweden
20 minutes from Vemdalasskalet (same pass). 385m vertical.
9 15km

Black Mountain USA
New Hampshire area with lodging in nearby Jackson.
4 143 acres

Blatten Switzerland
Mountainside hamlet above Naters, beside the Rhône near Brig. Small but tall Belalp ski area, with larger Aletsch area nearby.
1320m; slopes 1320–3100m
9 60km

Bled 654
Lakeside base in Slovenia.

Blue Cow Australia
Part of Perisher resort, Australia's highest and expanding ski area. Accessible only by tube train. Nearest town – Jindabyne. Six hours from Sydney.
1890m; slopes 1605–2035m
47 3075 acres

Blue Mountain Canada
Largest area in Ontario, with glorious views of Lake Huron. High-capacity lift system and 100% snowmaking.
230m; slopes 230–450m
15 275 acres

Blue River Canada
Base of world-famous Mike Wiegele heli-ski operation in Cariboo and Monashee mountains.

Bluewood USA
Particularly remote area even by American north-west standards. Worth a visit if you're in Walla Walla.
1355m; slopes 1355–1725m
3 530 acres

Bogus Basin USA
Sizeable area overlooking Idaho's attractive, interesting capital, Boise. Limited accommodation at the base.
1760m; slopes 1760–2310m
8 2600 acres

Bohinj Slovenia
Lakeside village near Bled set in a beautiful valley, with lovely views from its plateau area of short runs high above.
540m; slopes 540–1480m
6 23km
Balkan Holidays, Crystal

Bois-d'Amont France
One of five resorts that make up Les Rousses area in Jura region on the Swiss border.
1050m; slopes 1120–1680m
40 50km Lagrange

Boi Taull Spain
A typical Pyrenean resort set high above the Boi Valley, close to the stunning Aigues Tortes National Park. Good intermediate terrain.
slopes 2020–2750m
15 *44km*

Bolognola Italy
Tiny area in Macerata region near the Adriatic Riviera.
1070m; slopes 1070–1845m
5 *8km*

Bolton Valley USA
Resort near Stowe with mostly intermediate slopes.
465m; slopes 465–960m
6 *155 acres*

Bonneval-sur-Arc France
Unspoiled, remote old village in the Haute Maurienne valley. Pass to neighbouring Val d'Isère is closed in winter.
1800m; slopes 1800–3000m
11 *25km*

Bons 252
Rustic, unspoiled old hamlet linked to Les Deux-Alpes.

Boreal USA
Closest area to north Lake Tahoe town, Truckee. Limited slopes, best for novices.
2195m; slopes 2195–2375m
9 *380 acres*

Bormio Italy
An attractive old spa town, distinctly Italian and within day-trip distance from Livigno and Santa Caterina. The main slopes are a 15-minute walk from the centre, where a gondola goes to the hub at Bormio 2000, with fast lifts to the high point at 3010m. The mountain is confined, long (vertical of 800m) and narrow – mainly suited to intermediates. The men's downhill course is a tough red. The nursery slopes are snow-sure, but there are few progression runs. There's a good terrain park and ample mountain huts. There are more slopes in a separate area, with fast lifts from Le Motte or Isolaccia, on the other side of town. The resort has over 40 hotels, plus a wide choice of restaurants. Après-ski is quite lively.
1225m; slopes 1225–3010m
35 *110km* *Solo's*

Borovets 650

Bosco Chiesanuova Italy
Weekend day trippers' place near Verona. A long drive from any other resort.
1105m; slopes 1105–1805m
18 *20km*

Bosco Gurin Switzerland
Highest ski area in Ticino. The only German speaking village in the Italian canton.
1500m; slopes 1480–2400m
6 *30km*

Les Bottières France
Hamlet at the edge of the Sybelles area, with limited infrastructure and poor access to the main network – it takes three lifts to reach La Toussuire, before setting off for L'Ouillon. *1300m*

La Bourboule France
Spa and cross-country village with the Alpine slopes of Le Mont-Dore nearby. Spectacular extinct-volcano scenery.
850m; slopes 1050–1850m
17 *42km* *Lagrange*

Bourg-d'Oisans France
Pleasant valley town on main Grenoble-Briançon road. Cheap base for visits to Alpe-d'Huez and Les Deux-Alpes.

Bourg-St-Maurice 212
French valley town with a funicular to Les Arcs.

Bovec 654
Town linked to Kanin-Sella Nevea on the Italian border.

Boyne Highlands USA
Area with impressive, high-capacity lift system for weekend Detroit crowds. Fierce winds off Lake Michigan a major drawback.
225m; slopes 225–390m
10 *240 acres*

Boyne Mountain USA
Popular with weekend Detroit crowds. Not as windy as sister resort Boyne Highlands.
190m; slopes 190–340m
12 *115 acres*

Bozel France
Small town that, in good snow conditions, you can ski down to off-piste from Courchevel and catch a bus back. Also near access road for Champagny-en-Vanoise (La Plagne ski area). *860m*

Bramans France
Old cross-country village near Modane. Well placed for touring numerous nearby resorts such as Val Cenis and Valloire. *1200m* *1* *3km*

Bramberg Austria
Village near Pass Thurn (Kitzbühel area). Shares slopes with Neukirchen.
820m; slopes 820–2150m
15 *55km*

Brand 195
Family resort in the Alpenregion Bludenz

Les Brasses France
Collective name for six traditional hamlets with some of the closest slopes to Geneva, but best known for cross-country.
900m; slopes 900–1600m
14 *50km*

Braunwald Switzerland
Sunny but limited area near Zürich, a funicular ride above Linthal.
1255m; slopes 1255–1900m
9 *32km*

Breckenridge 557

Bregenzerwald 192

Brentonico Italy
Little resort just off Verona-Trento motorway, with linked slopes of La Polsa and San Valentino above.
1160m; slopes 1160–1520m
15 *35km*

Bressanone Italy
Valley town 20 minutes by free ski-bus from the lift base of Plose. *565m*

La Bresse France
Largest resort in the northerly Vosges mountains near Strasbourg. Three separate downhill areas (with a lot of snowmaking), but also extensive ski de fond and lots of other activities.
900m; slopes 900–1350m
24 *220 hectares*
Lagrange

Briançon 327
Part of the Grand Serre Chevalier region.

Brian Head USA
Utah area south of Salt Lake City, too far from Park City for a day trip.
2925m; slopes 2925–3445m
10 *500 acres*

Brides-les-Bains 282
Quiet spa town in valley below Méribel.

Bridger Bowl 589
Day-trip resort near Big Sky, Montana.
1855m; slopes 1855–2460m
6 *1200 acres*

Brigels–Andiast Switzerland
In the same valley as Laax/Flims. Access from two sunny villages. Mostly red runs.
1300m; slopes 1100–2420m
7 *75km*

Brighton USA
Linked with Solitude. Total acreage is half that of Alta/Snowbird (in the next valley), but attracts fewer people so the powder doesn't get tracked out in hours. Four fast chairs, including one serving the resort's maximum vertical of 530m on Clayton Peak. This and the slightly lower Mt Millicent are almost all expert terrain, but other lifts serve a wide spectrum of runs. The resort's boundaries are open, and there are excellent backcountry adventures. Accommodation is in the slope-side Brighton Lodge and some cabins.
2670m; slopes 2435–3200m
13 *2250 acres*

Brixen im Thale 173
Grossraum village that shares slopes with Söll and Ellmau.

Bromley USA
New York City weekend retreat, reputedly the warmest place to ski in chilly Vermont.
595m; slopes 595–1000m
9 *300 acres*

Bromont Canada
Purpose-built resort an hour east of Montreal, with one of the best small areas in eastern Canada, popular for its night skiing.
slopes 405–575m
6 *135 acres*

Bruck am Grossglockner Austria
Low beginners' resort, but also a quiet base from which to visit Zell am See. *755m*

Brundage Mountain USA
Remote, uncrowded Idaho area with glorious views across the lake towards Hell's Canyon. Mostly intermediate slopes. Also has a snowcat operation.
1760m; slopes 1760–2320m
5 *1300 acres*

Bruneck Italy
Town with gondola link into the Plan de Corones/Kronplatz area. Italian name is Brunico.

Brunico Italy
Town with gondola link into the Plan de Corones/Kronplatz area. Bruneck in German.

Bruson 502
Relaxing respite from Verbier's crowds.

Brusson Italy
Major cross-country village in the Aosta valley, near Antagnod. Sunny downhill slopes up a side valley at Estoul (Palasinaz ski area).
1330m *3* *17km*

Les Bugnenets–Savagnieres Switzerland
Very small area in the Jura mountains, north of Neuchatel. Short runs served by drag lifts. Valid with the Valais Ski Card.
slopes 1090–1440m
7 *30km*

Bukovel Ukraine
Ukraine's second highest resort.
slopes 900–1370m
14 *50km*

Burke Mountain USA
Uncrowded, isolated family resort in Vermont with mostly intermediate slopes. Great views from the top.
385m; slopes 385–995m
4 *130 acres*

Bürserberg 195
Valley town in the Alpenregion Bludenz.

Cairngorm 657
Scottish ski resort.
slopes 550–1100m
11 *37km*

Caldirola Italy
Genoese weekend day-tripper spot in a remote region off the motorway to Turin.
1010m; slopes 1010–1450m
3 4km

Cambre-d'Aze France
Quiet ski area in the Pyrenees with few British visitors. Good beginner and intermediate terrain. Forms part of the Neiges Catalan (10 resorts on one pass).
1640m; slopes 1640–2400m
17 35km

Camigliatello Italy
Tiny area on the foot of the Italian 'boot' near Cosenza. Weekend/day-trip spot.
1270m; slopes 1270–1750m
4 6km

Campitello 447
Village in Val di Fassa.

Campitello Matese Italy
The only slopes near Naples. Surprisingly large area when snowcover is complete. Weekend crowds.
1440m; slopes 1440–2100m
8 40km

Campo di Giove Italy
Highest slopes in L'Aquila region east of Rome.
1070m; slopes 1145–2350m
15 21km

Campodolcino Italy
Valley town with funicular up to Madesimo's slopes.
1070m; slopes 1545–2880m
6 8km

Campo Felice Italy
Easiest resort to reach from Rome, off Aquila motorway. One of the better lift systems in the vicinity.
1410m; slopes 1520–2065m
15 40km

Campo Imperatore Italy
One of the best of the areas east of Rome in L'Aquila.
1980m 8 20km

Canazei 447
Lively rustic village in the Sella Ronda.

Candanchu / Astún Spain
French border resort on Pau road set in some of the Pyrenees' most stunning scenery. Almost exclusively challenging open slopes.
1450m; slopes 1560–2400m
24 80km

Canillo 92
Small, quiet village linked to Soldeu.

Canmore Canada
Old frontier town on the way to Nakiska/Fortress, well placed for touring and an attractive alternative to Banff.

Cannon Mountain USA
One of several small New Hampshire resorts scattered along the Interstate 93 highway; a ski area and nothing more. High and steep by eastern standards.
605m; slopes 605–1260m
9 165 acres

Canyons 578

Cardrona New Zealand
Three large basins with slopes for all standards. Good snow record and childcare facilities. Super views. An hour from Queenstown.
1650m; slopes 1260–1860m
8 345 hectares

Carezza 447
Dense network of short lifts close to Val di Fassa.

Les Carroz-d'Arâches 258
An attractive, spacious village on the road up to Flaine.

Caspoggio Italy
Attractive, unspoiled village north-east of Lake Como, with easy slopes (and more at nearby Chiesa).
1100m; slopes 1100–2155m
8 22km

Castelrotto Italy
Picturesque village west of Sella Ronda circuit with small sunny Alpine area and good cross-country trails. *1060m*

Castel S Angelo Italy
Tiny area in Macerata region near Adriatic Riviera.
805m 4 2km

Castle Mountain Canada
Remote resort south of Calgary. Good proportion of intermediate and advanced terrain. Area on Haig Ridge provides beginner and intermediate terrain.
1410m; slopes 1410–2270m
6 1750 acres
Ski Safari

Catedral (Bariloche) Argentina
One of South America's most developed resorts, linked with Lado Bueno and 19 km from San Carlos de Bariloche. Sheltered intermediate slopes, but very crowded in peak season. Slopeside luxury lodgings available.
slopes 1030–2180m
39 103km

Cauterets 318

Cavalese 443
Unspoiled medieval town in Val di Fiemme, Trentino.

Caviahue Argentina
Mountain village at the foot of the Copahue Volcano, 357km from Neuquén City.
1645m; slopes 1645–2045m
8 37km

The Cedars Lebanon
The largest of Lebanon's ski areas, 130km inland from Beirut. Good, open slopes; a surprisingly long season.
1850m; slopes 2100–2870m 6

Ceillac France
Tight cluster of rustic old buildings near Serre-Chevalier. Not far from the highest village in Europe, St-Veran.
1600m; slopes 1600–2450m
7 25km

Celerina 491
Quiet village with links to St Moritz's slopes.

Cerkno Slovenia
Modern, family resort 50km from Ljubljana. Lifts include three fast chairs.
900m 8 18km

Cerler Spain
Very limited, purpose-built resort with a compact ski area similar to that of nearby Andorra's Arinsal.
1500m; slopes 1500–2630m
18 76km

Le Cernix France
Hamlet near Megève where Les Saisies' slopes link to those of Crest-Voland, part of the Espace Diamant to which our figures relate.
1250m; slopes 1000–2070m
84 179km

Cerrato Lago Italy
Very limited area near the coastal town of La Spezia.
1270m; slopes 1270–1890m
5 3km

Cerro Bayo Argentina
Limited area amid stunning scenery 10km from La Angostura, and 90km from San Carlos de Bariloche.
slopes 1050–1780m
12 200 hectares

Cerro Castor Argentina
The most southern ski runs in the world, on the Martial Glacier, Tierra del Fuego. Lodgings are in Ushuaia, the southernmost city in the world. Also plenty of cross-country skiing on the island.
195m 7 24km

Cerro Mirador Chile
Chile's most southerly snow-zone, located 8km outside Punta Arenas. Tiny but attractive woodland runs. No base lodging. *600m 2*

Cervinia 387

Cesana Torinese Italy
Little Italian village linking the Sauze d'Oulx, Sestriere and Sansicario side of the Milky Way to the Clavière, Montgenèvre side. *1350m*

Le Châble 502
Small village below Verbier.

Chaillol France
Cross-country base on the edge of the beautiful Ecrins National Park, near Gap. Small Alpine area.
1600m; slopes 1450–2000m
10 13km

Chamois Italy
Small area above Buisson, a few miles from Valtournenche (near Cervinia) – worth a look on bad-weather days.
1815m; slopes 1815–2270m
9 20km

Chamonix 227

Champagny-en-Vanoise 304
Charming village linking to the La Plagne network.

Champéry 459

Champex-Lac Switzerland
Lakeside hamlet tucked away in the trees above Orsières. A quiet, unspoiled base from which to visit Verbier's area.
1470m; slopes 1470–2220m
4 25km

Champfèr 491
Lakeside hamlet between St Moritz and Silvaplana.

Champoluc 412
Unspoiled village at one end of the Monterosa Ski area.

Champorcher Italy
Small village south of Aosta valley with tall but narrow ski area, mostly red runs on open slopes, with one black through the trees to the lift base at Chardonney.
1430m; slopes 1430–2500m
5 21km

Champoussin 459
Quiet village with links to the rest of the Champéry slopes.

Chamrousse France
Functional family resort near Grenoble, with good, sheltered slopes. Chairlifts and a cable car from three bases serve largely beginner and intermediate slopes.
1650m; slopes 1400–2250m
19 90km
Crystal, Erna Low, Lagrange, PowderBeds, Ski Collection, Ski France, Ski Independence, Thomson, Zenith

Chandolin 498
Village in the Val d'Anniviers.

Chantemerle 327
One of the villages making up Serre-Chevalier.

Chapa Verde Chile
60km north-east of Rancagua and 145km from Santiago.
1200m; slopes 1200–2500m
4 1200 hectares

Chapelco Argentina
Small ski area with full infrastructure of services 19km from sizeable town of San Martin de Los Andes. Accommodation in hotels 11km from the slopes.
slopes 1250–1980m
10 140 hectares

La Chapelle-d'Abondance 237
Unspoiled village 5km down the valley from Châtel.

Charlotte Pass Australia
Oldest and most remote resort in NSW, on a charming Alpine pass near Mt

Kosciusko. Reached only by snowcat from Perisher. Scenic chalets and five lifts. Nearest town Jindabyne. 6.5 hours from Sydney.
1765m; slopes 1850–2000m
5 123 acres

Chastreix Sancy France
Small family ski area near Mont Dore and Super-Besse. Limited but varied terrain. All draglifts.
1400m 7 16km

Château d'Oex Switzerland
Pleasant French-speaking valley town sharing a lift pass with neighbouring, but unconnected, Gstaad. Good rail links to other sectors. Low slopes. Famous for its Alpine Balloon festival.
950m; slopes 890–1630m
8 30km

Châtel **237**

Le Chatelard France
Small resort in remote Parc des Bauges between Lake Annecy and Chambéry.

Chiesa Italy
Attractive beginners' resort with a fairly high plateau of easy runs above the resort.
1000m; slopes 1700–2335m
16 50km

Le Chinaillon France
Chalet-style village at lift base above Le Grand-Bornand.
1300m; slopes 1000–2100m
29 90km PowderBeds

Chiomonte Italy
Tiny resort on the main road east of Bardonecchia and Sauze d'Oulx. A good half-day trip from either.
745m; slopes 745–2210m
6 10km

Chsea Algeria
Largest of Algeria's skiable areas, 135km south-east of coastal town of Alger in the Djur Djur mountains.
1860m; slopes 1860–2510m 2

Chur–Brambruesch Switzerland
Chur's local ski area a cable car and gondola ride from the town. *595m; slopes 1170–2200m 6 25km*

Churwalden Switzerland
Hamlet on fringe of Lenzerheide-Valbella area, linked via a slow chair. Four short local runs served by a quad and steep drag.
1230m; slopes 1230–2865m
35 155km

Claviere **292**
Village linked to Montgenèvre and the Milky Way ski area.

La Clusaz France
Genuine mountain village near Geneva that exudes rustic and Gallic charm. Attracts a lot of weekend visitors, so can be crowded. Buses also link with Le Grand Bornand. Together they offer over 200km slopes – covered by the area lift pass. The local slopes sprawl over five attractively wooded and varied sectors. All are below 2500m, so snow conditions are unreliable; but there is a lot of snowmaking. Good steep blacks and bumps on La Balme (the highest sector), as well as decent off-piste when conditions permit. There are challenging but wide blues, as well as gentle cruises and nursery slopes up the mountain. But there are still a lot of old chairs and drags. There's a park and pipe, plentiful rustic huts, and a few lively bars.
1100m; slopes 1100–2470m
54 132km
Alpine Answers, Classic Ski, Crystal, Independent Ski Links, Lagrange, Peak Retreats, Pierre & Vacances, PowderBeds, Ski Bespoke, Ski Famille, Ski France, Ski Weekend, Ski Weekender, Snowlife, Zenith

Les Coches **304**
Purpose-built village, linked to the La Plagne ski area.

Cogne Italy
One of Aosta valley's larger villages. Main resort in the Gran Paradiso national park. Worth a visit from nearby Pila. Limited, mostly red slopes. Major cross-country centre, with 70km trails.
1535m; slopes 1530–2250m
4 9km

Colfosco **423**
Smaller, quieter satellite of Corvara in the Sella Ronda.

Colle di Tenda Italy
Dour, modern resort. Shares a good area with much nicer Limone. Not far from Nice.
1400m; slopes 1120–2040m
33 80km

Colle Isarco Italy
Brenner Pass area – and the bargain-shopping town of Vipiteno is nearby.
1095m; slopes 1095–2720m
5 15km

Le Collet-d'Allevard France
Ski area of sizeable summer spa Allevard-les-Bains in remote region east of Chambéry-Grenoble road.
1450m; slopes 1450–2140m
11 35km

Collio Italy
Tiny area of short runs in a remote spot between lakes Garda and d'Iseo.
840m; slopes 840–1715m 14

Les Collons **502**
Near Thyon 2000 in the Verbier area.

Combloux **269**
Quiet, unspoiled alternative to linked Megève.

Les Contamines France
Largely unspoiled but sprawling chalet resort close to Megève and Chamonix, with a fair-sized intermediate area and a good snow record for its height. The main access lift is a shuttle-bus ride from the centre, with a few lodgings at its base. Most of the slopes are above the treeline and on both sides of the Col du Joly – from where a long red run descends over 1000m vertical. There's a good mix of blue and red runs, and substantial off-piste opportunities. Complete beginners are better off elsewhere though. Reports of the school are mixed too. The village is quiet with few amenities, but there are other sporting activities.
1160m; slopes 1160–2485m
24 120km
Alpine Answers, Chalet Kiana, Classic Ski, Holiday in Alps, Lagrange, Peak Retreats, Ski Expectations, Ski France

Copper Mountain USA
Modern, but pleasant purpose-built village with some of Colorado's best terrain. And good value by regional standards. Worthwhile outing from nearby resorts such as Vail. The Village at Copper is the main base, with smart condo lodging and fast chairs into the slopes. Two other bases are served by free shuttle-buses and with easier terrain above them. The slopes spread across two main peaks, Union and Copper, with an attractive mix of open and wooded areas. There is lots of expert terrain in the upper bowls, some seriously steep. There are top-to-bottom greens and excellent nursery slopes. The terrain park is well regarded. Queues are rarely a problem outside peak weekends. Limited off-slope diversions. Reports of the school are favourable. Nightlife livens up at weekends.
2925m; slopes 2960–3750m
22 2465 acres
Alpine Answers, AmeriCan Ski, American Ski Classics, Crystal, Erna Low, Independent Ski Links, Momentum, Ski Independence, Ski Safari, Skitracer, Skiworld, Supertravel, Thomson

Le Corbier France
A no-compromise functional resort centrally placed in the Sybelles area. The resort is purpose-built and compact, as well as being traffic-free – so it suits families very well. Nearly all of the lodging is slope-side apartments, some in a traditional style. There are bars and restaurants, but evenings are generally very quiet. Lifts link directly to St-Jean-d'Arves and La Toussuire, as well as a higher level connection to St-Sorlin. But progress can be slow – only seven fast chairs in the whole area. One belongs to Le Corbier and serves local slopes. The gentle terrain is mostly north-east facing and makes ideal cruising, if rather lacking in variety – though there's a black run from the top. Beginners have good slopes at resort level.
1550m; slopes 1100–2620m
72 310km
Erna Low, Pierre & Vacances, Rocketski, Ski France

Corno alle Scale Italy
Small resort in the Emilia Romagna region of the Apennines.
1355m; slopes 1355–1945m
9 36km

Coronet Peak New Zealand
Closest area to Queenstown (20 minutes). Good mix of bowls, chutes, varied level pistes. Biggest vertical is 462m. Relies on large snowmaking facility for good snow cover. Splendid views.
1230m; slopes 1230–1650m
7 690 acres

Corrençon-en-Vercors France
Charming, rustic village at foot of Villard-de-Lans ski area. Good cross-country, too.
1160m; slopes 1145–2170m
25 125km

Cortina d'Ampezzo **393**

Corvara **423**

Courchevel **242**

Courmayeur **398**

Cranmore USA
Area in New Hampshire with attractive town/resort of North Conway. Easy skiing. Good for families.
150m; slopes 150–515m
9 190 acres

Crans-Montana **462**

Crested Butte USA
One of the cutest old Wild West towns in Colorado, and the steep, gnarly terrain enjoys cult status among experts. It's a small area, but it packs in an astonishing mixture of perfect beginner slopes, easy cruising runs and expert terrain. Snowfall is modest by Colorado standards, but for those who like steep, ungroomed terrain, if the snow is good, it's idyllic. You can stay there or at the mountain, a couple of miles away, with its modern resort 'village'.
2860m; slopes 2775–3620m
16 1165 acres
AmeriCan Ski, Crystal, Ski Safari

Crest-Voland France
Attractive, unspoiled traditional village near Megève and Le Grand Bornand with wonderfully uncrowded intermediate slopes linked to Les Saises and beyond to Praz sur Arly, as part of the Espace Diamant region – to which our figures relate.
1035m; slopes 1000–2070m
84 179km

Crissolo Italy
Small, remote day-tripper area, south-west of Turin. Part of the Monviso ski area.
1320m; slopes 1745–2340m
4 20km

La Croix-Fry France
On the pass to La Clusaz. Couple of hotels and good gentle slopes. *1480m*

Les Crosets **459**
Micro-resort above Champéry in the Portes du Soleil.

Crystal Mountain USA
Area in glorious Mt Rainier National Park, near Seattle. Good, varied area given good snow/weather, but it's often wet. Lively at weekends.
1340m; slopes 1340–2135m
9 2300 acres

Cuchara Valley USA
Quiet little family resort in southern Colorado, some way from any other ski area.
2800m; slopes 2800–3285m
4 250 acres

Cutigliano Italy
Sizeable village near Abetone in the Apennines. Less than two hours from Florence and Pisa.
1125m; slopes 1125–1850m
9 13km

Cypress Mountain Canada
Vancouver's most challenging area, 20 minutes from the city and with 40% for experts. Good snowfall record but rain is a problem.
920m; slopes 910–1445m 5

Daemyeong Vivaldi Resort South Korea
One of the less ugly Korean resorts, 75km from Seoul.
10

La Daille **358**
Ugly apartment complex at the entrance to Val d'Isère.

Daisen Japan
Western Honshu's main area, four hours from Osaka.
800m; slopes 740–1120m 21

Damüls **192**
Village in Bregenzerwald.
1430m; slopes 700–2010m
31 105km

Davos **464**

Deer Mountain USA
South Dakota area close to 'Old West' town Deadwood and Mount Rushmore.
1825m; slopes 1825–2085m
4 370 acres

Deer Valley **580**

Les Deux-Alpes **252**

Les Diablerets Switzerland
Spacious chalet resort towered over by the Diablerets massif, with two areas of local slopes, plus Glacier 3000. A high-speed quad followed by a slow chair lead up to the red runs of the Meilleret area and the link to Villars. A gondola in the centre of town takes you to Isenau, a mix of blues and reds served by draglifts. From Isenau there's a red run down to Col du Pillon and the cable car to and from the glacier. On Glacier 3000, you'll find blue runs at over 3000m, stunning views and the long, black Combe d'Audon – a wonderful, usually quiet, run away from all the lifts with sheer cliffs rising up on both sides. Snow reliability away from the glacier is not great – especially on sunny Isenau.
1150m; slopes 1115–3000m
46 125km
Alpine Answers, Independent Ski Links, Lagrange, Momentum, Neilson, PowderBeds, Ski Club Freshtracks, Switzerland Travel Centre, Tracks European Adventures

Diamond Peak USA
Quiet, pleasant, intermediate area on Lake Tahoe, with lodging in Incline Village five minutes' drive away. Its narrow area consists of a long ridge served by one fast chair; there are great lake views from the run along the ridge and from the terrace of Snowflake Lodge. There are black runs off the ridge, but nothing seriously steep.
2040m; slopes 2040–2600m
6 655 acres

Dienten Austria
Quiet, tiny, picturesque village with a handful of traditional hotels and guest houses east of Saalbach and at the heart of the large, low-altitude Hochkönig area that spreads over a series of gentle peaks from Maria Alm to Mühlbach.
1070m; slopes 800–1900m
33 150km

Dinner Plain Australia
Attractive resort best known for cross-country skiing. Shuttle to Mt Hotham for Alpine slopes. Four hours from Melbourne.
1520m; slopes 1490–1520m

Discovery Ski Area USA
Pleasant area miles from anywhere except Butte, Montana, with largely intermediate slopes but double-black runs on the back of the mountain – and the chance of seriously good snow. Usually deserted. Fairmont Hot Springs (two huge thermal pools) are nearby.
1975m; slopes 1760–2485m
8 2,200 acres

Disentis Switzerland
Unspoiled old village in a pretty setting on the Glacier Express rail route near Andermatt. Scenic area with long runs.
1125m; slopes 1150–2830m
10 60km

Dobbiaco Italy
One of several little resorts in the South Tyrol near the Austrian border; a feasible day out from the Sella Ronda. Toblach is its German name.
1250m; slopes 1250–1610m
5 15km
Exodus, Headwater, Ramblers

Dodge Ridge USA
Novice/leisurely intermediate area north of Yosemite. The pass from Reno is closed in winter, preventing crowds.
2010m; slopes 2010–2500m
12 815 acres

Dolonne **398**
Quiet suburb of Courmayeur.

Donnersbachwald Austria
Small area in the Dachstein-Tauern region.
950m; slopes 950–1990m
4 25km

Donner Ski Ranch USA
One of California's first ski resorts, still family owned and operated.
2140m; slopes 2140–2370m
6 460 acres

Dorfgastein **111**
Quieter, friendlier alternative to Bad Gastein.

Doucy-Combelouvière France
Quiet hamlet tucked away in the trees at the foot of Valmorel's slopes, linked by easy green pistes, a fast chair and draglifts into the main sector. *1250m* *Lagrange*

Dundret Sweden
Lapland area 100km north of the Arctic Circle with floodlit slopes open through winter when the sun barely rises.
slopes 475–825m
7 15km

Durango Mountain Resort USA
Not a resort to cross the Atlantic to visit – it's a small area even by US standards. Directly above the resort is a steepish slope with a slow double chair off to the right serving gentle green runs. All link to the shady slopes that form the main part of the area, served by a row of three chairs with a vertical of not much over 350m. Snowcat skiing is said to operate from the top. The heart of the resort is Purgatory Village, a modern, purpose-built affair. Evening options in the 'village' are extremely limited. The city of Durango is worth visiting.
2680m; slopes 2680–3300m
11 1200 acres

Eaglecrest USA
Close to Yukon gold rush town Skagway. Family resort famous for its ski school.
365m; slopes 365–790m
3 640 acres

Eben im Pongau Austria
Part of Salzburger Sportwelt Amadé area that includes nearby St Johann, Wagrain, Flachau and Zauchensee.
855m; slopes 855–2185m
100 350km

Egg **192**
Village in Bregenzerwald.
565mm; slopes 1100–1400m
6 10km

Ehrwald Austria
Pleasant village with easy access to three small and varied ski areas, notably the Zugspitze glacier. Access to the slopes there is by cable car a couple of miles outside the resort at Obermoos. There are gentle nursery slopes and good open intermediate terrain – including a couple of genuine reds. Most are of limited extent. There's a half-pipe and three restaurants. Après-ski is fairly lively. The Zugspitz Arena lift pass covers all three sectors, plus the other resorts of the valley.
1000m; slopes 990–2960m
52 147km *Ski Famille*

El Colorado / Farellones Chile
Scattering of accommodation around a base station 40km east of Santiago, sharing Valle Nevado's ski area (to which our figures relate).
slopes 2430–3670m
43 113km

Eldora Mountain USA
Day-visitor resort with varied terrain (including plenty of steep stuff) close to Denver Boulder (45min by regular scheduled bus). All forest trails, but with some good glade areas. Crowded at weekends.
2795m; slopes 2805–3230m
12 680 acres

Elk Meadows USA
Area south of Salt Lake City, more than a day trip from Park City.
2775m; slopes 2745–3170m
6 1400 acres

Ellmau **114**

Elm Switzerland
One hour from Zürich, at the head of a quiet, isolated valley. Good choice of runs including a long black to the valley.
1020m; slopes 1000–2105m
🚡 *6* ⛷ *40km*

Encamp Andorra
Traffic-choked town with a gondola link to the Pas de la Casa slopes. Popular for its nightlife and low prices.

Enego Italy
Limited weekend day-trippers' area near Vicenza and Trento.
1300m; slopes 1300–1445m
🚡 *7* ⛷ *30km*

Engelberg 471

Entrèves 398
Cluster of hotels at the lift up to Courmayeur's slopes.

Escaldes Andorra
Central valley town, effectively part of Andorra la Vella.

Estoul Italy
Village in the Aosta valley up a side valley near Brusson. Sunny, easy red slopes.
1800m; slopes 1800–2235m
🚡 *2* ⛷ *9km*

Etna Italy
Scenic, uncrowded, short-season area on the volcano's flank, 20 minutes from Nickolossi. *1800m; slopes 1800–2350m* ⛷ *5km*

Evolène Switzerland
Charming rustic village in the Val d'Hérens. Small ski area in unspoiled, attractive setting south of Sion. Area lift pass gives access to the 4 Valleys.
1370m; slopes 1405–2680m
🚡 *7* ⛷ *42km*

Faak am See Austria
Limited area, one of five overlooking town of Villach.
560m; slopes 560–800m
🚡 *1* ⛷ *2km*

Fai della Paganella 443
Trentino village near Madonna.

Fairmont Hot Springs Canada
Major luxury spa complex ideal for a relaxing holiday with some gentle skiing thrown in. 🚡 *2* ⛷ *60 acres*

Faistenau Austria
Cross-country area close to Salzburg and St Wolfgang. Limited Alpine slopes.
785m; slopes 785–1000m
🚡 *3* ⛷ *3km*

Falcade 443
Trentino village south of the Sella Ronda.

Falera 479
Village with access to ski area shared by Flims and Laax.

Le Falgoux France
One of the most beautiful old villages in France, set in the very scenic Volcano National Park. Several ski areas nearby.
930m; slopes 930–1350m

Falkertsee Austria
Base area rather than a village, with bleak, open slopes in contrast to nearby Bad Kleinkirchheim.
1850m; slopes 1690–2310m
🚡 *5* ⛷ *15km*

Falls Creek Australia
Alpine-style modern family resort, 5 hours from Melbourne, near Mt Hotham. Fair-sized area of short intermediate runs. Access by snowcat to Mt McKay's steep slopes. Lavish spa resort nearby.
1600m; slopes 1500–1780m
🚡 *14* ⛷ *1115 acres*

La Feclaz France
One of several little resorts in the remote Parc des Bauges. Popular cross-country ski base. *1165m*

Feldberg 378
Small resort in the Black Forest. 🚡 *31* ⛷ *55*

Fernie 615

Fieberbrunn Austria
Atmospheric and friendly Tirolean village, sprawling along the valley road for 2km, but mostly set back from the road and railway. Its small but attractive area of wooded slopes is a bus ride away. One sector consists mainly of blue runs, the other mainly of easy reds, many below the treeline. Across a valley are separate lifts going up to the high point of 2020m on Hochhörndl – gondola down to 1284m accesses some good off-piste here. The resort is boarder-friendly, with a popular terrain park. Accommodation in the village is in hotels, and there is also lodging at the lift station.
800m; slopes 830–2020m
🚡 *11* ⛷ *43km*
🛏 *Crystal, Snowscape, Thomson*

Fiesch Switzerland
Traditional Rhône valley resort near Brig, with a lift up to Fiescheralp (2220m) part of the lovely Aletsch area; includes Bettmeralp to Riederalp.
1050m; slopes 1925–2870m
🚡 *35* ⛷ *100km*

Fiescheralp Switzerland
Mountain outpost of Fiesch, down in the Rhône valley. At one end of the beautiful Aletsch area extending across the mountain via Bettmeralp to Riederalp.
2220m; slopes 1925–2870m
🚡 *35* ⛷ *100km*

Filzmoos Austria
Charming, unspoiled, friendly village with leisurely slopes that are ideal for novices. Good snow record for its height. Quiet pistes, good grooming and decent nursery slopes.
1055m; slopes 1055–1645m
🚡 *8* ⛷ *32km*
🛏 *Inghams, Skitracer*

Fiss Austria
Nicely compact, quiet, traditional village sharing an extensive, sunny area with bigger Serfaus.
1435m; slopes 1200–2750m
🚡 *70* ⛷ *190km*
🛏 *Ski Bespoke*

Flachau Austria
Quiet, spacious village in a pretty setting at one end of an extensive three-valley lift network linking via Wagrain to Alpendorf. Central to an impressive lift system. On the Salzbuger Sportwelt lift pass.
925m; slopes 800–2185m
🚡 *64* ⛷ *200km*
🛏 *Ski Bespoke*

Flachauwinkl Austria
Tiny ski station beside Tauern autobahn. Centre of an extensive three-valley lift network linking Kleinarl to Zauchensee. Near similarly sized Flachau. All these resorts are covered by the Salzburger Sportwelt ski pass.
930m; slopes 800–2185m
🚡 *15* ⛷ *65km*

Flaine 258

Flims 479
Long-established resort sharing an area with Laax.

Flumet France
Surprisingly large traditional village, the main place from which to ski the Espace Diamant area, linked through to Les Saisies/ Crest Voland. Near Megève.
1000m; slopes 1000–2070m
🚡 *84* ⛷ *179km* 🛏 *Lagrange*

Flumserberg Switzerland
Collective name for the villages sharing a varied area an hour south-east of Zürich. Part of the wider Heidiland region. Mostly red and black runs, served by good network of fast lifts.
425m; slopes 1220–2220m
🚡 *16* ⛷ *65km*

Folgaria 443
Sizeable area east of Trento.

Folgarida 407
Small Trentino village linked to Madonna di Campiglio.

Foncine-le-Haut France
Major cross-country village in the Jura Mountains with extensive trails.
🛏 *Lagrange*

Fonni Gennaragentu Italy
Sardinia's only 'ski area' – and it's tiny. 🚡 *1* ⛷ *5km*

Font-Romeu 318

Foppolo Italy
Relatively unattractive but user-friendly village, a short transfer from Bergamo.
1510m; slopes 1610–2160m
🚡 *9* ⛷ *47km*

Forca Canapine Italy
Limited area near the Adriatic and Ascoli Piceno. Popular with weekend day-trippers.
1450m; slopes 1450–1690m
🚡 *11* ⛷ *20km*

Formazza Italy
Cross-country base with some downhill slopes. *1280m; slopes 1275–1755m* ⛷ *8km*

Formigal 643

Formigueres France
Small downhill and cross-country area in the Neiges Catalanes. There are 110km cross-country trails.
slopes 1700–2350m
🚡 *8* ⛷ *19km*

Le Fornet 358
Rustic old hamlet 3km up the valley from Val d'Isère.

Forstau Austria
Secluded hamlet above Radstadt–Schladming road. Very limited area (Fageralm) with old lifts, but nice and quiet.
930m; slopes 930–1885m
🚡 *7* ⛷ *14km*

La Fouly Switzerland
Small area near Martigny, with varied slopes, 10km of cross-country trails and a floodlit toboggan run.
1600m; slopes 1600–2200m
🚡 *3* ⛷ *20km*

La Foux-d'Allos France
Purpose-built resort that shares a good intermediate area with Pra-Loup (Val d'Allos ski area).
1800m; slopes 1800–2600m
🚡 *51* ⛷ *180km* 🛏 *Zenith*

Frabosa Soprana Italy
One of numerous little areas south of Turin, well placed for combining winter sports with Riviera sightseeing.
850m; slopes 860–1740m
🚡 *7* ⛷ *40km*

Frisco 557
Small town down the valley from Breckenridge.

Frontignano Italy
Best lift system in the Macerata region, near the Adriatic Riviera.
1340m; slopes 1340–2000m
🚡 *8* ⛷ *10km*

Fucine Italy
Old Trentino valley village near Marilleva/Folgarida.
980m

Fügen Austria
Unspoiled Zillertal village with road up to satellite Hochfügen – part of fair-sized Ski Optimal area, along with Kaltenbach.
550m
🛏 *Crystal, Lagrange, STC*

Fulpmes 189
Village in the Stubai valley.

Furano 658
Resort on Hokkaido island, Japan.

Fusch Austria
Cheaper, quiet place to stay when visiting Zell am See. Across a golf course from Kaprun and Schuttdorf.
805m; slopes 805–1050m
2 5km

Fuschl am See Austria
Attractive, unspoiled, lakeside village close to St Wolfgang and Salzburg, 30 minutes from its slopes. Best suited to part-time skiers who want to sightsee as well.
670m Inntravel

Gålå Norway
Base for downhill and cross-country skiing, an hour's drive north of Lillehammer.
930m; slopes 830–1150m
7 20km Inntravel

Gallio Italy
One of several low resorts near Vicenza and Trento. Popular with weekend day-trippers.
1100m; slopes 1100–1550m
11 50km

Galtür 122
Charming traditional village near Ischgl.

Gambarie d'Aspromonte Italy
Italy's second most southerly ski area (after Mt Etna). On the 'toe' of the Italian 'boot' near Reggio di Calabria.
1310m; slopes 1310–1650m 3

Gantschier Austria
No slopes of its own but particularly well placed for visiting all the Montafon areas. *700m*

Gargellen Austria
Quiet, tiny and secluded village tucked up a side valley in the Montafon area, with a small but varied piste network of blues and reds on Schafberg that is blissfully quiet. For experts there is lots of off-piste terrain plus ski routes, and there is a special day tour of Madrisa (Klosters). Snowmaking on the valley pistes is good, and you can ski to the door of some hotels.
1425m; slopes 1425–2300m
8 33km

Garmisch-Partenkirchen 380

Gaschurn Austria
A pleasant village in the Montafon area, bypassed by the valley traffic, with a gondola to the Nova area of slopes – the valley's largest, with 114km of pistes.This is generally the most challenging area in the valley, with many red runs, and blues that are not entirely easy. Most of the slopes are above the treeline, typically offering a very modest 300m vertical. There is lots of off-piste potential, including steep (and quite dangerous) slopes down into the central valley. Snowmaking covers almost half the area, including runs down to the valley. The NovaPark terrain park features a half-pipe and boardercross course. There are lots of mountain restaurants. It also links to the Hochjoch ski area (see St Gallenkirch).
1000m; slopes 655–2395m
61 219km
Ski Bespoke

Gaustablikk Norway
Small snow-sure Alpine area on Mt Gausta in southern Norway with plenty of cross-country. 15km

Gavarnie France
Traditional village and fair-sized ski area, with the longest green run in the Pyrenees. Grand views of the Cirque de Gavarnie.
1400m; slopes 1850–2400m
11 45km

Geilo Norway
Small, quiet, unspoiled community on the railway line from Bergen, on the coast, to Oslo. It provides all the basics of a resort – a handful of cafes and shops around the railway station, a dozen hotels more widely spread around the wide valley, children's facilities and a sports centre. Geilo is a superb cross-country resort. It's very limited for downhillers, and none of the runs is very difficult, but it does claim to have Scandinavia's only super-pipe.
800m; slopes 800–1180m
18 35km
Absolutely Snow, Headwater, Inntravel, Neilson

Gérardmer France
Sizeable lakeside resort in the northerly Vosges mountains near Strasbourg, with plenty of amenities. Limited downhill slopes nearby include one of almost 4km. Extensive ski de fond trails in the area.
665m; slopes 750–1150m
20 40km Lagrange

Gerlitzen Austria
Carinthia's central ski area. A worthwhile outing from Bad Kleinkirchheim. Gondola ride from the valley near Villach, with good views and varied but short runs.
500m; slopes 1000–1910m
15 26km

Gerlos 145
Village in the Zillertal Arena.

Gerlosplatte Austria
Inexpensive but fairly snow-sure area above the village of Krimml, linked to Gerlos, Königsleiten and Zell am Ziller to form a fair-sized intermediate area.

Les Gets 265

La Giettaz 269
Tiny village between La Clusaz and Megève.

Gitschtal / Weissbriach Austria
One of many little areas near Hermagor in eastern Austria, close to Italian border.
690m; slopes 690–1400m
4 5km

Glaris Switzerland
Hamlet base station for the uncrowded Rinerhorn section of the Davos slopes.
1460m; slopes 1460–2490m
5 30km

Glencoe 657
Scottish ski resort.
305m; slopes 305–1110m
7 20km

Glenshee 657
Scottish ski resort.
610m; slopes 610–1070m
22 40km

Going 114
Small area near Ellmau, linked to the huge SkiWelt area.

Goldegg Austria
Year-round resort famous for its lakeside castle. Limited slopes but Wagrain (Salzburger Sportwelt) and Grossarl (Gastein valley) are nearby.
825m; slopes 825–1250m
4 12km

Golden Canada
Small logging town, the place to stay when visiting Kicking Horse resort 15 minutes away. Also the launch pad for Purcell heli-skiing.

Golte Slovenia
Ski area in the East Karavante mountains, above Mozirje. Gondola to the slopes from Zekovec village. Mostly advanced runs.
7 18km

Gore Mountain USA
One of the better areas in New York State. Near Lake Placid, sufficiently far north to avoid worst weekend crowds. Intermediate terrain.
455m; slopes 455–1095m
9 290 acres

Göriach Austria
Hamlet with trail connecting into one of the longest, most snow-sure cross-country networks in Europe. *1250m*

Gortipohl Austria
Traditional village in the pretty Montafon valley.
920m; slopes 900–2395m
61 243km

Gosau Austria
Family-friendly resort, with straggling village. Plenty of pretty, if low, runs. Fast lifts mean queues are rare. Snow-sure Obertauern and Schladming are within reach.
755m; slopes 755–1800m
37 80km Crystal

Göstling Austria
One of Austria's easternmost resorts, between Salzburg and Vienna. A traditional village in wooded setting.
530m; slopes 530–1880m
8 18km

Götzens Austria
Valley village base for Axamer Lizum and Mutters, near Innsbruck. Gondola from village to Mutteralm and red run back down.
870m; slopes 830–2100m
4 15km Lagrange

Gourette-Eaux-Bonnes France
Most snow-sure resort in the French Pyrenees. Very popular with local families, so best avoided at weekends.
1400m; slopes 1400–2400m
14 30km

Grächen Switzerland
Charming chalet-village reached by tricky access road off the approach to Zermatt. A small area of open slopes, mainly above the trees and of red-run difficulty, reached by two gondolas – one to Hannigalp (2115m), the main focus of activity with a very impressive children's nursery area. The village has almost a score of hotels, mostly 3-star; most of the accommodation is in chalets and apartments.
1615m; slopes 1615–2865m
9 42km

Le Grand-Bornand France
Covered by the Aravis lift pass, and much smaller and even more charming than La Clusaz. The slopes can be accessed from either the outskirts of the village or from the satellite village of Le Chinaillon. There are worthwhile shady black runs on Le Lachat, and on the lower peak of La Floria. There are plenty of good cruising blue and red intermediate runs, and also good beginner slopes. And there are extensive cross-country trails in the Vallée du Bouchet and towards Le Chinaillon.
1000m; slopes 1000–2100m
29 90km
AmeriCan Ski, Erna Low, Lagrange, Peak Retreats, PowderBeds, Ski France, Ski Independence, Ski Weekender, Zenith

Grand Targhee 589
Powder skiing paradise an hour from Jackson Hole.
2439m; slopes 2260–3005m
5 2100 acres

Les Granges 212
Hamlet at the mid-station of the funicular up from Bourg to Les Arcs.

Grangesises Italy
Small satellite of Sestriere, with lifts up to the main slopes.

Granite Peak USA
One of the oldest areas in the Great Lakes region, and now one of the largest. New base village. Good selection of black runs on the upper mountain.
7 400 acres

Grau Roig 95
Mini-resort between Pas de la Casa and Soldeu.

La Grave 267

Great Divide USA
Area near Helena, Montana, best for experts. Mostly bowls; plus near-extreme Rawhide Gulch.
1765m; slopes 1765–2195m
6 720 acres

Gresse-en-Vercors France
Resort south of Grenoble. Sheltered slopes worth noting for bad-weather days.
1250m; slopes 1600–1750m
13 18km

Gressoney-la-Trinité 412
Village in Monterosa Ski area.

Gressoney-St-Jean Italy
Larger and lower of the two villages in the central valley of the Monterosa Ski area. Good for cross-country as well as downhill. Varied slopes and well-equipped nursery area.
1390m 7km
Alpine Answers

Grimentz 498
Village in the Val d'Anniviers.

Grindelwald 473

Grossarl 111
Secluded village in the Gastein valley.

Grossglockner area Austria
Two linked areas near Heiligenbluit, above the villages of Kals and Matrei. Remote position west of Bad Gastein. Uncrowded, fairly extensive slopes. Some long, varied runs.
1000m; slopes 1000–2620m
15 110km

Grosskirchheim Austria
Area near Heiligenblut, not linked but access to 55km slopes.
1025m; slopes 1025–1400m

Grouse Mountain Canada
The Vancouver area with the largest lift capacity. Superb city views from mostly easy slopes; night skiing.
880m; slopes 880–1245m
11 120 acres

Grünau Austria
Spacious riverside village in a lovely lake-filled part of eastern Austria. Nicely varied area, but very low.
525m; slopes 620–1600m
15 40km

Gryon 513
Village below Villars.

Gstaad Switzerland
Despite its exclusive reputation, an attractive, traditional village where anyone could have a relaxing holiday. Of the four sectors, the largest is above Saanenmöser and Schönried, reached by train. Snow-cover can be unreliable except on the Glacier des Diablerets, 15km away. Few runs challenge experts. Black runs rarely exceed red or even blue difficulty. There is off-piste potential. Given good snow, this is a superb area for intermediates, with long, easy descents in the major area. The nursery slopes at Wispile are adequate, and there are plenty of runs to progress to. Time lost on buses or trains is more of a problem than queues.
1050m; slopes 950–3000m
57 250km
Alpine Answers, Momentum, Oxford Ski Co, Powder Byrne, PowderBeds, Ski Bespoke, Ski Independence, Ski Weekend, Switzerland Travel Centre, White Roc

Gunstock USA
One of the New Hampshire resorts closest to Boston, popular with families. Primarily easy slopes. Lovley Lake Winnisquam views.
275m; slopes 275–700m
8 220 acres

Guthega Australia
Australia's most challenging and diverse slopes (at Perisher). Comfortable accommodation in the resort's only commercial lodge. Free shuttle from Jindabyne. 6.5 hours from Sydney.
1640m; slopes 1605–2035m
47 3075 acres

Guzet France
Charming cluster of chalets set in a pine forest at Guzet 1400. Three main sectors offer slopes for all levels.
1400m; slopes 1100–2100m
14 40km

Hafjell Norway
Main ski area for Lillehammer.
12 33km

Haider Alm Italy
Area in the Val Venosta in the South Tyrol close to Nauders. Malda Haider is its Italian name. 5 20km

Hakuba 658
European-style resort four hours from Tokyo.

Harper Mountain Canada
Small, family-friendly resort in Kamloops, British Colombia.
1100m; slopes 1100–1525m
3 400 acres

Harrachov Czech Republic
Closest resort to Prague, with enough terrain to justify a day trip. No beginner area.
650m; slopes 650–1020m
4 8runs

Hasliberg Switzerland
Four rustic hamlets on a sunny plateau overlooking Meiringen and Lake Brienz. Two of them are the bottom stations of a varied intermediate area.
1050m

Haus 164
Village next to Schladming.

Haystack USA
Minor satellite of Mount Snow, in Vermont, but with a bit more steep skiing.
580m; slopes 580–1095m
26 540 acres

Heavenly 535

Hebalm Austria
One of many small areas in Austria's easternmost ski region near Slovenian border. No major resorts in vicinity.
1350m; slopes 1350–1400m
6 11km

Heiligenblut Austria
Picturesque village in beautiful surroundings at the foot of the Grossglockner, west of Bad Gastein. Quiet, mainly red runs in two main areas. Lifts include three gondolas and a fast chair.
1300m; slopes 1300–2910m
12 55km

Heiterwang Austria
Small lakeside village with access to Berwang's slopes in the Zugspitz Arena. Bus ride to the lift station. Couple of local downhill slopes and popular cross-country venue.
995m 2 2km

Hemlock Resort Canada
Area 55 miles east of Vancouver towards Sun Peaks. Mostly intermediate terrain and with snowfall of 600 inches a year. Lodging is available at the base area.
1000m; slopes 1000–1375m
4 350 acres

Hemsedal 647

Heremence Switzerland
Quiet, traditional village in unspoiled attractive setting south of Sion. Verbier's slopes are accessed a few minutes' drive away at Les Masses.
1250m

Hermagor Austria
Main village base for the Nassfeld ski area in Carinthia.
600m; slopes 610–2000m
30 100km

High 1 Resort South Korea
Small ski area at the High 1 leisure complex, 250km from Seoul by train. 21km

Hinterglemm 158
One of the villages making up Saalbach-Hinterglemm.

Hintermoos Austria
Tiny village east of Saalbach and part of the large, low-altitude Hochkönig area that spreads over a series of gentle peaks linking Maria Alm to Mühlbach.
slopes 800–1900m
33 150km

Hintersee Austria
Easy slopes very close to Salzburg. Several long top-to-bottom runs and lifts sosize of the ski area is greatly reduced if the snowline is high.
745m; slopes 750–1470m
9 40km

Hinterstoder Austria
A very quiet valley village – neat but not overtly charming – spread along the road up the dead-end Stodertal in Upper Austria. The local Höss slopes are pleasantly wooded, less densely at the top, with splendid views. It's a small area, but has a worthwhile vertical of 1250m, and 450m above mid-mountain. A gondola from the main street goes up to the flat-bottomed bowl of Huttererböden (1400m), where there are very gentle but limited nursery slopes and lifts up to higher points. Most of the mountain is of easy red steepness. The run to the valley is a pleasant red with one or two tricky bits where it takes a quick plunge; it has effective snowmaking.
600m; slopes 600–1860m
14 36km

Hinterthal Austria
One of five villages in the varied Hochkönig area that spreads over a series of gentle peaks from Maria Alm to Mühlbach. The village is small – little more than a few four-star hotels and chalets, shops and bars – but it connects well with the main area via a newish gondola. There are good nursery slopes and some challenging reds.
990m; slopes 800–1900m
33 150km
Elevation Holidays

Hintertux / Tux valley 117

Hippach 145
Hamlet near a crowd-free lift into Mayrhofen's main area.

Grand Hirafu 658
Interlinked area in Niseko, Japan.

Hittisau 192
Village in Bregenzerwald.
800m; slopes 800–1600m
5 9km

Hochfügen Austria
High-altitude ski-station outpost of Fügen, part of Ski Optimal area linked with Kaltenbach. Best suited to intermediates.
1500m; slopes 560–2500m
35 155km

Hochgurgl **150**
Quiet village with connection to Obergurgl's slopes.

Hochkönig Austria
Varied area that spreads over four linked mountains from Maria Alm via Hinterthal and Dienten to Mühlbach.
800-1070m; slopes 800–1900m
33 150km

Hochpillberg Austria
Hamlet with fabulous views towards Innsbruck and an antique chairlift into varied terrain above Schwaz with good vertical of 1000m. Wonderfully safe for children; all accommodation within two minutes of lift.
1300m; slopes 1300–2100m
5 10km

Hochsölden **168**
Satellite above Sölden.

Hoch-Ybrig Switzerland
Purpose-built complex only 64km south-east of Zürich, with facilities for families.
1050m; slopes 1050–1830m
12 50km

Hochzillertal Austria
Along with Hochfugen forms the large Ski Optimal area above the valley village of Kaltenbach. Best suited to intermediates – but there is plenty of potential for off-piste too.
1500m; slopes 560–2500m
35 155km

Holiday Valley USA
Family resort in New York State, an hour's drive south-east of Buffalo.
slopes 485–685m
12 270 acres

Hollersbach Austria
Hamlet near Mittersill, over Pass Thurn from Kitzbühel, with a gondola up to the Resterhöhe above Pass Thurn.
805m; slopes 805–1000m
2 5km

Homewood USA
Uncrowded area near Tahoe City with the most sheltered slopes in the vicinity. Apart from one fast quad, most slopes are served by slow chairlifts, and the views are as much of an attraction as the slopes. Set right on the western shore of the lake, so access is quick and easy. The notably quiet slopes include plenty of short black pitches as well as cruisers.
1900m; slopes 1900–2400m
7 1260 acres

Hoodoo Ski Bowl USA
Small area in Oregon with short runs and limited vertical of around 300m. Some 65km from Bend (see Mount Bachelor).
1420m; slopes 1420–1740m
5 800 acres

Hopfgarten **173**
Small chalet village with lift link into the SkiWelt area.

Horseshoe Resort Canada
Toronto region resort with high-capacity lift system and 100% snowmaking. The second mountain – The Heights – is open to members only.
310m; slopes 310–405m
7 60 acres

Les Houches **227**
Varied area at the entrance to the Chamonix valley.

Hovden Norway
Big, modern luxury lakeside hotel in wilderness midway between Oslo and Bergen. Cross-country venue with some Alpine slopes.
820m; slopes 820–1175m
5 14km

La Hoya Argentina
Small uncrowded resort 15km from the town of Esquel.
slopes 1350–2150m
9 22km

Huez **202**
Charming old hamlet on the road up to Alpe-d'Huez.

Hunter Mountain USA
Popular New Yorkers' area so it gets very crowded at weekends.
485m; slopes 485–975m
14 230 acres

Hüttschlag Austria
Hamlet in a dead-end valley with lifts into the Gastein area at nearby Grossarl.
1020m; slopes 1020–1220m 1

Hyundai Sungwoo Resort South Korea
Modern high-rise resort, 140km from Seoul. Host to the 2009 World Snowboard Championships. *9*

Idre Fjäll Sweden
Collective name for four areas 490km north-west of Stockholm.
slopes 590–890m
30 28km

Igls Austria
Almost a suburb of Innsbruck – the city trams run out to the village – but it is a small resort in its own right. Its famous downhill race course is an excellent piste.
900m; slopes 900–2245m
9 7km
Lagrange

Iizuna Japan
Tiny area 2.5 hours from Tokyo.
slopes 1080–1480m 7

Incline Village USA
Large village on northern edge of Lake Tahoe – it is a reasonable stop-off if you are touring.

Indianhead USA
South Lake Superior area with the most snowfall in the region. Winds are a problem.
395m; slopes 395–585m
12 195 acres

Inneralpbach **107**
Village in Ski Juwel (Alpbachtal-Wildschönau).

Innerarosa Switzerland
The prettiest part of Arosa, with lifts into the slopes and a quiet, 'gentle' children"s area. *1800m*

Innichen Italy
Small resort in South Tyrol. San Candido in Italian.
1175m; slopes 1175–1580m
4 15km

Innsbruck Austria
Lively and interesting former Olympic city at Alpine crossroads, surrounded by small areas, each ideal for a day trip. Among them is the Stubai glacier. Area pass available.
575m; slopes 800–3210m
78 282km

Interlaken Switzerland
Large lakeside summer resort at entrance to the valleys leading to Wengen, Grindelwald and Mürren.
Crystal

Ischgl **122**

Ishiuchi Maruyama-Gala-Yuzawa Kogen Japan
Three resorts with a shared lift pass 90 minutes from Tokyo by bullet train and offering the largest ski area in the central Honshu region.
255m; slopes 255–920m 52

Isola 2000 France
A compact purpose-built resort 90km from Nice, which makes it great for short breaks and very convenient. The doorstep snow, high slopes and an improving range of amenities make it equally appealing to families and beginners; there are some excellent nursery slopes near the base. But the core of the resort village isn't pretty: mostly block-like and tatty apartment buildings. The slopes spread across three main sectors, with varied runs suiting confident intermediates best; most are above the treeline and often sunny, but the resort's southerly aspect means that the area can have masses of snow when it is in shorter supply elsewhere in the French Alps. And most slopes keep their snow well.
2000m; slopes 1840–2610m
22 120km
Erna Low, Lagrange, Pierre & Vacances, PowderBeds, Ski Collection, Ski France, Ski Solutions, Skitopia, Zenith

Iso Syöte Finland
Finland's most southerly fell region, 150km south of the Arctic Circle but receiving the most snow in the country. A family-friendly resort that suits beginners and intermediates best, since there are only two black runs. But there are two freeride areas. Most runs are short, with the longest 1200m and a maximum vertical of less than 200m. And all the lifts are drags. There's a terrain park, expanded children's nursery area, tubing, tobogganing, and igloo hotel. Cross-country is big here, with 120kms of trails. There's a choice of hotels and cabins.
430m; slopes 240–430m
9 21km
Crystal, Thomson

Itter **173**
Next to Söll.

Jackson USA
Classic New England village, and a major cross-country base. A lovely place from which to ski New Hampshire's Alpine areas.

Jackson Hole **595**

Jasná Slovakia
Largest ski area in Slovakia, in the Low Tatras mountains. Big children's area, terrain park, night skiing. Several tough 'freeride zones'.
slopes 1240–2005m
14 21km Zenith

Jasper Canada
Set in the middle of Jasper National Park, this low-key, low-rise little town appeals more to those keen on scenery and wildlife (and cross-country skiing) rather than piste miles. Could combine a stay with Whistler, Banff or Lake Louise. Snowfall is modest by North American standards and there is lots of steep terrain that needs good snow to be fun. Keen piste-bashers will cover all the groomed runs in half a day. There are excellent nursery slopes. Visitors have commented on few crowds and queues. There are 300km of cross-country trails. Most accommodation is out of town or on the outskirts and the local slopes are a 30-minute drive.
1695m; slopes 1695–2610m
8 1675 acres
American Ski Classics, Canadian Affair, Crystal, Crystal Finest, Frontier, Independent

Ski Links, Inghams, Momentum, Neilson, Ski Independence, Ski Safari, Ski Solutions, Skiworld, Virgin Snow

Jay Peak USA
Vermont resort near Canadian border with best snowfall record in the east. Tree-lined intermediate/advanced slopes – as many classified black as blue. Experts also have access to hike-in/out terrain in West bowl.
550m; slopes 550–1205m
🚡 *8* ⛷ *385 acres*
🛏 *American Ski Classics, Ski Safari*

Jochberg 129
Straggling village, 8km from Kitzbühel.

La Joue-du-Loup France
Slightly stylish little purpose-built a few km north-west of Gap. Shares a fair-sized intermediate area with Superdévoluy. A ski-in/ski-out, family-oriented resort; all accommodation is in good-value apartments and chalets; good choice of affordable restaurants. Easily reached using budget flights to Marseille.
1450m; slopes 1450–2450m
🚡 *22* ⛷ *100km*
🛏 *Lagrange, Ski Collection*

Jouvenceaux 418
Less boisterous base near Sauze d'Oulx.

Jukkasjärvi Sweden
Centuries-old cross-country resort with unique ice hotel rebuilt every December.

June Mountain USA
Small area near Mammoth, closed for the 2012/13 season.

Juns 117
Small village between Lanersbach and Hintertux.

Kals am Grossglockner Austria
Remote valley village north of Lienz. Now linked to Matrei.
1325m; slopes 975–2620m
🚡 *15* ⛷ *110km*

Kaltenbach Austria
One of the larger, quieter Zillertal areas, with plenty of high-altitude slopes, mostly above the treeline.
560m; slopes 560–2500m
🚡 *35* ⛷ *155km*

Kananaskis Canada
Small area near Calgary, nicely set in woods, with slopes at Nakiska.
slopes 1525–2465m
🚡 *12* ⛷ *605 acres*
🛏 *Frontier*

Kandersteg Switzerland
Good cross-country base set amid beautiful scenery near Interlaken. Easy, but limited, slopes. Popular with families.
1175m; slopes 1175–1900m
🚡 *7* ⛷ *14km*
🛏 *Headwater, Inntravel, Neilson*

Kanin 654

Kappl Austria
A 15-minute bus ride down the valley from Ischgl, and worth a visit. Both the village and the slopes are family-oriented, and delightfully quiet compared with Ischgl. The village, with a couple of dozen hotels and guest-houses, sits on a shelf 100m above the valley floor. The slopes – served by an access gondola from the roadside and fast quads above it – offer plenty of variety, with several tough reds. Most of the slopes are open, but the run down the gondola offers some shelter for bad-weather days.
1260m; slopes 1180–2690m
🚡 *9* ⛷ *40km*
🛏 *Interactive Resorts*

Kaprun Austria
A spacious but pleasant village a few minutes bus ride down the road from Zell am See, and with slopes on the snow-sure Kitzsteinhorn glacier. It makes a particularly good early- or late-season break. Buses to and from both resorts are often crowded at peak times; staying centrally may be best. Most slopes are on the glacier, but nearby Maiskogel also has a small intermediate area. The glacier slopes offer little challenge but there is off-piste with a guide, three ski routes and freeride workshops. The town has plenty of hotels, restaurants, a few lively bars and new Tauern Spa centre.
785m; slopes 755–3030m
🚡 *53* ⛷ *138km*
🛏 *Crystal, Crystal Finest, Inghams, Interactive Resorts, Ski Line, Skitracer, Snow Finders, Snowscape, STC, Thomson, Zenith*

Les Karellis France
Resort with slopes that are more scenic, challenging and snow-sure than those of better-known Valloire, nearby.
1600m; slopes 1600–2550m
🚡 *15* ⛷ *60km*

Kastelruth Italy
German name for Castelrotto.

Kasurila Finland
Siilinjarvi ski area popular with boarders. 🚡 5

Katschberg Austria
Cute hamlet above the road pass from Styria to Carinthia, by-passed by Tauern motorway. Non-trivial area of high intermediate slopes. Popular with families.
1640m; slopes 1065–2220m
🚡 *16* ⛷ *70km*
🛏 *Neilson*

Keystone USA
Sprawling condo-dominated resort below three varied mountains; the nearest thing to a proper village is a handy development near the gondola. Evenings are quiet, with limited restaurants/bars. The lift pass covers Breckenridge and nearby Arapahoe Basin. Fast lifts link all three mountains, with varied terrain including ungroomed steep bowls, forest glades and cat skiing. There's a beautifully groomed network of tree-lined blues and greens, and good nursery slopes. Reporters praise the school for small classes. There's a huge terrain park and super-pipe, floodlit skiing and tubing. A favourite hut is the table-service Alpenglow Stube.
2835m; slopes 2835–3650m
🚡 *20* ⛷ *3148 acres*
🛏 *Alpine Answers, AmeriCan Ski, American Ski Classics, Crystal, Erna Low, Independent Ski Links, PowderBeds, Ski Independence, Ski Safari, Skitracer, Snow Finders*

Kicking Horse 620

Killington 600

Kimberley Canada
Mining town turned twee mock Austro-Bavarian/English Tudor resort scenically set 2 hours from Banff. The terrain offers a mix of blue and black runs (and occasional green) and a vertical of 750m. The mainly forested runs are spread over two rather bland hills. There are only a few short double diamonds, but classification tends to understate difficulty, and many of the single diamonds are quite challenging. It has a reputation for good powder, although it doesn't get huge amounts by the standards of this region.
1230m; slopes 1230–1980m
🚡 *5* ⛷ *1800 acres*
🛏 *AmeriCan Ski, Frontier, Inghams, Ski Safari, Skiworld*

Kirchberg 129
Lively town close to Kitzbühel.

Kirchdorf Austria
Attractive village a bus ride from St Johann in Tirol, with good local beginner slopes.
640m 🛏 *Crystal, Thomson*

Kirkwood USA
Renowned for its powder, and has a lot to offer experts and confident intermediates, but it's limited for intermediates who are not happy to tackle black runs. It makes a great outing from South Lake Tahoe, though heavy snowfall may close the high-level passes to get there. Deep snow is part of the attraction, often reportedly better than Heavenly.
2375m; slopes 2375–2985m
🚡 *14* ⛷ *2300 acres*

Kitzbühel 129

Kleinarl Austria
Secluded traditional village up a pretty side valley from Wagrain, part of the three-valley lift network linking Flachauwinkl to Zauchensee – our figures relate to this area.
1015m; slopes 800–2185m
🚡 *15* ⛷ *65km*

Kleinwalsertal 378
Area in the German Alps.

Klippitztörl Austria
One of many little areas in Austria's easternmost ski region near Slovenian border.
1550m; slopes 1460–1820m
🚡 *6* ⛷ *25km*

Klösterle 195
Valley village in the Alpenregion Bludenz.

Klosters 477

Kobla 654
Slovenian village a bus ride from Vogel.

Kolasin 1450 Montenegro
Small ski area on Bjelasica Mountain above the town of the Kolasin, where you stay.
1450m 🚡 *5* ⛷ *20km*

Kolsass-Weer Austria
Pair of Inn-side villages with low, inconvenient and limited slopes.
555m; slopes 555–1010m
🚡 *3* ⛷ *14km*

Königsleiten 145
Quiet resort sharing area with Gerlos in the Zillertal Arena.

Konjiam South Korea
Purpose-built resort 40 minutes north of Seoul. The slopes suit beginners best, and offer the area's longest run at 1.8km. The base village has over 400 condos, a restaurant and spa, Popular with families.
🚡 *3* ⛷ *11 runs*

Kopaonik Serbia
Modern, sympathetically designed family resort in a pretty setting.
1770m; slopes 1110–2015m
🚡 *23* ⛷ *60km*
🛏 *BoardnLodge*

Koralpe Austria
Largest and steepest of many gentle little areas in Austria's easternmost ski region near the Slovenian border.
1550m; slopes 1550–2050m
10 25km

Korea Condo South Korea
A single condo complex built some way from the three slopes. 2

Kössen Austria
Village near St Johann in Tirol with low, scattered and limited local slopes.
600m; slopes 600–1700m
9 25km

Kötschach-Mauthen Austria
One of many little areas near Hermagor in eastern Austria, close to the Italian border.
710m; slopes 710–1300m
4 7km

Kranjska Gora **654**

Krimml Austria
Sunny area, high enough to have good snow usually. Shares regional pass with Wildkogel resorts (Neukirchen).
1075m; slopes 1640–2040m
9 33km

Krippenstein Austria
A mainly freeride resort on Dachstein glacier near Salzburg. Cable car from Obertraun in the valley. 30km off-piste routes and 11km long blue/red run. Shares lift pass with Annaberg-Gosau region.

Krispl-Gaissau Austria
Easy slopes very close to Salzburg. Several long top-to-bottom lifts mean the size of the area is greatly reduced if the snow line is high.
925m; slopes 750–1570m
11 40km

Kronplatz Italy
Distinctive ski area in South Tyrol, with amazingly efficient lifts from Brunico and San Vigilio di Marebbe. Plan de Corones is its Italian name.
1200m; slopes 1200–2275m
32 114km
Mountainsun

Krvavec **654**

Kühtai Austria
A collection of comfortable hotels beside a high road pass only 25km from Innsbruck – higher than equally snow-sure Obergurgl or Obertauern, and cheaper than either. Covered also by the standard Innsbruck pass. A modern gondola, three fast quads and a handful of drags serve red cruisers of about 500m vertical on either side of the road, plus some token black runs; not ideal for novices – few easy blues to graduate to. Very quiet in the week, but liable to weekend crowds if lower resorts around Innsbruck are short of snow. Limited mountain huts. Quiet in the evening, but for its size a reasonable selection of hotels.
2020m; slopes 800–2620m
12 44km
Crystal, Inghams, STC

Kusatsu Kokusai Japan
Attractive spa village with hot springs, three hours from Tokyo.
slopes 1250–2170m 13

Laax **479**

Le Lac Blanc France
Mini-resort with six-pack in the northerly Vosges mountains near Strasbourg. Extensive ski de fond trails.
830m; slopes 830–1235m
9 14km

Laces Italy
Village in the Val Venosta in the South Tyrol covered by the Ortler Skiarena pass.

Lachtal Austria
Second largest ski resort in the Styrian region NE of Salzburg.
1600m; slopes 1600–2100m
8 29km

Ladis Austria
Smaller alternative to Serfaus and Fiss, with lifts that connect into the same varied ski area.
1200m; slopes 1200–2750m
70 190km

Lagunillas Chile
83km south-east of Santiago. 494 acres

Le Laisinant **358**
Tiny hamlet down the valley from Val d'Isère.

Lake Louise **622**

Lake Tahoe USA
Collection of 14 ski areas spectacularly set on California-Nevada border – Heavenly and Squaw Valley best known in Britain.

Lamoura France
One of four villages that makes up the Les Rousses area in the Jura.
1120m; slopes 1120–1680m
40 40km

Landeck–Zams Austria
Small ski area in the Tirol region.
780m; slopes 816–2210m
7 22km

Lans-en-Vercors France
Village close to Villard-de-Lans and 30km from Grenoble. Highest slopes in the region; few snowmakers.
1020m; slopes 1400–1805m
16 24km

Lanslebourg France
One of the villages that makes up Val Cenis.

Lanslevillard France
One of the villages that makes up Val Cenis.

Laterns Austria
Small, low altitude resort in the Vorarlberg near Friedrichshafen. Two fast chairs serve mainly red runs and some ski routes.
900m; slopes 900–1785m
6 27km

Lauchernalp-Lötschental Switzerland
Small but tall and challenging slopes reached by cable car from Wiler in the secluded, picturesque, dead-end Lötschental, north of Rhône valley. Glacier runs above 3000m.
1970m; slopes 1420–3110m
6 33km

Lauterbrunnen **482**
Valley town with rail connection up to Mürren.

Le Lavancher **227**
Quiet village between Chamonix and Argentière.

Lavarone **443**
Areas east of Trento, good for a weekend day trip.

Leadville USA
Old mining town full of historic buildings. Own easy area (Ski Cooper) plus snowcat operation. Picturesque inexpensive base for visiting Copper Mountain, Vail and Beaver Creek.

Lech **137**

The Lecht **657**
Scottish ski resort.
640m; slopes 610–825m
13 20km

Lélex France
Family resort with pretty wooded slopes between Dijon and Geneva.
900m; slopes 900–1680m
29 50km

Las Leñas Argentina
European-style resort, 400km south of Mendoza, with varied, beautiful terrain and extensive off-piste. But it's a stormy place that can close the lifts for days. Lodgings at the foot of the slopes.
2240m; slopes 2240–3430m
13 64km Skiworld

Lenggries-Brauneck **378**
Bavarian resort south of Munich.
680m; slopes 700–1710m
18 34km

Lenk Switzerland
Traditional village sharing a sizeable area with Adelboden, and with its own separate slopes at Betelberg. Buses to lifts at Rothenbach, or to the six-pack from Buhlberg.
1070m; slopes 1070–2360m
56 185km

Lenzerheide Switzerland
The senior partner with Valbella in an extensive area of intermediate slopes in a pretty setting around a lake, all at a decent altitude. The slopes are on the two sides of the valley. The east-facing, morning-sun slopes are mainly fairly gentle. The west-facing slopes have more character, both in skiing and visual terms, including a run on the back of the dramatic peak of the Rothorn. There is considerable off-piste potential.
1470m; slopes 1230–2865m
35 155km
Alpine Answers, Crystal, Powder Byrne, Ski Safari, STC

Leogang **158**
Quiet village with link to Saalbach-Hinterglemm.

Lermoos Austria
Pleasant little village with 30km of shady intermediate slopes on Grubigstein, and a pass giving access to a variety of other areas in the locality, including the towering (and glacial) Zugspitze, on the border with Germany. The slopes offer splendid views of the mountain. The village is compact, with good family-friendly hotels. Fast lifts go from both ends, serving some worthwhile descents – including a fine black run and an area of ready-made moguls. The runs below mid-mountain are worthwhile blues and reds, with good nursery slopes at village level. Lots of cross-country trails along the flat valley.
1005m; slopes 990–2960m
52 147km

Lessach Austria
Hamlet with trail connecting into one of the longest, most snow-sure cross-country networks in Europe.
1210m 1

Leukerbad Switzerland
Major spa resort of Roman origin, spectacularly set beneath towering cliffs, which are scaled by a cable car up to high-altitude cross-country trails. The downhill slopes are on the opposite side of the valley, mainly above the treeline and of red gradient, though there are a couple of blacks including a World Cup downhill course, which descends from open slopes into the woods. Lifts include a six-pack.
1410m; slopes 1410–2700m
10 52km
Inntravel, Thomson

Leutasch Austria
Traditional cross-country village with limited slopes but a pleasant day trip from nearby Seefeld or Innsbruck.
1130m; slopes 1130–1605m
3 6km
Headwater, Inntravel

Levi **645**

Leysin Switzerland
This is a spread-out village, climbing up a wooded hillside. The lifts are to the east of the village and take you to a pretty mix of mainly red and blue runs. Itineraries from the top of Chaux de Mont provide the best options for experts, along with a heli-operation. There are nursery slopes at village level. The revolving Kuklos restaurant at La Berneuse has stunning views.
1250m; slopes 1300–2200m
14 60km
PowderBeds

Lienz Austria
Pleasant town in pretty surroundings.
675m; slopes 730–2280m
17 40km

Lillehammer Norway
Cultural fjordside town, 2 to 3 hours north of Oslo by train/car, with its two Olympic areas 15 and 35km away, poorly served by bus.
200m; slopes 200–1030m
10 25km

Limone Italy
Pleasant old town not far from Turin, with a pretty area, but far from snow-sure.
1010m; slopes 1030–2050m
15 80km

Lincoln USA
Sprawling New Hampshire town from which to visit Loon mountain.

Lindvallen-Högfjället Sweden
Two of the mountains that make up the four unlinked ski areas of Sälen.
800m; slopes 590–890m
46 85km

Le Lioran France
Auvergne village near Aurillac with a purpose-built satellite above. Spectacular volcanic scenery.
1160m; slopes 1160–1850m
24 60km

Livigno **403**

Lizzola Italy
Small base development in remote region north of Bergamo. Several other little areas nearby.
1250m; slopes 1250–2070m
9 30km

Loch Lomond Canada
Steep, narrow, challenging slopes near Thunder Bay on the shores of Lake Superior. Candy Mountain is nearby.
215m; slopes 215–440m
3 90 acres

Lofer Austria
Quiet, traditional village in a pretty setting north of Saalbach with a small area of its own, and Waidring's relatively snow-sure Steinplatte nearby.
640m; slopes 640–1745m
10 46km STC

Longchamp France
Dreary purpose-built resort with little to commend it over pretty Valmorel, with which it shares its ski area.
1650m

Loon Mountain USA
Small, smart, modern resort just outside Lincoln, New Hampshire. Mostly intermediate runs.
290m; slopes 290–910m
10 275 acres
Virgin Snow

Lost Trail USA
Remote Montana area, open only Thursday to Sunday and holidays. Mostly intermediate slopes.
2005m; slopes 2005–2370m
6 800 acres

Loveland USA
Exceptionally high and snowy slopes right next to highway I70, just east of the Continental Divide, easily reached from other Colorado resorts, especially Keystone.
3230m; slopes 3230–3870m
9 1365 acres

Luchon France
Sizeable village with plenty of amenities, with gondola (eight minutes) to its ski area at purpose-built Superbagnères.
630m; slopes 1440–2260m
16 35km Lagrange

Lurisia Italy
Sizeable spa resort, a good base for visits to surrounding little ski areas and to Nice.
750m; slopes 800–1800m
8 35km

Lutsen Mountains USA
In Minnesota, the largest ski area in between Vermont and Colorado, with panoramic views of Lake Superior. Four small linked hills offer surprisingly good and extensive terrain.
80m; slopes 80–335m
9 1000 acres

Luz-Ardiden France
Spa village below its ski area. Cauterets and Barèges nearby.
710m; slopes 1730–2450m
15 60km

Macugnaga Italy
Two quiet, pretty villages dramatically set at the head of a remote valley, over the mountains from Zermatt and Saas-Fee. Lifts run up to the foot of the Belvedere glacier. A chairlift rises very slowly from the village to Burky, in the middle of the small, woody area of gentle runs. There is an excellent nursery slope beside the village and a two-stage cable car going over sunny slopes to the Swiss border. Good, varied red runs down the 1100m vertical of the top cable car, and considerable off-piste possibilities given good snow.
1325m; slopes 1325–2800m
11 35km

Madesimo Italy
Lots of fast lifts but limited extent of slopes. Not ideal for a week, but the mountain has something for everyone and the system copes well with weekend visitors. The village spreads along both sides of a river, a couple of hours from Bergamo or Milan; a random mix of traditional buildings and narrow streets on one side and more modern development on the other, but with a good choice of mid-priced hotels. The slopes have an almost equal share of blue and red runs that make great intermediate territory, though there are a few notable challenges – including the classic Canalone ski route. For a resort with a respectable altitude and a generally quiet and queue-free mountain, it is worth considering.
1550m; slopes 1550–2945m
12 60km

Madonna di Campiglio **407**

Mad River Glen USA
Cult resort, co-operatively owned, with some tough ungroomed terrain, a few well-groomed intermediate trails and antique lifts. Snowboarding is banned.
485m; slopes 485–1110m
4 115 acres

La Magdelaine Italy
Close to Cervinia, and good on bad weather days.
1645m; slopes 1645–1870m
4 4km

Maishofen Austria
Cheaper place to stay when visiting equidistant Saalbach and Zell am See. *765m*

Malbun Liechtenstein
Quaint user-friendly little family resort, 16km from the capital, Vaduz. Limited slopes and short easy runs.
1600m; slopes 1595–2100m
6 21km

Malcesine Italy
Large summer resort on Lake Garda with a fair area of slopes, served by a revolving cable car.
1430m; slopes 1430–1830m
8 12km

Malga Ciapela Italy
Resort at the foot of the Marmolada glacier massif, with a link into the Sella Ronda. Cortina is nearby.
1445m; slopes 1445–3270m
8 18km

Malga Haider Italy
Small area in Val Venosta, close to Austrian border. Haideralm is its German name. *5 20km*

Mallnitz Austria
Village in a pretty valley close to Slovenia, with two varied areas providing a fine mix of wooded and open runs. Closest is Ankogel. The snow-sure Molltal Glacier is nearby, above Flattach.
1200m 15 88km

Mammoth Mountain **540**

Manigod France
Small valley village, sharing quiet, wooded slopes with La Clusaz – over the Col de la Croix-Fry.
1100m 132km

Marble Mountain Canada
Tiny area in the Humber Valley on Newfoundland. Good snow record by east coast standards. Splendid base lodge, and some slope-side lodging. Blomidon Cat Skiing operates nearby.
85m; slopes 10–545m
5 175 acres
Frontier

Les Marecottes Switzerland
Small area near Martigny. Valid with the Valais Ski Card.
1100m; slopes 1775–2200m
5 25km

Maria Alm Austria
Charming unspoiled village at one end of the varied Hochkönig area that spreads over a series of gentle peaks via Hinterthal and Dienten to Mühlbach. Maria Alm, though small, is one of the two largest villages in the area, and the most animated in the evening; it's a pretty place with a splendid old church boasting the highest spire in Salzburgerland. The Hochkönig area is best for adventurous intermediates, but for beginners there is a good local nursery slope. Experts can explore the ungroomed ski routes and the excellent off-piste. Snowboarders may find there are too many draglifts. Maria Alm also has its own small local area of slopes. There are 40km of cross-country trails in the area.
800m; slopes 800–1900m
33 150km
Interactive Resorts, Select Chalets

Mariapfarr Austria
Village at the heart of one of the longest, most snow-reliable cross-country networks in Europe. Sizeable Mauterndorf-St Michael Alpine area and Obertauern area are nearby.
1120m 5 30km

Mariazell Austria
Traditional Styria village with an impressive basilica. Limited slopes.
870m; slopes 870–1265m
5 11km

Maribor-Pohorje 654

Marilleva 407
Small Trentino resort linked with Madonna di Campiglio.

Le Markstein France
Long-standing small resort in the northerly Vosges region near Strasbourg, which has hosted World Cup slalom races. Extensive nordic trails.
slopes 770–1270m 10

Masella Spain
Friendly Pyrenean village linked with the slopes of La Molina to form the Alp 2500 area. Weekend crowds.
1600m; slopes 1600–2535m
31 121km

La Massana Andorra
Pleasant valley town linked by gondola to the Arinsal/Pal slopes and fairly convenient for trips to Arcalis.
slopes 1550–2563m
31 63km

Les Masses 502
A hamlet below Les Collons in the Verbier ski area.

Le Massif Canada
One of several small but developing areas near historic Québec City, dramatically set in a UNESCO World Bio Reserve overlooking the St Lawrence river; the views of the ice floes from the summit lodge are stunning. The varied but limited treelined slopes offer Eastern Canada's biggest vertical at 770m – including a couple of steep double-black diamond runs and some good intermediate cruising.
35m; slopes 35–805m
6 406 acres
AmeriCan Ski, Frontier, Ski Safari

Matrei in Osttirol Austria
Large market village south of Felbertauern tunnel. Mostly high slopes, linked to Kals on the other side of the hill.
1000m; slopes 975–2620m
15 110km
Zenith

Maurienne Valley France
A great curving trench with over 20 winter resorts, from pleasant old valley villages to convenience resorts purpose-built in the 1960s.

Mauterndorf Austria
Village near Obertauern with tremendous snow record.
1120m; slopes 1075–2360m
10 35km

Maverick Mountain USA
Montana resort with plenty of terrain accessed by few lifts. Cowboy Winter Games venue – rodeo one day, ski races the next.
2155m; slopes 2155–2800m
2 500 acres

Mayens de Riddes Switzerland
Hamlet at the base of lifts on the back of Verbier's Savoleyres sector, more often referred to as La Tzoumaz.
1500m

Mayens-de-Sion Switzerland
Tranquil hamlet off the road up to Les Collons – part of the Verbier area. *1470m*

Mayrhofen 145

Méaudre France
Small resort near Grenoble with good snowmaking to make up for its low altitude.
1000m; slopes 1000–1600m
10 18km

Megève 269

Meiringen Switzerland
An old town in the broad Haslital valley, a good outing from the nearby Jungfrau resorts or Interlaken and 90 minutes' drive from Zürich or Bern. High-speed lifts take you into the slopes, which are on a broad, sunny mountainside spread across two main sectors. The area is particularly suitable for beginners and confident intermediates – experts will find little to challenge them and early intermediates will find a lack of blue runs. The area is popular with boarders but there are some flat sections. There's a good choice of mountain restaurants, and the resort is great for families with kids' snow gardens, special restaurants and fun areas. There's a choice of hotels and plenty of apartments; most of the restaurants are hotel-based. Après-ski is lively up the mountain but quiet and relaxed in town later on. There's plenty to do off the slopes – including visiting the Sherlock Holmes museum, of course.
600m; slopes 1060–2435m
18 60km

Melchsee-Frutt Switzerland
Limited, but high and snow-sure bowl above a car-free village. Family-friendly.
1920m; slopes 1080–2255m
10 32km

Mellau 192
Village in Bregenzerwald.
700m; slopes 700–2000m
31 105km

Les Menuires 276

Merano 2000 Italy
Small ski area just outside Merano, with main lift base at Falzeben above Avelengo/Hafling.
2000m; slopes 2000–2240m
7 40km

Méribel 282

Métabief-Mont-d'Or France
Twin villages in the Jura region, not far from Geneva.
900m; slopes 880–1460m
22 42km

Methven New Zealand
Nearest town/accommodation to Mt Hutt, and helicopter base for trips to Arrowsmith range – good for intermediates as well as advanced.

Mieders 189
Village in the Stubai valley.

Mijoux France
Pretty wooded slopes between Dijon and Geneva. Lélex nearby.
1000m; slopes 900–1680m
29 50km

Mission Ridge USA
Area in dry region that gets higher-quality snow than other Seattle resorts but less of it. Good intermediate slopes.
1390m; slopes 1390–2065m
6 300 acres

Misurina Italy
Tiny village near Cortina. A cheap alternative base.
1755m; slopes 1755–1900m
4 13km

Mittenwald 378
Cute town in the Bavarian Alps. *915m*

Mittersill Austria
Valley-junction village south of Pass Thurn. A gondola runs from Hollersbach up to the Resterhöhe sector above Pass Thurn.
790m; slopes 1265–1895m
15 25km

Moena Italy
Large village between Cavalese and Sella Ronda resorts, ideally located for touring the Dolomites area.
1200m; slopes 1200–2500m
8 35km

La Molina Spain
Cheap, basic resort near Andorra, sharing a fair-sized, varied area with Masella to form Alp 2500.
1400m; slopes 1400–2535m
31 121km

Mölltal Glacier Austria
Little-known high glacier slopes above Flattach on the other side of the Tauern tunnel from Bad Gastein. Varied runs and fast lifts. Worthwhile excursion when the snowline is high. Summer skiing available.
2570m; slopes 695–3120m
8 53km

Molveno Italy
Lakeside village on the edge of the Dolomites, with a couple of lifts – but mostly used as a base to ski nearby Andalo.

Monarch USA
Wonderfully uncrowded area, a day trip from Crested Butte. Great powder. Good for all but experts.
3290m; slopes 3290–3645m
5 800 acres

Monesi Italy
Southernmost of the resorts south of Turin. Close to Monaco and Nice.
1310m; slopes 1310–2180m
5 38km

Le Monêtier 327
Quiet little village with access to Serre-Chevalier's slopes.

La Mongie 318

Montafon Austria
The 40km-long Montafon valley contains eleven resorts and four main lift systems. The valley is well worth a look. The biggest is the Nova area (linking Gaschurn and St Gallenkirch) and this is now linked to the Hochjoch area and Schruns. Gargellen and Golm are smaller ski areas in the valley.
655-1425m; slopes 655–2395m
61 219km
Crystal

Montalbert 304
Traditional village with access to the La Plagne network.

Mont Blanc Canada
Small locals' hill near Tremblant, with only 300m of vertical and no resemblance to the Franco-Italian item.
7 36

Montchavin 304
Attractive village on the fringe of La Plagne.

Mont-de-Lans 252
Low village near Les Deux-Alpes.

Le Mont-Dore France
Attractive traditional small town, the largest resort in the stunningly beautiful volcanic Auvergne region near Clermont-Ferrand.
1050m; slopes 1350–1850m
17 42km

Monte Bondone 443
Trento's local hill.

Monte Campione Italy
Tiny purpose-built resort, spread thinly over four mountainsides; 80% snowmaking helps to offset the low altitude.
1100m; slopes 1200–2010m
16 80km

Monte Livata Italy
Closest resort to Rome, popular with weekenders.
1430m; slopes 1430–1750m
8 8km

Monte Piselli Italy
Tiny area with the highest slopes of the many little resorts east of Rome.
2100m; slopes 2100–2690m
3 5km

Monte Pora Italy
Tiny resort near Lake d'Iseo and Bergamo. Several other little areas nearby.
1350m; slopes 1350–1880m
11 30km

Monterosa Ski **412**

Mont Gabriel Canada
Montreal area with runs on four sides of the mountain, though the south-facing sides rarely open. Two short but renowned double-black-diamond bump runs. 9

Montgenèvre **292**

Mont Glen Canada
Least crowded of the Montreal areas, so a good weekend choice.
680m; slopes 680–1035m
4 110 acres

Mont Grand Fonds Canada
Small area sufficiently far from Québec not to get overrun at weekends.
400m; slopes 400–735m 4

Mont Habitant Canada
Very limited area in the Montreal region but with a good base lodge. 3

Mont Olympia Canada
Small, two-mountain area near Montreal, one mostly novice terrain, the other best suited to experts. 6

Mont Orford Canada
Cold, windswept lone peak (no resort), worth a trip from nearby Montreal on a fine day.
slopes 305–855m
8 180 acres

Mont-Ste-Anne Canada
Quebec City's biggest and most varied local ski area. Wide choice of amenities at the base. The slopes are limited, but the vertical is a decent 625m. A gondola goes to the top, from where slopes span north and south sides of the mountain. The views are spectacular. Over a third of the area is classified black or double-black, so it's a good place for experts. The Beast (double black diamond) has one of the steepest pitches in the east at 65%. But there are decent intermediate trails too, adequate nursery slopes and an easy top-to-bottom green run. The Dual mountain lift pass is valid at Stoneham.
175m; slopes 175–800m
11 69km
AmeriCan Ski, Frontier, Ski Safari

Mont-St-Sauveur Canada
Perhaps the prettiest resort in Canada, popular with Montreal (60km) day trippers and luxury condo owners.

Mont Sutton Canada
Varied area with some of the best glade skiing in eastern Canada, including some for novices. Quaint Sutton village nearby.
9 175 acres

Moonlight Basin **590**
Quiet area of slopes linked to Big Sky, Montana.

Morgins **459**
Resort on the Swiss side of the Portes du Soleil circuit.

Morillon **258**
Valley village in the Flaine network.

Morin Heights Canada
Area in the Montreal region with 100% snowmaking. Attractive base lodge. 6

Morzine **296**

Les Mosses Switzerland
Peaceful scenic resort and area, best for a day trip from Villars or Les Diablerets. There's a terrain park, a few chalet-style hotel-restaurants, shops and a rather fine church. There are only draglifts to access the mainly red and blue runs. Prides itself on the number of activities on offer – such as ice-diving, a natural ice rink and an international dog-sled track.
1500m; slopes 1500–2200m
14 60km

Mottaret **282**
Purpose-built but reasonably attractive part of Méribel.

Mottarone Italy
Closest slopes to Lake Maggiore. No village – just a base area.
1200m; slopes 1200–1490m 25km

Les Moulins Switzerland
Village down the road from Château d'Oex with its own low area of slopes, part of the big Gstaad lift-pass area.
890m; slopes 890–3000m
58 250km

Mount Abram USA
Small, pretty, treelined area in Maine, renowned for its immaculately groomed easy runs.
295m; slopes 295–610m
5 170 acres

Mountain High USA
Best snowfall record and highest lift capacity in Los Angeles vicinity – plus 95% snowmaking. Mostly intermediate cruising.
2010m; slopes 2010–2500m
12 220 acres

Mount Ashland USA
Arty town in Oregon renowned for Shakespeare performances. Tiny ski area best for experts run by local charity.
1935m; slopes 1935–2285m
4 200 acres

Mount Bachelor USA
Extinct volcano in Oregon with a big ski area and runs on all sides. Higher elevation means better chance of good snow than many other resorts in north-west USA and average annual snowfall of 370 inches is more than any major Colorado resort. Good cruising and beginner terrain lower down and plenty to occupy experts, including treelined blacks and steep terrain on the south-facing slopes. No lodging at the base; stay 30 mins away at Sunriver Resort – a big lodge with bar, restaurant, chalet lodging and excellent spa – or in Bend, an attractive small town served by free shuttles.
1920m; slopes 1755–2765m
13 3680 acres
Ski Safari

Mount Baker USA
Almost on the coast near Seattle, yet one of the top resorts for snow (averages 600 inches a year). Plenty of challenging slopes. Known for spectacular avalanches.
1115m; slopes 1115–1540m
9 1000 acres

Mount Baldy Canada
Tiny area, but a worthwhile excursion from Big White. Gets ultra light snow – great glades/powder chutes.
slopes 1705–2150m
2 150 acres

Mount Baldy USA
Some of the longest and steepest runs in California. Only an hour's drive from Los Angeles so a day trip is feasible, but 20% snowmaking and antiquated lifts are major drawbacks.
1980m; slopes 1980–2620m
4 400 acres

Mount Baw Baw Australia
Small but entertaining intermediate area in attractive woodland, with great views. Closest area to Melbourne (150km).
1450m; slopes 1450–1560m
7 35 hectares

Mount Buffalo Australia
Site of Australia's first ski lift. Plateau area best suited to beginners. Short season. On-mountain accommodation. four hours from Melbourne.
1400m; slopes 1455–1610m
8 66 acres

Mount Buller Australia
Three hours from Melbourne and Victoria's largest ski area. Proper resort village, with with a 360-degree network of short runs on its isolated massif. Luxury hotel and spa.
1600m; slopes 1600–1790m
22 80km

Mount Dobson New Zealand
Mostly intermediate slopes in a wide, treeless basin near Mt Cook, with good snow-cover. Accommodation in Fairlie, 40 minutes away.
1610m; slopes 1610–2010m
3 990 acres

Mount Falakro Greece
Area two hours' drive from Salonica in northern Greece; almost as big as Parnassos, uncrowded and with good views. Has a fast quad.
1720m 8 22km

Mount Hood Meadows USA
The biggest and most varied ski area on Mt Hood in Oregon served by 11 lifts including five fast quads. Good beginner area, intermediate cruising, single black diamond runs in the centre of the main ski area and a big area of double black diamond runs roped off and entered through gates. Up to six terrain parks, depending on snow conditions. No accommodation at the base – stay at Timberline (see separate entry) half an hour away or Government Camp (near Mt Hood Skibowl, which also gets its own entry) 20 minutes away.
1635m; slopes 1375–2225m
11 2150 acres
Ski Safari

Mount Hood Skibowl USA
Small area of mainly tough gladed runs, offering the steepest and most extreme slopes in the Mount Hood area. Claims to be America's largest night skiing area with a lot of runs open up to 10/11pm nightly. Two floodlit terrain parks, tubing hills, snow bikes and snowmobiles. Just below Timberline ski area; stay there or in Government Camp at the foot of Skibowl's slopes, a sizeable settlement with a choice of lodgings and restaurants. Other local ski area is Mt Hood Meadows.
1075m; slopes 1075–1530m
7 960 acres

Mount Hotham Australia
Australia's highest ski village. Built on a ridge above the slopes. Intermediate and advanced skiing. Good snow record. Nearest town Bright, four hours from Melbourne.
1750m; slopes 1450–1845m
13 30km

Mount Hutt New Zealand
Steepest, most snow-sure area in NZ, with ocean views, but prone to bad weather; 100km from Christchurch, a tricky drive up from Methven.
slopes 1405–2085m
4 365 hectares

Mount Lemmon USA
Southernmost area in North America, close to famous Old West town Tombstone, Arizona. Reasonable snowfall.
2500m; slopes 2500–2790m
3 70 acres

Mount McKay Australia
Australia's steepest skiing accessed from Falls Creek, with genuine black-diamond terrain and snowcats.
1600m

Mount Pilio Greece
Pleasant slopes cut out of dense forest, only 15km from the holiday resort of Portaria above town of Volos.
1500m 3

Mount Rose USA
Much the highest base elevation in the Tahoe area – a good 600m above the lake – and with an annual snowfall average of 400 inches. The Chutes is a shady bowl mainly of serious double-diamond gradient on the front face of the slopes. But there are blue and easy black runs to the base and a wider, gentler, lightly wooded area. The slopes have a lot to offer, especially if staying in Heavenly – where the groomed stuff may be too dull and the ungroomed stuff too challenging.
2520m; slopes 2410–2955m
6 1200 acres

Mount Shasta Ski Park USA
Californian resort 300 miles north of San Francisco.
4 425 acres

Mount Snow USA
A one-peak resort, with a long row of lifts on the front face (two fast quads among them) serving easy and intermediate runs of just over 500m vertical. Separate area of black runs on the north face – including a couple of short but serious double blacks – served by a triple chair and a six-pack. And on the opposite side a small area of intermediate runs above Carinthia base, accessed by a third fast quad. Reputed to have some of the best terrain parks in the east. Lodgings at the base include a Grand Summit hotel.
580m; slopes 580–1095m
19 590 acres
Ski Safari

Mount Spokane USA
Little intermediate area near Spokane (Washington State).
1160m; slopes 1160–1795m
5 350 acres

Mount St Louis / Moonstone Canada
Premier area in Toronto region, spread over three peaks. Very high-capacity lift system and 100% snowmaking.
13 175

Mount Sunapee USA
Area in New Hampshire closest to Boston; primarily intermediate terrain.
375m; slopes 375–835m
10 230 acres

Mount Vermio Greece
Oldest ski base in Greece. Two areas in central Macedonia 60km from Thessaloniki. Barren but interesting slopes.
slopes 1420–2000m 7

Mount Washington Resort Canada
Scenic area on Vancouver Island with lodging in the base village. Impressive snowfall record but rain is a problem.
1110m; slopes 1110–1590m
6 970 acres
Frontier

Mount Washington Resort USA
One of several small resorts in New Hampshire scattered along the Interstate 93 highway. The slopes are on a single mountain face but highly rated, particularly by families, who relish the top-to-bottom easy trails on the main peak, Mt Rosebrook. There is a good mix of terrain, with West Mountain consisting mainly of double-diamond slopes. Snowmaking is comprehensive. There's a terrain park, half-pipe and boardercross. There are a few places to stay near the base, with the grand old Mount Washington hotel five minutes away.
480m; slopes 480–940m
8 435 acres

Mount Waterman USA
Small Los Angeles area where children ski free. The lack of much snowmaking is a drawback.
2135m; slopes 2135–2440m
3 210 acres

Mühlbach Austria
Sprawling village along the main road at one end of the Hochkönig area that spreads over a series of gentle peaks via Dienten to Maria Alm. The Hochkönig area is best for adventurous intermediates, but for beginners there is a good local nursery slope. Experts can explore the ungroomed ski routes and the excellent off-piste. Snowboarders may find there are too many draglifts. There are 40km of cross-country trails in the area.
855m; slopes 800–1900m
33 150km

Mühltal Austria
Small village halfway between Niederau and Auffach in the Wildschönau. No local skiing of its own.
780m; slopes 830–1905m
25 70km

Muhr Austria
Village by Katschberg tunnel well placed for visiting St Michael, Bad Kleinkirchheim, Flachau and Obertauern.
1110m

Muju Resort South Korea
Largest area in Korea and with a fair amount of lodging. Though it is the furthest resort from Seoul (four hours south) it is still overcrowded.
14

Mürren **482**

Mutters Austria
Charming rustic village near Innsbruck, at the foot of long slopes of 900m vertical that extend along the Götzens valley to Axamer Lizum. Good for families and beginners.
830m; slopes 830–2340m
4 15km

Myoko Suginohara Kokusai Japan
A series of small resorts two or three hours from Tokyo, which together make up an area of extensive slopes with longer, wider runs than normal for Japan. 15
Ski Safari

Naeba Japan
Fashionable resort with lots of accommodation two hours north of Tokyo. Crowded slopes.
900m; slopes 900–1800m 30

Nakiska Canada
Small area of wooded runs between Banff and Calgary, with emphasis on downhill speed. Unreliable snow, but state-of-the-art snowmaking and pancake-flat grooming.
1525m; slopes 1525–2260m
5 230 acres

Nasserein **180**
Quiet suburb of St Anton.

Nassfeld Ski Arena Austria
Carinthia's biggest: scenic and sunny area on the Italian border. Good intermediate slopes. Stay in Tröpolach, by the gondola, or larger Hermagor, further east.
1500m; slopes 610–2195m
30 110km
BoardnLodge, Interactive Resorts, Ski Line, STC

Nauders Austria
Spacious, traditionally Tirolean village tucked away only 3km from the Swiss border and almost on the Italian one. Its slopes start 2km outside the village (free shuttle-bus) and are mainly high and sunny intermediate runs spread over three areas. Lots of snowmaking. Not ideal for experts, though there is a lot of off-piste terrain. Not ideal for complete beginners either – the village nursery slopes are some way out. There are five cross-country trails amounting to 40km in all.
1400m; slopes 1400–2850m
24 120km

Nax Switzerland
Quiet, sunny village in a balcony setting overlooking the Rhône valley. Own little area and only a short drive from Veysonnaz. Handful of red and blue runs.
1300m 6 35km

Nendaz **502**
A sizeable family resort linked in to the Verbier ski area.

Neukirchen Austria
Quiet, pretty resort sharing slopes with Bramberg. Fairly snow-sure plateau at the top of its mountain.
855m; slopes 855–2150m
15 50km Crystal

Neustift **189**
Village in the Stubai valley.

Nevegal Italy
Weekend place near Belluno, south of Cortina.
1030m; slopes 1030–1650m
14 30km

Nevis Range **657**
Scottish ski resort.
90m; slopes 655–1220m
11 35km

Niederau **107**
Village in Ski Juwel (Alpbachtal-Wildschönau).

Niederdorf Italy
Cross-country village in South Tyrol. Villabassa in Italian.

Niseko **658**
Resort on Hokkaido island, Japan.

Niseko Village **658**
One of Niseko's three interlinked areas.

Nockberge Innerkrems Austria
Area just south of Katschberg tunnel.
1500m; slopes 1500–2020m
10 33km

Nordseter Norway
Cluster of hotels in deep forest north of Lillehammer. Some Alpine facilities but best for cross-country.
850m; slopes 1000–1090m
2 2km

Norefjell Norway
Norway's toughest run, a very steep 600m drop. 120km north-west of Oslo.
185m; slopes 185–1185m
10 23km

La Norma France
Traffic-free, purpose-built resort near Modane and Val Cenis.
1350m; slopes 1350–2750m
18 65km
AmeriCan Ski, Erna Low, Peak Retreats, Ski France

Norquay 605
Banff's quiet local hill.

North Conway USA
Attractive factory-outlet-shopping town in New Hampshire close to Attitash and Cranmore ski areas.

Northstar-at-Tahoe USA
Classic US-style mountain, with runs cut through dense forest and a pleasant base village that is still growing. The whole area is very sheltered and good for bad-weather days. A gondola and a fast quad go up to a lodge at Big Springs, only 160m above the village. From this point three fast chairs radiate to serve a broad bowl with some short steep pitches at the top, with easier blue runs lower down and around the ridges. From the ridge you can access the Backside, a steeper bowl with a central fast quad chair serving a row of easy black runs. Lookout Mountain has more black runs and a modest vertical of 390m.
1930m; slopes 1930–2625m
19 3000 acres
American Ski Classics, Ski Safari, Skiworld, Supertravel, Virgin Snow

Nôtre-Dame-de-Bellecombe France
Pleasant 'very French' village spoiled by the busy road. Inexpensive base from which to visit Megève, though it has fair slopes of its own. Queues and slow lifts can be a problem now it is linked to Les Saisies. Free bus to/from Crest Voland.
1150m; slopes 1035–2070m
84 175km
AmeriCan Ski, Erna Low, Lagrange, Peak Retreats

Nova Levante 443
Trentino village close to Bozen/Bolzano.

Nozawa Onsen Japan
Spa village with good hot springs three hours from Tokyo. The runs are cut out of heavy vegetation.
500m; slopes 500–1650m 21
Ski Safari

Nub's Nob USA
One of the most sheltered Great Lakes ski areas (many suffer fierce winds). 100% snowmaking; weekend crowds from Detroit. Wooded slopes suitable for all abilities.
275m; slopes 275–405m
8 245 acres

O2Resort South Korea
Built up the mountain in Gangwon province and with Korea's best snow. Slopes suit all levels and include a 3.2km long run. Facilities include: condos, youth hostel, fitness centre, spa and restaurants.
1420m 16runs

Oberammergau 378
Village in the Bavarian Alps.
835m

Oberau Austria
Pretty village in the Ski Juwel (Alpbachtal-Wildschönau) area – but least convenient for the slopes. *935m*
Inghams, Neilson

Obereggen 443
Tiny Trentino resort close to Bozen/ Bolzano.

Obergurgl 150

Oberjoch-Hindelang Germany
Small, low-altitude resort, particularly good for beginners.
850m; slopes 1140–1520m
12 32km

Oberlech 137
Car- and crowd-free family resort alternative to Lech.

Oberndorf Austria
Quiet hamlet with beginners' area and a chair connecting it to St Johann's undemanding ski area. *700m*

Oberperfuss Austria
Small village west of Innsbruck, with tall but limited slopes. On the Innsbruck lift pass.
820m; slopes 820–2000m
5 17km

Obersaxen-Mundaun-Lumnezia Switzerland
Several quiet villages above Ilanz, in the Vorderrhein Valley, near Laax. Sizeable area of mainly red and blue runs on four linked mountains. The main lifts are fast chairs.
1300m; slopes 1200–2310m
18 120km

Oberstaufen Germany
Three small areas: Steibis; Thulkirchdorf and Hochgrat. Within an hour of Friedrichschafen.
600m; slopes 860–1880m
30 45km

Oberstdorf 378
Town in the German Alps near the Austrian border.
815m; slopes 800–2220m
31 30km

Obertauern 155

Ochapowace Canada
Main area in Saskatchewan, east of Regina. It doesn't get a huge amount of snow but 75% snowmaking helps.
4 100 acres

Ohau New Zealand
Some of NZ's steepest slopes, with great views of Lake Ohau 9km away (where you stay). 320km south of Christchurch.
1500m; slopes 1425–1825m
3 310 acres

Okemo USA
Worthwhile and nicely varied intermediate area above the old Vermont town of Ludlow. Family oriented, with good child care. Comprehensive snowmaking and highly rated grooming.
345m; slopes 345–1020m
18 624 acres
American Ski Classics

Oppdal Norway
One of the larger Norwegian resorts, but very far north. Many runs are quite short.
715m; slopes 715–1020m
17 60km

Orcières-Merlette France
High, convenient family resort a few km north-east of Gap, Merlette being the ugly, purpose-built ski station above the village of Orcières (1450m). Snow-sure beginner area. Slopes have a good mix of difficulty spread over several mountain flanks, and expanded to open a cable car up to almost 3000m on Roche Brune.
1850m; slopes 1850–2725m
28 100km
Lagrange, Ski Collection, Ski France

Ordino Andorra
Rustic valley village near La Massana, on the way up to Andorra's best snow at Arcalis.

Orelle 368
Village in the Maurienne with access to Val Thorens.

Oropa Italy
Little area just off the Aosta–Turin motorway. An easy change of scene from Courmayeur.
1180m; slopes 1200–2390m
15km

Les Orres France
Friendly modern resort with great views and varied intermediate terrain, but the snow is unreliable, and it's a long transfer from Lyon.
1550m; slopes 1550–2720m
23 62km
Crystal, Lagrange, Ski Collection, Ski France

Orsières Switzerland
Traditional winter resort near Martigny. Close to Grand St Bernard resorts, including Champex-Lac. Well-positioned base from which to visit Verbier and the Chamonix valley. *900m*

Ortisei 432
Market town in Val Gardena.

Oslo Norway
Capital city with cross-country ski trails in its parks. Alpine slopes and lifts in Nordmarka region, just north of city boundaries.

Otre il Colle Italy
Smallest of many little resorts near Bergamo.
1100m; slopes 1100–2000m
7 7km

Ötz Austria
Village at the entrance to the Ötz valley with an easy/ intermediate ski area of its own and access to the Sölden, Kuhtai (sharing a lift pass) and Niederau areas.
820m; slopes 820–2200m
11 34km

Oukaimeden Morocco
Slopes 75km from Marrakech with a surprisingly long season.
2600m; slopes 2600–3260m
7 15km

Ovindoli Italy
One of the smallest areas in L'Aquila region east of Rome, but it has higher slopes than most and one of the better lift systems.
1375m; slopes 1375–2220m
9 10km

Ovronnaz Switzerland
Pretty village set on a sunny shelf above the Rhône valley, with a good pool complex. Limited area but Crans-Montana and Anzère are close.
1350m; slopes 1350–2080m
8 30km

Owl's Head Canada
Steep mountain rising out of a lake, in a remote spot bordering Vermont, away from weekend crowds.
7 90 acres

Oz-en-Oisans 202
Old village with satellite at the lifts into Alpe-d'Huez.

Pajarito Mountain USA
Los Alamos area laid out by nuclear scientists. Atomic slopes too – steep, ungroomed. Open Fridays, weekends and holidays. Fun day out from Taos.
2685m; slopes 2685–3170m
6 220 acres

Pal 90
Prettily wooded mountain linked with slopes of Arinsal.

Palandöken Turkey
Varied skiing area, transformed by three big hotels, overlooking the Anatolian city of Erzurum.
slopes 2150–3100m 4

Pampeago 443
Trentino area convenient for a trip from Milan.

Pamporovo 650

Panarotta Italy
Smallest of the resorts east of Trento. At a higher altitude than nearby Andalo, so worth a day out from there.
1500m; slopes 1500–2000m
6 7km

Panorama Canada
Home to one of North America's biggest verticals (1220m), with something for everyone on its quiet, wooded mountain. Small, purpose-built place at the foot of the slopes and on two levels. The upper 'village' is centred on a hot-pool complex, while the mostly condo accommodation in the lower area. The slopes rise steeply above the resort, but steepest at the top – with genuine blacks and two expert bowls (Taynton and Extreme Dream). Excellent terrain for adventurous intermediates too. More limited for novices. Heli-ski trips are available. There's a big park, pipe and floodlit mini-park. The school is 'very professional' and facilities for families good.
1160m; slopes 1160–2380m
9 2847 acres
American Ski Classics, Canadian Affair, Frontier, Neilson, Ski Independence, Ski Safari, Ski Solutions, Skiworld, Snow Finders

Panticosa Spain
Charming old Pyrenees spa village near Formigal with limited but varied slopes.
1500m; slopes 1500–2220m
16 35km
White Roc

Paradiski 302

Park City 582

Parnassos Greece
Biggest and best-organised area in Greece, 180km from Athens and with surprisingly good slopes and lifts.
slopes 1600–2300m
9 14km

Parpan Switzerland
Pretty village linked to the large intermediate area of Lenzerheide.
1510m; slopes 1230–2865m
35 155km

Partenen Austria
Traditional village in a pretty setting at the end of the Montafon valley. The slopes start at Gaschurn, and there are lots more in the vicinity.
1100m; slopes 700–2300m
25 100km

La Parva Chile
Only 50km east of Santiago and condoville for the capital's elite. A collection of apartments occupied mostly at weekends, linked with Valle Nevado and El Colorado (no area pass).
2750m; slopes 2430–3630m
43 113km

Pas de la Casa 92

Passo Costalunga Italy
Dense network of short lifts either side of the road over a pass, close to Val di Fassa, with links up from Nova Levante.

Passo Lanciano Italy
Closest area to Adriatic. Weekend crowds from nearby Pescara when the snow is good. *1305m; slopes 1305–2000m 13*

Passo Rolle 443
Small group of lifts in Trentino near San Martino di Castrozza.

Passo San Pellegrino Italy
Smallish ski area south of the Sella Ronda, with lifts each side of the pass road and links with the valley village of Falcade.
1920m; slopes 1150–2245m
19 75km

Passo Tonale 416

Pass Thurn 129
Road-side lift base for one of Kitzbühel's ski areas.

Passy-Plaine-Joux France
Small, quiet village 25km from Chamonix. Draglifts serve woody slopes best suited to novices.
1340m 6 12km

Pebble Creek USA
Small area on Utah-Jackson Hole route. Blend of open and wooded slopes.
1920m; slopes 1920–2530m
3 600 acres

Pec Pod Snezku Czech Republic
Collection of hamlets spread along the valley road leading to the main lifts and the very limited ski area.
770m; slopes 710–1190m
10 9km

Peisey 212
Small village linked to Les Arcs.

Peisey-Vallandry 212
Group of villages linked to Les Arcs and Paradiski area.

Pejo 443
Trentino spa resort near Madonna.

Penitentes Argentina
180km from Mendoza. Accommodation at the base.
10 300 hectares

Perelik Bulgaria
Development aiming to link Pamporovo with Mechi Chal.

Perisher / Smiggins Australia
Expanding resort with slopes on seven mountains, which between them offer plenty of short, intermediate runs. 30km from Jindabyne town, six hours from Sydney.
1640m; slopes 1680–2035m
47 3075 acres

Pescasseroli Italy
One of numerous areas east of Rome in L'Aquila region.
1250m; slopes 1250–1945m
6 25km

Pescocostanzo Italy
One of numerous areas east of Rome in L'Aquila region.
1395m; slopes 1395–1900m
4 25km

Pettneu Austria
Snow-sure beginners' resort with an irregular bus link to nearby St Anton.
1250m; slopes 1230–2020m
4 15km

Petzen Austria
One of many little areas in Austria's easternmost ski region near the Slovenian border.
600m; slopes 600–1700m
5 16km

Peyragudes France
Small Pyrenean resort with its ski area starting high above.
1600m; slopes 1600–2400m
17 60km
Lagrange, Ski Collection

Pfelders Italy
Resort near Merano in the South Tyrol covered by the Ortler Skiarena pass.
4 5km

Pfunds Austria
Picturesque valley village with no slopes but quick access to several resorts in Switzerland and Italy, as well as Austria.
970m

Phoenix Park South Korea
Golf complex with 12 trails in winter. Two hours (140km) from Seoul.
slopes 650–1050m 9

Piancavallo Italy
Uninspiring yet curiously trendy purpose-built village, an easy drive from Venice.
1270m; slopes 1270–1830m
17 45km

Piani delle Betulle Italy
One of several little areas near the east coast of Lake Como.
730m; slopes 730–1850m
6 10km

Piani di Artavaggio Italy
Small base complex rather than a village. One of several little areas near Lake Como.
875m; slopes 875–1875m
7 15km

Piani di Bobbio Italy
Largest of several tiny resorts above Lake Como.
770m; slopes 770–1855m
10 20km

Piani di Erna Italy
Small base development – no village. One of several little areas above Lake Como.
600m; slopes 600–1635m
5 9km

Piau-Engaly France
User-friendly St-Lary satellite in one of the best Pyrenean areas.
1850m; slopes 1420–2530m
17 65km Lagrange

Piazzatorre Italy
One of many little areas in the Bergamo region.
870m; slopes 870–2000m
5 25km

Pichl 164
Hamlet outside Schladming.

Pico USA
Low-key little family area (no resort village) close to Killington.
605m; slopes 605–1215m
9 160 acres

Piesendorf Austria
Cheaper, quiet place to stay when visiting Zell am See. Tucked behind Kaprun near Niedernsill.
780m 3 3km

Pievepelago Italy
Much the smallest and most limited of the Apennine ski resorts. Less than two hours from Florence and Pisa.
1115m; slopes 1115–1410m
7 8km

Pila Italy
Modern, purpose-built, car-free resort that's popular with families and school groups and is set above the old Roman town of Aosta – a 15-minute gondola ride away or reached by a 30-minute drive on a winding road. Chairlifts (some fast, most slow) and a cable car fan out to serve a fair-sized and interesting mix of well-groomed, snow-sure slopes. The treeline is high, at about 2300m, and most runs are below it, making this an excellent bad-weather resort. From the top heights there are grand views to Mont Blanc in the west and the Matterhorn in the east. There are runs for all standards, but mostly they are reds. The few blacks, above the treeline at the top of the area, don't amount to much, but there is quite a bit of off-piste. There are two short beginner lifts, but progression to longer runs means using a central run, which when the resort is busy is unpleasant. Like so many other Aosta Valley resorts, Pila is pretty quiet during the week but can be hectic at

weekends – and it does attract lots of British school groups.
1800m; slopes 1550–2740m
14 70km
Crystal, Interski, Pilaski, Ski Supreme, Ski Yogi, Thomson

Pinzolo 407
Trentino resort near Madonna.

Pitztal Austria
Long valley with good glacier area at its head, accessed by underground funicular.
1680m; slopes 880–3440m
12 68km Zenith

Pla-d'Adet France
Limited purpose-built complex at the foot of the St-Lary ski area (the original village is further down the mountain).
1680m; slopes 1420–2450m
32 80km Lagrange

La Plagne 304

Plan de Corones Italy
Distinctive ski area in South Tyrol, with amazingly efficient lifts from Brunico and San Vigilio di Marebbe. Better known by its German name, Kronplatz.
1200m; slopes 1200–2275m
32 103km

Plan-Peisey 212
Small development with link to Les Arcs.

Plose Italy
Varied area close to Bressanone, with the longest run in the South Tyrol.
560m; slopes 1065–2500m
11 40km

Poiana Brasov 653
Cheap, informal resort in Romania.
1020m; slopes 1020–1775m
9 14km

Pomerelle USA
Small area in Idaho on the Utah–Sun Valley route.
2430m; slopes 2430–2735m
3 300 acres

Pontechianale Italy
Highest, largest area in a remote region south-west of Turin. Day-tripper place.
1600m; slopes 1600–2760m
8 30km

Ponte di Legno 416
Attractive sheltered alternative to Passo Tonale.

Pontresina Switzerland
Small, sedate, sunny village with one main street, rather spoiled by the sanatorium-style architecture. All downhill skiing involves travel by car or bus, except the single long piste on Pontresina's own hill, Languard. It's cheaper to stay here than St Moritz.
1805m; slopes 1730–3305m
54 350km

Port-Ainé Spain
Small but high intermediate area in the Spanish Pyrenees near Andorra. Lifts include a six-pack; eponymous 3-star hotel at base.
1975m; slopes 1650–2440m
8 44km

Port del Comte Spain
High resort in the forested region of Lleida, north-west of Barcelona. The slopes spread across three linked sectors: El Sucre, El Hostal and El Estivella.
slopes 1700–2400m
15 40km

Porté Puymorens France
Little-known Pyrenean area close to Pas de la Casa in Andorra.
slopes 1600–2470m
12 45km

Porter Heights New Zealand
Closest skiing to Christchurch (one hour). Open, sunny bowl offering mostly intermediate skiing – with back bowls for powder.
1340m; slopes 1340–1950m
5 200 acres

Portes du Soleil 315

Portillo Chile
Luxury hotel 150km north-east of Santiago. Quiet snow-sure slopes used for training by US national ski team. Suits experts best.
2850m; slopes 2450–3310m
13 1200 acres
Crystal, Momentum, Scott Dunn, Skiworld

Powderhorn USA
Area in west Colorado perched on the world's highest flat-top mountain, Grand Mesa. Sensational views. Day trip from Aspen.
2490m; slopes 2490–2975m
4 300 acres

Powder King Canada
Remote resort in British Columbia, between Prince George and Dawson City. As its name suggests, it has great powder. Plenty of lodging.
880m; slopes 880–1520m
3 160 acres

Powder Mountain USA
Massive Utah area sprawled over six ridges, an hour and a quarter's drive from Salt Lake City. An ample 2,800 acres of its terrain is lift served, a mix of mainly north-facing slopes with enough green, blue and black runs to satisfy all abilities. You access the rest by snowcat or snowmobile tow, buses and hiking. It is the abundance of intermediate freeride terrain that makes it special. You can also stay in Ogden, 32km away.
2100m; slopes 2100–2740m
7 7000 acres

Pozza di Fassa 447
Pretty village in Val di Fassa.

Pragelato Italy
Inexpensive base, linked by cable car to Sestriere. Its own area is worth a try for half a day.
1535m; slopes 1535–2700m
6 50km
White Roc

Prägraten am Grossvenediger Austria
Traditional mountaineering/ski touring village in lovely setting south of Felbertauern tunnel. The Alpine ski slopes of Matrei are nearby.
1310m; slopes 1310–1490m
2 30km

Prali Italy
Tiny resort east of Sestriere – a worthwhile half-day trip.
1450m; slopes 1450–2500m
7 25km

Pralognan-la-Vanoise France
Unspoiled traditional village overlooked by spectacular peaks. Champagny (La Plagne) and Courchevel are close by.
1410m; slopes 1410–2355m
14 30km
Erna Low, Lagrange, Ski France

Pra-Loup France
Convenient, purpose-built family resort with an extensive, varied intermediate area linked to La Foux-d'Allos (Val d'Allos region).
1500m; slopes 1500–2600m
51 180km
Lagrange, Ski Collection, Ski France

Prati di Tivo Italy
Weekend day-trip place east of Rome and near the town of Teramo. A sizeable resort by southern Italy standards.
1450m; slopes 1450–1800m
6 16km

Prato Nevoso Italy
Purpose-built resort with rather bland slopes. Part of Mondolé ski area with Artesina.
1500m; slopes 1500–1950m
25 90km
Thomson

Prato Selva Italy
Tiny base development (no village) east of Rome near Teramo. Weekend day-trip place.
1370m; slopes 1370–1800m
4 10km

Le Praz 242
Lowest of the Courchevel resorts.

Les Praz 227
Quiet hamlet near Chamonix.

Praz-de-Lys France
Little-known snow-pocket area near Lake Geneva that can have good snow when nearby resorts (eg La Clusaz) do not.
1450m; slopes 1240–1965m
23 60km
Pierre & Vacances

Praz-sur-Arly France
Traditional village in a pretty, wooded setting just down the road from Megève. Sharing slopes with Notre Dame de Bellecombe and beyond to Crest Voland / Les Saises, to form the Espace Diamant.
1035m; slopes 1035–2070m
84 175km
Ski France

Predazzo Italy
Small, quiet place between Cavalese and the Sella Ronda resorts, with lift into modest area of slopes above Obereggen.
1015m; slopes 995–2205m
8 17km

Premanon France
One of four resorts that make up Les Rousses area in Jura region.
1050m; slopes 1120–1680m
40 Lagrange

La Presolana Italy
Large summer resort near Bergamo. Several other little areas nearby.
1250m; slopes 1250–1650m
6 15km

Les Prodains 222
Village at the foot of the cliffs on which Avoriaz sits.

Pucón Chile
Ski area on the side of the active Villarrica volcano in southern Chile, 800km south of Santiago. Lodgings are at Pucón village, 30 minutes away from the slopes.
1200m; slopes 1200–2440m
9 20runs

Puigmal France
Resort in the French Pyrenees with accommodation in nearby villages.
1830m; slopes 1830–2700m
12 34km

Puy-St-Vincent 316

Pyhä Finland
Expanding resort 150km north-east of Rovaniemi. Much of the area is in a National Park, with the 14 slopes on two sides of a part-wooded hill. Vertical is only 280m and there's no steep terrain but good off-piste. The best powder runs are on both sides of a long T-bar on the north side. Most pistes open for floodlit skiing. There's a well-developed terrain park, hosting regular competitions.
220m 8 Skiworld

The Pyrenees 318

Pyrenees 2000 France
Tiny resort built in a pleasing manner. Shares a pretty area of short runs with Font-Romeu. Impressive snowmaking.
2000m; slopes 1750–2250m
32 52km

Québec City Canada
French-speaking capital and old city with a number of ski areas a short drive away.
AmeriCan Ski, Crystal

Queenstown New Zealand
South Island's outdoor adventure capital, in a stunning lakeside setting. Two local resorts: the Remarkables and Coronet Peak. Treble Cone and Cardrona are easily reached by car. Typically commercialized but lively and relaxed, and where most people stay. The slopes are a 30-40 minute drive away. The Remarkables appeals mainly to families and beginners, while Coronet Peak is more satisfying to intermediates. Both resorts have challenges for experts too.
310m; slopes 1230–1945m
8 280 hectares

Radium Hot Springs Canada
Summer resort offering an alternative to the purpose-built slope-side resort of Panorama.
slopes 975–2155m
8 300 acres

Radstadt Austria
Unspoiled medieval town near Schladming, with its own small area and the Salzburger Sportwelt slopes accessed from nearby Zauchensee or Flachau.
855m; slopes 855–2185m
100 350km

Ragged Mountain USA
Family-owned ski area in New Hampshire.
9 200 acres

Rainbow New Zealand
Northernmost ski area on South Island. Wide, treeless area, best for beginners and intermediates. Accommodation at St Arnaud.
1440m; slopes 1440–1760m
5 865 acres

Ramsau am Dachstein Austria
Charming village overlooked by the Dachstein glacier. Renowned for cross-country, it also has Alpine slopes locally, on the glacier and at Schladming.
1200m; slopes 1100–2700m
18 30km

Ramundberget Sweden
Small, quiet, ski-in/ski-out family resort with very limited pistes but lots of cross-country. 22km

Rasos de Peguera Spain
The only resort in the Barcelona province. 14km from Berga. Ten pistes, mostly red classified.

Rauris Austria
Small village in a quiet, dead-end valley south-east of Zell, about 25km by road. Across the valley road from the village are nursery draglifts and a gondola accessing intermediate slopes with a vertical of 1250m.
950m; slopes 950–2200m
9 30km
Crystal, Neilson, Thomson

Ravascletto Italy
Resort in a pretty wooded setting near Austrian border, with most of its terrain high above on an open plateau.
920m; slopes 920–1735m
12 40km

Reallon France
Traditional-style village, with splendid views from above Lac de Serre-Ponçon.
1560m; slopes 1560–2115m
6 20km

Red Lodge USA
Picturesque Old West Montana town. Ideal for a combined trip with Big Sky or Jackson Hole.
1800m; slopes 2155–2860m
8 1600 acres

Red Mountain Canada
Up there with the likes of Fernie as a cult resort for expert skiers who can handle its steep terrain, wide glades and powder-filled bowls. While not big in European terms, it packs a lot of tough stuff into its two mountains. If that's your scene, get there quickly as the ski area has been developing. But it's still the black and double-black stuff that is the real attraction; it's marked on the map, but not on the mountain – so a guide may be necessary to explore it fully. There are long-term plans for a proper resort village at the base, but the small old mining town of Rossland is just 3km away.
1185m; slopes 1185–2075m
6 1685 acres
AmeriCan Ski, Frontier, Ski Independence, Ski Safari

Red River USA
New Mexico western town – complete with stetsons and saloons – with intermediate slopes above.
2665m; slopes 2665–3155m
7 290 acres

Reichenfels Austria
One of many small areas in Austria's easternmost ski region near the Slovenian border.
810m; slopes 810–1400m

Reinwald Italy
Resort near Merano in the South Tyrol covered by the Ortler Skiarena pass.

Reith im Alpbachtal **107**
Village in Ski Juwel (Alpbachtal-Wildschönau).

Reit im Winkl Germany
Southern Bavarian resort, straddling the German–Austrian border. Winklmoos ski area is best suited to intermediates.
750m; slopes 750–1800m
7 40km

The Remarkables New Zealand
Three bleak basins with great views of 'remarkable' jagged alps, 45 minutes from Queenstown. Popular with families and beginners, but some tougher terrain too. Big terrain park.
1580m; slopes 1580–1945m
6 545 acres

Rencurel-les-Coulumes France
One of seven little resorts just west of Grenoble. Unspoiled, inexpensive place to tour. Villard-de-Lans is the main resort.

Reschenpass Austria
Area in the Tirol right on the Swiss border; includes Schöneben and Haider Alm in Italy. Nauders is the main resort.
1520m 7 28

Rettenberg Germany
Small resort near Austrian border.
750m; slopes 820–1650m
15 40km

Reutte Austria
500-year-old market town with many traditional hotels, and rail links to nearby Lermoos.
855m; slopes 855–1900m
9 19km

Revelstoke **627**

Rhêmes Notre Dame Italy
Unspoiled village in the beautiful Rhêmes valley, south of Aosta. Courmayeur and La Thuile within reach. Handful of hotels and tiny amount of downhill – including two black runs.
1725m; slopes 1625–3605m
4 5km

Riederalp Switzerland
Pretty, car-free village high above the Rhône valley near Brig; part of the Aletsch Arena. Cable car or gondola from the valley village of Mörel. Quiet, friendly, uncrowded slopes.
1925m; slopes 1050–2870m
35 100km

Riefensberg **192**
Village in Bregenzerwald.
780m 14km

Rigi-Kaltbad Switzerland
Resort on a mountain rising out of Lake Lucerne, with superb all-round views, accessed by the world's first mountain railroad.
1440m; slopes 1195–1795m
4 9km

Riihivuori Finland
Small area with 'base' at the top of the mountain. 20km south of the city of Jyväskylä.
5

Riksgränsen Sweden
Unique Arctic Circle Alpine area not open until late February. You can use the slopes under the midnight sun (lift-served) from mid-May to June. 20 hours by train from Stockholm.
600m; slopes 600–910m
6 21km

Riscone Italy
Dolomite village sharing a pretty area with San Vigilio. Good snowmaking. Short easy runs.
1200m; slopes 1200–2275m
35 40km

Rittner Horn Italy
Resort near Merano in the South Tyrol covered by the Ortler Skiarena pass.
3 15km

Rivisondoli Italy
Sizeable mountain retreat east of Rome, with one of the better lift systems in the vicinity.
1350m; slopes 1350–2050m
7 16km

Roccaraso Italy
Largest of the resorts east of Rome – at least when snow-cover is complete.
1280m; slopes 1280–2200m
12 56km

Rohrmoos **164**
Suburb of Schladming, with vast area of nursery slopes.

La Rosière **321**

Rossland Canada
Remote little town 5km from cult powder paradise Red Mountain.

Rougemont Switzerland
Cute rustic hamlet just over the French/German language border near Gstaad, with local slopes and links to Gstaad's Eggli sector.
990m; slopes 950–3000m
58 250km

Les Rousses France
Group of four villages – Les Rousses, Premanon, Lamoura and Bois d'Amont – in the Jura mountains, 50km from Geneva airport.
1120m; slopes 1120–1680m
40 40km
Lagrange

Ruka Finland
80km south of the Arctic Circle, close to Kuusamo airport and the Russian border, in a region known for abundant and enduring snow. Lively, upbeat resort with a newly developed pedestrian village. Good but widely spread cabin lodging served by the ski bus. Slopes on two sides of a single low hill, with a mix of open and forest terrain, most floodlit and with snowmaking. None is particularly steep and the vertical very modest – but there is a new FIS racing piste. There's a terrain park and boardercross course. The cross-country scope is vast: 500km, of which 40km are floodlit.
200m *20* *20km*
Crystal, Crystal Finest, Skiworld, Thomson

Russbach Austria
Secluded village tucked up a side valley and linked into the Gosau-Annaberg Lungotz area. The slopes are spread over a wide area.
815m; slopes 780–1620m
33 *65km*

Rusutsu 658
Resort on Hokkaido, Japan.

Saalbach-Hinterglemm 158

Saalfelden Austria
Town ideally placed for touring eastern Tirol. Lift networks of Maria-Alm and Saalbach are nearby.
745m; slopes 745–1550m
3 *3km*

Saanen Switzerland
Cheaper and more convenient alternative to staying in Gstaad – but much less going on.
slopes 950–3000m
58 *250km*

Saanenmöser Switzerland
Small village with rail/road links to Gstaad. Scenic and quiet local slopes, with good mountain restaurants.
1270m; slopes 950–3000m
58 *250km*

Saas-Almagell Switzerland
Compact village up the valley from Saas-Grund, with good cross-country trails and walks, and a limited Alpine area.
1670m; slopes 1670–2400m
7 *12km*

Saas-Fee 486

Saas-Grund Switzerland
Sprawling valley village below Saas-Fee, with a separate small but high Alpine area.
1560m; slopes 1560–3200m
8 *35km*

Saddleback USA
Small area between Maine's premier resorts. High slopes by local standards.
695m; slopes 695–1255m
5 *100 acres*

Sahoro Japan
Ugly, purpose-built complex on snowy northern Hokkaido island, with a limited area.
610m; slopes 610–1030m
8 *15km* *Club Med*

Les Saisies France
Traditional-style cross-country venue, surrounded by varied four-mountain Alpine slopes. Now part of Espace Diamant. Easy runs, but some lift queues at peak times.
1650m; slopes 1035–2070m
84 *175km*
AmeriCan Ski, Classic Ski, Erna Low, Lagrange, Peak Retreats, PowderBeds, Ski Collection, Ski France, Ski Independence

Sälen Sweden
Well-developed family resort with extensive lift system, and some good off-piste for experts.
550m; slopes 550–950m
101 *144km*

Salt Lake City USA
Underrated base from which to ski Utah. 30 minutes from Park City, Deer Valley, The Canyons, Snowbird, Alta, Snowbasin. Cheaper and livelier than the resorts.
AmeriCan Ski, Crystal

Salzburg-Stadt Austria
A single, long challenging run off the back of Salzburg's local mountain, accessed by a spectacular lift-ride from a suburb of Grodig. *425m*

Samedan Switzerland
Valley town, just down the road from St Moritz. A run heads back to base from Corviglia-Marguns.
1720m; slopes 1730–3305m
54 *350km*

Samnaun 122
Shares large ski area with Ischgl.

Samoëns 325

San Bernardino Switzerland
Pretty resort south of the road tunnel, close to Madesimo.
1625m; slopes 1600–2525m
8 *35km*

San Candido Italy
Resort on the border with Austria on the road to Lienz. Innichen is its German name.
1175m; slopes 1175–1580m
4 *15km*

San Carlos de Bariloche Argentina
Year-round resort, with five areas nearby and the place to stay when skiing Cerro Catedral – 20 minutes away by bus. Once a quaint lakeside town, but now a substantial resort.
slopes 1030–2180m
39 *103km*

San Cassiano 423

Sandia Peak USA
The world's longest lift ride ascends from Albuquerque. Mostly gentle slopes; children ski free.
slopes 2645–3165m
7 *100 acres*

San Grée di Viola Italy
Easternmost of resorts south of Turin, surprisingly close to the Italian Riviera.
1100m; slopes 1100–1800m
30km

San Martin de los Andes Argentina
Sizeable town with accommodation, 19 km from the Chapelco ski area.

San Martino di Castrozza 443
Trentino village south of Val di Fassa.

Sansicario 418
Small, stylish resort in the Milky Way near Sauze d'Oulx.

San Simone Italy
Tiny development north of Bergamo, close to unappealing Foppolo area.
2000m; slopes 1105–2300m
9 *45km*

Santa Caterina Italy
Pretty, user-friendly village near Bormio, with a snow-sure novice and intermediate area.
1740m; slopes 1740–2725m
8 *25km*

Santa Cristina 432
Quiet village in Val Gardena.

Santa Fe USA
Interesting area only 15 miles from beautiful Santa Fe town. A tree-filled bowl with a good variety of terrain crammed into its small area. Ideal stopover en route from Albuquerque airport to Taos.
3145m; slopes 3155–3680m
7 *550 acres*

Santa Maria Maggiore Italy
Resort south of the Simplon Pass from the Rhône valley, and near Lake Maggiore.
820m; slopes 820–1890m
5 *10km*

San Vigilio di Marebbe / Kronplatz Italy
Pretty village in South Tyrol with lifts on two mountains, one being the quite impressive Plan de Corones / Kronplatz.
1200m; slopes 1200–2275m
32 *114km*

San Vito di Cadore Italy
Sizeable, alternative place to stay to Cortina. Negligible local slopes, though.
1010m; slopes 1010–1380m
9 *12km*

Sappada Italy
Isolated resort close to the Austrian border below Lienz.
1215m; slopes 1215–2050m
17 *21km*

Sappee Finland
Resort within easy reach of Helsinki, popular with boarders and telemarkers. Lake views. 7

Sarnano Italy
Main resort in the Macerata region near Adriatic Riviera. Valley village with ski slopes accessed by lift.
540m *9* *11km*

Le Sauze France
Fine area near Barcelonnette, sadly remote from airports.
1400m; slopes 1400–2440m
23 *65km*

Sauze d'Oulx 418

Savognin Switzerland
Pretty village with a good mid-sized area; a good base for the nearby resorts of St Moritz, Davos/Klosters and Laax.
1200m; slopes 1200–2715m
10 *80km*
Crystal

Scheffau 114
Rustic village not far from Söll.

Schia Italy
Very limited area of short runs – the only ski area near Parma. No village.
1245m; slopes 1245–1415m
7 *15km*

Schilpario Italy
One of many little areas near Bergamo.
1125m; slopes 1125–1635m
5 *15km*

Schladming 164

Schnalstal Italy
Valley and high ski area, in the Dolomites near Merano. Val Senales is its Italian name.
3210m; slopes 2110–3210m
12 *35km*

Schöneben Italy
Area in the Val Venosta in the South Tyrol, close to Austrian border and Nauders.
1520m *7* *28km*

Schönried Switzerland
A cheaper and quieter resort alternative to staying in Gstaad.
1230m; slopes 950–3000m
58 *250km*

Schoppernau 192
Village in Bregenzerwald.
860m; slopes 860–2060m
8 *44km*

Schröcken 192
Bregenzerwald village near Lech.
1260m; slopes 1260–2100m
15 *66km*

Schruns Austria
Pleasant little working valley town with a car-free centre at the heart of the Montafon region, with access to both the Hochjoch area (see St Gallenkirch) from a cable car near the centre of town and the Golm ski area (a few km away). At Golm four chairs and a drag serve easy blue and red slopes above the trees. A six-pack goes to the top of the area, linked via a ski tunnel to slopes on the back of the hill, including the Diabolo black run (the steepest in the valley). Snowmaking covers many of the upper slopes and the run to the valley. Ernest Hemingway ensconced himself in Schruns in 1925/26, and his favourite drinking table in the hotel Taube can be admired. Après-ski is not the big deal it is in many Austrian resorts, but a few places get quite lively.
700m; slopes 655–2395m
61 219km

Schüttdorf Austria
Ordinary dormitory satellite of Zell am See, with easy access to the shared ski area. Kids' area at the base.
755m; slopes 755–3030m
53 138km

Schwarzach im Pongau
Austria
Riverside village with rail links. There are limited slopes at Goldegg; Wagrain (Salzburger Sportwelt) and Grossarl (Gastein valley) are also nearby.
600m 4 12km

Schwarzenberg **192**
Village in Bregenzerwald.
700m; slopes 1145–1465m
9 24km

Schwaz Austria
Valley town beside the Inn with a lift into varied terrain shared with the village of Pill and its mountain outpost, Hochpillberg.
540m; slopes 540–2030m
6 10km

Schweitzer USA
Excellent family-friendly resort in northern Idaho, 85 miles from Spokane (Washington state) and 45 miles from Canada.
1220m; slopes 1229–1950m
10 2900 acres

Schwemmalm Italy
Resort near Merano in the South Tyrol covered by the Ortler Skiarena pass.
5 18km

Scopello Italy
Low area close to the Aosta valley, worth considering for a day trip in bad weather.
slopes 690–1700m
6 35km

Scuol Switzerland
Year-round spa resort close to Austria and Italy, with an impressive range of terrain.
1225m; slopes 1225–2780m
15 80km

Searchmont Resort Canada
Ontario area with modern lift system and 95% snowmaking. Fine Lake Superior views.
275m; slopes 275–485m
4 65 acres

Sedrun Switzerland
Sizeable roadside village east of the Oberalp Pass, and covered along with Andermatt by the Gotthard Oberalp lift pass. The most extensive piste skiing in the area. There's a good choice of red runs, a rewarding black and a 'freeride' route, plus plenty of scope for off-piste. At Milez there's a terrain park and family restaurant area. .
1450m; slopes 1450–2350m
10 50km

Seefeld Austria
Classic winter holiday resort, well designed in traditional Tirolean style, with a large pedestrian-only centre and lots of upmarket hotels (including three 5-stars). Lots of people come here to enjoy the superb cross-country trails and off-slope activities rather than the downhill skiing, but there are two main downhill sectors on the outskirts – Gschwandtkopf and Rosshütte – the latter served mostly by fast lifts. Both areas have intermediate runs of decent vertical; Rosshütte is more extensive, with a cable car across to the separate peak of Härmelekopf, and some worthwhile challenges for experts. There's a good long red run back to village level and a gentle nursery area too. But overall the terrain is far too limited to keep most folk entertained for a week's stay. You can always make excursions to Innsbruck, not far away and easily reached by train, or to the Stubai and Zugspitze glaciers.
1200m; slopes 1200–2100m
31 48km
Crystal, Inghams, Momentum, Neilson, Thomson

See im Paznaun Austria
Small family-friendly area in the Paznaun Valley, near Ischgl, with rustic old village set quietly 100m above the valley floor and main road.
1050m; slopes 1050–2300m
8 33km

Le Seignus-d'Allos France
Close to La Foux-d'Allos (which shares large area with Pra-Loup) and has own little area, too.
1400m; slopes 1400–2425m
13 47km

Seis Italy
German name for Siusi.

Sella Nevea Italy
Limited but developing resort in a beautiful setting on the Slovenian border, and now linked to Bovec-Kanin. Summer glacier nearby.
1140m; slopes 1190–2300m
12 30km

Sella Ronda **423**

Selva / Val Gardena **432**

Selvino Italy
Closest resort to Bergamo.
960m; slopes 960–1400m
9 20km

Selwyn Snowfields Australia
Popular with beginners and families. 6 hours from Sydney. Good lift system and cheaper passes than major Oz resorts.
1520m; slopes 1490–1615m
10 111 acres

Semmering Austria
Long-established winter sports resort set in pretty scenery, 100km from Vienna, towards Graz. Mostly intermediate terrain.
1000m; slopes 1000–1340m
5 14km

Semnoz France
Small, family and beginner focused resort above Lake Annecy with views of the lake and Mont Blanc.
1705m 11 18

Les Sept-Laux France
Improving family resort near Grenoble. Modern lift system – 90% of lifts having been replaced in recent years.
1350m; slopes 1350–2400m
21 120km
Zenith

Serfaus Austria
Virtually unknown in the UK, but it is a charming village of chalet-style buildings set on a sunny shelf and kept largely traffic-free by an underground railway to the lifts. Most of the accommodation is in hotels, frequented by well-heeled German families. It shares with Fiss and Ladis a broad area of high slopes, with long runs spanning several ridges – well-suited to mixed-ability parties and especially good for families. The vast kids' facilities at mid-mountain level and ample nursery slopes are key attraction. A lack of English speakers may be a drawback though.
1430m; slopes 1200–2800m
70 190km
Crystal, Crystal Finest, Ski Bespoke

Serrada Italy
Very limited area near Trento.
slopes 1250–1605m 5

Serre-Chevalier **327**

Sesto Italy
Dolomite village off the Alta Val Pusteria, surrounded by pretty little areas. Sexten is its German name.
1310m; slopes 1130–2200m
31 50km

Sestola Italy
Apennine village a short drive from Pisa and Florence with its pistes, some way above, almost completely equipped with snowmakers.
900m; slopes 1280–1975m
23 50km

Sestriere **439**

Seven Springs Mountain USA
Pennsylvania's largest resort.
slopes 220–2995m
18 494 acres

Sexten Italy
Dolomite village off the Hochpustertal, surrounded by pretty little areas. Sesto is its Italian name.
1310m; slopes 1130–2200m
31 50km

Shames Mountain Canada
Remote spot inland from coastal town of Prince Rupert and with impressive snowfall record. Deep powder.
670m; slopes 670–1195m
3 183 acres

Shawnee Peak USA
Small area near Bethel and Sunday River renowned for its night skiing. Spectacular views. Mostly groomed cruising.
185m; slopes 185–580m
5 225 acres

Shemshak Iran
Most popular of the three mountain resorts within easy reach of Tehran (60km).
3600m; slopes 2550–3050m 7

Shiga Kogen **658**
Largest area in Japan.

Showdown USA
Intermediate area in Montana forest north of Bozeman. 50km to the nearest hotel.
2065m; slopes 2065–2490m
4 640 acres

Sierra-at-Tahoe USA
A Colorado-style resort, with runs cut on densely wooded slopes. It claims an impressive average of 420 inches of snow. The slopes are spread over two flanks of Huckleberry Mountain. The fronts of both offer good intermediate cruising plus some genuine single-diamond blacks. The backside of Huckleberry has easier blue and green slopes. This is a natural day trip for those staying in South Lake Tahoe.
2210m; slopes 2025–2700m
14 2000 acres

Sierra Nevada **643**

Sierra Summit USA
Sierra Nevada area accessible only from the west. 100% snowmaking.
2160m; slopes 2160–2645m
8 250 acres

Silbertal Austria
Low secluded village in the Montafon valley, linked to Schruns. A good base for touring numerous areas.
890m; slopes 700–1450m
3 6km

Sillian Austria
A gondola and two fast quads serve this varied area in Austria's Hochpustertal region.
1100m 6 45km

Sils Maria 491
Lakeside village linked to the St Moritz Corvatsch slopes.

Silvaplana 491
Pretty village near St Moritz.

Silver Mountain USA
Northern Idaho area near delightful resort town of Coeur d'Alene. Best for experts, but plenty for intermediates too.
1215m; slopes 1215–1915m
6 1500 acres

Silver Star 629

Silverthorne USA
Factory outlet town on main road close to Keystone and Breckenridge. Good budget base for skiing those resorts plus Vail and Beaver Creek.
AmeriCan Ski

Silverton USA
Expert-only area in southern Colorado that used to be heli-ski country. Served by one lift. Avalanche transceiver, shovel and probe compulsory.
3170m; slopes 3170–3750m 1

Sinaia Romania
Dreary main-road town with a modest, open area of slopes. Recent investment in new lifts, included a gondola.
795m; slopes 795–2030m
10 20km
Mountain Tracks

Sipapu USA
Great little New Mexico area, with mostly treelined runs. Snow unreliable, but 70% snowmaking. Nice day out from Taos when conditions are good.
slopes 2500–2765m
4 70 acres

Siusi 432
Village west of the Sella Ronda circuit; Seis in German.

Siviez 502
A quieter, cheaper base for Verbier's Four Valleys circuit.

Sixt-Fer-a-Cheval 258
Village near Samoëns.

Sjusjøen Norway
Cluster of hotels in deep forest close to Lillehammer. Some Alpine facilities but better for cross-country.
885m; slopes 1000–1090m
2 2km
Exodus, Inntravel

Ski Apache USA
Apache-owned area south of Albuquerque noted for groomed steeps. Panoramic views. Nearest lodging in charming Ruidoso.
2925m; slopes 2925–3505m
11 750 acres

Ski Cooper USA
Small area close to historic Old West town of Leadville. Good ski/sightseeing day out from nearby Vail, Beaver Creek and Copper Mountain.
slopes 3200–3565m 4

Ski Juwel 107

Ski Windham USA
Two hours from New York City and second only to Hunter for weekend crowds. Decent slopes by eastern standards.
485m; slopes 485–940m
7 230 acres

Smugglers' Notch USA
French-style purpose-built family resort with sympathetic instructors, comprehensive childcare, child-friendly layout and long, quiet, easy runs. There are varied and satisfying slopes, spread over three hills, with a worthwhile vertical of 800m. It's a great area for beginners, but mileage-hungry intermediates should go elsewhere. Snowboarding is encouraged, and there are three impressive terrain parks and an Olympic-size super-pipe.
315m; slopes 315–1110m
8 1000 acres

Snowbasin USA
Underrated hill, usually with very good snow. No base village, but a worthwhile day out from Park City. The crowd-free slopes cover a lot of pleasantly varied terrain. This is a great mountain for experts – the Grizzly Downhill course drops 885m and is already claimed to be a modern classic. Between the race course and the area boundary is a splendid area of off-piste wooded glades and gullies. Middle Bowl is great terrain for the adventurous, with a complex network of blues and blacks. You have to stay in the town of Ogden on the Salt Lake plain in the backwater of Huntsville.
1965m; slopes 1965–2850m
11 3000 acres

Snowbird 587

Snowbowl (Arizona) USA
One of America's oldest areas, near Flagstaff, Arizona, atop an extinct volcano and with stunning desert views. Good snowfall record.
2805m; slopes 2805–3505m
5 135 acres

Snowbowl (Montana) USA
Montana area renowned for powder, outside lively town of Missoula. Intermediate pistes plus 700 acres of extreme slopes. Grizzly Chute is the ultimate challenge.
1520m; slopes 1520–2315m
4 1400 acres

Snowmass 562

Snow Park New Zealand
Dedicated terrain park across the valley from Cardrona. Features galore, including new 7m pipes. Budget lodging at the base. *1530m 1*

Snow Summit USA
San Bernardino National Forest ski area near Palm Springs. Lovely lake views. 100% snowmaking. High-capacity lift system for weekend crowds.
2135m; slopes 2135–2500m
12 230 acres

Snow Valley USA
Area quite near Palm Springs. Fine desert views. High-capacity lift system copes with weekend crowds better than nearby Big Bear.
2040m; slopes 2040–2390m
11 230 acres

Sochi Russia
Host of the 2014 Winter Olympic Games. Three developing areas: Gasprom, Rosa Khutor and Mountain Carousel. *520m 19 100km*
Crystal

Solda Italy
The other side of the Stelvio Pass from Bormio. Very long airport transfers. Sulden is German name.
1905m; slopes 1905–2625m
10 40km

Sölden 168

Soldeu 92

Soldier Mountain USA
Family resort in Central Idaho; backcountry snowcat tours.
slopes 1770–2195m
4 670 acres

Solitude USA
Smart, car-free mini-village linked with Brighton in the valley next to Alta and Snowbird. Most (not all) of the slopes are easy or intermediate, including a wide area served by the one fast quad. When open, the top lift accesses lots of steeps in Honeycomb Canyon, on the back of the hill, with a short quad to bring you back to the front face. Headwall Forest and Eagle Ridge also have good blacks. The resorts' boundaries are open, and there are good backcountry adventures to be had.
2490m; slopes 2435–3200m
13 2250 acres
American Ski Classics, Ski Safari

Söll 173

Solvista USA
Child-oriented resort close to Winter Park. Low snowfall record for Colorado.
2490m; slopes 2490–2795m
5 250 acres

Sommand France
Purpose-built base that shares area with Praz-de-Lys.
1420m; slopes 1200–1800m
22 50km

Sonnenkopf 195
Ski area above Klösterle in the Alpenregion Bludenz

Sorenberg Switzerland
Popular weekend retreat between Berne and Lucerne, with a high proportion of steep, low runs.
1165m; slopes 1165–2280m
16 50km

South Lake Tahoe USA
Tacky base for skiing Heavenly, with cheap lodging, traffic and gambling.

Spindleruv Mlyn
Czech Republic
Largest Giant Mountains region resort but with few facilities serving several little low areas.
715m; slopes 750–1310m
16 25km

Spital am Pyhrn Austria
Small village near Hinterstoder in Upper Austria, a bus ride from its limited intermediate slopes at Wurzeralm.
650m; slopes 810–1870m
8 20km

Spittal an der Drau Austria
Historic Carinthian town with a limited area at Goldeck starting a lift-ride above it. A good day trip from Bad Kleinkirchheim or from Slovenia.
555m; slopes 1650–2140m
8 30km

Spitzingsee Germany
Beautiful small lake (and village) an hour from Munich.
18 25km

Splugen Reinwald Switzerland
Small intermediate area south of Chur.
1485m; slopes 1455–2215m
6 30km

Sportgastein 111
Remote, high ski area at the top of the Badgastein valley.

Squaw Valley 545

Stafal 412
Isolated village with access to the Monterosa Ski area.

St Andra Austria
Valley-junction village ideally placed for one of the longest, most snow-sure cross-country networks in Europe. Close to the Tauern pass and to St Michael. *1045m*

St Anton 180

Starhill Resort South Korea
Purpose-built resort formerly called Cheonmasan, 30km north-east of Seoul. 8

Stari Vrh Slovenia
About 30 minutes from Ljubljana airport. Runs include a never-groomed black, three interesting reds and a winding blue virtually from top to bottom. *slopes 580–1200m*
5 12km

Stary Smokovec Slovakia
Spa town in the High Tatras mountains, with three small areas – Tatransky Lomica is the biggest. Funicular railway and snowmaking facilities.
1480m; slopes 1000–1500m
8 4km

St Cergue Switzerland
Limited resort in the Jura mountains, less than an hour from Geneva and good for families with young children.
1045m; slopes 1045–1680m
16 21km

St Christoph 180
Small village on Arlberg pass above St Anton.

St-Colomban-des-Villards France
Small resort in next side valley to La Toussuire. Series of drags link to the rest of the area, with a pretty run to return. *1100m*

Steamboat USA
A few miles from the old cattle town of Steamboat Springs, and famed for its powder snow. Huge investment continues to equip the slope-side base with modern lodging, shops and restaurants. The slopes are compact but varied, with pretty treelined runs rising to 3220m; many of them are ideal for novices. Fast chairs serve each area. The main attraction for experts is the glades, but also the steep chutes and bowls on the backside of the area. Much of the mountain is ideal cruising terrain, although there is limited vertical to be achieved. The nursery slopes at the base are excellent, revamped recently. And family facilities are splendid. Steamboat town has countless hotels, condos and restaurants.
2105m; slopes 2105–3220m
18 2965 acres
Alpine Answers, American Ski Classics, Crystal, Crystal Finest, Erna Low, Independent Ski Links, Momentum, Ski Bespoke, Ski Independence, Ski Line, Ski Safari, Skitracer, Skiworld, Supertravel, Thomson

Ste-Foy-Tarentaise 337

Steinach Austria
Pleasant market town with small area of slopes in picturesque surroundings, just off the autobahn up to the Brenner Pass, south of Innsbruck.
1050m; slopes 1050–2200m
6 25km

Stevens Pass USA
A day trip from Seattle, and accommodation 60km away in Bavarian-style town Leavenworth. Mostly intermediate slopes, with long expert runs on backside. Busy at weekends Jan to March.
1235m; slopes 1235–1785m
14 1125 acres

St-François-Longchamp France
Sunny, gentle slopes, with a couple of harder runs. Linked to Valmorel.
1400m Erna Low, Lagrange

St Gallenkirch Austria
Village in the Montafon strung along the main road and spoiled by traffic. A gondola goes up to Valisera on the west ridge of the Nova ski area (see Gaschurn) and a blue run comes back down to the gondola base. From the 2011/12 season a new gondola from the same area as the old one goes up the opposite side of the valley to Grasjoch on the Hochjoch ski area – but there is no piste back. Hochjoch is a fair-sized area of easy blue runs, with occasional red alternatives. Apart from the new gondola and one eight-pack, the lifts are slow chairs and drags. The blue/red run from Kreuzjoch down to Schruns is a notable 12km long and 1700m vertical (and includes a section through the longest ski tunnel in the world – 473m). Snowmaking covers almost half the runs.
900m; slopes 900–2370m
27 100km

St-Gervais 269
Small town sharing its ski area with Megève.

St Jakob am Arlberg Austria
Quiet St Anton village, beyond Nasserein. Depends on shuttle-bus to the slopes.
1295m

St Jakob in Defereggen Austria
Unspoiled traditional village in a pretty, sunny valley close to Lienz and Heiligenblut, and with a good proportion of high-altitude slopes.
1400m; slopes 1400–2525m
7 52km

St Jakob in Haus Austria
Snowy village with its own slopes (Buchensteinwand). Fieberbrunn, Waidring, St Johann are nearby.
855m; slopes 855–1500m
8 19km Inntravel

St-Jean-d'Arves France
Small, scattered community with 'friendly locals', set in the Sybelles area. The original old village, with the usual ancient church, is set across the valley from the slopes, which are at the mid-mountain hamlet of La Chal. Here, where a tasteful development of chalet-style buildings has been expanding, there are nursery slopes and the lift link to and piste back from Le Corbier. Not the best base to exploit the whole area, given the slow chair to Le Corbier, but a bus goes to St-Sorlin-d'Arves.
1550m 72 310km
Peak Retreats, Ski France, Thomson

St Jean d'Aulps France
Small village in Portes du Soleil area, with its own interesting slopes.
ChaletBook

St-Jean-de-Sixt France
Traditional hamlet, a cheap base for La Clusaz and Le Grand-Bornand (3km to both).
960m

St-Jean-Montclar France
Small village at the foot of thickly forested slopes. Good day out from nearby Pra-Loup.
1300m; slopes 1300–2500m
18 50km Zenith

St Johann im Pongau Austria
Bustling, lively working town with its own small area. An extensive three-valley lift network starts 4km away at Alpendorf, linking via Wagrain to Flachau – all part of the Salzburger Sportwelt ski pass area.
650m; slopes 800–2185m
64 200km Crystal

St Johann in Tirol Austria
Friendly valley town, an attractive place for beginners and leisurely part-timers – keen piste-bashers will ski all the local slopes in a day and need to go on to explore nearby resorts covered by the Kitzbüheler Alpenskipass as well. There is nothing here to challenge an expert. The main access lift is a 10-minute walk from the centre. It gets more snow than neighbouring Kitzbühel and the SkiWelt, and also has substantial snowmaking. Given good snow, St Johann is one of the best cross-country resorts in Austria – trails total 275km. The Park hotel is near the gondola and recommended by a reader.
650m; slopes 690–1700m
17 60km
Crystal, Ski Line, Skitracer, Snowscape, STC, Thomson

St Lary Espiaube 318
Satellite of St-Lary-Soulan in the Pyrenees.

St-Lary-Soulan 318

St Leonhard in Pitztal Austria
Village beneath a fine glacier in the Oetz area, accessed by underground funicular.
1250m; slopes 880–3440m
12 68km

St-Luc 498
Village in the Val d'Anniviers.

St Margarethen Austria
Valley village near Styria/Carinthia border, sharing slopes with higher Katschberg.
1065m; slopes 1065–2210m
16 70km

St Martin bei Lofer Austria
Traditional cross-country village in a lovely setting beneath the impressive Loferer Steinberge massif. Alpine slopes at Lofer.
635m; slopes 640–1745m
10 46km

St-Martin-de-Belleville 340

St Martin in Tennengebirge Austria
Highest village in the Dachstein-West region near Salzburg. It has limited slopes of its own but nearby Annaberg has an interesting area.
1000m; slopes 1000–1350m
4 5km

St-Maurice-sur-Moselle France
One of several areas near Strasbourg. No snowmakers.
550m; slopes 900–1250m
8 24km

St Michael im Lungau Austria
Quiet, unspoiled village in the Tauern pass snowpocket with an uncrowded but disjointed intermediate area. Close to Obertauern and Wagrain.
1075m; slopes 1065–2220m
16 70km

St Moritz 491

St-Nicolas-de-Véroce 269
Small hamlet in the Megève network.

St-Nicolas-la-Chapelle France
Small village close to larger Flumet, in the Val d'Arly.
1000m; slopes 1000–1600m
10 40km

St-Nizier-du-Moucherotte France
Unspoiled, inexpensive resort just west of Grenoble with no lifts of its own. Villard-de-Lans is the main resort.

Stoneham Canada
The closest resort to Québec City, around 20 minutes away. It also has its own small base 'village', with condo accommodation and an impressive lodge that has its own lively après-ski bar, restaurant and spas. But night owls should probably head for the city as the evenings are generally quiet in resort. Like most resorts in this region, the ski area is small. The slopes spread across three linked peaks, with mainly sheltered intermediate and beginner pistes. It suits families well and has a special nursery area equipped with a moving carpet. A key attraction is the resort's four terrain parks and half-pipe, regularly revamped and chosen to host the 2013 Snowboard World Championships.
210m; slopes 210–630m
7 326 acres
Frontier, Ski Safari

Stoos Switzerland
Small, unspoiled village an hour from Zürich. Weekend crowds. Splendid views of Lake Lucerne.
1300m; slopes 500–1935m
7 35km

Storlien Sweden
Small family resort amid magnificent wilderness scenery, one hour from Trondheim, 30 mins from Åre.
600m; slopes 600–790m
7 16km

Stowe 600

St-Pierre-de-Chartreuse France
Locals' weekend place near Grenoble. Unreliable snow.
900m; slopes 900–1800m
14 35km

Stratton USA
Something like the classic Alpine arrangement of a village at the foot of the lifts: a smart, modern development with a car-free shopping street. The slopes are mostly easy and intermediate, with some blacks and some short double-black pitches, spread widely around the flanks of a single peak, served by modern lifts. Stratton calls itself the 'snowboarding capital of the east', with no fewer than five terrain parks. The Suntanner Park has a super-pipe.
570m; slopes 570–1180m
14 660 acres

Strobl Austria
Close to St Wolfgang in a beautiful lakeside setting. There are slopes at nearby St Gilgen and Postalm.
545m; slopes 545–1510m
7 12km

St-Sorlin-d'Arves France
A refreshing contrast to the stark, functional resorts of Le Corbier and La Toussuire, with which it shares the extensive Les Sybelles ski area. And the resort accesses some of the most interesting slopes. The village is a picturesque collection of traditional buildings, alongside a more modern development that spreads out along the main road and has attracted some major tour operators. The local slopes form the biggest single sector of the linked network, with lifts serving two distinct mountains. Some of the most varied slopes in the whole area are here, and reached by fast quads to Les Perrons – which also has some of the best off-piste opportunities. There are leisurely cruising runs on La Balme.
1600m 72 310km
AmeriCan Ski, Crystal, Erna Low, Lagrange, Peak Retreats, Ski France, Ski Independence, Thomson

St Stephan Switzerland
Unspoiled old farming village at the foot of the largest sector of slopes in the area around Gstaad.
1000m; slopes 950–3000m
58 250km

Stubai valley 189

Stuben 180
Small, unspoiled village linked to St Anton.

St Veit im Pongau Austria
Spa resort with limited slopes at Goldegg; Wagrain (Salzburger Sportwelt) and Grossarl (Gastein valley) are nearby.
765m 4 12km

St-Veran France
Said to be the highest 'real' village in Europe, and full of charm. Close to Serre-Chevalier and the Milky Way. Snow-reliable cross-country skiing.
2040m; slopes 2040–2800m
15 30km

St Wolfgang Austria
Charming lakeside resort near Salzburg, some way from any slopes, best for a relaxing winter holiday with one or two days on the slopes.
540m; slopes 665–1350m
9 17km
Crystal, Skitracer, Thomson

Sugar Bowl USA
Exposed area north of Lake Tahoe with highest snowfall in California, best for experts. Lodging in Truckee but Squaw Valley nearby.
2100m; slopes 2100–2555m
8 1500 acres

Sugarbush USA
Dynamic resort in upper Vermont, with two mountains linked by fast chair, and something resembling a village at the foot of one of them. Good range of runs, including some real challenges.
480m; slopes 450–1245m
16 508 acres
Ski Safari

Sugarloaf USA
Developing Maine resort, 5 hours from Boston, with the Eastern US's best open terrain.
430m; slopes 405–1290m
15 1410 acres
American Ski Classics

Sulden Italy
The other side of the Stelvio Pass from Bormio. Very long airport transfers. Solda is its Italian name.
1905m; slopes 1905–2625m
10 40km

Summit at Snoqualmie USA
Four areas – Summit East, Summit Central, Summit West and Alpental – with interlinked lifts. Damp weather and wet snow are major drawbacks.
slopes 915–1645m
24 2000 acres

Sun Alpina Japan
Collective name for three ski areas four hours away from Tokyo. 21

Sundance USA
Robert Redford owned, tastefully designed family resort set amid trees in snow-sure Utah. It's a small, narrow mountain but the vertical is respectable, the setting is spectacular and there is terrain to suit all abilities. The lower mountain is easy-intermediate, the upper part steeper. There are 17km of cross-country trails, of varying difficulty.
1860m; slopes 1860–2515m
4 450 acres

Sunday River USA
One of the more attractive resorts in the East, four hours from Boston, best for intermediate cruisers. The slopes spread across eight peaks, but it's a small area. Only four of the chairs are fast quads but queues are not a problem – midweek, the resort is very quiet. Cross-country is big around here.
245m; slopes 245–955m
16 743 acres
American Ski Classics, Ski Independence, Ski Safari

Sunlight Mountain Resort USA
Quiet, small area 10 miles south of Glenwood Springs. Varied terrain with some serious glades.
2405m; slopes 2405–3015m
3 470 acres

Sun Peaks 631

Sunrise Park USA
Arizona's largest area, operated by Apaches. Slopes are spread over three mountains; best for novices and leisurely intermediates.
2805m; slopes 2805–3500m
12 800 acres

Sunshine Village 605
One-hotel mountain station in Banff's ski area.

Sun Valley 589
Purpose-built resort in Idaho.
1750m; slopes 1750–2790m
17 2054 acres

Suomu Finland
A lodge (no village) right on the Arctic Circle with a few slopes but mostly a ski-touring place.
140m; slopes 140–410m 3

Superbagnères France
Little more than a particularly French-dominated Club Med; best for a low-cost, low-effort family trip to the Pyrenees. Said to have good off-piste if the snow is good.
1880m; slopes 1440–2260m
16 35km
Lagrange

Super-Besse France
Purpose-built resort amid spectacular extinct-volcano scenery. Shares area with the spa town of Mont-Dore. Limited village.
1350m; slopes 1300–1850m
22 43km Lagrange

Superdévoluy France
Purpose-built but friendly family resort in a remote spot near Gap, with huge apartment blocks plus traditional chalets. Sizeable intermediate area shared with more appealing La Joue-du-Loup.
1450m; slopes 1450–2450m
22 100km
Crystal, Erna Low, Ski Collection

Super Espot Spain
Small area on the eastern edge of the Aigues Tortes National Park, close to the valley town of Sort.
slopes 1500–2500m
8 28km

Supermolina Spain
Dreary, purpose-built satellite of Pyrenean resort of La Molina, with a reasonable sized area of its own and linked to the slopes of Masella to form an area called Alp 2500.
1700m; slopes 1600–2535m
31 121km

Super St Bernard Switzerland
Swiss side of the Grand St Bernard tunnel to Italy. No resort – just a small beginner area and an old gondola rising to 850m; two black runs and lots of off-piste on a mainly north-facing and usually deserted mountain. You can also ski off-piste down the back to Italy but need transport back.
1950m; slopes 1950–2800m
3 25km

Les Sybelles France
A group of linked ski resorts in the Maurienne massif, forming an impressively large network.
1100m; slopes 1100–2620m
72 310km

Tahko Finland
Largest resort in southern Finland. Plenty of intermediate slopes in an attractive, wooded, frozen-lake setting.
9

Tahoe City USA
Small lakeside accommodation base for visiting nearby Alpine Meadows and Squaw Valley.

Talisman Mountain Resort Canada
One of the best areas in the Toronto region, but with a relatively low lift capacity. 100% snowmaking.
235m; slopes 235–420m 8

Tamsweg Austria
Large cross-country village with rail links in snowy region close to Tauern Pass and St Michael. *1025m*

La Tania 343

Taos 589
Isolated resort in New Mexico.
2805m; slopes 2805–3600m
13 1294 acres

Tärnaby-Hemavan Sweden
Twin resorts in north Sweden, offering downhill, cross-country and heliskiing. Own airport. *slopes 465–1135m*
13 44km

El Tarter 92
Relatively quiet, convenient alternative to Soldeu.

Tarvisio Italy
Interesting, animated old town bordering Austria and Slovenia. A major cross-country base with fairly limited Alpine slopes.
750m; slopes 750–1860m
12 15km

Täsch 520
The final road base on the way to car-free Zermatt.

Tauplitz Austria
Traditional village at the foot of an interestingly varied area north of Schladming. Few queues; decent lift system.
900m; slopes 900–2000m
18 40km

Telluride USA
An isolated resort in south-west Colorado, but a beautifully renovated old mining town with great Wild West charm and fairly dramatic mountain scenery. It's a friendly, small-scale resort, with a smartly developing slope-side base above it. Both have lifts into the ski area. Mountain Village has new luxury hotels and spa facilities. The slopes are limited in overall extent, but quite varied and with recently expanded expert terrain. Most runs are below the treeline, but the top lifts and bowls give great views. Queues are rarely a problem. Experts have some truly challenging terrain to play such as the Gold Hill Chutes, while there are splendid blue and greens runs for intermediates and beginners too – but it's not a resort for keen piste-bashers. There are three terrain parks. Nightlife revolves around the bars.
2665m; slopes 2665–3830m
18 2000 acres
Alpine Answers, AmeriCan Ski, American Ski Classics, Elegant Resorts, Momentum, Ski Bespoke, Ski Independence, Ski Safari, Ski Solutions, Skiworld

Temù Italy
Sheltered hamlet near Passo Tonale. Worth a visit in bad weather.
1155m; slopes 1155–1955m
4 5km

Tengendai Japan
Tiny area three hours by train and bus from Tokyo. One of Japan's best snow records, including occasional powder.
920m; slopes 920–1820m 4

Termas de Chillán Chile
Ski and spa resort 400km south of Santiago. Base village has lodgings or you can stay at Las Trancas a few minutes' drive away.
1650m; slopes 1600–2700m
9 46km Momentum

Termignon France
Traditional rustic village 6km down the Maurienne valley from Lanslebourg and the slopes of Val Cenis, to which it is linked. The local slopes are limited and served by slow lifts, but have the advantage of being extremely quiet.
1300m; slopes 1300–2500m
6 35km
Lagrange, Peak Retreats

Terminillo Italy
Purpose-built resort 100km from Rome with a worthwhile area when its lower runs have snow-cover.
1500m; slopes 1500–2210m
15 40km

Teton Village 595
Village at base of Jackson Hole's slopes.

Thollon-les-Mémises France
Attractive base for a relaxed holiday. Own little area and close to Portes du Soleil.
1000m; slopes 1600–2000m
19 50km

Thredbo Australia
Oz's best, 6 hours from Sydney; with long (and, in places, testing) runs, snowmaking, lots of accommodation and active nightlife.
1365m; slopes 1365–2035m
14 480 acres

Three Valleys

La Thuile 441

Thyon 2000 502
Mid-mountain resort above Veysonnaz in the Verbier area.

Tignes 347

Timberline (Palmer Snowfield) USA
Fair-sized area of largely intermediate slopes served by six lifts including four fast quads on Mt Hood in Oregon.
1800m; slopes 1510–2600m
6 1430 acres

Toblach Italy
Small resort in South Tyrol. Dobbiaco is its Italian name.
1250m; slopes 1250–1610m
5 15km

Togari Japan
One of several areas close to the 1998 Olympic site. Nagano, 2hr30 from Tokyo.
slopes 400–1050m 9

Torgnon Italy
Small village off the road up to Cervinia, good for bad-weather days. Some good cross-country loops.
1500m; slopes 1500–1965m
7 6km

Torgon Switzerland
Old village in a pretty wooded setting, with a connection to the Portes du Soleil. Still some steep draglifts.
1150m; slopes 950–2300m
197 650km

Le Tour 227
Charming hamlet at the head of the Chamonix valley.

La Toussuire France
Highest and most central of the Sybelles resorts, and convenient base for exploring the whole area. The centre has fairly dreary buildings, of apartments and hotels spreading widely from the car-free centre. But the local slopes have three of the seven fast chairs in the area, so access to Pte de L'Ouillon and the rest of the linked network is fairly quick. Two drags were installed in 2009 to reduce queues here too. Above the resort is a wide bowl with drags and chairs all around. Locally, the pistes are short cruisers with few challenges – but judged by a reporter as the most varied and snow-sure in the area. A splendid longer run goes to Les Bottières. There are gentle nursery slopes and good, easy progression runs. Eating out is inexpensive for France, but nightlife is dull.
1700m 72 310km
Erna Low, Lagrange, PowderBeds, Ski Collection, Ski France

Trafoi Italy
Quiet, traditional village in the Val Venosta in the South Tyrol on the Ortler Skiarena pass.
1570m; slopes 1570–2550m
4 10km

Treble Cone New Zealand
Plenty of good skiing opened up by two main lifts. Varied open terrain suitable for all levels. Great powder bowls. 2 hours from Queenstown.
1260m; slopes 1260–1960m
4 550 hectares

Tremblant 642

Trentino 443

Troodos Cyprus
Ski area on Mt Olympus, a 70-minute drive from Nicosia. Pretty, wooded slopes.
slopes 1730–1950m
4 5km

Tröpolach Austria
Small village at base of access gondola for Nassfeld ski area.
610m; slopes 610–2195m
30 110km

Trysil Norway
Extensive area, some distance from the town, spread around the conical Trysilfjellet, with some good, long runs of up to 4km. On the border with Sweden.
350m; slopes 350–1100m 24
Absolutely Snow

Tryvann Norway
Small area close to Oslo and popular with ocals. Vertical of 380m – are served by two drags and two chairs, one of them fast. 6

Tschagguns Austria
Village the Montafon valley – effectively a suburb of Schruns.
700m; slopes 700–2100m
13 32km

Tsugaike Kogen Japan
Sizeable resort four hours from Tokyo, three hours from Osaka. Helicopter service to the top station.
800m; slopes 800–1700m 26

Tulfes Austria
Hamlet on mountain shelf close to Innsbruck, with small main area above the trees and long runs back to base.
920m; slopes 920–2305m
7 22km

Turoa New Zealand
On the south-western slopes of Mt Ruapeha, with NZ's biggest vertical. Shares lift pass with Whakapapa. Mix of open, gentle and steeper runs. Good scope for off-piste.
slopes 1600–2320m
23 2590 acres

Turracherhöhe Austria
Tiny, unspoiled resort on a mountain shelf, with varied intermediate slopes above and below it. A good outing from Bad Kleinkirchheim.
1765m; slopes 1400–2205m
14 38km

Tyax Mountain Lake Resort Canada
Heli-skiing operation in the Chilcotin mountains – transfers from Whistler or Vancouver.

La Tzoumaz 502
Hamlet in Verbier's ski area.

Uludag Turkey
Surprisingly suave, laid-back, purpose-built resort near Bursa, south of Istanbul.
1750m; slopes 1750–2322m
14 15km

Unken Austria
Traditional village hidden in a side valley. Closest slopes to Salzburg.
565m; slopes 1000–1500m
4 8km

Untergurgl 150
Valley-floor alternative to staying in Obergurgl.

Unternberg Austria
Riverside village with trail connecting into one of the longest, most snow-sure cross-country networks in Europe. St Margarethen slopes close by. *1030m*

Unterwasser-Toggenburg Switzerland
Old but not especially attractive resort 90 minutes from Zürich. Fabulous lake and mountain views.
910m; slopes 900–2260m
17 60km

Uttendorf-Weiss-See Austria
Astute alternative to crowded Kaprun when the snowline is high.
805m; slopes 1485–2600m
8 23km

Vail 564

Valbella Switzerland
Convenient but ordinary village sharing intermediate Lenzerheide area.
1540m; slopes 1230–2865m
35 155km

Valberg France
Large Alpes-Maritimes resort (bigger than better-known Isola 2000) close to Nice.
1650m; slopes 1430–2100m
26 90km

Val Cenis France
A marketing concept rather than a place: its ski area is Val Cenis Vanoise and it comprises two quiet, friendly, traditional villages strung along the high and remote part of the Maurienne valley. There are lifts from several base stations, so convenience isn't a huge concern and queues are rare. Lanslebourg spreads along the RN6 road with no real focus, but lifts there have linked the slopes with those above Termignon further down the valley. Lanslevillard is the most captivating base, randomly arranged and with excellent nursery slopes. The mountain packs in more variety than you might expect for an area its size, with a good mix of open and treelined slopes and some decent vertical; most are north-facing, so snow reliability is quite good too. Beginners and intermediates will be best off here though.
1400m; slopes 1300–2800m
27 125km
AmeriCan Ski, Crystal, Erna Low, Lagrange, MGS, Peak Retreats, Ski Amis, Ski France, Ski Ici, Snowcoach, Thomson

Val d'Anniviers 498

Val di Fassa 447

Val d'Illiez 459
Peaceful, unspoiled village near Champéry.

Val d'Isère 358

Val Ferret Switzerland
Old climbing village near Martigny, with spectacular views. Own tiny area.
1600m 3 20km

Valfrejus France
Small and unusual modern resort on a narrow, shady shelf in the Maurienne valley – built in the woods, with the slopes higher up above the treeline. The focus is Plateau d'Arrondaz, with steep, open slopes above, offering genuine bumpy blacks with excellent snow (snowmaking on the lower runs is urgently required, though). There's a natural terrain park, and good off-piste is available above the main plateau. The nursery slopes are at mid-mountain and village levels. THere has been recent investment in new lifts.
1550m; slopes 1550–2740m
10 65km
Erna Low, Lagrange, PowderBeds, Ski Collection, Ski France

Val Gardena 432
Valley area of Selva, Ortisei and Santa Cristina.

Valgrisenche Italy
Small, peaceful village on the southern side of the Aosta valley. Established heli-ski centre – about 20 drop points. Intermediate runs, nursery area and a few cross-country loops.
1665m 4 12km

Vallandry 212
Satellite of Les Arcs.

Valle Nevado Chile
Developing purpose-built resort 46km east of Santiago. Varied, intermediate terrain.
3025m; slopes 2430–3670m
45 7000 acres
Crystal, Crystal Finest, Momentum, Skiworld

Valloire France
A compelling combination of an old mountain village with extensive slopes, branded as Galibier Thabor, and shared with the more modern two-part resort of Valmeinier. The village is the best known of the Maurienne valley resorts and retains a quiet, rustic charm of narrow streets, shops and restaurants set around a lively market square. The slopes spread widely across three sunny sectors, served by two gondolas out of the village, and are particularly good for intermediates wanting lots of gentle cruising and a sense of travel. Experts will find the challenges limited, although there is some decent off-piste opportunity towards Valmeinier.
1430m; slopes 1430–2595m
33 150km
AmeriCan Ski, Crystal, Erna Low, Lagrange, Peak Retreats, Pierre & Vacances, PowderBeds, Ski France, Ski Independence

Vallorcine 227
Backwater on road between Chamonix and Switzerland.

Vallter 2000 Spain
Small resort on the far eastern fringes of the Pyrenees, close to the Costa Brava.
slopes 1960–2535m
10 420 acres

Valmeinier France
Quiet, old mountain village with a modern purpose-built satellite where most people stay. Shares with Valloire the most extensive slopes in the Maurienne region, spreading widely over three mostly sunny sectors.
1500-1800m; slopes 1430–2595m 33 150km
Crystal, Erna Low, Lagrange, Pierre & Vacances, PowderBeds, Ski Collection, Ski France, Ski Ici, Ski Independence, Snowcoach

Valmorel France
The main resort in the Grand Domaine ski area, sharing slopes with St-François and Longchamp. The purpose-built village is prettily designed with a traffic-free centre, though lodging is broadly scattered among six 'hamlets' – mainly of simple hotels or apartments. The slopes offer a fair-sized area of varied skiing, with runs criss-crossing a number of minor valleys. Most are blue runs. Fast chairs serve the key links, but there are lots of slow drags. So, queues can be evident at peak times. The area appeals mainly to intermediates, and beginners. Few slopes are challenging, and there are good gentle greens for progression. Children are well catered for too. Nightlife is generally quiet and there is little off-slope diversion, although the slope-side cafe-bars are 'jolly'.
1400m; slopes 1250–2550m
46 152km
Alpine Answers, Chalet Valmorel, Club Med, Crystal, Erna Low, Interactive Resorts, Lagrange, Pierre & Vacances, PowderBeds, Ski France, Ski Independence, Ski Line, Ski Solutions, Ski Supreme, Skitracer

Val Senales Italy
Top-of-the-mountain hotel, the highest in the Alps, in the Dolomites near Merano.
3210m; slopes 2110–3210m
12 35km

Val Thorens 368

Valtournenche 387
Cheaper alternative to Cervinia.

Vandans Austria
Sizeable working village well placed for visiting all the Montafon areas. A gondola goes up directly from here into the Golm area.
655m; slopes 655–2085m
9 30km

Vars 375

Vasilitsa Greece
Resort in northern Greece, in the Pindos range, offering intermediate skiing.
1780m 8

Vaujany 202
Tiny village in the heart of the Alpe-d'Huez ski area.

Las Vegas Ski Resort USA
Tiny area formerly known as Lee Canyon, cut from forest 50 minutes' drive north-west of Las Vegas.
2595m; slopes 2595–2855m
4 200 acres

Velka–Raca Slovakia
Small resort near Oscadnica, with a modern lift system, including a 'chondola'.
630m; slopes 630–1050m
6 14km

Vemdalen Sweden
Twin areas of Björnrike and Vemdalsskalet (same pass) 20 minutes apart. 385m vertical.
18 28km

Vemdalsskalet Sweden
20 minutes from Björnrike (same pass). 385m vertical. Said to have hottest après-ski in Sweden.
18 28km

Venosc France
Captivating tiny village of cobbled streets, ancient church and craft shops with fast gondola to Les Deux-Alpes. *Peak Retreats*

Vent Austria
High, remote Oztal village known mainly as a touring base, with just enough lift-served skiing to warrant a day trip from nearby Obergurgl.
1900m; slopes 1900–2680m
4 15km

Ventron France
Small village near La Bresse in the northerly Vosges mountains near Strasbourg, with more ski de fond than downhill terrain.
630m; slopes 900–1110m
8 15km

Verbier **502**

Vercorin **498**
Cluster of chalets in the Val d'Anniviers.

Verditz Austria
One of several small, mostly mountain-top areas overlooking Villach.
675m; slopes 675–2165m
5 15km

Vex Switzerland
Major village in unspoiled, attractive setting south of Sion. Verbier slopes accessed nearby at Mayens-de-l'Ours.
900m

Veysonnaz **502**
Little old village within Verbier's Four Valleys network.

Vichères–Liddes Switzerland
Limited area near to Martigny. Part of the Grand St Bernard region, including Val Ferret and Champex-Lac. Valid with the Valais ski Card.
1350m; slopes 1350–2270m
4 15km

Vic-sur-Cère France
Charming village with fine architecture, beneath Super-Lioran ski area. Beautiful extinct-volcano scenery.
680m; slopes 1250–1850m
24 60km Lagrange

Viehhofen Austria
Cheaper place to stay when visiting Saalbach. 3km from the Schönleiten gondola, and there's a run back to the village from the Asitz section.
860m 1

Vigla-Pisoderi Greece
The longest run in Greece (over 2km), in an unspoiled setting 18km from the town of Florina in the north.
1600m 5

Vigo di Fassa **447**
Best base for the Val di Fassa.

La Villa **423**
Quiet Sella Ronda village.

Villabassa Italy
Cross-country village in South Tyrol. Niederdorf is its German name.

Villach-Dobratsch Austria
One of several small, mostly mountain-top areas overlooking the town of Villach.
900m; slopes 980–2165m
8 15km

Villar-d'Arêne France
Tiny area on main road between La Grave and Serre-Chevalier. Empty, immaculately groomed, short easy runs, plus a couple of hotels.
1650m

Villard-de-Lans France
Unspoiled, lively, traditional village west of Grenoble. Snow-sure, thanks to snowmaking.
1050m; slopes 1145–2170m
25 125km

Villard-Reculas **202**
Rustic village on periphery of Alpe-d'Huez ski area.

Villaroger **212**
Rustic hamlet with direct links up to Arc 2000.

Villars **513**

Villeneuve **327**
One of the villages making up the resort of Serre-Chevalier.

Vipiteno Italy
Bargain-shopping town close to Brenner Pass.
960m; slopes 960–2100m
12 25km

Virgen Austria
Traditional village in a beautiful valley south of the Felbertauern tunnel. Slopes at Matrei.
1200m; slopes 975–2620m
15 110km

Vitosha Bulgaria
Limited area of slopes and a few widely scattered hotels, 22km from Sofia, leading to crowds at weekends. The slopes are north-facing and have a decent snow record.
1810m; slopes 1515–2290m
12 29km

Vogel **654**

Vorarlberg **191**

Vorarlberg – Alpenregion Bludenz **195**

Vorarlberg – Bregenzerwald **192**

Vorderlanersbach **117**
Village with access to Mayrhofen's ski area.

Voss Norway
Well-equipped winter sports resort attractively set on a lake, with relatively limited Alpine slopes.
60m; slopes 150–945m
10 40km

Vuokatti Finland
Small mountain in a remarkable setting, surrounded on three sides by lots of little lakes. Good activity base. 8

Wagrain Austria
A towny little resort at the centre of a lift system that is typical of many in Salzburgerland – spreading widely across several low, partly wooded ridges. Flachau and Alpendorf/St Johann are at its extremities, and all these resorts are covered by Salzburger Sportwelt lift pass that our figures relate to. It's pleasant without being notably charming, and though it's a compact place the main lift bases are still a good walk apart. The slopes – wooded at the bottom, open higher up – are practically all easy/ intermediate stuff, but cover a huge area almost 15km across. The lift system is impressive, with a lot of fast chairs and gondolas. Despite the altitude, most of the upper slopes are fairly open. Some get too much sun for comfort, and snow reliability is not a strong point.
850m; slopes 850–2190m
64 200km

Waidring Austria
Quiet valley village north of Kitzbühel. Mainly gentle open and north-facing slopes, also accessible from Germany. Impressive lift system, but still prone to weekend queues.
780m; slopes 1230–1860m
10 35km

Waiorau Snow Farm New Zealand
Specialist cross-country base just over an hour from Queenstown. Spectacular views. Overnight huts.
1500m

Wald im Pinzgau Austria
Cross-country village surrounded by Alpine areas – Gerlos, Krimml and Neukirchen – and with Pass Thurn also nearby.
885m 50 160km

Wanaka New Zealand
Quiet, diffuse village in beautiful lakeside mountain setting close to four ski areas; the nearest is Treble Cone.

Warth **192**
Bregenzerwald village near Lech.
1500m; slopes 1260–2100m
15 66km

Waterville Valley USA
Compact New Hampshire area with runs dropping either side of a broad, gentle ridge rising 615m above the lift base. A couple of short but genuine double-black-diamond mogul fields, but most of the slopes are intermediate. The village is a Disneyesque affair a couple of miles away down on the flat valley bottom.
600m; slopes 600–1215m
12 255 acres

Watles Italy
Village in the Val Venosta in the South Tyrol covered by the Ortler Skiarena pass.
3 18km

Weinebene Austria
One of many gentle little areas in Austria's easternmost ski region near the Slovenian border. No major resorts in the vicinity.
1580m; slopes 1560–1835m
7 22km

Weissbach bei Lofer Austria
Traditional resort between Lofer and Saalfelden. No slopes of its own, but it's well placed for touring the Tirol. Kitzbühel, Saalbach, St Johann and Zell am See are nearby.
665m

Weissensee Naggeralm Austria
Little area in eastern Austria and the location of Europe's largest frozen lake, which is used for all kinds of ice sports, including ice-golf.
930m; slopes 930–1400m
5 6km

Weisspriach Austria
Hamlet on snowy pass near Obertauern that shares its area with Mauterndorf and St Michael.
1115m; slopes 1115 2050m
13 47km

Wengen **515**

Wentworth Canada
Long-established Nova Scotia area with largest accessible acreage in the Maritime Provinces. Harsh climate ensures good snow-cover despite low altitude.
55m; slopes 55–300m
6 150 acres

Werfen Austria
Traditional village spoiled by the Tauern autobahn, which runs between it and the slopes. Good touring to the Dachstein West region.
620m

Werfenweng Austria
Hamlet with the advantage over the main village of Werfen of being away from the autobahn and close to the slopes. Best for novices.
1000m; slopes 1000–1835m
9 25km
Thomson

Whakapapa/Turoa New Zealand
NZ's largest area, on a volcano close to Turoa with similarly superb views and shared pass. The Grand Chateau is a lovely old hotel in the tiny village 6km away.
1630m; slopes 1630–2320m
23 2590 acres

Whistler 633

Whitecap Mountains Resort USA
Largest, snowiest area in Wisconsin, close enough to Lake Superior and Minneapolis to ensure winds and weekend crowds.
435m; slopes 435–555m
7 500 acres

Whiteface Mountain USA
Varied area in New York State 15km from attractive lakeside resort of Lake Placid. 93% snowmaking ensures good snow-cover. Plenty to do off the slopes.
365m; slopes 365–1345m
10 211 acres
American Ski Classics

Whitefish Mountain Resort USA
Resort set close to the Canadian border and to Montana's Glacier National Park, this place has revamped its image in recent years. Lots of redevelopment has taken place, both on and off the slopes. Its 3,000 acres embrace a wide range of slopes that are not only impressively snowy but also blissfully devoid of people. There's easy cruising in dense forest around the base area, and steeper stuff higher up on 'gladed' slopes. There are two good terrain parks. There's lodging at the base and you can stay in the small town of Whitefish, a few miles away.
1360m; slopes 1360–2135m
13 3000 acres
Ski Safari

White Pass Village USA
Closest area to Mt St Helens. Remote and uncrowded during the week, with a good snowfall record. Some genuinely steep, expert terrain, as well as intermediate cruising.
1370m; slopes 1370–1825m
5 635 acres

Whitewater Canada
Renowned for powder (40% off-piste), food and weekend party atmosphere. Accommodation in the historic town of Nelson or a great day out from nearby Red Mountain.
1640m; slopes 1640–2040m 3
Frontier

Wildcat Mountain USA
New Hampshire area infamous for bad weather, but one of the best areas on a nice day. Lodging in nearby Jackson and North Conway.
slopes 600–1250m
4 225 acres

Wildhaus Switzerland
Undeveloped farming community in stunning scenery near Liechtenstein; popular with families and serious snowboarders. Shares its slopes with Unterwasser.
1050m; slopes 900–2260m
17 60km

Wildschönau 107
Part of Ski Juwel (Alpbachtal-Wildschönau).

Willamette Pass USA
Set in national forest near beautiful Crater Lake, Oregon. Small area of varied slopes. An average of 430 inches of snow a year – that's up there with Utah.
1560m; slopes 1560–2035m
6 550 acres

Williams USA
Tiny area above the main place to stay for the Grand Canyon.
slopes 2010–2270m
2 50 acres

Willingen Germany
Resort in Sauerland, east of Düsseldorf. 12

WindhamMountain USA
Boutique resort in the Catskill Mountains 2.5 hours from New York.
455m; slopes 455–945m
10 269 acres

Windischgarsten Austria
Large working village in Upper Austria with cross-country trails around and downhill slopes at nearby Hinterstoder and Spital am Pyrhn. *600m*

Winterberg Germany
Resort in Sauerland, east of Düsseldorf. 21

Winter Park 571

Wolf Creek USA
Remote area on a pass of the same name, with 'the most snow in Colorado' – 465 inches a year. One-third of the terrain is standard American trails through the trees; two-thirds is 'wilderness', served by a single lift. Great stop en route between Taos and Telluride. Stay in Pagosa Springs to the west, or South Fork to the east.
3140m; slopes 3140–3630m
6 1600 acres

Wolf Mountain USA
Utah cross-country area close to Salt Lake City. Powder Mountain and Snowbasin are nearby Alpine areas.
3 100 acres

Xonrupt France
Cross-country venue only 3km from nearest Alpine slopes at Gérardmer.
715m Lagrange

Yangji Pine Resort South Korea
Modern resort an hour (60km) south of Seoul, with runs cut out of dense forest. Gets very crowded. 6

Ylläs 645

Yong Pyong Resort South Korea
200km east of Seoul, close to the east coast, also known as Dragon Valley. The self-contained purpose-built resort village is centred on 200-room Dragon Valley Hotel. Modern lifts serve a small, mainly wooded slope area, with snowmaking on all its runs.
750m; slopes 750–1460m
15 20km

Zakopane Poland
An interesting old town 100km south of Kraków on the Slovakian border. Mostly intermediate slopes, branded as 14 small and fragmented sectors. Reported to have renovated its 70-year-old cable car.
830m; slopes 1000–1960m
60 60km

Zao Japan
Big area with unpredictable weather, four hours from Tokyo by train. Known for 'chouoh' – pines frozen into weird shapes. Hot springs.
780m; slopes 780–1660m 42

Zauchensee Austria
Purpose-built resort part of big three-valley lift network linking it via Flachauwinkl to Kleinarl – which our figures relate too. Also on the Salzburger Sportwelt ski pass.
855m; slopes 800–2185m
15 88km

Zell am See Austria
Lively old lakeside resort with a charming medieval centre, below a horseshoe-shaped mountain. A gondola from the edge of town goes up to the slopes. There are also lift stations at the suburb of Schüttdorf and Schmittental (1km west) in the centre of the horseshoe. The slopes offer an attractive mix of open and densely wooded lower runs; but they are very limited in extent, particularly when poor snow conditions low down limit you to the runs above mid-mountain. Keen, mileage-hungry intermediates should stay away. Experts have some short but genuinely black runs – more than in most resorts of this size – but off-piste is limited. Beginners may find the valley nursery areas crowded, but there are a few gentle blues up the mountain. There's a terrain park and lots of cross-country trails. The schools receive favourable reports. Accommodation choice is broad; mostly hotels. There are plenty of bars, cafes and discos, as well as non-hotel restaurants. Kaprun's glacier skiing is within reach.
755m; slopes 755–3030m
53 138km
BoardnLodge, Crystal, Crystal Finest, Erna Low, Inghams, Interactive Resorts, Neilson, Ski Club Freshtracks, Ski Line, Skitracer, Snow Finders, Snowscape, STC, Thomson, Zenith

Zell im Zillertal 145
Sprawling valley town with slopes on two mountains.

Zermatt 520

Zillertal Austria
Valley of ten ski resorts, of which the most well known is Mayrhofen.

Zinal 498
Village in the Val d'Anniviers.

Zug 137
Tiny village with Lech's toughest skiing.

Zugspitz Arena Austria
The name of Germany's highest mountain, and part of Austria's Zugspitz Arena over the border – a collection of small, gentle but low ski areas, with pretty villages.
990-1340m; slopes 990–2960m
55 148km

Zuoz Switzerland
An unspoiled village in a sunny setting just down the valley from St Moritz, with gentle slopes at village level and some more challenging runs higher up.
1715m; slopes 1720–2465m
5 15km
Inntravel

Zürs 137
High village on road to Lech.

Zweisimmen Switzerland
Limited but inexpensive base for slopes around Gstaad, with its own delightful little easy area too.
965m; slopes 950–3000m
58 250km